RPG II, RPG III, AND RPG/400 WITH BUSINESS APPLICATIONS

Second Edition

RPG II, RPG III, AND RPG/400 WITH BUSINESS APPLICATIONS

Stanley E. Myers
Professor
Norwalk State Technical College

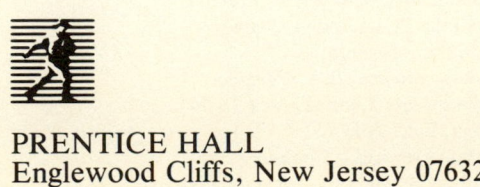

PRENTICE HALL
Englewood Cliffs, New Jersey 07632

Library of Congress Cataloging-in-Publication Data

Myers, Stanley E.
RPG II, RPG III, and RPG 400, with business applications / Stanley E. Myers.
p. cm.
Includes index.
ISBN 0-13-783077-7
1. RPG (Computer program language 2. Business—Data processing. I. Title. II. Title: RPG 2, RPG 3, and RPG 400, with business applications. III. Title: RPG two, RPG three, and RPG 400, with business applications.
HF5548.5.R2M927 1991
005.2'42—dc20 90-26008
CIP

Acquisition Editor: Marcia Horton
Editorial supervision: Cyndy Lyle Rymer
Cover design: Wanda Lubelska
Prepress buyer: Linda Behrens
Manufacturing buyer: Patrice Fraccio
Page layout: Maria S. Piper/Carol Ann Hyland

Printed in the United States of America

10 9 8 7 6

ISBN 0-13-783077-7

Prentice-Hall International (UK) Limited, *London*
Prentice-Hall of Australia Pty. Limited, *Sydney*
Prentice-Hall Canada Inc., *Toronto*
Prentice-Hall Hispanoamericana, S.A., *Mexico*
Prentice-Hall of India Private Limited, *New Delhi*
Prentice-Hall of Japan, Inc., *Tokyo*
Simon & Schuster Asia Pte. Ltd., *Singapore*
Editora Prentice-Hall do Brasil, Ltda., *Rio de Janeiro*

To my lioness, Candy

Contents

Preface

This book is a complete text, not a reorganization of any manufacturer's language manuals, that addresses the following versions of the popular RPG language:

1. RPG II language syntax and coding methods are discussed and presented in detail. Batch processing methods common to all manufacturer's RPG compilers (i.e., Digital Equipment Company, Data General, Bull, Hewlett-Packard, Prime, and so forth) are introduced. Interactive processing, unique to IBM's System/36 (or 34), is discussed in detail.
2. The syntax of RPG III, an enhanced version of the RPG II language, is incorporated in separate chapters or included as end-of-chapter supplements. Interactive processing, logic, syntax, and data base structure, unique to IBM's System/38, is covered.
3. RPG/400, introduced by IBM in 1988, supplements RPG II and RPG III with additional enhancements. The logic and syntax related to interactive processing is introduced. Because the coding for the control of physical files, logical files, display files, printer files, and subfiles is identical to the System/38, what is explained for one relates to the other computer configuration.

This text also offers the following advantages:

1. Any RPG compiler (micro, mini, or mainframe) may be used to complete the assignments in this text. However, the material in the chapters that include syntax unique to IBM's System/36, System/38, or AS/400 would not be relevant to other computer environments and may be skipped as elected.
2. Students will be able to write, compile, debug, and execute RPG programs after completing Chapter 2.
3. Over one hundred examples of RPG II, RPG III, or RPG/400 computer-executed programs support the learning of the language. Each program is supplemented with line-by-line explanation and/or separate figures.
4. Over a thousand figures are included in the text to illustrate the logic and syntax related to the RPG II, RPG III, and RPG/400 programming language.
5. Separate chapters address the interactive System/36, System/38, and AS/400 environments. Within the restrictions of any classroom environment, the instructor may elect to include or skip any chapter or subject and still maintain a logical sequence for the course.

6. Chapter Summaries, Questions, Exercises, and Laboratory Assignments are included at the end of every chapter. Summaries highlight the new material introduced in the chapter. Questions are designed to aid in the immediate recall of chapter materials. Exercises require that RPG syntax be translated on coding forms. At least two laboratory assignments (some chapters have ten) that range in difficulty from the simple to the complex, enhance the learning of the RPG language.
7. Comprehensive coverage of the creation, loading, and maintenance of Sequential, Indexed-Sequential, Direct, Addrout, and database files is convienently presented in separate chapters.
8. Emphasis is placed on the importance of data and its effect on program execution and final results.
9. The logic, syntax, and processing of database files, unique to IBM's System/38 and AS/400, is detailed separately in Chapters 19 through 24.
10. Structured RPG programming is emphasized throughout the book in order to stress the importance of writing programs that may be easily maintained and debugged. RPG structured operations are used in many of the program examples.

The text follows the sequence of subject matter outlined in the following chapters.

In order to familiarize the students to the world of the microcomputer, minicomputer, and mainframe environments, Chapter 1 introduces elementary computer concepts. The basic configuration of a computer system, batch and interactive, input and output devices, and media, is explained. An example RPG (II, III, or 400) source program and resultant output is illustrated. A lab assignment requires the student to enter, compile, and debug, execute a complete RPG program; build a data file and a procedure to control program execution.

Chapter 2 leaves the total computer environment and introduces specifics about the RPG (II, III, and 400) programming language. The sequence of steps followed for the completion of an RPG source program, which includes analysis of the problem, design of input and output requirements, formatting, coding, recording, compilation, debugging, and program execution, is explained. Completion of this chapter will provide the student with enough knowledge to write his or her first RPG program.

Chapter 3 further develops the student's knowledge of the RPG language syntax and coding procedures with an introduction to report headings. Also presented is the editing of numeric fields by edit codes and edit words. At this level, the student will be able to write RPG programs that generate reports which do not require calculations, subtotals, or totals. The function of the *First Page (1P)* and *Overflow Indicators (OA–OG* and *OV)* is discussed.

RPG operations that support the arithmetic functions addition, subtraction, multiplication, division, and square root are introduced in Chapter 4. The syntax and function of other special purpose operations, including *MVR, Z-ADD, Z-SUB, MOVE, MOVEL, SETON, SETOF,* and *DEFN* are also presented. In addition, the use of *Resulting, Field,* and *Last Record indicators (LR)* is detailed in this chapter.

Chapter 5 introduces the RPG syntax related to decision making, branching, and looping control within a program. Use of the *COMP (Compare)* operation for relational testing (equal to, greater than, or less than) is explained. Also presented is the logic and syntax of the *GOTO* operation that controls branching and looping routines. The function of the RPG III/400 *CABxx (Compare and Branch)* operation is shown.

Structured RPG III/400 operations *IF/ELSE, DO, DOW (DO While),* and *DOU (DO Until)* are introduced in Chapter 6. Use of these operations eliminates or reduces the need for the GOTO operation and the indicators generally required to logically condition calculation instructions.

Chapter 7 introduces the syntax for the *EXCPT (Except)* operation and *internal subroutines*. Both of these RPG features support structured programming procedures. Enhancements included in RPG III/400 for the support of these operations is separately discussed.

The structure and processing of *multiple record files*, common to the non-database environment, are discussed in Chapter 8. In addition, the function and syntax of *Data Structures* is explained.

Chapter 9 introduces the RPG syntax and procedures unique to the processing of reports that require subtotals. The logic and use of *Control Level Indicators* (L1–L9) in calculation and output instructions is detailed.

Table concepts and processing are introduced in Chapter 10. Emphasis is placed on methods of loading table data in the program cycle, alternative ways of organizing table data, and methods of processing.

Chapter 11 details the logic, syntax, and processing of *arrays*. Methods of loading arrays in the program cycle, organization of array data, and the editing of arrays on output are discussed. Also explained is array *LOKUP* with and without an index, simulated multidimensional array processing, and a binary search technique. The function and syntax of the *OCUR* operation, supported by RPG III/400, is shown.

Data validation procedures in a batch environment are introduced in Chapter 12. The RPG syntax and processing methods to control standard validity checks of input data is detailed in individual program examples.

Chapter 13 introduces basic disk file concepts and the creation and loading of *sequentially organized* disk files. Example programs that illustrate the syntax for adding records to an existing sequential disk file and how they are consecutively processed support the chapter material. The *packing* of numeric fields and *blocking* of records are explained.

Sequential file maintenance including inquiry, update, and record deletion are introduced in Chapter 14. *Matching Records, Chaining,* and the *READ,* operation are the three RPG methods discussed for the control of maintenance processing. Alternative methods for processing a sequential file between record limits is also presented.

Chapter 15 introduces the RPG syntax and procedures related to the creation, loading, and consecutive processing of *Indexed-Sequential* disk files. Two methods of processing this file organization type between key value *limits* are discussed.

The RPG syntax and procedures for file addition, inquiry, update, record deletion, and reorganization of Indexed-Sequential files are explained in Chapter 16. Two methods for the deletion of records are presented. Procedures for the building of *alternative* indexes is illustrated.

Chapter 17 presents the structure, creation, loading, and processing of *Direct Files*. All of the maintenance functions supported by this file organization type, including inquiry, update, and deletion, are explained and detailed in separate program examples. The RPG syntax and processing of *Addrout Files,* which are created from the output of a sort utility, are also discussed.

Chapter 18 addresses only the syntax for the creation of CRT screens and the interactive RPG II programs to process them in the IBM System/36 (and 34) environment(s). Throughout the chapter, modifications are made to an introductory interactive RPG "adds" program to support inquiry, update, and deletion processing.

Chapters related to the IBM System/38 and AS/400 environments begin with Chapter 19. The logic and structure of the *database* supported on those systems are discussed. Syntax for the creation of *keyed and non-keyed Physical Files* is explained.

Chapter 20 introduces the syntax unique to the creation of *Display Files* supported by the IBM System/38 and AS/400.

The RPG III/400 syntax and procedures for the processing of *Physical and Display Files* is explained in Chapter 21. Effective use of the RPG III/400 structured operations is shown in this chapter.

Chapter 22 introduces the processing logic and syntax related to *Logical Files*. The difference between the processing of *Nonjoin* and *Join Logical Files* is explained.

Chapter 23 details the syntax and processing logic associated with *Printer Files* unique to the software included with the System/38 and AS/400.

The processing logic and syntax related to *Subfiles* is explained in Chapter 24. Three program examples show how *Subfiles* may be used for data entry, inquiry, and update file maintenance.

TEACHING TIPS

This book may be used in any RPG course, at any level, and with any hardware environment. Because RPG is used as the primary high-level language on IBM minicomputers, the text places the most emphasis on that environment. However, RPG II is generic and what is learned for the IBM environment relates to the non-IBM. Note, however, that Chapter 18 addresses only the System/36 (or 34) environment(s) whereas Chapters 19–24 are written strictly for the IBM System/38 and AS/400. Consequently, the contents would not be applicable to different IBM or other manufacturer's mainframe or minicomputer hardware.

At the option of the instructor, the sequence of chapters, or those discussed, may depend on the background of the students or instructor. The suggested sequence for students in a two semester system with no previous computer course and/or work experience is to begin with Chapter 1 and continue through Chapter 9. Then, a second semester course would continue with Chapter 10 through 17.

Ideally every chapter in the book should be discussed. However, within time limitations this may not always be practical or possible. The decision to assign Chapter 18 and Chapters 19–24 may depend on the hardware used and/or course objectives. If students are entering, compiling, debugging, and executing an RPG program on an IBM System/36 (or 34), Chapter 18 should be studied and laboratory work assigned. On the other hand, if the student is learning in either the System/38 or AS/400 environment, study of Chapters 19 through 24 is a must.

For the professional RPG programmer who has no or little experience in the RPG III/400 environment, this book provides an excellent reference source. Not only is the syntax discussed, but detailed program examples that put all of the elements of database processing on the System/38 and AS/400 together. The syntax and processing logic of *Physical Files, Logical Files, Display Files, Printer Files, and Subfiles* is discussed. This text goes beyond the syntax of those unique file types and shows by many program examples how RPG controls the processing of each.

The following learning tools are available to users of this textbook:

1. An Instructor's Manual, which includes the answers to *all* questions, exercises, and laboratory assignments. Also included in the manual are teaching tips for each laboratory assignment.

2. A test bank is included in the manual and available on diskette.
3. Transparency masters of key figures in the textbook.
4. A source program for the first laboratory assignment from every chapter is available on diskette.
5. Coordinated with this text is an *IBM PC compatible RPG/400 compiler* that may be purchased for a nominal amount. Site license agreements are also available with attractive educational discounts.

Acknowledgments

I want to give special thanks to my wife, Candy, who had the patience and understanding to tolerate me in the writing of this text and supplemental Instructor's Manual.

Every art piece that required the completion of a form was done by her. More than often she identified and corrected errors in my original manuscript. Because she is highly skilled in the RPG language and IBM's AS/400 and System/38 computers, Candy's technical contributions to this text were invaluable.

The production of any text ultimately determines whether it results in a quality finished product. Without Prentice Hall's production editor, Cyndy Rymer, the job of revising, correcting, and coordinating could have been a difficult task. Her friendly, cooperative attitude and experience in working with frustrated authors made the activities of converting the manuscript into a textbook almost a pleasure.

In addition, Maria Piper and Carol Hyland from Prentice Hall's College Art Department deserve recognition. The readers of this book will appreciate how carefully they placed the figures as close as possible to the referencing text. With the hundreds of art pieces included it was a challenging task.

I also want to thank Marcia Horton, editor in chief, for having continued confidence in my writing skills.

Special recognition goes to the students at Norwalk State Technical College who classroom-tested the original manuscript over the last two years. Their comments and identification of topics that were not clearly presented have resulted in a book that will prove to be an excellent text and professional reference source.

I want to thank IBM for the initial development of the RPG computer language and their continued support and enhancements.

Personal thanks to each one of you.

Stan

RPG II, RPG III, AND RPG/400 WITH BUSINESS APPLICATIONS

chapter 1
The Data Processing Environment

Today, in most business and commercial establishments data is recorded, stored, and processed by computers. With the introduction of low-cost systems, such as the personal computer, almost all businesses have come to use computers to some extent. The typical environment is usually one or a combination of the following:

Nonprogramming

Use of preprogrammed software packages for all data processing applications and functions.

Programming

Design, writing, testing, and installation of user-developed application programs with a system-supported language, such as RPG II, RPG III, and RPG/400.

Maintenance of data bases and generation of reports by executing the user-developed software.

This book concentrates on the programming environment in which programs and systems are developed in the RPG II, RPG III, and RPG/400 languages.

THE PROGRAMMING AND SYSTEMS ENVIRONMENT

Nonmanagement professionals in the programming and systems environment are systems analysts, systems programmers, application programmers, computer operators, and data entry personnel. Management titles include manager of information services (MIS), data processing manager, manager of operations, project manager, and so forth.

In a large company the job responsibilities are usually clearly defined, and individuals perform duties within their responsibility center. On the other hand, medium and, especially, small companies often assign more than one function to employees. It is not uncommon to combine the systems programmer, analyst, and application programmer into one responsibility. Furthermore, on the low end of the spectrum, very small firms may not employ a systems or programming staff but contract with a consulting company instead.

DUTIES OF THE NONMANAGEMENT DATA PROCESSING PROFESSIONALS

Systems programmer is a job classification found in large user companies and in companies that manufacture hardware and vendor software. The primary function of a systems programmer is to configure the operating system to meet the specific needs of the manufacturer or vendor. This usually includes the structuring of present and future hardware and software configuration for optimum performance and flexibility.

Specific functions of a systems programmer include system software design, generation, and maintenance. File allocations and assignments are also typical job responbilities of this professional group.

Systems analysts are concerned with the design, development, and installation of software for an end user. They may or may not be programmers, but they are experienced in one or more application areas such as accounting, manufacturing, credit, banking, and the like. Because of an expertise in select fields, they work directly with the users and identify and translate their needs into program specifications that are submitted to the *application programmer*.

From the specifications developed by the systems analyst, application programmers write, test, and maintain programs required by users. A common function of this group is *maintenance programming*, which includes the modification of existing programs. This requires that supporting documentation must be developed for any program written and installed.

The primary objective of this textbook is to present the syntax and structure of the RPG II, RPG III, and RPG/400 language as a tool for the application programmer.

As was mentioned before, in the medium or small company, the functions of the systems analyst and application programmer are often integrated into one position that is commonly referred to as a *programmer/analyst*.

Again, the size of the firm will dictate how the computer operations staff is organized. In large companies, this department is often highly structured and mutually exclusive of the systems and the programming departments. Operations is responsible for job scheduling, throughput, timely output, and data base security. Knowing when and what disk pack or tape to mount, making paper changes, and following recovery procedures are some of the activities performed by operations. In small companies, this function is usually less formal and may be performed as an additional duty by an office worker trained as an operator.

The very important data entry function may be controlled in several ways. It may be a separate department with its own manager, or it may be a subset of another data processing function. On the opposite end of the spectrum, it may be only another job for the office staff. In any case, the department or individuals performing this function have the responsibility of ensuring that the data entered into the system is validated and accurate.

ELEMENTS OF A COMPUTER SYSTEM

Whether a computer system is a mainframe such as the IBM 4300 or 3000 series; a mini such as the IBM System 36, System 38, and AS/400; or a micro such as the IBM PC, Apple MacIntosh, or Texas Instruments PC it will consist of three basic hardware components: an input device(s), a central processing unit (CPU), and an output device(s).

Figure 1-1 shows a schematic of a computer installation supported by a CRT (cathode ray terminal), CPU, and line printer. Other hardware devices, such as

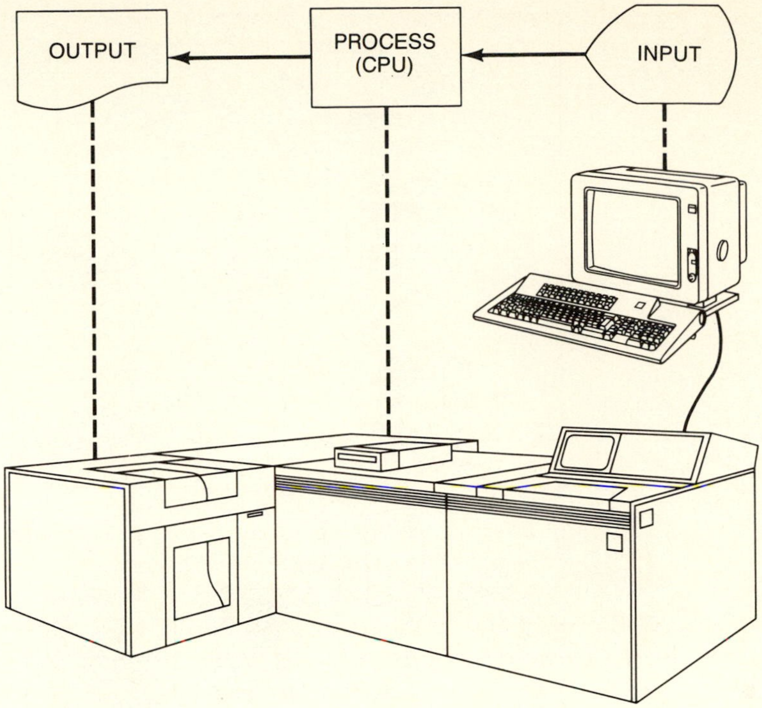

Figure 1-1 Hardware elements of a computer installation.

disk drives, diskette drives, and tape drives, support both input and output requirements.

Input/Output (I/O) Devices and Control

In addition to the I/O devices shown in Figure 1-1, others are identified in Figure 1-2. Notice that the CRT, diskette, disk, tape, and other devices may be used for both input and output (I/O).

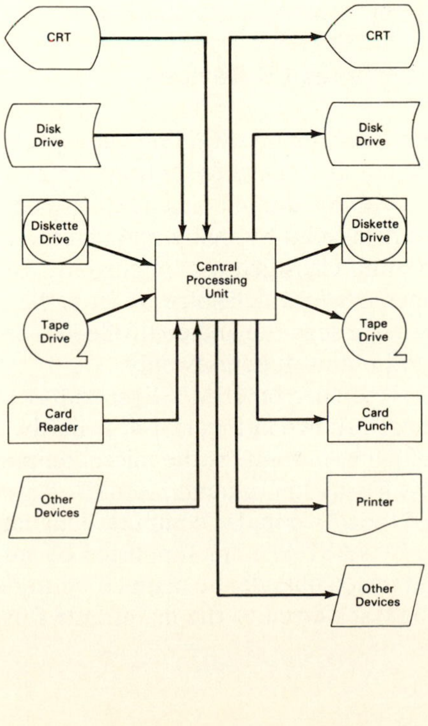

Figure 1-2 Input/output hardware devices.

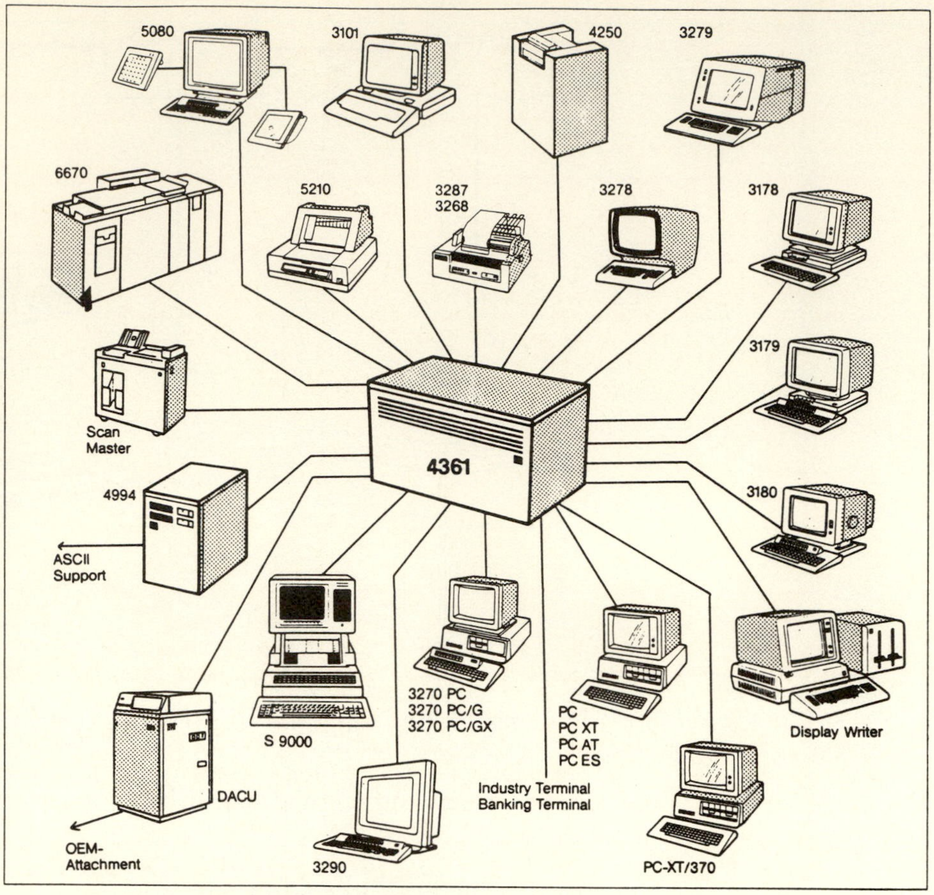

Figure 1-3 IBM's 4361 central processing unit shown with some of the available devices attached.

In Figure 1-3 some of the symbols from Figure 1-2 are translated into actual hardware units supported by IBM's popular 4361 computer system. Depending on the individual configuration, a mix of hundreds of input and output devices may be controlled by this system at the same time.

Role of Terminals (CRTs) as I/O Devices

An I/O device that has been important in the widespread use of computers is the CRT terminal, which may be connected to the central processing unit remotely by telephone lines or, within a limited distance, may be "hard-wired" directly to the CPU. Terminals are offered by many manufacturers in a variety of designs and features and are often classified as "intelligent" or "dumb." An intelligent terminal has limited memory to which software from the computer may be "downloaded" and processed in a separate and controlled environment. Dumb terminals are limited to input and output functions only.

A terminal that is popular on IBM's System/34s, 36s, and 38s, is the 5251 display unit and keyboard shown in Figure 1-4. A hardware unit that is being used extensively as an intelligent terminal is the microcomputer (IBM PC, COMPAC, Leading Edge, Tandy, Texas Instruments, Zenith, Xerox, and so forth).

Because most of today's popular computer languages (e.g., RPG, COBOL, FORTRAN, BASIC, C, PASCAL) are supported by microcomputers, programs may be developed and tested outside the main computer environment. Completed programs may then be transferred to the mainframe for production. Another ad-

Figure 1-4 IBM 5251 display unit and keyboard.

vantage of microcomputers is that many of the popular software packages (e.g., LOTUS 1,2,3, dBase III+, and Word Perfect) are supported only by microcomputers and are not available in a minicomputer or mainframe version.

Figure 1-5 shows an IBM PC model with two double-sided disk drives. This is only one of many configurations. Many of the hardware units from Figure 1-2 are supported by microcomputers.

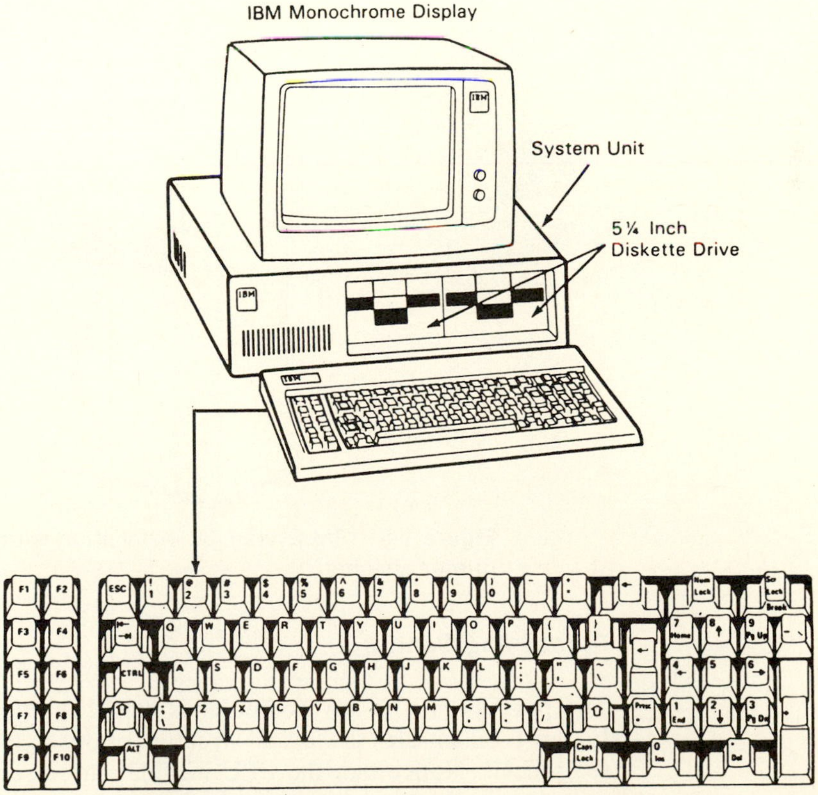

Figure 1-5 IBM PC configuration and keyboard.

Interactive Systems

Today's micro, mini, or mainframe computer systems support both *batch* and *interactive* processing. *Batch processing* refers to the submitting of jobs in batches and waiting until the operating system completes them. In this mode, the user has little or no control over processing.

After operating systems became more sophisticated, multiprocessing, timesharing, and multiprogramming environments could be supported—which led to *interactive processing* methods that allow the user to communicate directly with the computer instead of waiting for a job to finish, as is required in a batch environment.

One popular configuration of an interactive system is the IBM System/36 shown in Figure 1-6. Notice that the central processing unit supports four CRT terminals and a printer. Each terminal may be simultaneously used to access the same or different programs, data files, and other software, transparent to other users. The number of terminals or other hardware units that may be interfaced with any system is determined by the manufacturer of the computer hardware.

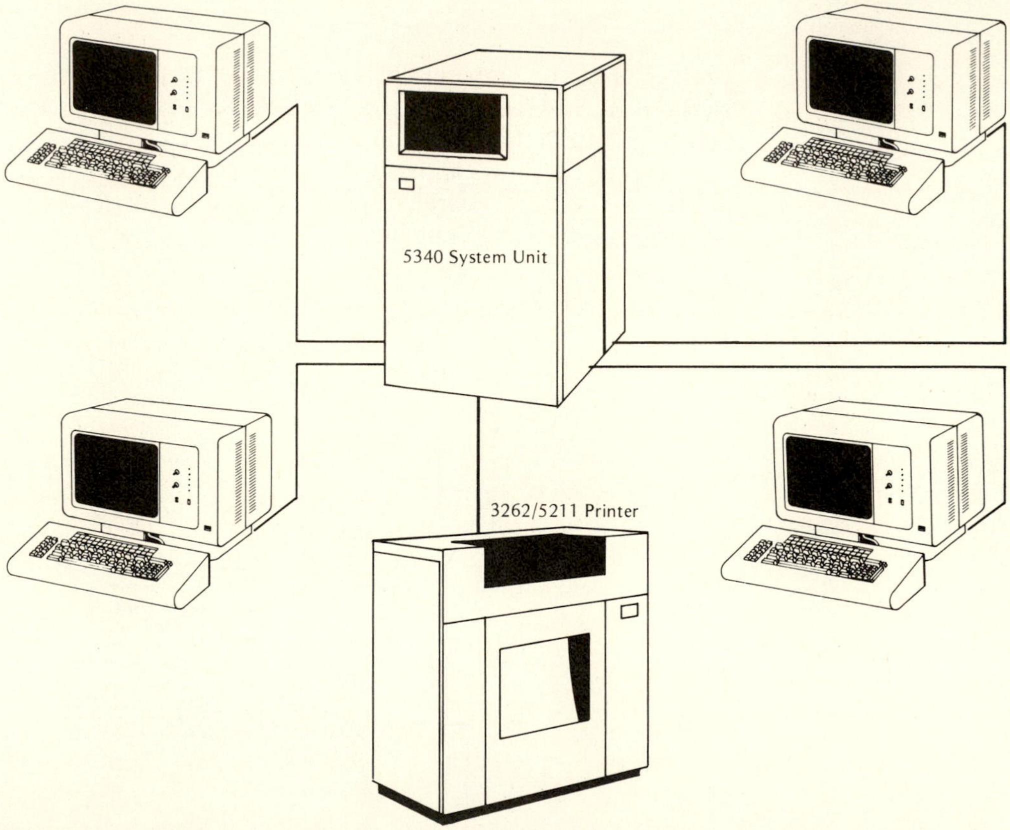

Figure 1-6 IBM System/36 installation with four terminals and a printer attached.

Processing Control

The process unit of any computer is called the central processing unit (CPU). Figure 1-7 illustrates the logical structure of this unit with input and output control referenced. Notice that the CPU includes three sections: memory, control, and arithmetic, which are discussed in the following paragraphs.

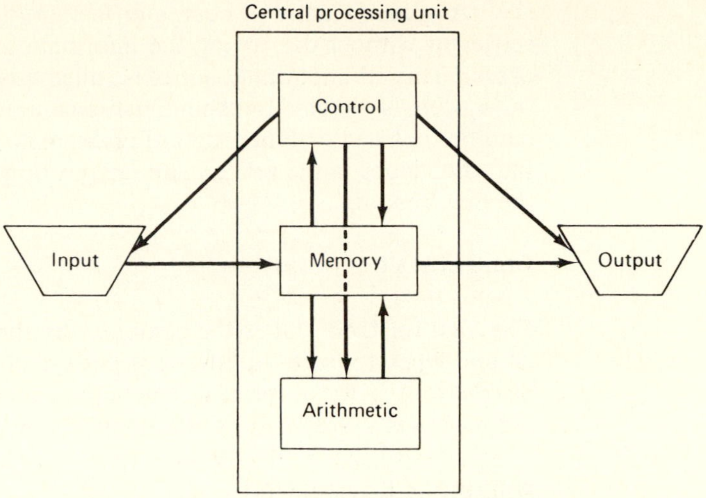

Figure 1-7 Components of a computer system.

Memory

The memory of early computers consisted of ferromagnetic cores that were expensive to produce or supplement. Today, memory is provided by microchips, which require less physical room and are relatively inexpensive. For example, an IBM PC with a 512K CPU is a fraction of the size and cost of an IBM 370 with the same storage.* This comparison does not imply that the PC has the same computer power as some larger machines; it is only an example of the technical progress made in real memory.

A 256K memory board for an IBM PC (or compatible) is shown in Figure 1-8. Notice that each of the rectangular elements provides 16K of storage.

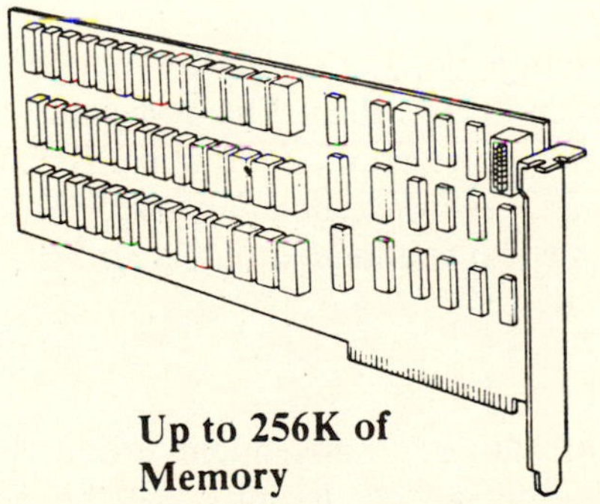

Figure 1-8 256K memory board for IBM PC (or compatible).

Memory supports two basic functions. First, when a system is IPLed (booted), system-supplied instructions are stored in memory to perform and control all processing functions. User-supplied instructions (program) are also stored in the CPU and are executed to perform some required task. Program instructions remain in storage until they are written over or the computer is turned off.

The second function of memory is to store data so it may be processed by a set of program instructions that have been previously stored. For example, data records are read one at a time into memory from some input device, stored, processed, and then output.

* K is an industry term that identifies memory capacity in bytes; 1K represents 1024 bytes. Hence, 512K is a multiple (512 × 1024), or 524,288 bytes. Memory capacities of non-microcomputer environments are often stated in megabytes (millions of bytes).

A unique feature of computer memory is that instructions and data may be retrieved without destroying the information stored at the related location (address). This all-important control is called *nondestructive readout process*. When the system is directed by the instructions, however, the values in the storage area may be replaced with new data. For example, when records are read from a data file, the values in the related storage positions are replaced with the values from the new record.

Control Unit

The Control Unit "takes the computer by the hand" and instructs it on what to do and when to do it. All the steps performed must be translated into executable instructions. After a set of instructions, called a *program*, is read into memory, the program is executed by the Control Unit.

Arithmetic/Logical Unit

Arithmetic functions and logical decisions are performed by this unit. When instructions demand computations or a decision, data stored in memory is transmitted to this unit where calculations and logical decision-making processes are performed. After a result has been determined, the value is transferred to memory and stored in a predetermined storage position. The phenomenal processing speeds of CPUs, which range from milliseconds (thousandths of a second) to picoseconds (trillionths of a second), have made repetitive and complex problem solving both practical and affordable.

A summary explanation of the concepts we have discussed should provide an insight into the control processes involved. As previously mentioned, the brains of any computer is the control unit, which provides the control to search, locate, and collect instructions and/or data that are stored in memory. The arithmetic unit performs any arithmetic or logic functions and transfers results back to the control unit.

Individual storage positions are referenced by addresses. A storage address may contain data or instructions. The computer distinguishes between types of information by a set of program instructions. Because instructions are stored and processed by computers in machine language (object code), high-level languages have been developed to enable computers to be a useful tool.

Output

After the input of data and subsequent processing, the results must be made available to an output device. Results may be printed, stored magnetically on disk, diskette, or tape or to any other output supported device.

COMPUTER LANGUAGES

As was mentioned earlier, the computer understands only a machine language that consists of only two "words": 1 and 0. A combination of these words represents an instruction. If programs were written at that level, instructions similar to 01011010000100000000000011000 would have to be formatted and would obviously be so difficult that computer use would be impossible for the average person to master.

The difficulty of writing computer programs in machine language encouraged users to find a simpler and more efficient way of using the computer's potential.

High-level languages such as ALGOL, APL, BAL, BASIC, C, COBOL, FORTRAN, PL–1, PASCAL, and RPG have been developed to provide an easier communication link between the user and the computer. These computer languages enable individuals to write programs in a form they understood. Now the computer, through a software package called a *compiler*, could translate a symbolic language such as RPG into the required machine language (in a format of 1s and 0s).

This book presents the syntax and structure of a widely used business programming language known by its memonic name RPG, an abbreviation for *Report Program Generator*.

BACKGROUND AND DEVELOPMENT OF RPG

Before the development of RPG, several computer languages were (and still are) popular, including FORTRAN and BAL. Because FORTRAN is algebraically structured and BAL only a step up from machine language, users in the business environment often found them difficult to use. In addition, other shortcomings, such as weak file control and difficult maintenance, led to the development of a computer language better suited to the business world.

In the early 1960s RPG was developed by IBM and has been continually improved into a powerful and versatile high-level computer language. The first major enhancement was RPG II, which included many new features not in RPG I—for example, array processing, interactive screen processing, and so forth.

IBM's last major changes to the compiler resulted in RPG/400, which now supports many of the features found in BASIC, FORTRAN, and COBOL. Structured operations including DO, DOU (do until), DOW (do while), and IF/ELSE are now supported. These recent changes have made RPG/400 (at the option of the programmer) less a *problem-oriented* language and more a *procedure-oriented* language (e.g., COBOL). All the previous features included in RPG II are fully supported by RPG/400. *Any reference to RPG II in this book also refers to RPG/400 unless otherwise stated.*

Most of the popular computer systems (including IBM PC compatible microcomputers) support an RPG II compiler. However, only IBM's AS/400 and System/38 support all the recent developments that are included in RPG III and RPG/400. Fortunately, however, all the other software manufacturers have followed IBM's standards for RPG II, which has resulted in the language being *machine-independent*.

WHAT DOES AN RPG PROGRAM LOOK LIKE?

Because RPG is a *column-oriented* (not free-form) programming language, standardized coding forms are used to write a program's syntax. The filled-in forms for an example program that reads, processes, and prints record values are illustrated in Figure 1-9.

An examination of the forms shown in Figure 1-9 shows the following features:

1. Different types of forms are used to define each logical section of an RPG program. A special form is provided for control options, file descriptions, input record descriptions, and output record descriptions. Other types of forms are introduced in subsequent chapters.

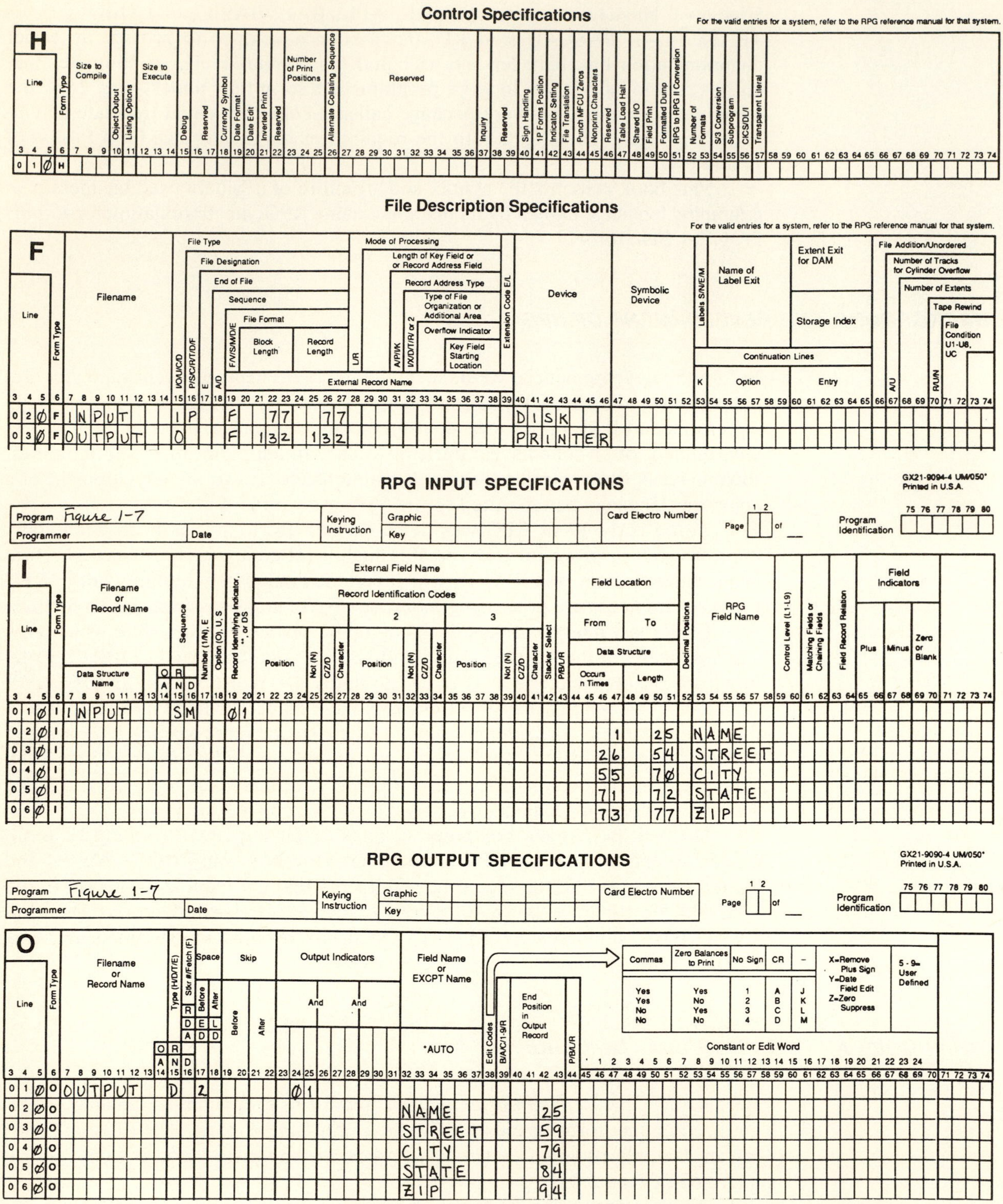

Figure 1-9 Filled-in coding forms for RPG example program.

2. The program's statements (instructions) must be arranged in an H, F, I, O *compilation order*.
3. Each type of form includes special-purpose fields that are not used in every program. For example, many of the fields in the Control Speci-

fications form refer to punch card systems and are no longer used in today's CRT/disk-controlled environment, but most of the fields included in the other types of forms are used when a processing function requires that they be specified.

The completed forms are referenced to enter and store the instructions (the RPG program) onto a storage media such as disk, tape, diskette, or punch cards. Today, a source program code is entered by a *text editor*, which may be unique to a computer's software, or by one of the popular word processing packages. Individual computer systems determine the method used to enter source code.

Source Listing

A copy of the source listing of the example program after it has been loaded on a storage media (disk in this example) and *compiled* is illustrated in Figure 1-10. Notice that, with the exception of the numbers across the top, no column references are included in the source listing.

```
... ... 1 ... ... 2 ... ... 3 ... ... 4 ... ... 5 ... ... 6 ... ... 7 ...
0001 H                                                                CH1P1
0002 FINPUT   IP  F  77  77           DISK                            CH1P1
0003 FOUTPUT  O   F 132 132           PRINTER                         CH1P1
0004 IINPUT   SM  01                                                  CH1P1
0005 I                                       1  25 NAME               CH1P1
0006 I                                      26  54 STREET             CH1P1
0007 I                                      55  70 CITY               CH1P1
0008 I                                      71  72 STATE              CH1P1
0009 I                                      73  77 ZIP                CH1P1
0010 OOUTPUT  D 2      01                                             CH1P1
0011 O                       NAME      25                             CH1P1
0012 O                       STREET    59                             CH1P1
0013 O                       CITY      79                             CH1P1
0014 O                       STATE     84                             CH1P1
0015 O                       ZIP       94                             CH1P1
```

Figure 1-10 Source listing of example RPG program.

After the program has been successfully compiled, an *object program* (machine language format) is generated that is automatically stored on disk. To execute the object program, its name must be included in a procedure (which includes control statements to reference the input file) that is executed to process the input data file and generate the printed report.

Relationship of Data File, Program, and Printed Report

The relationship of the data file, object program, and printed report controlled by the *execution phase* of program development is detailed in Figure 1-11. The top section of the figure shows the records in a data file that is stored on disk. This file is to be processed, consecutively, by the RPG program to generate the report shown at the bottom of the figure. The data file had to be previously built by an RPG (or other computer language) program, a sort utility, or a data entry utility such as IBM's DFU (Data File Utility) software package.

Notice the area identified as *object program*. This is output member created from the successful compilation of the source program. There are now two members stored in a library: the original source program and the object program.

The third section shown in Figure 1-11 is the printed report generated by execution of the object program.

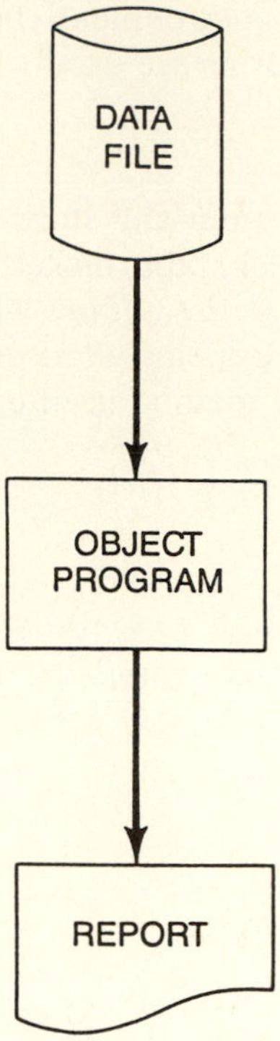

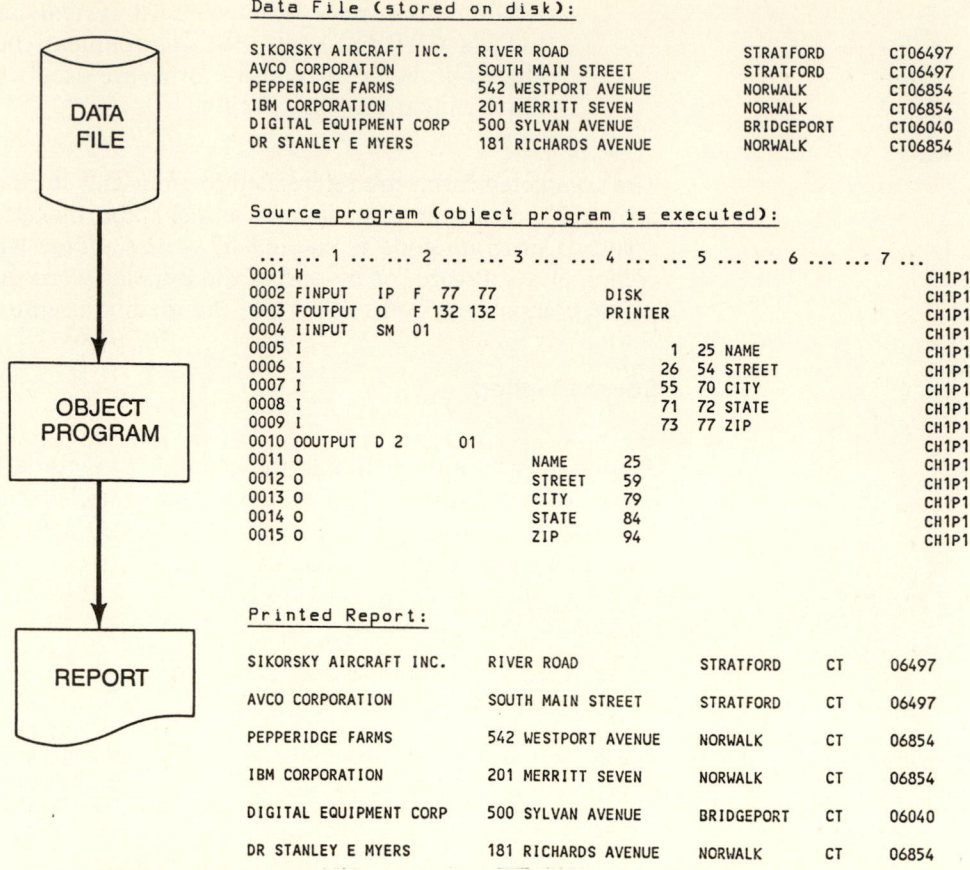

Data File (stored on disk):

```
SIKORSKY AIRCRAFT INC.   RIVER ROAD              STRATFORD     CT06497
AVCO CORPORATION         SOUTH MAIN STREET       STRATFORD     CT06497
PEPPERIDGE FARMS         542 WESTPORT AVENUE     NORWALK       CT06854
IBM CORPORATION          201 MERRITT SEVEN       NORWALK       CT06854
DIGITAL EQUIPMENT CORP   500 SYLVAN AVENUE       BRIDGEPORT    CT06040
DR STANLEY E MYERS       181 RICHARDS AVENUE     NORWALK       CT06854
```

Source program (object program is executed):

```
... ... 1 ... ... 2 ... ... 3 ... ... 4 ... ... 5 ... ... 6 ... ... 7 ...
0001 H                                                             CH1P1
0002 FINPUT    IP  F  77  77          DISK                         CH1P1
0003 FOUTPUT   O   F 132 132          PRINTER                      CH1P1
0004 IINPUT    SM  01                                              CH1P1
0005 I                                     1  25 NAME              CH1P1
0006 I                                    26  54 STREET            CH1P1
0007 I                                    55  70 CITY              CH1P1
0008 I                                    71  72 STATE             CH1P1
0009 I                                    73  77 ZIP               CH1P1
0010 OOUTPUT   D 2       01                                        CH1P1
0011 O                           NAME      25                      CH1P1
0012 O                           STREET    59                      CH1P1
0013 O                           CITY      79                      CH1P1
0014 O                           STATE     84                      CH1P1
0015 O                           ZIP       94                      CH1P1
```

Printed Report:

```
SIKORSKY AIRCRAFT INC.   RIVER ROAD            STRATFORD    CT    06497

AVCO CORPORATION         SOUTH MAIN STREET     STRATFORD    CT    06497

PEPPERIDGE FARMS         542 WESTPORT AVENUE   NORWALK      CT    06854

IBM CORPORATION          201 MERRITT SEVEN     NORWALK      CT    06854

DIGITAL EQUIPMENT CORP   500 SYLVAN AVENUE     BRIDGEPORT   CT    06040

DR STANLEY E MYERS       181 RICHARDS AVENUE   NORWALK      CT    06854
```

Figure 1-11 Relationship of the data file and generated report to example RPG program.

Procedure (or Run Unit)

A *procedure* (also called *run unit*), which includes job control (JCL, OCL, or CL) statements unique to each operating system, is created. Depending on the storage media available, the statements are in a source code format on disk, diskette, tape, or punch cards. Included in the procedure (run unit) is the object program's name. *Note that procedures are not compiled and are executed as source code.*

Because the structure of procedures and the format of control statements are unique to each computer system, a detailed explanation is not presented here. In a disk operating system, source programs, object programs, and procedures are stored on disk in an area allocated as the system, or user, *library*.

To understand the operation of the equipment in the student's environment, compilation, and execution procedures, it is recommended that Laboratory Assignments 1–1 and 1–2 be completed before continuing to the next chapter.

QUESTIONS

1-1. Name five job titles that may be found in a large data processing installation.

1-2. Explain the function of each job classification named in your answer to Question 1.

1-3. Name three basic elements of a computer system.

1-4. What is the function of each element?

1-5. Name five input devices.

1-6. Name five output devices.

1-7. What devices may be used for both input and output?

1-8. What input/output device has made interactive programming possible?

1-9. Explain the data entry function. Name three methods for the control of this function.

1-10. Name another term for the processing unit of a computer.

1-11. Name the logical parts of the unit to which Question 8 refers. In your own words explain each part's function.

1-12. How is the size of a computer's memory indicated?

1-13. A K of memory represents how many bytes?

1-14. How is 64,000 bytes of memory expressed?

1-15. What is the feature of a computer's memory that does not destroy a value in a storage position after it is accessed?

1-16. What are milliseconds? Picoseconds? How are these terms related to computers?

1-17. What are some of the functions the arithmetic unit of the processor performs?

1-18. Name five popular computer languages. Which are the most commonly used in the business environment?

1-19. What is a source program? Who writes it?

1-20. Name three mediums on which source program code may be stored.

1-21. Name three methods of entering and storing a source code onto the storage mediums you identified in Question 20.

1-22. What is the function of a compiler?

1-23. What is an object program? In what language format is it stored?

1-24. Explain program execution. What is executed? What is processed?

1-25. RPG is an abbreviation for what words?

1-26. For what purpose are coding forms used in RPG programming?

1-27. Name the RPG coding forms introduced in this chapter. Explain the function of each form.

1-28. What is a procedure? What is included in a procedure?

1-29. Define control statements.

1-30. What is a library? What is stored in a library?

1-31. Define a batch system. An interactive system. What advantages does one have over the other?

LABORATORY ASSIGNMENTS

Laboratory Assignment 1–1: BUILDING AND LOADING A DATA FILE

You may have a microcomputer, CRT, key-to-disk, key-to-diskette, or key-to-tape (cassette) recorders on the system available for lab work. You must become familiar with the unit before you can record source programs, data, and control statements.

After the instructor gives you directions on use of the equipment, build a file and enter the following data according to the field locations indicated. Prove the accuracy of your entered data by printing a listing of the file with the copy utility supplied with the system's software. If there are errors in the data, the output generated by the program will be incorrect. Data entry is a critical function in any data processing environment.

```
Name of company   positions  1-25
Street address    positions 26-54
City              positions 55-70
State             positions 71-72
Zip               positions 73-77
```

Data You Are to Record:

Name of company	Street address	City	State	Zip
SIKORSKY AIRCRAFT INC	RIVER ROAD	STRATFORD	CT	06497
AVCO CORPORATION	SOUTH MAIN STREET	STRATFORD	CT	06497
PEPPERIDGE FARMS	542 WESTPORT AVE	NORWALK	CT	06854
IBM CORPORATION	201 MERRIT SEVEN	NORWALK	CT	06854
DIGITAL EQUIPMENT CORP	500 SYLVAN AVENUE	BRIDGEPORT	CT	06040
your name here	(............ your address here ....)			

Note: Related data for each item must begin in the first position of its related field. Hence, for the first record, SIKORSKY AIRCRAFT INC will be stored beginning in column 1; RIVER ROAD beginning in column 26; STRATFORD, beginning in column 55; CT, beginning in column 71; and 06497, beginning in column 73.

Laboratory Assignment 1–2: KEYING AN RPG PROGRAM

Following are the filled-in coding forms for an RPG program that will process the data file built and loaded in Assignment 1–1. Refer to the forms and enter the instructions line by line onto the storage media supplied with your computer system. Your instructor will advise you on the procedures that must be followed.

The starting position of each instruction (line) is identified on the first coding form line. If a CRT-supported system (text editor) is used to enter the statements, the page and line numbers may be omitted. Keying the instructions may begin in column 6 with the related form letter. The RPG compiler will automatically supply sequence numbers in the source listing generated during compilation. The statement numbers are referenced in the debugging process where errors are located and corrected.

Refer again to the source listing shown in Figure 1-10. The numbers to the left of each statement were generated by the compiler. Because page and line numbers were not keyed by the programmer when instructions were entered, they are not included. If they had been entered, they would appear to the left of the compiler-supplied sequence numbers.

Filled-in RPG program coding forms:

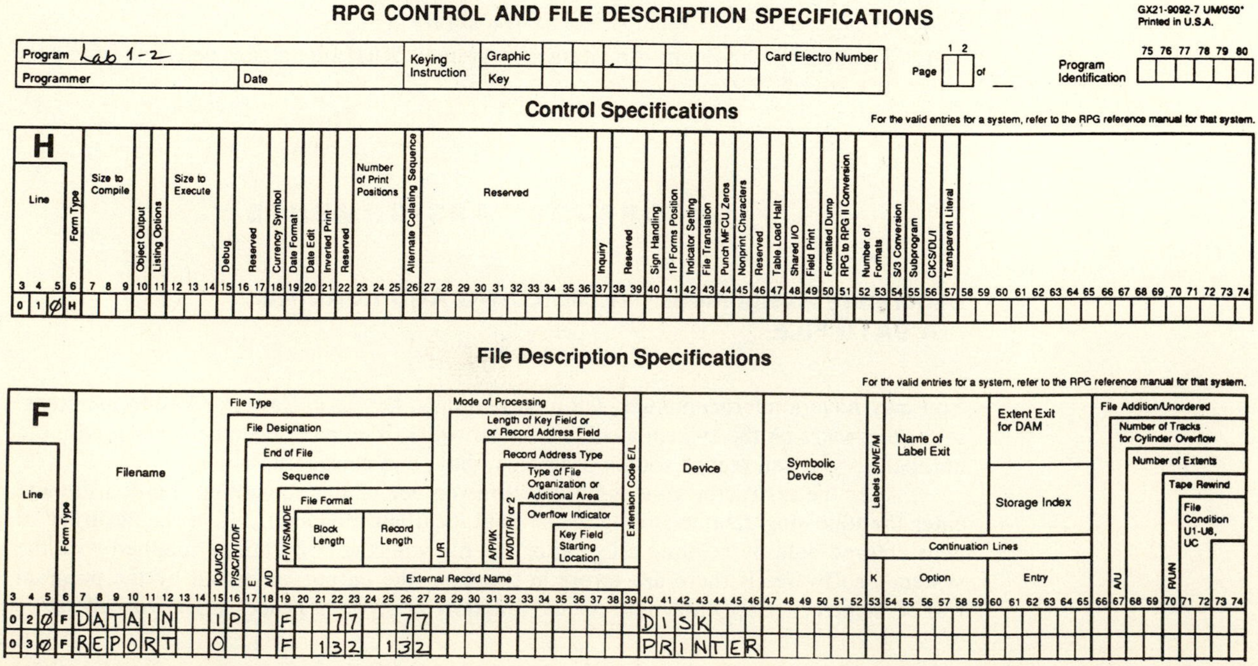

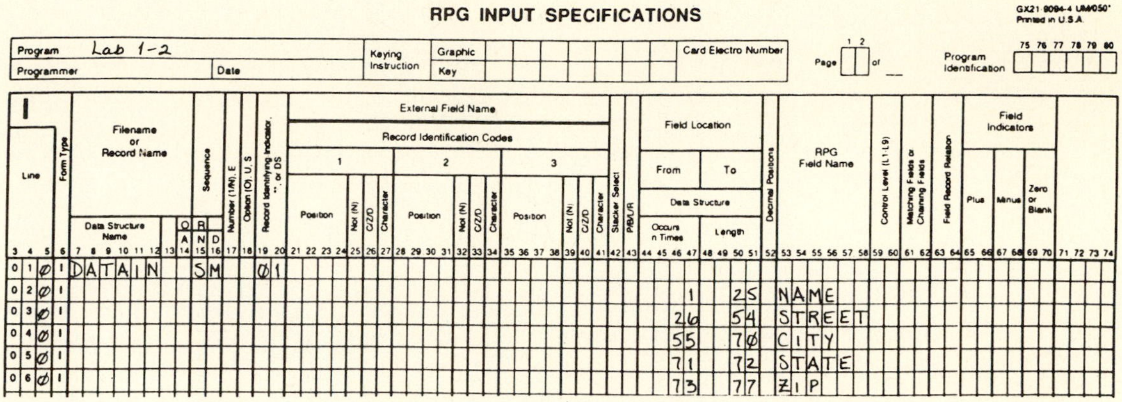

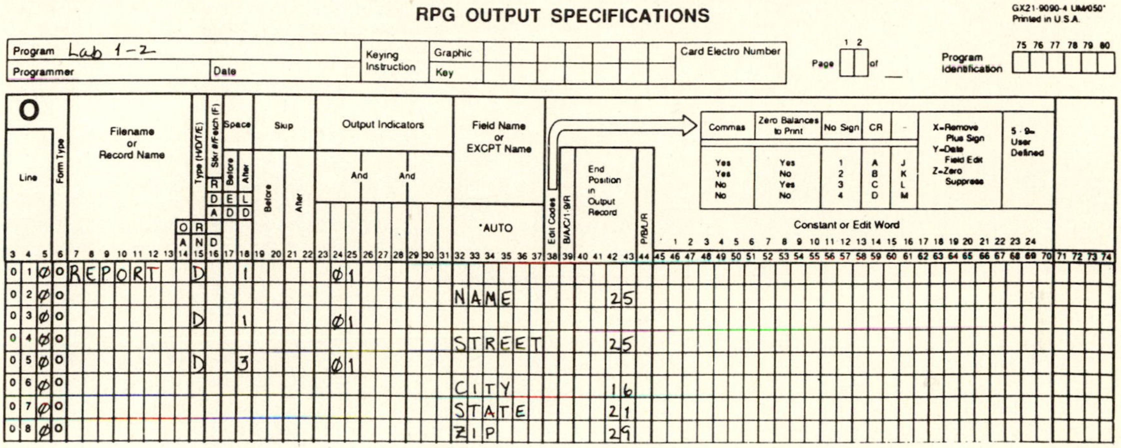

The completed program will include 17 instructions stored in a reserved disk area (your account) or on a diskette. After you have keyed the RPG program, your instructor will provide additional information for compilation, debugging, and execution procedures.

The completed lab assignment must include the following:

1. Copy of the data file you created in Laboratory Assignment 1.
2. Source program compilation listing (with no errors).
3. Printed report.

Your printed report must look like the following example:

```
SIKORSKY AIRCRAFT INC.
RIVER ROAD
STRATFORD            CT    06497

AVCO CORPORATION
SOUTH MAIN STREET
STRATFORD            CT    06497

PEPPERIDGE FARMS
542 WESTPORT AVENUE
NORWALK              CT    06854

IBM CORPORATION
201 MERRITT SEVEN
NORWALK              CT    06854

DIGITAL EQUIPMENT CORP
500 SYLVAN AVENUE
BRIDGEPORT           CT    06040

DR STANLEY E MYERS
181 RICHARDS AVENUE
NORWALK              CT    06854
```

chapter 2
Introduction to RPG Programming

PRELIMINARY PLANNING

Before an RPG source program can be written, preliminary planning steps must be completed. Specifically, initial planning should include the following:

1. Program specifications
2. The type and format of the data used for input
3. The design requirements of output
4. The processing logic for the program. Each of these steps is discussed in the following paragraphs.

Development of Program Specifications

In the business environment, programs are usually developed for an application requested by a user. Accounting, finance, sales, purchasing, inventory control, quality control, and engineering departments are typical users requesting program and system development. In a medium to large company, a systems analyst or programmer/analyst usually coordinates the user's needs with the data processing department. In a small firm, however, the experienced programmer may also serve as analyst. In any event, the analyst (or programmer) must translate the user's request into something tangible so that it may be understood by all interested parties.

The document used for this function is called *program specifications*. All the details and information needed to write an RPG application program should be included on the form. The test of well-written specifications is that the programmer does not constantly have to solicit additional information from the analyst or user.

Figure 2-1 illustrates the program specifications format used throughout this book. Data processing departments design their own formats on the basis of individual needs. Examination of the figure shows that the following information is included:

1. General Information. Space for application name, program, programmer, and relevant dates are provided.
2. Input requirements. Names of data files the program will access.
3. Processing requirements. Step-by-step details of what the program must do. Included may be formulas or mathematical procedures, data vali-

PROGRAM SPECIFICATIONS Page 1 of 1

Program Name GENERAL LEDGER REPORT Program-ID CH2P1 Written By S. Myers

Purpose Generate a report of GL accounts Approved By The Boss

Input files (directory names):

GLACTS (stored on disk)

Output files (directory names):

LISTING (printed on stock paper)

Processing Narrative:

Write an RPG program to print a listing of the accounts in the General Ledger of your company.

Input to the program:

An input file, GLACTS, is stored on disk which includes data records in the format shown in the attached layout form.

Processing:

Read the input file sequentially until end of file. For every record processed, print a detail line.

Output:

A printer spacing chart is attached which shows the format of the required report.

Note that the following are omitted from this report:

1. Headings
2. Page overflow control
3. Numeric fields and editing

After the program is compiled, executed, and the report printed, check the output for accuracy.

Figure 2-1 Specifications for General Ledger Report application program.

dation procedures, or general processing requirements of the application.

4. Output requirements. Type of output the program must generate. Included may be a printed report and/or data file loading or maintenance.

The specifications in Figure 2-1 show that a general ledger file (named GLACTS) stored on disk is to be processed sequentially for the purpose of generating a printed report.

DESIGN OF INPUT DATA

The planning and design of input data require an understanding of the general terms: file, record, field, column, byte, and bit. Figure 2-2 illustrates and explains four terms common to punch card terminology. Even though disks (or diskettes) have replaced punch cards as the storage media for data files, programs, and the like, the terminology specified in Figure 2-2 remains basically the same. For example, examine the disk terminology given in Figure 2-3 and notice that the terms

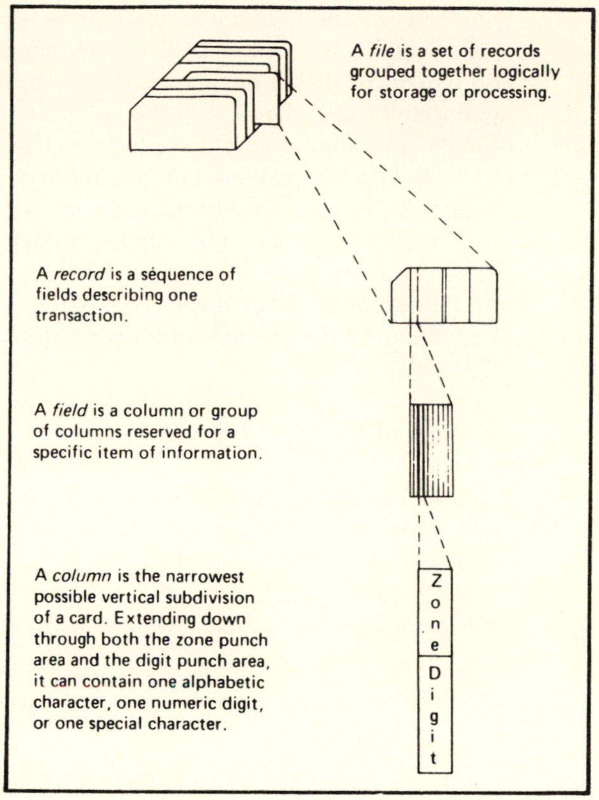

Figure 2-2 Punch card terminology.

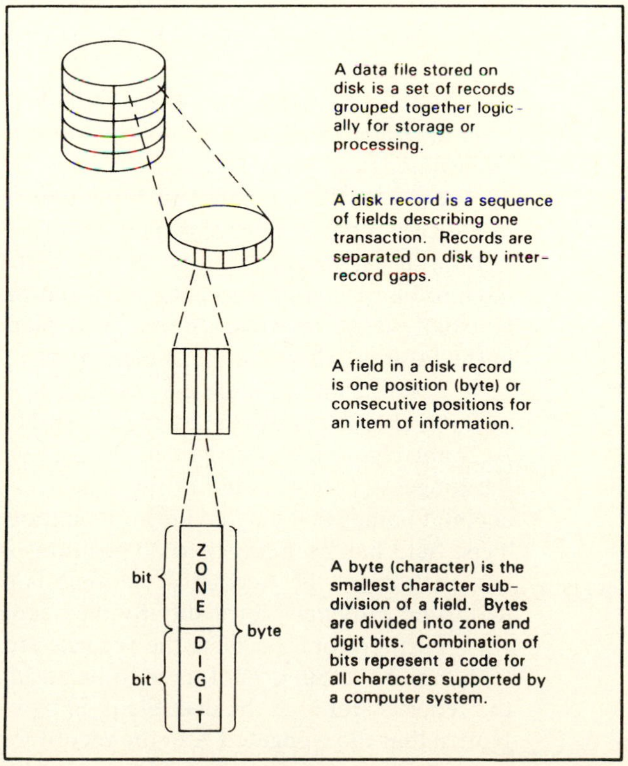

Figure 2-3 Terminology associated with data files stored on disk or diskette.

file, *record*, and *field* are identical to those used for the punch card environment. However, in lieu of tangible records, the data is recorded as magnetic impulses on a disk (or diskette) surface. The term *byte* (or character), instead of column, is normally associated with the smallest subdivision of records stored on disks. Similar to a card column, the byte is divided into *zone* and *digit bits*.

A data file may contain any number of records related to a common transaction. In fact, a file may include only one record—or thousands. Typical data files include information for employee payroll, merchandise inventory, sales transactions, checking or savings account activity, general ledger accounts, or any of the hundreds of other business activities. The maximum size of a data file may be limited by the computer hardware, including disk (diskette) storage and/or the CPU.

Design of Record Formats

Items to consider when designing data records are the required fields, their size and location in the record, the types of fields (whether numeric or alphanumeric), and record identification codes. This is an important step in the overall system design because a field size that is too small may cause high- or low-order truncation that would require extensive modifications to existing data files and related programs.

Data Record Documentation Forms

A tool that is useful when laying out the design of data recorded on punch cards is shown in Figure 2-4. Notice that six separate record designs may be formatted on the form. If the capacity of disk, diskette, or tape records is not greater than 80 bytes, the Multiple Record Layout Form (shown in Figure 2-4) may be used with files stored on that medium. The figure also shows the relationship of the source document information to the form and to the data records stored in a disk file.

In the example shown in Figure 2-4, the source information comes from the general ledger of a small proprietorship where the maximum size of each field is determined. After the sizes of Account Number, Account Name, and Account Type are established, they are formatted on the form by drawing a vertical line to indicate the boundaries of each field. A descriptive name for each field is then written in its related location. Notice that fields in the body of a record do not have to be placed next to each other but may be in any available positions. This is usually done, however, only if it is planned to add other fields to the format in the future. Otherwise, valuable storage space would be wasted in each record.

Refer again to Figure 2-4, and notice that the Account Number is formatted as three characters (bytes) by the assignment of columns 1 to 3 for this field. The Account Name has been given 27 bytes (columns 4 to 30), which is larger than the longest account name in the ledger. The analyst has provided for any new account names that may be longer than those presently used. Finally, the Account Type field has been assigned 20 positions (columns 31 to 50). Also, because the information for the Account Type field is not included in the General Ledger, it had to be provided—probably by the accounting department.

Furthermore, because the records are stored on disk, the unused positions (columns 51 to 80) do not have to be specified in the record format. The size of the records stored in the disk file is 50 bytes and not 80 as indicated by the form. Notice that the elongated X in the record format in Figure 2-4 indicates an unused area.

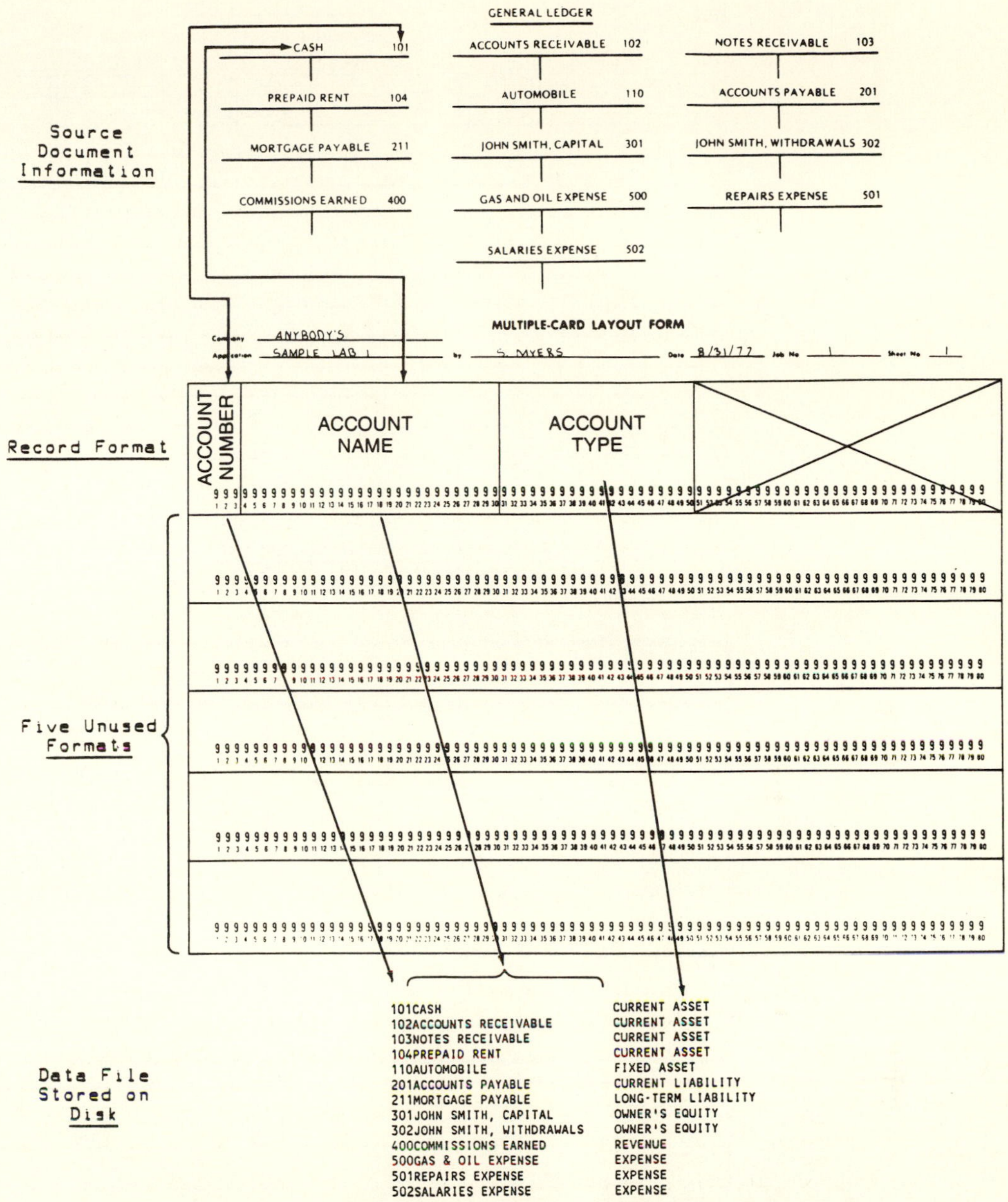

Figure 2-4 Relationship of source document information, record layout form, and data file records.

Depending on the disk hardware, record sizes are not limited to 80 bytes but may be formatted with lengths in the thousands of bytes. For example, the IBM System/36 computer supports disk-stored records up to 4096 bytes in length. Records input and output from a workstation (CRT) may be a maximum of 9999 bytes.

Other Record Documentation Forms

Figure 2-5 shows two other form designs for record layouts. The first type, the Proportional Record Layout Form, includes positions to support the format of a 1500-byte record. Areas are provided in the second type, identified as FILE DEFINITION, where the *attributes* of the data file, record formats, and fields may be

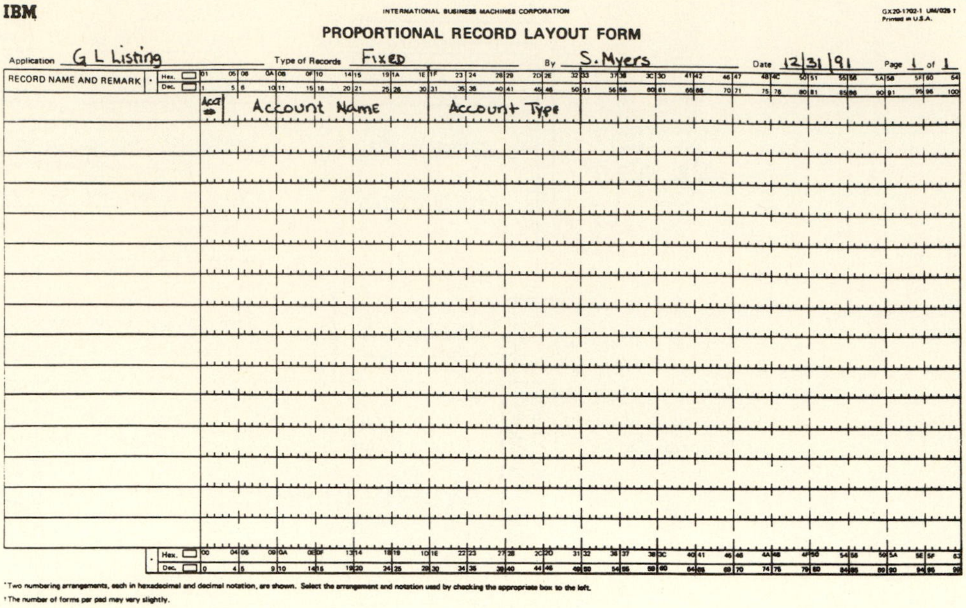

FILE DEFINITION			
SYSTEM Anybody's		DRAWN BY S, Myers	
FILE NAME GLACTS		DATE 12/31/92	REV. NO. 0
CREATED BY S. Myers		FILE TYPE Disk	
RECORD NAME None		KEY LENGTH none	
RECORDING MODE Fixed	ORGANIZATION Sequential	SEQUENCE Unordered	
RECORD SIZE 50 bytes	BLOCKING FACTOR 1	BLOCKSIZE 50 bytes	

FIELD DATA

FIELD NO.	FIELD NAME - DESCRIPTION	SIZE	CLASS C/P/Z/B	POSITION FROM	POSITION THRU	FORMAT/CONSTANT
1	Account Number	3	C	1	3	
2	Account Name	27	C	4	30	
3	Account Type	20	C	31	50	

Figure 2-5 Proportional Record Layout Form and File Definition Form.

specified. Because additional pages may be included as needed, the size of a record format on this type of form is unlimited. The new terms included on this form will be discussed when disk file processing is introduced in Chapter 13.

Because field locations, sizes, and field types are identified on any of the designs, record layout forms also serve as useful tools for the data entry function.

Data Entry

Also illustrated in Figure 2-4 is the relationship of the Multiple Card Layout Form to the records in the disk file. Regardless of the storage medium you must understand several important concepts when you enter data. First, alphabetic and alphanumeric data is usually stored *left-justified* in its related field. Consequently, the first character of the data item is entered in the first position of the assigned field area.

Numeric data must be *right-justified* in the assigned field. Hence, the data must be entered so that the low-order digit of the value is stored in low-order position of the field. Any unused *high-order* bytes are padded with zeros, or—in an RPG environment—they may be blanks.

Figure 2-6 illustrates the rules related to the entering of alphanumeric (alphabetic) and numeric data values. Notice that RPG does not distinguish between alphanumeric and alphabetic values. Any field not defined as numeric is processed as alphanumeric.

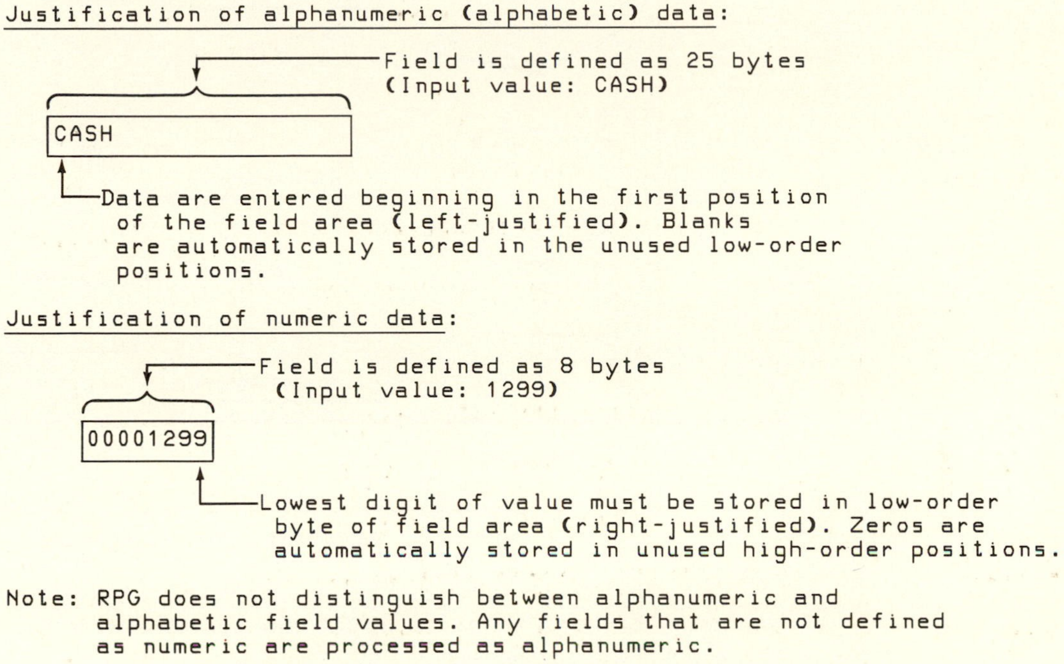

Figure 2-6 Justification rules for alphanumeric (alphabetic) and numeric data.

Some confusion often results as to when numeric data should be considered numeric for processing. Even though the data may consist solely of numbers, this does not necessarily indicate that the data must be defined as numeric. For example, the Account Number in Figure 2-6 contains numbers only. However, because it is not to be used in calculations, it may be defined as alphanumeric. This is an important processing consideration because the computer takes more time to process numeric values then alphanumeric values.

Methods of Entering Data

Figure 2-7 illustrates some of popular methods used for entering data onto common storage media. The trend today is to enter and access data by CRT-supported interactive screens controlled by a user program or a software utility. Many of the commonly used data validation functions (discussed in Chapter 12) are performed in this environment.

The location of the fields in the record defined in Figure 2-4 could have been formatted differently with, perhaps, Account Name first, then Account Number, followed by Account Type. Ideally, data records should be coordinated with the source document (i.e., time cards, invoices, sales slips, requisitions, etc.). To expedite data entry, information included at the beginning of a document should be entered first on a data record.

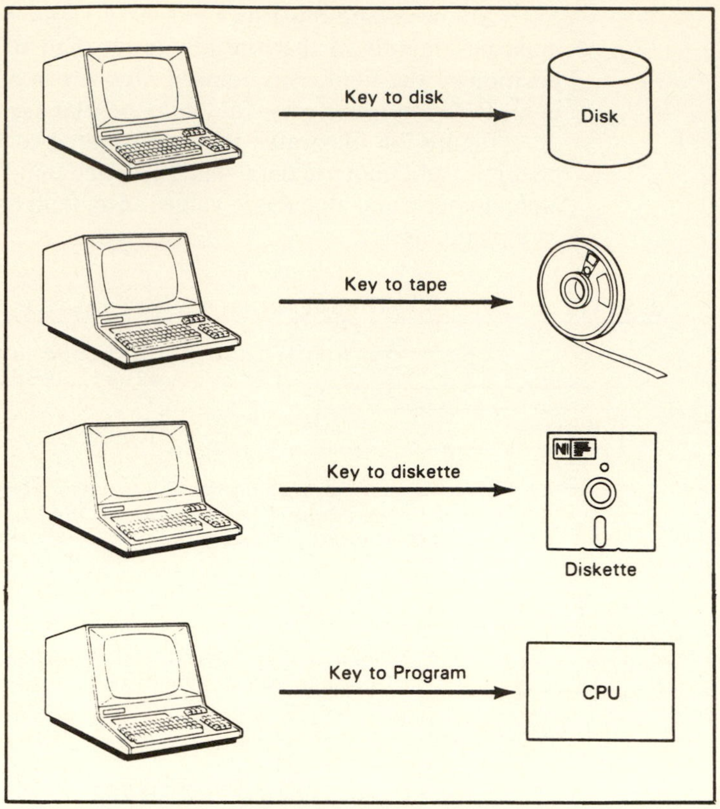

Figure 2-7 Methods of entering data.

Now that input requirements have been planned and documented, the format and design of the printed report for the introductory RPG program presented in this chapter will be discussed.

DESIGN OF PRINTED OUTPUT

Supplemental to the design of input data are output considerations. The form used for the design of reports is the Printer Spacing Chart. Examine Figure 2-8 and locate the large numbers 0, 1, 2, and so on and the smaller numbers that range from 0 to 9 in the lower row. These represent individual print positions that provide for the location and reference of characters, fields, and constants. For example, print position 49 is found within the large number 4 area under the small number 9 column. Only 82 print positions appear in the example shown in Figure 2-8. Standard Printer Spacing Charts provide for up to 144 columns to accommodate printers with 100, 120, 132, or 144 print positions.

Relationship of Printer Spacing Chart to Input Data

Refer to Figure 2-8 and locate the Xs entered in print positions 03 to 05, 15 to 41, and 49 to 68. The Xs represent the size of the variable data fields determined from the input record format. In the RPG programming environment, Xs represent both alphanumeric and numeric characters. Values that are defined as numeric are identified by edit symbols and are discussed in Chapter 4.

It is important to remember that the sizes of the data fields included in the Printer Spacing Chart were previously specified on a Record Layout Form. A field formatted on output should not be smaller than the related input data field.

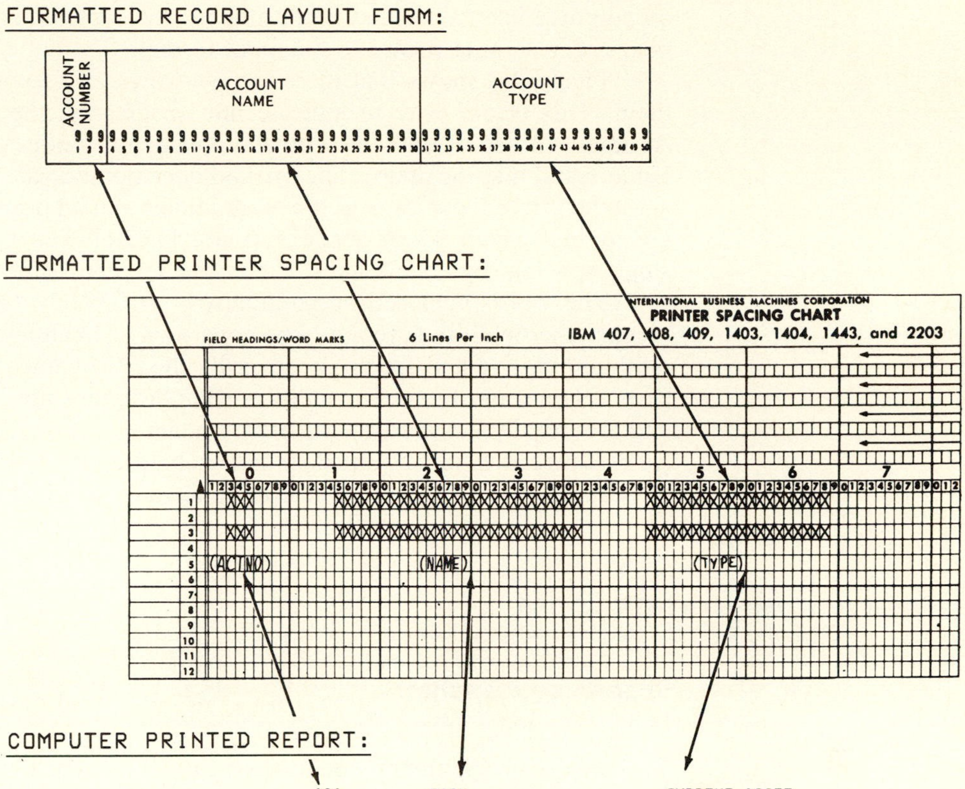


```
101    CASH                       CURRENT ASSET
102    ACCOUNTS RECEIVABLE        CURRENT ASSET
103    NOTES RECEIVABLE           CURRENT ASSET
104    PREPAID RENT               CURRENT ASSET
110    AUTOMOBILE                 CURRENT ASSET
201    ACCOUNTS PAYABLE           CURRENT LIABILITY
211    MORTGAGE PAYABLE           LONG-TERM LIABILITY
301    JOHN SMITH,CAPITAL         OWNER'S EQUITY
302    JOHN SMITH,WITHDRAWALS     OWNER'S EQUITY
400    COMMISSIONS EARNED         REVENUE
500    GAS & OIL EXPENSE          EXPENSE
501    REPAIRS EXPENSE            EXPENSE
502    SALARIES EXPENSE           EXPENSE
```

Figure 2-8 Relationship of record layout form to a Printer Spacing Chart and printed report.

Because of editing requirements (insertion of decimals, commas, signs, etc.), however, numeric output fields are usually larger. Also, other fields may be defined on output that were not included in an input record. These are also defined in the program and include the results of calculations, tests, and so forth.

Furthermore, notice that the output field locations are not related to the positions of the fields in the record format. For example, the layout form in Figure 2-8 indicates the field for Account Number located in columns 1 to 3; Account Name, columns 4 to 30; and Account Type 31 to 50. However, the Printer Spacing Chart shows that Account Number is to be printed in positions 3 to 5; Account Name, 15 to 41; and Account Type, 49 to 68. In other words, there does not have to be the same locational relationship between a field on input to the related field on output. Field values may be printed in any available print positions and in any field order without regard to the input format.

Figure 2-8 shows that there are two rows of Xs with a blank line between them. This is one way to indicate line spacing on the Printer Spacing Chart. Another is to show one line with a supplementary note for spacing instructions. Understand that the double line method does not indicate that only two data lines are to be printed, but informs the programmer that all print lines (for this example) are double-spaced. The absence of a blank line between rows of Xs would indicate single spacing; two blank lines, triple spacing; and so forth.

The words enclosed in parentheses—(ACTNO), (NAME), and (TYPE)—identify the fields and are not to be construed as headings or constants. They are only informative and are not necessarily the field names used in the source program. Names used to define fields in RPG programs are limited to six characters and are usually assigned by the programmer.

Notice that this report does not include headings. The syntax and control of headings in an RPG program will be introduced in Chapter 3.

OTHER DOCUMENTATION TOOLS

Supporting Flowcharts

In the RPG programming environment, flowcharts are often used to support the documentation of an application program. Included are:

1. System flowchart
2. Program flowcharts (processing logic)
3. Structure chart (introduced in Chapter 4)

Before these are discussed, an understanding of the symbols included in the standard flowchart template is essential. Figure 2-9 classifies the symbols for the related flowchart type.

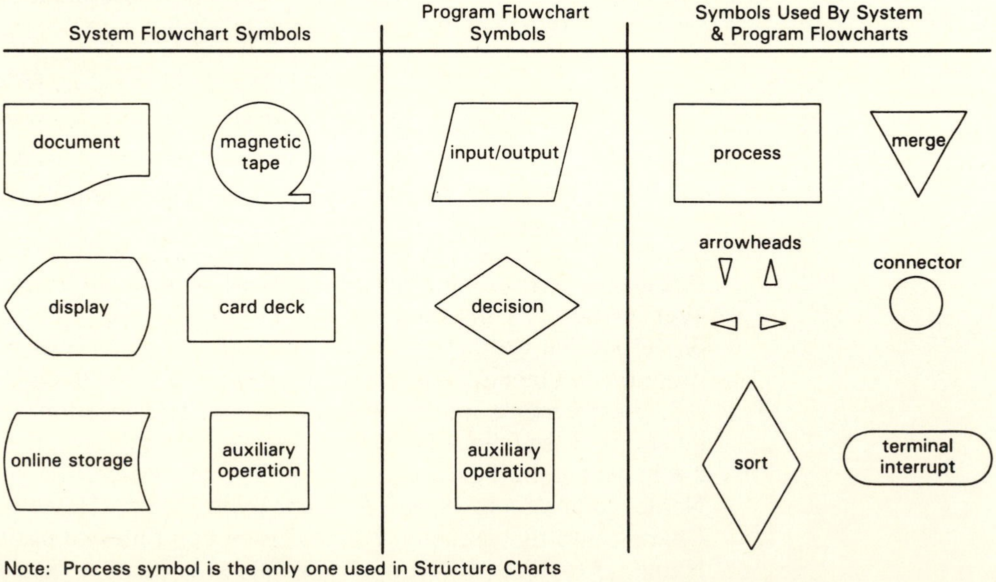

Figure 2-9 Relationship of symbols to flowchart type.

System Flowchart

The system flowchart is a useful documentation tool because it identifies all input to and output from a program. Three examples of this flowchart form are shown in Figure 2-10. Notice that they include the symbols classified in Figure 2-9 as those related to system flowcharts.

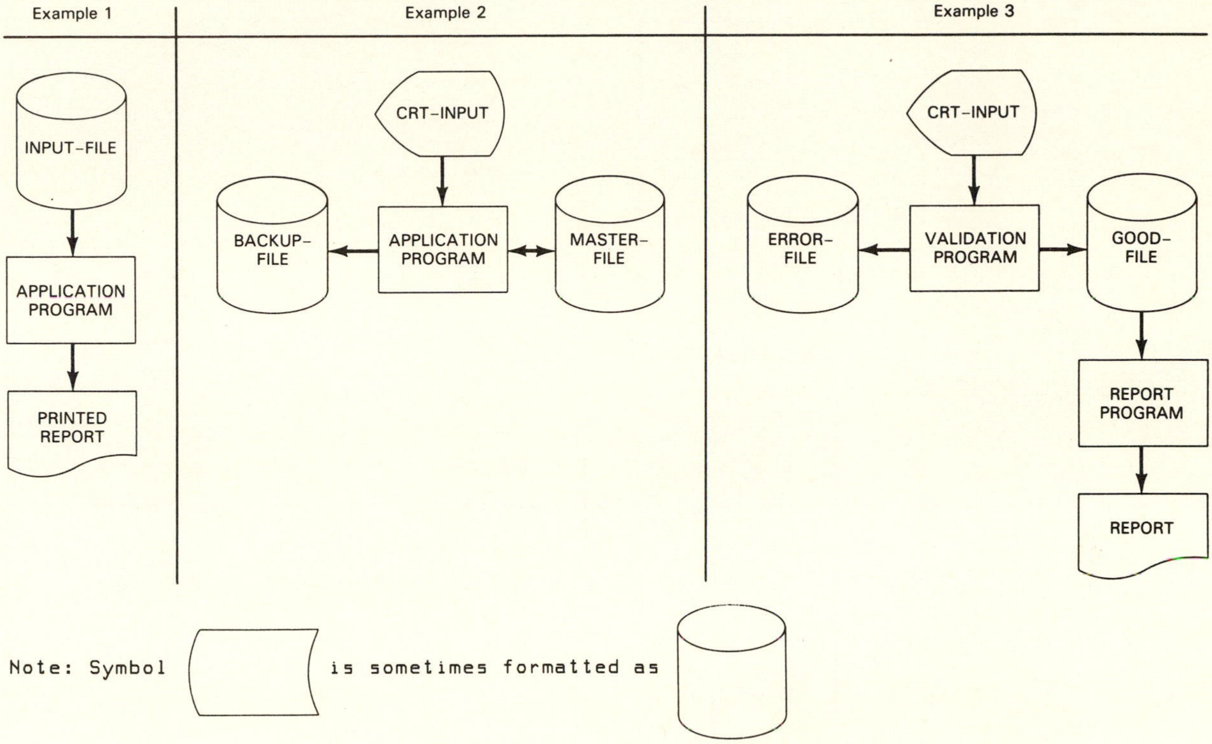

Figure 2-10 System flowchart examples.

Example 1 in Figure 2-10 indicates that one disk-stored file is input to a program with a printed report as output. Example 2 shows that input to the program is terminal (CRT) controlled and output is to two disk files. The double arrow to the master-file symbol shows that it is an update file, which is processed as an input and output file (called an I/O file).

Example 3 indicates that several functions are performed in the same run. Input data is entered via CRT, then validated by a program. Any error records are output to an error rejection file, and good records are stored in a separate file. The good records are then processed by a second program to generate a report.

It is not uncommon to process a large number of files by a group of related programs. In any case, the sequence of file processing and program execution is directed by control statements included in a *procedure* documented by a system flowchart.

The use and format of *structure charts* will be discussed when *internal subroutines* are introduced in Chapter 12.

Program Logic Flowcharts

Because RPG has a built-in processing cycle, program logic flowcharts relate only to the flow of statements included in the calculation coding. They may be developed at the individual statement level, or they may be less detailed and indicate

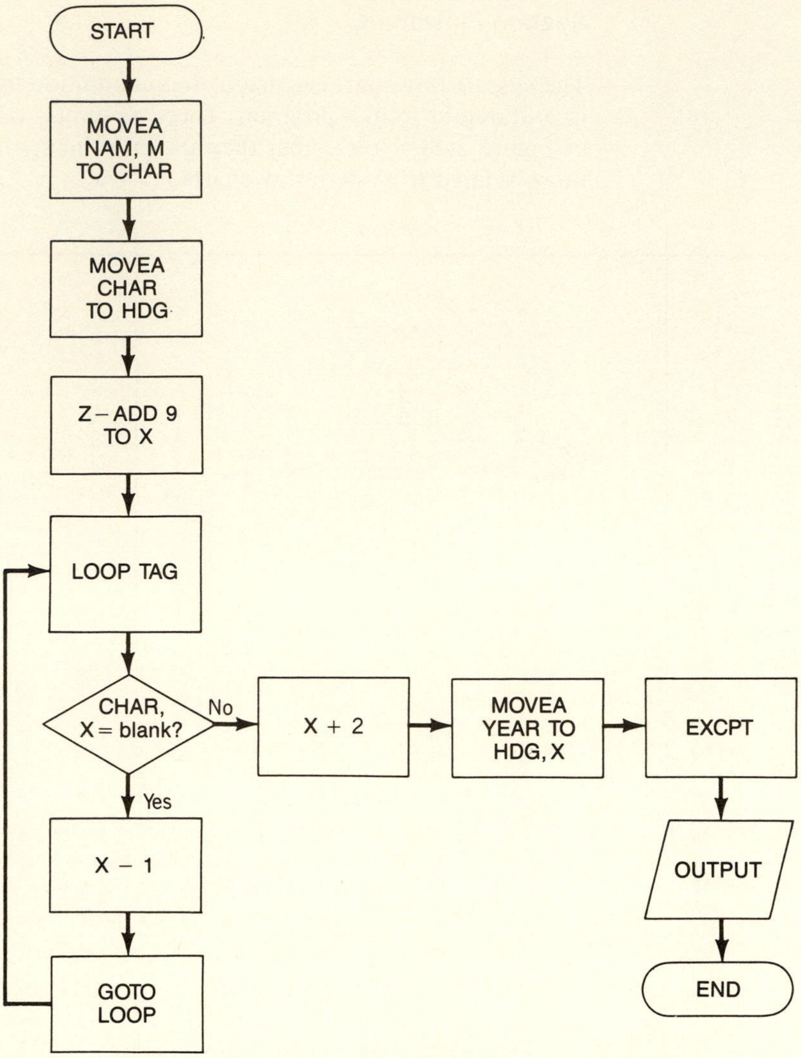

Figure 2-11 Processing logic flowchart example.

only the general flow of processing. Figure 2-11 illustrates an example of this type of flowchart formatted at the individual statement level. The flowchart illustrated is only hypothetical, so do not try to interpret the statements within each symbol. Notice, however, that each of the operations specified (i.e., MOVEA, Z-ADD, TAG, GOTO, EXCPT, etc.) will be explained in later chapters.

THE RPG PROGRAMMING LANGUAGE

RPG Program Cycle

During execution, an RPG program automatically follows a sequence of operations for each record that is processed. This built-in *program cycle* includes the following logical steps:

1. Reading input (READ)
2. Calculation processing (PROCESS)
3. Writing output (WRITE)

A flowchart that illustrates the RPG program cycle is presented in Figure 2-12. This processing and decision-making sequence is automatically followed for every input record read. Supplementing the flowchart is a detailed explanation of what RPG does at each step of the program cycle. Most of the terminology included in the symbols may not be familiar now. As subsequent chapters are discussed, however, each topic will be individually addressed.

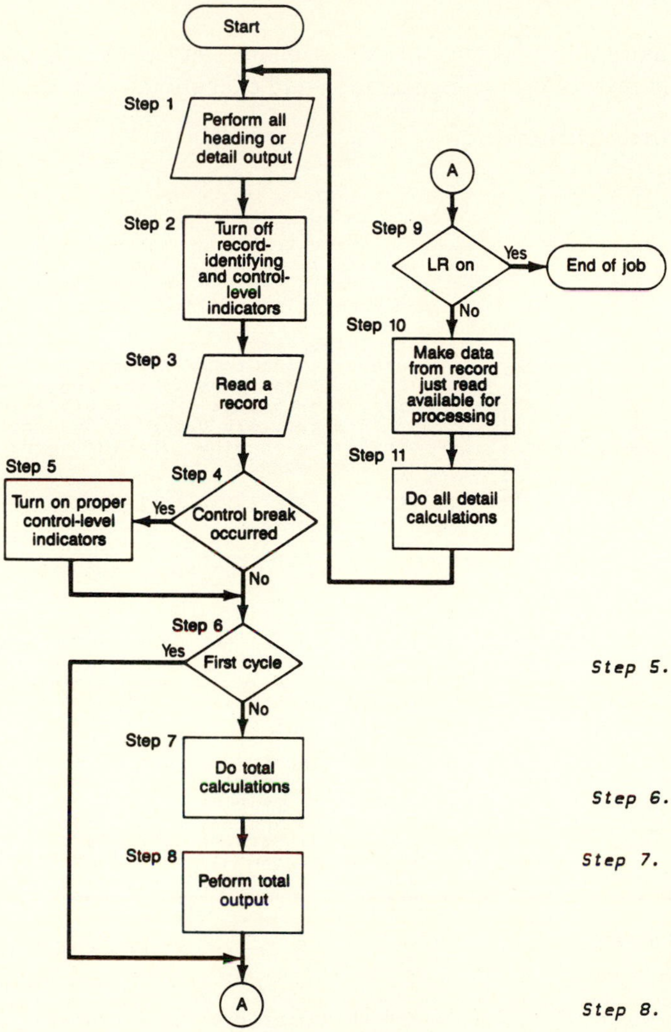

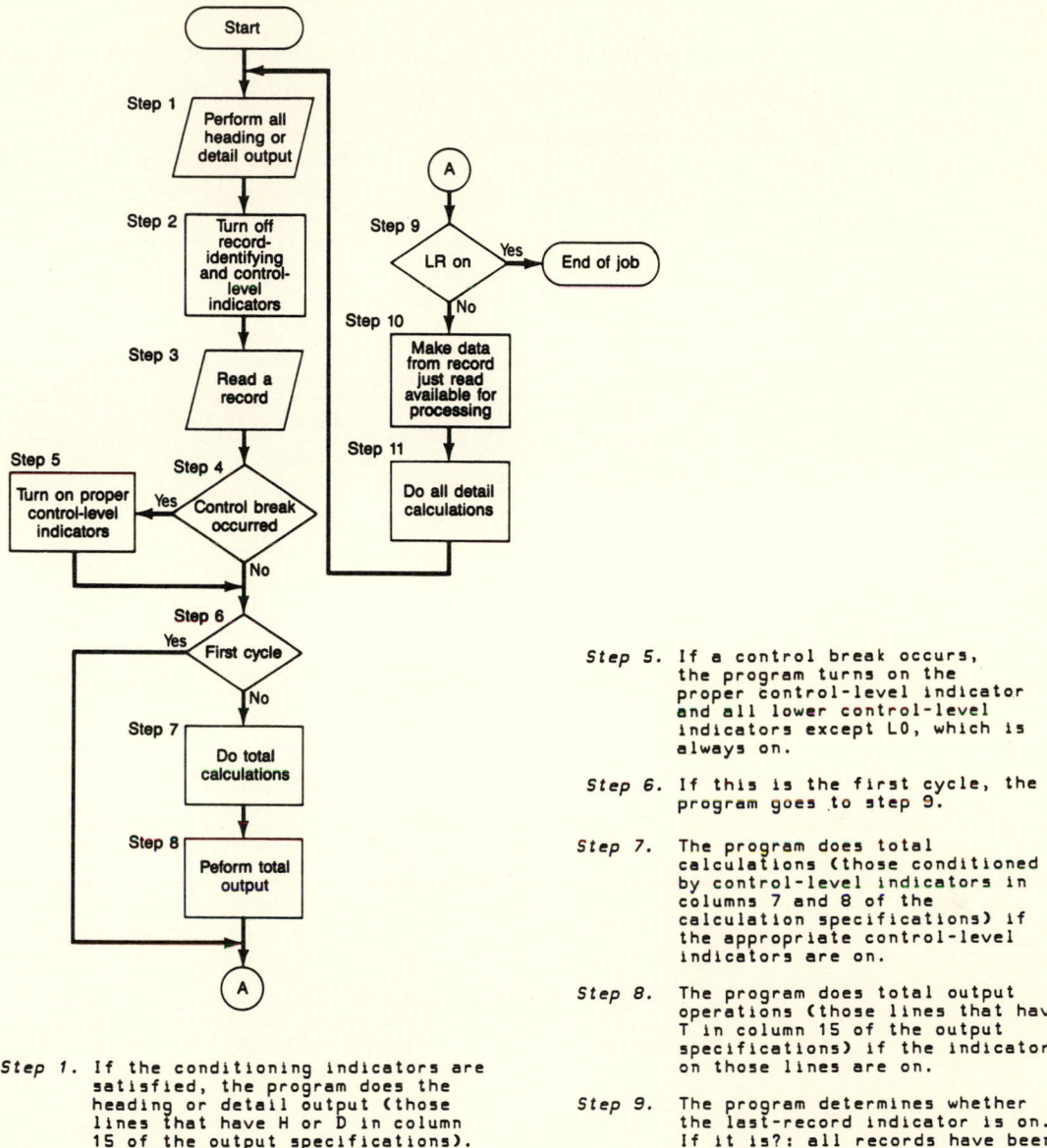

Step 1. If the conditioning indicators are satisfied, the program does the heading or detail output (those lines that have H or D in column 15 of the output specifications).

Step 2. The program turns off all control-level and record-identifying indicators.

Step 3. The program reads a record and turns on the appropriate record-identifying indicator.

Step 4. The program determines whether a control break occurred. (A control break occurs when the control field of the record just read differs from the control field of the previous record.)

Step 5. If a control break occurs, the program turns on the proper control-level indicator and all lower control-level indicators except L0, which is always on.

Step 6. If this is the first cycle, the program goes to step 9.

Step 7. The program does total calculations (those conditioned by control-level indicators in columns 7 and 8 of the calculation specifications) if the appropriate control-level indicators are on.

Step 8. The program does total output operations (those lines that have T in column 15 of the output specifications) if the indicators on those lines are on.

Step 9. The program determines whether the last-record indicator is on. If it is?: all records have been processed, and the programs ends.

Step 10. The program makes data from the record read at the beginning of the cycle (step 3) available for use in detail calculations and output.

Step 11. The program does all detail calculations (those not conditioned by control-level indicators in columns 7 and 8 of the calculation specifications) on the data from the record read at the beginning of the cycle.

Figure 2-12 RPG program cycle flowchart. (Courtesy of IBM)

RPG Program Coding (SYNTAX)

The functions involved in the development and processing of an RPG source program include:

1. Program generation
2. Program execution

Refer to Figure 2-13 and examine the sequence of operations included in the sections that discuss program generation and execution.

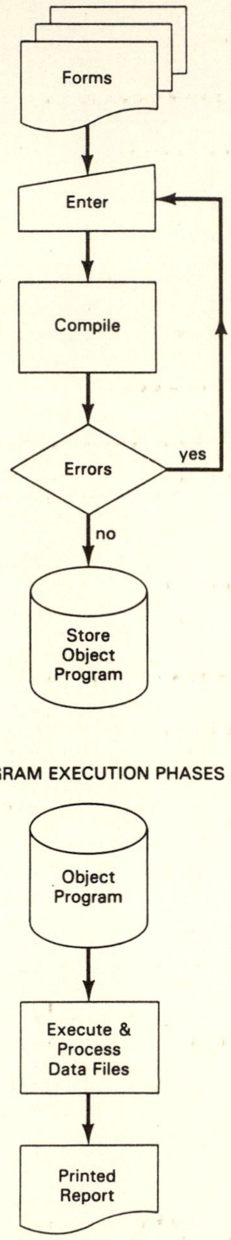

PROGRAM COMPILATION PHASES

1. Based on input, output, and logic requirements (program specifications, record layout(s), printer spacing chart(s), and flowcharts, an RPG source program is written on preprinted coding forms.
2. Completed coding forms are used as the reference for entering source program instructions. Code is entered by key-to-disk, key-to-tape, key-to-diskette machines, or interactively under the control of a word processing or other special purpose software utility package.
3. RPG source program is compiled in accordance with the procedures required by the hardware/software system used.
4. If the program has terminal errors, individual instructions must be corrected and the compilation step performed again. This phase may take several times until the program is free of syntax errors.
5. When the source program is free of terminal errors, an object program (also called member) is automatically generated. Depending on the computer system, this additional machine language copy of the source program may be permanently stored on disk or reside temporarily in the CPU, or both.

PROGRAM EXECUTION PHASES

1. RPG object program is executed by a sequence of control statements (usually stored in a procedure) unique to the operating system.
2. Any data files referenced in the program and control statements will be accessed and each input record will be processed under control of the program instructions.
3. Output as defined in the program (may be to printer, disk, tape, CRT, etc.) will be the result of program execution. Execution time errors may be identified in this phase which require additional corrections to the source program or procedure. For an error condition, compilation and execution steps described above would have to be repeated.

Figure 2-13 RPG program compilation and execution phases.

RPG CODING FORMS

The writing of RPG source programs requires the use of preprinted coding forms or a text editor that simulates the form designs (e.g., IBM's SEU (Source Entry Utility) software package). Because all source program entries must in a designated column, it is difficult to code in RPG without reference to the forms or related text editor. No attempt should be made, however, to memorize the format of each form. Some of the form types are special purpose and are seldom used in a program. In addition, many of the columns and fields in each form type are unique and are not required for all programs.

The five commonly used RPG coding forms are shown in Figure 2-14: the Control and File Description Specifications, Extension and Line Counter Specifications, Input Specifications, Calculation Specifications, and Output-Format Specifications. The function of each form is as follows:

1. Control and File Description Specifications. Only one Control Specification statement may be included in a program. Its function is to build a storage area for the object program in the CPU during program execution. The File Description instructions define the attributes of each file specified in the RPG program.

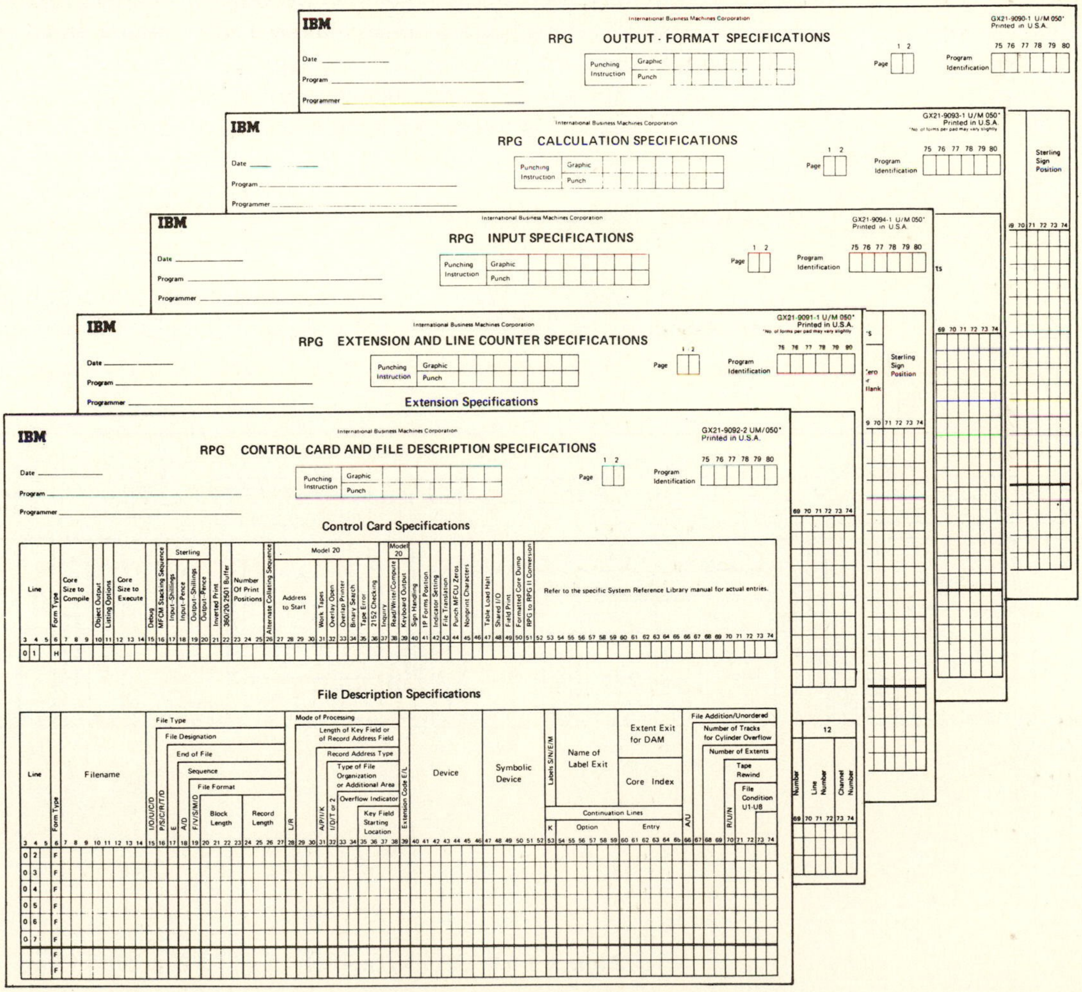

Figure 2-14 RPG Specifications Forms.

2. Extension and Line Counter Specifications. This form defines table, array, and select disk file processing attributes. The Line Counter Specifications (lower section) is used to define and control nonstandard page lengths.
3. Input Specifications. This form defines the attributes of the record types in a data file, including field names, field sizes, field types, testing, control fields, and so forth.
4. Calculation Specifications. Arithmetic operations, table lookup, array lookup, disk file processing functions, screen control, internal subroutines, and so forth are controlled by the instructions included in this form.
5. Output-Format Specifications. All output specified in the program is controlled by the instructions in this form. Output may be directed to a printer, disk, diskette, tape, CRT, or any combination of output devices supported by the related computer system.

When RPG source code is entered onto a storage medium, the instructions must be stored in an H, F, E, L, I, C, O *compilation order*. Any program instructions not in that order will be identified as *terminal errors* during the compilation phase of program development.

The syntax for Control and File Description, Input, and Output-Format Specifications is introduced in this chapter; Line Counter in Chapter 3; Calculations in Chapter 4; and Extension in Chapter 10. Because the use of each form is extensive, not all the related details are included in any one chapter. When appropriate, additional usage and syntax are introduced in other chapters.

Sections Common to All Forms

The circled numbers in Figure 2-15 identify the sections common to each type of form. An explanation of the numbered areas is included at the bottom of the figure.

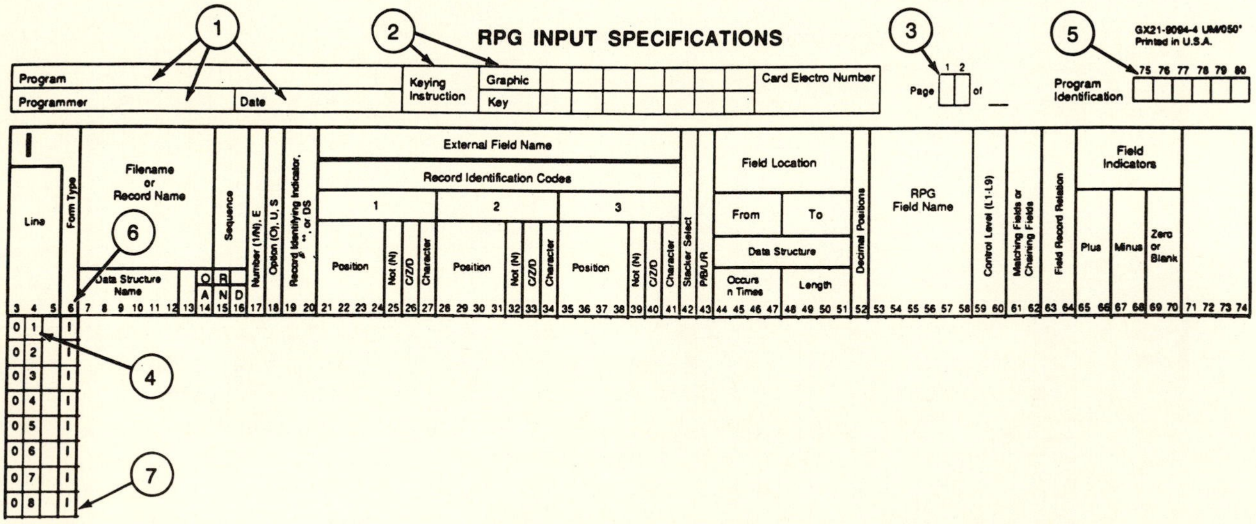

Figure 2-15 Areas common to all RPG coding forms.

Areas Common to All RPG Forms:

1. Lines for date, program name, and the programmer's name. This information is not included as instructions in the source program.

2. The punching instructions area helps a person other than the programmer who may be recording the source code, identify O's from 0's, I's from 1's, S's from 5's, and Z's from 2's. The character is entered in the top row and A (for alphanumeric) or N (for numeric) in bottom row. Hence, if the letter I was entered in the top row, A (for alphanumeric) would be specified in the bottom row. Entries in this area are not part of the source program.

3. The box labelled Page represents the form's page number. If used, this entry would be entered in columns 1 and 2 of each source program instruction followed by a related line number in columns 3 through 5. When punch cards were used to store the source code, this entry was important to maintain a sorted order of the instructions. However, with CRT controlled input, and the fact that RPG automatically generates sequence numbers that identify each statement, this entry is no longer necessary.

4. Another feature common to all forms is the line number. The extreme left-hand side of the form has the word Line entered. Note the numbers 3, 4, and 5 above their respective columns-these represent positions 3, 4, and 5 of an RPG instruction. Columns 3 and 4 are numbered starting with 01 for line 1, 02 for line 2, and so forth. Column 5 is blank so that instructions omitted in the initial coding of the program may be added at the bottom of the form and later inserted in their related location.

   When the line number is used with the page number, the first source program instruction will include 01010 in columns 1 through 5. Again, however, page and line number entries are no longer necessary when source code is stored/entered via CRT and stored on disk or diskette. In any case, the source program will compile without this entry.

5. The area identified as Program Identification (positions 75-80) is used to identify the program. Some computer systems (i.e. IBM's System/36 and 34) require that the program name *must* be entered in this field in the Control Card Specifications statement (H in column 6). The source and object members are stored in the user's library with this name supplemented with the letter S (source member) and O (object member) in the high-order position.

6. An entry must be made in column 6 of every RPG source program instruction. The related letters are preprinted on all the forms (column 6) to designate the entry for the specification type. For example, H represents a Control Card Specification instruction (only one for a program); F, File Description; E, Extension Specifications; L, Line Counter Specifications; I, Input Specifications; C, Calculation Specifications; and O, for Output-Format Specifications. *Any source program instruction missing the related letter in column 6, or not in the H, F, E, L, I, C, O compilation order, will generate a terminal error during compilation.*

   Note that if IBM's source entry utility (SEU) is used to enter the source code, the related form letter is automatically stored in column 6.

7. All of the specification forms include a bold line separating the prenumbered lines from lines that are not numbered. This area used to include instructions that may have been omitted from the initial coding sequence. When the source program is entered, the instruction is referenced and inserted in its intended location.

(*Continued*)

RPG SOURCE PROGRAM CODING

Figure 2-16 illustrates the completed coding forms for the introductory program detailed in the specifications given in Figure 2-1. Notice that only four forms are used—usually the minimum number required for any RPG program. Except for systems such as IBM's System/38 or AS/400 that are supported by a data base, the H, F, I, and O form instructions must be included in any RPG program. Extension (E), Line Counter (L), and Calculations (C) Specifications are not essential and are used only when the related processing control is needed. However, almost every RPG program requires some calculation control.

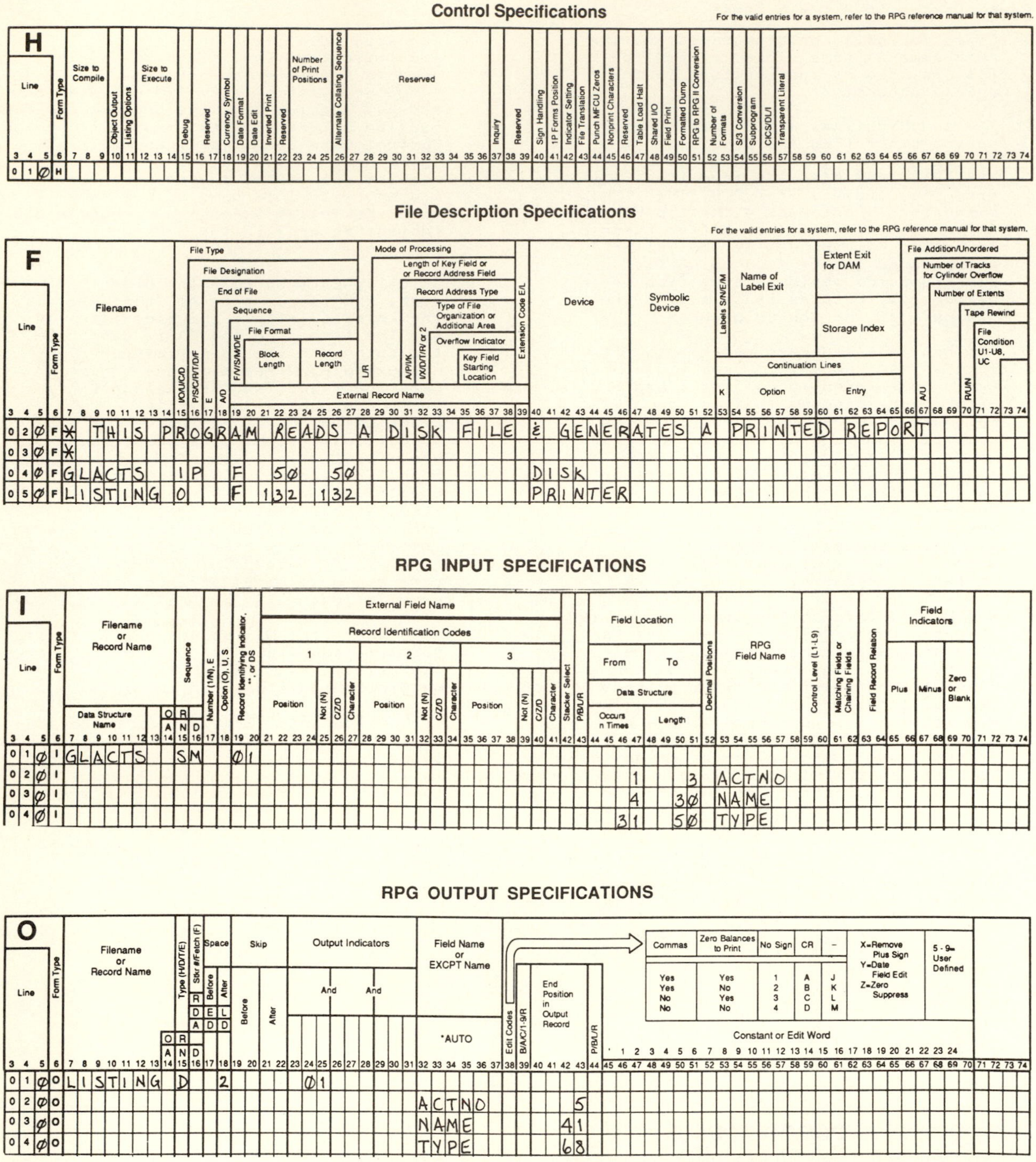

Figure 2-16 Filled-in RPG coding forms for example program.

A source listing of the program, generated from compilation, is shown in Figure 2-17. The row of numbers and dots across the top of the listing (supplied by some RPG compilers) provides a guide in the location of entries within each instruction. Observe that the source listing does not include column references for every type of specification. Also, included in this figure is the input file and output file relationship to the control sections of the RPG program.

Before we discuss the details of RPG source program coding, you must understand that not all the columns included in the form types are used in any

Input file (stored on disk):

```
101CASH                        CURRENT ASSET
102ACCOUNTS RECEIVABLE         CURRENT ASSET
103NOTES RECEIVABLE            CURRENT ASSET
104PREPAID RENT                CURRENT ASSET
110AUTOMOBILE                  FIXED ASSET
201ACCOUNTS PAYABLE            CURRENT LIABILITY
211MORTGAGE PAYABLE            LONG-TERM LIABILITY
301JOHN SMITH,CAPITAL          OWNER'S EQUITY
302JOHN SMITH,WITHDRAWALS      OWNER'S EQUITY
400COMMISSIONS EARNED          REVENUE
500GAS & OIL EXPENSE           EXPENSE
501REPAIRS EXPENSE             EXPENSE
502SALARIES EXPENSE            EXPENSE
```

Source program listing:

```
H                                                                CH2P1
* THIS PROGRAM READS A DISK FILE & GENERATES A PRINTED REPORT    CH2P1
*                                                                CH2P1
FGLACTS  IP  F  80  80            DISK                           CH2P1
FLISTING O   F 132 132            PRINTER                        CH2P1
IGLACTS  SM  01                                                  CH2P1
I                                       1   3 ACTNO              CH2P1
I                                       4  30 NAME               CH2P1
I                                      31  50 TYPE               CH2P1
OLISTING D  2     01                                             CH2P1
O                       ACTNO     5                              CH2P1
O                       NAME     41                              CH2P1
O                       TYPE     68                              CH2P1
```

Printed report:

```
101        CASH                          CURRENT ASSET

102        ACCOUNTS RECEIVABLE           CURRENT ASSET

103        NOTES RECEIVABLE              CURRENT ASSET

104        PREPAID RENT                  CURRENT ASSET

110        AUTOMOBILE                    FIXED ASSET

201        ACCOUNTS PAYABLE              CURRENT LIABILITY

211        MORTGAGE PAYABLE              LONG-TERM LIABILITY

301        JOHN SMITH,CAPITAL            OWNER'S EQUITY

302        JOHN SMITH,WITHDRAWALS        OWNER'S EQUITY

400        COMMISSIONS EARNED            REVENUE

500        GAS & OIL EXPENSE             EXPENSE

501        REPAIRS EXPENSE               EXPENSE

502        SALARIES EXPENSE              EXPENSE
```

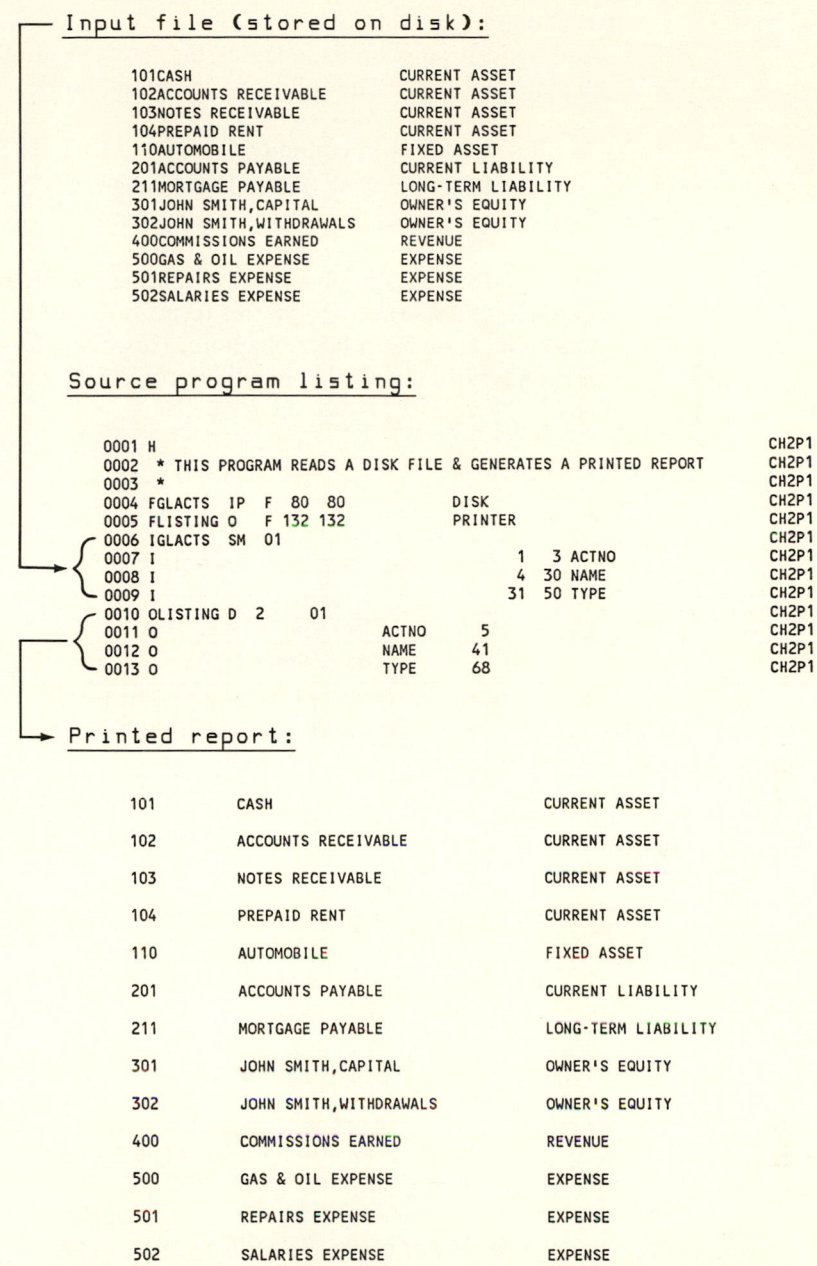

Figure 2-17 Source listing of example program and its relationship to the input file and printed report.

one program. In fact, many of the columns (fields) may be unique to an individual computer system or have a special purpose that is seldom used. Consequently, emphasis will be directed to those columns that control the processing feature currently being discussed and not to an entire specifications form.

The RPG syntax for each of the specification forms used in the example program is explained in the following paragraphs.

Control and File Description Specifications

Control Specifications. Refer again to Figure 2-16 and notice that the Control and File Description Specifications are included on one form.The top, or Control Specifications, describes the program and the computer system to the

RPG compiler. Only one Control Specification instruction is permitted in a program, and it must be included as the first executable statement (comments may be specified first). The following minimum entries are required:

1. Letter H in column 6.
2. Program name (limited to six characters) in columns 75 to 80. This entry may be optional on some systems.

Figure 2-18 identifies the required and some of the more commonly used (but optional) entries specified on this form. A few of the other special purpose entries will be introduced in later chapters. However, for a comprehensive explanation of each field, refer to the manufacturer's RPG language manual.

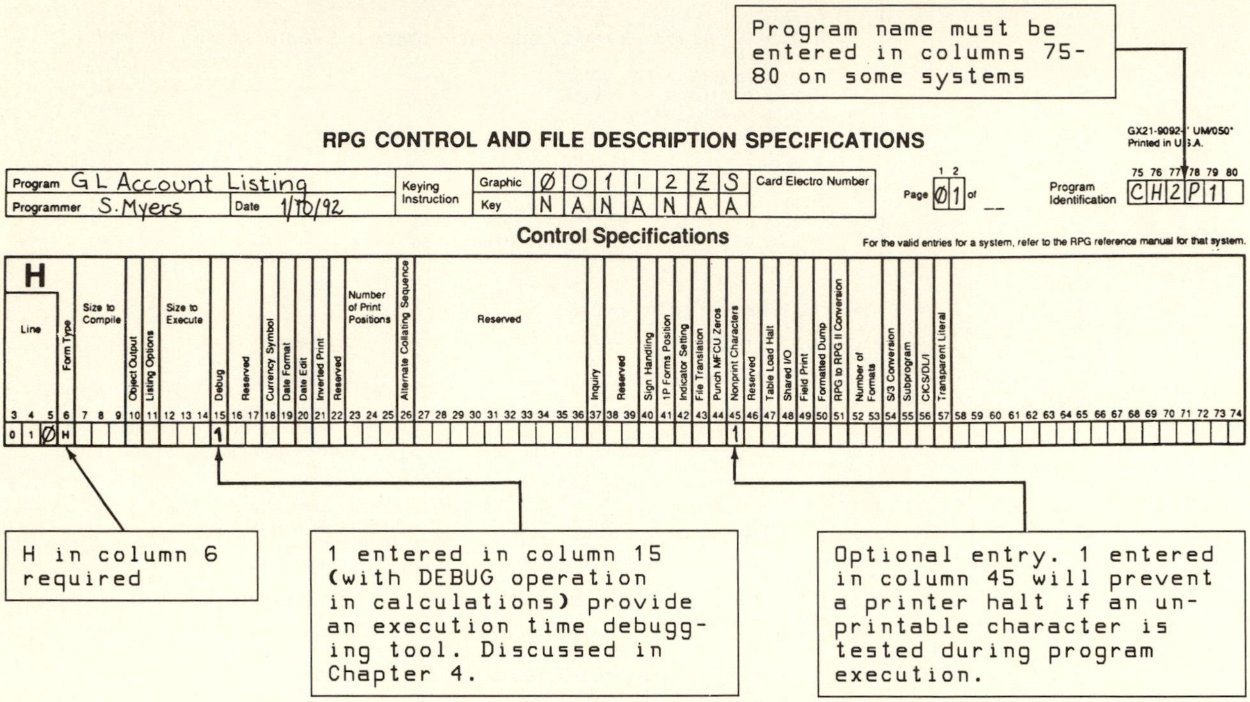

Figure 2-18 Required and commonly used optional entries for Control Specifications form.

File Description Specifications. The purpose of the File Description Specifications form is to define each file processed by the program. Specifically, the form does the following:

1. Names the input and output files processed by the program.
2. Indicates the file types (input, output, update, or combined). Only input and output file types are discussed in this chapter.
3. Designates the files as primary, secondary, full-procedural, chained, record address, table, or demand. (Only primary files are discussed in this chapter.)
4. Specifies the logical (RECORD LENGTH) and physical (BLOCK LENGTH) record lengths for each file.
5. Assigns the hardware devices that support each file.

The physical relationship of the example program's File Description entries to hardware devices and software items is shown in Figure 2-19.

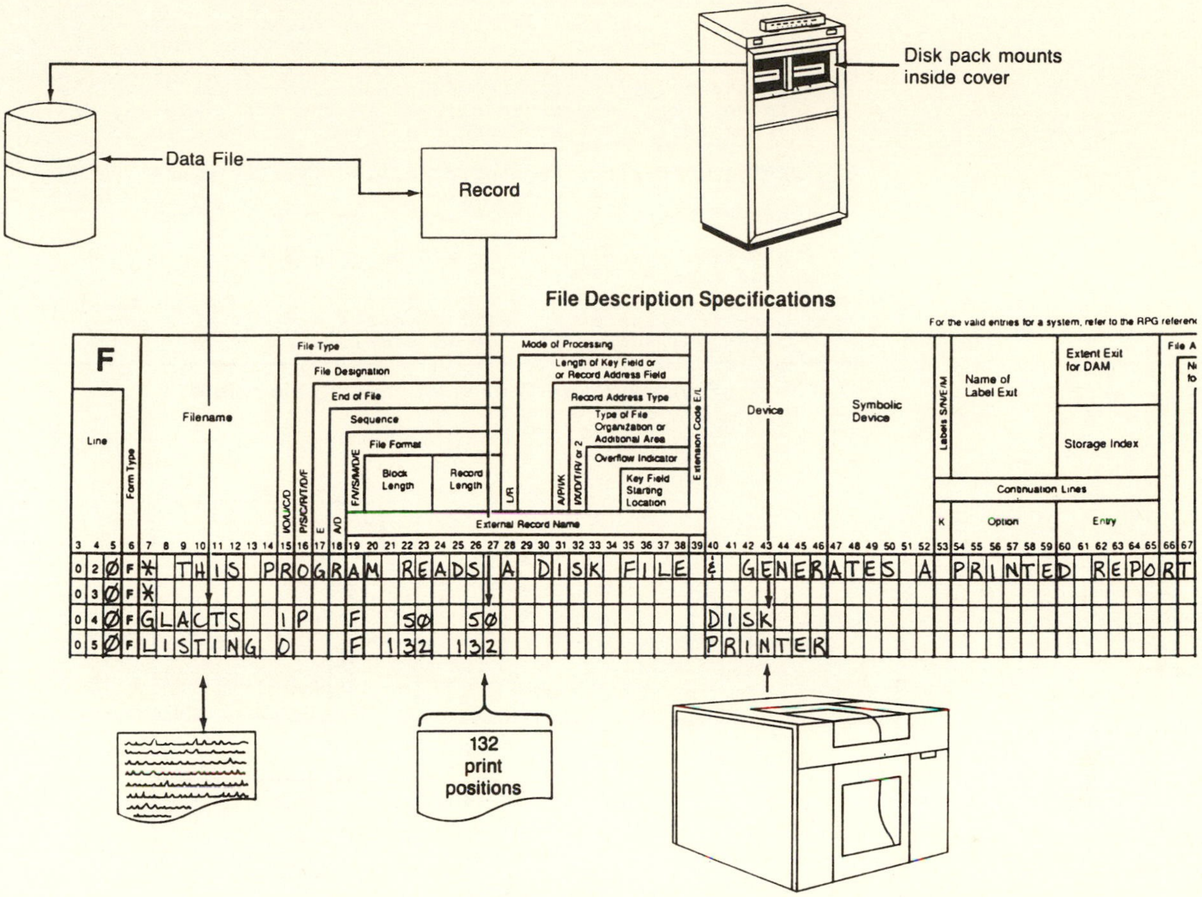

Figure 2-19 Relationship of File Description entries to hardware devices and software items.

Explanations of the coding rules for fields used in the File Description Specifications (Figure 2-19) for the example program are discussed in the following paragraphs.

Form Type (Column 6): The letter F must be entered in this position in every File Description instruction.

File Name (Columns 7–14): At least one input and one output file must be specified on this form. Notice in Figure 2-19 that the input file is named GLACTS and the output, LISTING. Any *programmer-supplied* name could be used here; however, the file name should be self-documenting. For example, a file name A1234 would not indicate the contents of the file to anyone except the programmer. The name GLACTS, however, does provide some hint of the application that the file supports. The rules for creating file names in an RPG program are detailed in Figure 2-20. Figure 2-21 shows examples of file names with an explanation of why the entry is correct or incorrect.

File Type (Column 15): The letters printed in the heading of this one column field indicate the following file types:

I Input file
O Output file
U Update file
C Combined file
D Display file

```
1. A file name may include no more than eight characters.

2. The first character of the file name must be alphabetic
   and entered left-justified (beginning in column 7) in the
   related field. Any other entries in the file name may be
   any combination of alphabetic and numeric characters.

3. Special characters are not permitted in a file name.

4. Imbedded blanks are not be permitted in a file name.

5. Every file specified in an RPG program must have a
   unique name.

Note: Any of these errors will generate a terminal error
      when the source program is compiled.
```

Figure 2-20 RPG rules for creating file names.

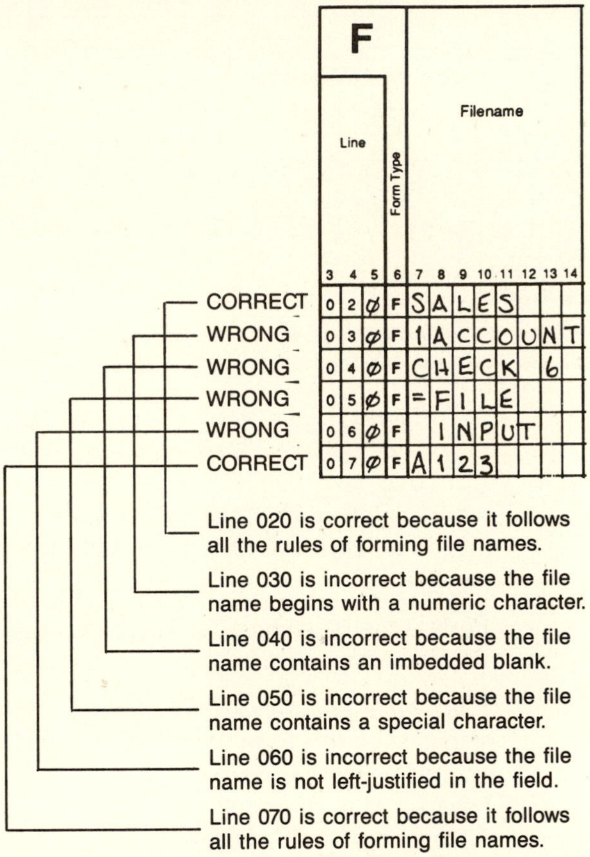

Figure 2-21 Examples of correct and incorrect file names.

Only disk input (I) and printer output (O) files are discussed now, reserving an explanation of the other file types for subsequent chapters.

Reexamine Figure 2-19 and notice that the letter I is entered in column 15 for the file GLACTS. This entry defines the file as input that contains data stored on the input device specified in the Device field (columns 40–46). The letter O entered in column 15 for the LISTING file defines it as an output file.

At least one input and output file must be used in any RPG program. However, more input and/or output files may be specified. The syntax and processing logic of programs that control multiple input and output files (*multifiles*) will be discussed in later chapters.

File Designation (Column 16): The letters included on the form for this field represent the following:

P Primary file	R Record address file
S Secondary file	T Table file
F Full-procedural file	D Demand file
C Chained file	Blank Output file

Only the file designations used in this chapter (primary and output) will be discussed now. The others will be explained in later chapters when the related subject is introduced.

The letter P, which designates the file as primary, is specified only with input files (letter I in column 15). An RPG program may have no more than one file defined as primary, however, for some processing modes, the RPG program does not have to have any primary file. With the exception of CRT and PRINTER files, the letter P may be specified with an input file supported by any other input device. For files defined as output (letter O in column 15), the file designation field must be blank.

Refer again to the example File Description form shown in Figure 2-19. In accordance with the rules previously explained, the letter P is entered in column 16 for the input file GLACTS and is blank for the output file, LISTING.

File Format (Column 19): This File Description entry indicates the format of the records in the data file. The entries commonly used are:

F Fixed format
V Variable format
E Externally defined (AS/400 and System/38)

Other letters (S, M, D) are also specified for this field, but they relate to formats that are not discussed in this textbook.

An F entered in column 19 indicates that all the record types (multiple record file) in the related file are the same length. If this entry is omitted, a warning error will be generated during compilation and F will be assumed.

The letter V is specified in this field for multiple record files that include record formats of varying lengths. Variable length records are not supported by all systems and are not commonly used.

The letter E indicates that the file is defined externally from the RPG program. This is unique to IBM's System/38 and AS/400 and will be discussed when that subject is introduced.

An examination of Figure 2-19 indicates that the letter F is entered for the input and output files. Because records directed to a printer must all be the same length (fixed), any files defined as PRINTER supported must always include an F in column 19.

Block Length (Columns 20-23): Block length refers to the *physical* size of the records stored in the file. Depending on how the data was loaded, the value specified in this field may be equal to or a multiple of the *logical* record size (following field). Blocking, which is specified when the file is initially created, will be discussed in detail when disk file processing concepts are introduced in Chapter 13.

Refer again to Figure 2-19 and notice that 50 is entered right-justified in this field and in the following Record Length field for the input file (GLACTS). Because blocking was not specified when GLACTS was created, this field must have the same value as the Record Length field.

Only the records in disk- and tape-stored files may be blocked; files controlled by PRINTER, WORKSTN, CONSOLE, CRT, and KEYBORD do not support this function. Notice that in accordance with this rule, the PRINTER file included in the example program (Figure 2-19) has 132 entered in both the Block Length and Record Length fields. With some computer systems the Block Length entry may be omitted; with others an entry must be made or a warning error will be generated in compilation of the source program. The length entered in the Block Length field must be identical to the size specified when the file was created, or an execution time error will be generated that will cause the program to cancel.

Record Length (Columns 24–27): The entry right-justified in this required field specifies the logical size of the records stored in the related data file. For unblocked disk- and tape-stored files, the record and block lengths will be the same. Refer back to Figure 2-19 and notice that 50 is entered as the record length for the input disk file and 132 for the output printer file.

Maximum record size is restricted by the input and output devices that

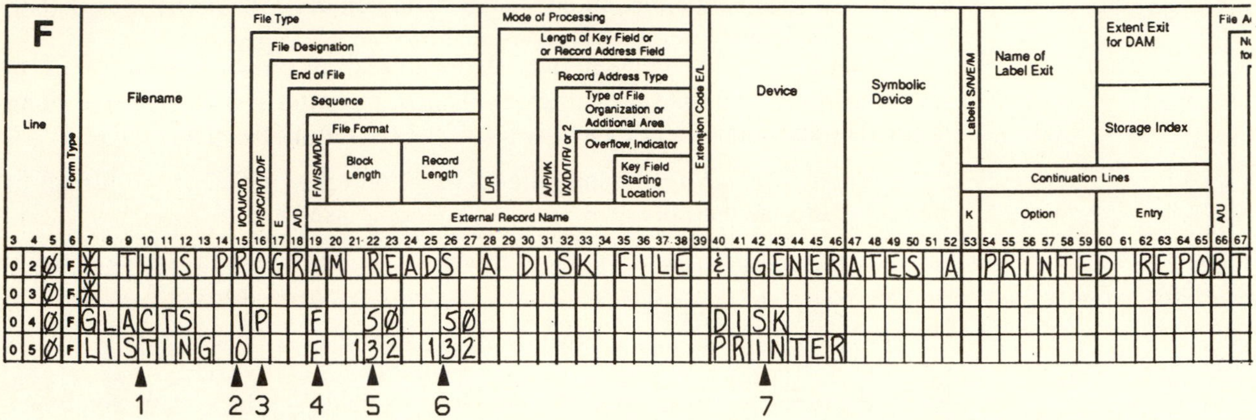

1. Programmer-supplied filenames do not have to be the same as those assigned to the stored disk or tape file. Control language (JCL, OCL, or CL) statements included in a procedure assign the file name used in program to name of the stored data file.

2. The letter I must be entered in column 15 for input files and O for output. Other optional entries will be introduced in later chapters.

3. The letter P indicates a primary file that may be assigned to only one input file. It may not be specified for output files.

4. The letter F in column 19 indicates the records are all the same length. Entry will be assumed if omitted.

5. For unblocked disk or tape files, the right-justified block length must be identical to the record length. Printer files must always be specified as unblocked. Blocking concepts are discussed in detail in Chapter 13.

6. This right-justified entry indicates the length of logical records stored in the file. The device assigned determines the maximum record length that may be specified.

7. DISK is used on many computer systems to identify disk stored data files and PRINTER for printer output files. Entry must be left-justified in the field.

Note: Other fields will be discussed when the related subject is introduced.

Figure 2-22 Summary of File Description entries specified in the example program.

control the file's I/O. For example, on IBM's System/36, DISK file records may be a maximum of 4096 bytes; WORKSTN file records, 9999; and depending on the width of printer, 198 for PRINTER files. If variable length records are included in a file, the maximum record length must be entered in this field.

Furthermore, the record size entered on this form for disk and tape files must be identical to the record size specified when the file was created. Any difference between the actual record size and that entered in the Record Length field will cause a *runtime* error when the program is executed. The File Description Specifications detailed in Figure 2-22 summarize all the entries used in this form for the example program.

Device (Columns 40–46): Look at Figure 2-22 and notice that DISK is entered left-justified in the Device field for the input file and PRINTER for the output file. These are standard device names used with IBM's System/34, System/36, System/38, and AS/400 for disk and printer assignments. For other computer systems, the related RPG language manual must be referenced to determine the requirements for device names.

Applications introduced later in the text will require WORKSTN, KEYBORD, CONSOLE, and CRT hardware device name assignments.

Comment Lines. An asterisk (*) entered in column 7 of any form type defines the instruction as a comment. The related form type letter in column 6 may be included or omitted. A reexamination of Figure 2-22 indicates that lines 020 and 030 are comment lines. Any number of comment lines may be included in a program, and because they provide for excellent documentation, their use is encouraged. Comment lines do require additional storage in the source program, but are not included in the object program generated from compilation.

Input Specifications

Unless the Extension Specifications (for tables, arrays, and a file processing function) or Line Counter Specifications (for control of variable form lengths) are included, the Input Specification instructions must follow the last File Description statement. Remember the required H, F, E, L, I, C, O order for the instructions included in an RPG program.

The function of the Input Specifications is to define the attributes of the records in a file. This includes the names, sizes, and types of the fields included in each record format; the sequence of the records; sign testing; and presence checking. With the exception of KEYBORD supported, externally (System/38 and AS/400) defined, table, record address, and address output files, all other files must be described on this form.

The Input Specifications form is divided into the following logical sections:

File and Record Identification Section (Columns 7–42): This section describes the input (or update) file(s), record types, and (for multiple record files) the order in which the records are processed.

Field Description Section (Columns 43–74): This section describes the names, sizes, and types of fields included in each record type. Entries in this section may not be included on the same line as a record description instruction but must be entered on the following coding lines.

Figure 2-23 illustrates the input specifications coding included for the example program. The entries shown are the minimum that must be specified on this form—the input file name, the record sequence, the record identifying indicator, and the location, name, and type of each field. Each of these field entries will be discussed in the following paragraphs.

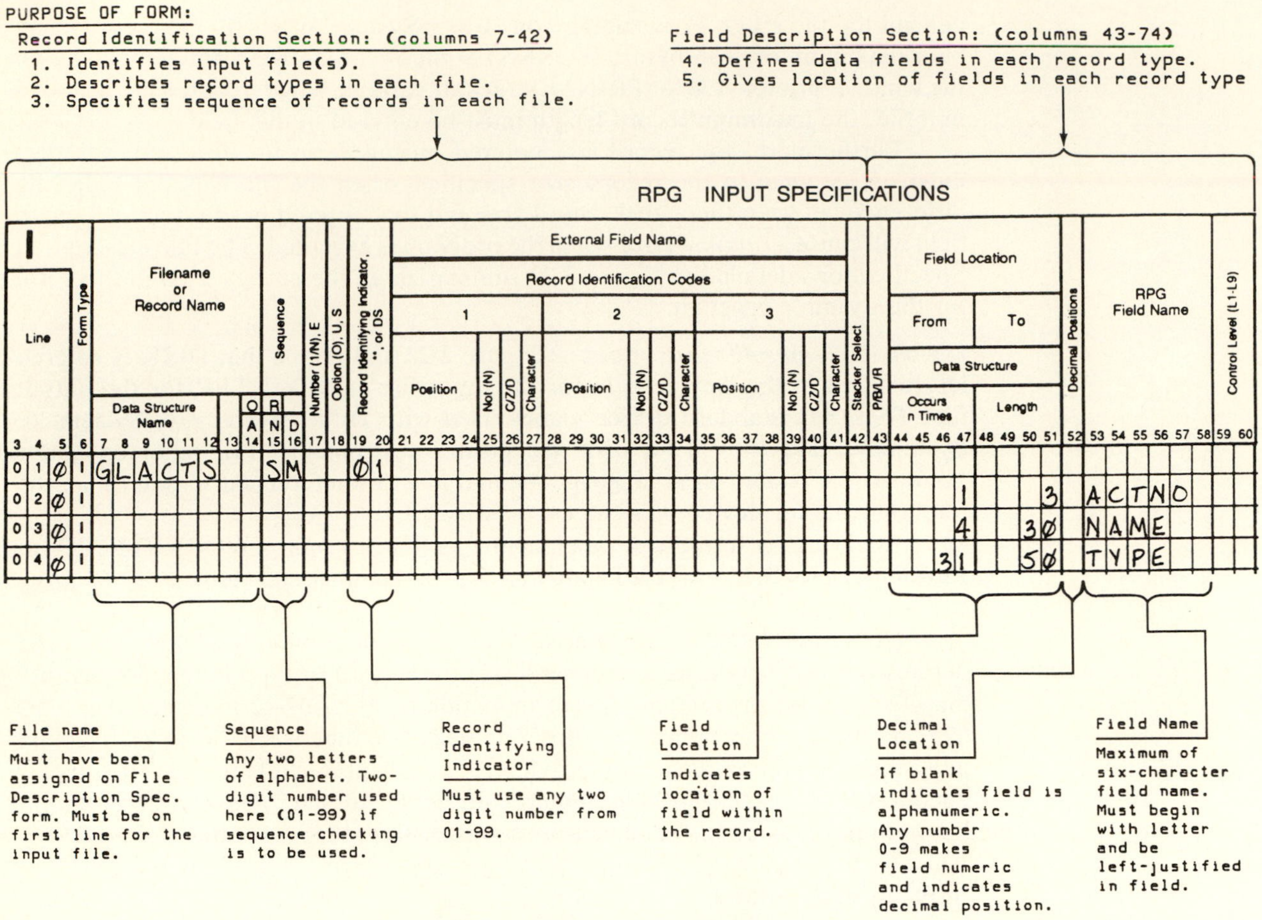

Figure 2-23 Input Specifications form for example program.

File name (Columns 7–14): The input file name is entered left-justified in this field and must be identical to the related file defined in the File Description Form. A terminal error would be generated in compilation if the names are not the same.

Examine Figure 2-23 and notice that the file name (GLACTS) is entered only on the *first line* and is *not repeated* on the following coding lines.

Sequence (Columns 15–16): A two-character entry must be placed in this field for every record type in the file. Depending on the requirements of the program, the entry may be either two alphabetic or two numeric characters. Any combination of two alphabetic letters should be used when

1. the file has only one record type, or,
2. when sequence checking (order of records in a multiple record file) is not required.

A two-number entry should be made when

1. the file includes more than one record type, and
2. the sequence checking of a multiple record file is required. This topic will be discussed in Chapter 8.

Look at Figure 2-23 and notice that the letters SM (author's initials) are entered in this field. Again, any two letters could have been specified. If this entry is omitted, a warning error will be generated in compilation and AA (default) will be assumed.

Record Identifying Indicator (Columns 19–20): Every record type in a file must be assigned a unique two-digit indicator from 01 through 99. The number, which is supplied by the programmer, may be considered as the numeric name assigned to the record format.

When a record is read from the file, the indicator assigned to the record type will turn on and remain on for the complete program cycle. After the last output instruction is executed, the Record Identifying indicator will be automatically turned off. Program control will then read another record, turn the indicator on, and continue the processing sequence until the end of the file is sensed.

The file processed contains 13 records, consequently, the 01 record identifying indicator assigned in the program (see Figure 2-23) will automatically be turned on and set off 13 times by RPG control. If there were 50,000 records in the file, the indicator would turn on and set off 50,000 times.

Record identifying indicators are used to *condition* calculation and output instructions. Depending on the status (*on* or *off*) of the indicator, they inform the computer when to execute any instructions conditioned by the related indicator. An explanation of the processing logic associated with Record Identifying Indicators is detailed in the example program's source listing in Figure 2-24.

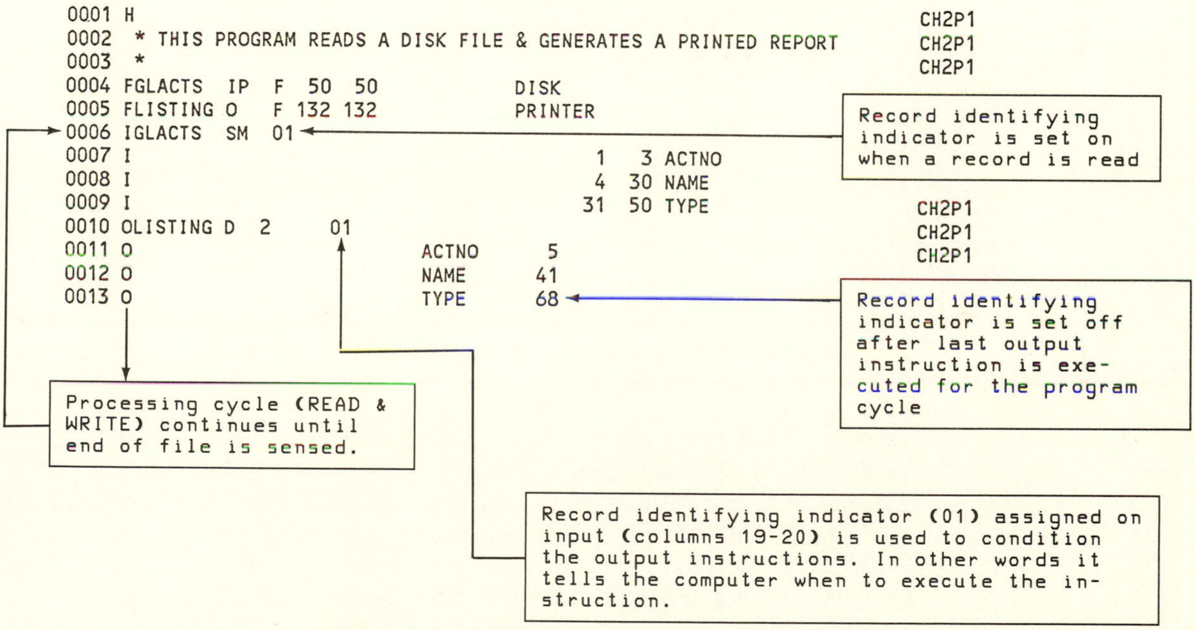

Figure 2-24 Record identifying indicator processing logic and control.

A thorough understanding of indicators (all classes) is important in RPG programming. As more complex programs are introduced, other indicator types will be presented and their logic and use discussed.

Field Location (Columns 44–51): This area is in the Field Description section of the input form and must be entered on a line different from Record Description entries. In Figure 2-25 the area is divided into two separate fields: the FROM field (columns 44–47) and the TO field (columns 48–51). The FROM field represents the beginning (high-order) position of the input field, and the TO field indicates the last (low-order) position.

Information for the field locations and lengths in the body of a data record is obtained from the related Record Layout form. The rules for developing field sizes are as follows:

1. FROM and TO field entries must be right-justified.
2. Alphanumeric fields may not be defined longer than 256 bytes.
3. Numeric fields may not be defined longer than 15 bytes.

The relationship of the Record Layout form and the entries in the Field Location fields is shown in Figure 2-25.

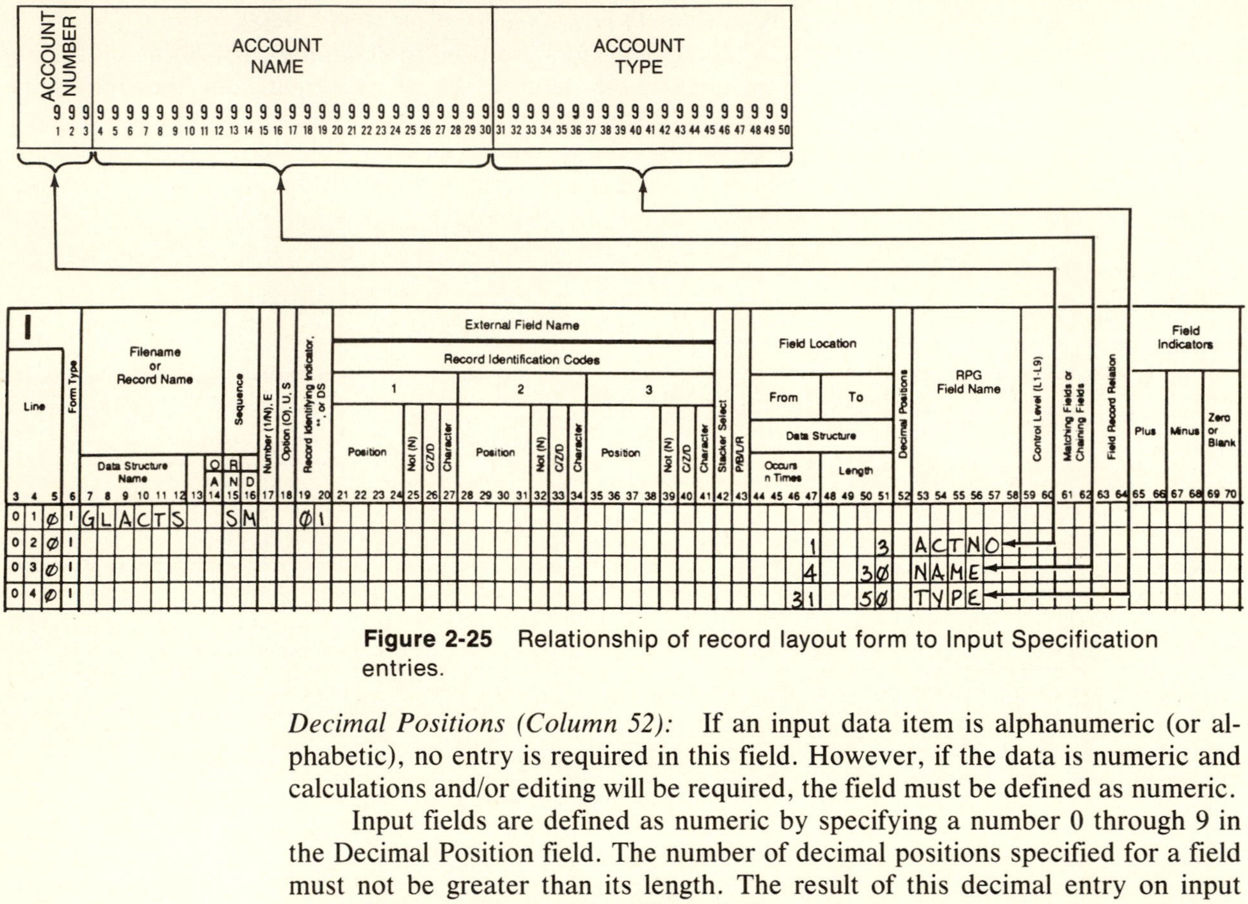

Figure 2-25 Relationship of record layout form to Input Specification entries.

Decimal Positions (Column 52): If an input data item is alphanumeric (or alphabetic), no entry is required in this field. However, if the data is numeric and calculations and/or editing will be required, the field must be defined as numeric.

Input fields are defined as numeric by specifying a number 0 through 9 in the Decimal Position field. The number of decimal positions specified for a field must not be greater than its length. The result of this decimal entry on input numeric data is illustrated in Figure 2-26.

Numeric data values stored on disk, tape, or diskette do not include an *explicit* or *implied decimal.* The decimal positions for a field are defined in the program and *implied* in the related CPU storage position during program execution. An implied decimal does not use a storage position; instead, it identifies its location in the body of a field (or literal) by a "tagging" process. A comprehensive discussion of the definition, editing, and processing of numeric fields is included in Chapters 3 and 4.

Field Name (Columns 53–58): The input field names specified on the Input Specifications form are programmer-supplied and must follow the syntax rules

Decimal Position Entry	*Value in disk field*	*Value CPU storage*	*Comments*
0	12345	12345▲	Integer value
2	12345	123▲45	Decimal value with 2 implied decimals
5	12345	▲12345	Decimal value with 5 implied decimals
blank	12345	12345	Alphanumeric value

Notes: In the last example, because the decimal position field is blank, the numeric value will be processed as alphanumeric. Calculation or editing may not be performed with that field.

Symbol ▲ indicates an implied decimal (not actual). With the exception of output edited numeric fields, actual decimals are not assigned to field storage in the CPU.

Figure 2-26 Storage result of decimal position assignments on input data.

detailed in Figure 2-27. If an output (or calculation) field name is not defined the same as a related input field name, two errors will be generated in compilation. First, because the input field was not specified as an output (or calculation) field, a warning error (UNREFERENCED FIELD) will be flagged for that condition. Second, because the related, but incorrect, output field was not defined on input, a terminal error (UNDEFINED FIELD) will also be generated.

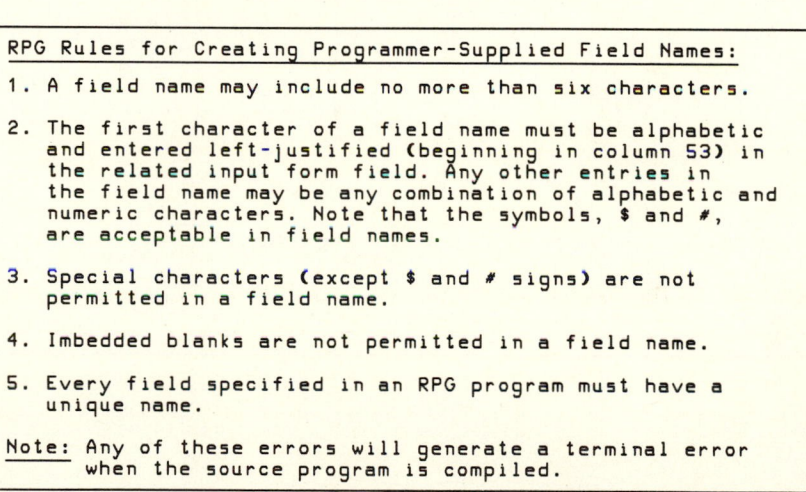

RPG Rules for Creating Programmer-Supplied Field Names:

1. A field name may include no more than six characters.
2. The first character of a field name must be alphabetic and entered left-justified (beginning in column 53) in the related input form field. Any other entries in the field name may be any combination of alphabetic and numeric characters. Note that the symbols, $ and #, are acceptable in field names.
3. Special characters (except $ and # signs) are not permitted in a field name.
4. Imbedded blanks are not permitted in a field name.
5. Every field specified in an RPG program must have a unique name.

Note: Any of these errors will generate a terminal error when the source program is compiled.

Figure 2-27 RPG rules for creating field names.

All the Input Specifications fields used in the example program have been explained. With the exception of the number of fields, they represent the minimum entries that must be included in a program that processes a disk-stored file and generates a printed report. The syntax and control of the input fields that have not been discussed are introduced in subsequent chapters.

Output-Format Specifications

Output to printers, disk, tape, diskette, CRTs, and so forth is controlled in an RPG program by the Output-Format Specifications form. Recall that the RPG compilation sequence (H, F, E, L, I, C, O) indicates that output instructions are included at the end of any program. The function of this specifications form is to:

1. Define and format output from the program.
2. Control the conditions under which the output is to occur.

Refer to Figure 2-28 and notice that the Output-Format Specifications form is divided into three logical processing sections, which are explained below.

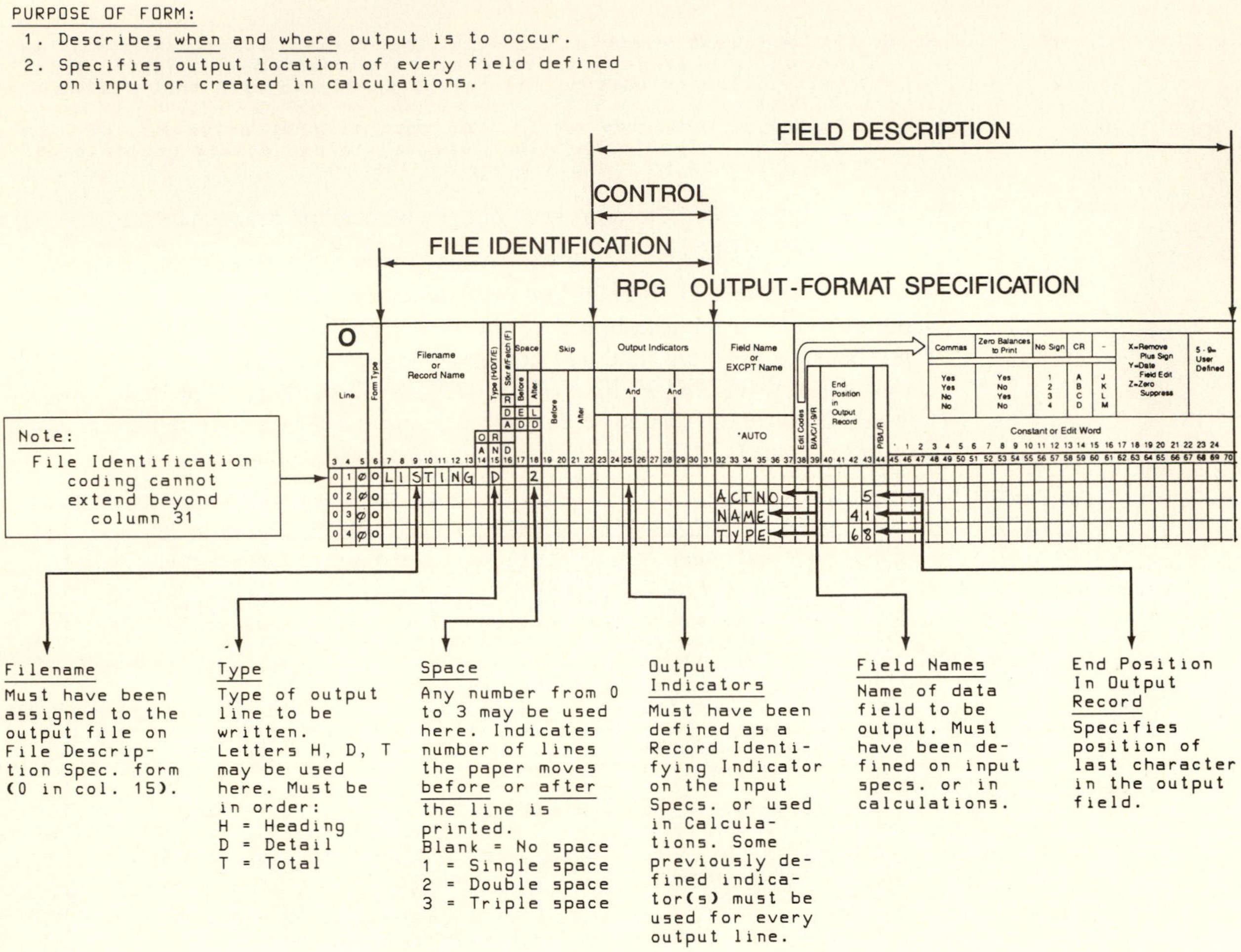

Figure 2-28 Detailed Output-Format Specifications form for example program.

File Identification Section (Columns 7–31): This section describes the following:

1. Output files (previously defined in File Description form.
2. Type of the output (H, D, T, and E).
3. Line spacing (before and after).
4. Top-of-page and other skipping control.
5. The conditions (indicator control) under which output will be executed.

Entries in this section may not extend beyond Column 31.

Control Section (Columns 23–31): Related indicators(s) previously defined on input, calculations, or as page control are entered in one or more of the fields in this section to inform the computer when to output an instruction. In RPG terminology, this process is referred to as the *conditioning of output*. In other words, on the basis of the indicator status (*on* or *off*), the output will or will not be executed.

Field Description Section (Column 23–74): This section describes the following:

1. Fields and constants included in the output record(s).
2. Where the field or constant values are to be placed in the output record(s).
3. Conditioning (indicator control) of record and/or field output.

Entries in this section must begin in column 23 and not be entered on the same line as a File Identification instruction.

Notice that the Control section (columns 23–31) is included in the File and Field Description sections. If the indicator(s) assigned (columns 19–20) conditions a record, then it is a File Identification entry. If the indicator(s) conditions a field or constant, then it is entered for Field Description control.

File Description Fields

Form Type (Column 6): The letter O must be entered in column 6 for every output instruction.

File Name (Columns 7–14): Any file name entered here must have been previously defined on the File Description form as an output file by specifying the letter O in column 15. Any difference in the two file names would result in a warning and terminal error. The file name must be left-justified in the field and *is not* repeated on the following output instructions. Examine Figure 2-28 and note how the file name, LISTING, is entered.

Type (Column 15): The H, D, T, and E entries that appear in this Output-Format Specifications field heading inform the computer on the timing of output. For any one output file, the line types must be assigned in an H, D, and T order. However, E line types may be specified in any order on the output form. The function of each type of line (column 15 entry) is explained as follows:

Heading line (H): Usually include constants and RPG reserved words. However, variable field data may also be output at heading time. This type of line is discussed in Chapter 3.

Detail line (D): Is assigned to line types that include variable data from an input record or from the result of calculations. Notice that same processing results occur if an output line is specified with an H or a D. In any case, however, H lines must precede any D (or T lines) to prevent a terminal error in compilation of the source program. Refer back to Figure 2-28 and notice that a D is entered in Column 15, indicating that output processing is executed at detail time.

Total line (T): End of file processing and control group total lines must be assigned this type of line. This subject is discussed in Chapters 4 and 9.

Exception line (E): Is controlled by an EXCPT operation in calculation and does not follow the normal RPG processing cycle. An explanation of this type of line is reserved for Chapter 7.

Space (Columns 17–18): This area includes two separate fields—*Before* (column 17) and *After* (column 18)—that control line spacing in the body of a report. A 3 is the largest number that may be specified in either field. Refer to Figure 2-28 and observe that a 2 is entered in the *After* field (column 18). This entry indicates that double spacing is to be included in the body of the report and that spacing control is to occur *after* the line is printed (output). Figure 2-29 explains the results of *Before* and *After* entries in the control of line spacing.

```
Example 1:

1 entered in column 17 (Before)

PREVIOUS LINE HERE
CURRENT LINE PRINTED HERE

Example 2:

2 entered in column 17 (Before)

PREVIOUS LINE HERE
         space
CURRENT LINE PRINTED HERE

Example 3:

3 entered in column 17 (Before)

PREVIOUS LINE HERE
         space
         space
CURRENT LINE PRINTED HERE

Example 4:

1 entered in column 18 (After)

CURRENT LINE PRINTED HERE
NEXT PRINT LINE

Example 5:

2 entered in column 18 (After)

CURRENT LINE PRINTED HERE
         space
NEXT PRINT LINE

Example 6:

3 entered in column 18 (after)

CURRENT LINE PRINTED HERE
         space
         space
NEXT PRINT LINE

Example 7:

It is possible to get a maximum of 5 spaces
between 2 print lines by specifying 3 in
the After field for one print line and a
3 in the Before field of the next line type
to be printed.

PREVIOUS LINE HERE
         space
         space
         space
         space
         space
NEXT LINE PRINTED HERE
```

Figure 2-29 Results of *Before* and *After* line spacing control.

Output Indicators (Columns 23–31): This area on the Output-Format Specifications includes three fields in which indicators are entered to control (condition) an output instruction. A conditioning indicator may be specified in any of the fields, and the field used is at the option of the programmer. The indicator(s) assigned must have been previously *defined* on the input form (or in calculations).

Any indicator specified but not defined would generate a terminal error during compilation. Figure 2-30 shows the relationship of the Record Identifying Indicator (01) assigned to the record type on the input form to its use on output. When a data record is read, the Record Identifying Indicator turns on and remains on until the last output instruction is executed, or tested. Then it is automatically turned off. This *on* and *off* condition of the indicator occurs for every record processed in the data file. If the 01 indicator had been omitted on the output form, the program would execute successfully.

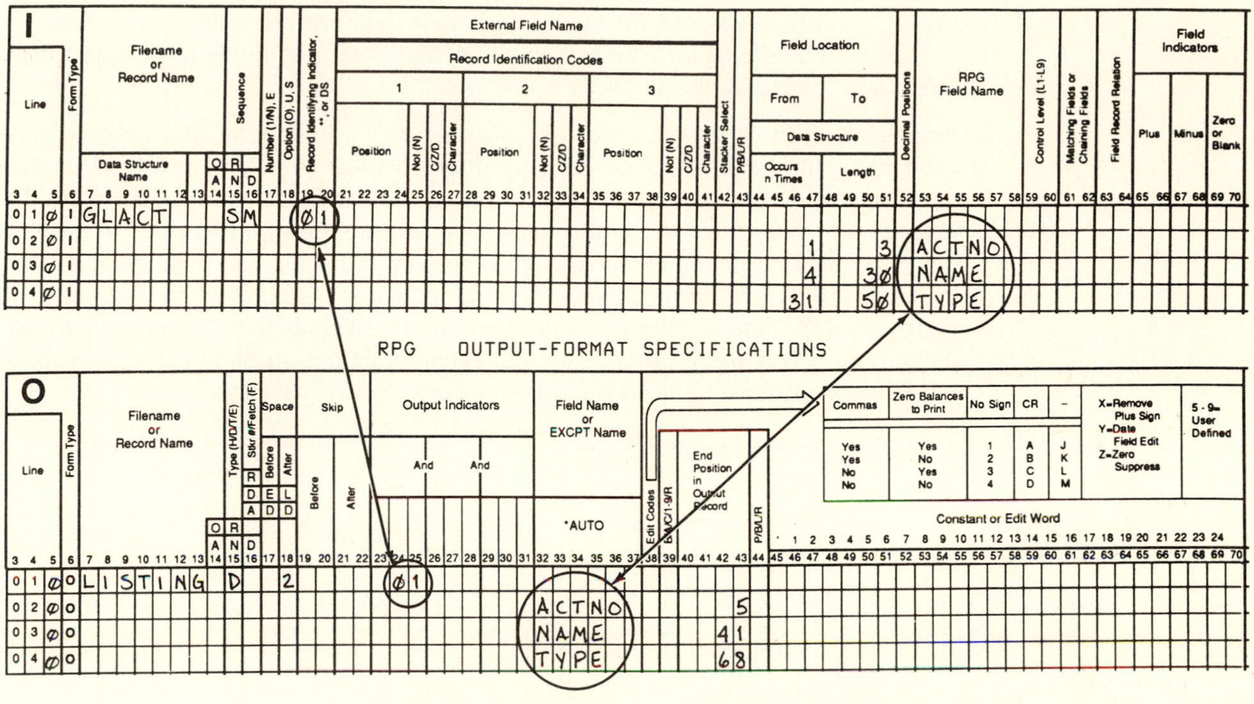

Figure 2-30 Relationship of Record Identifying Indicator assigned on Input Specifications to its use on output form.

However, the following two conditions would result:

1. Because the first processing cycle of RPG occurs before a record is read (see Figure 2-12, Step 1), any output not conditioned by an indicator will be executed. In the example program, this would cause two extra blank lines to be output (2 in the After field) before the first record from the data file was processed. RPG automatically pre-initializes alphanumeric fields to blanks on execution, so nothing would be printed during the first cycle.
2. A warning error would be generated in compilation, identifying that indicator 01 was UNREFERENCED.

Any of the available 01 to 99 indicators could have been assigned on input for the control of output. However, informal standards followed by many programmers have led to the functional assignment of these indicators. Often 01 to 20 are reserved for the input form, and 21 to 99 are grouped for calculations and other program control. Also, notice in Figure 2-30 that the fields defined on the input form are specified exactly the same on output. Any difference in a related field name results in two errors: a warning error identifying an UNREFERENCED input field and a terminal error for the UNDEFINED output field.

Field Name (Columns 32–37): The first entry for field names must begin on a line following the File Identification instruction. A terminal error is generated during source program compilation if this rule is not followed.

Field names entered in this area must have been defined in input or calculation specifications. Observe in Figure 2-30 that the input fields ACTNO, NAME, and TYPE are defined on the Input Specifications form and entered on the Output-Format form. Any misspelling of any field name on output will result in two errors in compilation time. A terminal error, UNDEFINED FIELD, will be generated for the undefined output field. A warning error, UNREFERENCED FIELD, will be generated for the related input field not referenced on output.

Subsequent chapters discuss how and when variable fields are created, defined, and loaded in calculations.

End Position in Output Record (Columns 40–43): Entries in this field, which must be right-justified, define the low-order position of the related field in the body of the output record. During output processing, the entire field value is placed in the output record by this entry. For printed reports, this entry identifies the print position of the last character in the output field. The placement of the example program's output fields in the output record is detailed in Figure 2-31. Notice that the line is not printed until all the field values have been moved into the output record (*buffer area*). This movement of data is automatically controlled in RPG and is transparent to the programmer.

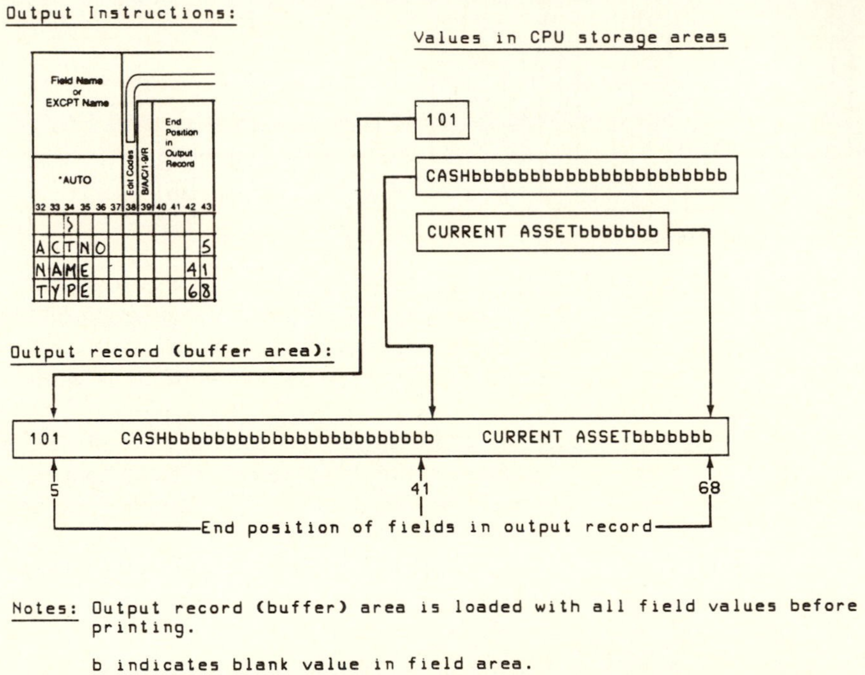

Figure 2-31 Relationship of input field values to output record (buffer area).

A *buffer area* is an input/output (I/O) storage area that is automatically built by the system for every input and output file during program execution. The I/O devices assigned in the program determine the minimum and maximum size of the buffer areas created.

Refer to Figure 2-32 and notice how the end position entries for the ACTNO, NAME, and TYPE fields specified on the output form relate to the last character

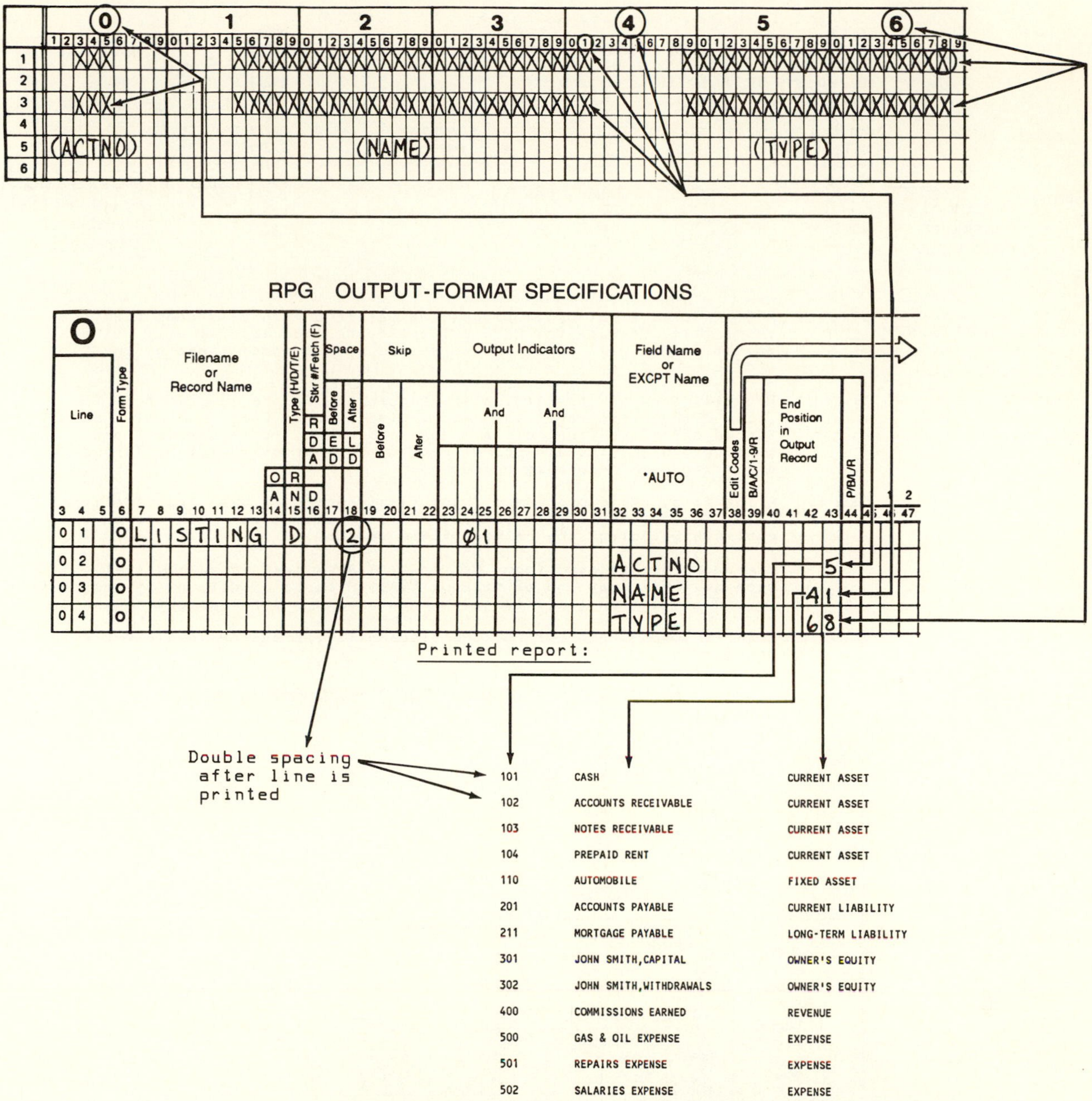

Figure 2-32 Relationship of fields locations in the print chart to output form end position entry and printed report.

of each field formatted on the printer spacing chart. For example, 5 is the print position of the last character for ACTNO value, 41 for NAME, and 68 for TYPE.

RPG Processing Cycle for Example Program

It has been previously explained (see Figure 2-12) that the execution of any RPG program is controlled by a built-in logic cycle. A subset of this cycle and the way it coordinates with the example RPG program is detailed in Figure 2-33.

```
... ... 1 ... ... 2 ... ... 3 ... ... 4 ... ... 5 ... ... 6 ... ... 7 ...
H                                                                   CH2P1
 * THIS PROGRAM READS A DISK FILE & GENERATES A PRINTED REPORT      CH2P1
 *                                                                  CH2P1
FGLACTS  IP  F  50  50          DISK                                CH2P1
FLISTING O   F 132 132          PRINTER                             CH2P1
IGLACTS  SM  01                                                     CH2P1
I                                          1   3 ACTNO              CH2P1
I                                          4  30 NAME               CH2P1
I                                         31  50 TYPE               CH2P1
OLISTING D  2      01                                               CH2P1
O                          ACTNO     5                              CH2P1
O                          NAME     41                              CH2P1
O                          TYPE     68                              CH2P1
```

Step 1: Perform all heading or detail output

Step 2: Turn off record-identifying and control-level indicators

Step 3: Read a record

Step 10: Make data from record just read available for processing

Step 1. RPG performs first cycle processing before a record is read from the input file. Because the Record Identifying Indicator 01 will not be on, no output will occur. Note that output is conditioned by the 01 indicator.

Step 2. RPG will turn off any indicators before any record is read from the file. A 1P (first page) indicator, discussed in Chapter 3, will be turned off after first cycle processing. Then, for subsequent processing cycles, the 01 Record Identifying Indicator will be turned off after each record is processed.

Step 3. After first cycle processing, the first record is read from the input file. Record Identifying Indicator 01 is automatically turned on which controls output of the related field values.

When a record is read from the input file, a test is automatically made by RPG for an end of file LR (Last Record) condition. If end of file is sensed, the LR indicator is turned on and program execution ends.

Step 10. Data is loaded into the related storage fields and available for output processing.

Figure 2-33 Example program's processing cycle.

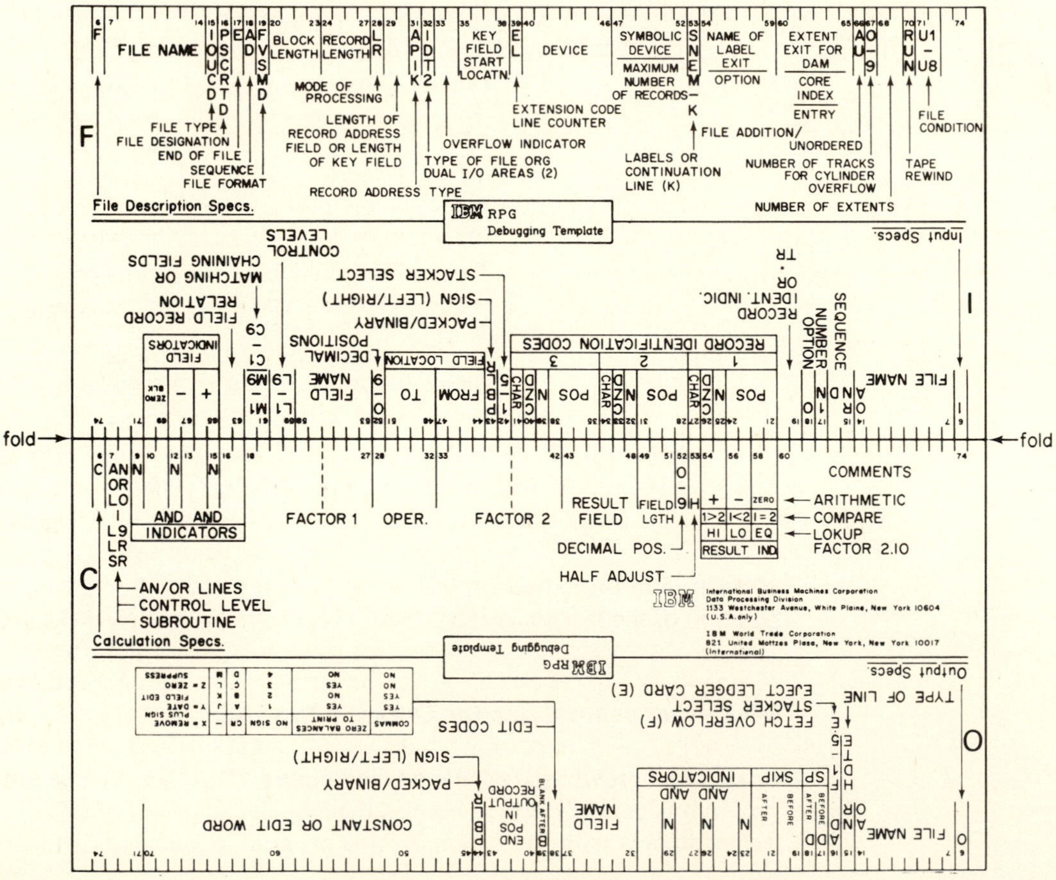

Figure 2-34 RPG debugging template.

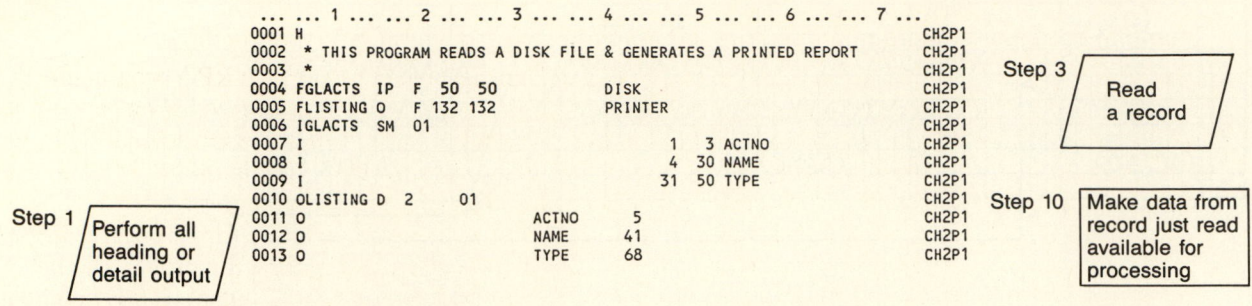

Debugging Aid

Specifying an entry in the wrong column is a common error in RPG programming. Because field and column references are not included on a source listing generated from compilation of the program, column entry errors are almost impossible to find without some aid. A tool, referred to as a *Debugging Template*, is available to locate the position of entries in a source listing. Examine the template shown in Figure 2-34 and notice that separate sections are included for File Description (F), Input (I), Calculations (C), and Output-Format (O) Specifications. The back of the form, which is not shown, has template sections for Control (H), Extension (E), Line Counter (L), Sort (S), Telecommunications (T), and Option (U) Specifications. Because S, T, and U specifications control processing functions are outside of an RPG program, they are not discussed in this textbook.

An example of how the template is used is illustrated in Figure 2-35. Notice that Column 6 on the template is aligned with the related specification letter F and that the form is placed horizontally along the line. A comparison of the columns on the Debugging Template with the source instruction will locate an incorrect entry.

```
... ... 1 ... ... 2 ... ... 3 ... ... 4 ... ... 5 ... ... 6 ... ... 7 ...
0001 H                                                                  CH2P1
0002  * THIS PROGRAM READS A DISK FILE & GENERATES A PRINTED REPORT     CH2P1
0003  *                                                                 CH2P1
0004 FGLACTS  IP  F  80  80            DISK                             CH2P1
0005 FLISTING O   F 132 132            PRINTER                          CH2P1
```

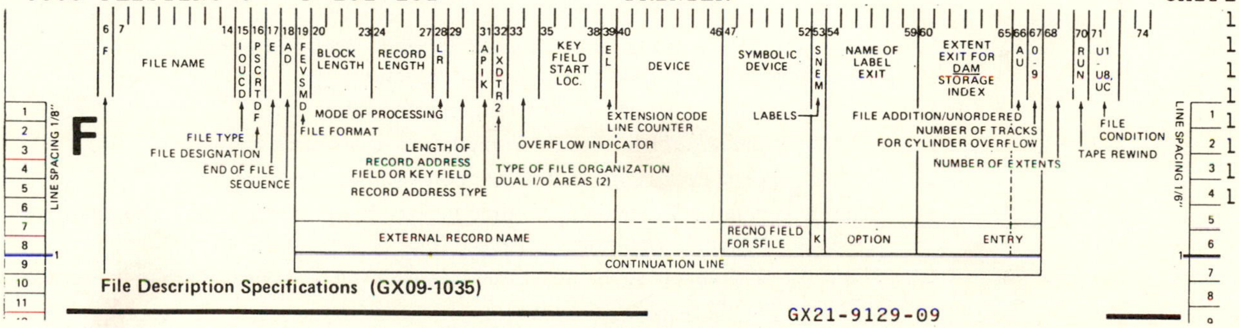

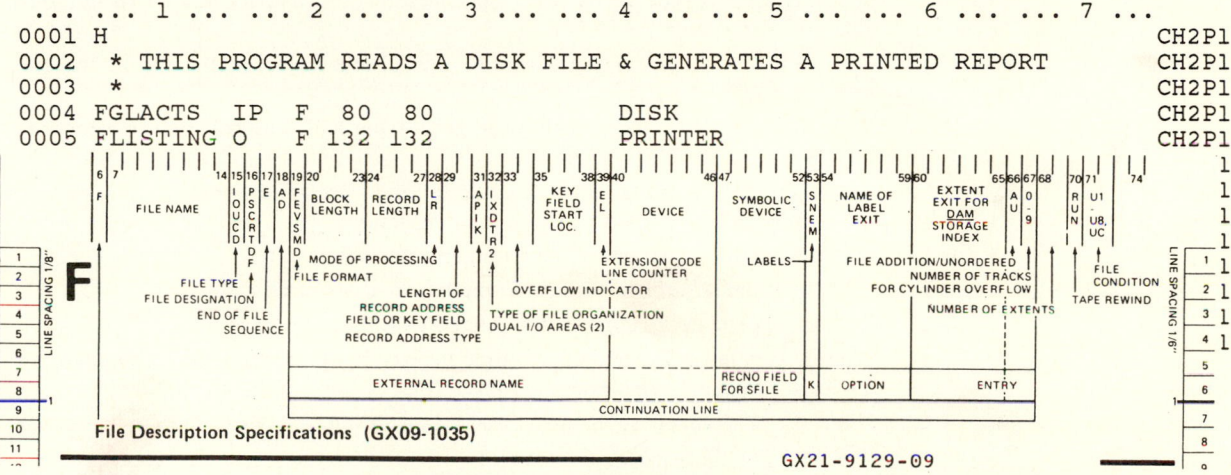

Figure 2-35 Example of how the debugging template is used.

SUMMARY

The preliminary planning steps and tools to develop an RPG program have been introduced in this chapter and will be used to support all the example programs presented in this text. Included were the preparation of program specifications, record layout forms, printer spacing charts, and system and program logic flowcharts.

A comprehensive discussion of the syntax for an RPG program that processes an input file and generates a printed report was presented. Entries in the Control, File, Input, and Output-Format Specifications needed to control the input and output processing requirements of the example program were explained.

The following chapters will supplement this introduction to RPG and address most of the important processing functions supported by this language.

QUESTIONS

2-1. Name four documentation tools that should be developed before an RPG application program is written.

2-2. What are some of the topics included in program specifications?

2-3. What is included in a data file? On what medium may a data file be stored? By what methods may data be loaded into a file?

2-4. What documentation tool is used to format data records? Are they all the same design? Explain.

2-5. What determines the size of a data record? Into what areas are data records subdivided? What may determine the location of these areas in the body of a record format?

2-6. The record areas answered in Question 2-5 may be further subdivided into what elements? Then, into what parts may those elements be segmented?

2-7. What documentation tool is used to format a printed report? What is the source of information for the size of the variable data included on this form?

2-8. What is the function of a system flowchart? Which flowchart symbols are applicable to its design?

2-9. Explain the purpose of a program logic flowchart. What flowchart symbols are used in this flowchart type? What RPG specifications are usually related to this flowchart?

2-10. What three basic processing functions are automatically performed in the RPG program cycle?

2-11. Refer to Figure 2-12 and explain what processing RPG controls before a record is read from a data file.

2-12. Assuming that the preliminary documentation is prepared, what are the steps required to prepare an RPG program for production?

2-13. On what medium may source programs be stored?

2-14. What may prevent the successful compilation of a source program?

2-15. Define the term *debugging* as it is related to RPG programming.

2-16. What is generated (other than a source listing) from the successful compilation of a source program? Where and in what format is this output stored?

2-17. Name the program phase that generates a printed report from a program that creates this type of output.

2-18. Refer to question 2-17 and explain what may prevent a successful completion of that phase.

2-19. Name six RPG specification forms.

2-20. What are the minimum number of form types that must be used for any RPG program?

2-21. What is the compilation order of an RPG program? What happens if this order is not followed?

2-22. Explain the minimum entries required on the Control Specifications form. What is the form's function?

2-23. In an RPG program, what is the function of the File Description Specifications instructions?

2-24. Refer to a File Description Specifications form and identify the minimum entries for an input file stored on disk. Also, identify the minimum entries required for an output printer file. Explain the significance of each of these entries.

2-25. Examine the file names that follow and identify which of the entries are incorrect and why the syntax is unacceptable.

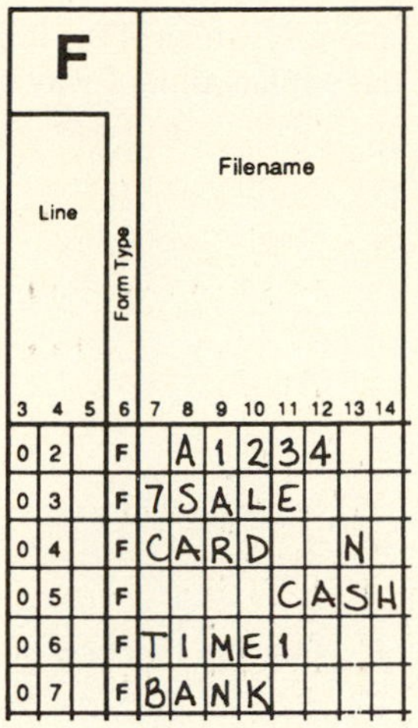

2-26. Refer to Question 2-25 and explain what type of error (if any) will be generated in program compilation if any of the file errors were included in the source instructions.

2-27. What is the function of the Input Specifications in an RPG program?

2-28. Refer to an Input Specifications form and identify the two logical sections. What is the processing function of each section? What are the general formatting restrictions for the sections?

2-29. What is the minimum number of files that must be specified in an RPG program?

2-30. Explain the entries in the following section of an Input Specifications form.

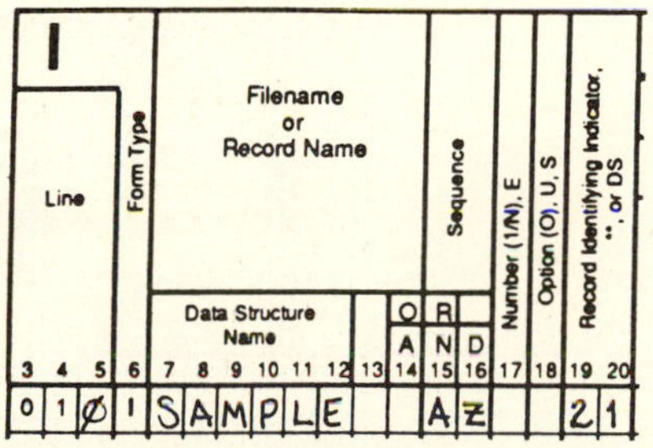

I
Line
Form Type
Filename or Record Name
Data Structure Name
Sequence
OR
AND
Number (1/N), E
Option (O), U, S
Record Identifying Indicator, **, or DS
3 4 5 6 7 8 9 10 11 12 13 14 15 16 17 18 19 20
0 1 Ø I SAMPLE AZ 21

2-31. What are Record Identifying Indicators? What is their function in an RPG program? Where are they defined and specified? When are they set on? When do they turn off?

2-32. Explain what is meant by the term *conditioning an instruction.*

2-33. Examine the following Input Specification instructions and determine if the RPG syntax is correct. Explain any entries that are incorrect.

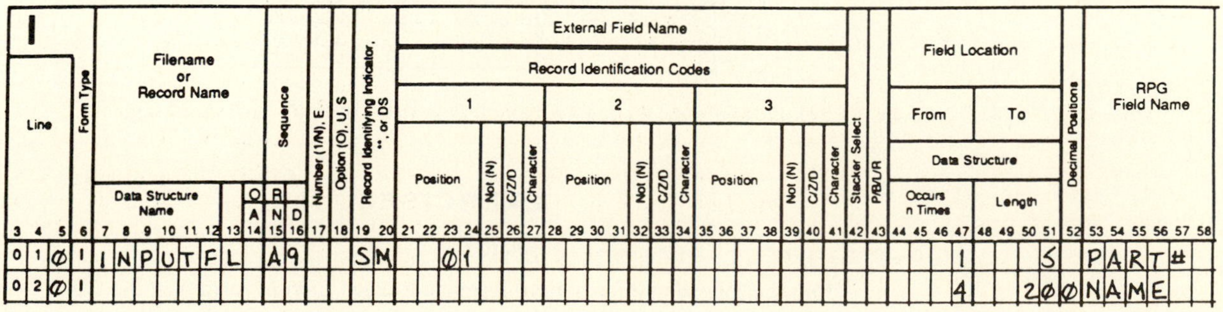

2-34. Identify which of the following field entries are incorrect. Support your answer with an explanation of why an entry is wrong.

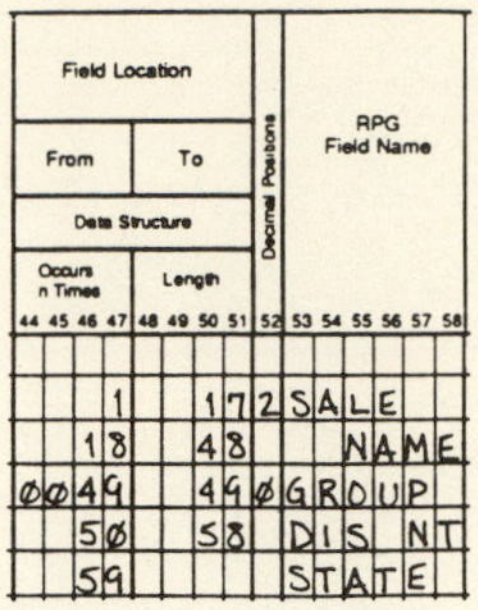

Field Location
From
To
Data Structure
Occurs n Times
Length
Decimal Positions
RPG Field Name
1 17 2 SALE
18 48 NAME
ØØ49 49Ø GROUP
5Ø 58 DIS NT
59 STATE

2-35. Explain the function of the Output-Format Specifications form.

2-36. Refer to an Output-Format Specifications form; identify the logical areas and explain their processing functions.

2-37. What entries may be specified in column 15 of the output form? Explain the meaning of each entry type. In what sequence must they be used?

2-38. If a 3 was specified in the Before field (column 17), how many blank spaces would be provided between two print lines?

2-39. Where in an RPG program is the indicator that is specified on the output form defined? What compilation errors (if any) will be generated if an indicator is correctly defined but is not referenced on output?

2-40. What does the entry in the End Position in Output Record field indicate? What is the source of this entry?

2-41. Examine the following output form and explain the function of each entry.

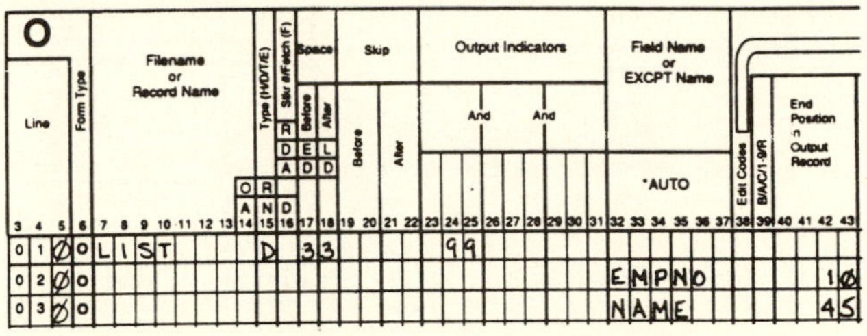

2-42. Identify and explain any errors in the following output form.

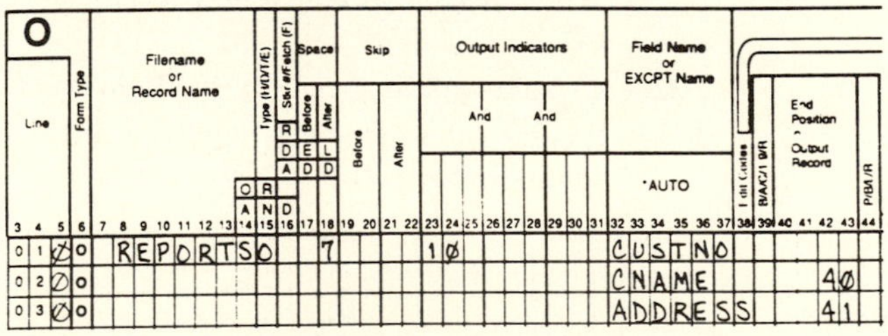

2-43. Explain how the Debugging Template is used in RPG programming.

EXERCISES

Note: Exercises 2-1 through 2-4 are related.

2-1. From the following information, format a Record Layout form (use the type of form available to you):

```
Part Name           20 alphanumeric characters
Part Number          4 alphanumeric characters
Warehouse Location   3 alphanumeric characters
```

2-2. Refer to Exercise 2-1, and format a Printer Spacing Chart. Place the fields on the chart according to the following *beginning* print position locations:

```
Part Number          11
Part Name            20
Warehouse Location   45
```

Indicate on the printer spacing chart that the report is to be double spaced.

2-3. Refer to Exercises 2-1 and 2-2 and write an RPG program to generate the required printed report. Provide your own file, device, and field names.

2-4. Refer to the RPG logic flowchart in Figure 2-12 and explain which steps the program you completed in Exercise 2-3 will execute for the following three conditions:

1. First cycle processing
2. For every record in the data file
3. When end of the input file is sensed

2-5. Debugging an RPG program. The following RPG program source listing includes terminal and warning errors. Refer to each error message; then locate the related error in the program; and, finally, indicate the necessary corrections.

```
Page  1   BABY/34  RPG II  Version 2.3  Unit 24/25    01-01-80  01:50  EX25

           ....+....1....+....2....+....3....+....4....+....5....+....6....+....7.

        1 0001 H                                                               EX25
        2 0002 H                                                               EX25
****-H102- More than one Control Specification encountered.


        3 0003 FDATA    I   F  70  80              DISK                        EX25
****-F007W-File Designation must not be blank with File Type of I, U or C.
****-F163- Record Length must not exceed Block Length.
        4 0004 FREPORT  OP  F 132 132              PRINTER                     EX25
****-F134- Output file requires a blank File Designation.
****-F138- Improper characteristics for use with a primary file.


        5 0005 IDATA    S9  SM                              1   9 STUNO        EX25
****-I095- Both Sequence characters in alpha sequence record must be alphabetic.
****-I100- Record Identifying Indicator must be 01-99, L1-L9, LR, H1-H9 or blank.
****-I090- Record identification and field specification may not share the same line.
****-I083- Columns 7-42 of field description should be blank.


        6 0006                                             10  35 SNAME        EX25
****-I101- Form Type following Input Specification must be I, C or O.


        7 0007 I                                               36 MARK         EX25
****-I107- From Position must be in the range 1-9999.


        8 0008 OREPORT  F 4       01                                           EX25
****-O102- Type must be H, D, T or E.
****-O146- Space Before must be 0-3 or blank.
        9 0009 O                          STUD#     10                         EX25
****-O106- Field Name has not been defined.
       10 0010 O                          SNAME     35                         EX25
****-O106- Field Name has not been defined.
       11 0011 O                          MARK                                 EX25
       12 /*
****-A108- The following field name was never given a length.
             MARK
       13 /*

             THE FOLLOWING INDICATORS WERE SPECIFIED BUT WERE NEVER
             USED TO CONDITION OPERATIONS

             01


             THE FOLLOWING INDICATORS APPEARED IN THIS PROGRAM

                  01
   1 Warning Errors
  15 Fatal Errors
```

<u>Note:</u> All source program entries are in the correct column locations. RPG source statements may be identified by the program name (EX25) in the right margin.

LABORATORY ASSIGNMENTS

All the following laboratory assignments require the following:

1. Printed report
2. Source program listing (generated from compilation)
3. System flowchart (include names of your input file and program in appropriate flowchart symbols)
4. Processing logic flowchart. Refer to RPG program flowchart in Figure 2-13, and include only those steps your program will execute.
5. Listing of the data file
6. Listing of the procedure (run unit) used for program execution. This will differ for individual computer systems.

Laboratory Assignment 2-1: ACTIVE EMPLOYEE LISTING

From the following record layout form and Printer Spacing Chart write an RPG program to generate the report shown.

Format of Input Data Records

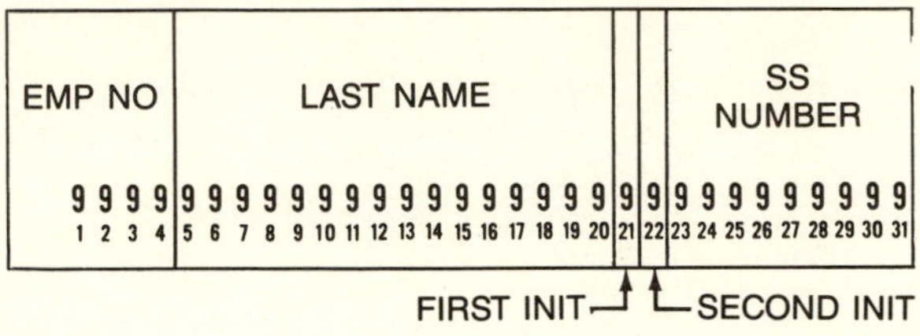

Report Design

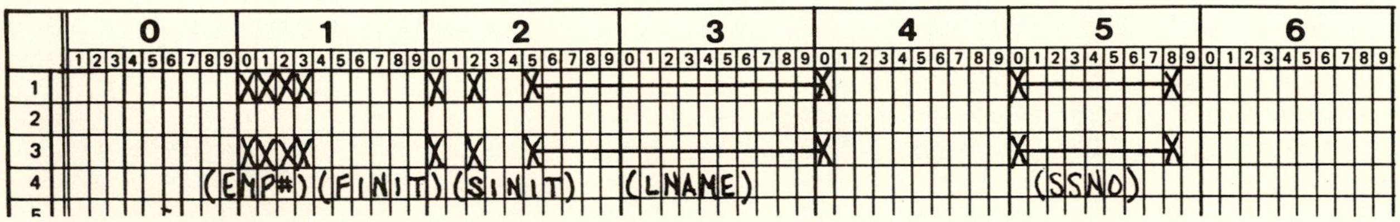

Input Data

Employee Number	Last Name	Initials 1st	Initials 2nd	Social Security Number
0001	WASHINGTON	G	G	017321799
0016	LINCOLN	A	T	018091864
0018	GRANT	U	S	018221885
0032	ROOSEVELT	F	D	018821945
0033	TRUMAN	H	S	018841973
0034	EISENHOWER	D	D	018901971
0039	CARTER	J		019771981
0040	REAGAN	R		020111989

Laboratory Assignment 2-2: EASTERN STATE REPORT LISTING

From the following information write an RPG program to generate the required report.

Format of Input Data Record. Format a record layout form based on the following field information. Then use the form as the document to complete the program's input specifications.

Field name	*Size*	*Type*
State name	20	Alphanumeric
State capital	25	Alphanumeric
State letters	2	Alphabetic
Largest city	25	Alphanumeric

Report Design. Complete a Printer Spacing Chart based on the following information. Indicate that the report is to be double spaced.

Field name	*Print position*
State letters	6–7
State name	16–35
State capital	46–70
Largest city	81–105

Input Data

State Name	State Capital	Letters	Largest City
MAINE	AUGUSTA	ME	PORTLAND
NEW HAMPSHIRE	CONCORD	NH	MANCHESTER
VERMONT	MONTPELIER	VT	BURLINGTON
MASSACHUSETTS	BOSTON	MA	BOSTON
CONNECTICUT	HARTFORD	CT	BRIDGEPORT
RHODE ISLAND	PROVIDENCE	RI	PROVIDENCE
NEW YORK	ALBANY	NY	NEW YORK
PENNSYLVANIA	HARRISBURG	PA	PHILADELPHIA
NEW JERSEY	TRENTON	NJ	NEWARK
DELAWARE	DOVER	DE	WILMINGTON
MARYLAND	ANNAPOLIS	MD	BALTIMORE
VIRGINIA	RICHMOND	VA	NORFOLK
WEST VIRGINIA	CHARLESTON	WV	HUNTINGTON
NORTH CAROLINA	RALEIGH	NC	CHARLOTTE
SOUTH CAROLINA	COLUMBIA	SC	COLUMBIA
GEORGIA	ATLANTA	GA	ATLANTA
FLORIDA	TALLAHASSEE	FL	JACKSONVILLE

Laboratory Assignment 2-3: CUSTOMER MAILING LIST

From the following record layout form and printer spacing chart write an RPG program to generate the report shown. Notice that three different output lines are printed for each record processed. Consequently, three separately formatted detail lines must be included in the program's output coding.

Format of Input Data Records

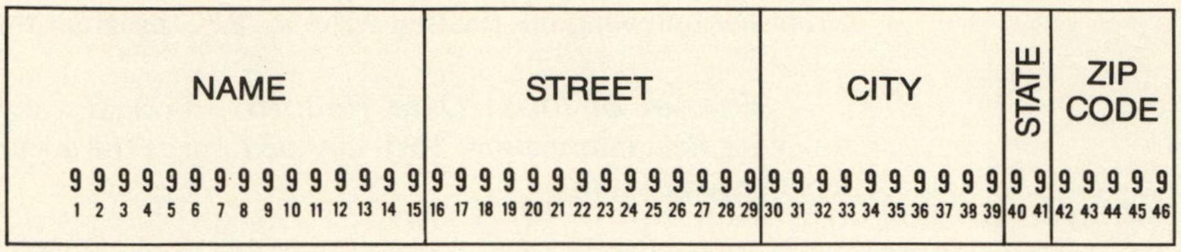

Report Design

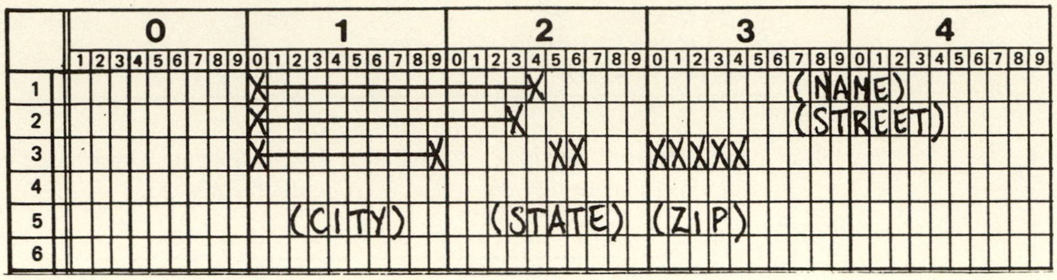

Note: Triple space between customer groups.

Input Data

Name	Street	City	State	Zip
ANDREW GUMP	1 SUN AVENUE	MIAMI	FL	08881
DICK TRACY	CELL 8	ALCATRAZ	CA	07770
BEETLE BAILEY	"A" COMPANY	FORT DIX	NJ	06666
CHARLIE BROWN	8 DOGHOUSE ST.	ANYWHERE	US	00000
MOON MULLINS	16 TIDE ROAD	LAKEVILLE	CT	06497
LI'L ABNER	80 PATCH LANE	DOG PATCH	SC	99999
YOUR NAME	YOUR ADDRESS	....	..	.....

chapter 3
Report Headings and Editing

Chapter 2 presented the RPG syntax and procedures required to print a report without headings, numeric data, or editing. Generally, however, reports do have headings and include numeric values that require editing for readability. This chapter discusses the RPG syntax and processing logic needed to provide for these important features.

Examine the report shown in Figure 3-1 and notice the following:

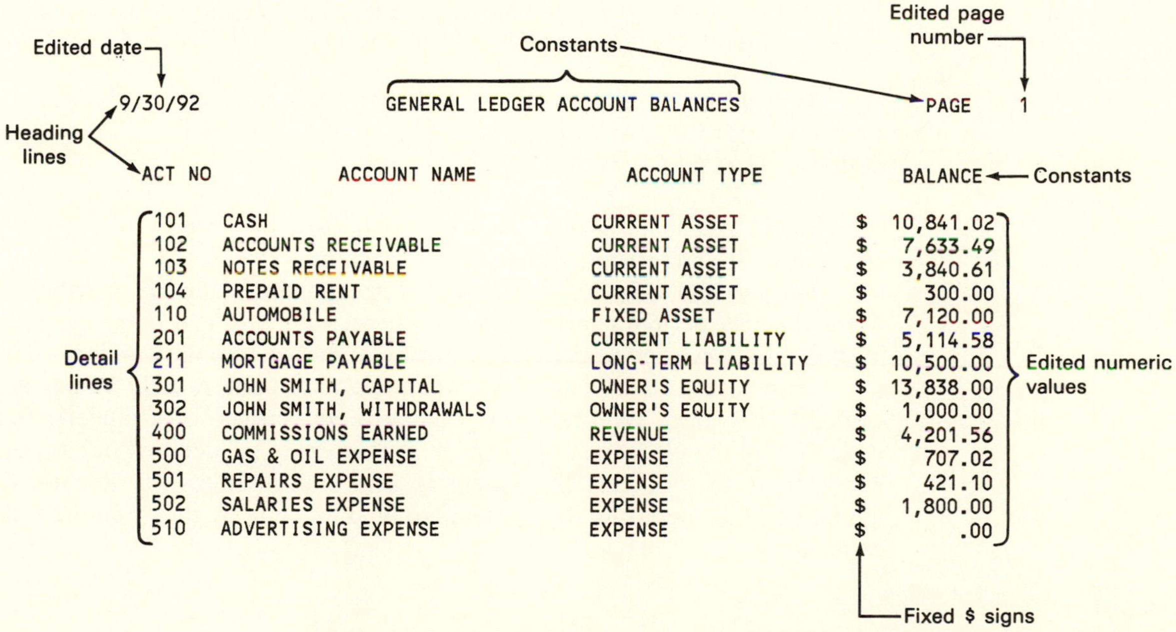

Figure 3-1 Printed report with two heading lines and edited numeric values.

1. The first heading line includes a date, constants, and page number.
2. The second heading line contains all constants.
3. The variable data (detail lines) are printed below the second heading line.
4. The variable spacing (triple, double, and single) is included in the body of the report.

5. All numeric fields (date, page number, and balance) are edited. Editing refers to zero suppression and the insertion of special characters in the body of a numeric value.
6. A fixed dollar sign ($) is printed before every edited balance value.

The printer spacing chart related to the report (Figure 3-1) is detailed in Figure 3-2. Notice that the first heading line contains the variable field UDATE; the constant GENERAL LEDGER ACCOUNT BALANCES; the constant PAGE; and the variable field for the page number, shown as XX0X.

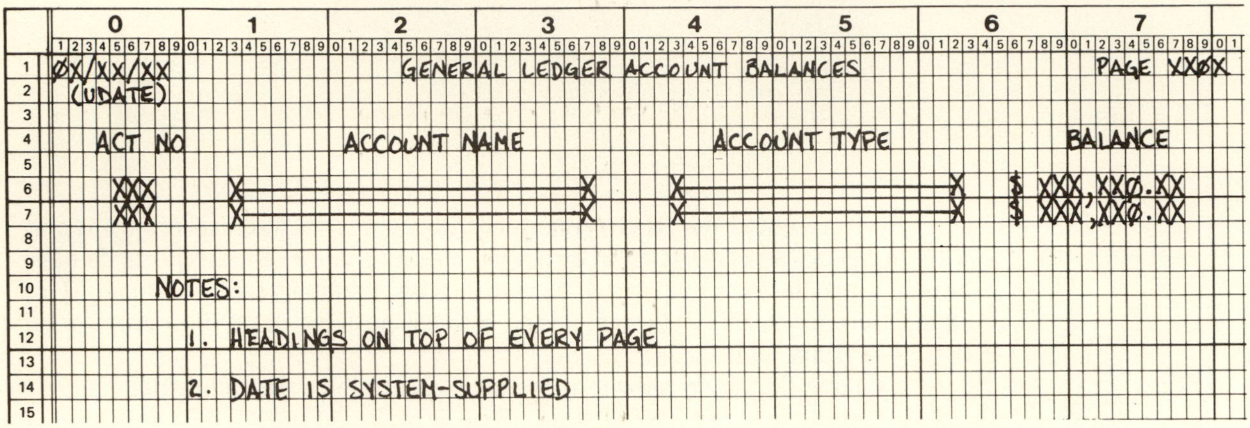

Figure 3-2 Printer spacing chart format with headings and numeric field editing requirements.

The variable field, identified as UDATE (positions 1–8), indicates that the system-supplied date is to be used for the report. Editing requirements for this field are indicated by the 0X/XX/XX format.

The XX0X after the constant PAGE is another RPG control feature that supplies an ascending page number on every page of a report. Page numbering starts at 0001 and increments to 9999.

The constants for the headings lines are coded in the RPG program to print every time the related instruction is executed. Variable field items are identified by the name enclosed in parentheses or by a related column heading.

In the RPG environment, alphanumeric and numeric field values are represented on a print chart with Xs. Editing requirements for a numeric field are indicated by the placement of insertion characters (e.g., decimal point, commas) in the body of the field. The extent of zero suppression in a numeric field is identified by a 0 (zero) in the appropriate field location as shown in the following example.

```
XXX,XX0.XX
      ↑
      └─Indicates where zero
          suppression ends
```

Examine Figure 3-2 and notice that UDATE and page number fields also include a 0 (zero) to represent the control of zero suppression. Included in the editing of the detail lines is a fixed dollar sign printed before each balance value.

Finally, required line spacing, triple after the first heading line, double after the second heading line, and single for the detail lines, is indicated on the print chart by the location of the related lines. Notice that the two identically formatted detail lines represent single spacing and *not* that the values from every input record are to be printed twice.

TYPES OF REPORT LINES

The specific types of lines that may be included in a printed report are classified as follows:

1. **Heading lines**. Print lines that include only constants and/or a combination of constants and variables. Depending on the report requirements, any number of heading lines may be specified in a program. They are designated in an RPG program by the letter H in column 15 of the output form.
2. **Detail lines**. Print lines that include values input into or generated by the program. Constants are often included in this type of line. A detail line is specified in an RPG program by the letter D in column 15 of the output form.
3. **Final total lines**. Print lines that are generated in an RPG program after the end of the data file is sensed. Referred to as *total time output processing*, which is controlled in an RPG program by specifying the letter T in column 15 of the output form. The syntax and logic associated with this line type will be discussed in Chapter 4.
4. **Control total lines**. Group totals that are printed in the body of a report. A comprehensive discussion of this type of line is presented in Chapter 9.

Notice that the use of H and D lines are only for documentation. Any line specified as H (heading) in an RPG program may be coded as D (detail), or vice versa, without generating a syntax error. However, the output records must be assigned in an H, D, and T order.

RPG SYNTAX FOR PAGE AND HEADING CONTROL

When a report extends to more than one page (most of them do), control must be included in an RPG program for this output processing. This is referred to as *page overflow*, which is performed in an RPG program by *skip* control. The logic for page overflow control is shown in Figure 3-3.

Note on Types of Printers

The page control shown in Figure 3-3 assumes that a *line printer* is used with continuous forms of paper. Line printers print a complete line in one stroke. The standard carriage width is 132 characters. Wider models are available, however.

Other popular types include the *serial* and *laser* printers. *Serial* printers, which are commonly used with microcomputers, print one character at a time across a line. They are usually multidirectional in that they print a line from left to right and then on the following line, print right to left. Like line printers, serial printers will also support printing on separate pages.

Laser printers differ from line and serial types of printers in that they format an entire page before printing. They are the fastest, have the best type quality, and offer a multitude of print types. Continuous forms paper, however, is not supported with laser printers; the output is printed on individual sheets.

Regardless of the type of printer used, the syntax and control of page overflow and spacing in the body of a report remains the same in an RPG program.

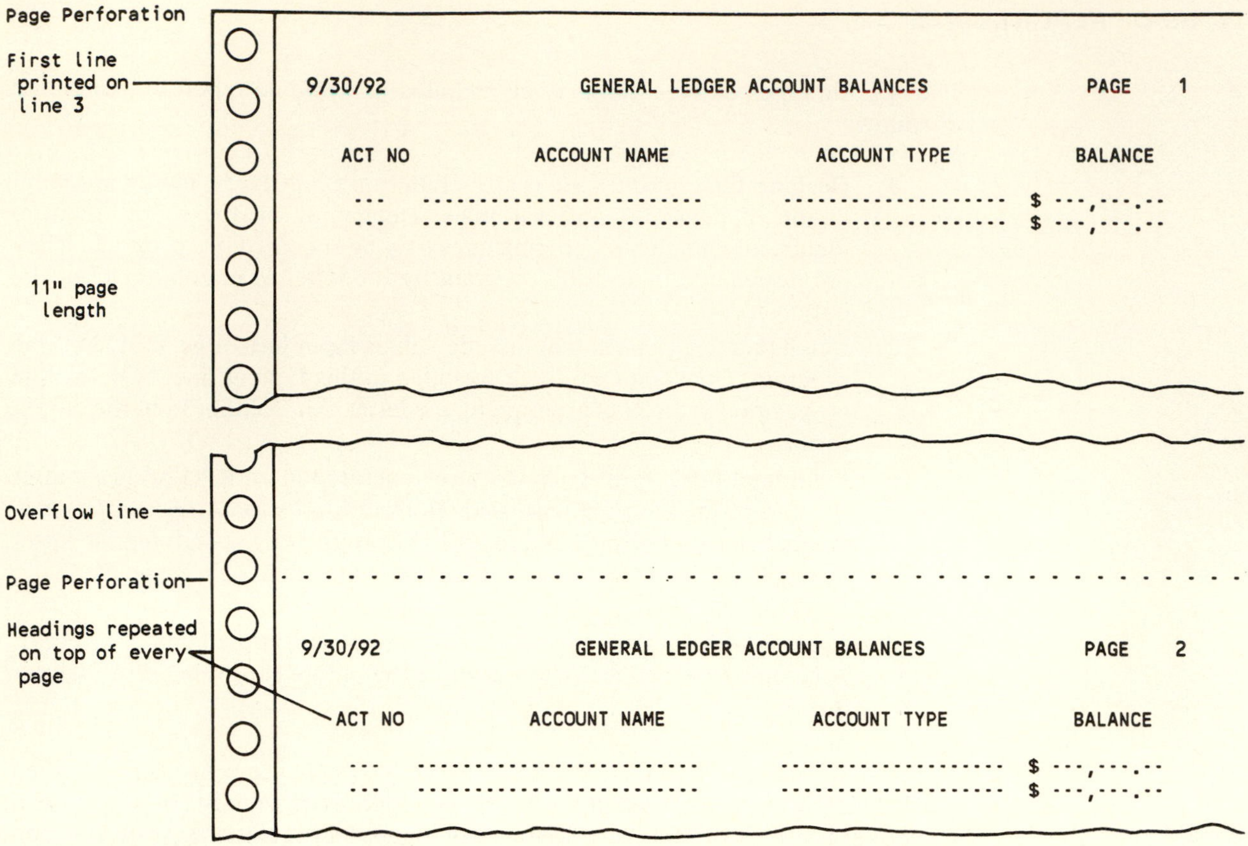

Notes:

1. Standard size (14 1/2" x 11") continuous forms paper is assumed.
2. Line printer is set for 6 lines per inch. Other option is 8 lines per inch.
3. Overflow line is established by the system when standard size paper is used.
4. First line of printing on line 3 is controlled in an RPG program by a Skip Before (or After) field entry in the output form.
5. The printing of headings on the top of every page is controlled by an one of the overflow indicators (OA through OG, or OV) entered in an indicator field on the output coding form.

Figure 3-3 Page overflow processing logic.

On most computer systems, the standard form length and the overflow line are set when the system is configured. For line printers, the standard size of continuous forms paper is usually 14½ by 11 inches.

FILE DESCRIPTION AND OUTPUT-FORMAT SPECIFICATIONS CODING FOR PAGE CONTROL

Top of Page Control

For printer- and CRT-supported output files, *spacing* refers to the advancing of one, two, or three lines at a time. Skipping refers to jumping from one print line to another. Examine the output form in Figure 3-4 and notice that the number 03 is entered in the *Skip Before* field (columns 19 and 20) of the first output instruction. During program execution, this entry will cause the paper to advance to the top of a new page and then begin printing on line 3. Any number from 01 to 99 may be entered in the Skip Before or After fields. For line numbers greater than

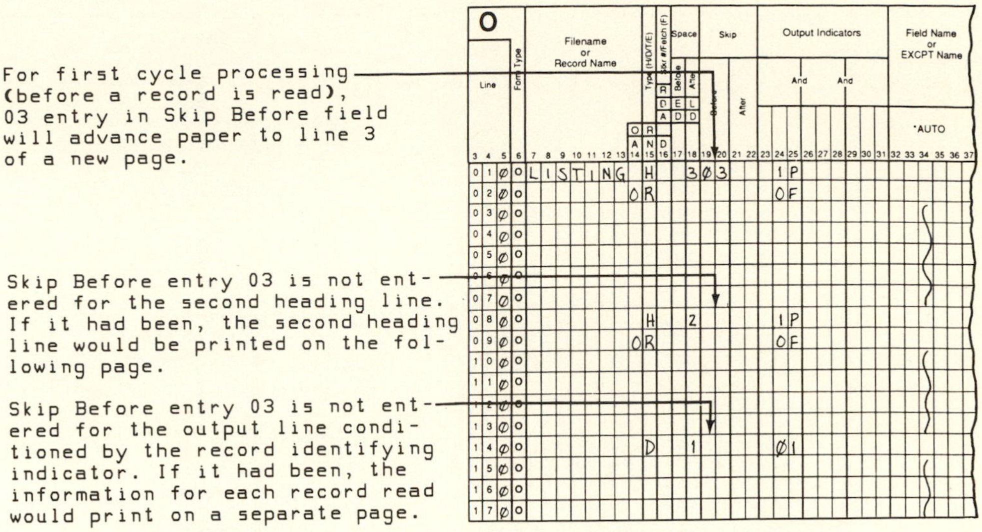
For first cycle processing (before a record is read), 03 entry in Skip Before field will advance paper to line 3 of a new page.
Skip Before entry 03 is not entered for the second heading line. If it had been, the second heading line would be printed on the following page.
Skip Before entry 03 is not entered for the output line conditioned by the record identifying indicator. If it had been, the information for each record read would print on a separate page.
Filename or Record Name
Space
Skip
Output Indicators
Field Name or EXCPT Name
LISTING
H
303
1P
OR
OF
H
2
1P
OR
OF
D
1
Ø1

Figure 3-4 Output-Format Specifications skipping control entry.

99, entries A0 to A9 will control skipping to lines 100 to 109; and entries B0 to B9, for skip control to lines 110 to 112 respectively. Notice that Skip Before controls skipping to the designated line *before* printing the record. Conversely, Skip After performs the skipping function *after* the current output record is printed.

Also, observe in Figure 3-4 that the 03 Skip Before entry is not made in the second heading or detail lines. If the entries had been specified, the second heading line would be printed on a separate page after the first heading line, and the information for every record read and processed would be printed on individual pages.

Some computer systems use a carriage control tape or forms buffer program to control Skipping. In this environment, the number of available channels (Skip) positions is limited to 12, with one of those reserved for page overflow control. For information regarding this type of page control, refer to the related operation manuals for the computer system.

First Page Control

A section of the RPG program logic flowchart is illustrated at the top of Figure 3-5. Notice that the heading (first cycle) processing is executed before the first record is read from an input file. Consequently, no Record Identifying Indicator has been turned on to condition output instructions. Because of this built-in processing cycle, RPG has provided a 1P (first page) indicator to control first cycle output. *After the last output instruction is tested, the 1P indicator is automatically set off and will never turn on again during program execution.*

The output form included in Figure 3-5 shows that the two heading lines are conditioned by a 1P indicator. Because UDATE and PAGE are RPG reserved words, their values are supplied by the system and are available at 1P time. Understand, however, that any field values from the data records will not be loaded in their related storage areas at first page time.

Furthermore, the detail line conditioned by the 01 indicator will not be executed during this first cycle processing. During the second cycle, when the first data record is read, the 1P lines are ignored, and the detail line conditioned with the 01 Record Identifying Indicator will be executed. This processing logic continues until end of the input file is sensed.

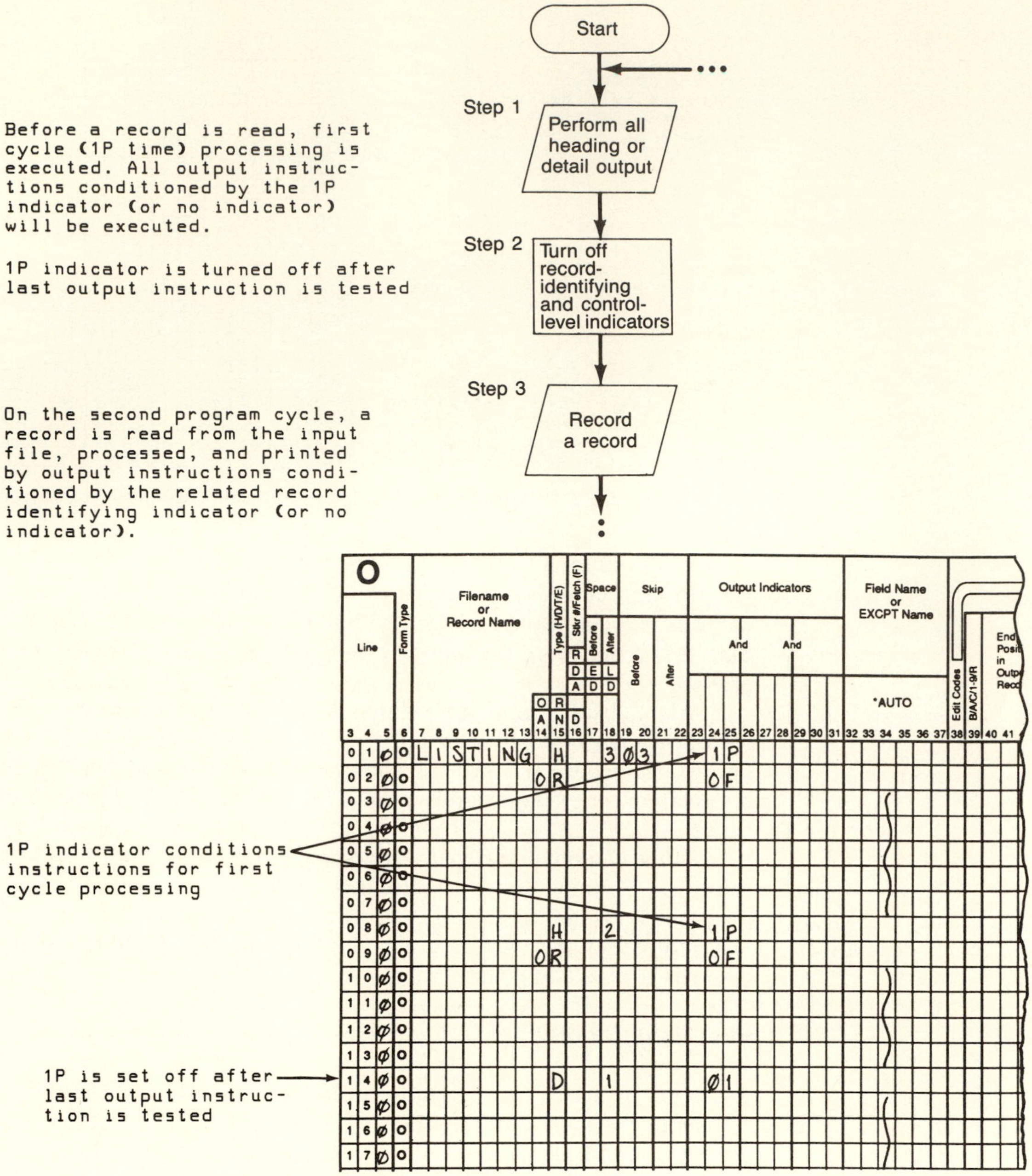
Start
Step 1
Perform all heading or detail output
Before a record is read, first cycle (1P time) processing is executed. All output instructions conditioned by the 1P indicator (or no indicator) will be executed.
1P indicator is turned off after last output instruction is tested
Step 2
Turn off record-identifying and control-level indicators
Step 3
Record a record
On the second program cycle, a record is read from the input file, processed, and printed by output instructions conditioned by the related record identifying indicator (or no indicator).
1P indicator conditions instructions for first cycle processing
1P is set off after last output instruction is tested
Filename or Record Name
Output Indicators
Field Name or EXCPT Name
LISTING H 3Ø3 1P
OR OF
H 2 1P
OR OF
D 1 Ø1

Figure 3-5 First cycle (1P time) processing logic and Output-Format Specification syntax.

Page Overflow Control

Indicators OA through OG and OV are preassigned indicators that control the page overflow function. Overflow indicators are automatically turned on when the overflow line for the type of form is sensed. For standard size paper, the line number on which page overflow is to execute is assigned when the system is generated. However, it may be modified by the Line Counter Specifications discussed at the end of this chapter.

Overflow indicators may not be used in an RPG program for any other processing function. The reason there are eight overflow indicators is that a program may support more than one printer file and each must be assigned to a different overflow indicator.

Examine the File Description Form in Figure 3-6, and notice that the OF indicator has been specified in the Overflow Indicator field (columns 33–34). This is where the Overflow Indicator is defined. If it is not entered here and specified in the output form, a terminal error (UNDEFINED INDICATOR) will be generated in compilation of the source program. Any of the other overflow indicators could have been used; the one selected is at the option of the programmer.

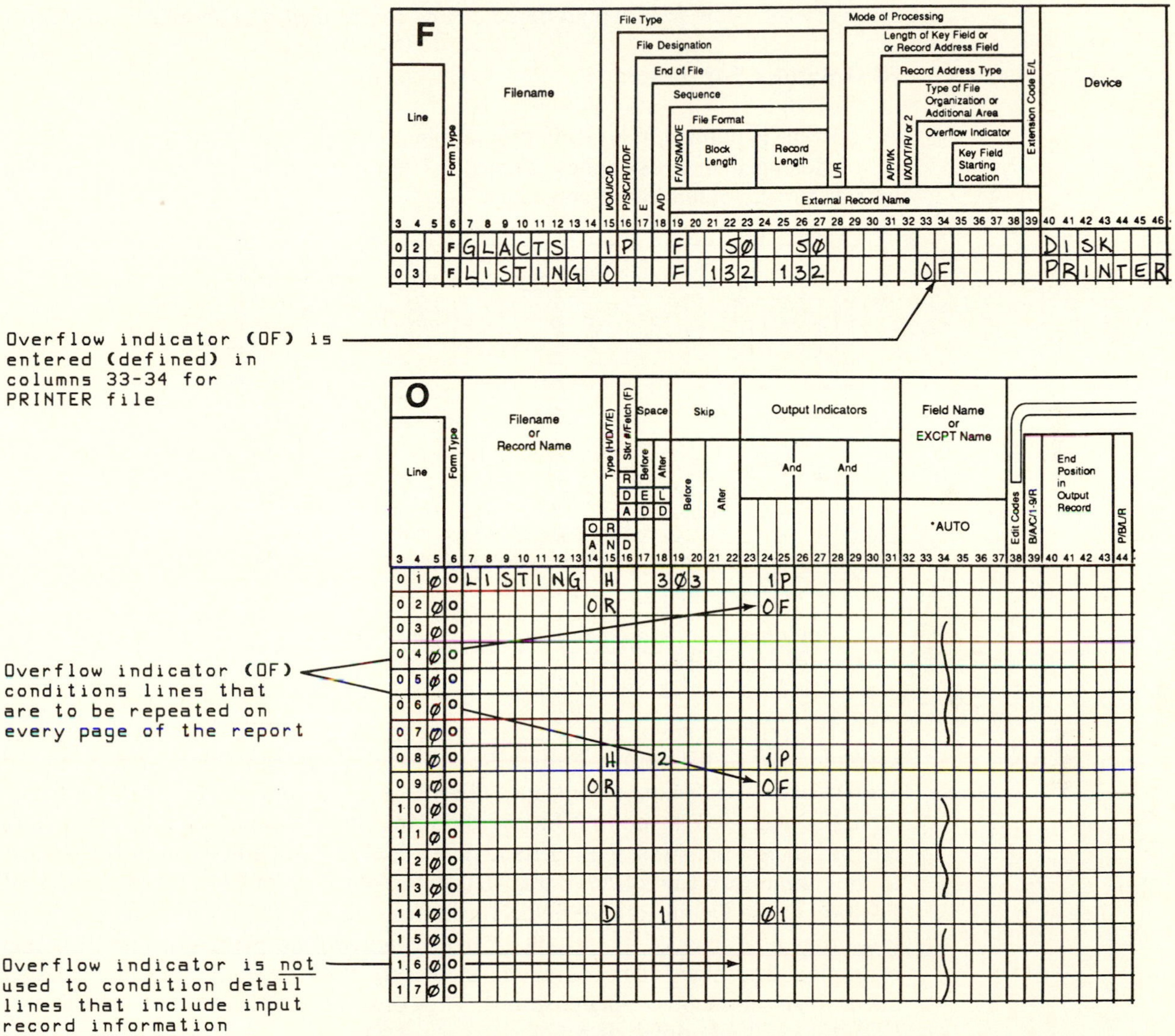
Overflow indicator (OF) is entered (defined) in columns 33-34 for PRINTER file
Overflow indicator (OF) conditions lines that are to be repeated on every page of the report
Overflow indicator is not used to condition detail lines that include input record information
0 2 F GLACTS IP F 50 50 DISK
0 3 F LISTING O F 132 132 OF PRINTER
0 1 Ø O LISTING H 3Ø3 1P
0 2 Ø O OR OF
0 8 Ø O H 2 1P
0 9 Ø O OR OF
1 4 Ø O D 1 Ø1

Figure 3-6 File Description and Output-Format entries for control of page overflow.

The output form shown in Figure 3-6 shows how the overflow indicator (OF) is used. Notice that it is included as an OR instruction that immediately follows the related 1P line. The OR entered in columns 14 and 15, on the same line with the OF indicator, specifies that the overflow instruction is in an "or" relationship with the 1P (or other indicator) instruction. If one of the two conditions is *true*, page overflow processing will be executed.

Skipping to the top of a new page (page overflow) is controlled by the sensing of the overflow line, which turns on the overflow indicator specified in the program. When this condition occurs, the overflow line is printed, the paper advances to the top of the next page, and the first heading line is printed. Notice that the Skip Before or After entry assigned to the related 1P instruction determines the line to which the paper advances on page overflow.

Further examination of Figure 3-6 indicates that an overflow instruction is not assigned to the detail line conditioned by the 01 Record Identifying Indicator. If it were, a detail line printed at the bottom of a page (overflow line) would be repeated on the following page. This repetition of information for a variable record on every overflow page would be confusing to the user and should be avoided.

RPG Syntax For Headings

A constant is defined in an RPG program in columns 45 to 70 of the output form by enclosing it in apostrophes. Figure 3-7 gives examples of valid and invalid entries for the definition of constants.

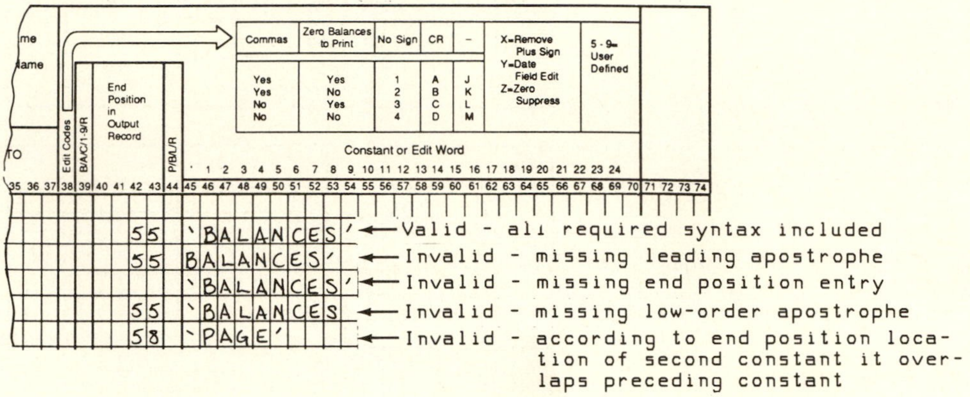

Figure 3-7 Examples of valid and invalid entries for the definition of constants.

The relationship of the constants and variable fields formatted in the printer spacing chart to the Output-Format Specifications coding is illustrated in Figure 3-8. Locate the heading constant, GENERAL LEDGER ACCOUNT BALANCES, included in the first line of the print chart. Notice that the letter T is entered in column 46 of the constant ACCOUNT. Now follow the arrowed line to the output form and observe that 46 is entered in columns 42 and 43 of the End Position in the Ouput Record field. This entry refers to the position in which the low-order character of a constant or field value will be placed (printed for this example). The high-order characters in the constant or field value are located accordingly in the preceding positions. The constant, GENERAL LEDGER ACCOUNT, will be printed as follows:

```
GENERAL LEDGER ACCOUNT
                     ↑
                     └print position 46
```

Refer to the print chart in Figure 3-8, and notice that the constant BALANCES ends in column 55. Trace the line that connects it to the output form, and observe that 55 is entered in the end position field. This entry will place the low-order S in BALANCES in print position 55 on output. Even though the space between ACCOUNT and BALANCES has not been included in either constant, the end

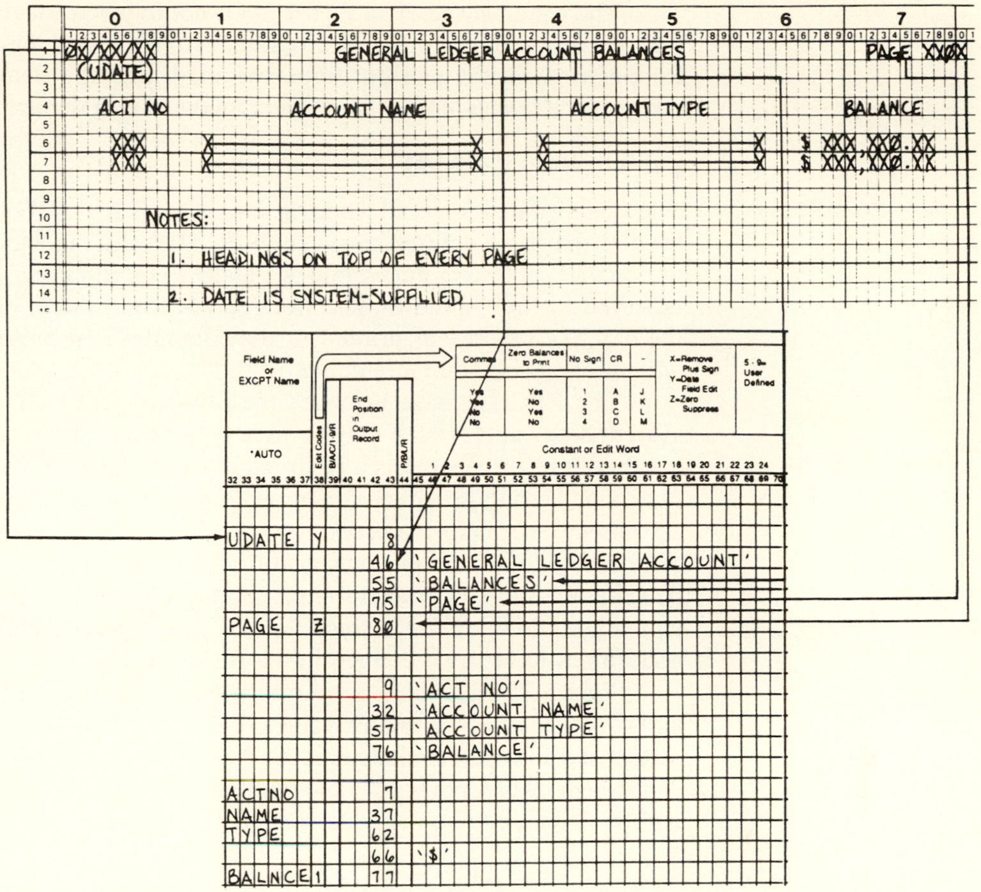

Figure 3-8 Relationship of printer spacing chart entries to output form instructions.

position entry (55) for BALANCES places this constant so that it begins one space after ACCOUNT. The result of this coding is as follows:

```
GENERAL LEDGER ACCOUNT BALANCES
                     ↑         ↑
  print position 46──┘         └─print position 55
```

If the end position for BALANCES had been specified as 53, a space would not be included after ACCOUNT; if 53, the B in BALANCES would overlap the T in ACCOUNT and the constant would print as follows:

```
GENERAL LEDGER ACCOUNBALANCES
                     ↑       ↑
  print position 46──┘       └─print position 53
```

Because the constants in the first heading line could not be entered on one line of output coding, BALANCES is included on a separate line. The end position references place a constant in its required horizontal location.

Included in this example are the RPG reserved field names for UDATE and PAGE. The values for these items are also positioned on output by their end position entries. This composite of instructions completes the output record (first heading line), which is controlled during processing by the related Record Description entries in columns 7 to 31.

The second heading line, which includes all constants, is coded on the output form by enclosing each constant in apostrophes and specifying the related end positions entry.

The example shown in Figure 3-8 is not to be construed as the only approach for the coding of headings in a program. Providing that the constants are enclosed in apostrophes, the end positions specified, and the items do not overlap, any coding style is acceptable. The format followed is at the option of the programmer.

System Date (UDATE)

The system date is entered when the computer is IPLed (booted). Some computers require that it be entered to successfully start the machine; for others it may be optional. The system date value is usually entered in the MMDDYY date format followed in the United States. For reports, the system date is used to indicate the date the report was printed. If the computer is not turned off, the date value will automatically be incremented.

The RPG language provides the reserved word UDATE for accessing the system date value, which may be used as a field entry in output and calculations. Furthermore, because it is a reserved word, it does not have to be defined in the program. During program execution, the system date is available at first cycle (1P) processing before a record is read. This feature enables the UDATE value to be included in heading lines conditioned by the 1P indicator. And UDATE may be separated into individual system month, day, and year values by the reserved words UMONTH, UDAY, and UYEAR, respectively. These are system-supplied and do not have to be defined in the program.

Figure 3-9 illustrates output form entries for UDATE, UMONTH, UDAY, and UYEAR and their related values. UDATE (or any date value) is usually edited so that slashes (/) are included in the printed format and the leading zero for months 01 through 09 is suppressed. The function and syntax of *edit codes* and *edit words* will be discussed in a separate section in this chapter.

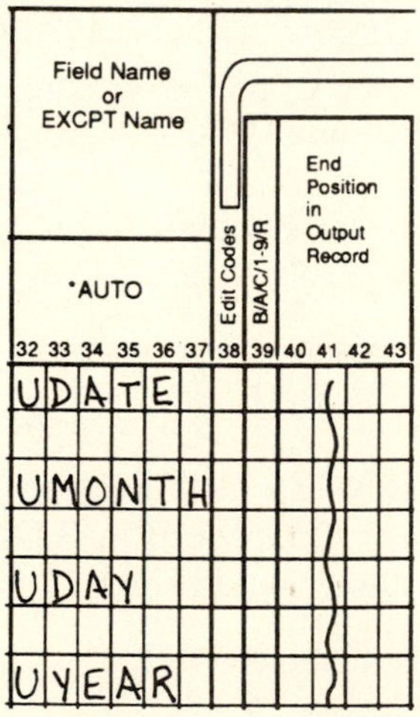

System-Supplied Value Extracted	System-Defined Field Size
093091	6
09	2
30	2
91	2

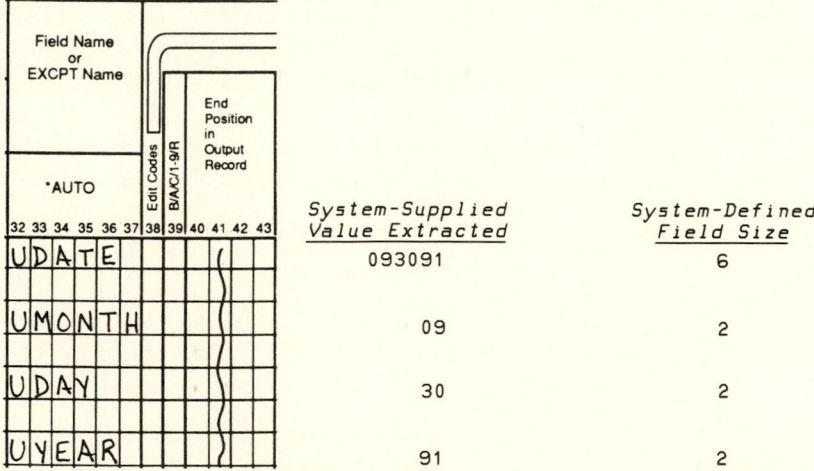

Figure 3-9 System date values provided by the RPG reserved words UDATE, UMONTH, UDAY, and UYEAR.

On some systems the UDATE format may be changed by an entry in column 19 of the Control Specifications. If column 19 is blank, an MMDDYY format is generated; if the letter D is specified, the format will be DDMMYY; and the letter Y will result in an YYMMDD format.

Page Numbering (PAGE)

PAGE is an RPG special word that controls the numbering of report pages. It is predefined as a four-byte numeric field with zero decimal positions (integer) that starts page numbering at 0001 and is automatically incremented for each page.

PAGE may also be defined from 1 to 15 bytes in input or calculations and may be initialized to a starting page number minus one. The incrementation of the page numbers will still be controlled automatically. Special RPG words, PAGE1 through PAGE7, are also provided so that pages of a report may be numbered differently, or so that they can be used in a program that supports more than one PRINTER file.

Figure 3-10 illustrates how PAGE is used in the example program and the values in the field for the first and second pages of the report. Use of the constant PAGE is optional and has no effect on the function of the special word PAGE.

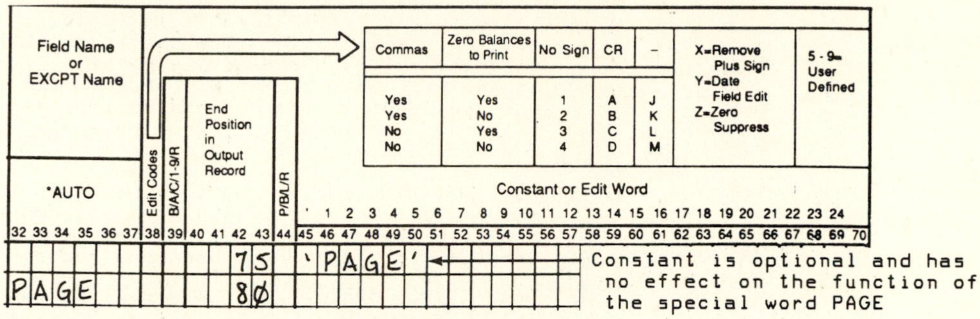

Value in PAGE for first page of report - 0001

Value in PAGE for second page of report - 0002

Figure 3-10 Syntax and processing results of the special word PAGE.

SUMMARY OF THIS SECTION

The example program source listing and related notes shown in Figure 3-11 summarizes the syntax and control for headings, page overflow, constants, and the special RPG words discussed in the previous paragraphs.

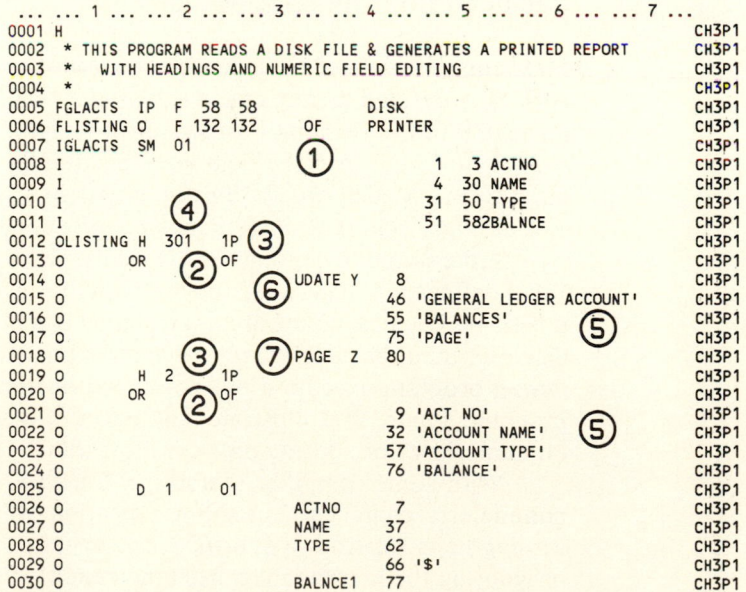

```
...  ... 1 ... ... 2 ... ... 3 ... ... 4 ... ... 5 ... ... 6 ... ... 7 ...
0001 H                                                              CH3P1
0002  * THIS PROGRAM READS A DISK FILE & GENERATES A PRINTED REPORT  CH3P1
0003  *   WITH HEADINGS AND NUMERIC FIELD EDITING                    CH3P1
0004  *                                                             CH3P1
0005 FGLACTS  IP  F  58  58           DISK                          CH3P1
0006 FLISTING O   F 132 132      OF   PRINTER                       CH3P1
0007 IGLACTS  SM  01                                                CH3P1
0008 I                         (1)          1   3 ACTNO             CH3P1
0009 I                                      4  30 NAME              CH3P1
0010 I               (4)                   31  50 TYPE              CH3P1
0011 I                                     51  582BALNCE            CH3P1
0012 OLISTING H  301    1P (3)                                      CH3P1
0013 O        OR     (2)OF                                          CH3P1
0014 O                    (6)UDATE Y   8                            CH3P1
0015 O                                46 'GENERAL LEDGER ACCOUNT'   CH3P1
0016 O                                55 'BALANCES'   (5)           CH3P1
0017 O                                75 'PAGE'                     CH3P1
0018 O               (3)  (7)PAGE  Z  80                            CH3P1
0019 O          H  2    1P                                          CH3P1
0020 O        OR     (2)OF                                          CH3P1
0021 O                                 9 'ACT NO'                   CH3P1
0022 O                                32 'ACCOUNT NAME'  (5)        CH3P1
0023 O                                57 'ACCOUNT TYPE'             CH3P1
0024 O                                76 'BALANCE'                  CH3P1
0025 O          D  1    01                                          CH3P1
0026 O                       ACTNO     7                            CH3P1
0027 O                       NAME     37                            CH3P1
0028 O                       TYPE     62                            CH3P1
0029 O                                66 '$'                        CH3P1
0030 O                       BALNCE1  77                            CH3P1
```

Figure 3-11 Example program summarization for the syntax and control of headings, page overflow, constants, and special RPG words.

1. Overflow indicator (OF) defined in columns 33-34 for the PRINTER file.

2. Overflow indicator (OF) specified on two heading lines. When the overflow line is sensed, the overflow indicator is set on, line printed, and control advances paper to the top of the next page. Any heading line conditioned with the OF indicator is printed.

3. First page indicator (1P) controls the printing of headings on the first report page. Because a record has not been read from the input file, any field values related to input records are not available at this time. Input and calculation instructions are ignored in first cycle processing.

4. Entry in the Skip Before field (columns 19-20) advances paper to the line specified (3 for this program) before printing the related line. An entry in the Skip After field (columns 21-22) will advance paper to the designated line after printing. Either of these controls also apply to overflow pages.

5. Constants are defined on the output form in columns 45-70 and must be enclosed in apostrophes. End position entry refers to the low-order character in constant, not the low-order apostrophe.

6. UDATE is an RPG special word that extracts the system-date from the computer as a six byte integer in an MMDDYY format. The date value may be accessed at 1P (first cycle) time.

7. PAGE is an RPG special word that provides automatic page numbering for a report. It is predefined as a four byte integer with a starting value of 0001. Incrementation is automatic and may be specified at 1P (first cycle) time.

(*Continued*)

NUMERIC FIELDS

Definition On Input Specifications

Fields may be defined as numeric in the Input or Calculation Specification forms. A field is defined as numeric on the input form by specifying a number from 0 through 9 in the Decimal Positions field (column 52). The decimal position entry *cannot be larger* than the field size specified in the FROM and TO fields in the input form. In addition, *the maximum size of a numeric field in RPG is 15 digits, and no more than 9 decimal positions may be assigned.*

A 0 entered in column 52 defines the field as an *integer*, and any digit from 1 to 9 defines it as a *decimal* number with the specified number of *implied* decimal positions. Decimal points are not included in a numeric field value stored on disk, diskette, tape, or punch card (*explicit* decimal), but they are *implied* in the CPU during program execution by the related decimal position entry assigned in the program. Figure 3-12 illustrates the effect of decimal position entry assignments on numeric values during program execution.

With some computer systems, if a field is defined as numeric but contains nonnumeric characters, program execution will abort (cancel) or halt. If processing halts (instead of aborting), the operator has the option of ending the job or ignoring the record that caused the condition and continuing to process. Some computer systems process the value as numeric by ignoring the zone area and

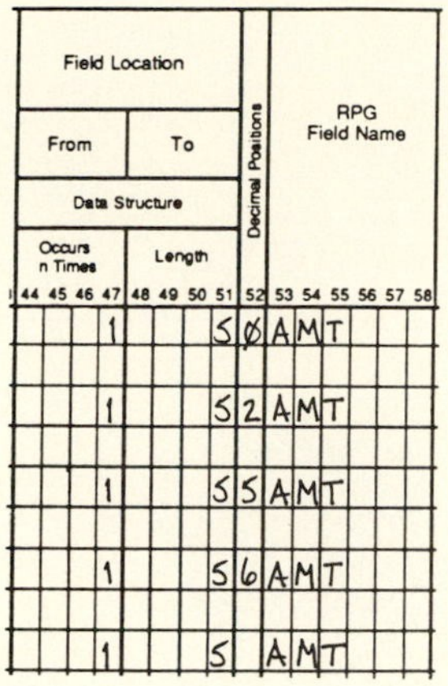

Decimal Position Entry	Value in Disk Field	Value CPU Storage	Comments
0	12345	12345▲	Integer value
2	12345	123▲45	Decimal value with 2 implied decimals
5	12345	▲12345	Decimal value with 5 implied decimals
6	12345	12345	Invalid - decimal entry greater than field length
blank	12345	12345	Alphanumeric value

Notes: In the last example, because the decimal position field is blank, the numeric value will be processed as alphanumeric. Calculation or editing may not be performed with that field.

Symbol ▲ indicates an implied decimal (not actual). With the exception of output edited numeric fields, actual decimals are not assigned to field storage in the CPU.

Figure 3-12 Effects of the decimal position assignments on numeric values during program execution.

processing only the digit section of the byte. Values that are defined as numeric should be validated before processing. The subject of data validation is discussed in Chapter 12.

Signed Numeric Values

In the RPG environment, an unsigned number is considered positive, and negative numbers must be explicitly signed as negative. To assign a number as negative on input, a minus sign must be included over the low-order digit. In the punch card environment, the embedded minus sign was included over the low-order byte by pressing a multipunch key, the minus sign, and then the required digit. However, because CRTs do not support this multipunch feature, other methods must be followed for entering negative data values.

For terminal input, some CRT keyboards have a special key (FIELD −) that when pressed will automatically store a minus sign over the low digit of the value. Many systems, however, do not support this feature, and negative values have to be tagged with a minus sign by substituting a special character in place of the low-order number. Figure 3-13 illustrates the character expression of numbers overpunched with a minus sign. Notice that the related character for positive numbers is also shown in the event an explicit plus sign is entered over the last digit. Remember that numbers not explicitly signed are processed as positive values.

Numeric Field Editing

Only fields that have been defined as numeric may be edited. *Editing* refers to the insertion, suppression, or replacement of characters within the body of a numeric value that is printed or displayed. Editing numeric fields is performed in RPG by Edit Codes and Edit Words. Each method is discussed separately in the following paragraphs.

NUMBER	POSITIVE	NEGATIVE
1	A	J
2	B	K
3	C	L
4	D	M
5	E	N
6	F	O
7	G	P
8	H	Q
9	I	R
0	{	}

Examples of Character Substitution for Negative Values:

Positive Value entry	*Negative Value entry*
12345	1234N
10000	1000}
03911	0391J

Figure 3-13 Alphabetic characters substituted for the low-order number to indicate a value is negative.

Edit Codes—Simple and Combination. All the available RPG edit codes are conveniently included in a table in the upper right-hand side of the Output-Format Specifications Form as shown in Figure 3-14. The heavy arrowed line from the Edit Codes field to the boxed-in edit code area indicates that they are entered in column 38. An examination of the table shows that Edit Codes 1, 2, 3, 4, A, B, C, D, J, K, L, M, X, Y, and Z are provided by RPG. With the exception of X, which is not used, each edit code provides a slightly different pattern. Edit Codes may be classified into two types: simple and combination.

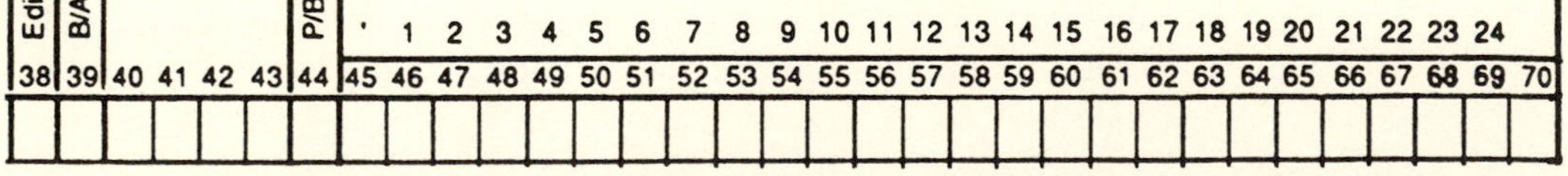

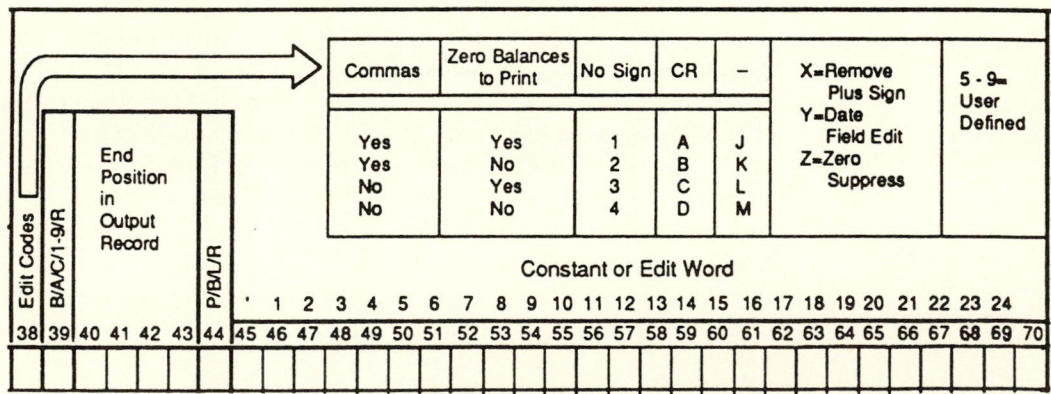

Figure 3-14 Table of available RPG edit codes included in the upper right-hand side of all Output-Format Specifications.

Simple Edit Codes (Y and Z): Simple Edit Codes, which include Y and Z, perform functions unique to the combination class of edit codes. Edit Code Y is usually used only to edit date fields (as suggested by the table notation) and performs the editing functions detailed in Figure 3-15.

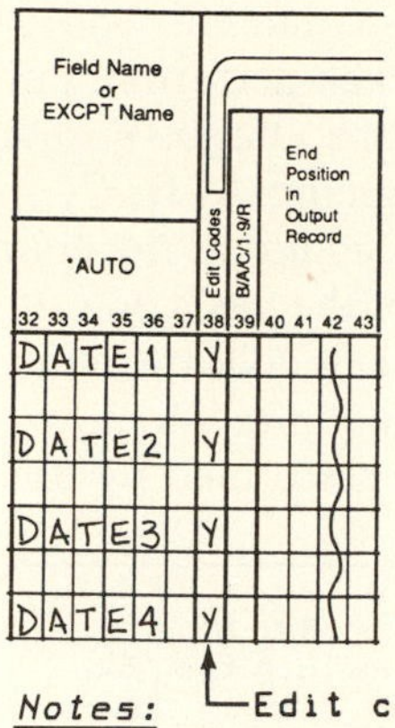

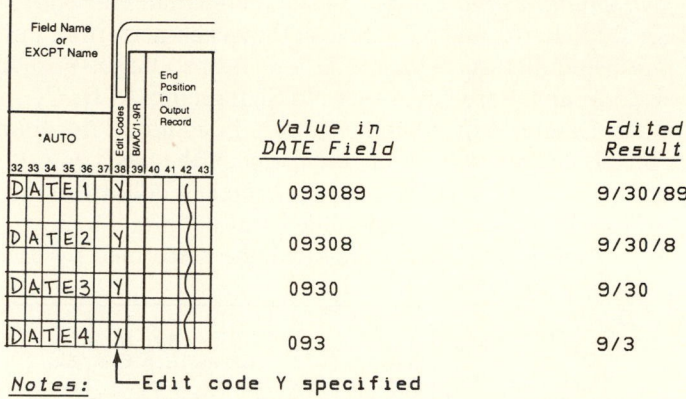

Value in DATE Field	*Edited Result*
093089	9/30/89
09308	9/30/8
0930	9/30
093	9/3

Notes: (Edit code Y specified)

1. Date items are usually defined as six integer fields. The other examples are included to show the results of editing different field sizes.

2. Regardless of the field size, the first slash (/) is inserted after the second high-order digit and the second after the fourth. Any zero suppression of a high-order 0 is performed after slash insertion.

3. A negative sign will not print if the field value is negative.

4. DATE1, DATE2, DATE3, and DATE4 are programmer-supplied names and are not incidental to the field sizes specified.

Figure 3-15 Edit results of the edit code Y (date edit code).

Edit Code Z performs only the suppression of leading zeros in a numeric field value. Any implied decimals defined for the related field is ignored when this Edit Code is specified, and the value is printed as an integer. The Z Edit Code is typically used with fields defined as integers (e.g., page numbers) that do not require commas and/or a decimal point for readability. Figure 3-16 illustrates the results of editing when the Edit Code Z is specified with a field.

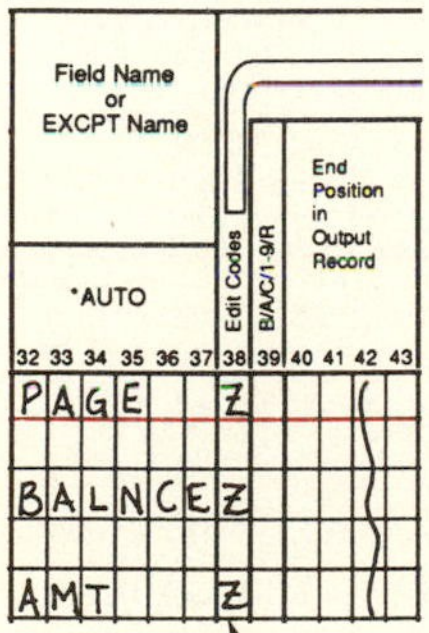

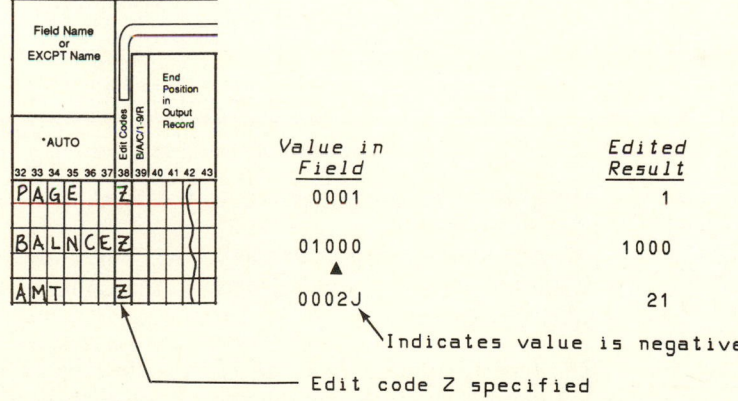

Value in Field	*Edited Result*
0001	1
01000 ▲	1000
0002J	21

0002J — Indicates value is negative

Edit code Z specified

Notes:

1. Only a zero suppression function is performed (shown in all of the above examples).

2. As shown in the second example, Implied decimal point position is ignored and field is output as an integer.

3. As shown in the third example, a negative sign is not printed if the value is negative.

Figure 3-16 Edit results for the edit code Z.

Combination Edit Codes: The combination edit codes include 1, 2, 3, 4, A, B, C, D, J, K, L, and M. Because they each perform a different edit function, they are listed as three separate groups in the Output-Format form table. Edit codes 1, 2, 3, and 4 are listed as a No-Sign group; A, B, C, and D as a CR group; and J, K, L, and M as the minus group. In addition, the columns for commas and for Zero Balances to Print identify some of the basic edit functions provided by each of the edit codes. All the combination edit codes will insert a decimal point in the edited output for decimal values, but not after the low-order digit for integers.

Figure 3-17 details the functions performed by each edit code.

Edit Code	Commas	Decimal Point	Sign for Negative Balance	Zero Suppress
1	Yes	Yes	No sign	Yes
2	Yes	Yes	No sign	Yes
3		Yes	No sign	Yes
4		Yes	No sign	Yes
A	Yes	Yes	CR	Yes
B	Yes	Yes	CR	Yes
C		Yes	CR	Yes
D		Yes	CR	Yes
J	Yes	Yes	- (minus)	Yes
K	Yes	Yes	- (minus)	Yes
L		Yes	- (minus)	Yes
M		Yes	- (minus)	Yes

Notes:

1. For integer numbers, none of the edit codes will print a decimal point after the low-order digit.
2. If edit codes 1 through 4 are specified for a field and the value is negative, a minus sign will not print.
3. If edit codes A through D are specified and the field is negative, the letters CR will be included after the low-order digit when printed or displayed. If the value is positive, two blanks will be included. When formatting output, these two additional positions must be considered.
4. If edit codes J through M are specified and the field is negative, a minus sign (-) will be included after the low- order digit when printed or displayed. If the value is positive, one blank will be included. When formatting output, this additional position must be considered.

Figure 3-17 Edit codes 1, 2, 3, 4, A, B, C, D, J, K, L, and M functions.

The processing results of the various edit codes are illustrated in Figure 3-18. Notice that the unedited value for each column is included horizontally on the first line, *Unedited*.

Dollar Signs ($) With Edit Codes: A dollar sign may be coded as floating or fixed. Figure 3-19 illustrates the syntax for each option when the dollar sign is used with an edit code. If a floating dollar sign is assigned and an Edit Code is not specified for the field, a terminal error is generated during program compilation.

Edit Words. Because Edit Codes are simple to use and their editing results are predetermined, they should be used whenever possible. Sometimes, however, they may not satisfy all editing requirements and an *Edit Word* must be specified. For example, the standard printed format of a social security number is 011–11–1111, in which the leading zero is not suppressed and hyphens are inserted in the body of the value. Because none of the Edit Codes provide for this pattern, an

Edit Code	Positive Number, 2 Decimal Positions	Positive Number, 0 Decimal Positions	Negative Number, 3 Decimal Positions	Negative Number, 0 Decimal Positions	Zero Balance, 0 Decimal Positions
Unedited	1234567	1234567	00012}	00012}	000000
1	12,345.67	1,234,567	.120	120	0
2	12,345.67	1,234,567	.120	120	
3	12345.67	1234567	.120	120	0
4	12345.67	1234567	.120	120	
A	12,345.67	1,234,567	.120CR	120CR	0
B	12,345.67	1,234,567	.120CR	120CR	
C	12345.67	1234567	.120CR	120CR	0
D	12345.67	1234567	.120CR	120CR	
J	12,345.67	1,234,567	.120-	120-	0
K	12,345.67	1,234,567	.120-	120-	
L	12345.67	1234567	.120-	120-	0
M	12345.67	1234567	.120-	120-	

} indicates low order position is a zero and that value is negative.

CR requires two low-order print positions. Spaces will still be allocated if value is positive.

- sign requires one low-order print position. Space will still be allocated if value is positive.

Figure 3-18 Processing results of the 1, 2, 3, 4, A, B, C, D, J, K, L, and M edit codes. (Courtesy of IBM.)

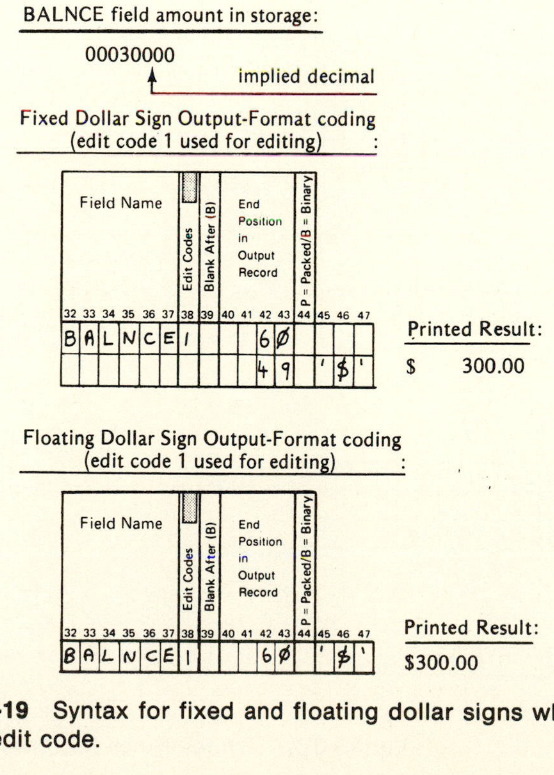

Figure 3-19 Syntax for fixed and floating dollar signs when used with an edit code.

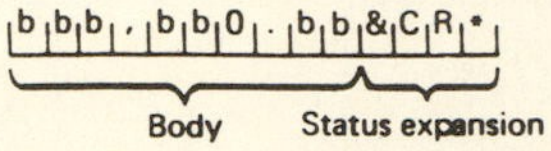

Rules for Forming an Edit Word:

1. An edit word must be enclosed in apostrophes.
2. A blank in the body of the edit word is replaced with the character from the corresponding position of the data field specified in *Field Name*.
3. An ampersand in the body or status portion causes a blank in the edited field. It remains unchanged in the expansion portion.
4. A zero is used for zero-suppression. It is placed in the rightmost position where zero suppression is to stop. It is replaced with the character from the corresponding position of the data field, unless that character is zero. Column 38 (edit codes) must be left blank.
5. If leading zeros are desired, the edit word must contain one more position than the field to be edited. A zero must be placed in the high-order position of the edit word.
6. An asterisk in the body of the edit word is used for asterisk protection and zero suppression. It is placed in the rightmost position where zero suppression is to stop. It is replaced with the non-zero character from the corresponding position of the data field. Each suppressed zero is replaced by an asterisk. An asterisk preceding a zero is interpreted as representing asterisk protection.
7. A dollar sign in the body of the edit word written immediately to the left of the zero-suppression code causes the insertion of a dollar sign in the position to the left of the first significant digit. This is the *floating dollar* sign. A dollar sign that is entered immediately after the initial single-quote mark is fixed (printed in the same location each time). This is the ***fixed dollar*** sign.
8. The decimal and commas are printed in the same relative positions they were written in the edit word.
If they are to the left of significant digits, they are blanked out or replaced by an asterisk.
9. All other characters used in the body of the edit word are printed if they are to the right of significant digits in the data field. If they are to the left of high-order significant digits in the data word, they are blanked out. If asterisk protection is used they are replaced by an asterisk.
10. The letters CR or the minus symbol in the status portion of the edit word are undisturbed if the sign in the data field is minus. If the sign is plus, CR and - are blanked out.
11. Characters to the right of the status portion of the edit word are undisturbed.
12. The edit word may be larger than the field to be edited.

	Constant or Edit Word (positions 1–16, columns 45–61)	*Field Value*	*Edited Result*	*Comments*
3	'Ø & & '	081189	8 11 89	Zero is placed in the body of the edit word to indicate where zero suppression is to end. & inserts a space in the body of the edited value.
5	'Ø - - '	012345678	012-23-5678	Extra high-order zero in edit word prevents suppression of leading zero in the value.
5	'Ø( )- - '	2039998888	(203)-999-8888	Extra high-order zero on edit word prevents suppression of the (in the value
6	' , *. '	00001000	****10.00	Leading zeros and comma are replaced with asterisks.
7	' , $Ø. '	0001499	$14.99	Zeros are suppressed and floating $ sign is printed next to first significant digit. Extra position must be included in edit word for $ sign.
7	'$, Ø. '	0001499	$ 14.99	Fixed dollar sign must be placed immediately after leading quote mark. Extra position must be included in edit word for $ sign.
8		1000000000	10,000,000.00	Comma and decimal point are printed in their relative edit word positions. These symbols will be suppressed when value is smaller.
10	' , Ø. &CR'	01894J	189.41 CR	Symbol CR will print only if value is negative. Spaces are still allocated if value is positive. End position entry for field refers to R in CR
10	' , Ø. -'	01894J	189.41-	Minus sign will print only if value is negative. Space is still allocated if value is positive. End position entry for field refers to the - sign.
11	' , Ø. &THANKS'	020187	201.87 THANKS	Entries specified to the right of the status section (see format on top of this figure) are printed without regard to the status value.
9				

Figure 3-20 Syntax Rules for forming edit words and coding examples.

Edit Word must be used. Other special editing functions, such as the insertion of blanks in the print pattern, or the addition of words at the end of the edited value, may be required. The syntax rules for forming edit words are detailed in Figure 3-20. Notice that rules 1, 2, and 4 are applicable to all Edit Word patterns and are not individually shown, but they are included in the coding examples in Figure 3-20.

Data Entry of Numeric Values. It was explained in Chapter 2 that numeric data must be stored right-justified in its related field position when entered. Because this concept cannot be overemphasized it is presented again as a timely review. Examine the top section of Figure 3-21 and observe what processing results occur if a numeric value is not stored right-justified. The value should be processed as 123.45, but if entered incorrectly, as shown in the figure, it will be processed as 12345.00.

```
Field defined as 7 long with 2 decimal positions

RPG initializes all numeric fields to zeros before processing.

Initialized value - 0000000
                         ▲
                              Implied decimal position

Numeric data entry in a disk environment that
does not support a data entry utility:

Valid Entry - 0012345      Processed as - 0012345
                                                ▲
                  zeros are entered beginning in the first position
                   in the field, and so on. Low-order digit of value
                   is stored in the low-order position of field

Invalid - 1234500      Processed as - 1234500
                                            ▲
                                        *********

Interactive data entry and screen utilities (software packages) usually support
one or more (optional) of the following features for the entry of numeric data:

Option 1:

       12345bb      (b's indicate blanks)

          data is entered starting at high-order position as follows:

After the value is entered, and the ENTER or FIELD EXIT key is pressed, the value
is automatically right-justified and zeros are stored in the unused high-order
bytes as:

      0012345
         ▲
              low-order position of field

Option 2:

      bb12345

              data is entered beginning at low-order position

Each digit is entered in low-order position. The next digit entered causes the
current low-order digit to move to the left by one position, and so on. After
last digit is entered, the value is stored in the correct format without any
other movement. Leading zeros are automatically included in stored value as:

      0012345
         ▲
```

Figure 3-21 Procedures for valid numeric data entry.

In an environment that does not support a data entry or screen utility, numeric values smaller than the field size are usually entered with the required leading zeros. However, as illustrated in Figure 3-21, the entry of numeric data in an interactive environment is simplified. Two optional methods are shown in the figure. Option 1 places the CRT cursor at the high-order position of the field; as digits are entered, the cursor moves to the right. After all the numbers are entered, pressing the ENTER or FIELD EXIT (available on some systems) key will automatically right-justify the value in its related storage area in the CPU. Option 2 places the CRT cursor at the low-order position of the field; as digits are entered, the number previously stored in the low-order position moves one space to the left. For either option, any unused high-order positions do not have to be filled with zeros. Zeros are automatically included when the value is moved from the screen field to the storage area. Today, most of the screen and data entry utilities support both options.

Numeric Field Definition and Editing in the Example Program. A source listing of the example program and its relationship to the printed report is shown in Figure 3-22. Notice the following:

```
... ... 1 ... ... 2 ... ... 3 ... ... 4 ... ... 5 ... ... 6 ... ... 7 ...
H                                                              CH3P1
 * THIS PROGRAM READS A DISK FILE & GENERATES A PRINTED REPORT CH3P1
 *   WITH HEADINGS AND NUMERIC FIELD EDITING                   CH3P1
 *                                                             CH3P1
FGLACTS  IP  F  58  58          DISK                           CH3P1
FLISTING O   F 132 132     OF   PRINTER                        CH3P1
IGLACTS  SM  01                                                CH3P1
I                                        1   3 ACTNO           CH3P1
I                                        4  30 NAME            CH3P1
I                                       31  50 TYPE
I                                       51  582BALNCE
OLISTING H  301    1P
O        OR        OF
                           UDATE Y   8
                                    46 'GENERAL LEDGER ACCOUNT' CH3P1
                                    55 'BALANCES'               CH3P1
                                    75 'PAGE'
                           PAGE  Z  80
           H  2    1P
O        OR        OF
O                                    9 'ACT NO'
O                                   32 'ACCOUNT NAME'           CH3P1
O                                   57 'ACCOUNT TYPE'           CH3P1
O                                   76 'BALANCE'                CH3P1
O          D  1    01                                           CH3P1
O                          ACTNO     7                          CH3P1
O                          NAME     37                          CH3P1
                           TYPE     62                          CH3P1
                                    66 '$'
                           BALNCE1  77
```

Field is defined as numeric by 2 entry in column 52

Edit code Y suppresses leading zero and inserts slashes in the system date value

Edit code Z suppresses leading zeros in page value

Fixed $ will print in position 66 for every detail record processed

BALNCE field is edited with edit code 1 which provides a decimal, zero suppression, commas, and .00 if the value is zero

```
9/30/92          GENERAL LEDGER ACCOUNT BALANCES               PAGE    1

     ACT NO          ACCOUNT NAME          ACCOUNT TYPE          BALANCE

      101   CASH                          CURRENT ASSET     $  10,841.02
      102   ACCOUNTS RECEIVABLE           CURRENT ASSET     $   7,633.49
```

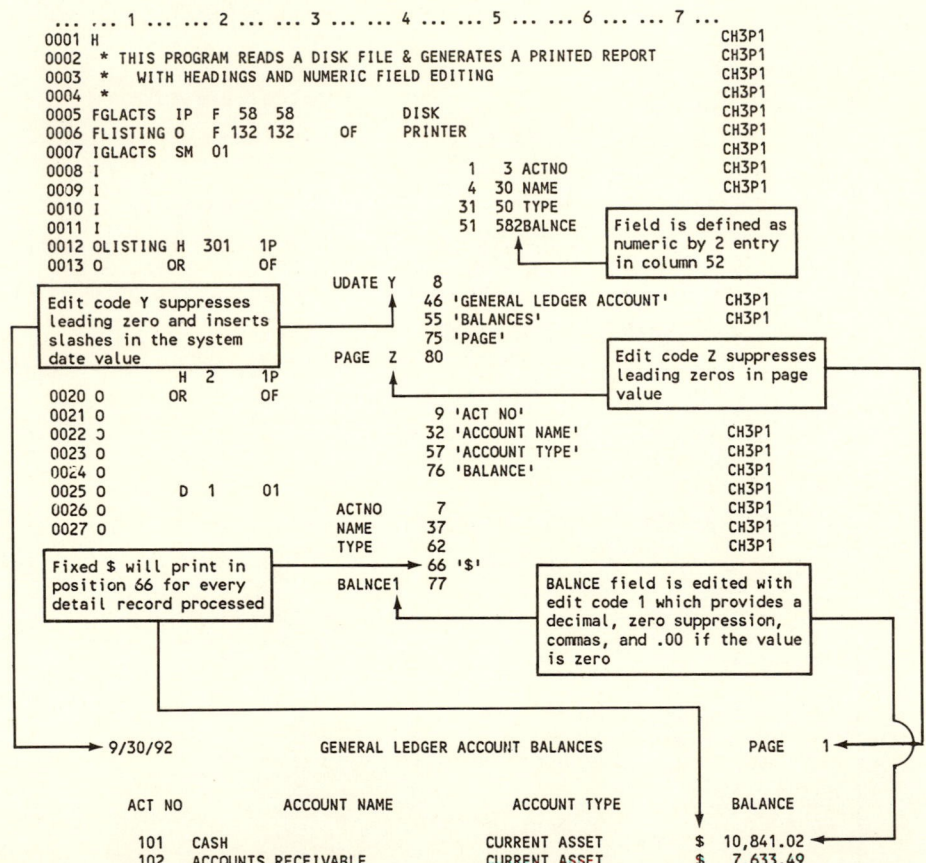

Figure 3-22 Example program source listing and its relationship to editing included in the printed report.

1. The field, BALNCE, is defined as numeric on input by the 2 entered in column 52 and is edited on output by the Edit Code 1 entry in Column 38.
2. The system date (UDATE) is edited by the edit code Y, which suppresses the leading zero and inserts two slashes.

3. The special word PAGE is edited by the edit code Z, which suppresses leading zeros in the page number.

RPG CONTROL FOR MODIFICATION OF FORM LENGTHS

The standard form length that is specified when the computer is configured is usually defined with a default length of 66 lines (printing at six lines per inch) with the default overflow on line 60. Printer adjustment at the top of the form will, however, determine the exact location of the page overflow line in the body of a printed report.

Special forms, such as labels, checks, invoices, transcripts, and so forth, are not often the standard paper length supported by a system. Consequently, procedures have been included in the RPG environment to modify a form length when needed. Two methods are available on most systems to modify the length of a form. One includes control by the control language (e.g., OCL, JCL, CL) supported. The other method controls variable form lengths directly in an RPG program by *Line Counter Specification* instructions. Because control languages are unique to each computer system, only the RPG method will be discussed.

A Line Counter Specifications form is detailed in Figure 3-23. Notice that this form is included at the bottom of the Extension Specifications and that the "L" instructions must be stored in the compilation order (H, F, E, L, I, C, O) required for all RPG programs.

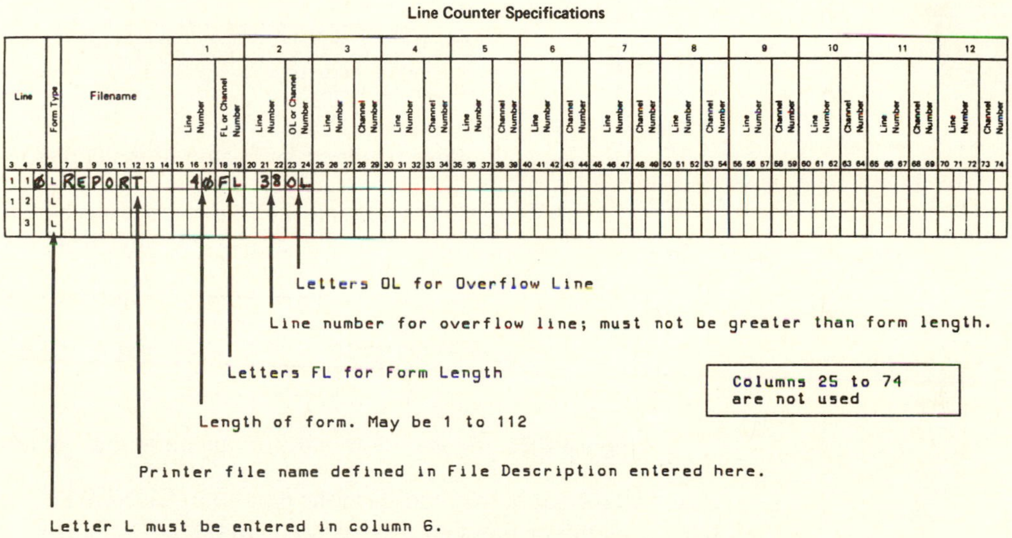

Figure 3-23 Line Counter Specifications and example entries for printers that use line (not channel) references.

The documentation and RPG syntax for an application program that generates customer mailing labels is presented to illustrate how the Line Counter Specifications is used to modify the standard page length and overflow line location.

Application Program—Customer Mailing Labels

Documentation

The specifications presented in Figure 3-24 describe the processing requirements for an RPG program that generates mailing labels.

PROGRAM SPECIFICATIONS Page 1 of 1

Program Name CUST MAILING LABELS Program-ID CH3P2 Written By S. Myers

Purpose Generate customer mailing labels Approved By The Boss

Input files (directory names):

CUSTMRS (stored on disk)

Output files (directory names):

LABELS (printed on pre-glued continuous labels)

Processing Narrative:

Write an RPG program to print customer mailing labels on pre-glued continuous labels.

Input to the program:

An input file, CUSTMRS, contains customer names and addresses in the format shown in the attached record layout form.

Processing:

Read the input file sequentially until end of file. For every record processed, print three detail lines on a mailing label form.

Output:

A printer spacing chart is attached which shows the output format for the mailing labels. Continuous forms labels are used which are separated by perforated lines.

The following must be included in the program to control the printing of the labels:

1. Line Counter Specifications must be included with a form length defined as 5 lines and overflow on line 4.
2. Printer must be set at 6 lines per inch.
3. One label per form is to be printed in the format detailed in the print chart.

Figure 3-24 Specifications for customer mailing label program.

A system flowchart indicating the files processed by the program is shown in Figure 3-25.

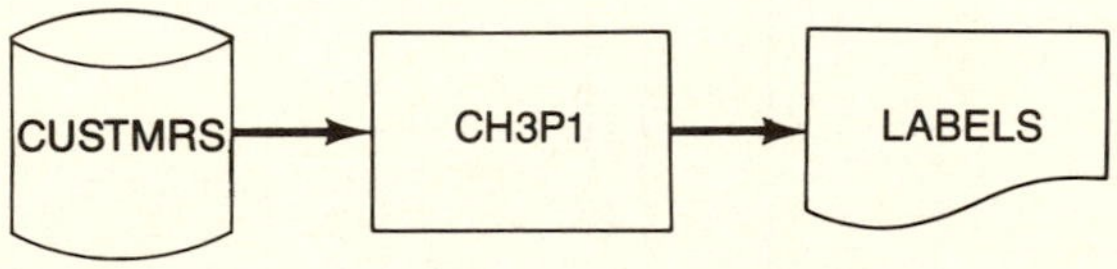

Figure 3-25 System flowchart for customer mailing label program.

The format of the records in the input file, CUSTMRS, is presented in Figure 3-26. A listing of the data file is also included at the bottom of the figure.

Record Layout Form

Data File Listing

```
PAUL CEZANNE          44 RUE PIGALLE    STAMFORD     CT06518
EDGAR DEGAS           10 ROSE TERRACE   WESTPORT     PA07777
BUCKMINISTER FULLER 999 PARK AVENUE     GREENWICH    CT06444
```

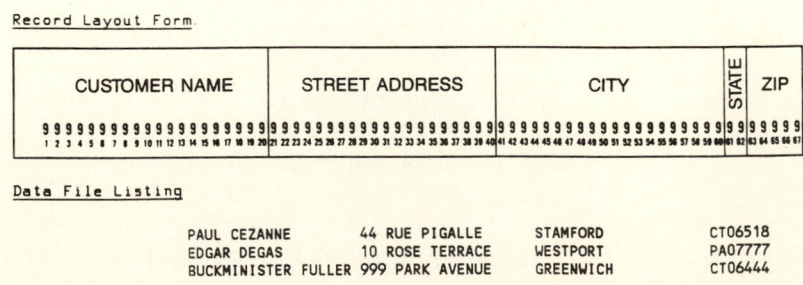

Figure 3-26 Record layout form and listing of the input file processed by the customer mailing label program.

The print format of the continuous form labels is shown in Figure 3-27. Notice that the individual label forms are 5 lines in length, printing is to begin on line 2 of each label, and page overflow occurs on line 4. Also shown in Figure 3-27 is a listing of the labels printed by the example program.

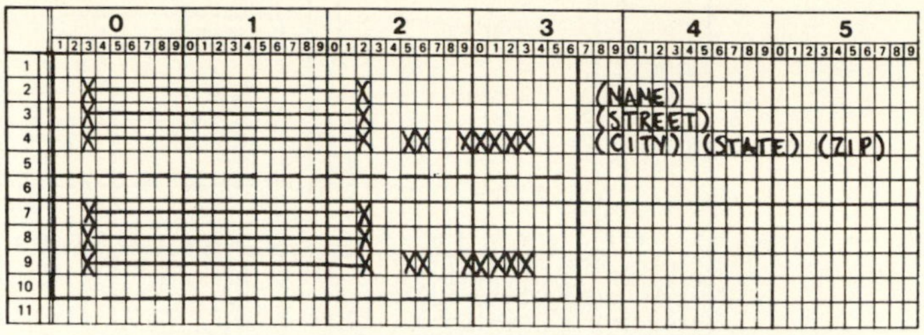

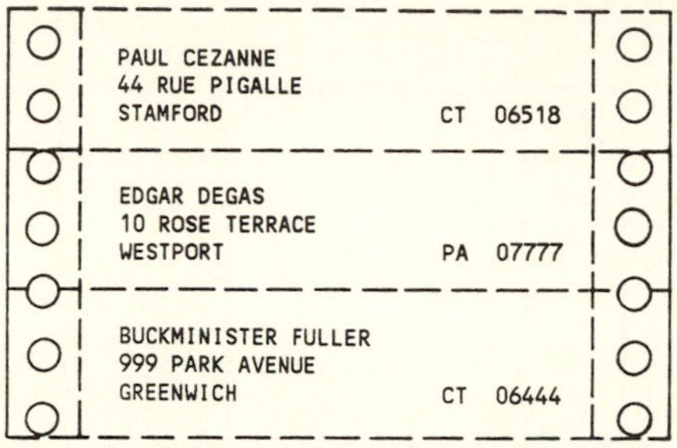

Figure 3-27 Printer spacing chart and printed labels for customer label program.

Source Program Coding for Customer Labels Program

The source program listing in Figure 3-28 identifies the syntax that controls the size and processing of the labels. Also included at the bottom of the figure is a listing of the labels with comments documenting the line references included in the Line Counter Specifications and Skip Before entries in the program.

The File Description and Line Counter Specifications entries that modify the standard form length and overflow line for the continuous form labels are detailed in Figure 3-29.

```
... ... 1 ... ... 2 ... ... 3 ... ... 4 ... ... 5 ... ... 6 ... ... 7 ...
0001  * PROGRAM PRINTS CONTINUOUS FORMS CUSTOMER MAILING LABELS
0002 H
0003 FCUSTMRS IP  F  67  67              DISK
0004 FLABELS  O   F 132 132              LPRINTER
0005 LLABELS    5FL  40L
0006 ICUSTMRS SM  03
0007 I                                        1  20 CNAME
0008 I                                       21  40 STREET
0009 I                                       41  60 CITY
0010 I                                       61  62 STATE
0011 I                                       63  67 ZIP
0012 OLABELS  D  102   03
0013 O                       CNAME      22
0014 O        D  1     03
0015 O                       STREET     22
0016 O        D  1     03
0017 O                       CITY       22
0018 O                       STATE      26
0019 O                       ZIP        33
```

L must be specified in column 53 of PRINTER file when Line Counter Spec. is included

PRINTER file name must be entered in cols 7-14. 5FL entries indicate a form length of 5 lines. 40L entries indicate that overflow is on line 4

02 entry (Skip Before) in cols 19-20 controls printing so that it begins on line 2 of every label

Printed Labels:

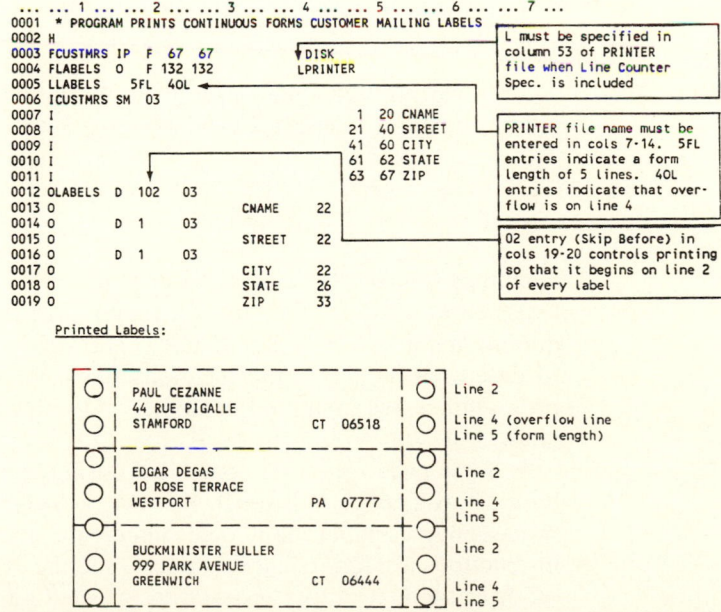

Figure 3-28 Detailed source program listing and printed labels with program related line reference comments.

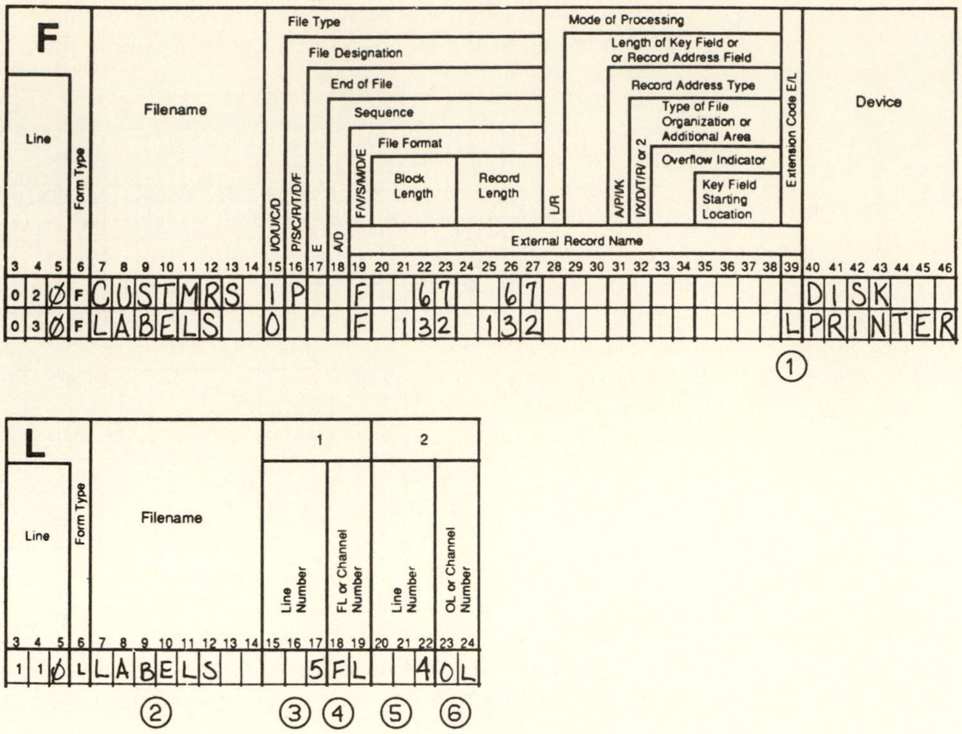

Notes:

Entry for File Description Specifications:

1. L must be specified in column 53 for PRINTER file.

Entries for Line Counter Specifications:

2. PRINTER file name (from File Description form) must be specified in columns 7-14.
3. Form length of 5 is specified right-justified in columns 15-17.
4. FL specified in columns 18-19 indicates form length.
5. Overflow at line 4 is specified right-justified in columns 20-22.
6. OL specified in columns 23-24 references overflow line.

Figure 3-29 File Description and Line Counter Specification that define the label size and overflow line.

SUMMARY

Headings (constants) in an RPG program are defined in Columns 45 to 70 of the Output-Format Specifications form and must be enclosed in apostrophes (single quotation marks). A printer spacing chart (or display screen) is usually referenced to determine end position locations for a constant or group of constants. The programmer has unlimited flexibility as to how the constants are coded in a program.

First page output is controlled during the first cycle of program execution by a 1P (first page indicator). Because a record has not been read at first cycle processing, variable input field values are not available. Input and calculation instructions are ignored at first cycle, and the 1P indicator is automatically turned off after the last output instruction is tested and/or executed.

Special RPG words that access a system-supplied date are UDATE, UMONTH, UDAY, and UYEAR. UDATE is in an MMDDYY format; the others extract the individual date elements as indicated. PAGE is another special RPG word that provides for automatic page numbering in a report. All the values in these reserved words are available at 1P (first cycle) time.

Top-of-page control is included in a program by a Skip Before or After entry on the output form. The entry refers to the exact line number that the paper will advance to before printing.

The repetition of headings on every page of a report is controlled by the overflow indicators OA to OG and OV. Overflow indicators are defined in the File Description form for the PRINTER file in columns 33 to 34. They are specified on the output form, usually in an OR relationship with another line type conditioned by some other indicator—1P, for example.

Fields are defined as numeric by entering a related number (for decimal positions) in column 52 of the input form. Integers are defined with a 0 entry and decimal numbers 1 to 9. The maximum size of a numeric field in RPG is 15 digits. In addition, a maximum of nine decimals may be assigned to a numeric field.

Only fields defined as numeric may be edited in RPG. Editing is performed by Edit Codes or Edit Words. The function of Edit Codes is predetermined and they are, therefore, easier to use. Edit Words, however, offer additional flexibility and must be used when an Edit Code will not meet the editing requirements.

For line printers, the standard form length is 66 lines with the overflow set on line 60 (assumes printer set at six lines per inch). This standard form length may be modified in an RPG program by the Line Counter Specifications. Any form size may be controlled directly by this RPG program control.

QUESTIONS

3-1. Where are report headings defined in an RPG program?

3-2. On a blank output form define the following report heading:
SALARIED EMPLOYEE PAYROLL INFORMATION

3-3. When does the 1P indicator turn on in an RPG program? What function does it perform? What variables are available at 1P (first cycle) time?

3-4. What is the function of the Skip Before and Skip After entries in an RPG program? How does skipping control differ from spacing?

3-5. Is skipping specified for every output record type? Explain your answer.

3-6. Explain the page overflow function.

3-7. What overflow indicators are provided by RPG? Where is an overflow indicator defined? Where is it specified? Is it assigned to every output record type?

3-8. What, if anything, is wrong with the following source program coding for a heading line? Note 10 is a Record Identifying Indicator.

Line	Form Type	Filename or Record Name	Type (H/D/T/E)	Stkr #/Fetch (F)	Space Before	After	Skip Before	After	Output Indicators And	And							
3 4 5	6	7 8 9 10 11 12 13	14	15 16	17 18		19 20	21 22	23 24 25	26 27	28	29	30	31			
0 1	O	BALANCE	H		7		1 2		1 Ø								
0 2	O		OR						OV								

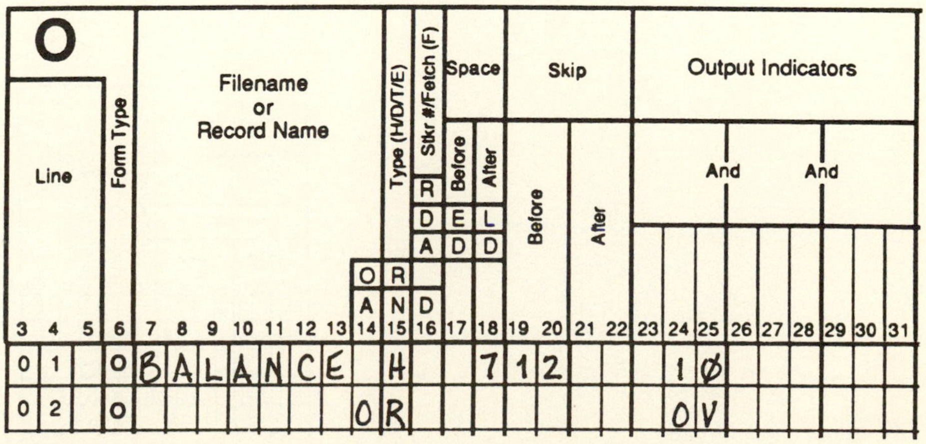

3-9. What is the RPG special word for the system date? In what format is it stored? Into what elements may it be subdivided? Are these values available for processing at 1P (first cycle) time?

3-10. Explain how page numbering is provided for in an RPG program that generates a report.

3-11. What, if anything, is wrong with the following partial output form coding for a heading line?

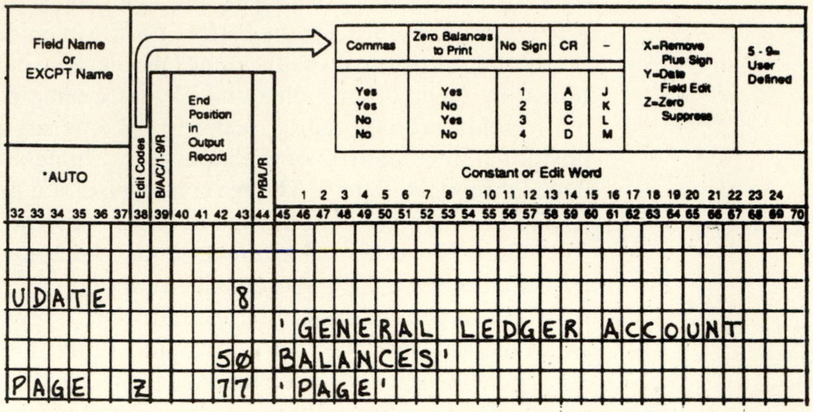

3-12. How and on which coding form are fields defined as numeric?

3-13. What is the maximum length of a numeric field supported by RPG? What is the maximum number of decimal positions that may be assigned to a numeric field? May the number of decimal positions assigned exceed the related field length?

3-14. Explain the alternative processing results that may occur when an alphanumeric field (value includes nonnumeric characters) is defined as numeric.

3-15. Define the term *implied decimal position*. What function does it perform in an RPG program?

3-16. Define the term *explicit decimal position*. Where is it specified in an RPG program?

3-17. Other that the Input Specifications, where else may fields be defined as numeric?

3-18. If editing is specified for a field that is not defined as numeric, what is the result during program compilation? What is the result during program execution?

3-19. Examine the following record layout form and the related Input Specifications coding. Explain any entries on the input form that are incorrectly defined.

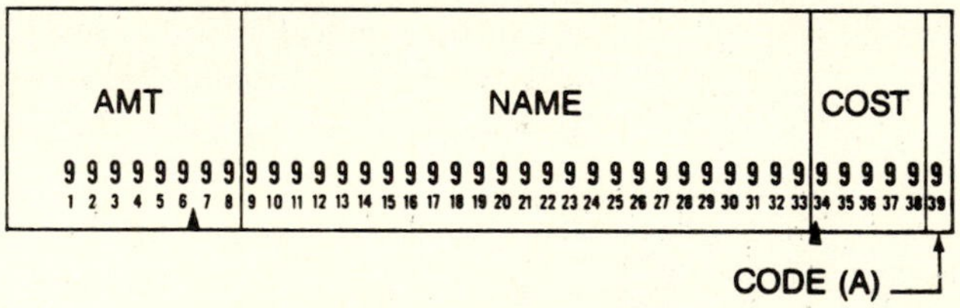

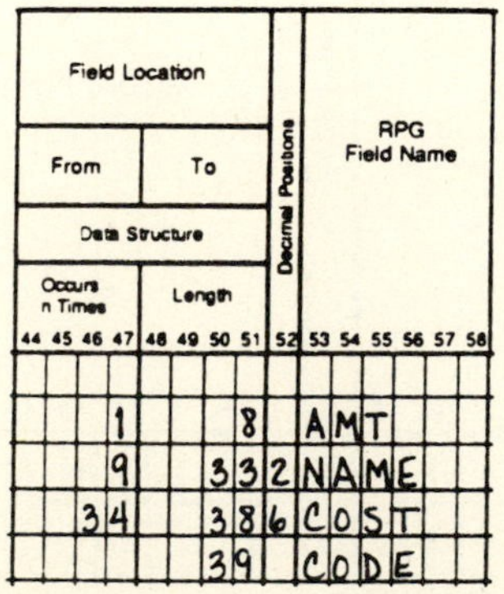

3-20. Explain the editing function. By what methods may it be controlled in an RPG program? How does syntax for the methods differ? What field types may be edited?

3-21. Determine the edited results for the following integers if the Y Edit Code is specified:

Value in Storage	Edited Result
081189	
0811	
08	
000000	
123189	

3-22. Determine the edited results for the following values when the Edit Code specified is assigned:

Value In Storage	Edit Code Specified	Edited Result
00000▲00	1	
00000▲00	2	
01234▲56	1	
10000▲00	3	
00000▲99	4	
20000▲0J	A	
02000▲00	B	
00010▲00	Z	
01245▲9}	K	

▲ Indicates implied decimal position

3-23. On the basis of the values in storage, format the edit words to generate the indicated edited results. For all *monetary* values, the format .00 is to be printed for decimal values and 0 for integers if the value is zero. In addition, for monetary values, include commas in the edit word if the size suggests them. Field sizes are indicated by the values in storage (first column).

Value In Storage	Edited Result	Required Edit Word (format on a blank output form)
012223456▲	012-22-3456	
0102▲90	1/01/89	
000010▲00	*****10.00	
000099▲44	$99.44	
2033334444▲	(203) 333 4444	
005000▲00	$ 5,000.00	
0001▲87N	18.75 CR	
0213500J▲	$ 2,135,001-	
00150▲00	150.00 DEBIT	

▲ Indicates implied decimal position in storage

3-24. Do the blank positions in an Edit Word pattern have to be *equal* to the related field size? Explain your answer.

3-25. When an Edit Code is used, how is a fixed dollar sign specified? How is a floating dollar sign specified? If an Edit Word is used, how is a fixed dollar sign specified? How is a floating dollar sign specified?

3-26. For line printers, what is the standard paper length for forms expressed in lines? On what line is page overflow set?

3-27. Which RPG specification forms are required to modify the standard paper length? Refer to the form(s), and identify the entries required.

EXERCISES

3-1. From the following record layout format and printer spacing chart, write the Input and Output Specifications coding. All input fields are integers.

FROM AGI	TO AGI	CON-TRIB	INT	TAX-ES	MED-CAL
9 9 9 9 9	9 9 9 9 9	9 9 9 9	9 9 9 9	9 9 9 9	9 9 9 9
1 2 3 4 5	6 7 8 9 10	11 12 13 14	15 16 17 18	19 20 21 22	23 24 25 26

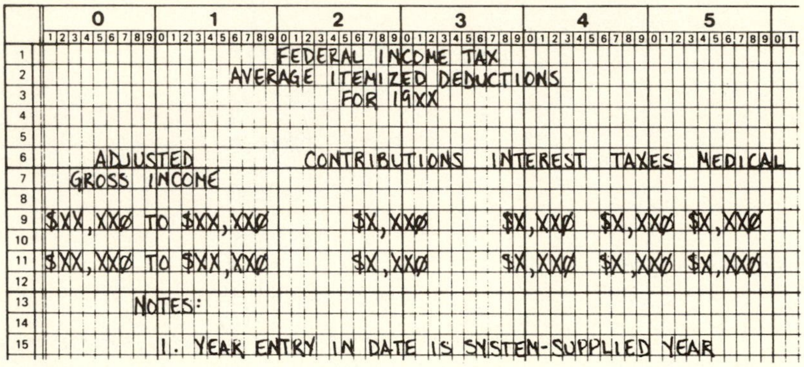

3-2. Examine the source program and related partial report listings, and determine what correction(s) must be made to eliminate the repetition of headings for every detail line.

```
... ... 1 ... ... 2 ... ... 3 ... ... 4 ... ... 5 ... ... 6 ... ... 7 ...
0001 H                                                              EX32
0005 FGLACTS  IP  F  80  80          DISK                           EX32
0006 FLISTING O   F 132 132     OF   PRINTER                        EX32
0007 IGLACTS  SM  01                                                EX32
0008 I                                    1   3 ACTNO               EX32
0009 I                                    4  30 NAME                EX32
0010 I                                   31  50 TYPE                EX32
0011 I                                   51  582BALNCE              EX32
0012 OLISTING H  301    1P                                          EX32
0013 O        OR        OF                                          EX32
0014 O                        UDATE Y   8                           EX32
0015 O                                 47 'GENERAL LEDGER ACCOUNT ' EX32
0016 O                                 55 'BALANCES'                EX32
0017 O                                 75 'PAGE'                    EX32
0018 O                        PAGE  Z  80                           EX32
0019 O          H  2    01                                          EX32
0020 O        OR        OF                                          EX32
0021 O                                  9 'ACT NO'                  EX32
0022 O                                 32 'ACCOUNT NAME'            EX32
0023 O                                 57 'ACCOUNT TYPE'            EX32
0024 O                                 76 'BALANCE'                 EX32
0025 O          D  1    01                                          EX32
0026 O                        ACTNO     7                           EX32
0027 O                        NAME     37                           EX32
0028 O                        TYPE     62                           EX32
0029 O                                 66 '$'                       EX32
0030 O                        BALNCE1  77                           EX32
```

```
12/31/92              GENERAL LEDGER ACCOUNT BALANCES              PAGE    1

  ACT NO          ACCOUNT NAME            ACCOUNT TYPE            BALANCE

   101   CASH                          CURRENT ASSET         $  10,841.02
  ACT NO          ACCOUNT NAME            ACCOUNT TYPE            BALANCE

   102   ACCOUNTS RECEIVABLE           CURRENT ASSET         $   7,633.49
  ACT NO          ACCOUNT NAME            ACCOUNT TYPE            BALANCE

   103   NOTES RECEIVABLE              CURRENT ASSET         $   3,840.61
  ACT NO          ACCOUNT NAME            ACCOUNT TYPE            BALANCE
```

3-3. Debug the following source program listing.

```
         ....+....1....+....2....+....3....+....4....+....5....+....6....+....7.

       1 0001 H                                                            EX33


       2 0002 FGLACTS  IP  F  58  58            DISK                       EX33
       3 0003 FLISTING O   F 132 132            PRINTER                    EX33


       4 0004 IGLACTS  SM  01                                              EX33
       5 0005 I                                        1   3 ACTNO         EX33
       6 0006 I                                        4  30 NAME          EX33
       7 0007 I                                       31  500TYPE          EX33
****-I114- The length of a numeric field must not exceed 15.
       8 0008 I                                       51  59 BALNCE        EX33
****-I110- To Position must not exceed record size.


       9 0009 OLISTING H  301   1P                                         EX33
      10 0010 O        OR       OF                                         EX33
****-0124- Overflow Conditioning Indicator was not defined in File Specifications.
      11 0011 O                          DATE  Y    8                      EX33
****-0106- Field Name has not been defined.
****-0113- Edit Code or Edit Constant must not be specified for an alphameric field.
      12 0012 O                                    47 'GENERAL LEDGER ACCOUNT '   EX33
      13 0013 O                                    55 'BALANCES            EX33
****-0109- Constant must have a terminating quote.
      14 0014 O                                    75 'PAGE'               EX33
      15 0015 O                          PAGE  Z   80                      EX33
      16 0016 O           H  2     1P                                      EX33
      17 0017 O        OR       OF                                         EX33
****-0124- Overflow Conditioning Indicator was not defined in File Specifications.
      18 0018 O                                     9 'ACT NO'             EX33
      19 0019 O                                    12 'ACCOUNT NAME'       EX33
      20 0020 O                                    57 'ACCOUNT TYPE'       EX33
      21 0021 O                                    76 'BALANCE             EX33
****-0109- Constant must have a terminating quote.
      22 0022 O           D  1     1P                                      EX33
      23 0023 O                          ACTNO      7                      EX33
      24 0024 O                          NAME      37                      EX33
      25 0025 O                          TYPE      62                      EX33
      26 0026 O                                    66 '$'                  EX33
      27 0027 O                          BALNCE1   77                      EX33
****-0113- Edit Code or Edit Constant must not be specified for an alphameric field.
      28 /*
      29 /*


           THE FOLLOWING INDICATORS WERE SPECIFIED BUT WERE NEVER
           USED TO CONDITION OPERATIONS

           01


           THE FOLLOWING INDICATORS WERE USED TO CONDITION OPERATIONS
           BUT WERE NEVER SET

           OF


           THE FOLLOWING INDICATORS APPEARED IN THIS PROGRAM

           01  1P  OF
   No Warning Errors
    9 Fatal Errors
```

LABORATORY ASSIGNMENTS

Laboratory Assignment 3-1: SALARIED EMPLOYEE REPORT

From the following record layout and printer spacing chart, write an RPG program to generate the report format:

Format of Input Data Records:

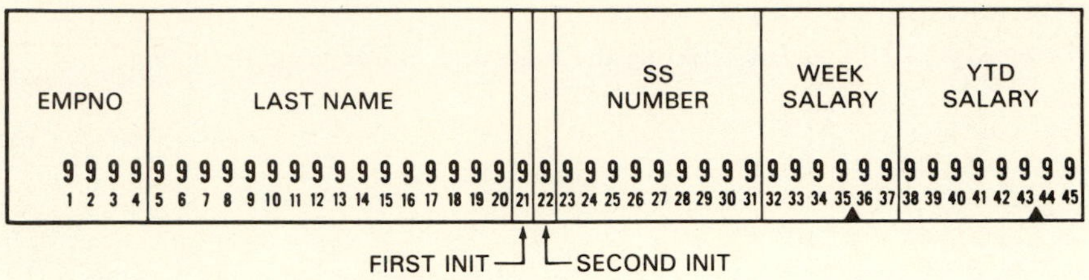

Report Design:

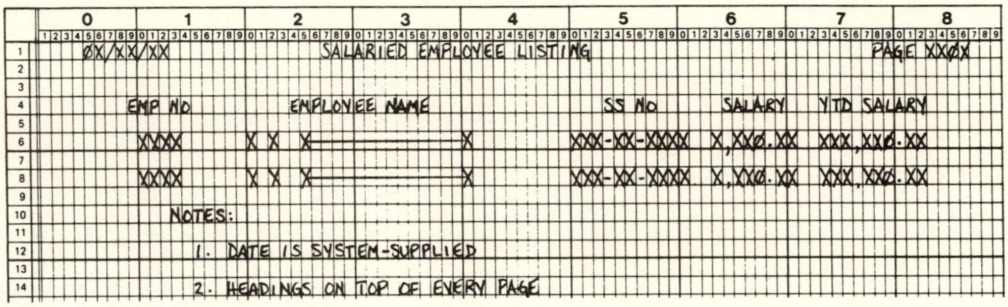

Input Data:

Employee Number	Last Name	Initials 1st	Initials 2nd	SS Number	Weekly Salary	YTD Salary
0001	WASHINGTON	G	G	010731799	080000	01600000
0016	LINCOLN	A	T	018091864	110000	00440000
0018	GRANT	U	S	018221885	051599	00051599
0032	ROOSEVELT	F	D	018821945	095000	00950000
0033	TRUMAN	H	S	018841973	099999	02999970
0034	EISENHOWER	D	D	018901971	140000	02940000
0039	CARTER	J		019771981	023000	00920000
0040	REAGAN	R		020111989	200000	02000000

Laboratory Assignment 3-2: DATA PERSONNEL SALARY LISTING

Write an RPG program to generate the report detailed in the formatted printer spacing chart. Refer to the record format for field sizes and types.

Format of Input Data Records:

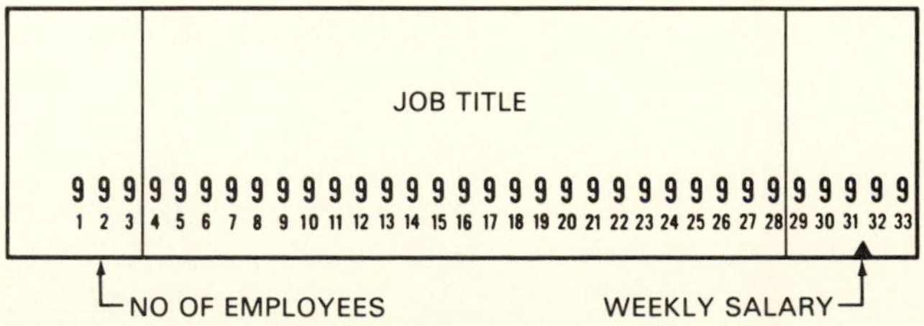

Report Design:

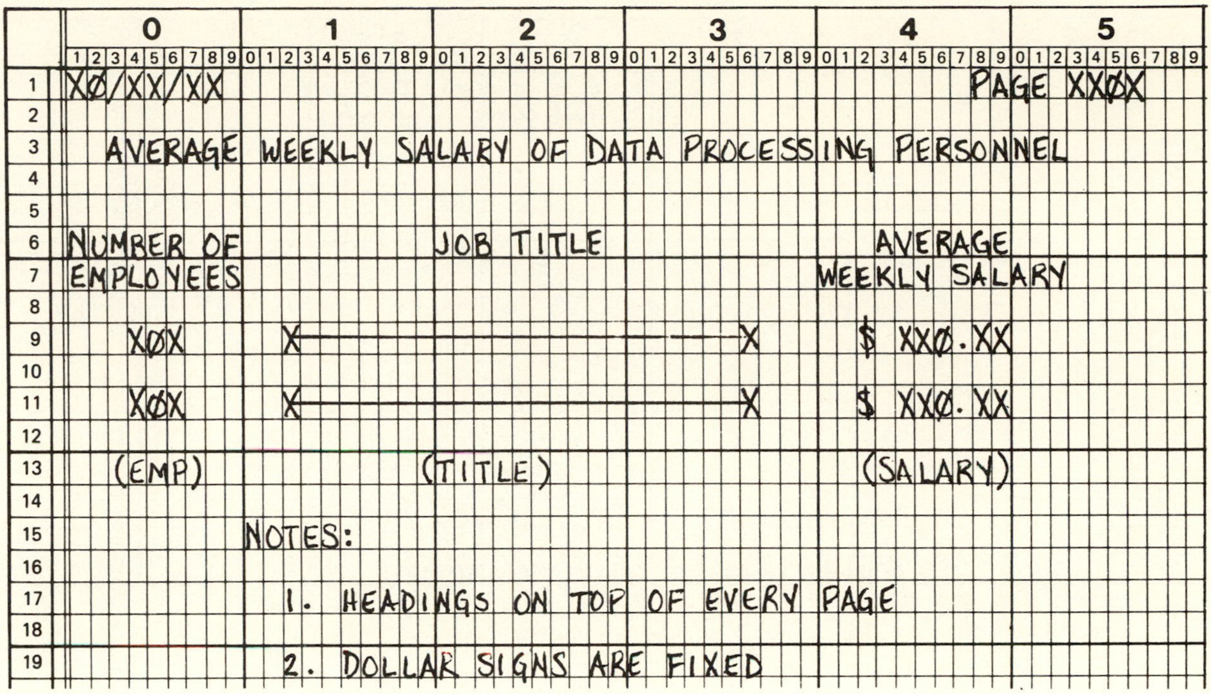

Input Data:

Job Title	Average Weekly Salary	Number of Employees
APPLICATION PROGRAMMERS	50000	010
SYSTEMS PROGRAMMERS	65000	003
COMPUTER OPERATORS	27500	008
SYSTEMS ANALYST	75000	004
DATA ENTRY CLERKS	25000	010
PROGRAMMER TRAINEES	30000	003
RECORDS CLERKS	22500	002
DATA PROCESSING MANAGER	82500	001
OPERATOR SUPERVISORS	45000	002

Laboratory Assignment 3-3: SINGLE TAXPAYERS TAX RATE SCHEDULE

Write an RPG program to generate the report detailed in the printer spacing chart. In your examination of the chart, notice that the dollar signs and percentage sign are included on only the first detail line. Program control must consider this requirement.

Format of Input Data Records (All input values are integers)

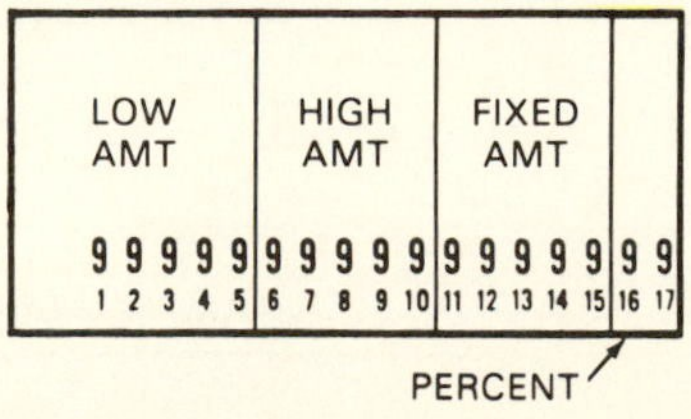

Report Design:

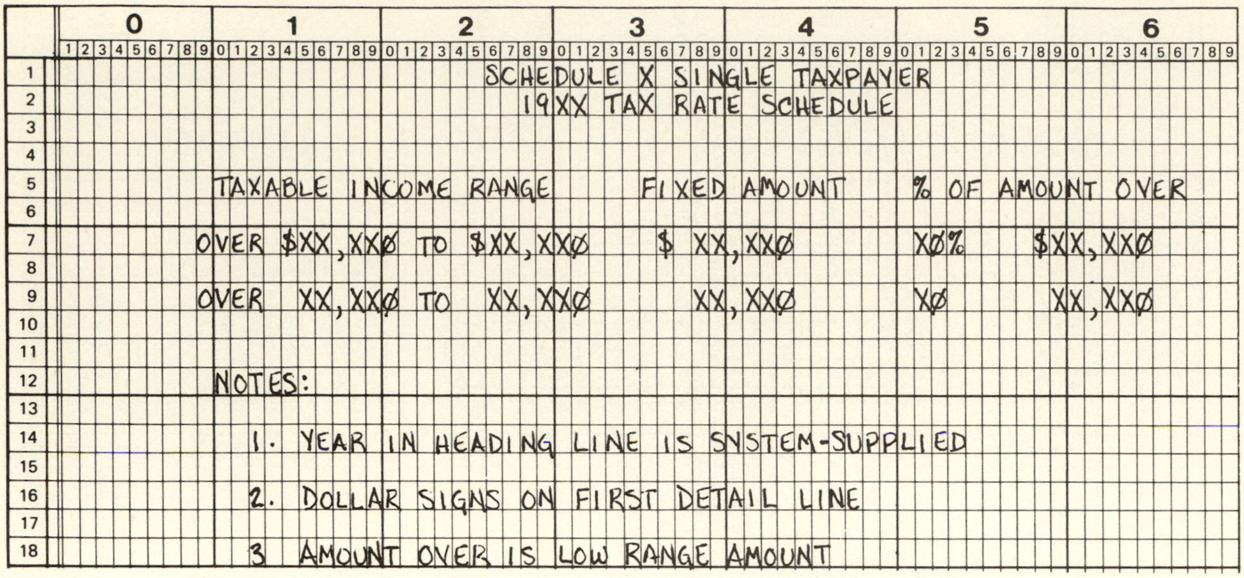

SCHEDULE X SINGLE TAXPAYER
19XX TAX RATE SCHEDULE
TAXABLE INCOME RANGE
FIXED AMOUNT
% OF AMOUNT OVER
OVER $XX,XXØ TO $XX,XXØ
$ XX,XXØ
XØ%
$XX,XXØ
OVER XX,XXØ TO XX,XXØ
XX,XXØ
XØ
XX,XXØ
NOTES:
1. YEAR IN HEADING LINE IS SYSTEM-SUPPLIED
2. DOLLAR SIGNS ON FIRST DETAIL LINE
3 AMOUNT OVER IS LOW RANGE AMOUNT

Input Data:

Taxable Income Range Over	Not over	Fixed Amount	Percent of Amount Over
00000	02300	00000	00
02300	03400	00000	11
03400	04400	00121	13
04400	08500	00251	15
08500	10800	00866	17
10800	12900	01257	19
12900	15000	01656	21
15000	18200	02097	24
18200	23500	02865	28
23500	28800	04389	32
28800	34100	06045	36
34100	41500	07953	40
41500	55300	10913	45
55300		17123	50

Laboratory Assignment 3-4: STUDENT ENROLLMENT REPORT

Write an RPG program form to generate the report detailed in the following printer spacing chart:

Format of the Input Data Records:
(SS NO, TEL NO, and TEST MARK are integers).

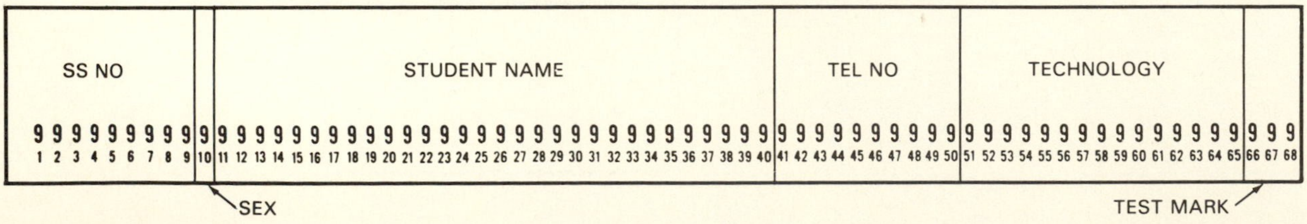

Report Design:

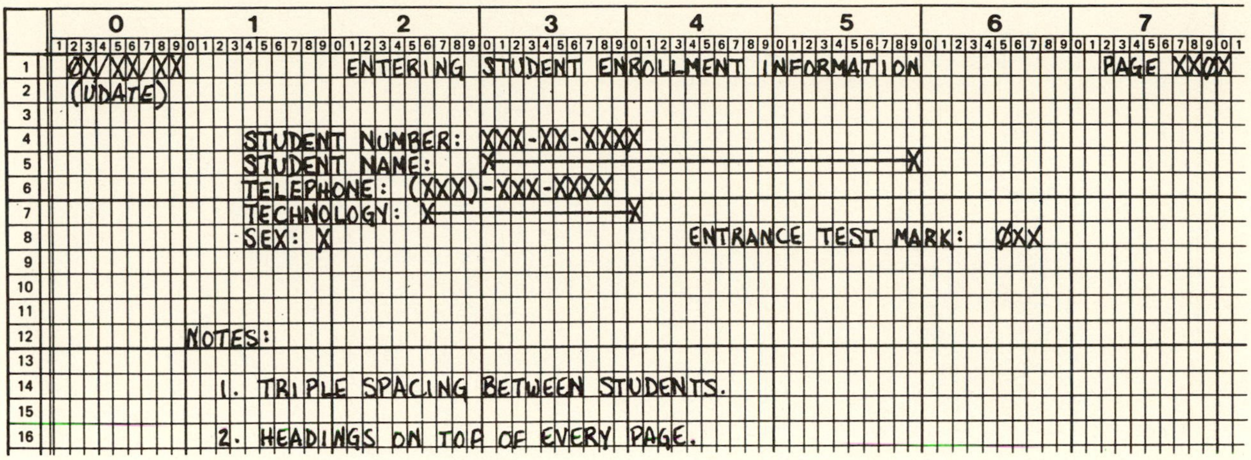

Input Data:

SS Number	Sex	Student Name	Telephone Number	Technology	Entrance Test Mark
011223333	M	LAMONT CRANSTON	2037778888	DATA	090
066445432	F	LOIS LANE	2129994322	CHEMISTRY	085
124111235	M	FRANK N STEIN	9142668413	ARCHITECTURAL	078
077889999	M	D R ACULA	9134445555	PREP PROGRAM	060
124111235	F	REDDI WATT	2033777865	MECHANICAL	100

chapter 4
RPG Calculations

This chapter introduces the syntax and processing logic for RPG calculations and related indicator control. All calculation instructions are included in the Calculations Specifications. The logical areas of this form and an explanation of their functions are detailed in Figure 4-1.

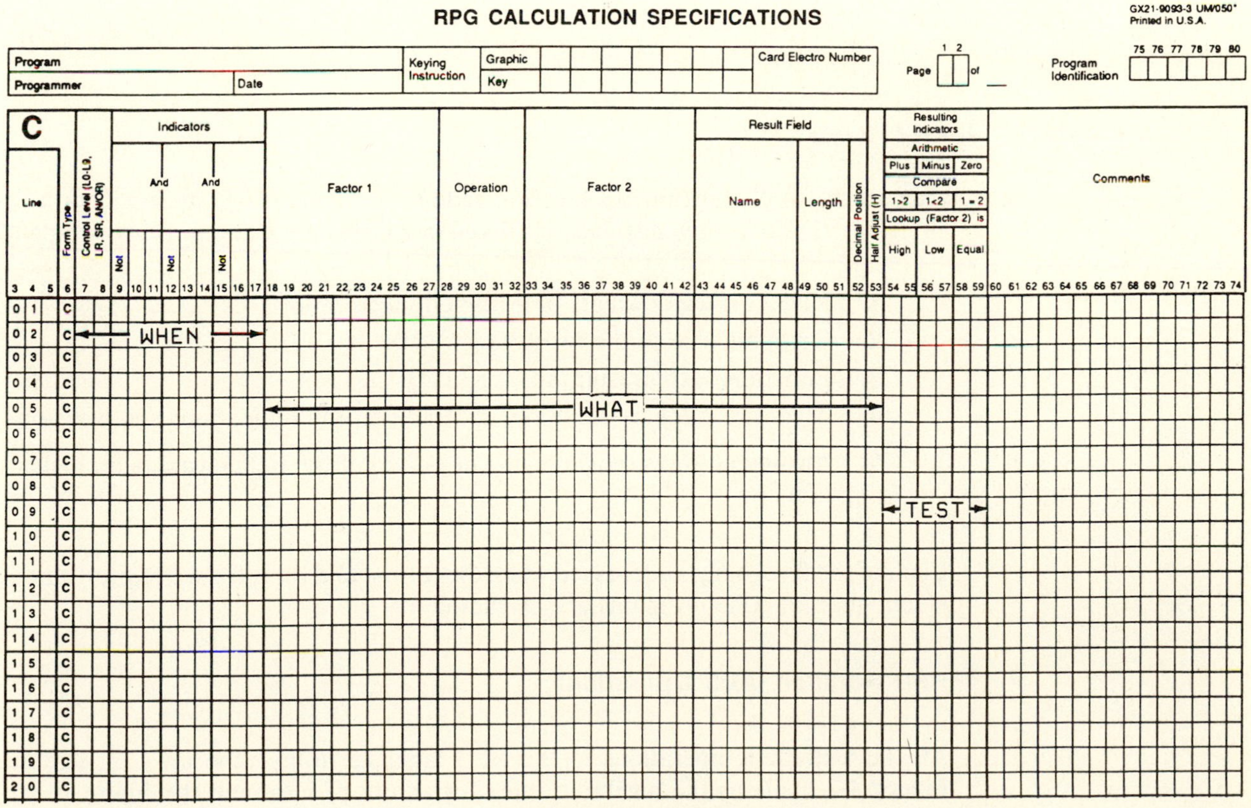

Figure 4-1 RPG Calculations specifications.

All calculation instructions must have a letter C in column 6.

Form Areas:

When (columns 7-17)

Conditioning indicator(s) are specified (only when needed) in this logical area. Columns 7-8 are for the Control Level Indicators L1-L9 that control total time processing; and for the LR indicator that controls last record (end-of-file) time processing. Control level indicator concepts are introduced in Chapter 8 and the LR indicator later in this chapter. Any RPG indicators (except 1P and LR) may be specified in columns 9-17 to condition an instruction.

What (columns 18-53)

This area includes fields labelled Factor 1, Operation, Factor 2, Result field, Field Length, Decimal Positions, and Half-Adjust. Their function is to inform the computer about the operation to be executed. Many operations are supported in the calculation specifications. This chapter only introduces the syntax and processing logic associated with arithmetic operations. Other chapters present the function of other operations.

Test (columns 54-59)

Refer to the form and notice that this area is labelled as Resulting indicators, followed by the heading Arithmetic, and then the fields for Plus, Minus, and Zero. Indicators (usually 01-99) are specified in one or more of these fields to test a result field value for positive, negative, and/or zero. Resulting indicator(s) are used to condition other calculations and/or output instructions. The programmer must determine what tests, if any, are to be made.

The heading labelled Compare and related fields, High, Low, and Equal, is used in decision making instructions which are introduced in the next chapter. The Lookup heading and fields are unique to table and array processing, and are discussed in Chapters 9 and 10, respectively.

Comments (columns 60-74)

Comments may be included in this area to support instructions. They do not require an asterisk in column 7 and do not have to be enclosed in apostrophes (quotes).

(Continued)

RPG ARITHMETIC OPERATIONS

Regardless of the arithmetic function (addition, subtraction, multiplication, or division), the following must be considered in an RPG programming environment:

1. RPG language formats of arithmetic instructions
2. Optimum size of the result (answer field)
3. Function of the result (answer field)
4. Algebraic rules for addition, subtraction, multiplication, and division
5. Arithmetic signs (positive and negative) of the fields used in an instruction

Each of the foregoing is addressed when the format and rules for writing arithmetic statements for RPG programs are discussed.

RPG Addition (ADD Operation)

All the arithmetic operations in the RPG language follow the laws of algebra. Figure 4-2 explains the algebriac rules for addition. Examine the figure to understand how the sum (answer) is affected by the various combinations of positive and negative signs.

	Rule 1	Rule 2	Rule 3	Rule 3	Rule 3
Addend	+2	-3	+5	+3	+8
Addend	+2	-3	-5	-9	-6
Sum	+4	-6	-0	-6	+2

Explanation of algebraic rules:

Rule 1: Addition of two positive values results in a positive value for the sum.

Rule 2: Addition of two negative values results in a negative value for the sum.

Rule 3: Addition of two values with different signs results in the difference in the positive and negative values and the sum carries the sign of the largest value. (see three Rule 3 examples above).

Figure 4-2 Algebriac rules for addition.

The ADD operation controls the addition function in RPG programs. Figure 4-3 details the syntax related to this operation.

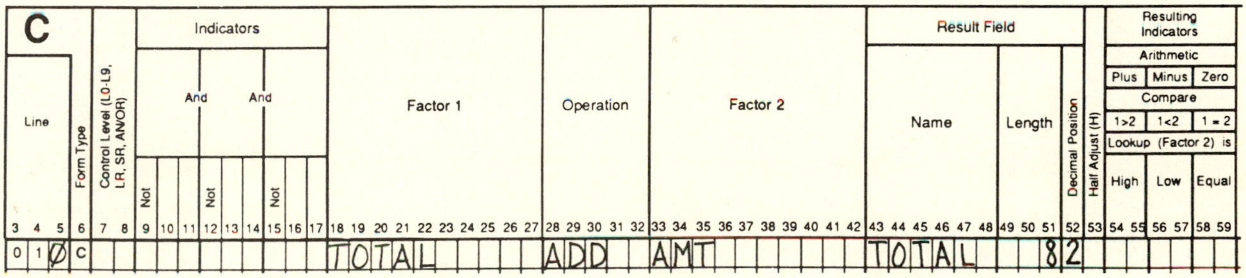

1. If a conditioning indicator is not specified, as in the example shown, the instruction will be executed for every record processed.

2. A field name (or numeric literal) must be left-justified in Factor 1.

3. ADD operation must left-justified in Operation field.

4. A field name (or numeric literal) must be left-justified in Factor 2.

5. A field name must be left-justified in Result Field area. It may be a Factor 1 or Factor 2 field name. For addition instructions that perform an accumulation function (i.e. record count), the result field name must be the same as the Factor 1 or 2 entry.

6. If the result field item was not previously defined on input or in some other calculations instruction, it must be defined in these fields (field length and decimal position entries)

Figure 4-3 RPG syntax for ADD instruction.

Four ADD instructions are illustrated in Figure 4-4. Notice that the field values *before* and *after* a statement is executed are shown for every example.

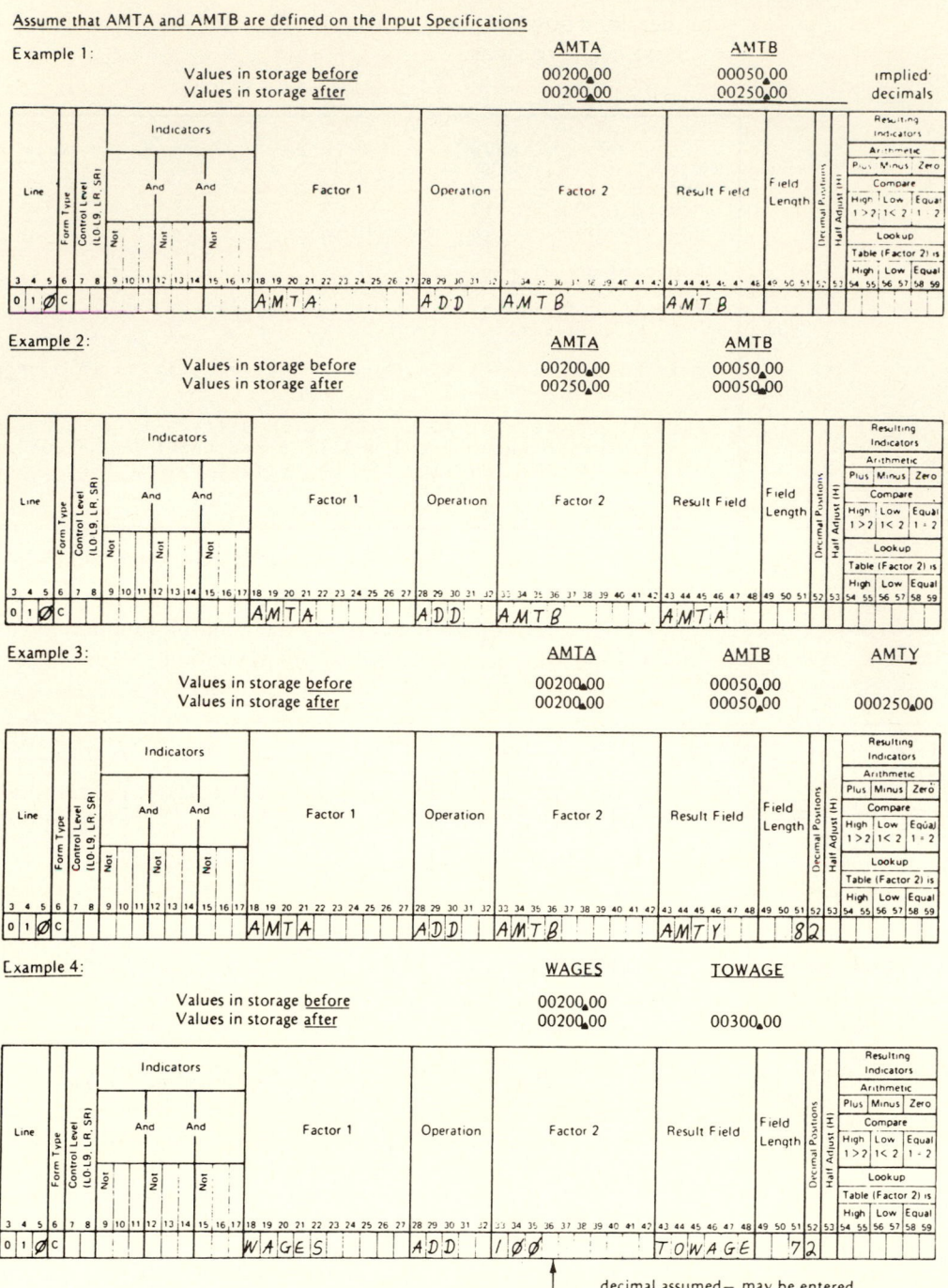

Assume that AMTA and AMTB are defined on the Input Specifications

Example 1:

	AMTA	AMTB	
Values in storage before	00200.00	00050.00	implied decimals
Values in storage after	00200.00	00250.00	

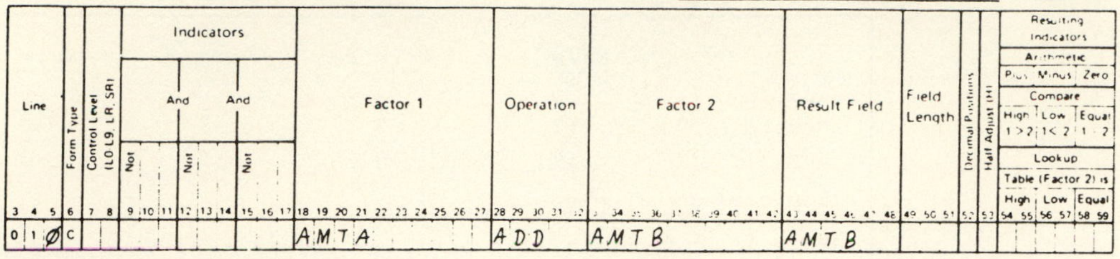

Example 2:

	AMTA	AMTB
Values in storage before	00200.00	00050.00
Values in storage after	00250.00	00050.00

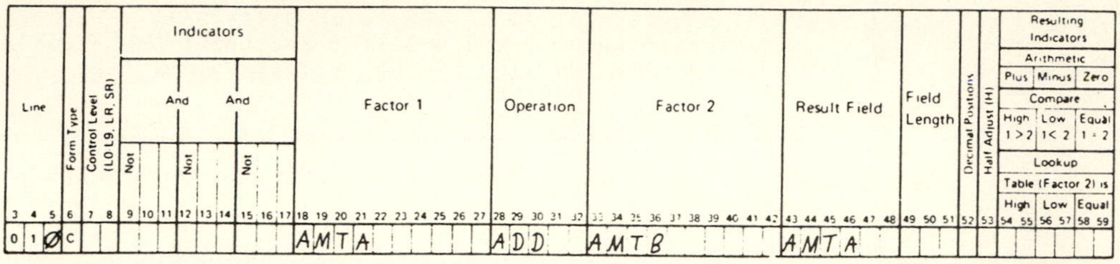

Example 3:

	AMTA	AMTB	AMTY
Values in storage before	00200.00	00050.00	
Values in storage after	00200.00	00050.00	000250.00

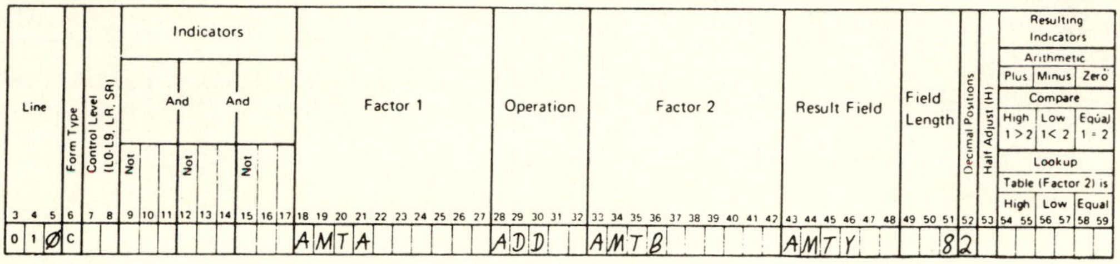

Example 4:

	WAGES	TOWAGE
Values in storage before	00200.00	
Values in storage after	00200.00	00300.00

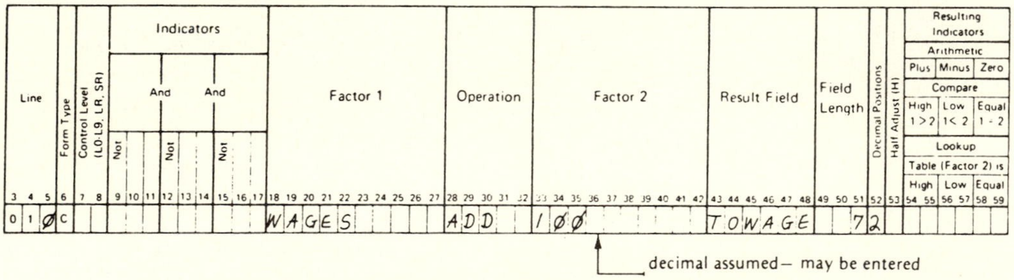

Figure 4-4 Coding examples of ADD instructions.

After you have examined Figure 4-4, notice the following features for the ADD operation:

1. Factor 1 and 2 entries may be specified in either field.
2. A Factor 1 or 2 field may be used as the Result Field. However, for accumulators, it is more efficient to specify the Factor 1 field entry as the Result Field.
3. If a Factor 1 or 2 field is specified as the Result Field, the original value is replaced with the sum.

4. Numeric literals may be specified (left-justified) in either Factor 1 or 2. A decimal point is required for decimal literals and optional for integers.
5. Numeric literals may not be specified in the Result Field.

The Result Field size (sum) should usually be defined at least one byte greater than the largest addend (Factor 1 or 2 entry). High-order or low-order truncation, depending on the related decimal locations, may result from any sum field that is defined as too small. The data processed will determine the optimum size of a sum field.

RPG Subtraction (SUB Operation)

The algebraic rules for subtraction are explained in Figure 4-5. RPG performs the subtraction function by the SUB operation. Unlike the ADD operation, it is important which field or numeric literal is specified in Factors 1 and 2. The syntax and rules for the SUB operation are detailed in Figure 4-6.

	Example 1	Example 2	Example 3	Example 4
Minuend	+7 = +7	+7 = +7	-7 = -7	-7 = -7
Subtrahend	+5 = -5	-5 = +5	-5 = +5	+5 = -5
Difference	+2	+12	-2	-12

General Algebraic Subtraction Rule:

Before subtraction, sign of the subtrahend is changed. Minuend and subtrahend are then added to compute the difference. Finally, the addition sequence follows the algebraic rules for addition explained in Figure 4-2.

Figure 4-5 Algebraic rules for subtraction.

RPG CALCULATION SPECIFICATIONS

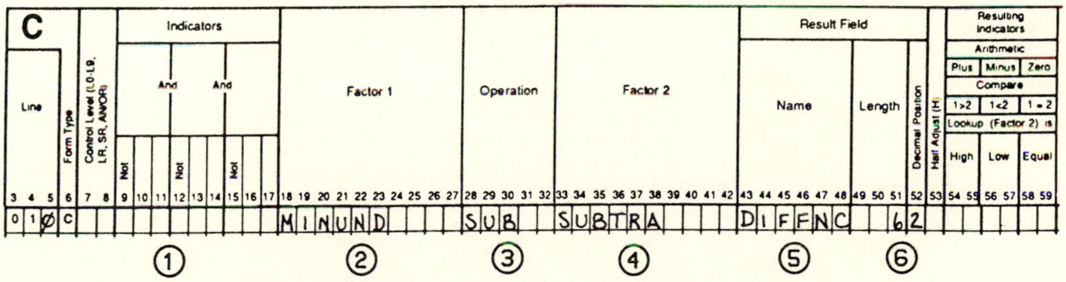

1. If a conditioning indicator is not specified, as in the example shown, the instruction will be executed for every record processed.

2. The minuend (field name or numeric literal) must be entered left-justified in Factor 1.

3. SUB operation must be left-justified in Operation field.

4. The subtrahend (field name or literal) must be entered left-justified in Factor 2.

5. The difference field name (not a numeric literal) must be entered left-justified in the Result Field.

6. If the Result Field item was not previously defined on input or in some other calculation instruction, it must be defined in these fields (field length and decimal position entries).

Figure 4-6 RPG syntax for SUB (subtraction) instructions.

Four SUB instructions are illustrated in Figure 4-7. Observe that the field values *before* and *after* a statement is executed are included for every example.

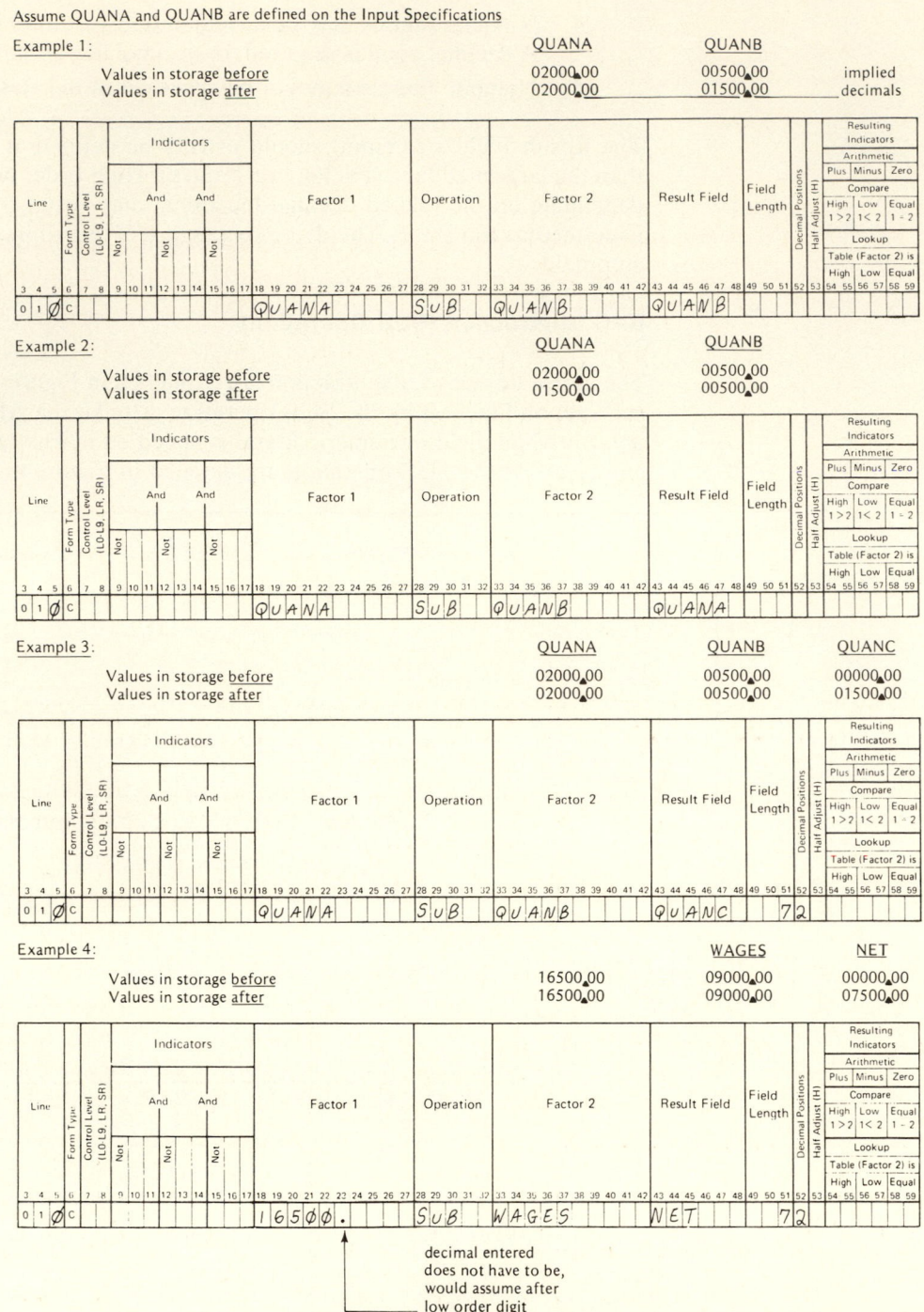

Assume QUANA and QUANB are defined on the Input Specifications

Example 1:

	QUANA	QUANB	
Values in storage before	02000‸00	00500‸00	implied
Values in storage after	02000‸00	01500‸00	decimals

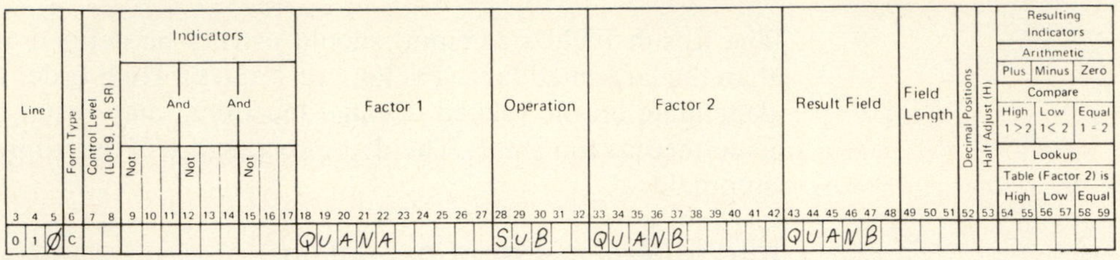

Example 2:

	QUANA	QUANB
Values in storage before	02000‸00	00500‸00
Values in storage after	01500‸00	00500‸00

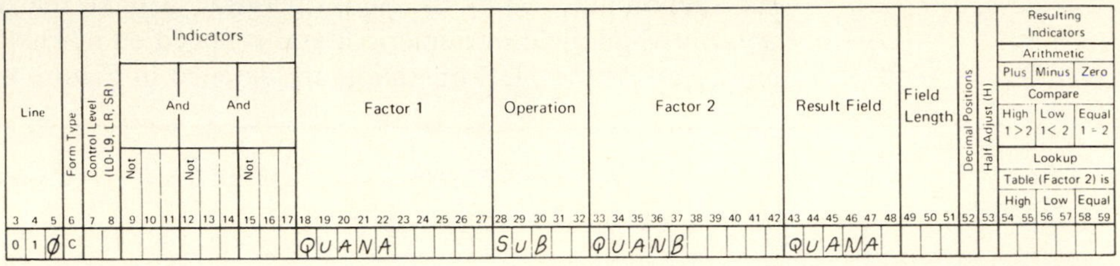

Example 3:

	QUANA	QUANB	QUANC
Values in storage before	02000‸00	00500‸00	00000‸00
Values in storage after	02000‸00	00500‸00	01500‸00

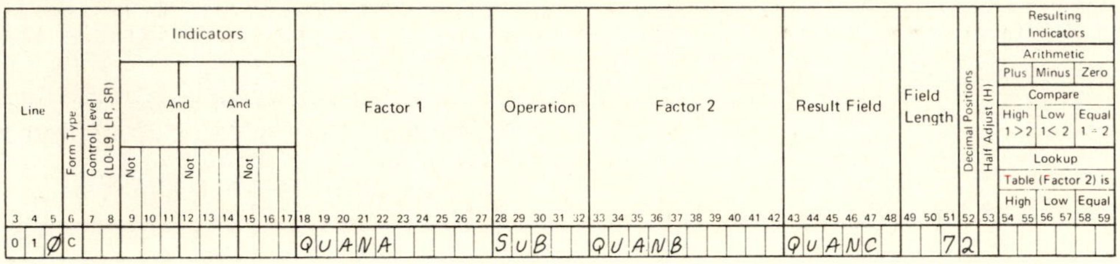

Example 4:

		WAGES	NET
Values in storage before	16500‸00	09000‸00	00000‸00
Values in storage after	16500‸00	09000‸00	07500‸00

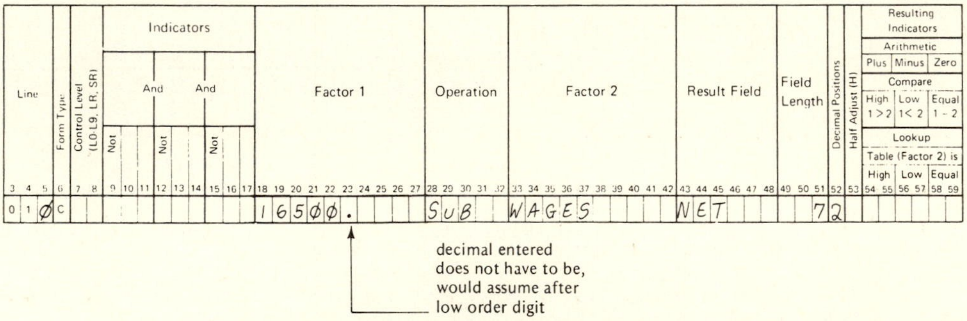

Figure 4-7 Coding examples of SUB instructions.

After you examine Figure 4-7, you should understand the following processing features for the SUB operation:

1. The field or literal used as the minuend (top number) must be specified in Factor 1.
2. A Factor 1 or 2 field may be used as the Result Field. However, to reduce processing time, it is more efficient to specify the Factor 1 field entry as the Result Field.

3. If a Factor 1 or 2 field is specified as the Result Field, the original value of that item is replaced with the value of the difference.
4. Numeric literals may be specified (left-justified) in either Factor 1 or 2. A decimal point is required for decimal literals and optional for integers.
5. Numeric literals may not be specified in the Result Field.

The Result Field size (difference) should usually be defined as same size as the largest of the Factor 1 or 2 entries. High-order or low-order truncation, depending on the related decimal locations, may occur if the difference field is not large enough to store the value of the answer.

RPG Multiplication (MULT Operation)

The algebraic rules for multiplication are explained in Figure 4-8. RPG performs the multiplication function by the MULT operation. The syntax and rules for this operation are presented in Figure 4-9.

	Rule 1	*Rule 1*	*Rule 2*	*Rule 2*
Multiplicand	+3	-3	+3	-3
Multiplier	+8	-8	-8	+8
Product	+24	+24	-24	-24

Explanation of Rules:

Rule 1: Multiplication of numbers with like signs results in a product with a positive value.

Rule 2: Multiplication of numbers with unlike signs results in a product with a negative value.

Figure 4-8 Algebraic rules for multiplication.

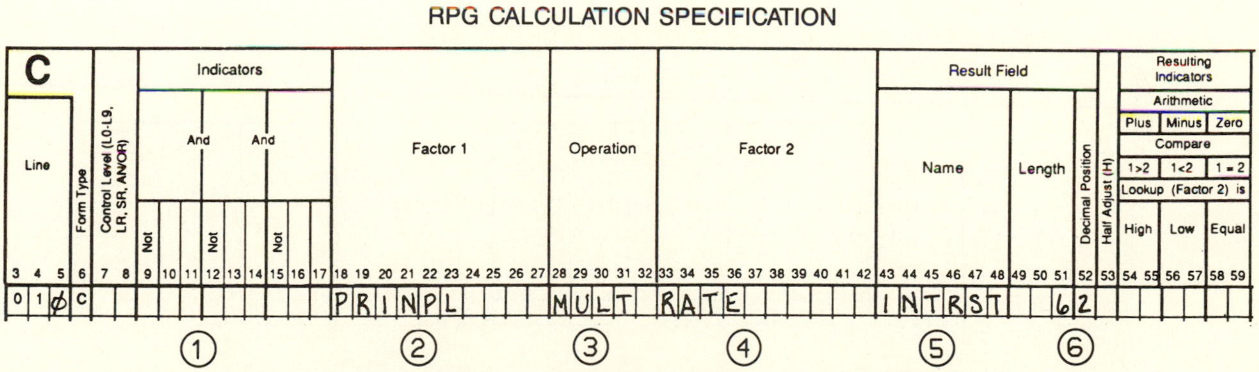

1. If conditioning indicator is not specified, as in the example shown, the instruction will be excecuted for every record processed.
2. Either the multiplicand or multiplier may be specified (left-justified) in Factor 1. For program efficiency, however, the smaller field (or numeric literal) should be entered in Factor 1.
3. MULT operation must be left-justified in Operation field.
4. Either the multiplicand or multiplier field name (or numeric literal) may be specified (left-justified) in Factor 2.
5. A field name for the product (may be a Factor 1 or 2 field name) must be entered left-justified in the Result Field.
6. If the Result Field item was not previously defined on input or in some other calculation instruction, it must be defined in these fields (field length and decimal position entries).

Figure 4-9 RPG syntax for MULT (multiplication) instructions.

Coding examples of the MULT operation that show before and after values of the Factor 1, Factor 2, and Result Field items are illustrated in Figure 4-10, a study of which shows the following RPG multiplication features:

1. Either Factor 1 or Factor 2 may be used for the multiplier or multiplicand. For program efficiency, however, the smaller field or literal should be specified in Factor 1.

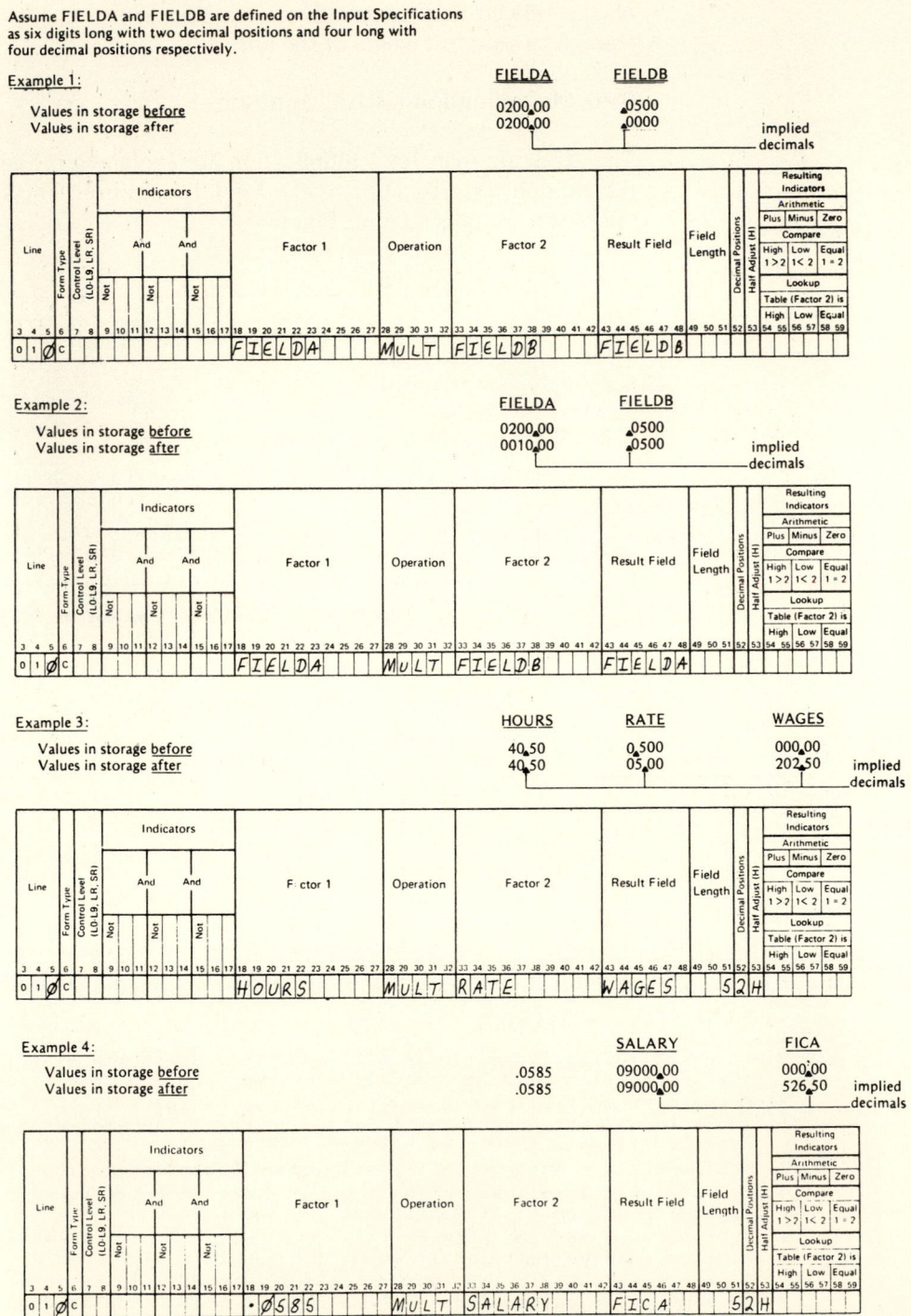

Assume FIELDA and FIELDB are defined on the Input Specifications as six digits long with two decimal positions and four long with four decimal positions respectively.

Example 1:

	FIELDA	FIELDB
Values in storage before	0200.00	.0500
Values in storage after	0200.00	.0000

implied decimals

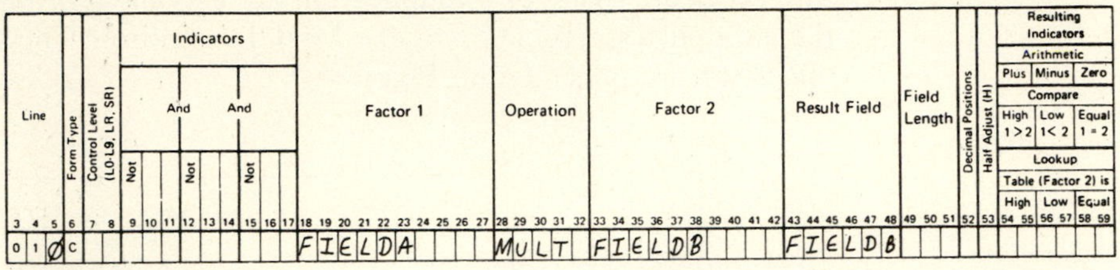

Example 2:

	FIELDA	FIELDB
Values in storage before	0200.00	.0500
Values in storage after	0010.00	.0500

implied decimals

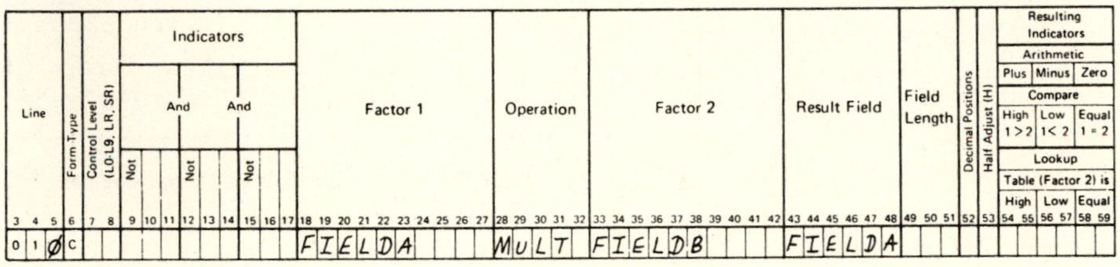

Example 3:

	HOURS	RATE	WAGES
Values in storage before	40.50	0.500	000.00
Values in storage after	40.50	05.00	202.50

implied decimals

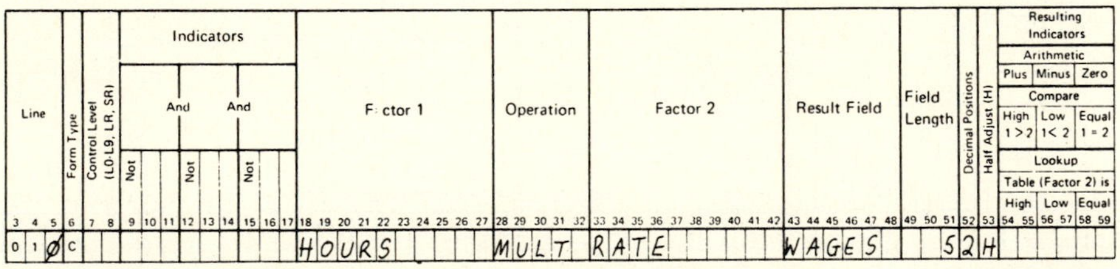

Example 4:

		SALARY	FICA
Values in storage before	.0585	09000.00	000.00
Values in storage after	.0585	09000.00	526.50

implied decimals

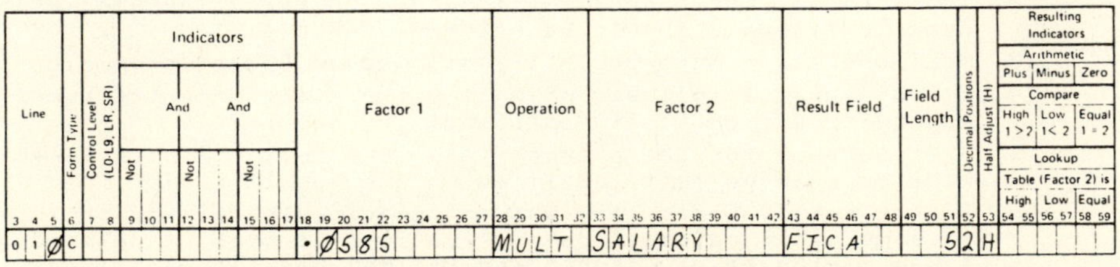

Figure 4-10 Coding examples of MULT instructions.

2. The Factor 1 or Factor 2 field may be used as the Result Field. For program efficiency, the Result Field should be the same as Factor 1.
3. When a Factor 1 or 2 field is specified as the Result Field, the original value of that item is replaced with decimal literals and optional for integers.
4. Numeric literals may not be specified as a Result Field.

For multiplication instructions, the optimum Result Field size (product) may be determined by the procedure illustrated in Figure 4-11.

```
Rule for Field Length Determination:

The maximum field length for the product of multiplication is the sum
of the number of digits in the multiplicand and multiplier fields
and/or numeric literal.

Rule for Decimal Position Determination:

The number of decimal positions for the product of the multiplication
is the sum of the number of decimal positions in the multiplicand and
multiplier fields and/or numeric literal.

Computation Routine:

Assume that FLD1, which is 8 digits in length with 2 implied decimals,
is multiplied by FLD2 defined as 5 digits long with 5 decimal
positions. The maximum size of the product may be determined by the
following routine:

                              Field or
                              Literal      Decimal
                               Size       Positions

FLD1                             8            2
FLD2                            +5           +5
                                ---          ---
Maximum product size            13            7

If rounding to zero decimal positions was specified, the product size
is computed as follows:

                               Field       Decimal
                               Size       Positions

Maximum product size            13            7
Less 5                          -7           -7
                                ---          ---
Rounded product size             6            0

Note: 7 must be subtracted from the field size and decimal position
      values.

Examples: (Assume value shown is related field size)

           FLD1        x        FLD2     =     Maximum Product Size

Values      200        x         50      =      10000
           ▲                    ▲               ▲
Values     200000      x         50             1000000
              ▲                 ▲                  ▲
Values     20000       x         50      =      1000000
              ▲                    ▲                 ▲
Values     20000       x         50      =      1000000
                ▲                  ▲                   ▲
▲ Indicates implied decimal
```

Figure 4-11 Procedures for the determination of optimum product size for multiplication.

RPG Division (DIV Operation)

The algebraic rules associated with division are explained in Figure 4-12. Division is performed in RPG by the DIV operation. The syntax of this operation is explained in Figure 4-13. Examples of this operation are shown in Figure 4-14. The following observations should be made from the coding examples in Figure 4-14.

1. A Factor 1 or Factor 2 field may be specified for the Result Field. However, because the divisor is often smaller than the dividend, its size may not be large enough to store the quotient (answer).
2. When more decimal positions are required than included in either Factor 1 or 2, a separate field should be specified for the Result Field.
3. Numeric literals may be specified in either Factor 1 or 2.

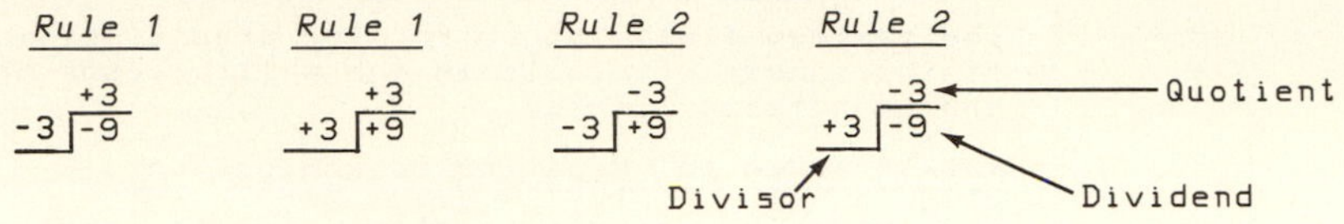

Explanation of rules:

Rule 1: Division of numbers with like signs results in a quotient with a positive value.
Rule 2: Division of numbers with unlike signs results in a quotient with a negative value.

Figure 4-12 Algebraic rules for division.

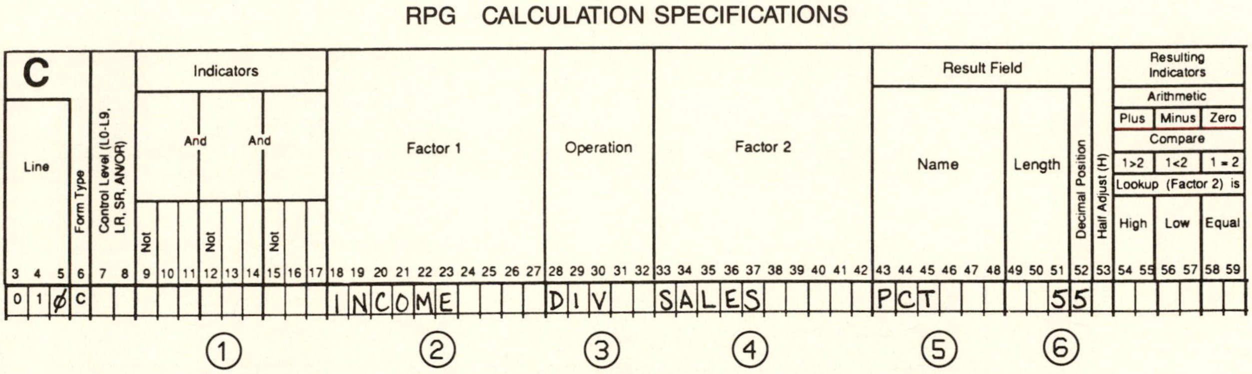

RPG CALCULATION SPECIFICATIONS
C
Line
Form Type
Control Level (L0-L9, LR, SR, AN/OR)
Indicators
And
And
Not
Not
Not
Factor 1
Operation
Factor 2
Result Field
Name
Length
Decimal Position
Half Adjust (H)
Resulting Indicators
Arithmetic
Plus
Minus
Zero
Compare
1>2
1<2
1 = 2
Lookup (Factor 2) is
High
Low
Equal
01Ø C
INCOME
DIV
SALES
PCT
5 5
1
2
3
4
5
6

1. If a conditioning indicator is not specified as in the example shown, the instruction will be executed for every record processed.

2. The dividend (field or numeric literal) must be entered left-justified in Factor 1.

3. DIV operation must be left-justified in Operation field.

4. The divisor (field or numeric literal) must be entered left-justified in Factor 2.

5. A field name for the quotient (may be a Factor 1 or 2 field name) must be entered left-justified in the Result Field.

6. If the Result Field item was not previously defined on input or in some other calculation instruction, it must be defined in these fields (field length and decimal position entries).

Figure 4-13 RPG syntax for the DIV (division) operation.

Example 1:

	GRPRFT	NETSAL
Value in storage before	1000000	20000000
Value in storage after	1000000	00000005

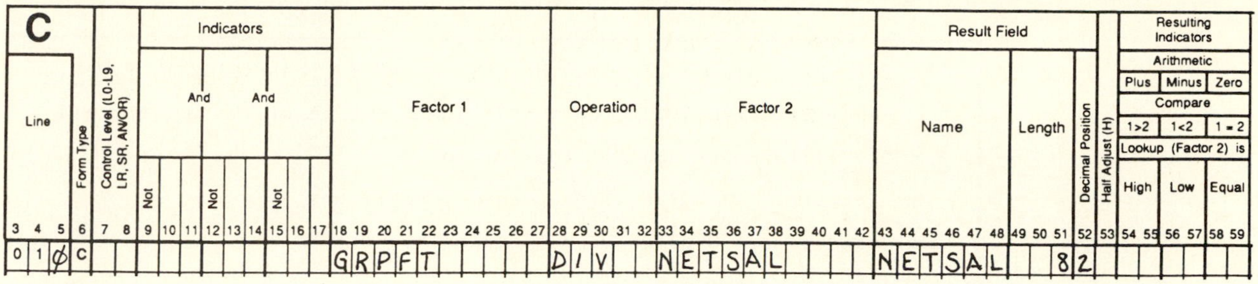
C
Indicators
Line
Form Type
Control Level (L0-L9, LR, SR, AN/OR)
And
And
Not
Not
Not
Factor 1
Operation
Factor 2
Result Field
Name
Length
Decimal Position
Half Adjust (H)
Resulting Indicators
Arithmetic
Plus Minus Zero
Compare
1>2 1<2 1=2
Lookup (Factor 2) is
High Low Equal
0 1 Ø C GRPFT DIV NETSAL NETSAL 8 2

Example 2:

	GRPFT	NETSAL	PERCNT
Value in storage before	1000000	20000000	00000
Value in storage after	1000000	20000000	05000

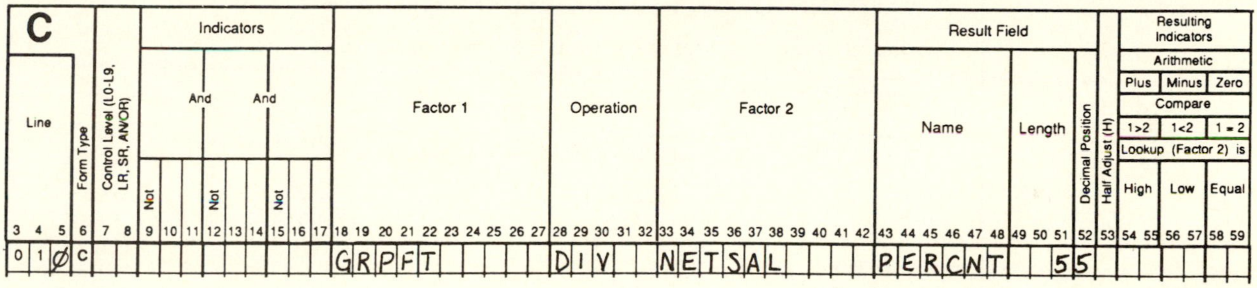
C
Indicators
Line
Form Type
Control Level (L0-L9, LR, SR, AN/OR)
And
And
Not
Not
Not
Factor 1
Operation
Factor 2
Result Field
Name
Length
Decimal Position
Half Adjust (H)
Resulting Indicators
Arithmetic
Plus Minus Zero
Compare
1>2 1<2 1=2
Lookup (Factor 2) is
High Low Equal
0 1 Ø C GRPFT DIV NETSAL PERCNT 5 5

Example 3:

	QTY	12	DOZ
Value in storage before	00288	12	0000
Value in storage after	00288	12	0024

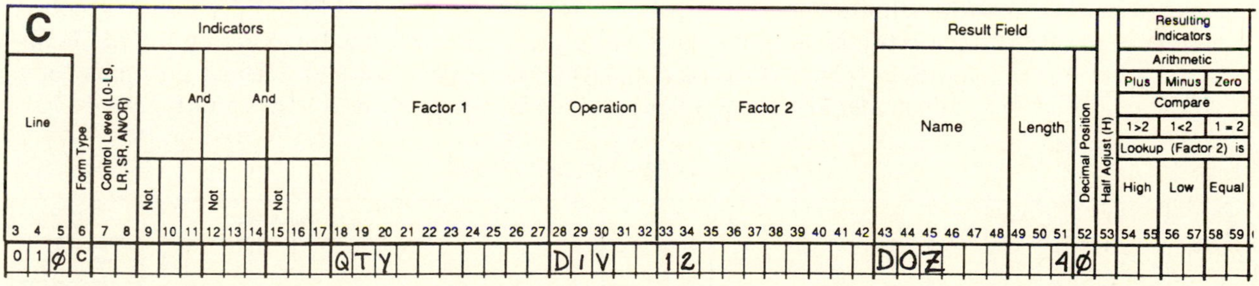

Note: Because the computer will not support division by zero, the divisor should always be tested in the program before the division instruction is executed. Some computer systems will ''abort'' program execution for a divide by zero error. Others will halt and give the operator a message requesting an action to either cancel the program or ignore the record and continue processing.

Figure 4-14 Coding examples of the DIV operation.

The optimum size of the quotient (answer) for a DIV instruction may be determined by the procedure explained in Figure 4-15. It is important to remember that computers will not support division by zero (the divisor cannot have a zero value). Some systems will immediately terminate program execution; others will halt and give the operator some control option.

```
The Optimum Quotient Size May Be Determined by the Following Formula

     Quotient size = Size of the dividend - Size of the divisor + 1

Example 1: (divisor smaller than dividend)

 Divisor size = 2 bytes with 0 decimal positions

 Dividend size = 6 bytes with 2 decimal positions

   Quotient size = 6 - 2 + 1

   Quotient size = 5

The decimal positions in the quotient will be equal to that
specified in the dividend

Example 2: (divisor larger than dividend)

Divisor size = 5 bytes with 0 decimal positions

Dividend size = 3 bytes with 0 decimal positions

   Quotient size = 3 - 5 + 1

   Quotient size = -1 (field must be specified as 1 long
                       with 1 decimal position)

When a larger value is divided into a smaller value, the quotient
size may be specified larger than the formula indicates. The
accuracy required will determine how many decimal positions are
assigned.
```

Figure 4-15 Procedure for determination of quotient size.

Move Remainder Operation (MVR)

Sometimes it may be necessary to store the remainder of a division instruction for subsequent processing. This function is performed in RPG by the MVR operation, which is detailed ‚n Figure 4-16. The size and decimal positions for a Remainder Field may be determined by the process illustrated in Figure 4-17.

RPG CALCULATION SPECIFICATIONS

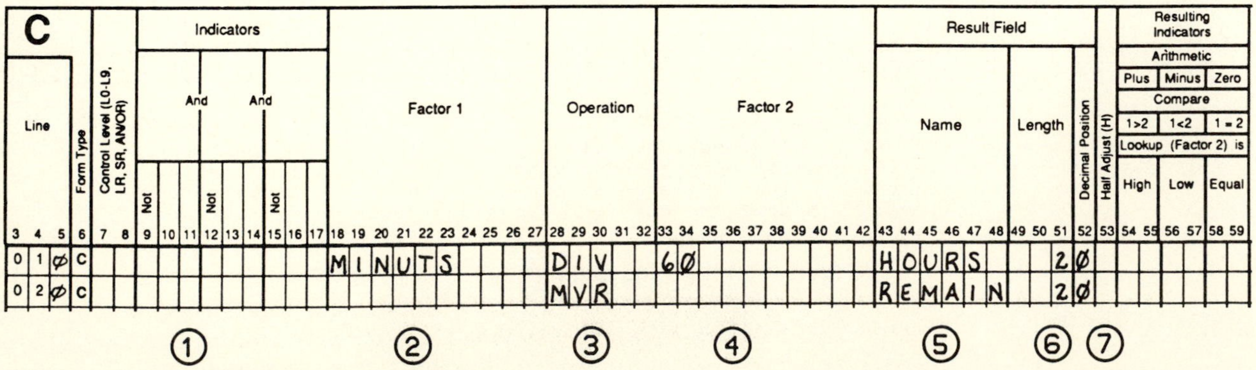

Figure 4-16 Syntax and rules for the MVR (Move Remainder) operation.

1. If a conditioning indicator is not specified, as in the example shown, the instruction will be executed for every record processed.

   When an indicator is specified for the DIV operation, the same one must be assigned to the related MVR instruction.

2. Factor 1 is not used with the MVR operation.

3. MVR must be entered left-justified in the Operation field.

4. Factor 2 is not used with the MVR operation.

5. A programmer-supplied field name (remainder field) must be specified left-justified in the Result Field. After processing, the value in the remainder field will have the same sign as the dividend.

6. Unless previously defined, the remainder field must be assigned a field length and decimal position entry.

7. Half Adjust (column 53) may be specified for the MVR operation's Result Field, but not for the quotient in the related DIV instruction.

The MVR Operation must immediately follow the related DIV instruction.

(*Continued*)

```
Division example:

                       173.07        Quotient
Divisor          52 | 900.000        Dividend
                      52
                      380
                      364
                      160
                      156
                       400
                       364
                        36 <-------- Remainder

Rules for the determination of quotient and remainder sizes:

1. The optimum quotient size may be determined by the following formula:

   Quotient size = Size of the dividend - Size of the divisor + 1

2. The optimum remainder size is equal to the size of the divisor.

   The number of decimal positions for a data-item defined as a remainder
   may be determined by the proof computation for division as shown below:

       173.07 <------------Quotient
    x      52 <------------Divisor
        34614
       86535          or     8999.64
       899964                    .36   Remainder is defined with 2 decimals to equal value of dividend
                             9000.00   Dividend

The determination of the decimal positions may also be determined by the following rule:

  The length of a data-item used as a remainder must be equal to the number of decimal
  positions included in the dividend; or the sum of the decimal positions in the divisor
  and quotient, whichever is greater.
```

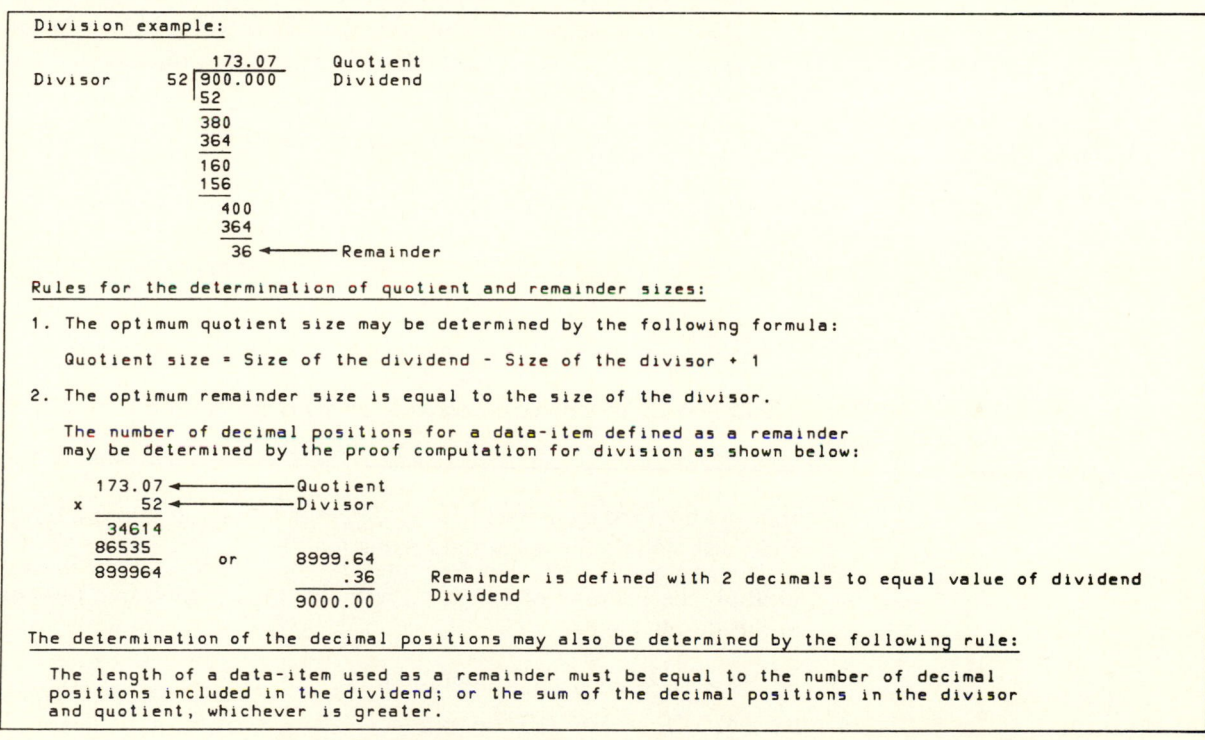

Figure 4-17 Process for determining the size and decimal positions for a remainder field.

Half Adjust (Rounding)

The RPG term *half adjust* refers to the mathematical procedure of rounding an answer to a final size. Half adjust may be used with any arithmetic operation and is specified for the instruction by entering the letter H in column 53. This function, which is explained in Figure 4-18, is automatically performed by the RPG compiler when it is specified in a statement.

```
Example of Half Adjust (rounding):

            Half adjust specified (H in column 53)
            Result Field defined as 6 long with 2 decimals
```

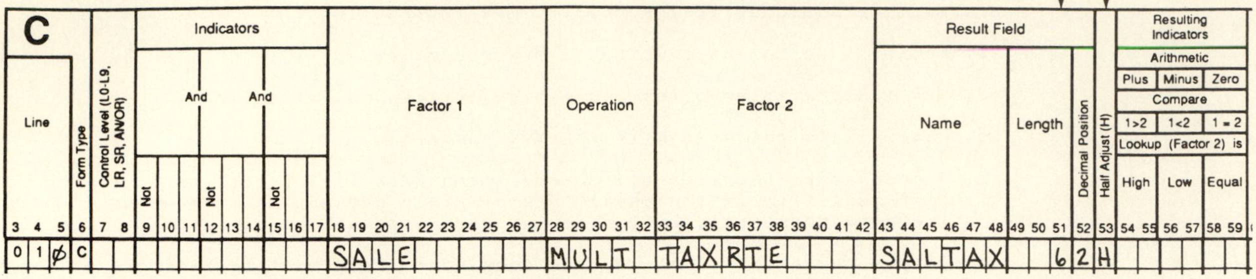

C
Indicators
Line
Form Type
Control Level (L0-L9, LR, SR, AN/OR)
And
And
Not
Not
Not
Factor 1
Operation
Factor 2
Result Field
Name
Length
Decimal Position
Half Adjust (H)
Resulting Indicators
Arithmetic
Plus
Minus
Zero
Compare
1>2
1<2
1=2
Lookup (Factor 2) is
High
Low
Equal
0 1 ø C
SALE
MULT
TAXRTE
SALTAX
6 2 H

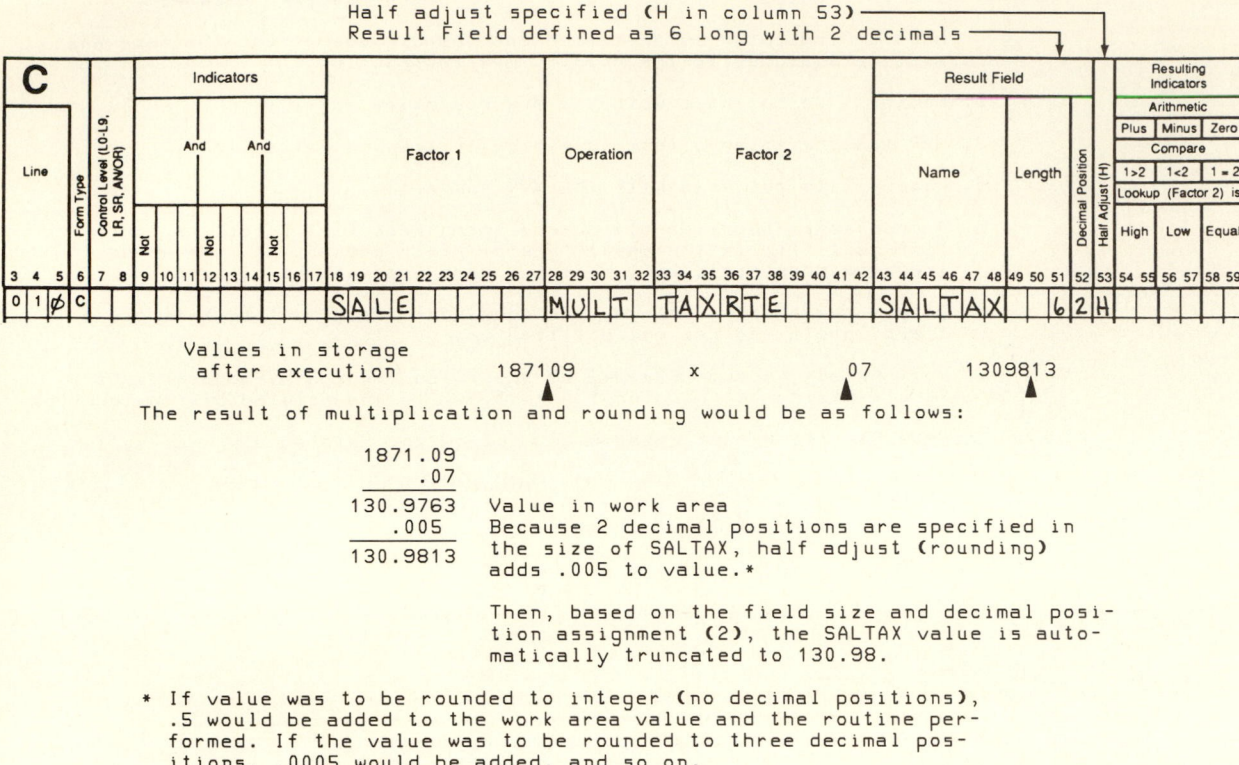

```
        Values in storage
         after execution          187109        x           07          1309813

The result of multiplication and rounding would be as follows:

              1871.09
                 .07
             130.9763   Value in work area
                .005    Because 2 decimal positions are specified in
             130.9813   the size of SALTAX, half adjust (rounding)
                        adds .005 to value.*

                        Then, based on the field size and decimal posi-
                        tion assignment (2), the SALTAX value is auto-
                        matically truncated to 130.98.

* If value was to be rounded to integer (no decimal positions),
  .5 would be added to the work area value and the routine per-
  formed. If the value was to be rounded to three decimal pos-
  itions, .0005 would be added, and so on.
```

Figure 4-18 The syntax and processing logic of half adjust (rounding).

INITIALIZATION OF NUMERIC FIELDS

A numeric field may be initialized to zeros in an RPG program by the following methods:

1. Subtract the field from itself. Hence, Factor 1, Factor 2, and the Result Field will include the same field name.
2. Multiply the Factor 1 or 2 field by zero and specify the same field name in the Result Field.
3. By the Z-ADD or Z-SUB operation.
4. By a MOVE or MOVEL operation.

Because methods 1 and 2 are obvious mathematical procedures, they are not discussed. The Z-ADD, Z-SUB, MOVE, and MOVEL operations are discussed in the following paragraphs.

The Z-ADD Operation

The Z-ADD operation is commonly used in RPG programs to initialize a Result Field to zeros or some other value. Figure 4-19 explains the syntax and function of this operation.

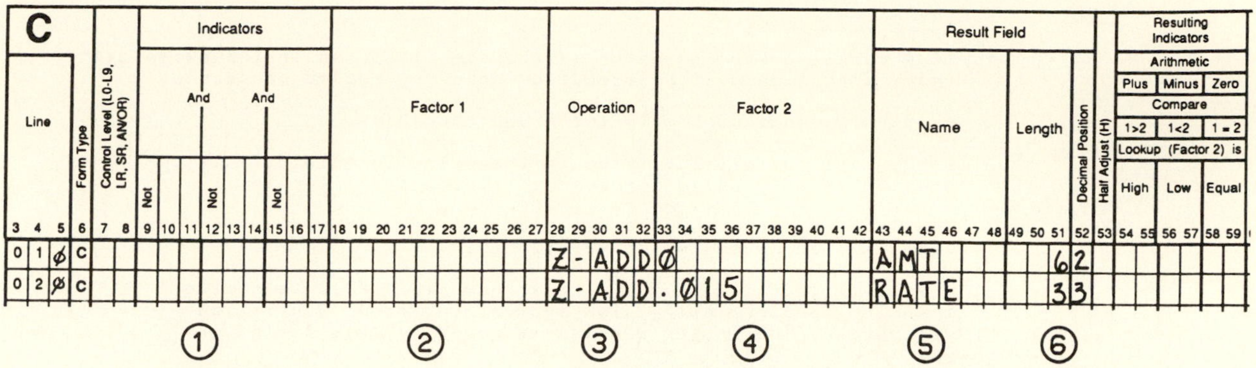

Syntax Rules:

1. If a conditioning indicator is not specified, as in the example shown, the instruction will be executed for every record processed.

2. Factor 1 is not used with the Z-ADD operation.

3. Z-ADD must be left-justified in the Operation field. This operation is only valid for numeric fields and literals.

4. Factor 2 may be a numeric field or literal. The value of this item will be moved to the Result Field.

5. A Result Field must be defined as numeric. If it is smaller than the Factor 2 entry, low and/or high order truncation will occur. The Factor 2 value is moved to this field.

6. Unless previously defined, the Result field item must be assigned field length and decimal position entries.

Processing Procedures:

The Z-ADD operation automatically performs the following two steps:

First, the Result Field value is initialized to zeros.

Then, the Factor 2 field value or literal is moved into the Result Field. Decimal alignment is performed during the move.

Figure 4-19 Syntax and function of the Z-ADD operation.

The Z-SUB Operation

The Z-SUB operation performs the same processing functions as Z-ADD with one exception. The value of the Factor 2 field or numeric literal value is automatically multiplied by -1 and the product is stored in the result field with a reversed sign. Figure 4-20 explains the syntax and processing logic of this operation.

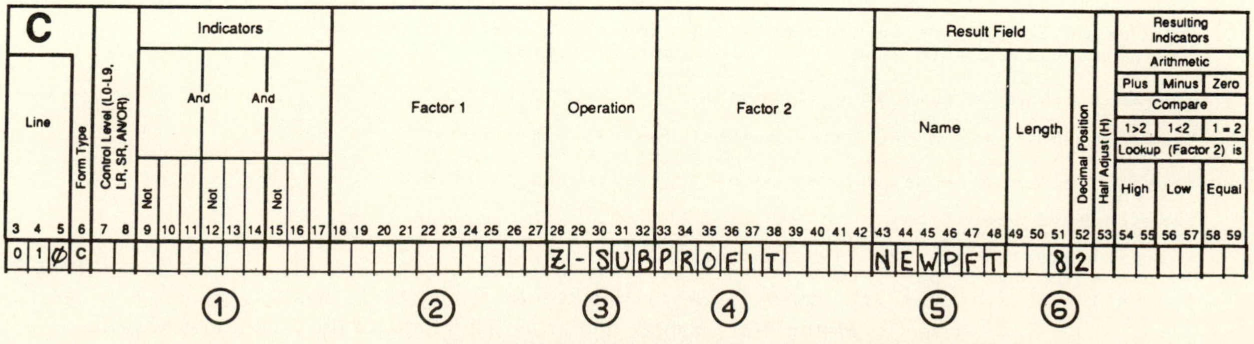

Figure 4-20 Syntax and function of the Z-SUB operation.

Syntax Rules:

1. If a conditioning indicator is not specified, as in the example shown, the instruction will be executed for every record processed.

2. Factor 1 is not used with the Z-SUB operation.

3. Z-SUB must be left-justified in the Operation field. This operation is only valid for numeric fields and literals.

4. Factor 2 may be a numeric field or literal. The value of this item will be moved to the Result Field.

5. A Result Field must be defined as numeric. If it is smaller than the Factor 2 entry, low and/or high order truncation will occur. The Factor 2 value is moved to this field.

6. Unless previously defined, the Result field item must be assigned field length and decimal position entries.

Processing Procedures:

The Z-SUB operation automatically performs the following two steps:

First, the Result Field value is initialized to zeros.

Then, the Factor 2 field value or literal is multiplied by -1 and the product is stored in the Result Field item. Decimal alignment is performed during the multiplication process.

(*Continued*)

The MOVE and MOVEL Operations

As was stated previously, the Z-ADD and Z-SUB operations are limited to numeric fields and literals. The MOVE and MOVEL operations, however, may also be used with alphanumeric fields and literals. The syntax and processing logic of these operations is explained in Figure 4-21.

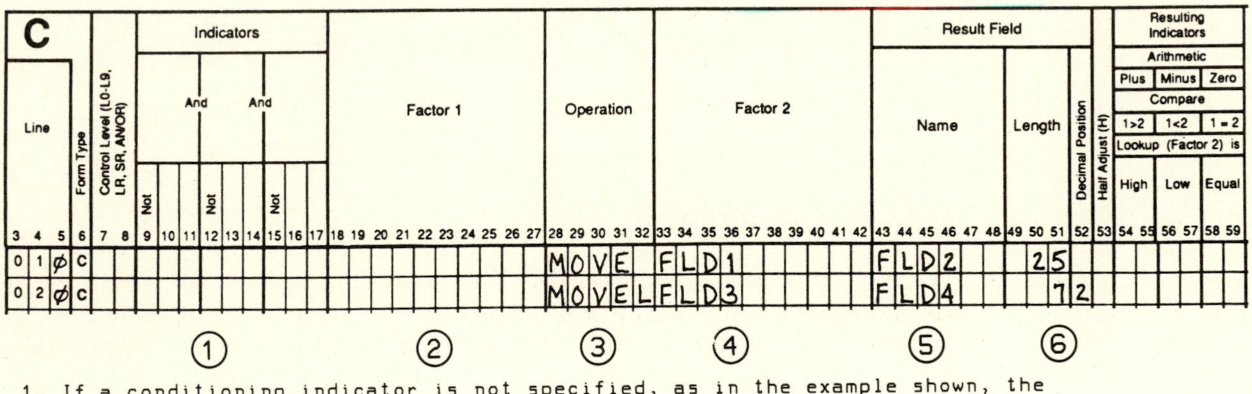

1. If a conditioning indicator is not specified, as in the example shown, the instruction will be executed for every record processed.

2. Factor 1 is not used with the MOVE or MOVEL operations.

3. MOVE or MOVEL must be left-justified in Operation field. Either operation may be specified with numeric or alphanumeric fields.

4. Factor 2 may be a numeric or alphanumeric field or literal.

   (refer to MOVE and MOVEL data movement features in item 5)

5. Result Field may be defined as numeric or alphanumeric field.

   For the MOVE Operation:

   Movement starts with the low-order bytes of the Factor 2 field or literal and are moved into the low-order positions of the Result Field. MOVE stops when all of the bytes from the Factor 2 item have been moved or when the Result Field is full.

Figure 4-21 Syntax and processing logic of the MOVE and MOVEL operations.

If the Result field is larger than the sending field (Factor 2), the excess high-order characters in the Result Field are unchanged. On the other hand, if the Result Field is smaller, the excess high-order characters from the Factor 2 item are truncated.

For the MOVEL Operation:

Movement starts with the high-order bytes of the Factor 2 field or literal and are moved into the high-order positions of the Result Field. MOVEL stops when all of the bytes from the Factor 2 item have been moved or when the Result Field is full.

If the Result field is larger than the sending field (Factor 2), the excess low-order characters in the Result Field are unchanged. On the other hand, if the Result Field is smaller, the excess low-order characters from the Factor 2 item are truncated.

6. Unless previously defined, the Result Field item must be assigned a field length, and if numeric, a decimal position entry.

Notes:

1. Decimal alignment is not performed for MOVE or MOVEL operations.
2. Numeric field or literals may be moved (MOVE or MOVEL) to alphanumeric fields, or literals may be moved to numeric fields. However, when an alphanumeric field or literal is moved to a numeric field, only the digit portion of each alphanumeric character is moved. This may cause subsequent execution time errors.

(*Continued*)

Coding examples and the before and after processing results for the MOVE operation are illustrated in Figure 4-22.

Example 1 - Sending and receiving fields the same size

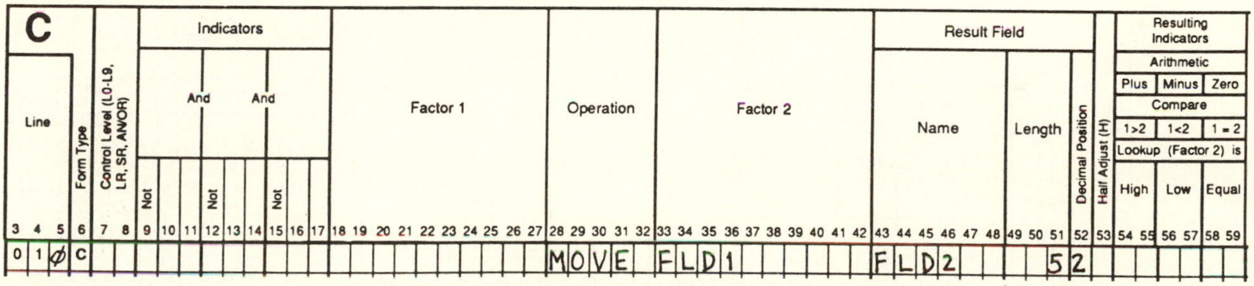

Field name:	FLD1	FLD2	Comments
Before MOVE:	12345	20000	
After MOVE:	12345	12345	Low-order digits of sending item are moved into low-order bytes of receiving field one by one.

Example 2: Sending field larger than receiving field

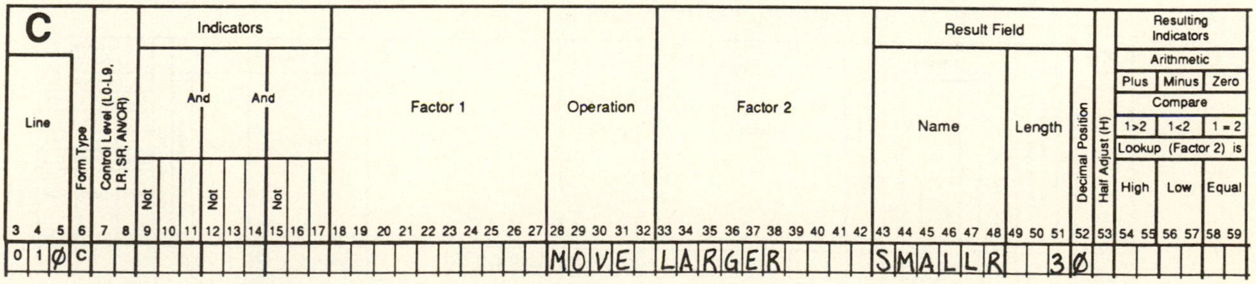

Field name:	LARGER	SMALLR	Comments
Before MOVE:	12345	200	
After MOVE:	12345	345	High-order digits of sending item value are truncated. MOVE stops when receiving field is full.

Figure 4-22 Examples of the MOVE operation with before and after processing results.

Example 3: Sending field smaller than receiving field (Alphanumeric to Alphanumeric)

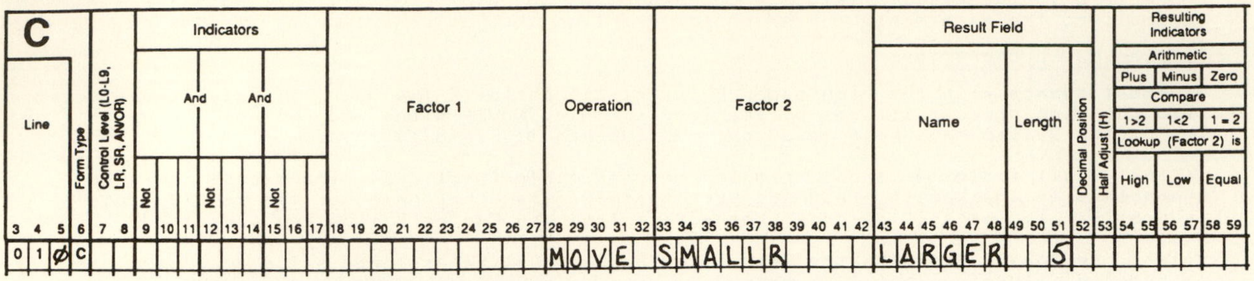

Field Name:	*SMALLR*	*LARGER*	*Comments*
Before MOVE:	ABC	DEFGH	
After MOVE:	ABC	DEABC	High-order digits in receiving item are not changed in the move. MOVE stops when all of the sending field digits are moved.

Notes:
1. Decimal alignment is not performed for numeric fields.
2. Alphanumeric field (or literal) may be moved to a numeric field or a numeric field (or literal) to an alphanumeric field.

(*Continued*)

Figure 4-23 illustrates coding examples of the MOVEL operation supported by the before and after results of processing.

Example 1 Sending and receiving fields the same size

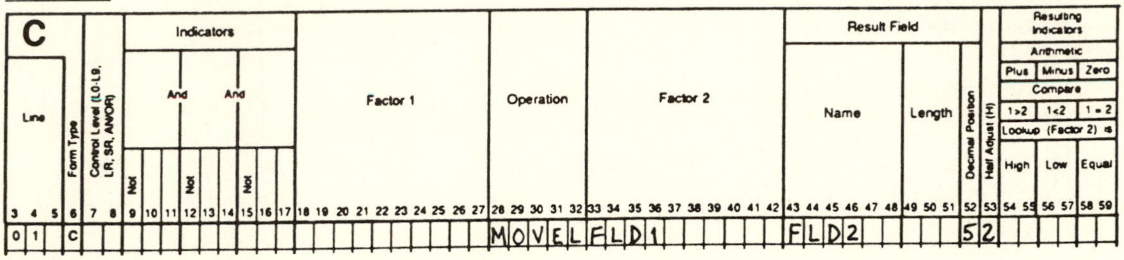

Field Name	*FLD1*	*FLD2*	*Comments*
Before MOVEL:	12345	20000	
After MOVEL:	12345	12345	High-order digits of sending item are moved into high-order bytes of receiving field one by one.

Example 2: Sending field larger than receiving field

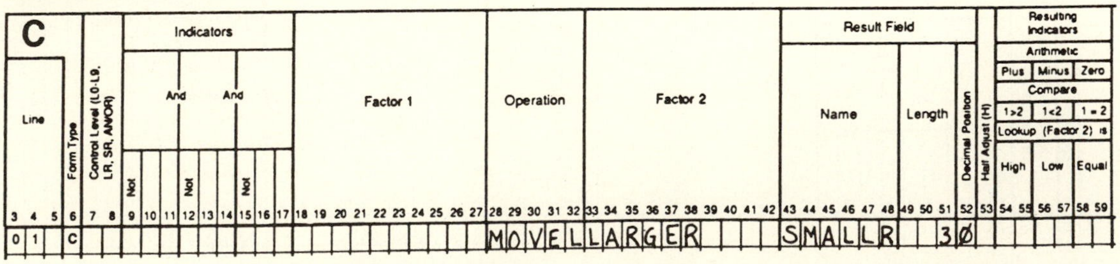

Field Name	*LARGER*	*SMALLR*	*Comments*
Before MOVEL:	12345	200	
After MOVEL:	12345	123	Low-order digits of sending item value are truncated. MOVEL stops when receiving field is full.

Figure 4-23 Examples of the MOVEL operation with before and after processing results.

Example 3: Sending field smaller than receiving field (Alphanumeric to Alphanumeric)

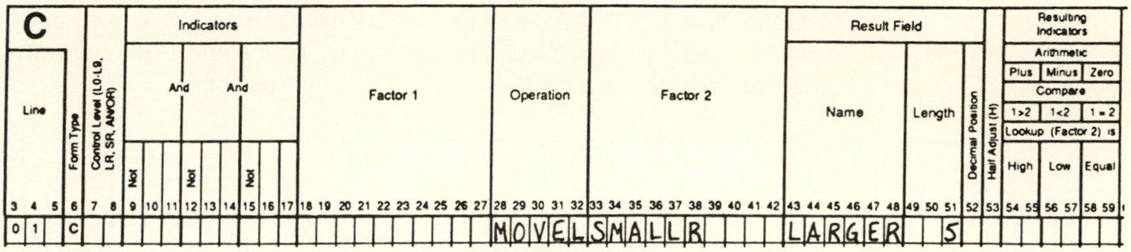

Field Name	*SMALLR*	*LARGER*	*Comments*
Before MOVEL:	ABC	DEFGH	
After MOVEL:	ABC	ABCGH	Low-order digits in receiving item are not changed in the move. MOVE stops when all of the sending field digits are moved.

Notes:

1. Decimal alignment is not performed for numeric fields.
2. Alphanumeric field (or literal) may be moved to a numeric field or a numeric field (or literal) to an alphanumeric field.

(Continued)

Figurative Constants

Figurative Constants, which include *BLANK/*BLANKS, *ZERO/*ZEROS, *HIVAL, *LOVAL, and *ALL'X . . . .', are *implied literals* that are assigned a predetermined value. They are referenced without regard to length and assume the size of the field to which they relate. An explanation of each Figurative Constant is presented in Figure 4-24.

***BLANK/BLANKS**	Indicates constant contains all blanks (spaces). May only be used with alphanumeric fields.
***ZERO/ZEROS**	Indicates constant contains all zeros. May be used with any field type.
***HIVAL**	Indicates constant contains the highest character in the collating character set of the computer. If the field compared (or result field) is numeric, *HIVAL is assumed to be nines. However, if it is alphanumeric, constant is assumed to be hexadecimal FFs.
***LOVAL**	Indicates constant contains the lowest character in the collating character set of the computer. If the field compared (or result field) is numeric, *LOVAL is assumed to be negative nines. However, if it is alphanumeric, constant is assumed to be hexadecimal zeros.
***ALL'X. . . '**	The character string X . . . etc., is repeated to the length equal to the Factor 1 or 2 field in a compare or the Result Field in a mathematical or MOVE or MOVEL operation. If compare (or result field) is numeric, all characters in X string must be numeric. No sign or decimal point may be used when string is numeric.

Figure 4-24 The processing features of figurative constants.

Examples of how Figurative Constants are used with the MOVE instruction are shown in Figure 4-25. Except for *BLANK/*BLANKS, each may be specified with a Z-ADD, Z-SUB, or any arithmetic operation. Any Figurative Constant may be included in a MOVE or MOVEL instruction.

Line (3-5)	Form Type (6)	Control Level (LO-L9, LR, SR, AN/OR) (7-8)	Indicators (9-17)	Factor 1 (18-27)	Operation (28-32)	Factor 2 (33-42)	Result Field Name (43-48)	Length (49-51)	Decimal Position (52)	Half Adjust (H) (53)	Resulting Indicators (54-59)
01	C			①	MOVE	*BLANKS	NAME	25			
02	C										
03	C			②	MOVE	*ZEROS	TOTAL	8	2		
04	C										
05	C			③	MOVE	*ALL'.'	DOTS	1Ø			
06	C										
07	C			④	MOVE	*HIVAL	EOF	6Ø			
08	C										
09	C			⑤	MOVE	*LOVAL	BEGIN	4Ø			

Explanation of Related Instructions:

1. Blanks (spaces) are moved into the 25 byte NAME field.
2. Zeros are moved into the TOTAL field.
3. The string value of . is moved into the DOTS field until it is filled. For this example, 10 periods will be moved into DOTS, resulting in a field value of .... (10 periods). Note that the X included in the syntax (Figure 4-24) is not specified in the figurative constant instruction.
4. If the receiving field is numeric, *HIVAL value is 9's. If alphanumeric, value is hexadecimal FF's. For this example, 9's are moved into the receiving field.
5. If the receiving field is numeric, *LOVAL is assumed to be negative 9's. If alphanumeric, the value is hexadecimal zeros. For this example, negative 9's are moved into the receiving field.

Figure 4-25 Examples of instructions with figurative constants.

Resulting Indicators

Refer to the calculation form shown in Figure 4-26, and locate the area (columns 54–59) entitled Resulting Indicators. Notice that it includes three headings: Arithmetic, Compare, and Lookup. This chapter discusses only the Arithmetic class of Resulting Indicators, reserving discussion of the Compare group for Chapter 5 and Lookup for Chapters 10 and 11.

Within the Arithmetic group of Resulting Indicators are three test fields: Plus, Minus, and Zero. The value of the Result Field item from any arithmetic function, Z-ADD, Z-SUB, MOVE, or MOVEL instruction may be tested for one, two, or three of the conditions.

The flowchart at the bottom of Figure 4-26 explains the processing logic for the Arithmetic Resulting Indicators included in the example instruction. Observe that the indicator "turned on" is used to condition a subsequent instruction. In this example, only calculations are conditioned by the related Resulting Indicator. Output record formats, fields, and/or constants, however, may also be conditioned

Line	Form Type	Control Level (L0-L9, LR, SR, AN/OR)	Indicators	Factor 1	Operation	Factor 2	Result Field Name	Length	Decimal Position	Half Adjust (H)	Resulting Indicators: Plus	Minus	Zero
01∅	C			SALES	SUB	RETRNS	NETSAL	8	2		1∅	11	12
02∅	C		1∅	NETINC	DIV	NETSAL	PCTPFT	4	4	H			
03∅	C		11		MOVE	'NET LOSS'	MSG	8					
04∅	C		12		MOVE	'NO PROFT'	MSG						

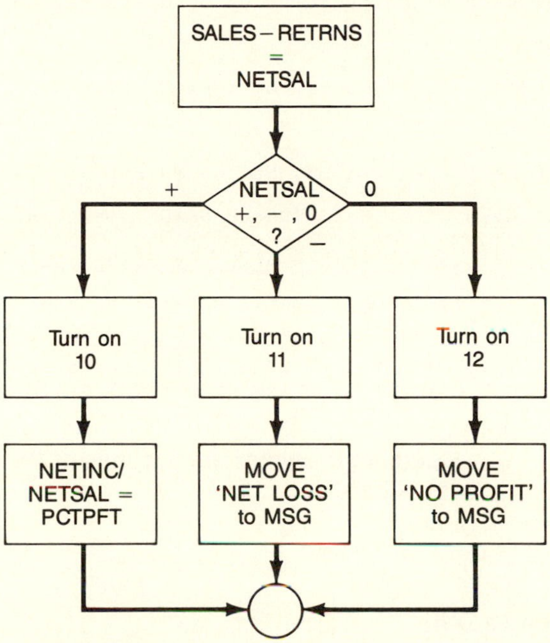

Figure 4-26 Processing logic of the Arithmetic class of Resulting Indicators.

by this indicator class. In the example shown in Figure 4-26, the indicators are specified in an ascending 10, 11, 12 order. This is not a requirement; any indicators may be assigned and in any order. However, to avoid uncertain processing results, a Record Identifying Indicator should not be specified as a Resulting Indicator.

SETON and SETOF Operations

The SETON operation is used to turn on the indicator(s) included in the Resulting Indicator fields. The indicator(s) is then used to condition one or more calculation and/or output instructions.

The SETOF operation is used to turn off the indicators included in the Resulting Indicator fields. This operation is often used as a housekeeping function to turn off all Resulting Indicators before the next record is processed. Because Record Identifying Indicators turn off automatically after the last output instruction for that processing cycle is tested and executed, they are seldom specified with a SETOF operation. Figure 4-27 explains the syntax and features of these operations.

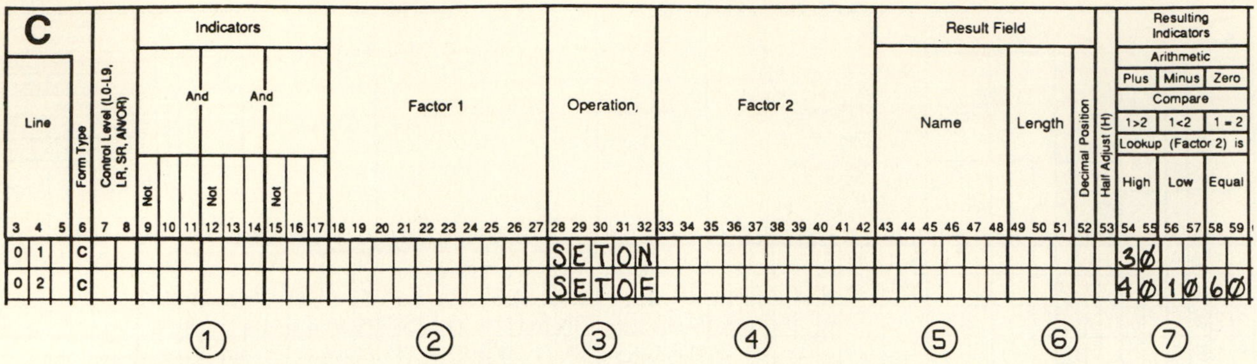

C			Indicators								Result Field				Resulting Indicators		
			And	And		Factor 1	Operation,	Factor 2							Arithmetic		
															Plus	Minus	Zero
															Compare		
Line	Form Type	Control Level (L0-L9, LR, SR, AN/OR)								Name	Length	Decimal Position	Half Adjust (H)		1>2	1<2	1 = 2
															Lookup (Factor 2) is		
			Not	Not	Not										High	Low	Equal
3 4 5	6	7 8	9 10 11	12 13 14	15 16 17	18 19 20 21 22 23 24 25 26 27	28 29 30 31 32	33 34 35 36 37 38 39 40 41 42		43 44 45 46 47 48	49 50 51	52	53		54 55	56 57	58 59
0 1	C						SETON								30		
0 2	C						SETOF								40	10	60

    ①   ②   ③   ④   ⑤   ⑥   ⑦

1. If a conditioning indicator is not specified, as in the example shown, the instruction will be executed for every record processed.

2. Factor 1 is not used with the SETON or SETOF operations.

3. SETON Operation:

   One, two, or three indicators may be turned on with a SETON operation.

   SETOF Operation:

   One, two, or three indicators may be turned off with a SETOF operation.

4. Factor 2 is not used with the SETON or SETOF operations.

5. Result Field is not used with the SETON or SETOF operations.

6. Field length and decimal position fields are not used with the SETON or SETOF operations.

7. Indicators specified with the SETON or SETOF operations may be included in any of the three Resulting Indicator fields. At last one indicator must be specified.

Figure 4-27 Syntax and features of the SETON and SETOF operations.

Recap to Date

The syntax and processing logic of the RPG operations ADD, SUB, MULT, DIV, MVR, Z-ADD, Z-SUB, MOVE, MOVEL, SETON, and SETOF have been introduced in this chapter. Figurative Constants and Resulting Indicators (Arithmetic) were also explained. Many of these RPG tools are used in the example application program that follows.

APPLICATION PROGRAM—PROFIT ANALYSIS OF SOUP BRANDS

Documentation

The specifications included in Figure 4-28 summarize the processing requirements for this example application program.

The system flowchart in Figure 4-29 indicates that one input disk file and one output printer file are processed by the program.

PROGRAM SPECIFICATIONS Page 1 of 1

Program Name PROFIT REPORT Program-ID CH4P1 Written By S. Myers

Purpose Determine profit/case for soup brands Approved By The Boss

Input files (directory names):

DAT4P1 (stored on disk)

Output files (directory names):

PRINTER (stock paper)

Processing Narrative:

Write a structured RPG program to generate a profit report.

Input to the program:

A soup inventory file (DAT4P1) is stored on disk which includes the record format shown in the supplemental record layout form.

Processing:

Read the soup inventory file consecutively and perform the following:

Detail Calculations:

For each record processed complete the following calculations:

Profit per case computation (in $):

Profit/case = Selling price/case - Cost/case

Percent of profit per case computation:

Step 1: $\text{Decimal profit} = \dfrac{\text{Profit/case}}{\text{Cost/case}}$

Step 2: Percent profit = Decimal profit x 100

Step 3: Add the percent profit (step 2) to an accumulator

Step 4: Add the number of records processed to an accumulator.

Total time calculations:

To compute the average profit of all the soup brands as follows:

$$\text{Average profit percent} = \frac{\text{Total profit percent (step 3)}}{\text{Record count (step 4)}}$$

Output:

The report design is detailed in a supplemental print chart.

Figure 4-28 Specifications for profit analysis of soup brands application program.

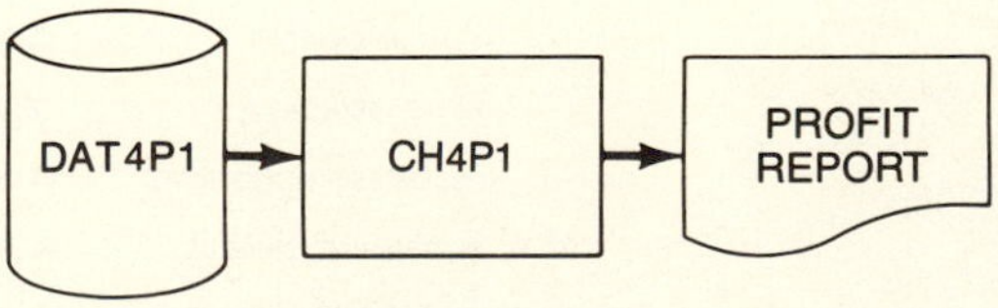

Figure 4-29 System flowchart for soup brand profit report application.

Included with the record layout form in Figure 4-30 is a listing of the input data file.

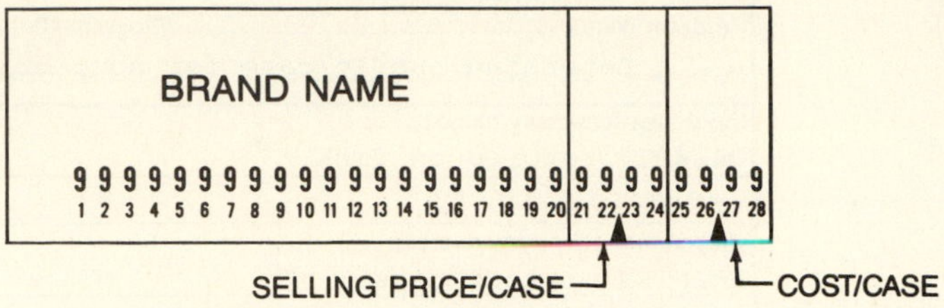

Data File Listing:

```
CAMPBELL TOMATO          06480504
LIPTON CHICKEN           14401188
HEINZ VEGETABLE          07920576
PROGRESSO MINESTRONE     17281224
PEPPERIDGE CHOWDER       14041116
STOP & SHOP TOMATO       14761044
A & P CHICKEN RICE       07200792
```

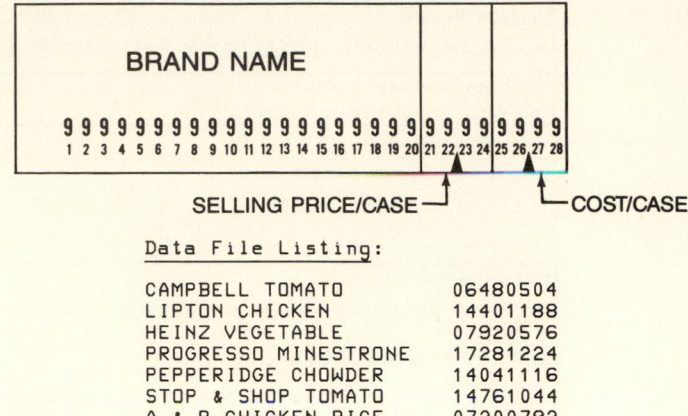

Figure 4-30 Input record layout form for soup brand profit report application.

The design of the report is illustrated in the printer spacing chart in Figure 4-31.

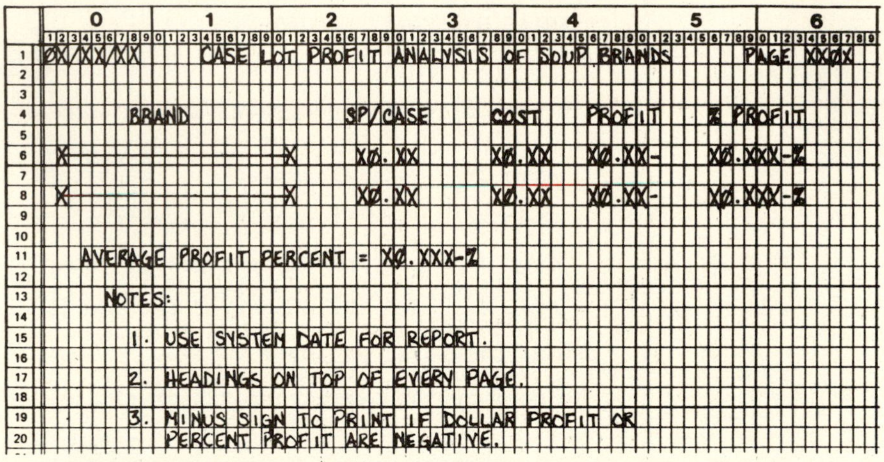

Figure 4-31 Printer spacing chart for soup brands profit report.

The report generated from the application program is shown in Figure 4-32.

```
11/30/92     CASE LOT PROFIT ANALYSIS OF SOUP BRANDS        PAGE    1

        BRAND                   SP/CASE    COST   PROFIT   % PROFIT

CAMPBELL TOMATO                  6.48      5.04    1.44    28.571 %
LIPTON CHICKEN                  14.40     11.88    2.52    21.212 %
HEINZ VEGETABLE                  7.92      5.76    2.16    37.500 %
PROGRESSO MINESTRONE            17.28     12.24    5.04    41.176 %
PEPPERIDGE CHOWDER              14.04     11.16    2.88    25.806 %
STOP & SHOP TOMATO              14.76     10.44    4.32    41.379 %
A & P CHICKEN RICE               7.20      7.92     .72-    9.090-%

  AVERAGE PROFIT PERCENT = 26.651 %
```

Figure 4-32 Soup brands profit report listing.

Source Coding for Soup Brands Profit Report Program

A commented source listing of the program that generates a soup brands profit report is detailed in Figure 4-33. In addition to the use of the arithmetic functions ADD, SUB, MULT, and DIV, the following new processing features are introduced:

1. Detail time calculations.
2. Total time (LR indicator) calculations.
3. Total time (T in column 15 for output record).

```
... ... 1 ... ... 2 ... ... 3 ... ... 4 ... ... 5 ... ... 6 ... ... 7 ...
 * THIS PROGRAM GENERATES A SOUP BRANDS PROFIT REPORT.                CH4P1
 *                                                                    CH4P1
H
FSOUPINV IP  F  80  80            DISK
FREPORT  O   F 132 132     OF     PRINTER
ISOUPINV SM  01
I                                        1  20 BRAND
I                                       21  242SP
I                                       25  282COST
C           SP        SUB  COST      PROFIT  42       $ PROFIT       CH4P1
C           PROFIT    DIV  COST      DECPCT  55       DECIMAL PCT    CH4P1
C           DECPCT    MULT 100       PERCNT  53H      PRINTABLE PCT  CH4P1
C           TOTPCT    ADD  PERCNT    TOTPCT  63       ACCUMULATE PCTSCH4P1
C           RECRDS    ADD  1         RECRDS  40       RECRD PROCESSEDCH4P1
CLR         TOTPCT    DIV  RECRDS    AVGPCT  53H      COMPUTE AVG PCTCH4P1
OREPORT  H  301   1P                                                 CH4P1
O       OR        OF                                                 CH4P1
O                         UDATE Y    8                               CH4P1
O                                   37 'CASE LOT PROFIT ANALYSIS'    CH4P1
O                                   52 'OF SOUP BRANDS'              CH4P1
O                                   62 'PAGE'                        CH4P1
O                         PAGE  Z   67                               CH4P1
O        H  2     1P                                                 CH4P1
O       OR        OF                                                 CH4P1
O                                   12 'BRAND'                       CH4P1
O                                   51 'SP/CASE    COST   PROFIT'    CH4P1
O                                   63 '% PROFIT'                    CH4P1
O        D  2     01                                                 CH4P1
O                         BRAND     21                               CH4P1
O                         SP     1  31                               CH4P1
O                         COST   1  42                               CH4P1
O                         PROFITJ   51                               CH4P1
O                         PERCNTJ   62                               CH4P1
O                                   63 '%'                           CH4P1
O        T 1      LR                                                 CH4P1
O                                   27 'AVERAGE PROFIT PERCENT ='    CH4P1
O                         AVGPCTJ   35                               CH4P1
O                                   36 '%'                           CH4P1
```

Fields used in arithmetic functions must be defined with required decimals

Detail time calculations

Total time calcs. (LR in columns 7-8 must follow detail time calcs.

Total time output (T in column 15) must follow detail time output

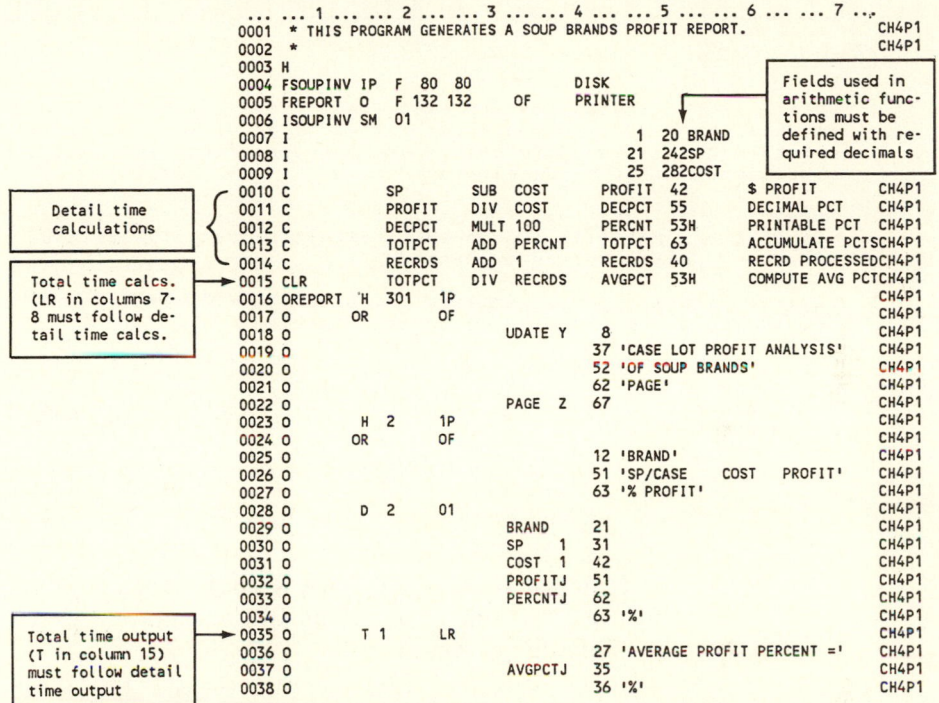

Figure 4-33 Source listing of the soup brands profit report program.

An examination of the source listing shows that File Description, Input, and Output-Format Specifications coding are similar to the RPG syntax discussed in previous chapters. The calculations, which are a new topic, are explained in the following paragraphs.

Calculation Specifications Coding

The calculation instructions included in the soup brand profit report program are shown in Figure 4-34. Notice that calculations are performed at *detail* and *total* times. *Detail time* calculations must be specified first and must include those statements either conditioned by an indicator(s) in columns 9 to 17 or not conditioned by any indicator. *Total time* calculations are those conditioned by an LR (Last Record) or Control Level indicator (discussed in Chapter 9) entered in columns 7 to 8. Any total time instructions must follow detail time, or a terminal error is generated during program compilation.

Line	Form Type	Control Level (L0-L9, LR, SR, AN/OR)	Indicators	Factor 1	Operation	Factor 2	Result Field Name	Length	Decimal Position	Half Adjust (H)	Resulting Indicators
01Ø	C			SP	SUB	COST	PROFIT	4	2		
02Ø	C			PROFIT	DIV	COST	DECPCT	5	5		
03Ø	C		①	DECPCT	MULT	1ØØ	PERCNT	5	3	H	
04Ø	C			TOTPCT	ADD	PERCNT	TOTPCT	6	3		
05Ø	C			RECRDS	ADD	1	RECRDS	4	Ø		
06Ø	C	LR		TOTPCT	DIV	RECRDS	AVGPCT	5	3	H	

② ③ ④ ⑤

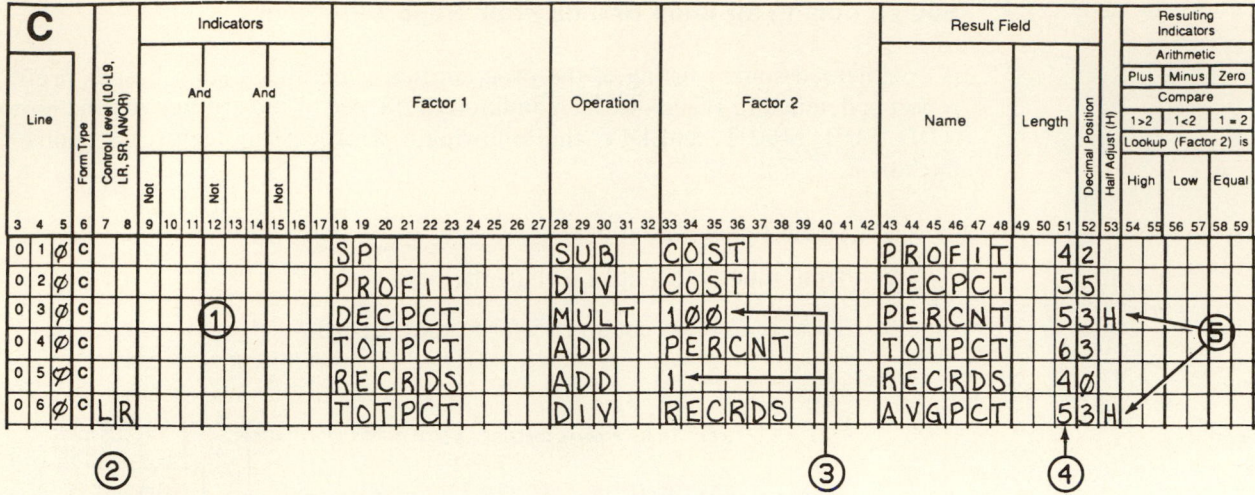

1. Detail time calculations are executed for every input record processed. Because there is only one input record type (01 Record Identifying Indicator) and Resulting Indicators are not specified, instructions are not conditioned by any indicator(s).

2. Total time calculations (LR indicator in columns 7-8) are executed when end of the input file is sensed. Instruction is only executed once and not for every detail record processed.

3. Numeric literals may be entered in Factor 1 or 2. Explicit decimal points may be omitted from integer literals.

4. Result field sizes are defined.

5. H in column 53 will round the Result Field values to designated decimal positions.

Figure 4-34 Calculation specifications for soup brand report program.

A line-by-line analysis of the results of each calculation instruction for the first data record processed is detailed in Figure 4-35. Observe that the statement conditioned with the LR (Last Record) indicator is not executed at detail time. Instructions conditioned by an LR indicator are executed only after the end of the input file is sensed.

Value of first record processed:

CAMPBELL TOMATO 06480504 (SP = 0648, COST = 0504)

Calculations:

						Values in items after execution: Factor 1	Factor 2	Result Field
0010 C	SP	SUB	COST	PROFIT	42	06▲48	05▲04	01▲44
0020 C	PROFIT	DIV	COST	DECPCT	55	01▲44	05▲04	▲28571
0030 C	DECPCT	MULT	100	PERCNT	53H	▲28571	100▲	28▲571
0040 C	TOTPCT	ADD	PERCNT	TOTPCT	63	000▲000	28▲571	028▲571
0050 C	RECRDS	ADD	1	RECRDS	40	0000▲	1▲	0001▲
0060 CLR	TOTPCT	DIV	RECRDS	AVGPCT	53H	28▲571	0001▲	00▲000

Because this example is for the first record processed, the instruction conditioned by the LR indicator (in columns 7-8) will not execute until end of file is sensed. Consequently, the result field has a zero value for this program cycle.

▲ Indicates implied decimal

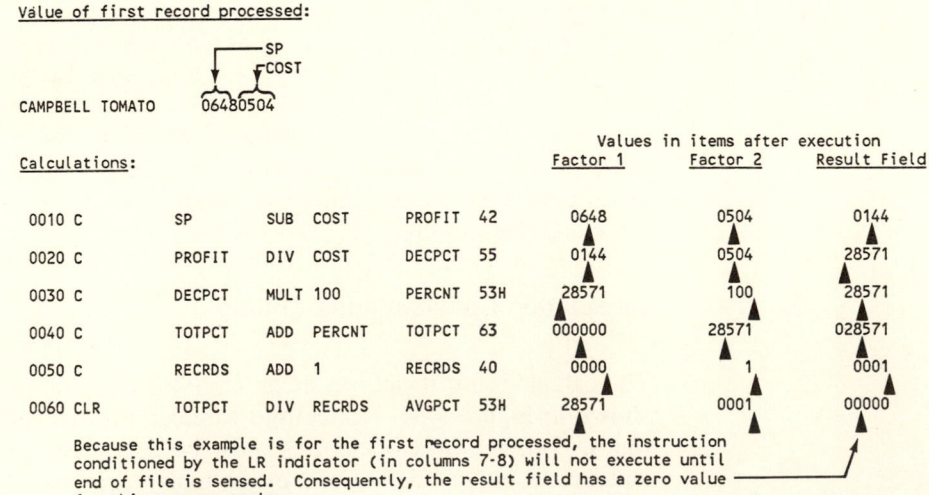

Figure 4-35 Step-by-step analysis of calculation instructions for first input record processed.

Last Record (Total Time) Calculations

When the end of an input data file is sensed, RPG automatically turns on the LR (Last Record) indicator, which is used to condition calculation and output instructions. The indicator may be specified only with total time calculations (LR entered in columns 7–8). If LR is incorrectly entered in columns 9 to 17 (detail time calculations), an error will *not* be generated in program compilation or execution. The instruction will be ignored, however. Figure 4-36 shows the syntax and processing results of total time calculations conditioned with an LR indicator.

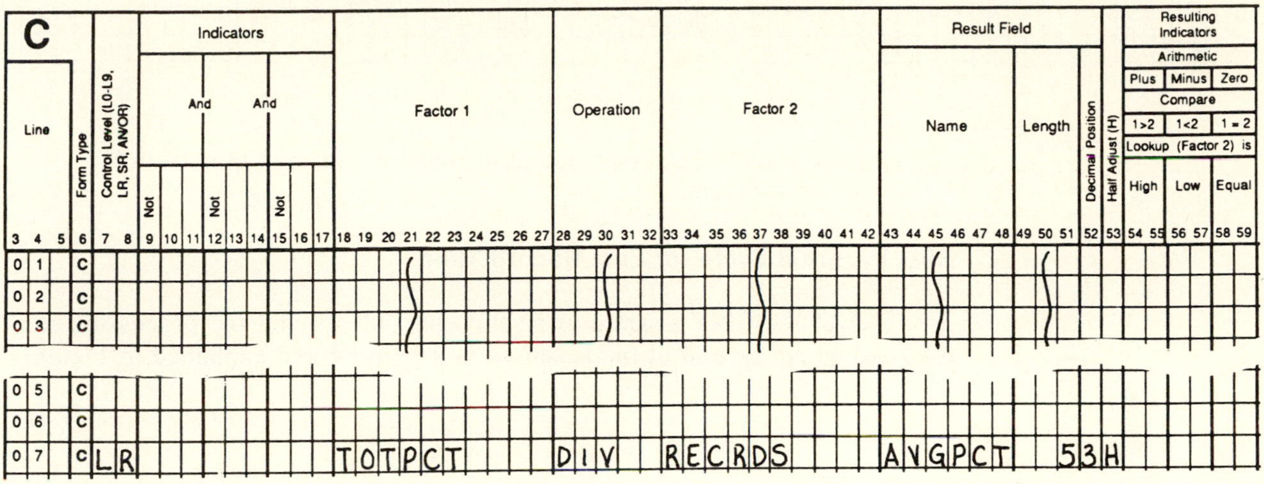

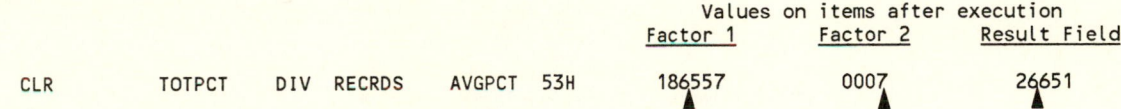

```
                                                    Values on items after execution
                                                    Factor 1     Factor 2      Result Field

CLR         TOTPCT    DIV  RECRDS    AVGPCT   53H   1865557        0007           26651
                                                       ▲              ▲              ▲

Features of LR total time calculations:

   1.  LR must be specified in columns 7 and 8.

   2.  Total time instructions must follow all detail time calculations.

   3.  Statements conditioned by the LR indicator are executed only when the end of the
       input data file is sensed which automatically turns on LR.

   4.  After the last output instruction conditioned by the LR indicator is executed,
       the job ends and control is returned back to the operating system.
```

Figure 4-36 Total time calculations included in the soup brands profit report program.

Last Record (Total Time Output)

For output control, an LR indicator may be specified only with total lines (letter T in column 15). In addition, total lines must follow all heading and detail lines for the related output file (often there is more than one). If an LR indicator is incorrectly included with a H or D line, it will be ignored during program execution. No errors will be generated in the compilation or execution phases. Figure 4-37 details the syntax for the total time output instructions included in the example program.

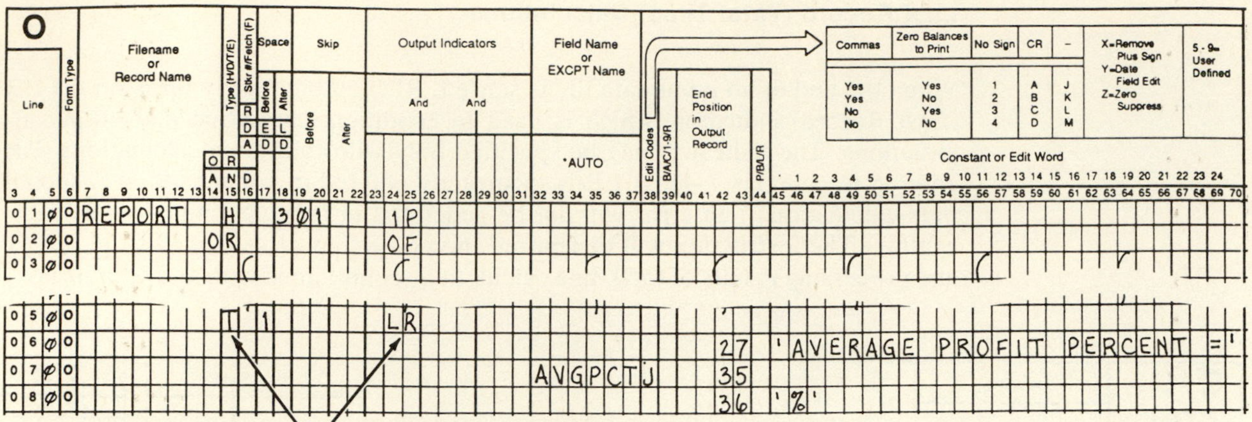

Output records conditioned by an LR indicator must be specified with total lines (T in column 15)

Figure 4-37 Total time output included in the soup brands profit report program.

RPG Program Cycle for Last Record Time

A subset of the RPG program cycle flowchart identifying the processing steps followed when the end of file is sensed is presented and explained in Figure 4-38.

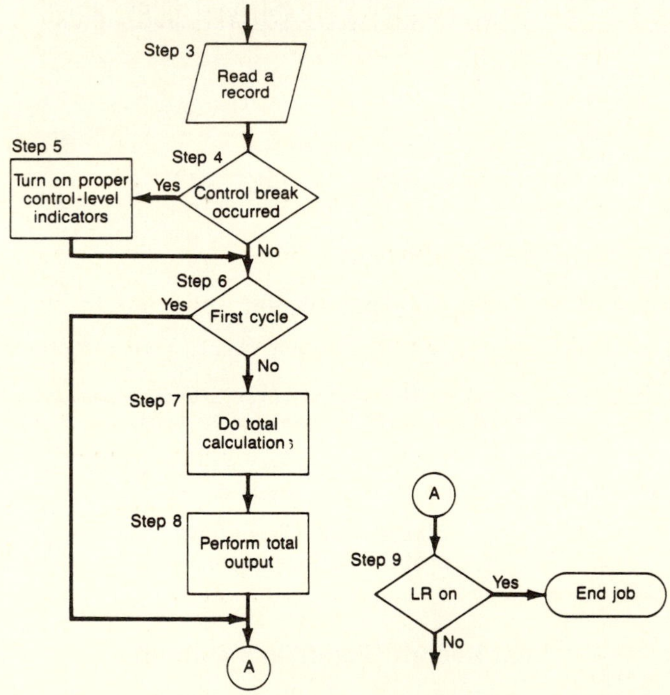

Explanation of Steps:

Step 3: A record is read from the input file.

Steps 4 and 5: If end of file is sensed, a control break is generated and the LR (Last Record) indicator is automatically turned on.

Figure 4-38 RPG program cycle processing when end of file is sensed (Last Record time). (Courtesy of IBM.)

```
Step 6:  Because end of file is not the first program cycle, the "NO" path is
         followed.

Step 7:  Any calculation instructions conditioned by an LR indicator specified
         in columns 7 and 8 are executed. Detail time calculations are ignored
         at Last Record time.

Step 8:  Any output instructions conditioned by an LR indicator at total time
         (T in column 15) are executed. Heading and detail time output (N or D
         in column 15) are ignored at Last Record time.

Step 9:  LR indicator is tested as "ON", job ends, and control is returned back
         to the operating system.
```

(*Continued*)

Program Summary

The soup brands profit report program introduced the use of the arithmetic functions ADD, SUB, MULT and DIV; numeric literals; and half adjust (rounding). In addition, total time calculations and output were included in program control. The syntax and processing logic of these new RPG items were explained in separate illustrations.

ADDITIONAL RPG FEATURES

The Square Root Operation (SQRT)

The square root of a number may be computed in an RPG program by the SQRT operation. Figure 4-39 explains the syntax associated with this function.

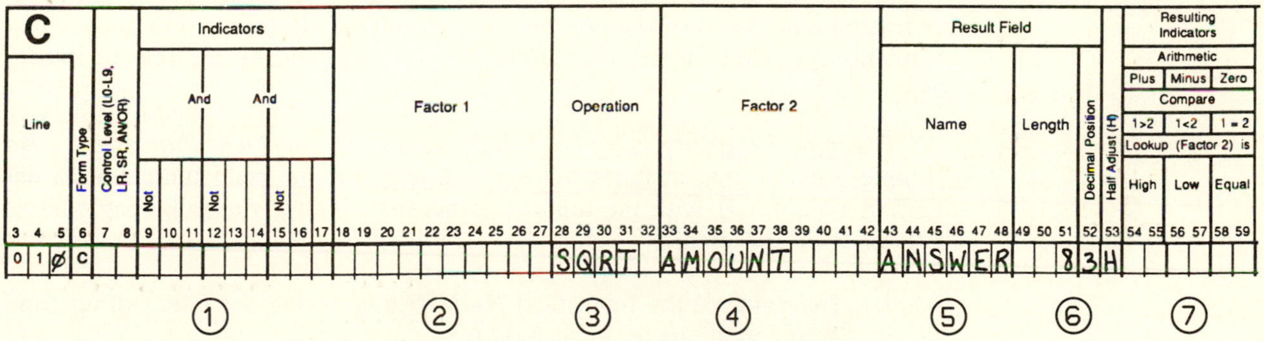


```
1. If a conditioning indicator is not specified, as in the example shown, the
   instruction will be executed for every record processed.

2. Factor 1 is not used with the SQRT operation.

3. SQRT must be left-justified in the Operation field.

4. Factor 2 entry must be a numeric field or literal and must be left-justified
   in the field.

   Factor 2 field or numeric literal value may not be negative. Program execution
   will, depending on the computer system, terminate or halt if the value is negative.

5. Result field entry must be a numeric field and must be left-justified.

6. Unless previously defined, the Result Field item must be assigned a field length and
   decimal position entry.

7. Resulting indicators may be used to check for a positive or zero result field value.
```

Figure 4-39 Syntax for the SQRT (square root) operation.

Field Indicators

Additional control of calculations and/or output is available to the programmer by the use of Field Indicators. Field Indicators are defined in columns 65 to 70 on the Input Specifications Form. Look at Figure 4-40 and notice that this field area is divided into three separate fields: Plus (columns 65–66), Minus (columns 67–68), and Zero (or Blank) (columns 69–70). The status of a numeric input field may be tested for Plus, Minus, or Zero, whereas an alphanumeric field may be tested only for a blank condition.

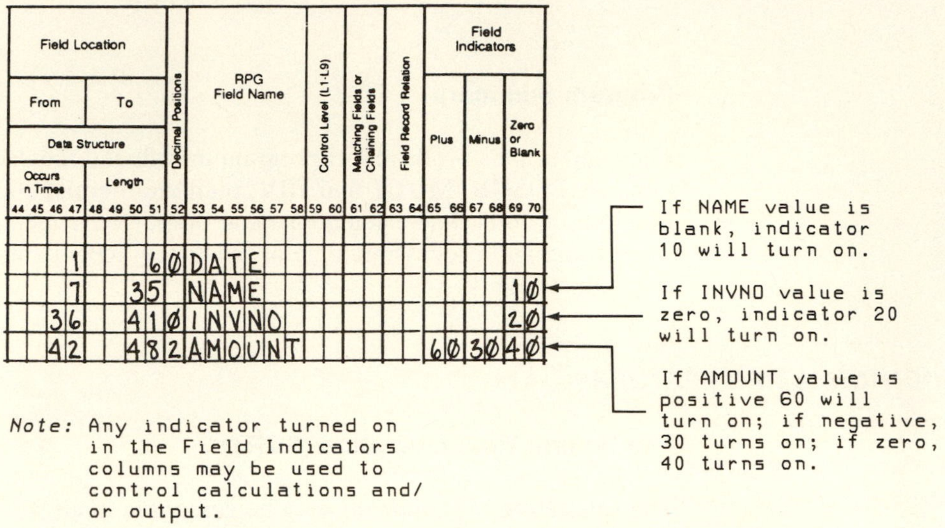

Figure 4-40 Examples of Field Indicator coding.

Because indicators in an RPG program require CPU storage and increase processing time, Field Indicators should be assigned only when some subsequent calculation or output instruction(s) requires conditioning by the related indicator(s).

Example Program Using the SQRT Operation and Field Indicators. An example program that includes the SQRT operation and Field Indicators is detailed in Figure 4-41 with the report it generated. Notice the following control features of this program:

1. The value of the input field NUMBER is tested for Plus, Minus, and Zero conditions by Field Indicators.
2. The SQRT instruction is conditioned by the 20 Field Indicator, which controls processing so that the statement is executed only when NUMBER is positive (Plus).
3. Field Indicators are assigned to output items (field and constants) so that they print only when the related indicator is on.

Not all the conditions (Plus, Minus, and Zero or Blank) have to be tested. For program efficiency, indicators of any type should be assigned only when absolutely necessary.

RPG Language Enhancements

Omission of Factor 1 Entry. If the Result Field name is the same as an entry in Factor 1 or 2, RPG coding may be modified as shown in Figure 4-42.

```
... ... 1 ... ... 2 ... ... 3 ... ... 4 ... ... 5 ... ... 6 ... ... 7 ...
 * THIS PROGRAM CALCULATES THE SQUARE ROOT OF INPUT NUMBERS.         CH4P2
 * FIELD INDICATORS ARE USED TO VALIDATE THE INPUT NUMBER VALUE      CH4P2
 * FOR PLUS, MINUS, AND ZERO.  THE SQRT STATEMENT AND OUTPUT MSGS    CH4P2
 * ARE CONDITIONED BY THE FIELD INDICATORS                           CH4P2
H                                                                    CH4P2
FNUMBERS IP  F   5   5            DISK                               CH4P2
FROOTS   O   F 132 132            PRINTER                            CH4P2
INUMBERS SM  01
I                                   1   5ONUMBER     202122
C  20              SQRT NUMBER    ROOT    83H
OROOTS   H  201   1P
O                                  47 'SQUARE ROOT OF NUMBERS'
O        H  1     1P
O                                  47 'NUMBER          SQUARE'       CH4P2
O        H  2     1P                                                 CH4P2
O                                  46 'ROOT'                         CH4P2
O        D  2     01                                                 CH4P2
O                       NUMBERJ   30                                 CH4P2
O                 20    ROOT  3   46                                 CH4P2
O                 21              55 'NUMBER NEGATIVE CHECK'         CH4P2
O                 21              60 'DATA'                          CH4P2
O                 22              56 'NUMBER ZERO CHECK DATA'        CH4P2
```

Instruction is executed only if NUMBER value is + (20 is turned on by input test.

If NUMBER value is +, 20 turns on; if -, 21 turns on; if 0, 22 turns on

Field indicators on output line with related item, control printing of value or constant

Record Identifying Indicator (01) is in and AND relationship with the Field Indicators 20, 21, and 22. Two indicators must be on for a related item to print. Note, however, because NUMBER is not conditioned by an indicator, its value will be printed for every input condition.

Printed Report:

```
        SQUARE ROOT OF NUMBERS

        NUMBER          SQUARE
                         ROOT

          144           12.000

         746-     NUMBER NEGATIVE CHECK DATA

       60,000          244.949

       92,000          303.315

            0     NUMBER ZERO CHECK DATA

       87,411          295.655
```

Figure 4-41 Source program and report listings for the Square Root example program.

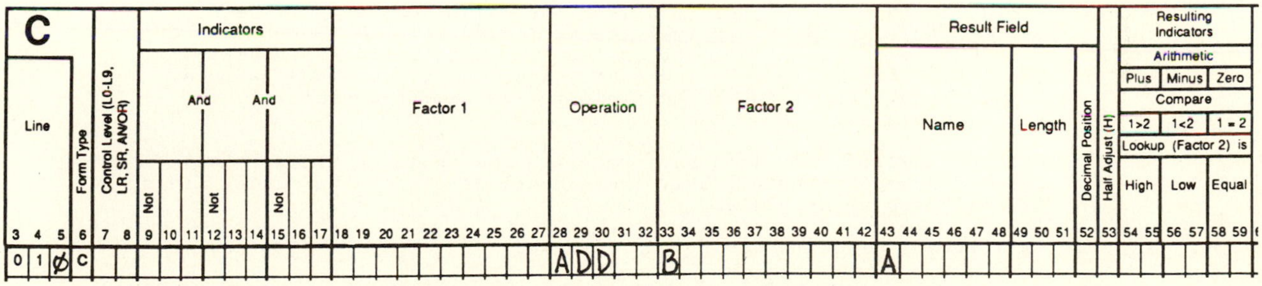

C
Line
Form Type
Control Level (L0-L9, LR, SR, AN/OR)
Indicators
And
And
Not
Not
Not
Factor 1
Operation
Factor 2
Result Field
Name
Length
Decimal Position
Half Adjust (H)
Resulting Indicators
Arithmetic
Plus
Minus
Zero
Compare
1>2
1<2
1 = 2
Lookup (Factor 2) is
High
Low
Equal
0 1 ø C
ADD
B
A

Factor 1 field entry may be omitted when result field is the same

Advantages:

1. Encourages the programmer to use Factor 1 as the Result Field when possible thereby reducing storage and decreasing in processing time.

2. Permits easier debugging because of less entries to examine.

3. Reduces coding.

Figure 4-42 RPG language enhancement—calculation coding when the result field is the same as the Factor 1 entry.

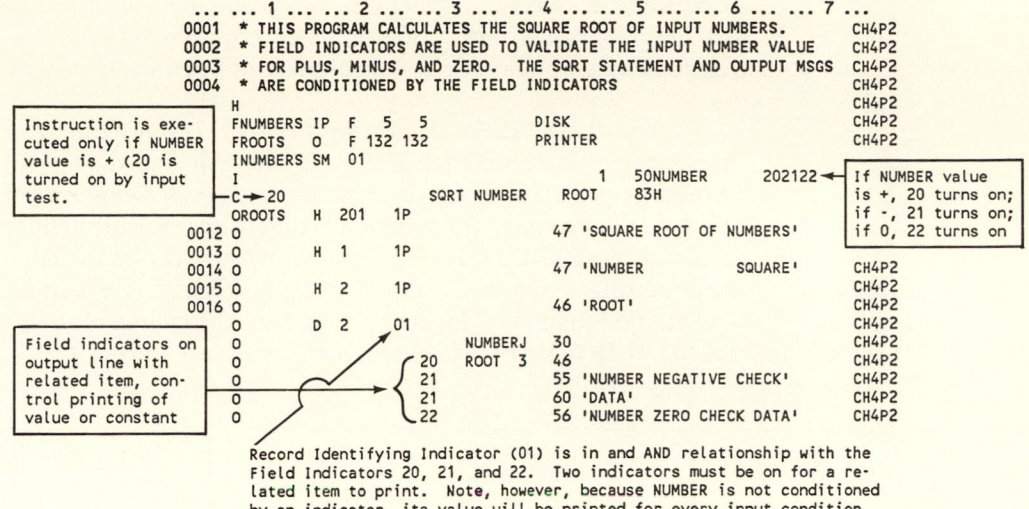

For some arithmetic instructions, however, the use of the Factor 1 entry as the Result Field may not be logical. Size requirements, or the need to retain the original value of the Factor 1 field, may not permit the use of this enhancement.

*The *LIKE DEFN (Field Definition).* The program examples presented in this chapter have defined all Result Fields in the related arithmetic statement. For large programs, however, where many result fields are defined, this approach may be inconvenient for program maintenance. Result Fields are more efficiently defined by *LIKE DEFN statements, which may be included in an internal subroutine (discussed in Chapter 5). *LIKE DEFN is executed as one of the first calculation functions. Figure 4-43 explains the syntax of this statement. Examples of the *LIKE DEFN statement are shown in Figure 4-44.

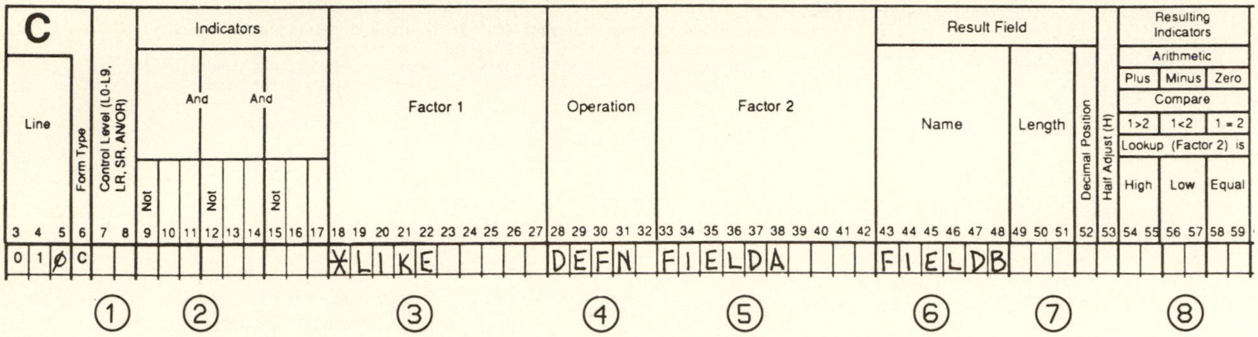

1. Control level indicator (L1-L9 and LR) may be entered in columns 7-8 (total time calculations).

2. Columns 9-17 are not used.

3. *LIKE must be specified left-justified in Factor 1.

4. DEFN must be left-justified in Operation field.

5. Factor 2 field name provides the attributes for the field being defined in the Result Field.

6. New field name must be left-justified in the Result Field.

7. Field length is not required unless the Result Field is to be defined smaller or larger than the Factor 2 field. A + in column 49 with a number right-justified in the field indicates an increase in the Result Field size. On the other hand, a - in column 49 with a number right-justified in the field indicates a decrease in the Result Field size.

   Original decimal position assignment in the Factor 2 field is not changed by + or - entry. Only the overall length of the Result Field is increased or decreased.

8. Resulting Indicators may not be assigned.

Figure 4-43 Syntax of the *LIKE DEFN (Field Definition) statement.

The DEBUG Operation

Programming errors may be classified into two types; *compile time* errors and *execution (or runtime) time* errors. Compile time errors are syntax errors that fall into one of the following broad categories:

1. Incorrect syntax such as placing an entry in the wrong field.
2. Undefined and unreferenced fields.

Line	Form Type	Control Level (L0-L9, LR, SR, AN/OR)	Indicators	Factor 1	Operation	Factor 2	Result Field Name	Length	Decimal Position	Half Adjust (H)	Resulting Indicators
01Ø	C			*LIKE	DEFN	NFLD1	NFLD2				
02Ø	C	*									
03Ø	C			*LIKE	DEFN	NFLD1	NFLD3	+ 1			
04Ø	C	*									
05Ø	C			*LIKE	DEFN	NFLD1	NFLD4	- 2			
06Ø	C	*									
07Ø	C			*LIKE	DEFN	AFLD1	AFLD2	- 1Ø			

Given:

NFLD1 is defined as a 7 position numeric field with 2 decimal positions

AFLD1 is defined as a 25 position alphanumeric field.

Related Result Field sizes:

1. NFLD2 is defined with the same attributes as NFLD1.
2. NFLD3 is defined as an 8 position numeric field with 2 decimal positions. One byte larger than NFLD1.
3. NFLD4 is defined as a 5 position numeric field with 2 decimal positions. Two bytes smaller than NFLD1.
4. AFLD2 is defined as a 15 byte alphanumeric field. Ten bytes smaller then AFLD1.

Figure 4-44 Coding examples of the *LIKE DEFN statement.

3. Specifying a field in calculations, or as edited output, that was not defined as numeric.
4. Undefined and unreferenced indicators.
5. Specifying total time before detail time in calculations and/or output.

Because these errors are identified on the source program listing, they are easily located.

Runtime errors that cause halts or abends during execution of a compiled program are usually logic errors and are more difficult to find. Some of the errors included in this category are the following:

1. Divide by zero
2. Conditioning of an instruction with the wrong indicator
3. Invalid numeric data
4. Never-ending (perpetual) loop (Chapter 5)
5. Unconditioned branch (Chapter 5)
6. Unidentified record type (Chapter 8)
7. Array index error (Chapter 11)
8. Incorrect output results

Some runtime errors may be difficult, if not impossible, to locate by standard procedures such as checking the program's syntax, studying the logic, and so forth. To expedite runtime debugging a DEBUG operation is available.

Source program coding for the DEBUG operation requires additional entries in the Control and Calculation Specifications. These entries are identified in Figure 4-45.

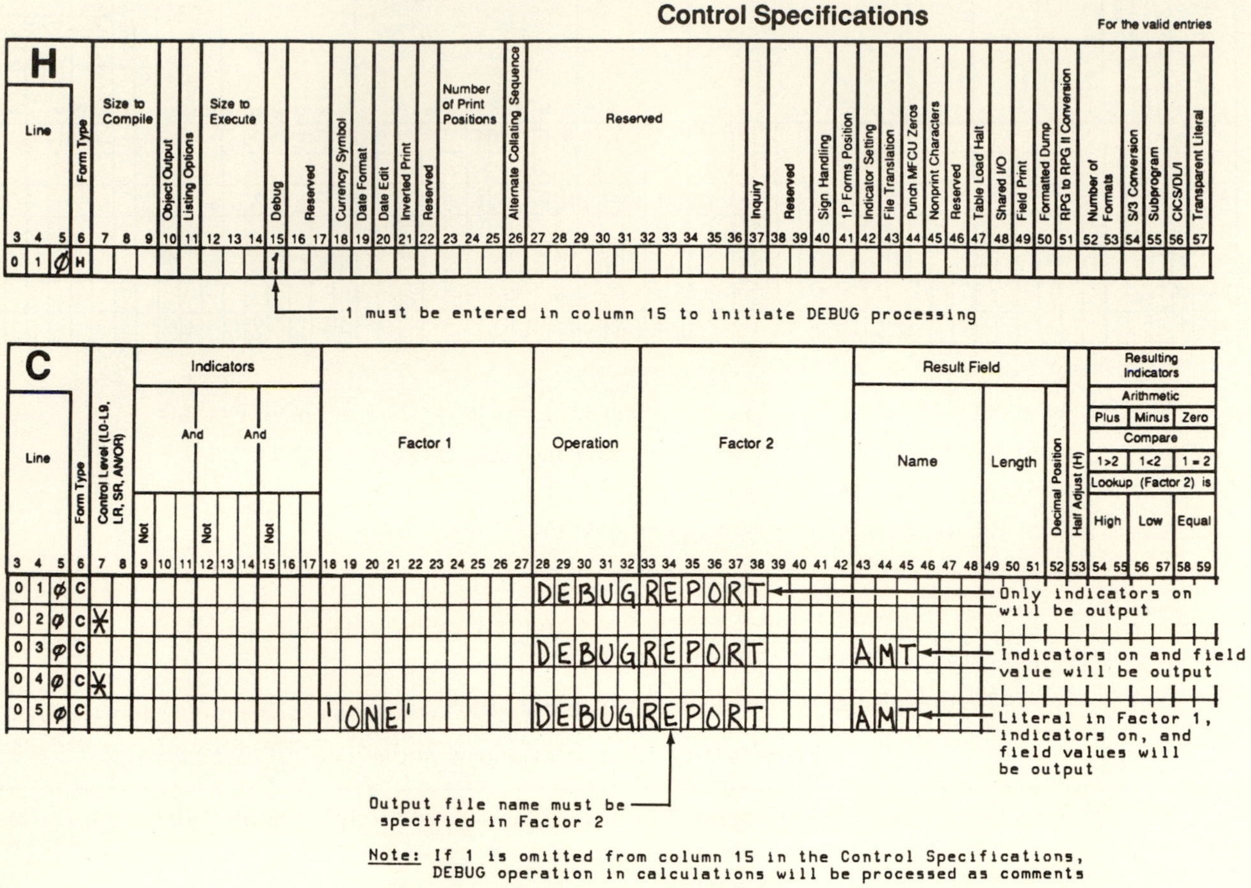

Figure 4-45 Control and Calculation Specification entries for DEBUG operation processing.

A source listing of the square root program modified with DEBUG operation is shown in Figure 4-46. Also included is a partial report listing that shows the output generated by two formats of the DEBUG operation. Notice for the format included on line 10 of the program that only the indicators that are "on" are identified. For the DEBUG format on line 12 of the program, indicators "on" and the value of the NUMBER field are printed. Also, note that an L0 (Level Zero) indicator is included on every DEBUG output line even though it was not assigned in the program. The *L0* indicator is turned on automatically by RPG, remains on for the duration of the program, and cannot be SETOF. It is used to condition total time calculation and output processing when a control level indicator is not specified in the program. L0 is a control level indicator that must be used with total time processing. Other control level indicators include L1 to L9, which are discussed in Chapter 9.

External Control of DEBUG Statements. When DEBUG operations are included in a program, the program must be recompiled, which can be time-consuming in a production environment, especially for large programs. A method to eliminate the need to compile a program during or after the debugging process is to use External Indicators (U1–U8).

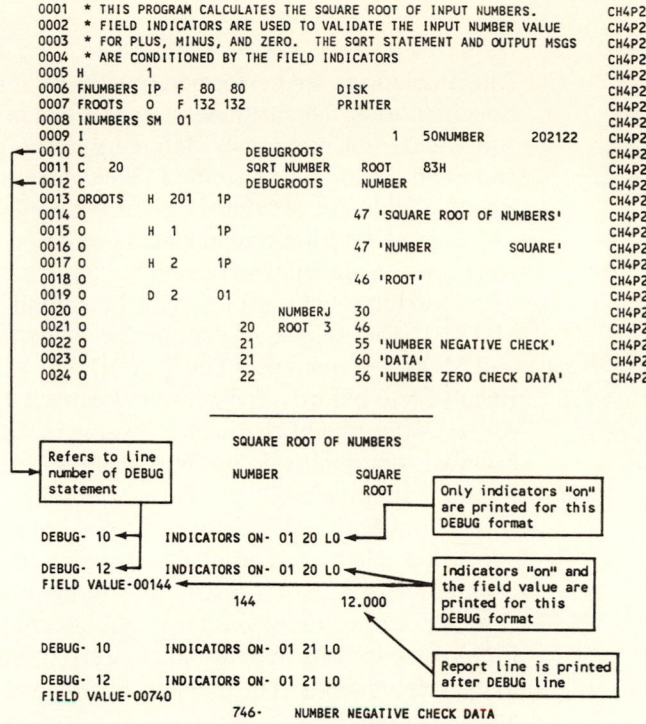

```
0001  * THIS PROGRAM CALCULATES THE SQUARE ROOT OF INPUT NUMBERS.         CH4P2
0002  * FIELD INDICATORS ARE USED TO VALIDATE THE INPUT NUMBER VALUE      CH4P2
0003  * FOR PLUS, MINUS, AND ZERO.  THE SQRT STATEMENT AND OUTPUT MSGS    CH4P2
0004  * ARE CONDITIONED BY THE FIELD INDICATORS                           CH4P2
0005 H        1                                                           CH4P2
0006 FNUMBERS IP  F  80  80            DISK                               CH4P2
0007 FROOTS   O   F 132 132            PRINTER                            CH4P2
0008 INUMBERS SM  01                                                      CH4P2
0009 I                                       1   50NUMBER      202122     CH4P2
0010 C                         DEBUGROOTS                                 CH4P2
0011 C   20                    SQRT NUMBER   ROOT    83H                  CH4P2
0012 C                         DEBUGROOTS    NUMBER                       CH4P2
0013 OROOTS   H  201   1P                                                 CH4P2
0014 O                                      47 'SQUARE ROOT OF NUMBERS'   CH4P2
0015 O        H  1     1P                                                 CH4P2
0016 O                                      47 'NUMBER          SQUARE'   CH4P2
0017 O        H  2     1P                                                 CH4P2
0018 O                                      46 'ROOT'                     CH4P2
0019 O        D  2     01                                                 CH4P2
0020 O                         NUMBERJ      30                            CH4P2
0021 O                    20   ROOT  3      46                            CH4P2
0022 O                    21                55 'NUMBER NEGATIVE CHECK'    CH4P2
0023 O                    21                60 'DATA'                     CH4P2
0024 O                    22                56 'NUMBER ZERO CHECK DATA'   CH4P2
```

```
                    SQUARE ROOT OF NUMBERS

                    NUMBER          SQUARE
                                     ROOT

DEBUG- 10     INDICATORS ON- 01 20 L0

DEBUG- 12     INDICATORS ON- 01 20 L0
FIELD VALUE-00144
                    144             12.000

DEBUG- 10     INDICATORS ON- 01 21 L0

DEBUG- 12     INDICATORS ON- 01 21 L0
FIELD VALUE-00740
                    746-    NUMBER NEGATIVE CHECK DATA
```

Refers to line number of DEBUG statement

Only indicators "on" are printed for this DEBUG format

Indicators "on" and the field value are printed for this DEBUG format

Report line is printed after DEBUG line

Figure 4-46 Example program with DEBUG included and report format generated.

The ON and OFF status of External Indicators is controlled by a switch statement included in the procedure that executes the program. Switch statements in IBM's System 34/36 environment are formatted as follows:

```
           Each number represents a U1 to U8 indicator,
            where 1 is on and 0 is off.
// SWITCH 10000000
           1 indicates that switch 1 is on. Zeros
             indicate that switches 2 to 8 are off.
```

Figure 4-47 shows how an External Indicator may be used to condition a DEBUG operation. After the program is debugged, the SWITCH statement is deleted from the procedure to prevent the DEBUG operations in the program from being executed, thus eliminating the need to recompile the program.

RPG CALCULATION SPECIFICATIONS

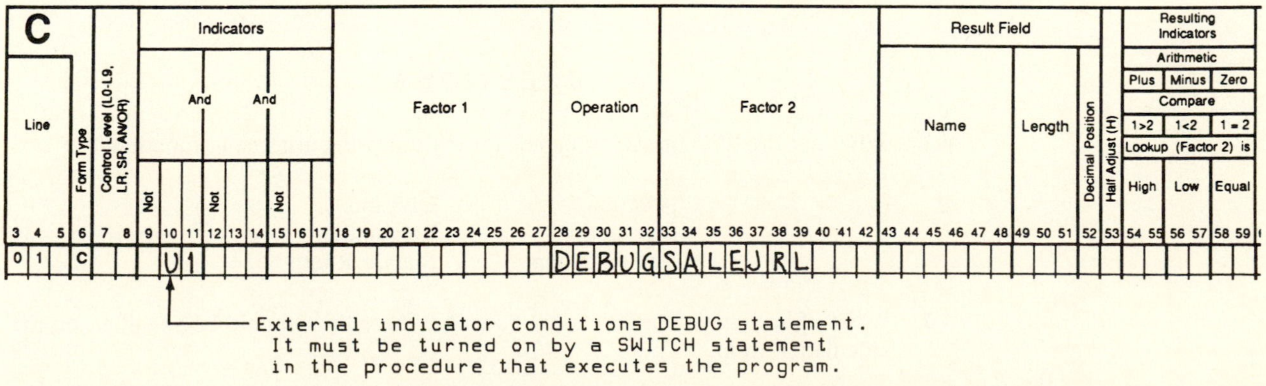

Figure 4-47 Conditioning of calculations with an External Indicator (U1–U8).

SUMMARY

All calculations are performed in RPG by instructions included in the Calculation Specifications. The arithmetic operations are ADD, SUB, MULT, and DIV. Result Fields not previously defined may be defined when the related calculation statement is initially specified. Field length and decimal position entries define Result Fields not previously defined on input.

An MVR (move remainder) operation may be used with DIV statement to save the remainder when needed.

Numeric field values may be initialized by Z-ADD, Z-SUB, MOVE, or MOVEL operations. Alphanumeric fields may be initialized only with MOVEL and MOVE statements. The Z-ADD and Z-SUB operations move zeros into the Result Field before moving in the Factor 2 value. However, the Z-SUB operation reverses the sign of the Factor 2 value in the Result Field value. The MOVE and MOVEL operations do not initialize the Result Field before the movement of the Factor 2 item value.

The LR (Last Record) indicator is automatically turned on during program execution when the end of the input file is sensed. It may be used to condition calculation and output instructions only at *total time*.

Resulting Indicators (arithmetic—columns 54–59) are used to test a Result Field value for Positive, Minus, or Zero by specifying one, two, or three indicators in the related fields. The indicator(s) are used to condition subsequent calculations and/or output.

The Figurative Constants *BLANK, *BLANKS, *ZERO, *ZEROS, *HIVAL, *LOVAL, *ALLX '. . . .' are unique in that they have predefined values. Each constant assumes the Result Field size.

The SQRT (Square Root) operation computes the square root of a number.

Field Indicators are specified in the Input Specifications in columns 65 to 70. An input field value may be tested for Plus, Minus or Zero (Blank for alphanumeric fields) by entering an indicator in one or more of the field positions. Field Indicators are used to condition related calculations and/or output instructions.

Debugging an RPG program at execution time may be controlled by the DEBUG operation. Depending on the format, DEBUG statements will output indicators and field values at the designated location in the program. External control of DEBUG statements may be specified by External Indicators (U1–U8), which are turned on by a SWITCH statement included in the procedure that executes the program.

Result Fields that are not defined on input may be more efficiently defined by *LIKE DEFN (Field Definition) statements than by any other method.

QUESTIONS

4-1. What are the RPG operation names for the following arithmetic functions?

Addition	Division
Subtraction	Remainder
Multiplication	Square Root

4-2. A list of arithmetic terms follows. Identify where they should be specified on the calculation form.

Quotient	Sum	Difference
Subtrahend	Divisor	Dividend

Product Addend Multiplier
Multiplicand Remainder

4-3. If a five-digit number with two decimals is multiplied by a four-digit number with four decimals, how large should the Result Field be and with how many decimals?

4-4. What sign will the Result Field carry after the following separate calculation statements?

	Factor 1 Value	Arithmetic Function	Factor 2 Value	Comment
(a)	+25	x	+4	Multiplication
(b)	-19	x	-5	Multiplication
(c)	-100	+	+50	Addition
(d)	+30	-	-35	Subtraction
(e)	+22	/	-2	Division
(f)	+12	x	-10	Multiplication
(g)	-500	/	-20	Division
(h)	-99	-	-9	Subtraction

4-5. Explain the rule for defining the size of the Result Field for a division statement.

4-6. What procedure should be followed for defining the size of a remainder?

4-7. Name some of the restrictions for a square root statement.

4-8. What is half adjusting? Where and how is it specified in an RPG program? Should it be included for every instruction?

4-9. Half adjust the following numbers to two decimal positions.

(a) 45.2891	(c) 99.9959	(e) 73.4444	(g) 26.789
(b) 18.134	(d) 100.56	(f) .4567	(h) 509.

4-10. For numeric literals that have a decimal value, is an explicit (actual) or implied decimal specified? Must a decimal be included with integer literals?

4-11. On a blank calculation form, write the instruction to multiply SALES by RATE and store the answer in TAX. The SALES field is defined as 7 digits with 2 decimal positions, and RATE is 3 digits long with 3 decimals. TAX is to be defined in the statement.

4-12. On a blank calculation form, enter the coding to divide QUANT by 12 and store the answer in DOZENS. QUANT is defined as 6 positions with 0 decimals. DOZENS is to be defined in the statement.

4-13. Refer to Question 12 and include an instruction to save the remainder in a field named REMAIN. The size of REMAIN must be determined.

4-14. In an RPG program, when does the LR indicator turn on? For conditioning of instructions, where is it specified in the calculation form? With which type of line must it be specified on output coding?

4-15. Examine the following calculations and explain if anything is wrong with the syntax.

Line (3-5)	Form Type (6)	Control Level (L0-L9, LR, SR, AN/OR) (7-8)	Indicators (9-17)	Factor 1 (18-27)	Operation (28-32)	Factor 2 (33-42)	Result Field Name (43-48)	Length (49-51)	Decimal Position (52)	Half Adjust (H) (53)	Resulting Indicators (54-59)
01Ø	C			TOTAL	ADD	SALES	TOTAL	9	2		
02Ø	C	LR		COUNT	ADD	1	COUNT	4	Ø		
03Ø	C		LR	TOTAL	DIV	COUNT	AVG	8	2		

4-16. In an RPG program, where are Resulting Indicators specified? What is their function?

4-17. May more than one Resulting Indicator condition a calculation or output instruction? May an instruction be conditioned by a Resulting Indicator and a Record Identifying Indicator?

4-18. What is the function of the SETON operation? What is the function of the SETOF operation? How many indicators may be controlled by one SETON or SETOF operation?

4-19. Explain the processing function of the Z-ADD operation.

4-20. Determine the Result Field value for each of the Factor 2 values after execution of a Z-ADD operation. The size of Factor 2 and the Result Field items are indicated by the beginning values.

```
               Beginning Values
       Factor 2                Result Field

       0 0 9 0 0              3 0 0 7 5
            ▲                      ▲

       1 0 0 0 0                  1 2 3
            ▲                          ▲

         0 7 5 0                0 0 0 0
        ▲                          ▲

         9 8 9 9                    2 5
                ▲                  ▲

       1 1 6 7 4 }            1 2 0 0 0 0
              ▲ ↑                    ▲
                └Indicates negative value

       ▲ Indicates implied decimal
```

4-21. How does the Z-SUB operation differ from Z-ADD? Refer to Question 4-20 and determine the Result Field values if a Z-SUB operation was specified.

4-22. Explain how the MOVE and MOVEL operations differ in processing. How do they differ from the function performed by the Z-ADD operation?

4-23. Determine the Result Field value for each of the MOVE statements. The size of the Factor 2 and Result Field items are indicated by the beginning values.

```
               Beginning Values
        Factor 2                Result Field

        1 2 3 4 5              1 0 0 0 0 0
             ▲                        ▲

        1 2 3 4 5                  0 0 0
             ▲                          ▲

          1 2 3 4               9 8 7 6 5 4
                 ▲                     ▲

        MOUSE                  MINNIEbbbbbb

     MIKE JACKSON                 PARTONb
```

▲ Indicates implied decimal.
b Indicates blank character.

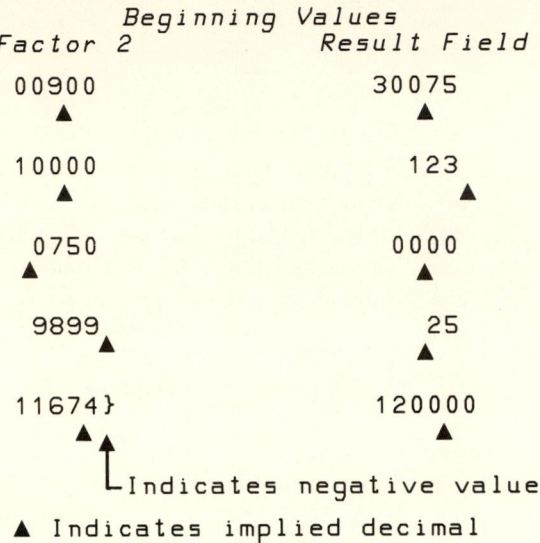

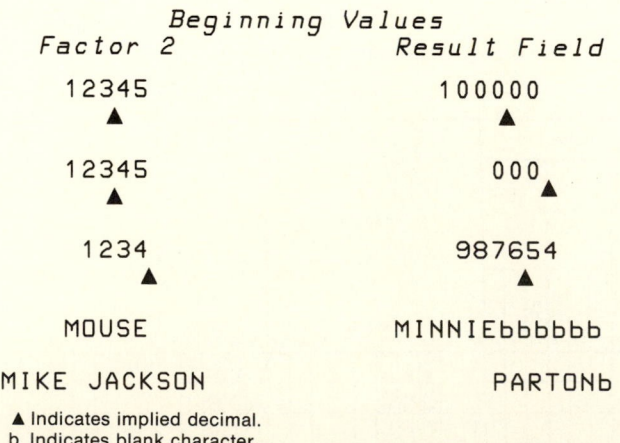

4-24. Refer to Question 4-23, and determine the Result Field values for the MOVEL operation.

4-25. Name the Figurative Constants and indicate the value supplied by each one. What is their function in an RPG program?

4-26. Where in an RPG program are Field Indicators specified? What is their programming function?

4-27. In addition to the calculation form, what other RPG specifications are used with the DEBUG operation? What entries are required?

4-28. Examine the Calculation Specifications instructions for the DEBUG operation alternatives given below and explain the meaning of the Factor 1, Operation, Factor 2, and Result Field entries.

Line	Form Type	Indicators	Factor 1	Operation	Factor 2	Result Field Name	Length	Resulting Indicators
01	C			DEBUG	OUTPUT			
02	C							
03	C			DEBUG	OUTPUT	FIELDA		
04	C							
05	C		'ONE'	DEBUG	OUTPUT			
06	C							
07	C		'TWO'	DEBUG	OUTPUT	FIELDT		

4-29. Examine the DEBUG statements shown in Question 4-28 and for each example explain what will be included on output.

4-30. What are External Indicators? Where are they defined? Give one example of how they may be used in an RPG program.

4-31. Using an RPG language enhancement, how may calculation instructions be shortened? Under what conditions should this method not be used?

4-32. What is the most efficient method to define fields that are not included in an input record?

4-33. On a calculation form, using the method identified in Question 4-32, write the instruction to define TOTAL 1 byte larger than AMOUNT. The AMOUNT field is defined as 7 bytes with 2 decimal positions. How many decimal positions will be defined for the TOTAL field after the operation is executed?

EXERCISES

4-1. Write the calculation instructions for the following formula:

$$I = \frac{D}{P} \times \frac{12}{T}$$

Input field sizes are:

Field Name	*Size*	*Decimals*
D	6	2
P	8	2
T	3	0

Note: I is to be defined as 5 long with 5 decimal positions and rounded.

Convert I from a XXXXX decimal value to a XX.XXX percentage format.

4-2. Refer to Exercise 4-1 and insert a DEBUG instruction in the place where you determine it is most appropriate for debugging purposes. Use the DEBUG format that gives a field value in addition to the indicators that are on.

4-3. Refer to Exercise 4-2, and modify it using RPG-enhanced coding methods.

4-4. Write the calculations for the following formula:

$$S = \sqrt{X^2} \qquad \text{(Note: } X \text{ is squared)}$$

where X = defined as 5 long with 0 decimal positions.

4-5. Write the calculations to accumulate a record count and a total for SALES. When end of file is sensed, divide the accumulated SALES total by the record count and store the answer in AVGSAL. SALES is an input field defined as 6 bytes with 2 decimals. A maximum of 50,000 records will be stored in the file.

4-6. Write the calculation coding for the following flowchart logic. Use Resulting Indicators to test the value of C.

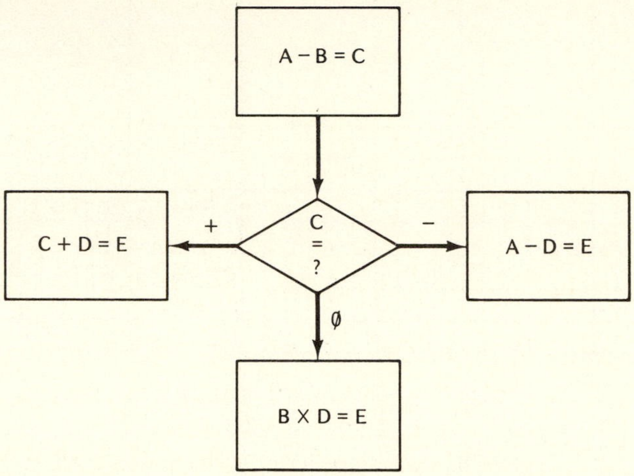

4-7. Complete the Input Specifications to test the value of FIELDA for Plus, Minus, and Zero. Then, from the following flowchart logic, complete the calculation coding.

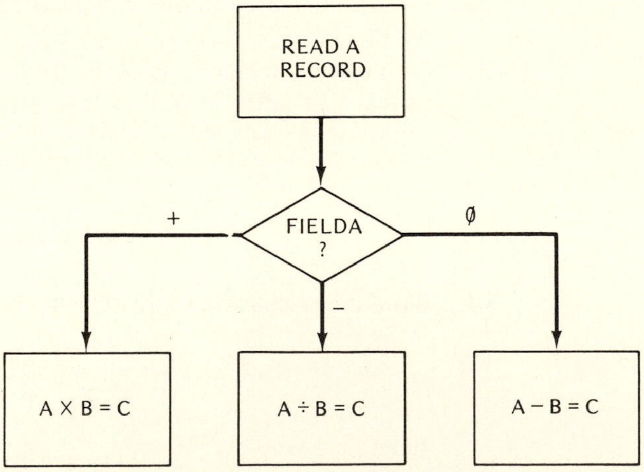

4-8. Write the calculation instructions for the following formula. Include the necessary tests to prevent the program from halting (or aborting on some systems) because of related minus and zero values.

$$\sqrt{\frac{X - Y}{Z}}$$

4-9. Debugging a source listing:

```
            ....+....1....+....2....+....3....+....4....+....5....+....6....+....7.
   1 0001 H
   2 0002 FSOUPINV IP  F  80  80          DISK
   3 0003 FREPORT  O   F 132 132     OF     PRINTER
   4 0004 ISOUPINV SM  01
   5 0005 I                                         1  20 BRAND
   6 0006 I                                        21  24 SP
   7 0007 I                                        25  282COST            10
   8 0008 C          SP        SUB  COST      PROFIT  42       $ PROFIT
****-C063- Operation Code requires a valid numeric Factor 1.
   9 0009 C  N11     PROFIT    DIV  COST      DECPCT  5        DECIMAL PCT
****-C193- Operation Code requires numeric Result Field with 0-9 Decimal Positions.
  10 0010 C          DECPCT    MULT 100       PERCNT           PRINTABLE PCT
  11 0011 C          TOTPCT    ADD  PERCNT    TOTPCT  63       ACCUMULATE PCTS
  12 0012 CLR        RECRDS    ADD  1         RECRDS  40       RECRD PROCESSED
  13 0013 C   LR     TOTPCT    DIV  RECRDS    AVGPCT  53H      COMPUTE AVG PCT
****-C190- Detail lines must come before last record (LR) lines.
  14 0014 OREPORT  H  301   1P
  15 0015 O       OR        OF
  16 0016 O                           UDATE Y    8
  17 0017 O                                     37 'CASE LOT PROFIT ANALYSIS'
  18 0018 O                                     52 'OF SOUP BRANDS'
  19 0019 O                                     62 'PAGE'
  20 0020 O                           PAGE  Z   67
  21 0021 O        H  2     1P
  22 0022 O       OR        OF
  23 0023 O                                     12 'BRAND'
  24 0024 O                                     51 'SP/CASE    COST   PROFIT'
  25 0025 O                                     63 '% PROFIT'
  26 0026 O        T  2     01
  27 0027 O                           BRAND     21
  28 0028 O                           SP    1   31
****-O113- Edit Code or Edit Constant must not be specified for an alphameric field.
  29 0029 O                           COST  1   42
  30 0030 O                           PROFITJ   51
  31 0031 O                           PERCNTJ   62
  32 0032 O                                     63 '%'
  33 0033 O        D 1      LR
  34 0034 O                                     27 'AVERAGE PROFIT PERCENT ='
  35 0035 O                           AVGPCTJ   35
  36 0036 O                                     36 '%'

****-A108- The following field name was never given a length.
           DECPCT
****-A108- The following field name was never given a length.
           PERCNT

           THE FOLLOWING INDICATORS WERE SPECIFIED BUT WERE NEVER
           USED TO CONDITION OPERATIONS

           10

           THE FOLLOWING INDICATORS WERE USED TO CONDITION OPERATIONS
           BUT WERE NEVER SET

           11

           THE FOLLOWING INDICATORS APPEARED IN THIS PROGRAM

           01  10  11  LR  1P  OF
 No Warning Errors
  6 Fatal Errors
```

LABORATORY ASSIGNMENTS

Laboratory Assignment 4-1: SALES JOURNAL

Write an RPG program to generate a Sales Journal that summarizes all of a month's sales on account.

Processing: Read the input file consecutively, and for every record processed perform the following calculations:

1. Test the Sales Amount field on input for a negative and zero value. If one of those conditions is tested *do not* perform any calculations for that record. Depending on the error condition, one of the two messages shown in the printer spacing chart that follows is to be printed with the transaction date, customer name, and invoice number from the related record.

For Valid Records:

2. Compute the sales tax by multiplying the sales amount by the numeric literal .0750.
3. Compute the total sale for the record by adding the sales tax to the sales amount.
4. Accumulate the sales amount, sales tax, and total sale into separate total fields.

Format of the Input Data:

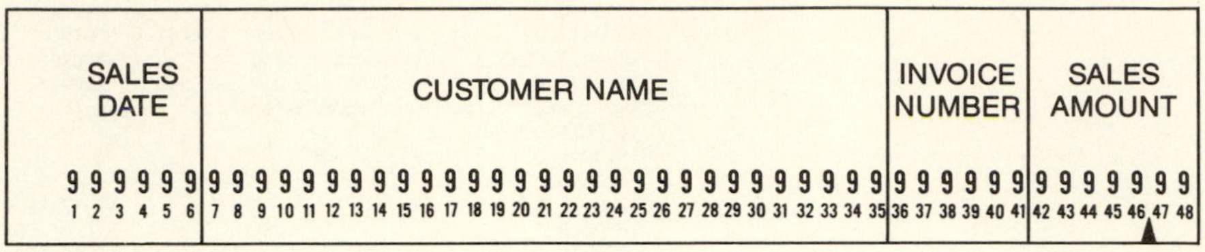

Report Design:

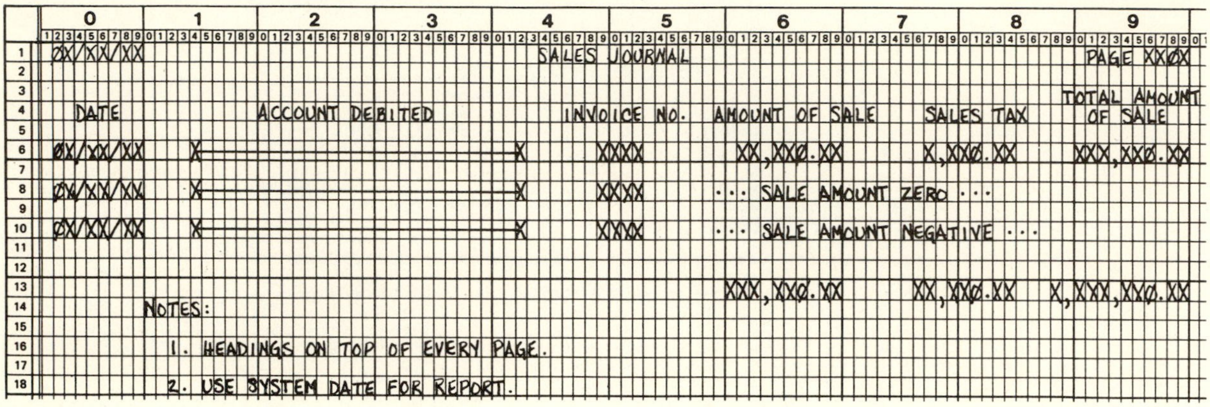

Input Data:

Sales Date	Customer Name	Invoice Number	Sales Amount
080192	HUDSON MOTOR CAR COMPANY	40000	0812000
080992	PACKARD COMPANY	40001	0000000
081192	THE HUPMOBILE COMPANY	40002	8570101
081692	THE TUCKER CAR COMPANY	40003	0002129
082192	AUBURN INCORPORATED	40004	004500J
082792	BRICKLIN LIMITED	40005	1068910
083092	THE LOCOMOBILE CAR COMPANY	40006	2140000
083192	STUDEBAKER CARS INCORPORATED	40007	0050500

Laboratory Assignment 4-2: COMPUTATION OF SIMPLE INTEREST

Simple interest is the rent paid to a lender for the privilege of borrowing money. It is charged on personal loans, car loans, installment loans, home mortgages, and so forth. The formula for computing simple interest is:

$$I = \frac{P \times R \times T}{365}$$

where I = Dollar amount of simple interest
P = Principal (amount borrowed) on which interest is computed
R = Annual interest rate expressed as a decimal
T = Number of days, months, or years for which the money will be loaned

Note: 365 is used as denominator in above formula if T (time) is in days. If time is in years, denominator may be one or no entry needed.

Processing: Include the formula for computing simple interest in an RPG program. Process the input file consecutively, and generate the report format shown in the supplemental printer spacing chart. Notice that the interest percentage value input must be multiplied by 100 for output.

Format of the Input Data:

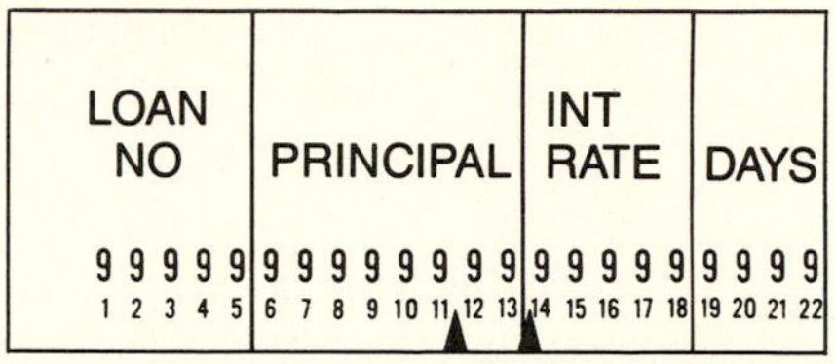

Report Design:

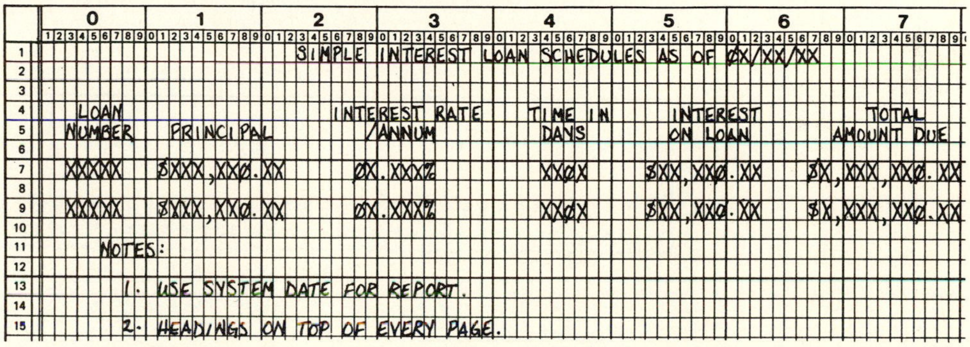

Input Data:

Loan #	Principal (P)	Interest Rate (R)	Time of Loan in Days (T)
10000	12000000	08500	0120
10001	00300000	07000	0185
10002	01025000	09100	0730
10003	00047500	10250	0090
10004	00100000	12125	0060
	2 dec. positions	5 dec. postions	0 dec. positions

Laboratory Assignment 4-3: GROSS PROFIT ANALYSIS REPORT

A computer supply company wants a gross profit report on their best-selling printers. The listed catalog selling prices are subject to trade discounts that range from the series 10%, 5%, 5% to 30%, 10%, 5%.

Trade discounts are computed as follows:
Assume a trade discount of 30%, 10%, 5%.

Step 1: Subtract each percentage point from 1.00.

$$1.00 - 0.30 = 0.70$$

$$1.00 - 0.10 = 0.90$$

$$1.00 - 0.05 = 0.95$$

Step 2: Determine equivalent trade discount by multiplying the percentages calculated in Step 1.

$$0.70 \times 0.90 \times 0.95 = 0.5985 \text{ (carry to four decimal places)}$$

Step 3: Multiply the catalog list price by the percentage derived from Step 2.

$$\$1{,}000 \times 0.5985 = 598.50 \text{ net selling price (rounded nearest cent)}$$

Step 4: Subtract the net selling price (Step 3) from the catalog list price to determine the trade discount.

Step 5: Determine the items's gross profit by subtracting cost from the net selling price calculated in Step 3.

Step 6: Calculate the percentage of gross profit (decimal expression) by dividing the gross profit (Step 5) by the net selling price (Step 3). *Include the control that prevents a divide-by-zero error.*

Step 7: Multiply the decimal percentage derived from Step 6 by 100 to calculate the percentage expression for printing.

Format of Data Records:

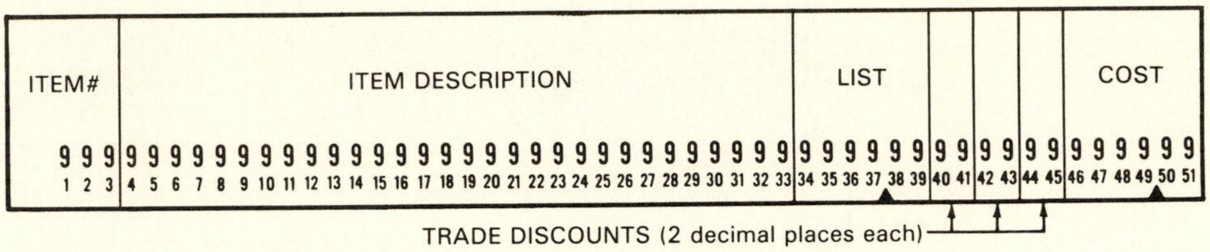

Report Design:

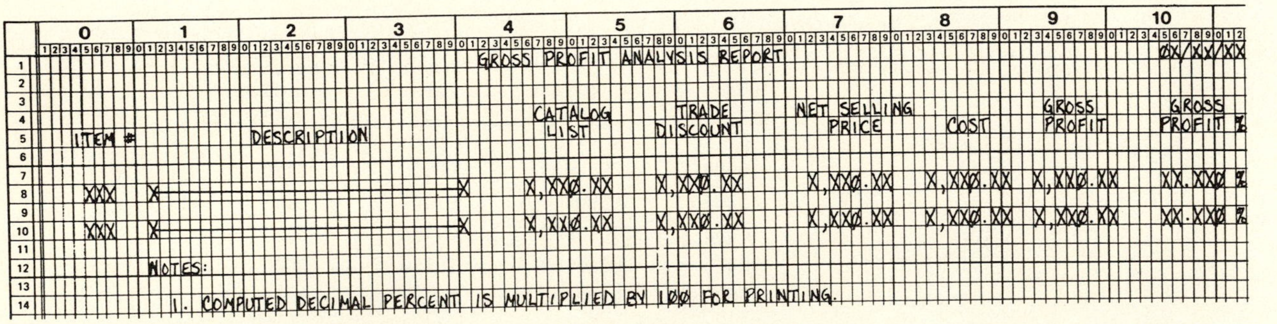

Input Data:

Item Number Col 1-3	Item Description 4-33	Catalog List 34-39	Trade Discount % 40-45	Cost 46-51
720	BROTHER JR-35 PRINTER	140000	30 10 05	061000
776	EXP-770 SILVER REED PRINTER	149500	25 10 05	073000
789	JUKI 6100 PRINTER	059900	10 05 05	037500
799	P12 DIABLO SYSTEMS PRINTER	069900	15 05 00	034500
820	H-P LASERJET+ PRINTER	349500	10 10 05	226800

Laboratory Assignment 4-4: DETERMINATION OF ECONOMIC ORDER QUANTITY

The costs of carrying an item in inventory include deterioration, obsolescence, handling, clerical labor, taxes, insurance, storage, and reasonable return on investment. These costs are weighted against the costs of inadequate inventory, which may lead to loss of sales, loss of customer goodwill, production stoppage, extra purchasing costs, and a higher item cost for small-quantity purchases. Because of these inventory considerations, companies often rely on mathematical models as guidelines for the decision-making process of determining how much to order and when. A useful quantitative tool is the economic order quantity formula, which calculates the optimum quantity to order of any one item.

Before an item's economic order quantity is calculated, the number of units needed annually, cost per order, unit cost of the item, and its carrying cost must be determined. Then, the following formula may be used:

$$\text{Economic Order Quantity} = \sqrt{\frac{2 \times \text{units needed annually} \times \text{ordering cost}}{\text{item unit cost} \times \text{inventory carrying cost \%}}}$$

or

$$\text{EOQ} = \sqrt{\frac{2 \times U \times OC}{UC \times ICC}}$$

Note: Round EOQ answer to a whole number.

Format of Data Records:

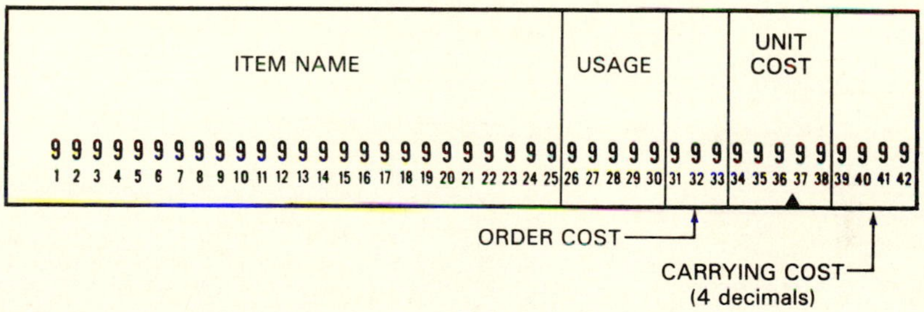

Report Design: Format a printer spacing chart according to the following general format:

```
0X/XX/XX      ECONOMIC ORDER QUANTITIES OF INVENTORY ITEMS     PAGE XX0X

          ITEM NAME               ANNUAL USAGE     EOQ      ORDER PER YEAR

XXXXXXXXXXXXXXXXXXXXXXXXX            XX,XX0       X,XX0          XX0

XXXXXXXXXXXXXXXXXXXXXXXXX            XX,XX0       X,XX0          XX0

Note:  Use system date for report.
```

Orders per year is determined by dividing annual usage by the economic order quantity computed. Round to a whole number.

Input Data:

Item Name Cols 1-25	Annual Usage 26-30	Order Cost 31-33	Unit Cost 34-38	Carrying Cost % 39-42
LEFT-HAND MONKEY WRENCH	10000	025	01250	0250
MEN'S DIESEL SHAVER	20000	018	01800	1000
ATOMIC TOOTHBRUSH	40000	020	11290	1400
FUEL-INJECTED LAWN MOWER	00200	050	29000	9000
LASER TOOTHPICKS	30000	024	00650	0856

chapter 5
Decision Making, Branching, and Looping with GOTO Operation Control

Decision making (without branching) may be controlled in an RPG program by the following two Calculation Specification methods:

1. The COMP (Compare) operation with indicators
2. IF and ELSE operations (Chapter 6)

The COMP operation is common to all RPG compilers with the IF/ELSE operations limited to IBM's System/36, 38, and AS/400 computer environments.

Regardless of the operation used in a decision-making statement, a relational test is made between a Factor 1 field value (or literal) and a Factor 2 field value (or literal). The tests that may be made with the COMP operation include an *equal to, less than, or greater than* condition. Tests with an IF statement include *equal to, less than, greater than, less than and equal to, greater than or equal to, and not equal to* conditions.

The test result from the comparison of the values in two fields or a field and a literal is controlled by the collating sequence of the computer. IBM systems support an Extended Binary Coded Decimal Interchange Code (EBCDIC) set and others, including IBM's personal computer series, an ASCII (American National Standard Code for Information Interchange) code structure. Figure 5-1 presents a partial listing of the two code sets. Any character lower in the hierarchy than another character will test as less than in relational (=, >, <) testing. Notice that a blank is the lowest character in both code sets, with 9 being the highest in EBCDIC and Z being the highest in ASCII.

```
EBCDIC                ASCII

      (blank)              (blank)        lowest
                      "                     |
  .                                         |
  <                   $                     |
  (                   :                     |
  +                   (                     |
  $                   )                     |
  *                   *                     |
  )                   +                     |
  ;                   ,                     |
  -                   -                     |
  /                   .                     |
  ,                   /                     |
  >                   0 thru 9              |
  :                   ;                     |
  =                   <                     |
  "                   =                     |
  A thru Z            >                     v
  0 thru 9            A thru Z            highest
```

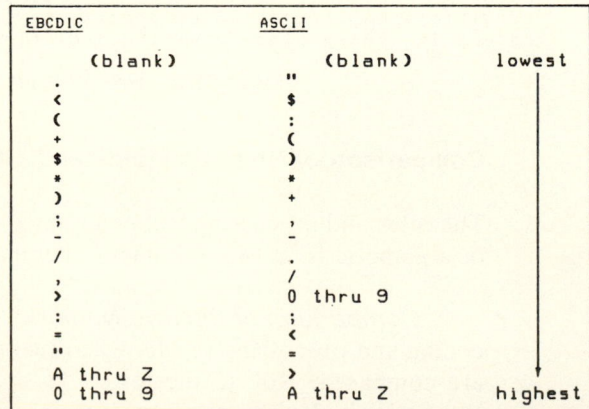

Figure 5-1 EBCDIC and ASCII code set collating sequences.

This chapter discusses the COMP operation. The structured IF/ELSE operations are discussed in Chapter 6.

THE COMP (COMPARE) OPERATION

The COMP operation is included in a calculation instruction that compares the value of a field or literal specified in Factor 1 with the value of the field or literal in Factor 2. Figure 5-2 details the syntax and rules related to the COMP operation.

RPG CALCULATION SPECIFICATIONS

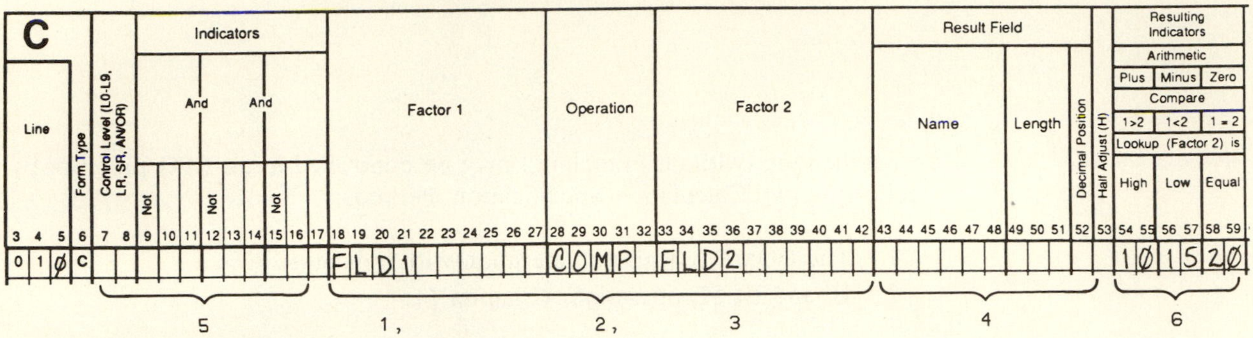

COMP Operations Syntax Rules:

1. Factor 1 and Factor 2 entries may be field names or literals that must be left-justified in their related calculation form field.

2. Factor 1 and Factor 2 must be defined as the same type, both numeric or both alphanumeric.

3. Factor 1 and Factor 2 field and/or literal sizes do not have to be the same. However, processing is more efficient if the items are the same size.

4. Result Field, Field Length, Decimal Positions, and Half Adjust fields are not used.

5. Conditioning indicators (columns 7-17) may be specified as required.

6. At least one indicator must be included in the Resulting Indicator fields. The value in the Factor 1 entry is compared to the value in the Factor 2 entry and the result may be tested for a greater than (1 > 2), less than (1 < 2), and/or equal to (1 = 2) condition(s). Depending on the program requirements; one, two, or all three relational conditions may be tested by specifying one or more indicators in the related Resulting Indicator field.

Figure 5-2 Syntax rules of the COMP operation.

Comparison of Numeric Fields and Literals

The rules and processing features related to the comparison of two numeric fields or a numeric field with a numeric literal are presented in Figure 5-3.

Comparison of Positive Numeric Field Values. Figure 5-4 illustrates the coding and processing results when two numeric fields that have positive values are compared. Not all the tests (>, <, =) have to be made for each COMP instruction. The program's processing logic will determine which test or tests have to be specified.

Features of Numeric Field/Literal COMP Statements

1. All numeric COMPares follow the laws of algebra where a positive (+) value is greater than a negative (-) value.

2. Numeric field or literal values are aligned at the implied decimal point. Any shorter field or literal positions are extended and filled with high or low-order zeros as needed to make the two values equal in length.

   Example:

Before COMP		During Execution of COMP Statement
FLD1 Value:	123456	123456
FLD2 Value:	11	001100

   Implied decimal

   Implied decimal points are aligned and zeros are added to high and low order positions of smaller field so that both items are equal for compare

3. Blanks in an item defined as numeric are replaced with zeros.

4. After the sign is tested, and if both values have the same sign (+ or -), a compare of the values begins at the the high-order byte and continues to the next low-order byte until one of the tested condition is true. When the condition tested is satisfied, execution of the COMP statement stops, and processing continues to the next executable statement.

   Example:

   123456
   001100

   Byte comparison begins at high-order byte and stops when test condition is satisfied

Figure 5-3 Rules and processing features related to numeric field/literal comparisons.

RPG CALCULATION SPECIFICATIONS

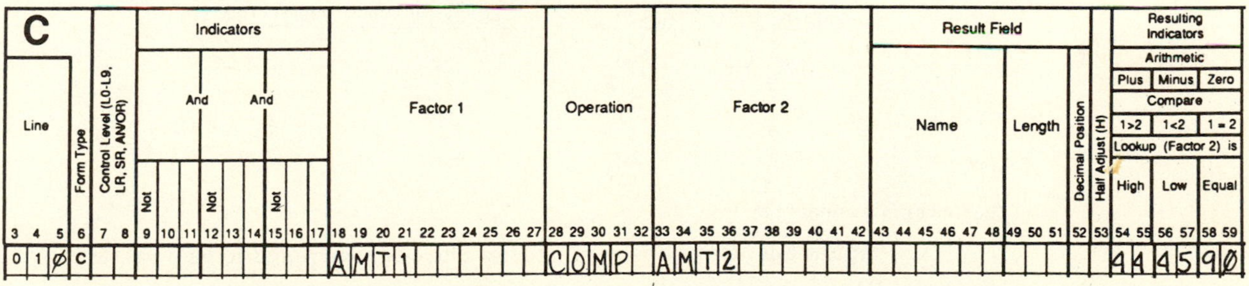

Values in Factor 1 and Factor 2:

	FACTOR 1	FACTOR 2	INDICATOR "ON"	CONDITION
Example 1	1234	1234	90	1 = 2
Example 2	1234	1235	45	1 < 2
Example 3	1234	1233	44	1 > 2

Figure 5-4 Comparison of positive numeric field values.

The test results for the COMP statement shown in Figure 5-4 are summarized as follows:

1. When the value in the Factor 1 field is *greater than* the value in the Factor 2 field, indicator 44 will turn on.
2. When the value in the Factor 1 field is *less than* the value in the Factor 2 field, indicator 45 will turn on.
3. When the value in the Factor 1 field is *equal to* the value in the Factor 2 field, indicator 90 will turn on.

The *Resulting Indicator* turned on is used to condition one or more calculation and/or output instructions. Any RPG indicator (except 1P and MR) may be specified in the Resulting Indicator fields. The sequence of the indicators has nothing to do with the related test. Notice, however, that uncertain processing results may occur if a *Record Identifying Indicator* is used in a COMP statement test.

Comparison of Positive and Negative Numeric Field Values. The COMP statement in Figure 5-5 illustrates the processing results when one of the field values is negative. Notice that only one Resulting Indicator is specified (columns 56–57). Depending on the test conditions required, indicators could have also been assigned in the High and Equal fields. As a general rule, however, the redundant assignment of indicators in any RPG program should be avoided.

RPG CALCULATION SPECIFICATIONS

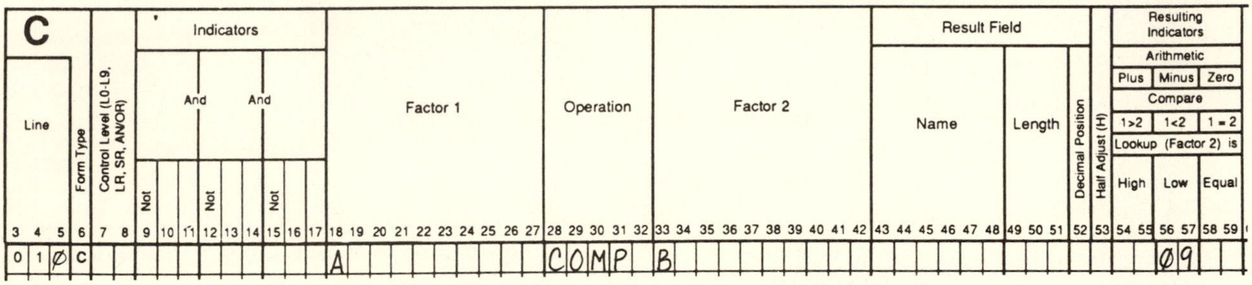

Values in Factor 1 and Factor 2:

	FACTOR 1	FACTOR 2	INDICATOR "ON"	CONDITION
Example 1	10}	100	09	1 < 2
Example 2	100	099	None	1 > 2
Example 3	100	100	None	1 = 2

Character for negative 0

Figure 5-5 Comparison of positive and negative numeric field values.

When the signs of the field/literal values are not the same, condition is immediately identified in the test and a byte-by-byte comparison is not executed. This process and the extension of smaller field/literal values in the execution of a COMP statement are controlled by the computer and are transparent to the programmer.

Comparison of a Numeric Field Value with a Numeric Literal. Figure 5-6 illustrates the comparison of a numeric field with a numeric literal. Numeric

RPG CALCULATION SPECIFICATIONS

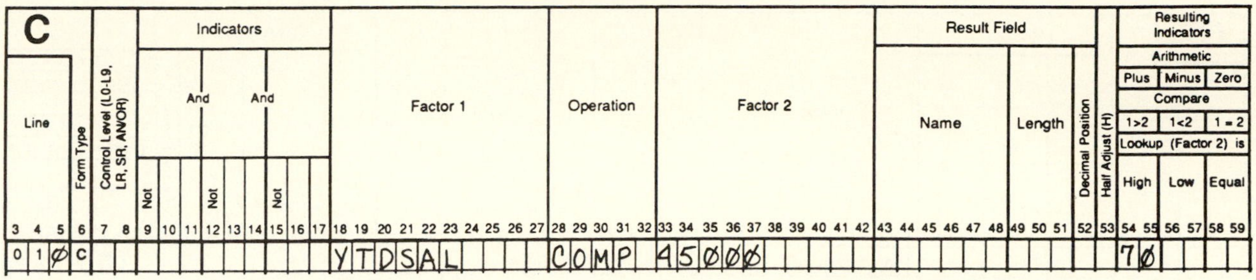

Values in Factor 1 and Factor 2:

	FACTOR 1	FACTOR 2	INDICATOR "ON"	CONDITION
Example 1	47000	45000	70	1 > 2
Example 2	20000	45000	None	1 < 2
Example 3	45000	45000	None	1 = 2

Figure 5-6 Comparison of a numeric field with a numeric literal.

literals are not enclosed in single quotes. If they are specified as an *integer*, they do not have to include the low-order decimal point. Program logic will determine whether the literal is entered in Factor 1 or 2. The comparison of two literals is supported by the RPG compiler, but it is not a logically structured statement.

Comparison of Alphanumeric Fields and Literals. The rules and processing features of the comparison of alphanumeric fields and literals are explained in Figure 5-7.

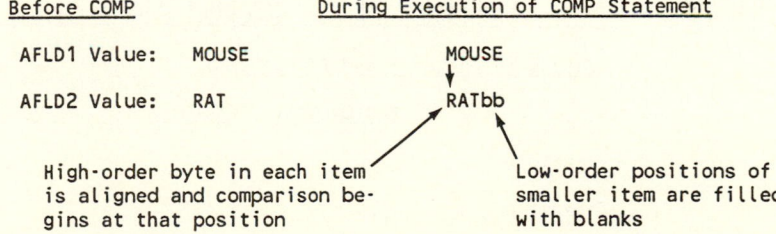

Features of Alphanumeric Field/Literal COMP Statements

1. Alphanumeric field or literal values are aligned at the their high-order bytes. Any shorter field or literal positions are filled with low-order blanks as needed to make the two values equal in length.

   Example:

Before COMP		During Execution of COMP Statement
AFLD1 Value:	MOUSE	MOUSE
AFLD2 Value:	RAT	RATbb

   High-order byte in each item is aligned and comparison begins at that position

   Low-order positions of smaller item are filled with blanks

2. Byte by byte comparison stops when test condition is satisified.

Figure 5-7 Rules and processing features related to alphanumeric field/literal comparisons.

Comparison of Two Alphanumeric Fields. The RPG syntax and processing results for the comparison of two alphanumeric fields are shown in Figure 5-8. All the possible tests have been included by the assignment of indicators in the Resulting Indicator fields. As previously stated, the logic of the program will determine whether one, two, or three indicators have to be specified. Often the same indicator may be used for two test conditions.

RPG CALCULATION SPECIFICATIONS

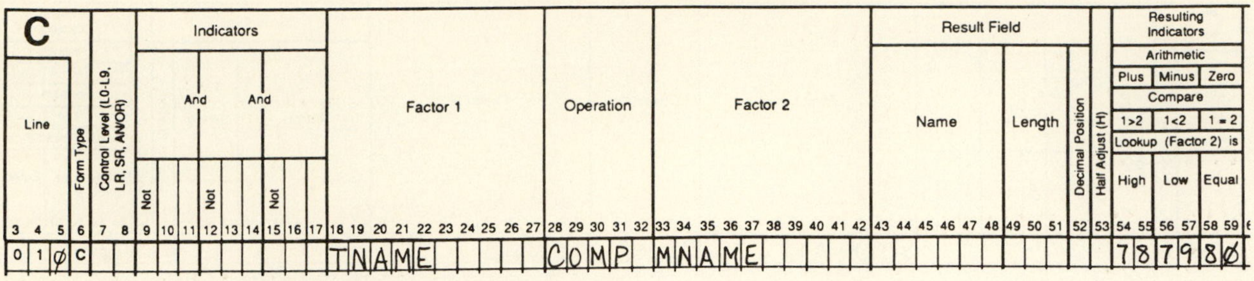

Values in Factor 1 and Factor 2:

	FACTOR 1	FACTOR 2	INDICATOR "ON"	CONDITION
Example 1	HENRY	HENRY	80	1 = 2
Example 2	HENRY	THOMAS	79	1 < 2
Example 3	HENRY	ADAMS	78	1 > 2

Figure 5-8 Comparison of an alphanumeric field with an alphnumeric field.

Comparison of an Alphanumeric Field with an Alphanumeric Literal. A COMP statement that compares an alphanumeric field with an alphanumeric literal is illustrated in Figure 5-9. Alphanumeric literals must be enclosed in single quotes, and the field included in the statement must be defined as alphanumeric. The test condition, or programmer's choice, will determine whether the literal is included in either Factor 1 or 2.

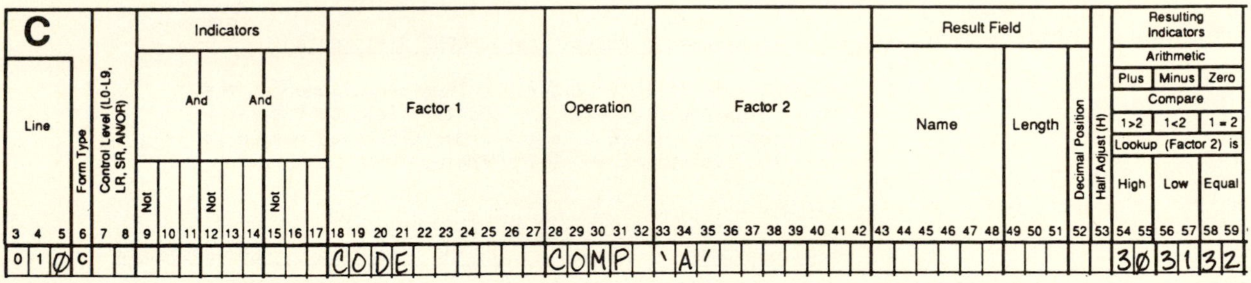

Values in Factor 1 and Factor 2:

	FACTOR 1	FACTOR 2	INDICATOR "ON"	CONDITION
Example 1	D	A	30	1 > 2
Example 2	D	T	31	1 < 2
Example 3	D	D	32	1 = 2

Figure 5-9 Comparison of an alphanumeric field with an alphnumeric literal.

All the characters supported by the *character set* of the related computer are valid for alphanumeric COMPares, whereas only the numbers 0 to 9 are valid for numeric comparisons when the fields and/or literal are defined as numeric. An application program that illustrates how the COMP statement is used in decision-making processes is detailed in the following sections.

APPLICATION PROGRAM—WEEKLY PAYROLL REPORT

Documentation

The specifications included in Figure 5-10 summarize the processing requirements for this example of an application program.

PROGRAM SPECIFICATIONS Page 1 of 1

Program Name WEEKLY PAYROLL RPT Program-ID CH5P1 Written By S. Myers

Purpose Generate a weekly payroll report Approved By The Boss

Input files (directory names):

DAT5P1 (stored on disk)

Output files (directory names):

PRINTER (stock paper)

Processing Narrative:

Write a structured RPG program to generate a weekly payroll report for day and night shift hourly employees.

<u>Input to the program</u>:

The data for each week's payroll information is stored on a disk file in the record format shown in the supplemental record layout form.

<u>Processing</u>:

Read the weekly payroll file consecutively and perform the following:

Step 1: Determine if the employee worked day or night shift. An additional 15% hourly rate bonus is added for nights.

Step 2: Convert minutes to hours. Any remainder less than 30 is considered .5 (1/2 hour) and if equal to or greater than 30 is processed as 1 hour.

Step 3: Compute regular pay as follows:
HOURLY RATE x HOURS WORKED = REGULAR PAY

Step 4: Determine if the employee worked overtime (over 35 hours).
HOURS WORKED - 35 = OVERTIME HOURS (if greater than 0)

Step 5: Compute overtime premium as follows:
HOURLY RATE/2 = OVERTIME PREMIUM RATE (rounded to 2 decimals)

Then:
OVERTIME HOURS x OVERTIME PREMIUM RATE = OVERTIME PAY

Step 6: Compute the employee's total week's pay as follows:
REGULAR PAY + OVERTIME PAY = TOTAL WEEK'S PAY

Step 7: Accumulate the hours worked, regular pay, overtime pay, and total pay amounts.

<u>Output</u>:

Complete the report detailed in the supplemental print chart.

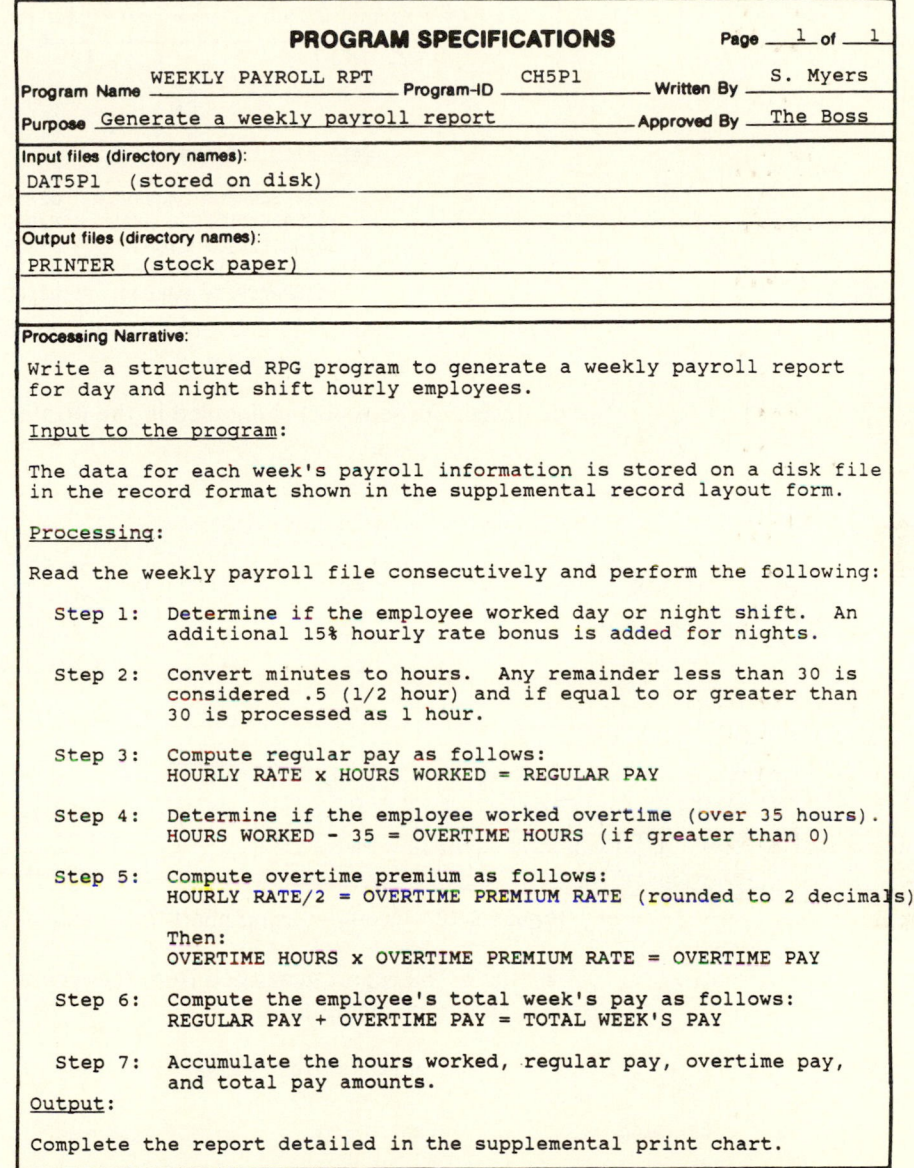

Figure 5-10 Specifications for weekly payroll report program.

The system flowchart shown in Figure 5-11 indicates that one data file stored on disk is input to the program and a printer file is output.

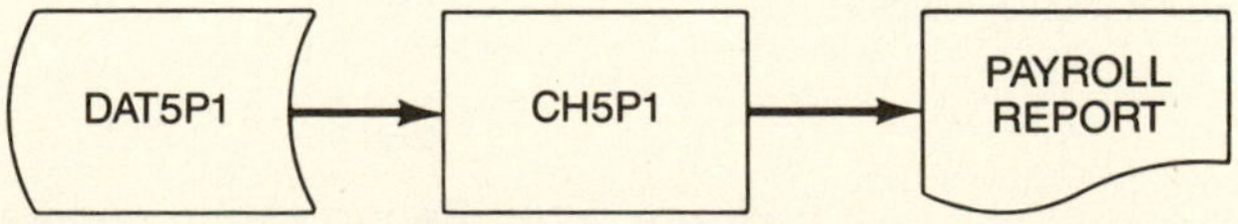

Figure 5-11 System flowchart for weekly payroll report program.

The format of the records in the input file and a listing of the input data file are illustrated in Figure 5-12.

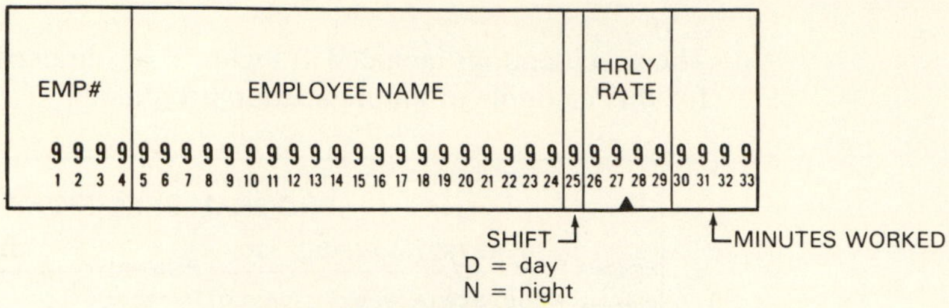

Data File Listing:

```
1234LEONARDO DA VINCI    D22502226
2345ALEXANDER G BELL     N20001800
3456ROBERT FULTON        D12752450
4567CHARLES GOODYEAR     N14252100
5678MARCHESE MARCONI     D15002130
```

Figure 5-12 Input record layout form and listing of data file for the weekly payroll report program.

The design of the report is detailed in the printer spacing chart in Figure 5-13.

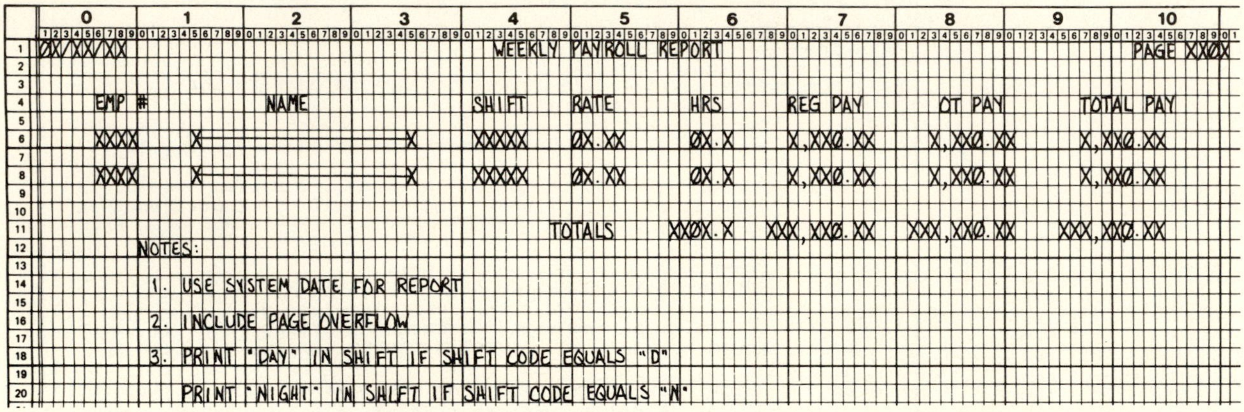

ØX/XX/XX
WEEKLY PAYROLL REPORT
PAGE XXØX
EMP #
NAME
SHIFT
RATE
HRS
REG PAY
OT PAY
TOTAL PAY
XXXX
XXXXX
ØX.XX
ØX.X
X,XXØ.XX
TOTALS
XXØX.X
XXX,XXØ.XX
NOTES:
1. USE SYSTEM DATE FOR REPORT
2. INCLUDE PAGE OVERFLOW
3. PRINT "DAY" IN SHIFT IF SHIFT CODE EQUALS "D"
PRINT "NIGHT" IN SHIFT IF SHIFT CODE EQUALS "N"

Figure 5-13 Printer spacing chart for weekly payroll report program.

A listing of the report generated from the weekly payroll report application program is shown in Figure 5-14.

```
10/14/92                          WEEKLY PAYROLL REPORT                              PAGE    1

   EMP #         NAME              SHIFT    RATE      HRS     REG PAY       OT PAY     TOTAL PAY

   1234     LEONARDO DA VINCI      DAY      22.50     37.5     843.75        28.13       871.88

   2345     ALEXANDER G BELL       NIGHT    23.00     30.0     690.00          .00       690.00

   3456     ROBERT FULTON          DAY      12.75     41.0     522.75        38.28       561.03

   4567     CHARLES GOODYEAR       NIGHT    16.38     35.0     573.30          .00       573.30

   5678     MARCHESE MARCONI       DAY      15.00     36.0     540.00         7.50       547.50

                                          TOTALS    179.5   3,169.80        73.91     3,243.71
```

Figure 5-14 Report listing generated from weekly payroll report program.

Source Coding for Weekly Payroll Report Program

A commented source listing of the program that generates a weekly payroll report is presented in Figure 5-15. The processing logic and each segment of the program are explained in supporting figures.

```
 * THIS PROGRAM GENERATES A WEEKLY PAYROLL REPORT FOR HOURLY EMPS     CH5P1
H                                                                    CH5P1
FDAT5P1  IP  F  33  33            DISK                               CH5P1
FPAYRPRT O   F 132 132    OF      PRINTER                            CH5P1
IDAT5P1  SM  01                                                      CH5P1
I                                        1   4 EMP#                  CH5P1
I                                        5  24 EMPNAM                CH5P1
I                                       25  25 SHIFT                 CH5P1
I                                       26  292HRRATE                CH5P1
I                                       30  330MINUTS                CH5P1
C                     SETOF                       101120TURN OFF IND.  CH5P1
C                     Z-ADDO         OTPAY              INIT. OTPAY  CH5P1
C           SHIFT     COMP 'D'                    10    > N SHIFT    CH5P1
C    10     HRRATE    MULT 1.15      HRRATE             NIGHT RATE   CH5P1
C           MINUTS    DIV  60        HRS     20         MINUTES TO HRS CH5P1
C                     MVR            REMAIN  20       11SAVE REMAINDER CH5P1
C    11               Z-ADDHRS       THRS    31         SAVE HRS     CH5P1
C   N11     REMAIN    COMP 30                     20  20TEST REM IF > 0CH5P1
 *                                                                   CH5P1
C    20     HRS       ADD  1         THRS               > = 30 MINUTES CH5P1
C   N20N11  HRS       ADD  .5        THRS               < 30 MINUTES CH5P1
C           THRS      MULT HRRATE    REGPAY  62         REGULAR PAY AMTCH5P1
 *                                                                   CH5P1
C           THRS      COMP 35                     20    HRS > 35?    CH5P1
C    20     THRS      SUB  35        OTHRS   31         OVERTIME HRS CH5P1
C    20     HRRATE    DIV  2         OTRATE  42H        OVERTIME RATE CH5P1
C    20     OTHRS     MULT OTRATE    OTPAY   62H        COMPUTE OT PAY CH5P1
 *                                                                   CH5P1
C           REGPAY    ADD  OTPAY     WEKPAY  62         REG + OT AMTS CH5P1
C           TOTHRS    ADD  THRS      TOTHRS  51         ACCUM TOT HRS CH5P1
C           TOTREG    ADD  REGPAY    TOTREG  82         ACCUM REG PAY CH5P1
C           TOTOT     ADD  OTPAY     TOTOT   82         ACCUM OT PAY CH5P1
C           TOTPAY    ADD  WEKPAY    TOTPAY  82         ACCUM TOTAL PAYCH5P1
OPAYRPRT H  3     1P                                                 CH5P1
O       OR        OF                                                 CH5P1
O                         UDATE Y    8                               CH5P1
O                                   64 'WEEKLY PAYROLL REPORT'       CH5P1
O                                  105 'PAGE'                        CH5P1
O                         PAGE  Z  110                               CH5P1
O        H  2     1P                                                 CH5P1
O       OR        OF                                                 CH5P1
O                                   10 'EMP #'                       CH5P1
O                                   25 'NAME'                        CH5P1
O                                   45 'SHIFT'                       CH5P1
O                                   53 'RATE'                        CH5P1
O                                   63 'HRS'                         CH5P1
O                                   76 'REG PAY'                     CH5P1
O                                   89 'OT PAY'                      CH5P1
O                                  105 'TOTAL PAY'                   CH5P1
O        D  2     01                                                 CH5P1
O                         EMP#       9                               CH5P1
O                         EMPNAM    34                               CH5P1
O                   N10             45 'DAY  '                       CH5P1
O                    10             45 'NIGHT'                       CH5P1
O                         HRRATE1   54                               CH5P1
O                         THRS  1   64                               CH5P1
O                         REGPAY1   77                               CH5P1
O                         OTPAY 1   90                               CH5P1
O                         WEKPAY1  104                               CH5P1
O        T 1      LR                                                 CH5P1
O                                   53 'TOTALS'                      CH5P1
O                         TOTHRS1   64                               CH5P1
O                         TOTREG1   77                               CH5P1
O                         TOTOT 1   90                               CH5P1
O                         TOTPAY1  104                               CH5P1
```

Figure 5-15 Source listing of the weekly payroll report program.

A processing logic flowchart that details each statement in the Calculation Specifications is presented in Figure 5-16. Notice that the *branching* around of one or more calculation instructions represents indicator control. If a related test condition (decision symbol in the flowchart) is true (Resulting Indicator turned on), one of two actions is performed. Either the next consecutive instruction is executed or it is ignored during the processing cycle. All the instructions in the Calculation Specifications are read in a consecutive order. If a statement is conditioned by an indicator, the status of the indicator (*on* or *off*) determines whether it is executed.

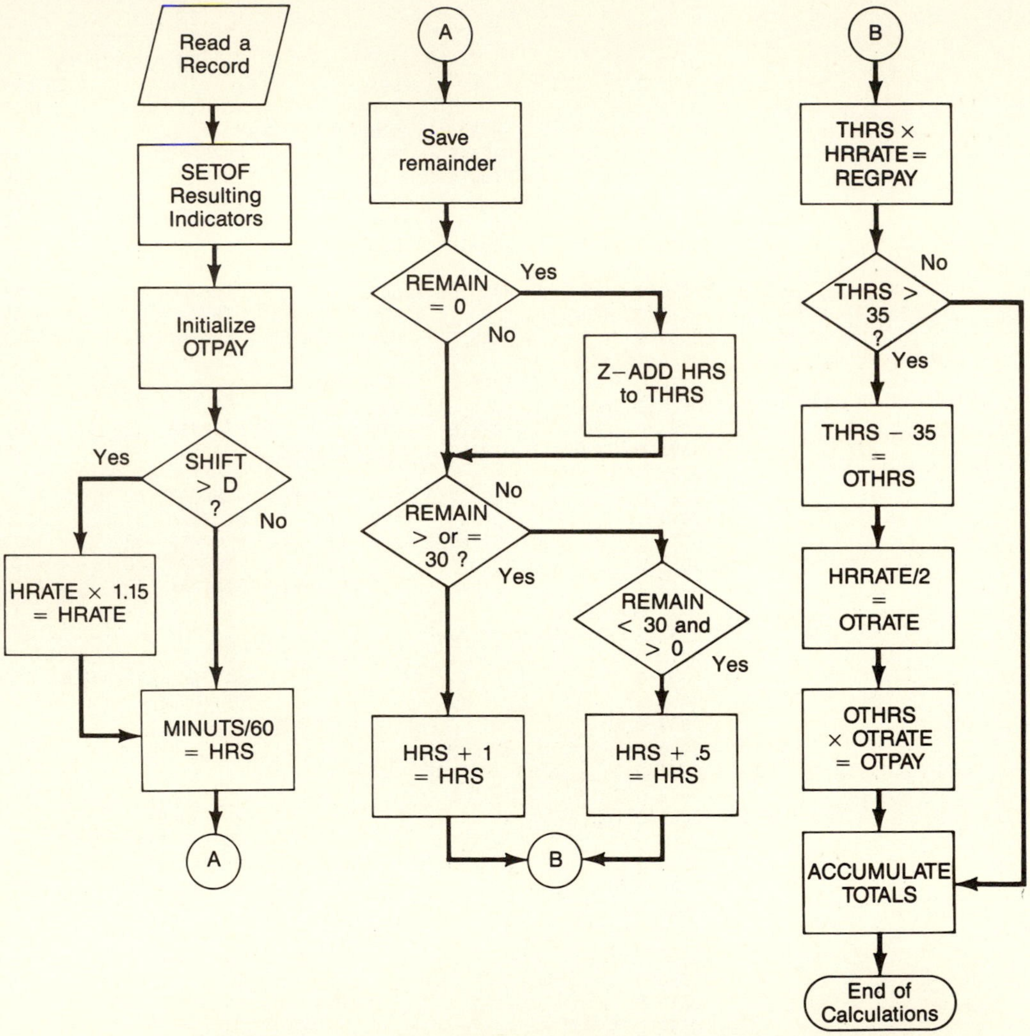

Figure 5-16 Processing logic flowchart of the calculation specifications for weekly payroll report program.

A line-by-line analysis of the results of each calculation instruction executed for the first record processed (EMP# 1234) is detailed in Figure 5-17. The example is for a day-shift employee with overtime hours (over 35 hours). Because lines 14, 17, and 20 are conditioned by indicators not turned on by this record (i.e., SHIFT = N, REMAIN = 0, REMAIN > or = 30), they are not executed. Furthermore, you should notice that many of the instructions are not conditioned by an indicator and will be executed for every record processed.

```
Value of first record processed:

                          Shift----+     +---Hrly Rate
                                   |    /  +-Minutes Worked
                                   |   /  /
1234LEONARDO DA VINCI              D22502226

                                                              Value in items after execution        Indicators(s)
                                                              Factor 1    Factor 2    Result Field    On
... ... 1 ... ... 2 ... ... 3 ... ... 4 ... ... 5 ... ... 6
0011 C                    SETOF               101120                                                 01
0012 C                    Z-ADDO      OTPAY                                           000000         01
0013 C          SHIFT     COMP 'D'            10             D           D                           01
0014 C  10      HRRATE    MULT 1.15   HRRATE                                                         01
0015 C          MINUTS    DIV  60     HRS                    2226        60           37             01
0016 C                    MVR         REMAIN     11                                   06             01
0017 C  11                Z-ADDHRS    THRS                                                           01
0018 C  N11     REMAIN    COMP 30             20 20          06          30                          01
0019 C*
0020 C  20      HRS       ADD  1      THRS                                                           01
0021 C  N20N11  HRS       ADD  .5     THRS                   37          5            375            01
0022 C          THRS      MULT HRRATE REGPAY                 375         2250         084375         01
0023 C*
0024 C          THRS      COMP 35             20             375         35                          01 20
0025 C  20      THRS      SUB  35     OTHRS                  375         35           025            01 20
0026 C  20      HRRATE    DIV  2      OTRATE                 2250        2            1125           01 20
0027 C  20      OTHRS     MULT OTRATE OTPAY                  025         1125         002813         01 20
0028 C*
0029 C          REGPAY    ADD  OTPAY  WEKPAY                 084375      002813       087188         01 20
0030 C          TOTHRS    ADD  THRS   TOTHRS                 00000       375          00375          01 20
0031 C          TOTREG    ADD  REGPAY TOTREG                 00000000    084375       00084375       01 20
0032 C          TOTOT     ADD  OTPAY  TOTOT                  00000000    002813       00002813       01 20
0033 C          TOTPAY    ADD  WEKPAY TOTPAY                 00000000    087188       00087188       01 20

Note: 01 is Record Identifying Indicator that turns on automatically when a record is read
```

Figure 5-17 Calculation instructions and results when a record for a day-shift employee with overtime hours is processed.

When there is only one record type in a file, it is not necessary and is inefficient to condition every instruction with a Record Identifying Indicator. As was mentioned before, the indiscriminant use of indicators should be avoided.

The accumulator fields on lines 29 through 33 are executed for every record processed, and the values are printed when LR is turned on when the end of the input file is sensed.

SUMMARY OF COMP OPERATION

The COMP operation with at least one Resulting Indicator entered in the >, <, or = field(s) controls a decision-making function in the calculation and/or output specifications instructions. Fields or literals specified in Factor 1 and Factor 2 must be the same type (alphanumeric or numeric), or a terminal error will be generated during program compilation. Because the COMP operation does not support branching, the next consecutive instruction will always be tested and then executed if it is not conditioned by an indicator or if the conditioning indicator(s) is on.

BRANCHING AND LOOPING

Branching

Branching may be defined as the transfer of control to a previous or to a subsequent instruction not immediately following the one executed. Branching is controlled in an RPG program by the GOTO and TAG operations. The syntax for these operations is detailed in Figure 5-18.

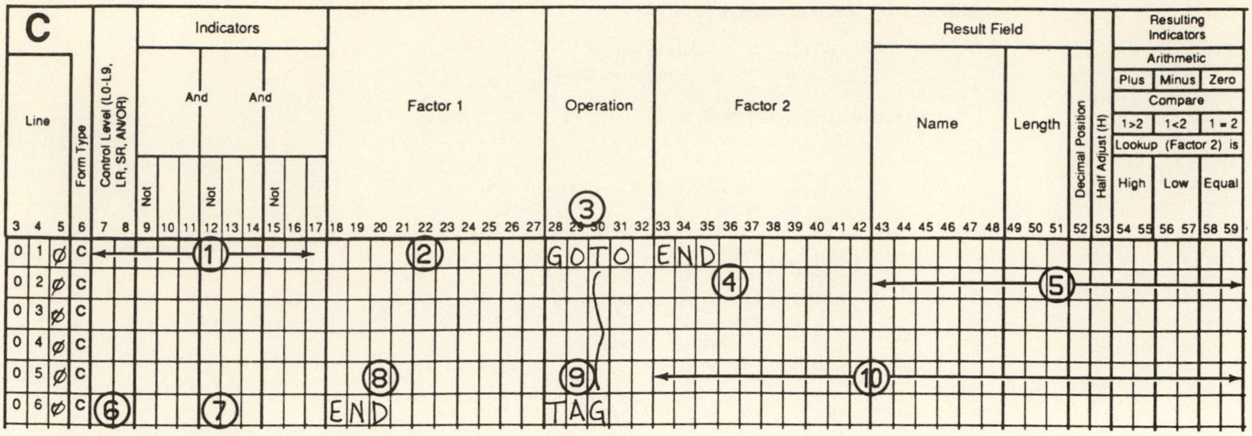

GOTO Operation Syntax Rules:

1. Total or detail time indicators may be used to condition a GOTO operation. If one or more indicators are specified, the instruction is referred to as a conditional GOTO. If no indicator control is included, the statement is called an unconditional GOTO.

2. Factor 1 is not used.

3. GOTO operation name must be left-justified in Operation field.

4. Factor 2 entry must be left-justified and a programmer-supplied name that meets RPG field naming convention requirements.

5. Other fields are not used.

TAG Operation Syntax Rules:

6. Control level indicators (L0-L9 and LR), entered in columns 7-8, may be specified with a TAG statement

7. Detail time indicators (columns 9-17) are not permitted.

8. Factor 1 entry must begin in column 18 and be identical to the Factor 2 entry of the related GOTO statement.

9. TAG operation name must be left-justified in the Operation field.

10. Other fields are not used.

Figure 5-18 RPG syntax for the GOTO and TAG operations.

More than one GOTO statement may reference the same TAG operation name (Factor 2 entry). However, each TAG statement must be specified with a different name (Factor 1 entry) and relate to at least one GOTO statement. The program's logic will determine whether a TAG statement is placed before or after the related GOTO statement(s).

The processing features and restrictions of the GOTO/TAG operations are explained in Figure 5-19.

Conditional and Unconditional GOTO Statements

Depending on the program logic, a GOTO statement may be *conditional* (specified with one or more conditioning indicators—columns 7 to 17) or *unconditional* (no conditioning indicators specified). The flowchart and supplemental RPG coding in Figure 5-20 illustrates the processing and syntax of a *conditional* GOTO statement.

<u>A GOTO Operation may specify a branch</u>:

1. To a previous or following operation.
2. From a detail time calculation instruction to another detail time calculation instruction.
3. From a total time calculation instruction to another total time calculation instruction.
4. Within an internal subroutine.

<u>However, a GOTO Operation may not be specified</u>:

1. From a detail time calculation instruction to a total time calculation instruction.
2. From total time calculations conditioned by L0-L9 to total time calculations conditioned by LR.
3. From an internal subroutine to a calculation instruction outside of the routine or vice versa.

Figure 5-19 Processing features and restrictions of the GOTO/TAG operations.

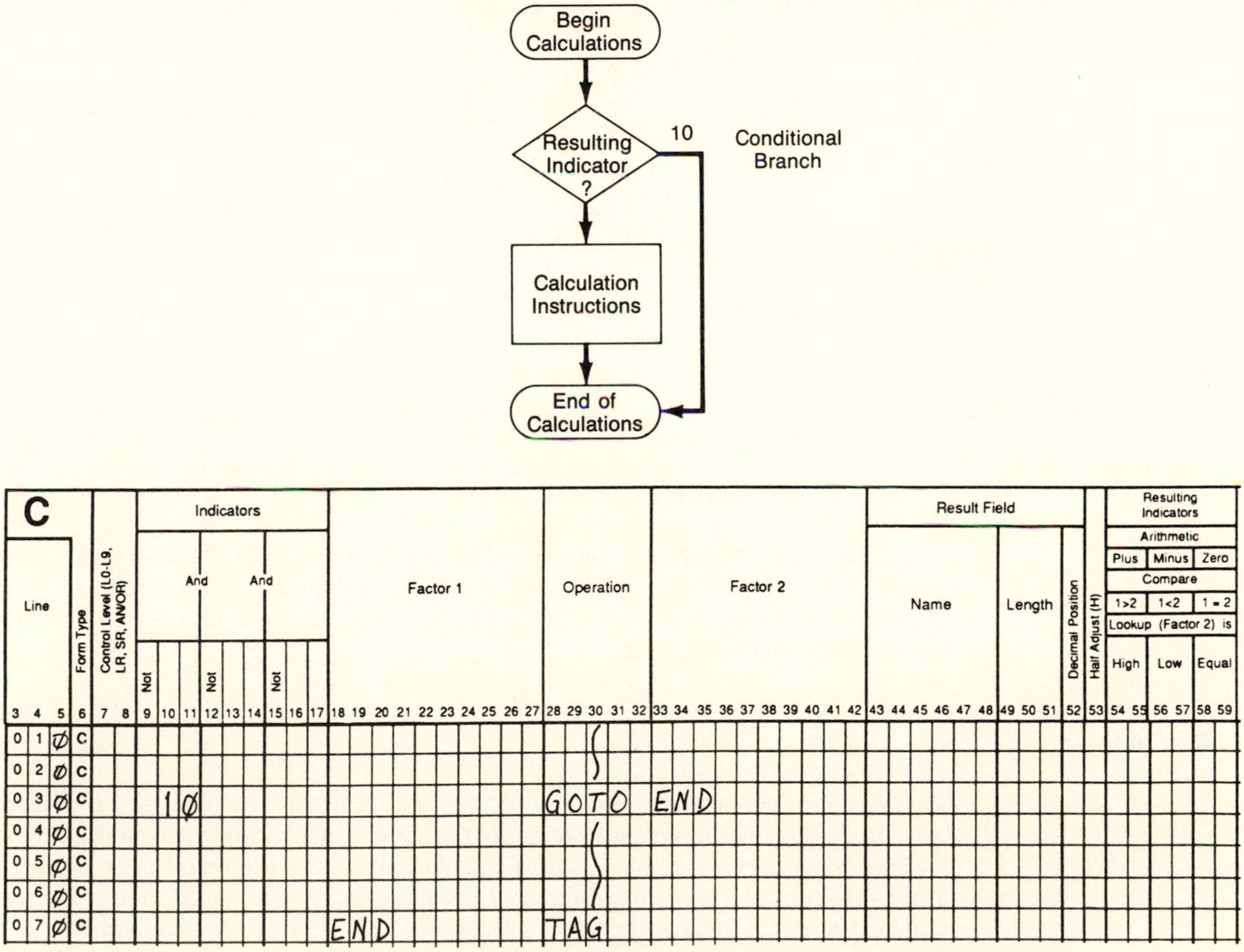

Figure 5-20 Processing logic and related RPG syntax for a conditional GOTO statement.

Both an unconditional and a conditional GOTO statement are included in the flowchart and RPG coding in Figure 5-21.

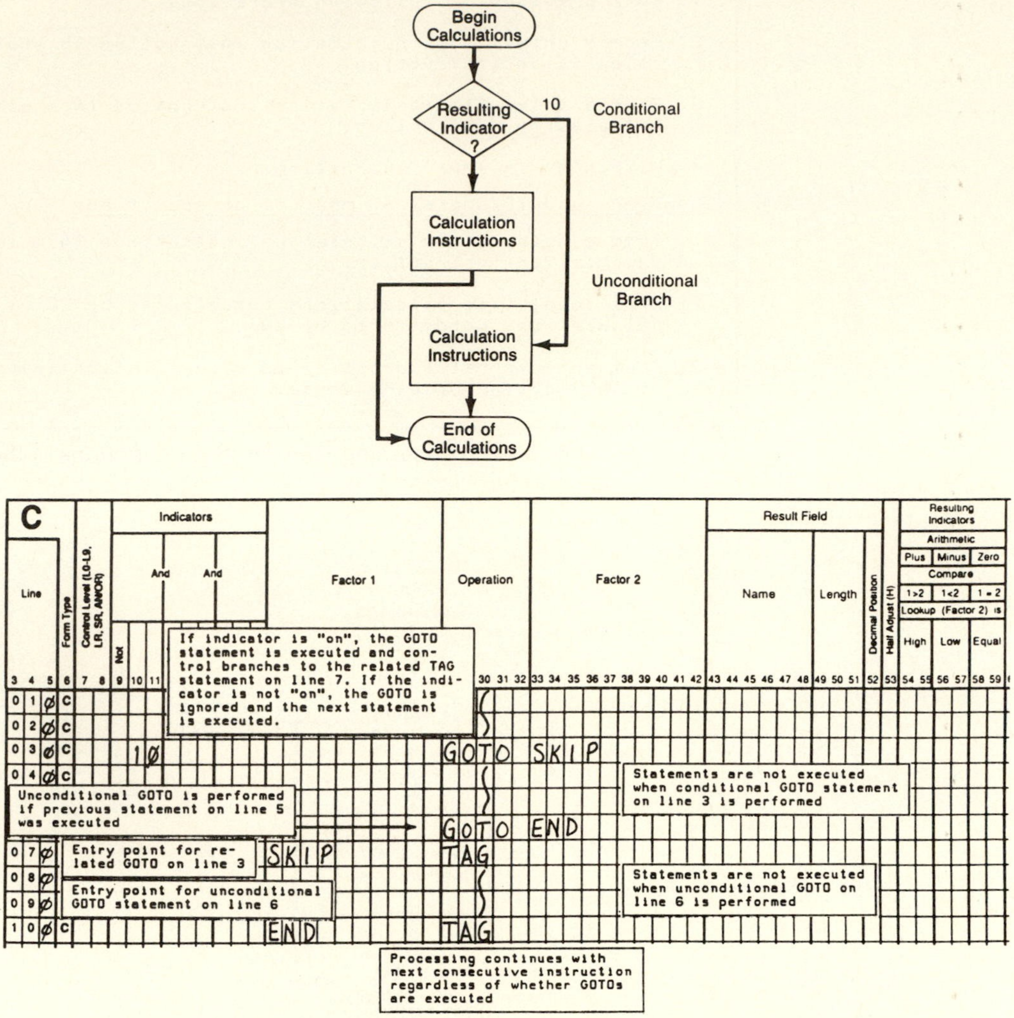

Figure 5-21 Processing logic and related RPG syntax for an unconditional GOTO statement.

The GOTO examples shown in Figures 5-20 and 5-21 illustrated the "forward" branching of program control. A GOTO statement may pass control back to a previously defined TAG statement. This processing logic will be explained in the following paragraphs.

LOOPING

Looping in a computer program is defined as the branching of program control to a preceding instruction and executing the same instructions one or more times. This process is required for *iterative* calculations where the result is determined after repeating the same instructions a predetermined number of times. Typical applications that require iterative processing are the raising of a number to a power, compound interest computation, mortgage payment calculations, depreciation of an asset, and so forth.

An application that raises any number to any power is presented in Figure 5-22 to illustrate how looping is controlled in an RPG program. The figure details

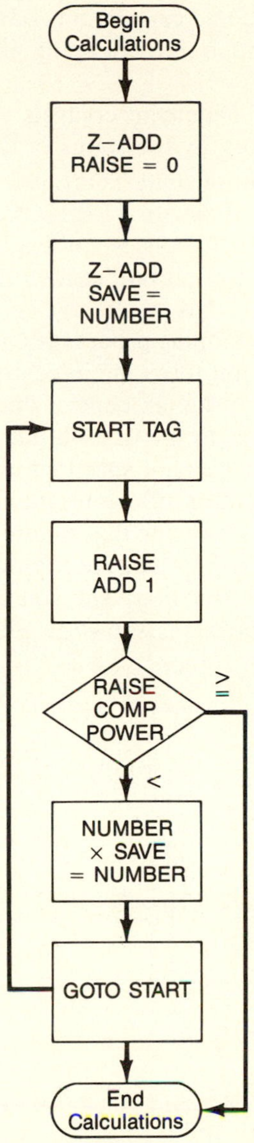

Line (3–5)	Form Type (6)	Control Level (L0-L9, LR, SR, AN/OR) (7–8)	Indicators (9–17)	Factor 1 (18–27)	Operation (28–32)	Factor 2 (33–42)	Result Field Name (43–48)	Length (49–51)	Decimal Position (52)	Half Adjust (H) (53)	Resulting Indicators High / Plus / 1>2 (54–55)	Low / Minus / 1<2 (56–57)	Equal / Zero / 1=2 (58–59)
01Ø	C				Z-ADD	Ø	RAISE	3	Ø				
02Ø	C				Z-ADD	NUMBER	SAVE	4	Ø				
03Ø	C			START	TAG								
04Ø	C			RAISE	ADD	1	RAISE						
05Ø	C			RAISE	COMP	POWER						12	
06Ø	C		12	NUMBER	MULT	SAVE	NUMBER						
07Ø	C		12		GOTO	START							

Figure 5-22 Processing logic and related calculation coding for a program that raises any number to any power.

the processing logic and calculation coding for this function. Notice the following coding features unique to the looping process:

1. A COMP statement controls whether the loop (GOTO statement) will be executed by the status of Resulting Indicator 12.
2. The conditional GOTO transfers control back to the TAG statement if Resulting Indicator 12 is on. When 12 is not on (i.e., when the value in the counter RAISE is *not less* than the value in POWER), control "falls through" to first output instruction and the detail line is printed.

Exit from the looping process is controlled by Resulting Indicator 12. When the COMP instruction turns the indicator on, the GOTO is performed; however, when 12 is not on, program control does not execute the GOTO statement and processing continues to the first output instruction.

If an indicator was not specified with the GOTO statement, an *infinite loop* would result. Execution of the program would have to be cancelled at the operator's console to terminate this condition. This is a common programming error that is usually caused by not specifying a conditional GOTO instruction for an iterative processing function. The source listing of the powers program and the printed report generated is shown in Figure 5-23.

Source Listing:

```
     ... ... 1 ... ... 2 ... ... 3 ... ... 4 ... ... 5 ... ... 6 ... ... 7 ...
0001 H                                                                  CH5P1
0002 FDATA5P1 IP  F  80  80            DISK                             CH5P1
0003 FPOWERS  O   F 132 132            PRINTER                          CH5P1
0004 IDATA5P1 SM  01                                                    CH5P1
0005 I                                       1   40NUMBER               CH5P1
0006 I                                       5   70POWER                CH5P1
0007 C                      Z-ADD0        RAISE   30       SET COUNTER     CH5P1
0008 C                      Z-ADDNUMBER   SAVE    30       SET MULTIPLIER CH5P1
0009 C            START     TAG                            ENTRY FOR LOOP CH5P1
0010 C            RAISE     ADD  1        RAISE            INCREMENT CTR  CH5P1
0011 C            RAISE     COMP POWER                 12  RAISE < POWER? CH5P1
     C    12      NUMBER    MULT SAVE     NUMBER           NEXT POWER     CH5P1
     C -->12                GOTO START                     LOOP TO LINE 10CH5P1
     OPOWERS  H   06    1P                                              CH5P1
     O        D 2       01                                              CH5P1
     O                          SAVE  Z  10                             CH5P1
     O                                   24 'RAISED TO THE'             CH5P1
     O                          POWER Z  28                             CH5P1
0019 O                                   37 'POWER IS'                  CH5P1
0020 O                          NUMBERZ  46                             CH5P1
```

GOTO is executed only if indicator 12 is "on". If the indicator was not specified, an infinite loop would occur.

Printed Report:

```
12 RAISED TO THE   2 POWER IS        144
 2 RAISED TO THE  20 POWER IS       8576
16 RAISED TO THE   3 POWER IS       4096
 9 RAISED TO THE   4 POWER IS       6561
```

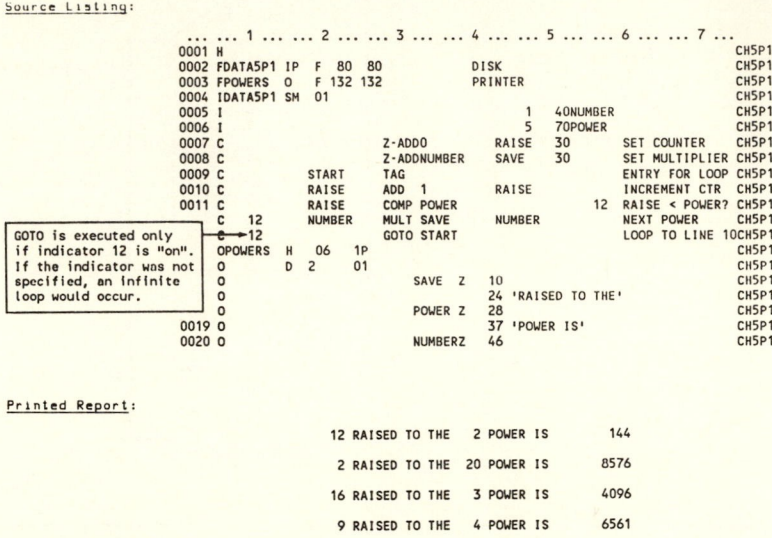

Figure 5-23 Source listing of the powers program and printed report generated.

Summary of GOTO/TAG Operations

Branching in RPG programs is controlled by the GOTO/TAG operations. Any number of GOTO statements may be related to one TAG instruction. Each TAG must be unique, however. A *conditional* GOTO statement is specified with one or more indicators (columns 7–19). An *unconditional* GOTO does not include any indicators.

Looping is a form of branching that is required in iterative processing—for example, raising a number to a power, compound interest computations, and so forth. The same instructions are executed more than once in a looping procedure. GOTO statements used to control looping are usually conditioned by one or more indicators to prevent an *infinite* loop from occurring. When an infinite loop occurs, program execution may have to be cancelled from the operator's console.

APPLICATION PROGRAM—COMPOUND INTEREST COMPUTATION

An application program that computes the daily compound interest of a principal amount is presented to reinforce the use of the COMP and GOTO/TAG operations and looping control. When interest is computed on the sum of the principal and the accumulated interest, it is called compound interest. The mathematics of compound interest is illustrated in Figure 5-24.

```
Problem:

     Calculate the amount of interest produced by $100 with
interest at 6% compounded annually for four years.

Solution:

      $100 X 6% = $   6.00  First year's interest
                  +100.00  Principal
                  $106.00  Balance - end of first year
      $106 X 6% = +   6.36  Second year's interest
                  $112.36  Balance - end of second year
   $112.36 X 6% = +   6.74  Third year's interest
                  $119.10  Balance - end of third year
   $119.10 X 6% = +   7.15  Fourth year's interest
                  $126.25  Balance - end of fourth year
                  -100.00  Balance at beginning
                  $ 26.25  Amount of compound interest
```

Figure 5-24 Mathematics of compound interest.

The step-by-step procedures shown in Figure 5-24 for computing the compound interest earned on a principal amount are controlled by the formula included in the program specifications in Figure 5-25. Because $(1 + i)^n$ is raised to the value of n, a looping procedure is required in the program.

PROGRAM SPECIFICATIONS Page 1 of 1

Program Name COMPOUND INTEREST RPT Program-ID CH5P2 Written By S. Myers

Purpose Report of interest on depositor's CDs Approved By The Boss

Input files (directory names):

DAT5P2 (stored on disk)

Output files (directory names):

PRINTER (stock paper)

Processing Narrative:

```
Write a structured RPG program to calculate the compound interest
earned on depositor's certificate of deposit and generate the report
detailed in the supplemental printer spacing chart.

Input to the program:
The data file, DATAP2, is stored on disk in the format shown in the
supplemental record layout form.

Processing:
Write the calculations for the following compound interest formula:
               n
   a = (i + 1)     Where:  a = Compound amount of $1
                           i = Annual interest rate (must be divided
                               by 365 or 366 for daily rate)
                           n = Number of interest periods

Step 1:   Compute the daily rate by dividing the annual rate by 365.

Step 2:   Add 1 to the daily rate computed in Step 1.

Step 3:   Save the result from Step 2 by moving it to another field.

Step 4:   Increment a counter and compare it with the number of inter-
          est periods input.  If the value in the counter is less than
          n, multiply the result field from Step 3 by the result field
          computed in Step 2 and store in the Step 3 field.  Loop and
          repeat this iterative process until the value in the counter
          is equal to the value of n.

Step 5:   After exit from the looping sequence, multiply the principal
          (input) by the compound amount of the $1 factor computed in
          Step 4 to determine the compound amount of the related prin-
          cipal.

Step 6:   Subtract the principal from the compound amount (Step 5) to
          determine the compound interest earened.

Step 7:   Multiply the daily and annual interest rates by 100 for the
          printing of the percent formats.
```

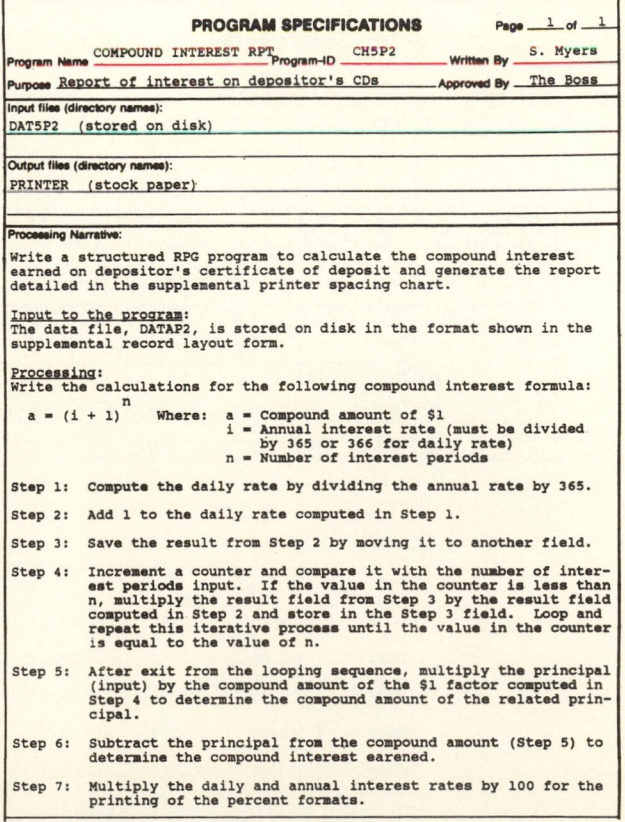

Figure 5-25 Specifications for compound interest report program.

The system flowchart in Figure 5-26 identifies the input and files processed by the compound interest report program.

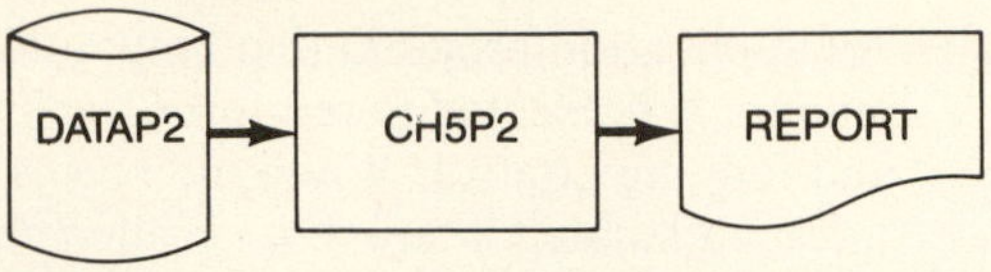

Figure 5-26 Systems flowchart for compound interest report application program.

The design of the records in the input file and a listing of the data are shown in Figure 5-27.

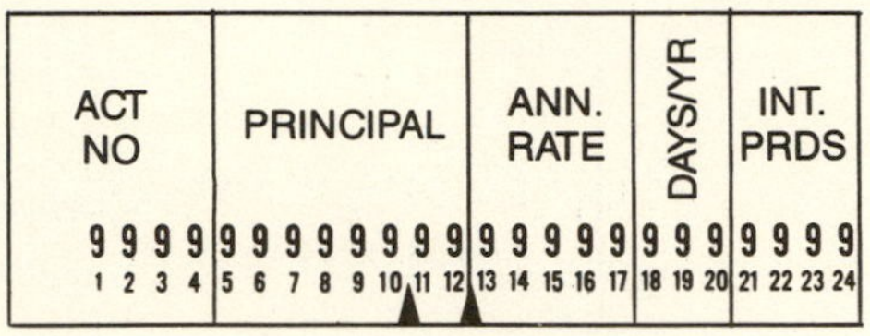

Data File Listing:

```
100000100000100003650365
200000100000100003650180
300000100000065003650365
400000100000065003650180
```

Figure 5-27 Design of the records in the input file and a listing of the data.

A printer spacing chart that details the report format is presented in Figure 5-28 with the report generated by the program.

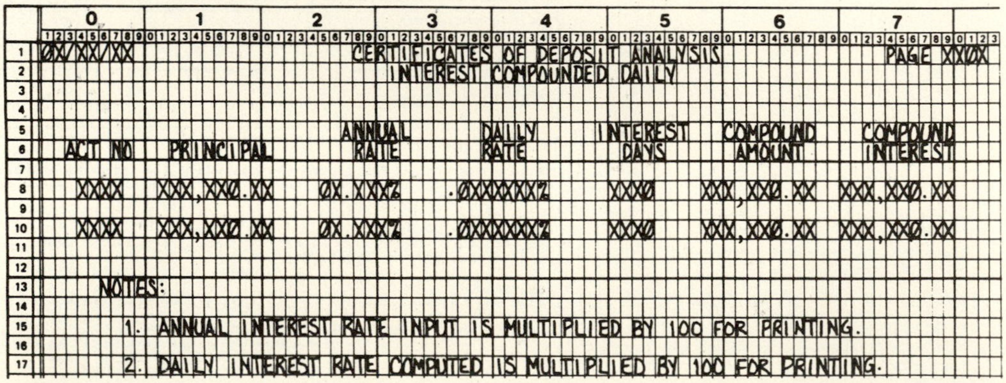


```
11/30/92                CERTIFICATES OF DEPOSIT ANALYSIS                PAGE    1
                           INTEREST COMPOUNDED DAILY

                         ANNUAL       DAILY      INTEREST    COMPOUND     COMPOUND
 ACT NO    PRINCIPAL      RATE         RATE        DAYS       AMOUNT      INTEREST

  1000      1,000.00    10.000%    .0273972%       365       1,105.16      105.16

  2000      1,000.00    10.000%    .0273972%       180       1,050.54       50.54

  3000      1,000.00     6.500%    .0178082%       365       1,067.15       67.15

  4000      1,000.00     6.500%    .0178082%       180       1,032.57       32.57
```

Figure 5-28 Report format and output generated by the compound interest program.

Source Coding for Compound Interest Program

A source listing of the compound interest program is detailed in Figure 5-29. Comments are included in the right-hand area of the calculation instructions to support the coding logic.

```
... ... 1 ... ... 2 ... ... 3 ... ... 4 ... ... 5 ... ... 6 ... ... 7 ...
H                                                                      CH5P2
FDATAP2  IP  F  24  24            DISK                                 CH5P2
FREPORT  O   F 132 132            PRINTER                              CH5P2
IDATAP2  SM  01                                                        CH5P2
I                                         1   4 ACCT#                  CH5P2
I                                         5  122PRINPL                 CH5P2
I                                        13  1751                      CH5P2
I                                        18  200YRDAYS                 CH5P2
I                                        21  240N                      CH5P2
C                          Z-ADD0      CTR     40         SET COUNTER  CH5P2
C                I         DIV  YRDAYS DARATE  99          DAILY RATE  CH5P2
C                DARATE    ADD  1      FACTOR 109         (1 + I)      CH5P2
C                          Z-ADDFACTOR HOLD   109         SAVE FACTOR  CH5P2
C                LOOP      TAG                            ENTRY FOR GOTO CH5P2
C                CTR       ADD  1      CTR                LOOP COUNTER CH5P2
C                CTR       COMP N                       90 CTR < N?    CH5P2
C   90           HOLD      MULT FACTOR HOLD               IF < MULTIPLY CH5P2
C   90                     GOTO LOOP                      IF < LOOP    CH5P2
C                PRINPL    MULT HOLD   CMPAMT  82H        COMPOUND AMT CH5P2
C                CMPAMT    SUB  PRINPL CH5P2  82          COMPOUND INT. CH5P2
C                DARATE    MULT 100    DAPCT   87         DAILY PCT    CH5P2
C                I         MULT 100    ANPCT   53         ANNUAL PCT   CH5P2
OREPORT  H  101   1P                                                   CH5P2
O                              UDATE Y    8                            CH5P2
O                                        49 'CERTIFICATES OF DEPOSIT'  CH5P2
O                                        58 'ANALYSIS'                 CH5P2
O                                        77 'PAGE'                     CH5P2
O                              PAGE  Z   82                            CH5P2
O        H  2     1P                                                   CH5P2
O                                        48 'INTEREST COMPOUNDED'      CH5P2
O                                        54 'DAILY'                    CH5P2
O        H  1     1P                                                   CH5P2
O                                        42 'ANNUAL      DAILY'        CH5P2
O                                        67 'INTEREST    COMPOUND'     CH5P2
O                                        79 'COMPOUND'                 CH5P2
O        H  2     1P                                                   CH5P2
O                                        20 'ACT NO   PRINCIPAL'       CH5P2
O                                        41 'RATE        RATE'         CH5P2
O                                        66 '  DAYS        AMOUNT'     CH5P2
O                                        79 'INTEREST'                 CH5P2
O        D  2     01                                                   CH5P2
O                              ACCT#      7                            CH5P2
O                              PRINPL1   20                            CH5P2
O                              ANPCT     31 '0 .   %'                  CH5P2
O                              DAPCT     43 '0.       %'               CH5P2
O                              N     Z   52                            CH5P2
O                              CMPAMT1   67                            CH5P2
O                              CMPINT1   79                            CH5P2
```

Figure 5-29 Source listing of compound interest program.

Calculation Coding Processing Logic and Syntax

The processing logic for the calculations specified in the compound interest program is identified in the flowchart in Figure 5-30. Also included at the bottom of the figure are the related instructions.

A line-by-line analysis of each calculation instruction after the looping is completed (i.e., the counter is equal to the number of interest periods) for the first record processed is detailed in Figure 5-31.

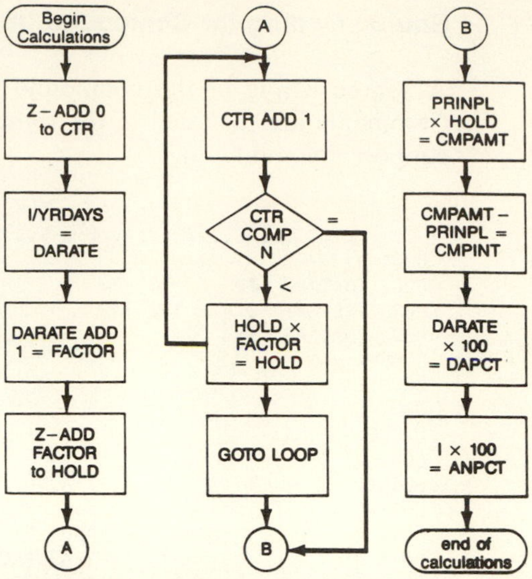

Line	Form Type	Control Level	Indicators	Factor 1	Operation	Factor 2	Result Field Name	Length	Decimal Position	Half Adjust (H)	Resulting Indicators: High	Low	Equal
01Ø	C				Z-ADDØ		CTR	4	Ø				
02Ø	C			I	DIV	YRDAYS	DARATE	9	9				
03Ø	C			DARATE	ADD	1	FACTOR	10	9				
04Ø	C				Z-ADD	FACTOR	HOLD	10	9				
05Ø	C			LOOP	TAG								
06Ø	C			CTR	ADD	1	CTR						
07Ø	C			CTR	COMP	N						9Ø	
08Ø	C		9Ø	HOLD	MULT	FACTOR	HOLD						
09Ø	C		9Ø		GOTO	LOOP							
10Ø	C			PRINPL	MULT	HOLD	CMPAMT	8	2	H			
11Ø	C			CMPAMT	SUB	PRINPL	CMPINT	8	2				
12Ø	C			DARATE	MULT	1ØØ	DAPCT	8	7				
13Ø	C			I	MULT	1ØØ	ANPCT	5	3				

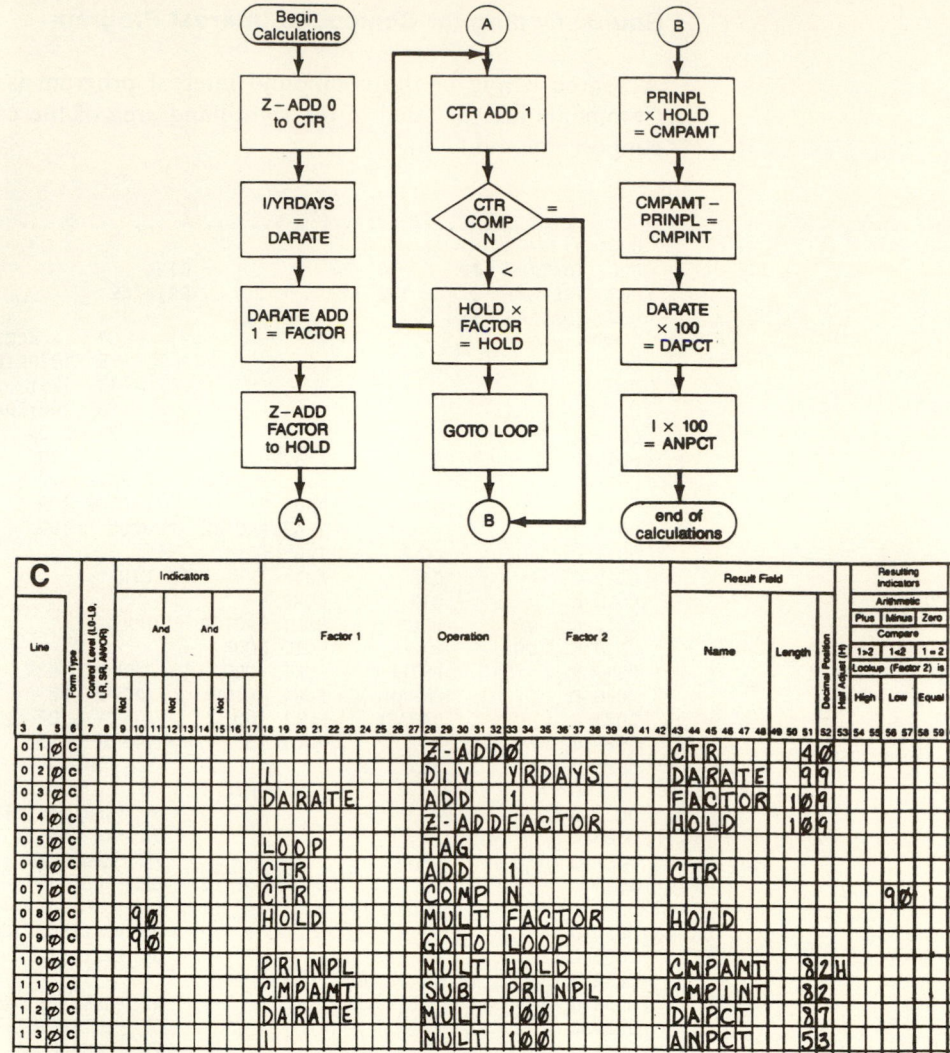

Figure 5-30 Processing logic flowchart and related calculations for compound interest program.

... ... 1 ... ... 2 ... ... 3 ... ... 4 ... ... 5 6	Value in items after execution: Factor 1	Factor 2	Result Field	Indicator(s) On
0010 C Z-ADDO CTR 40		0	0000	01
0011 C I DIV YRDAYS DARATE 99	10000	365	000273972	01
0012 C DARATE ADD 1 FACTOR 109	000273972	1	1000273972	01
0013 C Z-ADDFACTOR HOLD 109		1000273972	1000273972	01
0014 C LOOP TAG				01
0015 C CTR ADD 1 CTR	0365	1	0365	01
0016 C CTR COMP N 90	0366	365		01
0017 C 90 HOLD MULT FACTOR HOLD	1105155355	1000273972	1105155355	01
0018 C 90 GOTO LOOP				01
0019 C PRINPL MULT HOLD CMPAMT 82H	00100000	1105155355	00110516	01
0020 C CMPAMT SUB PRINPL CMPINT 82	00110516	00100000	00010516	01
0021 C DARATE MULT 100 DAPCT 87	000273972	100	0273972	01
0022 C I MULT 100 ANPCT 53	10000	100	10000	01

Figure 5-31 Line-by-line analysis of the calculation instructions after looping is completed for first record processed by compound interest program.

RPG III LANGUAGE ENHANCEMENT

CABxx Operation (Compare and Branch)

The CABxx operation is an RPG III enhancement that replaces the COMP and GOTO operation combination required to control conditional branching and looping. Advantages of this operation are the following:

1. One operation (CABxx) replaces two operations (COMP and GOTO).
2. Resulting Indicator tests (>, <, =) required with a COMP operation are eliminated.
3. Conditioning indicator(s) that control a conditional GOTO operation are eliminated.

The syntax related to the CABxx operation is explained in Figure 5-32.

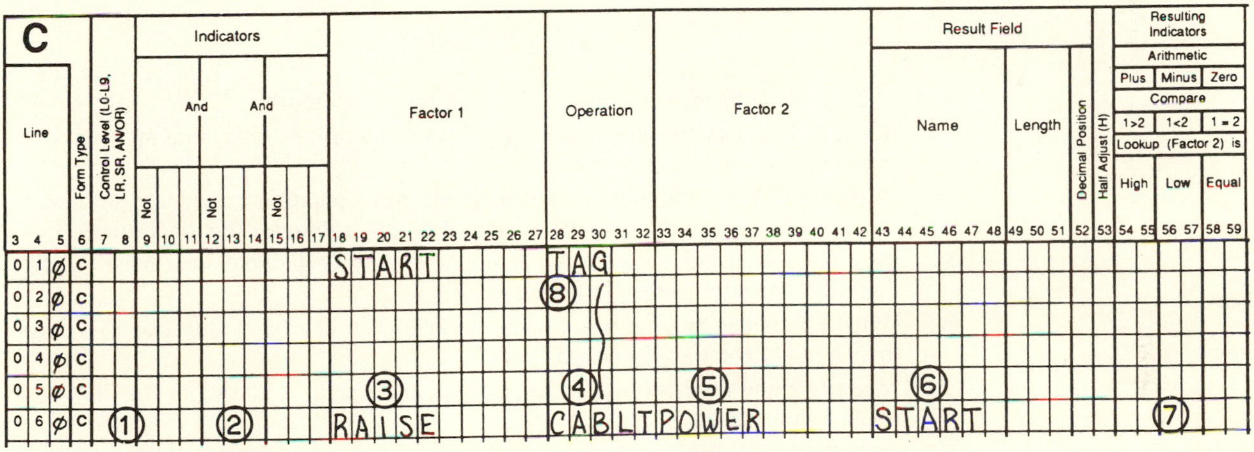

1. Indicator usage here is optional.

2. Indicator usage here is optional.

3. Factor 1 must contain an alphanumeric or numeric field or literal. Must be same type field or literal as included in Factor 2.

4. The CABxx operation takes the place of a separate COMP and GOTO. Both functions are performed with this operation. The xx in the CAB operation may have the following entries.
   - GT Factor 1 value greater than Factor 2 value.
   - LT Factor 1 value less than Factor 2 value.
   - EQ Factor 1 value is equal to Factor 2 value.
   - NE Factor 1 value is not equal to Factor 2 value.
   - GE Factor 1 value is greater than or equal to Factor 2 value.
   - LE Factor 1 value is less than or equal to Factor 2 value.

   In the example shown above, the value in RAISE is compared to the value in POWER; if less, then program control will branch to line 010. When values are equal, control will transfer to any instruction on line 060. The CABxx does not control looping: therefore, provision must be made in the instructions for an exit from the loop. Figure 5-33 illustrates how this operation is used for a branch and looping.

5. Factor 2 must contain an alphanumeric or numeric field or literal. Must be same type as the field or literal as included in Factor 1.

6. Name of TAG must be used in this field.

7. Indicator usage here is optional.

8. Entry instruction (TAG) for CABLT.

Figure 5-32 CABxx operation syntax rules.

The raising of a number to any power program previously presented with COMP and GOTO operations control has been modified in Figure 5-33 with the CABLT operation. Notice the absence of any *resulting* or *conditioning* indicators in calculations.

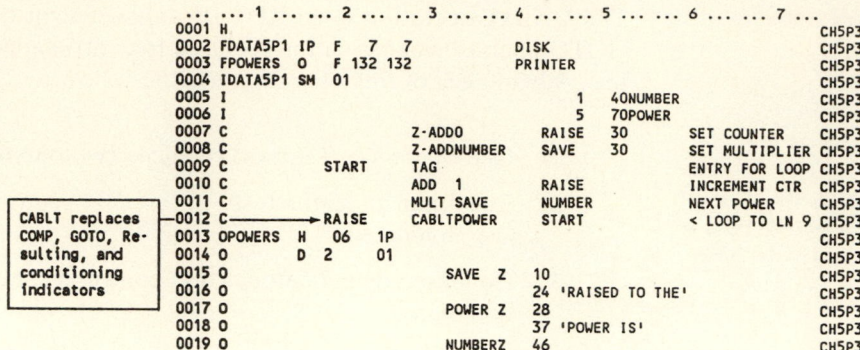

```
... ... 1 ... ... 2 ... ... 3 ... ... 4 ... ... 5 ... ... 6 ... ... 7 ...
0001 H                                                                 CH5P3
0002 FDATA5P1 IP  F   7   7              DISK                          CH5P3
0003 FPOWERS  O   F 132 132              PRINTER                       CH5P3
0004 IDATA5P1 SM  01                                                   CH5P3
0005 I                                           1   40NUMBER          CH5P3
0006 I                                           5   70POWER           CH5P3
0007 C                        Z-ADDO        RAISE   30      SET COUNTER     CH5P3
0008 C                        Z-ADDNUMBER   SAVE    30      SET MULTIPLIER  CH5P3
0009 C              START     TAG                           ENTRY FOR LOOP  CH5P3
0010 C                        ADD  1        RAISE           INCREMENT CTR   CH5P3
0011 C                        MULT SAVE     NUMBER          NEXT POWER      CH5P3
0012 C──────────────►RAISE    CABLTPOWER    START           < LOOP TO LN 9  CH5P3
0013 OPOWERS  H   06    1P                                             CH5P3
0014 O        D  2      01                                             CH5P3
0015 O                            SAVE  Z  10                          CH5P3
0016 O                                     24 'RAISED TO THE'          CH5P3
0017 O                            POWER Z  28                          CH5P3
0018 O                                     37 'POWER IS'               CH5P3
0019 O                            NUMBERZ  46                          CH5P3
```

CABLT replaces COMP, GOTO, Resulting, and conditioning indicators

Figure 5-33 Raising any number to any power program modified with the CABxx operation.

QUESTIONS

5-1. What RPG II operation controls relational test conditions?

5-2. Refer to a calculation specifications form, and identify the fields that are used with the operation named in Question 5-1.

5-3. What other operation must be specified with the operation named in Question 5-1? How many of the Question 5-1 operations may reference this operation?

5-4. Refer to a calculation specifications form and identify the fields that must be used with the operation named in Question 5-3.

5-5. What conditions may be tested with the operation named in Question 5-1? How many conditions must be tested?

5-6. Are there any restrictions for the Factor 1 and Factor 2 entries in the operation named in Question 5-1?

5-7. May fields with different sizes be compared? May numeric fields that have different decimal positions be compared?

5-8. If the previous question is true, explain the internal processing procedures executed for field/literal types of different sizes.

5-9. Examine the following *unrelated* lines of coding, and determine if and why the syntax is incorrect.

Field types:

STATE-alphanumeric YTDWAG-numeric SALAMT-numeric
CRLIMT-numeric BALANC-numeric TRSAMT-numeric

Line	Form Type	Factor 1	Operation	Factor 2	Result Field Name	Length	High 1>2 (54-55)	Low 1<2 (56-57)	Equal 1=2 (58-59)
01Ø	C	STATE	COMP	'CT'					2Ø
02Ø	C	STATE	COMP	CT					3Ø
03Ø	C	YTDWAG	COMP	'45ØØØ'			4Ø		4Ø
04Ø	C	SALAMT	COMP	CRLIMT					
05Ø	C	'NY'	COMP	1Ø				5Ø	
06Ø	C	BALANC	COMP	' '					6Ø
07Ø	C	TRSAMT	COMP	*ZEROS			7Ø		

5-10. Determine the result of the following comparisons using the EBCDIC character set first, then the ASCII character set. For all examples, assume that if both factor values are numeric, the items are defined as numeric. On the other hand, if the factor values are not the same type, the items are assumed to be defined as alphanumeric.

Factor 1	Factor 2	Relational Conditions 1 > 2, 1 < 2, 1 = 2
0585	0585	
9} (negative 90)	90	
00200	20000	
RPGbIII	RPGIII	
MYERS,S	MYERSbS	
NEW JERSEY	NEW YORK	
SMITH	SMITHY	
bbbBYTE	BYTEbbb	
ZZZZZZ	999999	
1111J (negative 11111)	00000	
bbbbbb	000000	

Note: Small letter b denotes blank value.

5-11. Define conditional branching. Define unconditional branching.

5-12. What, if anything, is wrong with the following *unrelated* lines of coding?

Line	Form Type	Control Level	Indicators	Factor 1	Operation	Factor 2	Result Field Name	Resulting Indicators (Equal, 58–59)
01Ø	C				GOTO		END	
02Ø	C				TAG	LOOP		
03Ø	C		1Ø	SKIP	TAG			
04Ø	C	L1		OVER	TAG			
05Ø	C				GOTO	JUMP	LOOP	
06Ø	C		Ø1		GOTO	AGAIN		1S

5-13. What, if anything, is wrong with the following *related* lines of coding?

Line	Form Type	Factor 1	Operation	Factor 2	Result Field Name	Length	Decimal Position	Half Adjust (H)
01Ø	C		GOTO	END				
02Ø	C	A	MULT	B	C	6	2	H
03Ø	C	C	DIV	D	E	5	2	
04Ø	C	END	TAG					

5-14. What is looping? How does it differ from branching? How is it controlled in an RPG program?

5-15. Define the term *infinite loop*. During program execution, what happens if an infinite loop is included?

5-16. Examine the following *related* calculations, and determine if they are valid. If invalid, how can they be corrected?

Line (3–5)	Form Type (6)	Control Level (L0-L9, LR, SR, AN/OR) (7–8)	Indicators (9–17)	Factor 1 (18–27)	Operation (28–32)	Factor 2 (33–42)	Result Field Name (43–48)	Length (49–51)	Decimal Position (52)	Half Adjust (H) (53)	Resulting Indicators (54–59)
01Ø	C			AGAIN	TAG						
02Ø	C			X	MULT	Y	Z				
03Ø	C			Z	ADD	S	T				
04Ø	C				GOTO	AGAIN					
05Ø	C			T	ADD	Q	P				

5-17. Explain the function of the CABxx operation.

5-18. What option(s) may be included in the xx entry of the CABxx operation?

5-19. As compared to conventional RPG syntax to control conditional branching, name some of the advantages of the CABxx operation.

5-20. Identify any errors in the following coding:

Line (3–5)	Form Type (6)	Control Level (L0-L9, LR, SR, AN/OR) (7–8)	Indicators (9–17)	Factor 1 (18–27)	Operation (28–32)	Factor 2 (33–42)	Result Field Name (43–48)	Length (49–51)	Decimal Position (52)	Half Adjust (H) (53)	Resulting Indicators (54–59)
01Ø	C			A	CABLG	B	C				
02Ø	C										
03Ø	C										
04Ø	C			B	TAG						

EXERCISES

5-1. Using conventional RPG coding, write the calculations to support the processing in the following flowchart.

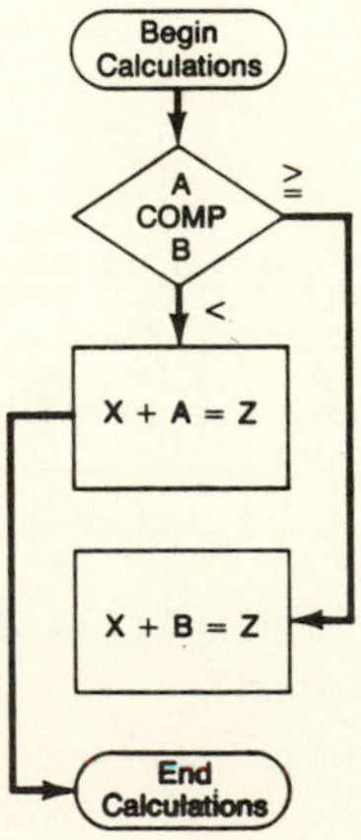

5-2. Refer to the flowchart in Exercise 5-1, and write the calculations using the CABxx operation(s).

5-3. Using conventional RPG coding (GOTO operation), write the calculations to support the following formula:

$$X = \left(\frac{Y^2}{Z^2}\right)^n$$

5-4. Refer to the formula in Exercise 5-3, and write (or modify if Exercise 5-3 was completed) the calculations using the CABxx operation.

5-5. Write the calculations using the GOTO operations(s) for the following flowchart:

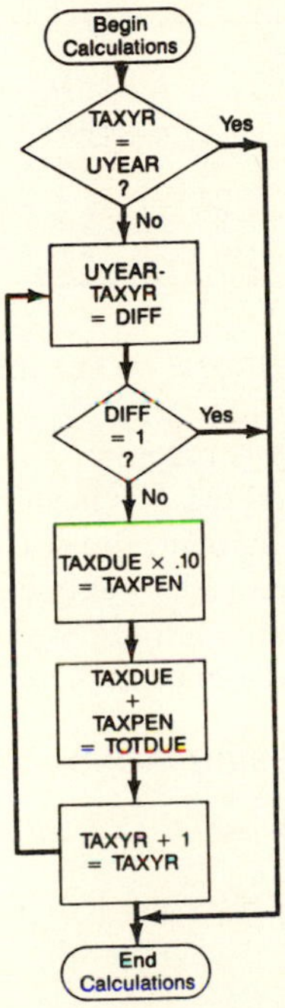

5-6. Refer to the flowchart in Exercise 5-5, and write (or modify if Exercise 5-5 was completed) the calculations to support the processing logic using CABxx operations.

5-7. Debugging a source listing (execution time errors): The following program does not have any compile errors but does include execution time errors. Examine the source listing, and identify and correct any errors.

```
... ... 1 ... ... 2 ... ... 3 ... ... 4 ... ... 5 ... ... 6 ... ... 7 ...
     H
     FNUMBERS IP  F   7   7            DISK
     FPOWERS  O   F 132 132            PRINTER
     INUMBERS SM  01
     I                                        1   40NUMBER
     I                                        5   70POWER
     C   01                GOTO OVER
     C                     Z-ADD0         RAISE   30
     C                     Z-ADDNUMBER    SAVE    30
     C           START     TAG
     C           RAISE     COMP POWER                 12   > TEST
     C           NUMBER    MULT SAVE      NUMBER
     C                     GOTO START
     C           OVER      TAG
     OPOWERS  H   06   1P
     O        D 2      01
     O                         SAVE  Z  10
     O                                  24 'RAISED TO THE'
     O                         POWER Z  28
     O                                  37 'POWER IS'
     O                         NUMBERZ  46
```

LABORATORY ASSIGNMENTS

Laboratory Assignment 5-1: PAYROLL REGISTER

A payroll register records the year-to-date and weekly payroll information for each employee. Federal income (YTDFWT) and social security taxes (YTDSS) are withheld to date and for the current week, and the related week's gross pay and net pay are always included. Other deductions (e.g., hospitalization, retirement, and union dues) may also be deducted from an employee's paycheck. From the record layout form, processing logic flowchart, and printer spacing chart presented, write an RPG program to generate the required report.

Format of Data Records:

SS#	EMPLOYEE NAME	YTD WAGES	YTD FWT	YTD SS	WEEK SALARY
9 9 9 9 9 9 9 9 9	9 9 9 9 9 9 9 9 9 9 9 9 9 9 9 9 9 9 9 9	9 9 9 9 9 9 9	9 9 9 9 9 9 9	9 9 9 9 9 9	9 9 9 9 9 9
1 2 3 4 5 6 7 8 9	10 11 12 13 14 15 16 17 18 19 20 21 22 23 24 25 26 27 28 29	30 31 32 33 34 35 36	37 38 39 40 41 42 43	44 45 46 47 48 49	50 51 52 53 54 55

Calculations: The logic flowchart that follows details the calculations required for the report. To simplify federal income tax computations, a constant rate of 20% is specified for this program. Refer to the first decision symbol in the flowchart, and notice that a relational test has been included to test if the YTDSS is less than $3,855.60. If it is less than this amount, the social security tax withheld for the current week's pay is computed; otherwise, this routine is ignored. The $3,855.60 figure was determined by multiplying the maximum wages subject to social security tax ($50,400) for 1990 by a rate of 7.65%. Both the maximum amount and the percentage are subject to change.

Processing Logic Flowchart:

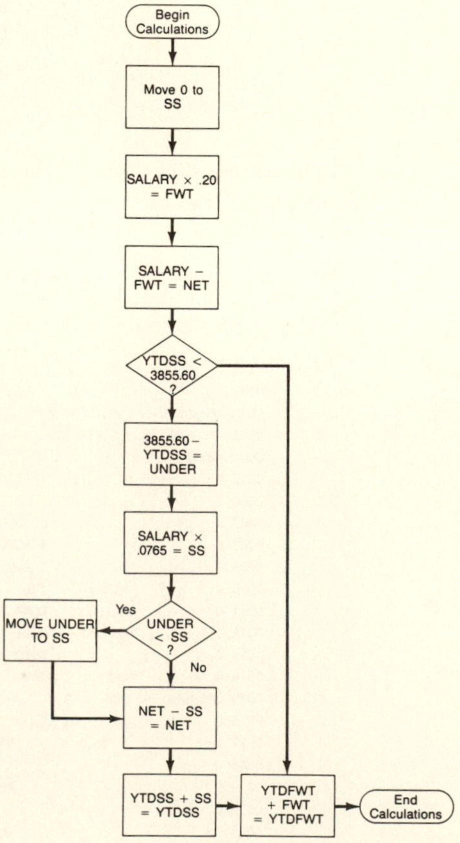

Report Design:

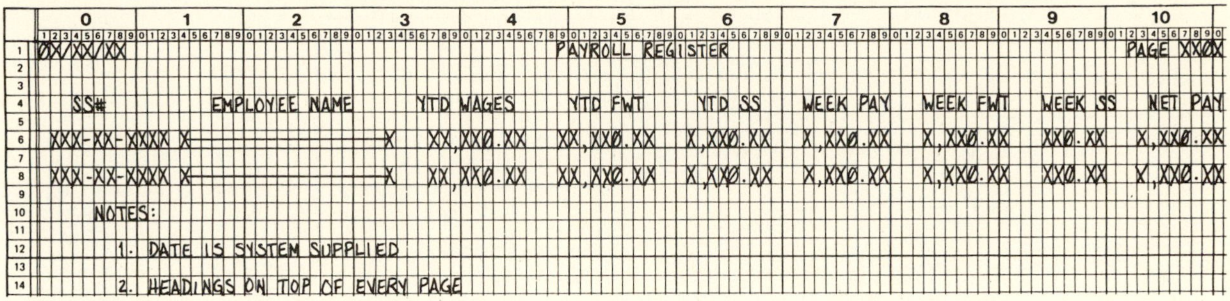

Input Data:

SS Number Cols 1-9	Employee Name 10-29	YTD Wages 30-36	YTD FWT 37-43	YTD SS 44-49	Weekly Salary 50-55
050446666	BETTY BURPO	0250000	0050000	019125	050000
001012345	DICK TRACY	4965000	0993000	379823	075000
100709876	SHERLOCK HOLMES	6000000	1200000	385560	100000
020324321	JAMES BOND	5000000	1000000	382500	080000
020400050	INSPECTOR GADGET	5040000	1008000	385560	090000
110889999	PERRY MASON	0011000	0002200	000842	027500

Note: YTD amounts do not include current week salary items

Laboratory Assignment 5-2: PRESENT VALUE OF A FUTURE AMOUNT

Fixed payment annuities require that a principal amount must be invested today to have a specific future amount, considering the current interest rate and period of the investment. The mathematical steps include the following:

Step 1. Compute the present worth of \$1 by dividing 1 by the compound amount of \$1, expressed by formula as:

$$PV = \frac{1}{(1 + i)^n}$$

where: PV = present value of \$1
i = interest rate per annum
n = number of interest periods

Notes: If interest is compounded more than yearly (i.e., monthly, weekly, or daily), the interest rate (i) must be divided by the number of interest periods per year. For accuracy, the answer must be carried to nine decimal positions. The total number of interest periods (n) is determined by multiplying the investment years by the interest payments per year.

Step 2. Determine the amount that must be invested today to have the required future annuity amount with the following formula:

$$P = S \times PV$$

where: P = amount that must be invested today to have future annuity
S = amount of future annuity
PV = present value of \$1

Format of Data Records:

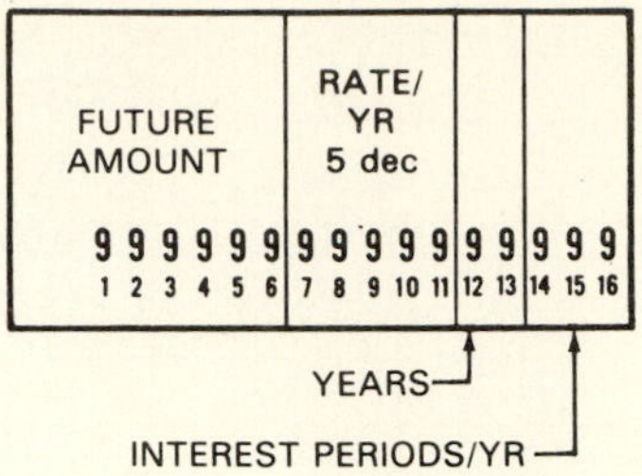

Report Design:

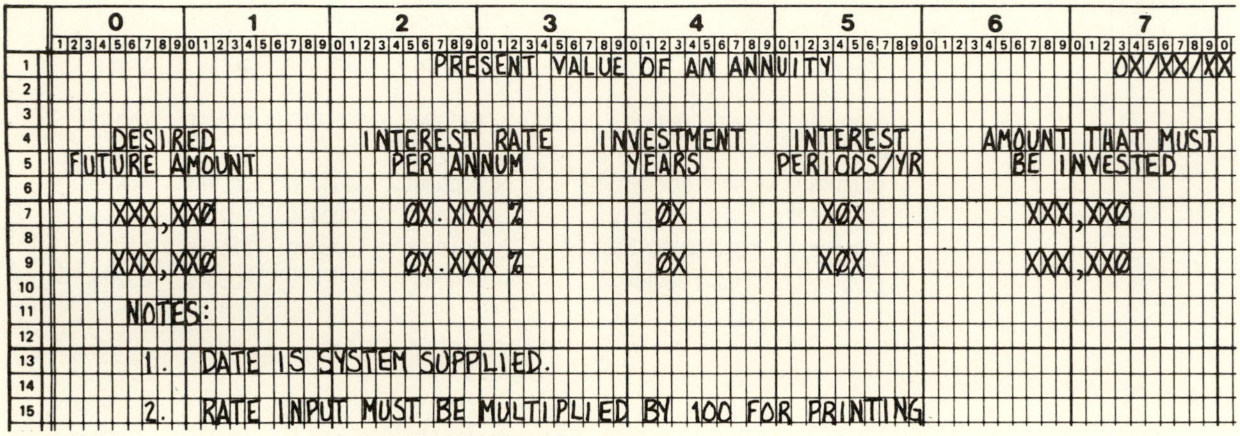
PRESENT VALUE OF AN ANNUITY
0X/XX/XX
DESIRED
FUTURE AMOUNT
INTEREST RATE
PER ANNUM
INVESTMENT
YEARS
INTEREST
PERIODS/YR
AMOUNT THAT MUST
BE INVESTED
XXX,XX0
0X.XXX %
0X
X0X
XXX,XX0
NOTES:
1. DATE IS SYSTEM SUPPLIED.
2. RATE INPUT MUST BE MULTIPLIED BY 100 FOR PRINTING

Input Data:

Desired Future Amount Cols 1-6	Interest Rate Per Annum 7-11	Investment Years 12-13	Interest Periods Per Year 14-16
100000	08000	10	001
100000	08000	10	012
100000	08000	10	365
100000	10000	10	001
100000	10000	10	012
100000	10000	10	365

Laboratory Assignment 5-3: STOCKBROKER'S COMMISSION REPORT

Write an RPG program to generate the stockbroker's commission report illustrated in the supplemental printer spacing chart.

Format of Input Records:

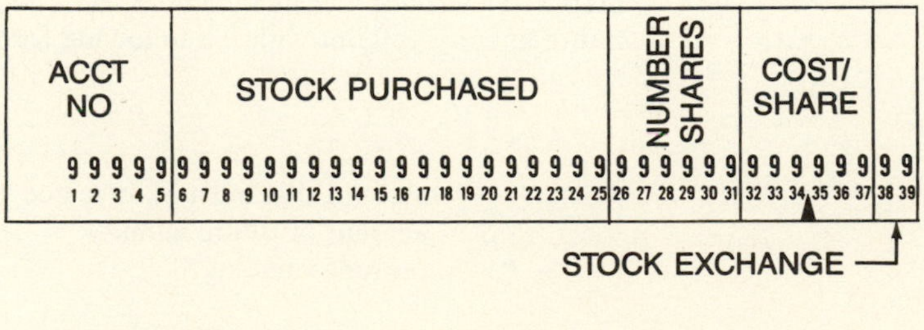

Calculations:

Step 1. Multiply the number of shares purchased by the cost per share (input values) to calculate the total dollars of stock purchased.

Step 2. Test the stock exchange input field to determine on which exchange the stock is listed. The stock exchange codes are as follows:

NY	New York Stock Exchange
AM	American Stock Exchange
OV	Over-the-Counter Exchange

Step 3. On the basis of the following individual stock exchange rates compute the broker commission on the total dollars of stock purchased:

NY 5.1% AM 4.2% OV 3.5%

Step 4. Accumulate separate totals for the number of transactions related to each stock exchange, and print at LR time.

Step 5. Test the stock exchange input field, and print the related code on each detail line as shown in the printer spacing chart.

Report Design:

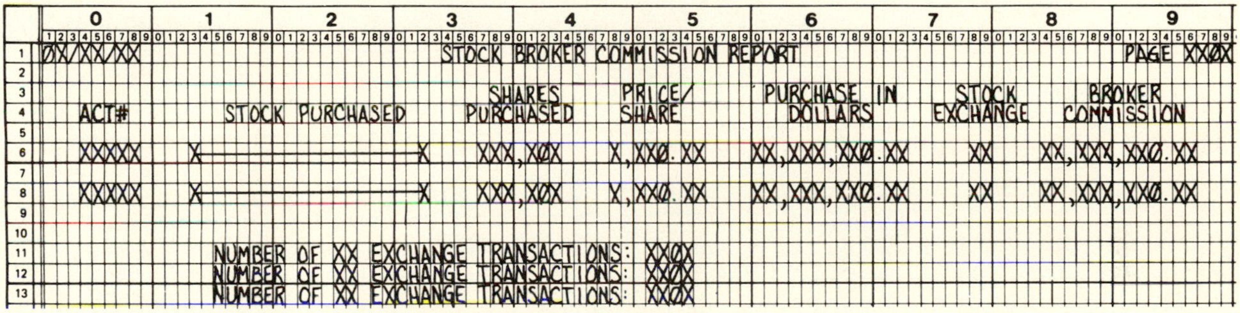

Input Data:

Acct # Col 1-5	Stock Purchased 6-25	Number of Shares 26-31	Cost/ Share 32-37	Stock Exchange 38-39
10000	IBM CORPORATION	001000	125500	NY
12000	STURM RUGER	000050	043000	OV
13000	BENQUET INC	010000	004250	NY
14000	BIC	000300	002600	AM
15000	BLACK & DECKER	001500	023750	OV
16000	TRANS-LUX	100000	009125	AM
17000	ALCIDE CORPORATION	025000	003125	OV
18000	PEOPLE'S BANK	004000	009500	OV
19000	XEROX	000100	051375	NY
20000	DU PONT	000300	088125	NY

chapter 6
Structured Operations IF/ELSE, DO, DOU, and DOW

RPG STRUCTURED OPERATIONS

The structured operations included in IBM's RPG III, RPG/400, and RPG II compilers are:

```
DO (Do)                          CASxx (Chapter 7)
DOWxx (Do While)                 IFxx (If/Then)
DOUxx (Do Until)                 ELSE (Else Do)
                     END (End)
```

Use of these operations in an RPG program provides the following advantages:

1. For many processing routines, they eliminate the unstructured use of GOTO statements, thereby providing better program maintenance and readability.
2. Fewer indicators have to be used in a program. This saves CPU storage, reduces processing time, and provides for easier maintenance.
3. The use of internal subroutines is encouraged because they support the design requirements of a well-structured RPG program. This subject is discussed in Chapter 7.
4. Syntax and processing logic closely follow that of many widely used and familiar high-level languages such as COBOL, BASIC, FORTRAN, and so forth.

First, the syntax and processing logic of the IFxx/ELSE operations will be introduced, followed by a discussion of the DO, DOU, and DOW operations.

IFxx/ELSE Operations

The *IFxx* (If/Then), the *ELSE* (Else/Do), and *END* operations, which are referred to as an *If-Then-Else* structure, are used to control conditional processing. The IFxx statement is used to evaluate a condition, and depending on whether the test is *true* or *false*, it will direct program control to a specific instruction in calculations. An ELSE statement, which must be related to an IFxx instruction, provides for an alternative action if the IFxx test is not true. Figure 6-1 explains the syntax associated with the IFxx and ELSE operations.

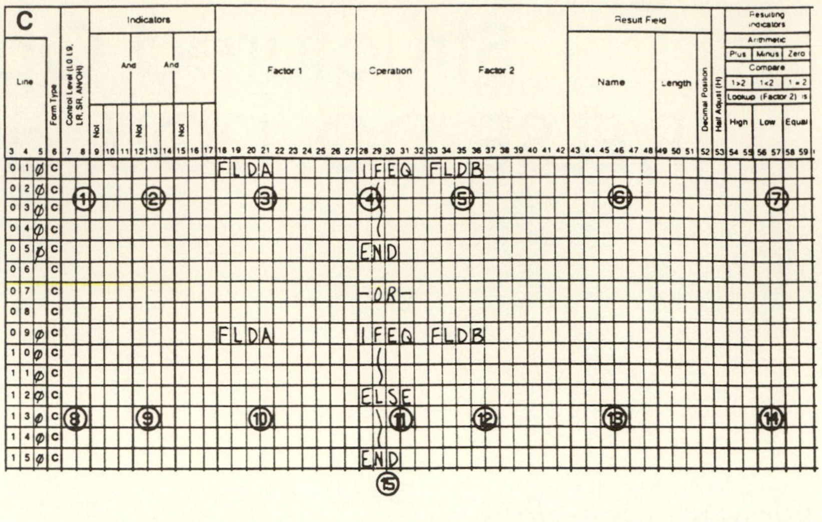

IFxx Rules:

1. Control level indicators (L1-L9 & LR) specified at Total Time are optional.

2. Indicators specified at Detail Time are optional.

3. Factor 1 must contain a literal, field name, array element, table name, or data structure subfield. Entry must be left-justified.

4. Operation IFxx must be left-justified in the Operation field. The xx option may have the following values:

xx Option	*Logical Test*
EQ	Value in Factor 1 is equal to value in Factor 2
GE	Value in Factor 1 is greater than or equal to value in Factor 2
GT	Value in Factor 1 is greater than value in Factor 2
LE	Value in Factor 1 is less than or equal to value in Factor 2
LT	Value in Factor 1 is less than value in Factor 2
NE	Value in Factor 1 is not equal to value in Factor 2

5. Required Factor 2 entry must be left-justified and may be a literal, field name, array element, table name, or data structure subfield name. The rules for comparison must be followed which requires that the Factor 1 and Factor 2 entries be the same type (alphanumeric or numeric).

6. Result field is not used and must remain blank.

7. Resulting Indicator fields are not used and must remain blank.

ELSE Rules:

8. A control level indicator (L1-L9 & LR) may be assigned to place the ELSE statement within a related control group. The entry has no function and is specified only for program documentation.

9. Detail time indicator fields must remain blank.

10. Factor 1 is not used.

11. ELSE operation name must be left-justified in the Operation field.

12. Factor 2 is not used.

13. Result field is not used.

14. Resulting Indicator fields are not used.

15. An END operation must terminate an IFxx group or an IFxx/ELSE group of statements. A control level indicator may be assigned to this operation to place it within a control group. No other fields are used for the END operation when related to IF/ELSE control.

Note: An IFxx operation *may be* specified without a related ELSE operation. However, an ELSE operation *may not* be assigned without a related IFxx statement.

Figure 6-1 Syntax rules for the IFxx and ELSE operations.

The conditional expression tested (xx entry) may be *simple* or *complex*. An IF statement that includes more than one test connected with an AND or OR relationship is considered complex. Those that include only one logical test are classified as simple. Figure 6-2 shows three flowcharts that detail the processing logic for simple IFxx statements that test for *true only*, *true and false*, and *false only* actions.

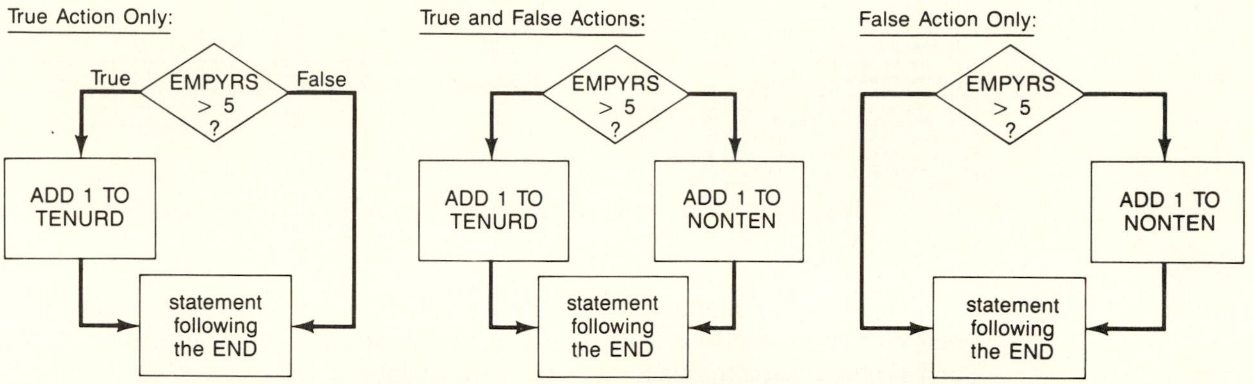

Figure 6-2 Processing logic flowcharts for simple IFxx statements.

The RPG IFxx statement coding to support the processing logic shown in the flowcharts in Figure 6-2 is detailed in Figure 6-3.

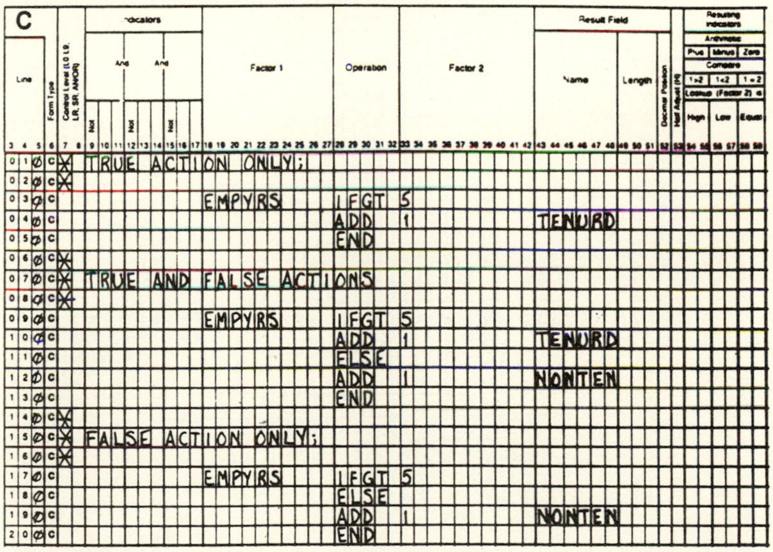

Figure 6-3 Simple IFxx/ELSE statement coding to control true only, true and false, and false action processing.

Complex IFxx Statements. A complex IFxx statement is one that includes two or more tests specified in an AND or OR relationship. When an AND relationship is included, all the conditions must be true to execute the action. For IFxx statements in an OR relationship, only one of the test conditions has to be true to execute the action. The processing logic and syntax related to a complex IFxx statement that includes one AND and two OR test relationships is shown in Figure 6-4.

Because there is no entry in Factor 1 (Figure 6-4) for the AND and OR statements, FLDA (Factor 1 entry) in the IFEQ (If equal) instruction is implied. Notice, however, that other fields or literals may be specified in Factor 1. Hence, the entry is not limited to the item defined in Factor 1 of the initial IFxx statement.

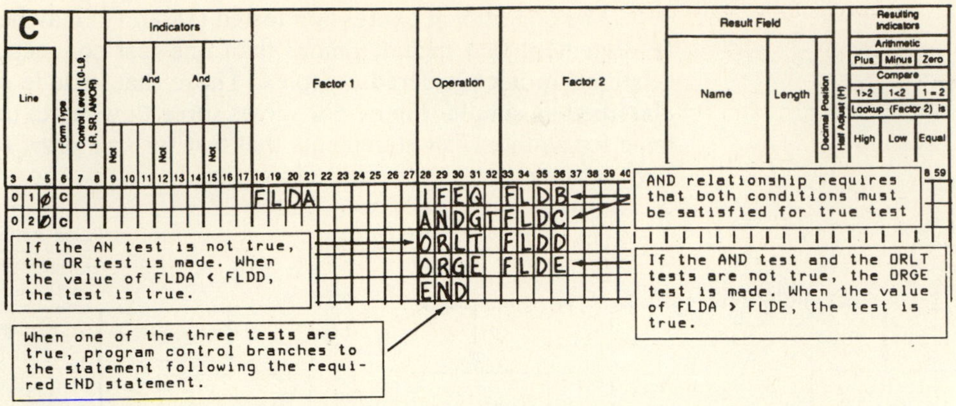

Figure 6-4 Processing logic and syntax related to complex IFxx statements.

Nested IFxx Statements. Nested IF statements are classified as those that pair more than one IFxx instruction with a single statement. The processing logic and syntax related to this form of IFxx statement are detailed in Figure 6-5.

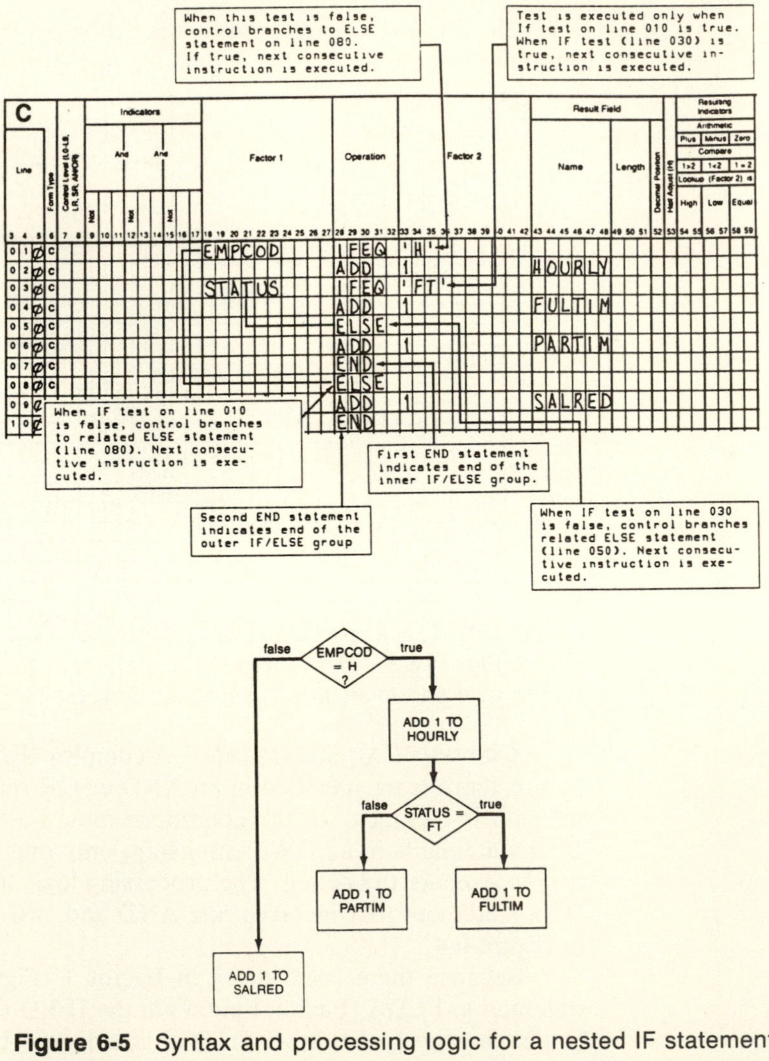

Figure 6-5 Syntax and processing logic for a nested IF statement example.

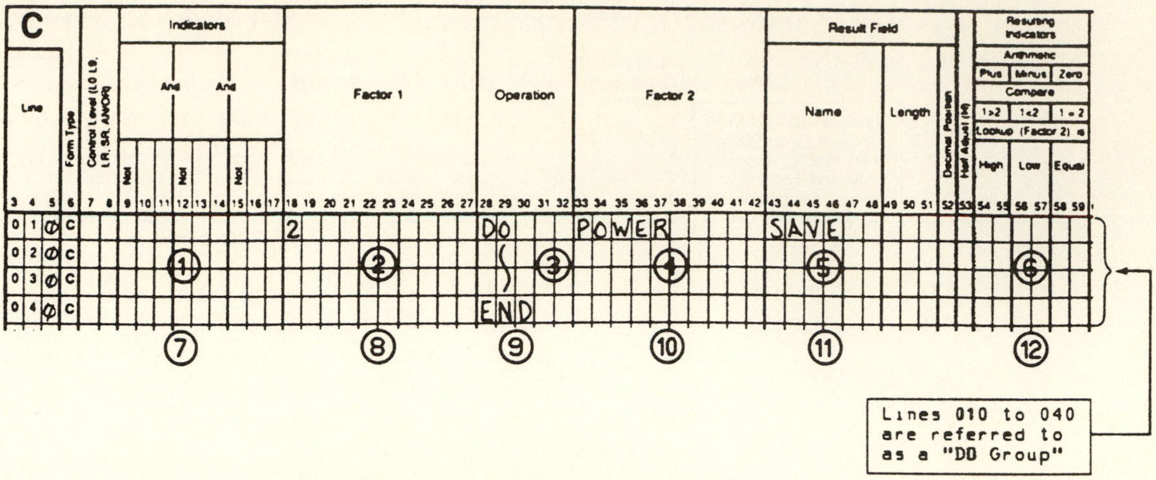

DO Operation:

1. Conditioning indicators may be specified at Total (columns 7-8) and/or Detail Time. If the indicator(s) specified is (are) not "ON", control will branch to the statement following the END instruction. Conditioning indicators specified are tested only when the DO statement is initially executed. For subsequent loops, the indicator status is ignored.

2. Factor 1 (starting value) entry is optional. It may include a numeric literal, field name, array element, table name, or data structure subfield. Any of these numeric entries must be defined as an integer (no decimal positions). The value stored in the Factor 1 entry initializes the index (Result Field entry) to its starting value. If the Factor 1 entry is omitted, the starting value of index will be 1.

3. The DO operation name must be left-justified in the Operation field. It provides for automatic looping and exit from the DO group when the index value (Result Field) is greater than the limit value (Factor 2 entry).

4. Factor 2 (limit value) entry is optional. It may include a numeric literal, field, name, array element, table name, or data structure subfield. Any of these numeric entries must be defined as an integer (no decimal positions). The value stored in the Factor 2 entry specifies the number of times the loop will be executed. If this entry is omitted, the limit value is 1. Note that the limit value must be equal to or greater than the starting value in the Factor 1 entry.

5. Result Field is optional. This entry may be a numeric field, array element, table name, or data structure subfield. When specified, it contains the index (counter) value which is automatically incremented by 1 or by the value included in Factor 2 of the related END statement. If this entry is omitted, the compiler will supply an index.

6. Resulting indicator fields are not used.

END Operation:

7. Optional conditioning indicator(s) may be assigned to an END statement which determine if the looping process is to continue. If an indicator(s) is assigned and it is ON, control will loop back to the DO statement. However, if the indicator is NOT ON, control will branch to the first executable instruction following the END operation.

8. Factor 1 is not used.

9. The required END operation marks the end of the DO group.

10. By default, the index will be incremented by 1. It may incremented with a different value by specifying a numeric literal, field, array element, table name, or data structure subfield in Factor 2.

11. Result Field is not used.

12. Resulting indicators are not used.

Notes:

1. The DO operation begins execution by moving the value from the Factor 1 entry (when specified) into the index item (Result Field). If a Factor 1 entry is not specified, 1 is moved into the index item.

2. When the index value (Result Field) is greater than the limit value (Factor 2), control branches to the first statement following the related END operation.

Figure 6-13 DO operation syntax and processing features.

```
SEQNBR *... ... 1 ... ... 2 ... ... 3 ... ... 4 ... ... 5 ... ... 6 ... ... 7 ... ... 8

   100  FNUMBERS IP  F   7   7           DISK                               CH6P2
   200  FPOWERS  O   F 132 132           PRINTER                            CH6P2
        INUMBERS     02                                                     CH6P2
        I                                       1   4ONO                    CH6P2
        I                                       5   7OPOWER
        C                      Z-ADDNO          SAVE     40       CREATE MULTPLER
        C ----------> 2        DO   POWER       RAISE             INIT INDEX TO 2
        C                      MULT SAVE        NO                RAISE TO POWER
        C                      END <--                            END OF DO GROUP
        OPOWERS  H  301    1P
  1100  O        D  2      02
  1200  O                       SAVE  Z   10
  1300  O                                 24 'RAISED TO THE'
  1400  O                       POWER Z   27
  1500  O                                 36 'POWER IS'
  1600  O                       NO    Z   42
```

When value in RAISE (index) is greater than POWER, looping ends and control passes to statement following the END

The END statement increments the index and returns control back to the DO statement where the test is made to continue or end looping

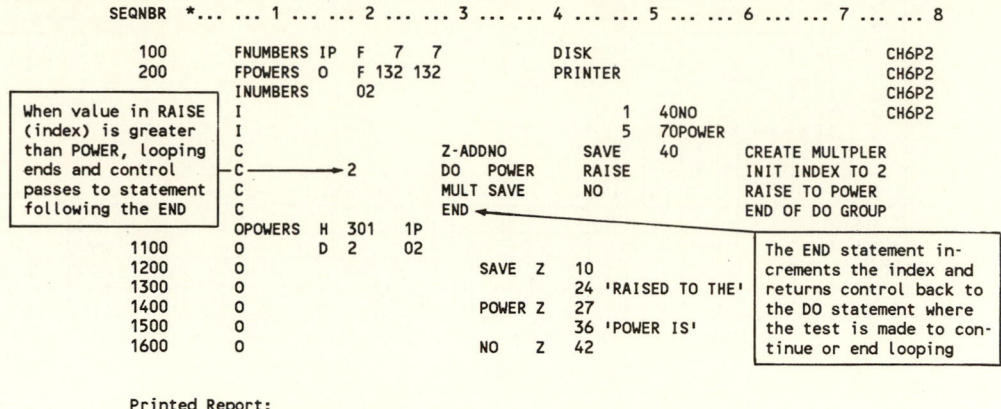

Printed Report:

```
12 RAISED TO THE  2 POWER IS   144

16 RAISED TO THE  3 POWER IS  4096

 9 RAISED TO THE  4 POWER IS  6561
```

Figure 6-14 Raising a number to a power example program with DO operation control.

DOUxx (Do Until) Operation

The DOUxx operation is another instruction that controls iterative processing. This operation differs, however, from the DO operation in that it requires a *programmer-supplied* counter to control exit from the looping sequence. The syntax and processing logic related to the DOUxx instruction are detailed in Figure 6-15.

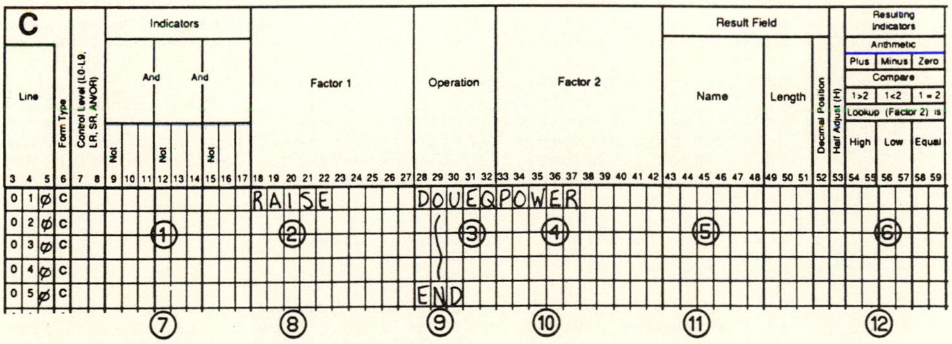

DOUxx Operation:

1. Conditioning indicators may be specified at Total (columns 7-8) and/or Detail Time. If the indicator(s) specified is (are not) "ON", control will branch to statement following the END instruction. The status of the indicator(s) is tested every time the DOUxx statement is executed.

2. Factor 1 entry is required. It may include a numeric literal, field name, array element, table name, or data structure subfield. The entries in Factor 1 and Factor 2 must follow the rules for COMParisons in that both must be the same type (alphanumeric or numeric).

3. The DOUxx operation executes the instructions within the group at least once. Subsequent looping depends on the status of the test specified in the DOUxx operation. Unlike the DO operation, the DOUxx operation does not include an automatic counter (index). Looping must be controlled by a programmer-supplied instruction(s) within the DOUxx group.

   The xx tests that may be specified in a DOUxx statement are identical to those available with the IF, CAB, and CAS statements which include EQ, GT, LT, GE, LE, NE.

   Note that the xx test is not made in the DOUxx statement, but in the END operation when that instruction is executed.

   When the condition (xx) specified in the DOUxx group is true, control will branch to the next executable statement following the associated END operation.

Figure 6-15 DOUxx operation syntax and processing features.

4. Factor 2 entry is required. It may include a numeric literal, field name, array element, table name, or data structure subfield. This entry must be the same type (alphanumeric or numeric) as the Factor 1 item.

5. Result Field is not used.

6. Resulting indicator fields are not used.

<u>END Operation</u>:

7. Optional conditioning indicator(s) may be assigned to END statement which determine if the looping process is to continue. If an indicator(s) is assigned and it is ON, control will loop back to the DOUxx statement. However, if the indicator is NOT ON, control will branch to the first executable instruction following the END operation.

8. Factor 1 is not used.

9. A required END operation marks the end of the DOUxx group. The xx test included in the DOUxx instruction is made by the END operation and not by the DOUxx operation. This processing logic supports the feature that the DOUxx group is always executed at least once.

10. Factor 2 is not used.

11. Result Field is not used.

12. Resulting indicators are not used.

(Continued)

The same *raising of a number to a power* application program that illustrated the processing logic of the DO operation has been modified in Figure 6-16 to support DOUxx statement processing. Notice that the relative test is made at the END operation and not at the DOUEQ statement. Consequently, *the DOUxx group will be processed at least once.*

```
SEQNBR *... ... 1 ... ... 2 ... ... 3 ... ... 4 ... ... 5 ... ... 6 ... ... 7 ... ... 8

   100     FNUMBERS IP  F   7   7          DISK                                CH6P3
   200     FPOWERS  O   F 132 132          PRINTER                             CH6P3
   300     INUMBERS     02                                                     CH6P3
   400     I                                       1   40NO                    CH6P3
           I                                       5   70POWER                 CH6P3
           C                      Z-ADDNO      SAVE    40       CREATE MULTPLERCH6P3
           C                      Z-ADD1       RAISE   30       INIT CTR TO 1  CH6P3
           C ------> RAISE        DOUEQPOWER                    COMP FOR = TESTCH6P3
           C                      MULT SAVE    NO               RAISE TO POWER CH6P3
           C                      ADD  1       RAISE            INCREMENT CTR  CH6P3
           C                      END <-----                    END OF DOU GRP CH6P3
           OPOWERS  H  301   1P
  1300     O        D  2     02
  1400     O                           SAVE  Z   10
  1500     O                                     24 'RAISED TO THE'
  1600     O                           POWER Z   27
  1700     O                                     36 'POWER IS'
  1800     O                           NO    Z   42
```

DOU group is executed at least once. When values in the two items are equal (EQ), control continues with statement following the END

The DOU test is made when the END statement is executed. If the test is false, control passes back to the DOU statement and the group is performed again. If the test is true, control passes to the statement following the END.

Printed Report:

```
12 RAISED TO THE  2 POWER IS   144

16 RAISED TO THE  3 POWER IS  4096

 9 RAISED TO THE  4 POWER IS  6561
```

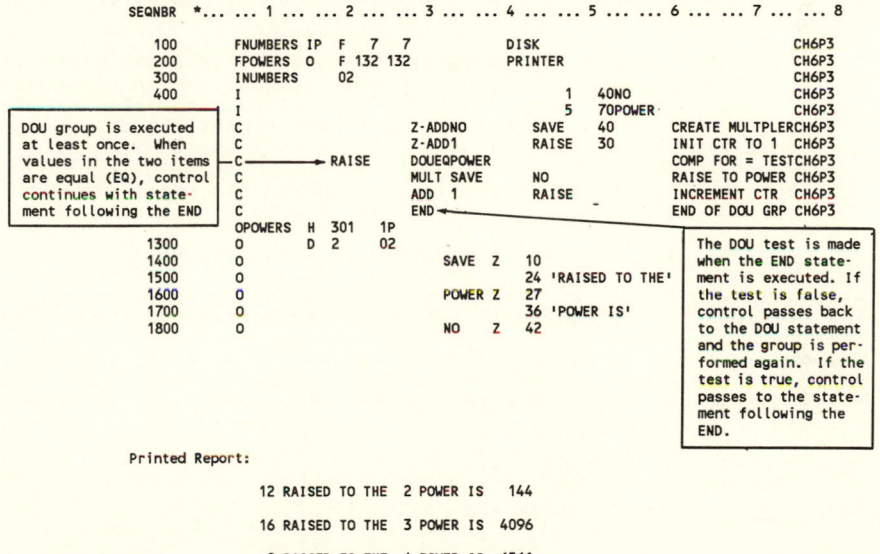

Figure 6-16 Raising a number to a power example program with DOUxx operation control.

DOWxx (Do While) Operation

The DOWxx structured operation processing differs from both DO and DOUxx. Similar to the DOUxx statement, a programmer-supplied counter must be included within the group to control an exit from the looping sequence. On the other hand, this operation differs from DOUxx in that the relational test [equal to (EQ), greater than (GT), greater than or equal to (GE), less than or equal to (LE), less than (LT), and not equal to (NE)] is made at the DOWxx statement and not at the related END operation. Consequently, the DOWxx group is performed only if the test (xx) condition is true, and not at least once as with the DOUxx operation. The syntax and processing features of the DOWxx operation are detailed in Figure 6-17.

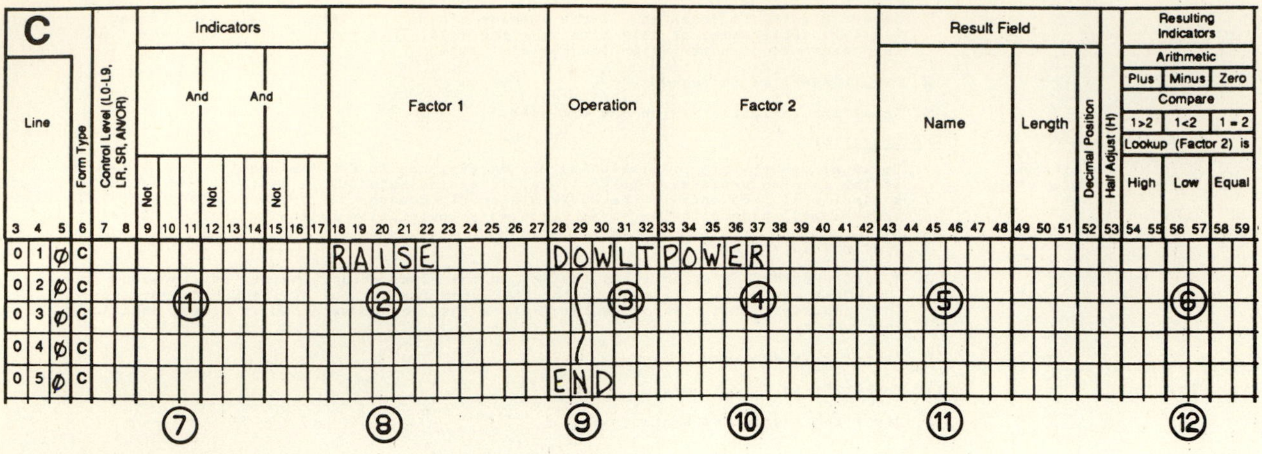

DOWxx Operation:

1. Conditioning indicators may be specified at Total (columns 7-8) and/or Detail Time. If the indicator(s) specified is (are not) "ON", control will branch to statement following the END instruction. The status of the indicator(s) is tested every time the DOWxx statement is executed.

2. Factor 1 entry is required. It may include a numeric literal, field name, array element, table name, or data structure subfield. The entries in Factor 1 and Factor 2 must follow the rules for COMParisons in that both must be the same type (alphanumeric or numeric).

3. The DOWxx operation executes the instructions within the group only if the relational xx test is true. Subsequent looping also depends on the status of the test specified in the DOWxx operation. Unlike the DO operation, and like the DOUxx the DOWxx does not include an automatic counter (index). Looping must be controlled by a programmer-supplied instruction(s) within the DOWxx group.

   The xx tests that may be specified in a DOWxx statement are identical to those available with the IF, CAB, and CAS statements which include EQ, GT, LT, GE, LE, NE.

   Note that the xx test is made in the DOWxx statement

   When the condition (xx) specified in the DOWxx group is true, control will branch to the next executable statement following the associated END operation.

4. Factor 2 entry is required. It may include a numeric literal, field name, array element, table name, or data structure subfield. This entry must be the same type (alphanumeric or numeric) as the Factor 1 item.

5. Result Field is not used.

6. Resulting indicator fields are not used.

END Operation:

7. Optional conditioning indicator(s) may be assigned to END statement which determine if the looping process is to continue. If an indicator(s) is assigned and it is ON, control will loop back to the DOWxx statement. However, if the indicator is NOT ON, control will branch to the first executable instruction following the END operation.

8. Factor 1 is not used.

9. A required END operation marks the end of the DOWxx group.

11. Result Field is not used.

12. Resulting indicators are not used.

Figure 6-17 DOWxx operation syntax and processing features.

A source listing of the example program that raises a number to a power, modified with DOUxx operation processing, is shown in Figure 6-18.

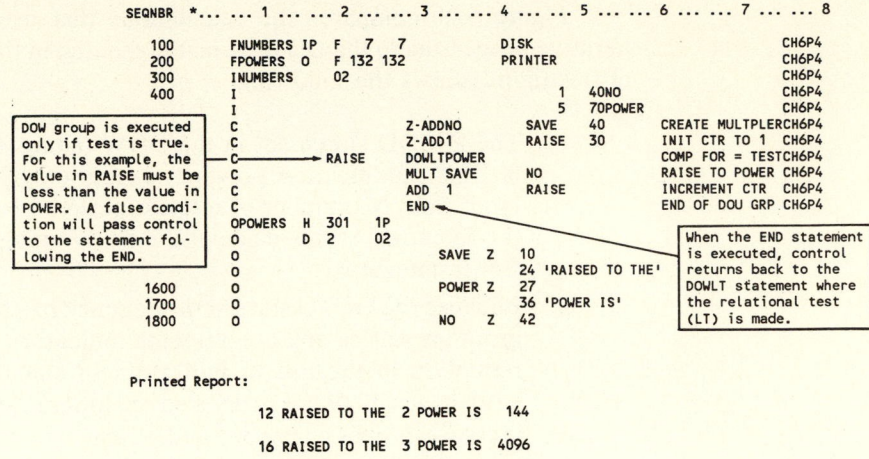

```
SEQNBR  *... ... 1 ... ... 2 ... ... 3 ... ... 4 ... ... 5 ... ... 6 ... ... 7 ... ... 8

       FNUMBERS IP  F   7   7            DISK                            CH6P4
       FPOWERS  O   F 132 132            PRINTER                         CH6P4
       INUMBERS     02                                                   CH6P4
       I                                        1   40NO                 CH6P4
       I                                        5   70POWER              CH6P4
       C                          Z-ADDNO       SAVE    40       CREATE MULTPLERCH6P4
       C                          Z-ADD1        RAISE   30       INIT CTR TO 1  CH6P4
       C           RAISE          DOWLTPOWER                     COMP FOR = TESTCH6P4
       C                          MULT SAVE     NO               RAISE TO POWER CH6P4
       C                          ADD  1        RAISE            INCREMENT CTR  CH6P4
       C                          END                            END OF DOU GRP CH6P4
       OPOWERS  H  301    1P
       O        D  2      02
       O                            SAVE  Z   10
       O                                      24 'RAISED TO THE'
       O                            POWER Z   27
       O                                      36 'POWER IS'
       O                            NO    Z   42
```

DOW group is executed only if test is true. For this example, the value in RAISE must be less than the value in POWER. A false condition will pass control to the statement following the END.

When the END statement is executed, control returns back to the DOWLT statement where the relational test (LT) is made.

Printed Report:

```
12 RAISED TO THE  2 POWER IS   144

16 RAISED TO THE  3 POWER IS  4096

 9 RAISED TO THE  4 POWER IS  6561
```

Figure 6-18 Raising a number to a power example program with DOUxx operation control.

APPLICATION PROGRAM—COMPOUND INTEREST COMPUTATION

A modified version of the compound interest computation program previously presented in Chapter 5 is shown in Figure 6-19. Notice that iterative GOTO processing has been replaced with DOW (Do While) statement control.

```
 ... ... 1 ... ... 2 ... ... 3 ... ... 4 ... ... 5 ... ... 6 ... ... 7 ...
  * THIS PROGRAM COMPUTES COMPOUND INTEREST USING THE DOW STRUCTURED  CH6P5
  * OPERATION..................                                       CH6P5
 H                                                                    CH6P5
 FDATA5P2 IP  F  24  24            DISK                               CH6P5
 FREPORT  O   F 132 132            PRINTER                            CH6P5
 IDATA5P2 SM  01                                                      CH6P5
 I                                        1   4 ACCT#                 CH6P5
 I                                        5  122PRINPL                CH6P5
 I                                       13  175I                     CH6P5
 I                                       18  200YRDAYS                CH6P5
 I                                       21  240N                     CH6P5
 C                    Z-ADD1        CTR     40       SET COUNTER      CH6P5
 C          I         DIV  YRDAYS   DARATE  99       DAILY RATE       CH6P5
 C          DARATE    ADD  1        FACTOR 109       (1 + I)          CH6P5
 C                    Z-ADDFACTOR   HOLD   109       SAVE FACTOR      CH6P5
  *                                                                   CH6P5
 C          CTR       DOWLTN                         DOW CTR < N      CH6P5
 C                    ADD  1        CTR              LOOP COUNTER     CH6P5
 C                    MULT FACTOR   HOLD             INCREASE HOLD    CH6P5
 C                    END                            ENDS DOW GROUP   CH6P5
  *                                                                   CH6P5
 C          PRINPL    MULT HOLD     CMPAMT  82H      COMPOUND AMT     CH6P5
 C          CMPAMT    SUB  PRINPL   CMPINT  82       COMPOUND INT.    CH6P5
 C          DARATE    MULT 100      DAPCT   87       DAILY PCT        CH6P5
 C          I         MULT 100      ANPCT   53       ANNUAL PCT       CH6P5
 OREPORT  H  101   1P                                                 CH6P5
 O                          UDATE Y    8                              CH6P5
 O                                    49 'CERTIFICATES OF DEPOSIT'    CH6P5
 O                                    58 'ANALYSIS'                   CH6P5
 O                                    77 'PAGE'                       CH6P5
 O                          PAGE  Z   82                              CH6P5
 O        H  2     1P                                                 CH6P5
 O                              -     48 'INTEREST COMPOUNDED'        CH6P5
 O                                    54 'DAILY'                      CH6P5
 O        H  1     1P                                                 CH6P5
 O                                    42 'ANNUAL      DAILY'          CH6P5
 O                                    67 'INTEREST    COMPOUND'       CH6P5
 O                                    79 'COMPOUND'                   CH6P5
 O        H  2     1P                                                 CH6P5
 O                                    20 'ACT NO   PRINCIPAL'         CH6P5
 O                                    41 'RATE        RATE'           CH6P5
 O                                    66 '  DAYS          AMOUNT'     CH6P5
 O                                    79 'INTEREST'                   CH6P5
 O        D  2     01                                                 CH6P5
 O                          ACCT#      7                              CH6P5
 O                          PRINPL1   20                              CH6P5
 O                          ANPCT     31 '0 .   %'                    CH6P5
 O                          DAPCT     43 '0.        %'                CH6P5
 O                          N     Z   52                              CH6P5
 O                          CMPAMT1   67                              CH6P5
 O                          CMPINT1   79                              CH6P5
```

Figure 6-19 Source listing of compound interest program modified with DOW operation control of iterative processing.

Figure 6-20 compares the calculations that use the GOTO statement for iterative processing to the DOW format presented in this chapter. An examination of this figure shows the following:

1. The Z-ADD statement in the DOW listing is initialized to 1 instead of 0. This modification prevents execution of the DOWLT group if the input field N (number of interest periods) has a value of 1. Recall that the relational test is made at the DOW statement and not at the related END statement.
2. Because the GOTO statement sequence has been replaced by a DOWLT group, resulting and conditioning indicators have been eliminated. The reduction in the use of indicators in calculation is one of the major advantages of all the structured operations. Indicators consume storage, increase processing time, and when used indiscriminately, make program maintenance more difficult.

```
0010 C                 Z-ADD0        CTR      40
0011 C       I         DIV  YRDAYS   DARATE  99
0012 C       DARATE    ADD  1        FACTOR 109
0013 C                 Z-ADDFACTOR   HOLD   109
0014 C       LOOP      TAG
0015 C       CTR       ADD  1        CTR
0016 C       CTR       COMP N                    90
0017 C  90   HOLD      MULT FACTOR   HOLD
0018 C  90             GOTO LOOP
0019 C       PRINPL    MULT HOLD     CMPAMT  82H
0020 C       CMPAMT    SUB  PRINPL   CH5P2  82
0021 C       DARATE    MULT 100      DAPCT   87
0022 C       I         MULT 100      ANPCT   53
```

```
0012 C                 Z-ADD1        CTR      40
0013 C       I         DIV  YRDAYS   DARATE  99
0014 C       DARATE    ADD  1        FACTOR 109
0015 C                 Z-ADDFACTOR   HOLD   109
0016 *
0017 C       CTR       DOWLTN
0018 C                 ADD  1        CTR
0019 C                 MULT FACTOR   HOLD
0020 C                 END
0021 *
0022 C       PRINPL    MULT HOLD     CMPAMT  82H
0023 C       CMPAMT    SUB  PRINPL   CMPINT  82
0024 C       DARATE    MULT 100      DAPCT   87
0025 C       I         MULT 100      ANPCT   53
```

Test is performed at the DOWLT statement

Conditioning indicators have been eliminated

END indicates end of DOWLT group. Control returns back to the DOWLT statement when the related END operation is sensed.

Resulting indicators have been eliminated

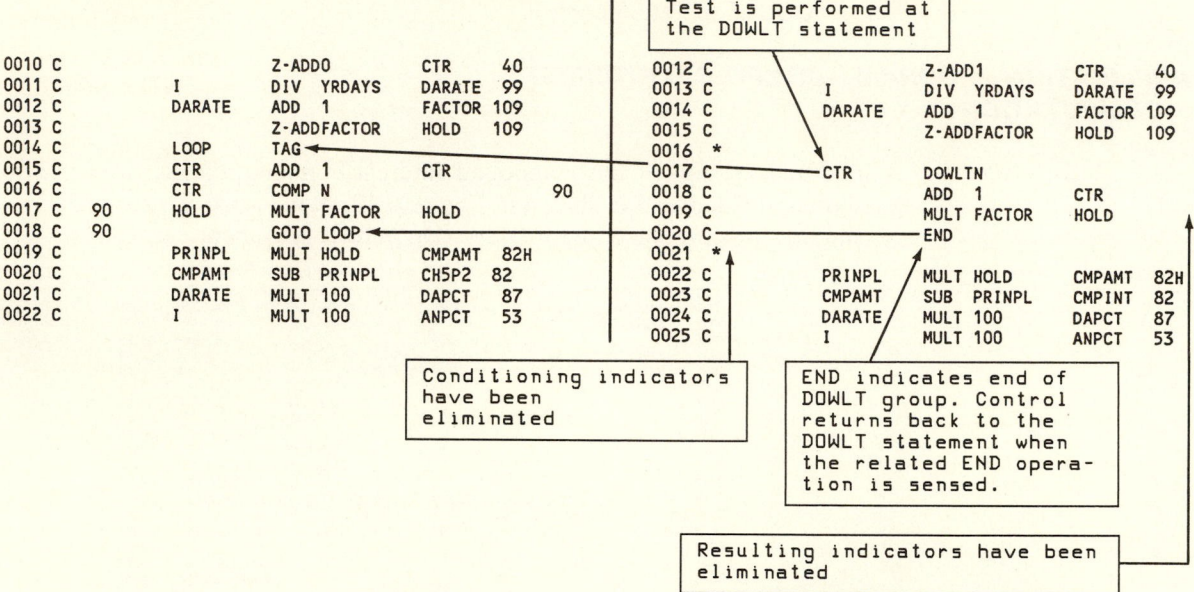

Figure 6-20 Comparison of GOTO to DOW statement coding for the control of iterative processing in the compound interest program.

The report generated by the compound interest program is shown in Figure 6-21.

```
11/30/92                 CERTIFICATES OF DEPOSIT ANALYSIS                  PAGE    1
                            INTEREST COMPOUNDED DAILY

                         ANNUAL        DAILY      INTEREST    COMPOUND    COMPOUND
  ACT NO   PRINCIPAL      RATE          RATE        DAYS       AMOUNT     INTEREST

   1000     1,000.00    10.000%    .0273972%        365       1,105.16      105.16

   2000     1,000.00    10.000%    .0273972%        180       1,050.54       50.54

   3000     1,000.00     6.500%    .0178082%        365       1,067.15       67.15

   4000     1,000.00     6.500%    .0178082%        180       1,032.57       32.57
```

Figure 6-21 Report generated by the compound interest program modified with a DOWLT structured operation.

SUMMARY

Structured RPG operations include DO (DO), DOWxx (Do While), DOUxx (Do Until), CASxx (Case Group), IFxx (If Then), ELSE (Else Do), and End (End). Operations IF, ELSE, DO, DOU, DOW, and END are discussed in this chapter. The syntax and processing logic of the CAS operation is introduced in Chapter 7.

The IF statement replaces the COMP statement for relational testing between the item in Factor 1 and the item in Factor 2. Tests supported include EQ (equal to), GE (greater than or equal to), GT (greater than), LE (less than or equal to), LT (less than), or NE (not equal to) conditions.

Linear and non-Linear IF statements include an ELSE statement that control one or more instructions related to a false action determined by the IF operation test.

Compound IF statements include AND (and) and/or OR (or) tests. AND (and) tests require that every relational test condition must be true for the statements controlled by the IF operation to be executed. OR relationships, however, require only that one test must be true for execution of the related statements.

An END operation must identify the end of an IF group. When two or more IF statements are specified in a linear format (nested), an END operation must be included for each IF operation.

Iterative processing is controlled by the structured operations DO, DOW, and DOU. The DO operation supports an index that is automatically incremented for every pass through the looping sequence, but the DOW and DOU operation require that a programmer-supplied counter be included to control exit from the loop.

The DOU statement tests the relational test condition at its related END operation. Consequently, the DOU group will always be executed at least once. However, the DOW operation performs the relational test at the DOW statement, and instructions within the DOW group are executed only if the specified test is true. DO, DOU, and DOW groups must be ended by an END statement. The relational tests supported are identical to those valid for the IF operation.

Any of the structured operations discussed in this chapter offer the following program advantages:

1. Replace the COMP operation and its required resulting indicators.
2. Eliminate or reduce the need for conditioning indicators.
3. Eliminate or reduce the use of GOTO statements that often result in poorly structured programs that are difficult to maintain.

QUESTIONS

6-1. Name six RPG structured operations. What programming advantages do they offer?

6-2. Explain the function of the IFxx and ELSE operations.

6-3. What variables may be specified in xx entry of the IFxx operation?

6-4. May an IFxx operation be specified without a related ELSE statement? May an ELSE operation be specified without a related IFxx statement?

6-5. What operation flags the end of an IF or IF/ELSE group?

Examine the following coding and answer Questions 6-6 to 6-9:

```
... ... 1 ... ... 2 ... ... 3 ... ... 4 ... ... 5 ... ... 6 ...

02010C             SEX       IFEQ 'F'
02020C                       ADD  1         FEMALE
02030C                       ELSE
02040C                       ADD  1         MALE
02050C                       END
02060C                        .
```

6-6. When the test on line 02010 is true, what instructions are executed?

6-7. When the test on line 02010 is false, what instructions are executed?

6-8. What is the function of the END statement? Is it required when the IF operation is specified without a related ELSE statement?

6-9. Name the structure of the IF/ELSE statement shown in the foregoing example.

6-10. Name any syntax restrictions related to the Factor 1 and Factor 2 entries of an IF statement.

6-11. In addition to the operation name, what other entries may be included with an ELSE statement?

Examine the following coding and answer Questions 6-12 to 6-16:

```
... ... 1 ... ... 2 ... ... 3 ... ... 4 ... ... 5 ... ... 6 ...

02010C             SEX       IFEQ 'F'
02020C             AGE       ANDLE21
02030C                       ADD  1         GROUP1
02040C                       ELSE
02050C                       ADD  1         GROUP2
02060C                       END
02070C                        .
```

6-12. When the relational tests on lines 02010 and 02020 are true, which instructions are executed?

6-13. When the test on line 02010 is true and the test on line 02020 is false, which instructions are executed?

6-14. When the test on line 02010 is false and the test on line 02020 is true, which instructions are executed?

6-15. Under what test conditions will the instructions on lines 02040 and 02050 be executed?

6-16. When is the instruction on line 02070 executed?

Examine the following coding and answer Questions 6-17 to 6-21:

```
... ... 1 ... ... 2 ... ... 3 ... ... 4 ... ... 5 ... ... 6 ...

02010C             CODE      IFEQ 'T'
02020C                       OREQ 'X'
02030C                       ADD  1         COUNT1
02040C                       ELSE
02050C                       ADD  1         COUNT2
02060C                       END
02070C                        .
```

6-17. When the relational tests on lines 02010 and 02020 are true, which instructions are executed?

6-18. When the test on line 02010 is true and the test on line 02020 is false, which instructions are executed?

6-19. When the test on line 02010 is false and the test on line 02020 is true, which instructions are executed?

6-20. Under what test conditions will the instructions on lines 02040 and 02050 be executed?

6-21. When is the instruction on line 02070 executed?

6-22. Name the RPG structured operations that support iterative processing. Identify the one that does not require a programmer-supplied counter for loop control.

Examine the following coding and answer Questions 6-23 to 6-27:

```
... ... 1 ... ... 2 ... ... 3 ... ... 4 ... ... 5 ... ... 6 ...

02010C           2         DO   INTPER    TIMES
02020C                     .
02030C                     .
02040C                     END  2
02050C                     .
```

6-23. Explain the function of the Factor 1 entry (numeric literal 2).

6-24. What is the function of the Factor 2 entry (INTPER)?

6-25. Explain the function of the Result Field entry (TIMES).

6-26. What is the function of the END operation and the numeric literal specified in Factor 2?

6-27. Under what conditions will an exit occur from the DO group?

6-28. Are any relational tests included with the DO operation?

6-29. How does the processing for the DOU (Do Until) operation differ from the DO operation?

Examine the following coding and answer Questions 6-30 to 6-32:

```
... ... 1 ... ... 2 ... ... 3 ... ... 4 ... ... 5 ... ... 6 ...

02010C           COUNT     DOUEQPERIDS
02020C                     .
02030C                     .
02040C                     END
02050C                     .
```

6-30. If the value in COUNT is equal to the value in PERIDS, when the DOUEQ statement is first tested, where does program control go?

6-31. In which statement is the xx (EQ) relational test made?

6-32. How is exit from the DOUEQ group controlled?

6-33. How does the processing logic for a DOWxx operation differ from a DOUxx operation?

Examine the following coding and answer Questions 6-34 to 6-36:

```
... ... 1 ... ... 2 ... ... 3 ... ... 4 ... ... 5 ... ... 6 ...

02010C           COUNT     DOWEQPERIDS
02020C                     .
02030C                     .
02040C                     END
02050C                     .
```

6-34. If the value in COUNT is equal to the value in PERIDS the first time the DOWEQ statement is tested, what statement is tested and what statement will be executed next?

6-35. In which statement is the xx (EQ) relational test made?

6-36. How is exit from the DOWEQ group controlled?

EXERCISES

6-1. From the following flowchart, write the necessary IF/ELSE statement(s) to support the processing logic:

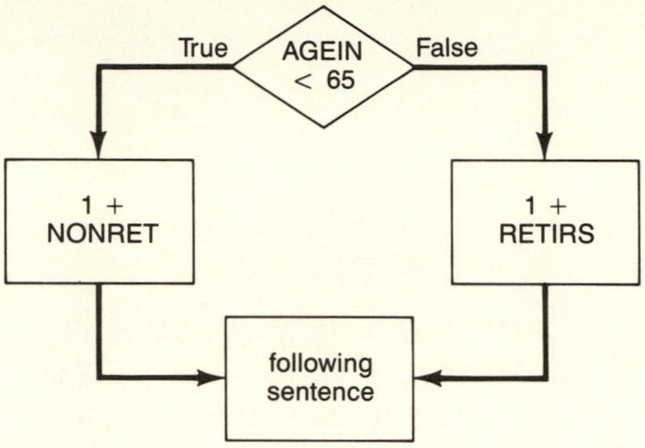

6-2. From the following flowchart, write the necessary IF/ELSE statement(s) to support the processing logic:

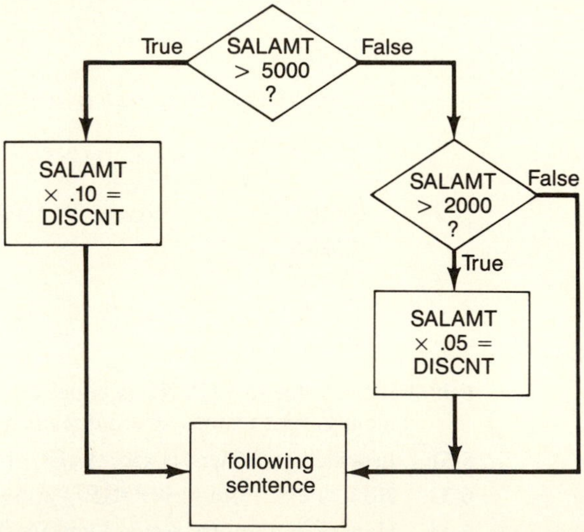

6-3 From the details given in the following two sentences, write the IF/ELSE statements to support the processing logic.

If TCODE is equal to 'UPD' or 'DEL' or 'CRD', add 1 to CHANGS. When TCODE is equal to 'ADD', add 1 to ADDS.

6-4. Write the instructions using the DO operation to support the following compound interest formula:

$$a = \frac{(1 + i)^n}{I}$$

where

a = compound interest of $1.00
i = annual interest rate
I = interest periods per year
n = total number of interest periods

Then: Compute the compound interest by the following two formulas:

1) Compound Amount = Principal × a (Compound interest of $1.00)
2) Compound Interest = Compound Amount − Principal

6-5. Refer to the compound interest formula in Exercise 6-4, and write the instructions using the DOU operation.

6-6. Modify the coding in Exercise 6-5 using the DOW operation.

LABORATORY ASSIGNMENTS

Laboratory Assignment 6-1: SALESMAN SALARY/COMMISSION REPORT

From the following documentation, write an RPG structured program to generate the report detailed in the supplemental print chart.

The Happy Sales Company pays its salesmen salary plus a commission on net sales. Payments are based on the following:

1. All sales employees are paid a base salary regardless of their sales. Those with less than two years' employment are paid a $600 monthly base salary. Employees with two or more years are guaranteed a $1,000 monthly salary.
2. Net sales over $2,000 are eligible for a commission that is added to the base salary. In any case, no commission is paid on the first $2,000 of net sales.

The commission amount is determined as follows:

1. Two or More Years' Employment. Twenty percent (0.20) commission is paid on net sales (sales − returns) over $2,000. Any commission sales over $30,000 are paid an additional 5% commission.
2. Less than Two Years' Employment. Twelve percent (0.12) commission is paid on net sales (sales − returns) over $2,000. Any commission sales over $25,000 are paid an additional 2% commission.

Summary:

Net Sales = Monthly Sales − Sales Returns
Commission Sales = Net Sales − $2,000

All commission computations are based on commission sales.

Format of the Input Records:

SAL NO	SALESMAN NAME		MONTHLY SALES	SALES RETURNS
9 9 9 9 9	9 9 9 9 9 9 9 9 9 9 9 9 9 9 9 9 9 9 9 9 9 9 9 9 9	9 9	9 9 9 9 9 9 9 9	9 9 9 9 9 9 9
1 2 3 4 5	6 7 8 9 10 11 12 13 14 15 16 17 18 19 20 21 22 23 24 25 26 27 28 29 30	31 32	33 34 35 36 37 38 39 40	41 42 43 44 45 46 47

YEARS EMPLOYED (positions 31–32)

Report Design:

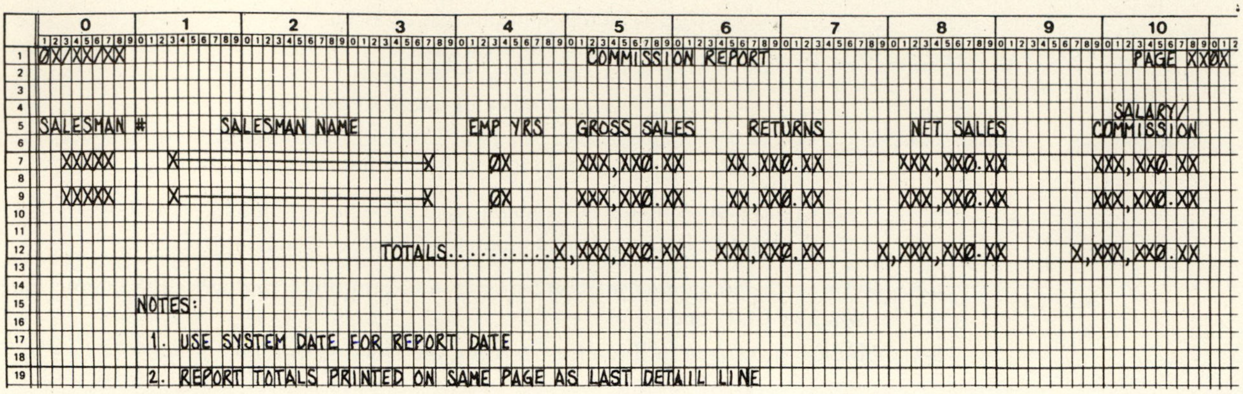

Input Data:

Salesman Number Cols 1-5	Name 6-30	Emp Yrs 31-32	Sales Amount 33-40	Sales Returns 41-47
11111	SIEGFRIED HOUNDSTOOTH	4	01125050	0100000
11112	FELIX GOODGUY	1	02800000	0000000
22222	OTTO MUTTENJAMMER	6	10000000	0000000
33333	HANS OFFENHAUSER	1	00250000	0070000
44444	BARNEY OLDFIELD	3	00190000	0000000
55555	WILLIAM PETTY	2	02200000	0000000

Laboratory Assignment 6-2: PAYROLL REGISTER

A payroll register records the year-to-date and weekly payroll information for each employee. Federal income and social security taxes withheld to date and for the current week are included in the report. In addition, the week's gross and net pay amounts are also specified. Other deductions, such as hospitalization, retirement, union dues, and so forth, are some of the other items that may be deducted from an employee's paycheck. From the record layout form, processing logic flowchart, and printer spacing chart that follows, write a structured RPG program to generate the required report.

Format of Data Records:

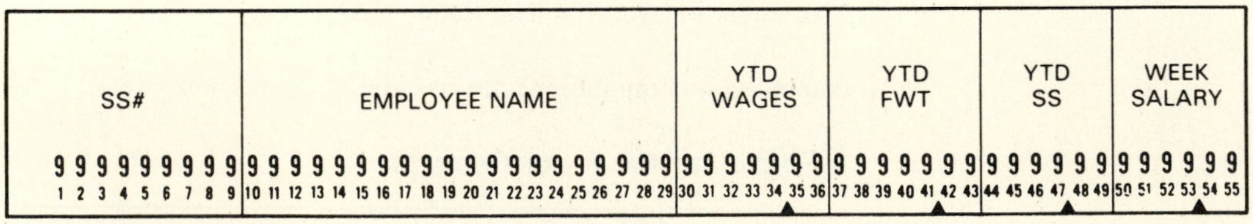

Calculations: The logic flowchart that follows details the calculations required for this application. To simplify federal income tax computations, specify a constant rate of 20%.

Refer to the first decision symbol in the flowchart, and notice that a relational test has been included to determine if the year-to-date (YTDSS) is less than $3,855.60 (maximum amount of social security that may be withheld for 1990). If it is less than that statutory amount, the social security tax withheld for the current week's pay is computed; otherwise the routine is ignored. The $3,855.60 constant was determined by multiplying maximum wages subject to social security tax ($50,400) for 1990 by a rate of 7.65%. The maximum amount and percentages are subject to change.

Processing Logic Flowchart:

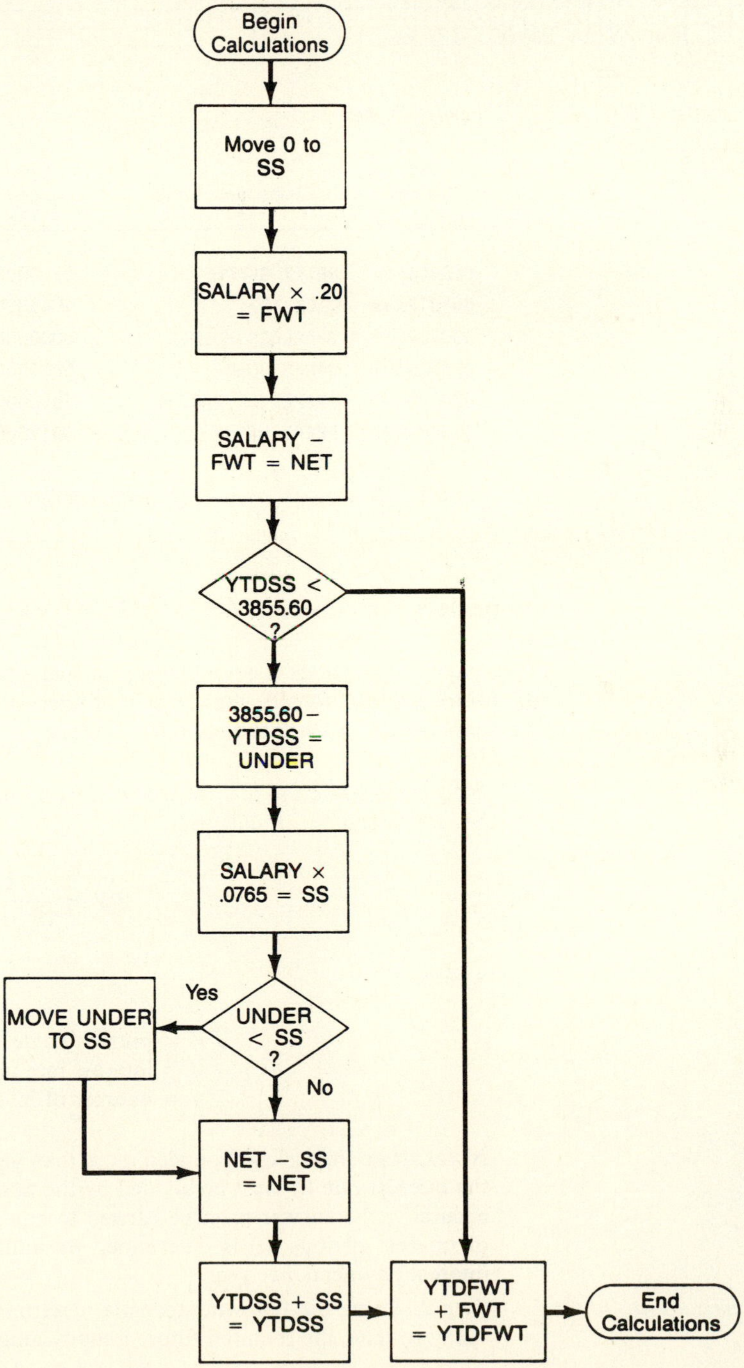

Report Design:

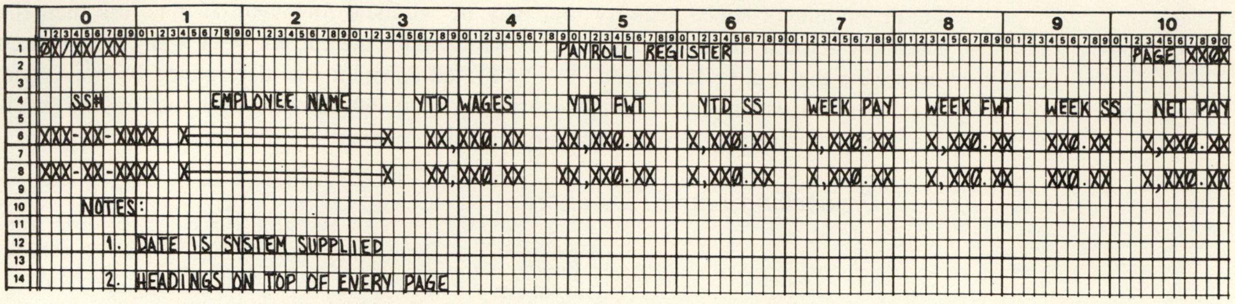
ØX/XX/XX
PAYROLL REGISTER
PAGE XXØX
SS#
EMPLOYEE NAME
YTD WAGES
YTD FWT
YTD SS
WEEK PAY
WEEK FWT
WEEK SS
NET PAY
XXX-XX-XXXX X X XX,XXØ.XX XX,XXØ.XX X,XXØ.XX X,XXØ.XX X,XXØ.XX XXØ.XX X,XXØ.XX
XXX-XX-XXXX X X XX,XXØ.XX XX,XXØ.XX X,XXØ.XX X,XXØ.XX X,XXØ.XX XXØ.XX X,XXØ.XX
NOTES:
1. DATE IS SYSTEM SUPPLIED
2. HEADINGS ON TOP OF EVERY PAGE

Input Data:

SS Number Cols 1-9	Employee Name 10-29	YTD Wages 30-36	YTD FWT 37-43	YTD SS 44-49	Weekly Salary 50-55
050446666	BETTY BURPO	0250000	0050000	019125	050000
001012345	DICK TRACY	4965000	0993000	379823	075000
100709876	SHERLOCK HOLMES	6000000	1200000	385560	100000
020324321	JAMES BOND	5000000	1000000	382500	080000
020400050	INSPECTOR GADGET	5040000	1008000	385560	090000
110889999	PERRY MASON	0011000	0002200	000842	027500

Note: YTD amounts do not include current week salary items

Laboratory Assignment 6-3: PRESENT VALUE OF A FUTURE AMOUNT

Fixed payment annuities require that a principal amount be invested today to have a specific future amount, considering the current interest rate and the period of the investment. The mathematical steps include the following:

Step 1: Compute the present worth of $1 by dividing 1 by the compound amount of $1, expressed by formula as:

$$PV = \frac{1}{(1 + i)^n}$$

where:

PV = present value of $1
i = interest rate per annum
n = number of interest periods

Notes: If interest is compounded more than yearly (i.e., monthly, weekly, or daily), the interest rate (i) must be divided by the number of interest periods per year. For accuracy, the answer must be carried to nine decimal positions. The total number of interest periods (n) is determined by multiplying the investment years by the interest payments per year.

Step 2: Using the following formula, determine the amount that must be invested today to have the required future annuity amount:

$$P = S \times PV$$

where:

P = amount that must be invested today to have future annuity
S = amount of future annuity
PV = present value of $1

Format of Data Records:

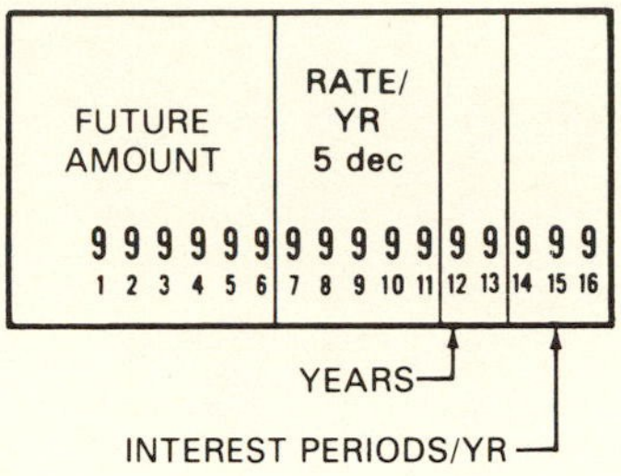

Report Design:

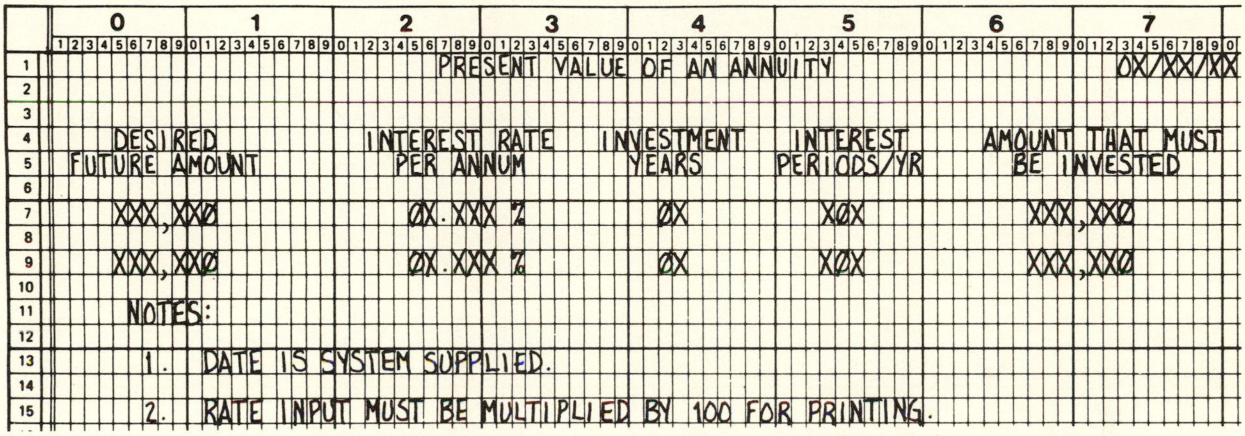

PRESENT VALUE OF AN ANNUITY
ØX/XX/XX
DESIRED
FUTURE AMOUNT
INTEREST RATE
PER ANNUM
INVESTMENT
YEARS
INTEREST
PERIODS/YR
AMOUNT THAT MUST
BE INVESTED
XXX,XXØ
ØX.XXX %
ØX
XØX
XXX,XXØ
NOTES:
1. DATE IS SYSTEM SUPPLIED.
2. RATE INPUT MUST BE MULTIPLIED BY 100 FOR PRINTING.

Input Data:

Desired Future Amount Cols 1-6	Interest Rate Per Annum 7-11	Investment Years 12-13	Interest Periods Per Year 14-16
100000	08000	10	001
100000	08000	10	012
100000	08000	10	365
100000	10000	10	001
100000	10000	10	012
100000	10000	10	365

chapter 7
The EXCPT Operation and Internal Subroutines

The EXCPT operation, which adds flexibility to RPG II, RPG III, and RPG/400 programs, is introduced in this chapter and use of the operation is shown in two application programs. First, the syntax and processing logic of the EXCPT operation are illustrated in an example program that prints the data in a record a predetermined number of times. Second, another example of EXCPT operation control is shown in an applications program that generates an electric billing report.

THE EXCPT (EXCEPTION) OPERATION

The syntax of the EXCPT operation is detailed in Figure 7-1. The processing logic of the EXCPT operation and its control of output are illustrated in Figure 7-2. Notice that the output instructions (exception output) controlled by the EXCPT operation must be specified with the letter E in the Type field (column 15). Any H (heading), D (detail), or T (total) time output is ignored when control from an

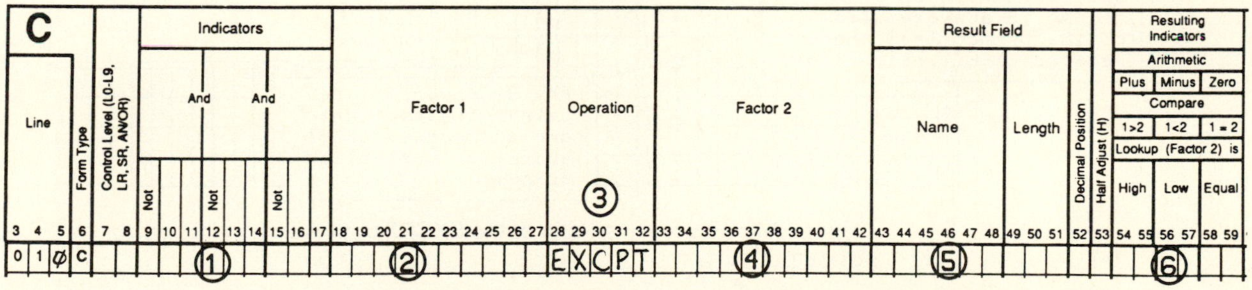

1. Total or Detail Time indicators may optionally be used to condition the EXCPT instruction.
2. Factor 1 is not used.
3. EXCPT operation name must be specified in the operation field.
4. Factor 2 is not used with non-IBM RPG compilers, but may be optionally used with RPG compilers installed on IBM's System/36, System/38, and the AS/400 model computers.
5. Result Field and Field Length fields are not used.
6. Resulting Indicators are not used.

Figure 7-1 EXCPT operation syntax.

EXCPT operation scans the output instructions. Also, E (exception) type of output may be included in any order and does not have to follow the H, D, T order required for other output types. Furthermore, any number of EXCPT operations may be included in a program.

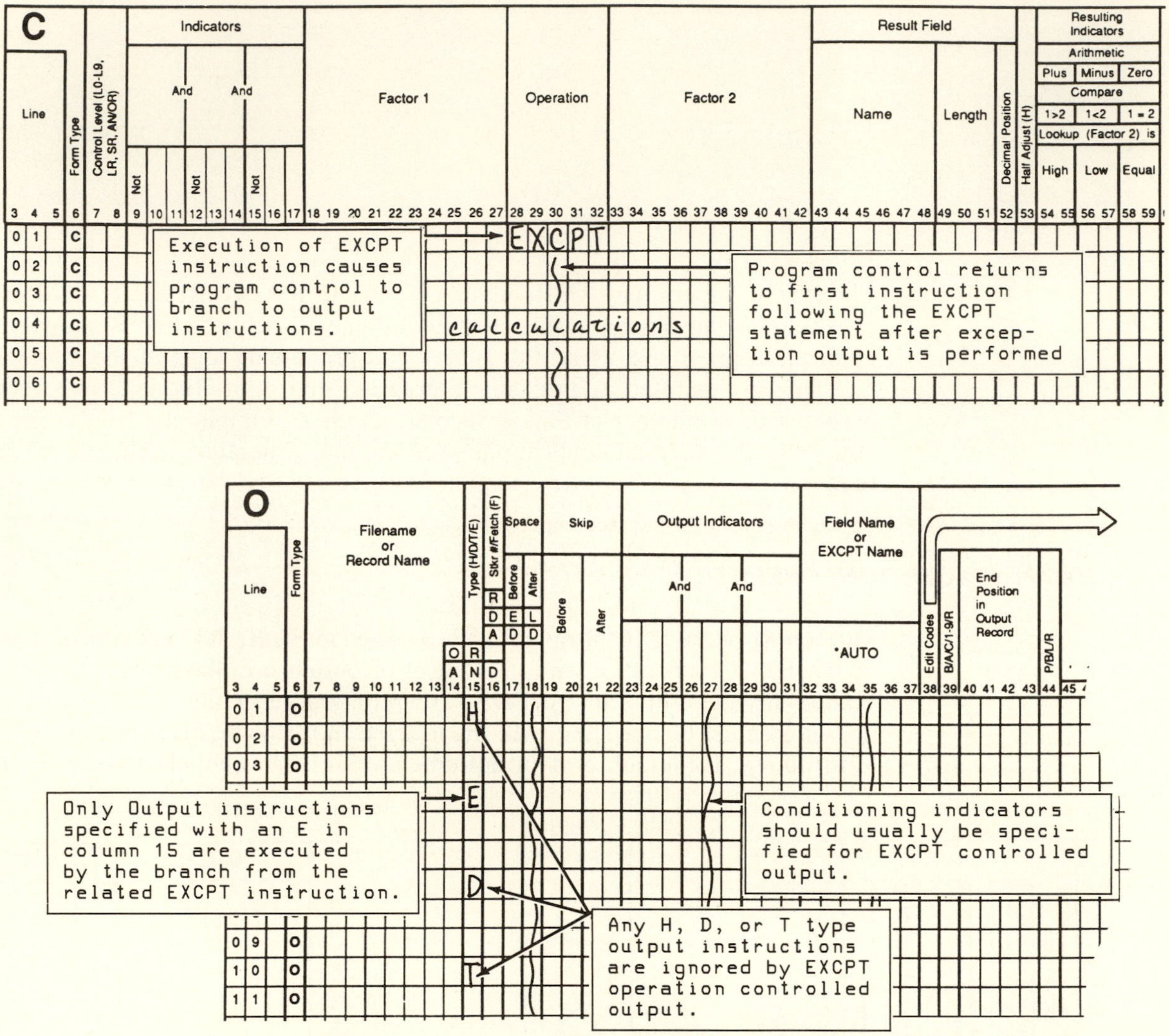

Figure 7-2 Processing logic of the EXCPT operation and its control of output.

APPLICATION PROGRAM—PRINTING CUSTOMER SHIPPING LABELS

The specifications for an RPG application program that prints shipping labels are detailed in Figure 7-3. The system flowchart for the customer shipping label program shown in Figure 7-4 indicates that one input disk file and one output printer file are processed by the program. The format of the records in the input file and a listing of the data are included in Figure 7-5. The design of the report is shown in the printer spacing chart in Figure 7-6 with the report (labels) generated by the program.

PROGRAM SPECIFICATIONS Page 1 of 1

Program Name MAILING LABELS Program-ID CH7P1 Written By S. Myers

Purpose Print three mailing labels per customer Approved By The Boss

Input files (directory names):

DAT7P1 (stored on disk)

Output files (directory names):

LABELS (on continuous label paper)

Processing Narrative:

Write a structured RPG program to print customer shipping labels.

Input to the program:

A customer address file (DATA7P1) is stored on disk in the format shown in the supplemental record layout form.

Processing:

Read the input file and for each record processed perform the following:

Provide for a looping sequence and include the EXCPT operation to control the printing of 3 labels for each customer. After the three labels are printed, program control must read another record from the customer address file and continue the process until the end of the input file is sensed.

Notice that a second address field is included in the input record format. This field must be tested, and if blank, the city, state, zip code values are to be printed on the third line and not the fourth. Consequently, for that condition, there will be three print lines for the label and not four.

Output:

Print three labels for each customer on the continuous forms. Individual labels have a length of 8 lines. Printing is to begin on line 2 with overflow specified on line 7. Set the printer at 6 lines per inch.

Figure 7-3 Specifications for program that prints customer shipping labels.

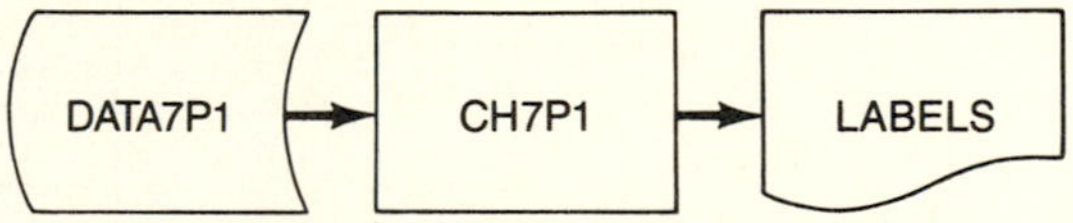

Figure 7-4 System flowchart for program that prints customer shipping labels.

CUST#	NAME	ADDRESS 1	ADDRESS 2	CITY	STATE	ZIP
9 9 9 9 9	9 9 9 9 9 9 9 9 9 9 9 9 9 9 9 9 9 9 9 9	9 9 9 9 9 9 9 9 9 9 9 9 9 9 9	9 9 9 9 9 9 9 9 9 9 9 9 9 9	9 9 9 9 9 9 9 9 9 9 9 9 9 9 9 9 9 9 9	9 9	9 9 9 9 9
1 2 3 4 5	6 7 8 9 10 11 12 13 14 15 16 17 18 19 20 21 22 23 24 25	26 27 28 29 30 31 32 33 34 35 36 37 38 39 40	41 42 43 44 45 46 47 48 49 50 51 52 53 54	55 56 57 58 59 60 61 62 63 64 65 66 67 68 69 70 71 72 73	74 75	76 77 78 79 80

Data File Listing:

```
10000ENRICO FERMI       10 NEUTRON LANE               CHICAGO             IL04010
20000EDWARD TELLER      ATOMIC LANE    PO BOX 239     LOS ALAMOS          NM08803
```

Figure 7-5 Input file's record format and listing of the data for the customer shipping labels program.

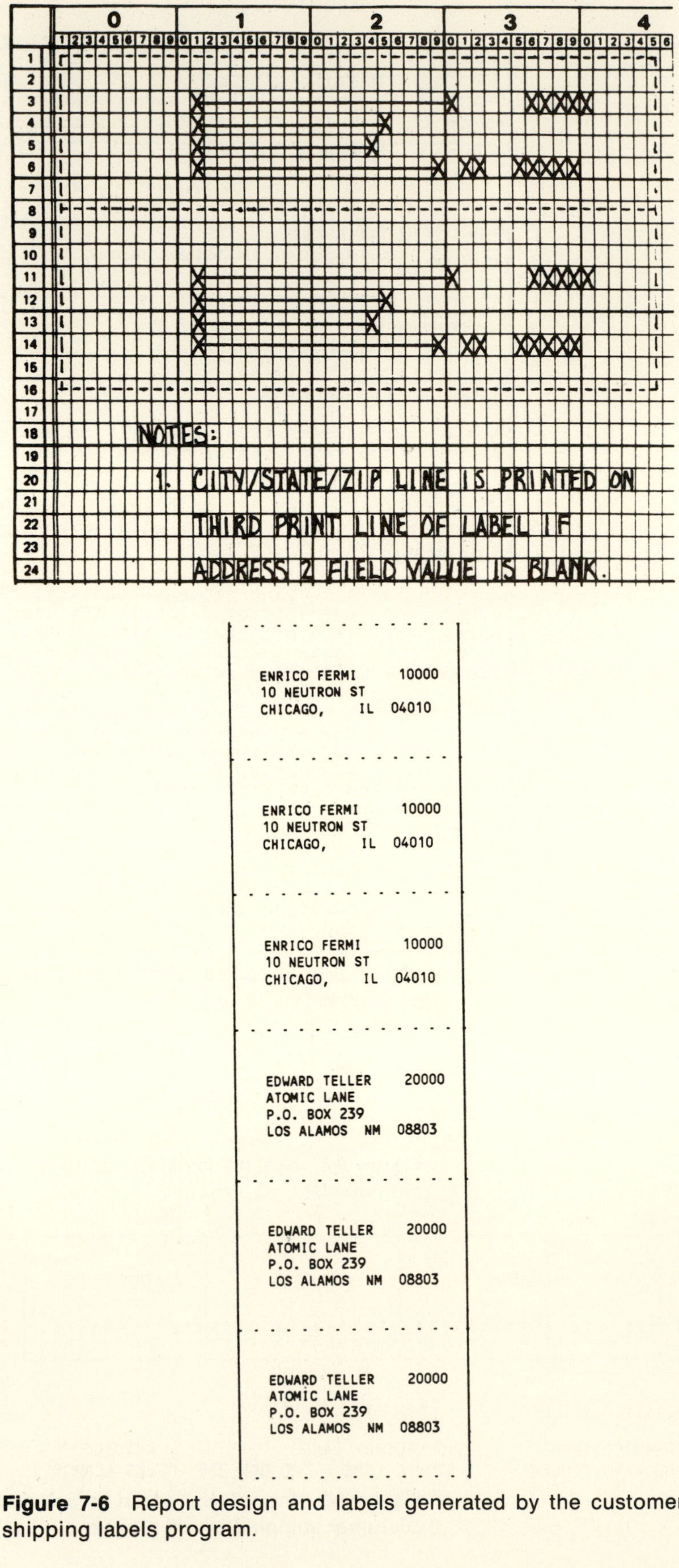

Figure 7-6 Report design and labels generated by the customer shipping labels program.

A flowchart that details the processing logic of the customer shipping label program is illustrated in Figure 7-7. Notice that the read and print symbols represent functions that are automatically performed by the RPG compiler. READ and WRITE operations are available in RPG, but they have not yet been introduced, and are, therefore, not included in this program.

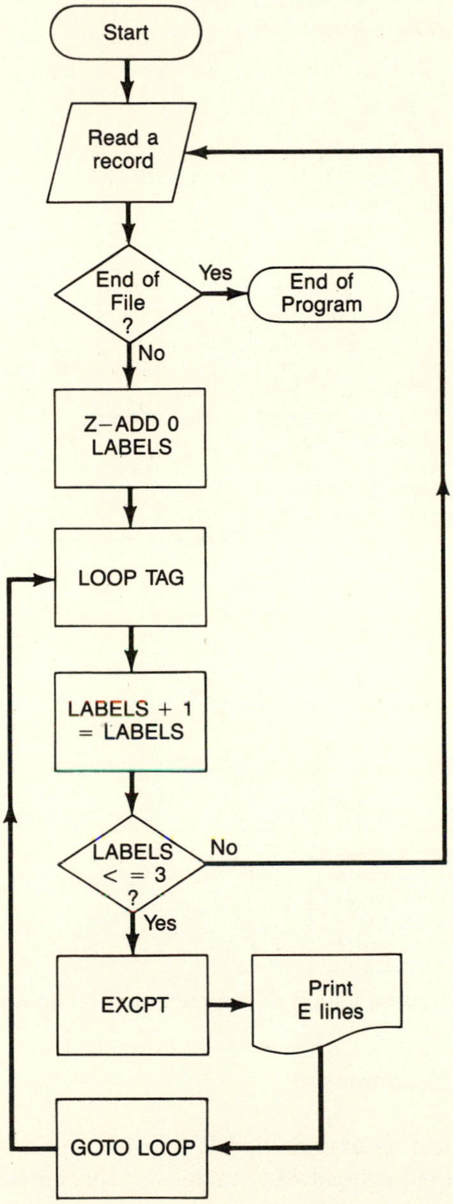

Figure 7-7 Processing logic flowchart for customer shipping labels program.

The source listing of the customer mailing labels program is presented in Figure 7-8. Notice the following features of this program:

1. Because the labels are a nonstandard forms length, a Line Counter Specifications instruction (line 4) is included to define a form (label) length of eight lines and page overflow on line 7. If necessary, refer to Chapter 3 for a review of the syntax related to this RPG form.
2. The RPG processing cycle is altered by the EXCPT operation.

3. The number of labels (three) to print for each customer is "hardcoded" in the program (line 16). Typically, however, the number of labels to print for each customer would be a variable input by CONSOLE, KEYBOARD, or interactive screen control. These methods for the input of data will be discussed separately in subsequent chapters.
4. Only E (exception) types of lines are specified for output. Before each label is printed, program control advances the printer to line 3 of the next continuous forms label.

```
... ... 1 ... ... 2 ... ... 3 ... ... 4 ... ... 5 ... ... 6 ... ... 7 ...
0001 H                                                           CH7P1
0002 FDATA7P1 IP  F  80  80            DISK                      CH7P1
   3 FLABELS  O   F 132 132           LPRINTER                   CH7P1
   4 LLABELS     8FL  70L                                        CH7P1
   5 IDATA7P1 SM  01                                             CH7P1
   6 I                                        1   5 CUST#        CH7P1
   7 I                                        6  25 NAME         CH7P1
0008 I                                       26  40 ADDRS1       CH7P1
0009 I                                       41  54 ADDRS2     10 CH7P1
0010 I                                       55  73 CITY         CH7P1
0011 I                                       74  75 STATE        CH7P1
0012 I                                       76  80 ZIP          CH7P1
0013 C                     Z-ADDO       LABELS  10       INIT.COUNTER CH7P1
0014 C           LOOP      TAG                                   CH7P1
0015 C           LABELS    ADD  1       LABELS           COUNTER CH7P1
  16 C           LABELS    COMP 3                   3030CTR < OR = 3? CH7P1
  17 C   30                EXCPT                    BRANCH TO OUTPTCH7P1
  18 C   30                GOTO LOOP                             CH7P1
  19 OLABELS  E  103   01                                        CH7P1
  20 O                          NAME      30                     CH7P1
  21 O                          CUST#     40                     CH7P1
0022 O        E  1     01                                        CH7P1
0023 O                          ADDRS1    25                     CH7P1
0024 O        E  1     01                                        CH7P1
0025 O                    N10   ADDRS2    24                     CH7P1
0026 O                     10   CITY      29                     CH7P1
0027 O                     10   STATE     32                     CH7P1
0028 O                     10   ZIP       39                     CH7P1
0029 O        E  1     01N10                                     CH7P1
0030 O                          CITY      29                     CH7P1
0031 O                          STATE     32                     CH7P1
0032 O                          ZIP       39                     CH7P1
```

L specs set page length & overflow line

EXCPT operation transfer program control to output

Looping continues until counter is > 3

E type output is controlled by execution of the EXCPT statement

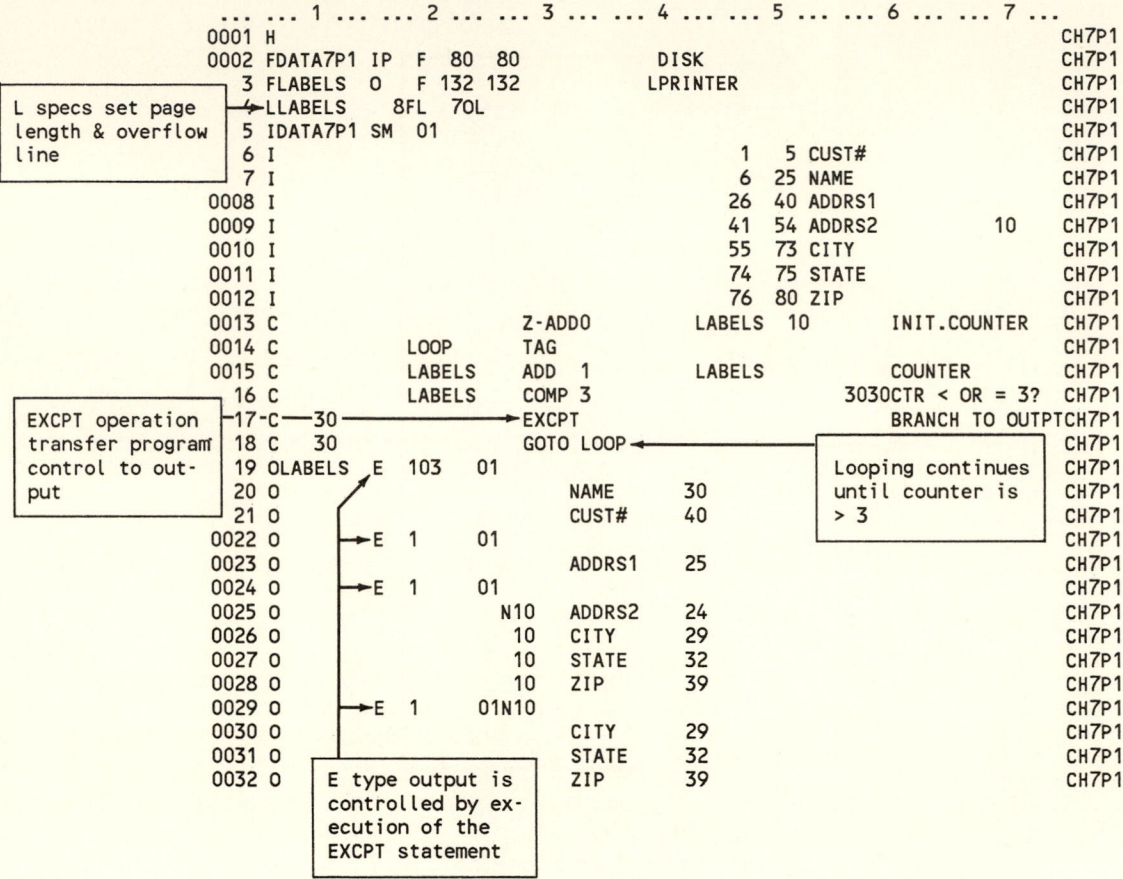

Figure 7-8 Source listing of the customer shipping labels program.

RPG Language Enhancement

In lieu of using indicators to condition E type (exception) output, an *EXCPT line name* may be specified instead. Advantages of this enhancement include the following:

1. Readability of the program is improved. Names are easier to reference than are indicators.
2. Reduces the number of indicators in an RPG program.

The syntax associated with this method is detailed in the modified source listing of the customer shipping label program shown in Figure 7-9. Currently, only RPG compilers installed on IBM's System/36, System/38, or AS/400 support this enhancement.

```
..... 1 ...... 2 ...... 3 ...... 4 ...... 5 ...... 6 ...... 7 ...
H                                                           CH7P2
FDATA7P1 IP  F  80  80            DISK                      CH7P2
FLABELS  O   F 132 132           LPRINTER                   CH7P2
LLABELS     8FL  7OL                                        CH7P2
IDATA7P1 SM  01                                             CH7P2
I                                         1   5 CUST#       CH7P2
I                                         6  25 NAME        CH7P2
I                                        26  40 ADDRS1      CH7P2
I                                        41  54 ADDRS2     10 CH7P2
I                                        55  73 CITY        CH7P2
I                                        74  75 STATE       CH7P2
I                                        76  80 ZIP         CH7P2
C                      Z-ADDO       LABELS  10     INIT.COUNTER CH7P2
C            LOOP      TAG                                  CH7P2
C            LABELS    ADD  1       LABELS         COUNTER  CH7P2
C            LABELS    COMP 3                               CH7P2
C   30                 EXCPTPLINE                           CH7P2
C   30                 GOTO LOOP                            CH7P2
OLABELS  E  103    01      PLINE                            CH7P2
O                          NAME      30                     CH7P2
O                          CUST#     40                     CH7P2
O        E  1      01      PLINE                            CH7P2
O                          ADDRS1    25                     CH7P2
O        E  1      01      PLINE                            CH7P2
O                 N10      ADDRS2    24                     CH7P2
O                  10      CITY      29                     CH7P2
O                  10      STATE     32                     CH7P2
O                  10      ZIP       39                     CH7P2
O        E  1      01N10   PLINE                            CH7P2
O                          CITY      29                     CH7P2
O                          STATE     32                     CH7P2
O                          ZIP       39                     CH7P2
```

Programmer-supplied name is entered in Factor 2. Name must be formatted in accordance with field name rules.

EXCPT name is entered left-justified in the Field Name columns on the same line as other Record Description entries.

When required, conditioning indicator(s) may be specified with the name specified for the EXCPT statement.

Figure 7-9 Modified source listing of the customer shipping labels program using EXCPT names for output.

Internal Subroutines

As programs become larger or more complex, they are usually difficult to debug and maintain. One method of keeping any program readable is to separate the calculations into *internal subroutines* (also called *modules*), which may or may not be independent of other coding. Ideally, any instructions related to a select program function should be included in a separate subroutine. The size and number of internal subroutines specified will depend on the program logic, program complexity, and/or the programmer's coding preferences. In addition, internal subroutines support the current trend of structured RPG programming where calculations are modularized and performed in a top-down sequence.

Internal Subroutine Operations. Internal subroutines are specified in the Calculation Specifications and include the following operation names:

EXSR—Causes program control to branch to the internal subroutine identified by the programmer-supplied name entered in Factor 2. The subroutine name must be formatted according the syntax related to field names.

BEGSR—Identifies entry point for the subroutine named in Factor 2 of the EXSR operation. The name specified in Factor 1 must be identical to the related EXSR instruction.

ENDSR—Indicates end of the internal subroutine. When this instruction is executed, program control branches to statement immediately following the related EXSR operation.

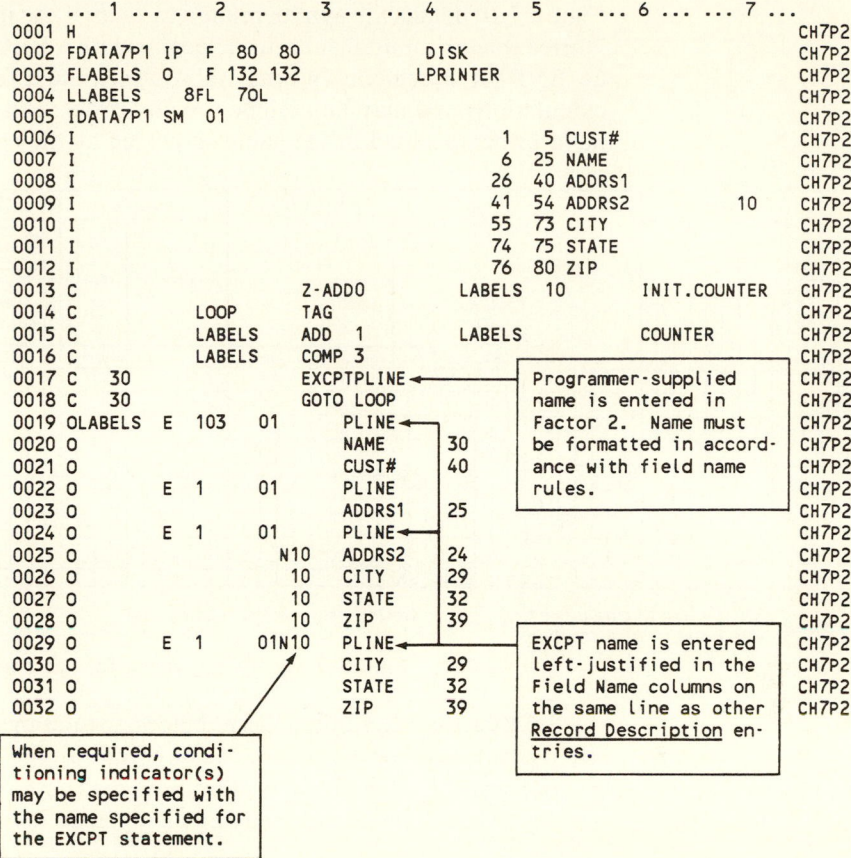

Figure 7-10 details the syntax related to each of the internal subroutine operations. Notice that an internal subroutine begins with a BEGSR instruction and ends with an ENDSR statement. Internal subroutines must follow all detail and total time calculations and may be assigned in any order. Furthermore, subroutines do not have to be specified in the same sequence as their related EXSR operations.

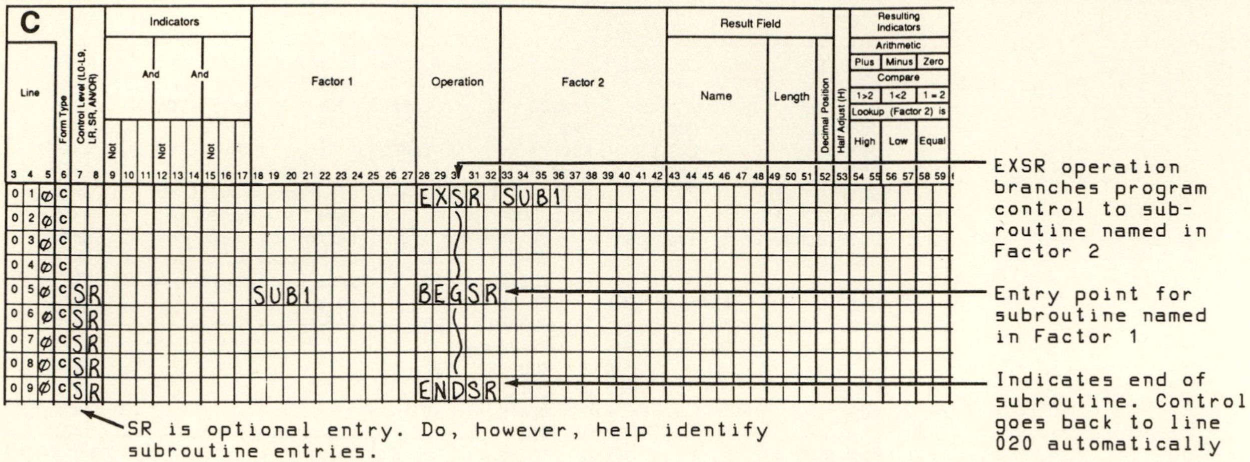

Figure 7-10 RPG syntax for internal subroutines.

Other than conditioning indicators at total or detail time, the entries shown are the only ones permitted for each operation. The SR entry that may be included in columns 7 and 8 with each subroutine instruction is optional on most computer systems. They may be omitted and/or replaced with control level indicators when required.

The rules related to the use of internal subroutines in an RPG program are given in Figure 7-11. The syntax related to rules 1, 6, 7, 8, and 9 is detailed in the instructions shown in Figure 7-12.

Internal Subroutine Rules:

1. Internal subroutine instructions must follow all detail and total time calculations.
2. Every subroutine must have a unique name.
3. The three operation codes; EXSR, BEGSR, and ENDSR must be used with each internal subroutine.
4. All RPG operations may be used within an internal subroutine.
5. Fields specified in a subroutine may be defined in the routine or outside of it.
6. Any RPG indicators (except 1P) may be entered in columns 7-17 (total and detail time) to condition instructions in the sub-routine.
7. A subroutine may branch to another subroutine by the EXSR operation. Program control will return back to the instruction following the related EXSR.
8. The GOTO operation may be used in an internal subroutine. However, a GOTO operation cannot be used to enter or exit from a subroutine.
9. The ENDSR operation (in lieu of a TAG statement) may be used as the entry point for a GOTO operation included in the routine.

Figure 7-11 Rules for the use of internal subroutines in an RPG program.

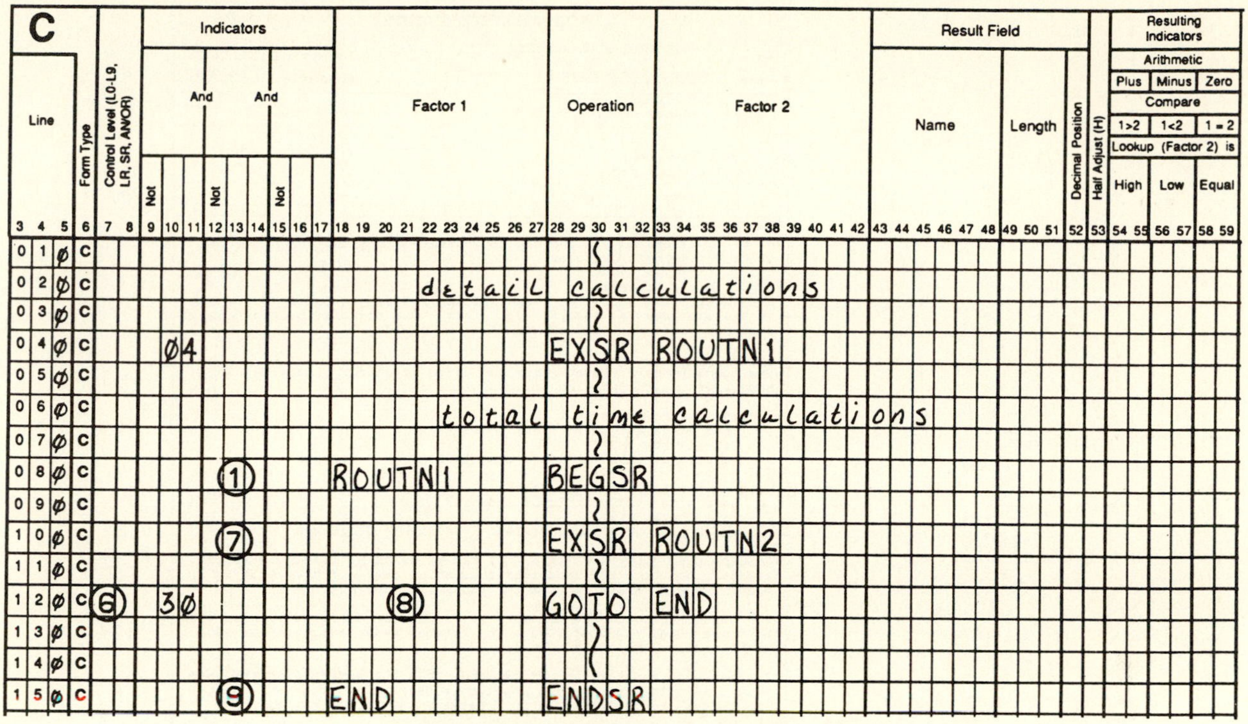

Line	Form Type	Control Level	Indicators	Factor 1	Operation	Factor 2
01Ø	C				}	
02Ø	C			detail	calculations	
03Ø	C				}	
04Ø	C		Ø4		EXSR	ROUTN1
05Ø	C				}	
06Ø	C			total	time	calculations
07Ø	C				}	
08Ø	C		(1)	ROUTN1	BEGSR	
09Ø	C				}	
10Ø	C		(7)		EXSR	ROUTN2
11Ø	C				}	
12Ø	C	(6)	3Ø	(8)	GOTO	END
13Ø	C				}	
14Ø	C				}	
15Ø	C		(9)	END	ENDSR	

Figure 7-12 Coding examples for syntax rules 1, 6, 7, 8, and 9.

An application program that illustrates how internal subroutines are effectively used in an RPG program follows. Understand, however, that internal subroutines are not a coding requirement but are used only to enhance the readability of a program and support and encourage structured design.

APPLICATION PROGRAM—ELECTRIC BILL REPORT

The specifications for an RPG program that generates a billing report for an electric company is presented in Figure 7-13. A system flowchart shown in Figure 7-14 indicates the input and output files processed by the program. A copy of the input file's record layout form and data are shown in Figure 7-15. The design of the report is shown in the printer spacing chart in Figure 7-16. The report generated by the electric billing report application program is presented in Figure 7-17.

Processing Logic for Program's Internal Subroutines

Figure 7-18 details the processing logic for the internal subroutines included in the program. Examine the source listing in Figure 7-19, and notice that on line 0058 *Detail time* output has been replaced by *Exception time* output (E in column 15), which is controlled by the EXCPT operation on line 0015. The EXCPT instruction is executed after all the calculations for an input record are completed and the results are ready for output. Heading lines and page overflow are controlled by generic RPG first page (1P) and page overflow (OF) indicator assignments. A step-by-step analysis of the instructions for the homeowner's and tax internal subroutines are detailed in Figure 7-20.

PROGRAM SPECIFICATIONS Page 1 of 1

Program Name ELECTRIC BILL REPORT Program-ID CH7P3 Written By S. Myers

Purpose Generate a electric bill report Approved By The Boss

Input files (directory names):
DAT7P3 (stored on disk)

Output files (directory names)
PRINTER (stock paper)

Processing Narrative:

Write a structured RPG program to generate a billing report for an electic company's customers.

Input to the program:
A customer file stored on disk includes records in the format shown in the supplemental record layout form. The file is to be processed consecutively until the end of file is sensed.

Processing:
The company has different base and usage rates for industrial and homeowners which detailed below:

Rates for Homeowners:
Base usage = 1000 kilowatt hours
Base charge = $40
Additional rate for usage over 1000 kwh = $.042/kwh

Rates for Industrial users:
Base usage = 5000 kilowatt hours
Base charge = $175
Additional rate for usage over 5000 kwh = $.035/kwh

Compare the input user field. If the value is H, branch to an internal subroutine for homeowner's calculations. If the value is I, branch to a separate routine for industrial users.

For either user, if the kilowatt hours used is equal to or less than the base usage (1000 or 5000), the related base charge (40 or 175) is billed for the month.

If more than the base amount is used, then the excess over the base amount is multiplied by the applicable base rate. The base charge and excess amount are added to determine the amount billed.

In addition, all users are subject to a tax based on $.015 per 100 kwh used. The tax is added to the amount billed. Add the total amount billed for each customer to an accumulator.

Output:

Complete the report detailed in the supplemental print chart.

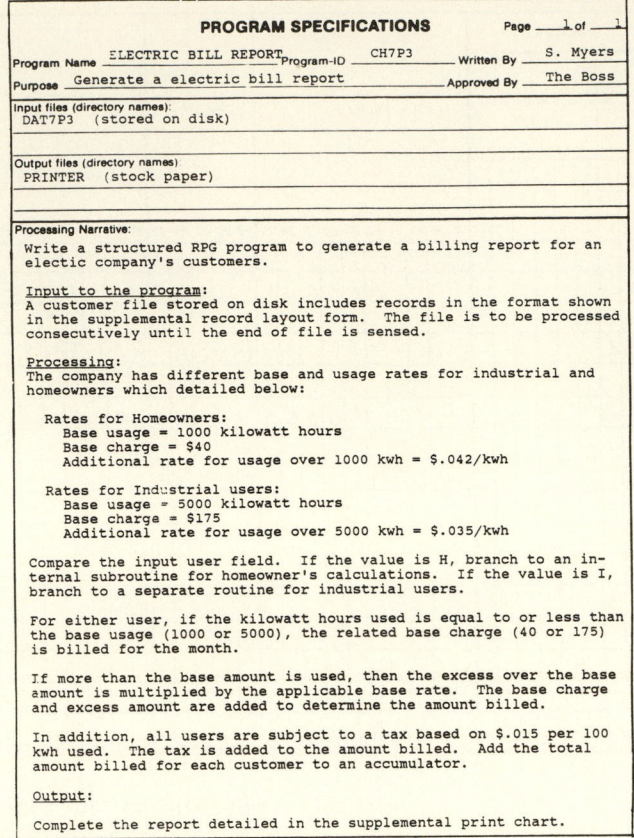

Figure 7-13 Specifications for an RPG program that generates an electric billing report.

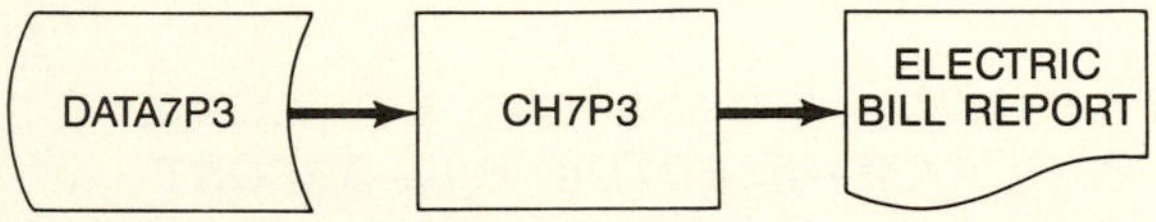

Figure 7-14 System flowchart for an RPG program that generates an electric billing report.

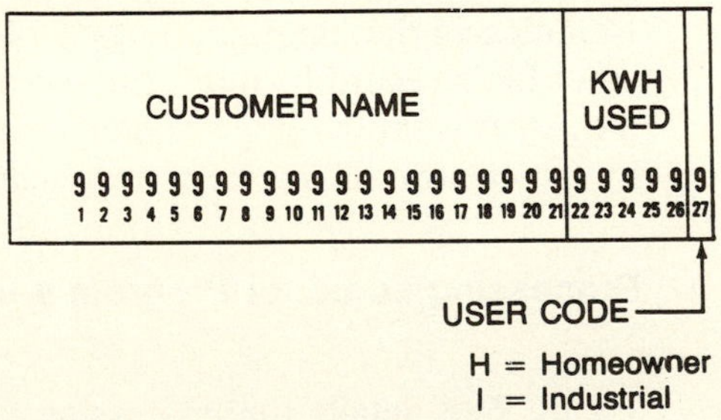

Data File Listing:

```
IVAN PATZIK          000945H
MANAGEMENT COMPANY   011000I
CHRIS LENTZ          001400H
TAYCO INCORPORATED   004500I
FRANZ ECKART         001050H
COMPUTER SERVICES CO150000I
```

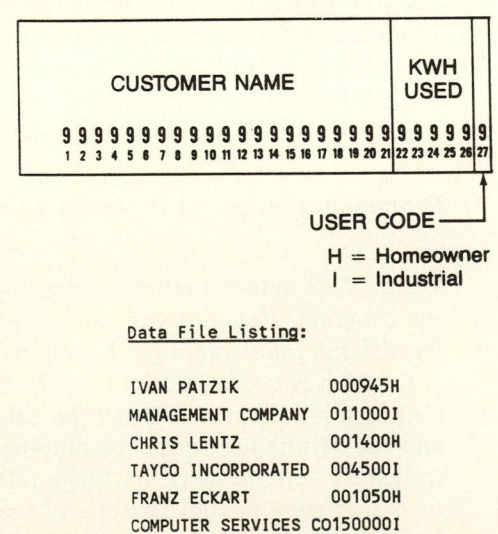

Figure 7-15 Record layout form and listing of the data file processed by the electric billing report.

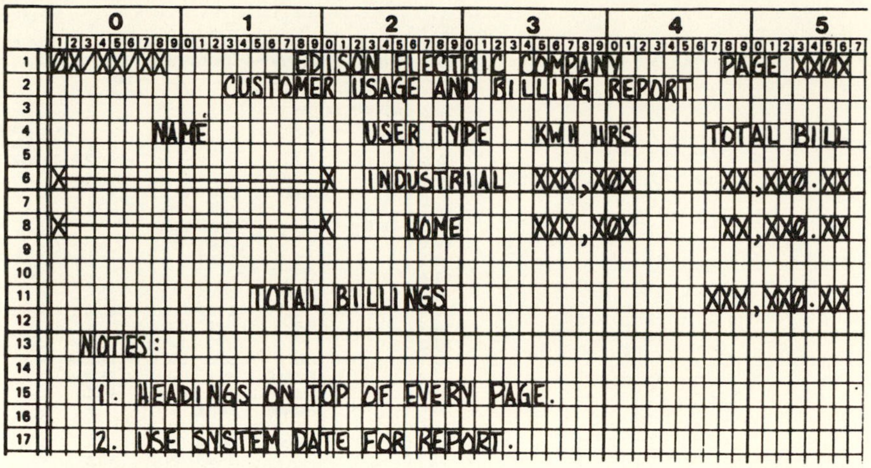

Figure 7-16 Printer spacing chart for report generated by the electric billing report program.

```
11/30/92            EDISON ELECTRIC COMPANY          PAGE    1
                  CUSTOMER USAGE AND BILLING REPORT

               NAME              USER TYPE   KWH HRS      TOTAL BILL

IVAN PATZIK                         HOME         945           40.14

MANAGEMENT COMPANY               INDUSTRIAL   11,000          386.65

CHRIS LENTZ                         HOME       1,400           57.01

TAYCO INCORPORATED               INDUSTRIAL    4,500          175.68

FRANZ ECKART                        HOME       1,050           42.25

COMPUTER SERVICES CO             INDUSTRIAL  150,000        5,272.50


                      TOTAL BILLINGS                        5,974.23
```

Figure 7-17 Report generated by electric billing report program.

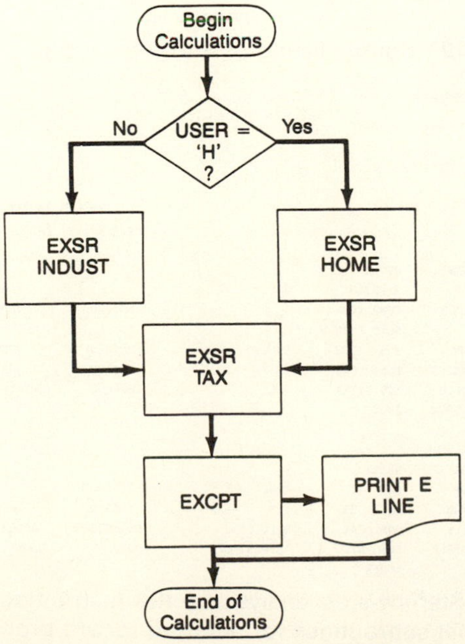

Figure 7-18 Processing logic for internal subroutines included in the electric billing report program.

```
... ... 1 ... ... 2 ... ... 3 ... ... 4 ... ... 5 ... ... 6 ... ... 7 ...
0001 H                                                                CH7P3
0002  * THIS PROGRAM COMPUTES AND GENERATES A BILLING REPORT FOR AN    CH7P3
0003  * ELECTRIC COMPANY'S CUSTOMERS....................               CH7P3
0004 FDATA7P3 IP  F  28  28            DISK                            CH7P3
0005 FBILLINGSO   F 132 132     OF     PRINTER                         CH7P3
0006 IDATA7P3 SM  01                                                   CH7P3
0007 I                                          1  20 CNAME            CH7P3
0008 I                                         21  260KWH              CH7P3
0009 I                                         27  28 USER             CH7P3
0010  *                                                                CH7P3
0011 C           USER      COMP 'H'                     10 USER TYPE?  CH7P3
0012 C   10                EXSR HOME                      HOMEOWNER SR CH7P3
0013 C  N10                EXSR INDUST                    INDUSTRIAL SR CH7P3
0014 C                     EXSR TAX                       TAX & TOTALS SRCH7P3
0015 C                     EXCPT                          PRINT E LINE CH7P3
0016  *                                                                CH7P3
0017 C           HOME      BEGSR                          BEGIN HOME SR CH7P3
0018 C                     Z-ADD40        BILL    72      BASE AMOUNT  CH7P3
0019 C           KWH       COMP 1000               1111 > 1000 KWH?    CH7P3
0020 C   11                GOTO ENDHOM                    < OR = BRANCH CH7P3
0021 C           KWH       SUB  1000      EXCESS  60      KWH > 1000   CH7P3
0022 C           EXCESS    MULT .042      EXTRA   72      > 1000 KWH $AMTCH7P3
0023 C           BILL      ADD  EXTRA     BILL            BASE + EXTRA CH7P3
0024 C           ENDHOM    ENDSR                          END HOME SR  CH7P3
0025  *                                                                CH7P3
0026 C           INDUST    BEGSR                          BEGIN INDUST SRCH7P3
0027 C                     Z-ADD175       BILL            BASE AMOUNT  CH7P3
0028 C           KWH       COMP 5000               1111 > 5000 KWH?    CH7P3
0029 C   11                GOTO ENDIND                    < OR = BRANCH CH7P3
0030 C           KWH       SUB  5000      EXCESS          KWH > 5000   CH7P3
0031 C           EXCESS    MULT  035      EXTRA           > 5000 KWH $AMTCH7P3
0032 C           BILL      ADD  EXTRA     BILL            BASE + EXTRA CH7P3
0033 C           ENDIND    ENDSR                          END INDUST SR CH7P3
0034  *                                                                CH7P3
0035 C           TAX       BEGSR                          BEGIN TAX SR CH7P3
0036 C           KWH       DIV  100       TKWH    40      KWH FOR TAX  CH7P3
0037 C           TKWH      MULT .015      TAX     62H     COMPUTE TAX  CH7P3
0038 C           BILL      ADD  TAX       BILL            ADD TAX TO BILLCH7P3
0039 C           TOTALB    ADD  BILL      TOTALB  82      ACCUM BILLS  CH7P3
0040 C                     ENDSR                          END TAX SR   CH7P3
0041  *                                                                CH7P3
0042 OBILLINGSH  101   1P                                              CH7P3
0043 O        OR       OF                                              CH7P3
0044 O                          UDATE Y    8                           CH7P3
0045 O                                    51 'PAGE'                    CH7P3
0046 O                          PAGE  Z   56                           CH7P3
0047 O                                    40 'EDISON ELECTRIC COMPANY' CH7P3
0048 O          H  2   1P                                              CH7P3
0049 O        OR       OF                                              CH7P3
0050 O                                    30 'CUSTOMER USAGE AND'      CH7P3
0051 O                                    45 'BILLING REPORT'          CH7P3
0052 O          H  2   1P                                              CH7P3
0053 O        OR       OF                                              CH7P3
0054 O                                    11 'NAME'                    CH7P3
0055 O                                    31 'USER TYPE'               CH7P3
0056 O                                    41 'KWH HRS'                 CH7P3
0057 O                                    56 'TOTAL BILL'              CH7P3
0058 O          E  2   01                                              CH7P3
0059 O                          CNAME     20                           CH7P3
0060 O                 10                 32 '   HOME   '              CH7P3
0061 O                N10                 32 'INDUSTRIAL'              CH7P3
0062 O                          KWH   2   41                           CH7P3
0063 O                          BILL  1   56                           CH7P3
0064 O          T 1    LR                                              CH7P3
0065 O                                    28 'TOTAL BILLINGS'          CH7P3
0066 O                          TOTALB1   56                           CH7P3
```

Figure 7-19 Source listing of the electric billing report program.

```
Value in record processed:

                KWH ───┐   ┌──USER
                       ▼   │
CHRIS LENTZ         001400H

Calculations:                                           Values in items after execution     Indicators
                                                        Factor 1   Factor 2   Result Field      On

0017 C          HOME     BEGSR                                                                01 10
0018 C                   Z-ADD40    BILL    72                          40^      0004^000     01 10
0019 C          KWH      COMP 1000                 1111   001400^     1000^                   01 10
0020 C    11             GOTO ENDHOM                                                          01 10
0021 C          KWH      SUB  1000  EXCESS  60            001400^     1000^      000400^      01 10
0022 C          EXCESS   MULT .042  EXTRA   72            000400^     ^042       00016^80     01 10
0023 C          BILL     ADD EXTRA  BILL                  0004^000    00016^80   00056^80     01 10
0024 C          ENDHOM   ENDSR

0035 C          TAX      BEGSR                                                                01 10
0036 C          KWH      DIV  100   TKWH    40            001400^      100^      0014^        01 10
0037 C          TKWH     MULT .015  TAX     62H             0014^     ^015       0000^21      01 10
0038 C          BILL     ADD  TAX   BILL                  00056^80    0000^21    00057^01     01 10
0039 C          TOTALS   ADD  BILL  TOTALS  82            00426^75    00057^01   00483^76     01 10
0040 C                   ENDSR
```

Figure 7-20 Step-by-step analysis of the instructions in the homeowner and tax internal subroutines for the third record processed.

RPG LANGUAGE ENHANCEMENT—CASxx AND END OPERATIONS

RPG syntax for internal subroutines has been enhanced by the addition of the CASxx and END operations. The CASxx (Case) operation conditionally controls an exit to an internal subroutine. Two functions, COMP (Compare) and EXSR (Exit to an internal subroutine) are included in this operation, which eliminates the need for the customary conditioning indicators. The syntax of the CASxx and required END operations is shown in Figure 7-21.

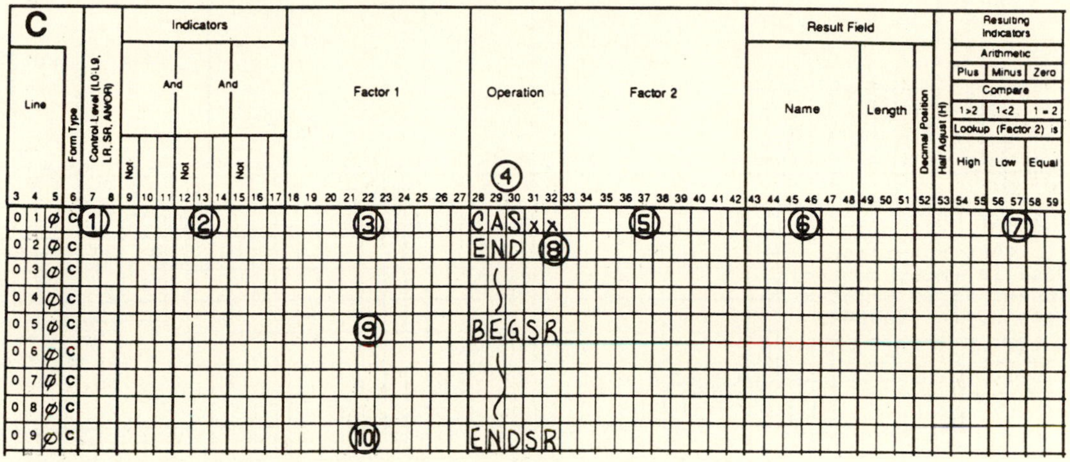

1. A total time indicator may condition a CASxx instruction.

2. Detail time indicators may condition a CASxx instruction.

3. Unless the xx entry in the CASxx operation is blank, a field name or literal must be entered in Factor 1. The items entered in this field must be the same type as the entry in Factor 2.

4. The CASxx operation name must be entered in the Operation field. Entries for the xx value may be:

   GT - Factor 1 is greater than Factor 2
   LT - Factor 1 is less than Factor 2
   EQ - Factor 1 is equal to Factor 2
   NE - Factor 1 is not equal to Factor 2
   GE - Factor 1 is greater than or equal to Factor 2
   LE - Factor 1 is less than or equal to Factor 2
   blanks - Factor 1 is not compared to Factor 2

5. A Factor 2 entry must include a literal or field name and be defined as the same type as the Factor 1 entry. If the xx entry in the CASxx operation is not blank, this field is required.

6. Programmer-supplied internal subroutine name must be left-justified in the Result Field.

7. Resulting indicators are required if the CASxx operation is specified without a relational test condition and the Factor 1 and 2 entries are included. Otherwise, they are optional.

8. Required END operation indicates the end of the single CASxx statement or group.

9. BEGSR operation indicates the beginning of an internal subroutine. Name specified in the Result Field of the CASxx operation must be entered in Factor 1. Internal subroutines must follow all detail and total time calculations.

10. ENDSR operation indicates the end of the internal subroutine. It may be used as a TAG statement for a GOTO or CABxx operation <u>within</u> the related subroutine.

<u>Notes</u>:

1. A single or group of CASxx statements must be terminated by an END operation.

2. After a CASxx operation is executed, control returns to the statement following the related END operation. Consequently, when a CASxx statement is executed, any following CASxx instructions will be ignored in the common Case group.

3. Only CASxx statements may be included in a Case group.

4. The normal placement of a CASbb (blanks) instruction (no test conditon specified) is after any other CASxx statements.

Figure 7-21 Syntax for the CASxx (Case) and END operations.

The processing logic related to a CASxx group is detailed in Figure 7-22. When a CASxx instruction within a *Case Group* is executed, any following CASxx statements will be ignored. Program control returns to the statement following the END operation, which must always terminate one or more CASxx instructions. This processing logic differs from the EXSR operation where program control returns to the statement immediately following the related EXSR.

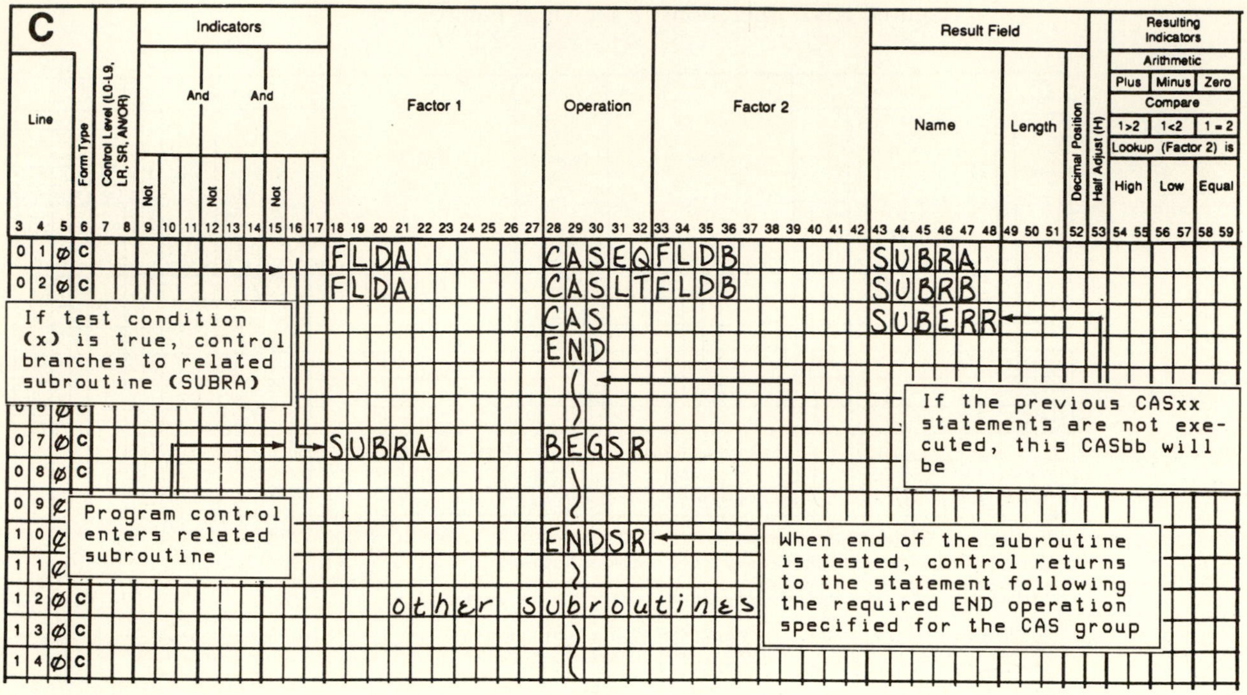

Figure 7-22 Processing logic of a CASxx group.

APPLICATION PROGRAM (ELECTRIC BILLING REPORT)— MODIFIED WITH RPG III/400 ENHANCEMENTS

The following RPG language enhancements that have been introduced in this and preceding chapters are included in the modified electric billing report program shown in Figure 7-23.

1. Elimination of Factor 1 entry when Result Field is specified with the same field name. (Chapter 4)
2. The EXCPT operation with an exception line name instead of one or more conditioning indicators for E output line control. (Chapter 7)
3. CABxx operation combines the functions of the COMP and GOTO operations into one statement. It eliminates the need for Resulting Indicator(s) required with the COMP statement that are used to condition a related GOTO instruction. (Chapter 6)
4. CASxx operation combines the functions of the COMP and EXSR operations into one statement. Also, it eliminates the need for one or more conditioning indicators to control a branch to an internal subroutine. (Chapter 7)

Remember that the language enhancements discussed are available only with RPG compilers installed on IBM's System/36, System/38, and AS/400 computers.

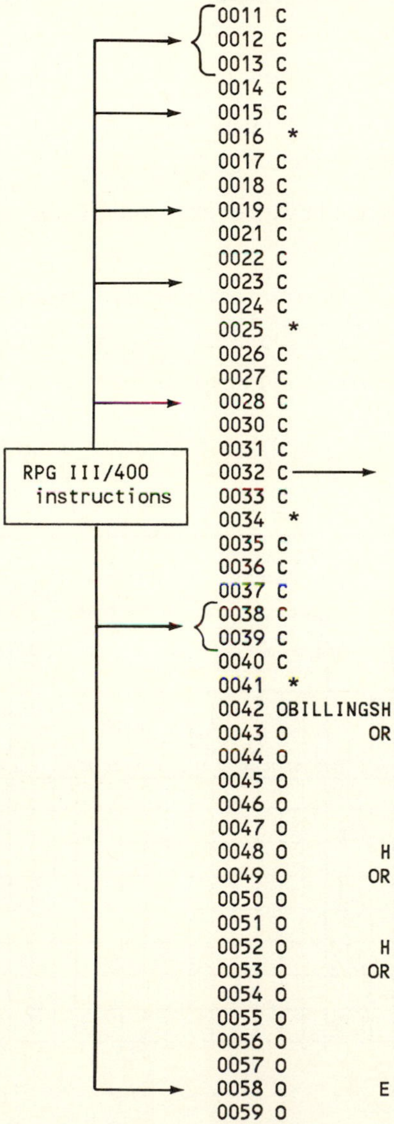

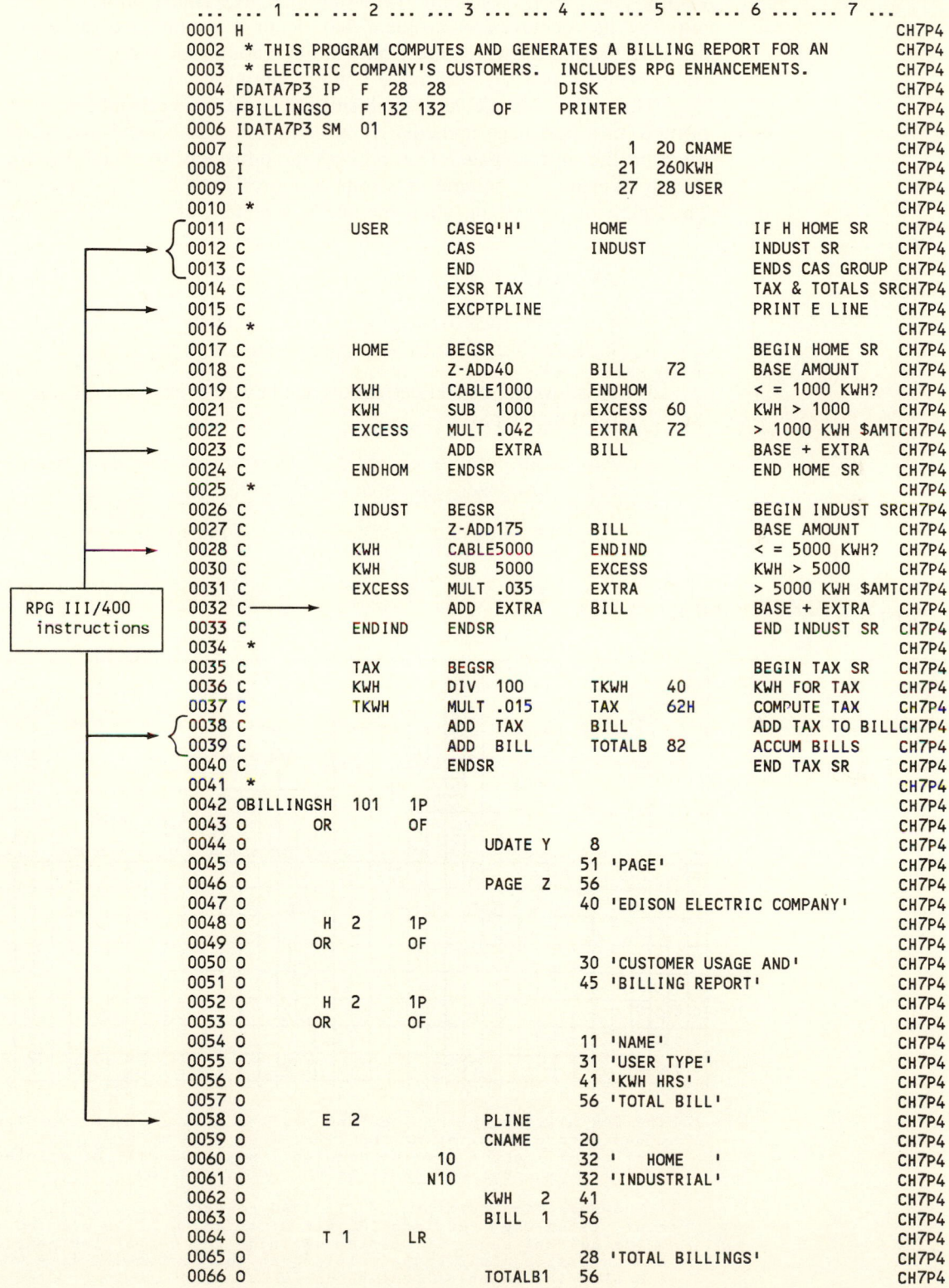

```
... ... 1 ... ... 2 ... ... 3 ... ... 4 ... ... 5 ... ... 6 ... ... 7 ...
0001 H                                                               CH7P4
0002  * THIS PROGRAM COMPUTES AND GENERATES A BILLING REPORT FOR AN   CH7P4
0003  * ELECTRIC COMPANY'S CUSTOMERS.  INCLUDES RPG ENHANCEMENTS.     CH7P4
0004 FDATA7P3 IP  F  28  28            DISK                          CH7P4
0005 FBILLINGSO   F 132 132     OF     PRINTER                       CH7P4
0006 IDATA7P3 SM  01                                                 CH7P4
0007 I                                        1  20 CNAME            CH7P4
0008 I                                       21  260KWH              CH7P4
0009 I                                       27  28 USER             CH7P4
0010  *                                                              CH7P4
0011 C           USER      CASEQ'H'       HOME              IF H HOME SR  CH7P4
0012 C                     CAS            INDUST            INDUST SR     CH7P4
0013 C                     END                              ENDS CAS GROUP CH7P4
0014 C                     EXSR TAX                         TAX & TOTALS SRCH7P4
0015 C                     EXCPTPLINE                       PRINT E LINE  CH7P4
0016  *                                                              CH7P4
0017 C           HOME      BEGSR                            BEGIN HOME SR  CH7P4
0018 C                     Z-ADD40        BILL     72       BASE AMOUNT   CH7P4
0019 C           KWH       CABLE1000      ENDHOM            < = 1000 KWH?  CH7P4
0021 C           KWH       SUB  1000      EXCESS   60       KWH > 1000    CH7P4
0022 C           EXCESS    MULT .042      EXTRA    72       > 1000 KWH $AMTCH7P4
0023 C                     ADD  EXTRA     BILL              BASE + EXTRA  CH7P4
0024 C           ENDHOM    ENDSR                            END HOME SR   CH7P4
0025  *                                                              CH7P4
0026 C           INDUST    BEGSR                            BEGIN INDUST SRCH7P4
0027 C                     Z-ADD175       BILL              BASE AMOUNT   CH7P4
0028 C           KWH       CABLE5000      ENDIND            < = 5000 KWH?  CH7P4
0030 C           KWH       SUB  5000      EXCESS            KWH > 5000    CH7P4
0031 C           EXCESS    MULT .035      EXTRA             > 5000 KWH $AMTCH7P4
0032 C                     ADD  EXTRA     BILL              BASE + EXTRA  CH7P4
0033 C           ENDIND    ENDSR                            END INDUST SR  CH7P4
0034  *                                                              CH7P4
0035 C           TAX       BEGSR                            BEGIN TAX SR  CH7P4
0036 C           KWH       DIV  100       TKWH     40       KWH FOR TAX   CH7P4
0037 C           TKWH      MULT .015      TAX      62H      COMPUTE TAX   CH7P4
0038 C                     ADD  TAX       BILL              ADD TAX TO BILLCH7P4
0039 C                     ADD  BILL      TOTALB   82       ACCUM BILLS   CH7P4
0040 C                     ENDSR                            END TAX SR    CH7P4
0041  *                                                              CH7P4
0042 OBILLINGSH  101   1P                                            CH7P4
0043 O       OR        OF                                            CH7P4
0044 O                         UDATE Y    8                          CH7P4
0045 O                                   51 'PAGE'                   CH7P4
0046 O                         PAGE  Z   56                          CH7P4
0047 O                                   40 'EDISON ELECTRIC COMPANY'  CH7P4
0048 O        H  2     1P                                            CH7P4
0049 O       OR        OF                                            CH7P4
0050 O                                   30 'CUSTOMER USAGE AND'     CH7P4
0051 O                                   45 'BILLING REPORT'         CH7P4
0052 O        H  2     1P                                            CH7P4
0053 O       OR        OF                                            CH7P4
0054 O                                   11 'NAME'                   CH7P4
0055 O                                   31 'USER TYPE'              CH7P4
0056 O                                   41 'KWH HRS'                CH7P4
0057 O                                   56 'TOTAL BILL'             CH7P4
0058 O        E  2             PLINE                                 CH7P4
0059 O                         CNAME     20                          CH7P4
0060 O                     10            32 '   HOME   '             CH7P4
0061 O                    N10            32 'INDUSTRIAL'             CH7P4
0062 O                         KWH   2   41                          CH7P4
0063 O                         BILL  1   56                          CH7P4
0064 O        T 1      LR                                            CH7P4
0065 O                                   28 'TOTAL BILLINGS'         CH7P4
0066 O                         TOTALB1   56                          CH7P4
```

Figure 7-23 Modified source listing (with RPG enhancements) of the electric billing report program.

Page Overflow Control for Exception Output

Fetch Overflow Feature. When page overflow is sensed during the program cycle, detail, total, and exception lines are printed on the page even after overflow has occurred. A problem may occur if a number of different types of lines are printed for which there may not be enough room on the page. This may cause printing over the perforated line on continuous forms paper.

To resolve this problem, the forms may be advanced and the overflow lines printed on a new page immediately after overflow is sensed instead of printing them on the current page. This process is controlled by specifying the letter F (Fetch Overflow) in column 16 of one or more H, D, T, or E type output lines. The following processing sequence occurs when Fetch Overflow is specified:

1. All total lines conditioned by an overflow indicator are printed.
2. Forms advance to the beginning line number of a new page as specified in the Skip Before or Skip After fields.
3. Heading and detail lines conditioned by an overflow indicator are printed on the new page.
4. Any detail, total, or exception lines specified with an F in column 16 of the record description area are printed.
5. Any remaining detail, exception, or total lines for the page are printed.

The syntax and processing logic of the Fetch Overflow feature is illustrated in Figure 7-24.

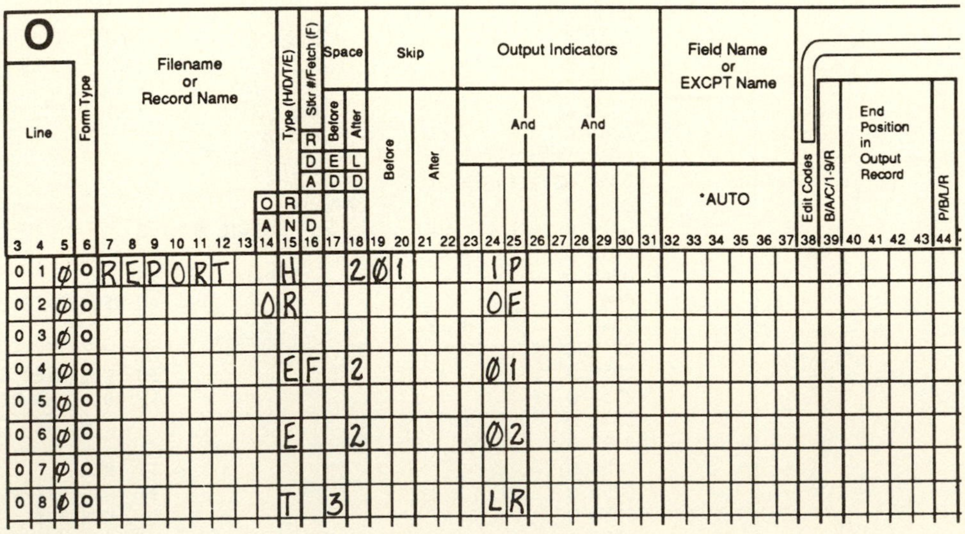

Line 040 will fetch the overflow routine only if page overflow is sensed before printing of the line. When this occurs, page overflow will occur and the heading line (010) will be printed on the following page before lines 040, 060, and 080.

If, however, the printing of line 040 caused page overflow to occur, lines 040, 060, and 080 (if L1 is on) will be printed on the current page. If printer was near the end of the page, this condition could cause printing on the perforated line which separates the pages of continuous forms paper.

Figure 7-24 Syntax and processing logic of the Fetch Overflow feature.

Program Control of Page Overflow

The automatic page overflow feature is unique to RPG and is controlled in other high-level languages (e.g., COBOL, FORTRAN, and BASIC) by programmer-supplied instructions. Sometimes this approach is desirable or required in an RPG program. In any case, it does give the programmer direct control over the overflow process and does not depend on the preset RPG logic cycle, which may not always give the expected result. The items needed for program-controlled page overflow include the following:

1. Field for lines per page—must be initialized with the page length value.
2. Field for lines used—must be initialized to a value greater than lines per page.

To support a structured programming environment, the instructions related to page overflow should be included in an internal subroutine. Also, all output should be performed by the EXCPT operation with no heading or detail lines. Figure 7-25 details the statements in an internal subroutine that controls program-controlled page overflow.

Line	Form Type	Indicators	Factor 1	Operation	Factor 2	Result Field Name	Length	Decimal Position	High (1>2)	Low (1<2)	Equal (1=2)
0 1	C	N20		Z-ADD	12	LPAGE	2	Ø			
0 2	C	N20		Z-ADD	13	LUSED	2	Ø			
0 3	C	N20		SETON					2Ø		
0 4	C		LUSED	COMP	LPAGE				21		21
0 5	C	21		Z-ADD	5	LUSED					
0 6	C			EXCPT							
0 7	C		LUSED	ADD	2	LUSED					

<u>Line Number</u>:

010 - The Z-ADD 12 statement defines the page length (LPAGE). For stock size paper, this value would be 66 if the printer is set at 6 lines per inch.

020 - The Z-ADD 13 statement initialized the line counter (LUSED) to a value greater than the previously defined page length. This action forces overflow to the top of a new page before the first line of the report is printed.

030 - The SETON operation turns on indicator 20 so that the statements on lines 010 through 030 will not be executed for every record processed. This indicator remains on for the execution of the program.

040 - The line counter (LUSED) is compared to the lines defined for a page (LPAGE). If the value in LUSED is equal to or greater than the value in LPAGE, indicator 21 is turned on. Two resulting indicator fields (i.e > and =) are specified because the value in LUSED may not under some conditions be equal to the value in LPAGE. This coding procedure addresses that contingency.

050 - Indicator 21, turned on if the value in LUSED was equal to or greater than LPAGE, is used to condition this instruction. When program-controlled page overflow is sensed, form is advanced, and the heading lines printed, five lines have been used on the new page. Consequently, LUSED must be initialized to a value of 5.

060 - The EXCPT operation controls the printing of heading or detail type output which are all defined as E type lines. If indicator 21 is turned on by the COMP statement on line 040, only the heading type output lines are printed. On the other hand, if 21 is not set on, only the detail type record will print.

070 - LUSED is incremented by 2 which controls the line spacing of the detail type output. This statement is executed under all conditions.

Figure 7-25 Calculations that support program-controlled page overflow.

The processing logic of program-controlled page overflow instructions explained in Figure 7-25 is given in the flowchart shown in Figure 7-26. The relationship of the instructions in the overflow subroutine to the output coding is illustrated in Figure 7-27. A listing of the report generated by the modified electric billing report program is presented in Figure 7-28. Notice that printing begins on line 1 of each page of the report. As explained in Chapter 3, this feature is controlled by a line number, or in some systems by a channel number, entry in the Skip Before field in the first record defined on the output form. Page length and overflow are defined in statements in a subroutine.

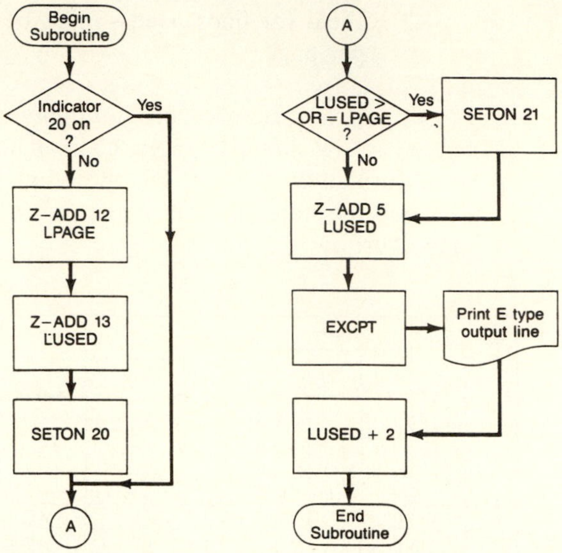

Figure 7-26 Processing logic flowchart for program-controlled page overflow subroutine.

```
... ... 1 ... ... 2 ... ... 3 ... ... 4 ... ... 5 ... ... 6 ... ... 7 ...
 .                         .
 .                         .
 .                         .
0016 C          OFSUB      BEGSR
0017 C   N20               Z-ADD12         LPAGE   20
0018 C   N20               Z-ADD13         LUSED   20
0019 C   N20               SETON                     20
0020 C          LUSED      COMP LPAGE                21  21
0021 C    21               Z-ADD5          LUSED
0022 C                     EXCPT
0023 C          LUSED      ADD  2          LUSED
0024 C                     ENDSR
 .                         .
 .                         .                                   CH7P5
0051 OBILLINGSE  101   21                                      CH7P5
0052 O                        UDATE Y    8                     CH7P5
0053 O                                  51 'PAGE'              CH7P5
0054 O                        PAGE  Z   56
0055 O                                  40 'EDISON ELECTRIC COMPANY'
0056 O          E  2   21
0057 O                                  30 'CUSTOMER USAGE AND'
0058 O                                  45 'BILLING REPORT'
0059 O          E  2   21
0060 O                                  11 'NAME'              CH7P5
0061 O                                  31 'USER TYPE'         CH7P5
0062 O                                  41 !KWH HRS'           CH7P5
0063 O                                  56 'TOTAL BILL'
0064 O          E  2   01
0065 O                        CNAME     20
0066 O                   10             32 '   HOME   '
0067 O                  N10             32 'INDUSTRIAL'
0068 O                        KWH   2   41
0069 O                        BILL  1   56                     CH7P5
0070 O          T 1    LR                                      CH7P5
0071 O                                  28 'TOTAL BILLINGS'    CH7P5
0072 O                        TOTALB1   56                     CH7P5
```

When value is LUSED is > or = value in LPAGE, indicator 21 is turned on to control printing of the exception lines that include heading constants.

EXCPT operation controls printing of all exception lines.

Exception lines conditioned by indicator 21 will print if test on line 0020 turned it on.

Exception line conditioned by Record Identifying indicator 01 will be executed for every record processed.

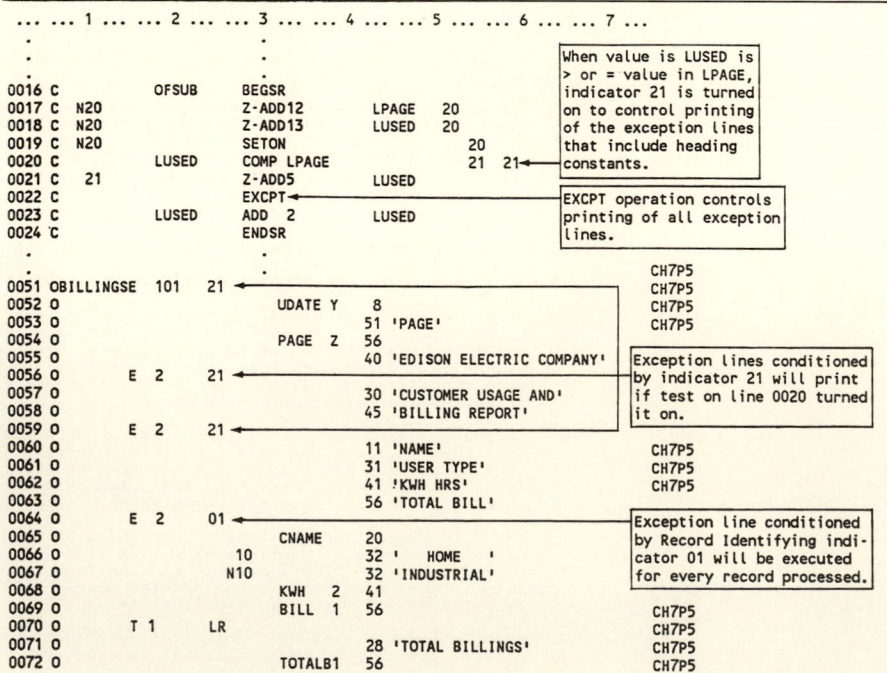

Figure 7-27 Relationship of instructions in the overflow subroutine with the output coding.

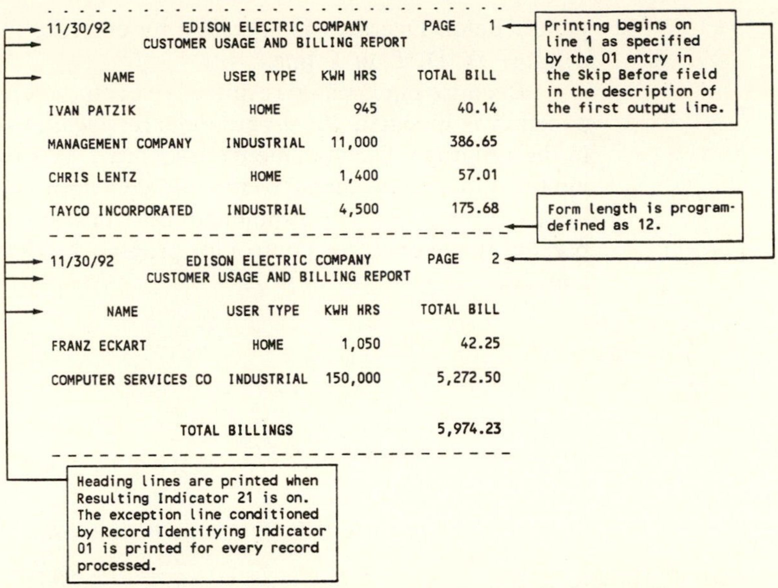

Figure 7-28 Printed report generated by the electric billing report program modified with program-controlled page overflow.

SUMMARY

The EXCPT (Exception) operation modifies the regular RPG logic cycle and causes output to be accessed directly from calculations. Output specification lines that support an EXCPT operation must be specified with an E in column 15. H, D, and T lines are ignored during exception time output. After the E output lines are executed, the program returns control back to the statement following the related EXCPT instruction. Any number of EXCPT operations may be included in a program. Standard RPG coding usually requires that E lines must be conditioned by one or more indicators. An enhancement to the RPG compiler supports the use of a programmer-supplied *exception line name* instead of indicators.

Internal subroutines logically group calculation statements into separate modules. They are specified in an RPG program by the three operations; EXSR (Exit to internal subroutine), BEGSR (Begin internal subroutine), and ENDSR (End internal subroutine). When the end of an internal subroutine is sensed, program control returns to the statement following the related EXSR operation and any detail or total time processing continues. When the first BEGSR statement is sensed without an EXSR controlled branch, all the subroutines are ignored and program control "falls through" to the output instructions.

Internal subroutine instructions must follow all detail and total time calculations. The order of the subroutines does not indicate the processing sequence, which is controlled by the order in which the EXSR statements are executed.

The CASxx operation is an RPG enhancement that combines the functions of the COMP and EXSR statements. One or more CASxx statements in a consecutive order are referred to as a Case Group, which must be terminated by an END operation. If more than one CASxx statement is included in a Case Group, and one is executed, the others are ignored. After the subroutine is executed, program control returns to the statement following the related END.

The Fetch Overflow feature adds additional control to the automatic page overflow cycle included in the RPG compiler. It resolves the problem that occurs when overflow is sensed and additional lines are specified for a page. Under that condition, lines may be printed over the page perforation on continuous forms paper. Fetch Overflow is specified by entering the letter F in column 16 in one or more H, D, T, or E lines.

Because unexpected results may occur when the regular RPG cycle for page overflow is specified, the programmer may want to directly provide for this control in the program. The statements associated with this procedure should ideally be included in an internal subroutine. Page length is defined in the coding that eliminates or overrides any form length or overflow line assignments. This procedure parallels page overflow control for programs written in other high-level computer languages.

QUESTIONS

7-1. Explain how the EXCPT operation processing differs from the regular RPG logic cycle.

7-2. What coding forms and related fields are used to control exception output?

7-3. After an EXCPT statement is executed and exception output performed, where does program control go?

7-4. How many EXCPT operations are permitted in any RPG program?

7-5. What is an exception type of line?

7-6. When exception output occurs, are heading, detail, or total time lines also executed if they are conditioned with the same indicator(s)? Explain the processing procedure.

7-7. Define internal subroutines. When should they be included in an RPG program?

7-8. In standard RPG, what are the operations that control the processing of an internal subroutine? Explain the function of each.

7-9. Where in the calculation specifications are internal subroutines located?

7-10. If more than one internal subroutine is included in a program, what controls the order in which they will be processed?

7-11. What is the sequence of processing after an internal subroutine is executed?

7-12. What RPG operations and indicators may be included in an internal subroutine?

7-13. Explain the function of the CASxx operation. What are its advantages?

7-14. What does the xx entry in the CASxx operation represent?

7-15. What is a Case Group? How is it terminated?

7-16. Explain the relationship tests indicated and the processing procedures followed for each of the following CASxx instructions:

Line (3–5)	Form Type (6)	Control Level (L0-L9, LR, SR, AN/OR) (7–8)	Indicators (9–17)	Factor 1 (18–27)	Operation (28–32)	Factor 2 (33–42)	Result Field Name (43–48)	Length (49–51)	Decimal Position (52)	Half Adjust (H) (53)	Resulting Indicators (54–59)
01Ø	C			FLDA	CASEQ	FLB	SUBR1				
02Ø	C			FLDA	CASGT	FLC	SUBR2				
03Ø	C				CAS		SUBR3				
04Ø	C				END						

7-17. What is the function of the Fetch Overflow feature? When should it be included in a program?

7-18. What coding forms and fields are used to specify Fetch Overflow?

7-19. Explain the term *program-controlled page overflow*. As compared to the RPG logic cycle controlled page overflow, what are its advantages and disadvantages?

7-20. What control items must be included in an RPG program to provide for program-controlled page overflow?

EXERCISES

7-1. From the following record layout form and printer spacing chart, write the Calculations and Output Specifications to generate the report illustrated. Create a loop in which FLDA is multiplied by FLDB and the product stored in FLDB until the value in a programmer-defined counter is equal to the input field NUM. Notice that the two heading lines are to be printed as H lines with page overflow included.

Record Design:

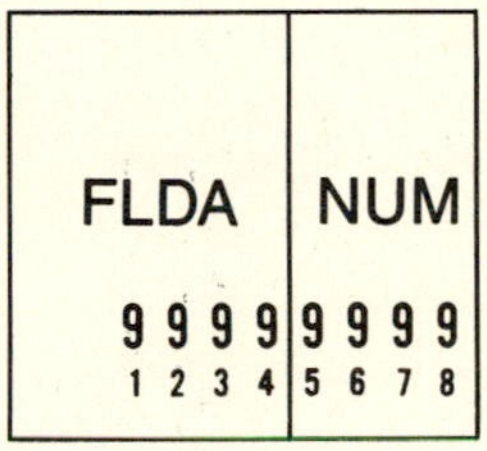

Report Design:

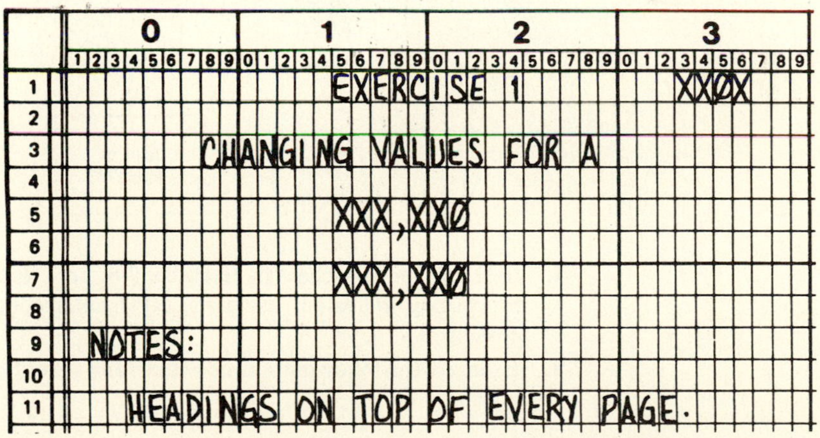

7-2. Refer to Exercise 7-1 and modify it so that all output (headings and page overflow) is controlled at exception time.

7-3. Refer to Exercise 7-2 and modify it to include all the relevant RPG language enhancements that have been discussed.

7-4. Refer to Chapter 5 and the source listing for the "Raising any number to any power" program in Figure 5-23. Modify the coding so that the power from each pass through the loop is printed instead of only the final answer.

7-5. From the following flowchart, write the calculations for the processing indicated.

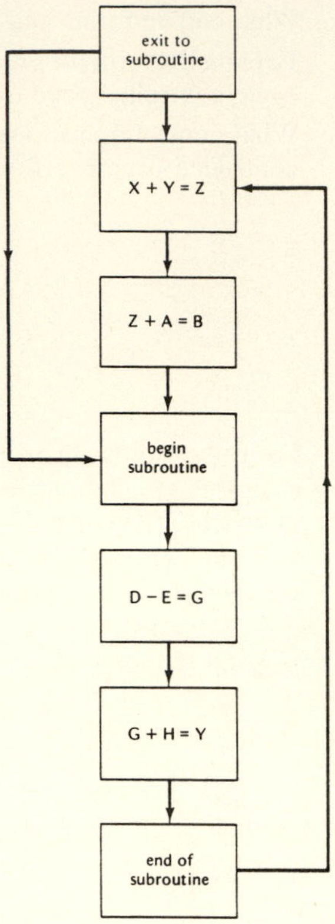

7-6. From the following flowchart, write the calculations for the processing indicated.

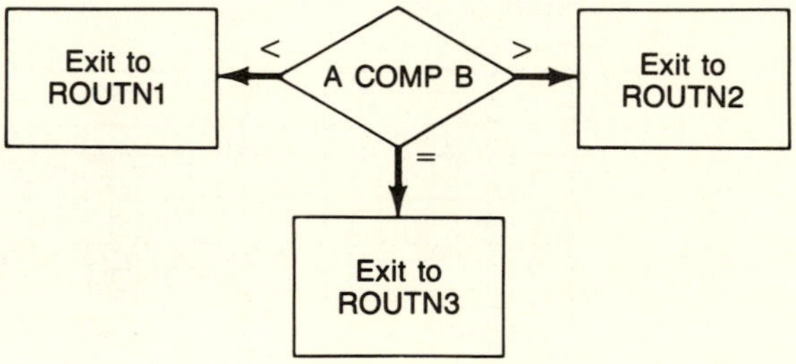

7-7. Refer to the flowchart in Exercise 7-6, and write the calculations to control the processing indicated, using the RPG enhancement for internal subroutine processing.

7-8. Examine the following source listing, and identify and correct any syntax and logic errors.

```
... ... 1 ... ... 2 ... ... 3 ... ... 4 ... ... 5 ... ... 6 ... ... 7 ...
0001 H                                                                EX78
0002  * THIS PROGRAM COMPUTES AND GENERATES A BILLING REPORT FOR AN      EX78
0003  * ELECTRIC COMPANY'S CUSTOMERS...................                 EX78
0004 FDATA7P3 IP  F  80  80            DISK                            EX78
0005 FBILLINGSO   F 132 132     OF     PRINTER                         EX78
0006 IDATA7P3 SM  01                                                   EX78
0007 I                                        1  20 CNAME              EX78
0008 I                                       21  260KWH                EX78
0009 I                                       27  28 USER               EX78
0010  *                                                                EX78
0011 C           USER      COMP 'H'                    10 USER TYPE?   EX78
0012 C     10              EXSR HOME                     HOMEOWNER SR  EX78
0013 C                     EXSR INDUST                   INDUSTRIAL SR EX78
0014 C           HOME      BEGSR                         BEGIN HOME SR EX78
```

```
0015 C   10                EXSR TAX                        TAX & TOTALS SREX78
0016 C   10                EXCPT                           PRINT E LINE   EX78
0017  *                                                                   EX78
0018 C                     Z-ADD40        BILL    72       BASE AMOUNT    EX78
0019 C           KWH       COMP 1000                   1111 > 1000 KWH?   EX78
0020 C   11                GOTO ENDHOM                     < OR = BRANCH  EX78
0021 C           KWH       SUB  1000      EXCESS  60       KWH > 1000     EX78
0022 C           EXCESS    MULT .042      EXTRA   72       > 1000 KWH $AMTEX78
0023 C           BILL      ADD  EXTRA     BILL             BASE + EXTRA   EX78
0024 C           ENDHOM    ENDSR                           END HOME SR    EX78
0025  *                                                                   EX78
0026 C           INDUST    BEGSR                           BEGIN INDUST SREX78
0027 C                     Z-ADD175       BILL             BASE AMOUNT    EX78
0028 C           KWH       COMP 5000                   1111 > 5000 KWH?   EX78
0029 C   11                GOTO ENDIND                     < OR = BRANCH  EX78
0030 C           KWH       SUB  5000      EXCESS           KWH > 5000     EX78
0031 C           EXCESS    MULT .035      EXTRA            > 5000 KWH $AMTEX78
0032 C           BILL      ADD  EXTRA     BILL             BASE + EXTRA   EX78
0033 C           ENDIND    ENDSR                           END INDUST SR  EX78
0034  *                                                                   EX78
0035 C           TAX       BEGSR                           BEGIN TAX SR   EX78
0036 C           KWH       DIV  100       TKWH    40       KWH FOR TAX    EX78
0037 C           TKWH      MULT .015      TAX     62H      COMPUTE TAX    EX78
0038 C           BILL      ADD  TAX       BILL             ADD TAX TO BILLEX78
0039 C           TOTALB    ADD  BILL      TOTALB  82       ACCUM BILLS    EX78
0040  *                                                                   EX78
0041 OBILLINGSH  101   1P                                                 EX78
0042 O       OR        OF                                                 EX78
0043 O                        UDATE Y   8                                 EX78
0044 O                                 51 'PAGE'                          EX78
0045 O                        PAGE  Z  56                                 EX78
0046 O                                 40 'EDISON ELECTRIC COMPANY'       EX78
0047 O        H  2     1P                                                 EX78
0048 O       OR        OF                                                 EX78
0049 O                                 30 'CUSTOMER USAGE AND'            EX78
0050 O                                 45 'BILLING REPORT'                EX78
0051 O        E  2     1P                                                 EX78
0052 O       OR        OF                                                 EX78
0053 O                                 11 'NAME'                          EX78
0054 O                                 31 'USER TYPE'                     EX78
0055 O                                 41 'KWH HRS'                       EX78
0056 O                                 56 'TOTAL BILL'                    EX78
0057 O        D  2     01                                                 EX78
0058 O                        CNAME    20                                 EX78
0059 O                  10             32 '   HOME   '                    EX78
0060 O                 N10             32 'INDUSTRIAL'                    EX78
0061 O                        KWH   2  41                                 EX78
0062 O                        BILL  1  56                                 EX78
0063 O        T 1      LR                                                 EX78
0064 O                                 28 'TOTAL BILLINGS'                EX78
0065 O                        TOTALB1  56                                 EX78
```

LABORATORY ASSIGNMENTS

Laboratory Assignment 7-1: STRAIGHT-LINE DEPRECIATION SCHEDULE

Write an RPG program to generate a report that details a depreciation schedule for a company's fixed assets. Depreciation is a tax deductible expense for assets that are used in the production of income. It may be defined as the "allocation of the cost of an asset over its useful life." Because of its simplicity and acceptance by the Internal Revenue Service, one of the most popular determinations of annual depreciation expense is the straight-line method, which is computed by the following formula:

$$\text{Annual Depreciation} = \frac{\text{Cost} - \text{Salvage (Trade-In)}}{\text{Estimated Useful Life}}$$

where:

Annual Depreciation = the amount of depreciation expense computed for each year of the asset's life.

Cost = the original cost of the asset plus any capital improvements.

Salvage Value (also called Trade-In) = the amount the asset will realize as scrap or trade-in at the end of its estimated useful life.

Estimated Useful Life = the expected life of the asset based on its estimated productivity. The tax laws have established useful life by general categories of assets. For example, autos and light-duty trucks are assigned a three-year life, whereas all other capital goods (machinery, equipment, and so forth) have a five-year life.

Format of Data Records:

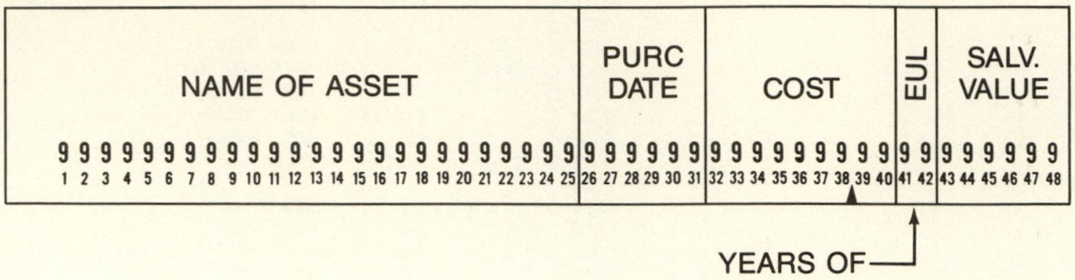

Processing: Read the input file and for every record processed, compute the annual depreciation expense for the asset based on the formula that has been given. Notice that the accumulated depreciation and book value must be computed each year for the life of the asset. The printer spacing chart indicates the field sizes for these items. The annual depreciation, accumulated depreciation, and book value amounts are rounded to the nearest dollar. Because of rounding, the book value after the last year's depreciation as calculated may not equal the cost of the asset. Any dollar difference must be added to the last year's annual depreciation amount, so the book value is zero for the last year.

Report Design: Page overflow is to be specified in the report for the two heading lines for the columns (i.e., YEAR, ANNUAL, ACCUMULATED, BOOK, and so forth) only and not for the first four report lines.

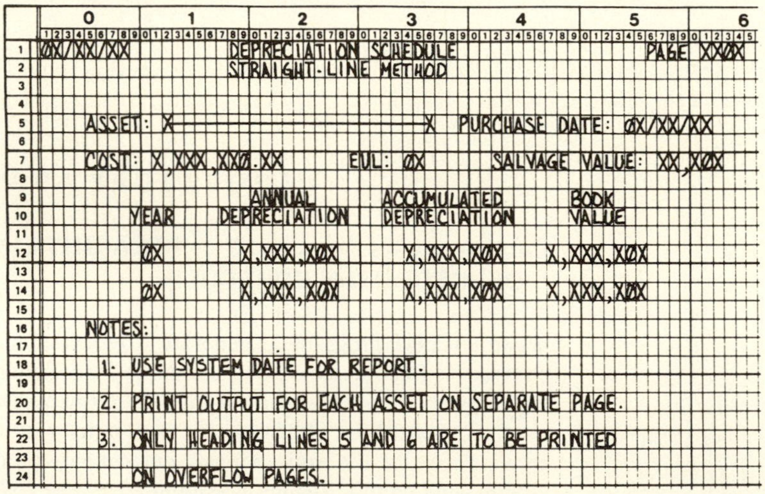
ØX/XX/XX DEPRECIATION SCHEDULE PAGE XXØX
STRAIGHT-LINE METHOD
ASSET: X X PURCHASE DATE: ØX/XX/XX
COST: X,XXX,XXØ.XX EUL: ØX SALVAGE VALUE: XX,XØX
ANNUAL ACCUMULATED BOOK
YEAR DEPRECIATION DEPRECIATION VALUE
ØX X,XXX,XØX X,XXX,XØX X,XXX,XØX
ØX X,XXX,XØX X,XXX,XØX X,XXX,XØX
NOTES:
1. USE SYSTEM DATE FOR REPORT.
2. PRINT OUTPUT FOR EACH ASSET ON SEPARATE PAGE.
3. ONLY HEADING LINES 5 AND 6 ARE TO BE PRINTED
ON OVERFLOW PAGES.

Input Data:

Asset Name Cols 1-25	Date of Purchase 26-31	Cost 32-40	EUL 41-42	Salvage Value 43-48
BPT MILLING MACHINE	051491	001500000	07	003000
IBM SYSTEM/38	021091	037500000	05	020000
IBM MEMORY TYPEWRITER	011191	000280000	03	000400
OFFICE FURNITURE	100191	000900000	10	000600
FACTORY BUILDING	061591	120000000	18	000000

Laboratory Assignment 7-2: ACRS AUTOMOBILE DEPRECIATION SCHEDULE

Beginning with the 1987 tax year, the federal tax laws require that special rates (referred to as ACRS rates) must be applied to automobiles used 50% or more for business purposes. The maximum depreciation deduction allowed each year for the life of an automobile is as follows:

```
Year 1   $2,560
Year 2    4,000
Year 3    2,450
Year 4    1,475 (this last amount is taken until
                 the asset is fully depreciated)
```

Under this method, a full year's depreciation may be taken regardless of when the asset was purchased. Also, salvage or trade-in value is ignored in the computations.

Format of Data Records:

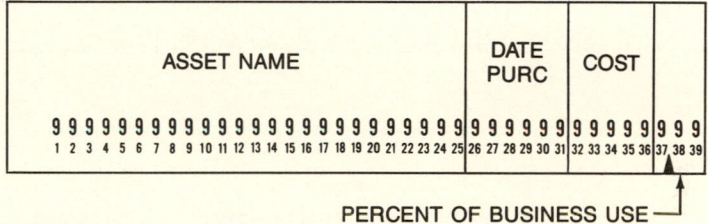

ASSET NAME	DATE PURC	COST	PERCENT OF BUSINESS USE
9999999999999999999999999	999999	99999	999
1 2 3 4 5 6 7 8 9 10 11 12 13 14 15 16 17 18 19 20 21 22 23 24 25	26 27 28 29 30 31	32 33 34 35 36	37 38 39

Processing: For each record processed, compute the annual depreciation using the statutory amounts given above. For assets used less than 100% for business, the annual limit must be multiplied by the related percentage of business use to compute the deductible depreciation expense for the year. The depreciation schedule for each asset must include all the years needed to fully depreciate the automobile to its allowable depreciable amount. The steps related to the determination of annual depreciation, accumulated depreciation, and remaining amount follow:

Step 1: Compute the depreciable amount:

Cost × Business Percentage = Depreciable Amount

Step 2: Initialize a Remainder Field with the depreciable amount value.

Step 3: Determine each year's depreciation by multiplying the year's factor (i.e., $2,560) by the business percentage.

Factor × Business Percentage = Year's Depreciation

Step 4: Determine if the remainder (Step 1) is less than the current year's depreciation (Step 3). If it is, move the remainder value to the year's depreciation field.

Step 5: Accumulate the current year's depreciation

Accumulated Depreciation + Year's Depreciation = Accumulated Depreciation

Step 6: Subtract accumulated depreciation from the depreciable amount.

Depreciable Amount − Accumulated Depreciation = Remaining Amount

Round the annual depreciation, accumulated depreciation, and remaining values to the nearest dollar.

The depreciation schedule is complete when the accumulated depreciation value is equal to the depreciable amount (i.e., when the remainder is zero).

Report Design:

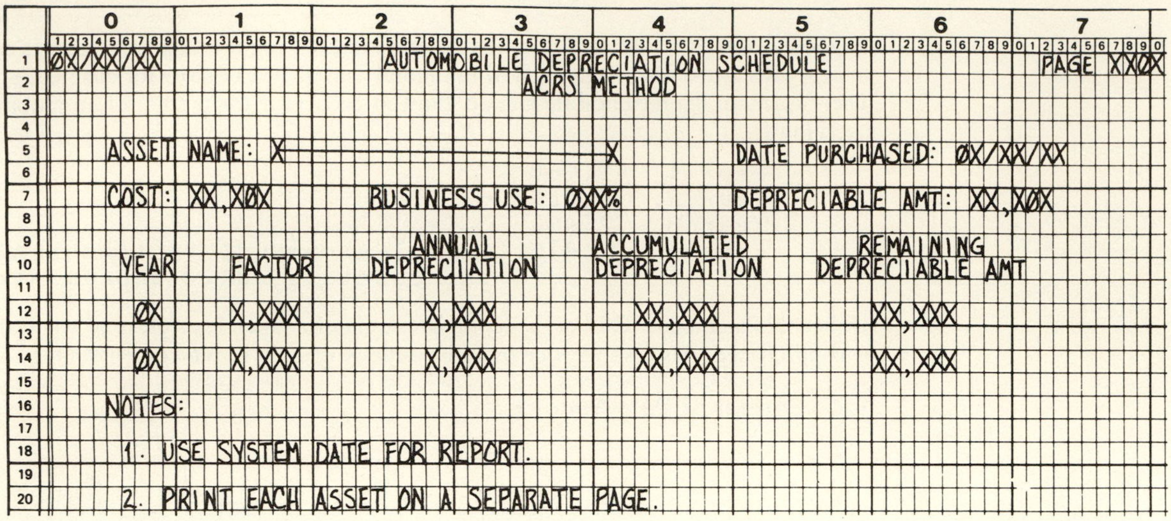
ØX/XX/XX
AUTOMOBILE DEPRECIATION SCHEDULE
PAGE XXØX
ACRS METHOD
ASSET NAME: X
X
DATE PURCHASED: ØX/XX/XX
COST: XX,XØX
BUSINESS USE: ØXX%
DEPRECIABLE AMT: XX,XØX
ANNUAL
ACCUMULATED
REMAINING
YEAR
FACTOR
DEPRECIATION
DEPRECIATION
DEPRECIABLE AMT
ØX
X,XXX
X,XXX
XX,XXX
XX,XXX
ØX
X,XXX
X,XXX
XX,XXX
XX,XXX
NOTES:
1. USE SYSTEM DATE FOR REPORT.
2. PRINT EACH ASSET ON A SEPARATE PAGE.

Input Data:

Automobile Name Cols 1-25	Date Purchased 26-31	Cost 32-36	Percent of Business Use 37-39
FORD TAURUS	011591	12500	100
TOYOTA MR-2	021791	15900	060
PONTIAC BONNEVILLE	030191	22000	080
BMW 351i	041991	33700	050

Laboratory Assignment 7-3: SALESPERSON COMMISSION REPORT

From the following information write a structured RPG program to generate the report detailed in the supplemental printer spacing chart.

The Happy Sales Company pays its salespersons a salary plus a commission on net sales. Salary and commission payments are based on the following:

1. All sales employees are paid a base salary regardless of their sales. Employees with less than two years' employment are paid a $600 monthly base salary. Those with two or more years are paid $1,000 a month.
2. Net sales (Monthly Sales − Sales Returns) over $2,000 are eligible for a commission that is added to the base salary. However, no commission is paid on the first $2,000 of net sales. The commission amount is determined as follows:

Employees with two or more years' employment are paid 20% commission on net sales over $2,000. Any net sales over $30,000 are paid at an additional 5% commission rate.

Employees with less than two years' employment are paid 12% commission on net sales over $2,000. Any net sales over $25,000 are paid at an additional 2% commission rate.

Format of Input Records:

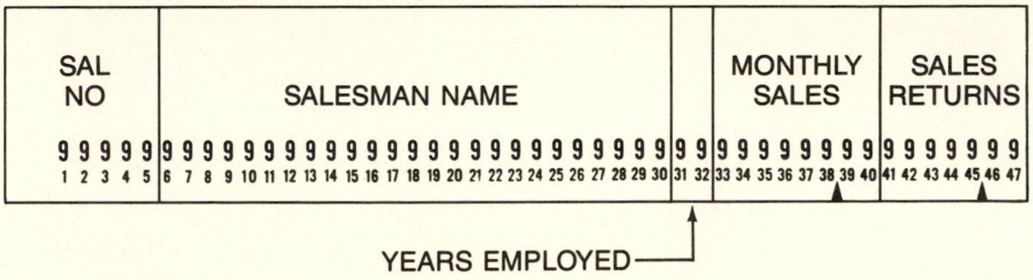

Report Design:

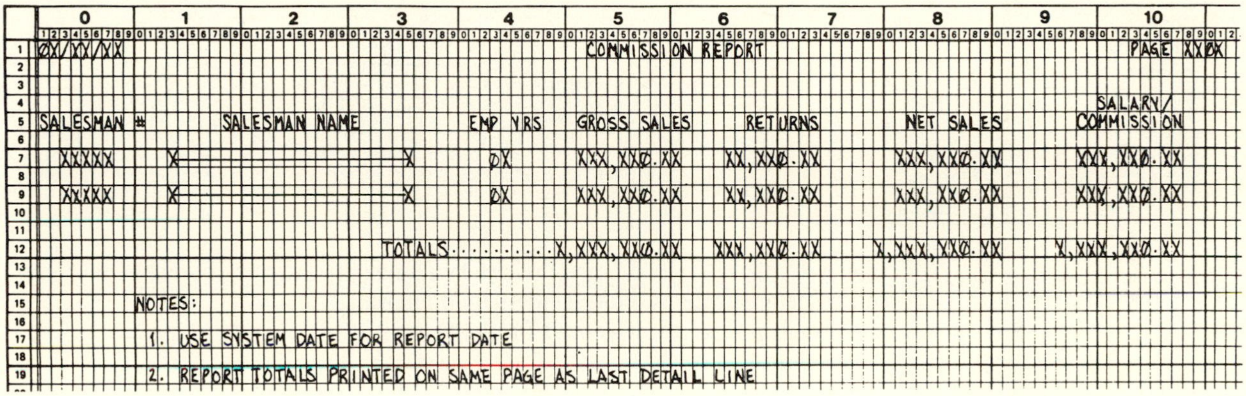

Input Data:

Salesman Number Cols 1-5	Name 6-30	Years Employed 31-32	Sales Amount 33-40	Sales Returns 41-47
11111	SIEGFRIED HOUNDSTOOTH	04	01125050	0100000
11112	FELIX GOODGUY	01	02800000	0000000
22222	OTTO MUTTENJAMMER	06	10000000	0000000
33333	HANS OFFENHAUSER	01	00250000	0070000
44444	BARNEY OLDFIELD	10	00190000	0000000
55555	WILIAM PETTY	02	02200000	0000000

Laboratory Assignment 7-4: MORTGAGE AMORTIZATION SCHEDULE

Banks and other lending institutions often provide the mortgagor with an amortization schedule of the monthly payments. For fixed-rate mortgages, the payments are the same for the life of the mortgage. Included in the schedule are details related to the amount of the payment and what part of it applies separately to the principal and interest. A new principal balance is computed after each payment, and the interest for the next period is calculated on that amount.

Format of the Input Records:

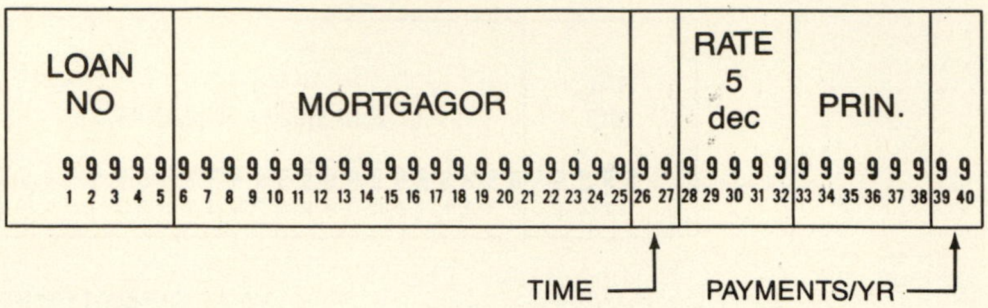

Calculations:

Step 1: Determine the constant fixed monthly payment from the following formula:

$$\text{Monthly Payment} = \frac{P}{\left(\dfrac{1 - \dfrac{1}{(1+i)^n}}{i}\right)}$$

where:

i = annual mortgage rate. Must be divided by number of interest payments per year to determine applications interest rate period month.
n = total number of payment periods for the year.
P = Balance of the mortgage principal.

Step 2: Calculate the interest amount of the monthly payment using the following formula for simple interest:

$$I = \frac{P \times R \times T}{12}$$

Where:

I = simple interest amount
P = principal amount. The balance of the principal will decline after each monthly payment
R = annual interest rate.
T = time for the life of the mortgage. If payments are monthly, is expressed as total number of months for the mortgage loan.
12 = Because payments are monthly, 12 is used as a denominator in formula.

Step 3: The amount of the monthly payment applicable to the payment of the principal (reduces the principal) is determined as follows:

Principal Payment = Monthly Payment − Interest Amount

Step 4: The end-of-month principal balance is determined by subtracting the monthly principal payment (Step 3) amount from the previous principal balance. The new balance is used for the next month's computation of the principal/interest parts of the monthly payment.

Report Design:

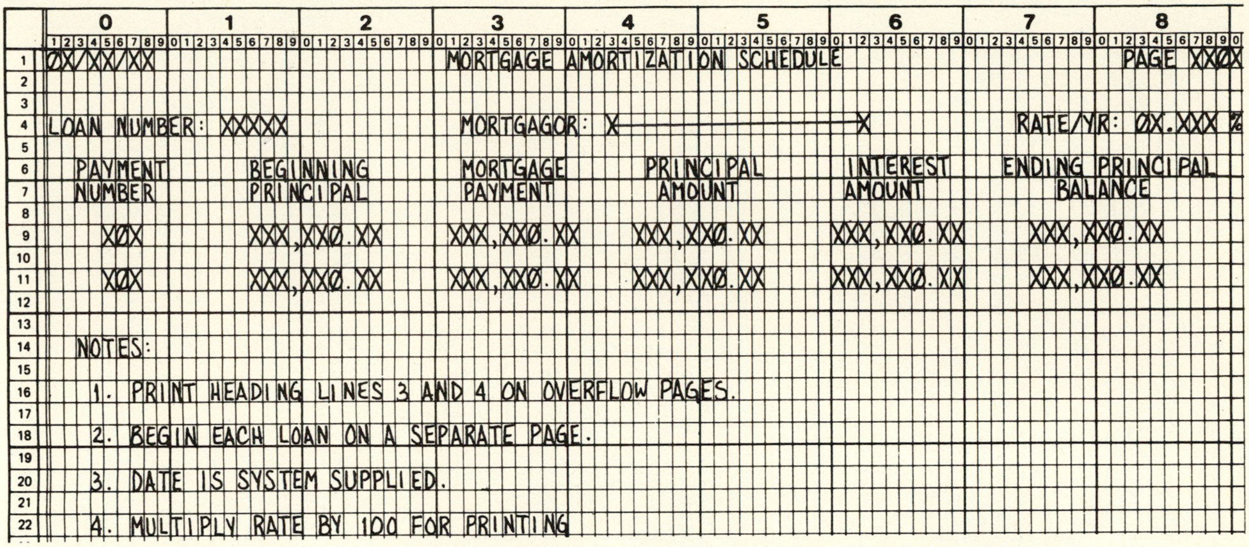
ØX/XX/XX
MORTGAGE AMORTIZATION SCHEDULE
PAGE XXØX
LOAN NUMBER: XXXXX
MORTGAGOR: X
X
RATE/YR: ØX.XXX %
PAYMENT NUMBER
BEGINNING PRINCIPAL
MORTGAGE PAYMENT
PRINCIPAL AMOUNT
INTEREST AMOUNT
ENDING PRINCIPAL BALANCE
XØX
XXX,XXØ.XX
XXX,XXØ.XX
XXX,XXØ.XX
XXX,XXØ.XX
XXX,XXØ.XX
XØX
XXX,XXØ.XX
XXX,XXØ.XX
XXX,XXØ.XX
XXX,XXØ.XX
XXX,XXØ.XX
NOTES:
1. PRINT HEADING LINES 3 AND 4 ON OVERFLOW PAGES.
2. BEGIN EACH LOAN ON A SEPARATE PAGE.
3. DATE IS SYSTEM SUPPLIED.
4. MULTIPLY RATE BY 100 FOR PRINTING

Input Data:

Loan# Cols 1-5	Mortgagor 6-25	Time of Loan (yrs) 26-27	Interest Rate 28-32	Principal 33-38	Payments per year 39-40
12345	HENRY W. LONGFELLOW	05	12500	020000	04
13333	EDGAR A. POE	30	12000	056000	12
22222	GEOFFREY CHAUCER	10	10000	060000	12
22333	JOHN MILTON	30	09500	200000	02

chapter 8
Multiple Record Data Files and Data Structures

Previous chapters presented example programs in which the input files included only one record format. Many applications, however, require that more than one record format be included in an input file. Figure 8-1 illustrates a Multiple Record Layout form formatted with three record designs. Data records with those formats will be included in an input data file processed by a Cash Receipts Journal application program discussed later. The elongated X areas in each record format represent unused positions included for the possible addition of new fields. In order to format the three record types with the same 80 bytes (fixed format), the X areas are a different size.

MULTIPLE RECORD IDENTIFICATION

An examination of Figure 8-1 shows that three types of records are formatted on the layout form. The first record design includes the data items (fields) related to miscellaneous (sundry) transactions; the second, the collection of an accounts receivable; and the third, cash sales receipts. Hence, each record type is a unique *physical record* format used to store a specific accounting transaction. Data based on the cash receipts transactions will be entered and stored on the related record type.

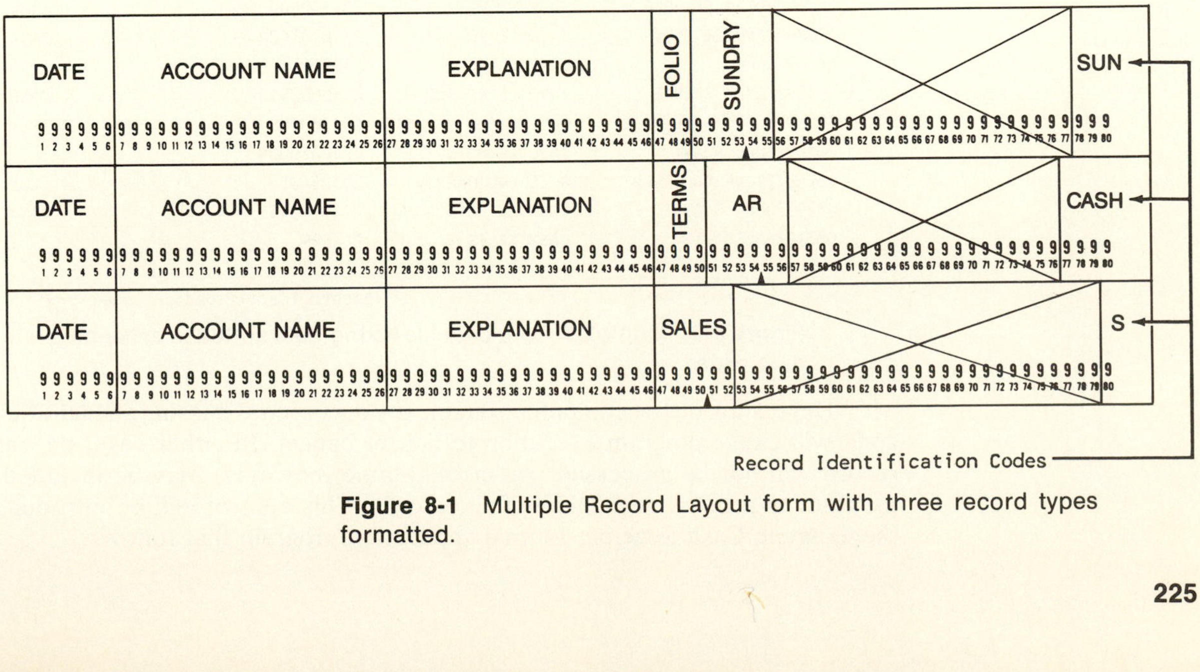

Figure 8-1 Multiple Record Layout form with three record types formatted.

When there is more than one record format in a data file, some method must be included in the program to identify each type for processing. This is controlled in RPG programs by Record Identification Codes, which are entered on every data record. Refer to Figure 8-1 and notice that the Record Identification Code, SUN, is entered in columns 78, 79, and 80 in the first record format. The second record type includes the letters C, A, S, H in columns 77, 78, 79, and 80, and the third record is identified by the letter S in column 80.

Record Identification Codes may be entered in any column(s) of a record format, not only in the last positions, as shown in Figure 8-1. Typically, Record Identification Codes are included in the first or last bytes of a record type. In any case, the placement of codes identifying the records in the data files that are supported by an individual application or by the whole computer installation should be consistent. Furthermore, any number of characters may be specified to identify a record type. However, in disk- or tape-stored data files, records are usually identified with only one character. This procedure saves disk storage space and reduces the amount of keying in the data entry process. Any characters supported by the character set of the computer may be used for Record Identification Codes.

STRUCTURE OF A MULTIPLE RECORD DATA FILE

Data may be entered and loaded to a data file in an unordered sequence. Before it is processed by a program, however, it often has to be sorted in some required sequence. Because accounting transactions are usually processed in an ascending date order, any related data file(s) must be sorted accordingly. The sort function is supported by a separate software program that is unique to every computer system that is *not* a subset of the RPG compiler. Consequently, all data files discussed in this text that have to be in a specific order for processing are assumed to have been previously sorted by a *sort utility program*.

A listing of the data file that includes the record formats shown in Figure 8-1 is presented in Figure 8-2. Notice two important features of the file: first, the records are sorted in an ascending order by date (columns 1–6) and second, each record type (except one) is identified with its related Record Identification Code.

```
080192TERRY LENTZ         INVOICE NO 100      1/10030000                  CASH
080292SALES               CASH SALES          075412                         S
080692NOTES PAYABLE       BANK LOAN           302200000                    SUN
080892CANDICE MYERS       INVOICE NO 101      2/10107422                  CASH
081092SALES               CASH SALES          000311                         S
081192KATHI SPENCE        INVOICE NO 102      2/10002510                  CASH
081292NOTES RECEIVABLE    COLLECTION OF NOTE  102080000                    SUN
081592BUGS BUNNY          INVOICE NO 103      1/10010000
082492STORE EQUIPMENT     SOLD EQUIPMENT      201034000                    SUN
082992JOHN BODINE         INVOICE NO 103      2/10228455                  CASH
083192SALES               CASH SALES          004529                         S

                                         Record Identification Codes
```

Figure 8-2 Multiple record data file listing-data sorted in ascending date order.

Depending on the computer system, any data record missing an identification code will cause program execution to halt or cancel. In either case, the related record will not be processed. An error routine, however, may be included in a program to process any unidentified records. This control will be introduced in the example Cash Receipts Journal application program that follows.

APPLICATION PROGRAM—CASH RECEIPTS JOURNAL

A Cash Receipts Journal is used to record the receipt of cash regardless of the source. In merchandising concerns, cash receipts result from cash sales recorded on cash registers and totaled for the day and from checks received in the mail from charge customers (Accounts Receivable). Other receipts of cash may be generated from loans, the sale of an asset, and so forth.

Documentation

The program specifications in Figure 8-3 explain the processing requirements for a program that generates a Cash Receipts Journal. The system flowchart illustrated in Figure 8-4 shows that one input and one output file are processed by the Cash Receipts Journal program (CH8Pl). For convenience, the record layout

PROGRAM SPECIFICATIONS Page 1 of 1

Program Name CASH RECEIPTS JRL Program-ID CH8P1 Written By S. Myers

Purpose Generate a CR Journal for a month's trans. Approved By The Boss

Input files (directory names):

DATA8P1 (stored on disk)

Output files (directory names):

PRINTER (stock paper)

Processing Narrative:

Write a structured RPG program to generate the Cash Receipts Journal illustrated in the supplemental printer spacing chart.

Input to the program:

A data file loaded with records for cash receipts transactions for a month is to be read consecutively until the end.

Processing:

The Record Identification Code included in the data records will determine the calculation and output requirements for each record. Each record type requires the following separate processes:

Record ID	Calculation Requirements	Output Requirements
SUN	Accumulate the sundry amounts	Print sundry amount in two output positions (see print chart).
S	Accumulate the cash sale amounts	Print cash sales amount in two output positions (see print chart).
CASH	Multiply the sales discount (first byte of TERMS field) by .01 to convert the value to a decimal percent. Then, multiply the accounts receivable input value by this percent to determine the sales discount. Subtract the sales discount from the accounts receivable value to determine the net cash received. Accumulate the accounts receivable, sales discount, and net cash amounts.	Print accts receivable, sales discount, and net cash values in their related output positions (see print chart).

Output: Complete the output coding to generate the report form detailed in the supplemental printer spacing chart. Accumulated totals are to be printed at LR time.

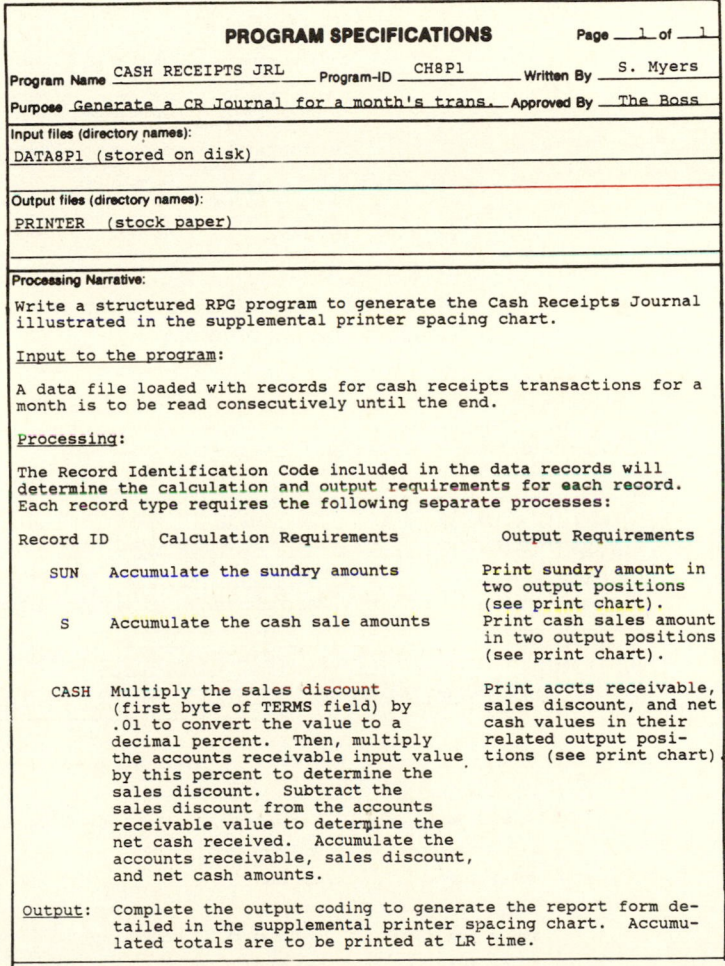

Figure 8-3 Specifications for program that generates a Cash Receipts Journal.

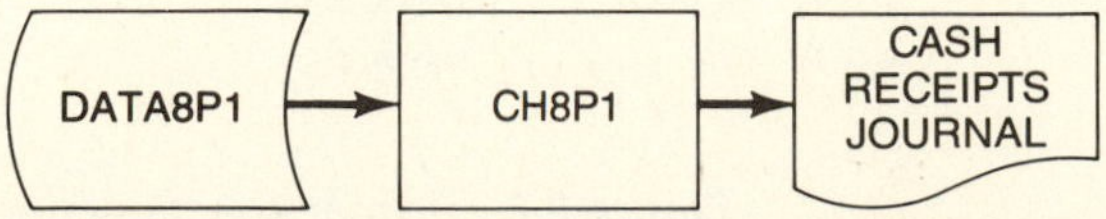

Figure 8-4 System flowchart for Cash Receipts Journal program.

forms and data file listing previously presented are illustrated again in Figure 8-5. A printer spacing chart that details the design of the Cash Receipts Journal is shown in Figure 8-6 supplemented by a listing of the report generated by the application program.

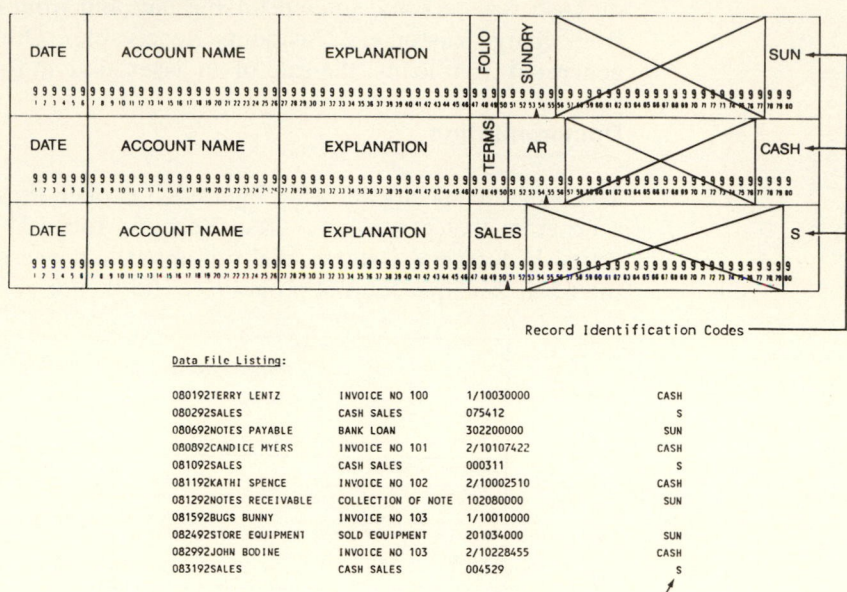

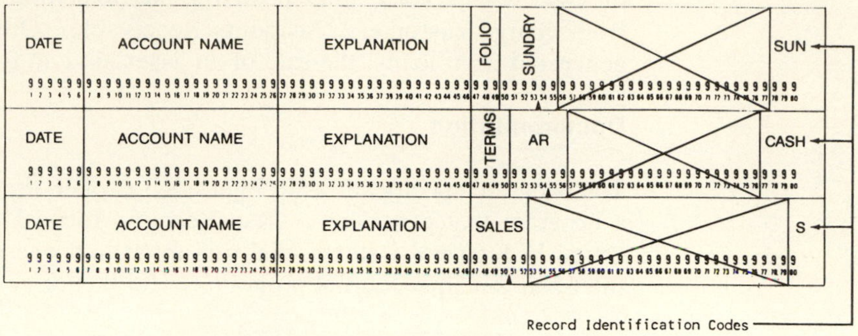

Data File Listing:

```
080192TERRY LENTZ          INVOICE NO 100      1/10030000              CASH
080292SALES                CASH SALES          075412                     S
080692NOTES PAYABLE        BANK LOAN           302200000                SUN
080892CANDICE MYERS        INVOICE NO 101      2/10107422              CASH
081092SALES                CASH SALES          000311                     S
081192KATHI SPENCE         INVOICE NO 102      2/10002510              CASH
081292NOTES RECEIVABLE     COLLECTION OF NOTE  102080000                SUN
081592BUGS BUNNY           INVOICE NO 103      1/10010000
082492STORE EQUIPMENT      SOLD EQUIPMENT      201034000                SUN
082992JOHN BODINE          INVOICE NO 103      2/10228455              CASH
083192SALES                CASH SALES          004529                     S
```

Record Identification Codes

Figure 8-5 Record layout forms and data file listing for the Cash Receipts Journal program.

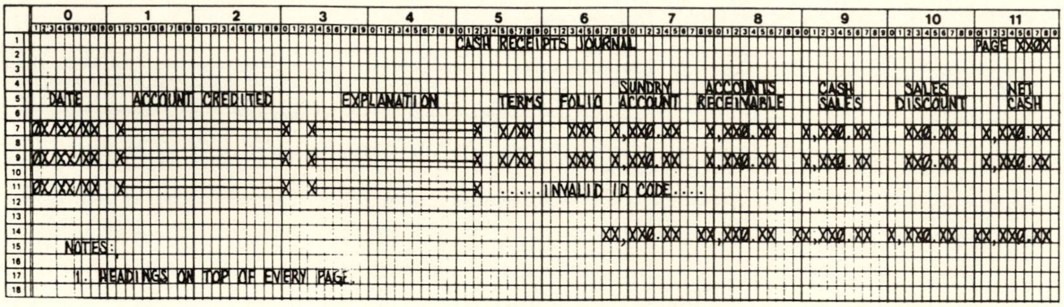

CASH RECEIPTS JOURNAL PAGE 1

DATE	ACCOUNT CREDITED	EXPLANATION	TERMS	FOLIO	SUNDRY ACCOUNT	ACCOUNTS RECEIVABLE	CASH SALES	SALES DISCOUNT	NET CASH
8/01/92	TERRY LENTZ	INVOICE NO 100	1/10			300.00		3.00	297.00
8/02/92	SALES	CASH SALES					754.12		754.12
8/06/92	NOTES PAYABLE	BANK LOAN		302	2,000.00				2,000.00
8/08/92	CANDICE MYERS	INVOICE NO 101	2/10			1,074.22		21.48	1,052.74
8/10/92	SALES	CASH SALES					3.11		3.11
8/11/92	KATHI SPENCE	INVOICE NO 102	2/10			25.10		.50	24.60
8/12/92	NOTES RECEIVABLE	COLLECTION OF NOTE		102	800.00				800.00
8/15/92	BUGS BUNNY	INVOICE NO 103	.....INVALID ID CODE....						
8/24/92	STORE EQUIPMENT	SOLD EQUIPMENT		201	340.00				340.00
8/29/92	JOHN BODINE	INVOICE NO 103	2/10			2,284.55		45.69	2,238.86
8/31/92	SALES	CASH SALES					45.29		45.29
					3,140.00	3,683.87	802.52	70.67	7.555.72

Figure 8-6 Printer spacing chart and report generated by the Cash Receipts Journal application program.

Source Program Coding—Cash Receipts Journal

A commented source listing of the program that generates a Cash Receipts Journal is illustrated in Figure 8-7. The input, calculations, and output format specifications related to this application program are discussed in the following paragraphs.

```
... ... 1 ... ... 2 ... ... 3 ... ... 4 ... ... 5 ... ... 6 ... ... 7 ...
 * THIS PROGRAM GENERATES A CASH RECEIPTS JOURNAL FROM AN INPUT      CH8P1
 * FILE THAT INCLUDES THREE RECORD FORMATS............               CH8P1
H                                                                    CH8P1
FDATA8P1 IP  F  80  80            DISK                               CH8P1
FCASHRJRLO   F 132 132     OF     PRINTER                            CH8P1
IDATA8P1 SM  01  78 CS  79 CU  80 CN                                 CH8P1
I                                        1   60DATE                  CH8P1
I                                        7  26 ACTNAM                CH8P1
I                                       27  46 EXPLAN                CH8P1
I                                       47  49 FOLIO                 CH8P1
I                                       50  552SUNDRY                CH8P1
I        SM  02  77 CC  78 CA  79 CS                                 CH8P1
I       AND      80 CH                                               CH8P1
I                                        1   60DATE                  CH8P1
I                                        7  26 ACTNAM                CH8P1
I                                       27  46 EXPLAN                CH8P1
I                                       47  50 TERMS                 CH8P1
I                                       47  470DISPCT                CH8P1
I                                       51  562ARAMT                 CH8P1
I        SM  03  80 CS                                               CH8P1
I                                        1   60DATE                  CH8P1
I                                        7  26 ACTNAM                CH8P1
I                                       27  46 EXPLAN                CH8P1
I                                       47  522CASHSL                CH8P1
I        NC  04                                                      CH8P1
I                                        1   60DATE                  CH8P1
I                                        7  26 ACTNAM                CH8P1
I                                       27  46 EXPLAN                CH8P1
C   01                EXSR SUNSR                      SUNDRY SR      CH8P1
C   02                EXSR CASHSR                     ACCTS REC SR   CH8P1
C   03                EXSR SSR                        CASH SALES SR  CH8P1
 *                                                                   CH8P1
C           SUNSR     BEGSR                                          CH8P1
C           TOTSUN    ADD  SUNDRY    TOTSUN  72       ACCUM SUN AMTS CH8P1
C           TOCASH    ADD  SUNDRY    TOCASH  72       ADD TO TOT CASHCH8P1
C                     ENDSR                                          CH8P1
 *                                                                   CH8P1
C           CASHSR    BEGSR                                          CH8P1
C           DISPCT    MULT .01       PCT     22       COMPUTE DEC PCTCH8P1
C           ARAMT     MULT PCT       SALDIS  62H      COMPUTE DIS AMTCH8P1
C           ARAMT     SUB  SALDIS    NETCSH  62       COMPUTE NET CASCH8P1
C           TOTDIS    ADD  SALDIS    TOTDIS  72       ACCUM DIS AMTS CH8P1
C           TOTAR     ADD  ARAMT     TOTAR   72       ACCUM AR AMTS  CH8P1
C           TOCASH    ADD  NETCSH    TOCASH           ACCUM CASH AMTSCH8P1
C                     ENDSR                                          CH8P1
 *                                                                   CH8P1
C           SSR       BEGSR                           BEGIN SALES SR CH8P1
C           TOTSAL    ADD  CASHSL    TOTSAL  72       ACCUM SALES AMTCH8P1
C           TOCASH    ADD  CASHSL    TOCASH           ADD TO TOT CASHCH8P1
C                     ENDSR                                          CH8P1
 *                                                                   CH8P1
OCASHRJRLH  301   1P                                                 CH8P1
O       OR        OF                                                 CH8P1
O                                   70 'CASH RECEIPTS JOURNAL'       CH8P1
O                                  113 'PAGE'                        CH8P1
O                         PAGE  Z  118                               CH8P1
O        H  1     1P                                                 CH8P1
O       OR        OF                                                 CH8P1
O                                   74 'SUNDRY'                      CH8P1
O                                   86 'ACCOUNTS'                    CH8P1
O                                   95 'CASH'                        CH8P1
O                                  106 'SALES'                       CH8P1
O                                  116 'NET'                         CH8P1
O        H  2     1P                                                 CH8P1
O       OR        OF                                                 CH8P1
O                                    6 'DATE'                        CH8P1
O                                   28 'ACCOUNT CREDITED'            CH8P1
O                                   47 'EXPLANATION'                 CH8P1
O                                   59 'TERMS'                       CH8P1
O                                   67 'FOLIO'                       CH8P1
O                                   75 'ACCOUNT'                     CH8P1
O                                   87 'RECEIVABLE'                  CH8P1
O                                   96 'SALES'                       CH8P1
O                                  108 'DISCOUNT'                    CH8P1
O                                  117 'CASH'                        CH8P1
O        D  2     01                                                 CH8P1
O       OR        02                                                 CH8P1
O       OR        03                                                 CH8P1
O       OR        04                                                 CH8P1
O                         DATE  Y    8                               CH8P1
O                         ACTNAM    30                               CH8P1
O                         EXPLAN    52                               CH8P1
O                    02   TERMS     58                               CH8P1
O                    01   FOLIO     65                               CH8P1
O                    01   SUNDRY1   75                               CH8P1
O                    01   SUNDRY1  118                               CH8P1
O                    02   ARAMT 1   86                               CH8P1
O                    02   SALDIS1  107                               CH8P1
O                    02   NETCSH1  118                               CH8P1
O                    03   CASHSL1   97                               CH8P1
O                    03   CASHSL1  118                               CH8P1
O                    04             78 '.....INVALID ID CODE....'    CH8P1
O        T 1      LR                                                 CH8P1
O                         TOTSUN1   75                               CH8P1
O                         TOTAR 1   86                               CH8P1
O                         TOTSAL1   97                               CH8P1
O                         TOTDIS1  107                               CH8P1
O                         TOCASH1  118                               CH8P1
```

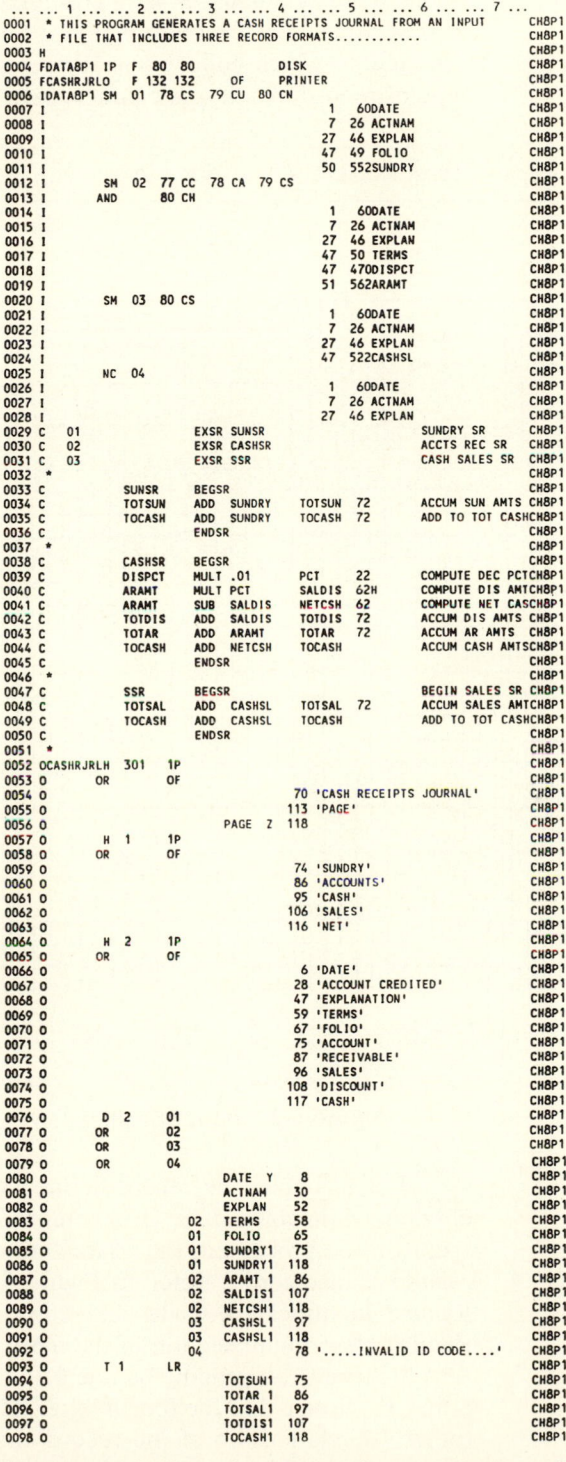

Figure 8-7 Source listing of program that generates a Cash Receipts Journal.

Input Specifications Coding—Cash Receipts Journal Program

The Input Specifications Form shown in Figure 8-8 indicates that new entries are specified for identifying the three record formats (01, 02, and 03) included in the data file. Locate line 010; notice that supplementing the file name, sequence letters, and the Record Identifying Indicator are entries in the Record Identification Codes fields (columns 21–41). This area of the input form consists of three identical sections. Each section includes four fields—Position, Not (N), C/Z/D, and Character—which collectively define the location, presence (or absence), and type of record identifying character(s).

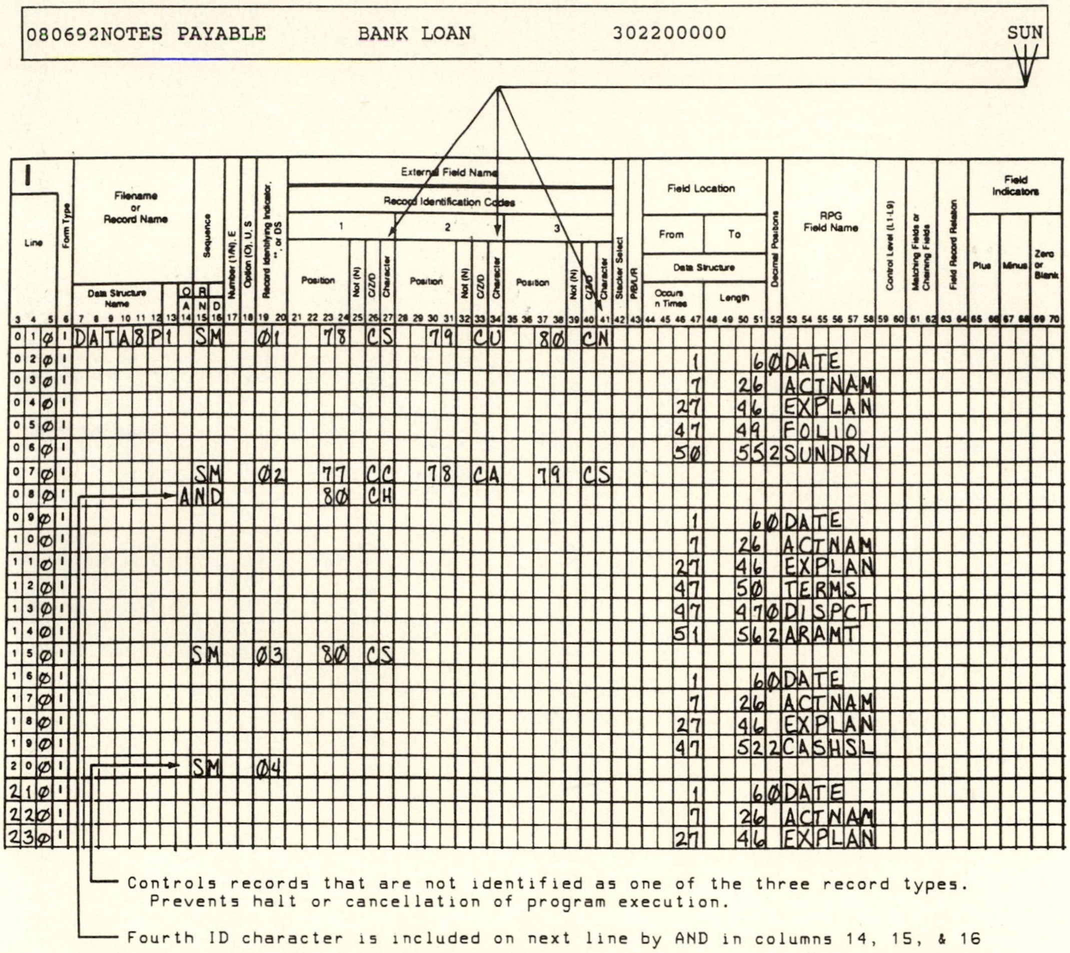

Figure 8-8 Input Specifications for Cash Receipts Journal program.

For example, the record defined with a 01 indicator is identified with the character S in column 78, U in column 79, and N in column 80. For that type of record to be processed, the characters must be entered in those columns of the related data records. Refer to Figure 8-8, and examine the relationship of the Record Identification Code characters in the data record to the entries in the Record Description section of the input form.

Record 02, beginning on line 070, is coded with the characters C and A and S and H. Notice that the fourth letter (H) is entered on line 080, which continues the AND relationship of the record codes. The letters A, N, D are entered in columns 14 to 16 of the statement as referenced in the column headings of the input form. Also notice that the file name is not repeated on the AND line.

Any number of characters may be used to code a record format. However, because they require storage positions and increase the probability of data entry errors, they should not be assigned indiscriminately.

Record type 03 defined on lines 150 to 190 is identified by the letter S in column 80.

The 04 type of record is commonly called a *catchall* record that is included to prevent halt or cancellation of program execution if an unidentified record is read. Omission of any record identification codes in the record description area controls the processing of any records that are not coded as one of the previously defined record types.

Any number of processing options may be specified for records with an incorrect identification code. For this program example, an error message is printed on the report indicating that the record has an invalid identification code. Another common method is to load the unidentified records to a disk or tape file to be reviewed after program execution is completed.

Field Positions of Record Identification

The function of the fields in the Record Identification Codes area of the input form are explained in Figure 8-9. Any rules or comments are common to any of the individual code areas.

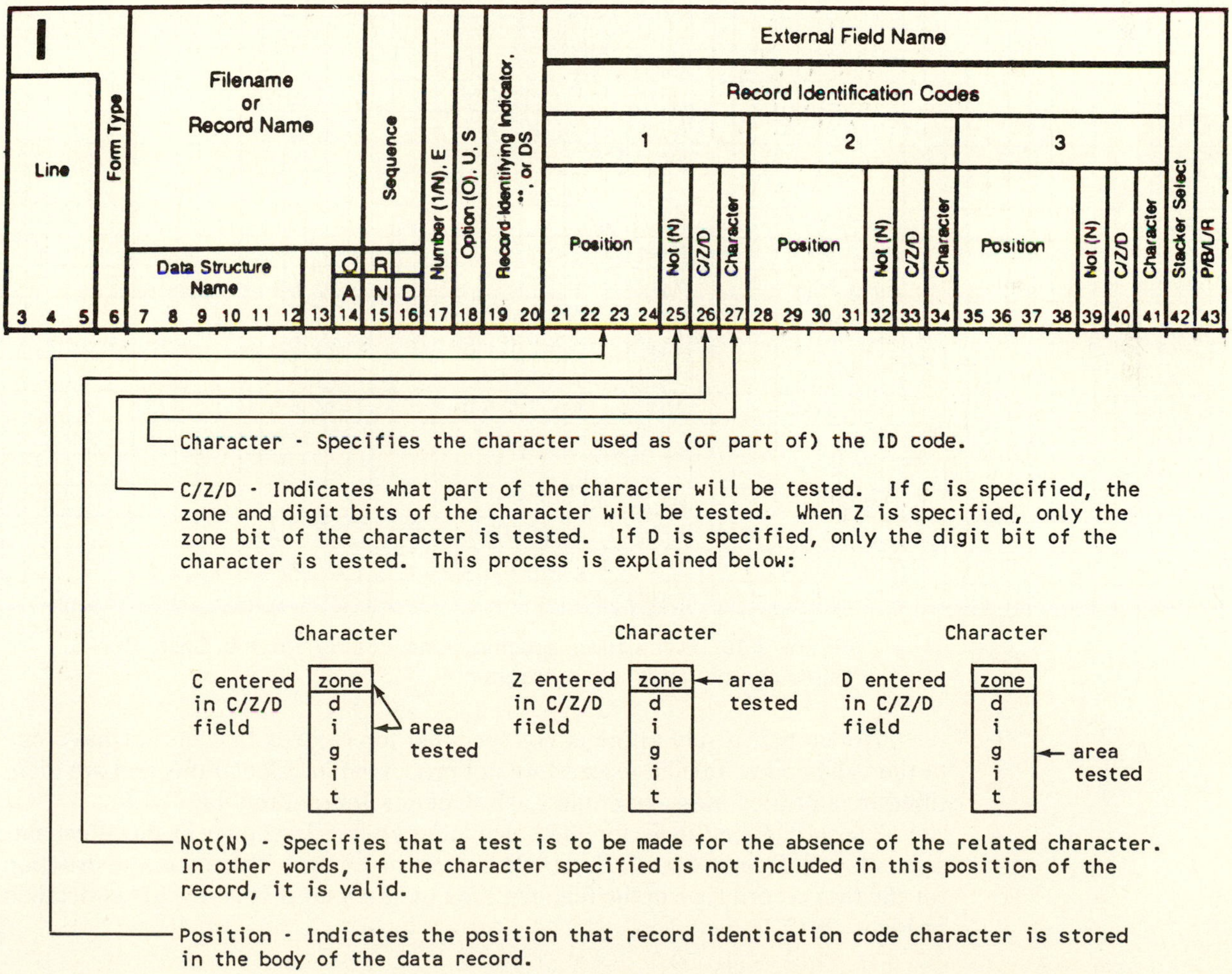

Figure 8-9 Functions of the Record Identification Code fields.

Calculation Specifications Coding—Cash Receipts Journal Program

Examine the Calculation Specifications coding in Figure 8-10, and notice that a structured format is used that incorporates an internal subroutine for each of the three valid types of records. A Record Identifying Indicator turned on by the test of a Record Identification Code controls exit to the related internal subroutine. If internal subroutines were not used, the related Record Identifying Indicator would have to be specified for each instruction of the record type. This procedure would also require that program control test every instruction for the ON or OFF condition of the indicator before execution, which would increase processing time.

Line (3–5)	Form Type (6)	Control Level (L0-L9, LR, SR, AN/OR) (7–8)	Indicators (9–17)	Factor 1 (18–27)	Operation (28–32)	Factor 2 (33–42)	Result Field Name (43–48)	Length (49–51)	Decimal Position (52)	Half Adjust (H) (53)	Resulting Indicators (54–59)
01Ø	C		Ø1		EXSR	SUNSR					
02Ø	C		Ø2		EXSR	CASHSR					
03Ø	C		Ø3		EXSR	SSR					
04Ø	C	*									
05Ø	C			SUNSR	BEGSR						
06Ø	C			TOTSUN	ADD	SUNDRY	TOTSUN	7	2		
07Ø	C			TOCASH	ADD	SUNDRY	TOCASH	7	2		
08Ø	C				ENDSR						
09Ø	C	*									
10Ø	C			CASHSR	BEGSR						
11Ø	C			DISPCT	MULT	.Ø1	PCT	2	2		
12Ø	C			ARAMT	MULT	PCT	SALDIS	6	2	H	
13Ø	C			ARAMT	SUB	SALDIS	NETCSH	6	2		
14Ø	C			TOTDIS	ADD	SALDIS	TOTDIS	7	2		
15Ø	C			TOTAR	ADD	ARAMT	TOTAR	7	2		
16Ø	C			TOCASH	ADD	NETCSH	TOCASH				
17Ø	C				ENDSR						
18Ø	C	*									
19Ø	C			SSR	BEGSR						
20Ø	C			TOTSAL	ADD	CASHSL	TOTSAL	7	2		
21Ø	C			TOCASH	ADD	CASHSL	TOCASH				
22Ø	C				ENDSR						

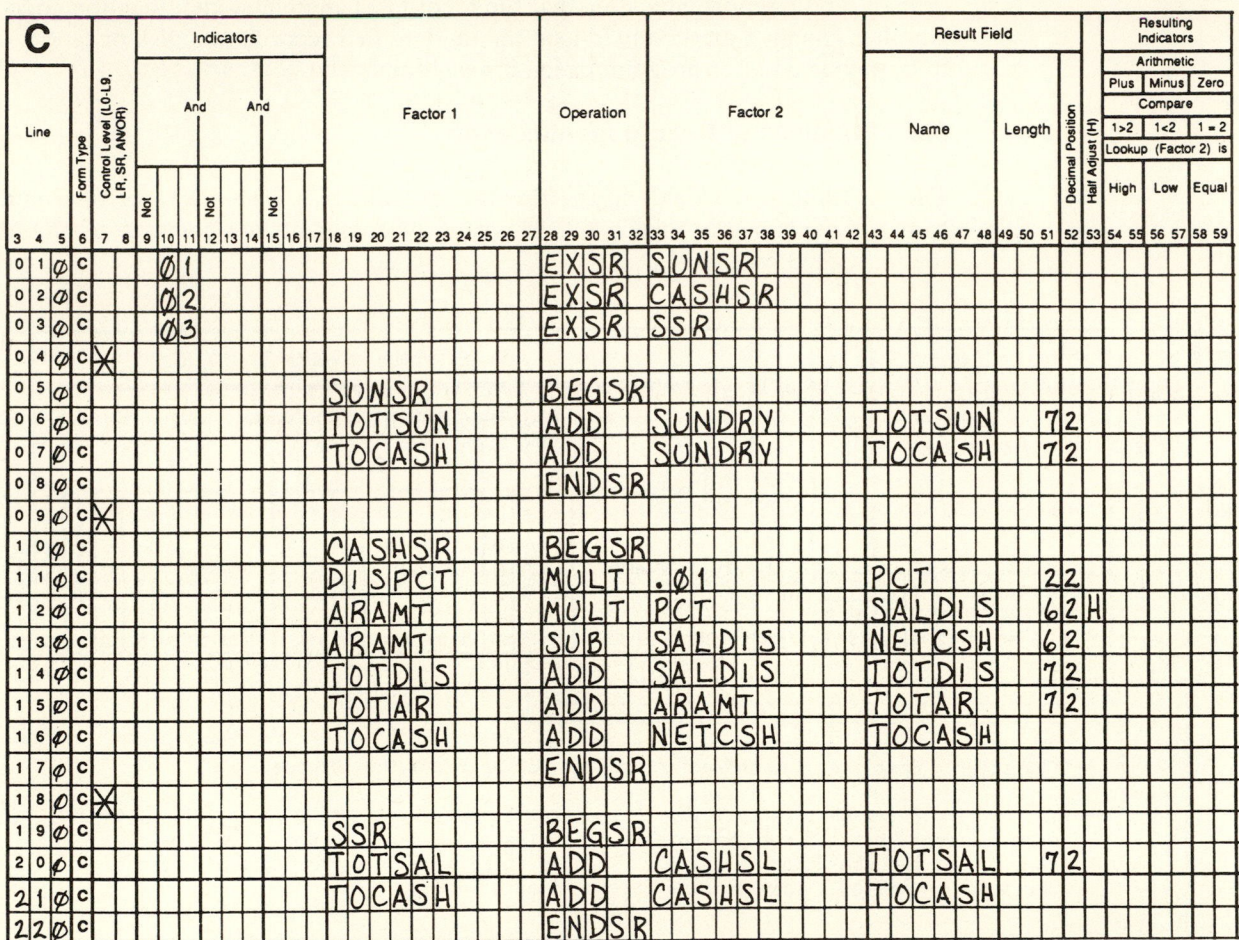

Figure 8-10 Calculation specifications coding for the Cash Receipts Journal application program.

Notice that a subroutine is not specified for records that do not have one of the valid codes. Invalid records are not processed in calculations and are identified by a printed message in the Cash Receipts Journal report.

The processing logic for the calculation coding is shown in the flowchart presented in Figure 8-11. A line-by-line analysis of each calculation instruction for the first record type in the file identified by the record code CASH is detailed in Figure 8-12.

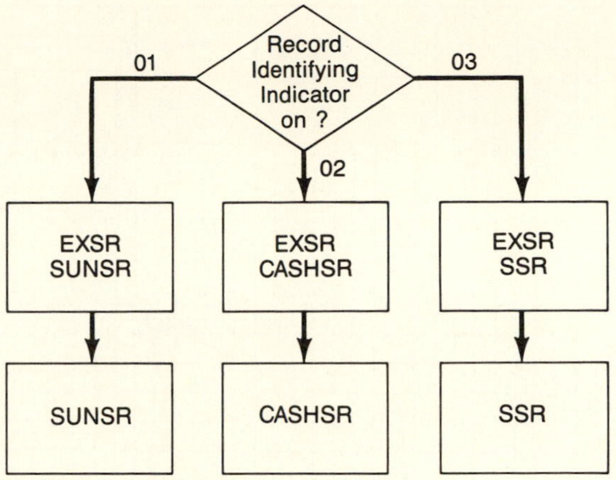

Figure 8-11 Processing logic flowchart for the control of calculations for the Cash Receipts Journal program.

First record processed - CASH Record Identification Code:

```
080189TERRY LENTZ          INVOICE NO 1001/10030000                      CASH
```

```
                                                          Value in items after execution      Indicator(s)
                                                        Factor 1      Factor 2   Result Field      On
... ... 1 ... ....2 ... ... 3 ... ... 4 ... ... 5 ... ... 6

0038 C          CASHSR    BEGSR
0039 C          DISPCT    MULT .01      PCT      22           1         .01          .02           02
0040 C          ARAMT     MULT PCT      SALDIS   62H     030000         .01        000300          02
0041 C          ARAMT     SUB  SALDIS   NETCSH   62      030000      000300        029700          02
0042 C          TOTDIS    ADD  SALDIS   TOTDIS   72     0000000     0000300       0000300          02
0043 C          TOTAR     ADD  ARAMT    TOTAR    72     0000000     0029700       0029700          02
0044 C          TOCASH    ADD  NETCSH   TOCASH          0000000     0029700       0029700          02
0045 C                    ENDSR
```

Note: DISPCT is a redefined one byte item of the first position of the input field TERMS.

Figure 8-12 Line-by-line analysis of the calculation instructions for first record processed in the data file by the Cash Receipts Journal program.

Output Specifications Coding—Cash Receipts Journal Program

Because the coding for heading and LR total lines are common to programs previously discussed, they are not detailed in the output form for the Cash Receipts Journal program shown in Figure 8-13. Examination of the coding indicates that detail output is conditioned by the four Record Identifying Indicators in an OR relationship. This control specifies that the related field/literal values are to be output for any of the record types defined on input. Included is the 04 indicator, which was assigned as a catchall format for records that were not coded by one of the three valid Record Identification codes.

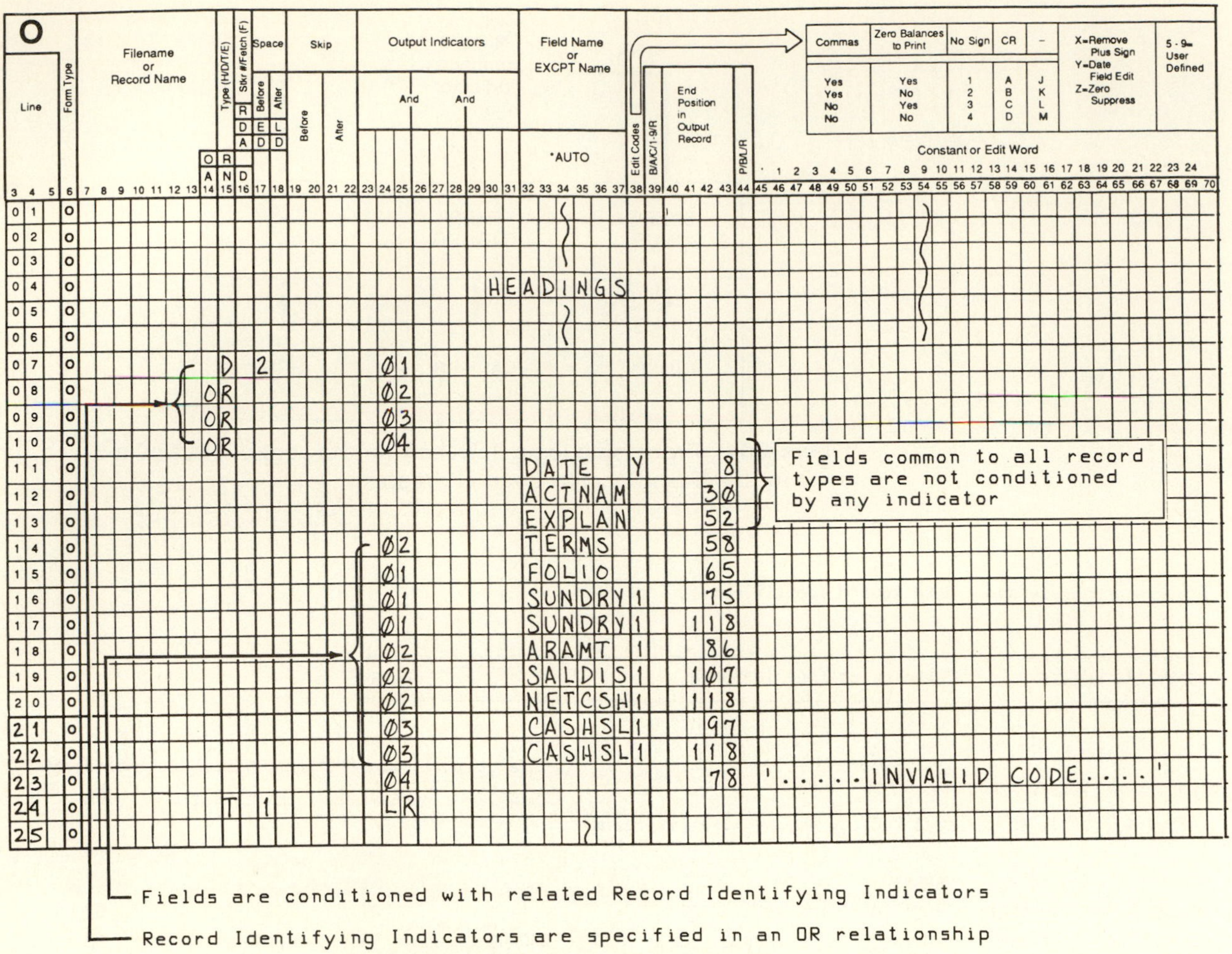

Figure 8-13 Output specifications coding (detail output) for the Cash Receipts Journal program.

Refer to the Field Description area for the detail time output. Notice that with the exception of the first three items (DATE, ACTNAM and EXPLAN), which are common to the four records, each field is conditioned by its related Record Identifying Indicator in columns 24 to 25 (notice that any of the other two indicator fields may have been used). For output records specified in an OR relationship, this coding procedure is necessary to control when and where a field value is to print.

Alternative Input and Output Coding—Cash Receipts Journal Program

Any number of possible coding methods may be specified in the input and output syntax for the control of multiple record file processing. For example, the Input Specifications coding for the Cash Receipts Journal program is modified in Figure 8-14 using an OR relationship (OR is entered in columns 14–15) to define the input record formats. Supplementing the OR statements are entries in the Field Record Relation area (columns 63–64) of the input form. Because the DATE, ACTNAM, and EXPLAN items are common to all the record types, Record Identifying Indicators do not have to be specified in the Field Record Relation field. However,

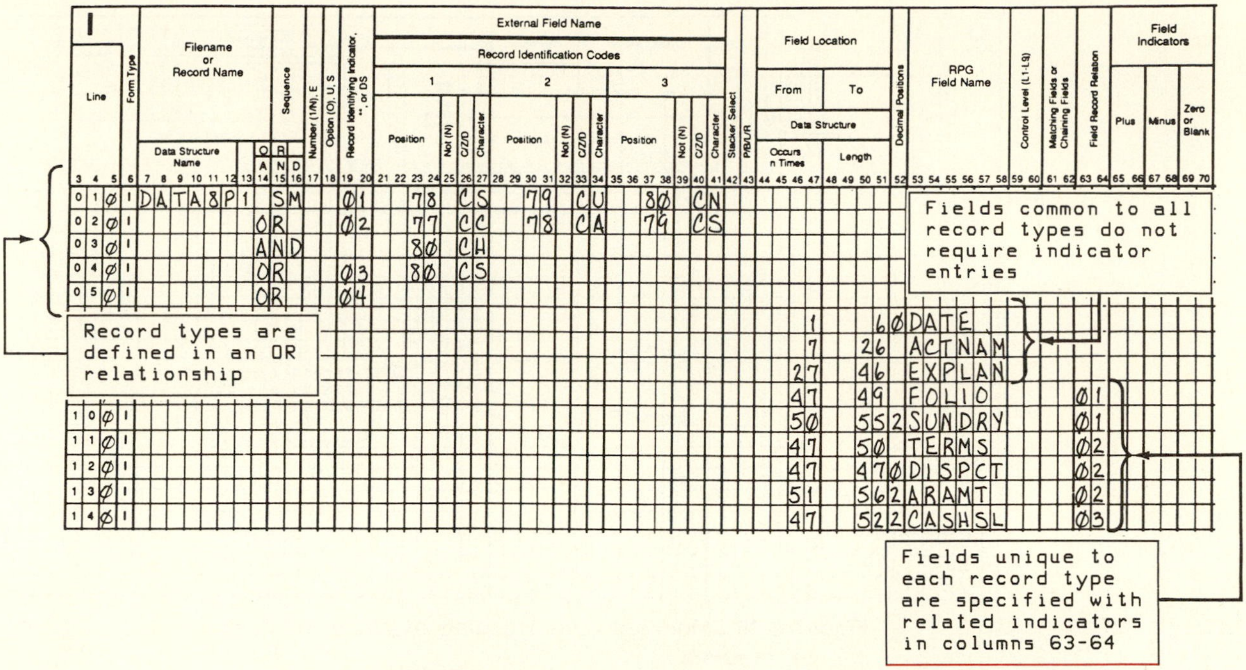

Figure 8-14 Modified input specifications coding for the Cash Receipts Journal program using OR relationship syntax.

the other fields are not common to each record type and are therefore assigned their related indicator in the Field Record Relation columns.

Use of the OR method for defining the record types on the input form for multiple record files has the following syntax and processing advantages:

1. Only one input record buffer area is created, which speeds processing and decreases the CPU storage that is allocated to process the file. Definition of separate record formats on input creates a separate buffer area for each record format.
2. Fewer instructions are required, which reduces the complexity of a program.

Disadvantages of the OR method for defining multiple record formats on input include the following:

1. After a record type is processed and if the next record read has a different format, the single buffer area is reformatted with the new record's fields and values. Consequently, if program control requires that the data from a previous record type has to be referenced after another format is read, the OR method for input should not be used.
2. When the fields in the records of a multiple record file are common to two or more record types and not to others, the syntax required may necessarily become repetitive and complex.

The program example specified the OR relationship of the output records and conditioned each of the independent fields with its related Record Identifying Indicators. Again, other methods may be used to code the output instructions for the data in variable record formats. For example, Figure 8-15 specifies the output coding for the four record types individually.

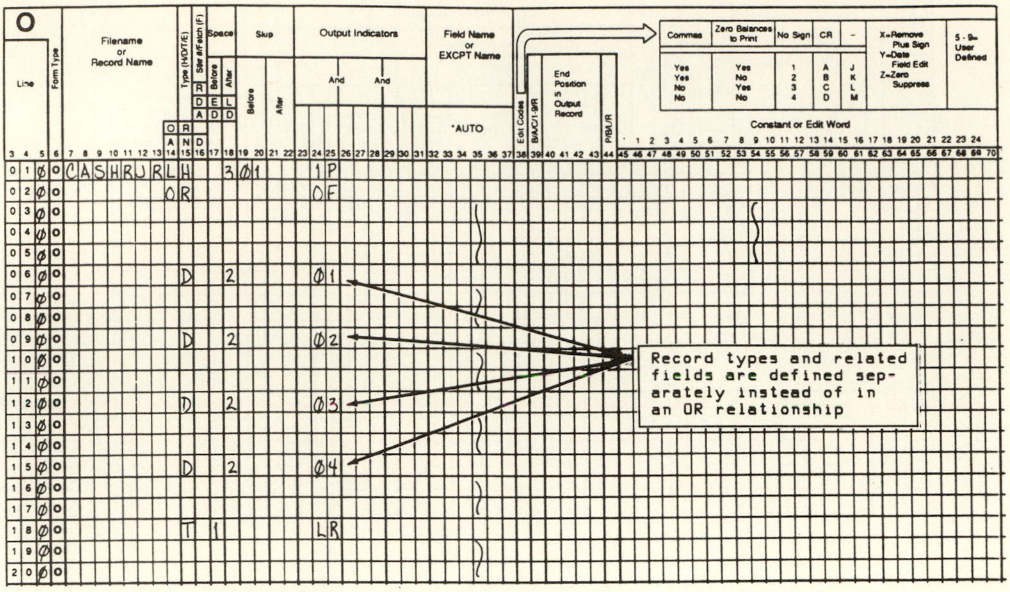

Figure 8-15 Modified output coding example for Cash Receipts Journal program.

MODIFIED CASH RECEIPTS JOURNAL PROGRAM—WITH RPG LANGUAGE ENHANCEMENTS

*INxx Keyword

With the exception of 1P, the ON or OFF condition of any indicator included in an RPG program may be tested during execution. *INxx keywords predefine one-byte alphanumeric fields for every indicator used in the program. The indicator specified in the xx positions may be tested for "1" (ON condition) or "0" (OFF condition). Figure 8-16 explains the syntax of the *IN keyword. The method by which the *INxx keyword is used in the Cash Receipts Journal program is illustrated in Figure 8-17. The keyword is not limited to relational testing but may be used as a general input, calculation, or output item.

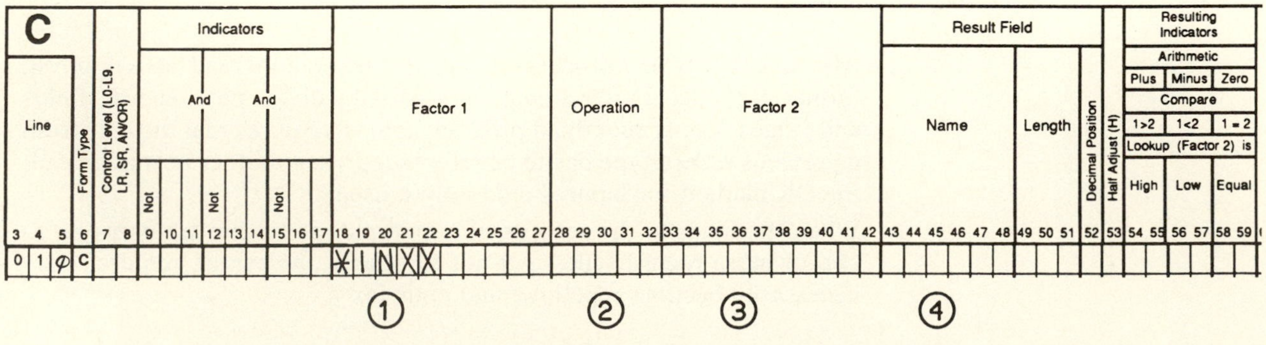

1. Any indicator (except 1P) included in an RPG program may be specified in the xx positions.
2. COMP, CABxx, CASxx, and IFxx operations may be used in the relational test of an *INxx statement.

Figure 8-16 Syntax of the *INxx keyword.

```
3. '1' must be entered in Factor 2 to test the indicator specified in
   the *INxx statement for an ON condition and '0' for an OFF
   condition.

4. The operation included in the Operation field will determine entry
   in the Result Field.

*INxx may also be specified in Factor 2 or the Result Field of calculations
or be used as an item in any other coding form field.
```

(*Continued*)

Line	Form Type	Control Level	Indicators	Factor 1	Operation	Factor 2	Result Field Name	Length	Decimal Position	Half Adjust	Resulting Indicators
010	C			*IN01	CASEQ	'1'	SUNSR				
020	C			*IN02	CASEQ	'1'	CASHSR				
030	C			*IN03	CASEQ	'1'	SSR				
040	C				END						

```
*IN01, *IN02, and *IN03 entries in Factor 1 of the three statements specify
the indicator to be tested.

The CASEQ operations in the Operation field test the status of the indicators
for an equal condition.

The '1' entries in Factor 2 specify that the tests are made for the On condition
of the indicators

The entries in the Result Field represent internal subroutine names and are
required with CASxx statements

The END operation is required to terminate the CAS group.

Note: When one of the test conditions is true, program control executes
      the internal subroutine and returns to the instruction following the
      END statement.
```

Figure 8-17 Use of *INxx keywords in the modified Cash Receipts Journal program.

The source listing of the modified Cash Receipts Journal program shown in Figure 8-18 includes the following RPG language enhancements:

1. CASxx operations (introduced in Chapter 7) replacing EXSR operations.
2. *INxx keyword discussed in the previous paragraphs.
3. Elimination of the Factor 1 entry in arithmetic statements when the Result Field is the same as the Factor 1 item. This coding method was introduced in Chapter 4.
4. Exception time replaces detail time output. This method is not an RPG language enhancement and could have been included in the previously discussed version of the program.

In addition, the previously discussed OR relationship method for input coding and the separate definition of the output records are included in the modified source program.

RPG III/400 syntax

```
... ... 1 ... ... 2 ... ... 3 ... ... 4 ... ... 5 ... ... 6 ... ... 7 ...
 * THIS PROGRAM GENERATES A CASH RECEIPTS JOURNAL FROM AN INPUT      CH8P2
 * FILE THAT INCLUDES THREE RECORD FORMATS - WITH RPG/400 SYNTAX      CH8P2
H                                                                    CH8P2
FDATA8P1 IP  F  80  80            DISK                               CH8P2
FCASHRJRLO   F 132 132      OF    PRINTER                            CH8P2
IDATA8P1 SM  01  78 CS  79 CU  80 CN                                 CH8P2
I       OR   02  77 CC  78 CA  79 CS                                 CH8P2
I       AND      80 CH                                               CH8P2
I       OR   03  80 CS                                               CH8P2
I       OR   04                                                      CH8P2
I                                        1   60DATE                  CH8P2
I                                        7  26 ACTNAM                CH8P2
I                                       27  46 EXPLAN                CH8P2
I                                       47  49 FOLIO       01        CH8P2
I                                       50  552SUNDRY      01        CH8P2
I                                       47  50 TERMS       02        CH8P2
I                                       47  470DISPCT      02        CH8P2
I                                       51  562ARAMT       02        CH8P2
I                                       47  522CASHSL      03        CH8P2
C           *IN01     CASEQ'1'       SUNSR            SUNDRY SR      CH8P2
C           *IN02     CASEQ'1'       CASHSR           ACCTS REC SR   CH8P2
C           *IN03     CASEQ'1'       SSR              CASH SALES SR  CH8P2
C                     END                             ENDS CAS GROUP CH8P2
C                     EXCPT                           TO E OUTPUT    CH8P2
 *                                                                   CH8P2
C           SUNSR     BEGSR                                          CH8P2
C                     ADD  SUNDRY    TOTSUN  72       ACCUM SUN AMTS CH8P2
C                     ADD  SUNDRY    TOCASH  72       ADD TO TOT CASHCH8P2
C                     ENDSR                                          CH8P2
 *                                                                   CH8P2
C           CASHSR    BEGSR                                          CH8P2
C           DISPCT    MULT .01       PCT     22       COMPUTE DEC PCTCH8P2
C           ARAMT     MULT PCT       SALDIS  62H      COMPUTE DIS AMTCH8P2
C           ARAMT     SUB  SALDIS    NETCSH  62       COMPUTE NET CASCH8P2
C                     ADD  SALDIS    TOTDIS  72       ACCUM DIS AMTS CH8P2
C                     ADD  ARAMT     TOTAR   72       ACCUM AR AMTS  CH8P2
C                     ADD  NETCSH    TOCASH           ACCUM CASH AMTSCH8P2
C                     ENDSR                                          CH8P2
 *                                                                   CH8P2
C           SSR       BEGSR                           BEGIN SALES SR CH8P2
C                     ADD  CASHSL    TOTSAL  72       ACCUM SALES AMTCH8P2
C                     ADD  CASHSL    TOCASH           ADD TO TOT CASHCH8P2
C                     ENDSR                                          CH8P2
 *                                                                   CH8P2
OCASHRJRLH  301   1P                                                 CH8P2
O       OR        OF                                                 CH8P2
O                                   70 'CASH RECEIPTS JOURNAL'       CH8P2
O                                  113 'PAGE'                        CH8P2
O                         PAGE  Z  118                               CH8P2
O        H  1     1P                                                 CH8P2
O       OR        OF                                                 CH8P2
O                                   74 'SUNDRY'                      CH8P2
O                                   86 'ACCOUNTS'                    CH8P2
O                                   95 'CASH'                        CH8P2
O                                  106 'SALES'                       CH8P2
O                                  116 'NET'                         CH8P2
O        H  2     1P                                                 CH8P2
O       OR        OF                                                 CH8P2
O                                    6 'DATE'                        CH8P2
O                                   28 'ACCOUNT CREDITED'            CH8P2
O                                   47 'EXPLANATION'                 CH8P2
O                                   59 'TERMS'                       CH8P2
O                                   67 'FOLIO'                       CH8P2
O                                   75 'ACCOUNT'                     CH8P2
O                                   87 'RECEIVABLE'                  CH8P2
O                                   96 'SALES'                       CH8P2
O                                  108 'DISCOUNT'                    CH8P2
O                                  117 'CASH'                        CH8P2
O        E  2     01                                                 CH8P2
O                         DATE  Y    8                               CH8P2
O                         ACTNAM    30                               CH8P2
O                         EXPLAN    52                               CH8P2
O                         FOLIO     65                               CH8P2
O                         SUNDRY1   75                               CH8P2
O                         SUNDRY1  118                               CH8P2
O        E  2     02                                                 CH8P2
O                         DATE  Y    8                               CH8P2
O                         ACTNAM    30                               CH8P2
O                         EXPLAN    52                               CH8P2
O                         TERMS     58                               CH8P2
O                         ARAMT 1   86                               CH8P2
O                         SALDIS1  107                               CH8P2
O                         NETCSH1  118                               CH8P2
O        E  2     03                                                 CH8P2
O                         DATE  Y    8                               CH8P2
O                         ACTNAM    30                               CH8P2
O                         EXPLAN    52                               CH8P2
O                         CASHSL1   97                               CH8P2
O                         CASHSL1  118                               CH8P2
O        E  2     04                                                 CH8P2
O                         DATE  Y    8                               CH8P2
O                         ACTNAM    30                               CH8P2
O                         EXPLAN    52                               CH8P2
O                                   78 '.....INVALID ID CODE....'    CH8P2
O        T  1     LR                                                 CH8P2
O                         TOTSUN1   75                               CH8P2
O                         TOTAR 1   86                               CH8P2
O                         TOTSAL1   97                               CH8P2
O                         TOTDIS1  107                               CH8P2
O                         TOCASH1  118                               CH8P2
```

Figure 8-18 Modified source listing of the Cash Receipts Journal program.

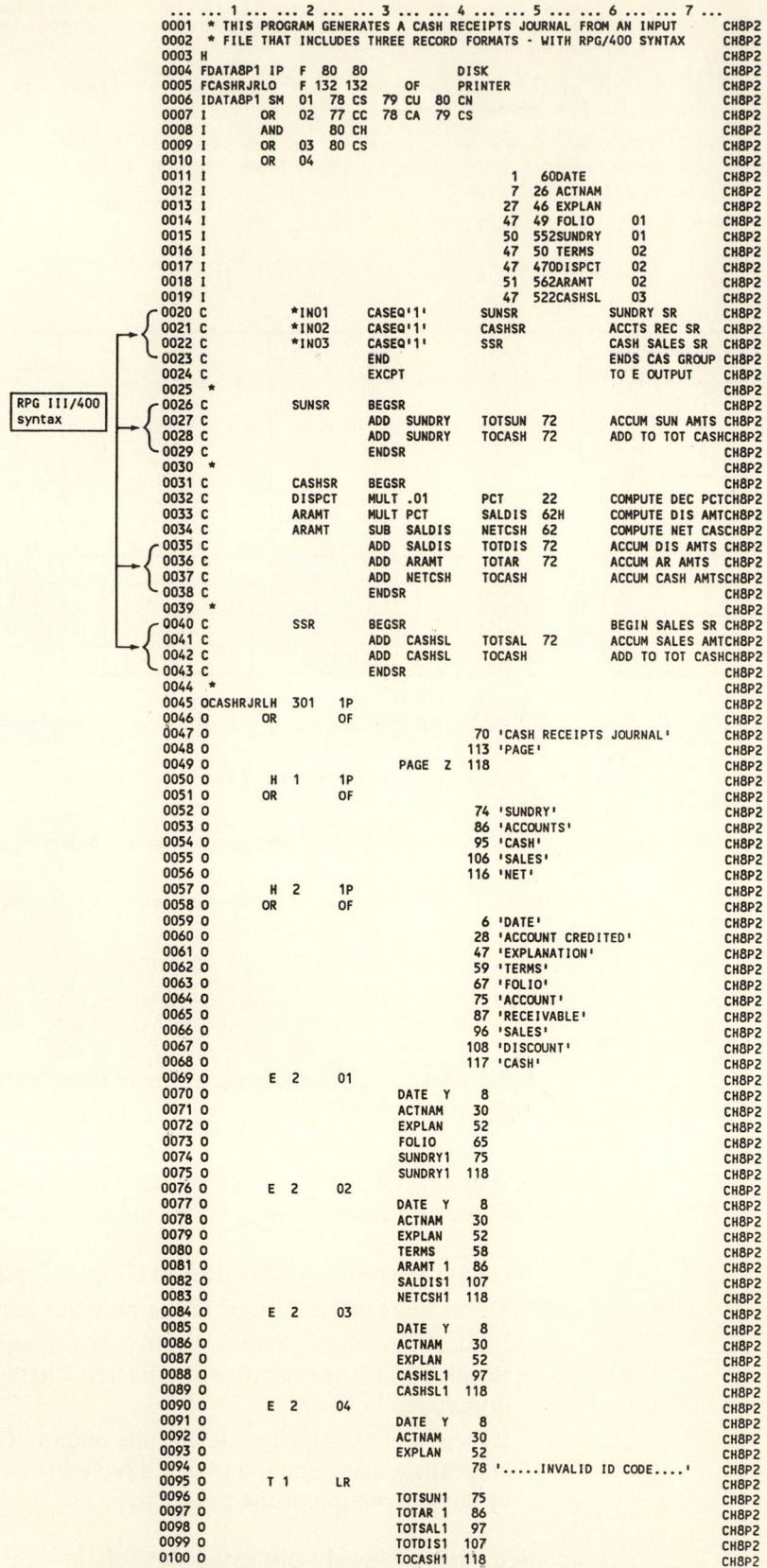

SEQUENCE CHECKING RECORD TYPES ON INPUT

Some applications that use multiple record data files require that the sequence of the input records be checked. Since the introduction of disk-supported sorting, however, this function is not as necessary as it was for data files stored on punch cards. Because sequence checking is an RPG feature that may be included in older programs and sometimes required for new applications, however, it is important that the subject be addressed. An application program that generates an income statement illustrates the syntax and processing logic related to the sequence checking of multiple record types on input.

APPLICATION PROGRAM—INCOME STATEMENT

Documentation

The specifications for the program that generates an income statement is presented in Figure 8-19. The system flowchart shown in Figure 8-20 indicates that one input file is processed by the program to generate an income statement on the printer.

PROGRAM SPECIFICATIONS Page 1 of 1

Program Name INCOME STATEMENT Program-ID CH8P3 Written By S. Myers

Purpose Generate an income statement Approved By The Boss

Input files (directory names):
DATA8P3 (stored on disk and sorted in ascending record identification code order - D, I, X)

Output files (directory names):
PRINTER (stock paper)

Processing Narrative:

Write an RPG structured program to generate the income statement shown in the supplemental printer spacing chart.

Input to the Program:

A data file stored on disk is to be processing consecutively until end of file is sensed. Included in the file are three records types with only one date and any number of income and expense records. The record are stored in the file in a Date, Income, and Expense record order (D, I, X).

Processing:

Sequence check the records and include the following tests:

1. The one date record must be the first processed.
2. Any number of income type records are to be processed second.
3. Any number of expense records are to be processed last.
4. All three record types are required.

Accumulate the amounts for the income and expense records. At LR time, compute the net income or loss by subtracting the total expenses from the total income and sign test the result. If the result is positive or zero, the constant NET INCOME is to be printed. If the result is negative, NET (LOSS) is to be printed with parent-thesis encompassing the dollar value.

Output:

Refer to the supplemental printer spacing chart and code the output accordingly. Note that page overflow is not to be provided.

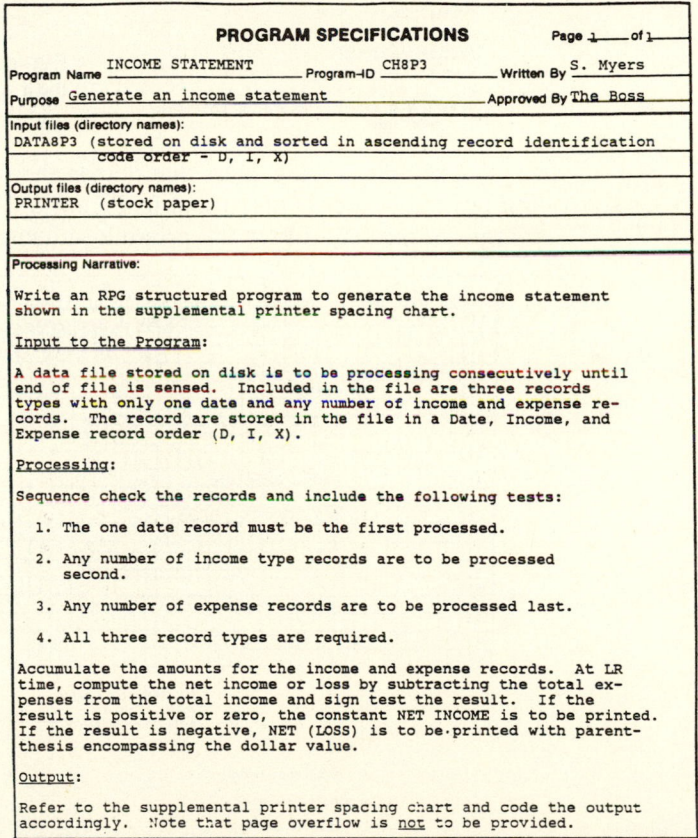

Figure 8-19 Specifications for a program that generates an income statement.

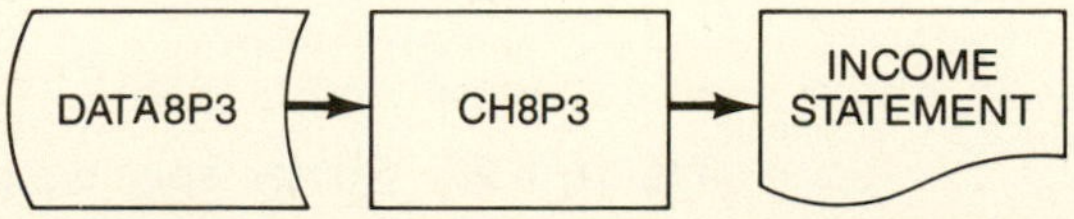

Figure 8-20 System flowchart for the income statement program.

Shown in Figure 8-21 are the record layout forms for the three record types in the file and a listing of the data. Notice that the records are in a D, I, and X identification code sequence. Data files must sometimes be sorted before processing to sequence the data in a required order.

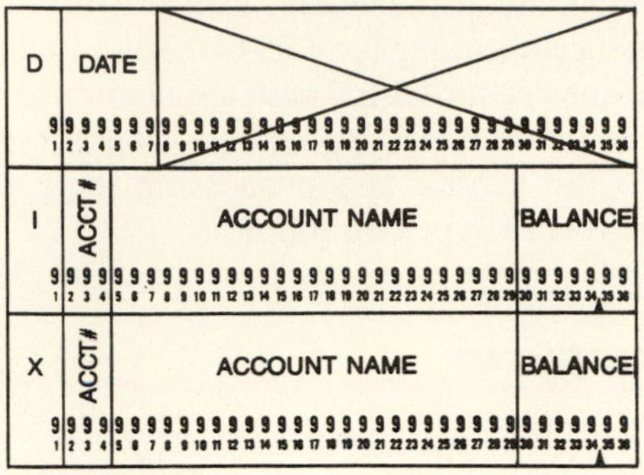

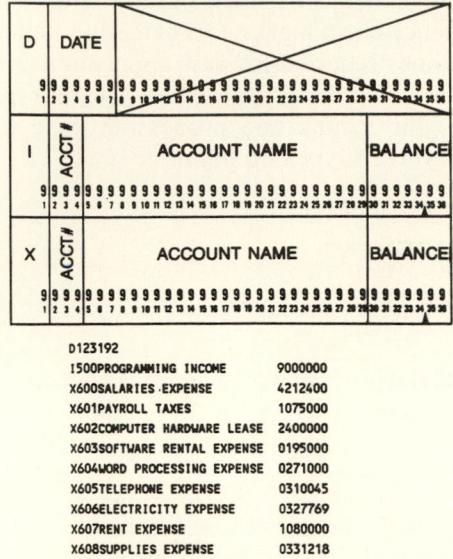

```
D123192
I500PROGRAMMING INCOME          9000000
X600SALARIES EXPENSE            4212400
X601PAYROLL TAXES               1075000
X602COMPUTER HARDWARE LEASE     2400000
X603SOFTWARE RENTAL EXPENSE     0195000
X604WORD PROCESSING EXPENSE     0271000
X605TELEPHONE EXPENSE           0310045
X606ELECTRICITY EXPENSE         0327769
X607RENT EXPENSE                1080000
X608SUPPLIES EXPENSE            0331218
X609MISCELLANEOUS EXPENSE       0200637
```

Records in ascending record identification code order

Figure 8-21 Record layout forms and data listing for file processed by the income statement program.

A printer spacing chart that details the design of the income statement and the printed output is illustrated in Figure 8-22. The comments in the right-hand margin of the report give the printing sequence of the input record types.

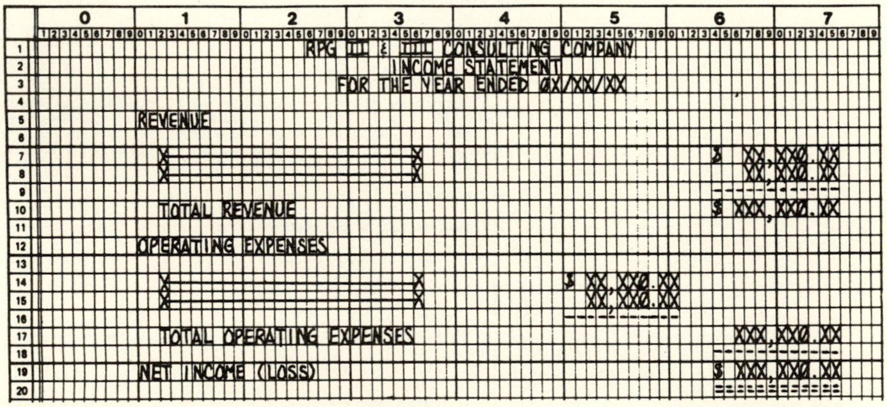


```
                  RPG II & III CONSULTING COMPANY
                        INCOME STATEMENT
                   FOR THE YEAR ENDED 12/31/92
REVENUE

  PROGRAMMING INCOME                              $ 90,000.00

OPERATING EXPENSES

  SALARIES EXPENSE                $ 42,124.00
  PAYROLL TAXES                     10,750.89
  COMPUTER HARDWARE LEASE           24,000.00
  SOFTWARE RENTAL EXPENSE            1,950.00
  WORD PROCESSING EXPENSE            2,710.00
  TELEPHONE EXPENSE                  3,100.45
  ELECTRICITY EXPENSE                3,277.69
  RENT EXPENSE                      10,800.00
  SUPPLIES EXPENSE                   3,312.18
  MISCELLANEOUS EXPENSES             2,006.37
                                   ----------
  TOTAL OPERATING EXPENSES                         104,031.58
                                                 ------------
NET (LOSS)                                       ($ 14,031.58)
                                                 ============
```

Date record processed first (FOR THE YEAR ENDED 12/31/92)

Revenue record processed second ($ 90,000.00)

Expense records processed third, fourth, etc.

Lines printed at LR time

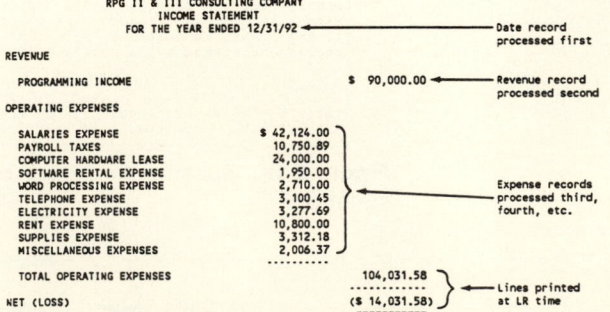

Figure 8-22 Printer spacing chart and printed report for the income statement program.

Source Coding—Income Statement Program

An examination of the source listing of the income statement program shown in Figure 8-23 indicates that File Description, Calculations, and Output coding are identical to the syntax common to the program previously discussed.

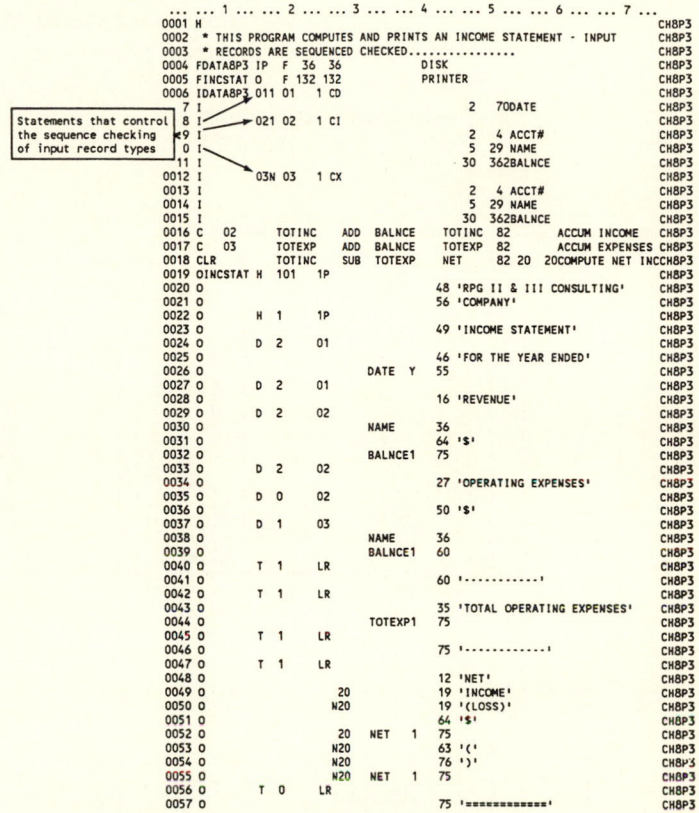

```
... ... 1 ... ... 2 ... ... 3 ... ... 4 ... ... 5 ... ... 6 ... ... 7 ...
H                                                                    CH8P3
 * THIS PROGRAM COMPUTES AND PRINTS AN INCOME STATEMENT - INPUT       CH8P3
 * RECORDS ARE SEQUENCED CHECKED................                      CH8P3
FDATA8P3 IP  F  36  36            DISK                               CH8P3
FINCSTAT O   F 132 132            PRINTER                            CH8P3
IDATA8P3 011 01    1 CD                                              CH8P3
I                                          2   70DATE                CH8P3
I        021 02    1 CI                                              CH8P3
I                                          2   4 ACCT#               CH8P3
I                                          5  29 NAME                CH8P3
I                                         30  362BALNCE              CH8P3
I        03N 03    1 CX                                              CH8P3
I                                          2   4 ACCT#               CH8P3
I                                          5  29 NAME                CH8P3
I                                         30  362BALNCE              CH8P3
C   02      TOTINC    ADD  BALNCE    TOTINC  82        ACCUM INCOME   CH8P3
C   03      TOTEXP    ADD  BALNCE    TOTEXP  82        ACCUM EXPENSES CH8P3
CLR         TOTINC    SUB  TOTEXP    NET     82 20  20COMPUTE NET INCCH8P3
OINCSTAT H  101   1P                                                 CH8P3
O                                 48 'RPG II & III CONSULTING'       CH8P3
O                                 56 'COMPANY'                       CH8P3
O        H  1     1P                                                 CH8P3
O                                 49 'INCOME STATEMENT'              CH8P3
O        D  2     01                                                 CH8P3
O                                 46 'FOR THE YEAR ENDED'            CH8P3
O                       DATE  Y   55                                 CH8P3
O        D  2     01                                                 CH8P3
O                                 16 'REVENUE'                       CH8P3
O        D  2     02                                                 CH8P3
O                       NAME      36                                 CH8P3
O                                 64 '$'                             CH8P3
O                       BALNCE1   75                                 CH8P3
O        D  2     02                                                 CH8P3
O                                 27 'OPERATING EXPENSES'            CH8P3
O        D  0     02                                                 CH8P3
O                                 50 '$'                             CH8P3
O        D  1     03                                                 CH8P3
O                       NAME      36                                 CH8P3
O                       BALNCE1   60                                 CH8P3
O        T  1     LR                                                 CH8P3
O                                 60 '-----------'                   CH8P3
O        T  1     LR                                                 CH8P3
O                                 35 'TOTAL OPERATING EXPENSES'      CH8P3
O                       TOTEXP1   75                                 CH8P3
O        T  1     LR                                                 CH8P3
O                                 75 '------------'                  CH8P3
O        T  1     LR                                                 CH8P3
O                                 12 'NET'                           CH8P3
O                    20           19 'INCOME'                        CH8P3
O                   N20           19 '(LOSS)'                        CH8P3
O                                 64 '$'                             CH8P3
O                    20 NET    1  75                                 CH8P3
O                   N20           63 '('                             CH8P3
O                   N20           76 ')'                             CH8P3
O                   N20 NET    1  75                                 CH8P3
O        T  0     LR                                                 CH8P3
O                                 75 '============'                  CH8P3
```

Statements that control the sequence checking of input record types

Figure 8-23 Source listing of the income statement program.

An examination of the Input Specifications Form shown in Figure 8-24 indicates that new coding entries are included on lines 010, 030, and 070 in columns 15, 16, and 17 (18 is not used for this application). The following paragraphs explain the syntax of these entries.

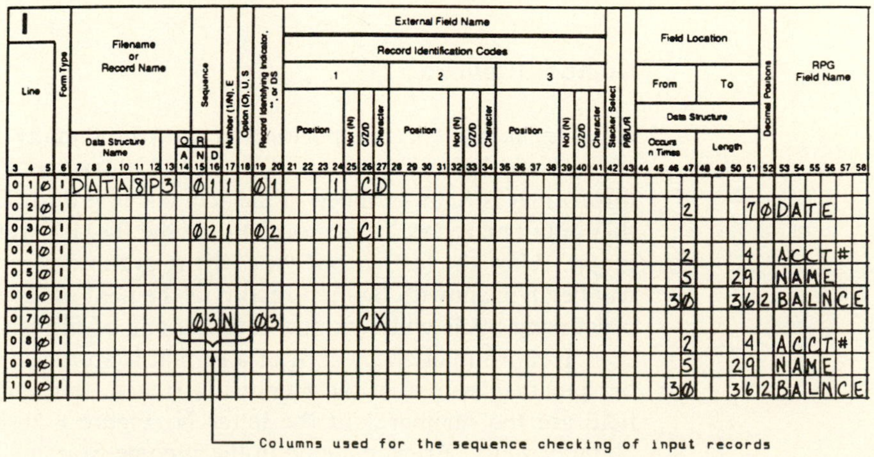

Figure 8-24 Input specifications coding for income statement program using the sequence checking of data records.

Sequence (Columns 15–16)

In lieu of two letters, a two-digit number, starting with the lowest value (01), must be entered in columns 15 to 16 of the input form for record types that are to be sequence checked. Figure 8-25 details the syntax related to this entry. Notice that the date record is read first, followed by the income record, and then the expense records. The Record Identification Code assigned to the record type will determine if the record is in the correct processing sequence. *When sequence checking is included in a program, any record out of the specified sequence will cause program execution to terminate.*

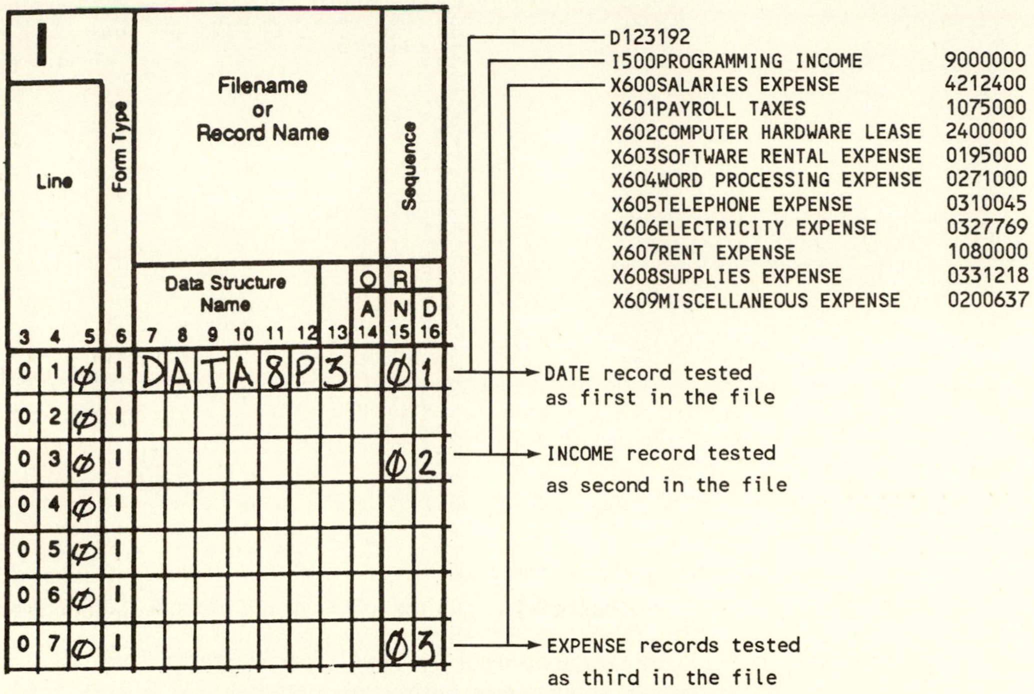

Figure 8-25 Entries required in the Sequence field when the sequence checking of three record types is specified.

Number (Column 17)

An entry is made in this position to show how many records of the related type are to be included in a group. A number 1 entry specifies that only one record of this format is to be included in the sequenced group. This entry does not indicate that only one record of the format is in the file; it is only a test for the sequenced group. After the last record type of the group is processed, sequence checking will begin again with the first record of the next group in the file. This testing and processing cycle will continue until the end of file is sensed.

If more than one record of a format is stored in a group, the letter N must be specified instead of the number 1. Hence, the only two valid entries for this field are the number 1 or the letter N. Figure 8-26 explains the syntax of the Number field entries included in the Income Statement program.

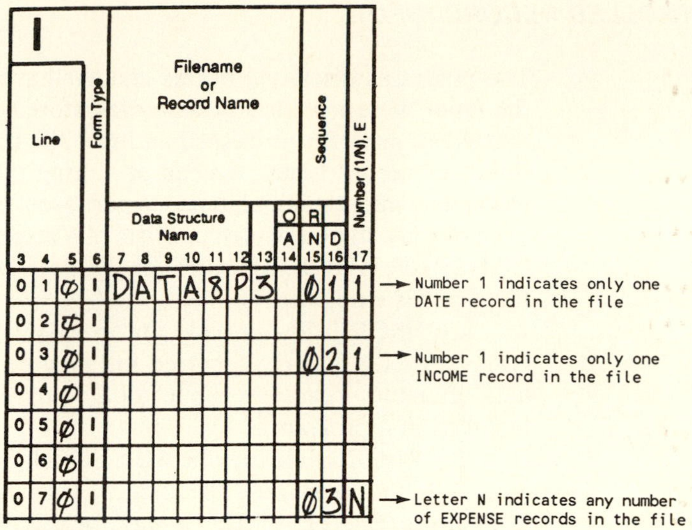

Figure 8-26 Entries required in the Number field when the sequence checking of three record types is specified.

Option (Column 18)

If a record type must be included in a sequenced group, this position must be blank. However, if the presence of the record type is optional, the letter O must be specified in this sequence test field. The syntax for this entry is shown in Figure 8-27. Because the Income Statement program requires that all record types be stored in the file, this position in all three formats is blank.

Again, it must be emphasized that sequence checking of multiple record files is not a common program procedure. It should be included only when it is absolutely necessary. Any additional program tests may cause program termination and resulting delays that will not be acceptable to the end users.

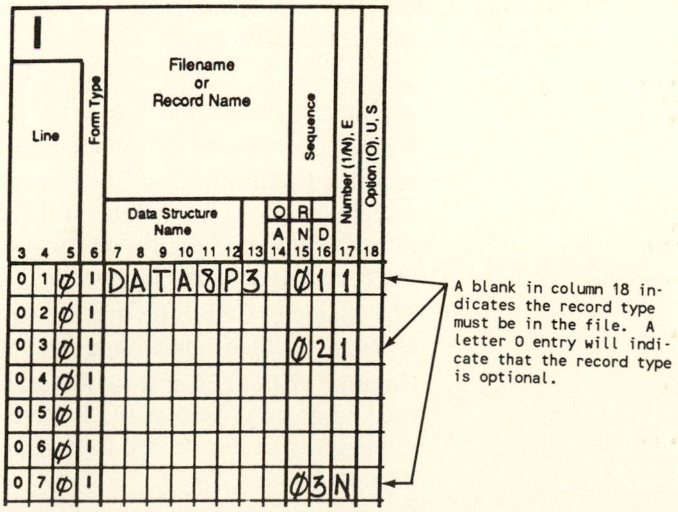

Figure 8-27 Entries required in the Option field when the sequence checking of three record types is specified.

CRT-CONTROLLED RECORD INPUT

The programs discussed in this chapter have indicated that all the record types for input were included in data files stored on disk. For example, the Income Statement program processed an input file that included a date record as one of the three record types. Instead of storing the date record in the file, it may be more convenient (for maintenance purposes) to input the date value to the program via a display station, which consists of a display screen and a keyboard supported CONSOLE, KEYBORD, CRT, or WORKSTN files. The features of each of these file types is explained.

CONSOLE files provide for an easy way to create simple-data entry programs. A CONSOLE supported file may be used only as an input file to input data after the program has executed. Only one CONSOLE defined file may be included in a program.

KEYBORD files may be used as both input and output files when the KEY and SET operations are specified. These two operations display prompts and provide for data entry. The syntax for this file control is introduced in Chapter 12.

A CRT file may be used only as an output file to display data or constants. Variable data cannot be input or changed at the keyboard.

WORKSTN (work station) files are combined files (both input and output). They support the display of constants and provide for the input, output, and protection of variable fields. Also, the same work station file may be referenced by more than one program, which is not true of CONSOLE, KEYBORD, or CRT files. Work station files are supported by software that is not included in an RPG compiler. The syntax of the work station software (Screen Format Generator) for the IBM System/34 and 36 computer series is discussed in Chapter 18; the IBM AS/400 and System/38 in Chapter 20. Other computer companies also have work station software that is unique to their systems.

The Income Statement program will be modified to support CONSOLE controlled input of the date value. Figure 8-28 illustrates the File Description coding for the CONSOLE file defined in the program and explains the syntax rules for this display station input method.

The Input Specifications coding for the modified Income Statement program using CONSOLE input is detailed in Figure 8-29. Notice the following Record Description coding features:

1. Alphabetic characters are entered in the Sequence field because sequence checking is not specified for the CONSOLE file.
2. A Record Identification Code position must be entered in column 1. If a second code is used, it must be defined in position 2. A maximum of two ID codes are permitted for a CONSOLE file. Also, no more than ten record types may be specified for this display station type of file.
3. The character C must be specified in column 26 (and 33 if a two-character code is specified) indicating that the complete character is tested.
4. Column 27 (and 34 if a two-character code is specified) must contain the character(s) used as the Record Identification code. The code value is assigned to the screen format and identifies it when the program is executed.
5. Columns 35 to 74 are not used.

Similar to disk- or tape-stored files, CONSOLE files also support the sequence checking function. However, because there is only one record type input (DATE

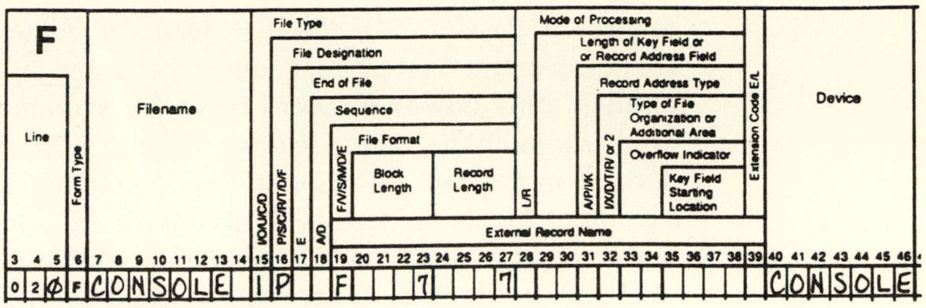

Field Name	*Columns*	
Filename	7-14	A programmer-supplied file name must be entered.
File Type	15-15	An I (for input file) must be specified in this field. CONSOLE supported files may only be defined as input.
File Designation	16-16	May include a P (primary), S (secondary), D (demand), or R (record address) to indicate how the program is to use the file. S files will be explained in this chapter and D and R files in later chapters.
End of File	17-17	May include an E if column 16 contains P, S, or R. It must be blank if column 16 includes D. E indicates that the program must process every record in the file before the program can end. Blank in this position indicates that the program can end whether every record in the file(s) are processed.
Sequence	18-18	May contain an A or a D if column 16 includes a P or S. A indicates that the program will check that the records are in an asceding value order. D will check that the records are in a descending value order. Blank indicates that the record sequence is not to be checked.
File Format	19-19	This column must contain an F which indicates that every record input has the same length (fixed and not variable lengths).
Block Length	20-23	The value specified in this field must be the same as the entry in the Record Length field or be blank.
Record Length	24-27	The record length must be equal to the total of the fields defined on the input form for this file. The record length may not be less than 2 or greater than 1518.
Device	40-46	CONSOLE must be entered as the device name.

Figure 8-28 File Description Specifications coding for the CONSOLE file included in the modified income statement program and general syntax rules.

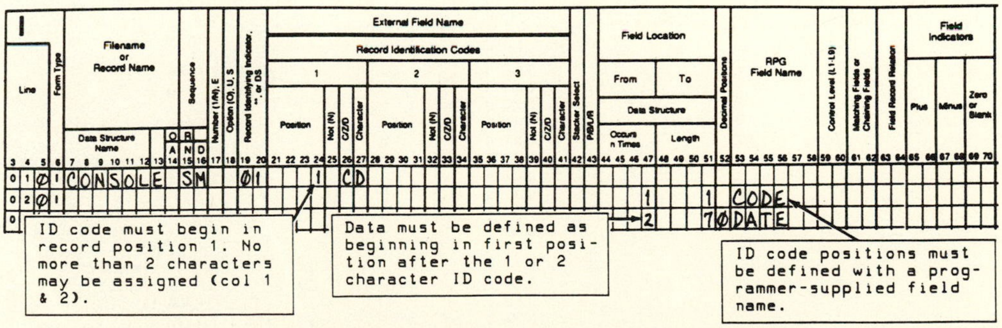

Prompts displayed on screen by CONSOLE file during program execution:

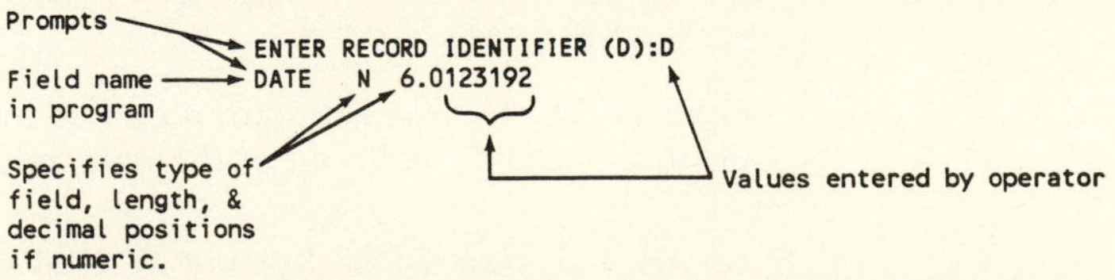

Figure 8-29 Input Specifications coding for the CONSOLE file included in the modified income statement program.

record) by the CONSOLE file, sequence checking is not included for this example. As in the original program, sequence checking is specified for the input file stored on disk, only now two record types are sequence checked and not three.

Examine the source listing in Figure 8-30, and notice that two input files are defined in the File Description Specifications. The CONSOLE file is defined as a *primary* file by the letter P in column 16, and the disk file (DATA8P3) is defined as a *secondary* file by the S in column 16. Only one input file may be defined as the primary file. Any other input (or update or combined) files processed by the program are considered secondary. If an input secondary file is not an update or combined file, the letter S must be specified in column 16. On some systems a primary file does not have to be explicitly defined. In that environment, the first secondary file specified in the File Description coding will automatically be assigned as the primary file.

```
... ... 1 ... ... 2 ... ... 3 ... ... 4 ... ... 5 ... ... 6 ... ... 7 ...
H
 * THIS PROGRAM COMPUTES AND PRINTS AN INCOME STATEMENT -
 * RECORDS ARE SEQUENCED CHECKED - DATE IS CONSOLE INPUT.
FCONSOLE IP  F   7   7            CONSOLE
FDATA8P3 IS  F  36  36            DISK
FINCSTAT O   F 132 132            PRINTER
ICONSOLE SM  01    1 CD                                        CH8P4
I                                       1   1 CODE
I                                       2  70DATE
IDATA8P3 011 02    1 CI
I                                       2   4 ACCT#
                                        5  29 NAME             CH8P4
                                       30  362BALNCE           CH8P4
         02N 03    1 CX                                        CH8P4
                                        2   4 ACCT#            CH8P4
I                                       5  29 NAME             CH8P4
I                                      30  362BALNCE           CH8P4
C   02       TOTINC    ADD  BALNCE    TOTINC  82      ACCUM INCOME   CH8P4
C   03       TOTEXP    ADD  BALNCE    TOTEXP  82      ACCUM EXPENSES CH8P4
CLR          TOTINC    SUB  TOTEXP    NET     82 20  20COMPUTE NET INCCH8P4
OINCSTAT H  101   1P                                           CH8P4
O                                   48 'RPG II & III CONSULTING'   CH8P4
O                                   56 'COMPANY'               CH8P4
O        H  1     1P                                           CH8P4
O                                   49 'INCOME STATEMENT'      CH8P4
O        D  2     01                                           CH8P4
O                                   46 'FOR THE YEAR ENDED'    CH8P4
O                         DATE  Y   55                         CH8P4
O        D  2     01                                           CH8P4
O                                   16 'REVENUE'               CH8P4
O        D  2     02
O                         NAME      36
O                                   64 '$'
O                         BALNCE1   75
O        D  2     02
O                                   27 'OPERATING EXPENSES'    CH8P4
O        D  0     02                                           CH8P4
O                                   50 '$'                     CH8P4
O        D  1     03                                           CH8P4
O                         NAME      36                         CH8P4
O                         BALNCE1   60                         CH8P4
O        T  1     LR                                           CH8P4
O                                   60 '-----------'           CH8P4
O        T  1     LR                                           CH8P4
O                                   35 'TOTAL OPERATING EXPENSES'  CH8P4
O                         TOTEXP1   75                         CH8P4
O        T  1     LR                                           CH8P4
O                                   75 '------------'          CH8P4
O        T  1     LR                                           CH8P4
O                                   12 'NET'                   CH8P4
O                     20            19 'INCOME'                CH8P4
O                    N20            19 '(LOSS)'                CH8P4
O                                   64 '$'                     CH8P4
O                     20  NET   1   75                         CH8P4
O                    N20            63 '('                     CH8P4
O                    N20            76 ')'                     CH8P4
O                    N20  NET   1   75                         CH8P4
O        T  0     LR                                           CH8P4
O                                   75 '============'          CH8P4
```

Two input files are defined. CONSOLE file as primary and DISK file as secondary

DATE value is defined and input via CRT

Sequence checking is specified for the two record types in the DISK file.

After input from the CONSOLE file is ended, report will be printed.

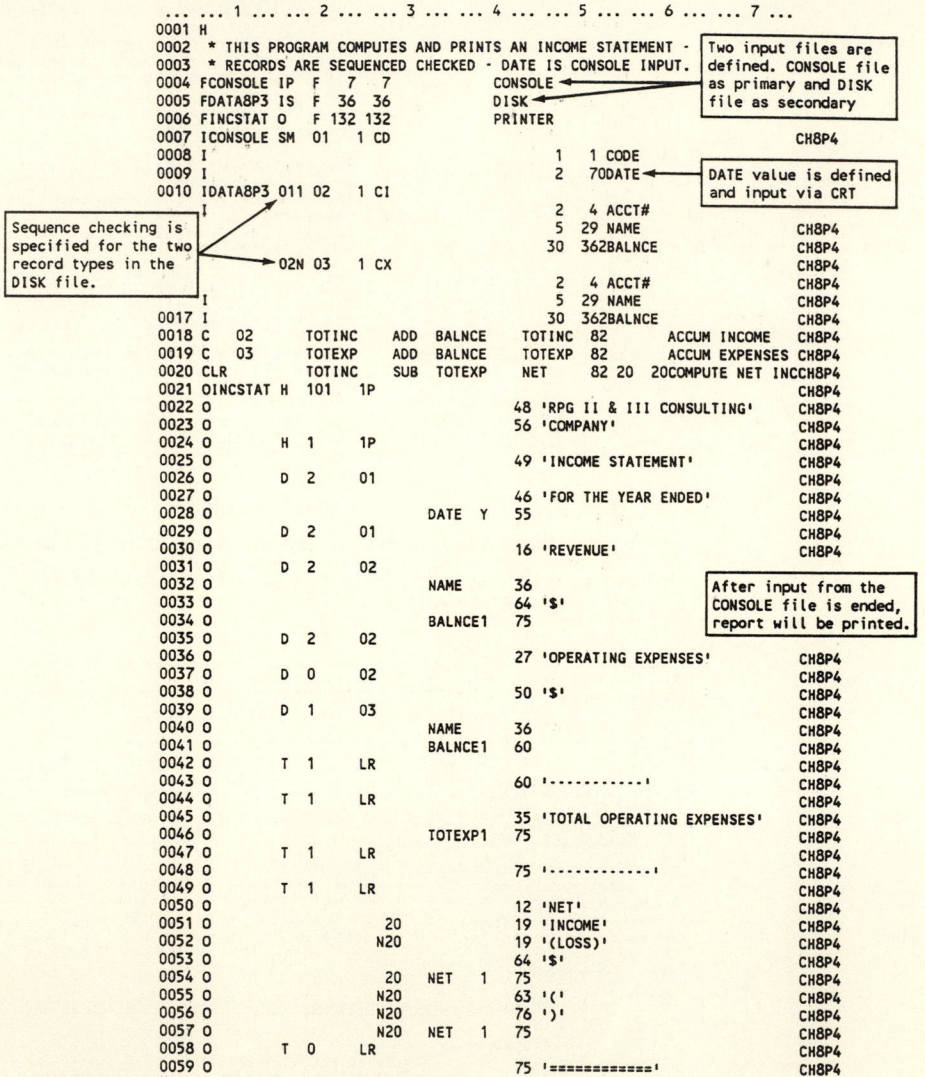

Figure 8-30 Source listing of modified income statement program using CONSOLE file input of the date value.

In an IBM System/34 or System/36 environment, exit from a CONSOLE file is controlled by pressing Command Key 24. Other systems may require a different exit procedure.

DATA STRUCTURES

A data structure is an area in storage that is built when a program that includes the related coding is executed. Data structures, which are defined in the Input Specifications, are used to accomplish the following:

1. Define an allocated area of storage in more than one format.
2. Subdivide an input field so that its elements may be referenced in more than one way.
3. Reorganize fields in an input record.
4. Special purpose data structures (SAVDS, Local data area, and File Information Data Structure (INFDS) that are used to control functions related to Work Station (WORKSTN) files. The related manufacturers's manuals should be referenced for the syntax and purpose of these three types of data structures.

The syntax and function of the first three of these data structures are explained in the following paragraphs.

Coding a Data Structure

Data structures are coded in the Input Specifications and must follow all other input instructions. The entries have two parts: the *data structure statement* and the *subfields*. Figure 8-31 details the syntax related to the both of these data structure areas.

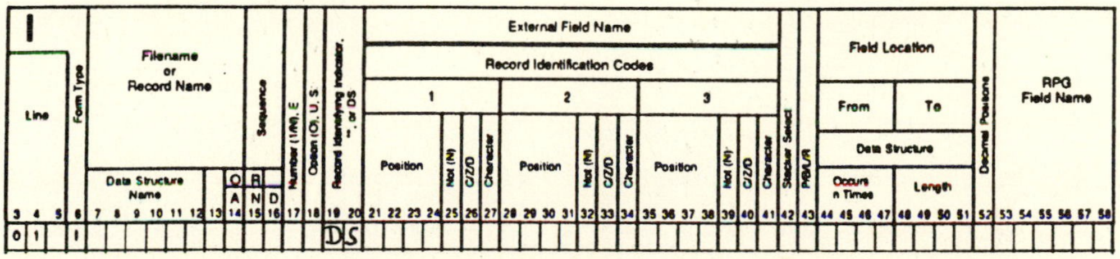

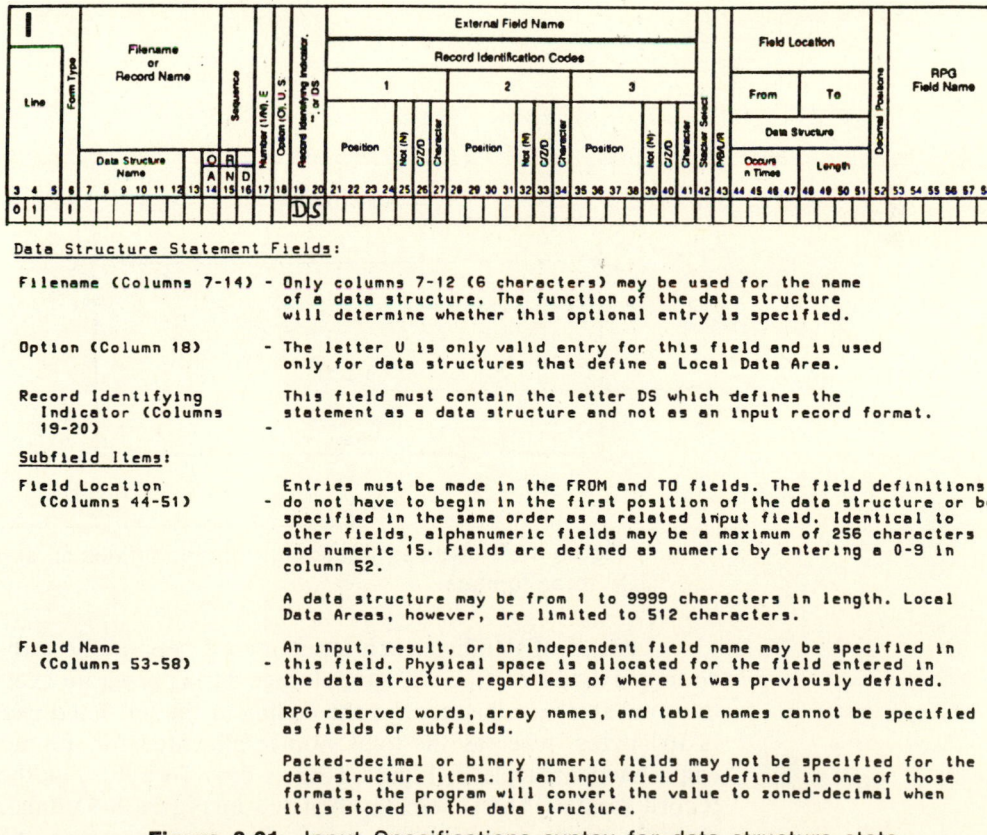

<u>Data Structure Statement Fields:</u>

Filename (Columns 7-14)	- Only columns 7-12 (6 characters) may be used for the name of a data structure. The function of the data structure will determine whether this optional entry is specified.
Option (Column 18)	- The letter U is only valid entry for this field and is used only for data structures that define a Local Data Area.
Record Identifying Indicator (Columns 19-20)	- This field must contain the letter DS which defines the statement as a data structure and not as an input record format.

<u>Subfield Items:</u>

Field Location (Columns 44-51)	- Entries must be made in the FROM and TO fields. The field definitions do not have to begin in the first position of the data structure or be specified in the same order as a related input field. Identical to other fields, alphanumeric fields may be a maximum of 256 characters and numeric 15. Fields are defined as numeric by entering a 0-9 in column 52. A data structure may be from 1 to 9999 characters in length. Local Data Areas, however, are limited to 512 characters.
Field Name (Columns 53-58)	- An input, result, or an independent field name may be specified in this field. Physical space is allocated for the field entered in the data structure regardless of where it was previously defined. RPG reserved words, array names, and table names cannot be specified as fields or subfields. Packed-decimal or binary numeric fields may not be specified for the data structure items. If an input field is defined in one of those formats, the program will convert the value to zoned-decimal when it is stored in the data structure.

Figure 8-31 Input Specifications syntax for data structure statement and subfields.

Data Structure Functions

Defining an Area of Storage in More Than One Format. An example of defining an area of storage in more than one format with a data structure is illustrated in Figure 8-32. This example redefines the Input Specifications for the Cash Receipts Journal program introduced at the beginning of this chapter (see Figure 8-8). For comparison, the original coding and data structure coding are included in the Figure 8-32.

Input Coding Without Data Structures

```
     ... ... 1 ... ... 2 ... ... 3 ... ... 4 ... ... 5 ... ... 6
     IDATA8P1 SM  01   78 CS  79 CU  80 CN
     I                                         1  60DATE
     I                                         7  26 ACTNAM
     I                                        27  46 EXPLAN
     I                                        47  49 FOLIO
     I                                        50  552SUNDRY
     I          SM  02   77 CC  78 CA  79 CS
     I         AND       80 CH
     I                                         1  60DATE
     I                                         7  26 ACTNAM
     I                                        27  46 EXPLAN
     I                                        47  50 TERMS
     I                                        47  470DISPCT
     I                                        51  562ARAMT
     I          SM  03   80 CS
     I                                         1  60DATE
     I                                         7  26 ACTNAM
     I                                        27  46 EXPLAN
     I                                        47  522CASHSL
```

Input Coding With Data Structures

```
     ... ... 1 ... ... 2 ... ... 3 ... ... 4 ... ... 5 ... ... 6
     IDATA8P1 SM  01   78 CS  79 CU  80 CN
     I                                         1  55 SUNREC
     I          SM  02   77 CC  78 CA  79 CS
     I         AND       80 CH
     I                                         1  56 CASREC
     I          SM  03   80 CS
     I                                         1  52 SALREC
     * DATA STRUCTURE CODING FOLLOWS....
     I                DS
     * SUN RECORD FIELDS.....
     I                                         1  55 SUNREC
     I                                         1  60DATE
     I                                         7  26 ACTNAM
     I                                        27  46 EXPLAN
     I                                        47  49 FOLIO
     I                                        50  552SUNDRY
     * CASH RECORD FIELDS.....
     I                                         1  56 CASREC
     I                                         1  60DATE
     I                                         7  26 ACTNAM
     I                                        27  46 EXPLAN
     I                                        47  50 TERMS
     I                                        47  470DISPCT
     I                                        51  562ARAMT
     * SALES RECORD FIELDS.....
     I                                         1  52 SALREC
     I                                         1  60DATE
     I                                         7  26 ACTNAM
     I                                        27  46 EXPLAN
     I                                        47  522CASHSL
```

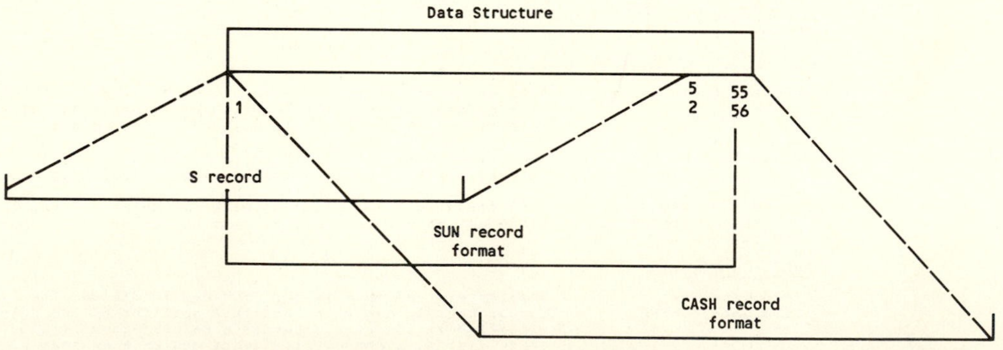

Figure 8-32 Data structure control that defines an area of storage in three formats.

Instead of defining each input record separately with conventional input coding, a data structure will save storage during program execution. For example, the total storage allocated for the coding in the left-hand example in Figure 8-32 is 163 bytes, whereas the total storage allocated for the data structure method (right-hand example in Figure 8-32) is only 56 bytes, or the size of the largest record format. The schematic included in Figure 8-32 illustrates how the three record formats use the same contiguous area of storage allocated to the data structure by the input coding.

Defining Subfields Within a Field. Parts of a field (subfields) may be defined by standard input coding, by the MOVEL and MOVE operations, or by a data structure. Figure 8-33 illustrates two coding examples of this data structure function. The first example includes the input field name, ACT#, in the Data Structure Name field (columns 7–12) with the subfields defined in the subfield area (columns 44–58). A limitation of this method is that the data structure name (ACT# in columns 7 to 14), cannot be used as a field in calculations. However, the subfield, ACTNO, which redefines the entire ACT# item, may be used as a Factor 1, Factor 2, or Result Field in calculations. The second example does not include an entry in the Data Structure Name field. Instead, the input field name is specified as a subfield and then redefined into its related elements.

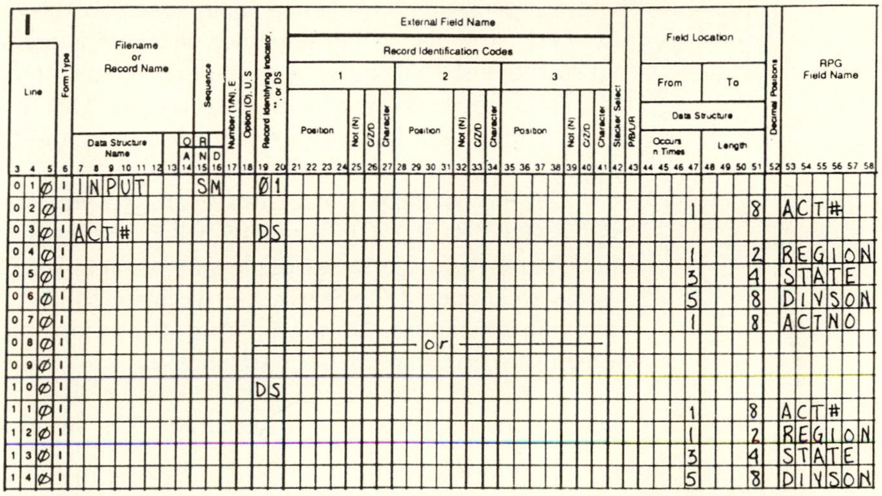

Line	Form Type	Filename / Data Structure	Sequence	Record Identifying Indicator, or DS	From	To	RPG Field Name
01Ø	I	INPUT	SM	Ø1			
02Ø	I				1	8	ACT#
03Ø	I	ACT#		DS			
04Ø	I				1	2	REGION
05Ø	I				3	4	STATE
06Ø	I				5	8	DIVSON
07Ø	I				1	8	ACTNO
08Ø	I	or					
09Ø	I						
10Ø	I			DS			
11Ø	I				1	8	ACT#
12Ø	I				1	2	REGION
13Ø	I				3	4	STATE
14Ø	I				5	8	DIVSON

Figure 8-33 Defining subfields within a field with a data structure.

Reorganizing Fields in an Input Record. Figure 8-34 shows a data structure format that is used to reorganize a field in an input record. The input DATE field is in an MMDDYY format, but processing logic requires that it be rearranged in a YYMMDD format. First, the input field is subdivided into its related elements (MM, DD, YY). The elements are individually rearranged and then defined as a new six-byte field. This is a more efficient approach than using a mathematical formula or MOVE and MOVEL operations to separate and reorganize the date elements.

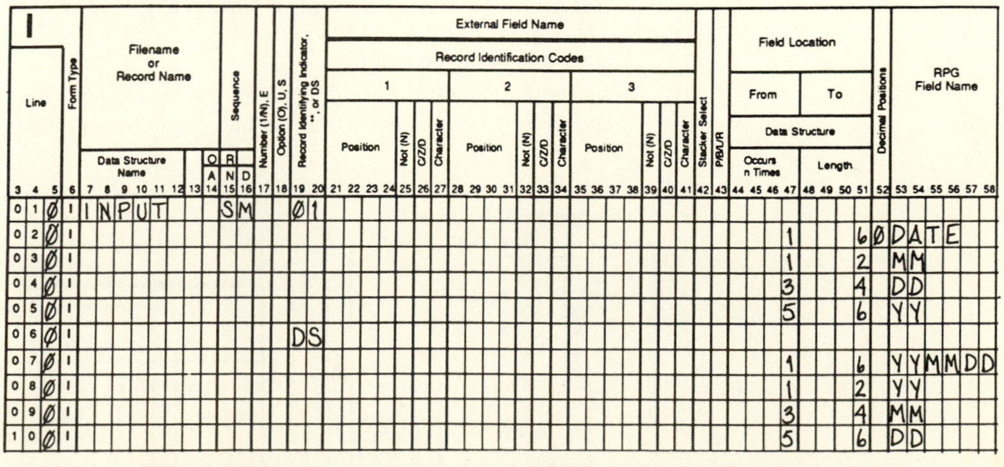

Line	Form Type	Filename	Sequence	Record Identifying Indicator, or DS	From	To	Decimal Positions	RPG Field Name
01Ø	I	INPUT	SM	Ø1				
02Ø	I				1	6	Ø	DATE
03Ø	I				1	2		MM
04Ø	I				3	4		DD
05Ø	I				5	6		YY
06Ø	I			DS				
07Ø	I				1	6		YYMMDD
08Ø	I				1	2		YY
09Ø	I				3	4		MM
10Ø	I				5	6		DD

Figure 8-34 Reorganizing the subfields in an input record with a data structure.

SUMMARY

Multiple record files are those that include more than one record format. Record Identification Codes, unique to each record type, identify the records for processing. A catchall record type that will prevent program halts or termination may be included in the input coding to process records that have an unidentified ID code.

Multiple record formats may be defined separately or in an OR relationship to each other. Record Identifying Indicators entered in the related Field Record Relation (columns 65–70) fields assign the field to a record type.

Sequence checking is used to check the sequence of a record group in a data file during program execution. Data files usually have to be sorted in some order before processing. Sorting is a standalone software utility that is not included in the RPG compiler. When sequence checking is included in a program, a record out of sequence will cause program execution to terminate.

The *INxx keyword is used to test the ON or OFF status of an indicator. Its function is not limited to relational testing and may be used as a field in an input, calculations, or output statement.

Display stations, which consist of a screen and a keyboard, support CONSOLE, KEYBORD, CRT, and WORKSTN files. CONSOLE files, discussed in this chapter, provide for a simple way to input data from a display station. The syntax to support CONSOLE files is included only in the File Description and Input Specifications. During program execution, prompts are displayed on the screen to request an operator's response.

A data structure is an area in storage that is built when a program that includes the related syntax is executed. Data structures are used to:

1. Define an allocated area of storage in one than one format.
2. Subdivide an input field so that its elements may be referenced in more than one way.
3. Reorganize fields in an input record.
4. Create a Local Data Area and build an Information Data Structure.
5. Define multiple occurrence of data that requires multidimensional processing. (Chapter 11)

Data structures are coded in the Input Specifications, are identified by the letters DS in columns 19 to 20, and must follow all other input coding.

QUESTIONS

8-1. Define a multiple record file.

8-2. What is the function of Record Identification Codes? Where are they specified in a source program? What is the minimum number of codes that must be specified for a record type?

8-3. Examine the following entries in the Record Identification Codes fields and explain the function of each.

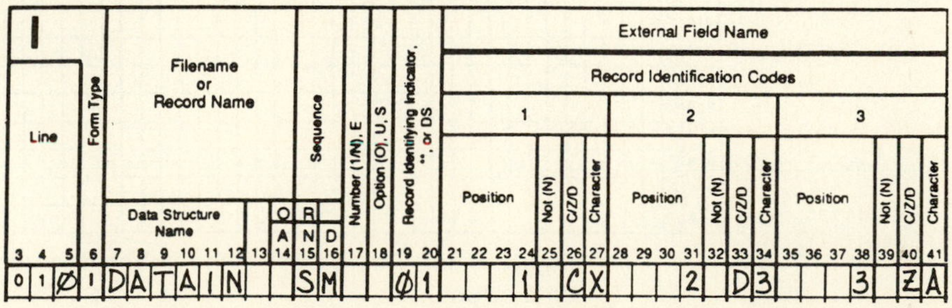

8-4. Refer to the input form in Question 3, and explain the logic related to the C/Z/D fields.

8-5. Refer to the coding in Question 3, and explain when the N fields should be specified.

8-6. When processing a multiple record file, how many Record Identifying Indicators may be on at the same time?

8-7. If the OR relationship method is used to define the input record formats, what coding procedure is used to identify which field belongs to which record format?

8-8. Name one advantage of using the OR relationship method to define input record format in a multiple record file as compared to defining the record formats independently. Name one disadvantage.

8-9. Examine the following partial input coding and explain the purpose of the indicator entries in columns 63 to 64.

Field Location From (44–47) / Data Structure Occurs n Times	Field Location To (48–51) / Data Structure Length	Decimal Positions (52)	RPG Field Name (53–58)	Control Level (L1-L9) (59–60)	Matching Fields or Chaining Fields (61–62)	Field Record Relation (63–64)
1	5		ACT#			
6	25		NAME			Ø1
26	4Ø		ADDRSS			Ø1
41	6Ø		CITY			Ø1
61	62		STATE			Ø1
63	67		ZIP			Ø1
6	9		INV#			Ø2
1Ø	14	Ø	QTY			Ø2
15	19	2	UCOST			Ø2

8-10. If all the record formats in a multiple record file are tested for their related Record Identification Codes and a record contains an invalid (or no) code, what are the processing results? How may this be prevented?

8-11. What is the purpose of sequence checking the records in a multiple record file?

8-12. Examine the following partial input coding form and explain the function of each entry:

Line (3–5)	Form Type (6)	Filename or Record Name / Data Structure Name (7–14)	Sequence (15–16)	Number (1/N), E (17)	Option (O), U, S (18)	Record Identifying Indicator, **, or DS (19–20)	RIC 1 Position (21–24)	Not (N) (25)	C/Z/D (26)	Character (27)	RIC 2 Position (28–31)	Not (N) (32)	C/Z/D (33)	Character (34)	RIC 3 Position (35–38)	Not (N) (39)	C/Z/D (40)	Character (41)	Stacker Select (42)	P/B/L/R (43)	Field Location From (44–47)	Field Location To (48–51)	Decimal Positions (52)
01Ø	I	ORDERS	Ø1	1		1Ø	1		C	S													
02Ø	I																						
03Ø	I																						
04Ø	I		Ø2	N		11	1		C	T													
05Ø	I																						
06Ø	I																						
07Ø	I		Ø3	N	O	12	1		C	R													
08Ø	I																						
09Ø	I																						

8-13. If sequence checking is specified in a program and a record is out of sequence, what are the processing results?

8-14. What is the function of the *INxx keyword? How may it be used in a program?

8-15. Explain the processing logic of the following instructions:

Line (3–5)	Form Type (6)	Control Level (7–8)	Indicators (9–17)	Factor 1 (18–27)	Operation (28–32)	Factor 2 (33–42)	Result Field Name (43–48)	Length (49–51)	Decimal Position (52)
01Ø	C			*IN2Ø	CASEQ	'1'	SUB1		
02Ø	C			*IN3Ø	CASEQ	'Ø'	SUB2		
03Ø	C				END				
04Ø	C				MOVE	'1'	*INLR		

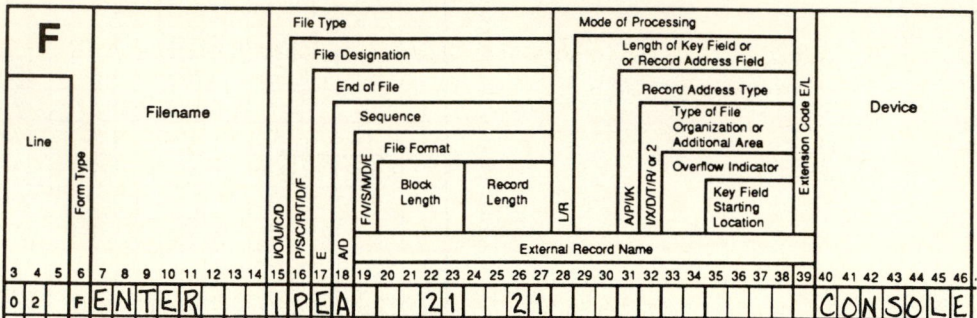

8-16. Name the hardware components of a display station.

8-17. What display station devices are supported by RPG? Explain the function of each.

8-18. Explain the function of the fields in the following coding example:

Line (3–5)	Form Type (6)	Filename (7–14)	File Type (15)	File Designation (16)	End of File (17)	Sequence (18)	File Format (19)	Block Length (20–23)	Record Length (24–27)	Device (40–46)
02	F	ENTER	I	P	E	A		21	21	CONSOLE

8-19. Examine the following coding example related to a CONSOLE file, and determine what will display on the screen.

Field Location From (44–47)	Field Location To (48–51)	Decimal Positions (52)	RPG Field Name (53–58)
1	1		CODE
2	7	Ø	ACTNO
8	19		LNAME

8-20. Refer to Question 19. Is the Record Identification Code entry required for CONSOLE supported files?

8-21. How is exit from a CONSOLE file controlled in an IBM System/34 or System/36 environment?

8-22. Define a data structure.

8-23. Name four functions for which data structures are used.

8-24. Where are data structures coded in an RPG program? How does the program distinguish a data structure from an input record definition?

EXERCISES

8-1. From the following record layout form, complete the Input Specifications coding. Define each record separately (*not* OR relationship format). Use INVENTY as the input file name.

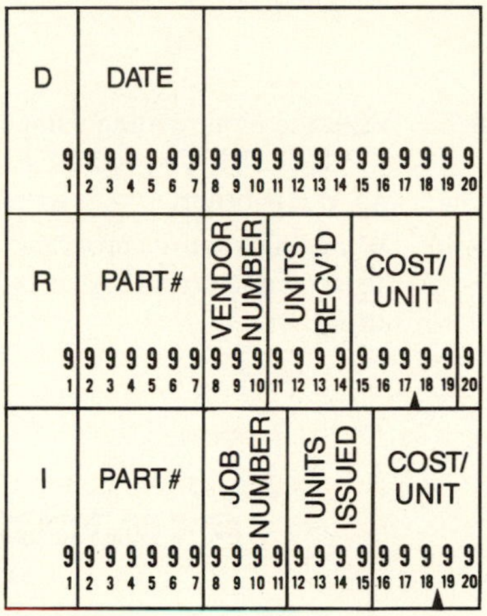

8-2. Rewrite the Input Specifications in Exercise 8-1 so that the records are defined in an OR relationship.

8-3. Rewrite the Input Specifications from the information in Exercise 8-1 using sequence checking for the R and I records. The R record type must be the first of the group. Also, any number of records (or none) may be included in the file for each record type. Only one D type record is in the file that is not part of the record group.

8-4. Refer to any of the previous exercises, and write the Calculation Specifications coding considering the following:

For the R records, compute the total cost for a part by multiplying the units received by the cost unit. Add the product to an accumulator.

For the I records, compute the cost of units issued by multiplying the units issued by the cost unit. Add the product to an accumulator.

8-5. Refer to Exercise 8-1 (or 8-2 or 8-3) and 8-4, and write the output coding for the report format shown in the following printer spacing chart.

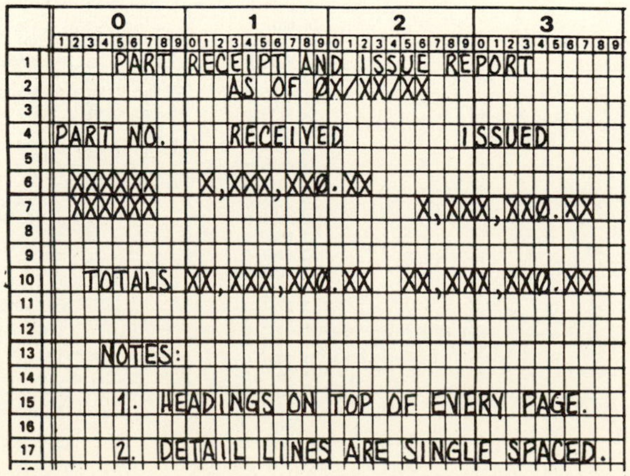

8-6. Write the File Description and Input Specifications coding to control the following CONSOLE input:

Field Name	Length	Decimal Positions	Field Type
SSNO	9	0	N
LNAME	6		A

8-7. Write the input coding using a data structure to redefine PARTNO, which consists of WH#, DEPT#, AISLE#, and BIN#, as KEY, in a BIN#, AISLE#, DEPT#, and WH# order.

8-8. Debugging a source program: Examine the following compilation listing, and correct the six fatal errors. Also, locate any logic errors that would result in incorrect output.

```
       ....+....1....+....2....+....3....+....4....+....5....+....6....+....7.

         1 0001 H                                                           CH7P3

         2 0002  * THIS PROGRAM COMPUTES AND PRINTS AN INCOME STATEMENT - INPUT     CH7P3
         3 0003  * RECORDS ARE SEQUENCED CHECKED...............                 CH7P3

         4      FCONSOLE IS  F   6   7            CONSOLE
****-F163- Record Length must not exceed Block Length.
         5 0004 FDATA7P3 IS  F  80  80            DISK                      CH7P3
         6 0005 FINCSTAT O   F 132 132            PRINTER                   CH7P3

         7 0006 ICONSOLE SM  01                                             CH7P3
****-1234- Invalid Record Identification Codes for a Console file in columns 21-34.
         8 0007 I                                  2   70DATE               CH7P3
         9 0008 IDATA7P3 02  02    1 CI                                     CH7P3
****-1096- First Sequence for numeric sequence records must be 01.
****-1092- Number must be 1 or N for numeric sequence records.
        10 0009 I                                  2   4 ACCT#              CH7P3
        11 0010 I                                  5  29 NAME               CH7P3
        12 0011 I                                 30  362BALNCE             CH7P3
        13 0012 I        012003    1 CX                                     CH7P3
****-1097- Sequence for numeric sequence record is out of numeric order.
****-1092- Number must be 1 or N for numeric sequence records.
        14 0013 I                                  2   4 ACCT#              CH7P3
        15 0014 I                                  5  29 NAME               CH7P3
        16 0015 I                                 30  362BALNCE             CH7P3

        17 0016 C          TOTINC    ADD  BALNCE    TOTINC  82       ACCUM INCOME   CH7P3
        18 0017 C          TOTEXP    ADD  BALNCE    TOTEXP  82       ACCUM EXPENSES CH7P3
        19 0018 CLR        TOTINC    SUB  TOTEXP    NET     82 20  20COMPUTE NET INCCH7P3

        20 0019 OINCSTAT H  101   02                                        CH7P3
        21 0020 O                                  48 'RPG II & III CONSULTING'    CH7P3
        22 0021 O                                  56 'COMPANY'             CH7P3
        23 0022 O        H  1     1P                                        CH7P3
        24 0023 O                                  49 'INCOME STATEMENT'    CH7P3
        25 0024 O        D  2     01                                        CH7P3
        26 0025 O                                  46 'FOR THE YEAR ENDED'  CH7P3
        27 0026 O                        DATE  Y   55                       CH7P3
        28 0027 O        D  2     01                                        CH7P3
        29 0028 O                                  16 'REVENUE'             CH7P3
        30 0029 O        D  2     02                                        CH7P3
        31 0030 O                        NAME      36                       CH7P3
        32 0031 O                                  64 '$'                   CH7P3
        33 0032 O                        BALNCE1   75                       CH7P3
        34 0033 O        D  2     02                                        CH7P3
        35 0034 O                                  27 'OPERATING EXPENSES'  CH7P3
        36 0035 O        D  0     02                                        CH7P3
        37 0036 O                                  50 '$'                   CH7P3
        38 0037 O        D  1     03                                        CH7P3
        39 0038 O                        NAME      36                       CH7P3
        40 0039 O                        BALNCE1   60                       CH7P3
        41 0040 O        T  1     LR                                        CH7P3
        42 0041 O                                  60 '-----------'         CH7P3
        43 0042 O        T  1     LR                                        CH7P3
        44 0043 O                                  35 'TOTAL OPERATING EXPENSES'   CH7P3
        45 0044 O                        TOTEXP1   75                       CH7P3
        46 0045 O        T  1     LR                                        CH7P3
        47 0046 O                                  75 '------------'        CH7P3
        48 0047 O        D  1     03                                        CH7P3
        49 0048 O                                  12 'NET'                 CH7P3
        50 0049 O                    20            19 'INCOME'              CH7P3
        51 0050 O                   N20            19 '(LOSS)'              CH7P3
        52 0051 O                                  64 '$'                   CH7P3
        53 0052 O                    20  NET    1  75                       CH7P3
        54 0053 O                   N20            63 '('                   CH7P3
```

```
55 0054 O                    N20            76 ')'                        CH7P3
56 0055 O                    N20    NET   1 75                            CH7P3
57 0056 O            T 0    LR                                            CH7P3
58 0057 O                                   75 '============'             CH7P3
59 /*
60 /*

         THE FOLLOWING INDICATORS APPEARED IN THIS PROGRAM

         01  02  03  20  LR  1P
No Warning Errors
 6 Fatal Errors
```

LABORATORY ASSIGNMENTS

Laboratory Assignment 8-1: SCHEDULE OF ACCOUNTS RECEIVABLE

From the following information, write a structured RPG program to generate a Schedule of Accounts Receivable.

Format of the Data Records:

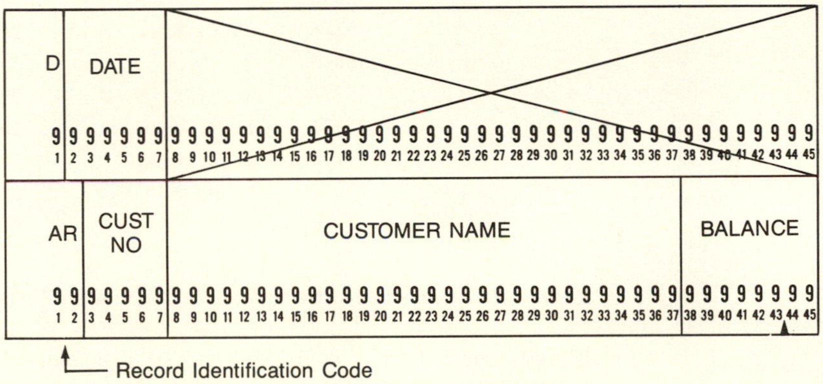

Any of the coding methods for defining records in a multiple record input file may be used for this program. (Do not use CONSOLE input).

Processing. Read the input file and accumulate the customer balances. Also, create a counter for the number of records processed.

Report Design:

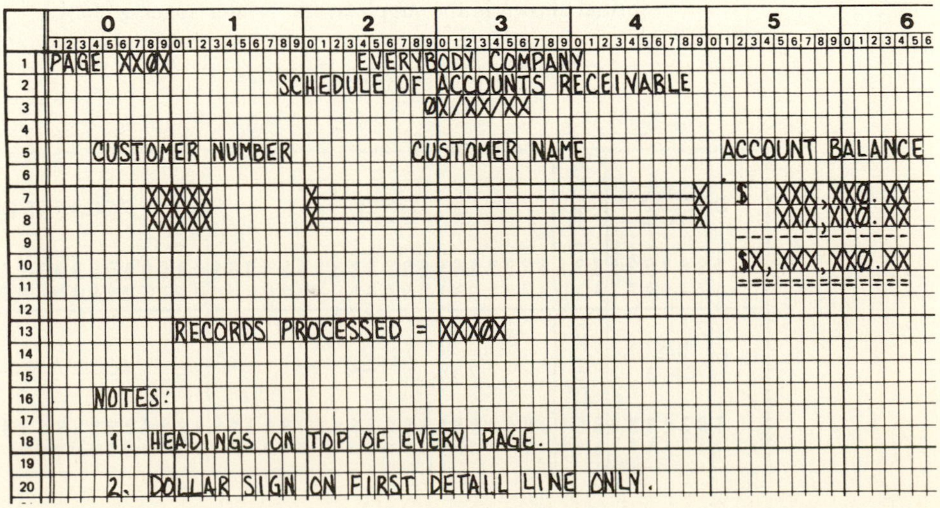

Input Data:

Record Type D (in column 1):

Use any six character date value (Cols 2-7)

Record Type AR (in columns 1 and 2):

Customer Number Cols 3-7	Customer Name 8-37	Account Balance 38-45
11111	ALWAYS ABLE	00219215
11121	MARY BEST	00051322
11444	I. M. CURRENT	00020010
12345	LARS DEFICIT	00797788
12356	HUGH DENT	00011154
13344	NEVER EARLY	00485673
14455	T. O. FATSO	00061487
15376	I. C. GUNN	01065936
16443	Y. HOLD	00004128
17777	I. ITCH	00613366
18123	H. I. JUMP	00032446
19996	E. Z. KIDD	00444444
20019	I. M. A. LUMOX	00056784

Laboratory Assignment 8-2: CONSOLE INPUT OF DATA

If Assignment 8-1 was completed, modify it to input the date value via CONSOLE and delete the date record from the data file. Otherwise, refer to the specifications in Assignment 8-1, and write the program to input the date value using the CONSOLE. Do not include the date record in the data file.

Laboratory Assignment 8-3: CASH DISBURSEMENTS JOURNAL

A Cash Disbursements Journal is used in an accounting system to record all cash disbursements. Individual columns are included in the journal when the business transactions for those accounts are numerous. Write a structured RPG program to generate the report format shown in the supplemental printer spacing chart.

Format of the Data Records:

S	CHECK DATE	CHECK#	PAYEE	ACCOUNT DEBITED	FOLIO	SUNDRY AMOUNT
9 1	9 9 9 9 9 9 2 3 4 5 6 7	9 9 9 8 9 10	9 9 9 9 9 9 9 9 9 9 9 9 9 9 9 9 9 9 9 9 11 12 13 14 15 16 17 18 19 20 21 22 23 24 25 26 27 28 29 30	9 9 9 9 9 9 9 9 9 9 9 9 9 9 9 9 9 9 9 9 31 32 33 34 35 36 37 38 39 40 41 42 43 44 45 46 47 48 49 50	9 9 9 51 52 53	9 9 9 9 9 9 54 55 56 57 58 59

P	CHECK DATE	CHECK#	PAYEE	ACCOUNT DEBITED	ACCTS PAYLE	DISNT PCT
9 1	9 9 9 9 9 9 2 3 4 5 6 7	9 9 9 8 9 10	9 9 9 9 9 9 9 9 9 9 9 9 9 9 9 9 9 9 9 9 11 12 13 14 15 16 17 18 19 20 21 22 23 24 25 26 27 28 29 30	9 9 9 9 9 9 9 9 9 9 9 9 9 9 9 9 9 9 9 9 31 32 33 34 35 36 37 38 39 40 41 42 43 44 45 46 47 48 49 50	9 9 9 9 9 51 52 53 54 55 56	9 9 9 57 58 59

Three Decimal Positions →

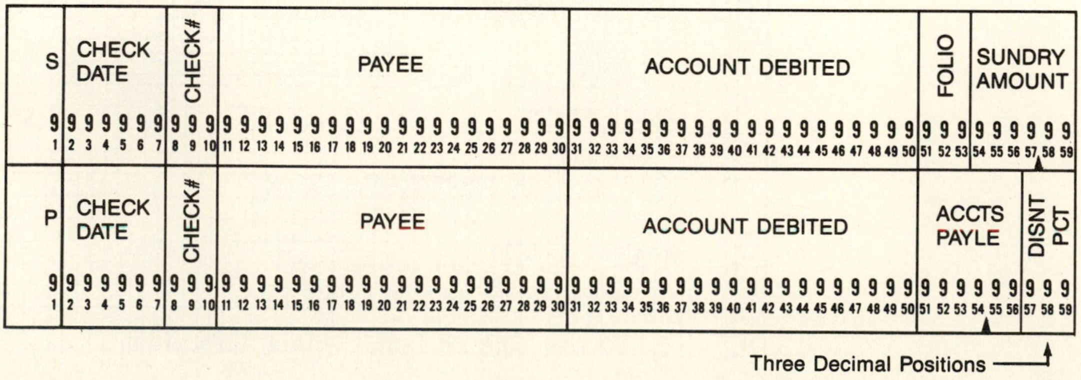

Processing. Refer to the print chart, and create fields for the column totals indicated in the print chart. For the records identified by the letter P (columns 1), the Accounts Payable amount must be multiplied by the related discount percent to calculate the Purchase Discount. The Purchase Discount amount is subtracted from the Accounts Payable amount to determine the net amount to be paid.

Report Design:

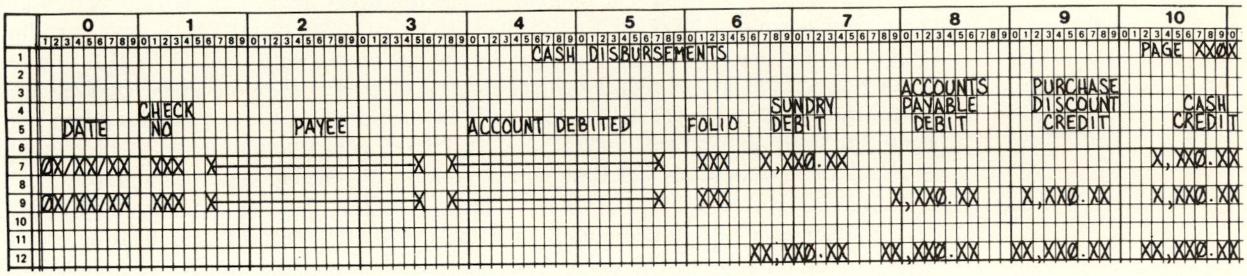

Input Data:

Data for records with ID code S:

Record ID Col 1	Check Date 2-7	Check# 8-10	Payee 11-30	Account Debited 31-50	Folio 51-53	Sundry Amount 54-59
S	011092	101	APEX REALTY	RENT EXPENSE	503	250000
S	012092	104	SAVO AND SONS	OFFICE EQUIPMENT	110	050000
S	012592	106	JERRY HALE	SALARIES EXPENSE	505	066000
S	013192	107	ELSIE TRUCKING CO	DELIVERY EXPENSES	590	005798

Data for records with ID code P:

Record ID Col 1	Check Date 2-7	Check# 8-10	Payee 11-30	Account Debited 31-50	Accounts Payable 51-56	Discount Percent 57-59
P	010292	098	EAST SALES CO	PURCHASES	100000	020
P	010392	099	ACME MFG CO	ACME MFG. CO.	200000	020
P	010492	100	SMITH AND SON INC	SMITH AND SON	030000	025
P	011592	102	ARIZONA SUPPLY CO	ARIZONA SUPPLY CO	095010	015
P	011892	103	WESTERN SUPPLY CO	WESTERN SUPPLY CO	089045	010
P	012192	105	MATCHLESS TOOL CO	MATCHLESS TOOL CO	060000	030

NOTE; DATA MUST BE LOADED IN THE FILE. IN ASCENDING DATE ORDER!!

Laboratory Assignment 8-4: AGING ACCOUNTS RECEIVABLE REPORT

Write a structured RPG program to generate the Aging Accounts Receivable report detailed in the supplemental printer spacing chart.

Format of the Data Records:

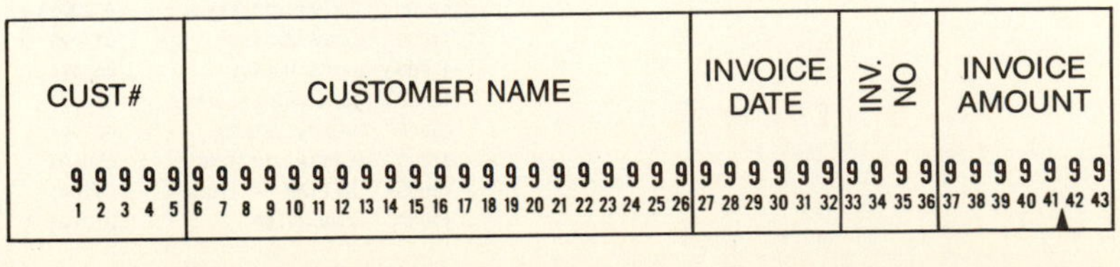

Note: Enter the report date, which is also used to determine the past-due status of the invoice, via CONSOLE input as a 080191 value. If CONSOLE input is not supported by your system, include a record with the 080191 value as the first record in the data file. In that case, include a record identification code in column 1 of the date record format. *Because the data file is provided, it is very important that the exact date value (080191) be entered as indicated.*

Processing. Read the input file, and for every record processed determime whether the account is NOT DUE, 1 to 30, 31 to 60, 61 to 90, or OVER 90 days past due. The procedures are as follows: Compare the invoice month with the CONSOLE entered month value. If the invoice month value is *equal to* or *greater than* the CONSOLE entered month, the account is NOT DUE. Move the invoice amount to its related column field (see print chart) and add the amount to a NOT DUE accumulator. If the invoice month value is *less than* the CONSOLE month, the following calculations are required:

1. Subtract the invoice month from the CONSOLE entered month to determine the difference. The result from this calculation is the number of months that the invoice month is less than the CONSOLE month value.
2. Build an iterative procedure, and add 30 to an accumulator for each integer in the difference value from Step 1. Exit the loop when the value in a counter is equal to the difference value.
3. After exit from the loop, subtract the invoice days from the accumulator (from Step 2) to determine days after the invoice date. Add 1 to this result field (to provide for the first day in the 080191 CONSOLE date). Then subtract 30 from that sum to provide for the company's 30-day credit period before an invoice is past due. A zero or negative difference indicates that the invoice is not due.
4. If the difference from Step 3 is not zero or negative, make the following comparisons and in each case move the invoice amount to its related column (see print chart) and add the amount to its column accumulator. Test the difference for the following:
   a. Greater than 90 days after the 30-day payment period.
   b. Greater than 60 days after the 30-day payment period.
   c. Greater than 30 days after the 30-day payment period.
   d. Greater than 1 day after the 30-day payment period.

Report Design:

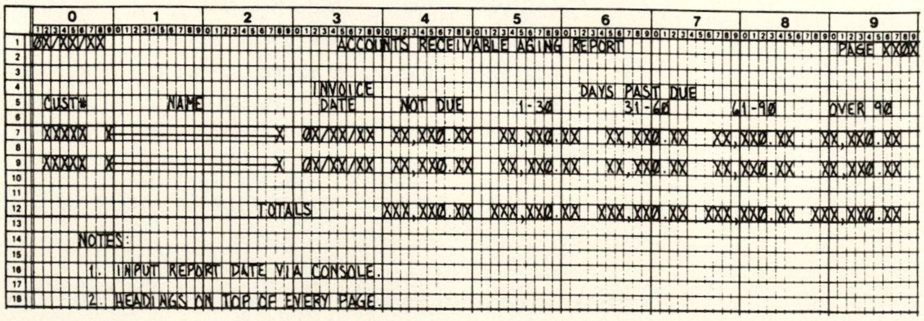

Input Data:

Cust# Col 1-5	Customer Name 6-26	Invoice Date 27-32	Invoice Number 33-36	Invoice Amount 37-43
10000	GEORGE WASHINGTON	072091	2000	0050000
11000	JOHN ADAMS	062991	1950	0110025
12000	THOMAS JEFFERSON	052091	1800	0005037
13000	JAMES MADISON	011091	1000	0003000
14000	JAMES MONROE	060191	1920	0645000
15000	JOHN QUINCY ADAMS	022891	1200	2500000
16000	ANDREW JACKSON	082991	2200	0043025
17000	MARTIN VAN BUREN	050191	1750	0019999
18000	WILLIAM HARRISON	041091	2145	0095000
19000	JOHN TYLER	070191	1960	0037585

chapter 9
Control Level Break Concepts and Processing

THE CONTROL LEVEL BREAK PROCESSING ENVIRONMENT

Record Identifying (01–99), Resulting, First Page (1P), Overflow (OA–OG and OV), Field Record Relation, Field, and Last Record (LR) indicators have been introduced and used in previous chapters. Another class of indicators, called Control Level (L1–L9), are included in the repertoire of indicators supplied by RPG. These indicators are commonly used for applications requiring subtotals within the body of reports. The previously discussed Last Record indicator (LR), which turns on automatically when end of file is sensed, is a control level indicator. However, LR provides for final totals only and does not control (except at last record time) the processing of subtotal calculations and/or output.

Detail Report with Subtotals

Figure 9-1 shows a report that includes subtotals for salesman groups. Notice that when the salesman number changes (from 1000 to 1100; 1100 to 1200; and so forth) a total line for the related salesman is printed. In addition, at end of file (LR time) the total for the last salesman group is printed before the TOTAL STORE SALES sum. An examination of the report shows that the data is in ascending order by date (minor field), which is within the ascending salesman number (major field) order. The logic of Control Level Break processing requires that the data file defined as input be sorted in ascending or descending order by control field(s) before processing.

Structure of the Data File

Figure 9-2 shows the data file that was processed for the report in Figure 9-1. Comments identify new terms associated with this environment including Control Field, Control Break, Control Group Totals, and Total Time.

Source Program Coding

A listing of the program that processed the file in Figure 9-2 and generated the report in Figure 9-1 is presented in Figure 9-3. Notice that input, calculations, and output coding include instructions unique to Control Level Break processing. The syntax and processing logic of each entry will be explained by separate illustrations.

```
                  WEEKLY SALES REPORT AS OF  9/30/91      PAGE    1

DATE        SALESMAN         WEEKLY SALES

9/08/91       1000               256.12 ]
9/15/91       1000             1,441.70 >    Control group
9/22/91       1000               384.20 ]    (same salesman number)
9/29/91       1000               302.44 ]

                    SALESMAN 1000 SALES..... 2,384.46 * <-- Control group total
                                                         (generated when sales-
9/08/91       1100               189.76 ]                 man number changes)
9/15/91       1100               500.38 >
9/22/91       1100             2,198.37 ]    Control group
9/29/91       1100               246.18 ]

                    SALESMAN 1100 SALES..... 3,134.69 * <-- Control group total

9/08/91       1200             1,612.55 ]
9/15/91       1200               800.00 >
9/22/91       1200               999.19 ]    Control group
9/29/91       1200             3,737.47 ]

                    SALESMAN 1200 SALES..... 7,149.21 * <-- Control group total

9/08/91       1300               645.33 ]
9/15/91       1300               301.76 >
9/22/91       1300             2,868.88 ]    Control group
9/29/91       1300             1,532.86 ]

                    SALESMAN 1300 SALES..... 5,348.83 * <-- Control group total

9/08/91       1400               184.79 ]
9/15/91       1400               733.74 >
9/22/91       1400               472.52 ]    Control group
9/29/91       1400             4,900.09 ]

                    SALESMAN 1400 SALES..... 6,291.14 * <-- Last control group total
                                                          generated at LR time

                    TOTAL STORE SALES....   24,308.33 ** LR total
```

Figure 9-1 Detail report with subtotals.

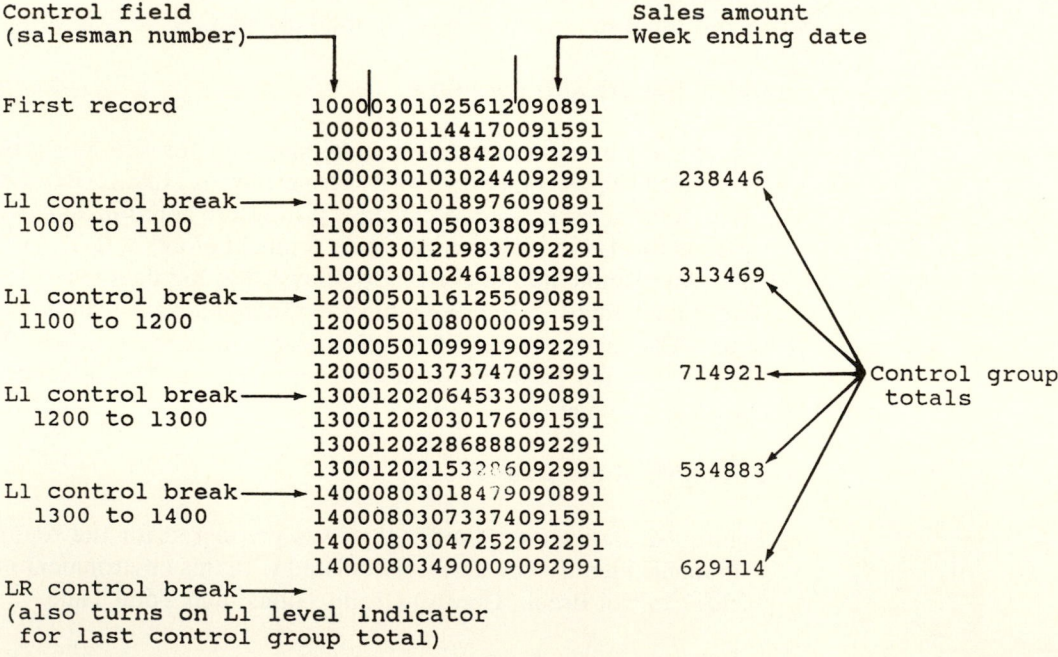

```
Control field                                   Sales amount
(salesman number)                               Week ending date

First record          10000301025612090891
                      10000301144170091591
                      10000301038420092291
                      10000301030244092991    238446
L1 control break ---> 11000301018976090891
 1000 to 1100         11000301050038091591
                      11000301219837092291
                      11000301024618092991    313469
L1 control break ---> 12000501161255090891
 1100 to 1200         12000501080000091591
                      12000501099919092291
                      12000501373747092991    714921 <-- Control group
L1 control break ---> 13001202064533090891                totals
  1200 to 1300        13001202030176091591
                      13001202286888092291
                      13001202153286092991    534883
L1 control break ---> 14000803018479090891
  1300 to 1400        14000803073374091591
                      14000803047252092291
                      14000803490009092991    629114
LR control break --->
(also turns on L1 level indicator
 for last control group total)
```

Notes:

1. File is sorted in ascending order by salesman number (major sort field) and date (minor sort field).

2. All control breaks are controlled at TOTAL TIME (T) with L1 control level indicator.

Figure 9-2 Listing of the data file processed for detail report with one control level break (subtotal).

```
... ... 1 ... ... 2 ... ... 3 ... ... 4 ... ... 5 ... ... 6 ... ... 7 ...
H                                                                   CH9P1
FSALSFILEIP  F  20  20          DISK                                CH9P1
FSALSRPT O   F 132 132     OF     PRINTER                           CH9P1
ISALSFILESM  01                                                     CH9P1
I                                       1   4 SALP# L1<-------------CONTROL FIELD
I                                       5   6 DEPT#                 CH9P1
I                                       7   8 STORE#                CH9P1
I                                       9  142SALAMT                CH9P1
I                                      15  200SALDAT                CH9P1
C           SALSUM    ADD  SALAMT    SALSUM  72       ACCUM SALP# SUMCH9P1
CL1         STASUM    ADD  SALSUM    STASUM  92       SAVE STATE SUM ---CTRL BRK CALC
OSALSRPT H  301    1P                                               CH9P1
O        OR        OF                                               CH9P1
O                                      42 'WEEKLY SALES REPORT AS'  CH9P1
O                                      45 'OF'                      CH9P1
O                          UDATE Y    54                            CH9P1
O                                      63 'PAGE'                    CH9P1
O                          PAGE  Z    68                            CH9P1
O         H  2     1P                                               CH9P1
O        OR        OF                                               CH9P1
O                                       6 'DATE'                    CH9P1
O                                      21 'SALESMAN'                CH9P1
O                                      41 'WEEKLY SALES'            CH9P1
O         D  1     01                                               CH9P1
O                          SALDATY     8                            CH9P1
O                          SALP#      19                            CH9P1
O                          SALAMT1    39                            CH9P1
O------>T 12       L1<--------------------------------------------CTRL BRK TOT
O                                      37 'SALESMAN'                CH9P1
O                          SALP#      42                            CH9P1
O                                      53 'SALES.....'              CH9P1
O                          SALSUM1B   62                            CH9P1
O                                      64 '*'                       CH9P1
O         T 1      LR                                               CH9P1
O                                      51 'TOTAL STORE SALES.....'  CH9P1
O                          STASUM1    62                            CH9P1
O                                      65 '**'                      CH9P1

--Total time output (T in column 15 and L1 assigned
    as the conditioning indicator)

--Total time calculations (L1 in columns 7 & 8)
```

Figure 9-3 Source listing of the program that generates a report with one control group total.

Input Specifications Coding

Detailed in the input form shown in Figure 9-4 is the syntax and logic related to Control Level Break processing. Because the SALP# field has a *Control Level Indicator (L1)* entered in columns 59 to 60, it is referred to as a *Control Field.* When the value in this field for the record currently being processed is different from the value in the field for the previous record, the L1 Control Level indicator is automatically turned on by RPG control. *Any calculations and output instructions conditioned by the L1 indicator are immediately executed, temporarily skipping any detail processing.* Detail calculations, followed by detail output, are returned to after all related level break processing is executed. Comparison of the current and previous record Control Field values is controlled by RPG; the programmer does not have to include this processing in the program.

Control Fields and Control Level Indicators

Control fields are specified on input by including a Control Level indicator in columns 59 and 60 of the input form. The features of Control Fields and Control Level indicators are outlined in Figure 9-5. "Split" control field concepts are not included; they will be introduced later in this chapter.

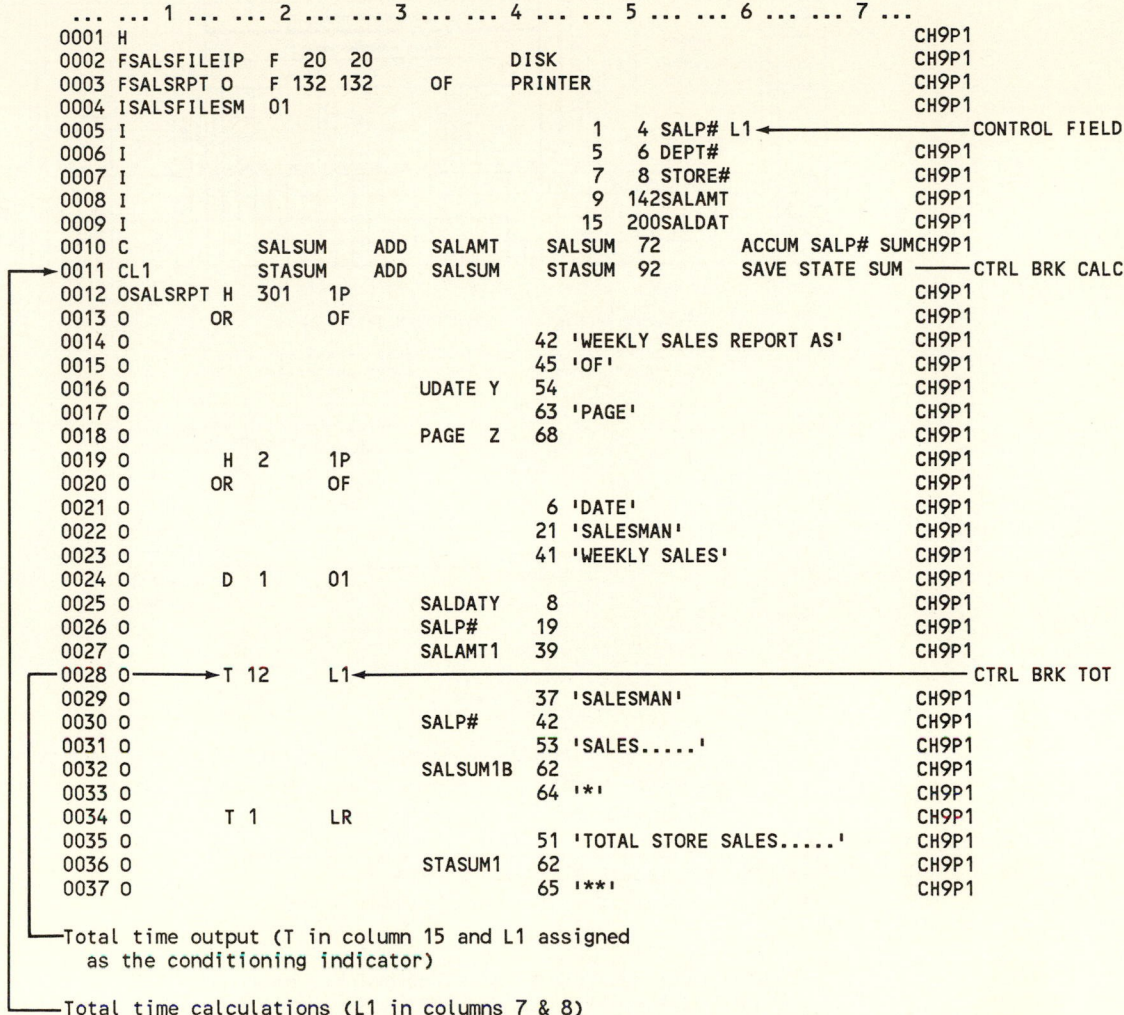

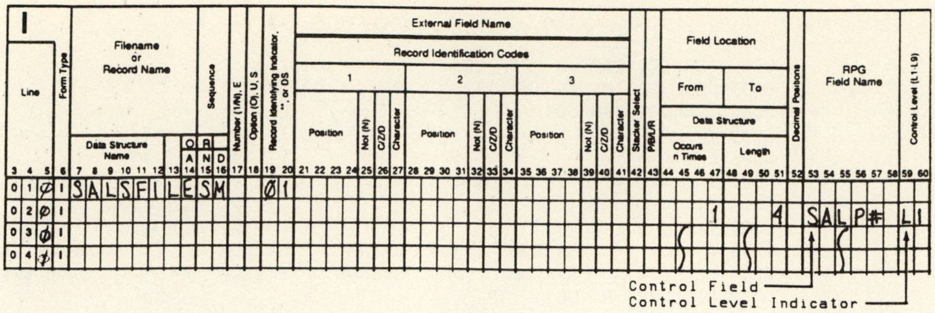

Processing Logic For Control Break:

SALP# value in current record processed: 1100
SALP# value in previous record processed: 1000

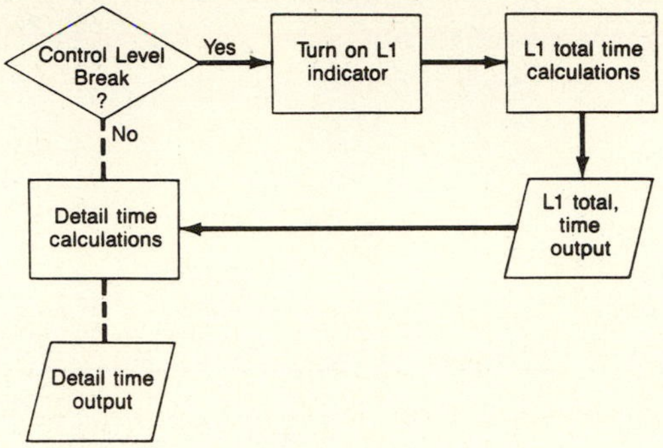

Note: Solid line indicates flowchart path when control break is sensed.

Figure 9-4 Input specifications coding for program that generates a report with one control group total.

Single Control Field Features:

1. Must be located in the same columns within an individual record format.
2. May be located in different columns within different record formats.
3. May be defined numeric or alphanumeric. Maximum numeric control field size is 15 bytes and alphanumeric 256.
4. If the same control field has been assigned the same control level in different record types or files, they must be defined as the same type (numeric or alphanumeric) and length. Same control field name may be specified in each record type.
5. Decimal positions are ignored when control field values are compared. All numeric fields are considered integers.
6. Signs are ignored when control field values are compared. All numeric fields are considered positive for control break testing.

Control Level Indicator (L1-L9) Features:

1. Nine control level indicators (L1-L9) are available in RPG.
2. A higher level indicator turns on all lower level indicators. For example, if L3 is turned on by program control, L2 and L1 will automatically set on.
3. At end of file, when LR is turned on, all lower level indicators used in the program are automatically set on.
4. L1 is commonly assigned to the lowest control field and L2, L3, etc. assigned in order as needed. For example, L1 would be assigned to employee number, L2 to department number, L3 to store and so forth.
5. L1-L9 may be assigned to control fields in any order providing the logic specified in item 4 (above) is followed.
6. A control level indicator turned on in calculations by the SETON or other operation does not set on any lower level indicator. For example, if L2 was turned on by a SETON statement, L1 would not automatically be turned on.

Figure 9-5 Control field and Control Level Indicator processing features.

Calculation Specifications Coding

Calculation statements that are conditioned by a Control Level indicator entered in columns 7 and 8 are executed at total time. Instructions conditioned by L1 to L9 in columns 10 to 11, or 13 to 14, or 16 to 17 are executed at detail time. The significance of these processing "times" is explained in the example program's calculations illustrated in Figure 9-5.

The processing logic shown in Figure 9-6 identifies the following four important features when a control break is sensed:

1. Detail time calculation is automatically skipped, and L1 total time calculation is executed.

C Line (3–5)	Form Type (6)	Control Level (L0-L9, LR, SR, AN/OR) (7–8)	Indicators (9–17)	Factor 1 (18–27)	Operation (28–32)	Factor 2 (33–42)	Result Field Name (43–48)	Length (49–51)	Decimal Position (52)	Half Adjust (H) (53)
01Ø	C			SALSUM	ADD	SALAMT	SALSUM	7	2	
02Ø	C	L1		STASUM	ADD	SALSUM	STASUM	9	2	

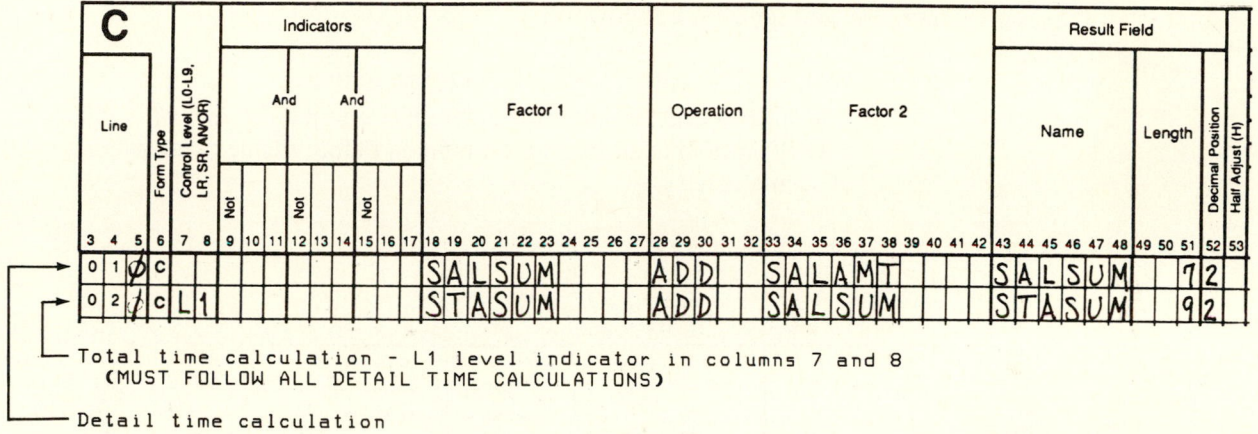

Total time calculation - L1 level indicator in columns 7 and 8
(MUST FOLLOW ALL DETAIL TIME CALCULATIONS)

Detail time calculation

Processing logic after control break is sensed:

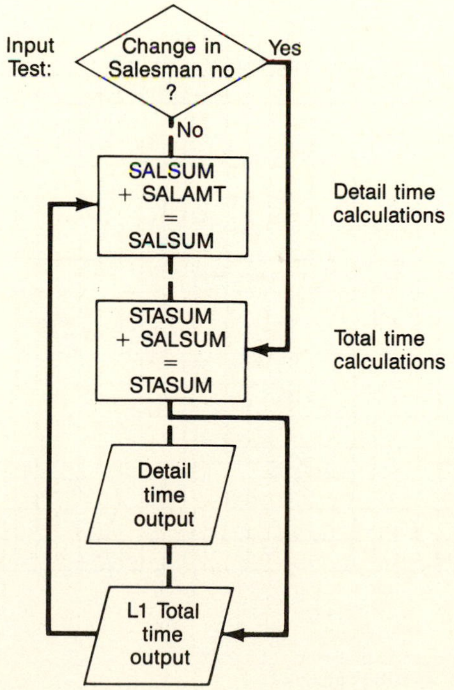

Note: Solid line indicates processing flow when a control break is sensed.

Figure 9-6 Example of one control break program calculations and processing logic when a control break is sensed.

2. Then, detail time output is skipped, and total time output is executed.
3. Program control returns to the Detail time calculation after total time output is executed.
4. After detail time calculation is executed, program control skips the total time calculation and executes detail time output.

The total time calculation statements must follow all detail time calculations, and total time output instructions must follow detail time output coding. A terminal error will result during program compilation if this rule is not followed.

Output Specifications Coding

Examine the partial output coding for the one control break example program in Figure 9-7 and notice the following:

1. L1 total time output follows detail time output.
2. The function of the letter B, entered in column 39, is to initialize the SALSUM field to zeros after output and before the next salesman group is accumulated.

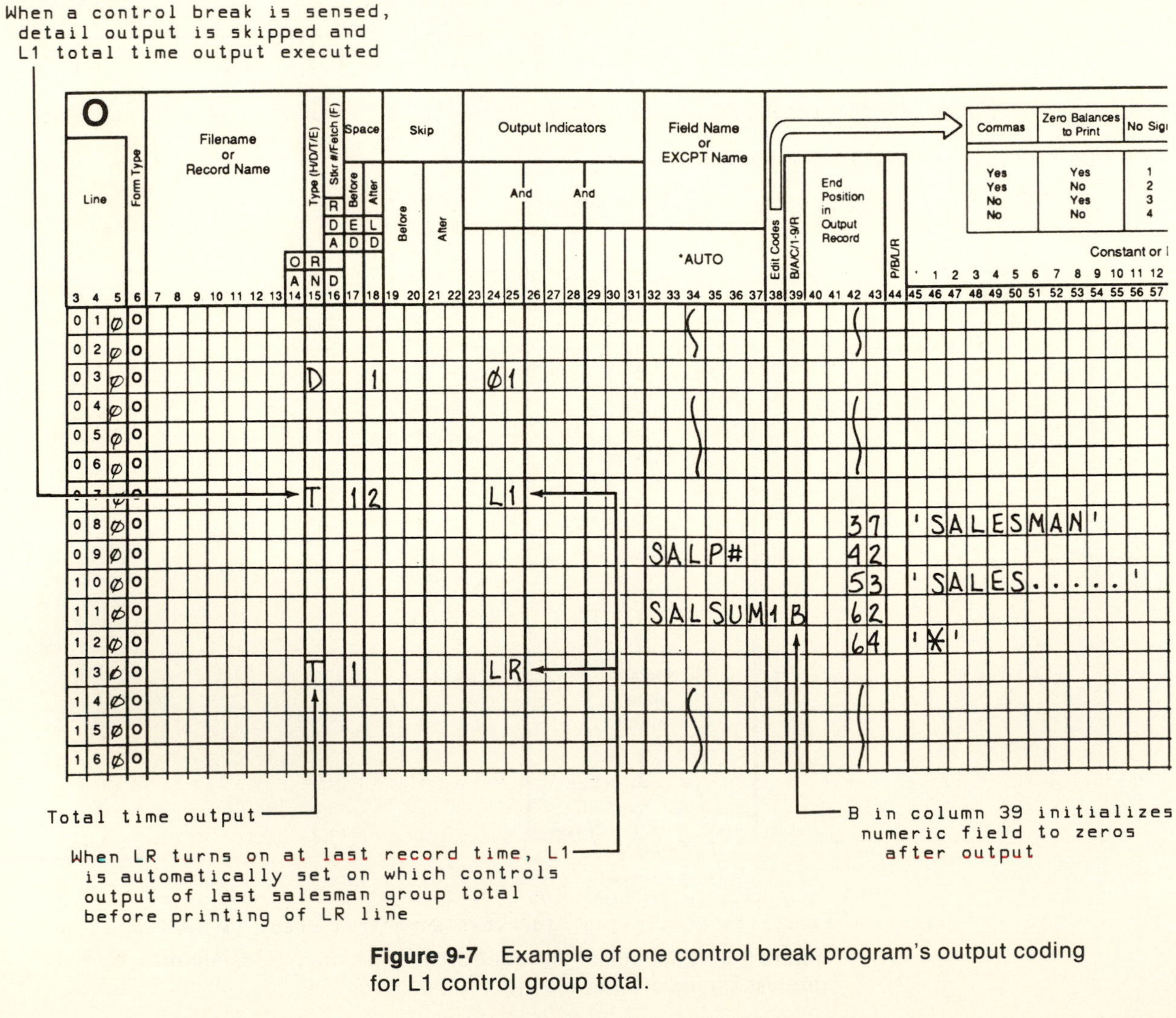

Figure 9-7 Example of one control break program's output coding for L1 control group total.

L1 Detail Time Processing—Calculation Control. All control break processing discussed has been addressed to total time calculations and output. Sometimes program logic requires that it be performed at detail time. For example, in the example program, B was specified in column 39 on the output form to initialize the accumulator, SALSUM, to zeros after printing. An alternative approach to clearing an accumulator requires the use of a calculation instruction that is conditioned with a related control level indicator at detail time. Figure 9-8 illustrates the coding for this method and the corresponding processing logic.

Line (3-5)	Form Type (6)	Control Level (L0-L9, LR, SR, AN/OR) (7-8)	Indicators (9-17)	Factor 1 (18-27)	Operation (28-32)	Factor 2 (33-42)	Result Field Name (43-48)	Length (49-51)	Decimal Position (52)	Half Adjust (H) (53)
01Ø	C		L1		Z-ADD	Ø	SALSUM	7	2	
02Ø	C			SALSUM	ADD	SALAMT	SALSUM			
03Ø	C	L1		STASUM	ADD	SALSUM	STASUM	9	2	

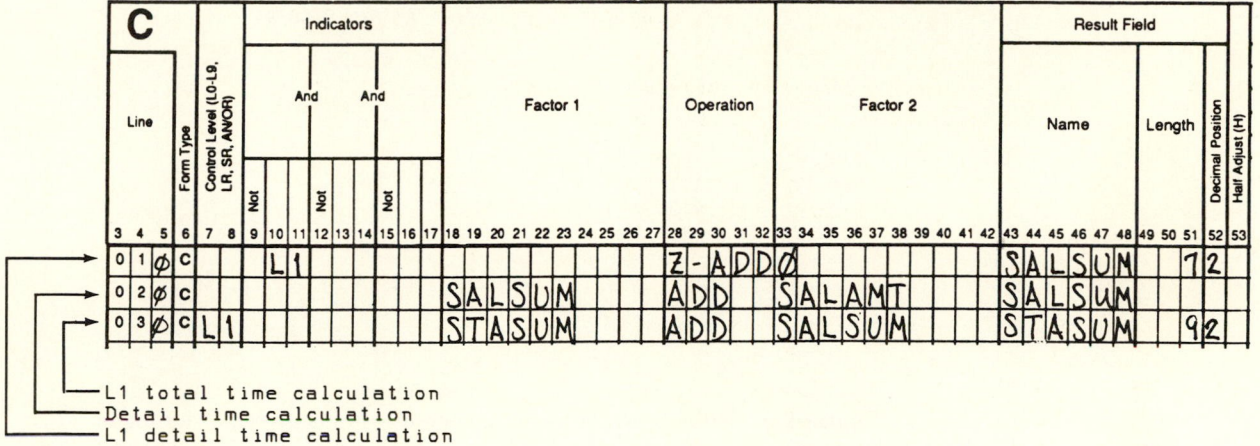

```
Line 01Ø — L1 detail time calculation
Line 02Ø — Detail time calculation
Line 03Ø — L1 total time calculation
```

```
Processing Logic of L1 Detail and Total Times:

  Salesman number:

                    1000................
L1 Detail Time ---> 1100................ <--- First record of new control group
                    1100................
                    1100................
L1 Total Time ----> 1100................ <--- Last record of control group
L1 Detail Time ---> 1200................ <--- First record of new control group
```

Notes:

1. First record (detail time) of a new control group is referenced by entering L1 in one of the indicator columns (10-11, or 13-14, or 16-17).

2. Last record (total time) of a control group is referenced by entering L1 in columns 7 and 8.

3. When there is only one record in a control group, detail and total time calculations will process the same record.

Figure 9-8 Detail and total time calculations and processing logic.

L1 Detail Time Processing—Output Control. A reexamination of the detail report in Figure 9-1 will show that more than one salesman group is included on a page. If, however, the application required that each salesman group be printed on a separate page, L1 detail time output control would be necessary. Figure 9-9 illustrates a report that prints salesman groups on separate pages.

Changes needed to the original program (Figure 9-3) are shown in the partial source listing in Figure 9-10. Only the output coding has to be modified to support the new report requirements.

```
                              WEEKLY SALES REPORT AS OF  9/30/91      PAGE    1

   DATE        SALESMAN        WEEKLY SALES

  9/08/91        1000              256.12
  9/15/91        1000            1,441.70
  9/22/91        1000              384.20
  9/29/91        1000              302.44

                                 SALESMAN 1000 SALES..... 2,384.46

- - - - - - - - - - - - - - - - - - - - - - - - - - - - - - - - - - - -

                              WEEKLY SALES REPORT AS OF  9/30/91      PAGE    2


   DATE        SALESMAN        WEEKLY SALES


  9/08/91        1100              189.76
  9/15/91        1100              500.38
  9/22/91        1100            2,198.37
  9/29/91        1100              246.18

                                 SALESMAN 1100 SALES..... 3,134.69

- - - - - - - - - - - - - - - - - - - - - - - - - - - - - - - - - - - -
                                        .
                                        .
```

Figure 9-9 Modified report with salesman groups on separate pages.

```
... ... 1 ... ... 2 ... ... 3 ... ... 4 ... ... 5 ... ... 6 ... ... 7 ...
                                .
                                .
                                .
0012 OSALSRPT D   301    L1                                      CH9P1
0013 O       OR          OF                                      CH9P1
0014 O                                 42 'WEEKLY SALES REPORT AS'   CH9P1
0015 O                                 45 'OF'                   CH9P1
0016 O                        UDATE Y  54                        CH9P1
0017 O                                 63 'PAGE'                 CH9P1
0018 O                        PAGE  Z  68                        CH9P1
0019 O           D  2    L1                                      CH9P1
0020 O       OR          OF                                      CH9P1
0021 O                                  6 'DATE'                 CH9P1
0022 O                                 21 'SALESMAN'             CH9P1
0023 O                                 41 'WEEKLY SALES'         CH9P1
0024 O           D  1    01                                      CH9P1
0025 O                        SALDATY   8                        CH9P1
0026 O                        SALP#    19                        CH9P1
0027 O                        SALAMT1  39                        CH9P1
0028 O           T 12    L1                                      CH9P1
0029 O                                 37 'SALESMAN'             CH9P1
0030 O                        SALP#    42                        CH9P1
0031 O                                 53 'SALES.....'           CH9P1
0032 O                        SALSUM1B 62                        CH9P1
0033 O                                 64 '*'                    CH9P1
0034 O           T 1     LR                                      CH9P1
0035 O                                 51 'TOTAL STORE SALES.....'   CH9P1
0036 O                        STASUM1  62                        CH9P1
0037 O                                 65 '**'                   CH9P1
```

L1 (instead of 1P) at D or H time (column 15) controls printing of each salesman control group on separate pages.

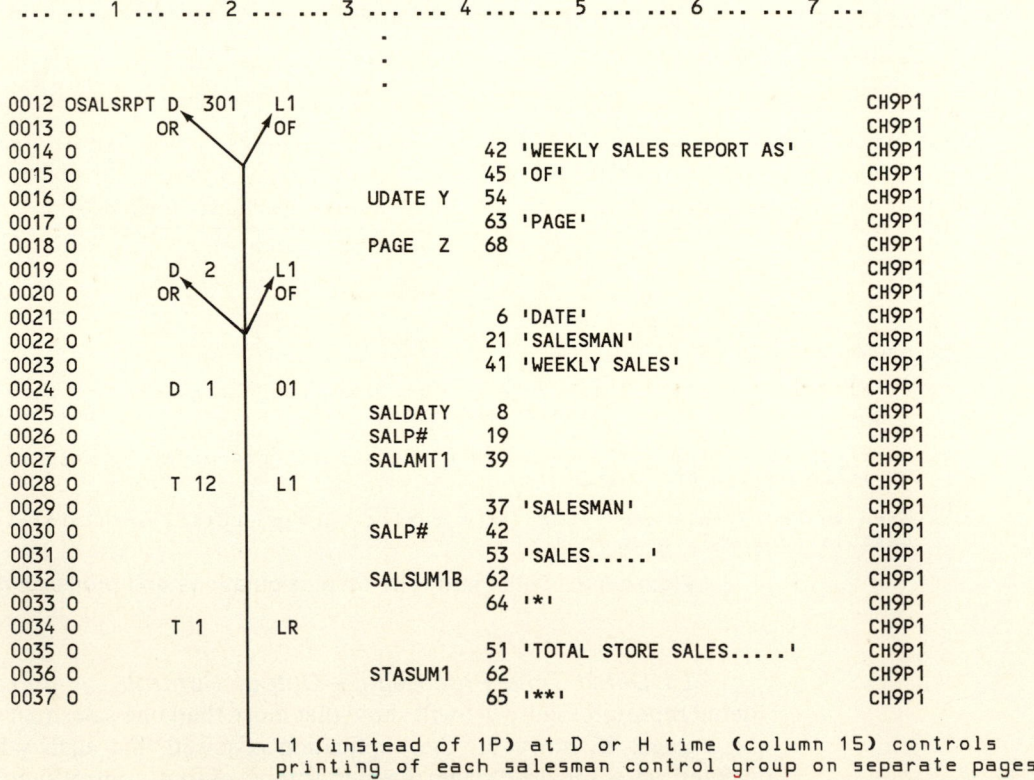

Figure 9-10 Modified program coding to control the printing of salesman groups on separate pages.

<u>Processing Logic</u>:

```
  first record in file    1000    Control break - detail time L1
                          1000
                          1000
                          1000
                          1100    Control break - detail time L1
                            .
                            .
```

<u>Notes:</u>
Because the control field (SALP#) was automatically initialized to blanks by RPG on execution, the first record processed in the file generates an L1 detail time (D in column 15) control break.

To eliminate a ''null'' break, RPG does not process the first record in the file as a total time control break. Again, this processing is automatically controlled by the RPG compiler and does not have to be considered by the programmer.

If this control was not provided, a total time L1 break would occur and print zeros for numeric field and blanks for alphanumeric fields - a ''null break''.

(Continued)

MULTIPLE CONTROL BREAK PROCESSING

The previous program examples have illustrated the processing logic and RPG syntax for single control breaks. Reports, however, often include more than one control break. An example of a report with three control breaks is illustrated in Figure 9-11. Each subtotal is identified with the appropriate Control Level In-

```
                    WEEKLY SALES REPORT AS OF  9/30/91                PAGE   1

 DATE       SALESMAN    DEPT    STORE      WEEKLY SALES

9/08/91       1000       03      01            256.12
9/15/91       1000       03      01          1,441.70
9/22/91       1000       03      01            384.20
9/29/91       1000       03      01            302.44

                                         SALESMAN 1000 SALES..... 2,384.46 *<----L1 total

9/08/91       1100       03      01            189.76
9/15/91       1100       03      01            500.38
9/22/91       1100       03      01          2,198.37
9/29/91       1100       03      01            246.18

                                         SALESMAN 1100 SALES..... 3,134.69 *<----L1 total
                                         DEPT 03  SALES.........  5,519.15 **<---L2 total

9/08/91       1200       05      01          1,612.55
9/15/91       1200       05      01            800.00
9/22/91       1200       05      01            999.19
9/29/91       1200       05      01          3,737.47

                                         SALESMAN 1200 SALES..... 7,149.21 *<----L1 total
                                         DEPT 05  SALES.........  7,149.21 **<---L2 total
                                         STORE 01  SALES........ 12,668.36 ***<--L3 total

9/08/91       1300       12      02            645.33
9/15/91       1300       12      02            301.76
9/22/91       1300       12      02          2,868.88
9/29/91       1300       12      02          1,532.86

                                         SALESMAN 1300 SALES..... 5,348.83 *<----L1 total
                                         DEPT 12  SALES.........  5,348.83 **<---L2 total
                                         STORE 02  SALES........  5,348.83 ***<--L3 total

9/08/91       1400       08      03            184.79
9/15/91       1400       08      03            733.74
9/22/91       1400       08      03            472.52
9/29/91       1400       08      03          4,900.09

                                         SALESMAN 1400 SALES..... 6,291.14 *<----L1 total
                                         DEPT 08  SALES.......... 6,291.14 **<---L2 total
                                         STORE 03  SALES......... 6,291.14 ***<--L3 total

                                         TOTAL SALES...........   24,308.33 ****  LR total
```

Figure 9-11 Detail report with multiple control groups.

dicator used in the program to condition the print line. Notice that SALESMAN SALES is an L1 total; DEPT SALES, an L2 total; and STORE SALES, an L3 total. Also, understand that when LR turns on, any Control Level Indicators included in the program are automatically set ON. This RPG feature provides for the output of the last control group before the TOTAL SALES line is printed.

The source listing of the program that generated the multiple control group report in Figure 9-11 is detailed in Figure 9-12.

```
... ... 1 ... ... 2 ... ... 3 ... ... 4 ... ... 5 ... ... 6 ... ... 7 ...
 * MULTIPLE CONTROL BREAK PROGRAM THAT GENERATES A REPORT WITH THREE CH9P2
 * CONTROL GROUP TOTALS - L1 SALESMAN, L2 DEPT, & L3 STORE          CH9P2
H                                                                   CH9P2
FSALSFILEIP  F  80  80            DISK                              CH9P2
FSALSRPT O   F 132 132     OF     PRINTER                           CH9P2
ISALSFILESM  01                                                     CH9P2
I                                         1   4 SALP# L1  ┐
I                                         5   6 DEPT# L2  ├ Control Fields
I                                         7   8 STORE#L3  ┘
I                                         9  142SALAMT              CH9P2
I                                        15  200SALDAT              CH9P2
C           SALSUM    ADD  SALAMT    SALSUM  72     ACCUM SALP# SUMCH9P2
CL1         DEPSUM    ADD  SALSUM    DEPSUM  82     ACCUM DEPT SUM CH9P2
CL2         STOSUM    ADD  DEPSUM    STOSUM  82     ACCUM STORE SUMCH9P2
CL3         STASUM    ADD  STOSUM    STASUM  92     ACCUM STATE SUMCH9P2
OSALSRPT H  301    1P                                               CH9P2
O        OR        OF                                               CH9P2
O                                  42 'WEEKLY SALES REPORT AS'      CH9P2
O                                  45 'OF'                          CH9P2
O                         UDATE Y  54                               CH9P2
O                                  78 'PAGE'                        CH9P2
O                         PAGE  Z  83                               CH9P2
O        H  1      1P                                               CH9P2
O        OR        OF                                               CH9P2
O                                   6 'DATE'                        CH9P2
O                                  21 'SALESMAN'                    CH9P2
O                                  29 'DEPT'                        CH9P2
O                                  38 'STORE'                       CH9P2
O                                  56 'WEEKLY SALES'                CH9P2
O        D  1      01                                               CH9P2
O                         SALDATY   8                               CH9P2
O                         SALP#    19                               CH9P2
O                         DEPT#    28                               CH9P2
O                         STORE#   36                               CH9P2
O                         SALAMT1  54                               CH9P2
O        T 21      L1 <──────────────────────────────────────────── L1 Group Total
O                                  52 'SALESMAN'                    CH9P2
O                         SALP#    57                               CH9P2
O                                  68 'SALES.....'                  CH9P2
O                         SALSUM1B 77                               CH9P2
O                                  79 '*'                           CH9P2
O        T  1      L2 <──────────────────────────────────────────── L2 Group Total
O                                  48 'DEPT'                        CH9P2
O                         DEPT#    51                               CH9P2
O                                  67 'SALES.........'              CH9P2
O                         DEPSUM1B 77                               CH9P2
O                                  80 '**'                          CH9P2
O        T  1      L3 <──────────────────────────────────────────── CH9P2 L3 Group Total
O                                  49 'STORE'                       CH9P2
O                         STORE#   52                               CH9P2
O                                  67 'SALES........'               CH9P2
O                         STOSUM1B 77                               CH9P2
O                                  81 '***'                         CH9P2
O        T 1       LR <──────────────────────────────────────────── CH9P2 LR Grand Total
O                                  66 'TOTAL SALES...........'      CH9P2
O                         STASUM1  77                               CH9P2
O                                  82 '****'                        CH9P2
```

Figure 9-12 Source listing of multiple control break program.

The data in the file listing shown in Figure 9-13 is identical to the one presented in Figure 9-2. However, now DEPT# and STORE# are used as control fields to generate subtotals for departments and stores. The file is sorted by STORE# (major sort field), DEPT# (first minor sort field), SALP# (second minor sort field), and SALDAT (third minor sort field). Correct sorting of the data file(s) is critical to control break processing. One record out of sequence would cause an unwanted control break, which would result in invalid calculations and output. The syntax and processing logic of each program segment are explained in the following paragraphs.

```
Control fields:

 STORE#-------------------------+
 DEPT#------------------------+ |
 SALP#---------------------+  | |
                           v  v v
First record         10000301025612090891
                     10000301144170091591
                     10000301038420092291
                     10000301030244092991
L1 control break---->11000301018976090891<---SALP# change from 1000 to 1100
                     11000301050038091591
                     11000301219837092291
                     11000301024618092991
L1 control break---->12000501161255090891<---SALP# change from 1100 to 1200
L2 control break     12000501080000091591    DEPT# change from 03 to 05
                     12000501099919092291
                     12000501373747092991
L1 control break---->13001202064533090891<---SALP# change from 1200 to 1300
L2 control break     13001202030176091591    DEPT# change from 05 to 12
L3 control break     13001202286888092291    STORE# change from 01 to 02
                     13001202153286092991
L1 control break---->14000803018479090891<---SALP# change from 1300 to 1400
L2 control break     14000803073374091591    DEPT# change from 12 to 08
L3 control break     14000803047252092291    STORE# change from 02 to 03
                     14000803490009092991
L1 control break---->.... end of file ...
L2 control break
L3 control break
LR control break

Notes:

 1. File is sorted in ascending order by STORE# (major field), DEPT#
    (first intermediate field), SALP# (second intermediate field),
    and SALDAT (minor field).

 2. All control level indicators specified in the program are turned on
    at LR time (end of file) which provides for the printing of the last
    control group.
```

Figure 9-13 Listing of the data file processed for a detail report with three control level breaks (subtotals).

Multiple Control Break Example Program

Input Specification. The input form coding for the multiple control break program and the processing logic are detailed in Figure 9-14.

The following input control is provided by the RPG compiler:

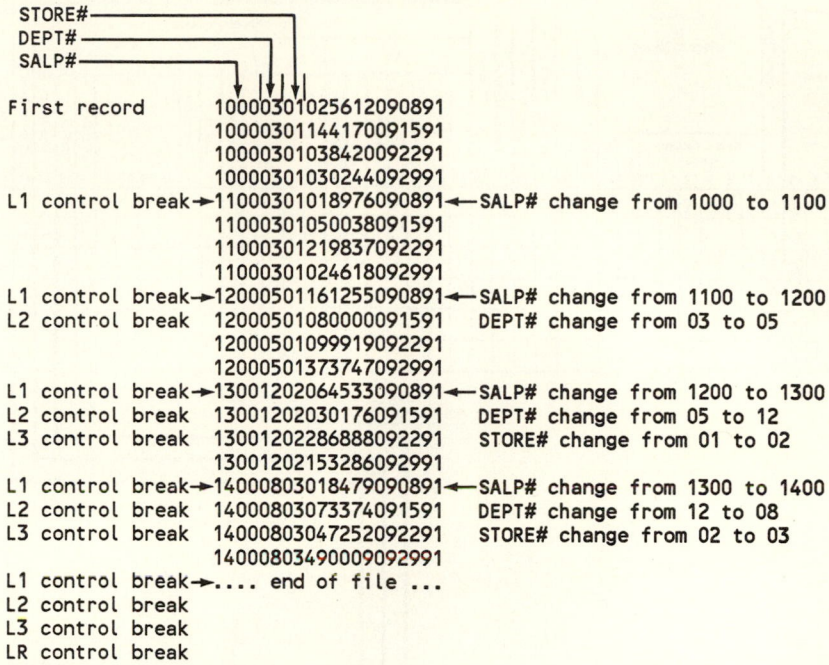

1. Creation of a holding area where the first record of a control group is stored.
2. Comparison of the current record's control field value with the previous record processed (in holding area).
3. Automatic set ON of control level indicators when a control break (change in control field value) is sensed.
4. Execution of related control break calculation and output instructions.
5. Return to detail time processing (calculations and output) of the record that generated the control break.

Each of these features would have to be provided by the programmer in other high-level languages such as COBOL, BASIC, and FORTRAN.

Further examination of Figure 9-14 indicates that the control level indicators were assigned in ascending order (i.e., L1, L2, L3). The location of the related

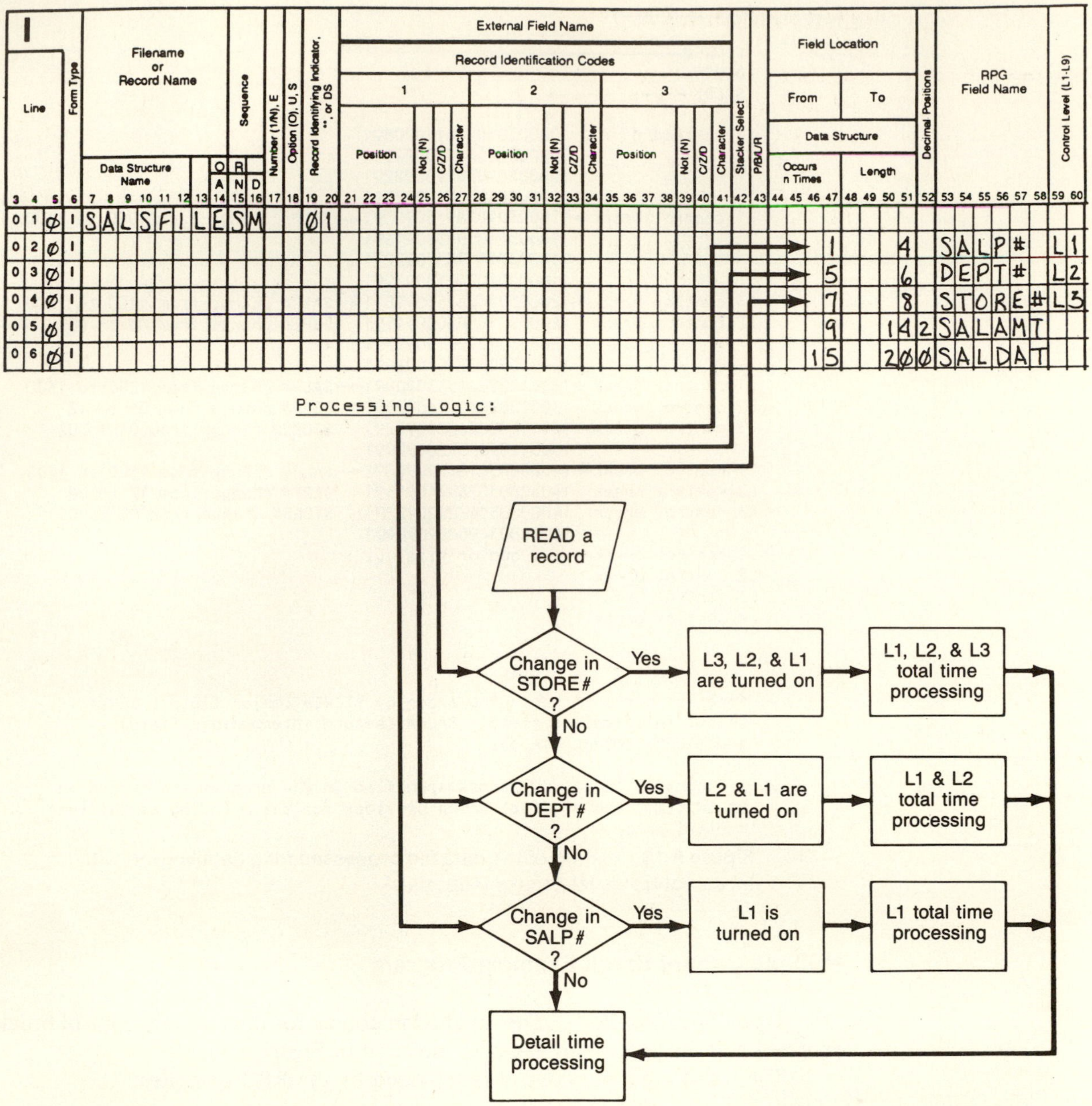

Figure 9-14 Input specifications coding for multiple control break program.

control field in a record format determines the order in which the indicators are specified. RPG does not require that any designated order be followed.

Calculation Specifications. The calculation form coding for the multiple control break program and related processing logic are presented in Figure 9-15. Remember, when Control Level Indicators are entered in columns 7 and 8 of the calculation form, the related statement is executed at *total time*. Statements conditioned by a level indicator entered in the other conditioning columns (10–11, 13–14, and 16–17), are performed at *detail time*. Also, any statement conditioned at *total time* (columns 7 and 8) must follow any detail calculations. This error will be identified as terminal in compilation of the source program.

Line (3–5)	Form Type (6)	Control Level (L0-L9, LR, SR, AN/OR) (7–8)	Indicators (9–17)	Factor 1 (18–27)	Operation (28–32)	Factor 2 (33–42)	Result Field Name (43–48)	Length (49–51)	Decimal Position (52)	Half Adjust (H) (53)
010	C			SALSUM	ADD	SALAMT	SALSUM	7	2	
020	C	L1		DEPSUM	ADD	SALSUM	DEPSUM	8	2	
030	C	L2		STOSUM	ADD	DEPSUM	STOSUM	8	2	
040	C	L3		STASUM	ADD	STOSUM	STASUM	9	2	

Processing logic:

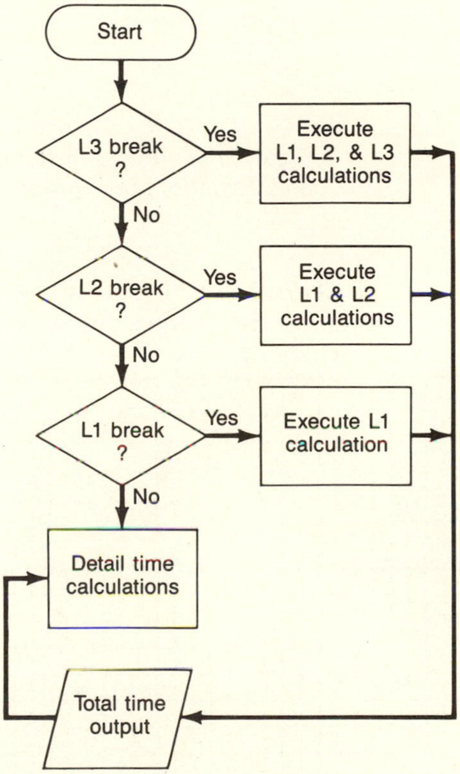

<u>Note:</u> Detail calculation is first statement on the form. However, as the flowchart indicates, it is not executed until all level break checks have been made and any L3, L2, and/or L1 calculations and output performed.

Figure 9-15 Calculation specifications for multiple control break program.

On IBM System/36, System/38, and AS/400 computers, the level indicators may be assigned in any order on the calculation form. Other systems require, however, that they be assigned in ascending order (L1, L2, L3, and so forth).

Figure 9-16 illustrates the calculation steps generated by the RPG compiler when an L2 control break is sensed. It is important to understand that on the basis of the illustrated calculations, all control totals are saved in the next higher subtotal before output. Otherwise, because of the necessary "blanking out" of the field after output to prevent incorrect accumulation of different control group totals, the value would be lost.

```
                                                                     Result Field values
Calculations:                                                        before and after the
                                                                     L2 break is sensed

                                                                     Before      After

0012 C       SALSUM   ADD SALAMT    SALSUM  72                       0313469     0313469
0013 CL1     DEPSUM   ADD SALSUM    DEPSUM  82                       0238446     0551915
0014 CL2     STOSUM   ADD DEPSUM    STOSUM  82                       0000000     0551915
0015 CL3     STASUM   ADD STOSUM    STASUM  92                       0000000     0000000

L2 break turns on L1 and adds current SALSUM total to previous DEPSUM total

Instruction conditioned by L2 adds new DEPSUM total to previous STOSUM total

The statement on line 0014 "saves" the DEPSUM total so that is will be included in
a subsequent L3 control group total.  Otherwise, it would be lost when control totals
are "blanked out" (B in column 39 in output statement) after printing.

Partial Report Listing (after first L2 break is sensed):

                                         .
                                         .

9/08/91      1100      03      01          189.76
9/15/91      1100      03      01          500.38
9/22/91      1100      03      01        2,198.37
9/29/91      1100      03      01          246.18

                        SALESMAN 1100 SALES..... 3,134.69 *      L1 total
                        DEPT 03  SALES.........  5,519.15 **     L2 total
```

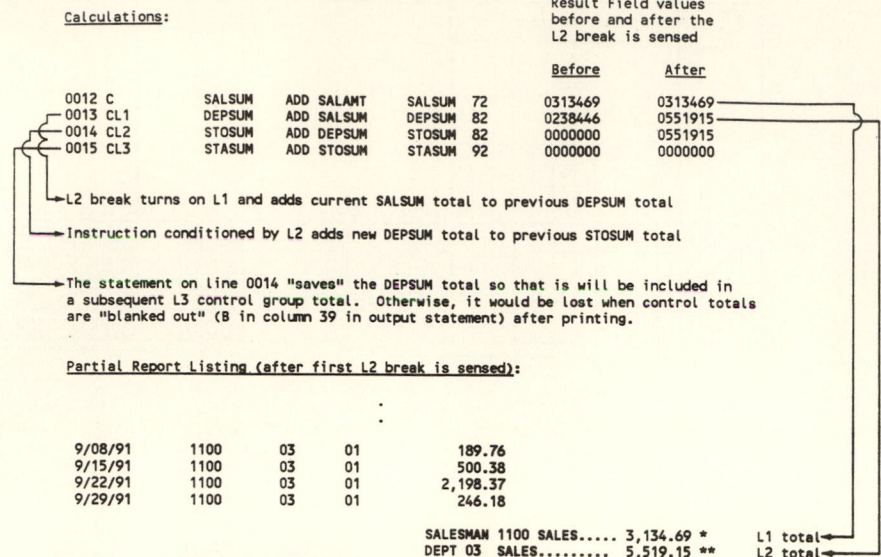

Figure 9-16 Relationship of calculations with printed report when an L2 control break program is sensed.

Output Specifications. A partial output form (heading line coding is not shown) for the multiple control break program is illustrated in Figure 9-17.

Line	Form Type	Type (H/D/T/E)	Space Before	Space After	Output Indicators	Field Name or EXCPT Name	Edit Codes	Blank After (B)	End Position in Output Record	Constant or Edit Word
01	O									
02	O									
03	O	T	2	1	L1					
04	O								52	'SALESMAN'
05	O					SALP#			57	
06	O								68	'SALES.....'
07	O					SALSUM	1	B	77	
08	O								79	'*'
09	O	T		1	L2					
10	O								48	'DEPT'
11	O					DEPT#			51	
12	O								67	'SALES........'
13	O					DEPSUM	1	B	77	
14	O								80	'**'
15	O	T	1	1	L3					
16	O								49	'STORE'
17	O					STORE#			52	
18	O								67	'SALES........'
19	O					STOSUM	1	B	77	
20	O								81	'***'
21	O	T	1		LR					
22	O								66	'TOTAL SALES:..........'
23	O					STASUM	1	B	77	
24	O								82	'****'

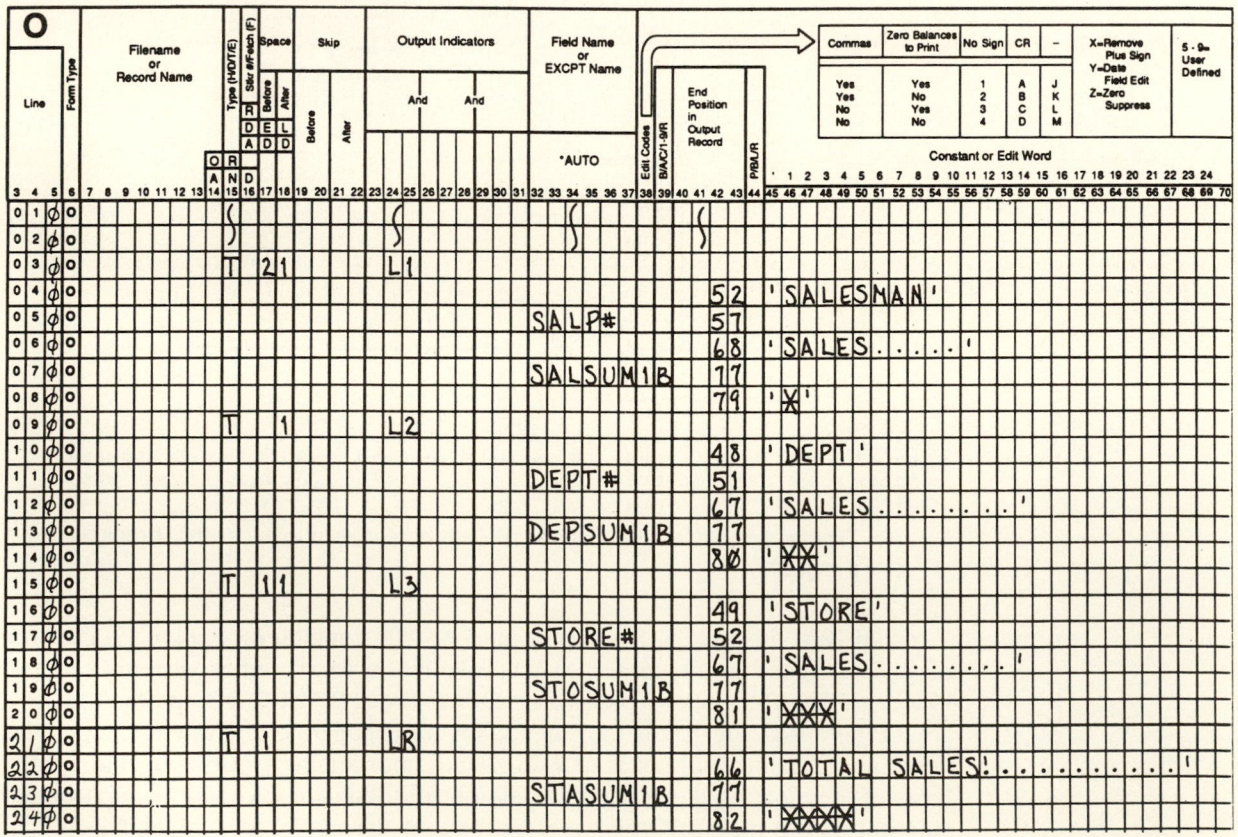

Figure 9-17 Output specifications for multiple control break program.

The processing logic for the output specifications is detailed in the flowchart in Figure 9-18.

Processing logic:

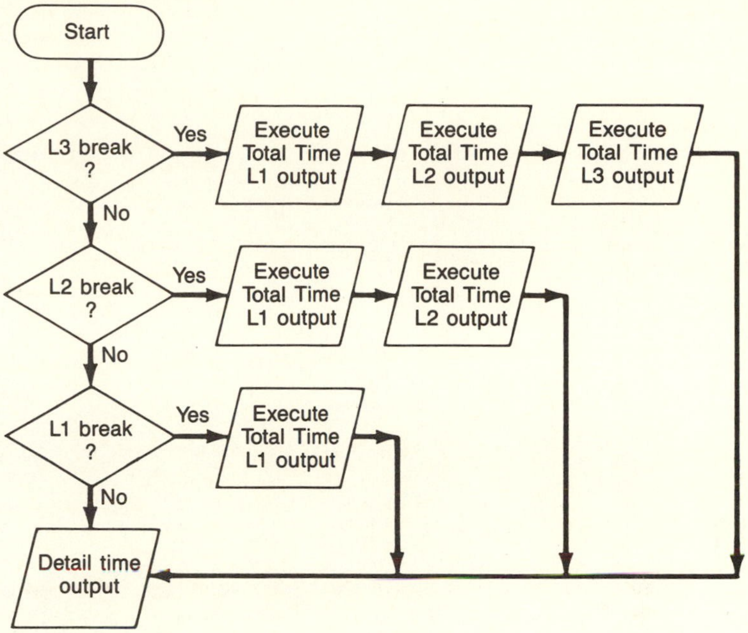

Note: Detail output must be specified before Total Time output. The related symbol, however, is included in the flowchart after Total Time output to illustrate the flow of processing and not the physical location of the program's instructions.

Figure 9-18 RPG controlled processing logic for output coding for multiple control break program.

Group Reports

The reports shown in Figures 9-1 and 9-11 are referred to as *Detail Reports* because the control field information is printed for every detail record within a group. Readability may be enhanced by including less information. Reports of this type are broadly classified as *Group* and *Summary*.

Figure 9-19 illustrates the report from Figure 9-11 modified as a *Group Report*. Notice that the control field information is printed for only the first record in a group when a control break is sensed and not for every detail record.

The changes needed in the example program to generate a group instead of a detail report are shown in the partial output form in Figure 9-20.

Summary Reports

Reports directed to higher levels of management usually include less detail information that those to lower management. In fact, the reports often include only group totals. In the RPG environment, these are called *Summary Reports*. Figure 9-21 illustrates a *Summary Report* generated from the same data file used for the other report formats previously discussed. Notice the absence of any detail lines and that each salesman, department, and store control group totals are summarized for easy reference.

An examination of partial source listing of the modified control break pro-

```
                    WEEKLY SALES REPORT AS OF  9/30/91                    PAGE   1

 DATE       SALESMAN    DEPT    STORE      WEEKLY SALES

9/08/91       1000       03      01           256.12
9/15/91                                     1,441.70
9/22/91                                       384.20
9/29/91                                       302.44

                                       SALESMAN 1000 SALES..... 2,384.46 *

9/08/91       1100                            189.76
9/15/91                                       500.38
9/22/91                                     2,198.37
9/29/91                                       246.18

                                       SALESMAN 1100 SALES..... 3,134.69 *
                                       DEPT 03  SALES.........  5,519.15 **

9/08/91       1200       05                 1,612.55
9/15/91                                       800.00
9/22/91                                       999.19
9/29/91                                     3,737.47

                                       SALESMAN 1200 SALES..... 7,149.21 *
                                       DEPT 05  SALES.........  7,149.21 **
                                       STORE 01  SALES........ 12,668.36 ***

9/08/91       1300       12      02           645.33
9/15/91                                       301.76
9/22/91                                     2,868.88
9/29/91                                     1,532.86

                                       SALESMAN 1300 SALES..... 5,348.83 *
                                       DEPT 12  SALES.........  5,348.83 **
                                       STORE 02  SALES........  5,348.83 ***

9/08/91       1400       08      03           184.79
9/15/91                                       733.74
9/22/91                                       472.52
9/29/91                                     4,900.09

                                       SALESMAN 1400 SALES..... 6,291.14 *
                                       DEPT 08  SALES..........  6,291.14 **
                                       STORE 03  SALES.........  6,291.14 ***

                                       TOTAL SALES...........    24,308.33 ****
```

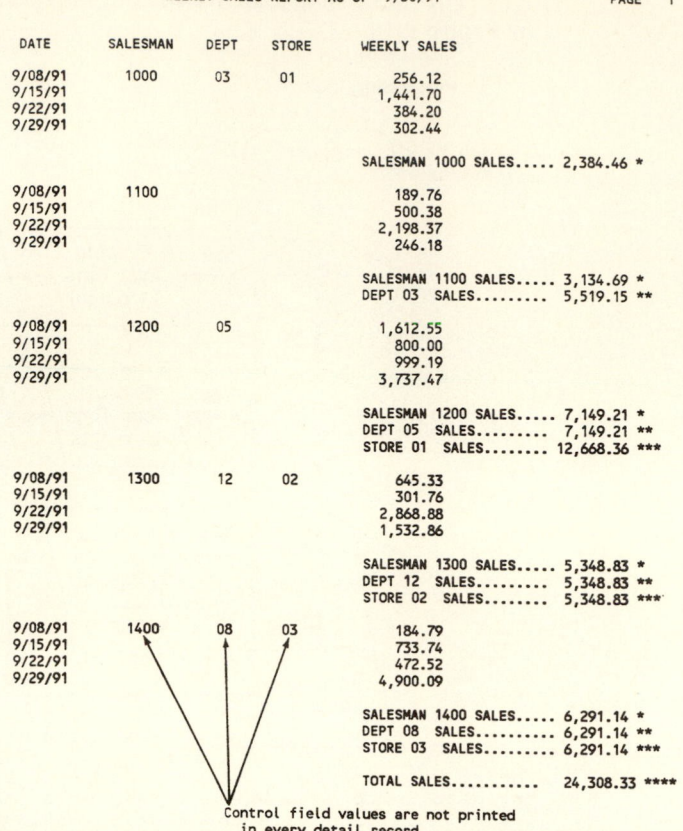

Control field values are not printed
in every detail record

Figure 9-19 Group report generated by modified multiple control break program.

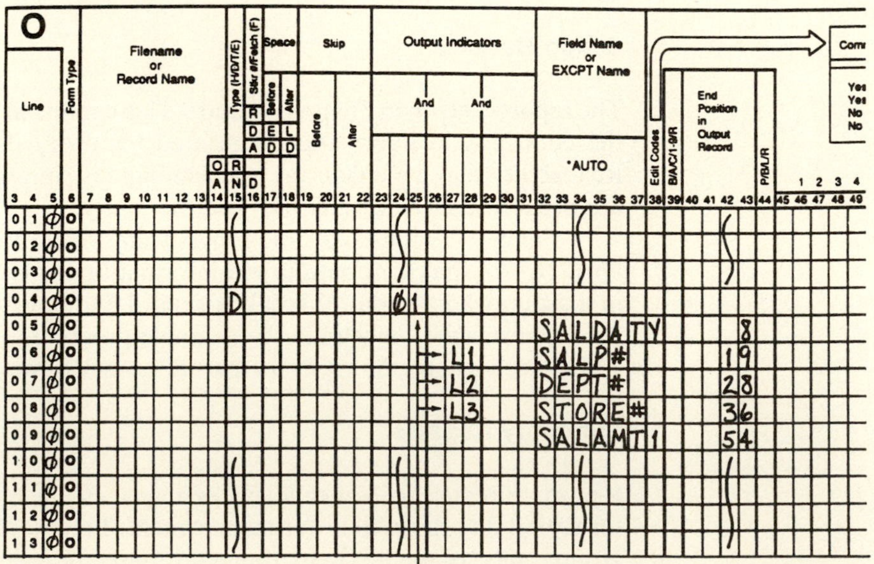

Specifying any control level indicator at detail time restricts printing of values to the first record in the control group. The level indicators in columns 27 and 28 are in an "AND" relationship with the Record Identifying indicator 01.

Output indicator columns 24-25 or 30-31 could have been used for the level indicators. Indentation does enhance readability and understanding of the program's syntax.

Figure 9-20 Partial output form for multiple control break program modified for group report format.

```
                 WEEKLY SALES REPORT AS OF  9/30/91                      PAGE   1

                              SALESMAN 1000 SALES..... 2,384.46 *

                              SALESMAN 1100 SALES..... 3,134.69 *
                              DEPT 03  SALES.........  5,519.15 **

                              SALESMAN 1200 SALES..... 7,149.21 *
                              DEPT 05  SALES.........  7,149.21 **
                              STORE 01  SALES........ 12,668.36 ***

                              SALESMAN 1300 SALES..... 5,348.83 *
                              DEPT 12  SALES.........  5,348.83 **
                              STORE 02  SALES........  5,348.83 ***

                              SALESMAN 1400 SALES..... 6,291.14 *
                              DEPT 08  SALES.......... 6,291.14 **
                              STORE 03  SALES......... 6,291.14 ***

                              TOTAL SALES...........   24,308.33 ****
```

Figure 9-21 Summary report generated by modified multiple control break program.

gram in Figure 9-22 indicates that the detail time coding lines have been deleted to support the Summary Report format. All other coding in the program is unchanged.

```
0016 OSALSRPT H  301    1P                                      CH9P3
0017 O        OR        OF                                      CH9P3
0018 O                                  42 'WEEKLY SALES REPORT AS'  CH9P3
0019 O                                  45 'OF'                 CH9P3
0020 O                        UDATE Y   54                      CH9P3
0021 O                                  78 'PAGE'               CH9P3
0022 O                        PAGE  Z   83                      CH9P3
0023 O         T 21     L1 <------------------------------------ Column headings and
0024 O                                  52 'SALESMAN'           CH9P3  Detail Time inst-
0025 O                        SALP#     57                      CH9P3  ructions deleted
0026 O                                  68 'SALES.....'         CH9P3
0027 O                        SALSUM1B  77                      CH9P3
0028 O                                  79 '*'                  CH9P3
0029 O         T  1     L2                                      CH9P3
0030 O                                  48 'DEPT'               CH9P3
0031 O                        DEPT#     51                      CH9P3
0032 O                                  67 'SALES.........'     CH9P3
0033 O                        DEPSUM1B  77                      CH9P3
0034 O                                  80 '**'                 CH9P3
0035 O         T  1     L3                                      CH9P3
0036 O                                  49 'STORE'              CH9P3
0037 O                        STORE#    52                      CH9P3
0038 O                                  67 'SALES........'      CH9P3
0039 O                        STOSUM1B  77                      CH9P3
0040 O                                  81 '***'                CH9P3
0041 O         T 1      LR                                      CH9P3
0042 O                                  66 'TOTAL SALES...........'  CH9P3
0043 O                        STASUM1   77                      CH9P3
0044 O                                  82 '****'               CH9P3
```

Figure 9-22 Partial output coding from multiple control break program modified for summary report format.

Split Control Fields

A control field that includes more than one field in a record is called a *Split Control Field*. It is defined by specifying the same control level indicator with two or more of a record's fields. An example of a Split Control Field is shown in the input form in Figure 9-23. Refer to the notes at the bottom of the figure for the rules associated with split control field usage.

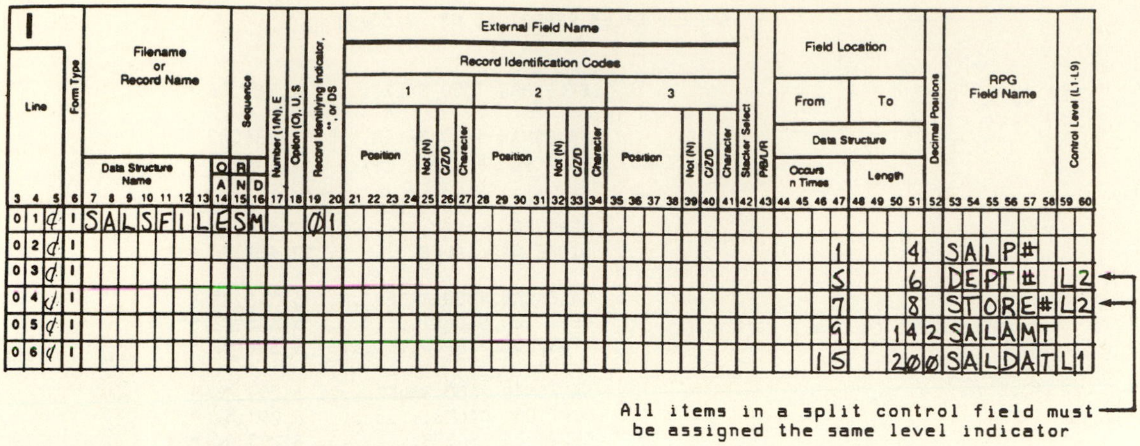

Notes:

1. Both items assigned L2 are processed as one control field.
2. If value changes in one or both of the fields, an L2 control break is generated.
3. Split control fields must be specified together. No other input specification lines may be entered between the fields. However, the fields do not have to be located next to each other in the data record.
4. If one field is defined as numeric, the whole split control field is processed as numeric.
5. The sum of a numeric split control field may not total more than 144 characters. The standard 15 byte length for the individual numeric fields must be followed.
6. If the names are different, a field may be split in some of the record types in a file and not others. The length of the split control field must, however, be the same for record types.
7. If the field names are different, the length of the elements of a split control field may be different for each record type. However, the total length of the related split control fields must be the same.

Figure 9-23 Split control field input specifications syntax.

A listing of a modified version of the previous control break programs that includes split control field processing is presented in Figure 9-24. The following changes have been included in this modified program:

1. The same data file used in this chapter's other program examples is specified as input. However, it has been resorted in a STORE# (major field), DEPT# (first minor), and SALDAT (second minor) order.
2. The input form defines STORE# and DEPT# as the elements of a Split Control Field.
3. Weekly sales amount for the same date (salesmen within the STORE/DEPT group) are added and are output when date changes (L1 control break).
4. Control Total for Store/Department is accumulated and output when the split control field value changes (L2 control break).
5. The report format shown in Figure 9-25 is modified with the following changes:
   a. Salesman headings, detail, and total output deleted.
   b. L1 control group total is sum for week ending date within the STORE/DEPT split field control group.
   c. L2 group total line for STORE#/DEPT# total.

```
... ... 1 ... ... 2 ... ... 3 ... ... 4 ... ... 5 ... ... 6 ... ... 7 ...
      * MULTIPLE CONTROL BREAK PROGRAM - DETAIL REPORT FORMAT                 CH9P4
      *                      SPLIT CONTROL FIELD                              CH9P4
     H                                                                        CH9P4
     FSALSFILEIP  F  20  20           DISK                                    CH9P4
     FSALSRPT O   F 132 132     OF    PRINTER                                 CH9P4
     ISALSFILESM  01                                                          CH9P4
     I                                        1   4 SALP#                     CH9P4
     I                                        5   6 DEPT# L2                  \ Split Control
     I                                        7   8 STORE#L2                  /  Field
     I                                        9  142SALAMT                    CH9P4
     I                                       15  200SALDATL1                  CH9P4
     C           DATSUM    ADD  SALAMT    DATSUM  82       DATE SUM           CH9P4
     CL1         STOSUM    ADD  DATSUM    STOSUM  92       STORE/DEPT SUM     CH9P4
     CL2         STASUM    ADD  STOSUM    STASUM  92       TOTAL SUM          CH9P4
     OSALSRPT H  301    1P                                                    CH9P4
     O        OR        OF                                                    CH9P4
     O                                  42 'WEEKLY SALES REPORT AS'           CH9P4
     O                                  45 'OF'                               CH9P4
     O                         UDATE Y  54                                    CH9P4
     O                                  78 'PAGE'                             CH9P4
     O                         PAGE  Z  83                                    CH9P4
     O          H  1    1P                                                    CH9P4
     O        OR        OF                                                    CH9P4
     O                                   6 'DATE'                             CH9P4
     O                                  21 'DEPT'                             CH9P4
     O                                  29 'STORE'                            CH9P4
     O                                  47 'WEEKLY SALES'                     CH9P4
     O          T  1    L1                                                    CH9P4
     O                         SALDATY   8                                    CH9P4
     O                         DEPT#    19                                    CH9P4
     O                         STORE#   28                                    CH9P4
     O                         DATSUM1B 46                                    CH9P4
     O          T 21    L2                                                    CH9P4
     O                                  46 'DEPT'                             CH9P4
     O                         DEPT#    49                                    CH9P4
     O                                  57 '- STORE'                          CH9P4
     O                         STORE#   60                                    CH9P4
     O                                  63 '...'                              CH9P4
     O                         STOSUM1B 75                                    CH9P4
     O                                  77 '*'                                CH9P4
     O          T  1    LR                                                    CH9P4
     O                                  61 'TOTAL SALES..'                    CH9P4
     O                         STASUM1  75                                    CH9P4
     O                                  78 '**'                               CH9P4
```

Figure 9-24 Source listing of example program using split control fields.

```
                    WEEKLY SALES REPORT AS OF  9/30/91                PAGE    1


DATE              DEPT   STORE        WEEKLY SALES

9/08/91            03     01              445.88
9/15/91            03     01            1,942.08
9/22/91            03     01            2,582.57
9/29/91            03     01              548.62

                                     DEPT 03 - STORE 01...     5,519.15 *

9/08/91            05     01            1,612.55
9/15/91            05     01              800.00
9/22/91            05     01              999.19
9/29/91            05     01            3,737.47

                                     DEPT 05 - STORE 01...     7,149.21 *

9/08/91            12     02              645.33
9/15/91            12     02              301.76
9/22/91            12     02            2,868.88
9/29/91            12     02            1,532.86

                                     DEPT 12 - STORE 02...     5,348.83 *

9/08/91            08     03              184.79
9/15/91            08     03              733.74
9/22/91            08     03              472.52
9/29/91            08     03            4,900.09

                                     DEPT 08 - STORE 03...     6,291.14 *

                                             TOTAL SALES..    24,308.33 **
```

Figure 9-25 Report generated by split control field program.

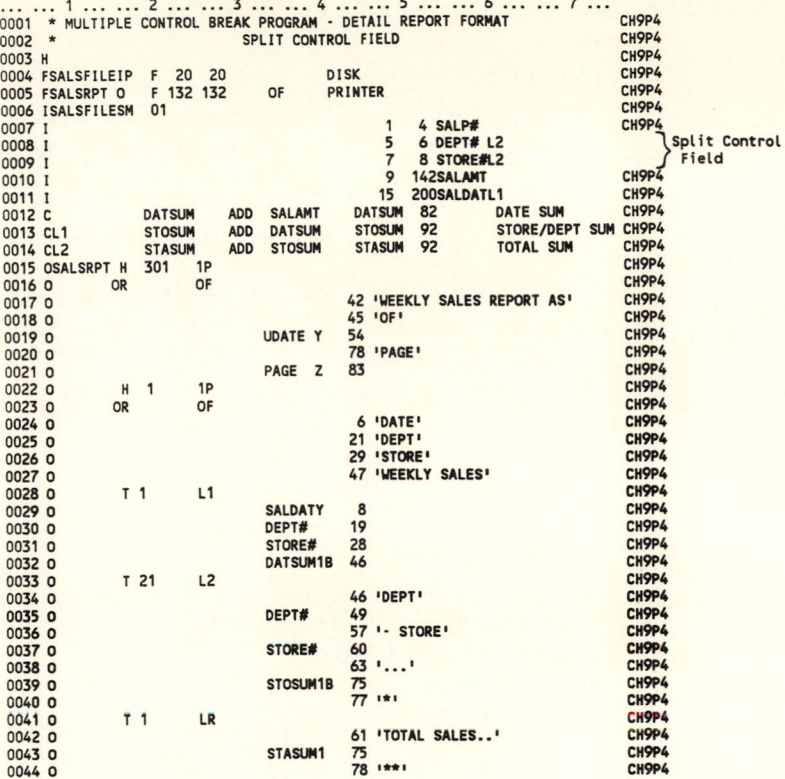

APPLICATION PROGRAM—CUSTOMER SALES INVOICES

Documentation

The specifications in Figure 9-26 explain the processing requirements for an application program that generates customer sales invoices. The system flowchart

PROGRAM SPECIFICATIONS Page 1 of 1

Program Name CUSTOMER INVOICES Program-ID CH9P5 Written By S. Myers

Purpose Customer Monthly Sales Invoices Approved By The Boss

Input files (directory names):

ACTFILE (stored on disk)

Output files (directory names):

INVOICES (Pre-printed invoice forms)

Processing Narrative:

Write a structured RPG program to print customer monthly sales invoices on pre-printed forms.

Input to the program:

A monthly sales file (ACTFILE), stored on disk, includes the sales transactions to customers for one month of the current year. A supplemental layout form details the format of the two record types in the file. The records are to be sequenced checked within a customer group with the "A" record first followed by any number of "P" records.

Assign L1 to the purchase number and L2 to the account number.

Processing:

Add the individual record amounts to a purchase order total field and print the value at total time L1.

When L1 is on, add the purchase order total to an invoice total and print at total time L2.

Output:

A supplemental "filled-in" invoice form is superimposed on a printer spacing chart for variable field locations. Note that all of the constants are pre-printed on the form; only the variables have to be defined in the program.

Figure 9-26 Specifications for an application program that generates customer sales invoices.

in Figure 9-27 indicates that one input disk and one output printer file are processed by the program. An examination of the record format in Figure 9-28 shows that

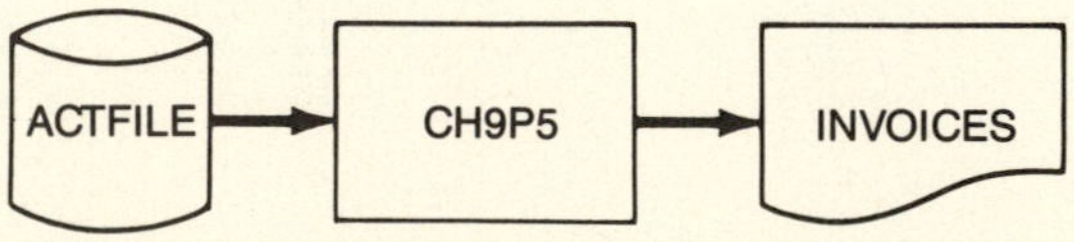

Figure 9-27 System Flowchart for customers sales invoice program.

two record types are included in the input file. The data file shown at the bottom of the figure has been sorted by customer number (major field) and purchase order number (minor field).

To locate the position of the variables in the body of the preprinted forms, a form has been superimposed on the printer spacing chart shown in Figure 9-29. The programmer has only to code for the variables (*X*s) and not the constants.

A	ACT #	CUSTOMER NAME	STREET	CITY	STATE	ZIP
9	9 9 9 9 9	9 9 9 9 9 9 9 9 9 9 9 9 9 9 9 9 9 9 9 9	9 9 9 9 9 9 9 9 9 9 9 9 9 9 9 9 9 9 9 9	9 9 9 9 9 9 9 9 9 9 9 9 9 9 9	9 9	9 9 9 9 9
1	2 3 4 5 6	7 8 9 10 11 12 13 14 15 16 17 18 19 20 21 22 23 24 25 26	27 28 29 30 31 32 33 34 35 36 37 38 39 40 41 42 43 44 45 46	47 48 49 50 51 52 53 54 55 56 57 58 59 60 61	62 63	64 65 66 67 68

P	ACT #	P.O. #	DATE	ITEM DESCRIPTION	AMOUNT	UNUSED
9	9 9 9 9 9	9 9 9 9	9 9 9 9 9 9	9 9 9 9 9 9 9 9 9 9 9 9 9 9 9 9 9 9 9 9	9 9 9 9 9 9 9	9 9 9 9 9 9 9 9 9 9 9 9 9 9 9 9 9 9 9 9 9 9 9 9 9
1	2 3 4 5 6	7 8 9 10	11 12 13 14 15 16	17 18 19 20 21 22 23 24 25 26 27 28 29 30 31 32 33 34 35 36	37 38 39 40 41 42 43	44 45 46 47 48 49 50 51 52 53 54 55 56 57 58 59 60 61 62 63 64 65 66 67 68

Data file listing:

```
A10000MANUEL LOPEZ        25 SUNSET BLVD      LOS ANGELES    CA09900
P100001234090591BOY'S WEAR          0007512
P100001234090591GIRL'S WEAR         0010060
P100001235091091MEN'S WEAR          0023799
A20000HENRY SNODGRAS      80 AIRPORT ROAD     STRATFORD      CT06497
P200001236091591WOMEN'S WEAR        0055000
P200001236091591SMALL APPLIANCES    0004989
P200001236091591GIRL'S WEAR         0001250
P200001237092091GARDEN TOOLS        0038900
P200001237092091MEN'S WEAR          0008000
```

Figure 9-28 Record layout forms and data listing of the input file processed by the customer sales invoice program.

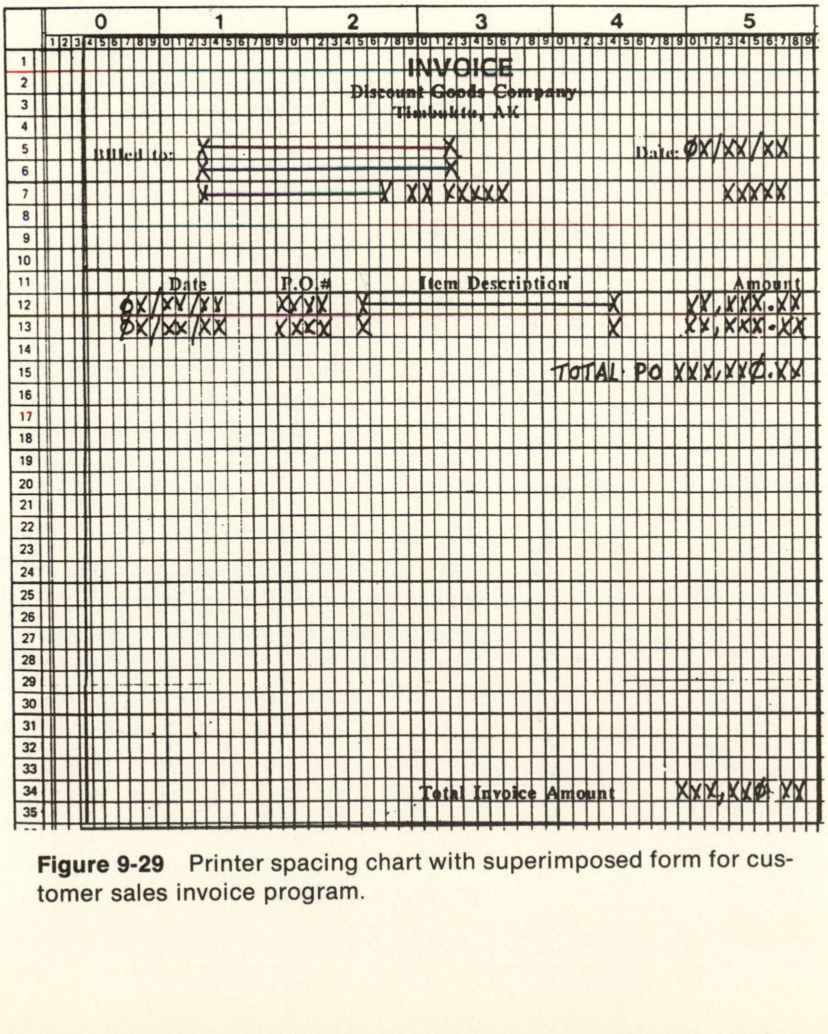

Figure 9-29 Printer spacing chart with superimposed form for customer sales invoice program.

The invoice generated by the customer sales invoice program is illustrated in Figure 9-30.

INVOICE
Discount Goods Company
Timbuktu, AK

Billed to: MARIA LOPEZ
25 SUNSET BLVD
LOS ANGELES CA 09900

Date: 9/30/91
10000

Date	P.O.#	Item Description		Amount
9/05/91	1234	BOY'S WEAR		75.12
9/05/91	1234	GIRL'S WEAR		100.60
			TOTAL PO	175.72
9/10/91	1235	MEN'S WEAR		237.99
			TOTAL PO	237.99
			Total Invoice Amount	413.71

Figure 9-30 Invoices generated by customer sales invoice application program.

Source Program

Examine the source listing of the customer sales invoice program in Figure 9-31, and notice the following:

1. A Line Counter Specification (line 0005) is included to define the preprinted form length and overflow line. IBM's System 34, 36's, 38's, and 400's require that line numbers be used for page skip control. Other systems may require channel numbers. Refer to Chapter 3 if you need a review of page control syntax and processing.
2. The calculation instruction on line 0020 is included to eliminate a total time L1 "null" break. Because two record types are included in the file and the PO# field is included only in the second record type, a total time L1 control break will be generated when the record type changes. This will cause an L1 total line with zeros to be printed before detail time. The instruction on line 0020 tests the field for zero (turns on 10 if zero), and conditions the output statement on line 0037 to print only if POAMT is not zero (L1 and N10 indicators).
3. Line numbers are included on the output lines 0022, 0027, and 0040 to control line skipping in the body of the form.
4. Detail time L2 controls advancing to the top of a new form when a change in ACT# is tested.

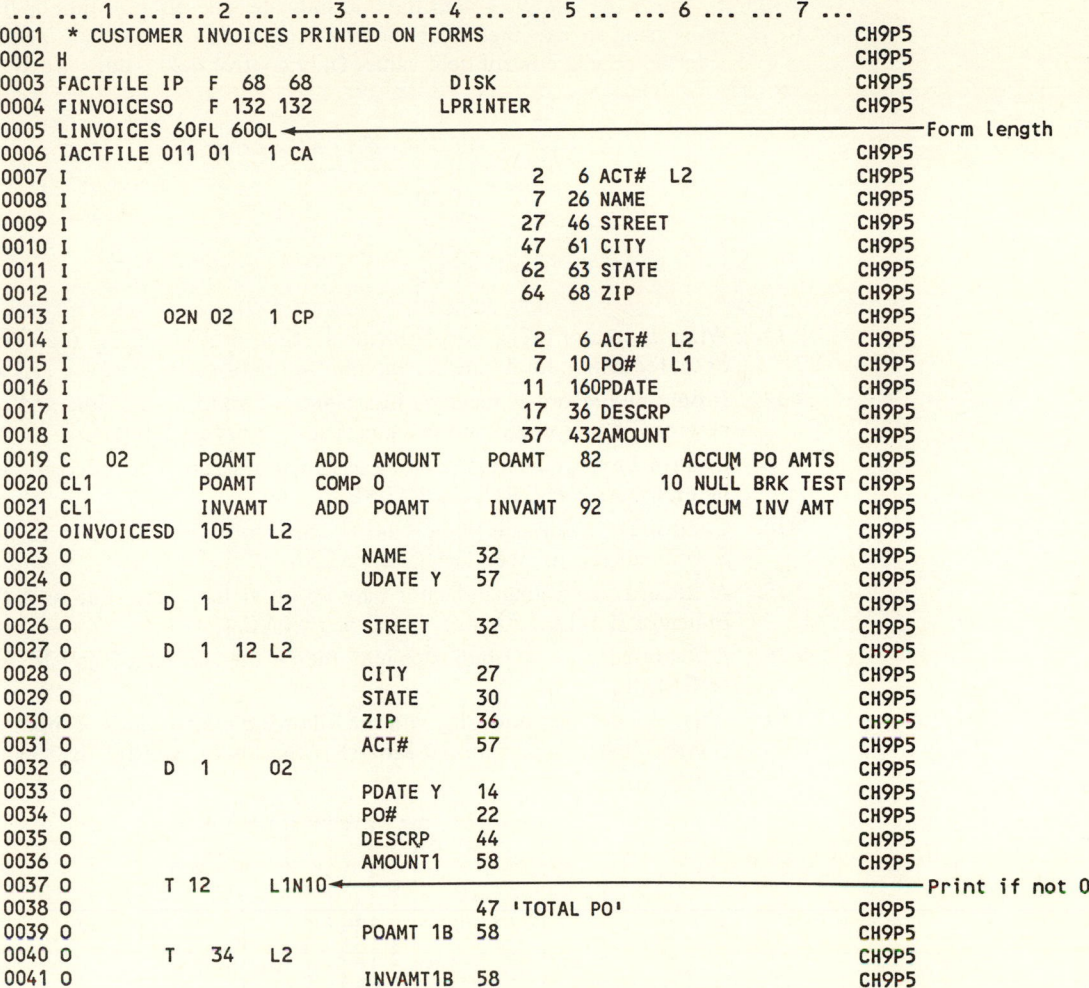

```
... ... 1 ... ... 2 ... ... 3 ... ... 4 ... ... 5 ... ... 6 ... ... 7 ...
0001  * CUSTOMER INVOICES PRINTED ON FORMS                              CH9P5
0002 H                                                                  CH9P5
0003 FACTFILE IP  F  68  68            DISK                             CH9P5
0004 FINVOICESO   F 132 132           LPRINTER                          CH9P5
0005 LINVOICES 60FL 600L<-------------------------------------------------Form length
0006 IACTFILE 011 01   1 CA                                             CH9P5
0007 I                                       2   6 ACT#  L2             CH9P5
0008 I                                       7  26 NAME                 CH9P5
0009 I                                      27  46 STREET               CH9P5
0010 I                                      47  61 CITY                 CH9P5
0011 I                                      62  63 STATE                CH9P5
0012 I                                      64  68 ZIP                  CH9P5
0013 I        02N 02   1 CP                                             CH9P5
0014 I                                       2   6 ACT#  L2             CH9P5
0015 I                                       7  10 PO#   L1             CH9P5
0016 I                                      11  160PDATE                CH9P5
0017 I                                      17  36 DESCRP               CH9P5
0018 I                                      37  432AMOUNT               CH9P5
0019 C   02        POAMT     ADD  AMOUNT    POAMT   82        ACCUM PO AMTS  CH9P5
0020 CL1           POAMT     COMP 0                        10 NULL BRK TEST  CH9P5
0021 CL1           INVAMT    ADD  POAMT     INVAMT  92        ACCUM INV AMT  CH9P5
0022 OINVOICESD  105   L2                                               CH9P5
0023 O                           NAME      32                           CH9P5
0024 O                           UDATE Y   57                           CH9P5
0025 O        D  1     L2                                               CH9P5
0026 O                           STREET    32                           CH9P5
0027 O        D  1  12 L2                                               CH9P5
0028 O                           CITY      27                           CH9P5
0029 O                           STATE     30                           CH9P5
0030 O                           ZIP       36                           CH9P5
0031 O                           ACT#      57                           CH9P5
0032 O        D  1     02                                               CH9P5
0033 O                           PDATE Y   14                           CH9P5
0034 O                           PO#       22                           CH9P5
0035 O                           DESCRP    44                           CH9P5
0036 O                           AMOUNT1   58                           CH9P5
0037 O        T 12     L1N10<----------------------------------------------Print if not 0
0038 O                                     47 'TOTAL PO'                CH9P5
0039 O                           POAMT 1B  58                           CH9P5
0040 O        T   34   L2                                               CH9P5
0041 O                           INVAMT1B  58                           CH9P5
```

Figure 9-31 Source listing of customer sales invoice program.

QUESTIONS

9-1. In an RPG program, how are subtotals controlled in the body of a report?

9-2. What are the Control Level Indicators? Where are they defined in an RPG program? On what coding forms may they be used to condition instructions?

9-3. What are Control Fields? Control Groups?

9-4. How should a data file that is processed by a program that includes control level breaks be organized?

9-5. What is generated when a Control Field value changes?

9-6. If L1, L2, and L3 are used in a program and L3 is turned on, what other Control Level Indicators are set on?

9-7. Refer to Question 9-6. When LR is turned on at end of file, what other indicators will be set on?

9-8. A Control Level Indicator entered in columns 7 and 8 of the calculation form processes the related instruction at __________ time.

9-9. A Control Level Indicator entered in columns 10 to 11, 13 to 14, or 16 to 17 processes the related instruction at __________ time.

9-10. Examine the following data file and indicate where detail time and total time L1 processing are executed. Answer by placing a DL1 and/or TL1, and/or TLR alongside the related control field value. Only control field values are shown.

```
1000   first record
1000
1000
2000
2000
3000
```

9-11. When a control break is sensed, detail time processing for the current record is executed before total time calculations are performed. Answer TRUE or FALSE.

9-12. If only one record is included in a Control Group, detail time and total time processing are performed on the same record. Answer TRUE or FALSE.

9-13. Control Level Indicators must be assigned in ascending order in the Input Specifications. Answer TRUE or FALSE.

9-14. Control Level Indicators must be assigned in ascending order in the Calculation Specifications. Answer TRUE or FALSE.

9-15. A Record Identifying Indicator may be on at the same time as a Control Break Indicator (L1–L9). Answer TRUE or FALSE.

9-16. A Record Identifying Indicator may the on the same time as LR. Answer TRUE or FALSE.

9-17. What, if anything, is wrong with the following related lines of input coding for the control fields assignments? EMPNO is the lowest control field and DIVISN the highest.

RPG Field Name (53–58)	Control Level (L1-L9) (59–60)	Matching Fields or Chaining Fields (61–62)	Field Record Relation (63–64)	Field Indicators: Plus (65–66)	Field Indicators: Minus (67–68)	Field Indicators: Zero or Blank (69–70)
EMPNO	L5					
SECTON	L4					
DEPT	L2					
DIVISN	L3					

9-18. What, if anything, is wrong with related lines of coding in the following calculation form? VOTERS is an input field and VOTOTL, COUNTY, DISTCT, and STATE are control group total fields.

Line (3–5)	Form Type (6)	Control Level (L0-L9, LR, SR, AN/OR) (7–8)	Indicators (9–17)	Factor 1 (18–27)	Operation (28–32)	Factor 2 (33–42)	Result Field Name (43–48)
01Ø	C		L1	VOTERS	ADD	VOTOTL	VOTOTL
02Ø	C		L3	VOTOTL	ADD	COUNTY	COUNTY
03Ø	C		L4	COUNTY	ADD	DISTCT	DISTCT
04Ø	C		L2	DISTCT	ADD	STATE	STATE

9-19. What, if anything, is wrong with the following calculation coding?

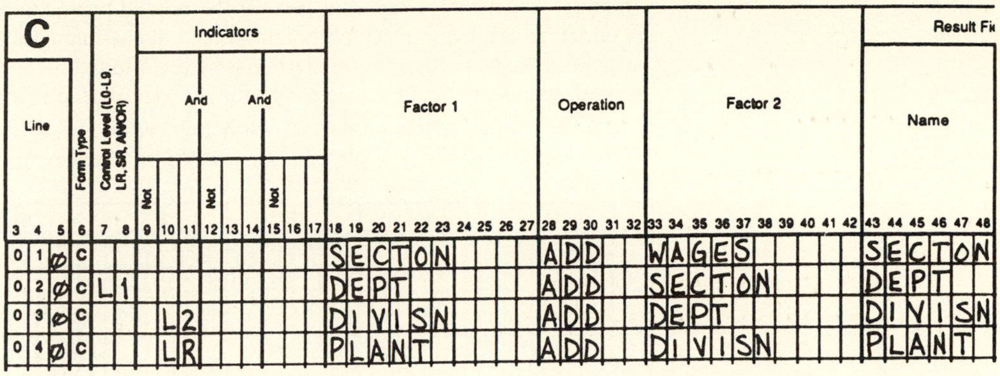
C
Line
Form Type
Control Level (L0-L9, LR, SR, AN/OR)
Indicators
Factor 1
Operation
Factor 2
Result Field
Name
01Ø C SECTON ADD WAGES SECTON
02Ø C L1 DEPT ADD SECTON DEPT
03Ø C L2 DIVISN ADD DEPT DIVISN
04Ø C LR PLANT ADD DIVISN PLANT

9-20. Name three classifications of reports. Explain their differences.

9-21. Examine the following partial output coding and determine what class of report will be generated.

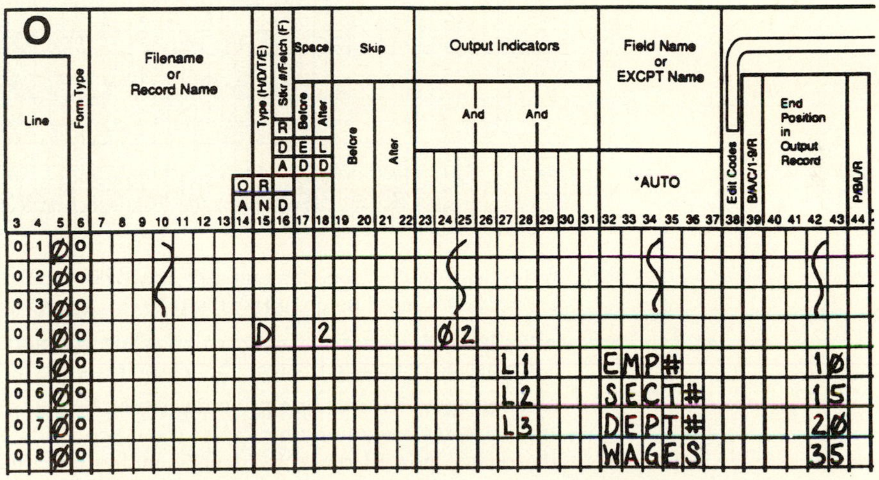
O
Line
Form Type
Filename or Record Name
Space
Skip
Output Indicators
Field Name or EXCPT Name
End Position in Output Record
04Ø O D 2 Ø2
05Ø O L1 EMP# 1Ø
06Ø O L2 SECT# 15
07Ø O L3 DEPT# 2Ø
08Ø O WAGES 35

9-22. If the output coding includes no detail time output, the report is classified as a __________ report.

9-23. Define a *Split Control* field.

9-24. Split Control fields must be entered in the input form next to each other. Answer TRUE or FALSE.

9-25. Split Control fields defined on input do not have to be physically next to each other in the logical record. Answer TRUE or FALSE.

9-26. The fields included in the Split Control field group must all be defined as the same type. Answer TRUE or FALSE.

EXERCISES

9-1. An input file (PARTS) includes data records in the following format: Write the Input Specifications to define the fields. Specify Job Number, Section Number, and Department Number as control fields. Define Job Number as the lowest control field and Department Number as the highest.

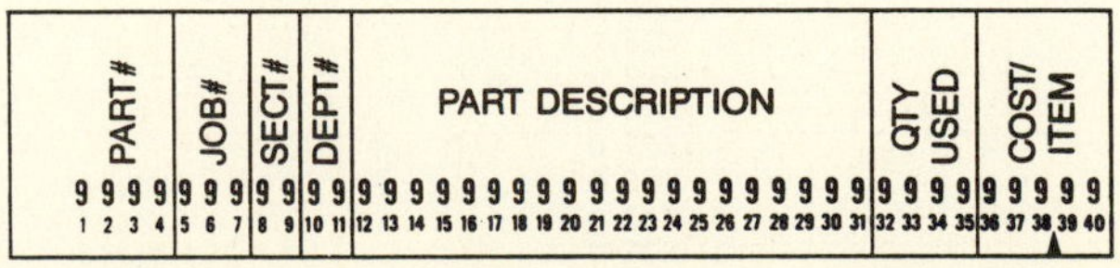
PART#
JOB#
SECT#
DEPT#
PART DESCRIPTION
QTY USED
COST/ ITEM

9-2. Refer to Exercise 9-1, and write the calculation coding. Item Cost is multiplied by Quantity to determine the total cost for the related part. The part's total cost amount is added to a job total, which is added to a department total. Execution of the instructions occurs when the related control level indicator is turned on. Refer to the printer spacing chart in Exercise 9-3 for the size of each Control Group field.

9-3. From the printer spacing chart shown below, write the output coding to generate a *Detail Report*. Refer to Exercises 9-1 and 9-2 for field names and sizes.

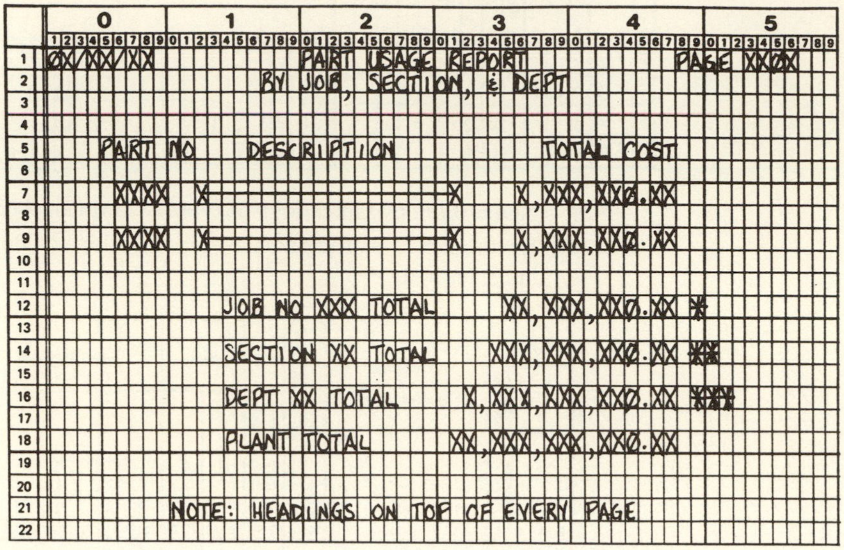

9-4. Refer to Exercise 9-3, and modify the RPG syntax to generate a *Group Report*. Exercise 9-3 must be completed before this exercise is started.

9-5. Refer to Exercise 9-3, and modify the coding to generate a *Summary Report*. Exercise 9-3 must be completed before this exercise is started.

9-6. Debugging an RPG source program: Given below is an RPG source program listing that includes execution time errors (no compilation errors). Examine the listing and the related printed report to identify and correct all errors.

Source Program Listing:

```
... ... 1 ... ... 2 ... ... 3 ... ... 4 ... ... 5 ... ... 6 ... ... 7 ...
0002 H                                                                 EX9#6
0003 FSALSFILEIP  F  20  20            DISK                            EX9#6
0004 FSALSRPT O   F 132 132      OF    PRINTER                         EX9#6
0005 ISALSFILESM  01                                                   EX9#6
0006 I                                      1   4 SALP# L1             EX9#6
0007 I                                      5   6 DEPT# L2             EX9#6
0008 I                                      7   8 STORE#L3             EX9#6
0009 I                                      9  142SALAMT               EX9#6
0010 I                                     15  200SALDAT               EX9#6
0011 CL1          SALSUM    ADD  SALAMT    SALSUM  72       ACCUM SALP# SUMEX9#6
0012 CL1          DEPSUM    ADD  SALSUM    DEPSUM  82       ACCUM DEPT SUM EX9#6
0013 CL2          STOSUM    ADD  DEPSUM    STOSUM  82       ACCUM STORE SUMEX9#6
0014 CL3          STASUM    ADD  STOSUM    STASUM  92       ACCUM STATE SUMEX9#6
0015 OSALSRPT H  301    1P                                             EX9#6
0016 O        OR        OF                                             EX9#6
0017 O                                 42 'WEEKLY SALES REPORT AS'     EX9#6
0018 O                                 45 'OF'                         EX9#6
0019 O                       UDATE Y   54                              EX9#6
0020 O                                 78 'PAGE'                       EX9#6
0021 O                       PAGE  Z   83                              EX9#6
0022 O          H  1    1P                                             EX9#6
0023 O        OR        OF                                             EX9#6
0024 O                                  6 'DATE'                       EX9#6
0025 O                                 21 'SALESMAN'                   EX9#6
0026 O                                 29 'DEPT'                       EX9#6
0027 O                                 38 'STORE'                      EX9#6
0028 O                                 56 'WEEKLY SALES'               EX9#6
0029 O          T 1     01                                             EX9#6
0030 O                       SALDATY    8                              EX9#6
0031 O                       SALP#     19                              EX9#6
0032 O                       DEPT#     28                              EX9#6
```

```
0033 O                          STORE#    36                       EX9#6
0034 O                          SALAMT1   54                       EX9#6
0035 O        T 21     L1                                          EX9#6
0036 O                                    52 'SALESMAN'            EX9#6
0037 O                          SALP#     57                       EX9#6
0038 O                                    68 'SALES.....'          EX9#6
0039 O                          SALSUM1   77                       EX9#6
0040 O                                    79 '*'                   EX9#6
0041 O        T  1     L2                                          EX9#6
0042 O                                    48 'DEPT'                EX9#6
0043 O                          DEPT#     51                       EX9#6
0044 O                                    67 'SALES.........'      EX9#6
0045 O                          DEPSUM1   77                       EX9#6
0046 O                                    80 '**'                  EX9#6
0047 O        T  1     L3                                          EX9#6
0048 O                                    49 'STORE'               EX9#6
0049 O                          STORE#    52                       EX9#6
0050 O                                    67 'SALES........'       EX9#6
0051 O                          STOSUM1B  77                       EX9#6
0052 O                                    81 '***'                 EX9#6
0053 O        D 1      LR                                          EX9#6
0054 O                                    66 'TOTAL SALES...........' EX9#6
0055 O                          STASUM1   77                       EX9#6
0056 O                                    82 '****'                EX9#6
```

Printed Report:

```
                  WEEKLY SALES REPORT AS OF  9/30/91              PAGE    1

 DATE      SALESMAN    DEPT    STORE     WEEKLY SALES

9/08/91      1000       03      01          256.12
9/15/91      1000       03      01        1,441.70
9/22/91      1000       03      01          384.20
9/29/91      1000       03      01          302.44

                                      SALESMAN 1000 SALES.....    302.44 *

9/08/91      1100       03      01          189.76
9/15/91      1100       03      01          500.38
9/22/91      1100       03      01        2,198.37
9/29/91      1100       03      01          246.18

                                      SALESMAN 1100 SALES.....    548.62 *
                                      DEPT 03  SALES.........     851.06 **

9/08/91      1200       05      01        1,612.55
9/15/91      1200       05      01          800.00
9/22/91      1200       05      01          999.19
9/29/91      1200       05      01        3,737.47

                                      SALESMAN 1200 SALES..... 4,286.09 *
                                      DEPT 05  SALES......... 5,137.15 **
                                      STORE 01  SALES........ 5,988.21 ***

9/08/91      1300       12      02          645.33
9/15/91      1300       12      02          301.76
9/22/91      1300       12      02        2,868.88
9/29/91      1300       12      02        1,532.86

                                      SALESMAN 1300 SALES..... 5,818.95 *
                                      DEPT 12  SALES......... 10,956.10 **
                                      STORE 02  SALES........ 10.956.10 ***

9/08/91      1400       08      03          184.79
9/15/91      1400       08      03          733.74
9/22/91      1400       08      03          472.52
9/29/91      1400       08      03        4,900.09

                                      SALESMAN 1400 SALES.....10,719.04 *
                                      DEPT 08  SALES..........21,675.14 **
                                      STORE 03  SALES.........21,675.14 ***
```

LABORATORY ASSIGNMENTS

Laboratory Assignment 9-1: CUSTOMER MONTHLY INVOICES

From the information included in the record layout forms and printer spacing chart, write an RPG program to generate the required report.

Format of Data Records:

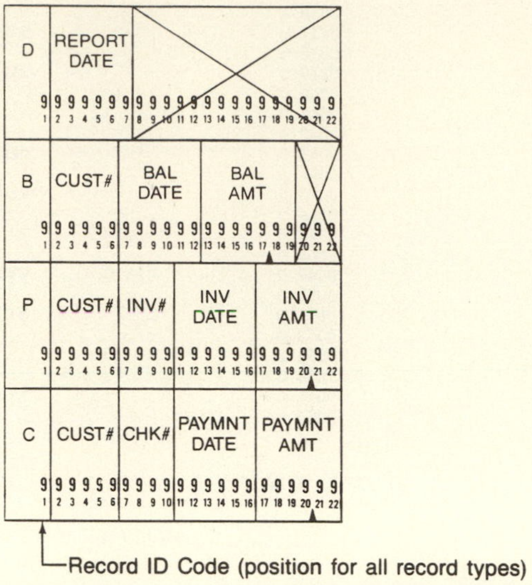

Processing: For each customer group, add any purchase amounts (record P) to the beginning balance and subtract payment amounts (record C) from the beginning balance. Print a detail line for the related transaction in the format shown in the print chart.

Accumulate the total purchases and total payments for a customer and print when the customer number changes (control level break). Also, accumulate totals for all purchases, payments, and ending balances. Refer to the print chart for related field sizes.

Report Design:

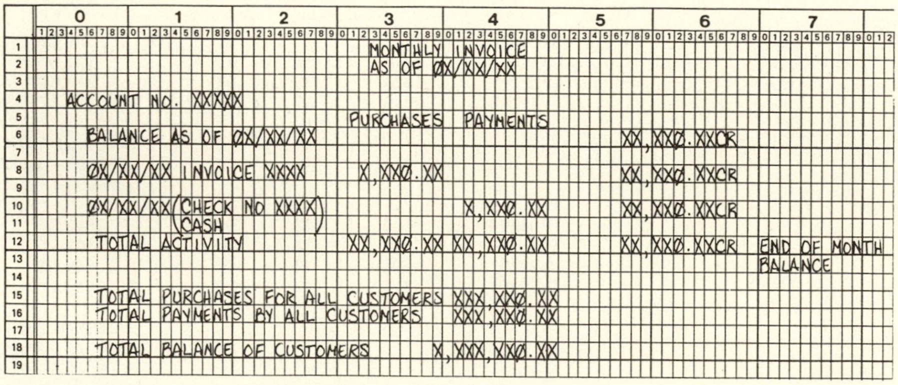

Input Data:

Date record (first in file):

ID Code	Report Date
D	093092

Balance records:

ID	Cust#	Balance Date	Balance Aamount	
B	11111	090192	0012010	
B	22222	090192	0287178	
B	33333	090192	0001045	
B	44444	090192	0000000	
B	55555	090192	000040}	(negative balance)

Sales records:

ID Code	Cust#	Invoice Number	Invoice Date	Invoice Amount
P	11111	0100	090192	030009
P	11111	0102	090492	005637
P	22222	0101	090392	025160
P	33333	0103	090592	010000
P	33333	0105	091892	070000
P	44444	0104	091092	061231
P	55555	0106	092892	041283

Payment on account records:

ID Code	Cust#	Check Number	Payment Date	Payment Amount
C	11111	0080	091592	042019
C	22222	0078	091292	287178
C	33333		092492	081500
C	44444	0099	092892	020179

Note: Blank value for check number indicates cash transaction.

Note: Data file must be sorted in ascending date order within each customer group. For example, the balance record for customer 11111 must be followed by his or her purchase and payment records in ascending date order.

Laboratory Assignment 9-2: VOTER REPORT BY TOWN AND STATE TOTALS

Write an RPG program to generate the report detailed in the supplemental printer spacing chart.

Format of Data Records:

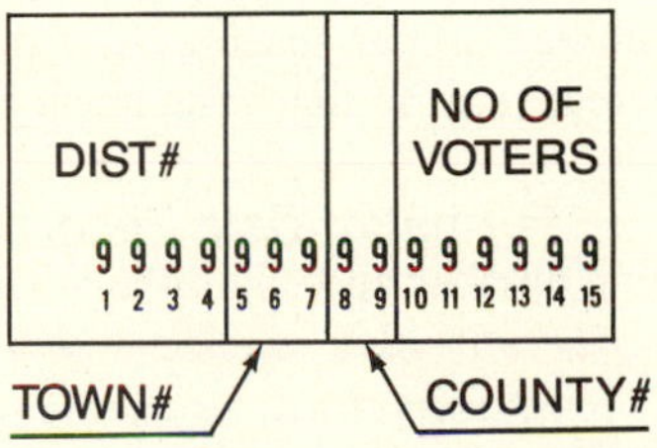

Note: A field is included for county number that is not referenced for this assignment. It is, however, required for the multiple control group report for Assignment 9-3.

Processing: Process the input file consecutively, and accumulate the number of voters in each district into a control total. Also, maintain a total for all the voters in the state that is to be printed after end of file is tested. Refer to the following printer spacing chart result field sizes. Print the report in a *detail* format.

Report Design:

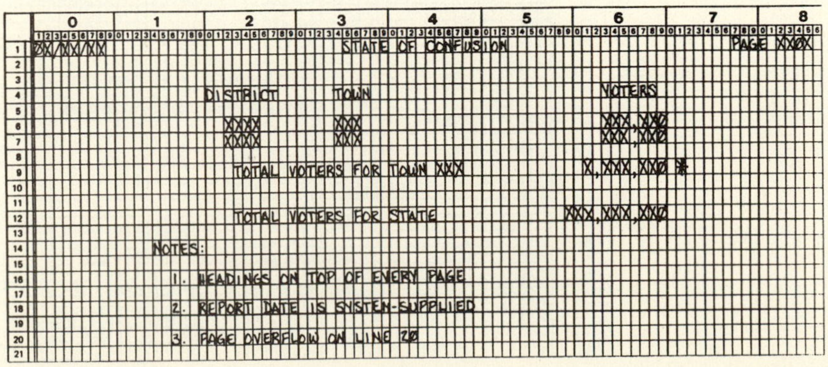

Because of the limited number of data records, page overflow control will not be tested. Therefore, with permission and procedures from the instructor, use the Line Counter form to change the page length to line 22 with page overflow on line 20. Printer type will determine whether line numbers or channel numbers are referenced.

Input Data:

District Number	Town Number	County Number	Number of Voters In District
1000	100	10	215625
1010	100	10	082784
1020	100	10	104716
1030	100	10	012899
1040	100	10	267004
2000	200	10	057800
2010	200	10	014111
2020	200	10	118923
2030	200	10	073807
3000	300	30	200749
3010	300	30	111111
4000	400	40	067242
4010	400	40	104338
4020	400	40	099917
4030	400	40	178615
4040	400	40	222234
4050	400	40	033845
4060	400	40	117871
4070	400	40	064899
4080	400	40	045348
4090	400	40	888888

Laboratory Assignment 9-3: VOTER REPORT BY TOWN, COUNTY, AND STATE TOTALS

If Assignment 9-1 was previously completed, supplement it to include the changes in the modified printer spacing chart shown below. On the other hand, if Lab 9-1 was not completed, refer to that assignment for input record format and data.

Format of Data Records: Refer to the record format in Assignment 9-2. Define town number and county number as the two control fields.

Processing: Read the file consecutively, and accumulate a town total. When the town number changes (L1 control break), add the accumulated town total to a county total field. Then, when the county number changes (L2 control break), add the accumulated county total to a state total. Print related output according to the report format detailed in the print chart.

Report Design:

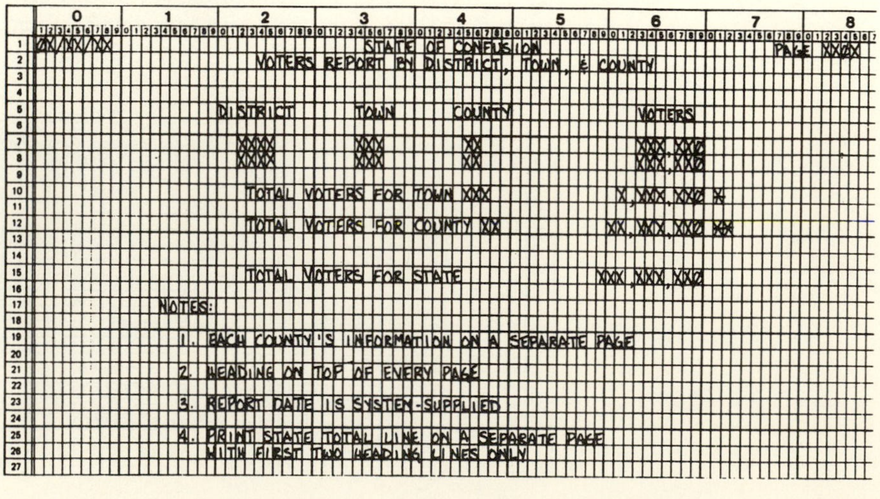

Note: Except for the second and third heading lines and county control group total, the report format is identical to Assignment 9-2. Report is to be completed in a *Detail* format.

Input Data: Use the data from Laboratory Assignment 9-2.

Laboratory Assignment 9-4: VOTER REPORT BY TOWN, COUNTY, AND STATE TOTAL (GROUP AND SUMMARY REPORTS)

Note: Assignment 9-2 or 9-3 must be completed before this assignment may be started.

Part A: Depending on which assignment was completed, modify Assignment 9-2 or 9-3 to generate a *Group* formatted report. If both were completed, modify Assignment 9-3.

Part B: Modify Assignment 9-2 or 9-3 to generate a summary report. Refer to the related print chart for the location of required control group totals. The third heading line and detail lines are not to be included in the summary report format.

Laboratory Assignment 9-5: MONTHLY SALES REPORT

Write an RPG program to generate the monthly sales report detailed in the printer spacing chart shown.

Format of Data Records: The two record formats shown below are included in the input file. It is important that the data be arranged in a *sorted* order with a salesman's month-to-date record (M) first, followed by the related daily sales records (S).

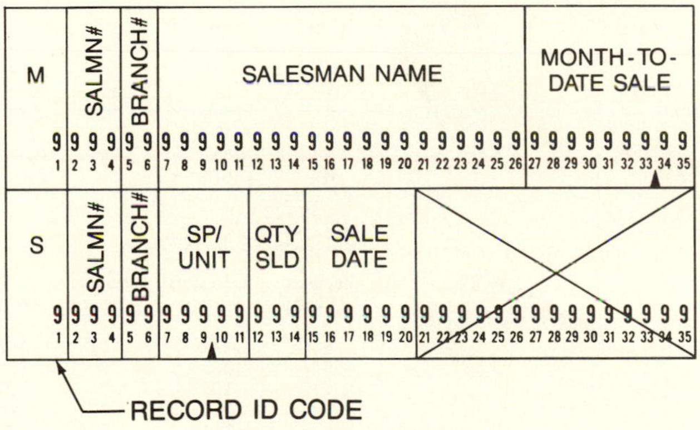

Processing: Process the input file consecutively, and for each "S" record multiply the selling price per unit by the quantity sold to determine the daily sales dollar amount. Add this amount to a weekly sales accumulator.

When the salesman number changes (L1 control break), add the accumulated week's total for the salesman to the month-to-date value from the "M" record and print the line as shown in the print chart. The salesman's weekly sales and monthly sales control group totals must be added to weekly and branch accumulators (see print chart). When the branch number changes (L2 control break), a branch's weekly and monthly totals are added to related company accumulators (see print chart).

Report Design: The week ending date value required in the second heading line is to be controlled by a screen prompt requesting an operator entry. CONSOLE or KEYBORD control must be included in the program to provide for interactive date entry. (Refer to Chapter 8 for CONSOLE syntax and to Chapter 12 for KEYBORD control.) However, if CRT controlled input is not available on the system used to execute this program, include the report date as the first record in the data file. Code it with a D in column 1 followed by the date in columns 2 to 7.

In either case use 113091 as the report date.

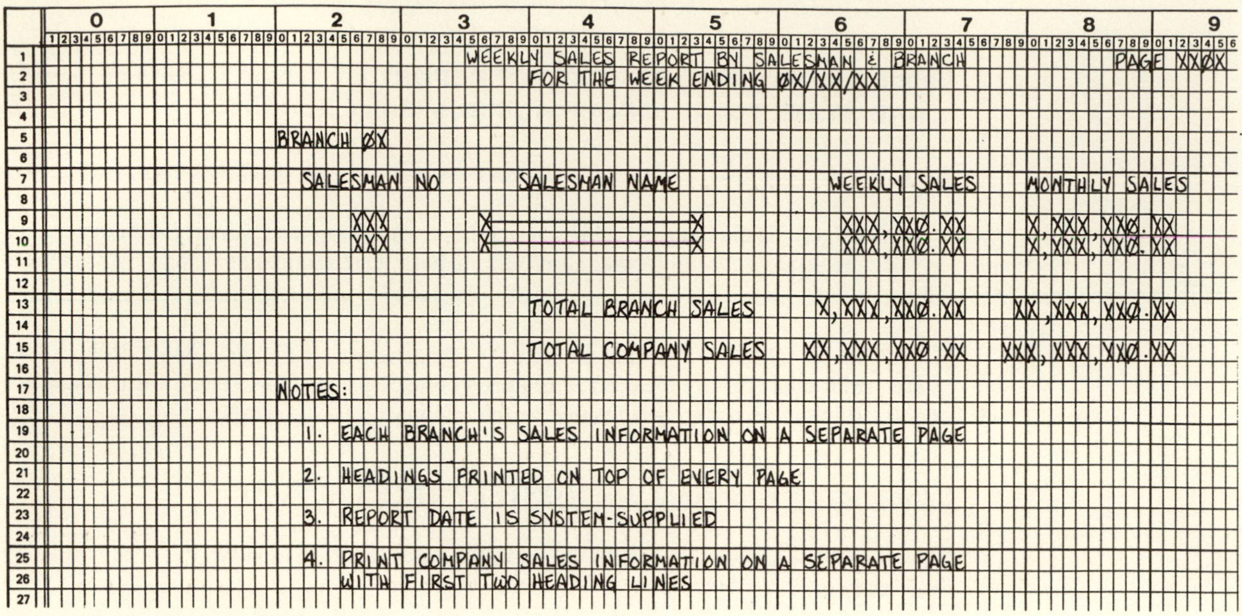

WEEKLY SALES REPORT BY SALESMAN & BRANCH
PAGE XXØX
FOR THE WEEK ENDING ØX/XX/XX
BRANCH ØX
SALESMAN NO
SALESMAN NAME
WEEKLY SALES
MONTHLY SALES
XXX
X—X
XXX,XXØ.XX
X,XXX,XXØ.XX
TOTAL BRANCH SALES
X,XXX,XXØ.XX
XX,XXX,XXØ.XX
TOTAL COMPANY SALES
XX,XXX,XXØ.XX
XXX,XXX,XXØ.XX
NOTES:
1. EACH BRANCH'S SALES INFORMATION ON A SEPARATE PAGE
2. HEADINGS PRINTED ON TOP OF EVERY PAGE
3. REPORT DATE IS SYSTEM-SUPPLIED
4. PRINT COMPANY SALES INFORMATION ON A SEPARATE PAGE WITH FIRST TWO HEADING LINES

Input Data:

Month-to-date Sales Records:

Record ID Code	Salesman Number	Branch Number	Salesman Name	Month-to-date Sales Amount
M	123	10	RICHARD H MACY	001232415
M	234	10	JOHN GIMBEL	000863579
M	345	10	JOHN WANAMAKER	001000000
M	456	20	BERT ALTMAN	000080000
M	567	20	ROGER PEET	003200000
M	678	30	JOHN PENNY	010856700

Daily Sales Records:

Record ID Code	Salesman Number	Branch Number	SP/Unit	Daily Qty Sold	Sales Date
S	123	10	10000	020	110191
S	123	10	00500	200	110391
S	123	10	60000	002	110491
S	234	10	09000	100	110291
S	345	10	01200	500	110191
S	345	10	50000	010	110491
S	456	20	02800	050	110291
S	456	20	14000	012	110691
S	567	20	35000	006	110391
S	678	30	01850	240	110191
S	678	30	09999	050	110491
S	678	30	01999	360	110691

Note: The sales date field is not included in the report or required in processing. Fields may be included in a data record format that are not used in every program that processes the file.

chapter 10
Table Concepts and Processing

In the RPG environment, a *table* may be defined as a list of data stored in memory. The storage positions for a table are built and loaded during program execution before any other input files are read and processed. Tables include relatively *fixed* data that is referenced by other data. Tax rates, transaction codes, pay grades, pay rates, month names, and so forth are examples of data commonly included in tables.

TABLE STRUCTURE

Argument and Function Tables

Figure 10-1 illustrates six examples of table structures. A single table is referred to in RPG as a Simple Table. A table may be processed as a standalone table or be used to relate to one or more other Simple Tables.

Illustration 1

Pay Code	Hourly Rate
A	500
B	550
C	610
D	675
E	735
F	800
Argument Table	Function Table

Related tables sorted in ascending order.

Illustration 2

Item Number	Price
1234	00056
5678	00188
9123	00239
8321	00751
1789	01051
Argument Table	Function Table

Smaller numeric table entries must be padded with high-order zeros. Both tables are in an unordered sequence.

Illustration 3

SS No.	Name
040000009	DROPOUT A
222222222	FAIL Y
789665555	HONORS HI
820801234	SUCCEED I
934202601	TOPP ON
Argument Table	Function Table

Smaller alphabetic (or alphanumeric) entries are padded with low-order blanks. SS No table is in ascending order and related Name table in unordered sequence.

Illustration 4

Taxable Amount	Fixed Amount	Tax Percent
035	0336	18
073	1020	21
202	3729	23
231	4396	27
269	5422	31
333	7406	35
Argument Table	Function Table 1	Function Table 2

Three tables that relate to each other. All sorted in ascending order.

Illustration 5

Item#	Brand
300	COCA COLA
500	SPRITE
400	7-UP
550	SLICE
600	FRESCA
900	HIRES ROOT BEER
100	WELCH'S GRAPE
Argument Table	Function Table

Item# table arranged in a "frequency" of processing order.

Illustration 6

Special Characters
&
*
#
:
@
?
/
Argument Table

Single table of special characters in unordered sequence

Notes:

1. Decimal points are not included in numeric table data, but implied in program (Extension form) when the table is defined.
2. Depending on the application, any table (when two or more are related) may be processed as an argument or function table.
3. Sorted order (ascending or descending) of any table processed as an argument table will control an "early exit" if the search argument value is not found.
4. Argument tables may be intentionally structured in an unordered sequence to place items that are more frequently accessed at the beginning of the table.

Figure 10-1 Examples of table structures.

Two new terms, *argument* and *function*, are introduced in Figure 10-1. An *argument table* is the one that is "looked up" by a data item called the *search argument.* A *function table* is one that relates physically and logically to an argument table. For example, the first entry in an argument table relates to the first entry in a corresponding function table. Any number of function tables may relate to an argument table; and, depending on the application, any table may be referenced as an argument or function table.

LOADING TABLES

Loading a table refers to the time in the program cycle when data is read, moved, and stored in the memory positions defined and built by an RPG program. Tables may be loaded at Compile (execution) Time or at Object (preexecution) Time. Figure 10-2 details the processing logic associated with loading a table at each time in the program cycle.

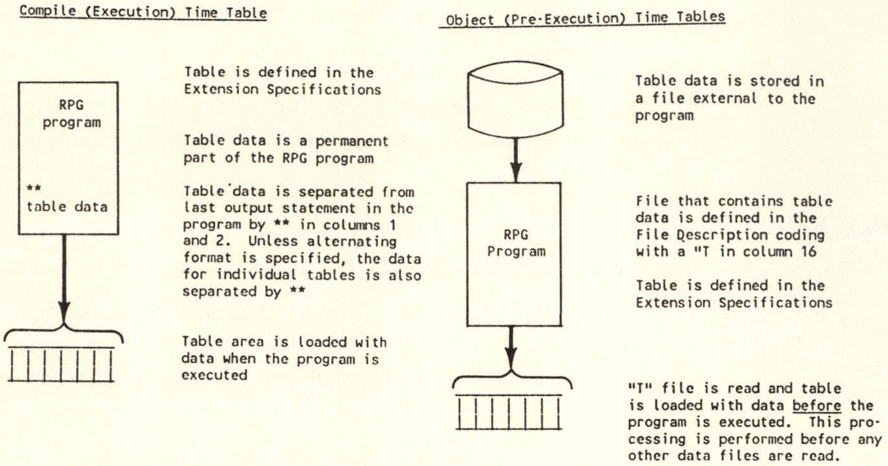

Figure 10-2 Processing logic for loading tables at Compile and Object Times.

TABLE DESCRIPTION

The number of table entries, size of an entry, type, and sequence (referred to as attributes) are specified in the Extension Specifications. This form allocates the table's total storage area before the loading of data. Refer to Figure 10-3 for an explanation of the fields used to define a table at Compile and Object Times. *Notice that all table names must begin with the letters TAB* with one, two, or three additional programmer-supplied characters (1–9, A–Z, #, $).

Extension Specifications

Line (3–5)	Form Type (6)	7–8	Record Sequence of the Chaining Field / Number of the Chaining Field (9–10)	From Filename (11–18)	To Filename (19–26)	Table or Array Name (27–32)	Number of Entries Per Record (33–35)	Number of Entries Per Table or Array (36–39)	Length of Entry (40–42)	P/B/L/R (43)	Decimal Positions (44)	Sequence (A/D) (45)	Table or Array Name (Alternating Format) (46–51)	Length of Entry (52–54)	P/B/L/R (55)	Decimal Positions (56)	Sequence (A/D) (57)	Comments (58–74)
01Ø	E					TAB1	12	12	2		Ø	A						COMPILE TIME
02Ø	E			TABLFILE		TAB2	1	12	9									OBJECT TIME
03Ø	E					TAB3	1	12	2		Ø	A	TAB4	9				COMPILE TIME
04Ø	E	*																ALTERNATING FORM

Figure 10-3 Fields used in the Extension Specifications to define tables at Compile and Object Times.

Explanation of Fields:

1. Extension instructions are identified by the letter E in column 6 and follow F specification statements.

2. Columns 7-10: Not used.

3. From Filename (Columns 11-18): Required for object (pre-execution) time tables. Related file must be defined in File Description as an input table file (I in column 15, T in column 16, and an E in column 39).

4. To Filename (Columns 19-26): If a copy of the table is required (to disk, tape, printer, or CRT), the related output file defined in File Description must be entered in this field. This option is commonly used when the table has been updated during processing and is to be verified.

5. Table Name (Columns 27-32): All table names must begin with the letters TAB. One, two, or three additional character(s) must be programmer-supplied (1-9, A-Z, #, $).

6. Number of Entries Per Record (Columns 33-35): Required entry that indicates how the table data is stored in the records. The number of table entries stored on a disk, diskette, or tape record depends on the maximum record size supported by the media.

7. Number of Entries Per Table (Columns 36-39): Required entry that builds (dimensions) the table with the number elements specified in this field. A 12 formats a twelve element table; 150, a one-hundred and fifty element table; and so forth.

8. Length of Entry (Columns 40-42): Required entry that defines the size of the table entries. Numeric table entries may be a maximum of 15 bytes and alphanumeric 256.

9. P = Packed/B = Binary (Column 43): If the numeric table data is stored in a zoned decimal format, this field is blank. When the table data is packed (internal decimal format), the letter P must be entered. Numeric table data that is stored as binary, must be identified by entering a B in this field (not a commonly used format).

10. Decimal Positions (Column 44): A blank in this field indicates the table is alphanumeric. A number 0-9 entered defines a table as numeric and assigns implied decimal positions for processing.

11. Sequence (A/D) (Column 45): If the table data is in an unordered sequence, this field must be blank. When the data is sorted in ascending order, the letter A may be entered. If the data is in a descending order, D may be entered. "Early exit" is provided for an unsuccessful equal lookup condition if the argument table data is in a sorted order.

12. Table Name (Alternating Format) (Columns 46-51): Alternating format indicates that two or more entries from two related tables are stored on each record. For example, one data entry for TAB1 followed by one data entry for TAB2. Number of Entries Per Record specifies how many "pairs" are included on a record.

13. Columns 52-57: Relate to attributes of alternating table. Refer to items 8, 9, 10 and 11 above for an explanation of these fields.

(Continued)

RPG SYNTAX FOR COMPILE TIME TABLES

Figure 10-2 indicated that Compile Time table data is an integral (hard-coded) part of an RPG program. The table data is included after a ** control statement entered in columns 1 and 2, and follows the last output (O) statement in the program. Unless an alternating sequence is specified, the data for two or more tables must also be separated by a ** statement. Figure 10-4 shows the relationship of the Extension form coding and the data for two Compile Time tables.

Extension Specifications Coding:

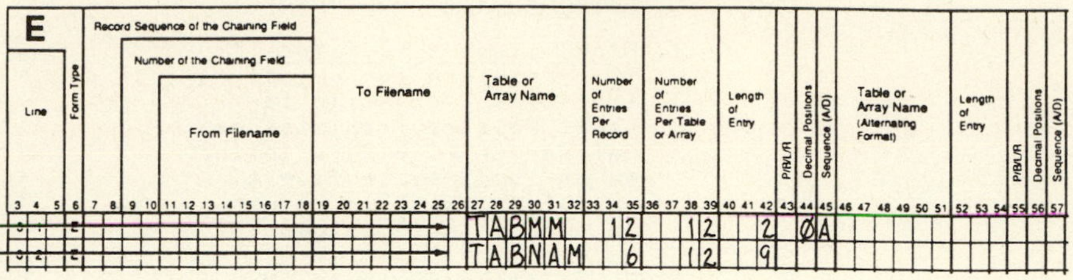

Extension Specifications
E
Line
Form Type
Record Sequence of the Chaining Field
Number of the Chaining Field
From Filename
To Filename
Table or Array Name
Number of Entries Per Record
Number of Entries Per Table or Array
Length of Entry
P/B/L/R
Decimal Positions
Sequence (A/D)
Table or Array Name (Alternating Format)
Length of Entry
P/B/L/R
Decimal Positions
Sequence (A/D)
TABMM 12 12 2 ØA
TABNAM 6 12 9


```
        .
        .
            (other RPG program statements)
        .
        .
    O                           (last output specifications statement)
**                              (delimits compile time table from program)
010203040506070809101112                  Compile time tables
**                                         separated by **
JANUARY  FEBRUARY MARCH    APRIL    MAY      JUNE      Data values for a table
JULY     AUGUST   SEPTEMBEROCTOBER  NOVEMBER DECEMBER   must be the same size.
                                                        Alphanumeric values
                                                        padded with low-order
                                                        blanks

Related table data must be entered in the order the tables are
specified in the Extension form

Note:  Table data items must be size of the elements defined in the
       Extension form.  Smaller numeric data is padded with high-order
       zeros and alphanumeric data is padded with low-order blanks.
```

Figure 10-4 Extension Specification syntax and related data for two Compile Time tables.

RPG SYNTAX FOR COMPILE TIME TABLES STORED IN AN ALTERNATING FORMAT

Figure 10-5 shows the table data from the previous figure rearranged in an alternating format with the modified Extension form coding.

Extension Specifications Coding:

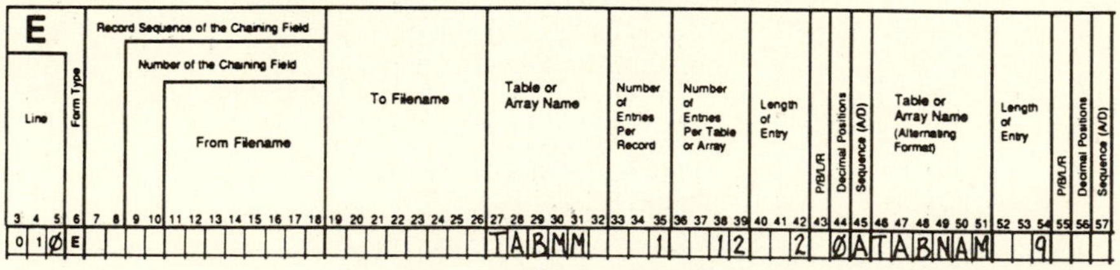


```
        .
        .
            (other RPG program statements)
        .
        .
     O<---------------------------(last output specifications statement)
**<-------------------------------(delimits compile time array from program)
01JANUARY
02FEBRUARY
03MARCH
04APRIL
05MAY
06JUNE           Alternating format specified in the Extension form as 12
07JULY           elements for each array and 1 entry per record for each
08AUGUST         table
09SEPTEMBER
10OCTOBER
11NOVEMBER
12DECEMBER
```

Figure 10-5 Extension Specification syntax and related data for two Compile Time tables arranged in an alternating format.

RPG SYNTAX FOR OBJECT TIME TABLES

Data for Object Time tables is stored externally from the program on disk, diskette, or tape files. The table is formatted and loaded with data (preexecution time) before the program is executed and any other data files are read. Tables remain in storage for the complete program cycle and, unless updated by the program, are not changed.

Figure 10-6 illustrates the syntax required in an RPG program to define Object Time tables when the data is stored on disk. The example assumes the same month number and name table data as in Figure 10-5. The File Description form must define the file that contains the table data. However, in addition to the usual entries (I in column 15, etc.), the letter T is entered in column 16 and E in column 39. T indicates to the program that the file is to be processed as a table file and that the tables are to be loaded before other input files are read. E specifies that the attributes of the table are defined in the Extension form instead of on the Input Specifications.

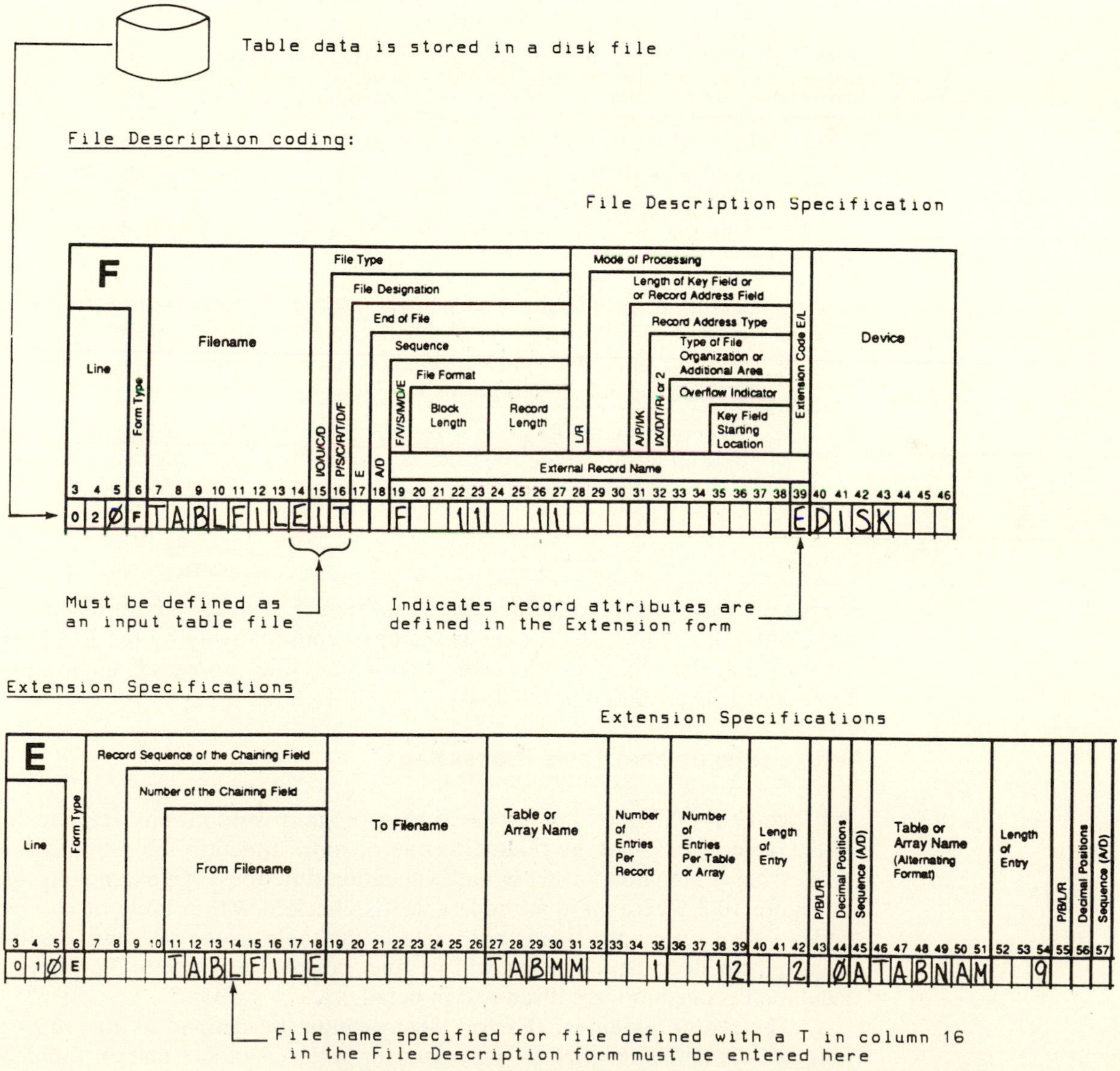

Figure 10-6 File Description and Extension Specification syntax for Object Time tables. Data arranged in an alternating format.

A limitation of table files is that a maximum of two tables (if an alternating format is used) may be included in one file. Additional files would need to be built and loaded if more than two tables were required.

FORMAT OF TABLE DATA

The records that store the data for Compile and Object Time tables must be formatted according to the rules explained in Figure 10-7. The decision on whether

```
1. Data must begin in first column of each record.

2. Entries for a table must be the same size.

3. Smaller numeric elements must be padded with high-order zeros and
   smaller alphanumeric elements must be padded with low-order blanks.

4. When alternating sequence is used for the data for two tables, the
   values for the tables must be included on a record based on the
   Number of Entries Per Record entry in the Extension form. Values
   may not be separated on two records.

5. Order of the data in a Compile Time table must relate to the Extension
   entry. The first table defined must have its data included first at
   the end of the program (after a ** statement), and so forth.
```

Figure 10-7 Rules for formatting the table data records for Compile and Object Time.

to use a Compile or Object Time table in a program generally depends on the following:

1. Compile Time tables are used when the table contains few entries, data is not likely to change, and/or data is not shared by other programs. The month/name tables previously shown are examples of the program data included in this type of table.
2. Object Time tables are used when tables contain many entries, data is frequently updated, and/or data is used by other programs.

PROCESSING TABLES

So far the RPG syntax to define tables has been explained without discussion of how tables are processed. A table is searched consecutively by the LOKUP operation, and depending on the table's structure, until an equal, high-range, or low-range test condition is satisfied.

Single (Standalone) Table Processing

An argument table may be processed by a program without any relationship to other tables, or it may be related to one or more function tables. Single table processing is commonly used in data validation functions. An example is shown in Figure 10-8 where an input code value is checked with a table of acceptable codes. When an input value is not found in the table, some alternative action is usually provided. This concept will be fully covered in Chapter 12 where data validation procedures are discussed in detail.

The search argument (Factor 1 entry) must be defined as the *same type* (numeric or alphanumeric) as the argument table (Factor 2 entry). Some RPG compilers also require that the size of the search argument and argument table be the same.

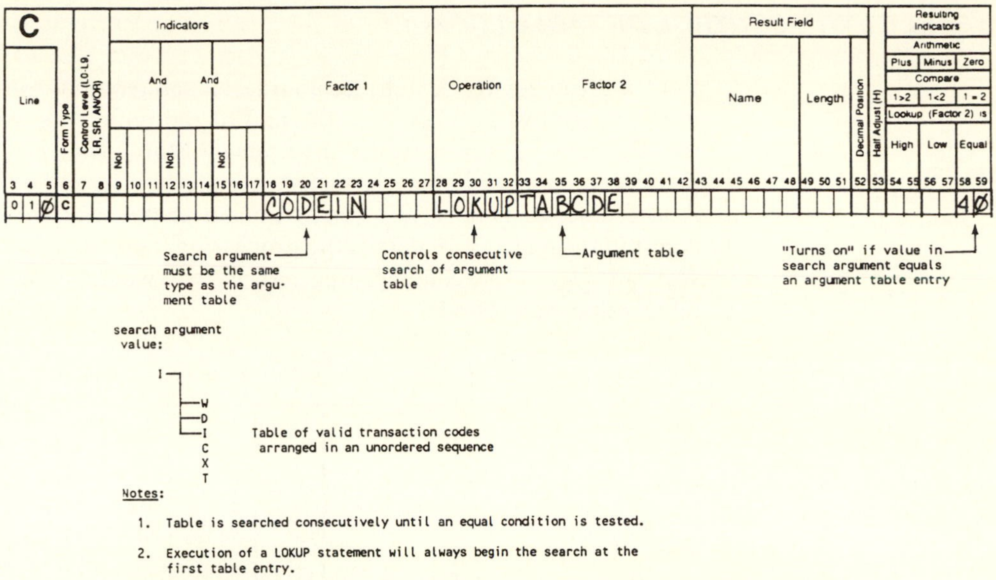

Figure 10-8 Syntax and processing logic for an equal lookup of one table.

Related Table Processing

In addition to single table processing, two or more tables may relate to each other. An argument table is searched, and when the lookup condition is satisfied, the related value from a function table is accessed. Figure 10-9 details the syntax and logic associated with the processing of three related tables.

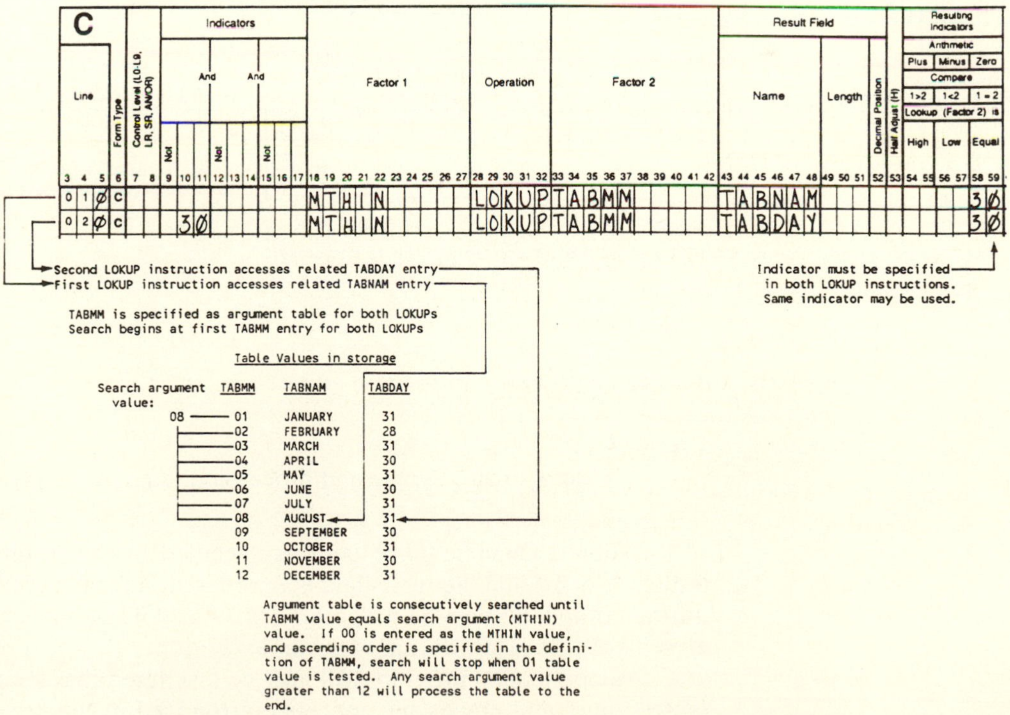

Figure 10-9 Syntax and processing logic for an equal "lookup" of related tables.

"EARLY EXIT" CONTROL OF TABLE LOOKUP

For an unsuccessful search, an unordered sequence of the table data will cause program control to process to the end of the table. For small tables this is not significant. It is, however, for large tables. More efficient processing is provided if the argument table data is sorted in either an ascending or descending order. A sorted order supports an "early exit" for an unsuccessful "equal" table lookup condition. Figure 10-10 details the processing logic of an "early exit." If the table was sorted in a descending order, early exit would be executed when a lower table value was tested.

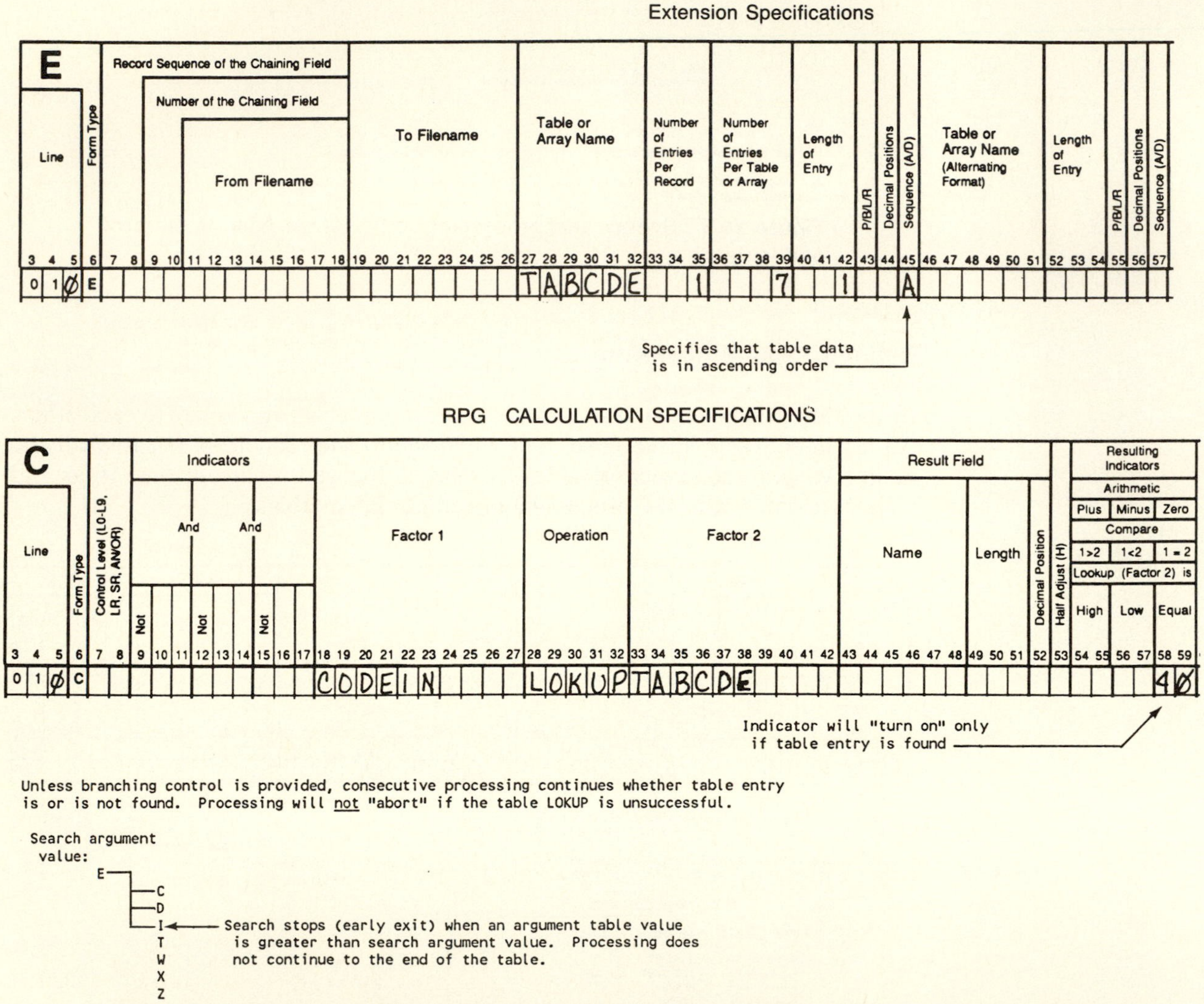

Figure 10-10 Syntax and processing logic for "early exit" control.

When a Compile Time table is specified in the Extension form as sorted (either A or D) and the table data is unordered, a terminal error will be generated during compilation of the program. For Object Time tables, however, sequence errors are "flagged" during program execution.

An application program will now be discussed that incorporates most of the table syntax and processing concepts introduced in the previous paragraphs.

APPLICATION PROGRAM—WEEKLY PAYROLL REPORT

Documentation

The specifications presented in Figure 10-11 explain the processing requirements for an application program that generates a weekly payroll report. The System

PROGRAM SPECIFICATIONS Page 1 of 1

Program Name WEEKLY PAYROLL REPORT Program-ID CH10P1 Written By S. Myers

Purpose Weekly payroll rpt for hourly employees Approved By The Boss

Input files (directory names):

DATA10P1

Output files (directory names):

PRINTER (stock paper)

Processing Narrative:

Write an RPG structured program to generate a weekly payroll report for day and night shift hourly employees.

Input to the Program:

The weekly payroll file includes the weekly payroll information for day and night shift hourly employees. A supplemental record layout form details the format of the data records.

Processing:

Provide for the following compile time tables in the program:

1. A table for month numbers and another for the related month name.
2. Tables for labor grades, day shift rates, and night shift rates.

Table data:

Labor Grades	Day Rates	Night Rates
A	0800	0900
B	1000	1150
C	1275	1525
D	1600	1800
E	1950	2300

Lookup the month number table with the month value from the first record processed to extract the related month name for the second heading line. Use day and year values from the same record for the third heading line.

Test the shift field for D or N and lookup the labor grade table to access the related shift rate. Two LOKUP statements must be provided; one to extract the day rates and the other for the night rates.

For a successful search of the grade table, compute the week's pay for the employee by multiplying the hours worked by the accessed rate table value. If the search is unsuccessful, print the error message ....LABOR GRADE NOT VALID.... . Refer to the print chart for the location of this message.

Add each employee's wages to an accumulator and print at LR time.

Output:

Refer to the supplemental printer spacing chart and code the output accordingly.

Figure 10-11 Specifications for an application program using tables that generates a weekly payroll report.

flowchart in Figure 10-12 indicates that one input disk file and one output printer file are processed by the program. Figure 10-13 details the record format of the input file. The Labor Grade field will be used as the *search argument* in the

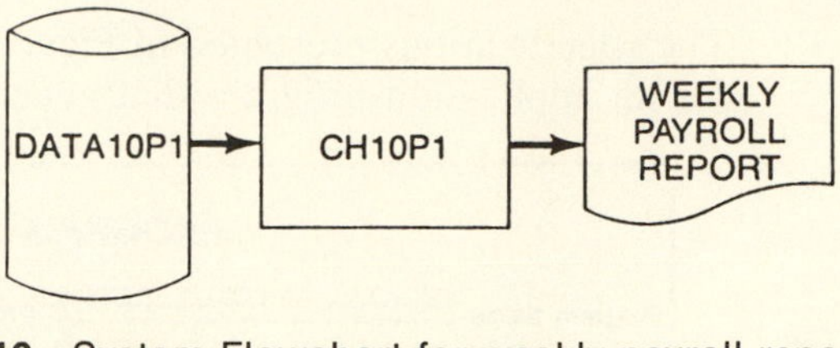

Figure 10-12 System Flowchart for weekly payroll report program.

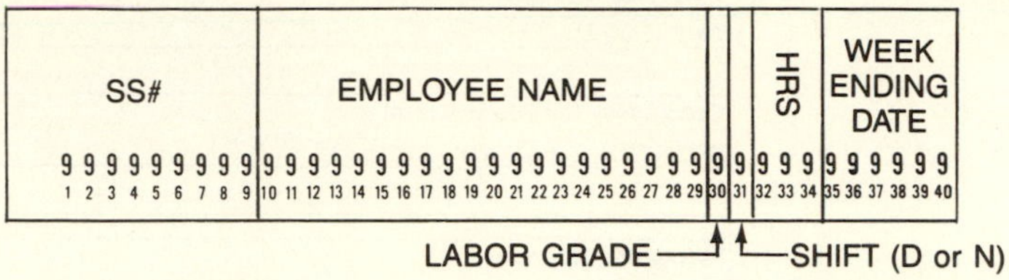

Figure 10-13 Record layout form for input file processed by the weekly payroll report program.

LOKUP operations. The design of the Weekly Payroll Report is shown in Figure 10-14, and the report generated by it is shown in Figure 10-15.

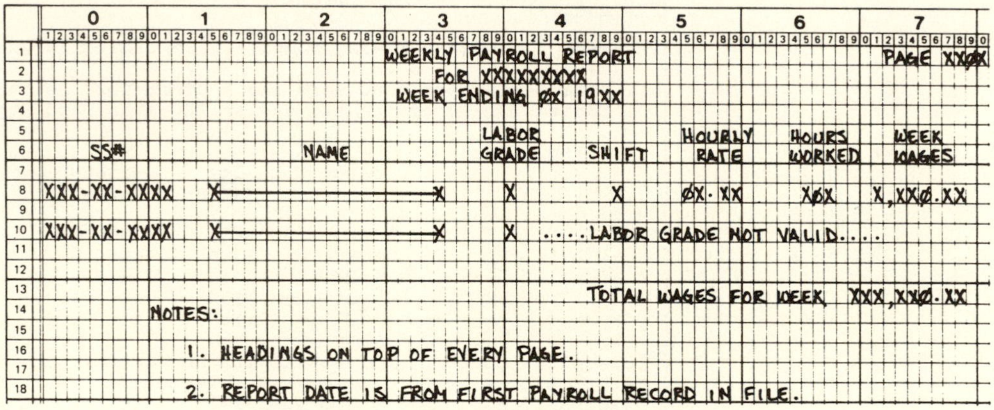

Figure 10-14 Design of Weekly Payroll Report.

```
                         WEEKLY PAYROLL REPORT                    PAGE    1
                              FOR SEPTEMBER
                          WEEK ENDING  9/16/92

                                      LABOR              HOURLY    HOURS    WEEK
      SS#              NAME           GRADE    SHIFT      RATE     WORKED   WAGES

011-11-1111   DONALD DRAKE              E        D        19.50      40     780.00

022-22-2222   LAMONT CRANSTON           A        N         9.00      32     288.00

033-33-3333   MICKEY MOUSE              C        D        12.75      37     471.75

044-44-4444   RICHARD TRACY             F    ....LABOR GRADE NOT  VALID....

055-55-5555   PAUL VALIANT              D        N        18.00      35     630.00

066-66-6666   MORTIMER SNERD            B        D        10.00      30     300.00

077-77-7777   ANDREW GUMP               E        N        23.00      40     920.00

                                          TOTAL WAGES FOR WEEK     3,389.75
```

Figure 10-15 Report generated by Weekly Payroll program.

Source Program Coding

Examine the source listing in Figure 10-16, and notice the following control for heading output:

> Because the 1P (first) cycle does not access data and the second heading line includes a variable (month name), the timing of that output must wait

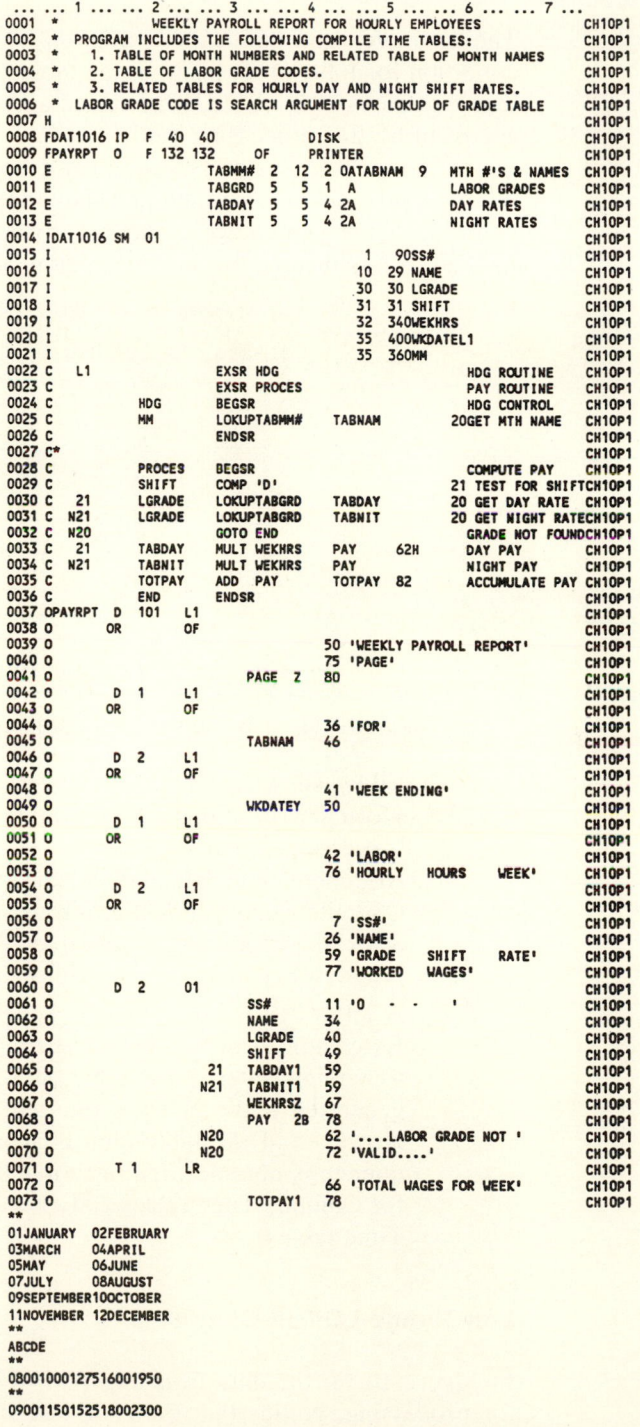

```
... ... 1 ... ... 2 ... ... 3 ... ... 4 ... ... 5 ... ... 6 ... ... 7 ...
0001 *            WEEKLY PAYROLL REPORT FOR HOURLY EMPLOYEES              CH10P1
0002 *  PROGRAM INCLUDES THE FOLLOWING COMPILE TIME TABLES:               CH10P1
0003 *    1. TABLE OF MONTH NUMBERS AND RELATED TABLE OF MONTH NAMES      CH10P1
0004 *    2. TABLE OF LABOR GRADE CODES.                                  CH10P1
0005 *    3. RELATED TABLES FOR HOURLY DAY AND NIGHT SHIFT RATES.         CH10P1
0006 *  LABOR GRADE CODE IS SEARCH ARGUMENT FOR LOKUP OF GRADE TABLE      CH10P1
0007 H                                                                    CH10P1
0008 FDAT1016 IP  F  40  40            DISK                               CH10P1
0009 FPAYRPT  O   F 132 132     OF     PRINTER                            CH10P1
0010 E                    TABMM#  2  12  2 0ATABNAM  9   MTH #'S & NAMES  CH10P1
0011 E                    TABGRD  5   5  1  A            LABOR GRADES     CH10P1
0012 E                    TABDAY  5   5  4 2A            DAY RATES        CH10P1
0013 E                    TABNIT  5   5  4 2A            NIGHT RATES      CH10P1
0014 IDAT1016 SM  01                                                      CH10P1
0015 I                                          1   90SS#                 CH10P1
0016 I                                         10  29 NAME                CH10P1
0017 I                                         30  30 LGRADE              CH10P1
0018 I                                         31  31 SHIFT               CH10P1
0019 I                                         32  340WEKHRS              CH10P1
0020 I                                         35  400WKDATEL1            CH10P1
0021 I                                         35  360MM                  CH10P1
0022 C   L1               EXSR HDG                        HDG ROUTINE     CH10P1
0023 C                    EXSR PROCES                     PAY ROUTINE     CH10P1
0024 C         HDG        BEGSR                           HDG CONTROL     CH10P1
0025 C         MM         LOKUPTABMM#    TABNAM         20GET MTH NAME    CH10P1
0026 C                    ENDSR                                           CH10P1
0027 C*                                                                   CH10P1
0028 C         PROCES     BEGSR                           COMPUTE PAY     CH10P1
0029 C         SHIFT      COMP 'D'                      21 TEST FOR SHIFTCH10P1
0030 C   21    LGRADE     LOKUPTABGRD    TABDAY         20 GET DAY RATE   CH10P1
0031 C  N21    LGRADE     LOKUPTABGRD    TABNIT         20 GET NIGHT RATECH10P1
0032 C  N20               GOTO END                        GRADE NOT FOUNDCH10P1
0033 C   21    TABDAY     MULT WEKHRS    PAY     62H      DAY PAY         CH10P1
0034 C  N21    TABNIT     MULT WEKHRS    PAY              NIGHT PAY       CH10P1
0035 C         TOTPAY     ADD  PAY       TOTPAY  82       ACCUMULATE PAY  CH10P1
0036 C         END        ENDSR                                           CH10P1
0037 OPAYRPT  D  101   L1                                                 CH10P1
0038 O        OR       OF                                                 CH10P1
0039 O                              50 'WEEKLY PAYROLL REPORT'            CH10P1
0040 O                              75 'PAGE'                             CH10P1
0041 O                    PAGE  Z   80                                    CH10P1
0042 O         D  1    L1                                                 CH10P1
0043 O        OR       OF                                                 CH10P1
0044 O                              36 'FOR'                              CH10P1
0045 O                    TABNAM    46                                    CH10P1
0046 O         D  2    L1                                                 CH10P1
0047 O        OR       OF                                                 CH10P1
0048 O                              41 'WEEK ENDING'                      CH10P1
0049 O                    WKDATEY   50                                    CH10P1
0050 O         D  1    L1                                                 CH10P1
0051 O        OR       OF                                                 CH10P1
0052 O                              42 'LABOR'                            CH10P1
0053 O                              76 'HOURLY   HOURS    WEEK'           CH10P1
0054 O         D  2    L1                                                 CH10P1
0055 O        OR       OF                                                 CH10P1
0056 O                               7 'SS#'                              CH10P1
0057 O                              26 'NAME'                             CH10P1
0058 O                              59 'GRADE    SHIFT    RATE'           CH10P1
0059 O                              77 'WORKED   WAGES'                   CH10P1
0060 O         D  2    01                                                 CH10P1
0061 O                    SS#       11 '0    -  -    '                    CH10P1
0062 O                    NAME      34                                    CH10P1
0063 O                    LGRADE    40                                    CH10P1
0064 O                    SHIFT     49                                    CH10P1
0065 O                 21 TABDAY1   59                                    CH10P1
0066 O                N21 TABNIT1   59                                    CH10P1
0067 O                    WEKHRSZ   67                                    CH10P1
0068 O                    PAY   2B  78                                    CH10P1
0069 O                N20           62 '....LABOR GRADE NOT '             CH10P1
0070 O                N20           72 'VALID....'                        CH10P1
0071 O         T 1     LR                                                 CH10P1
0072 O                              66 'TOTAL WAGES FOR WEEK'             CH10P1
0073 O                    TOTPAY1   78                                    CH10P1
**
01JANUARY  02FEBRUARY
03MARCH    04APRIL
05MAY      06JUNE
07JULY     08AUGUST
09SEPTEMBER10OCTOBER
11NOVEMBER 12DECEMBER
**
ABCDE
**
080010001275160019500
**
09001150152518002300
```

Figure 10-16 Source listing of Weekly Payroll Report program.

until the first record is processed. Exception (EXCPT) with the line counter method explained in Chapters 7 and 9 could have been used to control all output. However, for simplicity, the control of headings with the standard RPG logic cycle is used.

RANGE LOKUP CONTROL

The examples and application program presented have all used an *equal* test condition for table processing. Some tables, however, are structured in a format that requires a *range* LOKUP. Federal and state income tax tables are generally accessed by this processing method.

Figure 10-17 illustrates a state's tax tables used to determine the tax liability on dividends and interest income. The taxpayer's Adjusted Gross Income (AGI) determines the percentage of tax on dividends and interest income. No tax is applied to this income for any AGI below $54,000.

ADJUSTED GROSS INCOME

At Least	But Less Than	
$ 54,000	$ 58,000	1%
58,000	62,000	2%
62,000	66,000	3%
66,000	70,000	4%
70,000	74,000	5%
74,000	78,000	6%
78,000	82,000	7%
82,000	86,000	8%
86,000	90,000	9%
90,000	100,000	11%
100,000 AND OVER		12%

Low range — High range — Rate (function table)

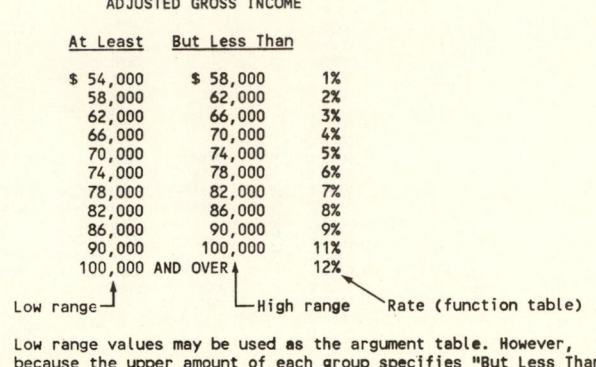

Low range values may be used as the argument table. However, because the upper amount of each group specifies "But Less Than", the values have to reduced by 1 to support high range processing.

Figure 10-17 Tax tables for a state's dividends and interest income.

The tables shown in Figure 10-17 require processing by *range* LOKUP control. Table format restrictions to support this processing method are the following:

1. Argument table data must be sorted in an ascending or descending order. Compile Time tables that are unordered will be flagged by a terminal error in compilation. Unordered Object Time will not be identified until program execution, which will then cause processing to abort.
2. A letter A (or D) should be specified in the sequence column of the Extension form for the related table. If sequence is not specified, an ascending order of the table data is assumed. A warning error will be generated if the entry is omitted and the data is in ascending order. However, if the table data is arranged in a descending order and sequence is not specified, a terminal error during compilation will result for Compile Time tables and execution time error will occur for Object Time tables.

Low Range LOKUP Control

In Figure 10-18, the data from Figure 10-17 has been formatted into two tables for processing. Notice that the At Least values (low range) have been used as the argument table data and the related percentages used for the function table entries. When low-range processing is specified, the high-range (But Less Than) values are not needed.

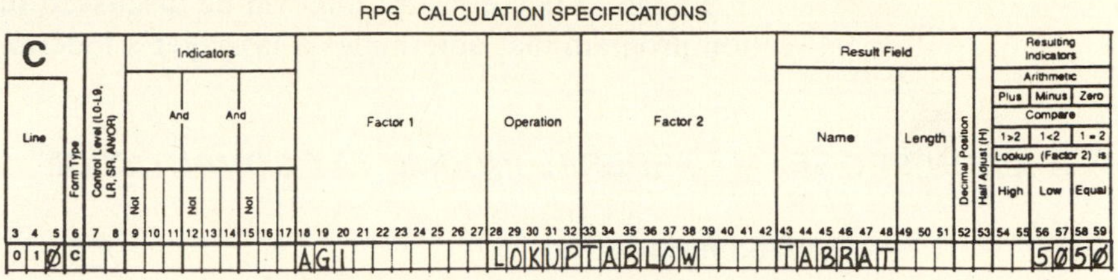


```
For low range LOKUP, same indicator must be entered in Low and Equal fields

Low Range LOKUP Processing Logic (Argument table must be in an A or D order)

Search argument    Low range    Rate
 value:              table      Table
        72000
                   54000         01
                   58000         02
                   62000         03
                   66000         04
                   70000 - - -   05
                   74000         06
                   78000         07
                   82000         08
                   86000         09
                   90000         11
                  100000         12
   argument table               function table

Table is searched consecutively until an equal or higher table value is found.
If a higher table value is tested, control "backs up" one entry.  Search for this
example will continue until table value 74000 is tested, then "back-ups" and points
to 70000 entry (and related function table entry) for processing.
```

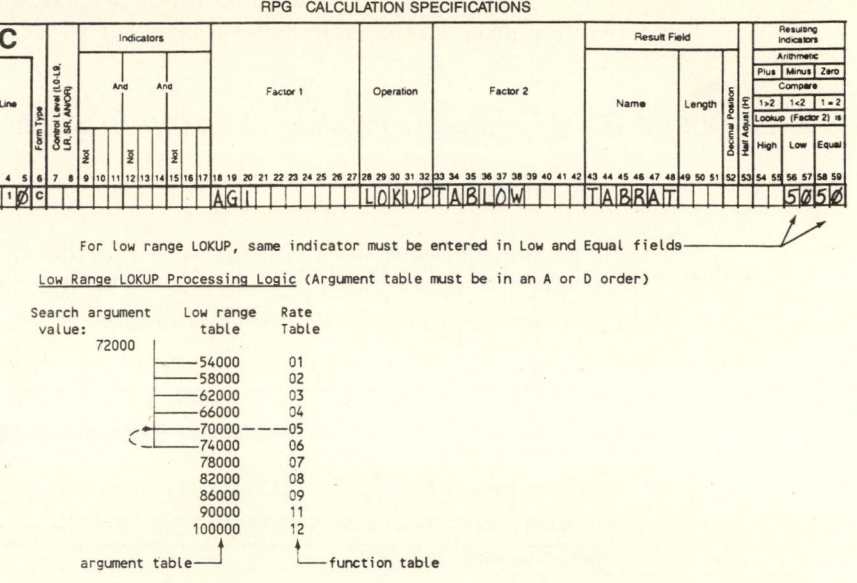

Figure 10-18 Structure of tables and processing logic for Low-Range LOKUP control.

High-Range LOKUP Control

An examination of Figure 10-19 shows that the data from Figure 10-17 has been reformatted for high-range table LOKUP processing. Notice that the But Less Than values have been reduced by 1 for each entry. Because the high amount of

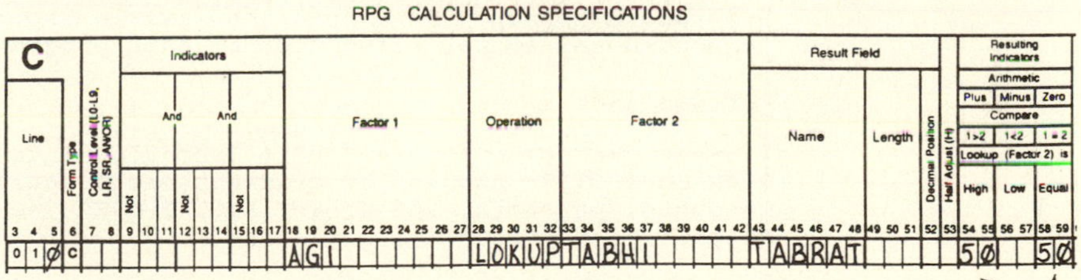


```
For high range LOKUP, same indicator must be entered in High and Equal fields

High Range LOKUP Processing Logic  (Argument table data must be in an A or D order)

Search argument   High range    Rate
 value:             table       Table
       72000
                   57999         01
                   61999         02
                   65999         03
                   69999         04      Because a "But less than" limit is specified
                 - -73999 - - -  05       for high range (see Figure 10-17), the value
                   77999         06       for each entry has to be modified with 1 less
                   81999         07       than related base table amount (i.e. from 58000
                   85999         08       to 57999).
                   89999         09
                   99999         11
                  999999         12      Needed for search argument values = or > 100,000
   argument table               function table

Table is searched consecutively until an equal to or higher table value is found.  Search
for this example will continue until table value 73999 is tested.  Then, any related function
table value may be accessed.  No additional movement of the "pointer" occurs with Higher/Equal
LOKUP.
```

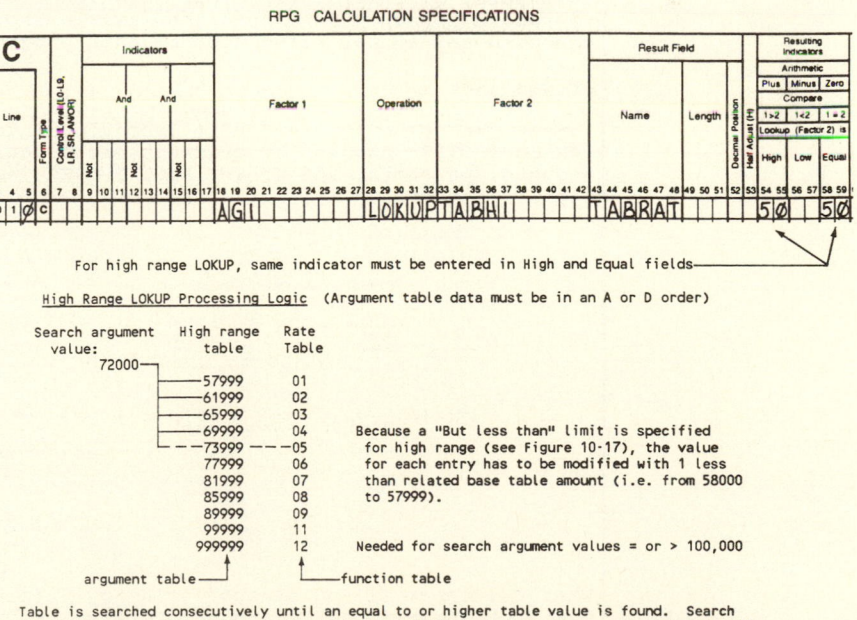

Figure 10-19 Structure of tables and processing logic for High Range LOKUP control.

a range relates to values less than those specified in Figure 10-17, the original table amounts must be reduced accordingly.

Range LOKUP processing will be discussed further in the following application program that determines a taxpayer's federal income tax liability.

APPLICATION PROGRAM—FEDERAL INCOME TAX COMPUTATION

Documentation

The specifications shown in Figure 10-20 detail the processing requirements for an application program that computes the federal income tax liability for taxpayers who have a filing status of Single, Married–Filing Jointly, Married–Filing Sep-

PROGRAM SPECIFICATIONS Page 1 of 1

Program Name FEDERAL TAX REPORT Program-ID CH10P2 Written By S. Myers

Purpose Federal Income Tax Liability Report Approved By The Boss

Input files (directory names):

DATA10P2 (stored on disk)

Output files (directory names):

PRINTER (stock paper)

Processing Narrative:

Write a structured RPG program to generate a Federal Income Tax Liability Report for individual taxpayers.

<u>Input to the program</u>:

The data file contains records with the information for individual taxpayers. The attached layout form identifies the fields included in record format. Note that the Taxable Income amount was previously computed and is not a function of this program.

<u>Processing</u>:

Format the following four Rate Schedules into 16 Compile Time tables (use OVER- amounts as argument table entries with related fixed amounts, percents, and OF THE AMOUNT OVER- as function tables for each filing status):

<u>Schedule X</u> - Single Taxpayers

If taxable income is

Over-	but not over-	The tax:	of the amount over-
$ 0	$17,850	.... 15%	$ 0
17,850	43,150	$ 2,677.50 + 28%	17,850
43,150	89,560	9,761.50 + 28%	43,150
89,560	......	.... 28%	0

Schedule Y - Married Taxpayers - Filing Separate Returns

If taxable income is

Over-	but not over-	The tax:	of the amount over-
$ 0	$ 14,875	.... 15%	$ 0
14,875	35,950	$ 2,231.25 + 28%	14,875
35,950	113,300	8,132.25 + 28%	35,950
113,300	....	.... 28%	0

<u>Schedule Y</u> - Married Taxpayers - Filing Joint Returns and Qualifying Widows and Widowers

If taxable income is

Over-	but not over-	The tax:	of the amount over-
$ 0	$ 29,750	.... 15%	$ 0
29,750	71,900	$ 4,462.50 + 28%	29,750
71,900	149,250	16,264.50 + 28%	71,900
149,250	....	.... 28%	0

<u>Schedule Z</u> - Heads of Household

If taxable income is

Over-	but not over-	The tax:	of the amount over-
$ 0	$ 23,900	.... 15%	$ 0
23,900	61,650	$ 3,585.00 + 28%	23,900
61,650	123,790	14,155.00 + 28%	61,650
123,790	....	.... 28%	0

Test the input filing status field for S (single), J (married-filing jointly), M (married-filing separately), and H (head of household) and execute a related subroutine to lookup the argument table.

Figure 10-20 Specifications for program that computes a taxpayer's federal income tax liability for every filing status.

The following calculations are required:

1. Lookup the appropriate low range table (OVER- amounts) with the taxable income input field and extract the fixed amount from the related function table.

2. Lookup the same low range argument table and extract the related "OF THE AMOUNT OVER-" value from the related function table.

3. Lookup the same low range argument table and extract the related percent value the related function table.

4. Subtract the "OF THE AMOUNT OVER-" amount (step 2) from the taxable income and store the difference in a work field.

5. Multiply the difference (step 4) by the table percent (step 3) and store in an output field for the tax due.

6. Add the fixed table amount (step 1) to the tax due field (step 5) to compute the total Federal Income Tax due for the taxpayer.

With the exception of the different tables, the six steps detailed above are identical for each filing status.

<u>Output</u>:

Generate the report shown in the attached printer spacing chart in accordance with the following considerations:

1. Use stock paper.
2. Headings on the top of every page.
3. Extract the tax year for second heading line from the first data record.

(Continued)

arately, or Head of Household. Input and output files processed by the program are identified in the system flowchart shown in Figure 10-21. The format of the records in the input file and a listing of the data are detailed in Figure 10-22. The

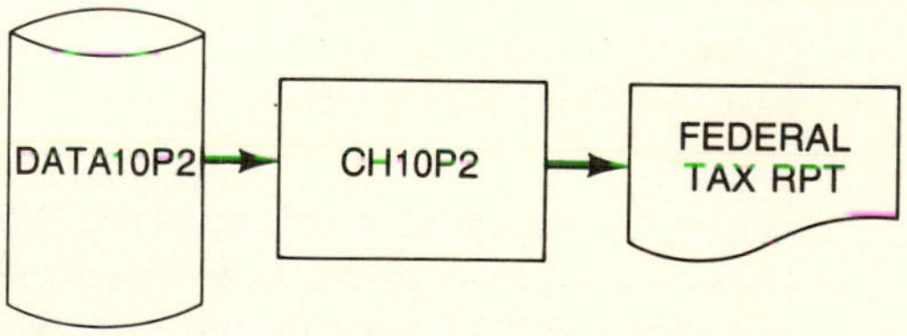

Figure 10-21 System flowchart for federal income tax report program.

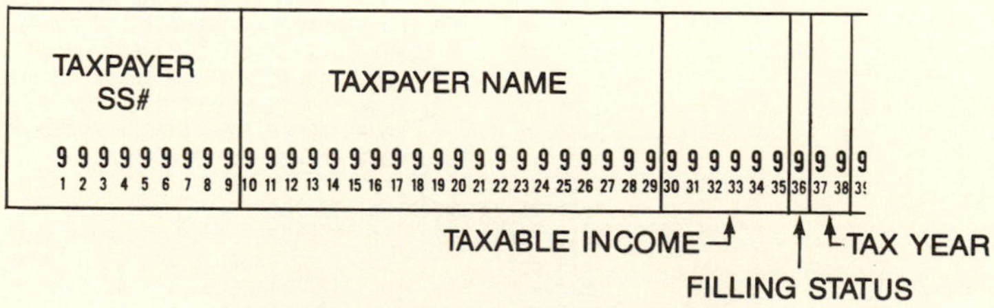


```
011111111DONALD & DAISY DRAKE050000J88
022222222LAMONT CRANSTON     080000H88
033333333MIKE & MINA MOUSE   200000J88
044444444RICHARD TRACY       010000M88
055555555PAUL VALIANT        023901H88
066666666MORTIMER SNERD      014875M88
077777777ANDREW GUMP         100000S88
```

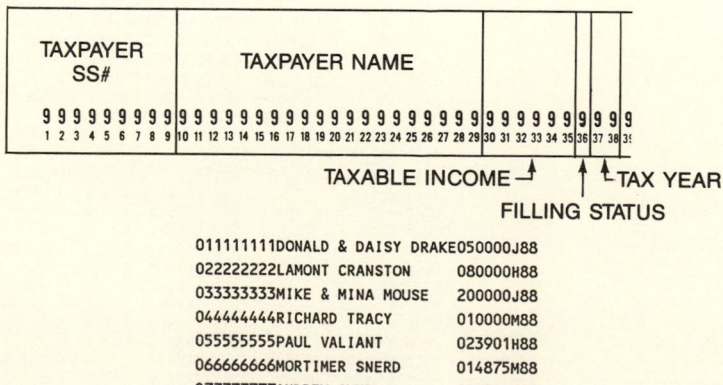

Figure 10-22 Record layout and listing of input file data processed by the federal income tax report program.

printer spacing chart in Figure 10-23 details the design of the report. A listing of the printed report generated by the program is shown in Figure 10-24.

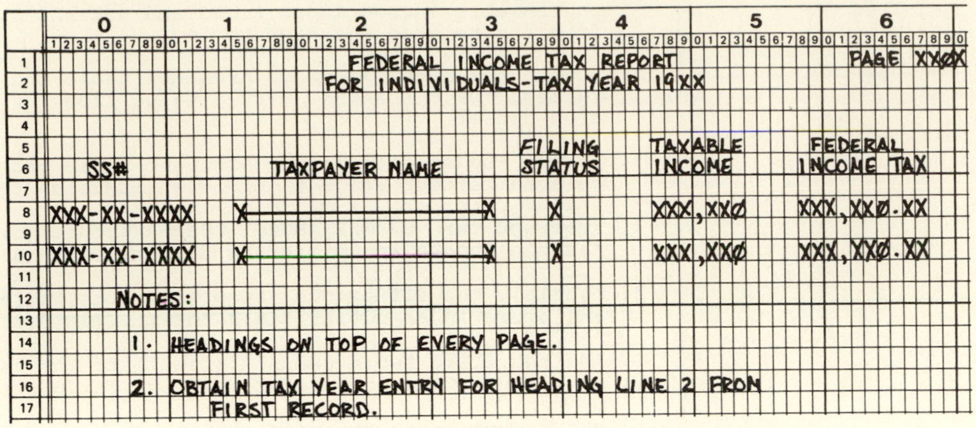

Figure 10-23 Design of the federal income tax report.

```
                        FEDERAL INCOME TAX REPORT              PAGE     1
                      FOR INDIVIDUALS-TAX YEAR 1988

                                           FILING   TAXABLE     FEDERAL
    SS#              TAXPAYER NAME         STATUS   INCOME     INCOME TAX

011-11-1111     DONALD & DAISY DRAKE         J       50,000     10,132.50

022-22-2222     LAMONT CRANSTON              H       80,000     19,293.00

033-33-3333     MIKE & MINA MOUSE            J      200,000     56,000.00

044-44-4444     RICHARD TRACY                S       10,000      1,500.00

055-55-5555     PAUL VALIANT                 H       23,901      3,585.28

066-66-6666     MORTIMER SNERD               M       14,875      2,231.25

077-77-7777     ANDREW GUMP                  S      100,000     28,000.00
```

Figure 10-24 Report generated by federal income tax report program.

Source Program Coding

A commented source listing of the federal income tax report application program is presented in Figure 10-25. Details related to the structure and processing logic are supported in separate illustrations.

```
... ... 1 ... ... 2 ... ... 3 ... ... 4 ... ... 5 ... ... 6 ... ... 7 ...
 *                    FEDERAL INCOME TAX REPORT                       CH10P2
 *       FOR INDIVIDUAL TAXPAYERS - FOR EVERY FILING STATUS           CH10P2
 *       16 COMPILE TABLE ARE DEFINED, WHICH INCLUDE:                 CH10P2
 *         1. FOUR TABLES FOR LOW RANGE AMOUNTS.                      CH10P2
 *         2. FOUR TABLES FOR FIXED AMOUNTS.                          CH10P2
 *         3. FOUR TABLES FOR FIXED TAX AMOUNTS.                      CH10P2
 *         4. FOUR TABLES FOR PERCENTS.                               CH10P2
H                                                                     CH10P2
FDATA10P2IP  F  38  38            DISK                                CH10P2
FTAXREPRTO   F 132 132     OF     PRINTER                             CH10P2
E                    TABS$   1   4  6 0ATABSF$  6 2 SINGLE LOW & FIX$CH10P2
E                    TABSLO  4   4  5 0             SINGLE LOW AMT   CH10P2
E                    TABSPT  4   4  2 2             SINGLE-PCT       CH10P2
E                    TABJ$   1   4  6 0ATABJF$  7 2 JOINT LOW & FIX$ CH10P2
E                    TABJLO  4   4  6 0             JOINT LOW AMT    CH10P2
E                    TABJPT  4   4  2 2             JOINT-PCT      : CH10P2
E                    TABM$   1   4  6 0ATABMF$  6 2 MAR-SEP INC & FIXCH10P2
E                    TABMLO  4   4  6 0             MAR-SEP LOW      CH10P2
E                    TABMPT  4   4  2 2             MAR-SEP PCT      CH10P2
E                    TABHH$  1   4  6 0ATABHF$  7 2 HH INC & FIXED$  CH10P2
E                    TABHLO  4   4  6 0             HH LOW AMT       CH10P2
E                    TABHPT  4   4  2 2             HH PCT           CH10P2
```

Figure 10-25 Source listing of federal income tax report program.

```
IDATA10P2SM  01                                                       CH10P2
I                                              1   90SS#              CH10P2
I                                             10  29 NAME             CH10P2
I                                             30  350TAXINC        10 CH10P2
I                                             36  36 STATUS           CH10P2
I                                             37  38 TAXYR            CH10P2
C  N11                 EXSR HDG                         HEADING ROUTINECH10P2
C  N10                 EXSR PROCES                      DETAIL PROCESNGCH10P2
C           HDG        BEGSR                                          CH10P2
C                      SETON                     11OF                 CH10P2
C                      ENDSR                                          CH10P2
 *                                                                    CH10P2
C           PROCES     BEGSR                                          CH10P2
C           STATUS     COMP 'S'                       20 SINGLE ?     CH10P2
C   20                 EXSR SSUB                         SINGLE ROUTINECH10P2
C   20                 GOTO END                                       CH10P2
C           STATUS     COMP 'J'                       20 JOINT RETURN? CH10P2
C   20                 EXSR JSUB                         JOINT ROUTINE CH10P2
C   20                 GOTO END                                       CH10P2
C           STATUS     COMP 'M'                       20 MAR-SEP RETURNCH10P2
C   20                 EXSR MSUB                         MAR-SEP ROUTINCH10P2
C   20                 GOTO END                                       CH10P2
C           STATUS     COMP 'H'                       20 HEAD OF HOUSE?CH10P2
C   20                 EXSR HSUB                         HEAD OF HOUSE CH10P2
C           END        ENDSR                                          CH10P2
 *                                                                    CH10P2
C           SSUB       BEGSR                             SINGLE SR    CH10P2
C           TAXINC     LOKUPTABS$     TABSF$        5050 GET FIXED AMT CH10P2
C  N50                 GOTO END1                                      CH10P2
C           TAXINC     LOKUPTABS$     TABSLO        5050 GET LOW AMT  CH10P2
C           TAXINC     LOKUPTABS$     TABSPT        5050 GET PCT      CH10P2
C           TAXINC     SUB  TABSLO    NET     82                      CH10P2
C           TABSPT     MULT NET       TAX     82H                     CH10P2
C           TAX        ADD  TABSF$    TAX            TAX DUE          CH10P2
C           END1       ENDSR                                          CH10P2
 *                                                                    CH10P2
C           JSUB       BEGSR                             M-JOINT SR   CH10P2
C           TAXINC     LOKUPTABJ$     TABJF$        5050 GET FIXED AMT CH10P2
C  N50                 GOTO END2                                      CH10P2
C           TAXINC     LOKUPTABJ$     TABJLO        5050 GET LOW AMT  CH10P2
C           TAXINC     LOKUPTABJ$     TABJPT        5050 GET PCT      CH10P2
C           TAXINC     SUB  TABJLO    NET                             CH10P2
C           TABJPT     MULT NET       TAX                             CH10P2
C           TAX        ADD  TABJF$    TAX               TAX DUE       CH10P2
C           END2       ENDSR                                          CH10P2
 *                                                                    CH10P2
C           MSUB       BEGSR                             M-SEP SR     CH10P2
C           TAXINC     LOKUPTABM$     TABMF$        5050 GET FIXED AMT CH10P2
C  N50                 GOTO END3                                      CH10P2
C           TAXINC     LOKUPTABM$     TABMLO        5050 GET LOW AMT  CH10P2
C           TAXINC     LOKUPTABM$     TABMPT        5050 GET PCT      CH10P2
C           TAXINC     SUB  TABMLO    NET                             CH10P2
C           TABMPT     MULT NET       TAX                             CH10P2
C           TAX        ADD  TABMF$    TAX               TAX DUE       CH10P2
C           END3       ENDSR                                          CH10P2
 *                                                                    CH10P2
C           HSUB       BEGSR                             HEAD HOUSE SR CH10P2
C           TAXINC     LOKUPTABHH$    TABHF$        5050 GET FIXED AMT CH10P2
C  N50                 GOTO END4                                      CH10P2
C           TAXINC     LOKUPTABHH$    TABHLO        5050 GET LOW AMT  CH10P2
C           TAXINC     LOKUPTABHH$    TABHPT        5050 GET PCT      CH10P2
C           TAXINC     SUB  TABHLO    NET                             CH10P2
C           TABHPT     MULT NET       TAX                             CH10P2
C           TAX        ADD  TABHF$    TAX               TAX DUE       CH10P2
C           END4       ENDSR                                          CH10P2
 *                                                                    CH10P2
OTAXREPRTH  101   OF                                                  CH10P2
O                                 42 'FEDERAL INCOME TAX '            CH10P2
O                                 48 'REPORT'                         CH10P2
O                                 65 'PAGE'                           CH10P2
O                        PAGE  Z  70                                  CH10P2
O        H  3     OF                                                  CH10P2
O                                 37 'FOR INDIVIDUALS-'               CH10P2
O                                 48 'TAX YEAR 19'                    CH10P2
O                        TAXYR    50                                  CH10P2
O        H  1     OF                                                  CH10P2
O                                 53 'FILING    TAXABLE'              CH10P2
O                                 65 'FEDERAL'                        CH10P2
O        H  2     OF                                                  CH10P2
O                                  6 'SS#'                            CH10P2
O                                 30 'TAXPAYER NAME'                  CH10P2
O                                 42 'STATUS'                         CH10P2
O                                 52 'INCOME'                         CH10P2
O                                 67 'INCOME TAX'                     CH10P2
O        DF 2     01                                                  CH10P2
O                        SS#      11 '0   -  -    '                   CH10P2
O                        NAME     34                                  CH10P2
```

(*Continued*)

```
0110 O                          STATUS    39                     CH10P2
0111 O                          TAXINC2   53                     CH10P2
0112 O                          TAX   1   67                     CH10P2
**
000000000000
017850267750
043150976150
089560000000
**
00000178504315000000
**
15282828
**
0000000000000
0297500446250
0719001626450
1492500000000
**
0000002975007190000000
**
15282828
**
000000000000
014875223125
035950813225
113300000000
**
0000001487503595000000
**
15282828
**
0000000000000
0239000358500
0616501415500
1237900000000
**
0000002390006165000000
**
15282828
```

(Continued)

Application Program's Processing Logic for Low-Range LOKUP

A listing of the four tables (TABJ$, TABJF$, TABJLO, and TABJPT) related to the Married–Joint Return filing status and the mathematical steps used to compute the tax liability are given in Figure 10-26. With the exception of having different tables, each of the other three filing statuses follow the same look-up logic and calculation procedures.

```
Processing logic for any filing status (Joint taxpayer's tables shown):

  Taxable                        TABJ$    TABJF$    TABJLO   TABJPT
    income:  050000 ───┐
                       ├──000000  0000000   000000    15
                  |──► ├──029750  0446250   029750    28
Table search continues └──071900  1626450   071900    28
 until higher value is    149250  0000000   000000    28
 tested, then control
 "backs-up" to previous
 entry. Argument and any
 one function table entry
 are available for process-
 ing.

The following steps are required to compute the tax due:

  Step 1: Subtract bracket low amount (TABJLO) from Taxable Income.

             50,000 - 29,750 = 20,250

  Step 2: Multiply difference from Step 1 by bracket percent (TABJPT).

             20,250 x .28 = 5,670

  Step 3: Add product from Step 2 to bracket fixed amount (TABJF$)
          for total tax amount due.

             5,670 + 4,462.50 = 10,132.50
```

Figure 10-26 Processing logic for program's low-range LOKUP control and mathematical steps to compute tax amount due.

Application Program's Calculation Statements

The calculation instructions included in the application program for one filing status (JOINT) are illustrated in Figure 10-27. Included in the right-hand margin are the field values after a statement is executed. Because the same steps are followed for every filing status, an understanding of the mathematics of one is sufficient.

```
Joint taxpayer's tables:

     Taxable                  TABJ$     TABJF$     TABJLO   TABJPT
       income:  050000 ──┐
                         ├── 000000    0000000     000000     15
                   |──►──├── 029750    0446250     029750     28
                   |─────└── 071900    1626450     071900     28
                             149250    0000000     000000     28

Calculations: (reference above tables for related table values)

                                                          Factor 1     Factor 2    Result Field
                                                           Value        Value        Value
...  ... 1 ... ... 2 ... ... 3 ... ... 4 ... ... 5 ... ... 6
     C          TAXINC    LOKUPTABJ$     TABJF$       5050   050000       029750      0446250
     C   N50              GOTO END
     C          TAXINC    LOKUPTABJ$     TABJLO       5050   050000       029750       029750
     C          TAXINC    LOKUPTABJ$     TABJPT       5050   050000       029750           28
     C          TAXINC    SUB  TABJLO    NET                 050000       029750     00020250
     C          TABSPT    MULT NET       TAX                     28     00020250     00005670
     C          TAX       ADD  TABJF$    TAX               00005670      0446250     01013250
                            .
                            .
```

Figure 10-27 Federal income tax report application program calculation statements to compute the tax amounts due for Married–Filing Jointly filing status.

In lieu of using low-range table look-up processing, the high-range may have been elected. The table values would have to be modified to include the upper amounts of the range bracket. Because the high values relate to a taxable income *not over* the amount shown, they may be used as given in the tables.

APPLICATION PROGRAM—FEDERAL INCOME TAX COMPUTATIONS MODIFIED WITH RPG III SYNTAX

The federal income tax program presented in Figure 10-28 has been modified to include RPG III syntax. Examine the listing and notice the following:

1. *INxx is used to test the on/off (1 or 0) condition of indicators.
2. CASxx (compare and branch to a subroutine) operations are used to control internal subroutine branching and processing.
3. IFxx operations are used to control unsuccessful table lookups.
4. Factor 1 entry is not used if the Result Field specifies the same item name.

```
... ... 1 ... ... 2 ... ... 3 ... ... 4 ... ... 5 ... ... 6 ... ... 7 ...
0001  *                     FEDERAL INCOME TAX REPORT                        CH10P3
0002  *     FOR INDIVIDUAL TAXPAYERS - FOR EVERY FILING STATUS               CH10P3
0003  *     16 COMPILE TABLE ARE DEFINED, WHICH INCLUDE:                     CH10P3
0004  *       1. FOUR TABLES FOR LOW RANGE AMOUNTS.                          CH10P3
0005  *       2. FOUR TABLES FOR FIXED AMOUNTS.                              CH10P3
0006  *       3. FOUR TABLES FOR FIXED TAX AMOUNTS.                          CH10P3
0007  *       4. FOUR TABLES FOR PERCENTS.                                   CH10P3
```

Figure 10-28 Source listing of federal income tax report program modified with RPG III syntax.

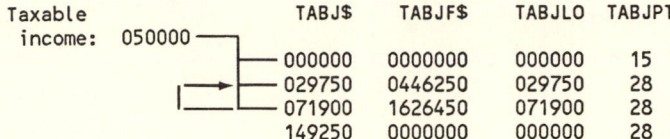

```
 ****************PROGRAM MODIFIED WITH RPG III/400 SYNTAX**************CH10P3
H                                                                     CH10P3
FDATA10P2IP  F  38  38            DISK                                CH10P3
FTAXREPRTO   F 132 132     OF     PRINTER                             CH10P3
E                    TABS$    1   4  6 0ATABSF$  6 2 SINGLE LOW & FIX$CH10P3
E                    TABSLO   4   4  5 0             LOW AMT          CH10P3
E                    TABSPT   4   4  2 2             SINGLE-PCT       CH10P3
E                    TABJ$    1   4  6 0ATABJF$  7 2 JOINT LOW & FIX$ CH10P3
E                    TABJLO   4   4  6 0             JOINT LOW AMT    CH10P3
E                    TABJPT   4   4  2 2             JOINT-PCT        CH10P3
E                    TABM$    1   4  6 0ATABMF$  6 2 MAR-SEP INC & FIXCH10P3
E                    TABMLO   4   4  6 0             MAR-SEP LOW      CH10P3
E                    TABMPT   4   4  2 2             MAR-SEP PCT      CH10P3
E                    TABHH$   1   4  6 0ATABHF$  7 2 HH INC & FIXED$  CH10P3
E                    TABHLO   4   4  6 0             HH LOW AMT       CH10P3
E                    TABHPT   4   4  2 2             HH PCT           CH10P3
IDATA10P2SM  01                                                       CH10P3
I                                        1   90SS#                    CH10P3
I                                       10  29 NAME                   CH10P3
I                                       30  350TAXINC         10      CH10P3
I                                       36  36 STATUS                 CH10P3
I                                       37  38 TAXYR                  CH10P3
C           *IN11     CASEQ'0'       HDG            HEADING ROUTINECH10P3
C                     END                                             CH10P3
C           *IN10     CASEQ'0'       PROCES         TAXINC NOT 0    CH10P3
C                     END                                             CH10P3
 *                                                                    CH10P3
C           HDG       BEGSR                                           CH10P3
C                     SETON                     11OF                  CH10P3
C                     ENDSR                                           CH10P3
 *                                                                    CH10P3
C           PROCES    BEGSR                                           CH10P3
C           STATUS    CASEQ'S'       SSUB           SINGLE ?        CH10P3
C           STATUS    CASEQ'J'       JSUB           JOINT RETURN?   CH10P3
C           STATUS    CASEQ'M'       MSUB           MAR-SEP RETURNSCH10P3
C           STATUS    CASEQ'H'       HSUB           HEAD OF HOUSE ?CH10P3
C                     END                                             CH10P3
C                     ENDSR                                           CH10P3
 *                                                                    CH10P3
C           SSUB      BEGSR                         SINGLE SR       CH10P3
C           TAXINC    LOKUPTABS$     TABSF$       5050 GET FIXED AMT CH10P3
C           *IN50     IFEQ '1'                                        CH10P3
C           TAXINC    LOKUPTABS$     TABSLO       5050 GET LOW AMT   CH10P3
C           TAXINC    LOKUPTABS$     TABSPT       5050 GET PCT       CH10P3
C           TAXINC    SUB  TABSLO    NET       82                     CH10P3
C           TABSPT    MULT NET       TAX       82H                    CH10P3
C                     ADD  TABSF$    TAX            TAX DUE         CH10P3
C                     END                                             CH10P3
C                     ENDSR                                           CH10P3
 *                                                                    CH10P3
C           JSUB      BEGSR                         M-JOINT SR      CH10P3
C           TAXINC    LOKUPTABJ$     TABJF$       5050GET FIXED AMT  CH10P3
C           *IN50     IFEQ '1'                                        CH10P3
C           TAXINC    LOKUPTABJ$     TABJLO       5050GET LOW AMT    CH10P3
C           TAXINC    LOKUPTABJ$     TABJPT       5050GET PCT        CH10P3
C           TAXINC    SUB  TABJLO    NET                              CH10P3
C           TABJPT    MULT NET       TAX                              CH10P3
C                     ADD  TABJF$    TAX            TAX DUE         CH10P3
C                     END                                             CH10P3
C                     ENDSR                                           CH10P3
 *                                                                    CH10P3
C           MSUB      BEGSR                         M-SEPARATE SR   CH10P3
C           TAXINC    LOKUPTABM$     TABMF$       5050 GET FIXED AMT CH10P3
C           *IN50     IFEQ '1'                                        CH10P3
C           TAXINC    LOKUPTABM$     TABMLO       5050 GET LOW AMT   CH10P3
C           TAXINC    LOKUPTABM$     TABMPT       5050 GET PCT       CH10P3
C           TAXINC    SUB  TABMLO    NET                              CH10P3
C           TABMPT    MULT NET       TAX                              CH10P3
C                     ADD  TABMF$    TAX            TAX DUE         CH10P3
C                     END                                             CH10P3
C                     ENDSR                                           CH10P3
 *                                                                    CH10P3
C           HSUB      BEGSR                         HEAD HOUSE SR   CH10P3
C           TAXINC    LOKUPTABHH$    TABHF$       5050 GET FIXED AMT CH10P3
C           *IN50     IFEQ '1'                                        CH10P3
C           TAXINC    LOKUPTABHH$    TABHLO       5050 GET LOW AMT   CH10P3
C           TAXINC    LOKUPTABHH$    TABHPT       5050 GET PCT       CH10P3
C           TAXINC    SUB  TABHLO    NET                              CH10P3
C           TABHPT    MULT NET       TAX                              CH10P3
C                     ADD  TABHF$    TAX            TAX DUE         CH10P3
C                     END                                             CH10P3
C                     ENDSR                                           CH10P3
 *                                                                    CH10P3
OTAXREPRTH  101   OF                                                  CH10P3
O                                    42 'FEDERAL INCOME TAX '         CH10P3
O                                    48 'REPORT'                      CH10P3
O                                    65 'PAGE'                        CH10P3
O                          PAGE  Z   70                               CH10P3
```

(Continued)

```
0096 O         H 3     OF                                              CH10P3
0097 O                                   37 'FOR INDIVIDUALS-'         CH10P3
0098 O                                   48 'TAX YEAR 19'              CH10P3
0099 O                        TAXYR      50                            CH10P3
0100 O         H 1     OF                                              CH10P3
0101 O                                   53 'FILING    TAXABLE'        CH10P3
0102 O                                   65 'FEDERAL'                  CH10P3
0103 O         H 2     OF                                              CH10P3
0104 O                                    6 'SS#'                      CH10P3
0105 O                                   30 'TAXPAYER NAME'            CH10P3
0106 O                                   42 'STATUS'                   CH10P3
0107 O                                   52 'INCOME'                   CH10P3
0108 O                                   67 'INCOME TAX'               CH10P3
0109 O         DF 2    01                                              CH10P3
0110 O                        SS#        11 '0   -  -    '             CH10P3
0111 O                        NAME       34                            CH10P3
0112 O                        STATUS     39                            CH10P3
0113 O                        TAXINC2    53                            CH10P3
0114 O                        TAX    1   67                            CH10P3
**
000000000000
017850267750
043150976150
089560000000
**
000001785043150000000
**
15282828
**
0000000000000
0297500446250
0719001626450
1492500000000
**
0000000297500719000000000
**
15282828
**
000000000000
014875223125
035950813225
113300000000
**
0000000148750359500000000
**
15282828
**
0000000000000
0239000358500
0616501415500
1237900000000
**
0000000239000616500000000
**
15282828
```

(*Continued*)

SUMMARY

In the programming environment, tables are lists of data stored in a computer's memory. A table may stand alone or relate to one or more other tables.

Tables are defined in Extension Specification instructions, which are entered in the program after the File Description statements. Tables may be defined as *Compile* (execution) Time or *Object* (preexecution) time. The data for Compile Time tables is stored in the program after the last output instruction and the delineating control statement **. Object Time table data is stored in a data file and requires that a table file be defined in the File Description Specifications by identifying it with the letter T in column 16.

Tables are always processed consecutively and are accessed by a LOKUP operation. The entry (literal or field name) in Factor 1, referred to as the search argument, must be the same type as the argument table entry in Factor 2. One related function table may be specified in the Result Field. If more than one function table is required for the application, additional LOKUP instructions must be provided.

For an equal LOKUP condition, an indicator must be specified in the equal field (columns 58–59) of the calculation instruction. When the value in the search argument (Factor 1) equals the value in the argument table (Factor 2), the indicator will be set on. A low-range table condition may be tested by including the same indicator in the Low and Equal fields. High-range conditions may be controlled by specifying the same indicator in the High and Equal fields. In either case, an argument table value is found even though an equal condition is not tested.

For processing efficiency, an early exit from an equal table LOKUP may be controlled by storing the table data in an ascending or descending order. Then, when a search argument is not found in a related argument table, table LOKUP is terminated before the table is searched to the end.

QUESTIONS

10-1. When should tables be included in an RPG program?

10-2. Name two business applications that require the use of tables.

10-3. On which RPG coding form are tables defined? Where are these instructions placed in the source program?

10-4. How is a table stored in memory?

10-5. When in the program cycle may tables be loaded with data? Where is the data stored (before processing) for each loading method?

10-6. Reference a blank Extension Specifications form. Identify and explain the function of the fields used to define a table. Indicate the fields used (and not used) for each loading method.

10-7. What new entries are needed in the File Description form to support each loading method? What new entries are needed on the input form to define and/or process tables?

10-8. What are some of the syntax rules regarding the assignment of a table name?

10-9. Define the following table terms:

```
SEARCH ARGUMENT   ARGUMENT TABLE
FUNCTION TABLE    LOKUP
```

10-10. Reference a blank calculation form, and answer the following:
   a. Entry in Factor 1 is referred to as the ________.
   b. Entry in Factor 2 is referred to as the ________.
   c. Entry in the Result Field is referred to as the ________.
   d. What are the minimum entries that must be specified with a LOKUP operation?
   e. How many tables may be accessed in one LOKUP operation?

10-11. Explain the rules for formatting table data.

10-12. What are alternating tables? How many tables may be defined in an alternating format?

10-13. Answer the following questions about table processing:
   a. Where in a table does a search begin?
   b. Does the search begin at the same table entry for successive LOKUP operations?
   c. Are tables consecutively or randomly processed?
   d. If the table data is in an unordered sequence and a search is unsuccessful, at which entry in the table does processing stop? Does this cancel program execution?

10-14. Explain the table processing term *early exit*. How is it provided for in an RPG program?

10-15. If a table is defined as sorted and the data is not in the required sequence, when is this error identified?

10-16. Explain the following table processing terms:

EQUAL look-up HIGH RANGE
LOW RANGE

10-17. What additional entries are needed in the Extension and Calculation forms to support low-range table processing? High-range table processing?

10-18. If a low-range LOKUP is specified, which table entry will be accessed if the search argument value is 07000? What table entry will be accessed if a high-range LOKUP is specified and the search argument value is 07000?

```
00000
02480
03670
04750
07010
09170
```

EXERCISES

10-1. Following are three simple tables that relate to one another. Format the TABCDE and TABSTA entries in an alternating format with one entry per record. Include all the related percentages on one record. Assuming they are Compile Time, format the tables (with required control statement(s)) as they would be entered in a program.

TABCDE	*TABSTA*	*TABTAX*
NJ	NEW JERSEY	6.0%
CT	CONNECTICUT	7.5%
NY	NEW YORK	7.0%
MA	MASSACHUSETTS	6.0%
VT	VERMONT	5.0%
NH	NEW HAMPSHIRE	3.0%

Note: TABCDE data must be sorted in ascending order.

10-2. Refer to Exercise 10-1, and complete the Extension and Calculation Specifications coding to define and access the three tables. Assume that the search argument STATE is defined as a two-byte alphanumeric input field.

10-3. Refer to Exercises 10-1 and 10-2, and include and/or make any additional changes to define and process the tables as Object Time.

10-4. Given below are a state's sales tax percentage tables. All sales over $1.07 are subject to a 7% sales tax. If the sales amount is:

Over:	*But Not Over:*	*The Tax Is:*
$ .00	$ .07	$ .00
.07	.21	.01
.21	.35	.02
.35	.49	.03
.49	.64	.04
.64	.78	.05
.78	.92	.06
.92	1.07	.07

Format the table entries so that all the entries for a table are included on one record. Assume that the tables are to be loaded at Compile Time. Use *low-range* processing for the amount of sales (argument) table.

10-5. Refer to Exercise 10-4, and complete the Extension and Calculations forms to define and process the tables. Assume SALES is the search argument item.

10-6. Refer to Exercise 10-3, and format the table data for *high-range* processing. Complete the Extension and Calculation forms to define and process the tables. Assume that the search argument is SALES.

Exercises 10-7 through 10-9 are related.

10-7. The following table gives the average property tax rates for several counties within a state. The names of the counties are in one column, and the average mill rate is in the second column.

Table data:

TABCNT	TABMIL
FAIRFIELD	40.6
HARTFORD	46.2
LITCHFIELD	36.5
MIDDLESEX	44.4
NEW HAVEN	39.7
NEW LONDON	37.9
TOLLAND	35.1

Arrange the tables in an alternating format with one entry per record. Assume that the tables are to be loaded at Compile Time, and complete the Extension form coding.

10-8. From the Extension form completed in Exercise 10-7, write the input and calculation instructions to define the input fields, process the tables, and compute the property tax liability.

Input Record Format:

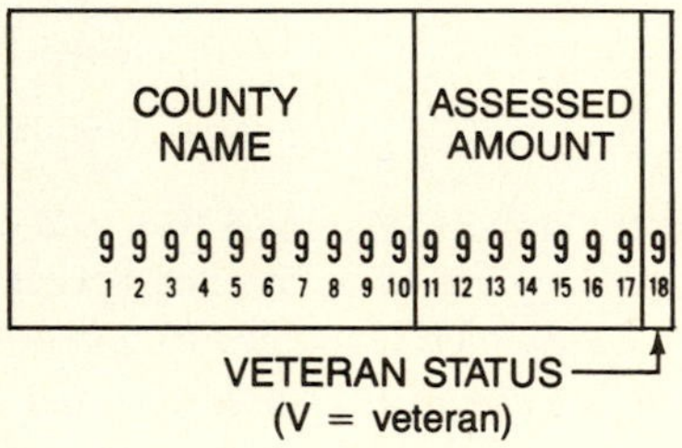

Calculations:

The following steps are required for the computation of the taxpayer's property tax liability:

a. Look up the TABCNT table to extract the mill rate from the related function table (TABMIL).

b. The mill rate indicates the dollar tax per thousand dollars of assessed tax amount. Divide the assessed value by \$1,000 to determine multiples of \$1,000.

Example:

$$\frac{\$60{,}000}{\$1{,}000} = 60 \text{ multiples of } \$1{,}000$$

c. Multiply the related TABMIL value by the multiple from Step 1 to determine the property tax liability.

Example:

Property tax liability = 60 × 40.6 (mill rate for FAIRFIELD) = $2,436

d. Veterans are eligible for a $1,000 tax exemption that is deducted before the multiples amount in Step b is determined. Using the same example, the property tax liability of a veteran is computed as follows:

$$(60{,}000 - 1{,}000)/1{,}000 \times 40.6 = \$2{,}395.40$$

The letter V in column 18 of the input record indicates that the taxpayer is a veteran and eligible for the exemption.

10-9. Refer to the input record format and completed Exercises 10-7 and 10-8. Write the output form statements from the following printer spacing chart:

Report Design:

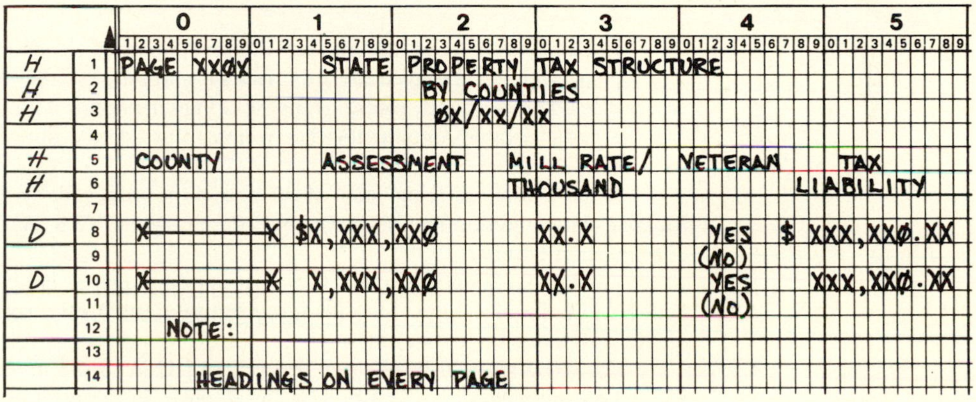

LABORATORY ASSIGNMENTS

Laboratory Assignment 10-1: WEEKLY SHIPPING REPORT

A company needs a weekly report of the shipping charges it incurs in a week. All deliveries are made FOB destination (seller pays the shipping cost).

Format of Data Records:

A file of customers that includes the summary information for every sales invoice is maintained. The format of the records follows:

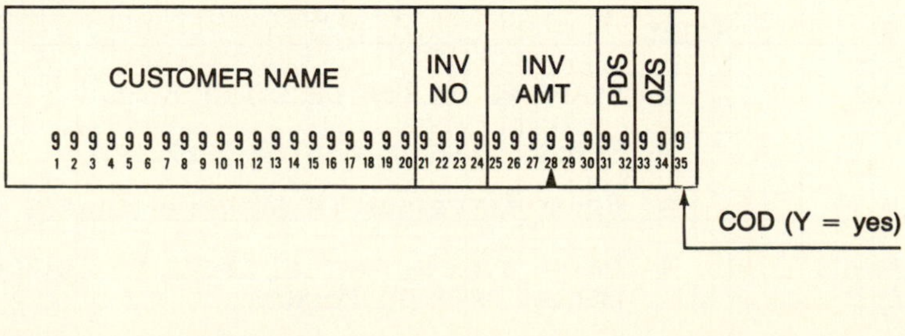

Table Data:
Include the following as Compile Time tables in the program:

Weight (PDS)	Rate (2 decimal positions)
01	129
02	137
03	146
04	154
05	163
06	171
07	180
08	188
09	197
10	205
11	214
12	222
13	231
14	239
15	248
16	256
17	265
18	273
19	282
20	290

Processing: Use the invoice shipping weight field as the search argument, and look up the weight table to access the related shipping charge. For any weights that are any ounces over a pound, round to the next higher pound. All shipments over 20 pounds are charged the table amount for that weight plus an additional 6 cents for each pound over 20.

A maximum shipping limit of 70 pounds is imposed by the parcel delivery firm. Identify this condition on the report by the message OVER WEIGHT, and skip any additional calculations.

For invoice amounts under $25, the shipping charge is absorbed by the buyer and added to the invoice total. Identify these transactions on the report by asterisks in place of the shipping charge amount.

For COD sales, a flat charge of $1.50 is added to the invoice on all invoices under $50. COD shipments are identified by the letter Y in the related input field.

Report Design:

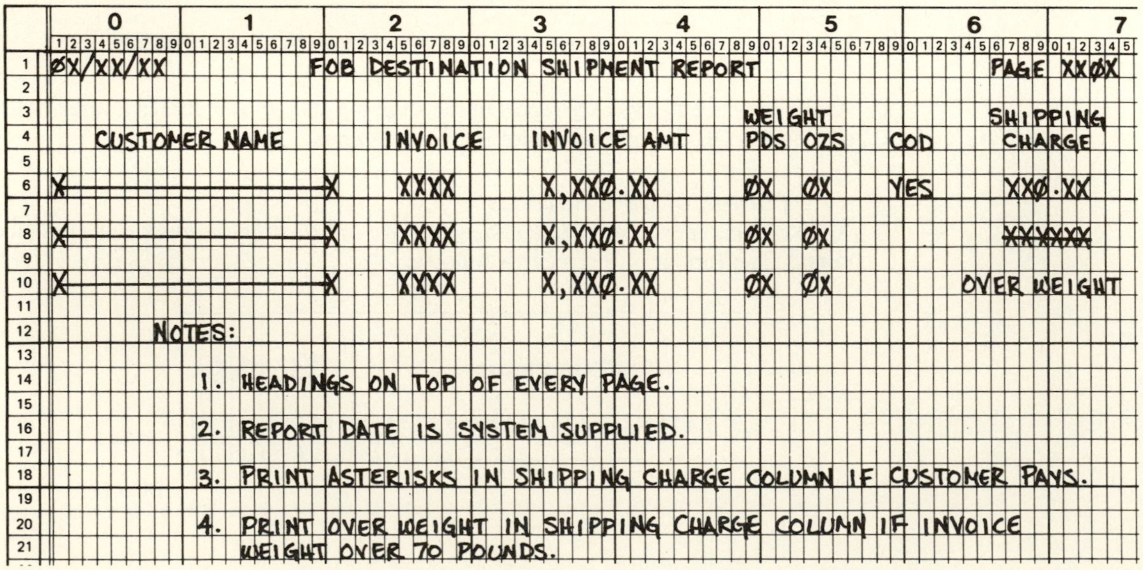
ØX/XX/XX
FOB DESTINATION SHIPMENT REPORT
PAGE XXØX
WEIGHT
SHIPPING
CUSTOMER NAME
INVOICE
INVOICE AMT
PDS OZS
COD
CHARGE
X————X XXXX X,XXØ.XX ØX ØX YES XXØ.XX
X————X XXXX X,XXØ.XX ØX ØX XXXXXX
X————X XXXX X,XXØ.XX ØX ØX OVER WEIGHT
NOTES:
1. HEADINGS ON TOP OF EVERY PAGE.
2. REPORT DATE IS SYSTEM SUPPLIED.
3. PRINT ASTERISKS IN SHIPPING CHARGE COLUMN IF CUSTOMER PAYS.
4. PRINT OVER WEIGHT IN SHIPPING CHARGE COLUMN IF INVOICE WEIGHT OVER 70 POUNDS.

Input Data:

Customer Name Cols 1-20	Invoice Number 21-24	Invoice Amount 25-30	Invoice Weight PD 31-32	OZ 33-34	COD 35
HENRY JACKSON	1234	002400	05	08	
DOROTHY PARTON	1235	010000	20	00	
ROBERT WARFIELD	1236	004500	08	09	Y
MARIO LANZA	1237	120000	70	00	Y
ENZIO PINZA	1238	245000	82	12	
NELSON EDDY	1239	001000	01	00	Y

Laboratory Assignment 10-2: FLEXIBLE BUDGET REPORT

A company has a flexible budget formula for its factory overhead expenses. Each expense item has a fixed dollar amount plus a variable rate based on the standard direct labor hours (hours budgeted for the level of production attained). The formula is expressed as:

Budget amount for overhead expense item = Fixed $ amount + (variable rate × std direct hrs)

At the end of each accounting period, the company wants to determine the flexible budget amount for each expense item and compare it with the actual dollars incurred to identify a *favorable* or *unfavorable variance*. A favorable variance occurs when the actual costs incurred for the expense are less than the budget allowance. An unfavorable variance results when the actual cost is more than the budget amount.

Format of Data Records:

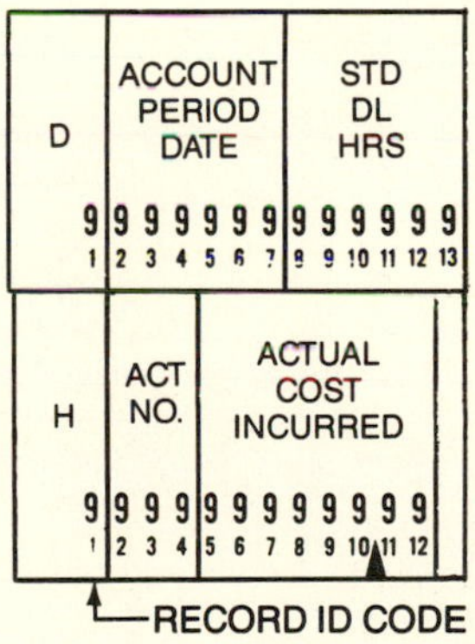

Table Data: Include the following data in Compile Time tables:

Account Number	Account Name	Fixed Amount	Variable Rate Per Direct Labor Hours (2 decimals)
600	INDIRECT LABOR	20000	015
601	FACTORY SUPPLIES	02000	100
602	FACTORY ELECTRICITY	03000	006
603	MACHINE REPAIR	01000	010
604	PLANT MAINTENANCE	04000	020
605	FACTORY HEATING OIL	02700	004
606	FACTORY CUSTODIAL	05000	010
607	TOOL CRIB LABOR	04500	011
608	COST CLERKS	04000	008

Processing: Use the Account Number field from the input records as the search argument, and look up the related Account Number table for an equal condition. Provide for an early exit if the account number is not found in the table.

If the table search is successful, multiply the standard direct labor hours input by the related variable rate table entry. Add this amount to the fixed amount table entry for the item for the total flexible budget amount allowed for the level of activity (standard direct labor hours input).

The favorable or unfavorable variance for each expense item is determined by subtracting the total flexible budget amount from the actual cost incurred. A positive difference indicates an unfavorable variance; a negative, favorable.

Examine the printer spacing chart, and notice that the letter F (favorable) or U (unfavorable) is printed alongside the variance amount. *Do not print a negative sign.*

Report Design:

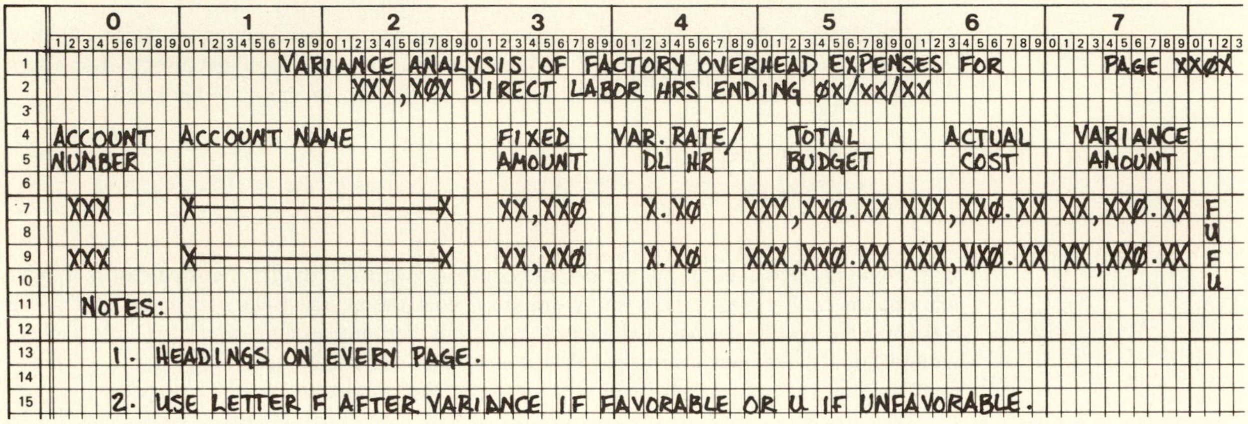
VARIANCE ANALYSIS OF FACTORY OVERHEAD EXPENSES FOR
PAGE XXØX
XXX,XØX DIRECT LABOR HRS ENDING ØX/XX/XX
ACCOUNT NUMBER
ACCOUNT NAME
FIXED AMOUNT
VAR. RATE/ DL HR
TOTAL BUDGET
ACTUAL COST
VARIANCE AMOUNT
XXX
X
XX,XXØ
X.XØ
XXX,XXØ.XX
XXX,XXØ.XX
XX,XXØ.XX
F
U
NOTES:
1. HEADINGS ON EVERY PAGE.
2. USE LETTER F AFTER VARIANCE IF FAVORABLE OR U IF UNFAVORABLE.

Input Data:

Date record data (one record and first in file):

Record ID Code Col 1	Accounting Period Date 2-7	Standard Direct Labor Hours 8-13
D	033192	050000

Actual Factory Expense Account Data:

Record ID Code Col 1	Account Number 2-4	Actual Cost Incurred 5-12
H	600	03000090
H	601	05100010
H	602	00550068
H	603	00840000
H	604	01500025
H	605	00850010
H	606	01000005
H	607	00950000
H	608	00705078
H	609	00420015

Laboratory Assignment 10-3: SALES DISCOUNT REPORT (GREGORIAN to JULIAN DATE CONVERSION)

The Stratford Company has a credit policy for all Accounts Receivable of 2/10, n/30, which is defined as follows:

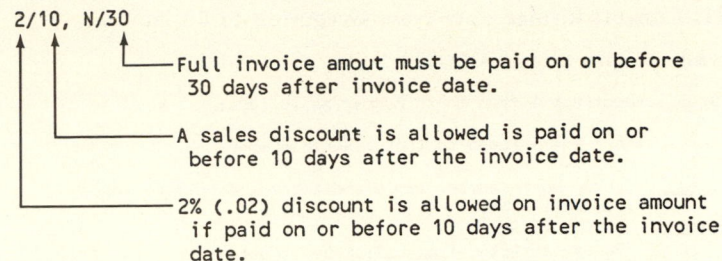

```
2/10, N/30
 ↑   ↑   ↑
 |   |   └──Full invoice amout must be paid on or before
 |   |       30 days after invoice date.
 |   |
 |   └──────A sales discount is allowed is paid on or
 |           before 10 days after the invoice date.
 |
 └──────────2% (.02) discount is allowed on invoice amount
             if paid on or before 10 days after the invoice
             date.
```

```
Example:                    Computation:
                                                                Therefore:
  Invoice date: 8/01/89     Invoice     Percent of              Amount paid is:
                            Amount   x  Discount    = $ Discount
  Date paid: 08/11/89                                            100.00 - 2.00 = 98.00
                            100.00   x     .02      =   2.00
```

Because the payment months and/or years may be different from the invoice month, the MMDDYY format cannot conveniently be used. Hence, Gregorian dates, such as 2/01/91, must be converted to a Julian format (032) for date comparisons and a customer's eligibility for a sales discount (payment within 10 days) or good credit rating (payment within 30 days). Julian dates refer to the relative day number in a year. For example, February 20 is the fifty-first (051) day of a year in the Julian format. Because of month and year changes, comparison of dates using Julian dates is more direct than using Gregorian dates.

The company needs the report detailed in the printer spacing chart that follows, which reflects the credit activity of their customers.

Format of Data Records:

CUST#	CUSTOMER NAME	INV#	GROSS INVOICE AMOUNT	INV DATE	PAYMNT DATE
9 9 9 9 9	9 9 9 9 9 9 9 9 9 9 9 9 9 9 9 9 9 9 9 9 9 9 9 9 9	9 9 9 9 9 9	9 9 9 9 9 9 9	9 9 9 9 9 9	9 9 9 9 9 9
1 2 3 4 5	6 7 8 9 10 11 12 13 14 15 16 17 18 19 20 21 22 23 24 25 26 27 28 29 30	31 32 33 34 35 36	37 38 39 40 41 ▲ 42 43	44 45 46 47 48 49	50 51 52 53 54 55

Table Data: Include the following data in Compile Time tables:

Month Number	Last day of month cumulative (Julian)	
00	000	entry needed for year changes
01	031	
02	059	non-leap year value
03	090	
04	120	
05	151	
06	181	
07	212	
08	243	
09	273	
10	304	
11	334	
12	365	non-leap year value

Computations: The following computations are required to convert an invoice date in Gregorian format (MMDDYY) to Julian format (DDD).

FIRST: Convert invoice date from Gregorian to Julian:

```
Given:  Invoice date is 4/27/89

  Step 1: Subtract 1 from month number as follows:

          4 - 1 = 3 (used to lookup Month Number Table)

  Step 2: Lookup Month Number table and extracted related value
          from Julian Day table:

          90 is extracted from Julian Day table.

  Step 3: Add month day to Julian table days:

          90 + 27 = 117

  Step 4: Add discount period to above total

          117 + 10 = 127 (Last day of discount period in Julian)
```

Invoice date has been converted from 4/27/89 to Julian day 127.

SECOND: Convert payment date from Gregorian to Julian (same computations).

```
Given:  Payment date is 5/07/89

  Step 1: Subtract 1 from month number as follows:

          5 - 1 = 4 (used to lookup Month Number Table)

  Step 2: Lookup Month Number table and extracted related value
          from Julian Day table:

          120 is extracted from Julian Day table.

  Step 3: Add month day to Julian table days:

          120 + 7 = 127
```

Note: Payment date conversion has one step less than invoice date because discount period is not added.

THIRD: Compare Julian payment date with Julian discount date.

```
IF greater, sales discount is not allowed.  If payment date
is = or < discount date, 2 % discount is allowed.  For this
example, discount is allowed because payment date of 127 =
invoice date of 127.
```

Leap Year Processing: When a year's number is divisible by 4, it is a leap year. If a leap year is tested, you must add 1 to the Julian payment days if the invoice is 2/29 or earlier and if the payment date is greater than 2/29. Other previously discussed calculations remain the same.

Year Change Processing: When the year changes, an additional calculation is required. Assume that the invoice date is 12/28/91. The Julian discount date is found to be 371, which is greater than 365. If the payment is made in the following year (1/05/92, for example), a valid comparison cannot be made. Therefore, the following additional computation must be included:

$$371 - 365 = 6$$

Payment on 1/05/92 would convert to a Julian day of 5. Then, a comparison of the payment date (5) with the discount date (6) is valid. Discount is allowed for this example (payment date is less than the discount date).

Report Design:

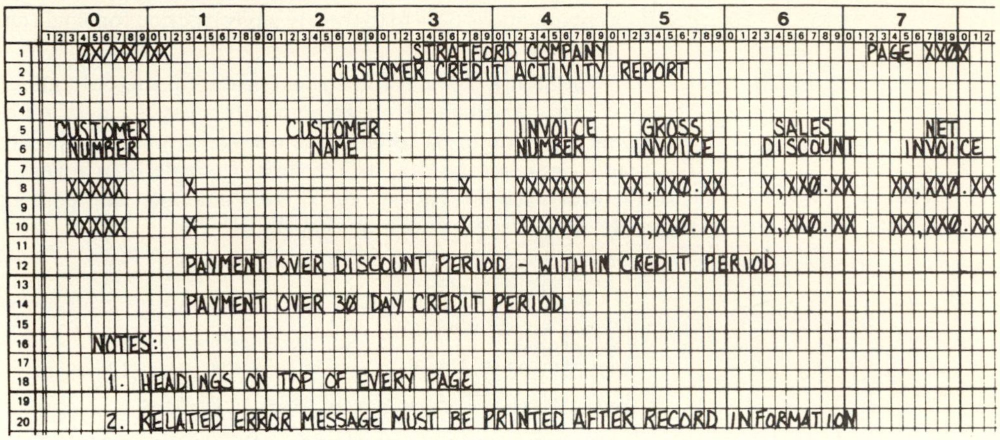

Input Data:

CUSTOMER NUMBER Cols 1-5	CUSTOMER NAME 6-30	INVOICE NUMBER 31-36	GROSS INVOICE 37-43	INVOICE DATE 44-49	PAYMENT DATE 50-55
13579	CARPENTER & SONS, INC.	678900	0822449	032989	040789
42337	SILVERSMITH & DAUGHTERS	678910	1455588	042589	050789
55550	JONES & GRANDPARENTS, LTD.	700000	2231344	050289	051289
66601	COPPERSMITH & FRIENDS	788888	0200000	053189	070589
77777	SHOEMAKER & SOLES	811112	0900010	122789	010590
80000	BLACKSMITH & PETS COMPANY	820000	0005000	122389	123189
85678	AUNTS & UNCLES, INC.	900000	2000000	122389	011090
90000	INLAWS & OUTLAWS COMPANY	944444	0071000	123089	020590

Laboratory Assignment 10-4: WEEKLY PAYROLL CHECKS

The XYZ Company needs a program to print salaried employee weekly payroll checks (with stubs) on preprinted check forms.

General Information: By federal law all employee wages are subject to federal withholding tax (FWT) and social security tax (FICA) deductions.

There are many acceptable methods of computing the federal income tax that must be withheld under the pay-as-you-earn system. The percentage method, which requires the use of tables, is popular on computerized systems. A table for single and married persons for a weekly payroll period (used for this program) follows.

Table Data:

Tables for Percentage Method of Withholding

(For Wages Paid After December 1988)

TABLE 1—If the Payroll Period With Respect to an Employee Is Weekly

(a) SINGLE person—including head of household:

If the amount of wages (after subtracting withholding allowances) is: Not over $21 . . . . . *The amount of income tax to be withheld shall be:* 0

Over—	*But not over—*		*of excess over—*
$21	—$378	15%	—$21
$378	—$885	$53.55 plus 28%	—$378
$885	—$2,028	$195.51 plus 33%	—$885
$2,028	. . . .	$572.70 plus 28%	—$2,028

(b) MARRIED person—

If the amount of wages (after subtracting withholding allowances) is: Not over $62 . . . . . *The amount of income tax to be withheld shall be:* 0

Over—	*But not over—*		*of excess over—*
$62	—$657	15%	—$62
$657	—$1,501	$89.25 plus 28%	—$657
$1,501	—$3,695	$325.57 plus 33%	—$1,501
$3,695	. . . .	$1,049.59 plus 28%	—$3,695

low range amount — fixed amount — percent amount

Earnings, number of exemptions, payroll period, marital status, and payroll period (weekly, biweekly, and so forth) determine the amount of federal income tax withheld. This program requires computations only for a weekly payroll period for single and married wage earners.

Processing: The mathematical procedures to determine the Federal Withholding Tax (FWT) to be withheld from an employee's pay are detailed in the following steps. To determine the FWT to be withheld for a wage earner, use the net amount from Step 1 as the search argument to look up the related (single or married) low-range amount table. Use the low-range (OVER–) values, fixed amounts, and percentages as the data for the three tables required for each marital status.

```
Weekly Salary: $ 450.00
Exemptions: 1
Marital Status: Single

Computations to determine Federal Income to withhold:

Step 1: The number of exemptions is multiplied by a statutory allowance of $ 38.46
        (for single/ weekly payroll period) and product subtracted from the week's wages.

                First:  1 x $ 38.46 = 38.46
                        ↑     ↑
             exemption──┘     └──statutory amt (single/weekly pay)

                Second: 450.00 - 38.46 = 411.54 net amount

Step 2: Use the net amount computed above as the search argument to lookup the low
        range amount table.  A code (S or M) in the input record will determine whether
        the single or married table is searched.  A low range lookup is to be specified.

Step 3: After a successful lookup, subtract the low range table value from the search
        argument to determine any excess amount.

                411.54 - 378.00 = 33.54
                           ↑
                           └──low range value of step

Step 4: Multiply the excess amount (Step 3) by the related percent table value to
        determine the extra amount.

                33.54 x .28 = 9.39  excess amt
                         ↑
                         └──rate table value

Step 5: Add the extra amount (Step 4) to the related fixed table amount to
        determine the Federal Income Tax to be withheld for the wage earner.

                53.55 + 9.39 = 62.94    FWT amt
                    ↑    ↑
          excess amt┘    └──fixed table amt

Step 6: Subtract FWT (Step 5) from week's gross wage to determine net wages
        before Social Security and other deductions.

                450.00 - 62.94 = 387.06    net wages
                     ↑    ↑
          gross wages┘    └──FWT
```

Currently, the social security tax (FICA) is computed at 7.65% on the first $50,400 paid to an employee. The gross weekly wages are multiplied by this rate to determine the FICA amount to be withheld. This amount is also subtracted from gross wages. The following must be considered in the computation of FICA:

1. If the year-to-date wages (before adding the current week) are greater than $50,400, no FICA tax is computed.

2. If the year-to-date wages are not $50,400 or greater, then it must be determined if all, or only a part, of the current week's wages is subject to this tax. For example, if the year-to-date wage is $50,200 and the current week's pay is $600, then only $200 will be subject to the FICA tax. Notice that there is no limit on FWT.

A data file that contains year-to-date and the current week's payroll information is stored on disk with records in the following format:

Format of Data Records:

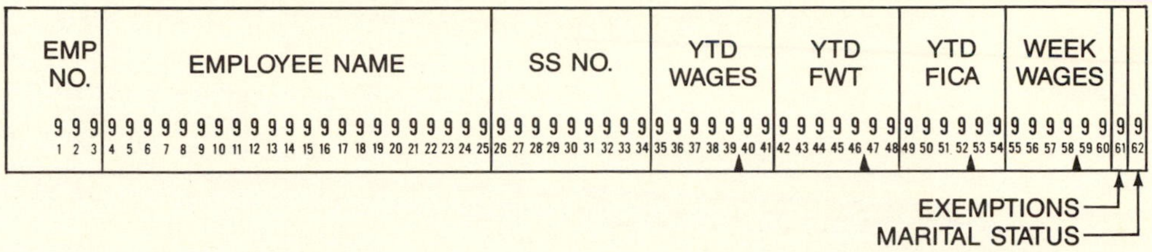

The week ending date and beginning check number (see print chart below) are to be entered by CONSOLE or KEYBORD controlled input. Use 083191 for the date and 1000 as the beginning check number.

Report Design: Output is printed on simulated preprinted check forms. *Assume that all the constants shown in the printer spacing chart are already printed.* The program is to output only the variable data. Control overflow so that one check (and stub) will print per page.

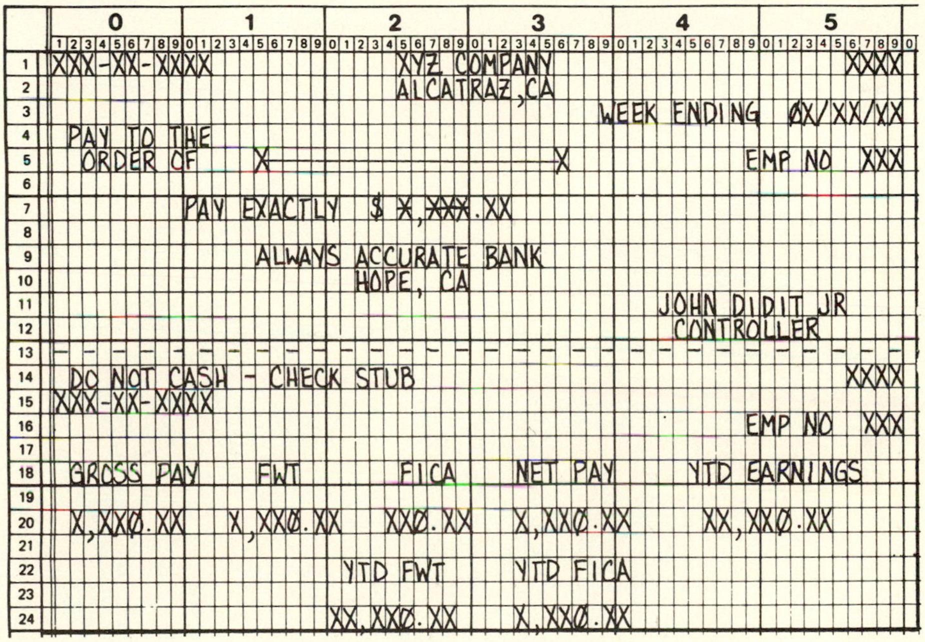

Correct alignment of variables may be determined by a transparency master supplied by the instructor or with a forms ruler.

Input Data:

Employee Number Col 1-3	Employee Name 4-25	SS Number 26-34	YTD Wages 35-41	YTD FWT 42-48	YTD SS 49-54	Week's Wages 55-60	Exemp- tions 61-61	Marital Status 62-62
111	ROBERT FULTON	040503871	5050000	1010000	385560	120000	2	M
222	THOMAS EDISON	030216532	3000000	0600000	229500	058000	1	S
333	ALEXANDER BELL	020315555	5020000	1004000	384030	080000	4	M
444	HENRY FORD	060548754	0046000	0009200	003060	008600	1	S

Note: YTD values are added before current week amounts are added.

chapter 11
Array Concepts and Processing

COMPARISON OF ARRAYS TO TABLES

Because arrays and tables are similar, you may be confused about when to use an array instead of a table or vice versa. Two broad considerations may help you to determine whether to use an array or a table in an RPG program:

1. The way the data for loading the array or table is arranged in the records.
2. The way the array or table will be processed.

The structural and processing differences of arrays and tables are explained in the comparison detailed in Figure 11-1.

Array Features	*Table Features*
1. Data used to load an input time array may be stored anywhere in the body of the records and need not be stored contiguously.	1. Data used to load tables must be stored beginning in the first byte of the input records. The data must be stored consecutively.
2. Arrays may be searched randomly by indexing. A specific element may be accessed without starting the search from the beginning of the array.	2. Tables must be consecutively searched, beginning with the first table entry for every look-up. Indexing is not supported for table processing.
3. All the elements in an array may be accessed at one time by specifying only the array name.	3. Only one table element may be accessed at a time. Reference to other entries requires additional look-ups.
4. During processing, elements in related arrays may be cross-referenced by indexing.	4. Three or more tables are related by successive look-ups.

Figure 11-1 Comparison of the structural and processing features of arrays and tables.

ARRAY STRUCTURE

As related to computers, an *array* may be defined as an arrangement of computer memory positions in one (or multiple) dimension with each position having the same attributes. Figure 11-2 illustrates the structures of a one- and a two-dimensional array.

One-Dimensional Array Defined as NAM

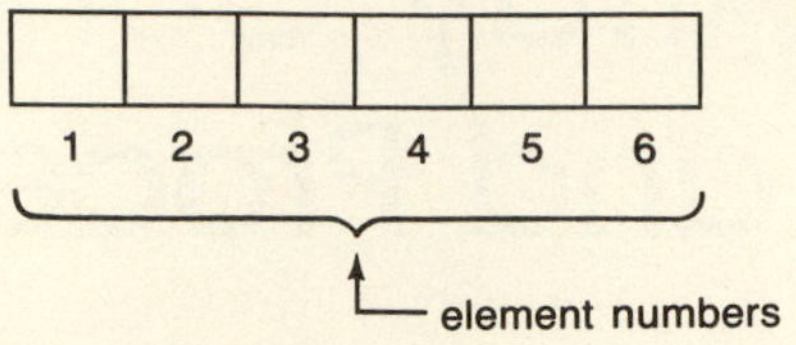

Notes:

1. Entire array may be processed by specifying the array name on input, calculations, and/or output specs.
2. Individual elements may be accessed by specifying the array name, comma, and either a numeric literal or variable field; as:

```
NAM,3   accesses third element
NAM,X   accesses element stored in X
   ↑↑
   │└──index
   │
   └───comma required
```

Two-Dimensional Array Defined as EGGS

COLUMNS

ROWS						
	1,1	1,2	1,3	1,4	1,5	1,6
	2,1	2,2	2,3	2,4	2,5	2,6

Notes:

1. Elements in a two-dimensional array are accessed by specifying two indexes. For example, if the third element in the second row was needed, one index with a value of 2 and a second with a value of 3 would be required in most high-level languages (BASIC, COBOL, etc).
2. Because RPG does not support multidimensional arrays, this processing may be simulated by storing all elements in a one-dimensional array. Calculation procedures must be provided to control multidimensional simulation.

Figure 11-2 Structure of one- and two-dimensional arrays.

One-Dimensional Arrays

The storage positions built for an array are referred to as *elements*. The array NAM, shown in Figure 11-2, was built with six elements. All the elements may be accessed at one time by specifying only the array name. Individual elements may be accessed by including a comma and a literal or variable field index with the array name. Program requirements will determine how the array is processed.

Multidimensional Arrays

Refer to Figure 11-2 for an example of a two- (multi-)dimensional array. This structure may be better understood if the array shown is thought of as an egg carton with two rows of six eggs each. In languages such as COBOL and BASIC, the third egg (column 3) from row 2 would be accessed by specifying two indexes. For example, the coding in COBOL would be:

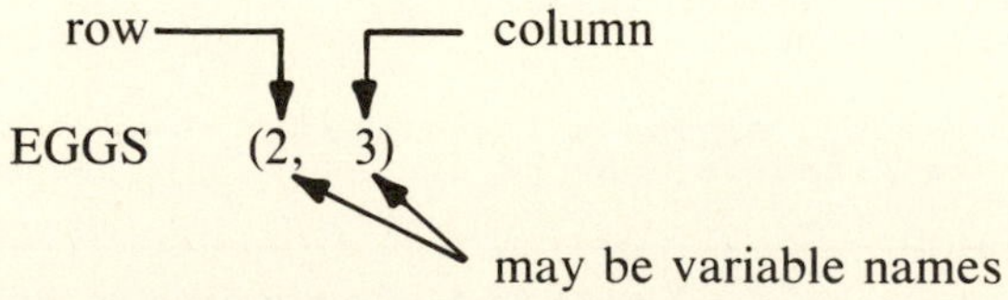

RPG *does not* directly support multidimensional arrays. This structure may be simulated by two methods, however. In an RPG II environment, a one-dimensional array is created and loaded with all the row and column data. Then, processing is controlled by calculations. If RPG III/400 (IBM System/38 and AS/400) is available, multidimensional array processing may be supported by the OCUR statement. An RPG II simulation method is explained at the end of this chapter followed by an OCUR example.

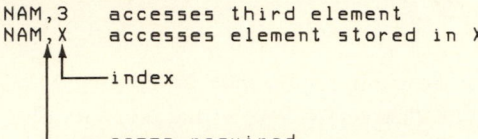

LOADING AN ARRAY

Loading an array refers to the time in the program cycle during which data is read, moved, and stored in the array elements built by the attributes defined in the Extension Specifications. Similar to tables, arrays may be loaded at Compile and Object (preexecution) Times. They may also be loaded at Input and Calculation Times (both being execution time). Figure 11-3 details the processing logic associated with loading an array at various times in the program cycle.

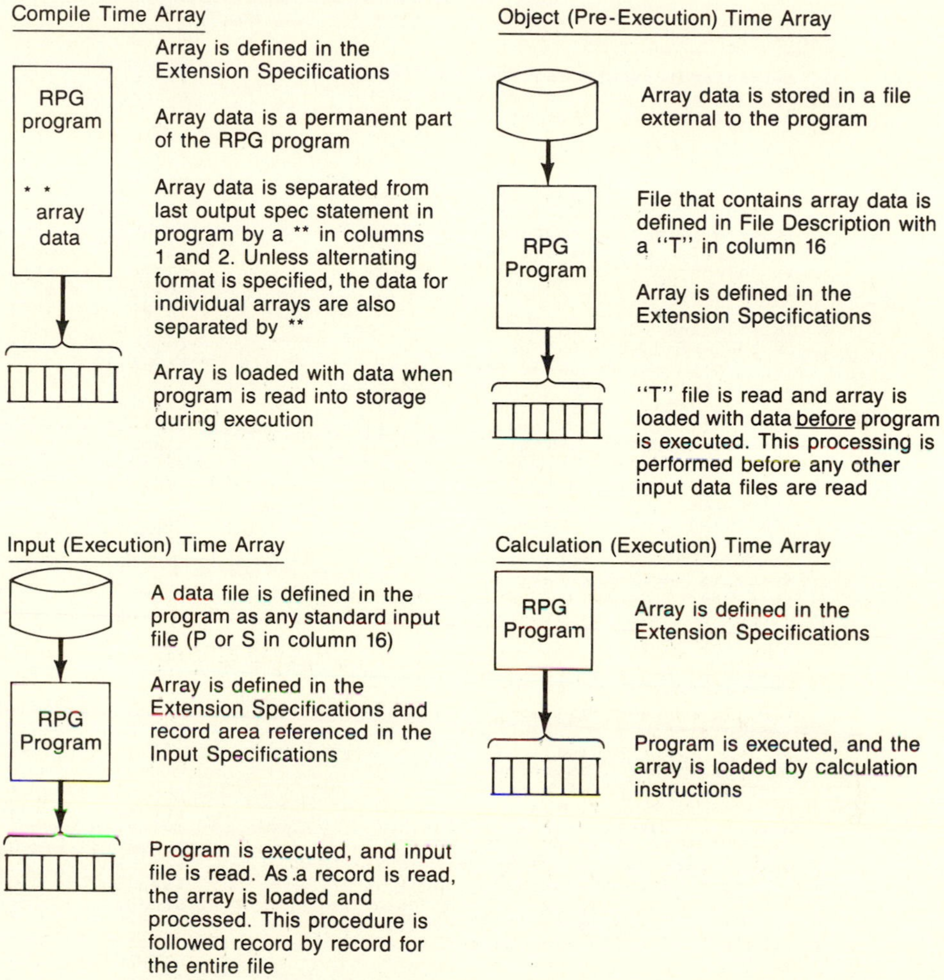

Figure 11-3 Processing logic for loading arrays at Compile, Object, Input, and Calculation Times.

ARRAY DESCRIPTION

Number of elements, size of the elements, type, and sequence (referred to as attributes) are specified in the Extension Specifications. This form allocates the array's total storage area before the loading of data. Refer to Figure 11-4 for an explanation of the fields used to define and load an array at Compile, Object, Input, and Calculation Times.

Line (3–5)	Form Type (6)	Record Sequence of the Chaining Field / Number of the Chaining Field (7–10)	From Filename (11–18)	To Filename (19–26)	Table or Array Name (27–32)	Number of Entries Per Record (33–35)	Number of Entries Per Table or Array (36–39)	Length of Entry (40–42)	P/B/L/R (43)	Decimal Positions (44)	Sequence (A/D) (45)	Table or Array Name (Alternating Format) (46–51)	Length of Entry (52–54)	P/B/L/R (55)	Decimal Positions (56)	Sequence (A/D) (57)	Comments (58–74)
01Ø	E				AR1	12	12	2		Ø	A						COMPILE TIME
02Ø	E		ARYFILE	REPORT	AR2	1	15Ø	8			D						OBJECT TIME
03Ø	E				AR3		25	1									INPUT TIME
04Ø	E				AR4		5	8		2							CALCULATION TIME
05Ø	E				AR5	1	2Ø	3				AR6	18				COMPILE ARRAYS/
06Ø	E	*															ALTERNATING FORM

Explanation of Fields:

1. Extension instructions are identified by the letter E in column 6 and follow F specification statements.

2. Columns 7-10: Not used.

3. From Filename (Columns 11-18): Required for object (pre-execution) time arrays. Related file must be defined in File Description as an input table file (I in column 15, T in column 16, and an E in column 39).

4. To Filename (Columns 19-26): If a copy of the array is required (to disk, tape, printer, or CRT), the related output file defined in File Description must be entered in this field. This option is typically used when the array has been updated during processing.

5. Array Name (Columns 27-32): Any programmer-supplied array name must be specified in this field. Unlike tables, array names must not begin with the letters TAB. If index processing of the array is required, name should be shortened to provide for the required comma and numeric literal or variable field name.

6. Number of Entries Per Record (Columns 33-35): This entry is required only for Compile and Object Time arrays. It indicates how the array data is stored in the records. Similar to tables, data must be entered beginning in the first column of the related records.

7. Number of Entries Per Array (Columns 36-39): This entry is required for all array types. It builds and dimensions the array with the number elements specified in this field. A 12 indicates a twelve element array; 150, a one-hundred and fifty element array; and so forth.

8. Length of Entry (Columns 40-42): This entry is required for all array types. It formats the size of the elements according to the value entered in this field. Numeric array elements may be a maximum of 15 bytes and alphanumeric 256.

9. P = Packed/B = Binary (Column 43): If the numeric array data is to be stored in a zoned decimal format, this field is blank. When the array data is packed (internal decimal format), the letter P must be entered. Numeric array data that is stored as binary, must be identified by entering a B in this field (not a commonly used format).

10. Decimal Positions (Column 44): A blank in this field indicates the array is alphanumeric. Number 0-9 entered defines array as numeric and assigns implied decimal positions.

11. Sequence(A/D) (Column 45): If the array data is in an unordered sequence, this field must be blank. When the data is sorted in ascending order, the letter A may be entered. If the data is in a descending order, D may be entered. Random processing of an array (LOKUP) is more efficient if the array data is in a sorted order.

12. Array Name (Alternating Format) (Columns 46-51): Similar to tables, alternating format indicates that two or more elements from related arrays are stored on each record. In other words, one data element for AR1 followed by one data element for AR2. Number of Entries Per array specifies how many "pairs" per record. Entry is used only with Compile and Object Time arrays.

13. Columns 52-57: Relate to attributes of alternating array. Refer to items 8, 9, and 10 above for an explanation of these fields.

Figure 11-4 Fields used in the Extension Specifications to define arrays for loading at Compile, Object, Input, and Calculation Times.

RPG SYNTAX FOR COMPILE TIME ARRAYS

It was previously indicated that *Compile Time* array data is an integral ("hard-coded") part of an RPG program. It must be included after a ** control statement entered in columns 1 and 2 and follow the last output (O) statement in the program. Unless alternating sequence is specified, the data for two or more arrays must also be separated by a ** control statement. Figure 11-5 shows the relationship of the Extension form coding and the data for two Compile Time arrays.

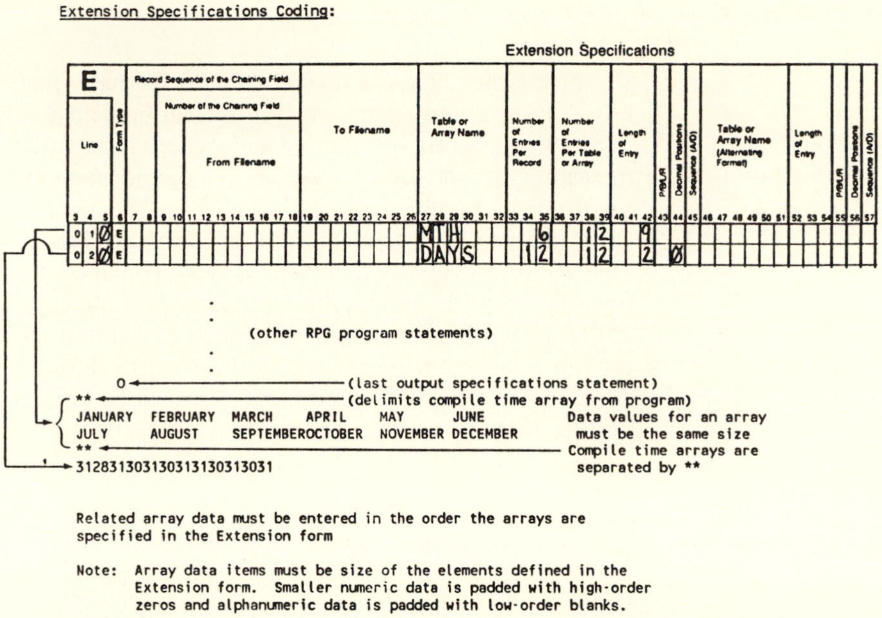

Figure 11-5 Extension Specification syntax and related data for two Compile Time arrays.

RPG SYNTAX FOR COMPILE TIME ARRAYS STORED IN AN ALTERNATING FORMAT

Figure 11-6 shows the array data from Figure 11-5 rearranged in an alternating format with the modified Extension form coding.

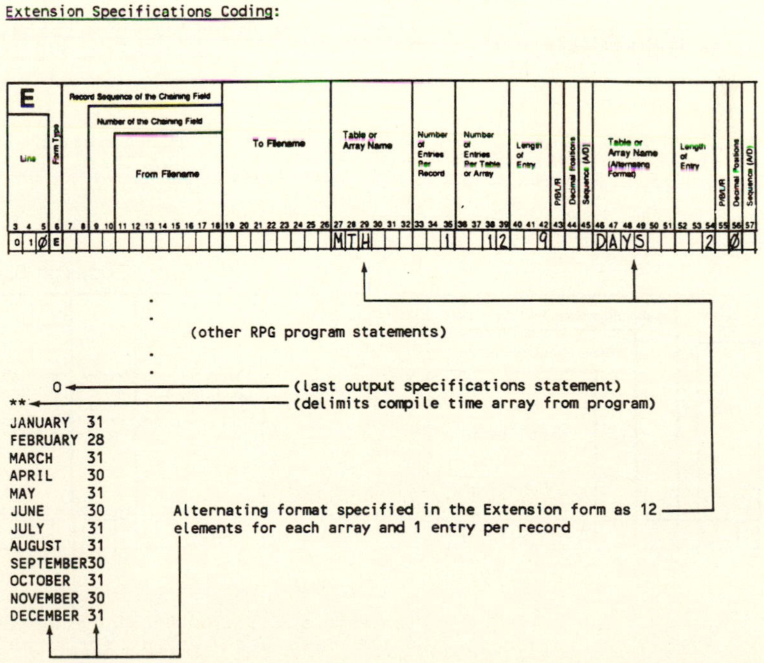

Figure 11-6 Extension Specification syntax and related data for two Compile Time array data arranged in an alternating format.

RPG SYNTAX FOR OBJECT TIME ARRAYS

Data for Object Time arrays is stored externally from the program on disk, diskette, or tape files. The array is formatted and loaded with data from the file *before* the program is executed and any other data files are read. The array remains in storage for the entire program cycle, and unless updated by the program, element values are unchanged.

Figure 11-7 illustrates the syntax required in an RPG program to support an Object Time array when the data is stored on disk. Notice that the File Description Specifications define the file that includes the array data as an input (I in column 15) table file (T in column 16). The E in column 39 indicates that the attributes for the records in the file are defined in the Extension and not the Input form. Also, notice that the related file name must be entered in the From Filename field on the Extension form.

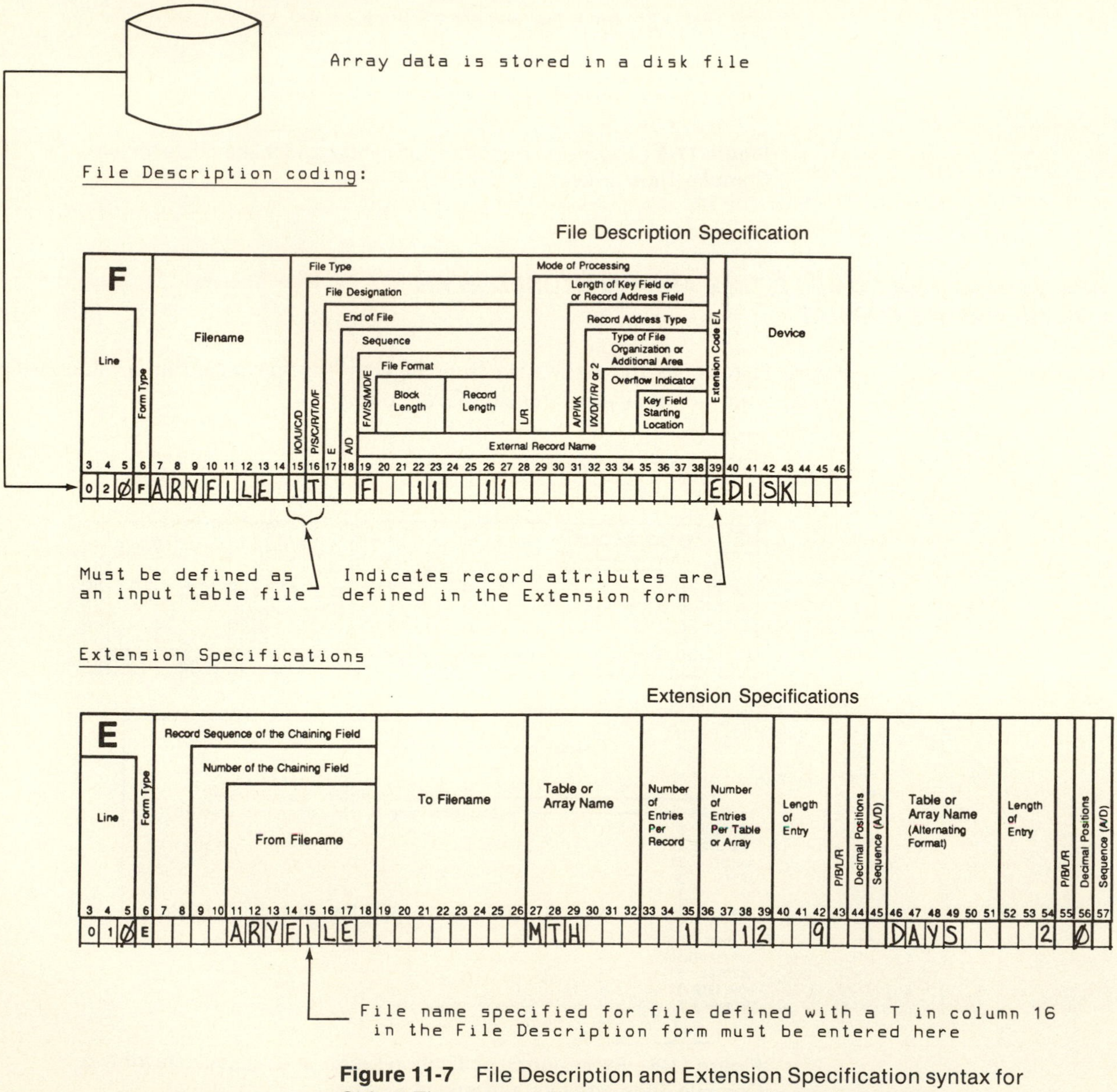

Figure 11-7 File Description and Extension Specification syntax for Object Time arrays. Data arranged in an alternating format.

FORMAT OF DATA FOR COMPILE AND OBJECT TIME ARRAYS

Data for the Compile and Object Time arrays must be formatted according to the rules explained in Figure 11-8.

```
1. Data must begin in first column of each record.

2. Elements for an array must be the same size.

3. Smaller numeric elements must be padded with high-order zeros and
   smaller alphanumeric elements must be padded with low-order blanks.

4. When alternating sequence is used for the data for two arrays, the
   values for the two arrays must be included on a record based on the
   Number of Entries Per Record entry in the Extension form. Values
   may not be separated on two records.

5. Order of the data in a Compile Time array must relate to the Extension
   entry. The first array defined must have its data included first at
   the end of the program (after a **), and so forth.
```

Figure 11-8 Rules for formatting the data records for Compile and Object Time arrays.

The decision to use a Compile or Object Time array in a program usually depends on the following:

1. Compile Time arrays are used when the array is small (i.e., having few elements), the data is not likely to change, and/or the data is not shared by other programs. The month name and the day arrays previously shown are an example of the type of information that may be included in this array classification.
2. Object Time arrays are used when an array is large (i.e., having many elements), the data frequently updated, and/or the data is used by other programs.

RPG SYNTAX FOR INPUT TIME ARRAYS

Like Object Time, the data for Input Time arrays are also stored on an external medium, such as disk, diskette, or tape. However, there are significant storage and processing differences that are identified in the comparison in Figure 11-9.

Input Time Array Features	*Object Time Array Features*
1. Data for the array may be stored in any field (or fields) in the body of the input records.	1. Data for the array must begin in column 1 of the input record (unless it relates to the data for the second array in an alternating sequence format).
2. Any number of arrays may be defined for an input file not defined as a table file.	2. A maximum of two arrays (alternating format) may be included in a file defined as an input table file.
3. Other fields in the record not defined as arrays may be formatted and processed.	3. Any data following array value(s) is ignored and not available for processing.
4. Array is built and loaded with data after the program is executed and first data record is read from a related input file.	4. Array is loaded with data from the entire file before any other processing occurs (pre-execution time).
5. Array data is changed for every record processed.	5. Array data remain unchanged (unless updated) for the complete program cycle.

Figure 11-9 Comparison of the storage and processing logic for Input and Object Time arrays.

Input Time arrays are used when the input data is to be manipulated for each record processed. Defining a field in the body of an input record as an array and validating each character as valid alphabetic is one example that requires the use of this array format.

Object Time arrays are frequently used for large groups of common data that is stored and referenced in processing. For example, a list of 500 acceptable account numbers stored as an Object Time array that will be subsequently validated by other data is an application of this array type.

The File, Extension, and Input Specification syntax to support Input Time array processing is detailed in Figure 11-10.

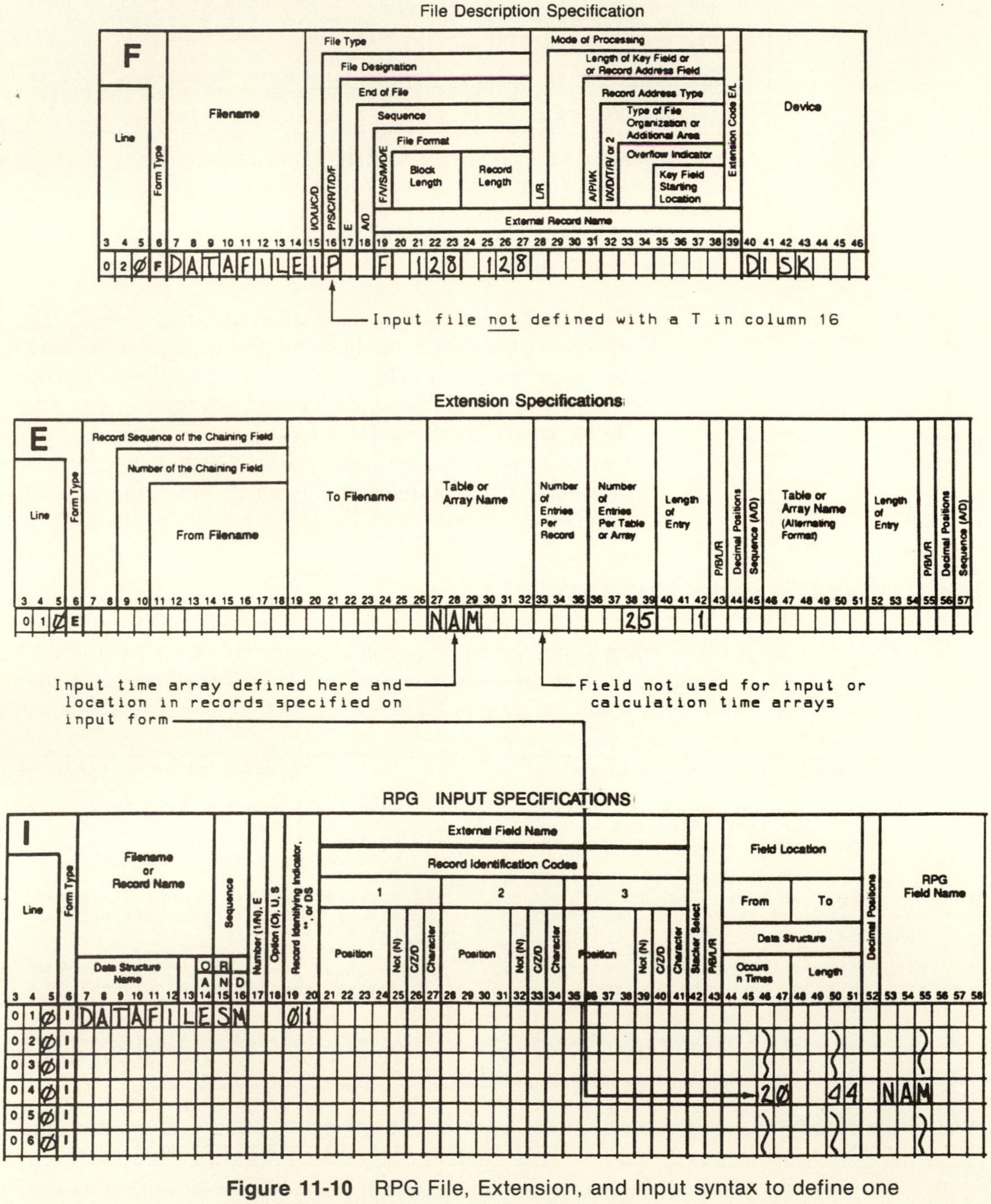

Figure 11-10 RPG File, Extension, and Input syntax to define one Input Time array.

RPG SYNTAX FOR CALCULATION TIME ARRAYS

Calculation time arrays are defined on the Extension form and loaded at execution time by statements in the Calculation form. Any of the arithmetic and Z-ADD, Z-SUB, SQRT, MOVE, MOVEL, MOVEA (discussed later) operations may be used to load a Calculation Time array. How and when the array is loaded will depend on the processing requirements. Figure 11-11 details the syntax for loading a Calculation Time array with the data from an Input Time array by an ADD operation.

Extension Specification

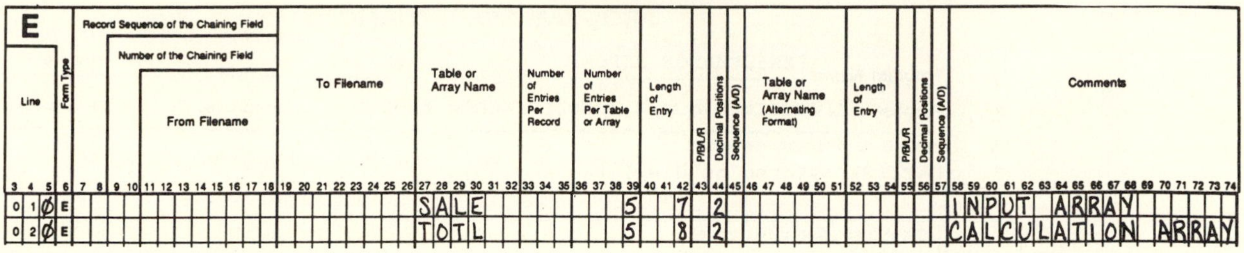
E
Record Sequence of the Chaining Field
Number of the Chaining Field
From Filename
To Filename
Table or Array Name
Number of Entries Per Record
Number of Entries Per Table or Array
Length of Entry
P/B/L/R
Decimal Positions
Sequence (A/D)
Table or Array Name (Alternating Format)
Length of Entry
Comments
0 1 Ø E SALE 5 7 2 INPUT ARRAY
0 2 Ø E TOTL 5 8 2 CALCULATION ARRAY

RPG CALCULATION SPECIFICATION

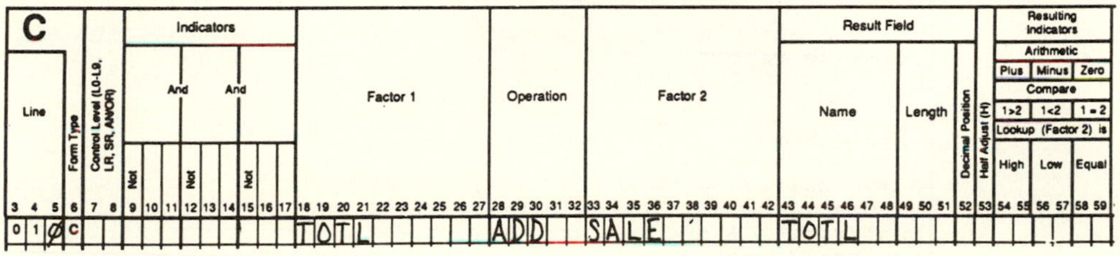
C
Line
Form Type
Control Level (L0-L9, LR, SR, AN/OR)
Indicators
And
And
Not
Factor 1
Operation
Factor 2
Result Field
Name
Length
Decimal Position
Half Adjust (H)
Resulting Indicators
Arithmetic
Plus Minus Zero
Compare
1>2 1<2 1=2
Lookup (Factor 2) is
High Low Equal
0 1 Ø C TOTL ADD SALE TOTL

Processing result of the ADD Statement:

```
SALE array   |1000000|0500000|0025099|0003933|0000999|

                 +       +       +       +       +

TOTL array   |1000000|0500000|0025099|0003933|0000999|
```

Assumes TOTL elements were zeros before execution of ADD statement

Note: The one ADD statement adds all of the element values from the SALE array to the TOTL array.
Same control may be used with any other arithmetic operation.

Figure 11-11 RPG Extension and Calculation syntax to define and load one Calculation Time array.

PROCESSING ARRAYS

The RPG syntax used to define all the array types has been explained in the preceding paragraphs without any discussion of how they are processed. Compile, Object, Input, or Calculation Time arrays may be processed consecutively or randomly. An entire array may be processed at one time, or individual elements may be randomly accessed. Extracting select elements from an array requires the use of indexes. This and other processing methods are explained in the following text and program examples. The first example of an application program illustrates the consecutive processing of one Input and one Calculation Time array.

APPLICATION PROGRAM—SALESPERSON MONTHLY PERFORMANCE REPORT

Documentation

The specifications presented in Figure 11-12 explain the processing requirements for the first application program that generates a Monthly Sales Performance Report by salesperson. The system flowchart in Figure 11-13 indicates that one input disk file and one output printer file are processed by the program.

PROGRAM SPECIFICATIONS Page 1 of 1

Program Name PERFORMANCE REPORT Program-ID CH11P1 Written By S. Myers

Purpose Salesperson Monthly Performance Report Approved By The Boss

Input files (directory names):
DAT11P1 (stored on disk)

Output files (directory names):
PRINTER (stock paper)

Processing Narrative:

```
Write a structured RPG program to generate a salesperson monthly per-
formance report.

Input to the program:

A monthly sales file (DAT11P1), stored on disk, includes the sales
transactions for the company salespersons for one month of the cur-
rent year. A supplemental layout form details the format of the
the input records

Processing:

Provide for an input time array and calculation time array in the
program. Define the weekly sales amount fields (four) as the input
time array data source. For every record processed cross-foot the
four weekly sales amounts to generate the total sales for the related
week. Add the four week sales amounts (defined as the input time
array) from every record to the four elements in the calculation time
array. At last record time cross-foot the calculation time array
element totals for the total company monthly sales.

Output:

Generate the report detailed in the attached printer spacing chart
in accordance with the following considerations:

     1. Use stock paper.
     2. Headings on the top of every page.
     3. Use system-supplied date for the report.
```

Figure 11-12 Specifications for an application program that processes an Input and a Calculation Time array consecutively.

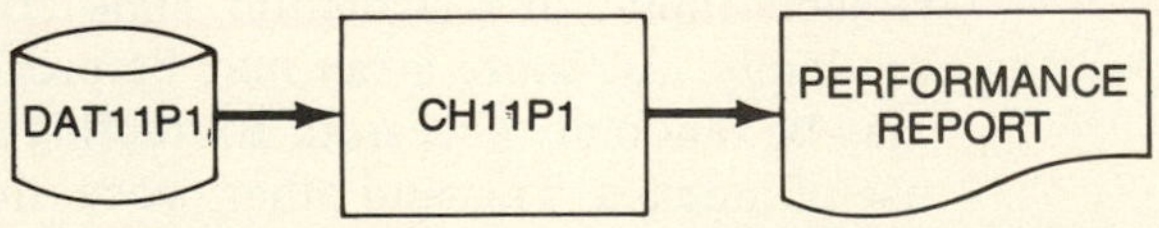

Figure 11-13 System flowchart for sales performance report program.

Figure 11-14 details the record format of the input file. The salesperson fields (columns 7 through 41) will be processed as a five-element Input Time array. The design of the Monthly Sales Performance Report is shown in Figure 11-15. The report generated by the program is detailed in Figure 11-16.

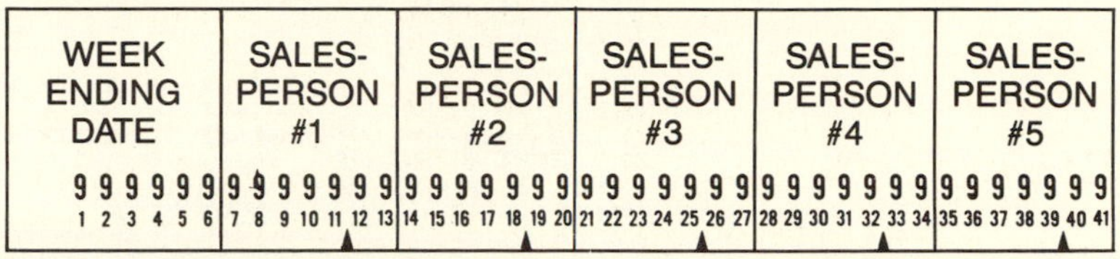

Figure 11-14 Record layout form for input file processed by sales performance report program.

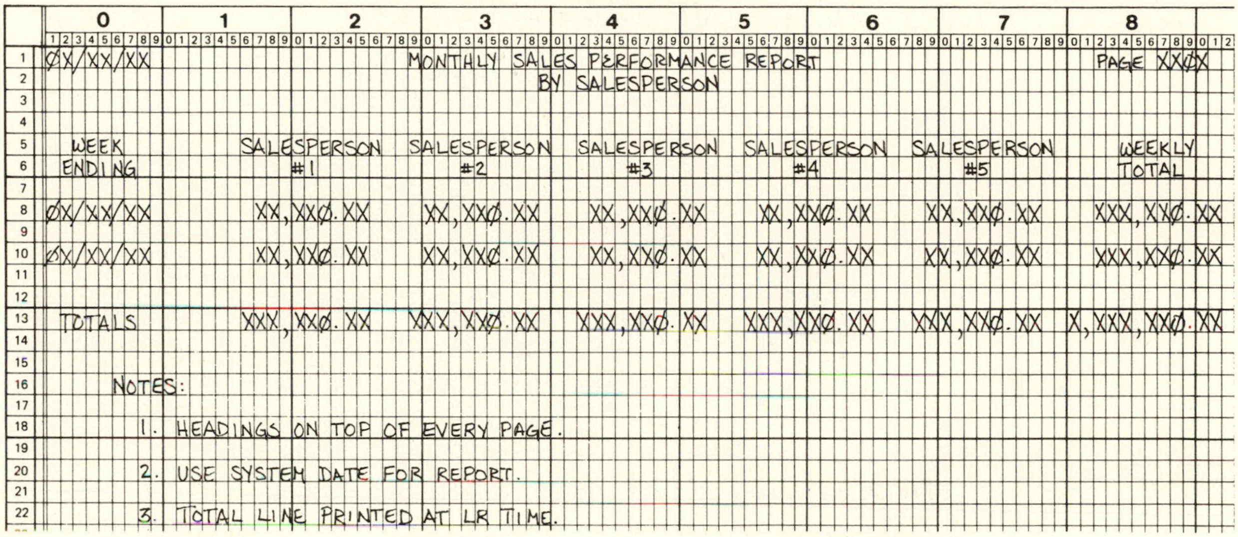

Figure 11-15 Design of Monthly Sales Performance Report.

```
6/30/91                MONTHLY SALES PERFORMANCE REPORT                    PAGE    1
                                 BY SALESPERSON
```

WEEK ENDING	SALESPERSON #1	SALESPERSON #2	SALESPERSON #3	SALESPERSON #4	SALESPERSON #5	WEEKLY TOTAL
6/04/91	80.00	145.30	351.40	124.00	52.24	752.94
6/11/91	543.00	570.00	5,800.01	585.00	630.00	8,128.01
6/18/91	90.00	400.00	525.00	535.00	7,540.00	9,090.00
6/25/91	500.00	453.00	120.99	850.00	860.00	2,783.99
6/30/91	120.00	123.00	140.00	1,508.00	30.00	1,921.00
TOTALS	1,333.00	1,691.30	6,937.40	3,602.00	9,112.24	22,675.94

Figure 11-16 Report generated by Monthly Sales Performance Report Program.

Source Program Coding

A source listing of the Monthly Sales Performance Report program is given in Figure 11-17. Syntax related to array processing is discussed in separate figures.

```
... ... 1 ... ... 2 ... ... 3 ... ... 4 ... ... 5 ... ... 6 ... ... 7 ...
0001  *************SALESPERSON MONTHLY PERFORMANCE REPORT***************  CH11P1
0002  * PROCESSING CONTROLLED BY 1 INPUT TIME & 1 CALCULATION TIME ARRAY  CH11P1
0003 H                                                                    CH11P1
0004 FDAT11P1 IP  F  41  41            DISK                               CH11P1
0005 FREPORT  O   F 132 132     OF     PRINTER                            CH11P1
0006 E                    SALS        5  7 2             INPUT TIME ARRAY CH11P1
0007 E                    TOTL        5  8 2             CALC TIME ARRAY  CH11P1
0008 IDAT11P1 SM  01                                                      CH11P1
0009 I                                        1   60WEDATE                CH11P1
0010 I                                        7  41 SALS                  CH11P1
0011 C                     XFOOTSALS      WEKTOT  82       WEEK'S TOTAL   CH11P1
0012 C           TOTL      ADD  SALS      TOTL             ACCUMULATE SALSCH11P1
0013 CLR                   XFOOTTOTL      MTHTOT  82       MONTH SALES    CH11P1
0014 OREPORT  H  101   1P                                                 CH11P1
0015 O       OR        OF                                                 CH11P1
0016 O                         UDATE Y    8                               CH11P1
0017 O                                   40 'MONTHLY SALES'               CH11P1
0018 O                                   59 'PERFORMANCE REPORT'          CH11P1
0019 O                                   85 'PAGE'                        CH11P1
0020 O                         PAGE  Z   90                               CH11P1
0021 O        H  3     1P                                                 CH11P1
0022 O       OR        OF                                                 CH11P1
0023 O                                   51 'BY SALESPERSON'              CH11P1
0024 O        H  1     1P                                                 CH11P1
0025 O       OR        OF                                                 CH11P1
0026 O                                    6 'WEEK'                        CH11P1
0027 O                                   39 'SALESPERSON  SALESPERSON'    CH11P1
0028 O                                   65 'SALESPERSON  SALESPERSON'    CH11P1
0029 O                                   89 'SALESPERSON     WEEKLY'      CH11P1
0030 O        H  2     1P                                                 CH11P1
0031 O       OR        OF                                                 CH11P1
0032 O                                    7 'ENDING'                      CH11P1
0033 O                                   34 '#1            #2'            CH11P1
0034 O                                   60 '#3            #4'            CH11P1
0035 O                                   88 '#5           TOTAL'          CH11P1
0036 O        D  2     01                                                 CH11P1
0037 O                         WEDATEY    8                               CH11P1
0038 O                         SALS      81 '  , 0.  &&&&'                CH11P1
0039 O                         WEKTOT1   91                               CH11P1
0040 O        T 1      LR                                                 CH11P1
0041 O                                    7 'TOTALS'                      CH11P1
0042 O                         TOTL      80 '   , 0.  &&&'                CH11P1
0043 O                         MTHTOT1   91                               CH11P1
```

Figure 11-17 Source listing of Monthly Performance Report program.

File Description and Extension Specifications Coding

Because Input Time or Calculation Time arrays do not require any changes in File Description coding, this form will not be discussed. On the other hand, any arrays included in an RPG program must be defined in the Extension form. The syntax for the two arrays used in this application program is shown in Figure 11-18.

Extension Specification

Line (3-5)	Form Type (6)	Record Sequence of the Chaining Field (7-8)	Number of the Chaining Field (9-10)	From Filename (11-18)	To Filename (19-26)	Table or Array Name (27-32)	Number of Entries Per Record (33-35)	Number of Entries Per Table or Array (36-39)	Length of Entry (40-42)	P/B/L/R (43)	Decimal Positions (44)	Sequence (A/D) (45)	Table or Array Name (Alternating Format) (46-51)	Length of Entry (52-54)	P/B/L/R (55)	Decimal Positions (56)	Sequence (A/D) (57)	Comments (58-74)
01Ø	E					SALS		5	7		2							INPUT TIME ARRAY
02Ø	E					TOTL		5	8		2							CALC TIME ARRAY

Figure 11-18 Extension form coding for Monthly Sales Performance Report program.

Input Specifications Coding

In addition to the definition of Input Time arrays in the Extension form, the arrays must also be specified in the input form. The coding for the SALS array is shown in Figure 11-19.

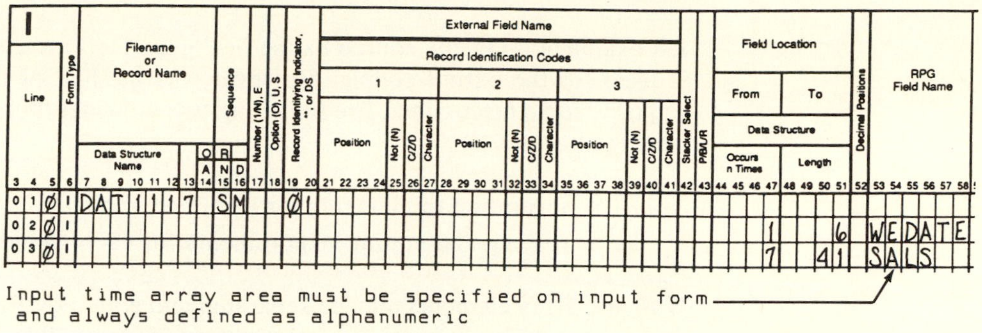

Figure 11-19 Input form coding for Monthly Sales Performance Report program.

Calculation Specifications Coding

The XFOOT Operation. The XFOOT operation, which is unique to numeric array processing, controls the addition function for a numeric array. All the elements are cross-footed (added) in one operation. Figure 11-20 shows one of the XFOOT statements used in the example program and explains the syntax related to this operation.

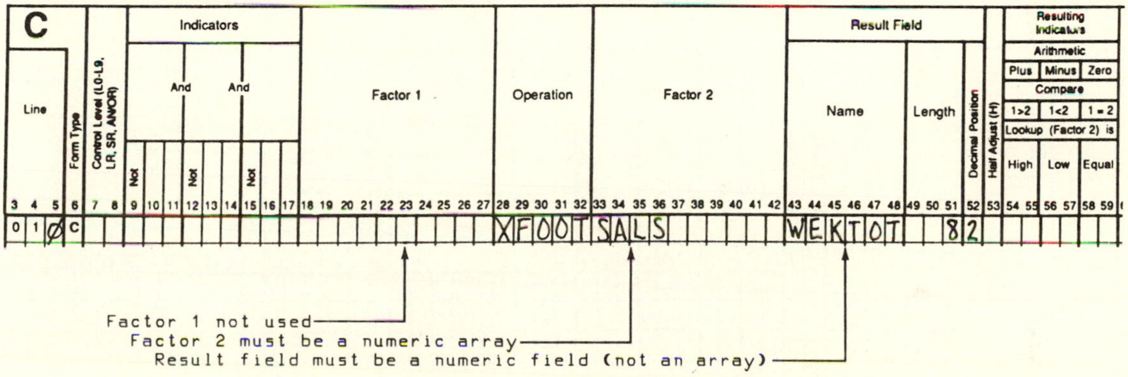

Figure 11-20 XFOOT operation syntax.

The calculation form instructions and results after processing one input record are illustrated in Figure 11-21.

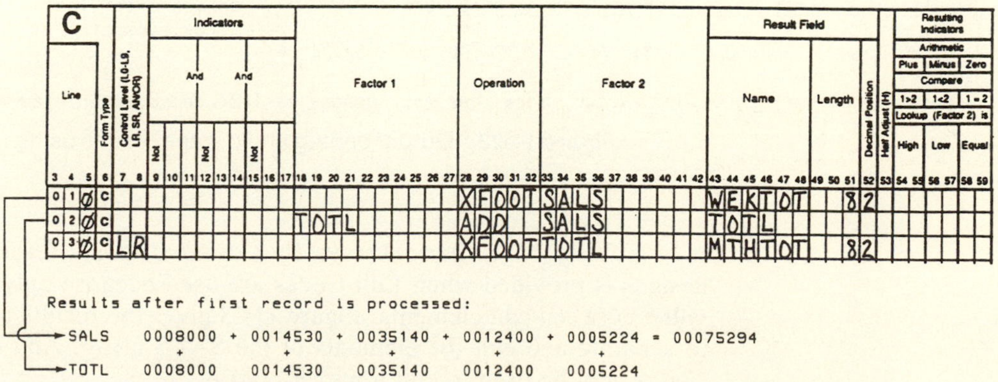

Figure 11-21 Calculations for Monthly Sales Performance Report program.

Output Specifications Coding

An examination of the source listing in Figure 11-17 reveals that familiar syntax is used for the output coding. However, the method of editing numeric arrays requires some discussion. The following two considerations must be given to the editing of arrays:

1. Separation of elements for printing (or display).
2. Spacing and editing requirements for each element.

Numeric array elements may be separated and edited by Edit Words, Edit Codes, or Indexing. The separation of alphanumeric arrays into individual elements is controlled only by indexing. However, because RPG does not support the editing of alphanumeric fields, this function cannot be included for arrays defined as being in this class. Each of these separation and editing functions is discussed in the following paragraphs.

Editing of Numeric Arrays By Edit Words. The coding to edit the SALS array using an Edit Word and processing results are shown in the partial output form in Figure 11-22. If a review of the syntax for Edit Words is needed, refer back to Chapter 3, pages 76–79.

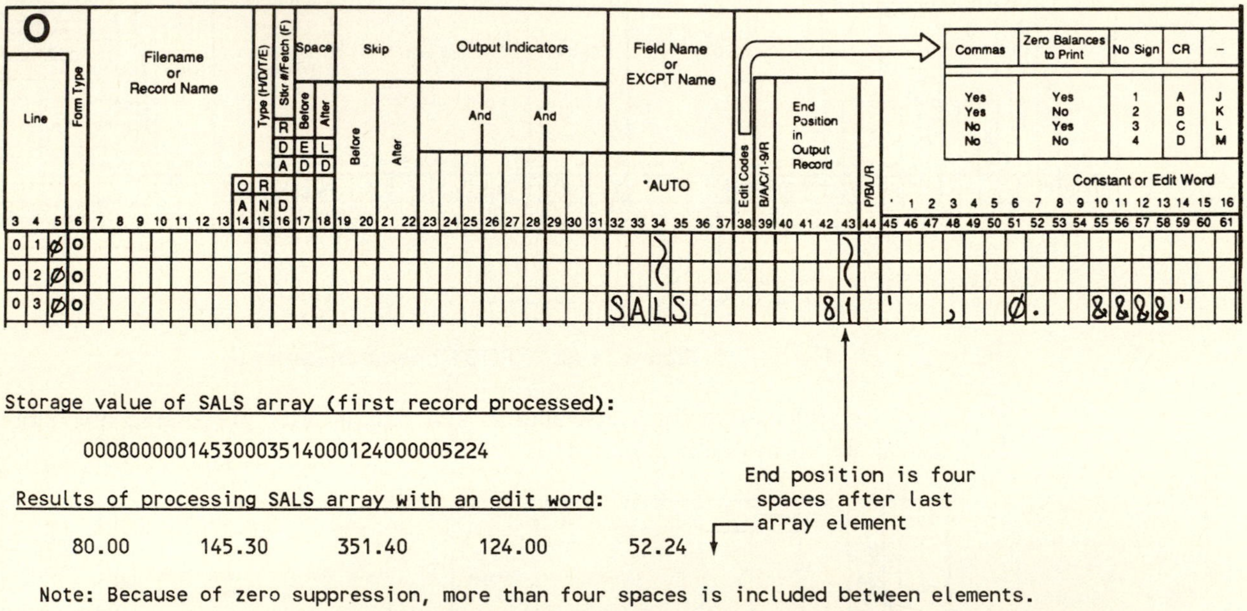

Storage value of SALS array (first record processed):

000800000145300035140001240000005224

Results of processing SALS array with an edit word:

80.00 145.30 351.40 124.00 52.24

End position is four spaces after last array element

Note: Because of zero suppression, more than four spaces is included between elements.

Figure 11-22 Output coding and printed results using an Edit Word.

Editing of Numeric Arrays By Edited Codes. Less flexibility in report designs is provided when Edit Codes are used because only two spaces are provided between edit elements. Figure 11-23 gives the results of using an Edit Code to separate and edit the elements of the SALS array. Any of the available Edit Codes may be used to edit a numeric array.

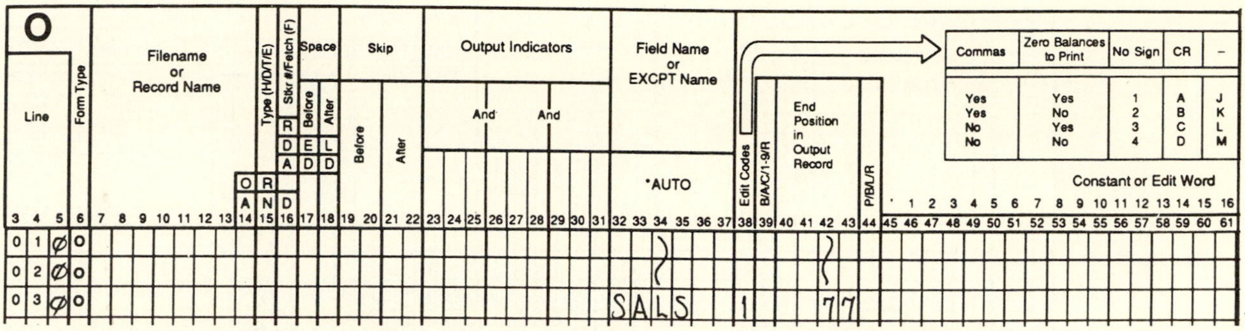

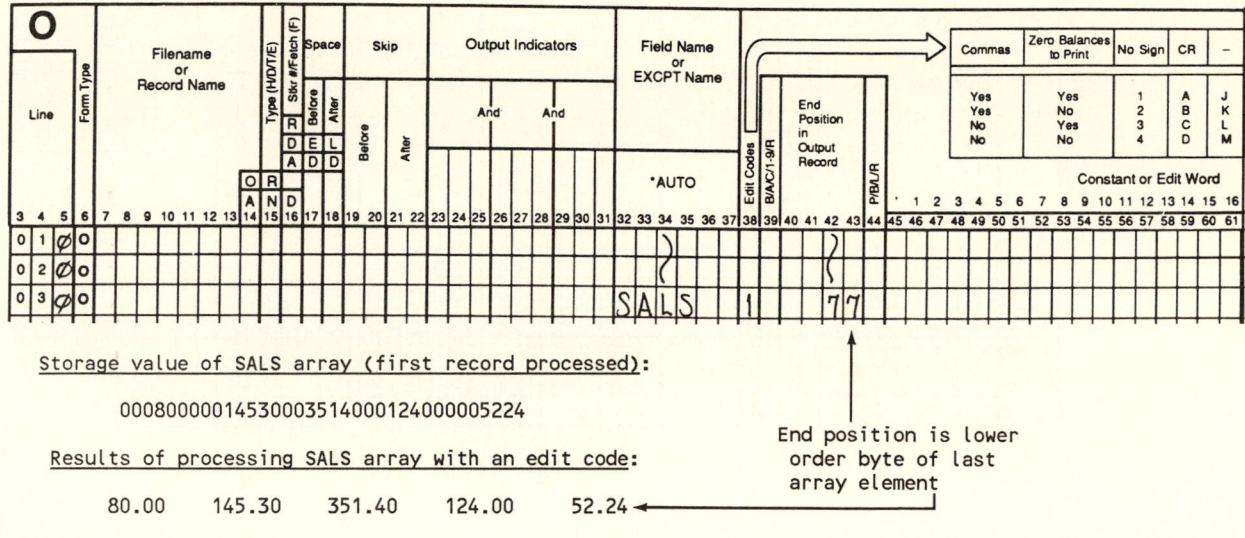

Storage value of SALS array (first record processed):

0008000001453000351400012400000 5224

Results of processing SALS array with an edit code:

80.00 145.30 351.40 124.00 52.24

End position is lower order byte of last array element

Edit codes automatically include two spaces before each element

Note: Because of zero suppression, more than two spaces is included between elements.

Figure 11-23 Output coding and printed results using an Edit Code.

Editing of Numeric and Alphanumeric Arrays By Indexing. The most flexibility in array element separation and editing is provided by the use of indexing. As related to array processing, indexing is the method by which individual array elements are randomly accessed. An index may be a numeric literal or field and must be used with an array name and comma, as shown in Figure 11-24.

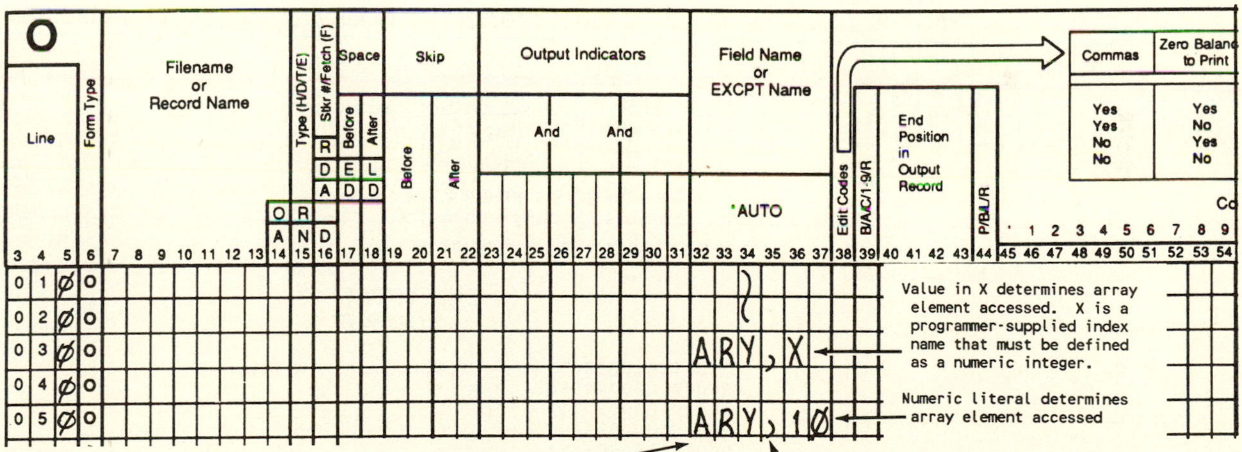

Value in X determines array element accessed. X is a programmer-supplied index name that must be defined as a numeric integer.

Numeric literal determines array element accessed

Array may be numeric or alphanumeric

Comma must be included

Figure 11-24 Output specifications formats for array indexing.

An examination of Figure 11-25 shows how indexing is used to separate the five SALS array elements so they may be individually edited and printed. With indexing, each array element is processed and controlled as a separate data-item.

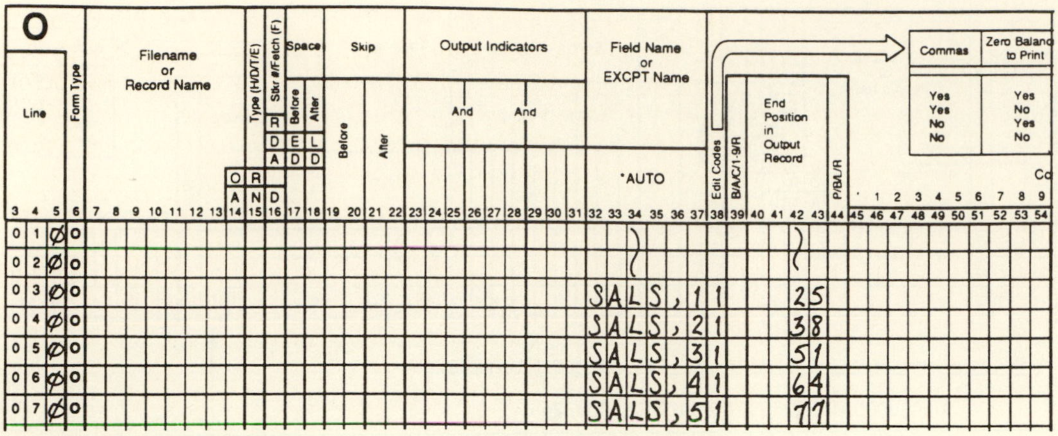

Storage value of SALS array (first record processed):

00080000014530003514000124000005224

Results of processing SALS array with indexing:

80.00 145.30 351.40 124.00 52.24

Indexing accesses each element separately and edits according to specified edit code

Figure 11-25 Output coding and printed results using indexing.

Loading Arrays From More Than One Input Record

The data for loading an array may not always be conveniently stored on one data record, as shown in the previous program example. Data may be scattered within or be included on more than one record. For example, the input file in Figure 11-26 shows that the sales data for the five salespersons for each week is now stored in five separate records. Hence, the data for the entire month is stored on 25 records instead of five, as in the file for the previous program. Also, notice that

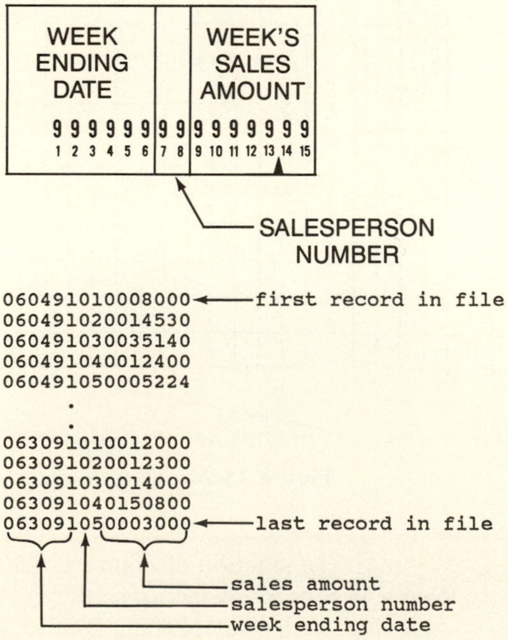

Figure 11-26 Modified record format and file listing of input array data stored on separate records.

the record format has been modified to include a salesperson number field. This addition is needed to determine which record for a related week belongs to what salesperson. Furthermore, if a sort of the file was required before processing, the salesperson number would be used as the *minor* sort field with week ending date used as the *major*. The following program modifications are necessary to load and process the arrays:

1. The SALS array is processed as a Calculation Time instead of an Input Time array. The related input form array reference is eliminated.
2. The SALS array is now loaded in calculations, and EXCPT (exception) output after the five elements are loaded. A counter is used to determine when the array is full (five elements loaded) and is to be *exception* printed.

A source listing of the modified program is shown in Figure 11-27.

```
... ... 1 ... ... 2 ... ... 3 ... ... 4 ... ... 5 ... ... 6 ... ... 7 ...
0001 *            SALESPERSON MONTHLY PERFORMANCE REPORT              CH11P2
0002 *      PROCESSING CONTROLLED BY 2 CALCULATION TIME ARRAYS        CH11P2
0003 *      ARRAY ELEMENT DATA STORED ON SEPARATE INPUT RECORDS       CH11P2
0004 H                                                                CH11P2
0005 FDAT11P2 IP  F  15  15           DISK                            CH11P2
0006 FREPORT  O   F 132 132     OF    PRINTER                         CH11P2
0007 E                     SALS       5  7 2            CALC TIME ARRAY  CH11P2
0008 E                     TOTL       5  8 2            CALC TIME ARRAY  CH11P2
0009 IDAT11P2 SM  01                                                  CH11P2
0010 I                                        1  60WEDATEL1           CH11P2
0011 I                                        7  80SALPR#             CH11P2
0012 I                                        9 152WEKSAL             CH11P2
0013 C          X          ADD  1        X       10     ADD 1 TO INDEX CH11P2
0014 C                     MOVE WEKSAL   SALS,X         LOAD ARRAY ELMTCH11P2
0015 C          X          COMP 5                     20 = ?          CH11P2
0016 C    20               XFOOTSALS     WEKTOT  82     CROSS-FOOT    CH11P2
0017 C    20    TOTL       ADD  SALS     TOTL           INCREMENT MTH CH11P2
0018 C    20               EXCPT                        PRINT LINE    CH11P2
0019 C    20               Z-ADDO        X              SET INDEX TO 0 CH11P2
0020 C    L1               MOVE WEDATE   DATE    60     SAVE WEEK DATE CH11P2
0021 CLR                   XFOOTTOTL     MTHTOT  82     MONTH SALES   CH11P2
0022 OREPORT  H  101   1P                                             CH11P2
0023 O       OR        OF                                             CH11P2
0024 O                       UDATE Y    8                             CH11P2
0025 O                                 40 'MONTHLY SALES'             CH11P2
0026 O                                 59 'PERFORMANCE REPORT'        CH11P2
0027 O                                 85 'PAGE'                      CH11P2
0028 O                       PAGE  Z   90                             CH11P2
0029 O        H  3     1P                                             CH11P2
0030 O       OR        OF                                             CH11P2
0031 O                                 51 'BY SALESPERSON'            CH11P2
0032 O        H  1     1P                                             CH11P2
0033 O       OR        OF                                             CH11P2
0034 O                                  6 'WEEK'                      CH11P2
0035 O                                 39 'SALESPERSON  SALESPERSON'  CH11P2
0036 O                                 65 'SALESPERSON  SALESPERSON'  CH11P2
0037 O                                 89 'SALESPERSON     WEEKLY'    CH11P2
0038 O        H  2     1P                                             CH11P2
0039 O       OR        OF                                             CH11P2
0040 O                                  7 'ENDING'                    CH11P2
0041 O                                 34 '#1             #2'         CH11P2
0042 O                                 60 '#3             #4'         CH11P2
0043 O                                 88 '#5           TOTAL'        CH11P2
0044 O        E  2     01                                             CH11P2
0045 O                       DATE  Y    8                             CH11P2
0046 O                       SALS      81 '  ,  0.  &&&&'             CH11P2
0047 O                       WEKTOT1   91                             CH11P2
0048 O        T 1      LR                                             CH11P2
0049 O                                  7 'TOTALS'                    CH11P2
0050 O                       TOTL      80 '   ,  0.  &&&'             CH11P2
0051 O                       MTHTOT1   91                             CH11P2
```

```
Processing result of statement 0014 after first record is processed:

Value in index X: 1

Data record value: 060488010008000

       SALS array value      |0008000|0000000|0000000|0000000|0000000|
```

Note: SALS array is built in storage according to attributes defined in the Extension form. Array elements are automatically initialized to zeros by the RPG compiler before first record is read.

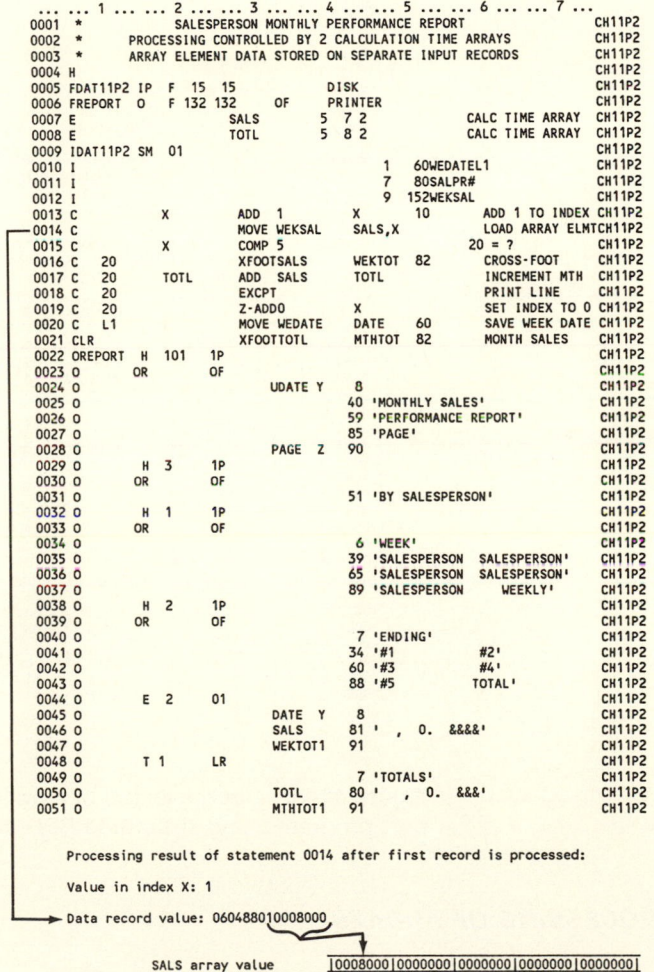

Figure 11-27 Source listing of modified Monthly Performance Report program and result of loading an array element using indexing.

MODIFIED PROGRAM USING RPG III STRUCTURED OPERATIONS

The Salesperson Monthly Performance Report program shown in Figure 11-27 is modified in Figure 11-28 to illustrate the use of RPG III structured operations. The new source listing now includes the following:

1. Data structure for the definition of work fields.
2. IF/ELSE operations to control decision-making processing.
3. Factor 1 entry omitted when specified as the Result Field.
4. EXCPT operation with name control.

```
... ... 1 ... ... 2 ... ... 3 ... ... 4 ... ... 5 ... ... 6 ... ... 7 ...
*          SALESPERSON MONTHLY PERFORMANCE REPORT                      CH11P3
*     PROCESSING CONTROLLED BY 2 CALCULATION TIME ARRAYS               CH11P3
*     ARRAY ELEMENT DATA STORED ON SEPARATE INPUT RECORDS              CH11P3
*     PROGRAM MODIFIED USING RPG III STRUCTURED OPERATIONS             CH11P3
H                                                                      CH11P3
FDAT1127 IP  F  15  15           DISK                                  CH11P3
FREPORT  O   F 132 132     OF    PRINTER                               CH11P3
E                    SALS       5  7 2             CALC TIME ARRAY    CH11P3
E                    TOTL       5  8 2             CALC TIME ARRAY    CH11P3
IDAT1127 SM  01                                                        CH11P3
I                                         1   60WEDATEL1               CH11P3
I                                         7   80SALPR#                 CH11P3
I                                         9  152WEKSAL                 CH11P3
I            DS                                                        CH11P3
I                                         1   82MTHTOT                 CH11P3
I                                         9   90X                      CH11P3
I                                        10  172WEKTOT                 CH11P3
I                                        18  230DATE                   CH11P3
C                     ADD  1         X                ADD 1 TO INDEX CH11P3
C                     MOVE WEKSAL    SALS,X           LOAD ARRAY ELMTCH11P3
C           X         IFEQ 5                          = 5 ?          CH11P3
C                     XFOOTSALS      WEKTOT           CROSS-FOOT SALSCH11P3
C                     ADD  SALS      TOTL             + MTH TOTALS   CH11P3
C                     EXCPTDETAIL                     PRINT WEEK INFOCH11P3
C                     Z-ADDO         X                SET INDEX      CH11P3
C                     END                                            CH11P3
C   L1                MOVE WEDATE    DATE             SAVE WEEK DATE CH11P3
CLR                   XFOOTTOTL      MTHTOT           MONTH SALES    CH11P3
OREPORT  H  101   1P                                                 CH11P3
O        OR       OF                                                 CH11P3
O                         UDATE Y    8                               CH11P3
O                                   40 'MONTHLY SALES'               CH11P3
O                                   59 'PERFORMANCE REPORT'          CH11P3
O                                   85 'PAGE'                        CH11P3
O                         PAGE  Z   90                               CH11P3
O          H  3   1P                                                 CH11P3
O        OR       OF                                                 CH11P3
O                                   51 'BY SALESPERSON'              CH11P3
O          H  1   1P                                                 CH11P3
O        OR       OF                                                 CH11P3
O                                    6 'WEEK'                        CH11P3
O                                   39 'SALESPERSON  SALESPERSON'    CH11P3
O                                   65 'SALESPERSON  SALESPERSON'    CH11P3
O                                   89 'SALESPERSON     WEEKLY'      CH11P3
O          H  2   1P                                                 CH11P3
O        OR       OF                                                 CH11P3
O                                    7 'ENDING'                      CH11P3
O                                   34 '#1          #2'              CH11P3
O                                   60 '#3          #4'              CH11P3
O                                   88 '#5         TOTAL'            CH11P3
O          E  2           DETAIL                                     CH11P3
O                         DATE  Y    8                               CH11P3
O                         SALS      81 '  ,  0.  &&&&'               CH11P3
O                         WEKTOT1   91                               CH11P3
O          T 1    LR                                                 CH11P3
O                                    7 'TOTALS'                      CH11P3
O                         TOTL      80 '   ,  0.  &&&'               CH11P3
O                         MTHTOT1   91                               CH11P3
```

Figure 11-28 Source listing of modified Monthly Performance Report program using structured RPG III operations.

RANDOM PROCESSING OF ARRAYS

Similar to tables, the access to individual array elements may be controlled by the LOKUP operation. However, there are major differences between array and table lookup processing, which are summarized in Figure 11-29. Array look-up may be performed *with* or *without* an index. The processing logic and syntax of each method are discussed in the following paragraphs.

Array LOKUP Features	Table LOKUP Features
1. Element values may be accessed positionally without a LOKUP operation.	1. Entry values may only be accessed by a LOKUP operation.
2. Any number arrays may be related by a common index. Result field is not used in array LOKUP operations.	2. Two tables may be related by entering second table name in the Result Field. Access to other related tables requires additional LOKUP operations.
3. Arrays may be random processed by using an index. Value is extracted directly.	3. Only consecutive table LOKUP is supported. Execution of a LOKUP operation starts processing at first entry in the table.
4. Relative location of an element may be determined by indexing.	4. Relative location of any table entry cannot be determined.
5. Multidimensional array processing may be simulated.	5. Only one-dimensional table processing may be performed.
6. Binary search of arrays may be programmer-coded.	6. Binary search is not available.
7. An equal or range condition LOKUP may be specified.	7. An equal or range condition LOKUP may be specified.
8. Search argument (Factor 1) must be defined the same type as the argument array (Factor 2)	8. Search argument (Factor 1) must be defined the same type as the argument table (Factor 2)

Figure 11-29 Comparison of array with table LOKUP processing.

ARRAY LOOKUP WITHOUT INDEXING

An array is processed without using an index when an element value does not have to be processed after it is found. Checking of a transaction code from an input record by a search of a Compile Time array of valid codes is one example of array lookup that does not require indexing. Figure 11-30 details the syntax and process logic of this type of array lookup.

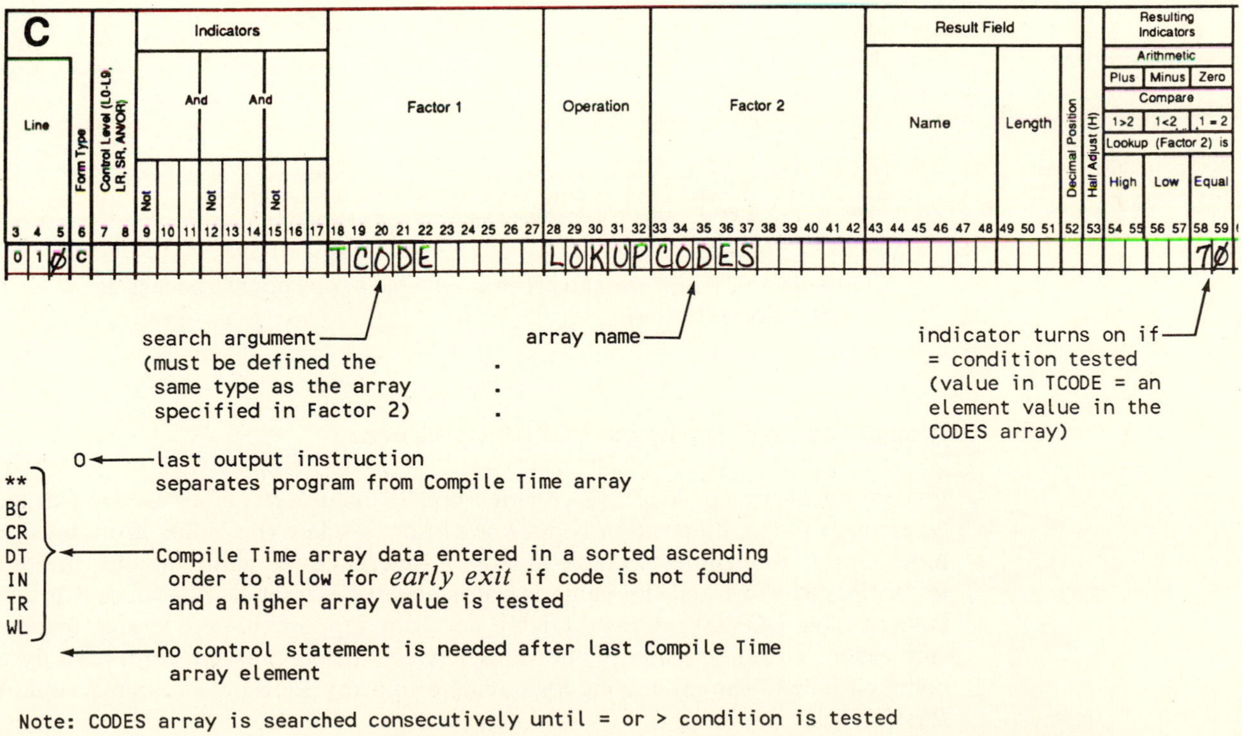

Figure 11-30 Syntax and processing logic of array LOKUP without indexing.

ARRAY LOOKUP BY INDEXING

Positional Processing Without the LOKUP Operation

Indexing must be used in an array lookup if an element value is to be extracted and used in subsequent processing. Access of an element is controlled by indexing, with or without the LOKUP operation (positional processing). An example of the processing of an array by the position of its elements (no LOKUP operation) is shown in Figure 11-31. A month name from the array is accessed for printing by specifying the array and index name. Assume for this example that the index name was previously defined as an Input Field.

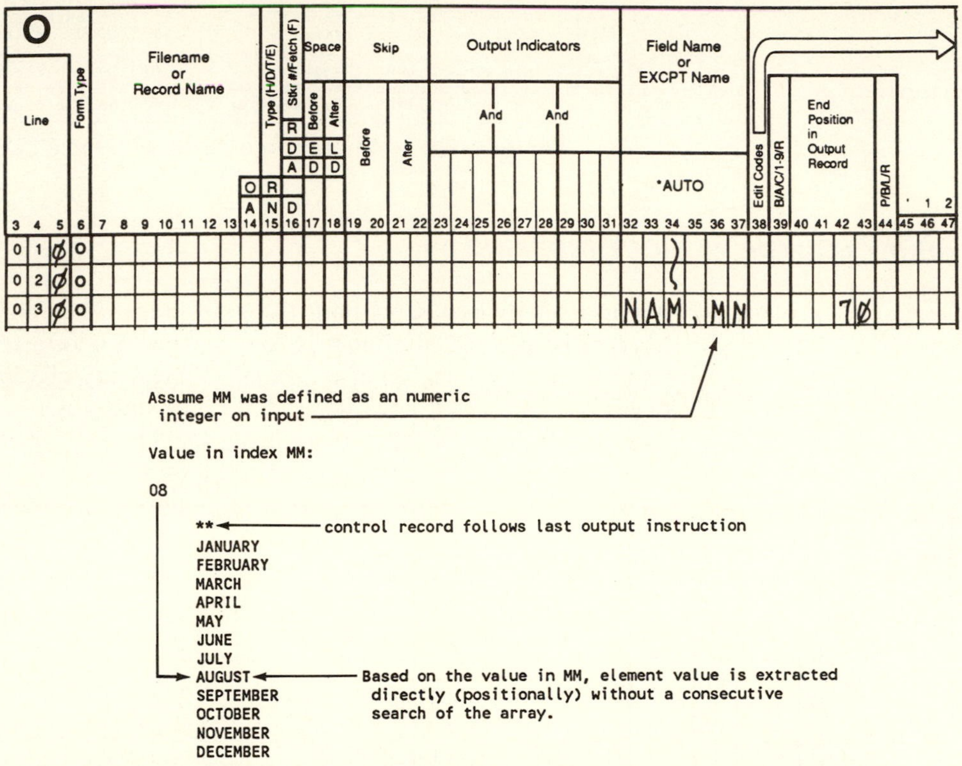

Figure 11-31 Syntax and processing logic to positionally access an array element.

Processing an Array by the LOKUP Operation

Processing an array by indexing with the LOKUP operation is often used to extract an element (when its position is not known) or to relate the values from two or more arrays. Remember, in table lookup, a function table name may be entered in the Result Field and the value is automatically extracted in a successful argument table LOKUP. Array LOKUP does not support this processing feature (see Figure 11-29), and any relationship between arrays must be controlled by a common index. The processing logic unique to array LOKUP is summarized in Figure 11-32.

1. Index must always be defined as a numeric integer.
2. Search of an array begins at the element specified as the value of the index.
3. Index is automatically incremented as array is consecutively searched for an equal or range condition.
4. Index is automatically initialized to 1 before next LOKUP of the array.
5. End of array control is automatically provided. Index is set back to 1 if the LOKUP is unsuccessful and control processed the array to the end.
6. An array element found is not retained from a LOKUP, but may be accessed by specifying the array name and index after the search condition is satisfied.

Figure 11-32 Array LOKUP operation with index processing features.

Illustrated in Figure 11-33 are the syntax and control for processing two related arrays by the LOKUP operation with indexing. Item numbers are stored in one Compile Time Array, and the related item name is stored in a second Compile Time array in an alternating format.

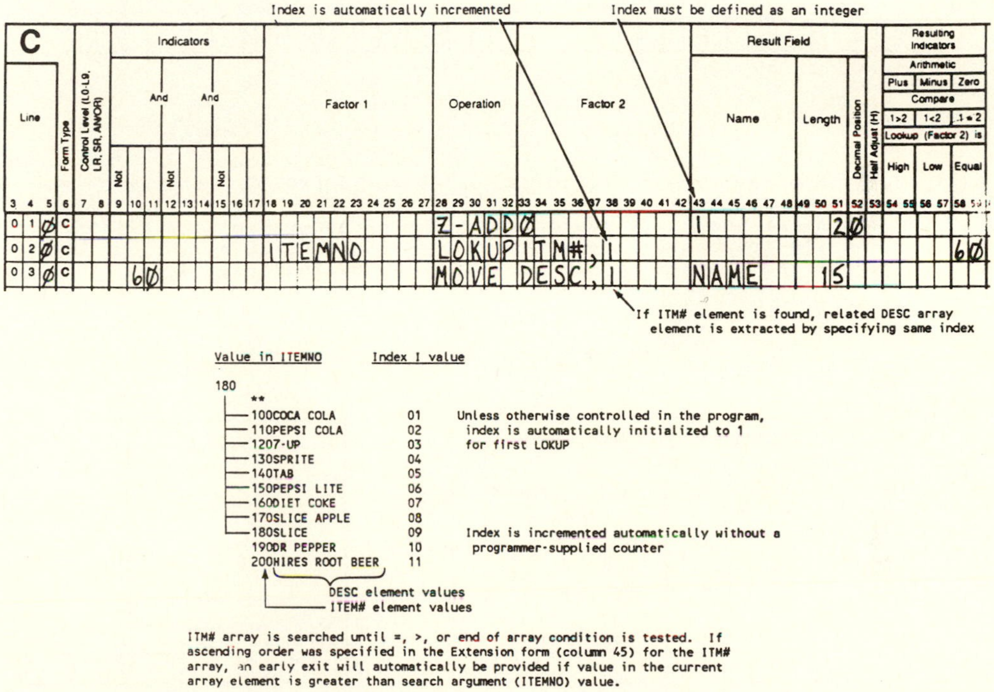

Figure 11-33 Syntax and logic for processing related arrays with the LOKUP operation and index control.

The Move Array (MOVEA) Operation

The values of individual array elements may be moved to another array element or to a field, or from a field to an array element by the MOVE and MOVEL operations. However, if a select *group* of array element values has to be moved or loaded, neither of these previously discussed operations will provide the necessary control. The MOVEA operation, which may be used only if Factor 2 and/or the Result Field is an array(s), is provided in RPG for this processing. Figure 11-34 gives the rules, syntax, and examples of the MOVEA operation.

```
Given:

    Array AR1: 5 - 1 byte elements
    Array AR2: 5 - 1 byte elements
    FIELD: 7 bytes

Rule 1: If array name and index is entered in FACTOR 2, movement of the
        data begins at that element and terminates when all of the
        elements in the array have been moved or when the field or
        array specified in the RESULT FIELD is filled.
```

Example:

```
    Before MOVEA          Value in AR12          Value in AR2
                             12345                  67890
```

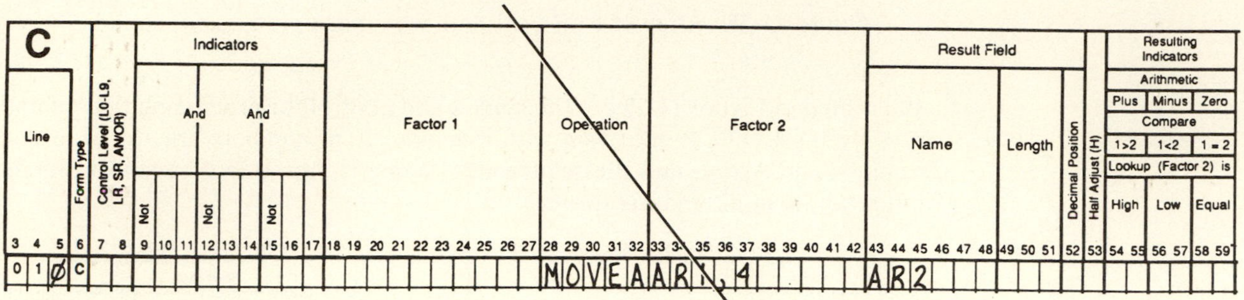


```
    After MOVEA           Value in AR1           Value in AR2
                             12345                  45890

Rule 2: If an array name or field is specified in FACTOR 2 and an array
        with an index is entered in the RESULT FIELD, movement of data
        begins at the first character of the array or field in FACTOR 2
        and starts loading the array in the RESULT FIELD at the
        specified element number as determined by the index value.
```

Example:

```
    Before MOVEA          Value in FIELD         Value in AR2
                             9999999                67890
```

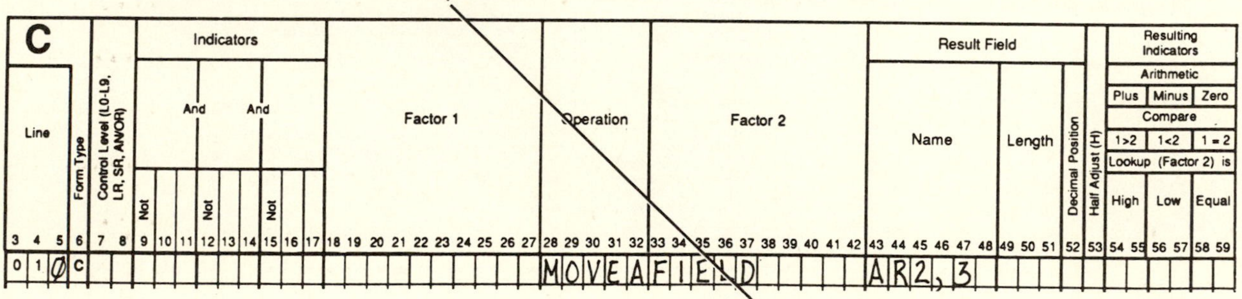


```
    After MOVEA           Value in FIELD         Value in AR2
                             9999999                67999
```

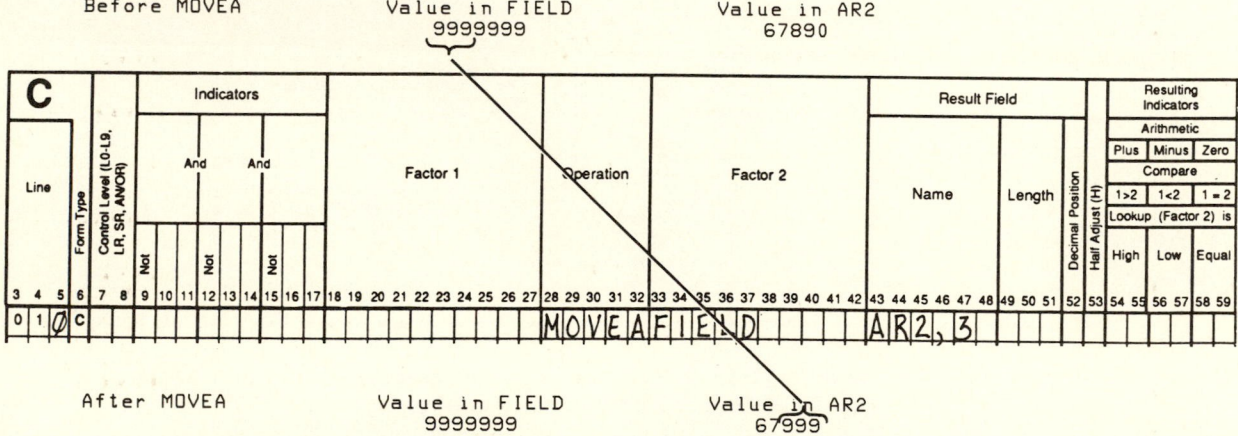

Figure 11-34 Rules, syntax, and examples of the MOVEA (Move Array) operation.

Identical to the MOVE and MOVEL operations, the MOVEA operation does *not* provide a decimal alignment relationship between the sending (Factor 2) and receiving fields (Result Field). The data is moved from an array to a field (or array), or from a field to an array according to the rules specified in Figure 11-34. The RPG compilers on IBM's System/36, 38, and 400 support the MOVEA operation with both alphanumeric and numeric arrays. Other manufacturers, however, may not support this operation for numeric arrays.

MOVEA PROCESSING EXAMPLE

Assume that the following heading is required in the body of a report:

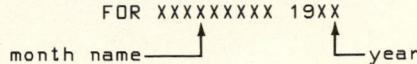

```
            FOR XXXXXXXXX 19XX
                        ↑      ↑
month name──────────────┘      └──year
```

The month name and year are variables that must be supplied during program execution. Month names are stored in a Compile Time array and the year is CONSOLE input. According to the format of this heading, the 19 of the year is to be printed one space from the last character of the month name. However, because month names vary in size, from three (MAY) to nine (SEPTEMBER), additional control must be included in the program to meet this requirement. Otherwise, the following printed output would result for shorter month names:

```
                    FOR MAY         1992

Instead of:

                    FOR MAY 1992
```

The following will be included in the program to support the required processing:

1. A Compile Time month name array is defined with 12 9-byte elements.
2. The related month name is extracted positionally from the month name array using a CONSOLE entered month number as the index.
3. The month name array element (accessed in Step 2) is moved to another array defined with 9 1-byte elements.
4. A loop is included to search the array (loaded in Step 3) elements to determine the length of the name.
5. MOVEA operations are used to build the segments of the required heading format.

The Extension and Calculation Specifications coding are shown in Figure 11-35.

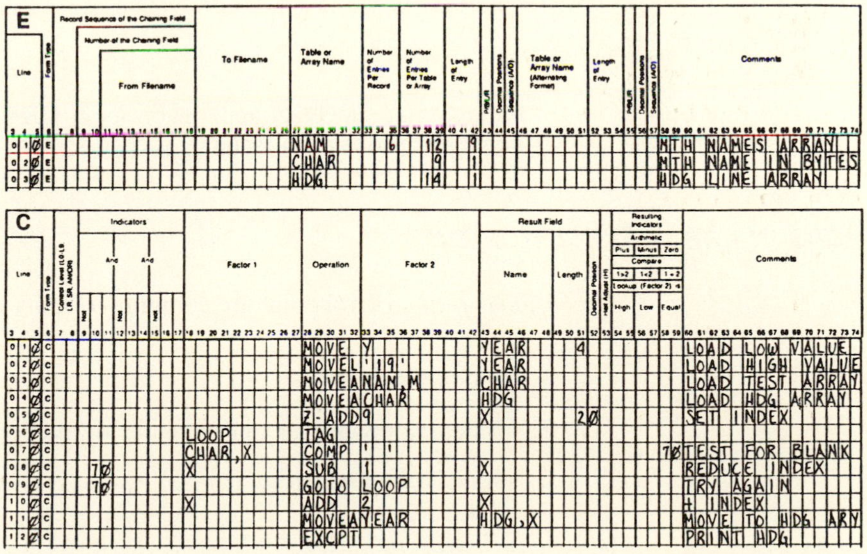

Line	Form Type	From Filename	To Filename	Table or Array Name	Number of Entries Per Record	Number of Entries Per Table or Array	Length of Entry	Comments
01Ø	E			NAM	6	12	9	MTH NAMES ARRAY
02Ø	E			CHAR		9	1	MTH NAME IN BYTES
03Ø	E			HDG		14	1	HDG LINE ARRAY

Line	Form Type	Indicators	Factor 1	Operation	Factor 2	Result Field Name	Length	Decimal Positions	Resulting Indicators (Equal)	Comments
01Ø	C			MOVE	Y	YEAR	4			LOAD LOW VALUE
02Ø	C			MOVEL	'19'	YEAR				LOAD HIGH VALUE
03Ø	C			MOVEA	NAM,M	CHAR				LOAD TEST ARRAY
04Ø	C			MOVEA	CHAR	HDG				LOAD HDG ARRAY
05Ø	C			Z-ADD	9	X	2	Ø		SET INDEX
06Ø	C		LOOP	TAG						
07Ø	C		CHAR,X	COMP	' '				7Ø	TEST FOR BLANK
08Ø	C	7Ø	X	SUB	1	X				REDUCE INDEX
09Ø	C	7Ø		GOTO	LOOP					TRY AGAIN
10Ø	C		X	ADD	2	X				+ INDEX
11Ø	C			MOVEA	YEAR	HDG,X				MOVE TO HDG ARY
12Ø	C			EXCPT						PRINT HDG

Figure 11-35 Extension and calculation coding for an application using MOVEA operations.

A logic flowchart, related instructions, and results after processing each statement are detailed in Figure 11-36. The field values included in the right-hand side of the instructions are after the first nonblank character was found in CHAR array (the low-order R in NOVEMBER).

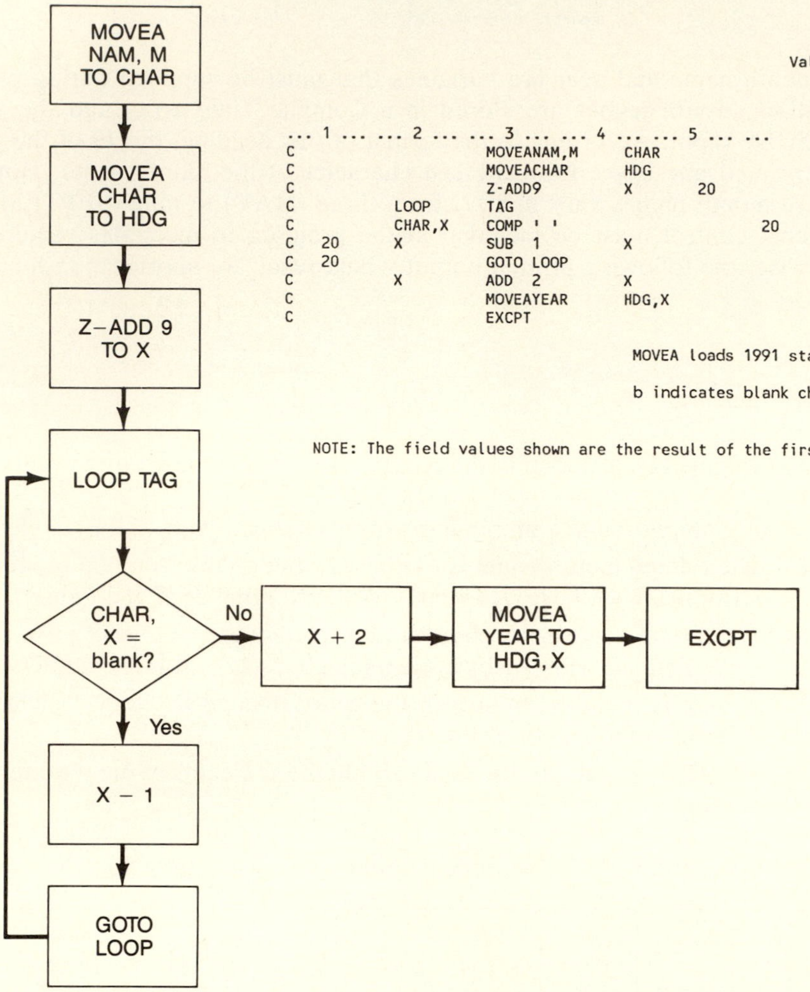


```
                                                    Values in fields after non-blank character
                                                        is found in search of CHAR array

                                                    Factor 1    Factor 2    Result Field
... 1 ... ... 2 ... ... 3 ... ... 4 ... ... 5 ... ...
C                      MOVEANAM,M    CHAR                       NOVEMBERb   NOVEMBERb
C                      MOVEACHAR     HDG                        NOVEMBERb   NOVEMBERb
C                      Z-ADD9        X       20                 9           09
C            LOOP      TAG
C            CHAR,X    COMP ' '                    20  R        b
C   20       X         SUB  1        X                 08       1           08
C   20                 GOTO LOOP
C            X         ADD  2        X                 08       2           10
C                      MOVEAYEAR     HDG,X                      1991        NOVEMBER 1991

C                      EXCPT

                                     MOVEA loads 1991 starting a 10th element (value in X)

                                     b indicates blank character

      NOTE: The field values shown are the result of the first pass in the GOTO LOOP sequence
```

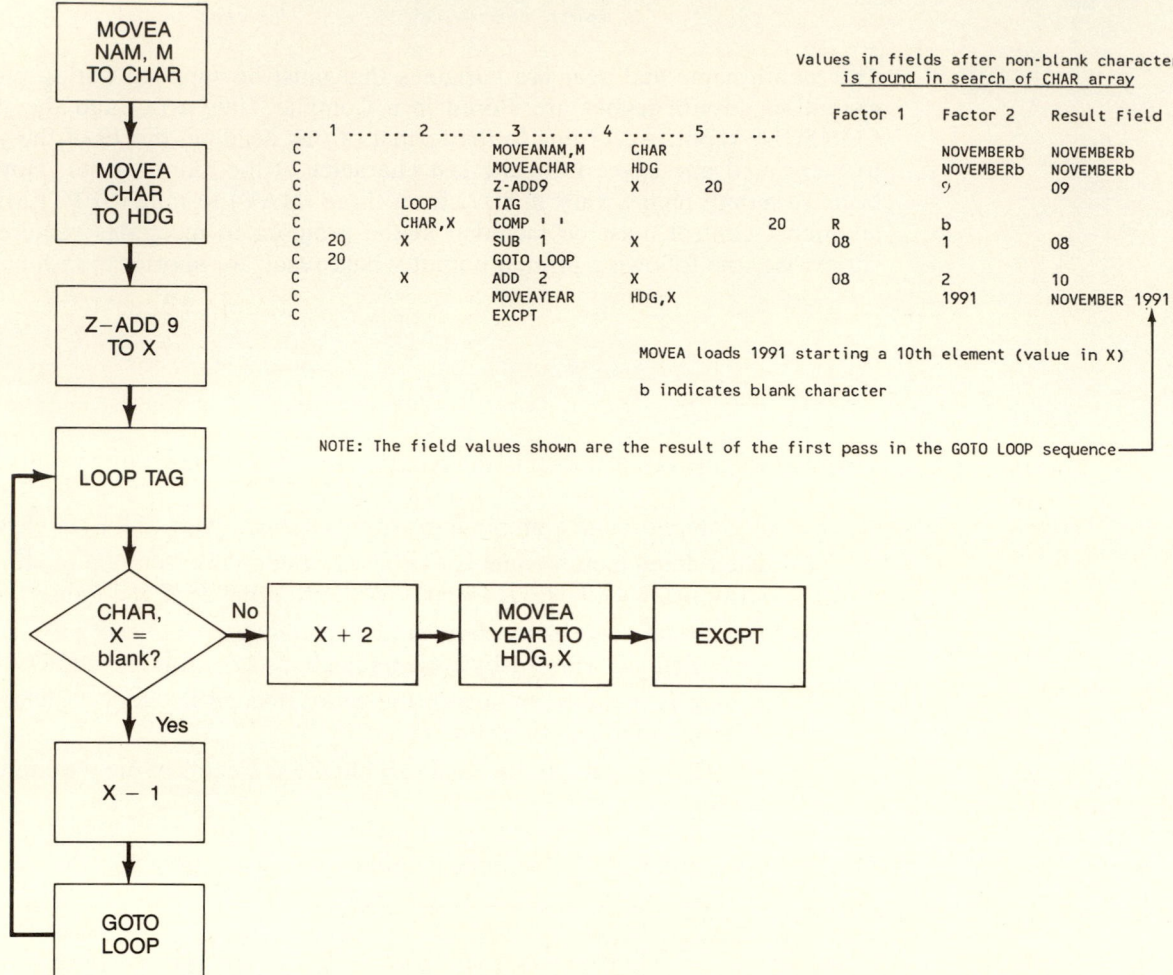

Figure 11-36 MOVEA application logic flowchart, related instructions, and processing results.

ERRORS IN ARRAY EXECUTION TIME

Execution (runtime) errors that are common to array processing are the following:

1. Index value zero.
2. Index value greater than number of elements in the array.
3. Index value negative.

Depending on the computer system, any of these array index errors is usually identified by an ARRAY INDEX ERROR or ARRAY INDEX OUT OF RANGE error message. The specific error (one of the three) may have to be determined by debugging.

APPLICATION PROGRAM—CANNED SODA INVENTORY REPORT

Many of the array features discussed in the previous paragraphs, such as LOKUP, indexing, related array access, and positional processing, are included in this application program.

Documentation

The specifications detailed in Figure 11-37 explain the processing requirement for this application program. The system flowchart in Figure 11-38 shows that one input disk file is processed by the program to generate the required report. The

PROGRAM SPECIFICATIONS Page 1 of 2

Program Name SODA INVENTORY RPT Program-ID CH11P4 Written By S. Myers
Purpose Generate a canned soda inventory report Approved By The Boss

Input files (directory names):
DAT1141 (stored on disk)

Output files (directory names):
PRINTER

Processing Narrative:

```
Write an RPG program to generate a canned soda inventory report.

Input to the program:

A canned soda inventory file (DAT1141), stored on disk, includes com-
pany assigned soda numbers and the related quantity in cans on hand.
A supplemental layout form details the record format of the input
file.

Processing:

Include the following four Compile Time arrays in the program:

   1.  Item numbers with the following values:

            100       130       160       190
            110       140       170       200
            120       150       180

   2.  Item descriptions with the following values:

         COCA COLA    SPRITE       DIET COKE    DR PEPPER
         PEPSI COLA   TAB          SLICE APPLE  HIRES ROOT BEER
         7-UP         PEPSI LITE   SLICE

   3.  Item cost with the following values:

         45      49      44      63
         47      51      48      56
         41      50      43

       Note: item number 100 relates to COCA COLA and 45; item
             number 110 to PEPSI COLA and 47; and so forth going
             to the and of one column and beginning at the first
             entry of the next....

   4.  One error message with the following value:

            ..ITEM NOT FOUND..
```

PROGRAM SPECIFICATIONS Page 1 of 2

Program Name SODA INVENTORY RPT Program-ID CH11P4 Written By S. Myers
Purpose Generate a canned soda inventory report Approved By The Boss

Input files (directory names):
DAT1141 (stored on disk)

Output files (directory names):
PRINTER

Processing Narrative:

```
Use ITEM NUMBER field from the input records as the search argument
to "lookup" (with indexing) the item number array for an equal condi-
tion.  If the input number is found in the item number array, use
the same index to access the related values from the item description
and cost arrays.  Multiply the input quantity by the cost array value
to determine total dollar amount on hand.

If an item number is not found, print the error message array value
in the location shown on the printer spacing chart.

Output:

Generate the report detailed in the attached printer spacing chart
in accordance with the following considerations:

      1.  Use stock paper.
      2.  Headings on the top of every page.
      3.  Use system-supplied date for the report.
```

Figure 11-37 Specifications for Canned Soda Inventory Report application program.

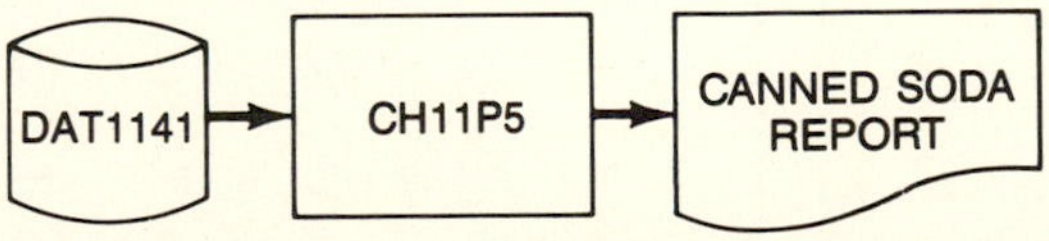

Figure 11-38 System flowchart for Canned Soda Inventory Report application program.

format of the records in the input data file is presented in Figure 11-39. Because all the arrays used in this program are Compile Time, none of the fields are processed as an Input Time array. A listing of the data file processed by the program is also included in Figure 11-39. The design of the Canned Soda Inventory Report is detailed in the printer spacing chart in Figure 11-40.

A printed report generated by the application program is presented in Figure 11-41.

Record format:

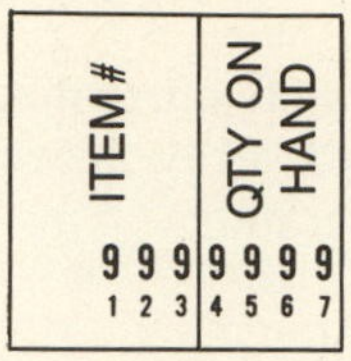

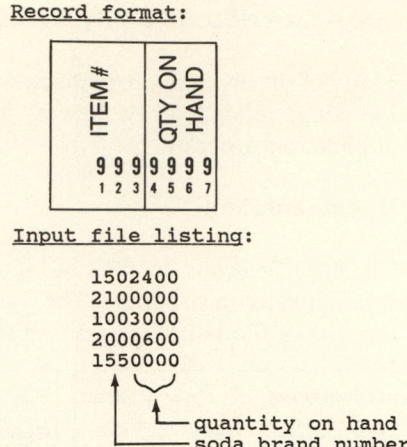

Input file listing:

```
1502400
2100000
1003000
2000600
1550000
```

quantity on hand
soda brand number

Figure 11-39 Record layout form and listing of the input file processed by the Canned Soda Inventory Report program.

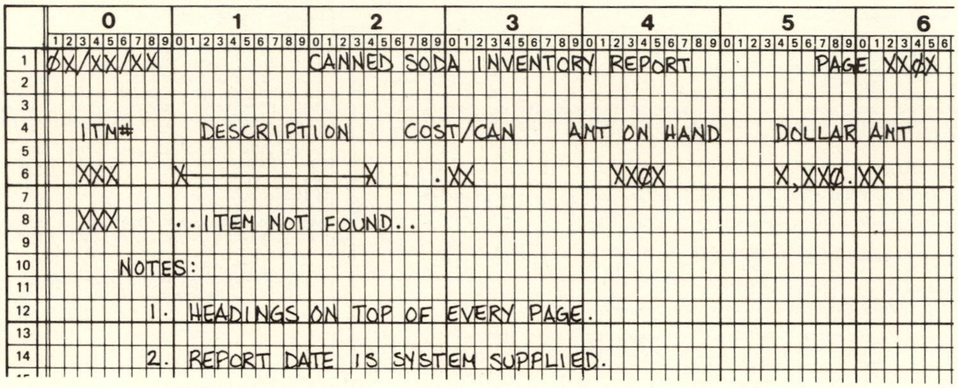

Figure 11-40 Design of the Canned Soda Inventory Report.

```
7/10/91          CANNED SODA INVENTORY REPORT          PAGE    1

 ITEM#     DESCRIPTION        COST/CAN   AMT ON HAND     DOLLAR AMT

 150      PEPSI LITE            .50          2400          1,200.00

 210      ..ITEM NOT FOUND..

 100      COCA COLA             .45          3000          1,350.00

 200      HIRES ROOT BEER       .56           600            336.00

 155      ..ITEM NOT FOUND..
```

Figure 11-41 Printed report generated by the Canned Soda Inventory program.

Source Program Coding

A source listing of the Canned Soda Inventory program is shown in Figure 11-42. Supplemental figures are used to explain the processing logic.

```
... ... 1 ... ... 2 ... ... 3 ... ... 4 ... ... 5 ... ... 6 ... ... 7 ...
*                         CANNED SODA INVENTORY REPORT                  CH11P4
*  THREE RELATED COMPILE TIME ARRAYS ARE INCLUDED FOR ITEM#, COST,      CH11P4
* AND DESCRIPTION. ONE ERROR MSG IS STORED IN A COMPILE TIME ARRAY      CH11P4
H                                                                       CH11P4
FDAT11P4 IP  F  80  80            DISK                                  CH11P4
FREPORT  O   F 132 132     OF     PRINTER                               CH11P4
E                         ITM#    1  11  3   DESC   15   ITEM#/DESCRIPTIONCH11P4
E                         COST   11  11  2 2             COST PER CAN   CH11P4
E                         MSG     1   1 18               ERROR MSG ARRAY CH11P4
IDAT11P4 SM  01                                                         CH11P4
I                                                  1   3 ITEMNO         CH11P4
I                                                  4   70QTY            CH11P4
C                          Z-ADD1         I        20                   CH11P4
C              ITEMNO      LOKUPITM#,I                    50            CH11P4
C   50         QTY         MULT COST,I    AMT      72                   CH11P4
C                          EXCPT                                        CH11P4
OREPORT  H  301   1P                                                    CH11P4
O        OR       OF                                                    CH11P4
O                              UDATE Y   8                              CH11P4
O                                       40 'CANNED SODA INVENTORY'      CH11P4
O                                       47 'REPORT'                     CH11P4
O                                       60 'PAGE'                       CH11P4
O                              PAGE  Z  65                              CH11P4
O            H  2     1P                                                CH11P4
O        OR       OF                                                    CH11P4
O                                       22 'ITEM#    DESCRIPTION'       CH11P4
O                                       49 'COST/CAN   AMT ON HAND'     CH11P4
O                                       63 'DOLLAR AMT'                 CH11P4
O            E  2     01                                                CH11P4
O                              ITEMNO    5                              CH11P4
O                         50   DESC,I   24                              CH11P4
O                         50   COST,I1  31                              CH11P4
O                         50   QTY   Z  45                              CH11P4
O                         50   AMT   1  61                              CH11P4
O                        N50            27 '..ITEM NOT FOUND..'         CH11P4
**
100COCA COLA
110PEPSI COLA
1207-UP
130SPRITE
140TAB
150PEPSI LITE
160DIET COKE
170SLICE APPLE
180SLICE
190DR PEPPER
200HIRES ROOT BEER
**
454741495150444843635 6
**
..ITEM NOT FOUND..
```

Figure 11-42 Source listing of Canned Soda Inventory Report program.

Extension Specifications Coding

The Extension coding and its relationship to the data in the Compile Time arrays are illustrated in Figure 11-43. It is common programming practice to include program-controlled (not system-supplied) error messages in a Compile Time array. A one-element array defined as MSG is included in this program to flag an ITEMNO (search argument) value that is not found in the ITM# array. As shown in Figure 11-42, the MSG arrray element is printed when indicator 50 is not on.

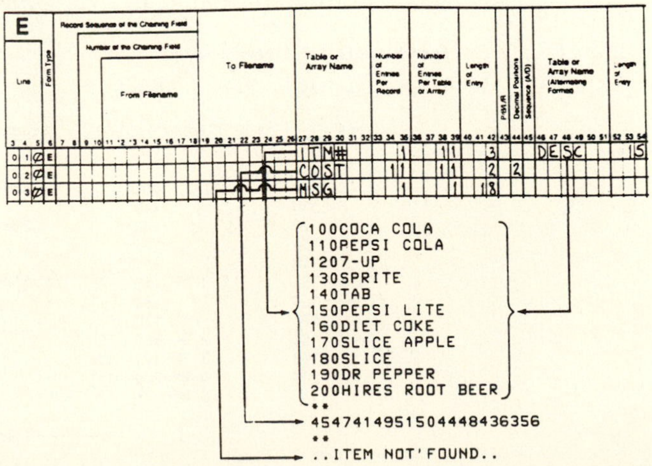

Figure 11-43 Extension form coding for the Canned Soda Inventory Report program and its relationship to the Compile Time array data.

Calculation Specifications Coding

An explanation of the calculation instructions after a successful lookup of the ITM# array and the access of related array elements is detailed in Figure 11-44.

```
Following illustration assumes ITEMNO 150 was input and processed:
                                                      Values in fields after execution
                                              Index I   Factor 1      Factor 2     Result Field
... 1 ... ... 2 ... ... 3 ... ... 4 ... ... 5 ... ... 6
C                       Z-ADD1        I       20        1                 1              1
C           ITEMNO      LOKUPITM#,I                50   6         150     150
C           QTY         MULT COST,I   AMT     72        6         2400    50             0120000
C                       EXCPT

ITM# array is searched consecutively until related item number is found

100COCA COLA
110PEPSI COLA
1207-UP
130SPRITE
140TAB
150PEPSI LITE <----------- DESC,I (6th element) is specified on output form to
160DIET COKE                 print related item description from DESC array
170SLICE APPLE
180SLICE
190DR PEPPER
200HIRES ROOT BEER
**
45474149515044484363356       50 (6th element) is referenced by COST,I <---
**
..ITEM NOT FOUND..
```

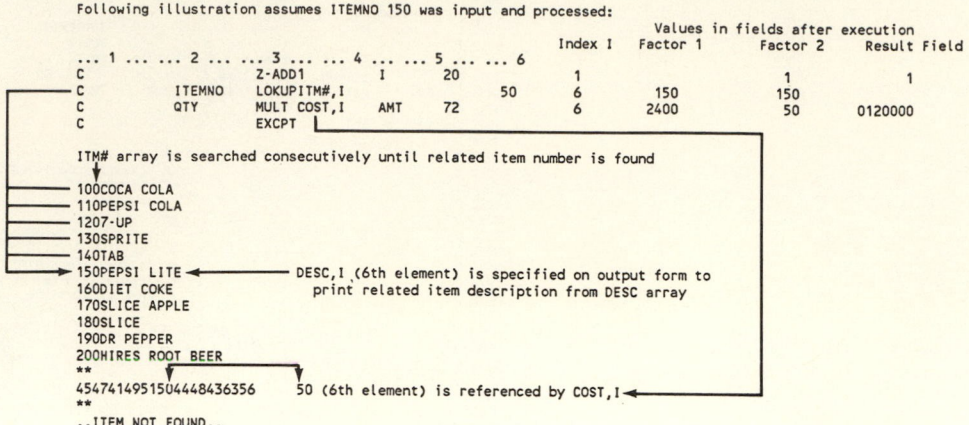

Figure 11-44 Calculations instructions and the result of array processing after a successful LOKUP.

BINARY SEARCH OF AN ARRAY

Array LOKUP procedures discussed in the previous paragraphs have addressed consecutive processing. For arrays that include 50 or more elements, processing time may be significantly reduced by using a *binary search*. For a comparison to be made between consecutive and binary array lookups, the previous application program is modified to support a binary search. The input data, arrays, element values, and report design remain the same.

Figure 11-45 details the steps followed in a binary search of the ITM# array. Even though there are only 11 elements in the array, the number of searches is reduced. For example, in a consecutive search of the ITM# array for item number 150, six elements must be tested before the equal lookup condition is satisfied. However, as shown in the figure, in a binary search the lookups are reduced to one. Furthermore, the number of lookups for item number 210, which is not in the array, is reduced from 12 to five. On the other hand, for elements located at

```
Search Logic for Binary Lookup:

ITEM# value    150              210              100              200              155

      Steps          I   Steps          I   Steps          I   Steps          I   Steps           I

             100                100          3 ►100   1            100                100
             110                110             110               110                110
             120                120          2 ►120   3            120                120
             130                130             130               130                130
             140                140             140               140                140
       1 ►   150     6    1 ►   150    6     1 ►150   6     1 ►   150    6   1 & 4 ►150    6
             160                160             160               160            3 ►160    7
             170                170             170               170                170
             180          2 ►   180    9        180         2 ►   180    9       2 ►180    9
             190          3 ►   190   10        190         3 ►   190   10          190
             200          4 ►   200   11        200         4 ►   200   11          200
                          5 ►         12
                                  \_______ Item number not found ______________/
I = array index
```

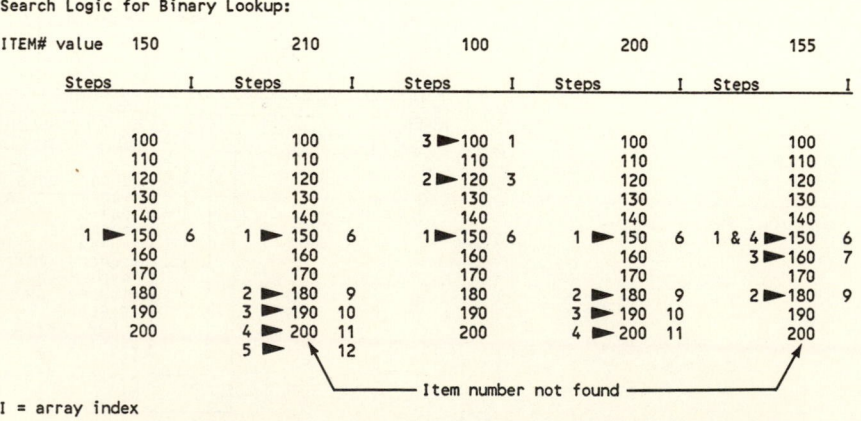

Figure 11-45 Processing steps for the binary search of the ITM# array for the modified Canned Soda Inventory Report program.

the beginning of the array, the number of searches may be increased. This process is illustrated in the lookup of item number 100, which requires three searches instead of one.

An examination of Figure 11-45 indicates that binary search control first divides the array in half; then, depending on whether the search argument value is lower or higher than the value of the middle array element, the control divides either the lower or upper remaining half. This halving (binary) process continues until one of the following conditions is satisfied:

1. The search argument value is equal to the argument array.
2. The index value (I) is equal to a low-range value.

A source listing of the binary lookup is shown in Figure 11-46. Comments in the right-hand side of the calculations explain the function of each instruction.

```
... 1 ... ... 2 ... ... 3 ... ... 4 ... ... 5 ... ... 6 ... ... 7 ...CH11P5
 *                    CANNED SODA INVENTORY REPORT                    CH11P5
 *  THREE RELATED COMPILE TIME ARRAYS ARE INCLUDED FOR ITEM#, COST,   CH11P5
 * AND DESCRIPTION. ONE ERROR MSG IS STORED IN A COMPILE TIME ARRAY   CH11P5
 *              ***** BINARY SEARCH OF ITEM# ARRAY *****              CH11P5
H                                                                     CH11P5
FDAT1141 IP  F  80  80            DISK                                CH11P5
FREPORT  O   F 132 132     OF     PRINTER                             CH11P5
E                   ITM#     1  11  3   DESC   15   ITEM#/DESCRIPTIONCH11P5
E                   COST    11  11  2 2             COST PER CAN      CH11P5
E                   MSG      1   1 18               ERROR MSG ARRAY   CH11P5
IDAT1141 SM  01                                                       CH11P5
I                                            1   3 ITEMNO             CH11P5
I                                            4   70QTY                CH11P5
 * FOLLOWING 2 INSTRUCTIONS SET UPPER & LOWER VALUES FOR 1ST SEARCH   CH11P5
C                    Z-ADD12        UP      20       ELEMENTS + 1     CH11P5
C                    Z-ADD0         LOW     20       SET LOW          CH11P5
C           AGAIN    TAG                                              CH11P5
C           UP       ADD  LOW       TOTAL   20                        CH11P5
C           TOTAL    DIV  2         I       20       COMPUTE INDEX    CH11P5
C           I        COMP LOW                      49 IF = NOT FOUNDCH11P5
C   49               GOTO END                                         CH11P5
C           ITEMNO   COMP ITM#,I              525150  > < =           CH11P5
C   52               Z-ADDI         LOW              RESET LOW VALUECH11P5
C   51               Z-ADDI         UP               RESET UPPER VALCH11P5
C  N50               GOTO AGAIN                                       CH11P5
C           COST,I   MULT QTY       AMT     62       COMPUTE $ AMT    CH11P5
C           END      TAG                                              CH11P5
C                    EXCPT                                            CH11P5
OREPORT  H  301   1P                                                  CH11P5
O       OR        OF                                                  CH11P5
                          UDATE Y    8                                CH11P5
O                                   40 'CANNED SODA INVENTORY'        CH11P5
O                                   47 'REPORT'                       CH11P5
O                                   60 'PAGE'                         CH11P5
O                         PAGE  Z   65                                CH11P5
O           H  2      1P                                              CH11P5
O          OR         OF                                              CH11P5
O                                   22 'ITEM#    DESCRIPTION'         CH11P5
O                                   49 'COST/CAN   AMT ON HAND'       CH11P5
O                                   63 'DOLLAR AMT'                   CH11P5
O           E  2      01                                              CH11P5
O                         ITEMNO     5                                CH11P5
O                     50  DESC,I    24                                CH11P5
O                     50  COST,I1   31                                CH11P5
O                     50  QTY   Z   45                                CH11P5
O                     50  AMT   1   61                                CH11P5
O                    N50  MSG,1     27                                CH11P5
**
100COCA COLA
110PEPSI COLA
1207-UP
130SPRITE
140TAB
150PEPSI LITE
160DIET COKE
170SLICE APPLE
180SLICE
190DR PEPPER
200HIRES ROOT BEER
**
4547414951504448436356
**
..ITEM NOT FOUND..
```

Figure 11-46 Source program listing of Canned Soda Inventory Report program modified for binary lookup.

The program's processing logic for a binary search is explained further in the flowchart presented in Figure 11-47.

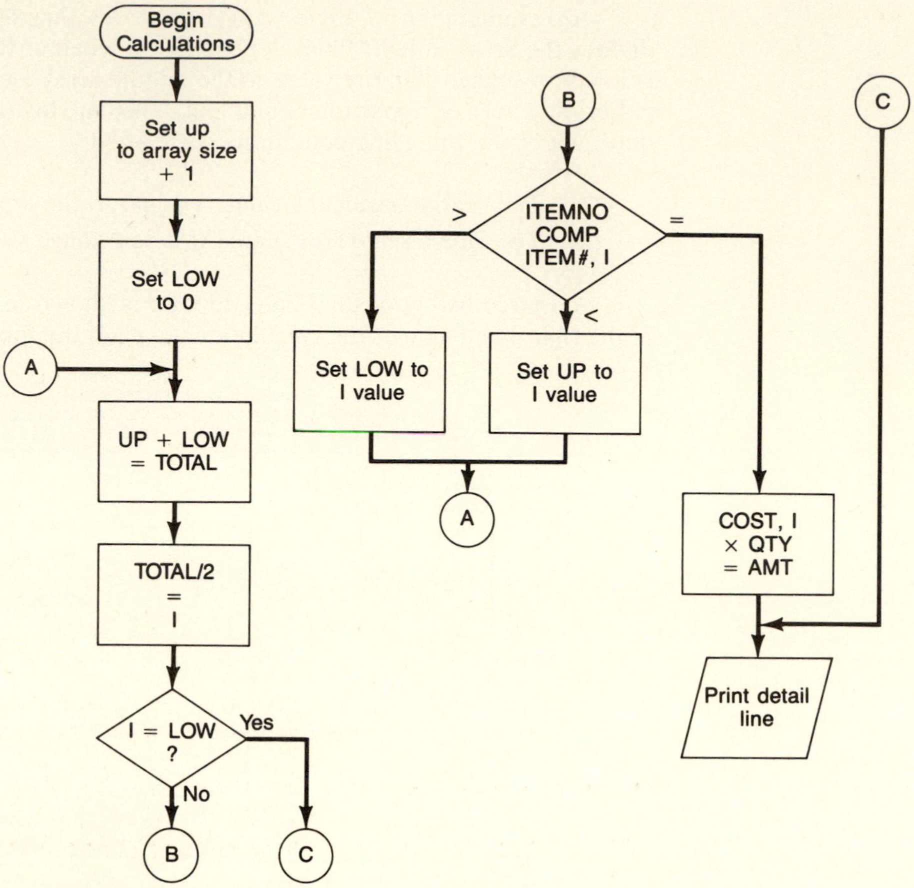

Figure 11-47 Processing logic flowchart for a binary search of ITEM# array in the modified Canned Soda Inventory Report program.

The report generated by this modified program is identical to that previously shown in Figure 11-41.

The following restrictions must be considered in any programs that support a binary search of arrays:

1. Argument array (the array searched) element values must be sorted in ascending order.
2. Only an equal lookup (not range) may be supported.

MULTIDIMENSIONAL ARRAY PROCESSING

Two-dimensional Array Structures

Multidimensional array structure and processing concepts were explained at the beginning of this chapter. It was emphasized that RPG does not directly support multidimensional arrays but that their structure may be simulated. This simulation method is explained in the following program example.

Assume that a company has three classes of hourly labor, each with a different rate for the day and night shifts. The logical structure of a typical two-dimensional array for the data is detailed in Figure 11-48. RPG processing for this example could be controlled by three separate arrays. However, a simulated two-dimensional environment may be created by specifying one array with supplemental calculation control. Figure 11-48 shows the logical two-dimensional array structure reformatted into the one-dimensional array necessary for RPG processing.

```
General two-dimensional structure example:

second dimension ---------> D    N

first dimension  |  1   |2000|2300|
                 |  2   |1700|1950| <------- GRADE 2/SHIFT N
                 v  3   |1400|1600|

Two-dimensional array shown above structured as a one-dimensional array in RPG:

 Related array data in program:

 shift letter    D    N    D    N    D    N

               |2000|2300|1700|1950|1400|1600|
                \____ ____/\____ ____/\____ ____/

   GRADE            1         2         3
```

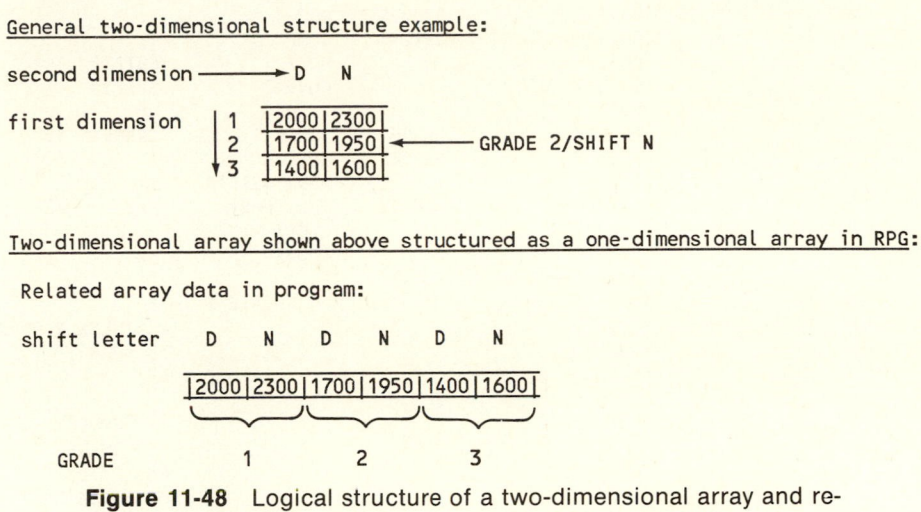

Figure 11-48 Logical structure of a two-dimensional array and reformatted one-dimensional structure for RPG processing.

Source Program—Simulated Two-Dimensional Array Processing. The source listing of the example program that simulates two-dimensional array processing is presented in Figure 11-49. Examine the listing, and notice the following:

1. One array is defined (RATE).
2. Alphanumeric SHIFT value is tested and the related number (1 or 2) is moved to a new field (SHIFT#).
3. GRADE value is modified and SHIFT# value is added to calculate index (I) value for related array element access.
4. Related array element value is accessed positionally by specifying array and index names (RATE, I).

The results of processing each statement in calculations when an input record includes a GRADE value of 3 and a SHIFT value of D is detailed in Figure 11-50. Notice that Factor 1, Factor 2, and the Result Field values (after the statement is executed) are included in the right-hand side of the figure.

A listing of the printed report generated by the program is illustrated in Figure 11-51. The array supplied the RATE value needed to compute the week's pay amount. All other variables in the report are input values. Notice that the calculations, which simulate two-dimensional array processing, are generic because any number of GRADE levels may be supported. Additional GRADEs will not change the two-dimensional structure. A three-dimensional array environment would require that the SHIFT value be divided into segments.

```
... ... 1 ... ... 2 ... ... 3 ... ... 4 ... ... 5 ... ... 6 ... ... 7 ...
 *               WEEKLY PAY COMPUTATION                           CH11P6
 *    BY SIMULATED TWO-DIMENSIONAL ARRAY PROCESSING               CH11P6
H                                                                 CH11P6
FDAT1147 IP  F  13  13            DISK                            CH11P6
FPAYREPT O   F 132 132            PRINTER                         CH11P6
E                    RATE    6   6 4 2              HRLY RATES    CH11P6
IDAT1147 SM  01                                                   CH11P6
I                                           1   9OSS#             CH11P6
I                                          10  100GRADE           CH11P6
I                                          11  11 SHIFT           CH11P6
I                                          12  130HRS             CH11P6
C                    EXSR PROCES                    PROCESSING    CH11P6
C          PROCES    BEGSR                                        CH11P6
C          SHIFT     COMP 'D'                     10DAY OR NIGHT? CH11P6
C   10               MOVE 1         SHIFT#  10      DAY SHIFT     CH11P6
C  N10               MOVE 2         SHIFT#          NIGHT SHIFT   CH11P6
 *                                                                CH11P6
C          GRADE     SUB  1         GRADE#  10      DECREASE GRADE CH11P6
C          GRADE#    MULT 2         I       10      PARTIAL INDEX CH11P6
C          I         ADD  SHIFT#    I               COMPLETE INDEX CH11P6
C          RATE,I    MULT HRS       PAY     62      COMPUTE PAY   CH11P6
C                    EXCPT                          PRINT LINE    CH11P6
C                    ENDSR                                        CH11P6
OPAYREPT H  201       1P                                          CH11P6
O                        UDATE Y    8                             CH11P6
O                                  42 'WEEKLY PAYROLL REPORT'     CH11P6
O                                  58 'PAGE'                      CH11P6
O                        PAGE  Z   63                             CH11P6
O        H  2     1P                                              CH11P6
O                                  11 'EMPLOYEE#'                 CH11P6
O                                  30 'GRADE    SHIFT'            CH11P6
O                                  48 'RATE/HR    HRS'            CH11P6
O                                  61 'WEEK PAY'                  CH11P6
O        E  2     01                                              CH11P6
O                        SS#       12 '0   -  -    '              CH11P6
O                        GRADE     19                             CH11P6
O                        SHIFT     28                             CH11P6
O                        RATE,I1   40                             CH11P6
O                        HRS   Z   47                             CH11P6
O                        PAY   1   60                             CH11P6
**
200023001700195014001600
```

Figure 11-49 Source listing of program that simulates two-dimensional array processing with a one-dimensional array.

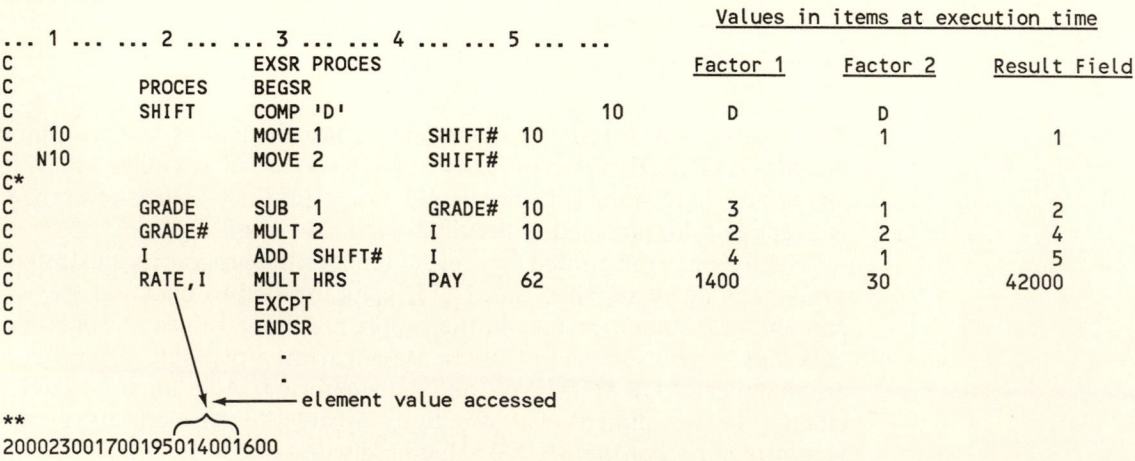

Values input:

GRADE = 3
SHIFT = D

```
... 1 ... ... 2 ... ... 3 ... ... 4 ... ... 5 ... ...
C                    EXSR PROCES
C          PROCES    BEGSR
C          SHIFT     COMP 'D'                     10
C   10               MOVE 1         SHIFT#  10
C  N10               MOVE 2         SHIFT#
C*
C          GRADE     SUB  1         GRADE#  10
C          GRADE#    MULT 2         I       10
C          I         ADD  SHIFT#    I
C          RATE,I    MULT HRS       PAY     62
C             \      EXCPT
C              \     ENDSR
                \      .
                 \     .
                  \<------- element value accessed
**               /\
200023001700195014001600
```

Values in items at execution time

Factor 1	Factor 2	Result Field
D	D	
	1	1
3	1	2
2	2	4
4	1	5
1400	30	42000

Figure 11-50 Field values after a record is read and a calculation instruction is executed.

7/30/91		WEEKLY PAYROLL REPORT			PAGE 1
EMPLOYEE#	GRADE	SHIFT	RATE/HR	HRS	WEEK PAY
011-11-1111	3	N	16.00	40	640.00
022-22-2222	1	D	20.00	35	700.00
033-33-3333	2	D	17.00	50	850.00
044-44-4444	3	D	14.00	30	420.00
055-55-5555	1	N	23.00	40	920.00
066-66-6666	2	N	19.50	25	487.50

Figure 11-51 Report generated by the simulated two-dimensional array program.

MULTIDIMENSIONAL PROCESSING WITH MULTIPLE DATA STRUCTURES

OCUR (SET/GT Occurrence of a Data Structure)

A direct method of accessing data that requires multidimensional processing is supported in RPG 400/III by a combination of data structures and the *OCUR* operation. Data structures build the *occurrences* (relative positions) of the data in storage, and an *OCUR* instruction must be specified to access the value of a select occurrence.

All the data for multiple occurrence data structures that are accessed by an *OCUR* operation must be loaded before the instruction is executed. The data for a data structure may be stored externally in a data file and loaded by *READ* operation control within a *DO group*. If a small number of records with fixed values are required for a multiple occurrence data structure, the data may be hard-coded in the program's calculations. For simplicity, this method is used in the program example discussed later in the chapter.

Figure 11-52 explains the syntax related to the *OCUR* operation. The input coding and storage results from building multiple occurrence data structures is shown in Figure 11-53.

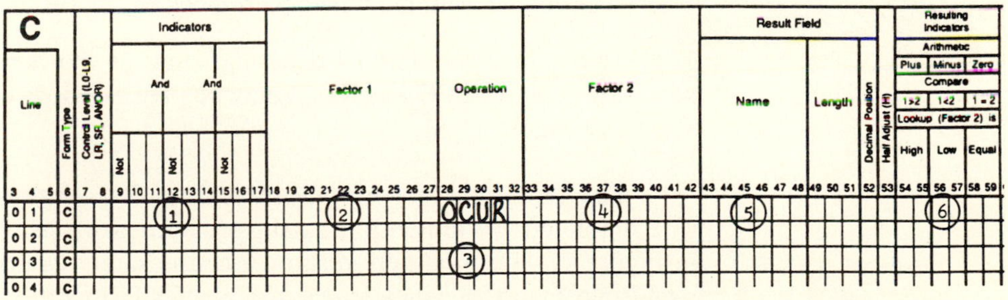

1. Indicators may be used to condition an OCUR instruction at total or detail time.
2. Factor 1 is an optional entry. If specified, its value must be a numeric literal or field with zero decimal positions; or a data structure name. This entry is used to set the occurrence (entry) of the data structure specified in Factor 2.
3. The OCUR operation must be left-justified in the Operation field.
4. A Factor 2 entry is required and must include the name of a multiple occurrence data structure.
5. A Result Field entry is optional. When used, it must be a numeric field defined with zero decimal positions. This field will contain the value in the current occurrence of the data structure referenced in Factor 2.
6. A resulting indicator may be specified in resulting indicator columns 56-57. The indicator is set on if the occurrence specified is outside of the range established by the data structure included in Factor 2.

Figure 11-52 OCUR (SET/GET Occurrence of a Data Structure) operation syntax.

Line	Form Type	Filename or Record Name / Data Structure Name	Record Identifying Indicator, or DS	Field Location From / Data Structure Occurs n Times	Field Location To / Data Structure Length	Decimal Positions	RPG Field Name
01Ø	I	DSTR1	DS	2Ø			
02Ø	I			1	5		FIELDA
03Ø	I			6	11		FIELDB
04Ø	I	DSTR2	DS	2Ø			
05Ø	I			1	4		FIELDC
06Ø	I			5	8		FIELDD

Format of the data structures occurrences in storage:

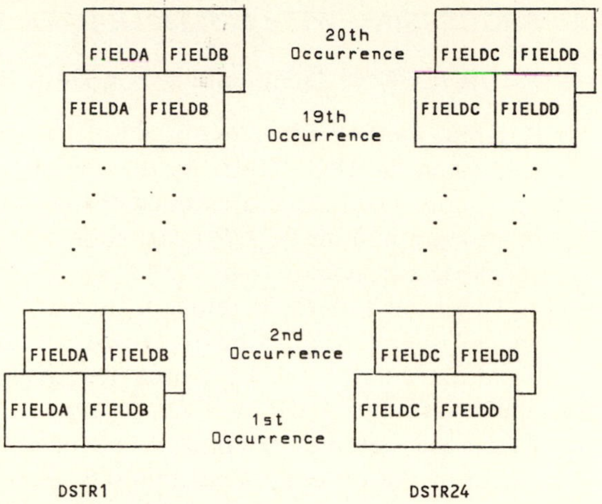

The 20 entry on line 1 of DSTR1 and line 4 of DSTR2 determine the number of occurrences for each data structure.

Figure 11-53 Input coding to define, and results of building, data structures with multiple occurrences for OCUR usage.

Calculation instructions detailing some of the methods by which the data structures defined in Figure 11-53 may be processed with an OCUR operation are shown in Figure 11-54.

Source Program—Multidimensional Processing with Data Structures. The simulated two-dimensional array program previously discussed and illustrated in Figure 11-48 is modified to show how the same results may be controlled with a multiple occurrence data structure and OCUR operation access. Examine Figure 11-55 and notice the following:

1. Only one multiple occurrence (3) data structure is specified, which defines the day and night pay rates for each labor grade.
2. An internal subroutine includes the hard-coded data to load the multiple occurrence data structure before the OCUR instruction is executed.
3. An OCUR operation accesses the occurrence of the data structure based on the value of the input field GRADE.

The report generated by the multiple occurrence data structure program is identical to that shown in Figure 11-49.

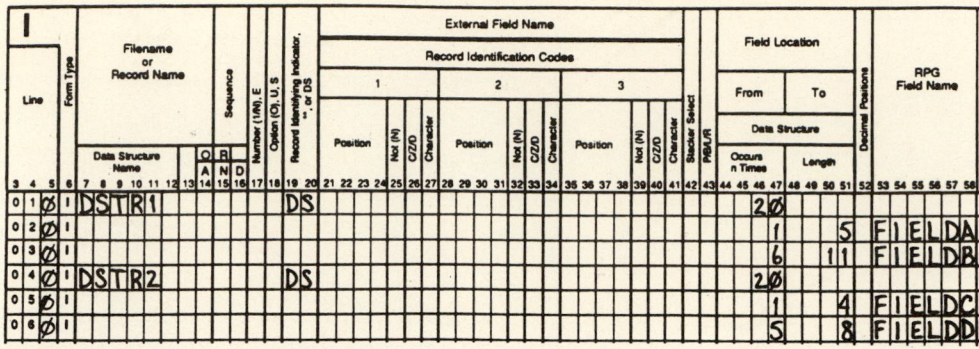

Line	Form Type	Control Level (L0-L9, LR, SR, AN/OR)	Indicators	Factor 1	Operation	Factor 2	Result Field Name	Length	Decimal Positions	Half Adjust (H)	Resulting Indicators High	Low	Equal
01Ø	C			1Ø	OCUR	DSTR1							
02Ø	C*												
03Ø	C			CODE	OCUR	DSTR2	FIELDD					9Ø	
04Ø	C*												
05Ø	C			DSTR2	OCUR	DSTR1							
06Ø	C*												
07Ø	C				OCUR	DSTR2	WORK1						
08Ø	C*												
09Ø	C			DSTR1	OCUR	DSTR2	WORK2						

Statement Number

010 Data structure DSTR1 is set to the tenth occurrence. FIELDA or FIELDB defined in DSTR1 would be available for processing.

030 The value in the CODE field (must be an integer) sets the occurrence in data structure DSTR2. If the value in CODE is within the limits of DSTR2, the value of FIELDD is accessed from DSTR2. Indicator 90, specified in columns 56-57, will be set on if the CODE value is zero or greater than the number of occurrences in data structure DSTR2.

050 Data structure DSTR1 is set to the current occurrence of DSTR2. If DSTR2 had been previously set to the eighteenth occurrence, DSTR1 would also be set to the same occurrence.

070 The current occurrence of DSTR2 is stored in WORK1. Any field specified in the Result Field of an OCUR instruction must be defined as an integer (0 decimal positions).

090 Data structure DSTR2 is set to the current occurrence of DSTR1. If DSTR1 had been previously set to the twelfth occurrence, DSTR1 would also be set to the same occurrence. The value of the DSTR2 occurrence is stored in the field WORK2.

Figure 11-54 OCUR operation processing examples.

```
... ... 1 ... ... 2 ... ... 3 ... ... 4 ... ... 5 ... ... 6 ... ... 7 ...
*                   WEEKLY PAY COMPUTATION                         CH11P7
*          WITH A MULTIPLE OCCURRENCE DATA STRUCTURE               CH11P7
H                                                                  CH11P7
FDAT11P6 IP  F      13            DISK                             CH11P7
FPAYREPT O   F     132            PRINTER                          CH11P7
IDAT11P6 SM  01
I                                        1   90SS#
I                                       10  100GRADE
I                                       11  11 SHIFT
I                                       12  130HRS
IRATES        DS                             3
I                                        1   42DAYRAT
I                                        5   82NITRAT                CH11P7
C           *IN10     CASEQ'0'       FIRST            CTRL SR BRANCH CH11P7
C                     END                             END CAS GROUP  CH11P7
C                     EXSR PROCES                                    CH11P7
C           PROCES    BEGSR                                          CH11P7
C           GRADE     OCUR RATES                      FIND SHIFT     CH11P7
C           SHIFT     IFEQ 'D'                        TEST FOR SHIFT CH11P7
C                     Z-ADDDAYRAT    RATE    42       MOVE ARY TO FLDCH11P7
C                     ELSE                            NOT DAY SHIFT  CH11P7
C                     Z-ADDNITRAT    RATE             MOVE ARY TO FLDCH11P7
C                     END                             ENDS IF/ELSE   CH11P7
C           HRS       MULT RATE      PAY     62       COMPUTE PAY    CH11P7
C                     EXCPT                                          CH11P7
C                     ENDSR                                          CH11P7
 *                                                                   CH11P7
C           FIRST     BEGSR                           SR TO LOAD DS  CH11P7
C           1         OCUR RATES                      FIND 1ST OCURRNCH11P7
C                     MOVE 20002300  RATES            LOAD 1ST OCURRNCH11P7
C           2         OCUR RATES                      FIND 2ND OCURRNCH11P7
C                     MOVE 17001950  RATES            LOAD 2ND OCCURNCH11P7
C           3         OCUR RATES                      FIND 3RD OCCURNCH11P7
C                     MOVE 14001600  RATES            LOAD 3RD OCURRNCH11P7
C                     MOVE '1'       *IN10            SETON 10 INDCATCH11P7
C                     ENDSR                           ENDS SR        CH11P7
OPAYREPT H  201   1P                                                 CH11P7
O                        UDATE Y    8                                CH11P7
O                                  42 'WEEKLY PAYROLL REPORT'        CH11P7
O                                  58 'PAGE'                         CH11P7
O                        PAGE  Z   63                                CH11P7
O        H  2     1P                                                 CH11P7
O                                  11 'EMPLOYEE#'                    CH11P7
O                                  30 'GRADE     SHIFT'              CH11P7
O                                  48 'RATE/HR        HRS'           CH11P7
O                                  61 'WEEK PAY'                     CH11P7
O        E  2     01                                                 CH11P7
```

3 entry right-justified in columns 44-47 defines the data structures as a multiple occurrence type with 3 occurrences

Figure 11-55 Source listing of a program that processes a multiple occurrence data structure with an OCUR operation.

```
0048 O                    SS#       12 '0  -  -   '        CH11P7
0049 O                    GRADE     19                     CH11P7
0050 O                    SHIFT     28                     CH11P7
0051 O                    RATE  1   40                     CH11P7
0052 O                    HRS   Z   47                     CH11P7
0053 O                    PAY   1   60                     CH11P7
```

Sequence Number	
0004 - 0005	One input data file stored on disk and one output printer file is defined in the program. Note that block size entries are not supported by IBM's AS/400 or System/38.
0006 - 0010	The fields included in the record format of the DAT11P6 input file are defined in these statements.
0011 - 0013	On line 0011, the multiple occurrence data structure name (RATES) is specified in the data structure field (columns 7-14). DS, which defines the entry as a data structure, is entered in columns 19-20. The number 3, right-justified in the FROM field (line 0011), specifies how many multiple occurrences of RATES are to be loaded in storage. On lines 0012 and 0013, each RATES entry is redefined into the two fields, DAYRAT and NITRAT.
0014 - 0015	When indicator 10 is "off", the CASEQ instruction controls branching to the internal subroutine PROCES. Because indicator 10 is SETON in the internal subroutine, this instruction is only executed once. A required END operation indicates the end of the CAS group.
0016 - 0017	The EXSR instruction transfers control to the internal subroutine PROCES. This procedure is executed for every record read. The BEGSR operation indicates the beginning of the subroutine.
0018	The OCUR operation causes the value in GRADE (1, 2, or 3) to access the related occurrence in the data structure RATES. The multiple occurrence data structure name, from which the data is to be accessed, must be specified in Factor 2.
0019 - 0023	The value of the input field SHIFT is tested for 'D' by the IFEQ statement on line 0019. If the test is true, the DAYRAT occurrence defined in the data structure is moved into the work field RATE. If the test on line 0019 is not true, instructions 0021 and 0022 are executed in which the NITRAT occurrence defined in the data structure is moved into the work field RATE. The END operation, required with any IF or IF/ELSE instruction, ends the IF/ELSE statement group.
0024	The input field HRS is multiplied by the RATE field to determine the PAY amount. Based on the IF/ELSE test, RATE will include either the day or night rate for the related labor grade.
0025	The EXCPT operation controls output of each detail line.
0026	The ENDSR operation indicates the end of the internal subroutine PROCES.
0028 - 0034	The instructions on lines 0029, 0031, and 0033 point to the occurrence in which the following related hard-coded data (lines 0030, 0032, and 0034) is to be moved. For a large amount or variable data, this would be impractical. In that scenario, the data would be stored in one or more data files, and loaded to the multiple occurrence data structure by a looping procedure controlled by a DO group before an OCUR instruction was executed.
0035 - 0036	This MOVE statement turns on indicator 10 which prevents this subroutine from being executed again. Note that the CASEQ instruction on line 0014 is executed only if indicator 10 is "off". ENDSR indicates the end of the internal subroutine.
0037 - 0053	Heading output is controlled at 1P time. Detail output is controlled at exception time.

(*Continued*)

ARRAY SORTING

Array data may be sorted by the following methods:

Object and Input Time Arrays

1. External from the program by the system's sort utility.
2. Internal in the program by the SORTA operation.

Compile and Calculation Time Arrays

1. Internal in the program by the SORTA operation.

Because sort utility syntax is different for every system and is not related to the RPG language, only the sorting of arrays by the SORTA operation is discussed.

The SORTA Operation

During program execution, arrays may be sorted in either an ascending or descending order by the SORTA operation. Figure 11-56 details the Extension and Calculation Specifications coding for the SORTA operation.

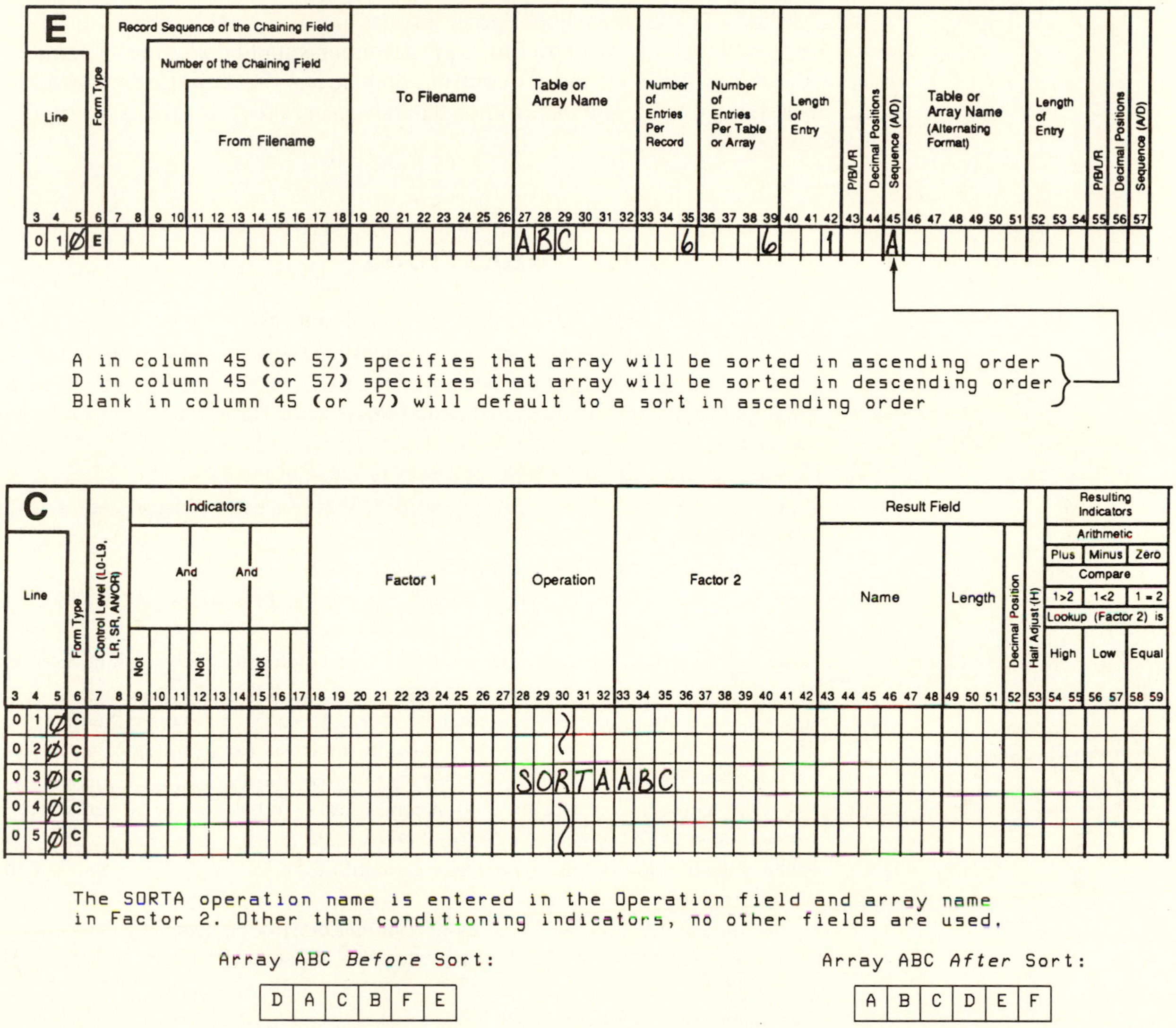

Figure 11-56 Extension and calculation syntax for the SORTA operation.

SUMMARY

Arrays may be defined as Compile, Object, Input, and Calculation Time in an RPG program. Similar to tables, an array element may be accessed by a LOKUP operation. However, a related array cannot be entered in the Result Field. If related arrays are to be processed together, an index from a previous LOKUP must be used to extract an element value from another array. In addition, arrays may be accessed positionally and randomly by indexing.

Arrays are defined in an RPG program in the Extension Specifications. If the Entries Per Record is omitted, the array is identified as either Input or Calculation Time. When the entry is specified, the array is defined as Compile or Object Time.

Individual elements of a numeric array may be edited by Edit Codes, Edit Words, or indexing. Alphanumeric array elements may be edited only by indexing.

RPG does not support a *binary search*. Such a search may be controlled by a programmer-supplied routine, however.

In addition, multidimensional array processing is not supported by RPG; however, it may also be simulated by a programmer-supplied routine. Enhancements included in RPG/400 and III control applications that require multidimensional processing by multiple occurrence data structures that are accessed by the OCUR operation.

QUESTIONS

11-1. What is an array in the RPG programming environment?

11-2. Describe the logical structure of a one-dimensional array and then, of a two-dimensional array. How many dimensions does RPG support for arrays?

11-3. What factors should be considered in deciding whether to use arrays or tables in a program?

11-4. Compare the processing features of arrays to those of tables.

11-5. On which RPG coding form are arrays defined? Where are these instructions placed in an RPG program?

11-6. When may arrays be loaded in the program cycle?

11-7. Refer to Question 11-6, and explain where the array data is stored and the loading process for each method.

11-8. Refer to Question 11-6, and explain under what conditions each loading method should be used.

11-9. Reference a blank Extension Specifications form. Identify and explain the function of the fields used to define an array. Indicate the fields used (and not used) with each loading method.

11-10. Do array names have to begin with special letters? What should be considered when specifying the length of an array name?

11-11. What is the function of the ** control statement in the format of array data? With which array type is it used?

11-12. By what methods may the elements of a numeric array be separated and edited for printed output? How may the elements of an alphanumeric array be separated for output?

11-13. How may an array be processed?

11-14. What is the function of the XFOOT operation? May it be used to control all the arithmetic functions?

Examine the following calculation instruction and answer Questions 11-15 and 11-16:

C Line (3–5)	Form Type (6)	Control Level (L0-L9, LR, SR, AN/OR) (7–8)	Indicators (9–17)	Factor 1 (18–27)	Operation (28–32)	Factor 2 (33–42)	Result Field Name (43–48)	Length (49–51)	Decimal Position (52)	Half Adjust (H) (53)	Resulting Indicators: Arithmetic Plus / Compare 1>2 / Lookup High (54–55)	Minus / 1<2 / Low (56–57)	Zero / 1=2 / Equal (58–59)
01Ø	C				XFOOT	AMT	FINAL						

11-15. The Factor 2 entry must be a: (a) field name; (b) array name; (c) either a field or array name.

11-16. The Result Field entry must be a: (a) field name; (b) array name; (c) either a field or array name.

11-17. What arithmetic operations may be used with numeric arrays? Are all the elements accessed in one instruction, or does each element have to be individually processed?

11-18. As related to array processing, what is an index? How must an index be defined? Where may an index be defined?

11-19. Name and explain the common (execution time) processing errors associated with the processing of arrays by indexes.

11-20. Explain the meaning of the following field name entry on the output form: NAME,X

11-21. What is the function of the LOKUP operation for arrays? How does it differ from table LOKUP processing?

11-22. Define positional array processing. Does this type of array access require a LOKUP operation?

11-23. When an array is processed with the LOKUP operation, how is the index incremented?

11-24. If three arrays, MTH, NAM, and DAYS, are related for processing and X is specified as the index, how many LOKUP instructions are needed for control? If MTH is the argument array, how are the related values from NAM and DAYS accessed?

11-25. How does MOVEA operation processing differ from the MOVE and MOVEL operation?

11-26. Refer to the following MOVEA instructions and determine the value in the Result Field item after the move is executed. Array or field sizes are indicated by values in Factor 2 and Result Field.

Entries		Values in		
Factor 2	Result Field	Factor 1 before MOVEA	Result Field before MOVEA	Result Field after MOVEA
ARY1	ARY2	123456	789000	________
FIELD	LAST,6	DONALD	DUCK,bbbbbb	________
STAT,3	NAM,7	CTNYNJ	DEVONbbb	________
AMT	FIELD	010000	9999999	________
AMT,3	FIELD	001400	88	________

Note: Items defined as a field (not an array) are specified as FIELD.

11-27. Explain the processing logic of a binary search of an array. What are two restrictions concerning the array that must be considered to support a binary search?

11-28. Refer to the array presented below and determine how many elements would be tested if the search argument value is 700 and binary search processing is used:

100
200
300
400
500
600
700

How many elements would be tested if a binary search was not used?

11-29. Refer to the two-dimensional array presented below, and reformat the data so that they may be processed as a one-dimensional array.

MODEL	D	S
1	1200	1000
2	1350	1175
3	1600	1450
4	1200	1790

11-30. How is the sorted order (ascending or descending) of the array data specified for the SORTA operation? May all array types be sorted by this operation?

EXERCISES

11-1. Complete the File Description, Extension, and Input form coding from the following information: A disk file named Census includes data records in the following format:

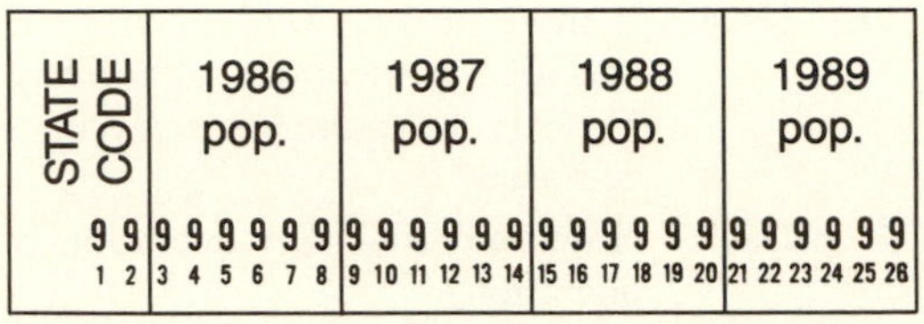

The fields in columns 3 to 26 are to be defined as the location of the data for an Input Time array.

11-2. Refer to your coding for Exercise 11-1, and complete the Calculation and Output Specifications from the information included in the following partial printer spacing chart. (*Note:* Heading line is included only to identify fields and is not to be coded.)

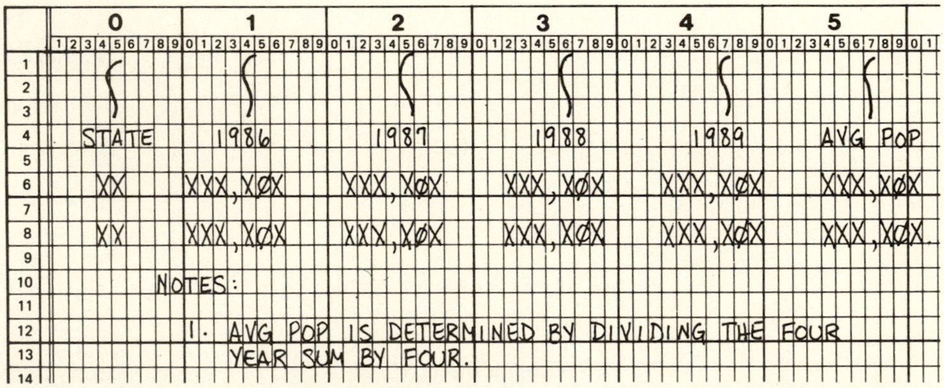

STATE
1986
1987
1988
1989
AVG POP
XX
XXX,XØX
NOTES:
1. AVG POP IS DETERMINED BY DIVIDING THE FOUR
YEAR SUM BY FOUR.

11-3. Modify the coding from Exercises 11-1 and 11-2 to load the array at Object Time.

11-4. Format the following data for three Compile Time arrays.
STAT and NAM array data is to be arranged in an alternating format with two entries in each record. The data for the TAX array is to be included on one record.

STAT	NAM	TAX
CT	CONNECTICUT	075
MA	MASSACHUSETTS	050
NH	NEW HAMPSHIRE	000
NJ	NEW JERSEY	060
NY	NEW YORK	070
VT	VERMONT	030

three decimal positions

11-5. Refer to Exercise 11-4 and complete the Extension form coding to define the arrays.

11-6. Refer to Exercise 11-5 and complete the calculations to process the arrays. Assume the search argument name is STATE and that STAT is the argument array. For a successful search, multiply the related value from the TAX array by the Input Field SALES, and store the product in TAX$.

11-7. Refer to Exercises 11-5 and 11-6, and write the output instructions (Field Name field only) to print the NAM and TAX values. Ignore any other output coding.

11-8. An input time array, ADDR, is defined in a program as 25 bytes. Each input data record includes one field for city, state, and zip code. Because city names are not all the same length, the location of the state letters and zip code in the field will not always be the same. Two examples of this are shown below:

RYE, NY 07710
STRATFORD, CT 06497

Write the calculations to extract the zip code from the array using indexing, looping, and the MOVEA operation.

11-9. Refer to Exercise 11-8, and write the calculations to extract state letters (not zip codes).

LABORATORY ASSIGNMENTS

Laboratory Assignment 11-1: FACTORY OVERHEAD BUDGET

Write an RPG program using arrays to generate the report shown in the Printer Spacing Chart below. The format of the input records is shown below.

Format of Data Records:

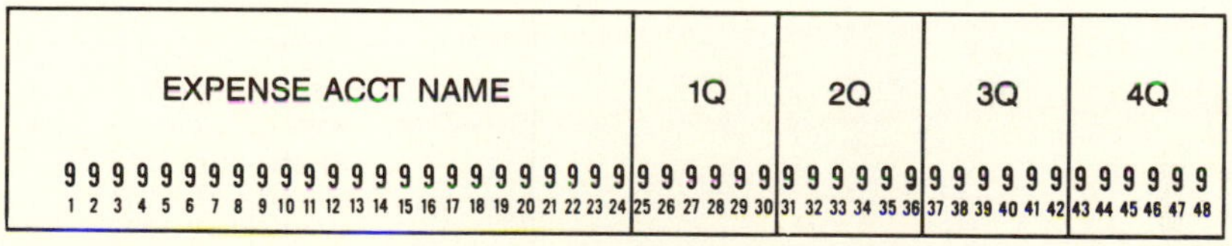

Define the four quarter fields (columns 25 through 48) as an Input Time array.

Calculations: For every record processed, the expense account's quarterly amounts are to be cross-footed to calculate the sum for the year. In addition, the quarterly amounts are added for quarter sums and at end of file, cross-footed for a grand total.

Design of Printed Report:

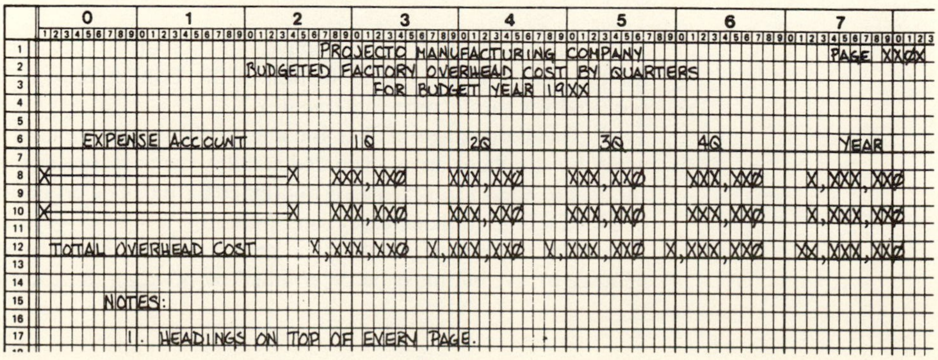

Input Data:

Account Name (col 1-24)	1Q (col 25-30)	2Q (col 31-36)	3Q (col 37-42)	4Q (col 43-48)
INDIRECT LABOR	250000	190000	201910	186750
FACTORY SUPPLIES	086000	070000	103480	093100
HEAT, LIGHT, POWER	067440	079000	080500	071330
SUPERVISION	150000	150000	165000	167000
MAINTENANCE	090000	087000	089000	077900
TAXES AND INSURANCE	110000	110000	110000	110000
DEPRECIATION	125000	125000	125000	125000

Laboratory Assignment 11-2: INCOME STATEMENT BY QUARTERS

Write an RPG program for the Income Statement shown in the attached Printer Spacing Chart. Seven - four element arrays must be defined: Sales, Cost of Goods Sold, Gross Profit, Operating Expenses, Net Income, Decimal Percentage of Net Income to Sales, and the expressed Percentage of Net Income to Sales. Sales, Cost of Sales, and Operating Expense arrays are to be loaded at Input Time. The other arrays must be loaded in Calculations. In addition, the expressed Percentage of Net Income to Sales is calculated by multiplying the Decimal Percentage of Net Income to Sales array by 100.

Format of Data Records:

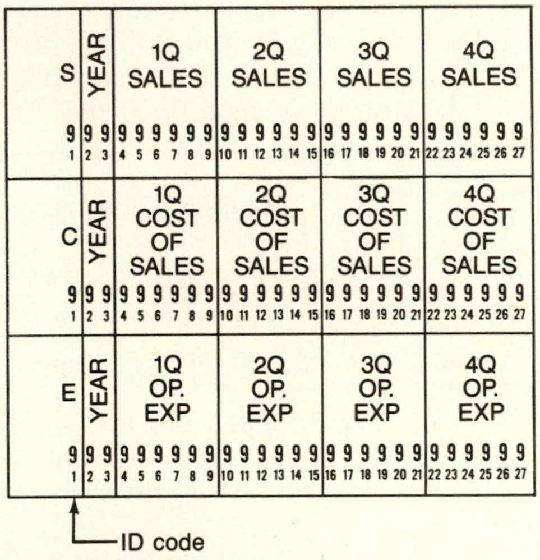

Calculations: The elements in each array (quarterly amounts) are cross-footed for the year totals. An examination of the Printer Spacing Chart gives the mathematics required for the Income Statement.

The Percentage of Net Income to Sales is computed by dividing the Net Income array by the Sales array. The decimal answer is stored in the Decimal Percentage of Net Income to Sales array, which is multiplied by 100. The products are stored in the Percentage of Net Income to Sales array, and printed.

The percentage for the total column cannot be calculated by cross-footing the percentage array, but must be determined by dividing the total net income by total sales.

Report Design:

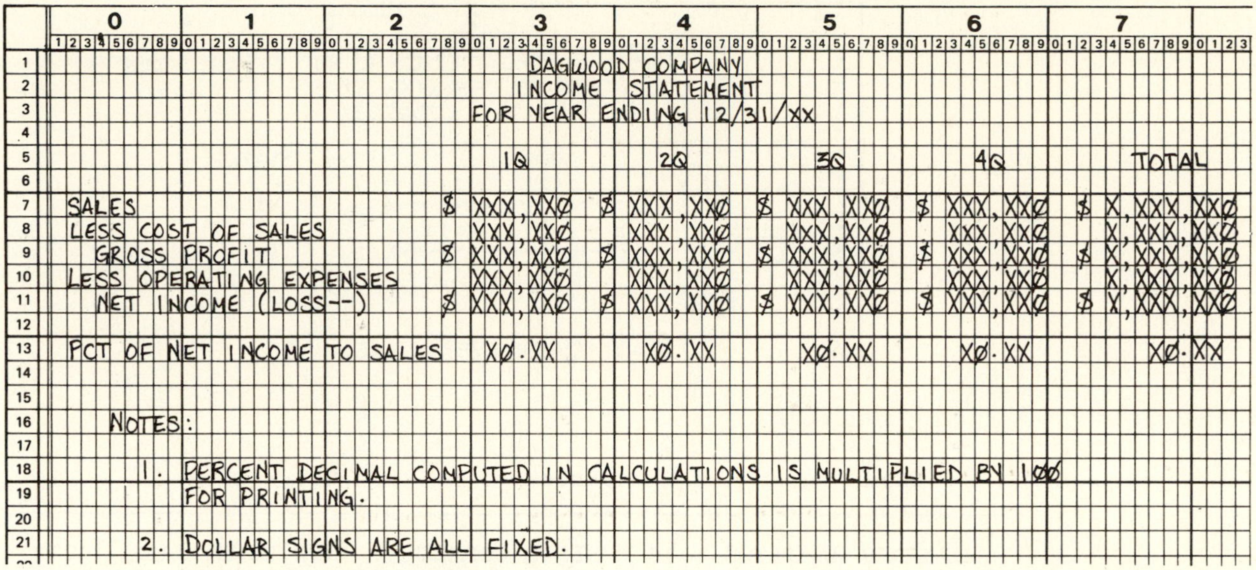

DAGWOOD COMPANY
INCOME STATEMENT
FOR YEAR ENDING 12/31/XX
1Q
2Q
3Q
4Q
TOTAL
SALES
LESS COST OF SALES
GROSS PROFIT
LESS OPERATING EXPENSES
NET INCOME (LOSS--)
PCT OF NET INCOME TO SALES
NOTES:
1. PERCENT DECIMAL COMPUTED IN CALCULATIONS IS MULTIPLIED BY 100
FOR PRINTING.
2. DOLLAR SIGNS ARE ALL FIXED.

Input Data:

ID Code col 1	Year 2-3	1Q 4-9	2Q 10-15	3Q 16-21	4Q 22-27
S	92	200000	175000	210000	309000
C	92	100000	092000	120000	209000
E	92	070000	052000	089000	105000

Laboratory Assignment 11-3: EXTRACTING THE STATE CODE FROM A CITY/STATE FIELD

Write an RPG program to generate the report shown in the attached Printer Spacing Chart below. A City/State field is included in the record format below. Because the city names are different lengths, the state letters will not be in the same location for every record.

Format of Data Records:

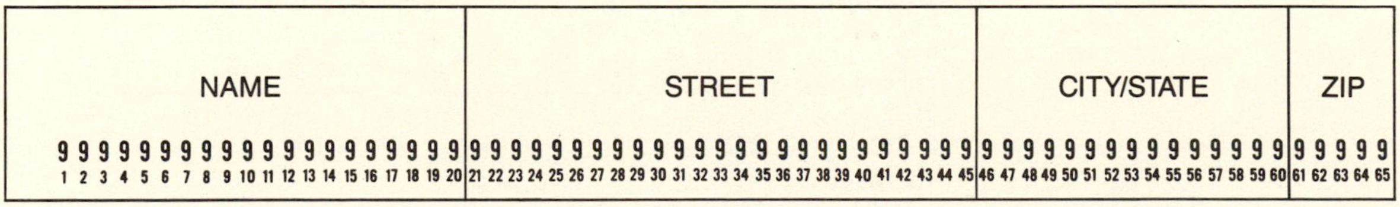

Processing: Define the City/State data field as an Input Time array, and write the calculations to extract the two-letter state code for the report requirements.

Report Design:

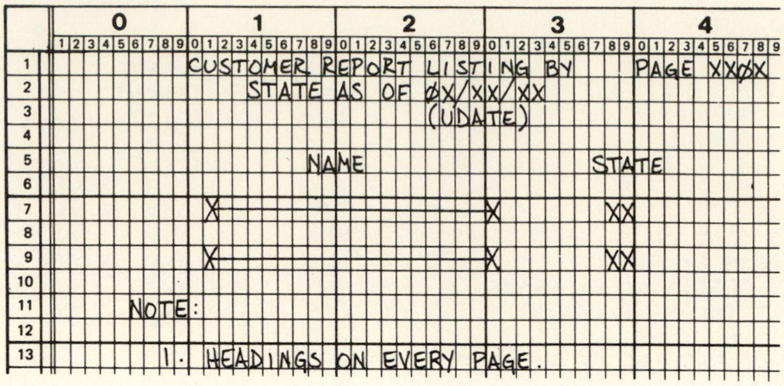

Input Data:

Name 1-20	Street 21-45	City/State 46-60	Zip 61-65
ALEXANDER HAMILTON	10 RESERVE STREET	NEW YORK, NY	07701
THOMAS JEFFERSON	30 SKYLINE DRIVE	MONTICELLO, VA	05555
JOHN JAY	44 CONSTITUTION PLACE	RYE, NY	07744
GEORGE WASHINGTON	1 APPLE TREE LANE	MT VERNON, VA	04444
FRANKLIN ROOSEVELT	1 FDR BOULEVARD	HYDE PARK, NY	06000

Laboratory Assignment 11-4: EVENING ADJUNCT FACULTY SCHEDULES

A college has a small evening division that employs five adjunct faculty. Classes are held Monday through Thursday and are assigned over three periods. Administration wants a schedule of the classroom assignments for each professor.

Format of Input Records:

NAME	MONDAY			TUESDAY			WEDNESDAY			THURSDAY		
	1	2	3	1	2	3	1	2	3	1	2	3
9999999999 1 2 3 4 5 6 7 8 9 10	999 11 12 13	999 14 15 16	999 17 18 19	999 20 21 22	999 23 24 25	999 26 27 28	999 29 30 31	999 32 33 34	999 35 36 37	999 38 39 40	999 41 42 43	999 44 45 46

Note: Professor names are to be defined in one array and related assignment information in a second array.

Input Data:

Day.........	M			T			W			TH		
Period......	1	2	3	1	2	3	1	2	3	1	2	3
Name												
PLATO	D08						D12	D12				
SOCRATES		D10			D10							
CHAUCER			D05			D06						D06
BACON										D12	D12	
HOMER					D09			D09			D12	D12

Note: If a room is not assigned for that day/period, the appropriate number of spaces are to be included in that position.

Processing: Use the professor name field as the search argument for an equal lookup of the name array. If the lookup is successful, extract the related day/room data from the related array. The day letter must be converted to a number for processing.

Compile Time Array Data (3 arrays):

Professor's Name 1-15	Course Number 16-21	Course Name 22-51
PLATO	DP 116	INTRODUCTION TO PROGRAMMING
SOCRATES	DP 125	INTRODUCTION TO RPG
CHAUCER	DP 135	ADVANCED RPG
BACON	DP 215	COBOL I
HOMER	DP 225	COBOL II

Report Design:

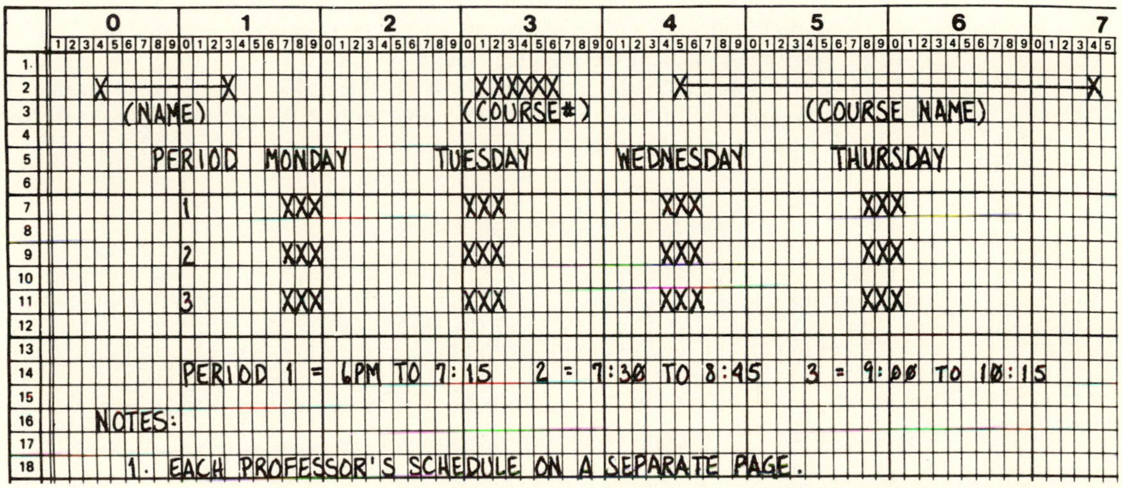

Laboratory Assignment 11-5: SHIPPING CHARGE REPORT (Array Lookup)

A company wants a weekly report of the shipping charges for invoice items sold FOB destination. The following array's data is to be included in the program as two Compile Time arrays:

Array Data:

Weight	Rate (2 decimal positions)
01	129
02	137
03	146
04	154
05	163
06	171
07	180
08	188
09	197
10	205

Format of the Data Records:

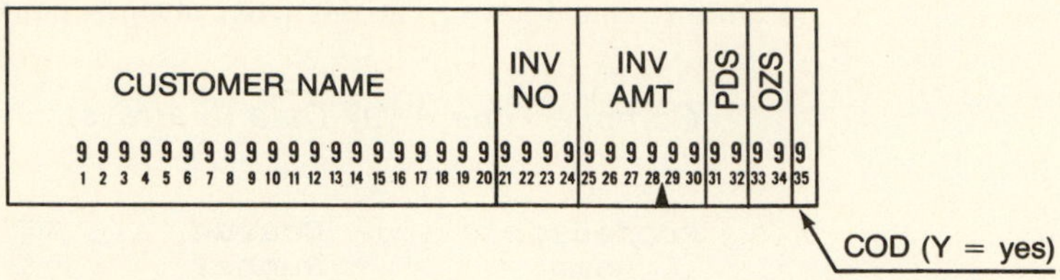

Processing: Use the invoice shipping pounds as the search argument to look up the weight array. For a successful lookup, extract the related rate from the shipping charge array. Increase any shipping weights over a pound to the next higher pound. Any shipping weights over 10 pounds are charged the array amount for 10 pounds plus an additional 6 cents for each pound over 10.

A maximum shipping weight limit of 20 pounds is imposed by the parcel delivery firm. Any packages over that weight cannot be shipped. Identify this on the report by the message OVER WEIGHT.

For any invoice amounts under $25, the shipping charge is added to the invoice amount. Because the customer is paying the shipping charge for this condition, print asterisks in place of the shipping charge amount.

For COD sales, a flat charge of $2.50 is added to the invoice on sales less than $50. Regardless of who pays the COD charge, print YES in the COD column (see print chart) if the shipment is COD.

Report Design:

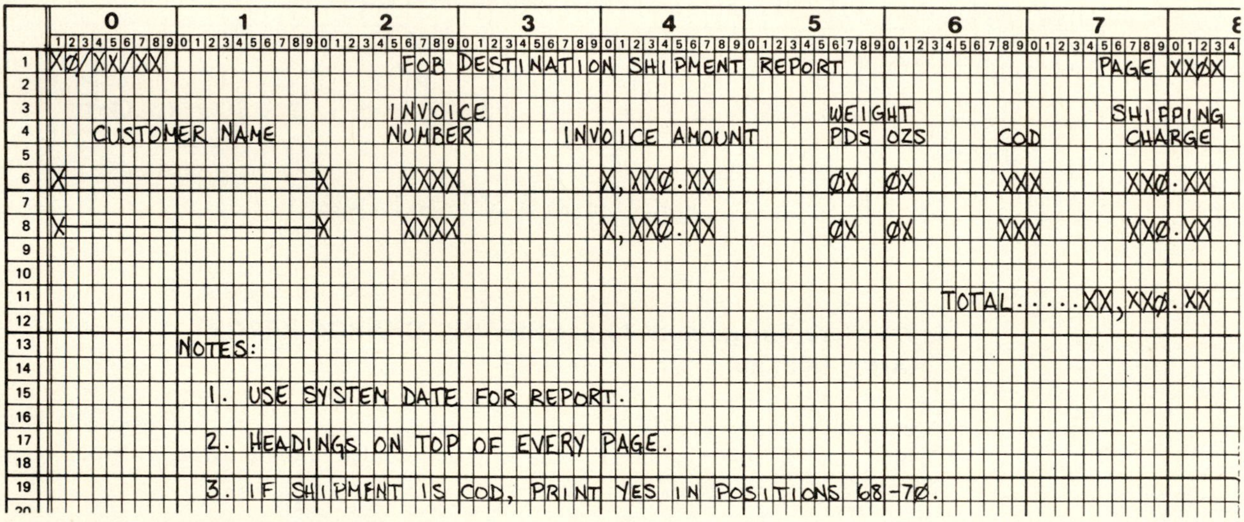

XØ/XX/XX
FOB DESTINATION SHIPMENT REPORT
PAGE XXØX
CUSTOMER NAME
INVOICE NUMBER
INVOICE AMOUNT
WEIGHT PDS OZS
COD
SHIPPING CHARGE
XXXX
X,XXØ.XX
ØX
XXX
XXØ.XX
TOTAL.....XX,XXØ.XX
NOTES:
1. USE SYSTEM DATE FOR REPORT.
2. HEADINGS ON TOP OF EVERY PAGE.
3. IF SHIPMENT IS COD, PRINT YES IN POSITIONS 68-7Ø.

Input Data:

Customer Name 1-20	Invoice Number 21-24	Invoice Amount 25-30	Shipping Weight PD 31-32	Shipping Weight OZ 33-34	COD 35-35
HENRY JACKSON	1234	002400	05	08	
DOROTHY PARTNER	1235	010000	10	00	
ROBERT WARFIELD	1236	004500	09	09	Y
MARIO LANZA	1237	120000	20	00	Y
ENZIO PINZA	1238	245000	20	12	
NELSON EDDY	1239	001000	01	00	Y

Laboratory Assignment 11-6: SHIPPING CHARGE REPORT (Binary Lookup)

If Assignment 11-6 was completed, modify it to process the arrays with a binary search. If it was not completed, refer to the documentation for Assignment 11-5 and write the program using a binary search.

Laboratory Assignment 11-7: MAILING LABELS

A mail-order company needs a program written to generate mailing labels for the shipment of goods to their customers. The labels are gummed and mounted on standard size (14½ inch × 11 inch) continuous forms paper in the format shown in the Printer Spacing Chart shown on the following page.

Processing: Define four element arrays for the following input fields:

1. CUSTOMER NAME
2. STREET
3. APARTMENT NUMBER (or other second address information)
4. CITY/STATE/ZIP (all items in one array)

After an input record is read, move the field values into their related arrays. A counter must be incremented for use as an index to load the input record values into their individual array elements. When the counter is equal to 4, (four elements in each array loaded), output a detail line of labels and initialize the counter back to 0 before the next group of four customer records are processed. Because the counter may not always be equal to four when the end of file is sensed, the printing of the last line of labels must be separately controlled.

Notice in the following record layout form that there are two address fields. ADDRESS 2 is for supplemental information such as apartment number, office number, blank value, and the like. If the input value for this field is blank, the CITY/STATE/ZIP line will be printed on the third line so that a blank line will not be included after the ADDRESS 1 value. If the ADDRESS 2 field is not blank, all four lines are to be printed for the label.

Format of Data Records:

CUSTOMER NAME	ADDRESS 1	ADDRESS 2	CITY-STATE-ZIP
9 9 9 9 9 9 9 9 9 9 9 9 9 9 9 9 9 9	9 9 9 9 9 9 9 9 9 9 9 9 9 9 9 9 9 9	9 9 9 9 9 9 9 9 9 9 9	9 9 9 9 9 9 9 9 9 9 9 9 9 9 9 9 9 9 9 9 9 9 9 9 9 9 9 9 9 9 9
1 2 3 4 5 6 7 8 9 10 11 12 13 14 15 16 17 18	19 20 21 22 23 24 25 26 27 28 29 30 31 32 33 34 35 36	37 38 39 40 41 42 43 44 45 46 47	48 49 50 51 52 53 54 55 56 57 58 59 60 61 62 63 64 65 66 67 68 69 70 71 72 73 74 75 76 77 78

Input Data:

Name 1-18	Address 1 19-26	Address 2 27-47	City/State/Zip 48-78
KAREL APPEL	20 AMSTERDAM AVE	APT 35	NEW YORK, NY 074500000
GEORGES BRAQUE	300 ST CLAIR ST		NEW JERSEY, NJ 055011234
PAUL CEZANNE	44 RUE PIGALLE	BLDG 10	STAMFORD, CT 065180010
MARC CHAGALL	222 QUAIL AVENUE		BRIDGEPORT, CT 066661000
EDGAR DEGAS	10 ROSE TERRACE		WESTPORT, PA 077770000
MAX ERNST	1 FRANKFURT DRIVE	LOT 14	FRANKFORT, KY 055510111
BUCKMINSTER FULLER	999 PARK AVENUE	APT 201	NEW YORK, NY 075500000
JULIO GONZALEZ	101 SMITH LANE		GREENWICH, CT 064440000
HECTOR HYPPOLITE	888 PEACHTREE AVE		ATLANTA, GA 033322200
PIERRE JEANERET	90 CHATEAU DRIVE		GENEVA, NY 077774000
WASSILY KANDINSKY	13 WARSAW LANE		LOS ANGELES, CA 099900000
CHARLES CORBUSIER	10 PARIS PLACE		ENGLEWOOD CLIFFS, NJ 076320000
PABLO PICASSO	1784 BASTILLE BLD		FRANCE, KY 088800000

Format of the Labels:

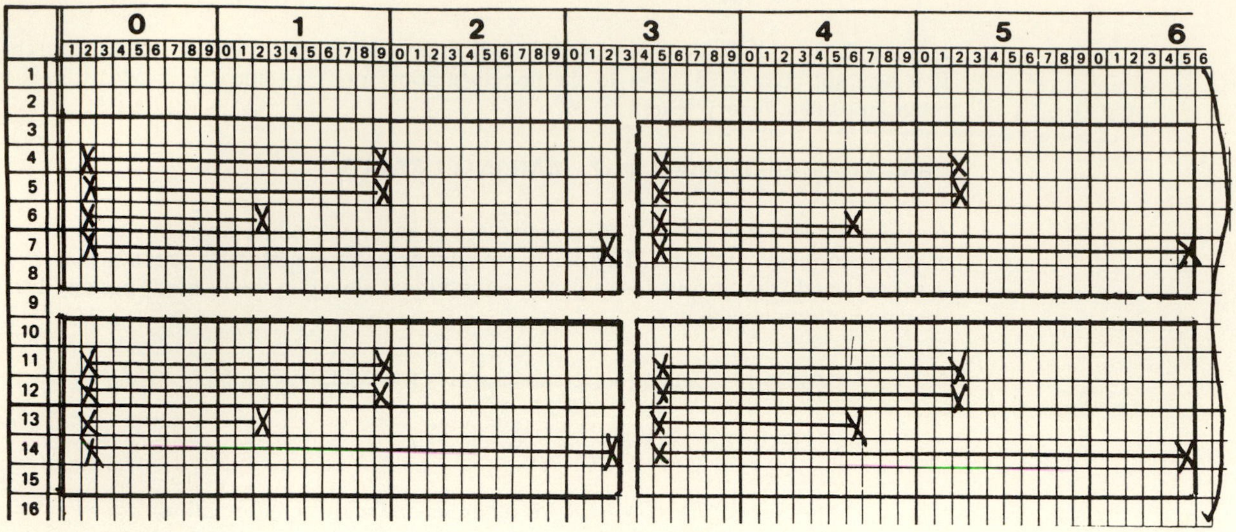

Note: Four labels are printed per line (one label per customer).

chapter 12
Data Validation Concepts and Processing

One of the most important functions associated with the data processing environment is insuring the accuracy of the data. Regardless of how well structured or efficient application programs are, if the input data is not accurate, the end results will usually be unacceptable. Once "bad" data is loaded in a file, it is often difficult to correct. For example, if invalid data was included in a daily transaction file used to update a master file, it would ultimately filter throughout the system, thus making subsequent corrections difficult.

DATA VALIDATION METHODS

The procedures for maintaining the accuracy of data are referred to as *data validation*. Whether the data entry environment is batch or interactive will determine how data is validated on input. Validation functions may be implemented by one or a combination of the following procedures:

Batch Procedures External to a Data Entry Program

Data is entered from source documents directly onto such storage media as diskettes, disks, or magnetic tape by a related hardware unit. Most of these recording machines also support a separate verification function. Verification in this environment requires that an operator reference the source documents and duplicate the keying process. In this mode, the machine does not record data but compares what is already stored with what is currently being keyed. The machine locks to indicate any differences found. Then, the value is checked to determine whether the original data or the currently keyed value is incorrect.

Batch Procedures Internal to a Data Entry Program

Data is entered from source documents directly onto the storage medium by the related hardware device. The file created and loaded is then processed by an RPG entry program to validate the data. Controls are included in the program to load records with errors to an error *rejection* or *abeyance* file. An error rejection file stores the record information for identification only, whereas the records loaded to an error abeyance file may be subsequently corrected by an update program or system utility.

Interactive Procedures Internal to a Data Entry Program

Data is entered via a CRT screen controlled by an RPG program. Some validation procedures may be supported by the screen generator software, whereas others are in the program. Popular software utilities are available, such as SDA and SEU, that provide for the design, syntax, and control of interactive screens. The standalone screens are interfaced with an RPG program with syntax and procedures unique to the computer system. See Chapters 18, 20, and 21 for interactive processing methods.

Often, not every data entry error can be identified by the procedures just discussed. Additional validation may be provided by batch total checks, edit listings, and feedback from users.

Internal Data Validation in a Batch Environment

The following procedures are commonly included in an RPG data validation program in a batch processing environment:

1. Data type testing
   a. Numeric or alphabetic
   b. Arithmetic signs or zeros
2. Data field checking
   a. Presence or absence of data
   b. Justification of data
   c. Acceptability of data
   d. Relationship to other data
   e. Structure of the data

Each of these validation processes is separately explained and supported by standalone programs, and then is integrated into a single comprehensive data validation program.

DATA TYPE TESTING

Input data may be tested for numeric or alphabetic class but not for alphanumeric class because all characters supported by a computer may be considered alphanumeric. Numeric testing and alphabetic testing are individually discussed in the following paragraphs.

Numeric Field Testing

For a field value to pass a numeric test, all the characters must be numeric (0–9). Numeric value testing should be performed before any calculation or editing is executed with the item. On some computer systems (IBM's System/34 and System/36) only the digit bit of the byte is read. Consequently, any characters that are not 0 through 9 will be processed as numeric. For example, the letter A would be processed as a valid number 1. However, on other systems, such as IBM's System/38 and AS/400, any numeric field that did not contain valid numeric characters would cause program execution to terminate when the value was processed. Consequently, routines should be included in data validation programs to test numeric fields to prevent undesirable results or program termination. Refer to Figure 12-1 for examples of valid and invalid field values.

Input Field Value	Explanation
0009999	Valid numeric
1200.00	Decimal is not a numeric character
A345000	Letter is not a numeric character
123	Blank is not a numeric character
002400J	Valid numeric (low order letter represents -1)

Note: Field is defined as 7 bytes with 2 implied decimals.

Figure 12-1 Examples of valid and invalid numeric values.

TESTN Operation

In a batch processing environment, numeric field validation may be controlled in an RPG program by the TESTN operation. Figure 12-2 explains the syntax of this operation. Notice that the field specified in the Result Field must be defined as alphanumeric. If the value passes the numeric test (TESTN), then it may be moved to a numeric field. If the field tested is defined on input, it may be specified as alphanumeric with one name and then redefined as numeric with another.

Line (3–5)	Form Type (6)	Control Level (7–8)	Indicators (9–17)	Factor 1 (18–27)	Operation (28–32)	Factor 2 (33–42)	Result Field Name (43–48)	Length (49–51)	Decimal Positions (52)	Half Adjust (53)	Resulting Indicators High (54–55)	Low (56–57)	Equal (58–59)	Comments (60–74)
01	C				TESTN		FLDA	4			30			NUMERIC TEST
02	C				TESTN		FLDB	4				31		LEADING BLANKS
03	C				TESTN		FLDC	4					32	ALL BLANKS
04	C				TESTN		FLDD	4			30	31	32	ALL TESTS
05	C				TESTN		FLDE	4			30	31	32	
06	C				TESTN		FLDF	4			30			

Fields are all defined as 4 bytes and values are:

FLDA = 1234	FLDC = bbbb	FLDE = b1b4
FLDB = b234	FLDD = A234	FLDF = 0000

Note: b indicates blank character

Indicators turned on by individual TESTN operation:

1 Indicator 30 is set on because FLDA contains all numeric characters.

2 Indicator 31 is set on because FLDB contains a leading blank.

3 Indicator 32 is set on because FLDC contains all blanks.

4 All indicators set off because FLDD contains an invalid numeric character (letter A).

5 All indicators set off because FLDE contains a blank after a digit.

6. Indicator 30 is set on because FLDD contains all numeric characters (zeros are valid numbers for this test).

Figure 12-2 TESTN operation syntax.

The example program in Figure 12-3 shows how the TESTN operation is used as a data validation function. Notice that all three tests (numeric, leading blanks, and all blanks) are included in the program. The application, however, may require that only one or two of the tests be specified.

```
... ... 1 ... ... 2 ... ... 3 ... ... 4 ... ... 5 ... ... 6 ... ... 7 ...
  * EXAMPLE NUMERIC VALIDATION PROGRAM                                  FIG123
H                                                                       FIG123
FIN      IP  F    8   8            DISK                                 FIG123
FOUT     O   F   80  80            PRINTER                              FIG123
E                   MSG     1   3 22                 ERROR MSGS         FIG123
IIN      SM  01                                                         FIG123
I                                         1   8 ALPQTY                  FIG123
C                        SETOF                  62                      FIG123
C                        EXSR NUMSUB                                    FIG123
C             NUMSUB     BEGSR                                          FIG123
C                        TESTN          ALPQTY     101112ALPHA FLD TEST FIG123
C   N10N11N12            MOVE 1         X      10      VALUE NOT NUM    FIG123
C    11                  MOVE 2         X              LEADING BLANKS   FIG123
C    12                  MOVE 3         X              ALL BLANKS       FIG123
C   N10                                                                 FIG123
COR 11                                                                  FIG123
COR 12                   SETON                  62                      FIG123
C* IF ALPHA FIELD TESTS AS NUMERIC, VALUE IS MOVED TO NUMERIC ITEM      FIG123
C   N62                  MOVE ALPQTY    NUMQTY  82                      FIG123
C                        EXCPT                                          FIG123
C                        ENDSR                                          FIG123
OOUT     H  301   1P                                                    FIG123
O                                     45 'NUMERIC VALIDATION'           FIG123
O        E  2     01                                                    FIG123
O                      N62   NUMQTY1   30                               FIG123
O                       62   ALPQTY    30                               FIG123
O                       62   MSG,X     55                               FIG123
**
QTY NOT NUMERIC
QTY HAS LEADING BLANKS
QTY IS BLANK
```

Figure 12-3 Example numeric data validation program.

A copy of the data file processed by the example numeric validation program and related report are presented in Figure 12-4.

```
Data File Listing:          Printed report:

                                 NUMERIC VALIDATION


 01450000                   01450000

 J1234500                   J1234500    QTY NOT NUMERIC

                                        QTY IS BLANK

   100000                     100000    QTY HAS LEADING BLANKS

 00099.99                   00099.99    QTY NOT NUMERIC

 12500000                   12500000
```

Figure 12-4 Data file listing and report for the numeric validation program.

Because the TESTN operation is not supported by all computer systems, procedures similar to those used in the alphabetic validation program shown in Figure 12-6 may be followed. The only major modification would be to substitute the Compile Time alphabetic character array with an array of valid numeric values.

Alphabetic Value Testing

Valid alphabetic characters include the character blank and the letters A through Z. Few field values are purely alphabetic. For example, names of individuals, places, and things often include nonalphabetic characters (e.g., the apostrophe in O'Brien). The two-letter state code abbreviations, (e.g., NY, CT, PA) are, however, one example of a field value that should always test as alphabetic.

Examples of valid and invalid alphabetic values are presented in Figure 12-5.

Input Field Value	Explanation
CT	Valid alphabetic value
Y	Blank is valid alphabetic value
12	Numbers are not alphabetic
9.	Special characters are not alphabetic

Note: field is defined as two byte alphanumeric

Figure 12-5 Examples of valid and invalid alphabetic values.

The RPG language does not provide a method for defining alphabetic values; fields are specified as either numeric or alphanumeric. Also, because a separate operation is not available for the testing of alphabetic values, other controls must be used. One method for testing alphabetic values in an RPG program is by array processing, which is detailed in the program example in Figure 12-6. A listing of the data file and printed output generated by the program are shown in Figure 12-7.

```
 ... ... 1 ... ... 2 ... ... 3 ... ... 4 ... ... 5 ... ... 6 ... ... 7 ...
0001  * EXAMPLE ALPHABETIC VALIDATION PROGRAM                             FIG126
0002 H                                                                    FIG126
0003 FIN      IP  F  20  20            DISK                               FIG126
0004 FOUT     O   F  80  80            PRINTER                            FIG126
0005 E                    NAME       20  1               INPUT ARRAY      FIG126
0006 E                    CODE   27  27  1               ALPHA CHARS ARRAYFIG126
0007 E                    MSG     1   1 20               ERROR MSG ARRAY  FIG126
0008 IIN      SM  01                                                      FIG126
0009 I                                        1  20 NAME                  FIG126
0010 C                     EXSR NAMSUB                                    FIG126
0011 C           NAMSUB    BEGSR                                          FIG126
0012 C                     Z-ADD0         X      20                       FIG126
0013 C           LOOP      TAG                                            FIG126
0014 C           X         ADD  1         X                               FIG126
0015 C           NAME,X    LOKUPCODE                     60 = LOOKUP      FIG126
0016 C           X         COMP 20                     61   <  TEST       FIG126
0017 C   60 61             GOTO LOOP                                      FIG126
0018 C                     EXCPT                                          FIG126
0019 C                     ENDSR                                          FIG126
0020 OOUT     H  301   1P                                                 FIG126
0021 O                                   40 'ALPHABETIC VALIDATION'       FIG126
0022 O        E  2     01                                                 FIG126
0023 O                         NAME      30                               FIG126
0024 O                   N60   MSG,X     55                               FIG126
**
 ABCDEFGHIJKLMNOPQRSTUVWXYZ
**
VALUE NOT ALPHABETIC
```

Figure 12-6 Example of an alphabetic data validation program.

Data File Listing	Report Listing	
	ALPHABETIC VALIDATION	
SEAN O'BRIEN	SEAN O'BRIEN	VALUE NOT ALPHABETIC
DOCTOR FRANKENSTEIN	DOCTOR FRANKENSTEIN	
KING HENRY THE 5	KING HENRY THE 5	VALUE NOT ALPHABETIC
COUNT VON-LUCKNER	COUNT VON-LUCKNER	VALUE NOT ALPHABETIC
JOSE' GONZALEZ	JOSE' GONZALEZ	VALUE NOT ALPHABETIC
SIDNEY GREENSTREET	SIDNEY GREENSTREET	

Figure 12-7 Data file listing and printed report for the alphabetic validation program.

Sign Testing

Sign testing is a data validation function that checks a numeric field for positive or negative value. Also included in this function is the testing of a numeric value for zero(s). This test is important in insuring that data is correctly signed before being used in file maintenance or report generation. For example, if a master file was updated by the addition of daily transactions, any transaction amount that was incorrectly specified as negative would cause the value to be subtracted and not added.

Sign testing may be performed on input and/or in calculations. Because the testing of Result Fields for positive, negative, and zero values was discussed in Chapter 4, only the sign testing of Input Fields is considered here.

Input control of sign testing is performed by indicators included in the plus, minus, and zero fields (columns 65 to 70) of the Input Specifications. Figure 12-8 shows examples of sign testing a numeric field on input. Only one, or a combination, of the tests may be specified for any input item.

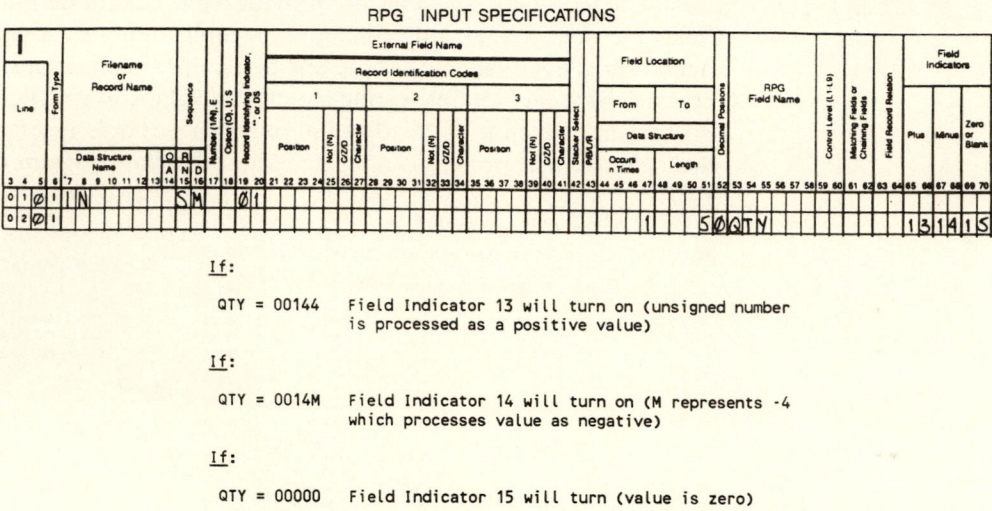

RPG INPUT SPECIFICATIONS

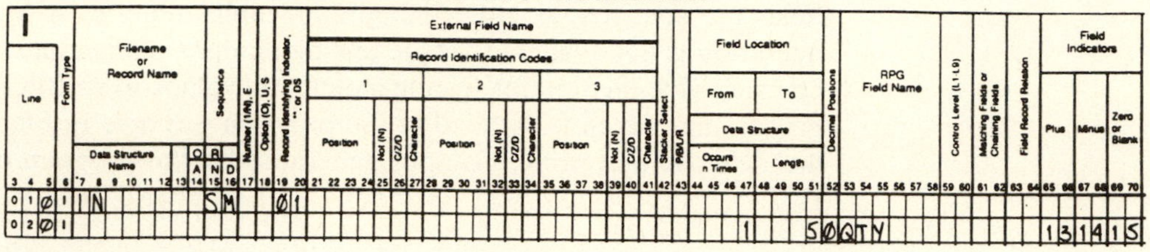

<u>If:</u>

```
QTY = 00144    Field Indicator 13 will turn on (unsigned number
               is processed as a positive value)
```

<u>If:</u>

```
QTY = 0014M    Field Indicator 14 will turn on (M represents -4
               which processes value as negative)
```

<u>If:</u>

```
QTY = 00000    Field Indicator 15 will turn (value is zero)
```

Figure 12-8 Sign testing control of an input field.

A program that illustrates sign testing of input fields is shown in Figure 12-9.

```
... ... 1 ... ... 2 ... ... 3 ... ... 4 ... ... 5 ... ... 6 ... ... 7 ...
 * EXAMPLE SIGN TESTING VALIDATION PROGRAM                       FIG129
H                                                                FIG129
FIN      IP  F   5   5          DISK                             FIG129
FOUT     O   F 132 132          PRINTER                          FIG129
E                   MSG     1   3 22                             FIG129
IIN      SM  01                                                  FIG129
I                                     1  50QTY          131415   FIG129
C                    EXSR SIGNSU                                 FIG129
C              SIGNSU   BEGSR                                    FIG129
C   13               MOVE 1         X       20      POSTIVE VALUE FIG129
C   14               MOVE 2         X               NEGATIVE VALUE FIG129
C   15               MOVE 3         X               ZERO VALUE   FIG129
C                    EXCPT                                       FIG129
C                    ENDSR                                       FIG129
OOUT     H  3     1P                                             FIG129
O                                  45 'SIGN TEST VALIDATION'     FIG129
O        E  2     01                                             FIG129
O                        QTY    J  30                            FIG129
O                        MSG,X     55                            FIG129
**
VALUE POSITIVE
VALUE NEGATIVE
VALUE ZERO
```

Figure 12-9 Example sign testing data validation program.

The data file processed by the sign testing program and the report that is generated are detailed in Figure 12-10.

Data file listing:	Printed Report:	
	SIGN TEST VALIDATION	
00000	0	VALUE ZERO
00144	144	VALUE POSITIVE
0001K	12-	VALUE NEGATIVE

Figure 12-10 Data file listing and report generated by sign validation program.

CHECKING DATA FIELDS

Included in data testing are procedures for the validation of data for presence, absence, justification, acceptability, relationship, and structure.

Presence of Data

This data validation function is performed to insure that a value other than all zeros (for numeric items) or all blanks (for alphanumeric items) is stored in the field. Presence testing checks that all data for the record has been entered into the related fields. This function is used only to validate that something has been entered in the assigned field positions and does not check the accuracy of the data.

Absence of Data

Unused fields are sometimes included in a record format to allow for uncertainties about the format's size when it was designed. These field positions may be used in validation programs to check for the justification of any field values that are located before and/or after the unused area. For example, if an unused record area did not test as blank, that would indicate that the preceding, or following, or both field values were incorrectly justified.

When an RPG program is executed, zeros are stored in all numeric fields before any data record is processed. Consequently, a justification test for numeric fields is not valid. If, however, an unused area exists before or after a numeric field, an absence test of the area may provide for a justification test for the numeric field.

Justification Checking

Alphanumeric (and alphabetic) data is usually left-justified in a related field, and any subsequent processing assumes this positioning. The justification of data is typically performed only on the high-order byte(s) of alphanumeric fields. For the reasons stated previously, numeric fields are not justification tested.

Figure 12-11 shows a record format and stored data that include presence, absence, and justification errors. An example program that processes the data record in Figure 12-11 is presented in Figure 12-12. Following the same structured

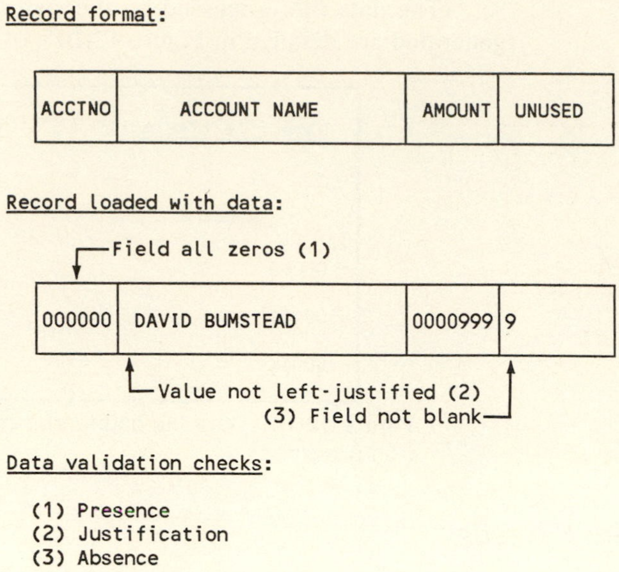

Figure 12-11 An example record that includes presence, absence, and justification validation errors.

format as in all of the programs previously discussed in this chapter, a separate internal subroutine is provided for each validation test.

```
... ... 1 ... ... 2 ... ... 3 ... ... 4 ... ... 5 ... ... 6 ... ... 7 ...
0001  * EXAMPLE PROGRAM THAT INCLUDES PRESENCE, ABSENCE, AND JUSTIFICATIONF1212
0002 H                                                                    F1212
0003 FIN      IP  F  50  50            DISK                               F1212
0004 FOUT     O   F 132 132            PRINTER                            F1212
0005 E                   MSG     1   3 23                ERROR MSGS       F1212
0006 IIN      SM  01                                                      F1212
0007 I* INDICATOR 16 TURNS ON IF ACCT NO IS ZEROS                         F1212
0008 I* INDICATOR 17 TURNS ON IF NAME FIELD IS NOT LEFT JUSTIFIED         F1212
0009 I* INDICATOR 18 TURNS ON IF UNUSED AREA IS NOT BLANK                 F1212
0010 I                                         1   50ACCTNO       16      F1212
0011 I                                         6  25 NAME                 F1212
0012 I                                         6   6 FIRST        17      F1212
0013 I                                        26  322AMT                  F1212
0014 I                                        33  40 UNUSED       18      F1212
0015 I                                         1  50 RECORD               F1212
0016 C                    SETOF                    60                     F1212
0017 C                    EXSR VALSUB                                     F1212
0018 C*                                                                   F1212
0019 C          VALSUB    BEGSR                                           F1212
0020 C   16               MOVE 1         X       10      PRESENCE MSG     F1212
0021 C   16               EXSR OUTSUB                                     F1212
0022 C   17               MOVE 2         X               JUSTIFY MSG      F1212
0023 C   17               EXSR OUTSUB                                     F1212
0024 C  N18               MOVE 3         X               ABSENCE MSG      F1212
0025 C  N18               EXSR OUTSUB                                     F1212
0026 C                    ENDSR                                           F1212
0027 C*                                                                   F1212
0028 C* 60 SETON AFTER FIRST ERROR LINE IS PRINTED SO RECORD DATA WILL    F1212
0029 C* NOT PRINT FOR OTHER ERROR MSG LINES........                       F1212
0030 C*                                                                   F1212
0031 C          OUTSUB    BEGSR                                           F1212
0032 C                    EXCPT                                           F1212
0033 C  N60               SETON                    60    AFTER 1ST ERRORF1212
0034 C                    ENDSR                                           F1212
0035 OOUT     H  101   1P                                                 F1212
0036 O                                  56 'PRESENCE, ABSENCE, AND'       F1212
0037 O                                  75 'JUSTIFY VALIDATION'           F1212
0038 O* FOLLOWING LINE PRINTS FOR FIRST ERROR TESTED IN RECORD            F1212
0039 O        E 21     01N60                                              F1212
0040 O                          RECORD    60                              F1212
0041 O                          MSG,X     93                              F1212
0042 O* FOLLOWING LINE PRINTS FOR ANY OTHER ERRORS TESTED IN RECORD       F1212
0043 O        E  1     60                                                 F1212
0044 O                          MSG,X     93                              F1212
**
ACCT NO IS ZERO
NAME NOT LEFT-JUSTIFIED
UNUSED AREA NOT BLANK
```

Figure 12-12 An example program for presence, absence, and justification validation tests.

Figure 12-13 shows the input file processed and the report generated by the program in Figure 12-12. Because the record for Lamont Cranston does not include presence, absence, or justification errors, it is not printed.

```
Data File Listing:

00000 DAVID BUMSTEAD      00009999
20000LAMONT CRANSTON      0010000
30000 HOMER GOMEZ         0450000
40000RENE RENAULT         70000000
00000LORD SMEDLEY         1234000


Printed Report:
                                  PRESENCE, ABSENCE, AND JUSTIFY VALIDATION


00000 DAVID BUMSTEAD      00009999                                     ACCT NO IS ZERO
                                                                       NAME IS NOT LEFT-JUSTIFIED
                                                                       UNUSED AREA NOT BLANK


30000 HOMER GOMEZ         0450000                                      NAME NOT LEFT-JUSTIFIED


40000RENE RENAULT         70000000                                     UNUSED AREA NOT BLANK


00000 LORD SMEDLEY        1234000                                      ACCT NO IS ZERO
                                                                       NAME NOT LEFT-JUSTIFIED
```

Figure 12-13 Data file processed and report generated by validation program that tests for presence, absence, and justification of data.

ACCEPTABILITY OF DATA

Range Checking

The verification of month, day, and year values in a transaction date is a common function of range check validation. A customer's eligibility for a cash discount, as in terms 2/10, N/30 (2% discount if paid for within 10 days after the invoice date), determination of delinquent accounts, and so forth are some of the applications that require date testing. The program listing in Figure 12-14 controls month, day, year, and leap year validation. Date element processing includes the following procedures:

1. The transaction month number is checked to insure that it is not 0 or greater than 12.
2. If the month number is valid, the transaction day value is checked with a Compile Time array of valid days for a related month. Because this routine will not be executed if the month number is invalid, error messages will not print for invalid month and day tests.
3. The transaction year is valid if it is equal to the current (UYEAR) or following year.
4. A routine executed only for February (02) is included for leap year computations.

```
... ... 1 ... ... 2 ... ... 3 ... ... 4 ... ... 5 ... ... 6 ... ... 7 ...
      * RANGE VALIDATION OF TRANSACTION DATE ELEMENTS (MM DD YY)          F1214
      * 1. MONTH (MM) IS TESTED FOR > 00 AND < 13.                        F1214
      * 2. DAY (DD) IS TESTED BY INDEXING AN ARRAY OF VALID MAXIMUM NUMBERF1214
      *    OF DAYS IN A MONTH.  LEAP YEAR TEST & ADJUSTMENT INCLUDED.     F1214
      *    DAY ROUTINE IS NOT EXECUTED IF MONTH NUMBER IS INVALID.        F1214
      * 3. YEAR (YY) IS VALID IF CURRENT OR FOLLOWING YEAR                F1214
      * 4. INDICATOR 20 CONTROLS ALL ERROR TESTING & OUTPUT.              F1214
     H                                                                    F1214
     FIN      IP  F  80  80            DISK                               F1214
     FOUT     O   F 132 132            PRINTER                            F1214
     E                    DAY    12  12  2 0             DAYS ARRAY       F1214
     E                    MSG     1   3 13               ERROR MSG ARRAY  F1214
     IIN      SM  01                                                      F1214
     I                                          1  60DATE                 F1214
     I                                          1  20MM                   F1214
     I                                          3  40DD                   F1214
     I                                          5  60YY                   F1214
     C                     EXSR MMTEST                                    F1214
     C  N20                EXSR DDTEST                                    F1214
     C                     EXSR YYTEST                                    F1214
     C*                                                                   F1214
     C* VALID MONTH NUMBER TEST - > 00 AND = OR < 12                      F1214
     C           MMTEST    BEGSR                                          F1214
     C           MM        COMP 00                       20 = 0 ?         F1214
     C  N20      MM        COMP 12                   20     > 12 ?        F1214
     C   20                MOVE 1          X       10      INVALID MTH    F1214
     C   20                EXSR OUTSUB                                    F1214
     C                     ENDSR                                          F1214
     C*                                                                   F1214
     C* DAY VALIDATION TEST: LEAP AND NON-LEAP YEAR CONTROL               F1214
     C           DDTEST    BEGSR                                          F1214
     C                     Z-ADDDAY,MM    MDAYS   20                      F1214
     C           MM        COMP 02                       20 FEB ?         F1214
     C   20                EXSR LEPSUB                                    F1214
     C           DD        COMP MDAYS                20                   F1214
     C   20                MOVE 2          X               INVALID DAYS   F1214
     C   20                EXSR OUTSUB                                    F1214
     C                     ENDSR                                          F1214
     C*                                                                   F1214
     C* LEAP YEAR TEST SUBROUTINE                                         F1214
     C           LEPSUB    BEGSR                                          F1214
     C           YY        DIV  4          QUOT    11      LEAP MATH      F1214
     C           QUOT      COMP 0                        20LEAP YR TEST   F1214
     C   20      MDAYS     ADD  1          MDAYS             + 1 IF LEAP YR F1214
     C                     ENDSR                                          F1214
     C*                                                                   F1214
     C* YEAR TEST: MUST = OR NO MORE THAN 1 > UYEAR                       F1214
     C           YYTEST    BEGSR                                          F1214
     C           YY        COMP UYEAR                  20   < BAD YR      F1214
     C  N20      UYEAR     ADD  1          NYR     20      ADD 1 TO UYEAR F1214
     C  N20      YY        COMP NYR                  20     > INVALID YY  F1214
     C   20                MOVE 3          X                              F1214
     C   20                EXSR OUTSUB                                    F1214
     C                     ENDSR                                          F1214
     C*                                                                   F1214
     C* ERROR MSG CONTROL - DATE IS PRINTED ON 1ST ERROR MSG LINE ONLY    F1214
     C* 01 SETOF SO DATE WILL NOT PRINT FOR 2ND OR 3RD ERROR MSGS         F1214
     C           OUTSUB    BEGSR                                          F1214
     C                     EXCPT                                          F1214
     C   01                SETOF                     01                   F1214
     C                     SETOF                     20                   F1214
     C                     ENDSR                                          F1214
     OOUT     H  101   1P                                                 F1214
     O                                 30 'DATE ELEMENT VALIDATION'       F1214
     O                         UDATE Y 40                                 F1214
     O        E 21     01                                                 F1214
     O                         DATE  Y 20                                 F1214
     O                         MSG,X   34                                 F1214
     O        E  1     20N01                                              F1214
     O                         MSG,X   34                                 F1214
**
312831303130313130313031
**
INVALID MONTH
INVALID DAY
INVALID YEAR
```

Figure 12-14 An example program for date element validation.

The data file processed by the date validation program and report listings generated are shown in Figure 12-15. Notice that transaction dates that pass the three validation tests (month, day, and year) are not printed. In addition, if a date includes errors for month and day, an error message will not print for the invalid day because that routine is not executed if the month value is incorrect.

```
Data File Listing:          Printed Report:

                               DATE ELEMENT VALIDATION     1/01/88

     013286                            1/32/86 INVALID DAY
                                               INVALID YEAR

     023088                            2/30/88 INVALID DAY

     123089                           13/30/89 INVALID MONTH

     013190                            1/31/90 INVALID YEAR

     003087                            0/30/87 INVALID MONTH
                                               INVALID YEAR
```

Figure 12-15 Data file processed and report generated by date element validation program.

Check Digits

Many account or customer numbers are large (Master Card has 16 digits), which often causes transposition or substitution errors on data entry. This problem may be controlled by including a check digit in the body of the number. Common methods used to develop and validate check digits are Modulus-10 and Modulus-11. Because Modulus-11 provides more control over transposition and substitution errors (it identifies over 95%), it is the method discussed.

The mathematical steps for the development of a check digit are detailed in Figure 12-16. The program that creates a check digit by the mathematical pro-

```
Steps for the development of a check digit:

Given:  Customer account number = 83327089

Step 1: Multiply constants (starting low-order) 2,3,4,5,6,7.
        (start with 2 again for larger number)

                                   8   3   3   2   7  0   8   9
                                  x3  x2  x7  x6  x5 x4  x3  x2

Step 2: Cross-foot products -     24 + 6 + 21 + 12 + 35 + 0 + 24 + 18 = 140

Step 3: Divide sum by 11 -             12
                                  11 | 140
                                       11
                                        30
                                        22
                                         8   Remainder

Step 4: Subtract remainder (8) from 11 -

                                   11 - 8 = 3  Check Digit

Step 5: Check Digit is included as an extra digit in account number. It may be
        included anywhere in the number, however, computations must consider
        it as the low-order digit.

                                   833270893
                                           └─Check Digit
```

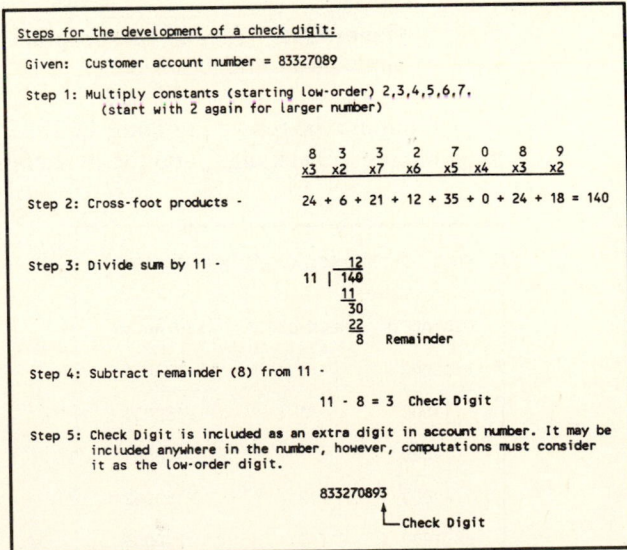

Figure 12-16 Mathematical steps for the development of a check digit by the Modulus-11 method.

cedures outlined in Figure 12-16 and builds a new account number with the digit included in the low-order byte is shown in Figure 12-17.

```
... ... 1 ... ... 2 ... ... 3 ... ... 4 ... ... 5 ... ... 6 ... ... 7 ...
  * PROGRAM THAT DEVELOPS CHECK DIGITS FOR ACCOUNT NUMBERS & BUILDS    F1217
  * A NEW ACCOUNT NUMBER WITH CHECK DIGIT IN LOW-ORDER BYTE            F1217
H                                                                      F1217
FIN      IP  F   5   5             DISK                                F1217
FOUT     O   F 132 132             PRINTER                             F1217
E                      ACT#      5  1 0            INPUT ARRAY         F1217
E                      SUM       5  2 0            CALC ARRAY          F1217
IIN      SM  01                                                        F1217
I                                        1   5 ACT#         10         F1217
I* INPUT ARRAY IS REDEFINED AS A FIELD FOR BUILDING NEW ACCT#          F1217
I                                        1   50ALACT#                  F1217
C* STEPS IN RIGHT-HAND MARGIN RELATED TO MATH STEPS IN FIGURE 12-16    F1217
C                       EXSR TOTSUB                  COMPUTE DIGIT     F1217
C                       EXSR BLDSUB                  MOVE TO ACCT#     F1217
C             TOTSUB    BEGSR                                          F1217
C                       Z-ADD5         X         50  ARRAY INDEX       F1217
C                       Z-ADD2         N         20  MULTIPLIER        F1217
C*                                                                     F1217
C             LOOP      TAG                                            F1217
C             ACT#,X    MULT N         SUM,X         STEP 1            F1217
C             X         SUB  1         X          20 - ARRAY INDEX     F1217
C   N20       N         ADD  1         N              + MULTIPLIER     F1217
C   N20                 GOTO LOOP                    IF INDEX NOT 0    F1217
C*                                                                     F1217
C                       XFOOTSUM       TOTAL     40  STEP 2            F1217
C*                                                                     F1217
C             TOTAL     DIV  11        QUOT      30  STEP 3            F1217
C                       MVR            REMAIN    30  STEP 3            F1217
C             11        SUB  REMAIN    DIGIT     10  STEP 4            F1217
C                       ENDSR                                          F1217
C*                                                                     F1217
C             BLDSUB    BEGSR                                          F1217
C*                                                                     F1217
C* NEW ACCT# IS BUILT - OLD LOADED IN HIGH-ORDER BYTES & CHECK         F1217
C* DIGIT LOADED TO LOW-ORDER BYTE..............................        F1217
C                       MOVELALACT#    ACCTNO    60  STEP 5            F1217
C                       MOVE DIGIT     ACCTNO        STEP 5            F1217
C                       EXCPT                                          F1217
C                       ENDSR                                          F1217
C*                                                                     F1217
OOUT     H  301   1P                                                   F1217
O                                     29 'MODULUS-11 CHECK DIGIT'      F1217
O                                     41 'COMPUTATION'                 F1217
O        H  2     1P                                                   F1217
O                                     15 'OLD ACCT#'                   F1217
O                                     29 'CHECK DIGIT'                 F1217
O                                     42 'NEW ACCT#'                   F1217
O        E  2     01                                                   F1217
O                         ALACT#      13                               F1217
O                         DIGIT       24                               F1217
O                         ACCTNO      41                               F1217
```

Figure 12-17 An example program that creates a check digit by the Modulus-11 method.

Examine the report in Figure 12-18, and notice that the old account number, the computed check digit, and the new composite account number are separately

```
MODULUS-11 CHECK DIGIT COMPUTATION

OLD ACCT#   CHECK DIGIT   NEW ACCT#

  12000          6          120006
  13000          1          130001
  14000          7          140007
  15000          2          150002
  21000          5          210005
  30000          4          300004
  40000          9          400009
```

Figure 12-18 Report generated by check digit creation program.

shown. The length of the new number is six bytes. Hence, all subsequent programs must specify that size.

The mathematical steps to validate an account number that includes a check digit in the low-order byte are detailed in Figure 12-19.

```
Validation with Modulus-11 Check Digit Control:
                                                                Check Digit
                                                                     ↓
Given:  Customer account number in low-order byte = 833270893 *

        * number from Step 5 of Figure 12-16

  Step 1: Multiply by constants (starting low-order) 3,2,7,6,5,4,3,2,1

          Note: In validation, low-order multiplier begins with 1 and
                continues with normal Modulus-11 digit assignment
                                                                  Check Digit
                                                                       ↓
                      8    3    3    2    7    0    8    9    3
                     x3   x2   x7   x6   x5   x4   x3   x2   x1

  Step 2: Cross-foot - 24 + 6 + 21 + 12 + 35 + 0 + 24 + 18 + 3 = 143

  Step 3: Divide sum by 11

                                      13
                                   11)143
                                      11
                                       33
                                       33
                                        0   Remainder

  Step 4: If remainder is 0, number is valid.
```

Figure 12-19 Mathematical steps to validate a number that includes a check digit in the low-order byte.

Figure 12-20 shows a program that validates account numbers by the Modulus-11 method. To expedite an understanding of the calculations, the steps from Figure 12-19 are specified in the right-hand margin of the related instructions.

```
... ... 1 ... ... 2 ... ... 3 ... ... 4 ... ... 5 ... ... 6 ... ... 7 ...
 * PROGRAM THAT VALIDATES ACCOUNT NUMBERS BY MODULUS-11 METHOD      F1220
H                                                                   F1220
FIN      IP  F   6   6           DISK                               F1220
FOUT     O   F 132 132           PRINTER                            F1220
E                  ACT#        6  1 0              INPUT ARRAY      F1220
E                  SUM         6  2 0              CALC ARRAY       F1220
E                  MSG      1  1 13                MSG ARRAY        F1220
IIN      SM  01                                                     F1220
I                                     1    6 ACT#                   F1220
C* STEPS IN RIGHT-HAND MARGIN RELATED TO MATH STEPS IN FIGURE 12-19 F1220
C                   Z-ADD0        Y       10        ARRAY INDEX     F1220
C                   EXSR TOTSUB                     COMPUTE DIGIT   F1220
C         TOTSUB    BEGSR                                           F1220
C                   Z-ADD6        X       10        ARRAY INDEX     F1220
C                   Z-ADD1        N       10        MULTIPLIER      F1220
C*                                                                  F1220
C         LOOP      TAG                                             F1220
C         ACT#,X    MULT N        SUM,X             STEP 1          F1220
C         X         SUB  1        X               20 - ARRAY INDEX  F1220
C   N20   N         ADD  1        N                 + MULTIPLIER    F1220
C   N20             GOTO LOOP                       IF INDEX NOT 0  F1220
C*                                                                  F1220
C                   XFOOTSUM      TOTAL   40        STEP 2          F1220
C*                                                                  F1220
C         TOTAL     DIV  11       QUOT    30        STEP 3          F1220
C                   MVR           REMAIN  30        STEP 3          F1220
C         REMAIN    COMP 0                    20    STEP 4          F1220
C    20             MOVE 1        Y                                 F1220
C    20             EXCPT                                           F1220
C                   ENDSR                                           F1220
C*                                                                  F1220
OOUT     H  301    1P                                               F1220
O                                33 'MODULUS-11 CHECK DIGIT'        F1220
O                                44 'VALIDATION'                    F1220
O        E  2      20                                               F1220
O                       ACT#     18                                 F1220
O                       MSG,Y    43                                 F1220
**
ACCT# INVALID
```

Figure 12-20 An example program that validates account numbers by the Modulus-11 check digit method.

The report generated in Figure 12-21 identifies the account numbers that did not pass the Modulus-11 test. An examination of the data file listing in Figure 12-21 shows that 130001 and 150002 were the only valid numbers processed. For convenience, the same account numbers developed in Figure 12-18 are used. Obviously, five of them were modified with incorrect check digits to test the function of the program in Figure 12-20.

```
Data File Listing                  Printed Report

                       MODULUS-11 CHECK DIGIT VALIDATION

  120005
  130001                 120005              ACCT# INVALID
  140009
  150002                 140009              ACCT# INVALID
  200001
  300005                 200001              ACCT# INVALID
  400000
                         300005              ACCT# INVALID

                         400000              ACCT# INVALID
```

Figure 12-21 Data file listing and error report generated by the Modulus-11 validation program.

Limit Checking

Limit checking is a validation function that controls a maximum (and sometimes minimum) value for a variable item. The maximum credit allowed to a customer or maximum sales amount for a department are examples of this test. If this function was included as a validation procedure, any customer who attempted to charge a purchase would have the transaction rejected if his or her credit limit had been reached. This process would be better controlled in an interactive environment, where decisions may be made at the time of the purchase. In a batch processing mode, the information would be available only after the fact.

Relationship of Data

When possible, additional validation of data may be made by relating it to other data. For example, if a hospital charged maternity fees to a male patient, this would obviously indicate that the relationship of the service to the individual's sex had not been checked. Another application might require that some transaction codes relate to positive amounts and others to negative.

The data file and report listings in Figure 12-22 show the result of following limits and relationship validation tests included in the example program in Figure 12-23:

1. Valid department numbers are 1 2 3.
2. Individual department sales have the following limits:

Dept #	*Maximum Sale Allowed*
1	1,000.00
2	3,000.00
3	200.00

3. Valid transaction codes and their functions are:

Code	Function	Valid Sign For Code
S	Sale	+
C	Credit	−

Note: If code is S, value must be positive; or if code is C, value must be negative to be acceptable as a valid transaction.

Data File Listing

```
112000}S  (} = negative 0)
225000JC  (J = negative 1)
4330000C
1000999X
3025000S

Note: 225000JC is a valid record
```

Printed Report

```
TRANSACTION CODE & SALES AMOUNT LIMIT VALIDATION

1   S   1,200.00-   SIGN NOT VALID FOR CODE

4   C   3,300.00    SIGN NOT VALID FOR CODE
                    INVALID DEPT NUMBER

1   X       9.99    CODE NOT VALID

3   S     250.00    SALES AMT OVER DEPT LIMIT
```

Figure 12-22 Data file processed and report generated by example limits/relationship validation program.

The limits/relationship validation program listing is detailed in Figure 12-23. Comments in the beginning of the program and the right-hand margin of the calculation form explain the processing logic.

```
... ... 1 ... ... 2 ... ... 3 ... ... 4 ... ... 5 ... ... 6 ... ... 7 ...
 * RANGE CHECK OF AMT & CODE/SIGN RELATIONSHIP VALIDATION              F1223
 * VALID CODES ARE S AND C                                             F1223
 *   IF CODE = S, TRANSACTION AMT MUST BE POSITIVE                     F1223
 *   IF CODE = C, TRANSACTION AMT MUST BE NEGATIVE                     F1223
 * VALID DEPT#'S ARE 1, 2, OR 3                                        F1223
 *   IF DEPT# IS NOT VALID, LIMIT CHECK IS NOT PERFORMED               F1223
H                                                                      F1223
FIN      IP  F    8   8          DISK                                  F1223
FOUT     O   F 132 132           PRINTER                               F1223
E                    CODES   2   2  1            CODE ARRAY            F1223
E                    DEPT    3   3  1 0          DEPT# ARRAY           F1223
E                    LIMT    3   3  6 2          LIMIT ARRAY           F1223
E                    MSG     1   4 25            ERROR MSG ARRAY       F1223
IIN      SM  01                                                        F1223
I                                        1   10DEPT#                   F1223
I                                        2   72AMT        2021         F1223
I                                        8   8 CODE                    F1223
C                     EXSR CODSUB                  CHECK CODE          F1223
C                     EXSR SALSUB                  SALES LIMIT         F1223
C*                                                                     F1223
C              CODSUB BEGSR                                            F1223
C              CODE   LOKUPCODES                 22 IN ARRAY ?         F1223
C  N22                SETON                 20                         F1223
C  N22                MOVE 1        X      10      NOT FOUND           F1223
C  N22                GOTO OVER                                        F1223
C   20         CODE   COMP 'S'              2020 + & S ?               F1223
C   21         CODE   COMP 'C'              2020 - & C ?               F1223
C   20                MOVE 2        X      10                          F1223
C              OVER   TAG                                              F1223
C   20                EXSR OUTSUB                                      F1223
C                     ENDSR                                            F1223
C*                                                                     F1223
C              SALSUB BEGSR                                            F1223
C                     Z-ADD1        N      10        ARRAY INDEX       F1223
C              DEPT#  LOKUPDEPT,N                21 IN ARRAY ?         F1223
C  N21                SETON                 20                         F1223
C   20                MOVE 3        X              NOT FOUND           F1223
C   20                GOTO END                                         F1223
```

Figure 12-23 An example program that controls limits and relationship validation functions.

```
C           AMT       COMP LIMT,N               20    LIMT ARRAY     F1223
C   20                MOVE 4         X                > DEPT LIMIT   F1223
C           END       TAG                                            F1223
C   20                EXSR OUTSUB                                    F1223
C                     ENDSR                                          F1223
C*                                                                   F1223
C           OUTSUB    BEGSR                                          F1223
C                     EXCPT                            ERROR OUTPUT  F1223
C   01                SETOF                     01    AFTER 1ST ERRORF1223
C                     SETOF                     20                   F1223
C                     ENDSR                                          F1223
OOUT     H  101    1P                                                F1223
O                                    28 'TRANSACTION CODE & SALES'   F1223
O                                    52 'AMOUNT LIMIT VALIDATION'    F1223
O*                                                                   F1223
O* RECORD INFO & 1ST ERROR MSG ARE PRINTED BY THIS OUTPUT CONTROL    F1223
O        E 2      01                                                 F1223
O                         DEPT#       5                              F1223
O                         CODE       10                              F1223
O                         AMT    J   22                              F1223
O                         MSG,X      50                              F1223
O*                                                                   F1223
O* OTHER ERROR MSGS FOR RECORD ARE PRINTED BY THIS OUTPUT CONTROL    F1223
O        E 1      20N01                                              F1223
O                         MSG,X      50                              F1223
**
CS
**
123
**
100000300000020000
**
CODE NOT VALID
SIGN NOT VALID FOR CODE
INVALID DEPT NUMBER
SALES AMT OVER DEPT LIMIT
```

(*Continued*)

Correspondence Checking

In inquiry or update maintenance, key fields are used to find a select record from a master file. If the corresponding key value is found in the master file, the required processing is performed. However, processing a record based on one field value may not provide enough control. Sometimes another field must be used to insure that the correct record is accessed. For example, a wrong social security number may be assigned to a payroll transaction. It may be a valid social security number but not related to the correct employee. Consequently, subsequent processing of that record would access the wrong payroll account. Errors of this type can be reduced through the use of correspondence checking. In addition to the social security number, another field value from the transaction record may be used to check with a related field from a master file (or table).

An example of correspondence checking is detailed in Figure 12-24. An Object (preexecution) Time table includes valid social security numbers, and a

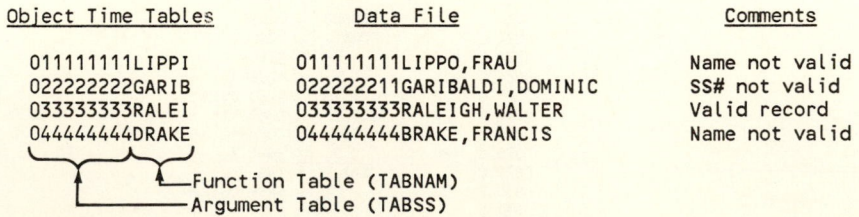

```
Object Time Tables        Data File                     Comments

 011111111LIPPI           011111111LIPPO,FRAU           Name not valid
 022222222GARIB           022222211GARIBALDI,DOMINIC    SS# not valid
 033333333RALEI           033333333RALEIGH,WALTER       Valid record
 044444444DRAKE           044444444BRAKE,FRANCIS        Name not valid
 \_______/\___/
     |      └──Function Table (TABNAM)
     └─────────Argument Table (TABSS)

Processing Logic:

Social security number from the data file is used as the search argument
to lookup the argument table (TABSS).  The function table (TABNAM) value,
accessed if the search is successful, is compared with first five char-
acters of the NAME field from data file.
```

Figure 12-24 Object Time table values and data records processed by correspondence checking program.

second table contains the first five characters of employee names. The records in the data file include the social security number and the complete employee name. As records from the data file are processed, the social security number is used to look up the related argument table. If the lookup is successful, the function table and first five bytes of the transaction record's name field are compared. When an equal condition is indicated, the transaction corresponds to the related employee.

The report generated by the example correspondence checking program is shown in Figure 12-25. Program control performs correspondence checking only for records for which the social security was found in the argument table. Any others are identified on the report by the error message: SS# NOT FOUND IN TABLE.

```
                    SS#/NAME CORRESPONDENCE VALIDATION

011-11-1111   LIPPO,FRAU                NAME DOES NOT CORRESPOND WITH SS#

022-22-2111   GARIBALDI,DOMINIC         SS# NOT FOUND IN TABLE

044-44-4444   BRAKE,FRANCIS             NAME DOES NOT CORRESPOND WITH SS#
```

Figure 12-25 Report generated by correspondence checking program.

A detailed source listing of the example correspondence checking program is presented in Figure 12-26.

```
... ... 1 ... ... 2 ... ... 3 ... ... 4 ... ... 5 ... ... 6 ... ... 7 ...
 * SS#/NAME CORRESPONDENCE VALIDATION.  SS# & FIRST 5 CHARACTERS    F1226
 * OF LAST NAME FROM TRANSACTION FILE ARE CHECKED WITH OBJECT TIME  F1226
 * TABLES.  TABSS CONTAINS SS#'S & TABNAM THE FIRST 5 CHARACTERS    F1226
 * OF LAST NAMES.  IF SS# IS NOT FOUND IN ARGUMENT TABLE, NAME      F1226
 * COMPARISON IS NOT EXECUTED.....                                  F1226
H                                                                   F1226
FNAMES   IT  F  14  14            EDISK                             F1226
FIN      IP  F  29  29             DISK                             F1226
FOUT     O   F 132 132             PRINTER                          F1226
E    NAMES          TABSS    1   4  9 0ATABNAM  5   SS# & NAME TABLESF1226
E                   MSG      1   2 33               ERROR MSGS      F1226
IIN      SM  01                                                     F1226
I                                       1   90SS#                   F1226
I                                      10  29 NAME                  F1226
I                                      10  14 FIRST5                F1226
C                    EXSR CORSUB                                    F1226
C          CORSUB    BEGSR                                          F1226
C          SS#       LOKUPTABSS     TABNAM          70SS# FOUND?    F1226
C  N70               MOVE 1         X        20       SS# NOT FOUND F1226
C  N70               GOTO END                                       F1226
C          TABNAM    COMP FIRST5                    70CORRESPOND ?  F1226
C  N70               MOVE 2         X                 DO NOT CORRES F1226
C          END       TAG                                            F1226
C  N70               EXCPT                            ERROR OUTPUT  F1226
C                    ENDSR                                          F1226
OOUT     H  301   1P                                                F1226
O                                  43 'SS#/NAME CORRESPONDENCE'     F1226
O                                  54 'VALIDATION'                  F1226
O        E  2     01N70                                             F1226
O                       SS#        15 '0   -  -   '                 F1226
O                       NAME       38                               F1226
O                       MSG,X      75                               F1226
**
SS# NOT FOUND IN TABLE
NAME DOES NOT CORRESPOND WITH SS#
```

Figure 12-26 Example correspondence checking program listing.

Batch Total Validation

Batch totals, which indicate a total amount for a group of source documents, are usually developed by a user department such as sales, payroll, accounting, and so forth. The batch total is entered when the program that processes the transaction file is executed. Transaction amounts are accumulated, and at the end of file the batch total is compared with the transaction file total. If the totals are equal, the amounts recorded are considered correct. However, if they are not equal, either the batch total is incorrect or the transaction file data is.

An example program is used to explain batch total validation processing. A batch number and total are input to the program by screen prompts and *KEYBORD* control. Figure 12-27 shows the screen prompts after the responses are entered.

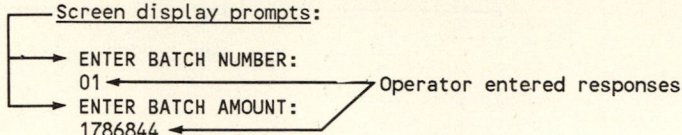

```
Screen display prompts:

  → ENTER BATCH NUMBER:
    01 ←                       Operator entered responses
  → ENTER BATCH AMOUNT:
    1786844 ←

Note: Numeric amount must be entered without editing
```

Figure 12-27 KEYBORD controlled prompts and input of variables for batch total validation program.

Input control of variables via the CRT are controlled in RPG by CONSOLE, KEYBORD, or interactive screens. CONSOLE input limits the prompt messages to related field names. KEYBORD input, which is used in the example program, provides for more detailed prompt messages. Ideally, an interactive screen should be created to support any screen input or output. It would provide more design options and processing flexibility. However, because screen generators are unique to every computer system, a generic approach is used here. Chapters 18, 20, and 21 discuss interactive screen syntax and processing for the IBM System/36, System/38, and AS/400 computer systems.

Figure 12-28 explains the RPG syntax requirements to support screen prompt displays and variable field entry by KEYBORD control.

CRT entry by KEY control requires that the KEYBORD file be defined as Input (I in column 15) and Primary or Demand file (P or D in column 16). If Primary is specified, provisions must be made in the program to turn on LR. If Demand is specified, a file other than KEYBORD will be specified as primary and automatically control the turning on of LR at end of file.

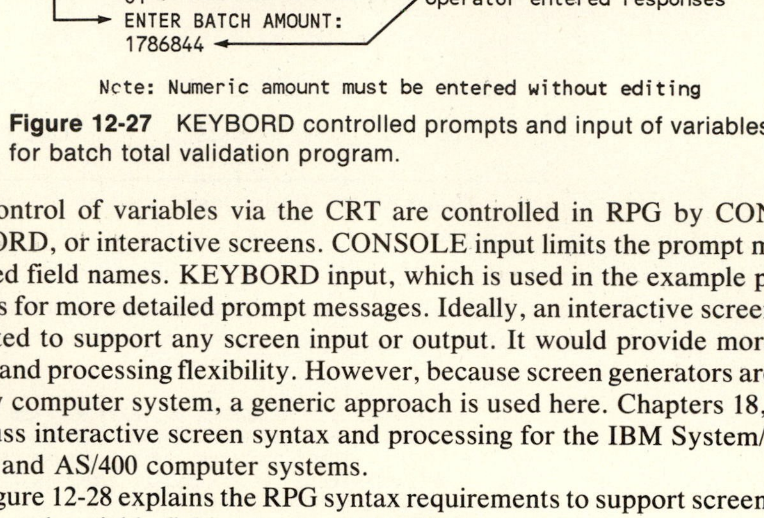

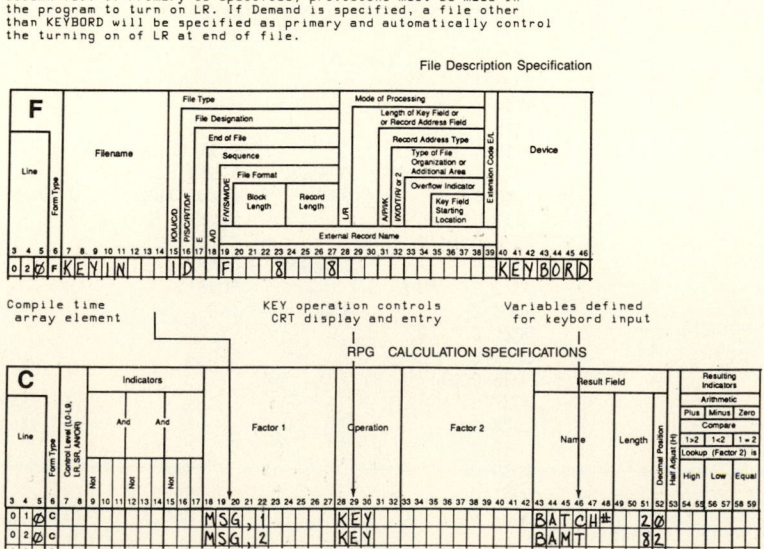

Figure 12-28 RPG program statements for KEYBORD control of prompts and variable field entries.

The data file processed and the report generated by the batch total validation program are shown in Figure 12-29. Notice that the report shows that the batch total equals the total of the accumulated transaction amounts. Any value other than zero in the DIFFERENCE IN AMTS ITEM would indicate that either the batch total was incorrect, or more likely, that the transaction amounts were recorded with errors.

```
Data File Listing                                      Printed Report

                                                   BATCH TOTAL VALIDATION

11111MORTIMER SNORD           0500000          BATCH NUMBER:  1
22222DAFFY MOOSE              0002299
33333BUGS RABBIT              1200000          BATCH AMT ENTERED:    17,868.44
44444SYLVESTER D DOG          0084545
                                               TOTAL AMT PROCESSED: 17,868.44

Note: Record amounts total 17,868.44           DIFFERENCE IN AMTS:         .00
```

Figure 12-29 Data file processed and report generated by batch total validation program.

A detailed source listing of the batch total validation program is presented in Figure 12-30. As explained in Figure 12-27, the keybord controlled prompts are stored in a Compile Time array instead of as Factor 1 literals. Because an alphanumeric literal entered in Factor 1 is limited to eight characters, error message arrays are commonly used for this function.

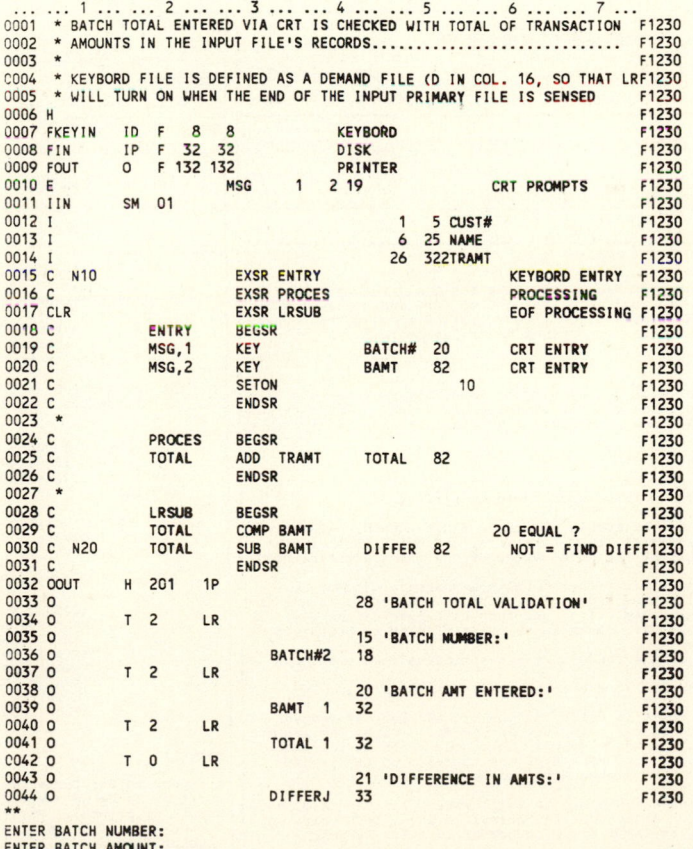

```
... ... 1 ... ... 2 ... ... 3 ... ... 4 ... ... 5 ... ... 6 ... ... 7 ...
  * BATCH TOTAL ENTERED VIA CRT IS CHECKED WITH TOTAL OF TRANSACTION  F1230
  * AMOUNTS IN THE INPUT FILE'S RECORDS.............................  F1230
  *                                                                   F1230
  * KEYBORD FILE IS DEFINED AS A DEMAND FILE (D IN COL. 16, SO THAT LRF1230
  * WILL TURN ON WHEN THE END OF THE INPUT PRIMARY FILE IS SENSED     F1230
 H                                                                    F1230
 FKEYIN   ID  F   8   8             KEYBORD                           F1230
 FIN      IP  F  32  32             DISK                              F1230
 FOUT     O   F 132 132             PRINTER                           F1230
 E                    MSG     1   2 19                CRT PROMPTS     F1230
 IIN      SM  01                                                      F1230
 I                                          1   5 CUST#               F1230
 I                                          6  25 NAME                F1230
 I                                         26  322TRAMT               F1230
 C   N10                EXSR ENTRY                    KEYBORD ENTRY   F1230
 C                      EXSR PROCES                   PROCESSING      F1230
 CLR                    EXSR LRSUB                    EOF PROCESSING  F1230
 C             ENTRY    BEGSR                                         F1230
 C             MSG,1    KEY           BATCH#  20      CRT ENTRY       F1230
 C             MSG,2    KEY           BAMT    82      CRT ENTRY       F1230
 C                      SETON                   10                    F1230
 C                      ENDSR                                         F1230
  *                                                                   F1230
 C             PROCES   BEGSR                                         F1230
 C             TOTAL    ADD  TRAMT    TOTAL   82                      F1230
 C                      ENDSR                                         F1230
  *                                                                   F1230
 C             LRSUB    BEGSR                                         F1230
 C             TOTAL    COMP BAMT                   20 EQUAL ?        F1230
 C   N20       TOTAL    SUB  BAMT     DIFFER  82      NOT = FIND DIFFF1230
 C                      ENDSR                                         F1230
 OOUT     H  201   1P                                                 F1230
 O                                   28 'BATCH TOTAL VALIDATION'      F1230
 O        T  2     LR                                                 F1230
 O                                   15 'BATCH NUMBER:'               F1230
 O                          BATCH#2  18                               F1230
 O        T  2     LR                                                 F1230
 O                                   20 'BATCH AMT ENTERED:'          F1230
 O                          BAMT  1  32                               F1230
 O        T  2     LR                                                 F1230
 O                          TOTAL 1  32                               F1230
 O        T  0     LR                                                 F1230
 O                                   21 'DIFFERENCE IN AMTS:'         F1230
 O                          DIFFERJ  33                               F1230
**
ENTER BATCH NUMBER:
ENTER BATCH AMOUNT:
```

Figure 12-30 Example batch total validation program.

Other Data Validation Functions

Many other functions, procedures, and combinations may be included in a program to control data validation. Record identification codes and sequence checking are only a few of the many other validation processes available. Both of these were discussed in Chapter 7.

Data Validation in an Interactive Environment

In an IBM System/38 or AS/400 environment, many of the data validation processes identified and discussed as being program controlled in this chapter are, instead, supported by interactive screens. Specifically, procedures such as numeric field testing, justification, mandatory entry, mandatory fill, Modulus-11 computations, range testing, value testing, and so forth are controlled by the syntax of a screen utility named Screen Design Aid (SDA). External definition of the screen syntax reduces the complexity of RPG programs, which expedites debugging and subsequent maintenance.

APPLICATION PROGRAM—DATA VALIDATION OF AN ACCOUNTS RECEIVABLE TRANSACTION FILE

To illustrate how the validation processes discussed in this chapter are used in file edit processing, an application program that incorporates many of them is given. The program specifications shown in Figure 12-31 explain the data vali-

PROGRAM SPECIFICATIONS Page 1 of 2

Program Name FILE VALIDATION Program-ID CH12P1 Written By S. Myers
Purpose Validation of AR transactions Approved By The Boss

Input files (directory names):
DATA12P1 (stored on disk)

Output files (directory names):
PRINTER

Processing Narrative:

Write a structured RPG program to validate the field values in the records of an accounts receivable transaction file and generate a report of the records that include errors. All fields in the records are to be validated for the conditions described below.

Input to the program:

The accounts receivable transaction file (DATA12P1) includes the sales transactions for the first quarter of the current year. The data was originally recorded from the invoices onto diskette and then loaded to disk without any validation.

Processing:

The following validation functions are to be performed:

1. ACCOUNT NUMBER by the Modulus-11 check digit method. Hint: Define input field as an input time array and build an iterative procedure to support the mathematics of the check digit method.

2. NAME for left-justification and valid alphabetic characters. Include a compile time array of alphabetic characters (blank and ' are to be considered valid) and test each byte of the field with the array values. Both tests are always to be performed.

3. Perform the following tests on the transaction date elements:

   a. MONTH must not be less than 01 or grèater than 12.

   b. Only if the MONTH is valid, is the transaction day tested. Starting with January, include in a compile time, the maximum number of days in each month. Using the month as the index, lookup the array to check that the transaction day is not greater than the related array value (maximum days).

   When the transaction month is 2 (February), a leap year test must be made. Instead of the normal 28 days, leap years support 29 days as the maximum number of days for February.

PROGRAM SPECIFICATIONS Page 2 of 2

Program Name Program-ID Written By
Purpose Approved By

Input files (directory names):

Output files (directory names):

Processing Narrative:

   To test for leap year, divide the transaction year by 2. If the remainder is zero, a leap year is indicated. A value of 1 must be added to the array value to indicate the maximum number of days in February for a leap year before the day test is executed. Note: move the array element to a separate field so it will not increment each time a 02 month transaction date is tested.

   c. Transaction year must not be less than current year (UYEAR) or greater than the following year (UYEAR + 1).

4. Transaction amount is to be checked for a valid numeric value. If the test is valid, then the amount is to be further tested for a positive value. Any negative amount is to be considered invalid.

5. Test record positions 40 through 50 for blanks. If not blank, it will indicate that the amount value (preceeding high-order field) was not justified correctly.

6. Include the following error messages in a compile time array:

   ACCOUNT NUMBER NOT VALID
   NAME NOT-LEFT-JUSTIFIED
   NAME CONTAINS INVALID CHARACTER
   INVALID MONTH
   INVALID DAY
   INVALID YEAR
   AMOUNT NOT NUMERIC
   AMOUNT NEGATIVE
   AMT HAS JUSTIFICATION ERROR

Output:

A report in the format detailed in the supplemental printer spacing chart is to be generated. Only records that have validation errors are to be printed. Notice that the record's data is only printed on the line with the first error message, and is not repeated on subsequent lines.

Figure 12-31 Specifications for batch edit program.

dation functions that are included in the example program. Notice that the text specifies that a structured RPG program is to be written. This requires that internal subroutines and the EXCPT operation be used in the program's structure.

System Flowchart

The system flowchart in Figure 12-32 shows that a data file stored on disk is input to the batch edit program and a printed report is output. Instead of directly printing, output is often stored on one or more disk files that are subsequently processed. This topic will be discussed when disk file organization methods are introduced in Chapter 13 through 19.

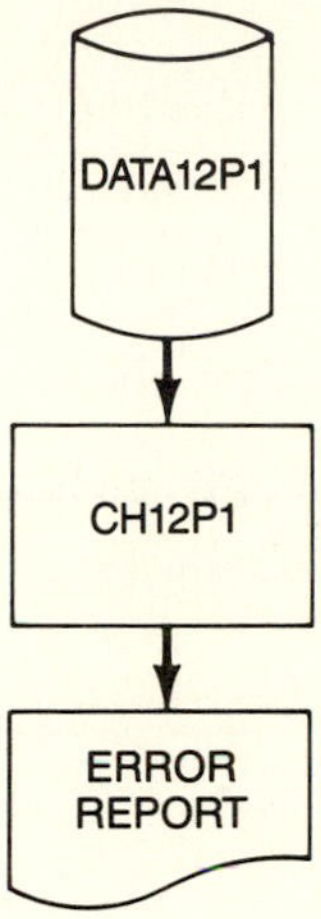

Figure 12-32 System flowchart for batch edit application program.

Input Record Format

Figure 12-33 shows the format of the input records. Notice that an unused field (columns 40–50) is included in the format. Additional unassigned fields are sometimes specified in a record to provide for any uncertainties. This procedure is often more convenient than reformatting the records after the file is loaded.

ACT #	NAME	DATE	AMT	UNUSED
9 9 9 9 9 9	9 9 9 9 9 9 9 9 9 9 9 9 9 9 9 9 9 9 9 9	9 9 9 9 9 9	9 9 9 9 9 9 9	9 9 9 9 9 9 9 9 9 9 9
1 2 3 4 5 6	7 8 9 10 11 12 13 14 15 16 17 18 19 20 21 22 23 24 25 26	27 28 29 30 31 32	33 34 35 36 37 38 39	40 41 42 43 44 45 46 47 48 49 50

Data file listing:

```
120006 ALEXANDER DUMAS     00309000025000
130000HAROLD ROBBINS       022988002390}
140007GEOFREY CHAUCER      0332890789000
210005WILLIAM SHAKESPEARE  0228890010000
300004JACQUELINE SUSAN     0131870056007
```

Figure 12-33 Input file record format and data file for batch edit application program.

Report Design

Figure 12-34 shows that the image of the input records is printed—not the individual fields. Also notice that the record's data is not repeated when there is more than one validation error for the record. Furthermore, only records that include edit errors are to be printed.

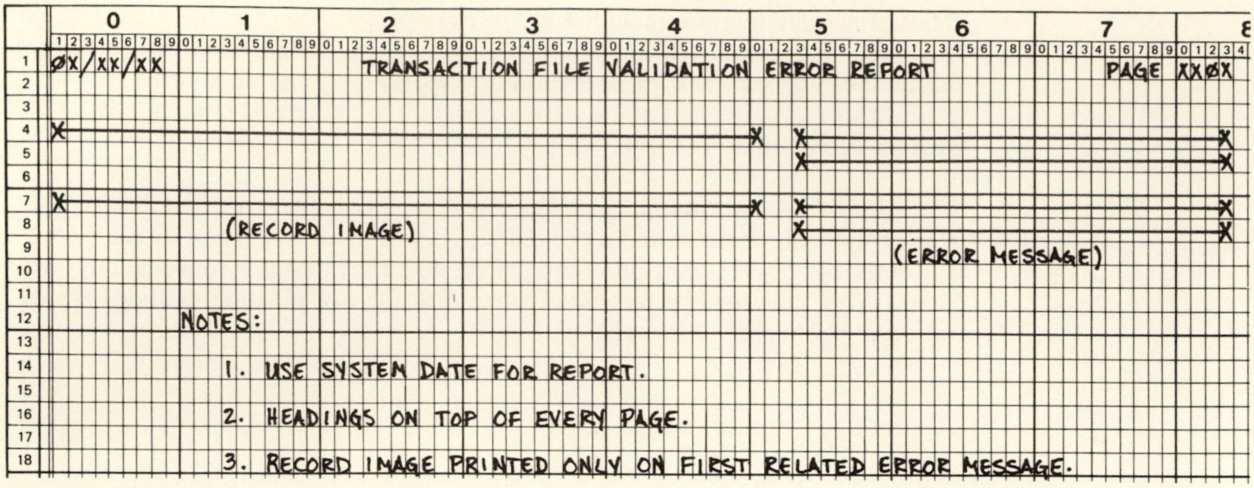

Figure 12-34 Error report design for batch edit application program.

The report generated by the batch edit program is presented in Figure 12-35.

```
8/11/88            TRANSACTION FILE VALIDATION ERROR REPORT            PAGE    1
                                                                          CH12P1

120006 ALEXANDER DUMAS    00309200025000        NAME NOT LEFT-JUSTIFIED
                                                INVALID MONTH
                                                INVALID YEAR
                                                AMT HAS JUSTIFICATION ERROR

130000HAROLD ROBBINS      022988002390}         ACCOUNT NUMBER NOT VALID
                                                AMOUNT NEGATIVE

140007GEOFREY CHAUCER     0332890789000         INVALID DAY

300004JACQUELINE SUSAN    013187005600T         INVALID YEAR
                                                AMOUNT NOT NUMERIC
```

Figure 12-35 Report generated by batch edit application program.

Program Structure

The structure chart in Figure 12-36 shows the structure of the program's calculation instructions. Each rectangle indicates an internal subroutine assigned to a specific validation function. Notice that MAINSU, included at the first level, controls all second level processing, which controls third level routines.

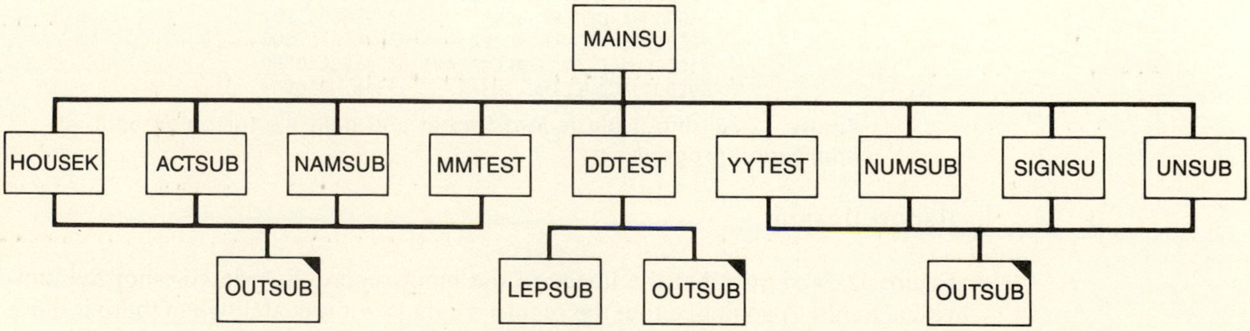

Figure 12-36 Structure chart for batch edit application program.

Processing Logic

The processing logic for the batch edit application program is shown in the flowchart in Figure 12-37. The rectangles segmented by the two inner vertical lines indicate internal subroutines.

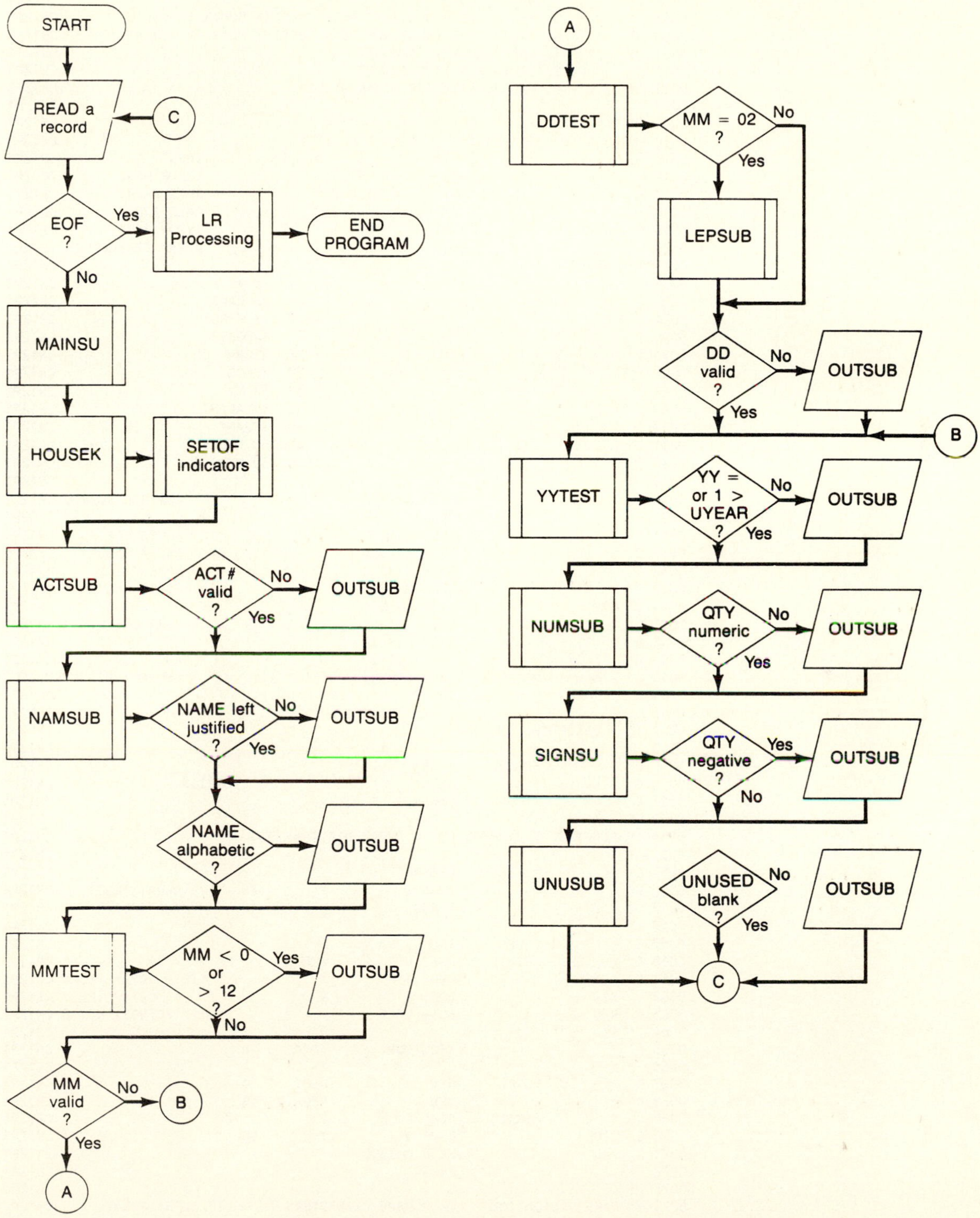

Figure 12-37 Processing logic flowchart for batch edit program.

A source listing of the data validation program is presented in Figure 12-38.

```
... ... 1 ... ... 2 ... ... 3 ... ... 4 ... ... 5 ... ... 6 ... ... 7 ...
 *          **** TRANSACTION FILE FIELD VALIDATION ****             CH12P1
 *  VALIDATION FUNCTIONS PERFORMED:                                 CH12P1
 *        1. ACCT# VALIDATION BY MODULUS-11 METHOD                  CH12P1
 *        2. NAME JUSTIFICATION                                     CH12P1
 *        3. VALID ALPHABETIC CHARACTERS (AND ') IN NAME            CH12P1
 *        4. VALID MONTH                                            CH12P1
 *        5. VALID DAY (THIS TEST MADE ONLY IF MONTH IS VALID)      CH12P1
 *        6. VALID YEAR (MUST NOT BE < CURRENT YEAR OR > NEXT YEAR) CH12P1
 *        7. VALID NUMERIC AMOUNT                                   CH12P1
 *        8. VALID POSITIVE AMOUNT                                  CH12P1
 *        9. UNUSED AREA FOR BLANK VALUE                            CH12P1
H                                                                   CH12P1
FDATA12P1IP  F  50  50            DISK                              CH12P1
FERRORS  O   F 100 100      OF      PRINTER                         CH12P1
E                    ACT#       6  1 0              INPUT ARRAY     CH12P1
E                    MSG     1  9 31                ERROR MSGS      CH12P1
E                    DAY    12 12  2 0              DAYS ARRAY      CH12P1
E                    SUM        6  2 0              CALC ARRAY      CH12P1
E                    NAME      20  1                INPUT ARRAY     CH12P1
E                    CODE   28 28  1                ALPHA CHARACTERSCH12P1
IDATA12P1SM  01                                                     CH12P1
I                                        1   6 ACT#                 CH12P1
I                                        7  26 NAME                 CH12P1
I                                        7   7 FIRST          14    CH12P1
I                                       27  320DATE                 CH12P1
I                                       27  280MM                   CH12P1
I                                       29  300DD                   CH12P1
I                                       31  320YY                   CH12P1
I                                       33  39 ALAMT                CH12P1
I                                       33  392AMT         15       CH12P1
I                                       40  50 UNUSED         16    CH12P1
I                                        1  50 RECORD               CH12P1
 *                                                                  CH12P1
C                     EXSR MAINSU                 CONTROL SUBROUTCH12P1
C           MAINSU    BEGSR                                         CH12P1
C                     EXSR HOUSEK                 HOUSEKEEPING      CH12P1
C                     EXSR ACTSUB                 ACCT# CHECK       CH12P1
C                     EXSR NAMSUB                 NAME CHECK        CH12P1
C                     EXSR MMTEST                 MONTH CHECK       CH12P1
C  N20                EXSR DDTEST                 DAY CHECK         CH12P1
C                     EXSR YYTEST                 YEAR CHECK        CH12P1
C                     EXSR NUMSUB                 AMT CHECKS        CH12P1
C   15 17             EXSR SIGNSU                 AMT SIGN CHECK    CH12P1
C  N16                EXSR UNUSUB                 UNUSED AREA CHKCH12P1
C                     ENDSR                                         CH12P1
 *                                                                  CH12P1
 * HOUSKEEPING ROUTINE                                              CH12P1
 *                                                                  CH12P1
C           HOUSEK    BEGSR                                         CH12P1
C                     SETOF                    202160               CH12P1
C                     ENDSR                                         CH12P1
 *                                                                  CH12P1
 * ACCT# TEST BY MODULUS-11 CHECK DIGIT METHOD                      CH12P1
 *                                                                  CH12P1
C           ACTSUB    BEGSR                                         CH12P1
C                     Z-ADD6         X        20  ARRAY INDEX       CH12P1
C                     Z-ADD1         N        10  MULTIPLIER        CH12P1
 *                                                                  CH12P1
C           LOOP      TAG                                           CH12P1
C           ACT#,X    MULT N         SUM,X                          CH12P1
C           X         SUB  1         X          20 - ARRAY INDEX    CH12P1
C  N20      N         ADD  1         N            + MULTIPLIER      CH12P1
C  N20                GOTO LOOP                   IF INDEX NOT 0    CH12P1
 *                                                                  CH12P1
C                     XFOOTSUM       TOTAL    40                    CH12P1
 *                                                                  CH12P1
C           TOTAL     DIV  11        QUOT     30                    CH12P1
C                     MVR            REMAIN   30                    CH12P1
C           REMAIN    COMP 0                    20                  CH12P1
C   20                MOVE 1         Y        10                    CH12P1
C   20                EXSR OUTSUB                                   CH12P1
C                     ENDSR                                         CH12P1
 *                                                                  CH12P1
 * NAME VALIDATION - LOKUP NAME CHARACTERS IN VALID ALPHA ARRAY     CH12P1
 *                                                                  CH12P1
```

Figure 12-38 Source listing of batch edit application program.

```
C         NAMSUB    BEGSR                                            CH12P1
C   14              MOVE 2        Y                                  CH12P1
C   14              EXSR OUTSUB                                      CH12P1
C                   Z-ADDO        X                                  CH12P1
C         AGAIN     TAG                                              CH12P1
C         X         ADD  1        X                                  CH12P1
C         NAME,X    LOKUPCODE                        20 = LOOKUP     CH12P1
C  N20              MOVE 3        Y                    CHAR NOT FOUND CH12P1
C  N20              EXSR OUTSUB                                      CH12P1
C  N20              GOTO OVER                                        CH12P1
C         X         COMP 20                        21  < TEST        CH12P1
C   21              GOTO AGAIN                         CHECK NEXT CHARCH12P1
C         OVER      ENDSR                                            CH12P1
 *                                                                   CH12P1
 * VALID MONTH NUMBER TEST - > 00 AND = OR < 12                      CH12P1
 *                                                                   CH12P1
C         MMTEST    BEGSR                                            CH12P1
C         MM        COMP 00                          20 = 0 ?        CH12P1
C  N20    MM        COMP 12                      20    > 12 ?        CH12P1
C   20              MOVE 4        Y                    INVALID MTH   CH12P1
C   20              EXSR OUTSUB                                      CH12P1
C                   ENDSR                                            CH12P1
 *                                                                   CH12P1
 * DAY VALIDATION TEST: LEAP AND NON-LEAP YEAR CONTROL               CH12P1
 *                                                                   CH12P1
C         DDTEST    BEGSR                                            CH12P1
C                   Z-ADDDAY,MM   MDAYS   20           MOVE ARAY VALUECH12P1
C         MM        COMP 02                          20 FEB ?        CH12P1
C   20              EXSR LEPSUB                        LEAP YR SR    CH12P1
C         DD        COMP MDAYS                   20    DAYS > ARRAY ? CH12P1
C   20              MOVE 5        Y                    INVALID DAY   CH12P1
C   20              EXSR OUTSUB                                      CH12P1
C                   ENDSR                                            CH12P1
 *                                                                   CH12P1
 * LEAP YEAR TEST SUBROUTINE                                         CH12P1
 *                                                                   CH12P1
C         LEPSUB    BEGSR                                            CH12P1
C         YY        DIV  4        QUOTNT  11           LEAP MATH     CH12P1
C         QUOTNT    COMP 0                           20 LEAP YR TEST CH12P1
C   20    MDAYS     ADD  1        MDAYS                + 1 IF LEAP YR CH12P1
C                   ENDSR                                            CH12P1
 *                                                                   CH12P1
 * YEAR TEST: MUST = OR NO MORE THAN 1 > UYEAR                       CH12P1
 *                                                                   CH12P1
C         YYTEST    BEGSR                                            CH12P1
C         YY        COMP UYEAR                     20  < BAD YR      CH12P1
C  N20    UYEAR     ADD  1        NYR     20           ADD 1 TO UYEAR CH12P1
C  N20    YY        COMP NYR                     20    > INVLAID YY  CH12P1
C   20              MOVE 6        Y                    INVALID YR    CH12P1
C   20              EXSR OUTSUB                                      CH12P1
C                   ENDSR                                            CH12P1
 *                                                                   CH12P1
 * TEST FOR VALID NUMERIC AMOUNT VALUE                               CH12P1
 *                                                                   CH12P1
C         NUMSUB    BEGSR                                            CH12P1
C                   TESTN         ALPQTY           17  NUMERIC TEST  CH12P1
C  N17              MOVE 7        Y                    NOT NUMERIC   CH12P1
C  N17              EXSR OUTSUB                                      CH12P1
C                   ENDSR                                            CH12P1
 *                                                                   CH12P1
 * TEST AMT FOR INVALID NEGATIVE VALUE ONLY IF AMT TESTS AS NUMERIC  CH12P1
 *                                                                   CH12P1
C         SIGNSU    BEGSR                                            CH12P1
C                   MOVE 8        Y                    NEGATIVE VALUE CH12P1
C                   EXSR OUTSUB                                      CH12P1
C                   ENDSR                                            CH12P1
 *                                                                   CH12P1
 * ROUTINE FOR UNUSED AREA IS PERFORMED IF FIELD DID NOT TEST BLANK  CH12P1
 *                                                                   CH12P1
C         UNUSUB    BEGSR                                            CH12P1
C                   MOVE 9        Y                    NOT BLANK     CH12P1
C                   EXSR OUTSUB                                      CH12P1
C                   ENDSR                                            CH12P1
 *                                                                   CH12P1
 * ALL ERROR OUTPUT IS CONTROLLED BY THIS SUBROUTINE................ CH12P1
 * 60 SETON AFTER FIRST ERROR LINE IS PRINTED SO RECORD DATA WILL    CH12P1
 * NOT PRINT FOR OTHER ERROR MSG LINES.........                      CH12P1
 *                                                                   CH12P1
```

(*Continued*)

```
C           OUTSUB    BEGSR                                             CH12P1
C                     EXCPT                                             CH12P1
C   N60               SETON                     60     AFTER 1ST ERRORCH12P1
C                     ENDSR                                             CH12P1
 *                                                                      CH12P1
OERRORS  H  101    1P                                                   CH12P1
O        OR        OF                                                   CH12P1
O                          UDATE Y    8                                 CH12P1
O                                    38 'TRANSACTION FILE'              CH12P1
O                                    62 'VALIDATION ERROR REPORT'       CH12P1
O                                    78 'PAGE'                          CH12P1
O                          PAGE  Z   83                                 CH12P1
O        H  1      1P                                                   CH12P1
O        OR        OF                                                   CH12P1
O                                    83 'CH12P1'                        CH12P1
O        E  11     01N60                                                CH12P1
O                          RECORD    50                                 CH12P1
O                          MSG,Y     80                                 CH12P1
O        E  1      60                                                   CH12P1
O                          MSG,Y     80                                 CH12P1
**
ACCOUNT NUMBER NOT VALID
NAME NOT LEFT-JUSTIFIED
NAME CONTAINS INVALID CHARACTERS
INVALID MONTH
INVALID DAY
INVALID YEAR
AMOUNT NOT NUMERIC
AMOUNT NEGATIVE
AMT HAS JUSTIFICATION ERROR
**
312831303130313130313031
**
 'ABCDEFGHIJKLMNOPQRSTUVWXYZ
```

(*Continued*)

Modified Batch Edit Program with RPG III Coding

A source listing of the batch edit application previously presented is modified in Figure 12-39 with RPG III syntax. The following RPG III coding procedures unique to IBM's System/38 and AS/400 are included in the program:

1. The input file is defined as a *primary* (P in column 16) and *program defined* (F in column 19) file in the File Description instruction.
2. Structured operations including IF, ELSE, DO, CAS, and CAB are included in the calculations.

```
... ... 1 ... ... 2 ... ... 3 ... ... 4 ... ... 5 ... ... 6 ... ... 7 ...
*             **** TRANSACTION FILE FIELD VALIDATION ****             CH12P2
* **************** MODIFIED WITH RPG III/400 SYNTAX ***************   CH12P2
*  VALIDATION FUNCTIONS PERFORMED:                                    CH12P2
*        1. ACCT# VALIDATION BY MODULUS-11 METHOD                     CH12P2
*        2. NAME JUSTIFICATION                                        CH12P2
*        3. VALID ALPHABETIC CHARACTERS (AND ') IN NAME               CH12P2
*        4. VALID MONTH                                               CH12P2
*        5. VALID DAY (THIS TEST MADE ONLY IF MONTH IS VALID)         CH12P2
*        6. VALID YEAR (MUST NOT BE < CURRENT YEAR OR > NEXT YEAR)    CH12P2
*        7. VALID NUMERIC AMOUNT                                      CH12P2
*        8. VALID POSITIVE AMOUNT                                     CH12P2
*        9. UNUSED AREA FOR BLANK VALUE                               CH12P2
H                                                                     CH12P2
FDATA12P1IP  F  50  50            DISK                                CH12P2
FERRORS  O   F 100 100     OF     PRINTER                             CH12P2
E                    ACT#        6  1 0            INPUT ARRAY        CH12P2
E                    MSG     1   9 31              ERROR MSGS         CH12P2
E                    DAY    12  12  2 0            DAYS ARRAY         CH12P2
E                    SUM         6  2 0            CALC ARRAY         CH12P2
E                    NAME       20  1              INPUT ARRAY        CH12P2
E                    CODE   28  28  1              ALPHA CHARACTERS   CH12P2
```

Figure 12-39 Source listing of batch edit application program modified with RPG III/400 (System/38 and AS/400 coding).

```
0022 IDATA12P1SM  01                                                  CH12P2
0023 I                                            1   6 ACT#          CH12P2
0024 I                                            7  26 NAME          CH12P2
0025 I                                            7   7 FIRST         CH12P2
0026 I                                           27  320DATE          CH12P2
0027 I                                           27  280MM            CH12P2
0028 I                                           29  300DD            CH12P2
0029 I                                           31  320YY            CH12P2
0030 I                                           33  39 ALAMT         CH12P2
0031 I                                           40  50 UNUSED        CH12P2
0032 I                                            1  50 RECORD        CH12P2
0033  *                                                               CH12P2
0034 C                    EXSR MAINSU                 CONTROL SUBROUTCH12P2
0035 C          MAINSU    BEGSR                                       CH12P2
0036 C                    EXSR HOUSEK                 HOUSEKEEPING    CH12P2
0037 C                    EXSR ACTSUB                 ACCT# CHECK     CH12P2
0038 C                    EXSR NAMSUB                 NAME CHECK      CH12P2
0039 C                    EXSR MMTEST                 MONTH CHECK     CH12P2
0040 C          *IN20     CASEQ'0'       DDTEST       DAY CHECK       CH12P2
0041 C                    END                                         CH12P2
0042 C                    EXSR YYTEST                 YEAR CHECK      CH12P2
0043 C                    EXSR NUMSUB                 AMT CHECKS      CH12P2
0044 C          AMT       IFLT .00                    AMT SIGN CHECK  CH12P2
0045 C          *IN17     ANDEQ'1'                                    CH12P2
0046 C                    EXSR SIGNSU                                 CH12P2
0047 C                    END                                         CH12P2
0048  *                                                               CH12P2
0049 C          UNUSED    CASNE*BLANK    UNUSUB       UNUSED AREA CHKCH12P2
0050 C                    END                                         CH12P2
0051 C                    ENDSR                                       CH12P2
0052  *                                                               CH12P2
0053  * HOUSKEEPING ROUTINE                                           CH12P2
0054  *                                                               CH12P2
0055 C          HOUSEK    BEGSR                                       CH12P2
0056 C                    MOVE '0'       *IN20        SETOFF IND.     CH12P2
0057 C                    MOVE '0'       *IN21        SETOFF IND.     CH12P2
0058 C                    MOVE '0'       *IN60        SETOF IND.      CH12P2
0059 C                    ENDSR                                       CH12P2
0060 C                    ENDSR                                       CH12P2
0061  *                                                               CH12P2
0062  * ACCT# TEST BY MODULUS-11 CHECK DIGIT METHOD                   CH12P2
0063  *                                                               CH12P2
0064 C          ACTSUB    BEGSR                                       CH12P2
0065 C                    Z-ADD6         X        20  ARRAY INDEX     CH12P2
0066 C                    Z-ADD1         N        10  MULTIPLIER      CH12P2
0067  *                                                               CH12P2
0068 C          X         DOWGT0                                      CH12P2
0069 C          ACT#,X    MULT N         SUM,X                        CH12P2
0070 C          X         SUB  1         X          20 - ARRAY INDEX CH12P2
0071 C          X         IFNE 0                      TEST INDEX      CH12P2
0072 C                    ADD  1         N            INCREMENT N     CH12P2
0073 C                    END                         ENDS IF         CH12P2
0074 C                    END                         ENDS DOW GROUP  CH12P2
0075  *                                                               CH12P2
0076 C                    XFOOTSUM       TOTAL    40                  CH12P2
0077  *                                                               CH12P2
0078 C          TOTAL     DIV  11        QUOT     30                  CH12P2
0079 C                    MVR            REMAIN   30                  CH12P2
0080 C          REMAIN    IFNE 0                      REMAIN 0 ?      CH12P2
0081 C                    MOVE 1         Y        10                  CH12P2
0082 C                    EXSR OUTSUB                                 CH12P2
0083 C                    END                                         CH12P2
0084 C                    ENDSR                                       CH12P2
0085  *                                                               CH12P2
0086  * NAME VALIDATION - LOKUP NAME CHARACTERS IN VALID ALPHA ARRAY   CH12P2
0087  *                                                               CH12P2
0088 C          NAMSUB    BEGSR                                       CH12P2
0089 C          NAME1     IFEQ *BLANK                 VALUE SPACES?   CH12P2
0090 C                    MOVE 2         Y                            CH12P2
0091 C                    EXSR OUTSUB                                 CH12P2
0092 C                    ELSE                        NAME NOT SPACESCH12P2
0093  *                                                               CH12P2
0094 C                    DO   20        X                            CH12P2
0095 C          NAME,X    LOKUPCODE                 20 = LOOKUP       CH12P2
0096 C  N20               END                         END DO GROUP    CH12P2
     C                    END                         END LINE 89 IF
0097  *                                                               CH12P2
0098 C          *IN20     IFEQ '0'                                    CH12P2
```

(Continued)

```
C                    MOVE 3         Y               CHAR NOT FOUND CH12P2
C                    EXSR OUTSUB                                   CH12P2
C                    END                                           CH12P2
C                    ENDSR                                         CH12P2
 *                                                                 CH12P2
 * VALID MONTH NUMBER TEST - > 00 AND = OR < 12                    CH12P2
 *                                                                 CH12P2
C           MMTEST   BEGSR                                         CH12P2
C           MM       IFEQ *ZERO                     MM = 0?        CH12P2
C           MM       ORGT 12                        > 12 ?         CH12P2
C                    MOVE 4         Y               INVALID MTH    CH12P2
C                    EXSR OUTSUB                                   CH12P2
C                    MOVE '1'       *IN20           SETON IND.     CH12P2
C                    ELSE                                          CH12P2
C                    MOVE '0'       *IN20           SETOFF IND.    CH12P2
C                    END                            ENDS IF/ELSE   CH12P2
C                    ENDSR                                         CH12P2
 *                                                                 CH12P2
 * DAY VALIDATION TEST: LEAP AND NON-LEAP YEAR CONTROL             CH12P2
 *                                                                 CH12P2
C           DDTEST   BEGSR                                         CH12P2
C                    Z-ADDDAY,MM    MDAYS   20      MOVE ARAY VALUECH12P2
C           MM       CASEQ02        LEPSUB           FEB ?         CH12P2
C                    END                            ENDS CAS       CH12P2
C           DD       IFGT MDAYS                     DAYS > ARRAY ? CH12P2
C                    MOVE 5         Y               INVALID DAY    CH12P2
C                    EXSR OUTSUB                                   CH12P2
C                    END                                           CH12P2
C                    ENDSR                                         CH12P2
 *                                                                 CH12P2
 * LEAP YEAR TEST SUBROUTINE                                       CH12P2
 *                                                                 CH12P2
C           LEPSUB   BEGSR                                         CH12P2
C           YY       DIV  4         QUOTNT  11      LEAP MATH      CH12P2
C           QUOTNT   IFEQ *ZERO                      LEAP YR TEST  CH12P2
C                    ADD  1         MDAYS           + 1 IF LEAP YR CH12P2
C                    END                                           CH12P2
C                    ENDSR                                         CH12P2
 *                                                                 CH12P2
 * YEAR TEST: MUST = OR NO MORE THAN 1 > UYEAR                     CH12P2
 *                                                                 CH12P2
C           YYTEST   BEGSR                                         CH12P2
C           UYEAR    ADD  1         NYR     20      ADD 1 TO UYEAR CH12P2
C           YY       IFLT UYEAR                     < BAD YR       CH12P2
C           YY       ORGT NYR                       > INVALID YY   CH12P2
C                    MOVE 6         Y               INVALID YR     CH12P2
C                    EXSR OUTSUB                                   CH12P2
C                    END                                           CH12P2
C                    ENDSR                                         CH12P2
 *                                                                 CH12P2
 * TEST FOR VALID NUMERIC AMOUNT VALUE                             CH12P2
 *                                                                 CH12P2
C           NUMSUB   BEGSR                                         CH12P2
C                    TESTN          ALAMT       17  NUMERIC TEST   CH12P2
C           *IN17    IFEQ '0'                                      CH12P2
C                    MOVE 7         Y               NOT NUMERIC    CH12P2
C                    EXSR OUTSUB                                   CH12P2
C                    ELSE                           VALID NUMERIC  CH12P2
C                    MOVE ALAMT     AMT     72      MOVE TO NUM FLDCH12P2
C                    END                            ENDS IF/ELSE   CH12P2
C                    ENDSR                                         CH12P2
 *                                                                 CH12P2
 * TEST AMT FOR INVALID NEGATIVE VALUE ONLY IF AMT TESTS AS NUMERIC CH12P2
 *                                                                 CH12P2
C           SIGNSU   BEGSR                                         CH12P2
C                    MOVE 8         Y               NEGATIVE VALUE CH12P2
C                    EXSR OUTSUB                                   CH12P2
C                    ENDSR                                         CH12P2
 *                                                                 CH12P2
 * ROUTINE FOR UNUSED AREA IS PERFORMED IF FIELD DID NOT TEST BLANK CH12P2
 *                                                                 CH12P2
C           UNUSUB   BEGSR                                         CH12P2
C                    MOVE 9         Y               NOT BLANK      CH12P2
C                    EXSR OUTSUB                                   CH12P2
C                    ENDSR                                         CH12P2
 *                                                                 CH12P2
 * ALL ERROR OUTPUT IS CONTROLLED BY THIS SUBROUTINE................ CH12P2
 * 60 SETON AFTER FIRST ERROR LINE IS PRINTED SO RECORD DATA WILL  CH12P2
```

(Continued)

```
0177  * NOT PRINT FOR OTHER ERROR MSG LINES.........                     CH12P2
0178  *                                                                   CH12P2
0179 C           OUTSUB    BEGSR                                          CH12P2
0180 C           *IN60     IFEQ '0'                                       CH12P2
0181 C                     EXCPTFIRST                                     CH12P2
0182 C                     MOVE '1'       *IN60      60    AFTER 1ST ERRORCH12P2
0183 C                     ELSE                                           CH12P2
0184 C                     EXCPTSECOND                                    CH12P2
0185 C                     END                                            CH12P2
0186 C                     ENDSR                                          CH12P2
0187  *                                                                   CH12P2
0188 OERRORS  H  101    1P                                                CH12P2
0189 O       OR         OF                                                CH12P2
0190 O                         UDATE Y    8                               CH12P2
0191 O                                   38 'TRANSACTION FILE'            CH12P2
0192 O                                   62 'VALIDATION ERROR REPORT'     CH12P2
0193 O                                   78 'PAGE'                        CH12P2
0194 O                         PAGE  Z   83                               CH12P2
0195 O          H  1    1P                                                CH12P2
0196 O       OR         OF                                                CH12P2
0197 O                                   83 'CH12P2'                      CH12P2
0198 O          E 11           FIRST                                      CH12P2
0199 O                         RECORD    50                               CH12P2
0200 O                         MSG,Y     80                               CH12P2
0201 O          E  1           SECOND                                     CH12P2
0202 O                         MSG,Y     80                               CH12P2
**
ACCOUNT NUMBER NOT VALID
NAME NOT LEFT-JUSTIFIED
NAME CONTAINS INVALID CHARACTERS
INVALID MONTH
INVALID DAY
INVALID YEAR
AMOUNT NOT NUMERIC
AMOUNT NEGATIVE
AMT HAS JUSTIFICATION ERROR
**
312831303130313130313031
**
 'ABCDEFGHIJKLMNOPQRSTUVWXYZ
```

(*Continued*)

For convenience, the report previously shown is presented again in Figure 12-40.

```
8/11/88              TRANSACTION FILE VALIDATION ERROR REPORT            PAGE    1
                                                                            CH12P2

120006 ALEXANDER DUMAS     00309200025000         NAME NOT LEFT-JUSTIFIED
                                                  INVALID MONTH
                                                  INVALID YEAR
                                                  AMT HAS JUSTIFICATION ERROR

130000HAROLD ROBBINS       022988002390}          ACCOUNT NUMBER NOT VALID
                                                  AMOUNT NEGATIVE

140007GEOFREY CHAUCER      0332890789000          INVALID DAY

300004JACQUELINE SUSAN     013187005600T          INVALID YEAR
                                                  AMOUNT NOT NUMERIC
```

Figure 12-40 Report generated by data validation program (RPG III/400).

SUMMARY

Data validation is important in the batch and or interactive mode to insure that data entered into a computerized system is accurate. The hardware and software restrictions of the computer installation usually determine when and how data are validated. Data may be validated by batch procedures external to a program, by batch procedures internal to a program, or by interactive procedures internal to a program.

Validation procedures may be broadly classified as data type testing and data field checking.

Data type testing includes the testing of numeric fields for valid numeric characters (0–9) and may be supported in a batch program by the TESTN operation or interactively by screen control. Because RPG does not have syntax unique to alphabetic testing, it may be supported by including a Compile Time array of valid alphabetic characters in the program. Then, any characters that are not usually considered alphabetic (the single quote mark, for example) may be included as valid in the testing procedure. Sign testing may be controlled by testing input fields with Field Indicators (columns 65–70) or Result Fields in calculations with Resulting Indicators (columns 54–59). Included in sign testing is the check of a numeric field for a zero value. This is an important test for fields that are used as a divisor in a divide instruction. Depending on the computer system, any attempt to divide a value by zero will either cause a termination or a halt of program execution.

Data field checking includes the presence or absence, justification, acceptability, relationship, and structure of data. The *presence of data* checking assures that something has been entered in the related field. On the other hand, the absence of data check determines if nothing is entered into the field area. *Justification* validation is usually performed only on alphanumeric fields to test if the value is entered beginning in the high-order position. The *acceptability of data* includes range checking, testing of a check digit, limit checking, correspondence checking, and the validation of a batch total.

QUESTIONS

12-1. Define data validation.

12-2. How may data validation procedures be implemented in a computer environment?

12-3. Explain how each of the data validation procedures named in Question 12-2 may be controlled in a computer environment.

12-4. What is the purpose of an error rejection or abeyance file?

12-5. Name and explain the validation functions included in data type testing.

12-6. By what coding methods may input data be validated as numeric?

12-7. What characters in a computer's character set are considered numeric?

12-8. Examine the following instruction and explain the function of each resulting indicator:

C Line (3–5)	Form Type (6)	Control Level (L0-L9, LR, SR, AN/OR) (7–8)	Indicators: Not, And, Not, And, Not (9–17)	Factor 1 (18–27)	Operation (28–32)	Factor 2 (33–42)	Result Field Name (43–48)	Length (49–51)	Decimal Position (52)	Half Adjust (H) (53)	Resulting Indicators: Arithmetic Plus / Compare 1>2 / Lookup (Factor 2) is High (54–55)	Minus / 1<2 / Low (56–57)	Zero / 1=2 / Equal (58–59)
01∅	C				TESTN		AMT				2∅	21	22

12-9. How must the Result Field specified in the TESTN operation in Question 12-8 be defined?

12-10. Explain the validation procedure(s) that may be included in an RPG program for testing a field vaue as alphabetic.

12-11. Name the methods by which sign testing may be implemented in an RPG program.

12-12. During processing, where is the sign of a number stored in a computer's memory? In a hexadecimal copy listing (over-and-under format) generated in an IBM mainframe or minicomputer environment, where is the sign identified?

12-13. When is it important to check a field value for zero?

12-14. What are some of the data validation functions that may be included in data field checking?

12-15. How is the presence of data checking implemented in an RPG program?

12-16. How is the absence of data checking supported in an RPG program?

12-17. Is justification checking usually performed on numeric or alphanumeric data (or both)? Explain your answer.

12-18. What data validation functions are related to the acceptability of data testing?

12-19. Identify an application in which range checking is applicable.

12-20. Refer to Question 12-19, and explain how the application may be controlled in an RPG program.

12-21. Explain the function of a check digit. Where is it usually stored in the related field value?

12-22. Use the Modulus-11 method to create a check digit for account numbers 12000 and 123456.

12-23. Use the Modulus-11 check digit method to determine if account numbers 130003 and 77003 are valid.

12-24. Name an application in which limit checking may be used. How is it implemented in an RPG program?

12-25. Give an example of correspondence checking. How may it be controlled in an RPG program?

12-26. What is a batch total? How may it be controlled in an RPG program?

EXERCISES

The following partial input specifications defines a record format to be used in the solution of Exercises 12-1 through 12-6:

Field Location From (Data Structure: Occurs n Times) 44–47	Field Location To (Data Structure: Length) 48–51	Decimal Positions 52	RPG Field Name 53–58	Control Level (L1-L9) 59–60	Matching Fields or Chaining Fields 61–62	Field Record Relation 63–64	Field Indicators Plus 65–66	Field Indicators Minus 67–68	Field Indicators Zero or Blank 69–70
1	6	Ø	CUST#						
7	26		NAME						
27	33	2	SALAMT						
34	39	Ø	DATE						

12-1. Write the instruction to test CUST# as a valid numeric value. If the value does not test numeric, move array element 1 (i.e., MSG,1) to the output field MESAGE.

12-2. Redefine the input coding so that CUST# may be used in a Modulus-11 test. The check digit is stored in the low-order byte.

12-3. Refer to Exercise 12-2 and write the calculations to control the Modulus-11 check digit method of validation. If CUST# does not check as valid, move array element 2 (i.e., MSG,2) to the output field MESAGE.

12-4. Include the necessary coding in an RPG program to check NAME as valid alphabetic. In addition to the usual alphabetic characters, assume that the single quote mark (') and hyphen (−) are considered valid for this application. If the field value does not check as alphabetic, move array element 3 (i.e., MSG,3) to the output field MESAGE.

12-5. Write an RPG instruction to check SALAMT as valid numeric. If the field value does not pass the test, move array element 4 (i.e., MSG,4) to the output field MESAGE. If the field value passes the numeric test, write the instruction(s) to check that the value does not exceed $1,000. If the amount is over the limit, move array element 5 (i.e., MSG,5) to the output field MESAGE.

12-6. Write the necessary RPG instructions to test the DATE field. The month value must be within the range of 01 to 12, and the day value must not exceed the maximum number of days for the related month. A leap year test must be included in this test. The year value is acceptable if it is equal to or one year less than UYEAR. If month is tested as invalid, the other DATE tests are not to be executed. When an error is tested, move array element 6 (i.e., MSG,6) to the field MESAGE.

LABORATORY ASSIGNMENTS

Laboratory Assignment 12-1: BATCH VALIDATION OF SAVINGS ACCOUNT TRANSACTIONS

A bank wants a program created that will ensure the accuracy of all daily savings account transactions before updating a depositor's account. The validation checks that the program is to perform on the input data are the following.

1. Transaction code
2. Transaction amount
3. Transaction date

Details related to each of these are explained in the following paragraphs. When a validation error is found, no further checks are to be performed, and any subsequent processing for that record is to be discontinued. The related error message is to be printed on the report with the record information.

Transaction Code Validation. The valid transactions codes are:

D - Deposit **W - Withdrawal** **I - Interest Credit**
A - Debit Adjustment **C - Credit Adjustment**

Any other code value is to be considered invalid.

Transaction Amount Validation. The following tests are to be performed on the transaction amount:

1. Valid numeric
2. Invalid zero value
3. If transaction code is D, I, or C, the amount must be positive.
4. If transaction code is W or A, the amount must be negative.

Transaction Date Validation. The following functions are to be performed, in the sequence presented, for transaction date validation.

Valid Month Number Test:

1. Test the transaction month number to determine if it is greater than 0 and less than 13.

Days in a Month Test:

1. If the transaction month test is passed, look up an array for the maximum number of days for the related month.
2. If the transaction month is equal to 02 (Feb), divide the year element of the date by 4 and test the remainder value. If the remainder is zero (indicates a leap year), add 1 to the array value 28. (*Note*: Move the array value to a work field. Changing the array value will store the new value for the entire run.)
3. If transactions days is not zero, compare it with the array value from step 1 or 2. Transactions days are invalid if they are zero or greater than the related array value.

Transaction Year Validation

The year value in the transaction date must be equal to the report year, which is to be input by either CRT control or as the first record in the data file.

Array Data

Days in a Month Array. Processed positionally with the transaction month value as the index.

```
31 2831 3031 3031 31 3031 3031
```

Error Message Array. Processed positionally with the related error number as the index value.

```
INVALID TRANSACTION CODE
TRANSACTION AMOUNT NOT NUMERIC
TRANSACTION AMOUNT ZERO
CODE INDICATES AMOUNT MUST BE POSITIVE
CODE INDICATES AMOUNT MUST BE NEGATIVE
TRANSACTION MONTH INVALID
TRANSACTION DAYS INVALID
TRANSACTION YEAR INVALID
```

Input of Report Date. Input a report date value of 022992 by CONSOLE, KEYBORD, or INTERACTIVE SCREEN control. If interactive processing is not available on your system, include the value on a separate record with the letter X in column 1 and the date in columns 2 to 7, which must be loaded as the first record in the file.

Format of the Input Data Records:

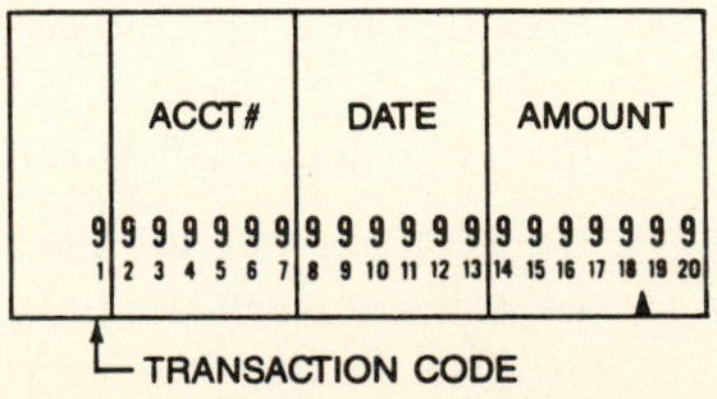

Input Data:

Transaction Code Col 1	Account Number 2-7	Transaction Date 8-13	Transaction Amount 14-20
D	100000	020192	0084000
W	200000	023192	1250000
T	300000	021092	0009250
A	400000	023092	002456P
I	500000	021592	090000Y
C	600000	020191	0067899
D	700000	021192	0000000
W	800000	023092	001209M
D	900000	022892	000250}
D	910000	130892	0100000
C	980000	022992	0070000

Report Design:

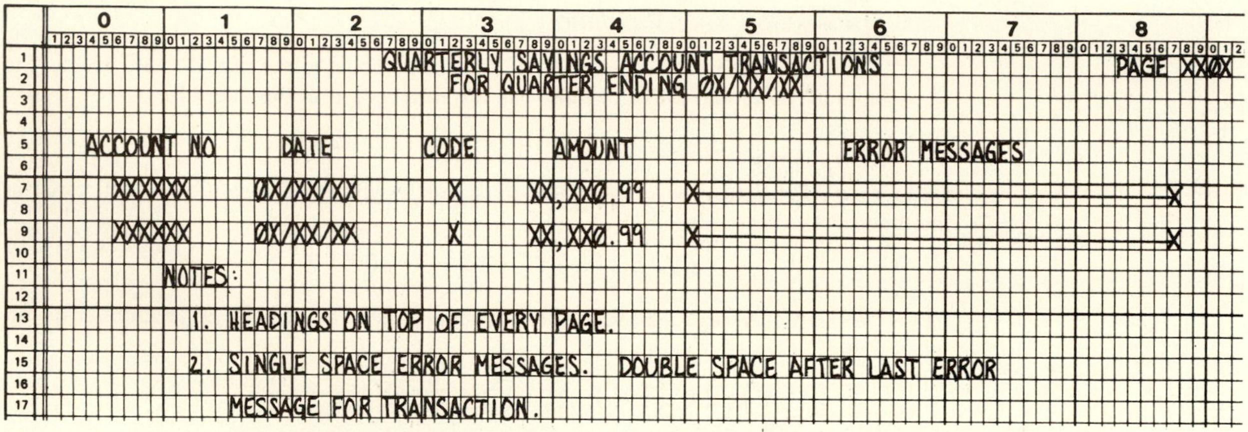

Laboratory Assignment 12-2: BATCH VALIDATION OF ITEM PURCHASES

A company requests a program to batch validate item purchases before accounts payable and general ledger accounts are updated.

Format of the Input Data Records:

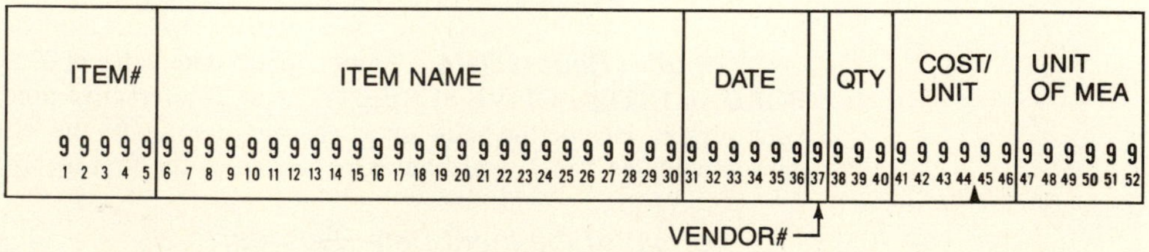

Processing. The program must control the following validation functions:

Item Number Validation:

1. Test for numeric value.
2. If the numeric test is passed, use the Modulus-11 check digit method to validate that the item number is correct.

Item Name Validation:

1. Test that the name value is alphabetic. Blank, hyphen, comma, and A through Z are to be considered valid alphabetic.
2. Test the field value for left-justification.

Vendor Number Validation:

Include the following table of valid vendor numbers in the program and provide lookup control: 124568

Quantity Validation:

Test for numeric value.

Cost Per Item Validation:

Test for numeric value.

Total Purchase Cost:

If the quantity and cost per item are numeric, test that the product of quantity times cost per unit is not over 2000.

The program is to be written so that every test is made and program execution does not cancel as the result of a validation error.

Error Control. The following error messages are to be printed in the area identified on the supplemental printer spacing chart.

```
ITEM NUMBER NOT NUMERIC
ITEM NUMBER DOES NOT CHECK
ITEM NAME NOT ALPHABETIC
ITEM NAME NOT LEFT-JUSTIFIED
VENDOR NUMBER NOT VALID
QUANTITY PURCHASED NOT NUMERIC
COST PER ITEM NOT NUMERIC
TOTAL COST EXCEEDS $2,000
```

Hint: Error message printing should begin after all the validation tests are completed for a record. When an error is identified, an array may be loaded with the related error message number. Then, after all the tests are made, the array may be processed and any error messages associated with the record must be printed.

Report Design:

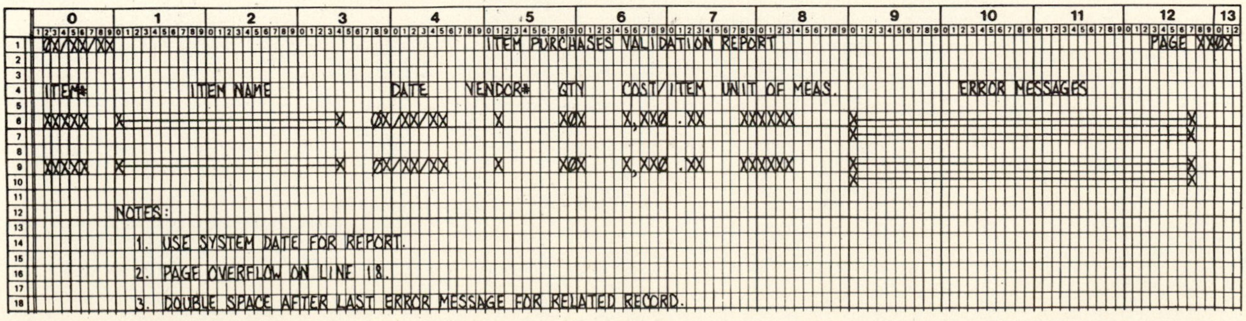

Input Data:

Item Number Col 1-5	Item Name 6-30	Purchase Date 31-36	Vendor Number 37	Quantity 38-40	Cost Per Item 41-46	Unit of Measure 47-52
11184	BLACK TRUFFLES	040192	1	024	008500	JAR/OZ
11206	SHARK FIN SOUP	040592	4	120	001000	CAN/OZ
11304	PICKLED TRIPE	041092	3	036	000400	JAR/OZ
11509	SMOKED PHEASANT	041592	8	012	001200	CAN/PK
11606	BLACK CAVIAR	041892	5	060	003900	CAN/OZ
11703	CHOCOLATE-COVERED ANTS	042092	6	048	000650	CAN/OZ
11800	SEA WATER KEL9 SPROUTS	042892	2	144	002.00	JAR/OZ
T2009	REINDEER MILK YOGURT	043092	9	01X	000700	JAR/QT

chapter 13

Disk File Concepts and Sequential File Processing

DISK FILE CONCEPTS

Previous chapters have discussed the RPG language syntax associated with the processing of data files and printed output. Depending on your installation, you recorded and stored input data on diskette, disk, or magnetic tape. Because disks have become the standard for the storage of data, the file structures and processing details associated with this medium will be explained.

Disks have become an important medium of storage for the following reasons:

1. Less physical room is occupied by data files stored on disk than on diskette or magnetic tape.
2. Data files stored on disk can be processed faster than files stored on tape or diskette.
4. Records may be added to an existing disk file and maintain a sequential order.
5. Disk-stored data files support the immediate random access required for on-line systems.
6. In addition to data files, source and object programs, procedures, screen formats, operating systems, utility software, and application software may be stored and immediately accessed.
7. All types of file organization, including sequential, indexed-sequential, direct, and data base management systems, are supported.
8. Disk areas may be deleted or written over and used to store other information.

DISK FILE TERMINOLOGY

Terms associated with disk hardware includes the following:

Disk Drive: The hardware unit that holds the disk pack(s) and controls the operation of the disk. Figure 13-1 shows the outside structure of an IBM 3340 disk drive unit commonly installed on many medium to large IBM computer systems.

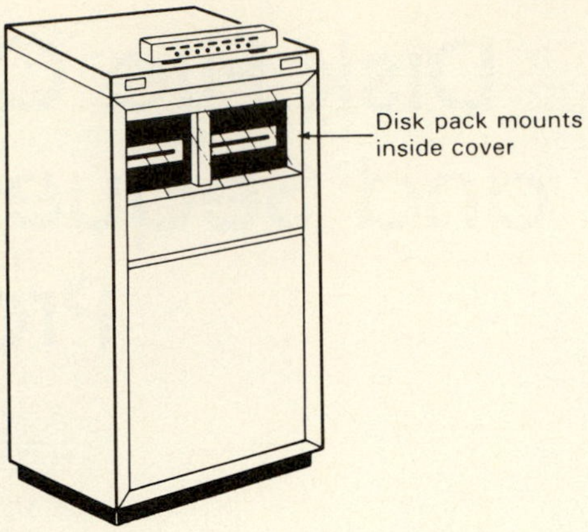

Figure 13-1 IBM 3340 disk drive unit.

Disk Pack: A self-contained portable unit that encases the magnetic disk (platters). Some disk drives include fixed disks that are an integral part of the unit and are not removable.

Volume: Refers to a disk pack, diskette, or reel of magnetic tape.

Data Set: Another name for a data file. A data set may occupy only a small area on a disk pack or be large enough to include more than one disk pack or fixed disk drive.

DISK STRUCTURE

Figure 13-2 shows the internal features of the 3348 disk pack used on the 3340 drive unit (Figure 13-1). The mechanical configuration is not shown—only the logical areas important to a programmer.

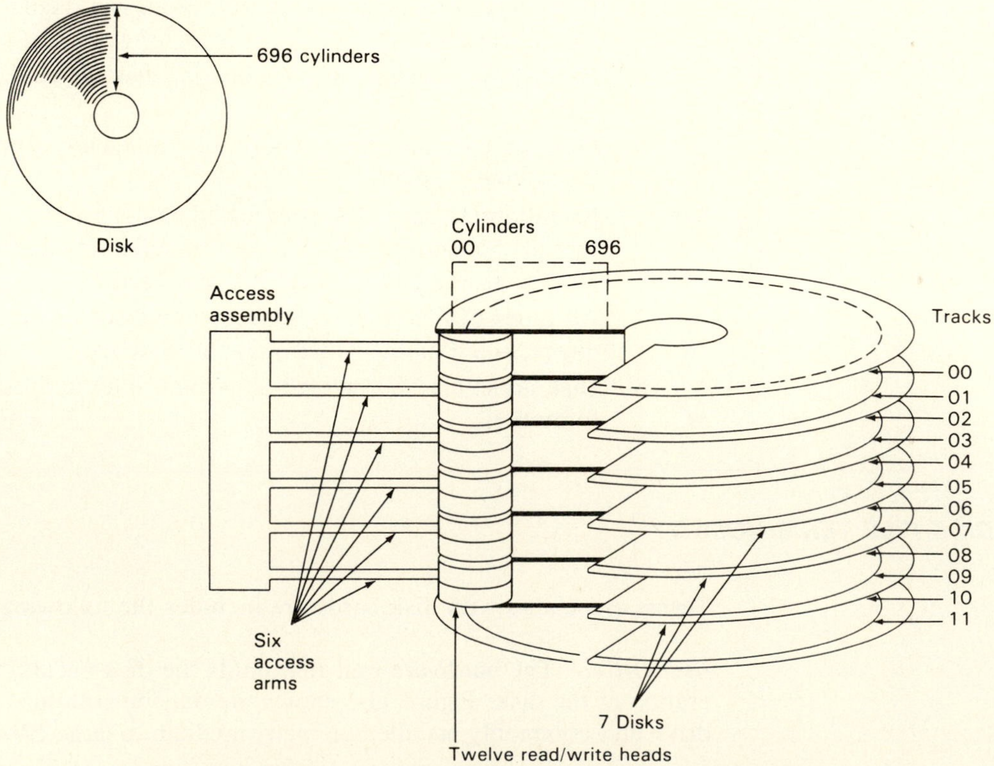

Figure 13-2 Logical areas of an IBM 3348 disk pack.

The inside structure of the 3348 disk pack contains seven magnetic disks (platters) and six arms, each with two read/write heads. Instructions from the CPU cause the arms to move horizontally and the read/write head vertically to a specified location (cylinder/track) on the disk. This mechanically and electrically controlled process is referred to as *seek time*. Except for the number of magnetic platters, this structure is common to all disk and diskette drives.

All disk packs and diskettes are defined into logical areas called *cylinders* and *tracks*:

Cylinders. Cylinders are conceptual areas determined by the horizontal movement of the read/write heads. Refer to Figure 13-2 and locate the two vertical dotted lines extending through all the platters. One line represents the fixed location of cylinder 000 and the other, cylinder 696. This disk pack design has a total of 699 cylinders—696 that are normally used and three extras in the event 1 to 3 become defective. Notice, however, that data is not referenced as being written on a cylinder but on a platter surface called a *track*.

Tracks. Examine Figure 13-2 and notice that each cylinder is divided into areas called tracks (platter surfaces). For this disk pack model, there are seven platters with track surfaces numbered 00 to 11. The top and bottom surfaces of the first and last platters are not used. Therefore, for each cylinder, 12 writing surfaces (tracks) are available for storage. Data is written on the track surfaces as magnetic impulses and may be written over any number of times. Figure 13-3 illustrates the way data records are stored on a track surface. On most systems,

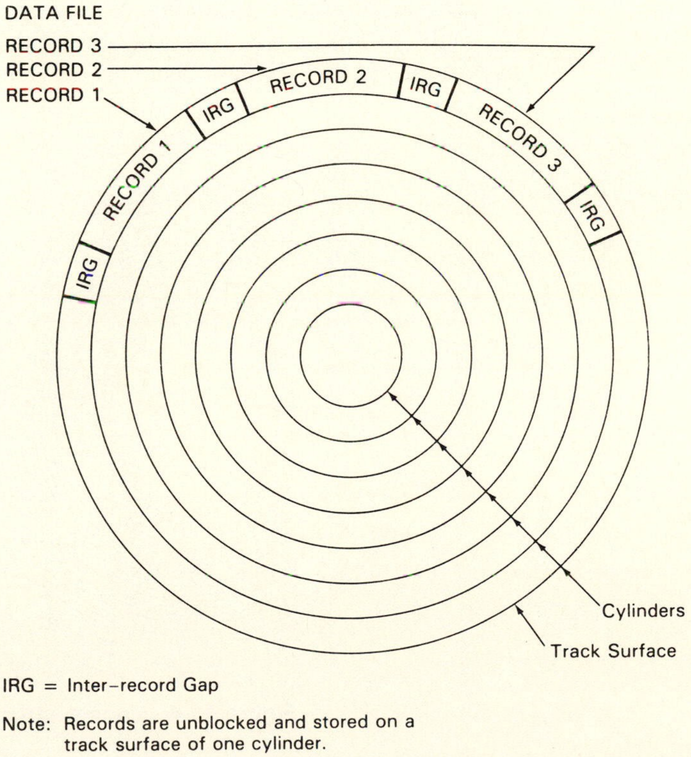

Figure 13-3 Illustration of the way records are stored on a track surface.

data is stored in a contiguous format occupying consecutive tracks. However, on IBM's System/38 and AS/400 elements of the data file may be on more than one disk drive. This configuration is controlled by the system software and not by the programmer.

The disk pack/drive configuration discussed is not the only type available. Some configurations have only one disk platter (diskette) and in turn have fewer cylinders and tracks for storage. Other designs include more platters with correspondingly larger storage capacity. For most scenarios, the type of disk pack and drive installed will depend upon need and its availability with the related computer system.

DISKETTES

Diskettes are made in three sizes: The 8-inch diskette is used with mainframe and minicomputers; the 5¼-inch and the 3½-inch are used with microcomputers. The 8-inch and 5¼-inch diskettes are thin flexible magnetic disks enclosed in a protective composition paper jacket. The 3½-inch diskettes are permanently encased in a hard plastic container.

Diskettes are made in single-sided or double-sided and single-density, double-density, and high density formats. A double-sided diskette stores information on both sides (i.e., both track surfaces) of the diskette, whereas a single-sided diskette stores on only one side. Double-density and high-density diskettes store the data closer together and thereby have more storage capacity then a single density design.

Figure 13-4 shows that a diskette is divided into cylinder and track areas similar to the disk pack illustrated in Figure 13-2. In addition, diskettes are further subdivided into sector locations. Notice that there are 77 cylinders, starting with 00. Only 75 are active, however, the other two being reserved in the event a maximum of two cylinders becomes defective.

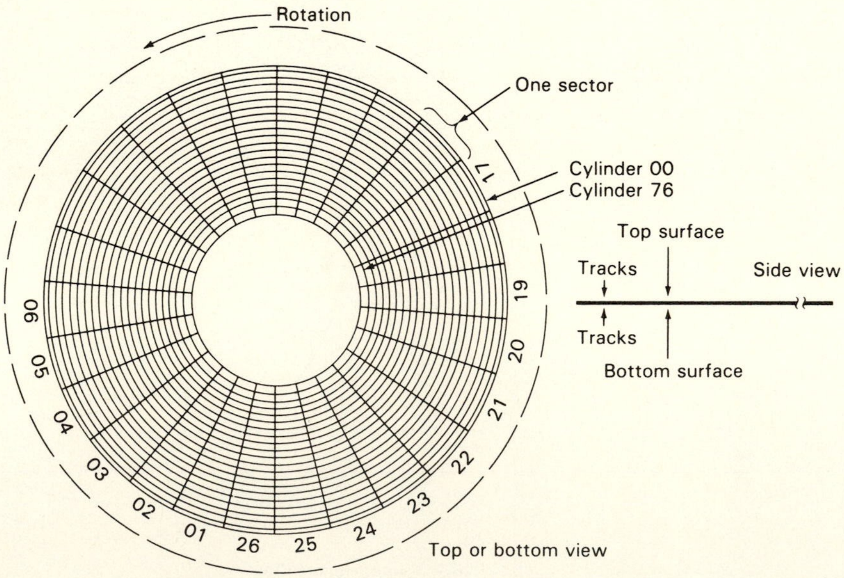

Figure 13-4 Logical structure of a diskette.

An examination of Figure 13-4 shows that each cylinder has two track surfaces. The number of sectors per cylinder depends on its location on the diskette. For example, cylinder 00 (outside cylinder) has 26 sectors, each with 256 bytes of storage. Other cylinders are divided into 8 or 26 sectors. Identical to disk packs, information is written on the track surfaces. The sector structure and number of cylinders on a diskette is different for $5\frac{1}{4}$-inch and $3\frac{1}{2}$-inch diskettes. All types have only two tracks per cylinder, however.

With the exception of knowing the storage capacity of any diskette, the structure of this storage medium is usually transparent to the user. When processing data to and from this storage medium, reference does not have to be made to a select cylinder, track, or sector location. The computer system will store and locate information automatically.

METHODS OF DISK FILE ORGANIZATION

Data files stored on disk or diskette may be organized as sequential, indexed-sequential, and direct. Figure 13-5 illustrates the physical areas of each type of file organization.

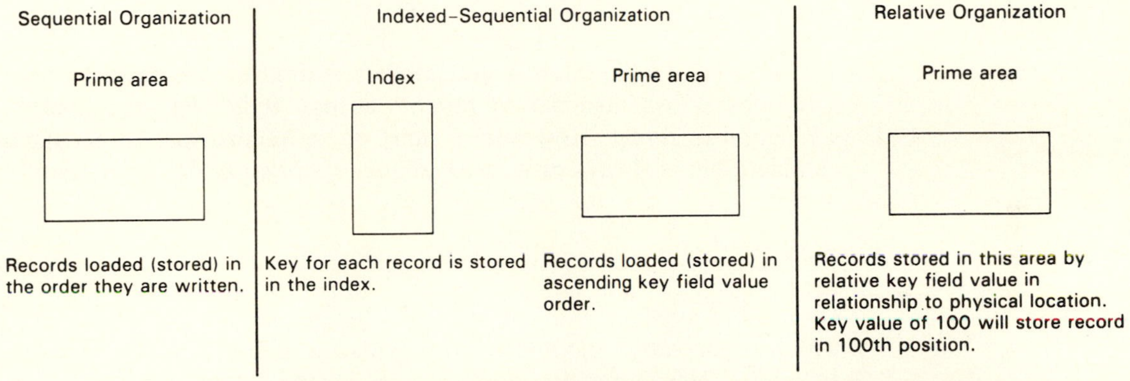

Figure 13-5 Physical areas of sequential, indexed-sequential, and direct data file organization methods.

The IBM System/38 and AS/400 supports a data base environment in which any file that includes data is referred to as a *physical file*. An indexed-sequential file is defined as a *keyed file*, and a sequential file is identified as a *nonkeyed file*. Logical files may be created that contain no data but build *access paths* to one or more physical files so that they may be processed in various field orders and record formats.

The file organization method used usually depends on how the data file is to be subsequently processed. Consider the following when selecting an organization method for the storage of a data file:

1. Master or transaction file
2. Volatility
3. Activity
4. Size of the file

Master or Transaction File

A master file contains information of a permanent nature. General ledger, accounts receivable, and merchandise inventory are typical examples of master files. With the exception of control or key field values, which identify the record, other field information may be updated. Because they are frequently updated (randomly processed) with a limited number of transactions, indexed-sequential or direct file organizations offer the most efficient processing.

On the other hand, because transaction files include original source document information that is less permanent, they are usually organized as sequential files. The data is generally used to update or add to an existing master file. For example, information from source documents (invoices, time cards, etc.) may be entered by workstation input and loaded directly into a sequentially organized disk file. Then, an edit report is generated to verify the data and correct errors before the information is used to update some master file.

Volatility

If a file undergoes frequent updates, additions, and deletions (high volatility), it is more efficient to organize it as indexed-sequential or direct. Both of these file types support faster random processing as compared to sequential.

Activity

The activity of a file refers to the number of times it is accessed in a program. If a file has a low incidence of random access, it is best organized as indexed-sequential or direct. However, if most of the records are to be updated or the complete file is always processed, sequential organization may reduce runtime.

Size of File

On smaller systems with limited disk storage, the size of a file may determine which organization method to use. Because of the separate indexes, indexed-sequential files do require more storage. Their random processing and self-maintenance features override any disadvantages, however.

File Organization Summary

If processing time is a major consideration in the determination of which method to use for a data file, direct organization has the advantages of both *sequential and indexed-sequential*. It requires less storage space than the same size indexed-sequential file, provides for faster *random access* than indexed sequential or sequential, and does not usually have to be *sorted* or *reorganized* before processing. However, as will be explained in Chapter 17, the maintenance problems associated with direct files may more than outweigh their advantages.

Any of the file organization methods may allow the file to be processed sequentially (one record at a time until the end of file) or randomly. Only indexed-sequential and direct files actually *random process* where, based on a *key* or *relative record number* value, a select record may be accessed without a consecutive record-by-record search.

How a data file is processed usually depends on the application. For example, when customer invoices are printed, the file is processed consecutively from the first record to the last. On the other hand, changes to individual customer records require random processing.

Now that an introduction to basic file concepts has been presented, the remainder of this chapter explains the RPG syntax and procedures for the loading to, consecutive processing of, and addition of records to a sequential disk file.

SEQUENTIAL FILE ORGANIZATION PROCESSING

Sequential disk file processing includes the following activities:

1. Creation (building) of the file (allocation of space on a disk pack for the file).
2. Loading of data records to the file.
3. Consecutive processing of the file.
4. Addition of records to an existing file.
5. Inquiry (random) processing.
6. General file maintenance including:
   a. Update of field values
   b. Deletion of records
   c. Sorting

The RPG syntax, logic, and procedures for items 1, 2, 3, and 4 are discussed in this chapter. Items 5 and 6 will be introduced in Chapter 14.

APPLICATION PROGRAM—CREATING AND LOADING A SEQUENTIAL DISK FILE

A transaction file of item purchases is used as the data base for the programs introduced in this chapter and Chapter 14 to illustrate the processing methods related to sequential files.

Documentation

A transaction file of item purchases is used as the data base for the application programs that illustrate each method of sequential file processing. The specifications for the first example program that creates (builds) and loads a sequential disk file are detailed in Figure 13-6.

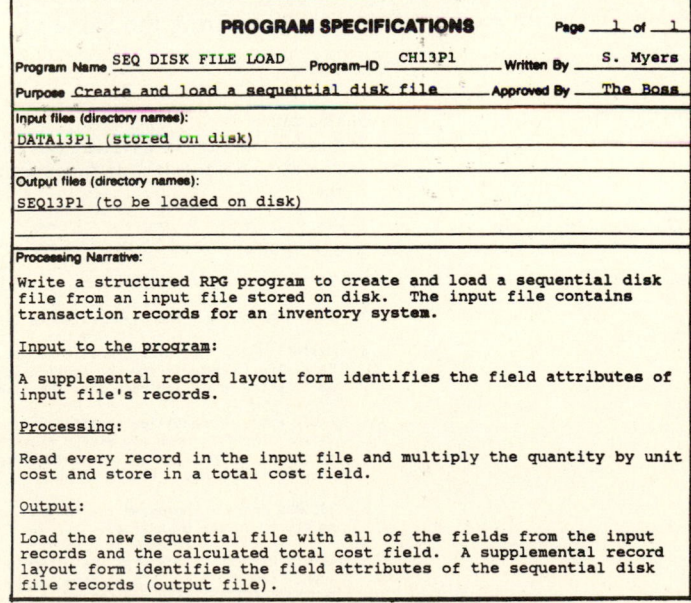

PROGRAM SPECIFICATIONS Page 1 of 1

Program Name SEQ DISK FILE LOAD Program-ID CH13P1 Written By S. Myers

Purpose Create and load a sequential disk file Approved By The Boss

Input files (directory names):

DATA13P1 (stored on disk)

Output files (directory names):

SEQ13P1 (to be loaded on disk)

Processing Narrative:

Write a structured RPG program to create and load a sequential disk file from an input file stored on disk. The input file contains transaction records for an inventory system.

Input to the program:

A supplemental record layout form identifies the field attributes of input file's records.

Processing:

Read every record in the input file and multiply the quantity by unit cost and store in a total cost field.

Output:

Load the new sequential file with all of the fields from the input records and the calculated total cost field. A supplemental record layout form identifies the field attributes of the sequential disk file records (output file).

Figure 13-6 Specifications for a program that creates and loads a sequential disk file.

The specifications indicate that a data file stored on disk is used to load a sequential disk file in a different record format. Other media such as magnetic tape, diskette, and work stations are other devices by which input data may be entered for processing. Chapter 18 presents the syntax and controls for entering data interactively on IBM's System/34 and System/36 computers, and Chapter 21 details the processes needed to enter data interactively on IBM's System/38 and AS/400.

Why create a disk file when the data is already stored on another medium? As previously explained, the advantages of disk storage, as compared to magnetic tape, encourage the transfer of data to this storage medium. On the other hand, diskettes offer many of the advantages of disk packs, so why transfer data stored on that medium to disk? This question may be answered by identifying the following diskette restrictions:

1. A limited amount of data may be stored on one diskette. Some formats store more than 2 million bytes. When large data files are supported, however, many diskettes would have to be used for storage of the file—which would be inconvenient and time consuming.
2. Many systems do not support direct processing from diskette. Consequently, the entire diskette file must be loaded to the system's fixed disk(s) and then processed. Files are backed up to diskettes by a SAVE utility and reloaded to the hard disk by a RESTORE utility. The names of these utilities may differ for each computer system.

Job Control Language

Disk space is allocated for any disk file by *Operation Control Language* (referred to as *OCL*, *JCL*, or *CL*), which is unique to every computer system. An example of the OCL statements required in an IBM System/34 or System/36 environment to create and load a sequential disk file from another disk file is detailed in Figure 13-7. The statements are included in a procedure that is built and stored in a system or user library. Procedures in the System/34 and System/36 environments are executed by simply entering the name via a workstation.

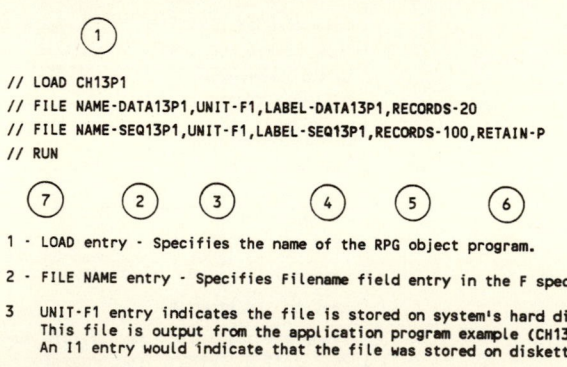

```
        (1)
// LOAD CH13P1
// FILE NAME-DATA13P1,UNIT-F1,LABEL-DATA13P1,RECORDS-20
// FILE NAME-SEQ13P1,UNIT-F1,LABEL-SEQ13P1,RECORDS-100,RETAIN-P
// RUN
(7)     (2)     (3)         (4)      (5)       (6)
```

```
1 - LOAD entry - Specifies the name of the RPG object program.

2 - FILE NAME entry - Specifies Filename field entry in the F specs.

3   UNIT-F1 entry indicates the file is stored on system's hard disk.
    This file is output from the application program example (CH13P1).
    An I1 entry would indicate that the file was stored on diskette.

4 - LABEL entry - Identifies the names (labels) of the disk stored
    files.  The file name may differ from the related file name
    specified in the F specs in the RPG program.  In this example
    they are the same.

5 - RECORDS entry - Indicatea the maximum number of records that to
    be stored in the disk file.

6 - RETAIN-P entry - Indicates the retention status for the file.  P
    identifies the file as a permanent file the may only be deleted
    by the DELETE utility and not accidently written over.

7 - RUN entry - Indicates the end of the procedure.
```

Figure 13-7 OCL statements in a procedure to create and load a sequential disk file in the IBM System/34 and System/36 environments.

The syntax available with OCL (i.e., JCL or CL) supports many of the functions common to high-level languages. Decision making, branching, looping, and the passing of values from one program or procedure to another one are some of the many controls supported.

To load a sequential file interactively in the System/38 and AS/400 environment, no OCL, referred to as *Control Languages* (CL) is required. However, when more than one program is included in a job stream, CL programs are required. They function the same as a procedure on other systems.

The system flowchart illustrated in Figure 13-8 shows that a diskette-stored file is input to and a disk file is output from the program.

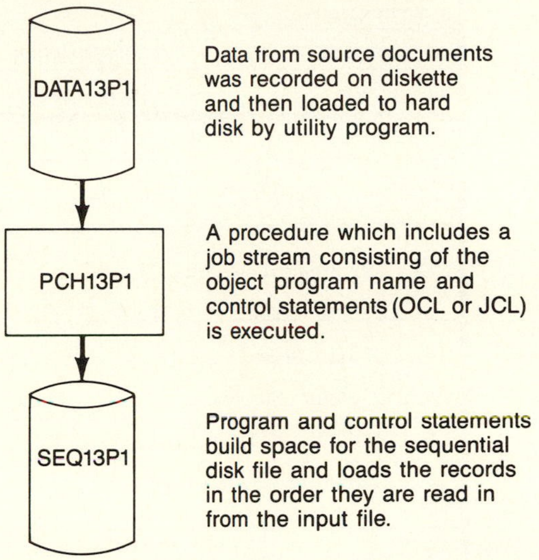

Figure 13-8 System flowchart for an application program that creates and loads a sequential disk file.

A record layout form and a listing of the records stored in the diskette input file is shown in Figure 13-9.

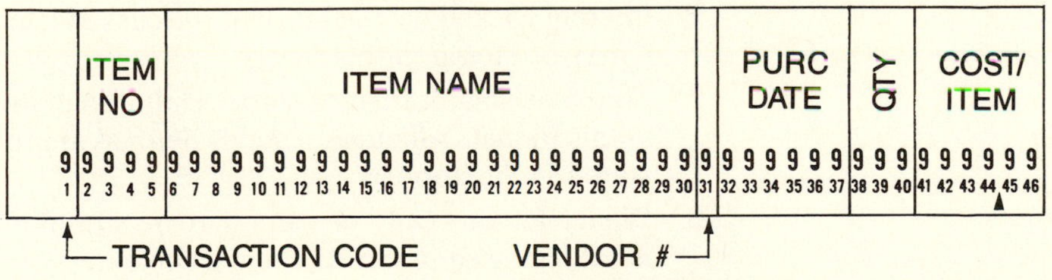


```
First Record——>0001BOUNTY PAPER TOWELS       6110190144000040
               0002MARCAL PAPER TOWELS       6110190360000041
               0004VANITY FAIR PAPER TOWELS  9110390060000039
               0007KLEENEX PAPER TOWELS      1111090048000045
               0008SCOTT'S PAPER TOWELS      4111590240000050
               0010HUDSON PAPER TOWELS       7112590072000054
               0011NORTHERN PAPER TOWELS     2112890120000060
               0015A & P PAPER TOWELS        1113090480000029
               ↑                                            ↑
               └—Transaction code byte                      └—Record length 46 bytes
```

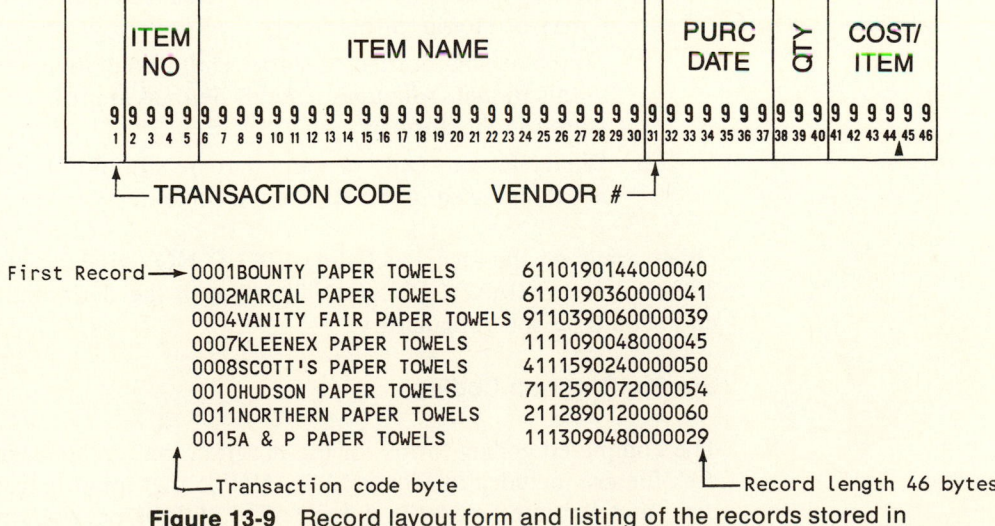

Figure 13-9 Record layout form and listing of the records stored in the diskette input file.

A different type of form that documents not only the record and field attributes but also the file is shown in Figure 13-10. Some of the terms, including

KEY LENGTH, RECORDING MODE, and BLOCKING, will be discussed as additional RPG syntax for the processing of disk files is introduced. Included in this new form is a CLASS column that specifies the type of field stored and that is explained below:

FILE DEFINITION

SYSTEM Yours		DRAWN BY S. Myers
FILE NAME SEQ13P1		DATE 10/19/91 REV. NO. 0
CREATED BY S. Myers		FILE TYPE Disk
RECORD NAME None		KEY LENGTH None
RECORDING MODE Fixed	ORGANIZATION Sequential	SEQUENCE Asc. by Item#
RECORD SIZE 55 bytes	BLOCKING FACTOR 1	BLOCKSIZE 55 bytes

FIELD DATA

FIELD NO.	FIELD NAME - DESCRIPTION	SIZE	CLASS C/P/Z/B	POSITION FROM	POSITION THRU	FORMAT/CONSTANT
1	Transaction Code	1	C	1	1	D if deleted
2	Item Number	4	C	2	5	Control Field
3	Item Name	25	C	6	30	
4	Vendor Number	1	C	31	31	
5	Purchase Date	6	Z	32	37	
6	Quantity Purchased	3	Z	38	40	Integer
7	Cost Per Item	6	Z	41	46	2 decimals
8	Amount (Qty x Cost)	9	Z	47	55	2 decimals

Figure 13-10 File definition form for the sequential disk file created and loaded by the application program.

C Character (alphanumeric) field. Any character in the collating sequence is supported

P Internal packed decimal format (discussed later). Only the numbers 0 to 9 may be stored in this format.

Z Zoned decimal format numeric. Only the numbers 0 to 9 may be stored in this format. All numeric fields defined in previous chapters have been stored in this format.

B Binary format. Only integers may be stored in this format. This format is seldom used in the RPG environment.

Other areas on the form, including FIELD NO., FIELD NAME, SIZE, POSITION, and FORMAT/CONSTANT, relate to the definition of individual fields and should be self-explanatory.

Source Program Coding

The completed coding forms for the program that creates and loads a sequential disk file are included in Figure 13-11. Notice that input is from disk, output is to disk, and a printed report is not specified. All the previous programs in the text have directed output to the printer. This is not a requirement, and because the printer is a slow device, printing should be specified only when absolutely necessary.

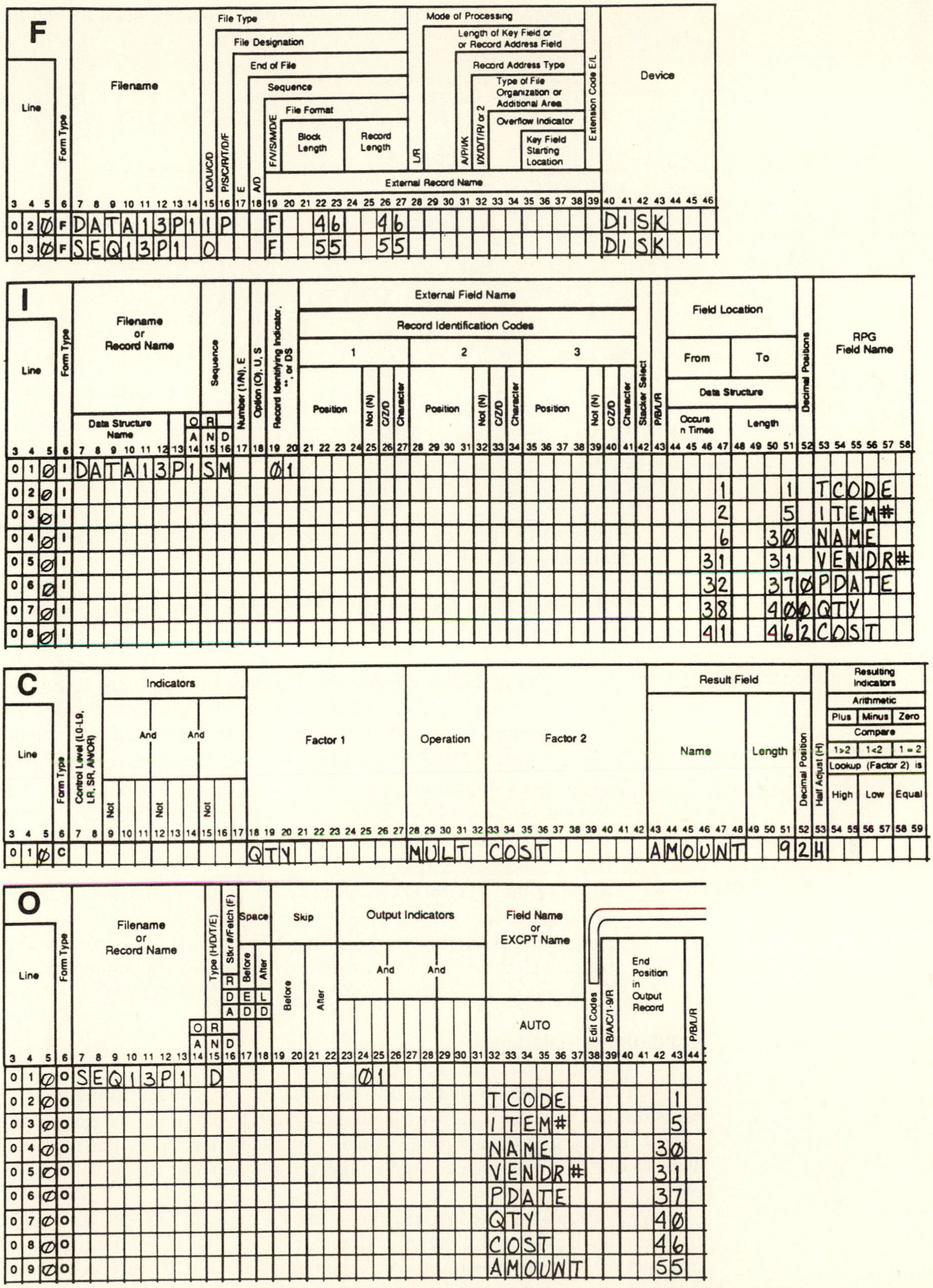

Figure 13-11 Completed coding forms for program that creates and loads a sequential disk file.

A commented source listing of the program coding detailed in Figure 13-11 is given in Figure 13-12.

```
... ... 1 ... ... 2 ... ... 3 ... ... 4 ... ... 5 ... ... 6 ... ... 7 ...
 *  THIS PROGRAM CREATES & LOADS A SEQUENTIAL FILE FROM A DISK FILE  CH13P1
 * THE RECORD FORMAT OF THE OUTPUT FILE IS DIFFERENT FROM THE INPUT  CH13P1
H                                                                    CH13P1
FDATA13P1IP  F  46  46           DISK                                CH13P1
FSEQ13P1 O   F  55  55           DISK                                CH13P1
IDATA13P1SM  01                                                      CH13P1
I                                          1   1 TCODE               CH13P1
I                                          2   5 ITEM#               CH13P1
I                                          6  30 NAME                CH13P1
I                                         31  31 VENDR#              CH13P1
I                                         32  370PDATE               CH13P1
I                                         38  400QTY                 CH13P1
I                                         41  462COST                CH13P1
C           QTY       MULT COST      AMOUNT  92H                     CH13P1
OSEQ13P1 D        01                                                 CH13P1
O                          TCODE      1                              CH13P1
O                          ITEM#      5                              CH13P1
O                          NAME      30                              CH13P1
O                          VENDR#    31                              CH13P1
O                          PDATE     37                              CH13P1
O                          QTY       40                              CH13P1
O                          COST      46                              CH13P1
O                          AMOUNT    55                              CH13P1
```

Figure 13-12 Source listing of program that creates and loads a sequential disk file.

The following three features should be noted when loading, adding to, or updating a disk-stored data file.

1. Line spacing and skipping control cannot be specified. If any of these printer controls are included in the program for an output file stored on disk, terminal errors will be generated during program compilation.
2. Editing should not be specified for numeric fields. This function will not cause any compilation or execution time errors when loading or adding records to the data file. However, during program execution, when the file is subsequently processed, any numeric fields that were previously edited will be tested as invalid and cause a runtime halt or abort.
3. Because the RPG processing cycle executes output instructions at 1P time before any record is read from an input file, output to a disk file should be conditioned by one or more indicators. Otherwise, in the loading or adding process a blank record (blanks for alphanumeric and zeros for numeric fields) will be output and stored in the file.

Validation of File Load

The fact that a program that loads a disk file did not cancel during execution is no assurance that the data was loaded correctly. A wrong end position on the output specifications could cause a field value to overlap a previous numeric field. This would result in an execution time error when the file was subsequently processed.

Validation of the file load may be done by writing an RPG program to process the file after it is loaded. Any invalid numeric data would be identified by a halt or abort of program execution. Alphanumeric values that were not loaded correctly would be either high- or low-order truncated or include more spaces than originally defined for the field. This method of validating the loading of a file requires that many RPG programs have to be written to check each file.

Utility programs such as DITTO (IBM 370/4300 series), DISPLAY (IBM System/34/36 series), and CPYF (IBM System/38 and AS/400) provide for the listing of a data file in varying formats. Figure 13-13 shows a *hexadecimal* listing (EBCDIC code) of the sequential file created by the example program. The output shown is referred to as an *over-and-under* format. Individual field values are identified on the listing by vertical lines and letters that are interpreted in a supplemental legend. Notice that these are not part of the utility listing and are included here only for readability.

```
Field legend:
                    a - blank space          e - purchase date
                    b - part number          f - quantity (packed)
                    c - part name            g - cost    (packed)
                    d - vendor number        h - amount  (packed)

Ruler is supplied by utility to reference location of each character

RCDNBR  *... ... 1 ... ... 2 ... ... 3 ... ... 4 ... ... 5 ...
                                                              Values inter-
   1    |0001|BOUNTY PAPER TOWELS      |6|110290|144|000040|000005760|<--preted here
       4|FFFF|CDEDEE4DCDCD4EDECDE444444|F|FFFFFF|FFF|FFFFFF|FFFFFFFFF|<--Zone area
       0|0001|2645380717590366532000000|6|110290|144|000040|000005760|<--Digit area

   2    |0002|MARCAL PAPER TOWELS      |6|110190|360|000041|000014760|
       4|FFFF|DCDCCD4DCDCD4EDECDE444444|F|FFFFFF|FFF|FFFFFF|FFFFFFFFF|<--Zone area
       0|0002|4193130717590366532000000|6|110190|360|000041|000014760|<--Digit area

       a  b           c                d    e    f     g       h

Notes:

   F in low-order byte of a numeric field indicates a positive value.
   On some systems the letter C is specified for a positive value.

   D in low-order byte of a numeric field indicates a negative value.

   4 }  indicates a blank value
   0 }
```

Figure 13-13 IBM EBCDIC hexadecimal listing (over-and-under format) of the sequential file created by the example program.

A side-by-side ASCII code hexadecimal listing generated on a non-IBM computer system or on an IBM PC compatible is shown in Figure 13-14. Observe that the value of each byte is interpreted in its character format in the right-hand

```
write

Legend:

A - Blank value (20)
B - Item number (30303031) or 0001 (3's represent unused zone bit value)
C - Item name (42 4F55 4E54 5920 .......) or BOUNTY PAPER TOWELS
D - Vendor number (36) or 6
E - Date (31 3130 3139 30) or 110190
F - Qty (31 3434) or 144
G - Cost (3030 3030 3430 or 000040
H - Amount (3030 3030 3537 3630) or 000005760

            A    B                   C
0000      2030 3030 3142 4F55   4E54 5920 5041 5045  D  * 0001BOUNTY PAPE*
0010    E 5220 544F 5745 4C53  F2020 2020 2020 3631  G  *R TOWELS      61*
0020    H 3130 3139 3031 3434   3030 3030 3430 3030     *1019014400004000*
0030      3030 3035 3736 3020   3030 3032 4D41 5243     *0005760 0002MARC*
0040      414C 2050 4150 4552   2054 4F57 454C 5320     *AL PAPER TOWELS *
0050      2020 2020 2036 3131   3031 3930 3336 3030     *     61101903600*
0060      3030 3034 3130 3030   3031 3437 3630 2030     *00041000014760 0*
```

Figure 13-14 Non-IBM (ASCII code) hexadecimal listing (side-by-side format) of the sequential file created by the example program.

margin. Also, instead of the records being individually printed as in the over-and-under format illustrated in Figure 13-13, they are presented in a continuous format.

A regular (nonhexadecimal) listing may also be generated by many of the named utilities. However, if the numeric fields are in an *internal packed decimal format* (discussed later in the chapter), the values would be unreadable. Consequently, a hexadecimal listing must be used if the packed numeric values are to be interpreted.

APPLICATION PROGRAM—ALTERNATIVE SYNTAX TO SAVE STORAGE AND DECREASE PROCESSING TIME

A procedure called *blocking* may be specified in an RPG program to save storage and decrease processing time. *Blocking* may be defined as the placing together of logical records in a group (physical record) instead of individually for storage on a direct access device, diskette, or magnetic tape. Two new terms, *logical record* and *physical record*, introduced in the blocking definition are defined as follows:

Logical Record: The field or fields defined as the record size in the RECORD LENGTH field of the File Description Specifications form.

Physical Record: Is the same size as a logical record in an unblocked file. In a data file that was created with a blocking factor greater than one, its length is a multiple of the logical record size. Maximum block size depends on the storage device and/or computer system used. For example, for data files created on an IBM System/34 or 36, block sizes in multiples of 256 bytes are the most efficient because these systems automatically build the buffer areas for disk and tape files in multiples of that constant.

Some systems (IBM System/38 and AS/400 for example) control the blocking process automatically, and any indicated blocking factor will be ignored by the system.

When records are written on a disk, diskette, or magnetic tape, in an unblocked format, space exists between each of the logical records. This is commonly called an *inter-record gap* (**IRG**), which consumes storage that could be used for data. Blocking eliminates the inter-record gap between the logical records, thereby saving storage. However, there will be *interblock gaps* (**IBG**) between each physical record.

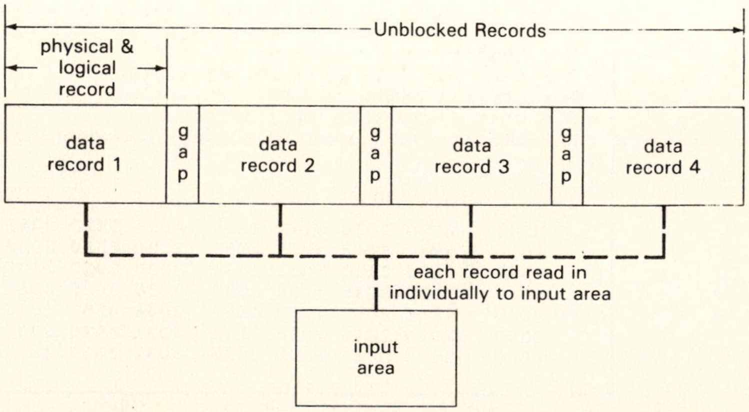

Figure 13-15 Format and processing logic of unblocked logical records.

In addition, blocking also reduces processing time because the logical records are read as a block and not individually into an input *buffer area* (one is built during program execution for every input and output file). Consequently, fewer "trips" have to be made into the storage device to locate and extract the records. After the records are stored in the buffer area, they are processed one at a time at CPU speed (nanoseconds). Figure 13-15 illustrates the structure and processing logic related to unblocked records.

The format for blocked records is shown in Figure 13-16. Notice that four *logical* records are included in one *physical* record. A *blocking factor* of four was chosen randomly to illustrate the blocking process. The computer system and/or hardware restrictions determine the optimum block size.

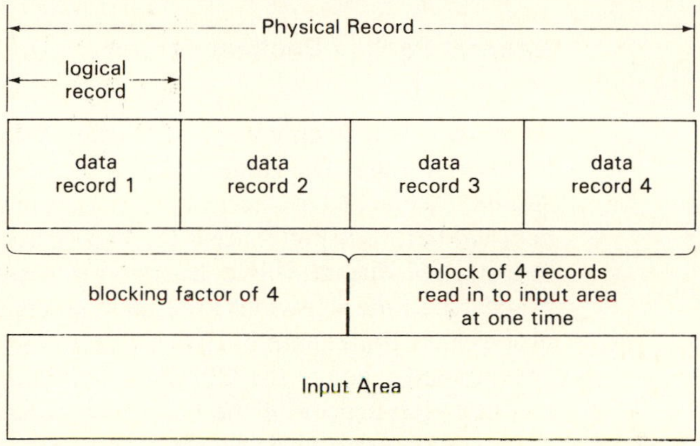

Figure 13-16 Format and processing logic of block records.

RPG Syntax for Blocking

The only coding entry in an RPG program to define blocking is entered in the Block Length field (columns 20–23) of the File Description Specifications form. Examine Figure 13-17 and notice that columns 20 to 23 of the output file specify 240, which indicates a blocking factor of 5 (record size of 48 × 5). Assuming that this program was executed on an IBM System/34 or System/36, the 240-byte block size would correspond closely to the 256-byte output buffer area built by the

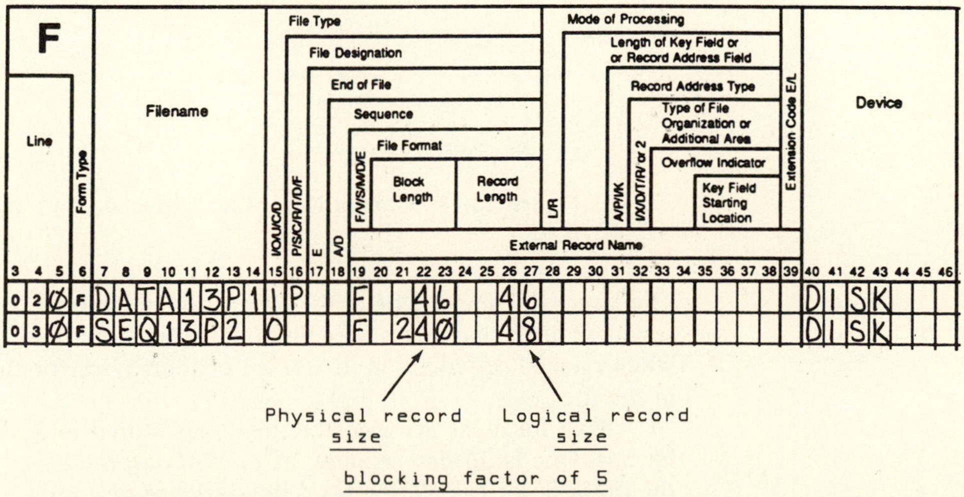

Figure 13-17 File Description form for sequential file load program modified for blocking and packing.

system software for the file. If a blocking factor of 6 had been specified, a block size of 288 bytes would be built and the system would allocate a 512-byte output buffer area. To some extent, this would reduce processing efficiency. Blocking may be specified only for data files stored on disk, diskette, or magnetic tape. Printer or workstation files do not support blocking. When a file created with blocking is subsequently processed, the exact block size must be referenced or a data exception error will occur that terminates program execution.

Observe in Figure 13-17 that the Record size (columns 24–27) has changed from the original program size of 55 bytes to 48 bytes. The shorter record size is the result of *packing* the numeric fields. Packing is discussed in the following paragraphs.

Internal Packed Decimal Format

All numeric fields may be packed when loaded to disk, diskette, or magnetic tape to save storage. On some systems (e.g., IBM 3000, 4300, 370, System/38 and AS/400) unpacked numeric data is automatically converted to *internal packed decimal* before being processed. Therefore, if the numeric data is already stored in a packed format, this conversion process will not be required, thus reducing processing time. However, not all systems pack numeric data in the CPU before processing. For example, IBM's System/34 and System/36 models store and process numeric data in the CPU in a *zoned decimal format* (*unpacked*) and require a conversion process if the data is in internal packed decimal format.

Unless otherwise specified, all numeric values are stored in a zoned decimal format. Except for the sign (positive or negative) position, stored numeric values do not use the zone area of a byte, only the digit segment. However, when packing is specified, the zone area is also used to store digits, which reduces the size of the field. Figure 13-18 shows a comparison of a three-digit numeric field in unpacked and packed formats. Notice that one byte of storage is saved by packing.

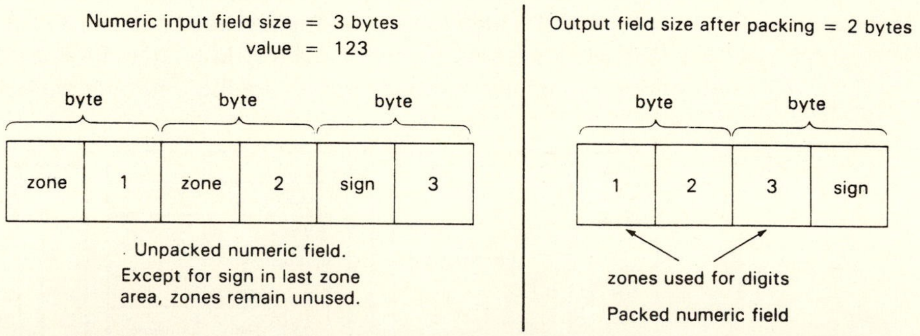

Figure 13-18 Comparison of an unpacked and a packed numeric field.

The larger the numeric field, the more storage is saved. For example, a nine-byte social security number stored in zone decimal format is reduced to five bytes when packed, a reduction in storage of four bytes for this field in every record in the file.

Two formulas are available for fields stored in an internal packed decimal format. One is for determining the *packed output size of an unpacked field*, and the other is for calculating *the unpacked size of a packed input field*. Figure 13-19 explains the formulas and illustrates their functions.

Formula for determining the size of a packed output field:

$$\text{Packed field size} = \frac{N+1}{2}$$

N= Unpacked field size

Example:

Unpacked field size = 4 bytes (digits)

Substituting: $\frac{4+1}{2} = 2.5$ or 3 as the size of the packed output field

Note: Any remainder increases whole number by 1

Formula for determining the output size of a packed input field:

$$\text{Unpacked field size} = (2 \times N) - 1$$

N= Packed field size

Example:

Packed field size = 3 bytes (digits)

Substituting: $(2 \times 3) - 1 = 5$ the unpacked output field size

Note: The original field size was 4 before packing and unpacking the packed field increases the unpacked size by 1 byte. This feature must be considered when editing and in calculations.

A *rule of thumb* is to make any unpacked numeric fields an *odd number length.* This will utilize all of the available positions in the packed field, and is more efficient.

Figure 13-19 Formulas for determining the input and output sizes when packing is specified.

RPG Syntax for Processing Numeric Fields Defined as Internal Packed Decimal

A numeric field loaded to disk, diskette, or magnetic tape is specified as being stored in an internal packed decimal format by entering a P in column 44 of the Output Specifications. Figure 13-20 shows the letter P entered in column 44 of the QTY, COST, and AMOUNT fields. The fields must have been previously defined as numeric, or a terminal error will result during program compilation. An alphanumeric field *cannot* be packed.

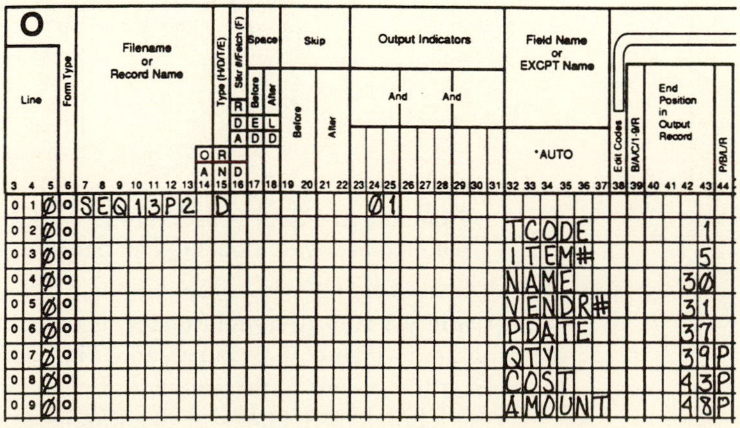

Figure 13-20 Output Specification syntax to specify that a numeric field value is to be stored in an internal packed decimal format on output.

QTY was defined on input as a three-byte numeric field and will be stored as a two-byte packed value on the output device. COST was defined as six bytes on input and will be stored as four bytes.

AMOUNT was defined as nine bytes in calculations and will be stored as five bytes. Notice that a numeric field must be at least three bytes in length to pack. A two-byte numeric field specified as packed will still require two bytes of storage. The output field sizes were determined by the first formula in Figure 13-19.

Notice also that the end positions for QTY, COST, and AMOUNT are 39, 43, and 48, respectively, which provides room for the exact packed size of each output field. It is very important that the end position for each field be determined accurately. If, for example, the end position for COST was incorrectly specified as 42, the value for that field would overlap the QTY value. The sign and low-order digit of QTY would be replaced with the two high-order digits in COST. Then, because the sign of the value was overwritten, subsequent processing of the file would generate an invalid numeric data error that would cause program execution to terminate or, on some systems, halt.

The commented source listing of the program that loads a sequential disk file is shown in Figure 13-21.

```
... ... 1 ... ... 2 ... ... 3 ... ... 4 ... ... 5 ... ... 6 ... ... 7 ...
 *  THIS PROGRAM CREATES & LOADS A SEQUENTIAL FILE FROM A DISK FILE  CH13P2
 * THE RECORD FORMAT OF THE OUTPUT FILE IS DIFFERENT FROM THE INPUT  CH13P2
 * BLOCKING AND PACKING IS SPECIFIED FOR OUTPUT SEQUENTIAL FILE      CH13P2
H                                                                    CH13P2
FDATA13P1IP  F  46  46          DISK                                 CH13P2
FSEQ13P2 O   F 240  48          DISK                                 CH13P2
IDATA13P1SM  01                                                      CH13P2
I                                        1   1 TCODE                 CH13P2
I                                        2   5 ITEM#                 CH13P2
I                                        6  30 NAME                  CH13P2
I                                       31  31 VENDR#                CH13P2
I                                       32  370PDATE
I                                       38  400QTY
I                                       41  462COST
C           QTY       MULT COST      AMOUNT  92H
OSEQ13P2 D        01
O                        TCODE     1                                 CH13P2
O                        ITEM#     5                                 CH13P2
O                        NAME     30                                 CH13P2
O                        VENDR#   31                                 CH13P2
O                        PDATE    37                                 CH13P2
O                        QTY      39P                                CH13P2
O                        COST     43P                                CH13P2
O                        AMOUNT   48P                                CH13P2
```

Fields must be defined as numeric if packing is specified on output

P in column 44 packs numeric value on output. Field must be at least 3 bytes to pack.

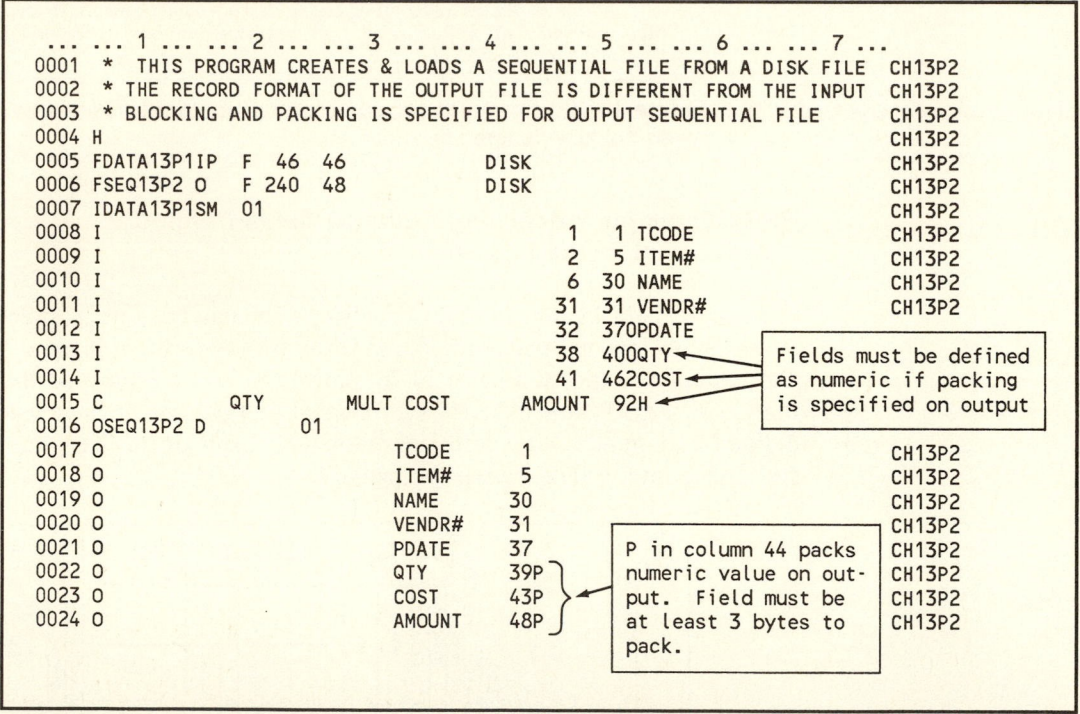

Figure 13-21 Source listing of the program that loads a sequential file modified with blocking and packing.

A utility listing (over-and-under hexadecimal format) of the file loaded by the program in Figure 13-21 is presented in Figure 13-22. Notice that the packing function stores a digit in the *zone bit* of each byte in the field area.

One method of reading a packed numeric field value is to start in the *zone* area of the first position of the field and then continue with the *digit* value directly under it. Then, the third number is read in the second zone position and the number under it, and so on until the end of the field. The end of a packed field is identified by an F (or C on some systems) if the value is positive, or a D if it is negative,

```
Field legend:
              a - blank space         e - purchase date
              b - part number         f - quantity (packed)
              c - part name           g - cost     (packed)
              d - vendor number       h - amount (packed)

Ruler is supplied by utility to reference location of each character

RCDNBR  *... ... 1 ... ... 2 ... ... 3 ... ... 4 ... ...    Alphanumeric &
                                                            unpacked numeric
   1     |0001|BOUNTY PAPER TOWELS     |6|110290|  |   |    |<-- values interpreted
        4|FFFF|CDEDEE4DCDCD4EDECDE44444|F|FFFFFF|14|000|00070|<-- Zone area
        0|0001|26453807175903665320000|0|611029|04F|004F|0056F|<-- Digit area

   2     |0002|MARCAL PAPER TOWELS     |6|110190|  |   |    |
        4|FFFF|DCDCCD4DCDCD4EDECDE44444|F|FFFFFF|30|001|00170|<-- Zone area
        0|0002|41931307175903665320000|0|611019|06F|004F|0046F|<-- Digit area

        a b           c               d   e   f   g   h

Notes:

  F in low-order digit bit of a packed numeric field indicates
    a positive value.
  On some systems the letter C is used to indicate a positive value.

  D in low-order digit bit of a packed numeric field indicates a
    negative value.

  4}  indicates a blank value
  0}
```

Figure 13-22 Utility listing (over-and-under hexadecimal format) of the sequential file after packing is specified.

in the digit position of the low-order byte. Methods of reading a packed numeric field are illustrated in Figure 13-23.

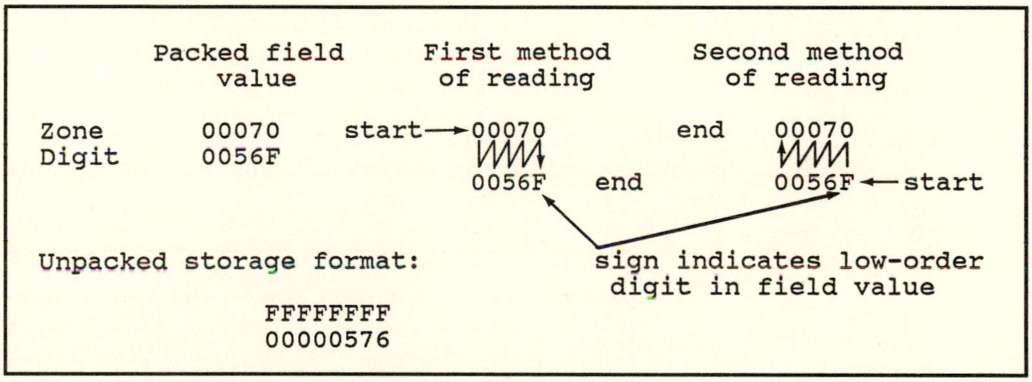

Figure 13-23 Methods of reading a packed numeric field value.

A second method of reading a packed field value is also shown in Figure 13-23. This method begins at the digit area of the low-order byte and reads up and down like the first method previously described. Before any field value is read, reference must be made to the documentation or source program to determine its exact location and size.

APPLICATION PROGRAM—CONSECUTIVE PROCESSING OF A SEQUENTIAL DISK FILE

Documentation

Specifications for an application program that consecutively processes a sequential disk file are explained in Figure 13-24. The system flowchart in Figure 13-25 indicates that one input and one output file are processed by the program.

PROGRAM SPECIFICATIONS Page 1 of 1

Program Name SEQ DISK FILE LIST Program-ID CH13P3 Written By S. Myers

Purpose Generate a report listing of a seq file Approved By The Boss

Input files (directory names):

DATA13P2 (stored on disk)

Output files (directory names):

REPORT (Printer file)

Processing Narrative:

Write a structured RPG program to consecutively process the sequential file specified and generate a report.

Input to the program:

A supplemental record layout form identifies the field attributes of input file's records.

Processing:

Read the sequential file consecutively and print an output line for every record processed. Test the transaction code field and if it includes the letter D, do not process the record.

Output:

A supplemental printer spacing chart details the format of the report. Include instructions in the program to access and print the system TIME value.

Figure 13-24 Specifications for a program that consecutively processes a sequential disk file.

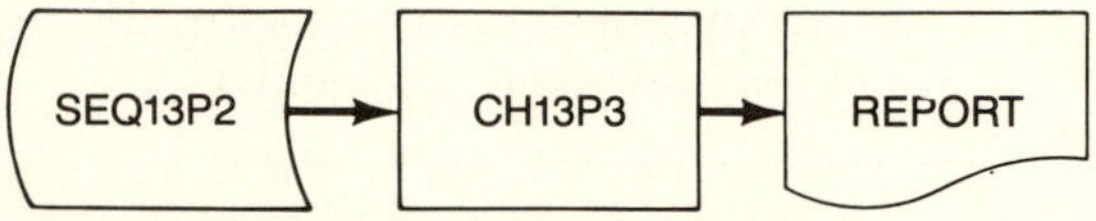

Figure 13-25 System flowchart for application program that consecutively processes a sequential disk file.

Figure 13-26 details the file, record, and field attributes of the sequential disk file loaded by the second example program (with blocking and packing) previously discussed in this chapter.

FILE DEFINITION

SYSTEM Yours		DRAWN BY S. Myers
FILE NAME SEQ13P2		DATE 11/01/90 REV. NO. 0
CREATED BY S. Myers		FILE TYPE Disk
RECORD NAME none		KEY LENGTH none
RECORDING MODE Fixed	ORGANIZATION Sequential	SEQUENCE Unordered
RECORD SIZE 48 bytes	BLOCKING FACTOR 5	BLOCKSIZE 240 bytes

FIELD DATA

FIELD NO.	FIELD NAME - DESCRIPTION	SIZE	CLASS C/P/Z/B	POSITION FROM	POSITION THRU	FORMAT/CONSTANT
1	Transaction code	1	C	1	1	letter D if deleted
2	Item number	4	C	2	5	
3	Item name	25	C	6	30	
4	Vendor number	1	C	31	31	
5	Purchase date	6	Z	32	37	
6	Quantity on hand	3	P	38	39	0 decimal positions
7	Cost per unit	6	P	40	43	2 decimal positions
8	Dollar amount on hand	9	P	44	48	2 decimal positions

Figure 13-26 File definition of the sequential disk file input by the program that processes it consecutively.

A printer spacing chart that details the report design is shown in Figure 13-27.

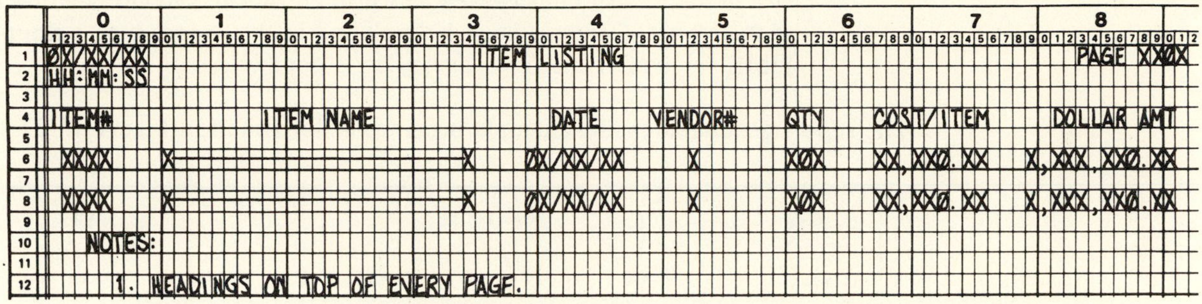

Figure 13-27 Printer spacing chart for program that processes a sequential disk file consecutively.

Source Program Coding

A source listing of the program that processes a sequential disk file consecutively is presented in Figure 13-28. In accordance with the documentation, the following controls are included in the program:

1. The block size that was specified when the file was created must be entered in the Block Length field of the File Description form. If an incorrect block size is used, the program will terminate during execution.
2. Fields that were specified as packed when the file was created must be defined as packed on the input form by including the letter P in column 43 with the field definition. If this entry is omitted and the field is stored in an internal packed decimal format, an invalid numeric data error will be generated and program execution will terminate.

```
... ... 1 ... ... 2 ... ... 3 ... ... 4 ... ... 5 ... ... 6 ... ... 7 ...
 * THIS PROGRAM PROCESSES A SEQUENTIAL FILE CONSECUTIVELY          CH13P3
H                                                                  CH13P3
FSEQ13P2 IP  F 240  48          DISK                               CH13P3
FREPORT  O   F 132 132     OF   PRINTER                            CH13P3
ISEQ13P2 SM  01                                                    CH13P3
I                                        1   1 TCODE               CH13P3
I                                        2   5 ITEM#               CH13P3
I                                        6  30 NAME                CH13P3
I                                       31  31 VENDR#              CH13P3
I                                       32  370PDATE               CH13P3
I                                     P 38  390QTY                 CH13P3
I                                     P 40  432COST                CH13P3
I                                     P 44  482DLRAMT              CH13P3
C   10                SETOF                     10   STOP HDG REPEATCH13P3
C  N11                TIME                HHMMSS  60     GET SYSTEM TIMECH13P3
C  N11                SETON                     1011  CTRL FOR TIME  CH13P3
C           TCODE     COMP 'D'                      20DELETED RECORD?CH13P3
OREPORT  H  101   1P                                               CH13P3
O       OR        OF                                               CH13P3
O                         UDATE Y    8                             CH13P3
O                                   46 'ITEM LISTING'              CH13P3
O                                   86 'PAGE'                      CH13P3
O                         PAGE  Z   91                             CH13P3
O        H  2     10                                               CH13P3
O       OR        OF                                               CH13P3
O                         HHMMSS     8 '  :  :  '                  CH13P3
O        H  2     10                                               CH13P3
O       OR        OF                                               CH13P3
O                                    5 'ITEM#'                     CH13P3
O                                   26 'ITEM NAME'                 CH13P3
O                                   44 'DATE'                      CH13P3
O                                   55 'VENDOR#'                   CH13P3
O                                   62 'QTY'                       CH13P3
O                                   75 'COST/ITEM'                 CH13P3
O                                   90 'DOLLAR AMT'                CH13P3
O        D  2     01N20                                            CH13P3
O                         ITEM#      5                             CH13P3
O                         NAME      34                             CH13P3
O                         PDATE Y   46                             CH13P3
O                         VENDR#    52                             CH13P3
O                         QTY    1  62                             CH13P3
O                         COST   1  75                             CH13P3
O                         DLRAMT1   91                             CH13P3
```

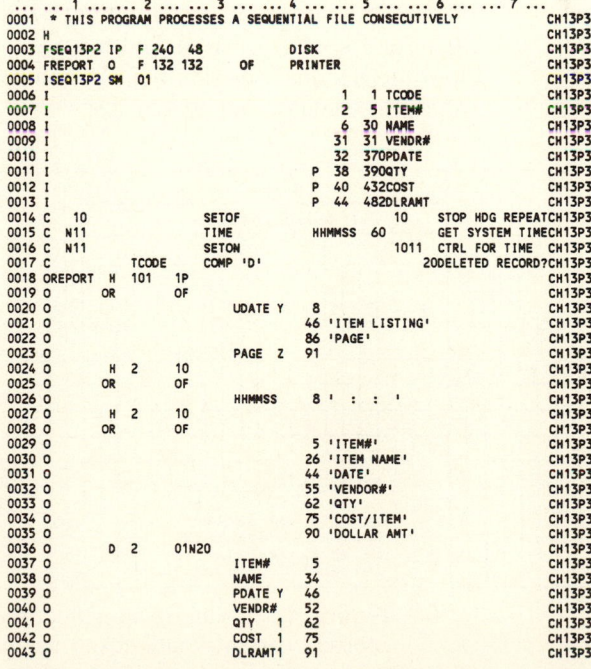

Figure 13-28 Source listing of the program that processes a sequential file consecutively.

3. A test must be made for records that are tagged for deletion. If the letter D is tested in the code field, the record is not to be printed.
4. System time is to be accessed and printed on the second heading line of the report. Controls must be included in the program to output the TIME value after the first page cycle is completed.

The report generated by the example program is illustrated in Figure 13-29.

11/30/90 ITEM LISTING PAGE 1
2:47:38

ITEM#	ITEM NAME	DATE	VENDOR#	QTY	COST/ITEM	DOLLAR AMT
0001	BOUNTY PAPER TOWELS	11/01/90	6	144	.40	57.60
0002	MARCAL PAPER TOWELS	11/01/90	6	360	.41	147.60
0004	VANITY FAIR PAPER TOWELS	11/03/90	9	60	.39	23.40
0007	KLEENEX PAPER TOWELS	11/10/90	1	48	.45	21.60
0008	SCOTT'S PAPER TOWELS	11/15/90	4	240	.50	120.00
0010	HUDSON PAPER TOWELS	11/25/90	7	72	.54	38.88
0011	NORTHERN PAPER TOWELS	11/28/90	2	120	.60	72.00
0015	A & P PAPER TOWELS	11/30/90	1	480	.29	139.20

Figure 13-29 Report generated by program that processes a sequential file consecutively.

Input Specification Syntax

The Input Specification coding form for the example program is shown separately in Figure 13-30. Because the fields were packed when the file was initially loaded (see File Definition form, Figure 13-26), they must be defined as packed by the letter P in column 43 with the other related field attributes. Also, notice that an input field specified as packed must be defined as numeric by entering the appropriate decimal position digit in column 52. If any of these entries is omitted, program execution will terminate.

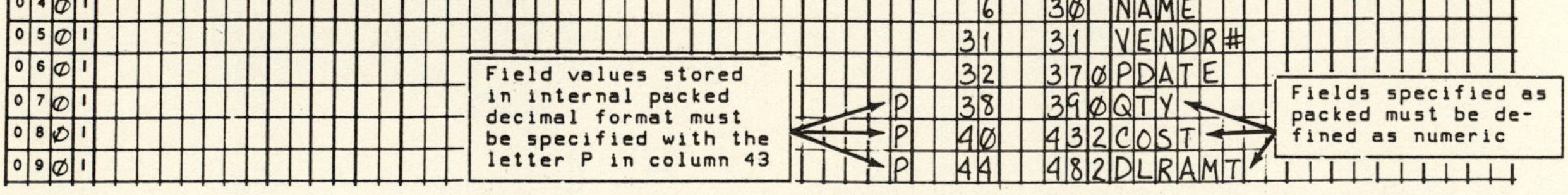

Line	Form Type	Filename or Record Name	Sequence	Record Identifying Indicator	P/B/L/R	From	To	Decimal Positions	RPG Field Name
01	I	SEQ13P2	SM	01					
02	I					1	1		TCODE
03	I					2	5		ITEM#
04	I					6	30		NAME
05	I					31	31		VENDR#
06	I					32	37	0	PDATE
07	I				P	38	39	0	QTY
08	I				P	40	43	2	COST
09	I				P	44	48	2	DLRAMT

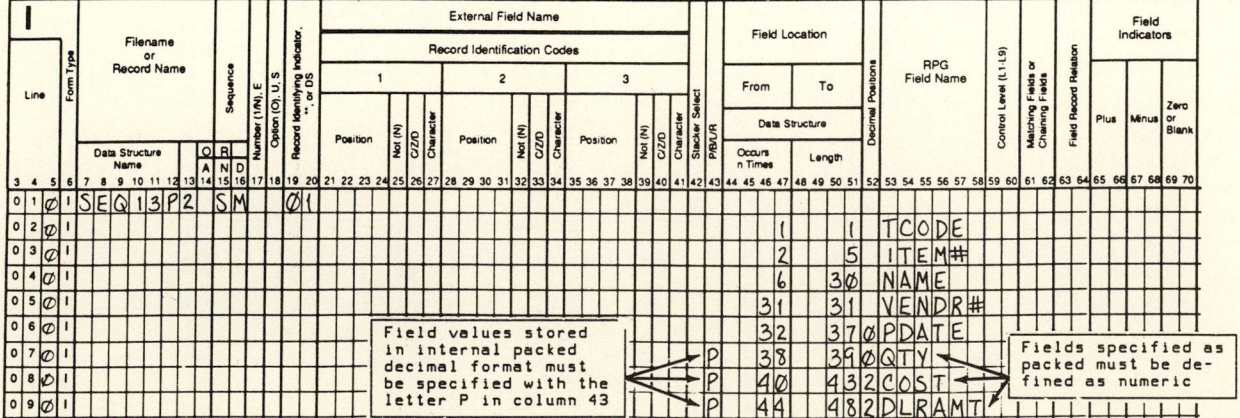

Figure 13-30 Input specifications syntax to define input fields stored in an internal packed decimal format.

System Time

Refer back to the printed report in Figure 13-29, and notice that the *System Time* is included on the second heading line. Unlike other RPG reserved words, such as PAGE, UDATE, UDAY, UMONTH, and UYEAR, the value for the System Time is not available at 1P (First Page) time. Instead, Time (stored in an HHMMSS format) must be accessed by a calculation statement that also requires that the related output instructions in a printed report be conditioned by an indicator other than 1P. Figure 13-31 explains the calculation statements needed to access the System Time value, control its output, and supplemental output statements.

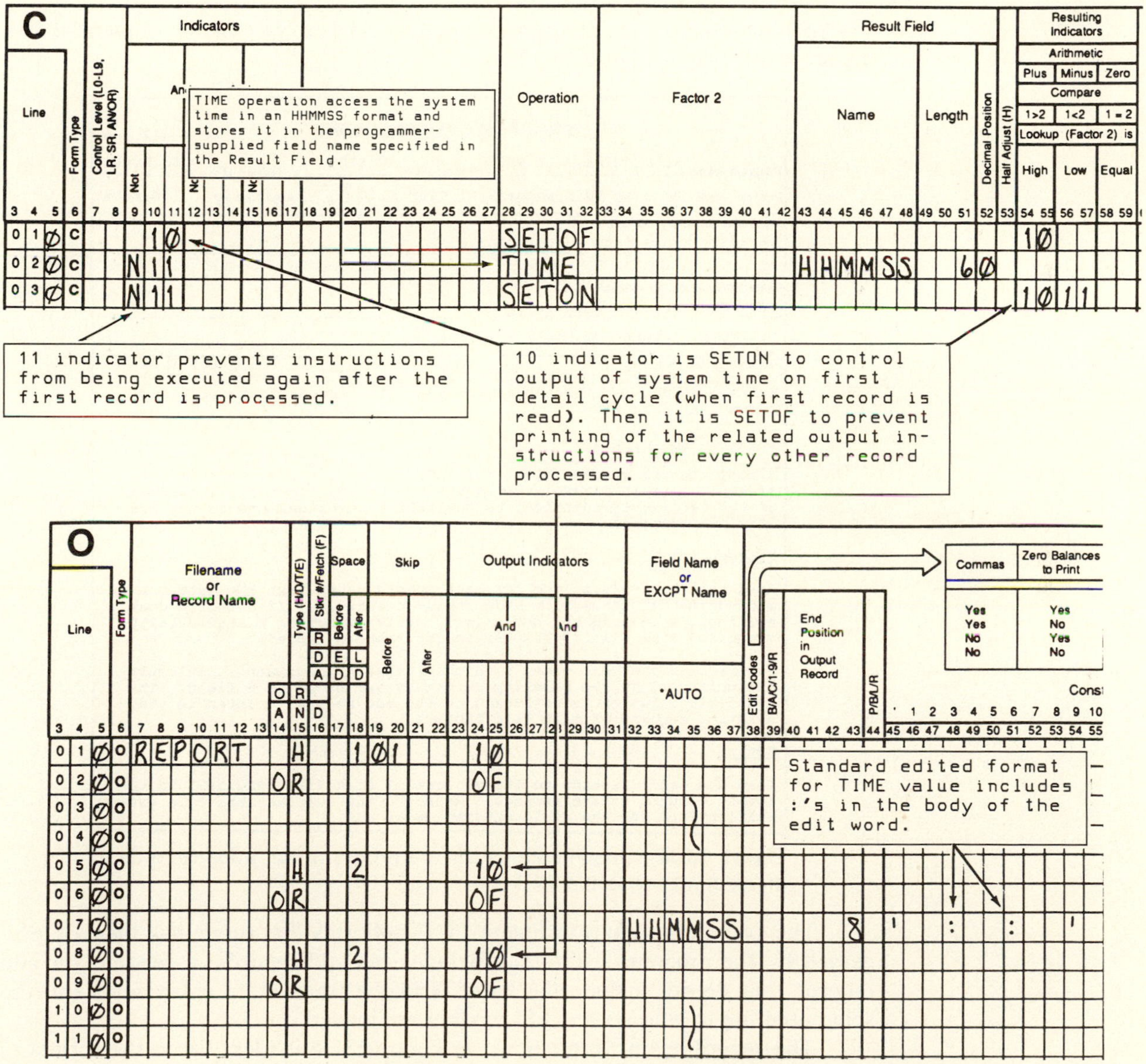

Figure 13-31 RPG syntax to access System Time (TIME) and control its output.

APPLICATION PROGRAM—SEQUENTIAL FILE ADDITION

File addition is a maintenance function that adds data records to an existing file. The add records are loaded after the previously stored last record. On input, the add records do not have to be in a sorted order. However, depending on a control field value, add records may destroy the sorted integrity of the existing sequential file and the file may have to be sorted before processing.

On some computer systems, disk storage space must be explicity defined by specifying the maximum number of records, blocks, or tracks for the data file. Consequently, consideration must be given to the number of possible additions to the file. Other systems do not require that space be allocated but, instead, dynamically (automatically) provide storage space on disk.

Documentation

The specifications for the program that adds records to an existing sequential disk file are explained in Figure 13-32.

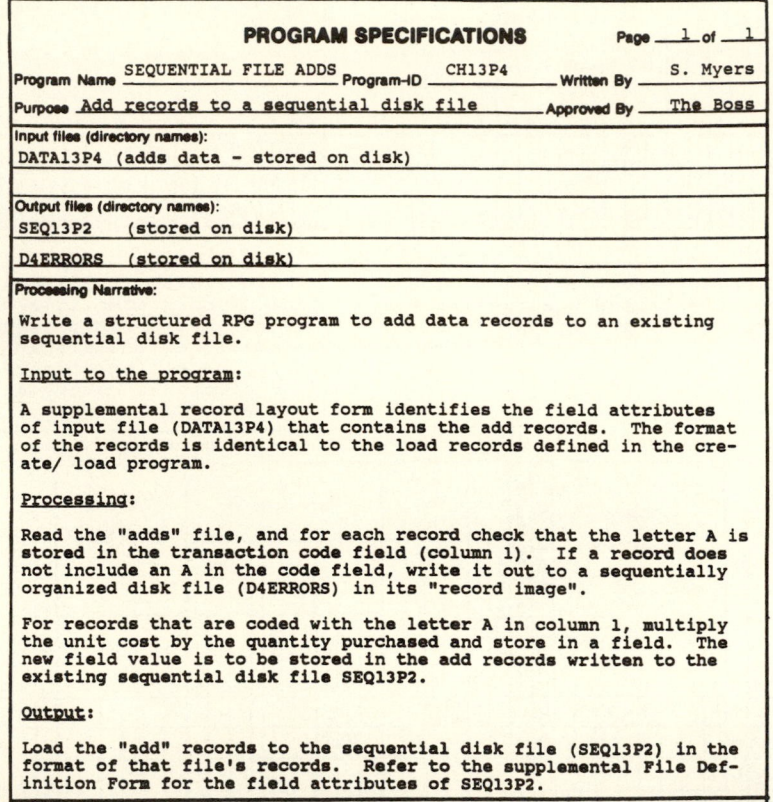

PROGRAM SPECIFICATIONS Page 1 of 1

Program Name SEQUENTIAL FILE ADDS Program-ID CH13P4 Written By S. Myers

Purpose Add records to a sequential disk file Approved By The Boss

Input files (directory names):

DATA13P4 (adds data - stored on disk)

Output files (directory names):

SEQ13P2 (stored on disk)

D4ERRORS (stored on disk)

Processing Narrative:

Write a structured RPG program to add data records to an existing sequential disk file.

Input to the program:

A supplemental record layout form identifies the field attributes of input file (DATA13P4) that contains the add records. The format of the records is identical to the load records defined in the create/ load program.

Processing:

Read the "adds" file, and for each record check that the letter A is stored in the transaction code field (column 1). If a record does not include an A in the code field, write it out to a sequentially organized disk file (D4ERRORS) in its "record image".

For records that are coded with the letter A in column 1, multiply the unit cost by the quantity purchased and store in a field. The new field value is to be stored in the add records written to the existing sequential disk file SEQ13P2.

Output:

Load the "add" records to the sequential disk file (SEQ13P2) in the format of that file's records. Refer to the supplemental File Definition Form for the field attributes of SEQ13P2.

Figure 13-32 Specifications for the program that adds records to an existing sequential disk file.

The system flowchart in Figure 13-33 indicates that three disk files are processed by the program: a file that includes the add records; a second, for add records that do not include the letter A in the transaction code field; and the sequential file to which valid add records are loaded.

The record layout form shown in Figure 13-34 is identical to the format of the load records previously presented in Figure 13-9. In addition, unless the file is to include multiple record formats (discussed in Chapter 8), the original record format in the master file will be the same for any records added. A listing of the data file that contains the add records is also included in Figure 13-34.

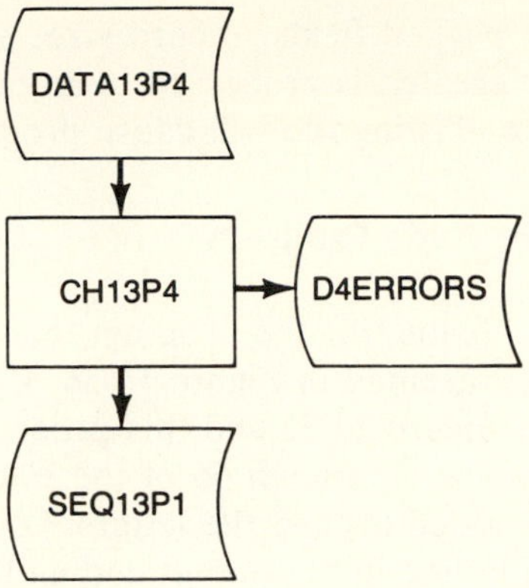

Figure 13-33 System Flowchart for program that adds records to an existing sequential disk file.

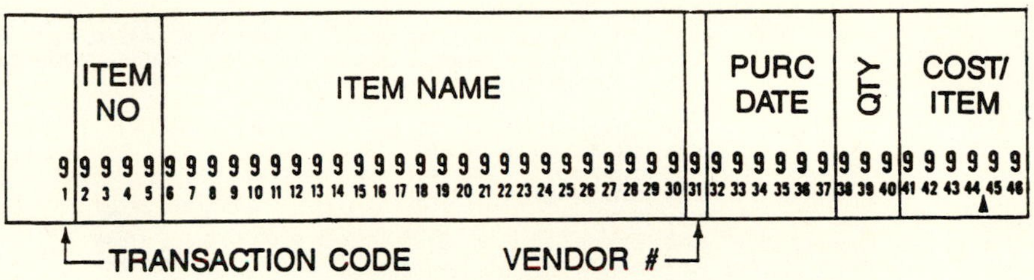


```
ADDS Data File Listing:

A0019ECONOMY PAPER TOWELS     4112890120000022
 0016STOP & SHOP PAPER TOWELS 2112990480000032
A0003GRAND UNION PAPER TOWELS 6113090240000039
A0005BRAVO PAPER TOWELS       7113090720000028

    Letter A in transaction code field
    identifies valid "add" record
```

Figure 13-34 Format of the add records and listing of the file that contains the add data.

A previously presented File Definition form that details the file, record, and field attributes of the master sequential disk file is shown again in Figure 13-35.

FILE DEFINITION

SYSTEM Yours		DRAWN BY S. Myers
FILE NAME SEQ13P2		DATE 11/01/90 REV. NO. 0
CREATED BY S. Myers		FILE TYPE Disk
RECORD NAME none		KEY LENGTH none
RECORDING MODE Fixed	ORGANIZATION Sequential	SEQUENCE Unordered
RECORD SIZE 48 bytes	BLOCKING FACTOR 5	BLOCKSIZE 240 bytes

FIELD DATA

FIELD NO.	FIELD NAME - DESCRIPTION	SIZE	CLASS C·P·Z/B	POSITION FROM	POSITION THRU	FORMAT/CONSTANT
1	Transaction code	1	C	1	1	letter D if deleted
2	Item number	4	C	2	5	
3	Item name	25	C	6	30	
4	Vendor number	1	C	31	31	
5	Purchase date	6	Z	32	37	
6	Quantity on hand	3	P	38	39	0 decimal positions
7	Cost per unit	6	P	40	43	2 decimal positions
8	Dollar amount on hand	9	P	44	48	2 decimal positions

Figure 13-35 File definition form for master sequential disk file.

It is important that packed fields, record size, and block size be exact when a data file previously created is processed in any mode. Any difference in any of these items from the existing file will cause program execution to terminate.

RPG Syntax for the Adds Program

The source program listing for the program that adds records to an existing sequential disk file is presented in Figure 13-36. If a comparison is made between the load program in Figure 13-22 and this program, it will be seen that the only changes are the letter *A in column 66* of the File Description Specifications for the output file (one added to) and the letters *ADD in columns 16, 17, and 18* on the record description line in the output coding for the file.

```
... ... 1 ... ... 2 ... ... 3 ... ... 4 ... ... 5 ... ... 6 ... ... 7 ...
 * THIS PROGRAM ADDS RECORDS TO AN EXITING SEQUENTIAL FILE, TESTS     CH13P4
 * FOR A VALID TRANSACTION CODE, AND LOADS INVALID RECORDS OUT TO     CH13P4
 * ANOTHER SEQUENTIAL (ERROR) FILE                                    CH13P4
H                                                                     CH13P4
FDATA13P4IP  F  46  46            DISK                                CH13P4
FSEQ13P2 O   F 240  48            DISK                   A            CH13P4
FD4ERRORSO   F  46  46            DISK                   ↑            CH13P4
IDATA13P4SM  01    1 CA                                               CH13P4
I                                        1   1 TCODE                  CH13P4
I                                        2   5 ITEM#                  CH13P4
I                                        6  30 NAME
I                                       31  31 VENDR#
I                                       32  370PDATE
I                                       38  400QTY
I                                       41  462COST
I              SM  02
I                                        1  46 IMAGE
C              QTY        MULT COST      AMOUNT  92H
OSEQ13P2 DADD←        01                                              CH13P4
O                        TCODE     1                                  CH13P4
O                        ITEM#     5                                  CH13P4
O                        NAME     30                                  CH13P4
O                        VENDR#   31                                  CH13P4
O                        PDATE    37                                  CH13P4
O                        QTY      39P                                 CH13P4
O                        COST     43P                                 CH13P4
O                        AMOUNT   48P                                 CH13P4
OD4ERRORSD            02                                              CH13P4
O                        IMAGE    46                                  CH13P4
```

In File Des. definition, letter A must be entered in column 66 for the output file and the letters ADD in columns 16, 17, and 18 of the Output Specs. for the related file.

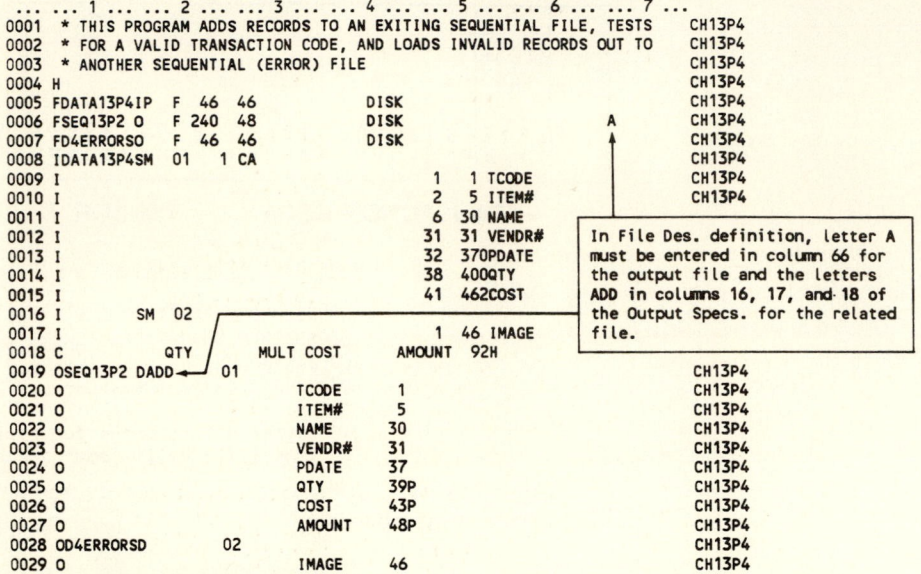

Figure 13-36 Source listing of the program that adds records to an existing sequential disk file.

Examine the report listing (generated by program CH13P3) in Figure 13-37 and observe that the add records are stored at the end of the file without regard to control field value (ITEM#).

11/30/90 ITEM LISTING PAGE 1
4:29:06

ITEM#	ITEM NAME	DATE	VENDOR#	QTY	COST/ITEM	DOLLAR AMT
0001	BOUNTY PAPER TOWELS	11/01/90	6	144	.40	57.60
0002	MARCAL PAPER TOWELS	11/01/90	6	360	.41	147.60
0004	VANITY FAIR PAPER TOWELS	11/03/90	9	60	.39	23.40
0007	KLEENEX PAPER TOWELS	11/10/90	1	48	.45	21.60
0008	SCOTT'S PAPER TOWELS	11/15/90	4	240	.50	120.00
0010	HUDSON PAPER TOWELS	11/25/90	7	72	.54	38.88
0011	NORTHERN PAPER TOWELS	11/28/90	2	120	.60	72.00
0015	A & P PAPER TOWELS	11/30/90	1	480	.29	139.20
0019	ECONOMY PAPER TOWELS	11/28/90	4	120	.22	26.40
0003	GRAND UNION PAPER TOWELS	11/30/90	6	240	.39	93.60
0005	BRAVO PAPER TOWELS	11/30/90	7	720	.28	201.60

Valid add records were loaded at end of the master file. Invalid add record (letter A missing in column 1) were written to a sequentially organized error file.

Figure 13-37 Report listing of the sequential disk file after records have been added.

In lieu of the report format shown in Figure 13-37, a hexadecimal listing of the file could have been generated by a utility program (e.g., COPY, DITTO, or DISPLAY). Unless a report program exists for the file, a utility listing is usually more convenient to use to validate the result of any maintenance to the file.

A side-by-side ASCII hexadecimal listing of the error file (D4ERRORS) is shown in Figure 13-38. Only one invalid record (the letter A missing in column 1) was included in the adds file, which has its values printed in the right margin of the listing. Controls in the program loaded the invalid records to the error file in a record image; hence, no packing was specified for the numeric fields.

```
0000   2030 3031 3653 544F  5020 2620 5348 4F50    * 0016STOP & SHOP*
0010   2050 4150 4552 2054  4F57 454C 5320 3231    * PAPER TOWELS 21*
0020   3132 3939 3034 3830  3030 3030 3332 0000    *12990480000032..*
```

Figure 13-38 Side-by-side ASCII hexadecimal listing of the error file loaded by the adds program.

SUMMARY

The most popular media for the storage of data and software are disks and diskettes. They support faster processing times and are relatively inexpensive compared to the amount of data they store. Files stored on disk or diskette may be randomly processed, whereas files stored on magnetic tape are restricted to consecutive processing.

The internal structure of a disk pack or diskette is divided into cylinders and tracks. Records are written concentrically on the track surfaces.

Disk file organization methods include sequential, indexed-sequential, and direct. How the data will be processed usually determines the organization method used. Master files are typically indexed-sequential, and transaction files are sequential. Direct files have limited use in an application environment but are used extensively in many software packages.

Sequential files may be loaded in an unordered sequence and include any number of duplicate records. After a file is loaded, the process should be validated by printing a utility listing of some of the records to insure that they are stored in the required format.

Data records may be loaded into a file in a blocked or unblocked format. In an unblocked file, logical records and physical records are the same size. When blocking is specified, a physical record includes two or more logical records. Blocking reduces processing time and saves disk storage. The block size must be specified when the file is created, and the size is entered in the Block Length field of the related file definition in the File Description form. The block length must be an exact multiple of the record length. To determine the optimum block size, refer to the manufacturer's manuals. When a file is created with blocking, any subsequent reference to that file in programs must specify the same block length. Otherwise, an error that terminates program execution will result.

Fields defined as numeric may be stored in an internal packed decimal format when stored on a disk pack, diskette, or magnetic tape. Packing saves storage by storing digits in the otherwise unused zone area of a numeric value. The letter P must be entered in column 44 of the output form for the related field. If the value is positive, an F (or C) will be stored in the digit area of the low-order byte. Negative values are identified by the letter D.

When a file is subsequently processed, any fields that were defined as packed when the file was created must be specified as stored in this format by entering the letter P in column 43 with the other input field attributes. If this entry is omitted when the value is stored as packed, an invalid numeric data error will be generated during program execution.

After a sequential file is initially loaded, add records are stored at the end of the file. An RPG program that controls the add function must include the letter A in column 66 for a file defined as an output adds file. In addition, the letters ADD must be entered in columns 16, 17, and 18 in the output file's record description area.

QUESTIONS

13-1. What types of software may be stored on disk packs or diskettes?

13-2. Name some of the advantages of using disk packs or diskettes for storage instead of magnetic tape.

13-3. What are the logical areas of a disk pack? What are the logical areas of a diskette?

13-4. On which of the logical areas on a disk pack are data records stored?

13-5. How many of the areas named in Question 13-3 are included on the 3348 disk pack illustrated in Figure 13-2?

13-6. How many of the areas named in Question 13-3 are included on the diskette format illustrated in the chapter?

13-7. As compared to disk packs, what are the advantages of using diskettes for storage? What are some of the disadvantages?

13-8. Name the methods of organizing disk files.

13-9. Explain the structure of each of the file types named in Question 13-8.

13-10. What are the processing advantages of the file types named in Question 13-8? What are their processing disadvantages?

13-11. In reference to file processing, explain the term *volatility*.

13-12. Name the minimum number of coding forms needed to create and load a sequential disk file.

13-13. As compared to printer files, what are some of the coding restrictions when loading a sequential disk file? Which of these restrictions will cause an error(s)? When will the error(s) be identified?

13-14. Sequential disk files must be loaded with data records in what order? What determines the order in which the records are loaded?

13-15. Define *blocking*. Name two advantages of blocking. What storage medium supports blocking?

13-16. Define *blocking factor*. What determines the optimum size of the blocking factor?

13-17. Where is blocking specified in an RPG program?

13-18. If the fixed record size in a file is 256 bytes and a blocking factor of 10 is specified, what is the block length?

13-19. If the record size for a data file is 200 bytes and the block size specified is 2000 bytes, which of the two sizes is the logical record and which the physical record?

13-20. If a data file is created with blocking, do programs that process the file have to reference the same block size? Explain.

13-21. Define the term *internal packed decimal format*. What types of fields may be packed?

13-22. What are the advantages of the internal packed decimal format?

13-23. Name the coding form(s) and field(s) that specify a field value is to be stored in an internal packed decimal format on output.

13-24. What coding form(s) and field(s) must be used to define an input field as stored in an internal packed decimal format?

13-25. If a field value was specified as packed when it was initially loaded to a file, what happens if it is not defined as packed when it is subsequently processed as an input field?

13-26. Determine the packed output size of the following unpacked fields: 6, 2, 7, 3, and 4 bytes.

13-27. Determine the unpacked size of the following packed input fields: 4, 2, 3, and 5.

13-28. In an over-and-under hexadecimal format, indicate how a date value of 123192 will be stored in an internal packed decimal format. What is the edited result if the edit Y is used to edit the field value? How may this problem be avoided?

13-29. Ideally, should the fields that are to be stored in an internal packed decimal format be defined in an even or odd length? Explain your answer.

13-30. Where in a sequential disk file are new records added? What provision must be made when a file is created if the addition of new records is anticipated? Do all computer systems require this control?

13-31. What coding forms, fields, and entries are required in a program to support file addition?

13-32. May duplicate records of the same control field value be loaded to a sequential disk file?

EXERCISES

Exercises 13-1 through 13-5 are related.

13-1. Write the File Description and Input Specifications to create a sequential disk file from the following information:

```
Input File:    TRANSACT
Output file:   SEQDISK
Printer File:  LISTING
```

The format of the records in the TRANSACT file is shown in the following record layout form:

CUST #	CUSTOMER NAME	ADDRESS	CITY	STATE	ZIP	CREDIT MAX.	CI
9 9 9 9	9 9 9 9 9 9 9 9 9 9 9 9 9 9 9 9 9 9 9 9 9 9 9 9 9 9	9 9 9 9 9 9 9 9 9 9 9 9 9 9 9 9 9 9 9 9	9 9 9 9 9 9 9 9 9 9 9 9 9 9 9	9 9	9 9 9 9 9	9 9 9 9 9 9	9 9
1 2 3 4	5 6 7 8 9 10 11 12 13 14 15 16 17 18 19 20 21 22 23 24 25 26 27 28 29 30	31 32 33 34 35 36 37 38 39 40 41 42 43 44 45 46 47 48 49 50	51 52 53 54 55 56 57 58 59 60 61 62 63 64 65	66 67	68 69 70 71 72	73 74 75 76 77 78	79 80

RECORD ID CODE (CI)

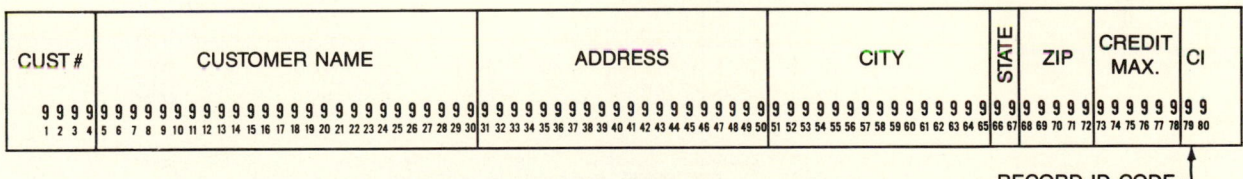

Determine the SEQDISK record size, considering that the Zip Code and Credit Limit fields are to be packed. This output file is to be created with a blocking factor of 10. Check the input records for the record identification code CI, and provide for the necessary control to prevent the program from cancelling if a record is not coded correctly.

13-2. From the information included in Exercise 13-1, write the calculations to accumulate the number of records loaded on disk, the number of unidentified records, and the total records read.

13-3. Refer to Exercises 13-1 and 13-2 and write the Output Specifications to create and load the sequential disk file (SEQDISK). Load the file in the same field sequence as the input file (TRANSACT). The Zip Code and Credit Limit fields are to be specified as packed, however. Also provide for a Delete Field in the first byte of the records.

13-4. Refer to the information in Exercises 13-1 and 13-2, and write the output specifications to generate the following report.

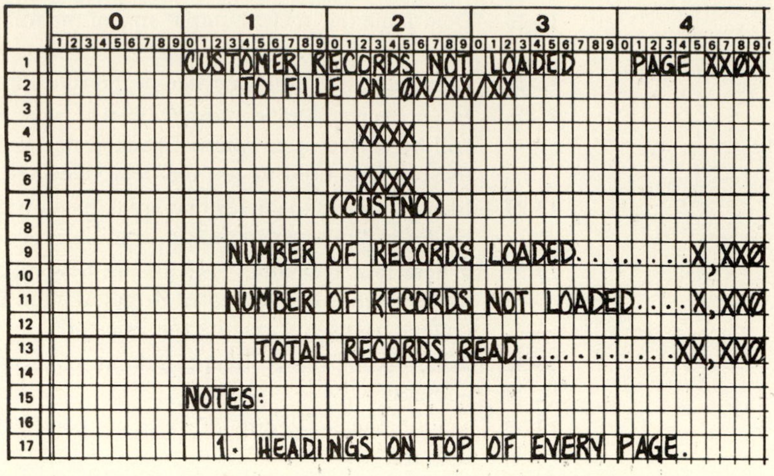
CUSTOMER RECORDS NOT LOADED
PAGE XXØX
TO FILE ON ØX/XX/XX
XXXX
XXXX
(CUSTNO)
NUMBER OF RECORDS LOADED.........X,XXØ
NUMBER OF RECORDS NOT LOADED....X,XXØ
TOTAL RECORDS READ..........XX,XXØ
NOTES:
1. HEADINGS ON TOP OF EVERY PAGE.

13-5. Refer to Exercises 13-1 and 13-3, and write the File Description and Input Specifications to process the previously created and loaded sequential disk file (SEQDISK) consecutively.

13-6. Modify your coding in Exercises 13-1 and 13-3 to control record addition to the previously created sequential disk file.

13-7. The following program listing includes six errors, three of which are identified as being terminal. Locate the six errors and explain how they may be corrected.

```
        ....+....1....+....2....+....3....+....4....+....5....+....6....+....7.

     1 0001 H                                                                 EX137


     2 0002 FDATA13P1IP  F  46  46            DISK                            EX137
     3 0003 FSEQ13P1 O   F 241  46            DISK                            EX137


     4 0004 IDATA13P1SM  01                                                   EX137
     5 0005 I                                       1   1 TCODE               EX137
     6 0006 I                                       2   5 ITEM#               EX137
     7 0007 I                                       6  30 NAME                EX137
     8 0008 I                                      31  31 VENDR#              EX137
     9 0009 I                                      32  370PDATE               EX137
    10 0010 I                                      38  40 QTY                 EX137
    11 0011 I                                      41  462COST                EX137


    12 0012 C           QTY       MULT COST      AMOUNT  92H                  EX137
****-C063- Operation Code requires a valid numeric Factor 1.


    13 0013 OSEQ13P1 D  2                                                     EX137
    14 0014 O                          TCODE      1                           EX137
    15 0015 O                          ITEM#      5                           EX137
    16 0016 O                          NAME      30                           EX137
    17 0017 O                          VENDR#    31                           EX137
    18 0018 O                          PDATE     37                           EX137
    19 0019 O                          QTY       39P                          EX137
****-0143- Field Type must be blank for an alphameric Field Name.
    20 0020 O                          COST      43P                          EX137
    21 0021 O                          AMOUNT    47P                          EX137
****-0110- End Position must not exceed the file record length.
    22 /*
    23 /*


            THE FOLLOWING INDICATORS WERE SPECIFIED BUT WERE NEVER
            USED TO CONDITION OPERATIONS

            01


            THE FOLLOWING INDICATORS APPEARED IN THIS PROGRAM

            01
No Warning Errors
 3 Fatal Errors
```

LABORATORY ASSIGNMENTS

Note: For all of these lab assignments, the input data must have been loaded in a file by your instructor, or you must create and load the file by the build utility supported by your system.

Laboratory Assignment 13-1: CREATION OF A SAVINGS ACCOUNT MASTER SEQUENTIAL DISK FILE

Write an RPG program to create a master file of new depositors for a savings bank.

Format of Input Records:

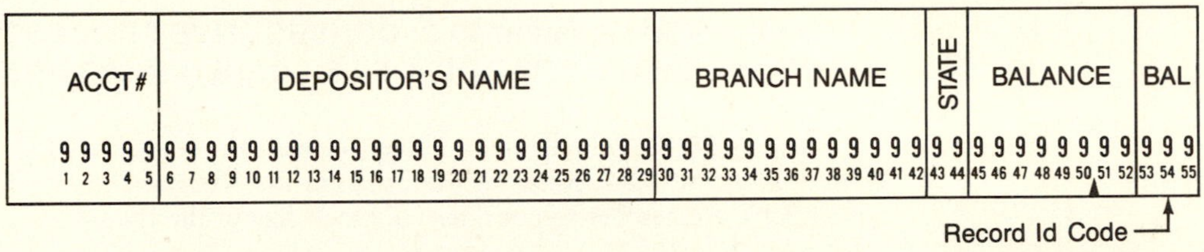

Processing: For every record processed, check the Account Balance field for zero. If it tests as zero, the record is not to be loaded to the master file. Instead, invalid records are to be loaded in an input record image to a sequentially organized error file.

Input is to be coded so that any unidentified records do not cancel program execution. Records not having the valid record identification code (BAL) are also to be loaded to the error file in their input record image.

Calculations: Provide for accumulator fields for the number of records with zero balances, the number with the incorrect record ID code, and the total number of records in the input file. See the supplemental printer spacing chart for the related field sizes.

Output. Load the records to the master file in the same field order as the input format. Pack the Account Balance field, and provide for a delete code position in the first byte of the records. Load the records with a blocking factor of 16.

Records that are tested with errors are to be loaded to a second sequential disk file in the input record image. After program execution, print a hexadecimal listing of the error file with the utility supplied with your system.

The following printer spacing chart details the format of the required report. Notice that the variable fields under the column headings represent account numbers.

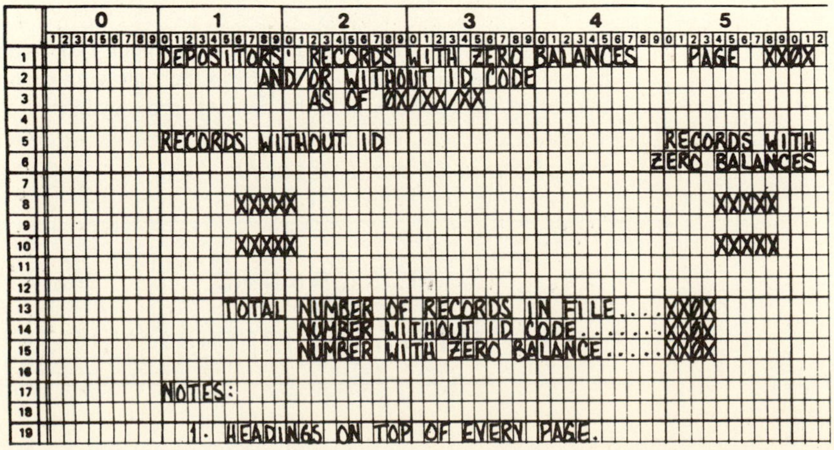

Input Data:

Account Number Col 1-5	Depositor's Name 6-29	Branch Name 30-42	State 43-44	Account Balance 45-52	ID Code 53-55
64321	HENRY FORD	DETROIT	MI	21584519	BAL
55114	LOUIS CHEVROLET	TARRYTOWN	NY		
88397	WALTER P. CHRYSLER	SAN DIEGO	CA	01000000	BAL
74891	BENJAMIN DODGE	CHICAGO	IL	04100000	
91784	WILLIAM BRICKLIN	TORONTO	ND	09000000	BAL
49814	JOHN STUDEBAKER	KANSAS CITY	KA		BAL
34444	STANLEY STEAMER	BUFFALO	NY	37100000	BAL

Laboratory Assignment 13-2: CONSECUTIVE PROCESSING OF THE SEQUENTIAL DISK FILE LOADED IN ASSIGNMENT 13-1

Write an RPG program to consecutively process the sequential disk file created and loaded in Assignment 13-1. Refer to the program for Assignment 13-1 for field attributes and locations. Remember to consider the block size of the file.

Calculations: Accumulate the balance amount for each depositor for a total balance of all depositors.

Report Design:

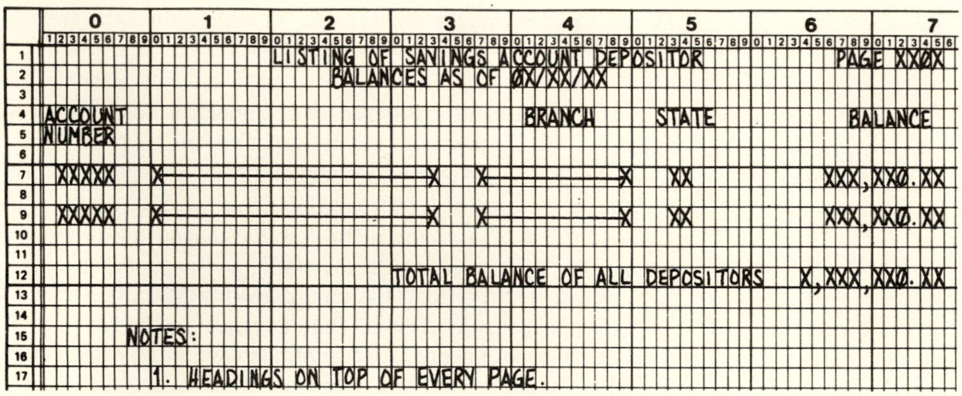

Laboratory Assignment 13-3: ADDING RECORDS TO A SEQUENTIAL DISK FILE

Modify the program completed for Assignment 13-1 to add records to the file. The input format of the add records is shown in the following record layout form. Calculations and the report instructions must be deleted from Assignment 13-1 for this assignment.

Format of Input Records:

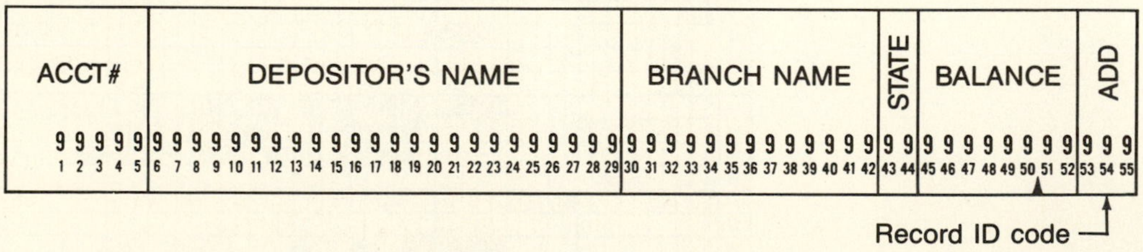

Processing: Check the record identification code for the letter ADD. Include controls in the program that will not cancel execution if an invalid code is tested in an input record. Also, test the balance field on input for a zero value.

Output: Records that include an invalid record identification code or have a zero balance are to be loaded to the same error file that was created and loaded in Assignment 13-1. Valid records are to be added to the existing sequentially organized master file built in Assignment 13-1.

No printed report is required for this assignment. After execution, check the results of your add program by your system's copy utility (in HEX format) or by executing Assignment 13-2 (if it was completed).

Adds Data:

Account Number Col 1-5	Depositor's Name 6-29	Branch 30-42	State 43-44	Account Balance 45-52	ID Code 53-55
11111	HARVEY HUPMOBILE	BRIDGEPORT	CT	00250000	ADD
92222	JON LESLIE	NORMAL	IL	00059800	
55555	DAVE CLEVELAND	TRENTON	NJ	34000000	ADD
88888	GEORGE HUDSON	FRANKFORT	KY	04000000	ADD
44444	MERCEDES GARCIA	BERLIN	NY	00000000	ADD

Laboratory Assignment 13-4: CREATION OF A CUSTOMER MASTER SEQUENTIAL DISK FILE

Create and load a customer master sequential disk file from the following input record formats:

Format of the Input Records:

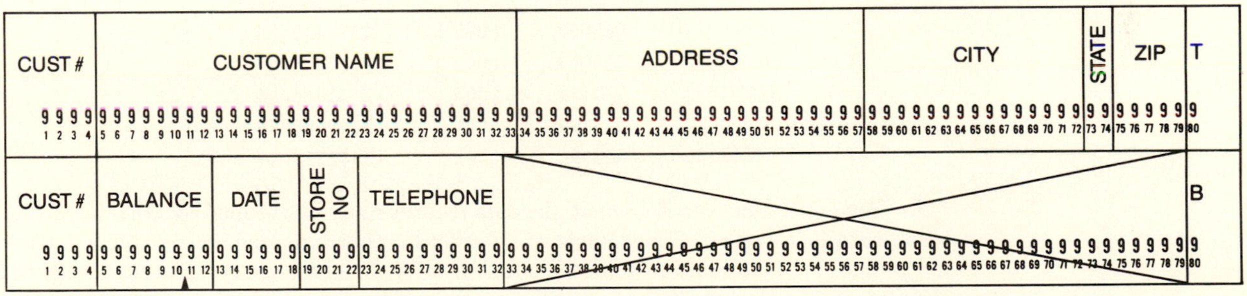

Processing: One disk record is to be created from the two input record types for each customer. Sequence check the record group on input. Pack the zip code, account balance, store number, and telephone number fields on output. Starting with the first record of the group, load the fields in the order that is specified in the input records. Do not repeat the customer number!

Provide for a delete code field in the first byte of each master file record, and store the letter M in the last byte. Store the system date (UDATE) instead of the date included in the input data to each master file record loaded. Specify a blocking factor of 5 when loading the master file.

Calculations: Provide for a count field of the total number of records processed. See the print chart for the recommended field size.

Output: In addition to the sequential output file, the program is to generate the report shown in the following print chart.

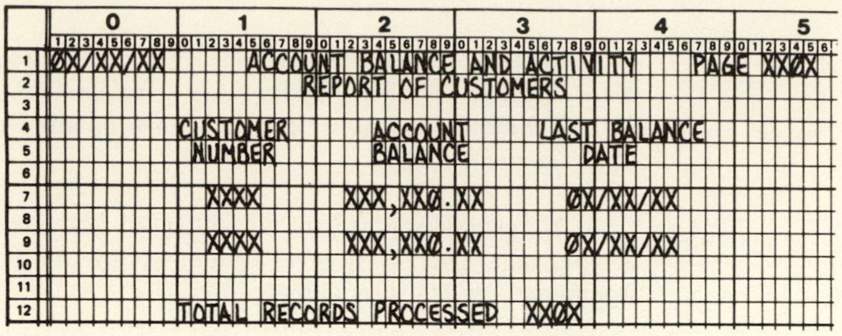

Input Data:

Record Type Coded With Character T in Column 80:

Cust# Col 1-4	Customer Name 5-33	Address 34-57	City 58-72	State 73-74	Zip 75-79
1234	JOHN FIRESTONE	20 TYRE LANE	AKRON	OH	05456
2345	WILLIAM GOODYEAR	19 TUBE ROAD	DETROIT	MI	06606
3456	JAMES GOODRICH	81 VALVE TERRACE	CHICAGO	IL	04404
4567	CLAUDE MICHELIN	1 PARIS PALCE	FRANCE	PA	06611
5678	ANTHONY PIRELLI	33 FIAT BLVD	ROME	NY	06608
6789	TOYO KOGO	12 HIROSHIMA ROAD	TOKYO	CA	06666

Record Type Coded With Character B in Column 80:

Cust# Col 1-4	Balance 5-12	Balance Date 13-18	Store# 19-22	Telephone# 23-32
1234	00018112	083190	0001	2022889999
2345	01041879	063090	0005	2127445555
3456	12000000	043090	0002	2063334441
4567	00091822	073190	0003	2136666666
5678	01800000	053190	0004	2015558888
6789	00045600	083190	0002	2142221111

Note: When the input file is created, the data records must be grouped together according to the customer number. For example, the T record for customer number 1234 will precede the B record for the same customer, and so forth for the other groups. Because sequence checking is to be included in the program, an incorrect order will cause program execution to cancel.

Laboratory Assignment: 13-5: ADDING RECORDS TO THE SEQUENTIAL FILE CREATED AND LOADED IN ASSIGNMENT 13-4

Modify Assignment 13-4 to control the addition of records to the master sequential disk file.

Format of Input Data: Use the input record format(s) from Lab 13-4.

Processing: Follow the processing requirements specified for Assignment 13-4.

Output: Refer to the source program listing for Assignment 13-4 for the record format of the master sequential file. The add records are to be loaded in exactly the same format as those in the existing master file.

Report Design: Use the report format from Assignment 13-4. After this program is executed, check the validity of the record addition by a utility listing of the file in a hexadecimal format. Highlight the records that were added to the file, and verify the packed field positions.

Adds Data:

Record Type Coded With Character T in Column 80:

Cust# Col 1-4	Customer Name 5-33	Address 34-57	City 58-72	State 73-74	Zip 75-79
1000	HENRY YOKOHOMA	1 RIM ROAD	FRANKFORT	KY	03330
7777	OSCAR ROYAL	88 PATCH PLACE	SASEBO	CA	09990

Record Type Coded With Character B in Column 80:

Cust# Col 1-4	Balance 5-12	Balance Date 13-18	Store# 19-22	Telephone# 23-32
1000	01000000	101590	0001	2094387777
7777	00098015	103190	0003	2143334567

chapter 14
Sequential Disk File Maintenance with Matching Records, Chain and Read Operations

MAINTENANCE FUNCTIONS

Sequential files are usually transactions files that include data to update one or more master files. Consequently, before an update process is executed, the data in the transaction file must be edited and modified accordingly. This requires that one or more of the following maintenance functions support a transaction file organized as sequential:

Addition: Previously discussed in Chapter 13.

Inquiry: Randomly extracting a record from a file but not changing any field values.

Update: Randomly extracting a record from a file and changing one or more field values.

Deletion: Randomly extracting a record from a file and tagging the record as deleted, or logically deleting the record.

Limits: Processing the file within two control field value limits.

In the example programs in this chapter, each of these maintenance functions is controlled by the *Matching Records Method, Chaining Method*, and/or by the *READ operation*.

APPLICATION PROGRAM—FILE INQUIRY

Documentation

The specifications for the program that controls inquiry processing of the Item Master file created and loaded in Chapter 13 (CH13P2, Figure 13-21) are detailed in Figure 14-1. *Inquiry* is a random processing function that extracts select records from a file. For sequentially organized files, the Matching Records Method, the READ operation, or the CHAIN operation may be used to control file inquiry. The first example program introduced in this chapter uses the Matching Records Method to control the file inquiry function.

The system flowchart shown in Figure 14-2 shows that an input file is sorted to generate a new output file. When the Matching Records Method (or READ operation) is used to process a file, the data must be in ascending or descending order by one or more Control Field value(s). Further examine Figure 14-2, and notice that the file created as output from the sort is input to the application

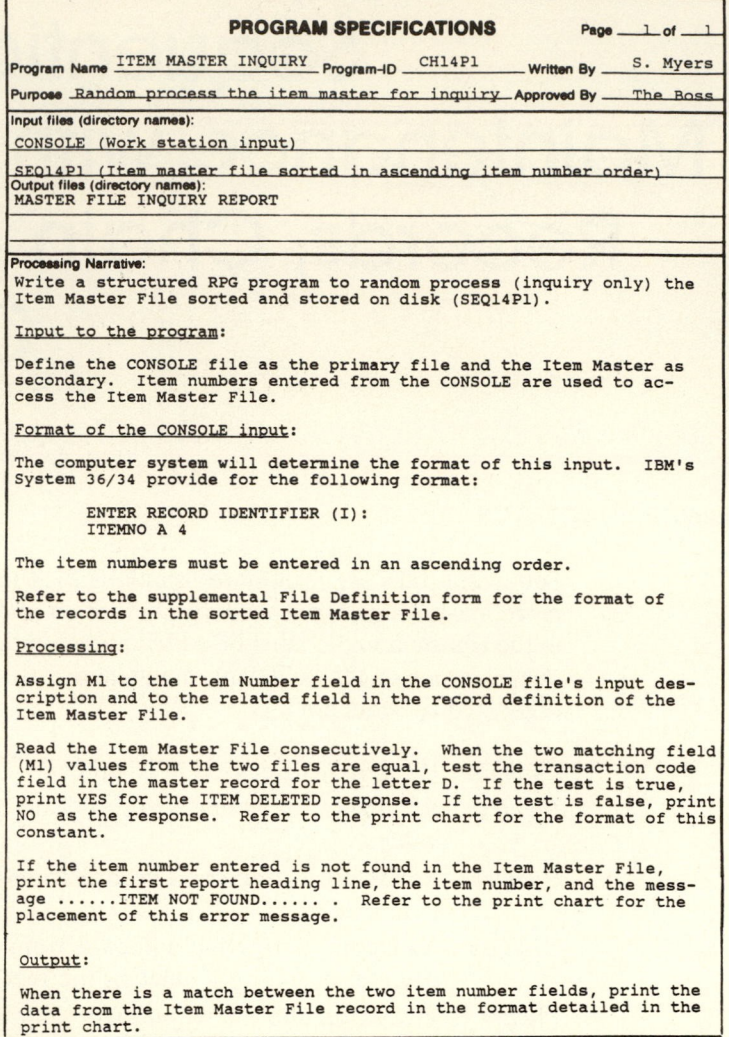

PROGRAM SPECIFICATIONS Page 1 of 1

Program Name ITEM MASTER INQUIRY Program-ID CH14P1 Written By S. Myers

Purpose Random process the item master for inquiry Approved By The Boss

Input files (directory names):

CONSOLE (Work station input)

SEQ14P1 (Item master file sorted in ascending item number order)

Output files (directory names):

MASTER FILE INQUIRY REPORT

Processing Narrative:

Write a structured RPG program to random process (inquiry only) the Item Master File sorted and stored on disk (SEQ14P1).

Input to the program:

Define the CONSOLE file as the primary file and the Item Master as secondary. Item numbers entered from the CONSOLE are used to access the Item Master File.

Format of the CONSOLE input:

The computer system will determine the format of this input. IBM's System 36/34 provide for the following format:

```
ENTER RECORD IDENTIFIER (I):
ITEMNO A 4
```

The item numbers must be entered in an ascending order.

Refer to the supplemental File Definition form for the format of the records in the sorted Item Master File.

Processing:

Assign M1 to the Item Number field in the CONSOLE file's input description and to the related field in the record definition of the Item Master File.

Read the Item Master File consecutively. When the two matching field (M1) values from the two files are equal, test the transaction code field in the master record for the letter D. If the test is true, print YES for the ITEM DELETED response. If the test is false, print NO as the response. Refer to the print chart for the format of this constant.

If the item number entered is not found in the Item Master File, print the first report heading line, the item number, and the message ......ITEM NOT FOUND...... . Refer to the print chart for the placement of this error message.

Output:

When there is a match between the two item number fields, print the data from the Item Master File record in the format detailed in the print chart.

Figure 14-1 Specifications for an application program that controls inquiry of an Item Master sequential disk file.

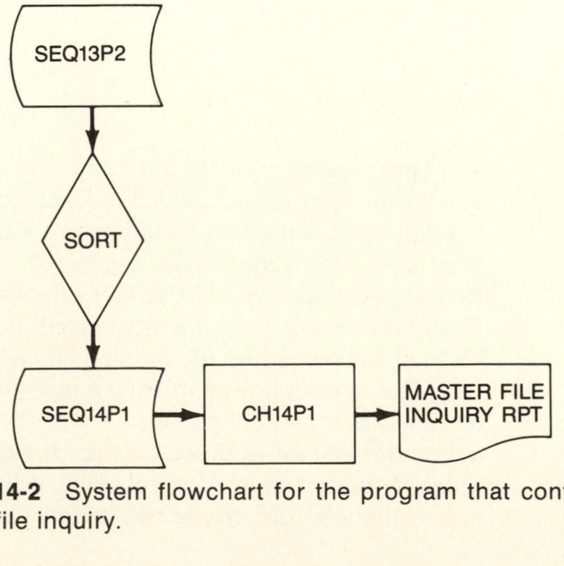

Figure 14-2 System flowchart for the program that controls Item Master file inquiry.

program. All these functions may be included in and controlled by one procedure (command file).

Sorting data files is performed by a *SORT/MERGE utility* that is usually included with the system software. The syntax for this software is unique to every system. In fact,within the IBM family of computers, the SORT/MERGE syntax for the 370/4300 series is completely different from the System/3X models. Consequently, the coding to support the sort function in Figure 14-2 is not discussed in this text.

Unlike COBOL, most RPG compilers do not support a *program-controlled (internal) sort*. Instead, the SORT statements must be included in a procedure. To a limited extent (only one sort field), however, IBM's 370/4300 series of computers do support an internal sort that requires the statements to be hard-coded in an RPG program (S specifications).

The file definition form for the Item Master file is presented in Figure 14-3. This file is processed randomly by item numbers entered by CONSOLE controlled input. This file is input to the sort; the output file generated has exactly the same file, record, and field attributes.

FILE DEFINITION

SYSTEM Yours		DRAWN BY S. Myers
FILE NAME SEQ13P2		DATE 11/01/90 REV. NO. 0
CREATED BY S. Myers		FILE TYPE Disk
RECORD NAME none		KEY LENGTH none
RECORDING MODE Fixed	ORGANIZATION Sequential	SEQUENCE Unordered
RECORD SIZE 48 bytes	BLOCKING FACTOR 5	BLOCKSIZE 240 bytes

FIELD DATA

FIELD NO.	FIELD NAME - DESCRIPTION	SIZE	CLASS C/P/Z/B	POSITION FROM	POSITION THRU	FORMAT/CONSTANT
1	Transaction code	1	C	1	1	letter D if deleted
2	Item number	4	C	2	5	
3	Item name	25	C	6	30	
4	Vendor number	1	C	31	31	
5	Purchase date	6	Z	32	37	
6	Quantity on hand	3	P	38	39	0 decimal positions
7	Cost per unit	6	P	40	43	2 decimal positions
8	Dollar amount on hand	9	P	44	48	2 decimal positions

Figure 14-3 Item Master file definition (input to the sort).

The data for the CONSOLE input file and the Item Master file is shown in Figure 14-4. Item numbers from the CONSOLE file are entered one at a time via keyboard input. The list is shown only to identify all the item numbers that are entered.

```
Primary File              Secondary File (Sequential Master File)
CONSOLE Input                        (Stored On Disk)

First ITEM#
 input ---->0002    0001BOUNTY PAPER TOWELS       6110190144000040000005760 <-- First Record
            0005    0002MARCAL PAPER TOWELS       6110190360000041000014760
            0008   A0003GRAND UNION PAPER TOWELS 6113090240000039000009360
            0011    0004VANITY FAIR PAPER TOWELS 9110390060000039000002340
            0013   A0005BRAVO PAPER TOWELS        7113090720000028000020169
             ^      0007KLEENEX PAPER TOWELS      1111090048000045000002160
             |      0008SCOTT'S PAPER TOWELS      4111590240000050000012000
             |      0010HUDSON PAPER TOWELS       7112590072000054000003888
             |      0011NORTHERN PAPER TOWELS     2112890120000060000007200
             |      0015A & P PAPER TOWELS        1113090480000029000013920
             |     A0019ECONOMY PAPER TOWELS      4112890120000022000002640
             |      ^
             |      |___ File is sorted in ascending item number order
             |
             |__________Data must be input by CONSOLE control in ascending
                        item number order
```

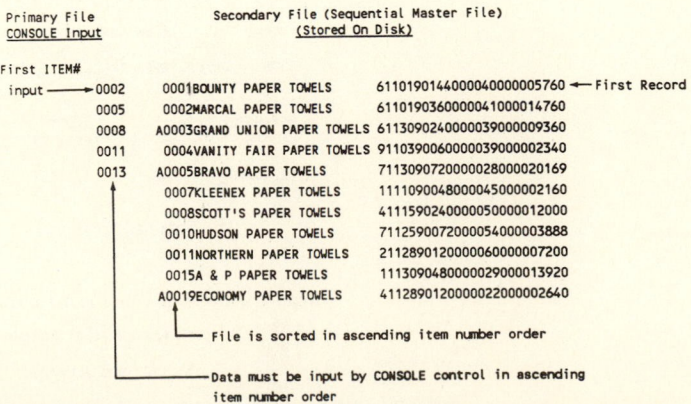

Figure 14-4 Listings of CONSOLE data and Item Master file.

The Matching Records method for processing files requires that the related files be sorted in the same order. Therefore, because the Item Master file has been sorted in ascending item number order, the data input by the CONSOLE must also be entered in the same order. An error that terminates program execution will be generated if an item number is entered out of sequence. If the master file had been sorted in descending sequence, the CONSOLE data would also have to be input in the same order.

The report format detailed in Figure 14-5 indicates the following controls:

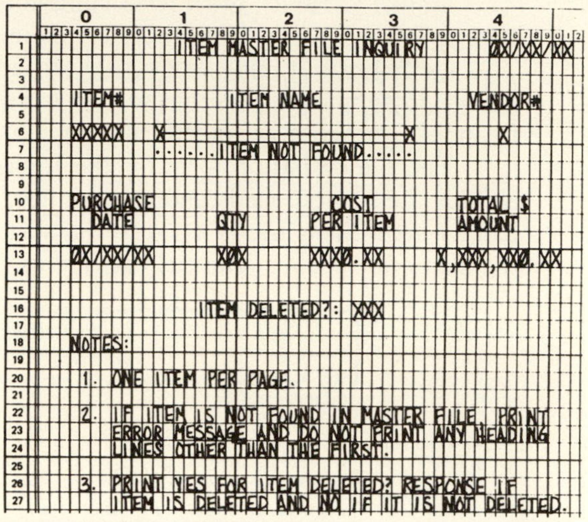

Figure 14-5 Report design for the Item Master inquiry program.

1. The information for each item is printed on a separate page.
2. An error message is generated if the CONSOLE entered item number is not found in the Item Master file.
3. The status of the transaction code field will determine whether a YES or NO response is entered for the ITEM DELETED?: constant.

A report generated when a matching record is found in the Item Master file is shown in Figure 14-6. To find a matching item in the Item Master file, item number 0005 is entered by an operator via a CONSOLE file. Also included at the bottom of Figure 14-6 is the error message report printed if a matching item number is not found in the Item Master file.

Report generated when a matching record is found:

```
                ITEM MASTER FILE INQUIRY       11/30/90

ITEM#           ITEM NAME                      VENDOR#

0005    BRAVO PAPER TOWELS                         7

PURCHASE                  COST            TOTAL $
  DATE        QTY       PER ITEM          AMOUNT

12/14/90      840          .28               238.00

                ITEM DELETED?: NO
```

Report generated when a matching record is not found:

```
                ITEM MASTER FILE INQUIRY       11/30/90

        ......ITEM NOT FOUND......
```

Figure 14-6 Reports printed when a matching item number is found in the Item Master file and when one is not found.

Matching Records Concepts

Matching Records may be used to control the following file processing functions:

1. On the basis of one or more matching fields, check the ascending or descending order of an input file.
2. Process the records in one or more files by one or more matching files in the records included in an input file.
3. Inquiry (random process) the records in one or more input files by one or more matching fields in an input file.
4. Update or delete (random process) the records in one or more update files by one or more matching fields in an input file.

Matching Records processing may be specified with any of the file organization types (sequential, indexed-sequential, and direct) and with any file combination.

RPG Syntax for Matching Records

To specify that Matching Records processing is to be used in a program, entries are required on both the File Description and Input Specification forms.

File Description Coding. In addition to the File Description coding previously discussed, Figure 14-7 explains the syntax required for matching records processing. If any of the files included in the Matching Records processing are not in the specified order, program execution will terminate when the first out-of-order record is read. Files used for this function must be defined as Input, Update, or Combined or I, U, or C in the File Type field (column 15).

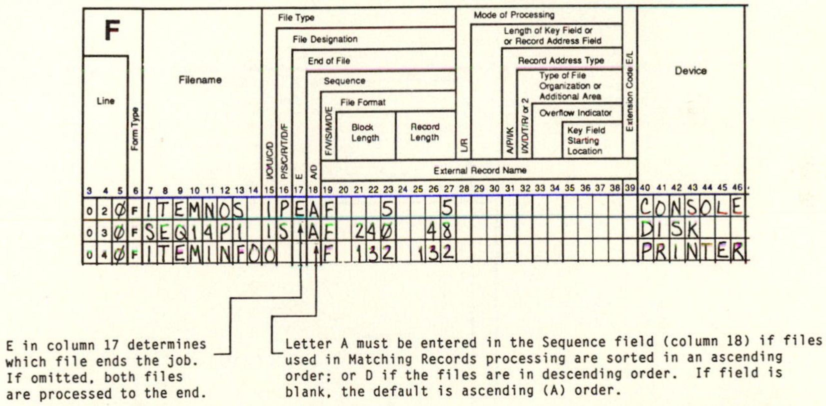

Figure 14-7 File Description coding to support Matching Records Processing.

Input Specifications Coding. Matching Records processing is controlled by specifying one or more *matching fields* on the Input Specifications. Input fields are designated as matching by the assignment of M1 to M9 in columns 61 and 62 in the input coding. If one matching field is used to match the files, M1 is assigned to the related fields; if two matching fields are assigned, then M1 and M2 must be specified; and so forth to a maximum of nine (M9) matching fields. When the values in two matching fields from two files are equal, an MR (Matching Record) indicator is automatically turned on to condition subsequent calculations and/or output.

The Input Specifications in Figure 14-8 explain the syntax related to matching records processing when one matching field is specified.

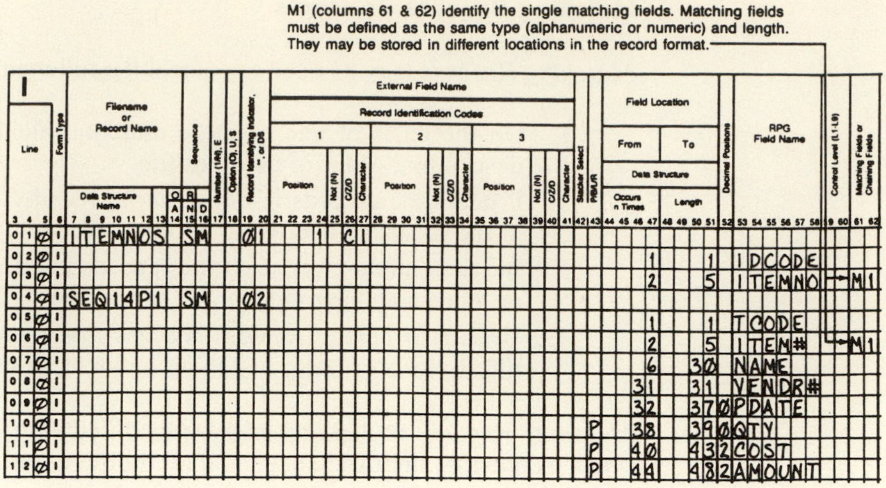

Figure 14-8 Input Specifications to support Matching Records processing when one matching field is specified.

Notice that M1 through M9 identify only the matching input fields and are not indicators. MR is the only indicator directly related to Matching Records processing. Record Identifying, Resulting, and Control Level Indicators may be specified with the MR indicator to condition calculation and output instructions.

The matching records processing logic used when two input (or update or combined) files are accessed by one matching field is detailed in the flowchart shown in Figure 14-9.

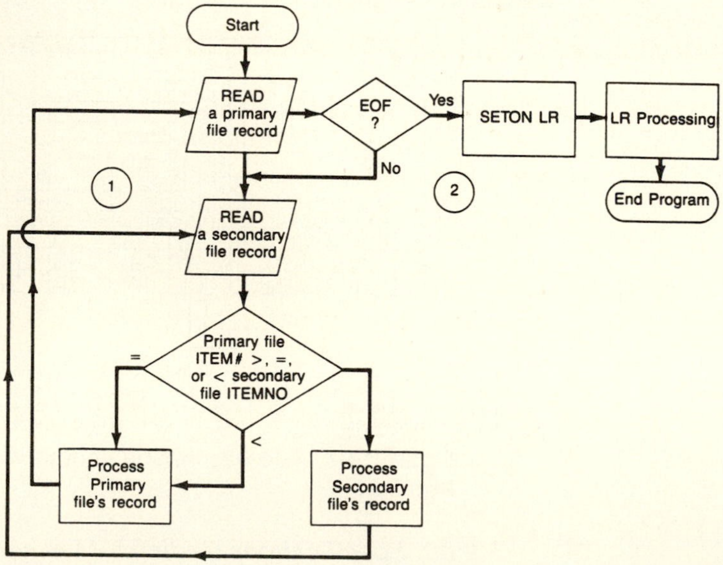

Notes:

1. One record is read from each file before matching records processing is executed. If matching records was not specified in the program, all of the records from the primary file would be processed before a record was read from the secondary file.

2. If E (END OF FILE) is specified in column 17 of the File Description Specifications for one of the files, job will end when end of that file is tested. Because E was specified for the primary file (CONSOLE), job will end when the operator enters the related end of file control command key. If E was not specified for any of the files used in Matching Records processing, both files will be processed to the end before job is ended.

Figure 14-9 Matching records processing logic used when two files are accessed by one matching field.

Exactly how the records from two files are processed under matching records control is further detailed in Figure 14-10. Because the files are sorted in an ascending item number order, the processing logic is identical to that shown in the flowchart in Figure 14-9.

```
        Primary File              Secondary File (Sequential Master File)
        CONSOLE Input                        (Stored On Disk)

First ITEM#
 Input ——►0002          0001BOUNTY PAPER TOWELS      61101901440000400000005760◄——First Record
          0005          0002MARCAL PAPER TOWELS      6110190360000041000014760
          0008         A0003GRAND UNION PAPER TOWELS 6113090240000039000009360
          0011          0004VANITY FAIR PAPER TOWELS 9110390060000039000002340
          0013         A0005BRAVO PAPER TOWELS       7113090720000028000020169
                        0007KLEENEX PAPER TOWELS     1111090048000045000002160
                        0008SCOTT'S PAPER TOWELS     4111590240000050000012000
                        0010HUDSON PAPER TOWELS      7112590072000054000003888
                        0011NORTHERN PAPER TOWELS    2112890120000060000007200
                        0015A & P PAPER TOWELS       1113090480000029000013920
                       A0019ECONOMY PAPER TOWELS     4112890120000022000002640

Processing Order:

Rule 1:  If the files are in ascending matching field(s) order and there is no
         match, the record with the lowest matching field value is processed first.

                    Primary File                  Secondary File

                     0002                         0001◄————No match will process
                                                           this record first. An-
                                                           other record is read
                                                           from this file

Rule 2:  If files are in ascending matching field(s) order and there is a match between
       • matching field(s) values, the primary record is selected for processing first.

                    Primary File                  Secondary File

  Match processes ►0002                          0002◄——After primary record is
  primary record                                        processed, this record
  first, then next                                      will be processed if
  record is read                                        value is lower than
  from primary file                                     primary record matching
                                                        file value

  Record order in which the files are processed (P preceding the item number indicates
  primary file record and S secondary).

     S0001, P0002, S0002, S0003, S0004, P0005, S0005, S0007, P0008, S0008, S0010, P0011,
     S0011, P0013, S0015, and S0019

  Note:  If the files were sorted in a descending order, the record with the highest
         value in the matching field would be processed first.
```

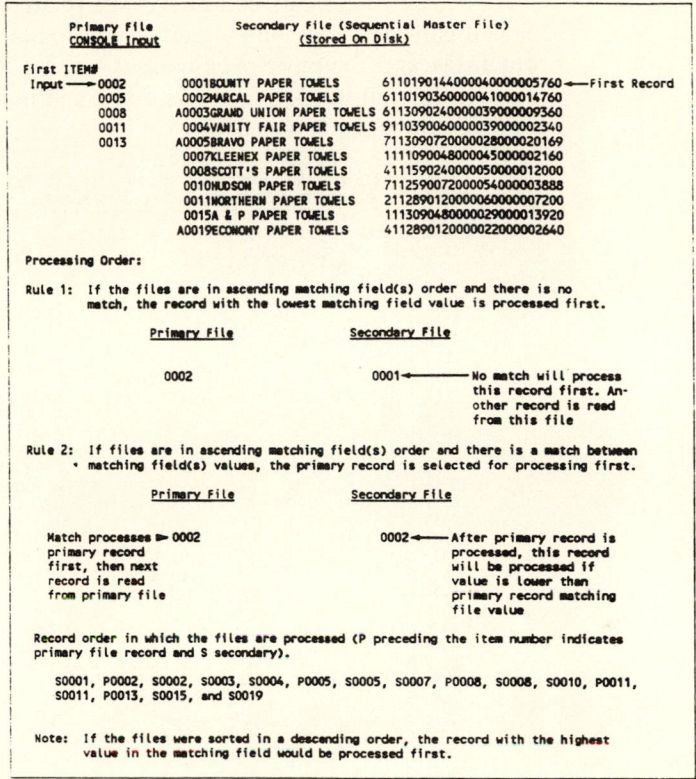

Figure 14-10 Processing sequence of the two input files processed by the master file inquiry program.

Matching Record Syntax Rules

Figure 14-11 lists the rules unique to matching record processing.

```
 1. One or more fields or entire records may be used in a match.

 2. A maximum of nine match fields may be specified in a program by the
    assignment of M1 through M9 to the related fields.

 3. All match fields must be the same length and type. In other words,
    the fields assigned M1 must be the same; the fields assigned M2,
    identical, etc. However, the size and type of each match group (M1,
    M2, and M3) may differ.

 4. The match fields may be in different locations in each of the file's
    records. Field names in the related records do not have to be the same.

 5. When numeric fields that include decimal positions are matched, they
    are processed as integers-not decimal numbers.

 6. The sign of a match field value is ignored. Negative numbers are
    processed as positive. Packed fields may be specified in a match
    but not binary.

 7. When one or more matching field values included in two or more files
    are equal (match), the MR (matching record) indicator is automatically
    turned on. The MR indicator may be used to condition subsequent calcu-
    lations and/or output.

 8. M1 through M9 are usually assigned according to the largest match field.
    For example, M1 would be assigned to TOWN, M2 to COUNTY, and M3 to STATE
    if those three fields were used in a match between two or more files.

 9. If more than one matching field is specified, they are treated as one
    continuous field in a descending sequence. Meaning that the M3 field
    value would be placed in the high order position of the continuous field,
    M2 the middle, and the M1 value stored in the low-order bytes. All of the
    matching field values must be in one group when equal the related fields
    in the other matching group to turn on the MR indicator.

10. Not all files or records within a file input by a program have to be
    included in the matching record process.
```

Figure 14-11 Matching Record Processing Rules.

Source Program for Item Master File Inquiry

A source listing of the Item Master File Inquiry program is presented in Figure 14-12. The syntax unique to Matching Records processing is identified by comments. The matching records syntax related to the File Description and Input Specifications forms has already been explained in Figures 14-6 and 14-7. Calculations and Output Specifications coding that supports matching record processing related to file inquiry is discussed in the following paragraphs.

```
... ... 1 ... ... 2 ... ... 3 ... ... 4 ... ... 5 ... ... 6 ... ..
 * THIS PROGRAM PROCESSES A SEQUENTIAL DISK FILE RANDOMLY FOR
 * INQUIRY USING THE MATCHING RECORDS METHOD.................
H
FITEMNOS IP AF   5   5             CONSOLE
FSEQ14P1 IS AF 240  48             DISK
FITEMINFOO   F 132 132             PRINTER
IITEMNOS SM  01   1 CI                                          CH14P1
I                                      1   1 IDCODE
I                                      2   5 ITEMNO  M1
ISEQ14P1 SM  02
I                                      1   1 TCODE
I                                      2   5 ITEM#   M1
I                                      6  30 NAME
I                                     31  31 VENDR#
I                                     32  370PDATE
I                                   P 38  390QTY                CH14P1
I                                   P 40  432COST               CH14P1
I                                   P 44  482AMOUNT             CH14P1
C   MR 02   TCODE     COMP 'D'                  10              CH14P1
OITEMINFOD  301   MR 02                                         CH14P1
O       OR        01NMR                                         CH14P1
O                                   37 'ITEM MASTER FILE INQUIRY'   CH14P1
O                           UDATE Y 51                          CH14P1
O          D  2   MR 02
O                                    8 'ITEM#'
O                                   27 'ITEM NAME'
O                                   48 'VENDOR#'
O          D      MR 02
O       OR        01NMR
O                           ITEMNO   7
O                 02 MR     NAME    36
O                 02 MR     VENDR#  45
O                 01NMR             36 '.....ITEM NOT FOUND.....'   CH14P1
O          D 11   MR 02                                         CH14P1
O                                   11 'PURCHASE'               CH14P1
O                                   32 'COST'                   CH14P1
O                                   47 'TOTAL $'                CH14P1
O          D  2   MR 02                                         CH14P1
O                                    9 'DATE'                   CH14P1
O                                   20 'QTY'                    CH14P1
O                                   34 'PER ITEM'               CH14P1
O                                   46 'AMOUNT'                 CH14P1
O          D  3   MR 02                                         CH14P1
O                           PDATE Y 11                          CH14P1
O                           QTY   Z 20                          CH14P1
O                           COST  1 33                          CH14P1
O                           AMOUNT1 51                          CH14P1
O          D  0   MR 02                                         CH14P1
O                                   29 'ITEM DELETED?:'         CH14P1
O                    10             33 'YES'                    CH14P1
O                   N10             33 'NO '                    CH14P1
```

E in column 17 of primary file indicates that processing will stop when end of this file is tested.

Matching fields that relate the primary and secondary files. When the field values are equal, MR indicator is automatically turned on.

MR amd 02 (secondary file indicator) condition output for a matching record condition. NMR and 01 (primary file indicator) condition output for a "no match" condition.

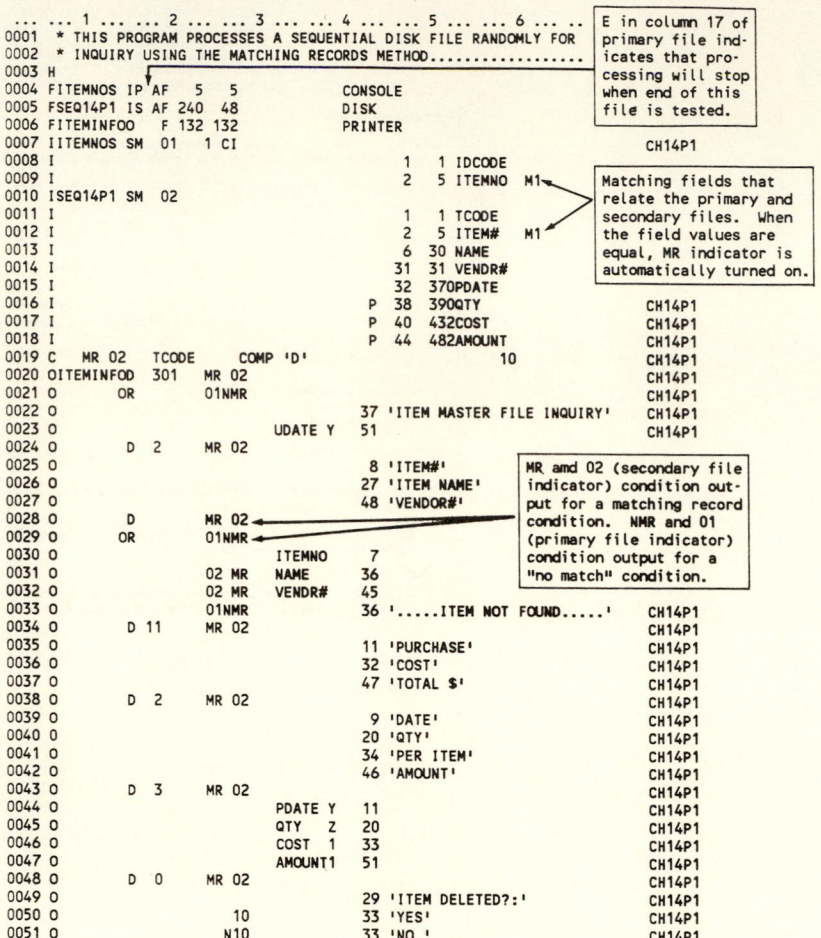

Figure 14-12 Source listing of the Item Master File Inquiry program.

Calculation Coding for Inquiry Program

The one calculation instruction included in the Item Master File Inquiry program is shown in Figure 14-13. Examine the coding and notice that the statement is executed only if both the MR and 02 indicators are on. Indicator 02 must be used because this is the record (item master file) from which the data is to be extracted when a match is tested. If indicator 01, assigned to the primary file (CONSOLE), was specified instead, or if MR was used alone, uncertain processing results could occur.

An understanding of when an indicator is on and why it is important is necessary to the use of matching records as a processing alternative. Any doubts about what indicators are on during the processing cycle for any program may be checked by the use of one or more DEBUG operations.

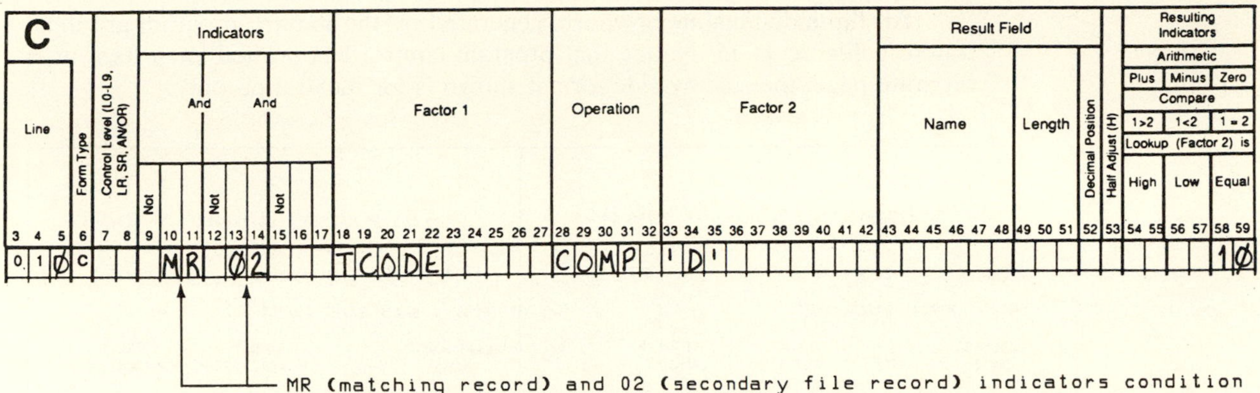

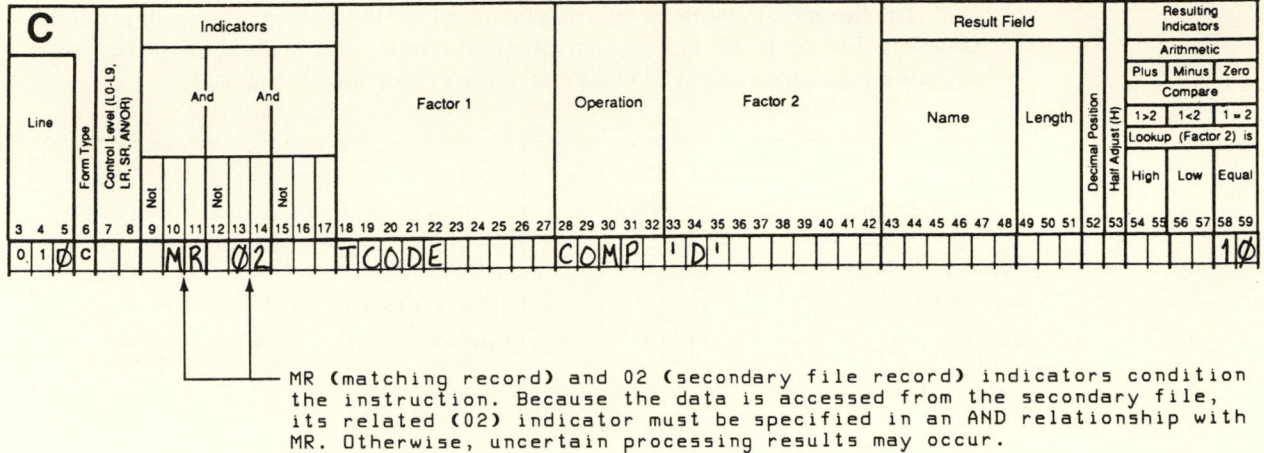

MR (matching record) and 02 (secondary file record) indicators condition the instruction. Because the data is accessed from the secondary file, its related (02) indicator must be specified in an AND relationship with MR. Otherwise, uncertain processing results may occur.

COMP test is included to check the status of the transaction code field. Result of test determines whether YES or NO is printed for the ITEM DELETED response on the report.

Figure 14-13 Calculation instruction included in the Item Master File Inquiry program.

Output Coding for Inquiry Program

The same reasoning for the assignment of the MR and 02 indicators to condition the calculation instruction applies to output control. However, an examination of the output coding in Figure 14-14 also indicates that two detail lines are conditioned by the 01 and NMR indicators to provide for alternative processing if a *no-match condition occurs*.

```
0020 OITEMINFOD  301 ->MR 02                                         CH14P1
0021 O        OR        01NMR<-                                      CH14P1
0022 O                                  37 'ITEM MASTER FILE INQUIRY'   CH14P1
0023 O                         UDATE Y  51                              CH14P1
0024 O          D  2  ->MR 02                                        CH14P1
0025 O                                   8 'ITEM#'                      CH14P1
0026 O                                  27 'ITEM NAME'                  CH14P1
0027 O                                  48 'VENDOR#'                    CH14P1
0028 O          D     ->MR 02                                        CH14P1
0029 O        OR        01NMR<-                                      CH14P1
0030 O                         ITEMNO    7                              CH14P1
0031 O                ->02 MR  NAME     36                              CH14P1
0032 O                ->02 MR  VENDR#   45                              CH14P1
0033 O                  01NMR<-         36 '.....ITEM NOT FOUND.....'   CH14P1
0034 O          D 11    MR 02                                        CH14P1
0035 O                                  11 'PURCHASE'                   CH14P1
0036 O                                  32 'COST'                       CH14P1
0037 O                                  47 'TOTAL $'                    CH14P1
0038 O          D  2  ->MR 02                                        CH14P1
0039 O                                   9 'DATE'                       CH14P1
0040 O                                  20 'QTY'                        CH14P1
0041 O                                  34 'PER ITEM'                   CH14P1
0042 O                                  46 'AMOUNT'                     CH14P1
0043 O          D  3  ->MR 02                                        CH14P1
0044 O                         PDATE Y  11                              CH14P1
0045 O                         QTY   Z  20                              CH14P1
0046 O                         COST  1  33                              CH14P1
0047 O                         AMOUNT1  51                              CH14P1
0048 O          D  0  ->MR 02                                        CH14P1
0049 O                                  29 'ITEM DELETED?:'             CH14P1
0050 O                     10           33 'YES'                        CH14P1
0051 O                    N10           33 'NO '                        CH14P1
```

MR and 02 indicators condition output when a match is found between the matching fields

01 and NMR indicators condition output when a match is not found between the matching fields

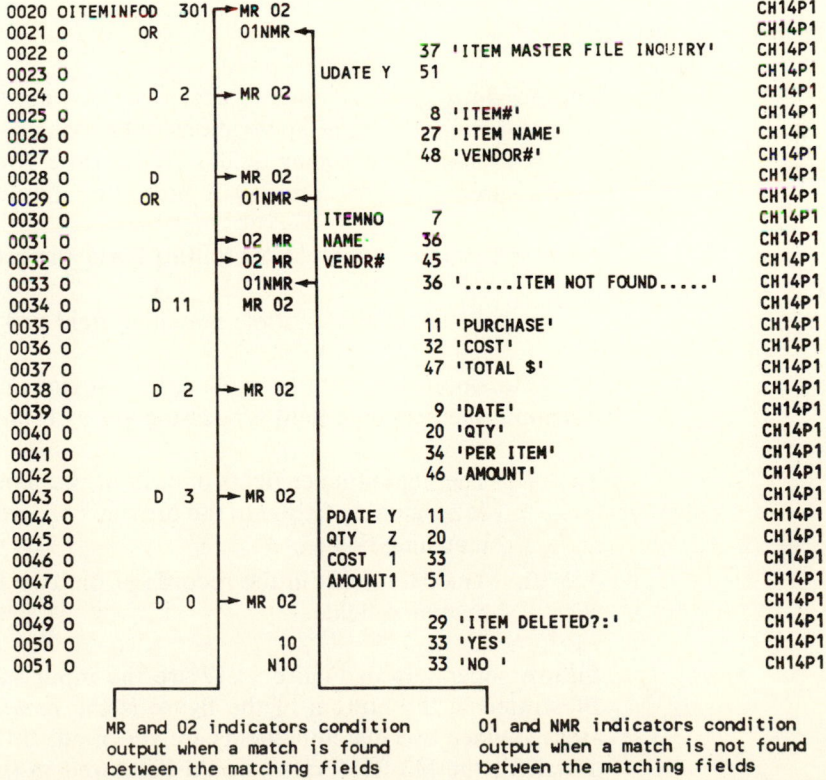

Figure 14-14 Output coding for the Item Master File Inquiry program.

All the individual item reports generated by the inquiry program are illustrated in Figure 14-15. Notice that program control has printed each item on a separate page; the side-by-side format shown is for illustration only.

```
          ITEM MASTER FILE INQUIRY        12/30/90

ITEM#          ITEM NAME                VENDOR#

0002   MARCAL PAPER TOWELS                 6

PURCHASE                  COST          TOTAL $
 DATE         QTY       PER ITEM        AMOUNT

11/01/90      360          .41              147.60

            ITEM DELETED?: NO
```

```
          ITEM MASTER FILE INQUIRY        12/30/90

ITEM#          ITEM NAME                VENDOR#

0005   BRAVO PAPER TOWELS                  7

PURCHASE                  COST          TOTAL $
 DATE         QTY       PER ITEM        AMOUNT

11/30/90      144          .28               40.32

            ITEM DELETED?: NO
```

```
          ITEM MASTER FILE INQUIRY        12/30/90

ITEM#          ITEM NAME                VENDOR#

0011   NORTHERN PAPER TOWELS               2

PURCHASE                  COST          TOTAL $
 DATE         QTY       PER ITEM        AMOUNT

11/28/90      120          .61               73.20

            ITEM DELETED?: NO
```

```
          ITEM MASTER FILE INQUIRY        12/30/90

0013      .....ITEM NOT FOUND.....
```

Figure 14-15 Item reports generated by the Item Master File Inquiry program.

MULTIPLE MATCHING FIELDS

The previous program random accessed the item master file (inquiry) with one matching field. For some applications, it may be necessary to process two or more files with multiple matching fields. To illustrate how multiple matching fields are used in processing, the previously presented inquiry program is modified.

Source Coding—Multiple Matching Field Program

A source listing of the multiple matching field program is detailed in Figure 14-16.

The only modifications made to the previous matching field program to support multiple matching field processing are as follows:

1. The item number fields in each of the input file records are assigned as M2 matching fields. In the previous program, they were specified as M1 matching fields.
2. The date fields in the records of the two input files are assigned as M1 matching fields.

Shown separately in Figure 14-17 are the input specifications for the program. Illustrated at the bottom of the figure is the *concatenated* structure created in storage when two matching fields are specified. If three matching fields had been assigned, the M3 field value would be stored in the high-order positions of the *composite* field, M2 in the middle position, and M1 in the low-order position.

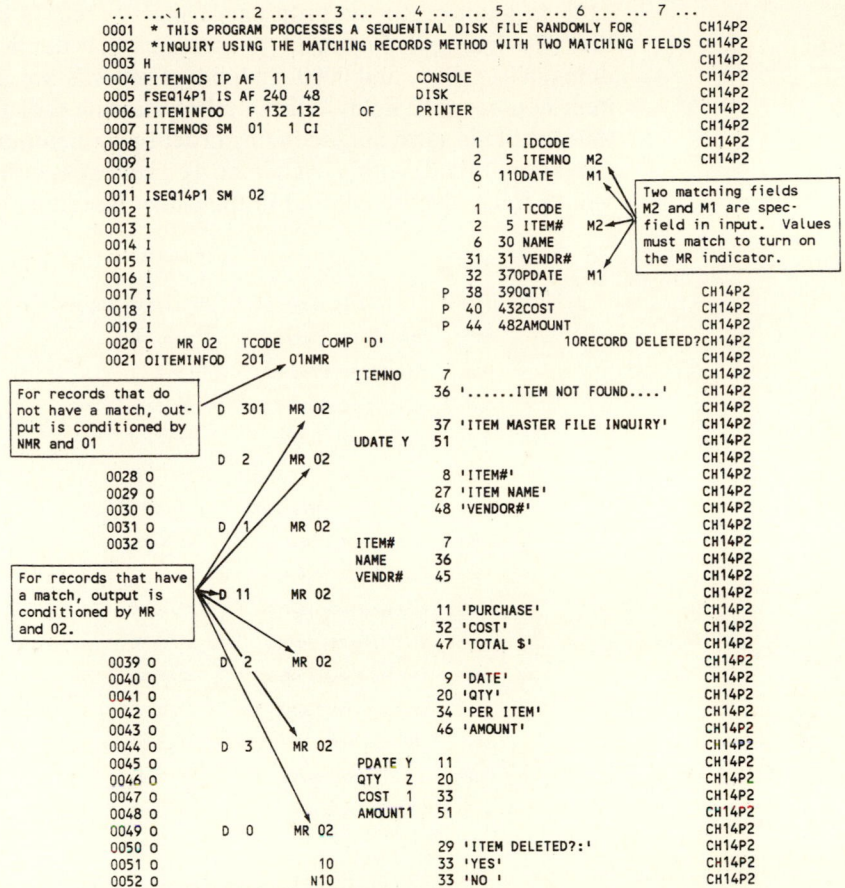

```
... ...\1 ... ... 2 ... ... 3 ... ... 4 ... ... 5 ... ... 6 ... ... 7 ...
0001  * THIS PROGRAM PROCESSES A SEQUENTIAL DISK FILE RANDOMLY FOR       CH14P2
0002  *INQUIRY USING THE MATCHING RECORDS METHOD WITH TWO MATCHING FIELDS CH14P2
0003 H                                                                   CH14P2
0004 FITEMNOS IP AF  11  11           CONSOLE                            CH14P2
0005 FSEQ14P1 IS AF 240  48           DISK                               CH14P2
0006 FITEMINFOO   F 132 132     OF    PRINTER                            CH14P2
0007 IITEMNOS SM  01   1 CI                                              CH14P2
0008 I                                        1   1 IDCODE               CH14P2
0009 I                                        2   5 ITEMNO  M2           CH14P2
0010 I                                        6  110DATE    M1
0011 ISEQ14P1 SM  02
0012 I                                        1   1 TCODE
0013 I                                        2   5 ITEM#   M2
0014 I                                        6  30 NAME
0015 I                                       31  31 VENDR#
0016 I                                       32  370PDATE   M1
0017 I                                     P 38  390QTY                  CH14P2
0018 I                                     P 40  432COST                 CH14P2
0019 I                                     P 44  482AMOUNT               CH14P2
0020 C   MR 02    TCODE     COMP 'D'                 10RECORD DELETED?CH14P2
0021 OITEMINFOD  201   01NMR                                             CH14P2
                                 ITEMNO     7                            CH14P2
                                           36 '......ITEM NOT FOUND....' CH14P2
           D  301   MR 02                                                CH14P2
                                           37 'ITEM MASTER FILE INQUIRY' CH14P2
                                 UDATE Y   51                            CH14P2
           D  2     MR 02                                                CH14P2
0028 O                                      8 'ITEM#'                    CH14P2
0029 O                                     27 'ITEM NAME'                CH14P2
0030 O                                     48 'VENDOR#'                  CH14P2
0031 O     D  1     MR 02                                                CH14P2
0032 O                           ITEM#      7                            CH14P2
                                 NAME      36                            CH14P2
                                 VENDR#    45                            CH14P2
           D 11     MR 02                                                CH14P2
                                           11 'PURCHASE'                 CH14P2
                                           32 'COST'                     CH14P2
                                           47 'TOTAL $'                  CH14P2
0039 O     D  2     MR 02                                                CH14P2
0040 O                                      9 'DATE'                     CH14P2
0041 O                                     20 'QTY'                      CH14P2
0042 O                                     34 'PER ITEM'                 CH14P2
0043 O                                     46 'AMOUNT'                   CH14P2
0044 O     D  3     MR 02                                                CH14P2
0045 O                           PDATE Y   11                            CH14P2
0046 O                           QTY   Z   20                            CH14P2
0047 O                           COST  1   33                            CH14P2
0048 O                           AMOUNT1   51                            CH14P2
0049 O     D  0     MR 02                                                CH14P2
0050 O                                     29 'ITEM DELETED?:'           CH14P2
0051 O                     10              33 'YES'                      CH14P2
0052 O                    N10              33 'NO '                      CH14P2
```

Two matching fields M2 and M1 are spec-field in input. Values must match to turn on the MR indicator.

For records that do not have a match, output is conditioned by NMR and 01

For records that have a match, output is conditioned by MR and 02.

Figure 14-16 Source listing of multiple matching field program.

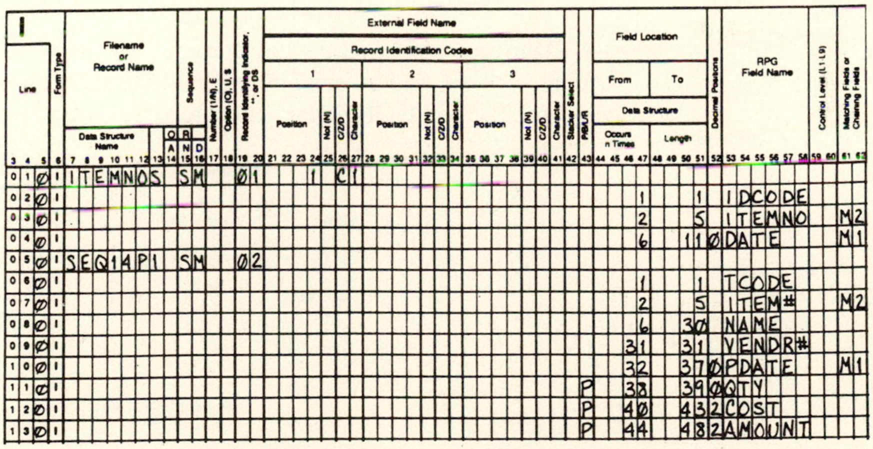

ITEMNOS File		SEQ13P1 File	
Matching Fields	Values	Matching Fields	Values
ITEMNO	0005	ITEM#	0005
DATE	121490	PDATE	121490

Matching field values are concatenated in storage with M2 value high-order bytes and M1 value in low-order bytes as follows:

```
0005121490                  0005121490
↑   ↑                       ↑   ↑
|   └─DATE                  |   └─PDATE
└─────ITEMNO                └─────ITEM#
```

Figure 14-17 Input specifications coding and matching field storage structure for the multiple matching field program.

In addition to the program changes, records have been added to the data file. The listing in Figure 14-18 indicates that duplicate records are included for items 0001, 0005, and 0008. Individual records are accessed from the file by the item number (M2 field) and the purchase date (M1 field) data items. Also notice that the file is sorted in ascending order by item number (major field) and purchase date (minor field) within each item. To prevent a runtime abort or halt, CONSOLE values must also be entered in the same ascending order.

12/30/90 ITEM LISTING PAGE 1
51:22

ITEM#	ITEM NAME	DATE	VENDOR#	QTY	COST/ITEM	DOLLAR AMT
0001	BOUNTY PAPER TOWELS	11/01/90	6	144	.40	57.60
0001	BOUNTRY PAPER TOWELS	12/22/90	6	840	.43	361.20
0001	BOUNTY PAPER TOWELS	12/05/90	6	960	.42	403.20
0002	MARCAL PAPER TOWELS	11/01/90	6	360	.41	147.60
0003	GRAND UNION PAPER TOWELS	11/30/90	6	240	.39	93.60
0004	VANITY FAIR PAPER TOWELS	11/03/90	9	60	.39	23.40
0005	BRAVO PAPER TOWELS	11/30/90	7	720	.28	201.60
0005	BRAVO PAPER TOWELS	12/14/90	7	120	.31	37.20
0007	KLEENEX PAPER TOWELS	11/10/90	1	48	.45	21.60
0008	SCOTT'S PAPER TOWELS	11/15/90	4	240	.50	120.00
0008	SCOTT'S PAPER TOWELS	12/20/90	4	480	.51	244.80
0010	HUDSON PAPER TOWELS	11/25/90	7	72	.54	38.88
0011	NORTHERN PAPER TOWELS	11/28/90	2	120	.60	72.00
0015	A & P PAPER TOWELS	11/30/90	1	480	.29	139.20
0019	ECONOMY PAPER TOWELS	11/28/90	4	120	.22	26.40

File is sorted in ascending order by item number (major field) and purchase date (minor field) within each related item.

Figure 14-18 Input data file processed by multiple matching fields program.

Two reports generated by the multiple matching fields program are shown in Figure 14-19. Again, remember that the item number and purchase date values were entered via CONSOLE input to access the related master records.

```
               ITEM MASTER FILE INQUIRY      12/31/90

ITEM#            ITEM NAME                 VENDOR#

0001     BOUNTY PAPER TOWELS                  6

PURCHASE                    COST           TOTAL $
  DATE          QTY       PER ITEM         AMOUNT

11/01/90        144          .40               57.60

                 ITEM DELETED?: NO
 - - - - - - - - - - - - - - - - - - - - - - - - - - -
               ITEM MASTER FILE INQUIRY      12/31/90

ITEM#            ITEM NAME                 VENDOR#

0005     BRAVO PAPER TOWELS                   7

PURCHASE                    COST           TOTAL $
  DATE          QTY       PER ITEM         AMOUNT

12/14/90        120          .31               37.20

                 ITEM DELETED?: NO
```

Figure 14-19 Reports generated by multiple matching fields program.

APPLICATION PROGRAM—FILE UPDATE WITH MATCHING RECORDS METHOD

Documentation

The specifications presented in Figure 14-20 explain the input, processing, and output requirements for an application program that updates a sequential disk file by the matching records method.

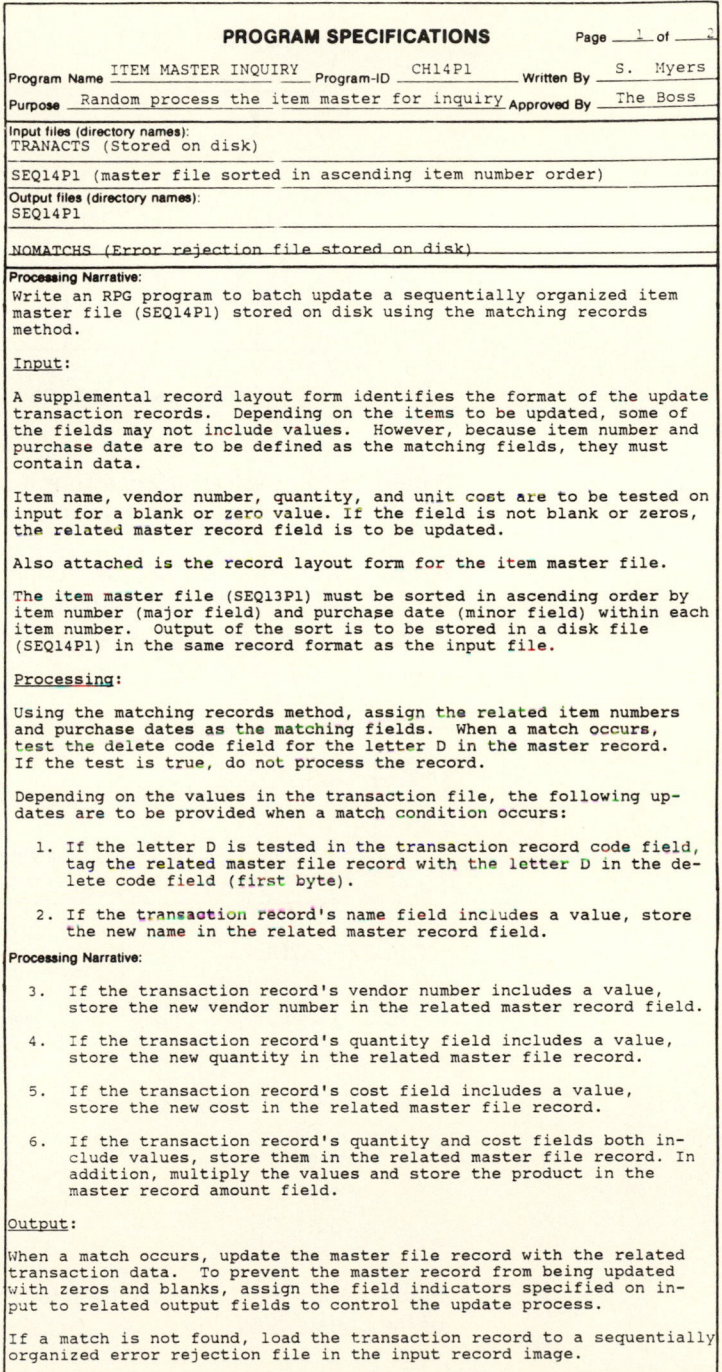

PROGRAM SPECIFICATIONS Page 1 of 2

Program Name ITEM MASTER INQUIRY Program-ID CH14P1 Written By S. Myers

Purpose Random process the item master for inquiry Approved By The Boss

Input files (directory names):
TRANACTS (Stored on disk)

SEQ14P1 (master file sorted in ascending item number order)

Output files (directory names):
SEQ14P1

NOMATCHS (Error rejection file stored on disk)

Processing Narrative:

Write an RPG program to batch update a sequentially organized item master file (SEQ14P1) stored on disk using the matching records method.

Input:

A supplemental record layout form identifies the format of the update transaction records. Depending on the items to be updated, some of the fields may not include values. However, because item number and purchase date are to be defined as the matching fields, they must contain data.

Item name, vendor number, quantity, and unit cost are to be tested on input for a blank or zero value. If the field is not blank or zeros, the related master record field is to be updated.

Also attached is the record layout form for the item master file.

The item master file (SEQ13P1) must be sorted in ascending order by item number (major field) and purchase date (minor field) within each item number. Output of the sort is to be stored in a disk file (SEQ14P1) in the same record format as the input file.

Processing:

Using the matching records method, assign the related item numbers and purchase dates as the matching fields. When a match occurs, test the delete code field for the letter D in the master record. If the test is true, do not process the record.

Depending on the values in the transaction file, the following updates are to be provided when a match condition occurs:

1. If the letter D is tested in the transaction record code field, tag the related master file record with the letter D in the delete code field (first byte).
2. If the transaction record's name field includes a value, store the new name in the related master record field.

Processing Narrative:

3. If the transaction record's vendor number includes a value, store the new vendor number in the related master record field.
4. If the transaction record's quantity field includes a value, store the new quantity in the related master file record.
5. If the transaction record's cost field includes a value, store the new cost in the related master file record.
6. If the transaction record's quantity and cost fields both include values, store them in the related master file record. In addition, multiply the values and store the product in the master record amount field.

Output:

When a match occurs, update the master file record with the related transaction data. To prevent the master record from being updated with zeros and blanks, assign the field indicators specified on input to related output fields to control the update process.

If a match is not found, load the transaction record to a sequentially organized error rejection file in the input record image.

Figure 14-20 Specifications for an application program that updates a sequential disk file by the matching records method.

The system flowchart in Figure 14-21 indicates that the item master file is sorted and that the output file generated is processed by the update program. A transaction disk file includes the data that is used to *batch* update the item master file. The double-headed arrow connecting the file to the program indicates that the item master file (SEQ14P1) is an input and output (I/O) file. A matched item master file record is accessed by the program, modified, and then stored back in its same disk location.

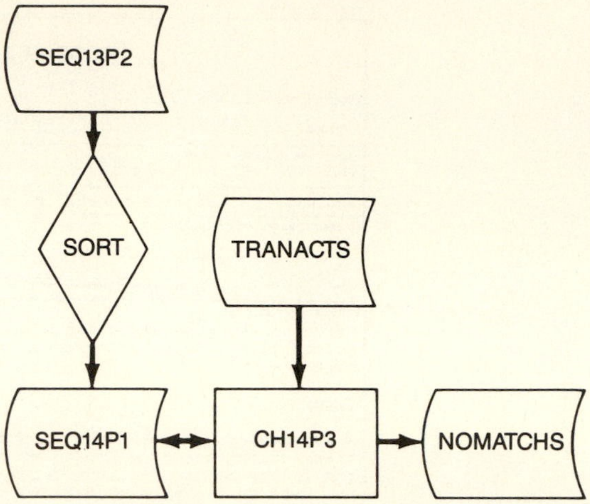

Figure 14-21 System flowchart for a program that batch updates the item master file by the matching records method.

A record layout form for the transaction file and a listing of the update data are included in Figure 14-22. Other than the matching fields (item number and purchase date), data included is only in fields that are to update the related master record.

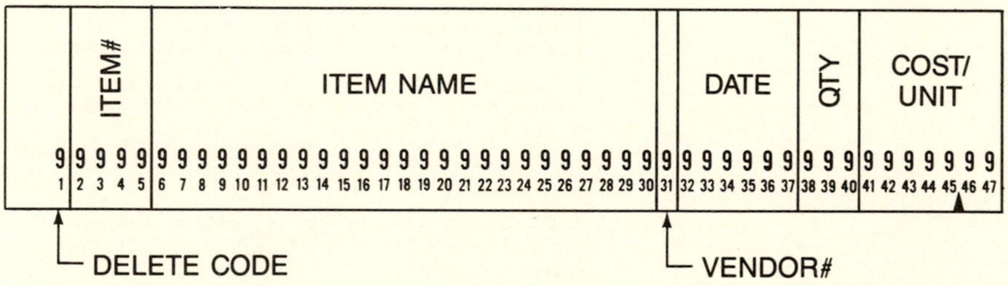


```
       Code  Item#         Name          Vendor#  Date    Qty   Cost
Cols   1-1   2-5           6-30          31-31    32-37   38-40 41-47

             0001  BOUNTY PAPER TOWELS            122290
       D     0003                                 113090
             0005                                 113090  144
             0007                                2 111090
             0011                                 112890        0000061
             0019                                 112890  108   0000023
```

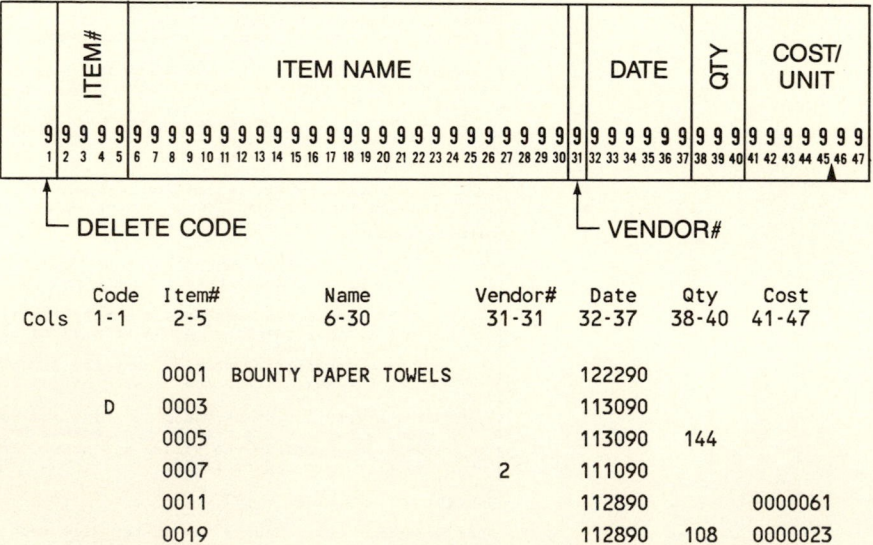

Figure 14-22 Record layout form for the transaction file and listing of the update data.

The file definition of the item master file is presented in Figure 14-23. Notice that item number and purchase date are to be specified as the matching fields in the program.

FILE DEFINITION

SYSTEM Yours		DRAWN BY S. Myers	
FILE NAME SEQ14P1		DATE 12/31/90	REV. NO. 0
CREATED BY S. Myers		FILE TYPE Disk	
RECORD NAME None		KEY LENGTH None	
RECORDING MODE Fixed	ORGANIZATION Sequential	SEQUENCE Soted (A order)	
RECORD SIZE 48 bytes	BLOCKING FACTOR 5	BLOCKSIZE 240 bytes	

FIELD DATA

FIELD NO.	FIELD NAME - DESCRIPTION	SIZE	CLASS C/P/Z/B	POSITION FROM	POSITION THRU	FORMAT/CONSTANT
1	Delete Code	1	C	1	1	D if deleted
2	Item Number	4	C	2	5	M2 field
3	Item Name	25	C	6	30	
4	Vendor Number	1	C	31	31	
5	Purchase Date	6	Z	32	37	M1 field
6	Quantity	3	P	38	39	0 decimal positions
7	Cost Per Unit	7	P	40	43	2 decimal positions
8	Dollar Amount	9	P	44	48	2 decimal positions

Figure 14-23 File definition of the item master file—file to be updated by matching records program.

Source Program Coding

A source program listing of the program that updates a sequential file by the matching records method is shown in Figure 14-24. The syntax related to update processing is detailed in separate figures.

```
... ... 1 ... ... 2 ... ... 3 ... ... 4 ... ... 5 ... ... 6 ... ... 7 ...
 * THIS PROGRAM BATCH UPDATES A SEQUENTIAL DISK FILE BY THE          CH14P3
 * MATCHING RECORDS METHOD WITH TWO MATCHING FIELDS                  CH14P3
H                                                                    CH14P3
FTRANACTSIP AF  47  47            DISK                               CH14P3
FSEQ14P1 US AF 240  48            DISK                               CH14P3
FNOMATCHSO   F  47  47            DISK                               CH14P3
ITRANACTSSM  01                                                      CH14P3
I                                        1   1 TCODE                 CH14P3
I                                        2   5 ITEMNO  M2            CH14P3
I                                        6  30 TNAME           20    CH14P3
I                                       31  31 TVENDR          21    CH14P3
I                                       32  370TDATE   M1            CH14P3
I                                       38  400TQTY            22    CH14P3
I                                       41  472TCOST           23    CH14P3
I                                        1  47 RECORD                CH14P3
ISEQ14P1 SM  02                                                      CH14P3
I                                        1   1 CODE                  CH14P3
I                                        2   5 ITEM#   M2            CH14P3
I                                        6  30 NAME                  CH14P3
I                                       31  31 VENDR#                CH14P3
I                                       32  370PDATE   M1            CH14P3
I                                    P  38  390QTY                   CH14P3
I                                    P  40  432COST                  CH14P3
I                                    P  44  482AMOUNT                CH14P3
C                     SETOF                     1011                 CH14P3
C   MR 02   CODE      COMP 'D'                      10MSTR REC DEL?  CH14P3
C   MR 02   TCODE     COMP 'D'                      11DELETE TRANS?  CH14P3
C   10                                                               CH14P3
COR 11                GOTO END                                       CH14P3
C   MR 02N22COST      MULT TQTY      AMOUNT           QTY CHANGE     CH14P3
C   MR 02N23TCOST     MULT QTY       AMOUNT           COST CHANGE    CH14P3
C   MR 02N22                                          COST AND QTY   CH14P3
CANN23      TCOST     MULT TQTY      AMOUNT           CHANGE         CH14P3
C           END       TAG                                            CH14P3
OSEQ14P1 D        02 MR                                              CH14P3
O                    11           1 'D'                              CH14P3
O                   N20   TNAME     30                               CH14P3
O                   N21   TVENDR    31                               CH14P3
O                   N22   TQTY      39P                              CH14P3
O                   N23   TCOST     43P                              CH14P3
O                         AMOUNT    48P                              CH14P3
ONOMATCHSD       NMR 01                                              CH14P3
O                         RECORD    47                               CH14P3
```

Figure 14-24 Source listing of the program that updates a sequential disk file by the matching records method.

File Description Coding

The File Description Specifications form in Figure 14-25 shows that three files are processed by the program. A primary file (TRANACTS) contains the transaction data, an item master file (SEQ14P1) includes records that are to be updated, and an output file (NOMATCHS) contains transaction records that do not have a matching master file record.

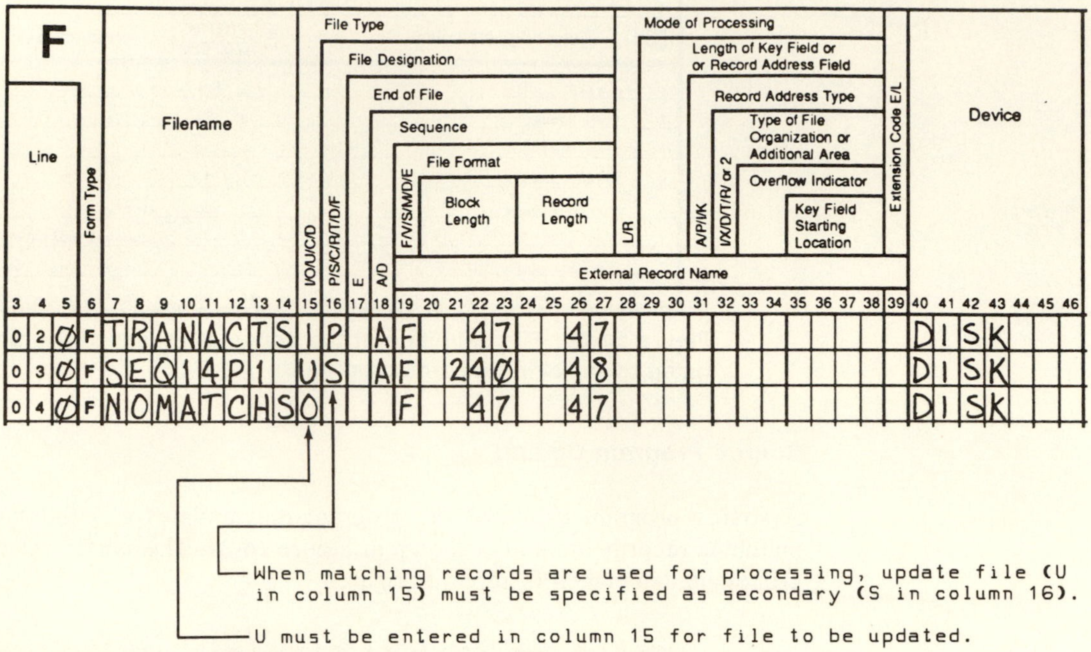

Figure 14-25 File Description Specifications coding for the program that updates a sequential disk file by matching records.

Two important syntax rules that must be followed when a file is to be updated by the matching records method follow:

1. The file must be defined as an update file by specifying the letter U in column 15. This entry indicates that the file is processed as both an input and output file. Consequently, no other file has to be defined as an output file (O in column 15) when one or more files are defined as update to meet minimum processing requirements.
2. The file specified as an update file (U in column 15) must be defined as a secondary file (S in column 16). Otherwise, uncertain processing results may occur.

Input Specifications Coding

Figure 14-26 illustrates the input coding included in the example update program. An examination of the input coding in Figure 14-26 indicates that the item number fields in the two record formats are specified as M2 matching fields and the purchase date items specified as M1 fields. When the matching field values in the transaction and master file records match, indicator MR will automatically turn on. The MR indicator, and the 02 Record Identifying Indicator assigned to the

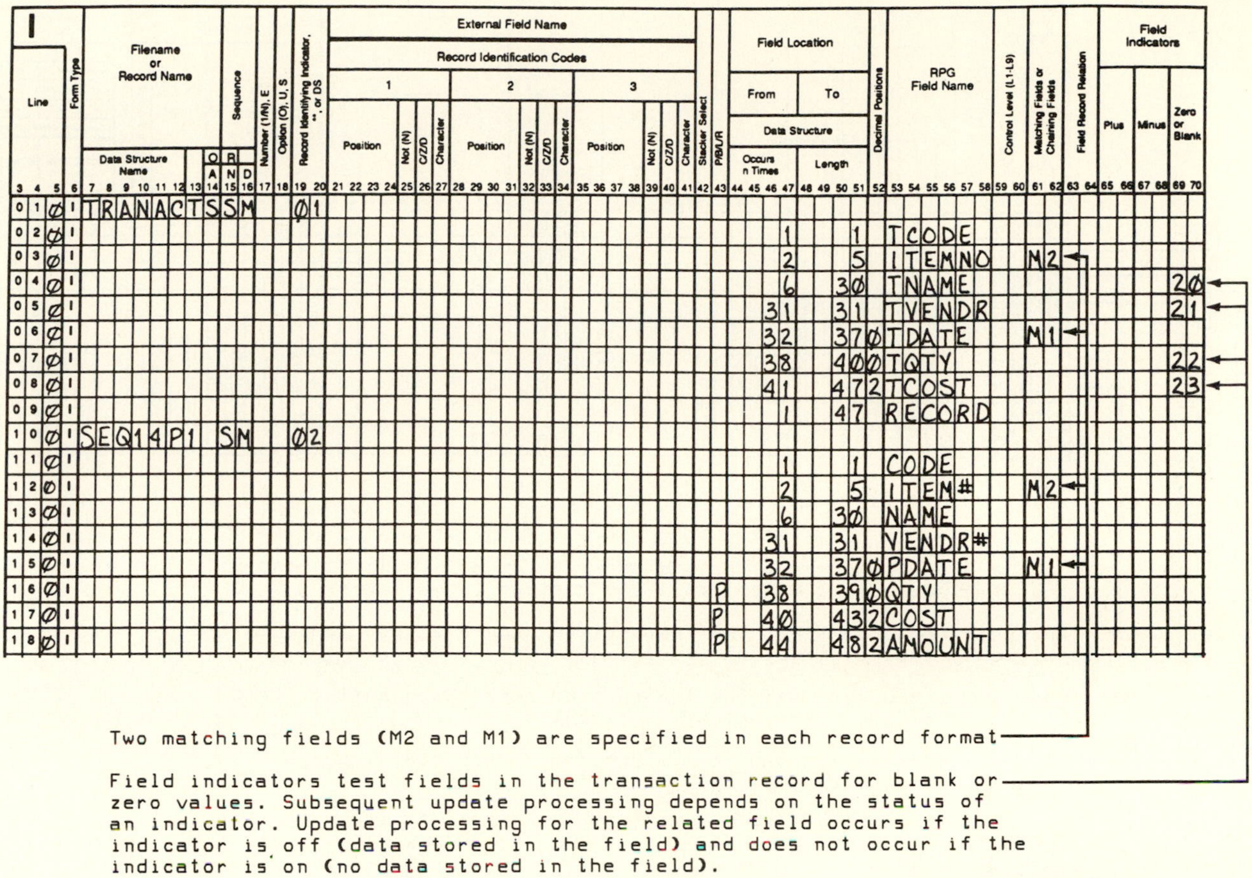
Two matching fields (M2 and M1) are specified in each record format
Field indicators test fields in the transaction record for blank or zero values. Subsequent update processing depends on the status of an indicator. Update processing for the related field occurs if the indicator is off (data stored in the field) and does not occur if the indicator is on (no data stored in the field).

Figure 14-26 Input Specifications coding for the program that updates a sequential disk file by matching records.

master file record format, are used to condition calculation and output instructions.

Field indicators (columns 69–70, blank or zero test) 20, 21, 22, and 23 are included in the definition of TNAME, TVENDR, TQTY, and TCOST fields. When the related field value is zero or blank, the assigned indicator is turned on to condition subsequent calculations and output.

Because QTY, COST, and AMOUNT were packed when the master file was created and loaded, they must be defined as packed (P in column 43) on input. A runtime error, identified as *invalid numeric data*, will be generated if this entry is not made for input fields that were originally loaded as packed.

Calculation Specifications Coding

The calculation instructions included in the item master update program are detailed in Figure 14-27. Notice that with the exception of the GOTO statement, all the statements are conditioned with the MR and 02 indicators. In addition, one or more related Field Indicators have been included. Again, it must be emphasized that the 02 Record Identifying Indicator assigned to the master record and not the 01 indicator specified for the transaction file record format is included with the MR indicator. Otherwise, the master record before or after the one that should be updated may instead be changed.

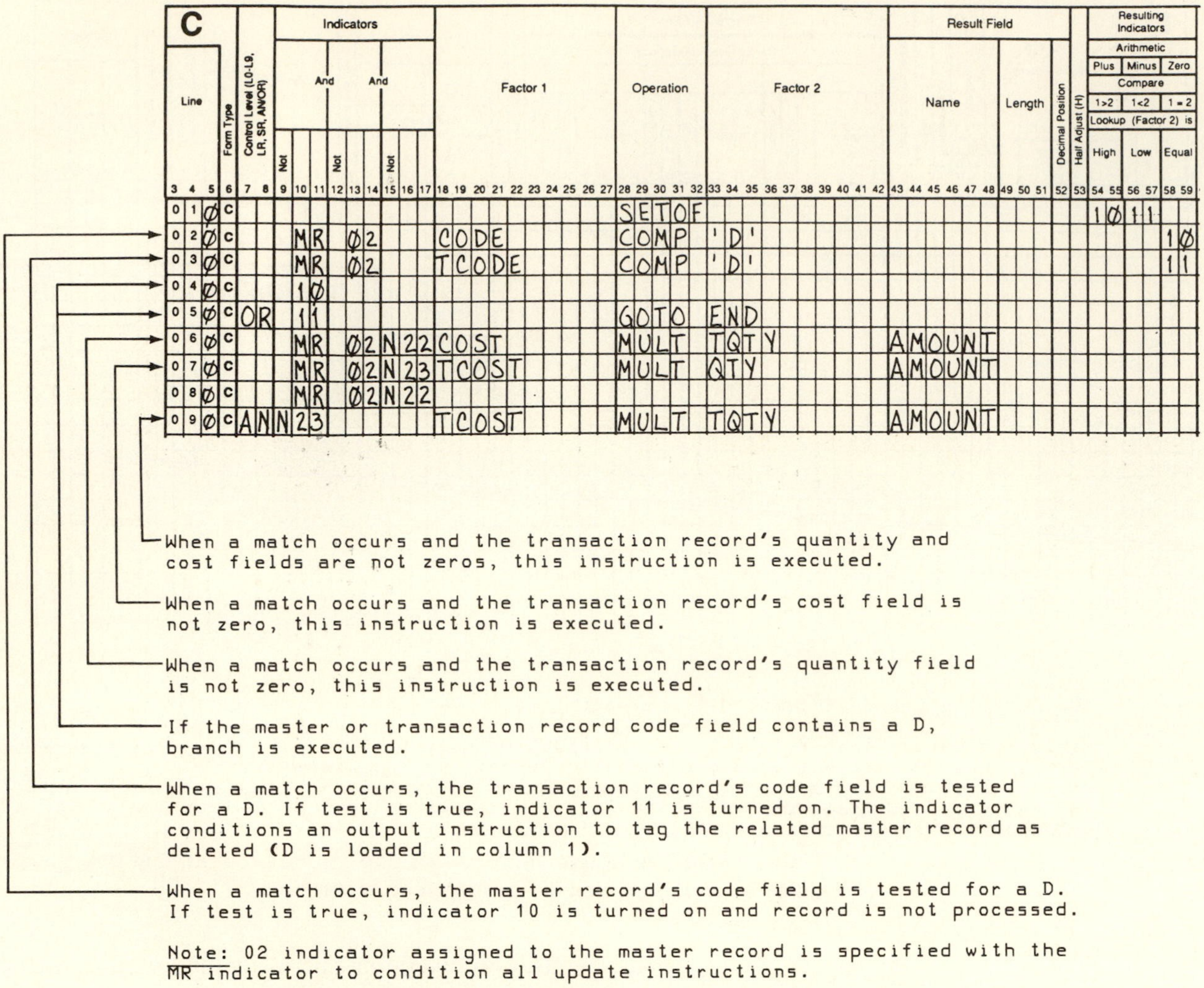

Figure 14-27 Calculation Specifications coding for the program that updates a sequential disk file by matching records.

Output Specifications Coding

The update program's output coding is explained in Figure 14-28. Master file updating is controlled by the MR and 02 indicators in the record description fields and the NOT condition (i.e., N21) of the *Field Indicators* that were specified on input. This control prevents zeros and blanks from being stored in the master record in the update process when the related transaction record's field contains no values.

Another sequential file is specified on output, which is loaded with transaction records that do not have a matching master record. Records are loaded to this file in their input record image.

Record Deletion

Refer back to Figure 14-28 and notice that record deletion is controlled in the program by the Resulting Indicator (11) turned on by a COMP statement which tested the transaction code field for the letter D.

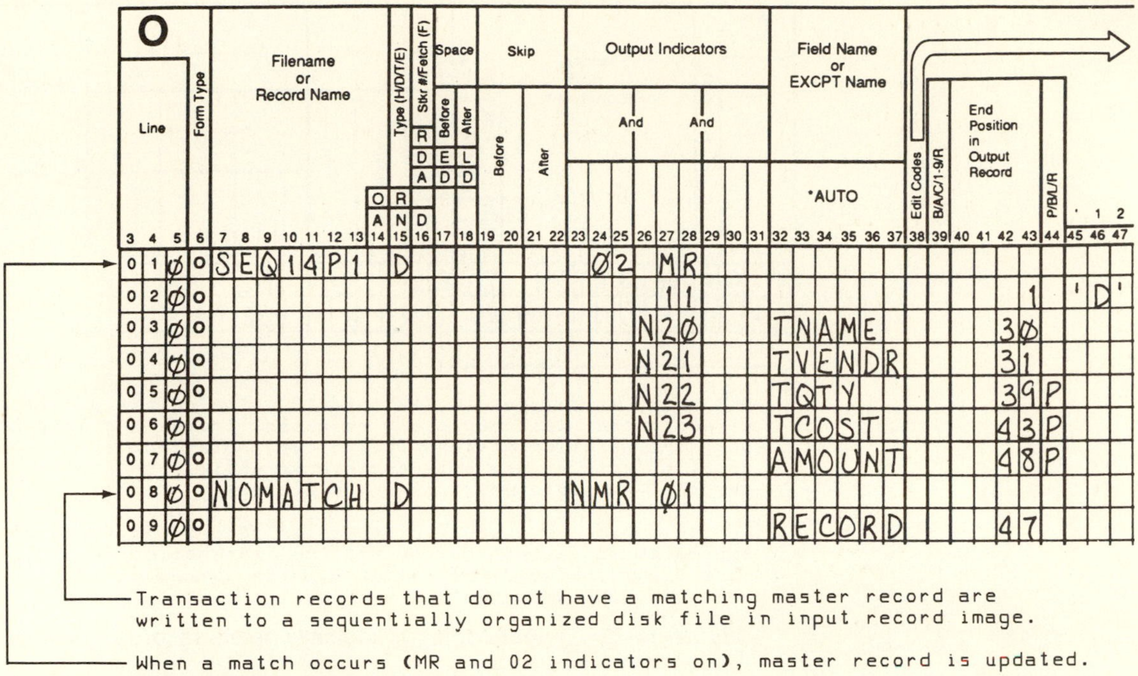

Transaction records that do not have a matching master record are written to a sequentially organized disk file in input record image.

When a match occurs (MR and 02 indicators on), master record is updated.

Indicator control is as follows:

11 - Master record is tagged for deletion
N20 - Master record name field is updated with transaction data
N21 - Master record vendor field is updated with transaction data
N22 - Master record quantity field is updated with transaction data
N23 - Master record cost field is updated with transaction data
- Amount field is either updated or rewritten for all conditions

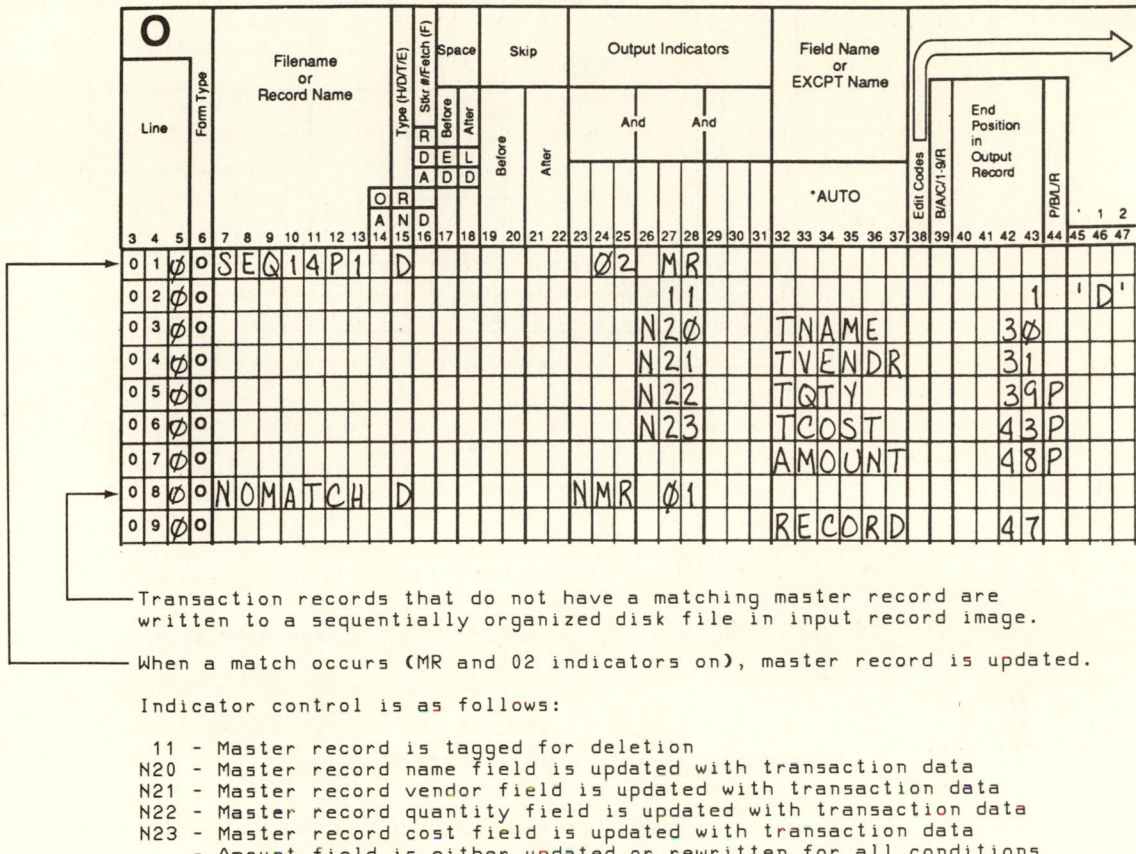

Figure 14-28 Output Specifications coding for the program that updates a sequential disk file by matching records.

Tagging records for deletion is in effect an update process. The related record has to be found and a delete character moved to the allocated delete field in the record. The deletion method shown in the output coding in Figure 14-28 stores the constant D (hard-coded) in the delete field position in the master record. This is in lieu of specifying the transaction record's code field as an output item.

An alternative to the deletion of records by the tagging method is to *logically delete* them. Depending on the computer system, two methods are available. One requires the DELET operation, which is available only on IBM's System/38s and AS/400s series of computers. A record is deleted by storing a *null byte* in the first position of the related record. This operation will be discussed further in Chapter 21.

The other method for the logical deletion of records requires a DEL entry in columns 16, 17, and 18 in the record description coding of an output instruction. Deleted records are filled with hexadecimal FFs. Figure 14-29 illustrates how the output coding from Figure 14-28 must be modified to support logical deletion by the DEL entry. It is important that the correct indicator control be included with the DEL entry, or every record in the file could be deleted when a consecutive mode of processing is specified.

Records logically deleted by DELET operation or DEL output entry are not physically removed from the file but are identified as deleted by one of the procedures previously explained. Records that are logically deleted are no longer available for processing however. With the tagging method, deleted records may still be accessed.

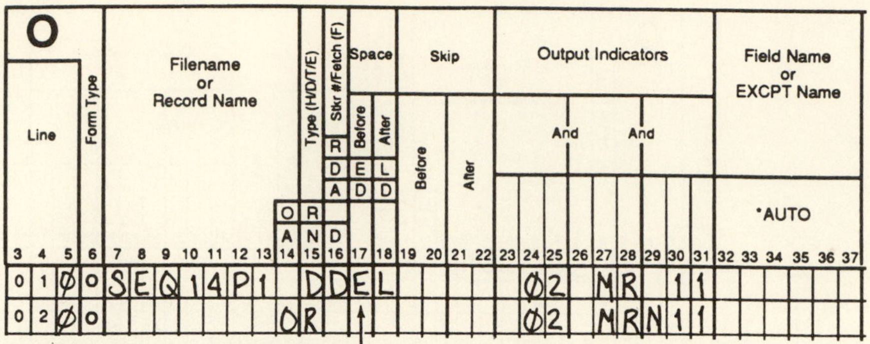

DEL entry in columns 16, 17, and 18 will logically delete a record that was previously accessed. Indicators control when the deletion process will occur. Note that field description entries are not required or valid when a record description statement includes a DEL entry.

For this program example, the master record was found by the matching records method and the transaction record's code field included the letter D which turned on 11 in a previous COMP statement.

Figure 14-29 Output coding to logically delete records by the DEL entry.

Processing Results of the Update Program

The processing results of the matching records update program are shown in the comparative listings in Figure 14-30. Records that have been updated are identified by the arrowheads at the right of each listing. Also notice that the one record that was tagged as deleted (0003 GRAND UNION . . .) is not printed in the updated listing. The program that generated the reports tests the delete code field in the master record; if the letter D is stored in the field, the record is not printed. If the record had been logically deleted, this test would not have been necessary.

Listing of the item master file *before* updating

12/31/90 ITEM LISTING PAGE 1
3:35:57

ITEM#	ITEM NAME	DATE	VENDOR#	QTY	COST/ITEM	DOLLAR AMT	
0001	BOUNTY PAPER TOWELS	11/01/90	6	144	.40	57.60	
0001	BOUNTY PAPER TOWELS	12/05/90	6	960	.42	403.20	
0001	BOUNTRY PAPER TOWELS	12/22/90	6	840	.43	361.20	◄
0002	MARCAL PAPER TOWELS	11/01/90	6	360	.41	147.60	
0003	GRAND UNION PAPER TOWELS	11/30/90	6	240	.39	93.60	
0004	VANITY FAIR PAPER TOWELS	11/03/90	9	60	.39	23.40	
0005	BRAVO PAPER TOWELS	11/30/90	7	720	.28	201.60	◄
0005	BRAVO PAPER TOWELS	12/14/90	7	120	.31	37.20	
0007	KLEENEX PAPER TOWELS	11/10/90	1	48	.45	21.60	◄
0008	SCOTT'S PAPER TOWELS	11/15/90	4	240	.50	120.00	
0008	SCOTT'S PAPER TOWELS	12/20/90	4	480	.51	244.80	
0010	HUDSON PAPER TOWELS	11/25/90	7	72	.54	38.88	
0011	NORTHERN PAPER TOWELS	11/28/90	2	120	.60	72.00	◄
0015	A & P PAPER TOWELS	11/30/90	1	480	.29	139.20	
0019	ECONOMY PAPER TOWELS	11/28/90	4	120	.22	26.40	◄

Figure 14-30 Listings of the item master file before and after updating.

Update data

	Code	Item#	Name	Vendor#	Date	Qty	Cost
Cols	1-1	2-5	6-30	31-31	32-37	38-40	41-47
		0001	BOUNTY PAPER TOWELS		122290		
	D	0003			113090		
		0005			113090	144	
		0007		2	111090		
		0011			112890		0000061
		0019			112890	108	0000023

Listing of the item master file *after* updating

12/31/90 ITEM LISTING PAGE 1
3:02:49

ITEM#	ITEM NAME	DATE	VENDOR#	QTY	COST/ITEM	DOLLAR AMT	
0001	BOUNTY PAPER TOWELS	11/01/90	6	144	.40	57.60	
0001	BOUNTY PAPER TOWELS	12/05/90	6	960	.42	403.20	
0001	BOUNTY PAPER TOWELS	12/22/90	6	840	.43	361.20	◄
0002	MARCAL PAPER TOWELS	11/01/90	6	360	.41	147.60	
0004	VANITY FAIR PAPER TOWELS	11/03/90	9	60	.39	23.40	
0005	BRAVO PAPER TOWELS	11/30/90	7	144	.28	40.32	◄
0005	BRAVO PAPER TOWELS	12/14/90	7	120	.31	37.20	
0007	KLEENEX PAPER TOWELS	11/10/90	2	48	.45	21.60	◄
0008	SCOTT'S PAPER TOWELS	11/15/90	4	240	.50	120.00	
0008	SCOTT'S PAPER TOWELS	12/20/90	4	480	.51	244.80	
0010	HUDSON PAPER TOWELS	11/25/90	7	72	.54	38.88	
0011	NORTHERN PAPER TOWELS	11/28/90	2	120	.61	73.20	◄
0015	A & P PAPER TOWELS	11/30/90	1	480	.29	139.20	
0019	ECONOMY PAPER TOWELS	11/28/90	4	108	.23	24.84	◄

(*Continued*)

RANDOM PROCESSING OF A SEQUENTIAL DISK FILE BY THE CHAIN OPERATION

Regardless of the mode of processing (consecutive or random) used, the matching records method processes a file in a consecutive order (i.e., one record after the other). True random processing of a sequential disk file may be controlled by defining the file as a *chained file* with record access provided by a CHAIN operation. This method *does not* require that the transaction file or master file be in any matching or control field order (ascending or descending).

Records are accessed by *relative record number* and not by a control, matching, or key field stored in the body of the records. A relative record number may be defined as the record's position related to the beginning of the file. For example, a record with a relative record number of 5 is stored in the fifth record slot in the file; one with a relative record number of 100 is stored in the hundreth position, and so forth.

The problem with this sequential file processing method is that the relative record number may not represent the identifying field for the record. For example, look at Figure 14-31 and notice that not all the item numbers, which have been used in the previous program examples to access the item master file, relate to their relative positions. With the exception of the first two records, in which the item numbers 0001 and 0002 correspond with their relative positions in the file, the others do not. Consequently, to random process the file by relative record number, either the item numbers must correspond exactly with the relative record positions or the exact location of each record in the file must be known.

```
Relative
Record#

  1   0001BOUNTY PAPER TOWELS        6110190144000040
  2   0002MARCAL PAPER TOWELS        6110190360000041
  3   0004VANITY FAIR PAPER TOWELS   9110390060000039
  4   0007KLEENEX PAPER TOWELS       1111090048000045
  5   0008SCOTT'S PAPER TOWELS       4111590240000050
  6   0010HUDSON PAPER TOWELS        7112590720000054
  7   0011NORTHERN PAPER TOWELS      2112890120000060
  8   0015A & P PAPER TOWELS         1113090480000029
```

Figure 14-31 Relationship of relative record numbers to records stored in the item master file.

Source Program Coding

A source listing of the program that random processes a sequential disk file by the **CHAIN**ing method is presented in Figure 14-32. The syntax for each of the coding forms that supports the random processing of a sequential disk file by the chaining method will be discussed separately in the following paragraphs.

```
... ... 1 ... ... 2 ... ... 3 ... ... 4 ... ... 5 ... ... 6 ... ... 7 ...
      * THIS PROGRAM PROCESSES A SEQUENTIAL DISK FILE RANDOMLY FOR       CH14P4
      * INQUIRY USING THE CHAINING METHOD............................    CH14P4
     H                                                                   CH14P4
     FITEMNOS IP  F   5   5            CONSOLE                           CH14P4
     FSEQ13P1 IC  F 240  48R           DISK                              CH14P4
     FITEMINFOO   F 132 132            PRINTER                           CH14P4
     IITEMNOS SM  01   1 CI                                              CH14P4
     I                                         1   1 IDCODE              CH14P4
     I                                         2   50RECRD#              CH14P4
     ISEQ13P1 SM  02                                                     CH14P4
     I                                         1   1 TCODE               CH14P4
     I                                         2   5 ITEM#               CH14P4
     I                                         6  30 NAME                CH14P4
     I                                        31  31 VENDR#              CH14P4
     I                                        32  370PDATE               CH14P4
     I                                      P 38  390QTY                 CH14P4
     I                                      P 40  432COST                CH14P4
     I                                      P 44  482AMOUNT              CH14P4
     C           RECRD#    CHAINSEQ13P1                99   GET THE RECORD CH14P4
     C  N99      TCODE     COMP 'D'                   10RECORD DELETED?CH14P4
     OITEMINFOD  301  N99 02                                             CH14P4
     O       OR         99                                               CH14P4
     O                                    37 'ITEM MASTER FILE INQUIRY'  CH14P4
     O                         UDATE Y    51                             CH14P4
     O        D  2    N99 02                                             CH14P4
     O                                     8 'ITEM#'                     CH14P4
     O                                    27 'ITEM NAME'                 CH14P4
     O                                    48 'VENDOR#'                   CH14P4
     O        D       N99 02                                             CH14P4
     O       OR         99                                               CH14P4
     O                         ITEM#       7                             CH14P4
     O                N99      NAME       36                             CH14P4
     O                N99      VENDR#     45                             CH14P4
     O                  99                36 '......ITEM NOT FOUND....'  CH14P4
     O        D 11    N99 02                                             CH14P4
     O                                    11 'PURCHASE'                  CH14P4
     O                                    32 'COST'                      CH14P4
     O                                    47 'TOTAL $'                   CH14P4
     O        D  2    N99 02                                             CH14P4
     O                                     9 'DATE'                      CH14P4
     O                                    34 'PER ITEM'                  CH14P4
     O                                    46 'AMOUNT'                    CH14P4
     O        D  3    N99 02                                             CH14P4
     O                         PDATE Y    11                             CH14P4
     O                         QTY   Z    20                             CH14P4
     O                         COST  1    33                             CH14P4
     O                         AMOUNT1    51                             CH14P4
     O        D  0    N99 02                                             CH14P4
     O                                    29 'ITEM DELETED?:'            CH14P4
     O                    10              33 'YES'                       CH14P4
     O                   N10              33 'NO '                       CH14P4
```

Figure 14-32 Source listing of a program that random processes a sequential disk file by the chaining method.

File Description Coding—Sequential File Random Access Program

Shown in Figure 14-33 is a detailed explanation of the File Description entries required to support the random processing of a sequential disk file by the **CHAIN**-ing method.

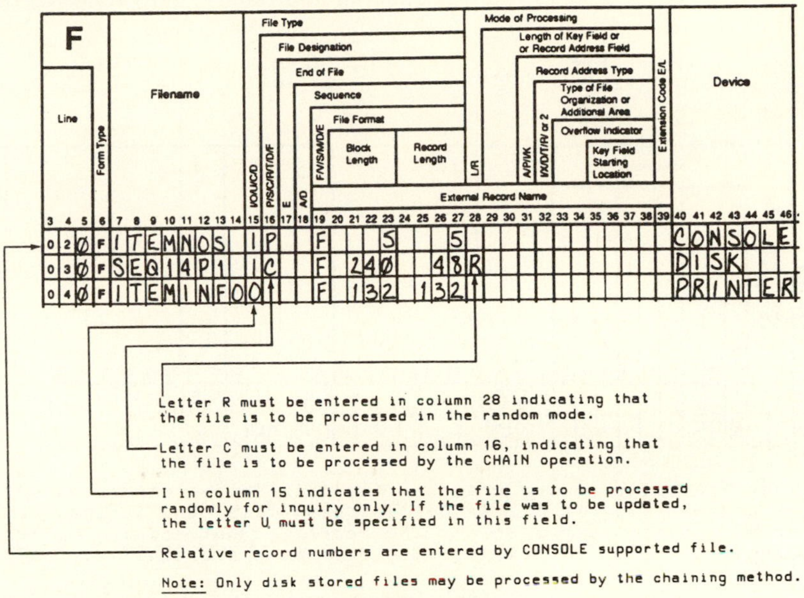

Figure 14-33 File Description Specifications coding for a program that processes a sequential disk file randomly.

Input Specifications Coding

An examination of the input coding in Figure 14-34 for this application program indicates that the relative record numbers used to random access the sequential disk file are CONSOLE (interactively) entered. The syntax for the other input instructions is identical to the rules previously discussed.

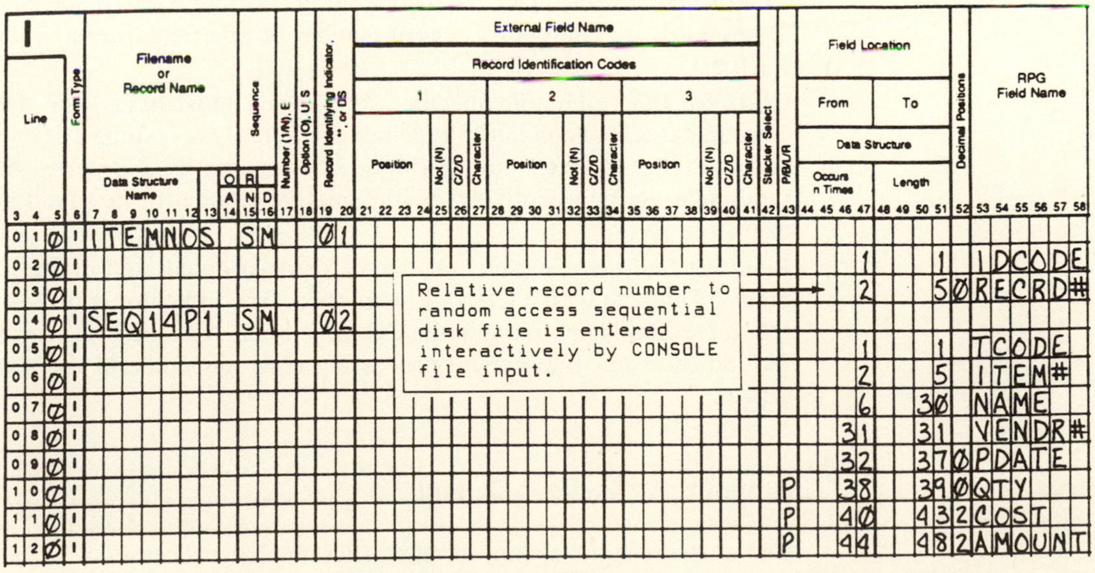

Figure 14-34 Input Specifications coding for a program that processes a sequential disk file randomly.

Calculation Specifications Coding

Look at the calculations coding for the example program in Figure 14-35, and notice the new terminology associated with the chaining method of random processing any disk file. As will be discussed in later chapters, the random processing of indexed-sequential and relative files requires the same coding procedures.

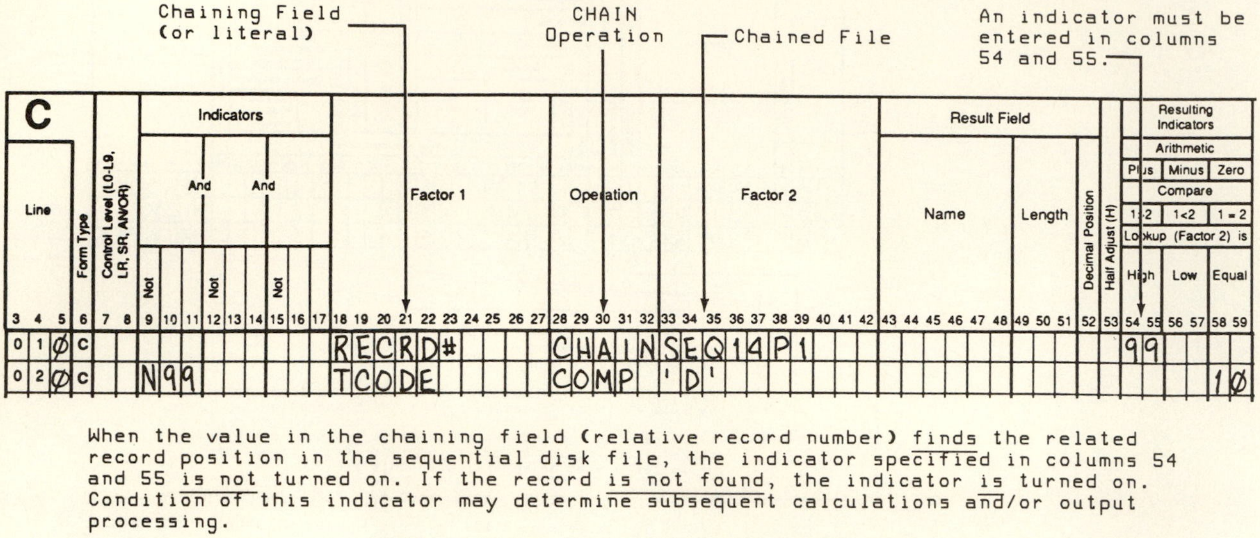
Chaining Field (or literal)
CHAIN Operation
Chained File
An indicator must be entered in columns 54 and 55.
C
Indicators
Line
Form Type
Control Level (L0-L9, LR, SR, AN/OR)
And
And
Not
Not
Not
Factor 1
Operation
Factor 2
Result Field
Name
Length
Decimal Position
Half Adjust (H)
Resulting Indicators
Arithmetic
Plus Minus Zero
Compare
1>2 1<2 1=2
Lookup (Factor 2) is
High Low Equal
01Ø C RECRD# CHAIN SEQ14P1 99
02Ø C N99 TCODE COMP 'D' 1Ø
When the value in the chaining field (relative record number) finds the related record position in the sequential disk file, the indicator specified in columns 54 and 55 is not turned on. If the record is not found, the indicator is turned on. Condition of this indicator may determine subsequent calculations and/or output processing.

Figure 14-35 Calculation Specifications coding for a program that processes a sequential disk file randomly.

The new terms associated with the **CHAIN**ing method of random processing disk files follow.

CHAINing Field: The field or literal entered in Factor 1. It must be defined with the same attributes as the relative, control, or key field, in the CHAINed file (file name entered in Factor 2).

CHAIN Operation: The CHAIN operation accesses a file (name entered in Factor 2) randomly by the relative record number or key field (literal) value specified in Factor 1.

CHAINed File: The file specified in Factor 2 must have been defined as input (I) or update (U in column 15); include the letter C in column 16 (File Designation) and the letter R in column 28 (Mode of Processing). A chained file is accessed randomly (not consecutively) by the relative number or key field value specified in Factor 1.

Resulting Indicator Control: An indicator must be entered in the High field (columns 54 and 55) with a CHAIN instruction. The indicator is turned on only if the related record is not found in the CHAINed file. A successful search will not turn the indicator on. Subsequent processing often depends on the status of this indicator.

Output Specifications Coding

The partial output coding for the program that processes a sequential disk file randomly (inquiry) by relative record number is shown in Figure 14-36. Output instructions for a successful chain are conditioned by an N99 and 02 (Record

Identifying Indicator assigned to the CHAINing file). To prevent output at 1P time, the 02 Record Identifying Indicator is included in an AND relationship with the N99 indicator. Unless the related indicator is on, a negative indicator (specified with an N) used alone is processed as a "no" indicator. Consequently, at least one positive indicator (one without an N) should be included with any negative indicator.

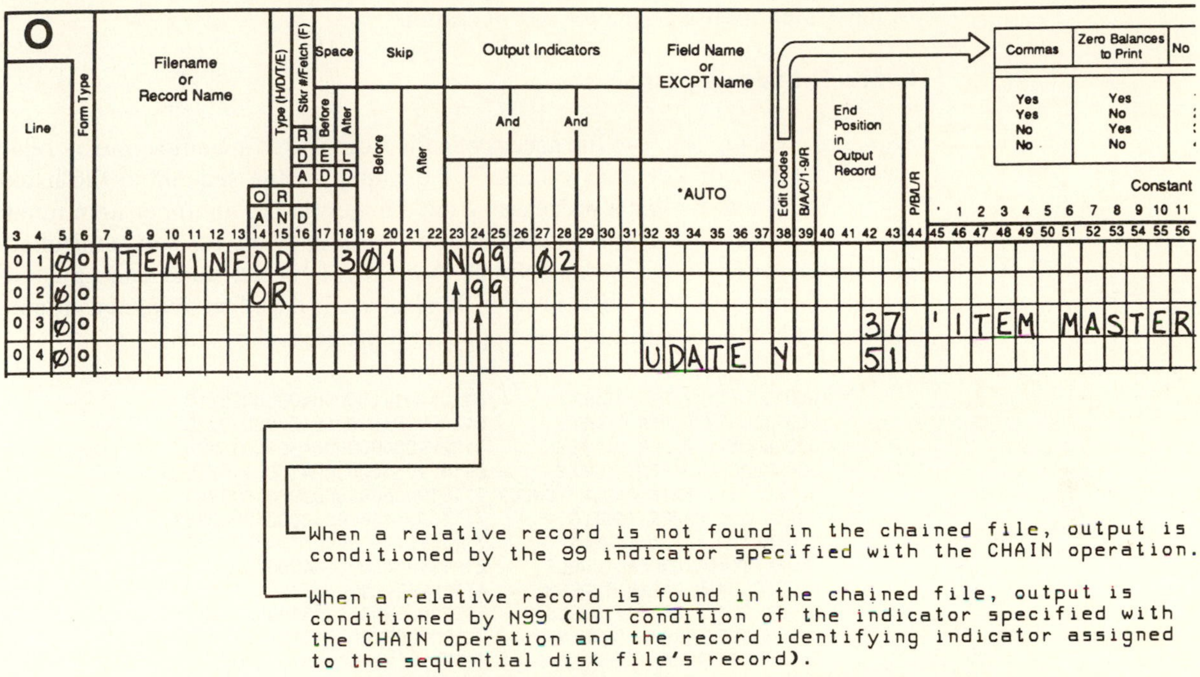
O
Line
Form Type
Filename or Record Name
Type (H/D/T/E)
Stkr #/Fetch (F)
Space
Before
After
Skip
Before
After
Output Indicators
And
And
Field Name or EXCPT Name
*AUTO
Edit Codes
B/A/C/1-9/R
End Position in Output Record
P/B/L/R
Commas
Zero Balances to Print
No
Constant
0 1 0 O ITEMINFO D 3 0 1 N99 02
0 2 0 O OR 99
0 3 0 O 37 'ITEM MASTER
0 4 0 O UPDATE N 51
When a relative record is not found in the chained file, output is conditioned by the 99 indicator specified with the CHAIN operation.
When a relative record is found in the chained file, output is conditioned by N99 (NOT condition of the indicator specified with the CHAIN operation and the record identifying indicator assigned to the sequential disk file's record).

Figure 14-36 Output Specifications coding for a program that processes a sequential disk file randomly.

Two reports generated by this program are presented in Figure 14-37. Recall that the relative record numbers used to random process the sequential disk file were entered interactively by CONSOLE file controlled input. Because the file is randomly accessed, the relative record numbers may be entered in an unordered sequence.

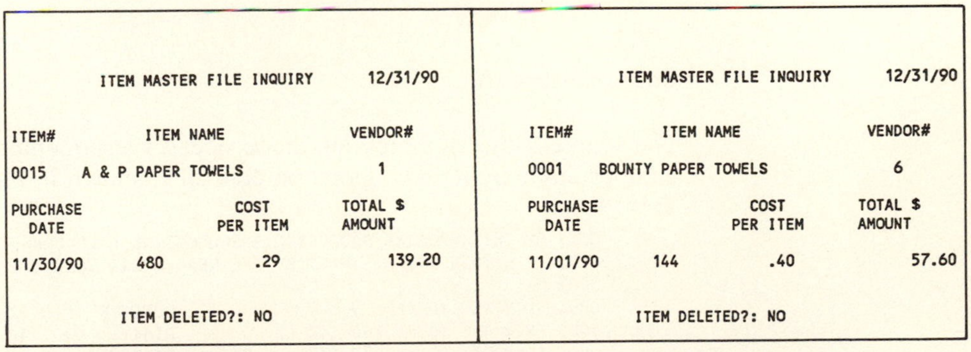

ITEM MASTER FILE INQUIRY 12/31/90

ITEM#	ITEM NAME		VENDOR#
0015	A & P PAPER TOWELS		1
PURCHASE DATE		COST PER ITEM	TOTAL $ AMOUNT
11/30/90	480	.29	139.20

ITEM DELETED?: NO

ITEM MASTER FILE INQUIRY 12/31/90

ITEM#	ITEM NAME		VENDOR#
0001	BOUNTY PAPER TOWELS		6
PURCHASE DATE		COST PER ITEM	TOTAL $ AMOUNT
11/01/90	144	.40	57.60

ITEM DELETED?: NO

Figure 14-37 Reports generated by the program that processes a sequential disk file randomly (inquiry).

Only an inquiry program has been presented to illustrate the random processing of a sequential disk file by relative number. Understand that other maintenance functions such as file updating and limits processing may be controlled by the CHAINing method.

CONSECUTIVE PROCESSING OF A SEQUENTIAL DISK FILE BY THE READ OPERATION

Another method of processing a sequential file consecutively is by the READ operation. This operation reads a record from the related input file during calculation time instead of at input time, as provided by the normal RPG processing cycle. A program that processes a sequential disk file *within limits* is presented to illustrate one use of the READ operation.

Limits Processing Logic

Limits processing refers to the access of a file from and to specific control, relative record number, or key field values. For example, if the sequential file listed in Figure 14-38 is to be limits processed from a lower and to an upper item number, the related values would be entered and the reading of the records controlled *on demand by a READ operation*. Notice that this file is the same one updated by the update program (CH14P3) previously discussed. It will be defined as the input file to be limits processed by this application program.

```
0001BOUNTY PAPER TOWELS          61101901440000040000005760
0001BOUNTY PAPER TOWELS          61205909600000042000040320
0001BOUNTY PAPER TOWELS          61222908400000043000036120
0002MARCAL PAPER TOWELS          61101903600000041000014760
0004VANITY FAIR PAPER TOWELS 91103900600000039000002340
0005BRAVO PAPER TOWELS           71130901440000028000004032
0005BRAVO PAPER TOWELS           71214901200000031000003720
0007KLEENEX PAPER TOWELS         21110900480000045000002160
0008SCOTT'S PAPER TOWELS         41115902400000050000012000
0008SCOTT'S PAPER TOWELS         41220904800000051000024480
0010HUDSON PAPER TOWELS          71125900720000054000003888
0011NORTHERN PAPER TOWELS        21128901200000061000007320
0015A & P PAPER TOWELS           11130904800000029000013920
0019ECONOMY PAPER TOWELS         41128901080000023000002484
```

```
Records are to be limits processed from item number 0002 to 0010.  Any range may be
specified providing the lower value is entered first.  If another range is required
during the same run, the next lower range must be higher than the previous upper range.
Otherwise, the run must be ended and the program executed again.
```

Figure 14-38   Listing of a sequential file processed by the READ operation.

Source Program

The source listing of a program that processes a sequential disk file between item number limits by READ operation control is shown in Figure 14-39.

```
0001  * THIS PROGRAM PROCESSES A SEQUENTIAL FILE CONSECUTIVELY
0002  * WITHIN ITEM# LIMITS BY THE READ OPERATION.................
0003 H
0004 FLIMITS  IP  F   9   9            CONSOLE
0005 FSEQ14P1 ID  F 240  48            DISK
0006 FREPORT  O   F 132 132      OF    PRINTER
0007 ILIMITS  SM  01    1 CI
0008 I                                  1    1 IDCODE
0009 I                                  2    5 LOW#
0010 I                                  6    9 HIGH#
0011 ISEQ14P1 SM  02
0012 I                                  1    1 TCODE
```

Figure 14-39   Source listing of a program that processes a sequential file between limits by the READ operation.

```
I                                           2   5 ITEM#
I                                           6  30 NAME
I                                          31  31 VENDR#
I                                          32  370PDATE
I                                        P 38  390QTY
I                                        P 40  432COST
I                                        P 44  482DLRAMT
C                      TIME           HHMMSS  60       GET SYSTEM TIME
C                      SETON                     10    CTRL FOR TIME
C                      EXCPT                           PRINT HDG LINES
C                      SETOF                     10    SETOF HDG IND.
 *
 * LOOPING PROCESS CONTROLS READING OF RECORDS FROM THE FILE.
 * OUTPUT BEGINS WHEN LOW# FROM CONSOLE FILE IS = AN ITEM# IN THE
 * DEMAND FILE.  READING OF FILE STOPS WHEN HIGH# IN CONSOLE FILE IS
 * < AN ITEM# IN THE DEMAND FILE (SEQ14P1).  WHEN END OF FILE IS
 * SENSED, CALCULATIONS ARE SKIPPED OVER........
C           AGAIN      TAG
C                      READ SEQ14P1                  90READ A RECORD
C   90                 EXCPT                           PRINT ERROR MSG
C   90                 GOTO END                        BRANCH IF EOF
C  N20      LOW#       COMP ITEM#                  2020 < OR = TESTS
C   20      HIGH#      COMP ITEM#                202120 > < = TESTS
C   20      TCODE      COMP 'D'                      30DELETED RECORD?
C   20N30              EXCPT                           OUTPUT RECORD
C  N21                 GOTO AGAIN                      GO & READ AGAIN
C           END        TAG
OREPORT  H  101     1P
O       OR          OF
O                              UDATE Y    8
O                                        46 'ITEM LISTING'
O                                        86 'PAGE'
O                              PAGE  Z   91
O        EF 2       10
O                              HHMMSS     8 ' :  :  '
O        EF 2       10
O                                         5 'ITEM#'
O                                        26 'ITEM NAME'
O                                        44 'DATE'
O                                        55 'VENDOR#'
O                                        62 'QTY'
O                                        75 'COST/ITEM'
O                                        90 'DOLLAR AMT'
 *
 * RECORD INFO IS PRINTED IF LOW# = ITEM# OR HIGH# IS > OR
 * = ITEM# AND RECORD IS NOT DELETED AND FILE IS NOT AT END
 *
O        E  2       20N30N90
O                              ITEM#      5
O                              NAME      34
O                              PDATE Y   46
O                              VENDR#    52
O                              QTY   1   62
O                              COST  1   75
O                              DLRAMT1   91
 *
 * ERROR MESSAGE PRINTED WHEN LOW# OR HIGH# INPUT IS > LAST ITEM#
 * IN THE FILE..................
 *
O        E  2       90
O                              LOW#       5
O                                         8 'OR'
O                              HIGH#     13
O                                        38 '......BEYOND END OF FILE'
O                                        44 '......'
```

(Continued)

The File Description, Calculation, and Output coding for the example program are explained in the following paragraphs. Because input coding is not affected by use of the READ operation, it will not be separately discussed. Reference may be made to the source listing in Figure 14-39 for the syntax related to the Input Specification entries.

File Description Syntax

Figure 14-40 shows the File Description entries for the example program that processes a sequential disk file between limits. Notice that the input file that is to be processed by the READ operation must be defined as a *demand file* by specifying the letter D in column 16. No other changes are required in this form to support demand file processing.

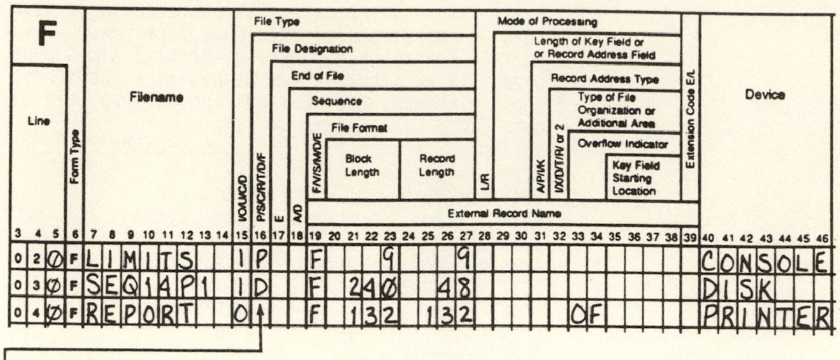

Processing a file (input, update, or combined) with the READ operation requires that the file be defined as a DEMAND file (D in column 16).

Figure 14-40 File Description coding for a program that processes a sequential file between limits by the READ operation.

Calculation Specifications Syntax

The RPG syntax for the READ operation is explained in Figure 14-41.

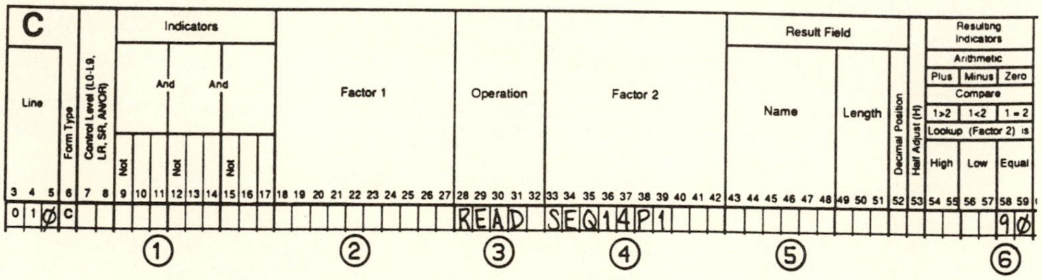

1. Total time (columns 7-8 or detail time (columns 9-17) may be used to condition a READ statement.

2. Factor 1 is never used.

3. READ operation must be specified in the operation field. It controls the reading of records from the related demand at calculation instead of input time.

4. The name of the file that was defined as a Demand file (D in column 16 of the FD form) or a full-procedural file (F in column 16) must be specified in Factor 2.

5. Result fields are never used.

6. In order to test for an end-of-file condition, an indicator must be specified in the equal field of the Resulting Indicator area. With WORKSTN files, an indicator may also be assigned in columns 56-57, which will turn on if a keyboard error occurs.

Figure 14-41 RPG Syntax for the READ operation.

Calculation instructions included in the program that limits processes a sequential disk file by the READ operation are detailed in Figure 14-42. For this application, the consecutive reading of the file is controlled by including the READ operation in a loop. Each pass through the loop outputs a record by the EXCPT operation or prints an error message if the end of the demand file is sensed.

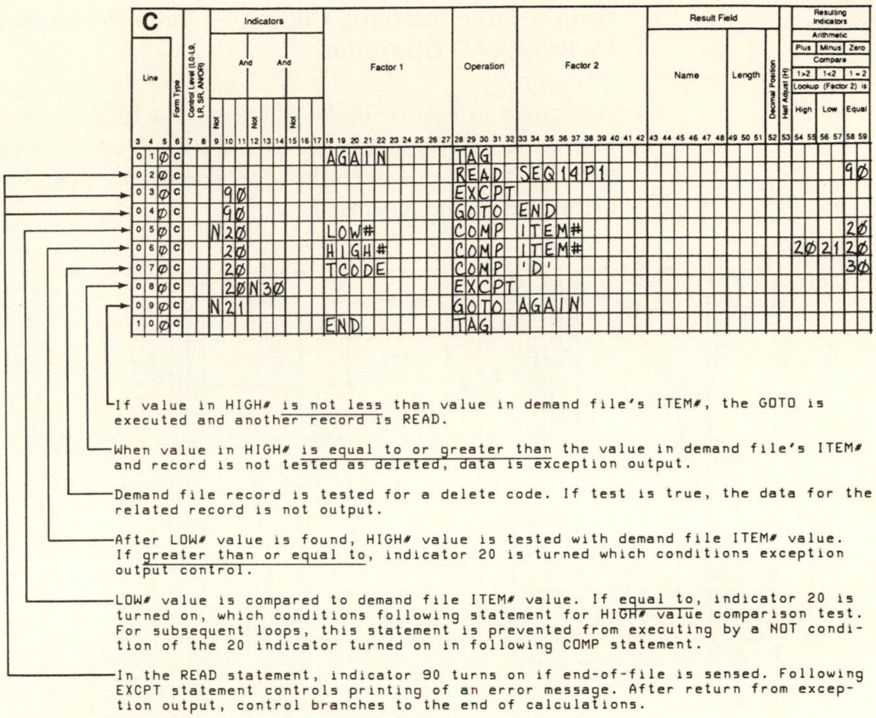
C
Line
Form Type
Control Level (L0-L9, LR, SR, AN/OR)
Indicators
And
And
Not
Factor 1
Operation
Factor 2
Result Field
Name
Length
Decimal Positions
Half Adjust (H)
Resulting Indicators
Arithmetic
Plus Minus Zero
Compare
1>2 1<2 1=2
Lookup (Factor 2) is
High Low Equal
01 C AGAIN TAG
02 C READ SEQ14P1 90
03 C 90 EXCPT
04 C 90 GOTO END
05 C N20 LOW# COMP ITEM# 20
06 C 20 HIGH# COMP ITEM# 20 21 20
07 C 20 TCODE COMP 'D' 30
08 C 20N30 EXCPT
09 C N21 GOTO AGAIN
10 C END TAG
If value in HIGH# is not less than value in demand file's ITEM#, the GOTO is executed and another record is READ.
When value in HIGH# is equal to or greater than the value in demand file's ITEM# and record is not tested as deleted, data is exception output.
Demand file record is tested for a delete code. If test is true, the data for the related record is not output.
After LOW# value is found, HIGH# value is tested with demand file ITEM# value. If greater than or equal to, indicator 20 is turned which conditions exception output control.
LOW# value is compared to demand file ITEM# value. If equal to, indicator 20 is turned on, which conditions following statement for HIGH# value comparison test. For subsequent loops, this statement is prevented from executing by a NOT condition of the 20 indicator turned on in following COMP statement.
In the READ statement, indicator 90 turns on if end-of-file is sensed. Following EXCPT statement controls printing of an error message. After return from exception output, control branches to the end of calculations.

Figure 14-42 Calculation coding for a program that processes a sequential file between limits by the READ operation.

Processing Logic

The flowchart in Figure 14-43 details the processing logic supported by the calculation instructions.

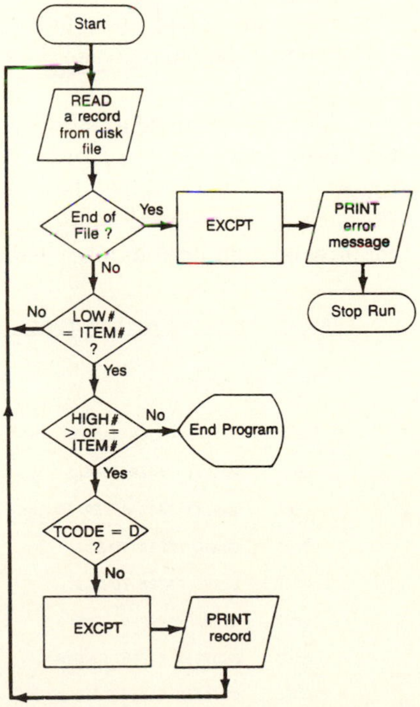
Start
READ a record from disk file
End of File ?
Yes
EXCPT
PRINT error message
Stop Run
No
LOW# = ITEM# ?
No
Yes
HIGH# > or = ITEM#
No
End Program
Yes
TCODE = D ?
No
EXCPT
PRINT record

Figure 14-43 Processing logic supported by the calculations included in a program that processes a sequential file by the READ operation.

Output Specifications Coding—Limits Processing by the READ Operation

As shown in Figure 14-44, detail output for the report is controlled by *exception output*. Iterative processing of the READ operation requires EXCPT output control. Every pass through the loop generates a print line of data or an error message if the end of file is sensed.

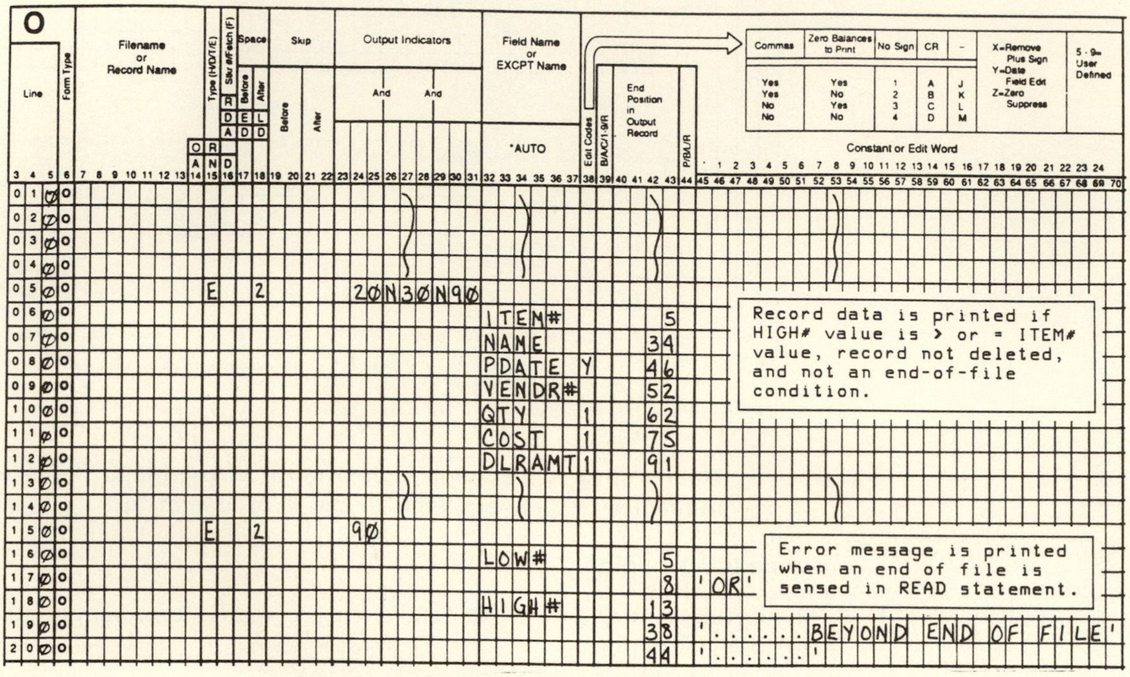

Figure 14-44 Output coding for a program that processes a sequential file between limits by the READ operation.

Three reports generated by the program are presented in Figure 14-45. The first prints a range of records from item number 0002 through 0010. A second report shows the results when the low-range item number value is found but not the high-range value. Finally, the third listing is a report generated when neither the low or high item number values are found in the file.

Report for item number range from 0002 through 010:

12/31/90 ITEM LISTING PAGE 1
50:32

ITEM#	ITEM NAME	DATE	VENDOR#	QTY	COST/ITEM	DOLLAR AMT
0002	MARCAL PAPER TOWELS	11/01/90	6	360	.41	147.60
0004	VANITY FAIR PAPER TOWELS	11/03/90	9	60	.39	23.40
0005	BRAVO PAPER TOWELS	11/30/90	7	144	.28	40.32
0005	BRAVO PAPER TOWELS	12/14/90	7	120	.31	37.20
0007	KLEENEX PAPER TOWELS	11/10/90	2	48	.45	21.60
0008	SCOTT'S PAPER TOWELS	11/15/90	4	240	.50	120.00
0008	SCOTT'S PAPER TOWELS	12/20/90	4	480	.51	244.80
0010	HUDSON PAPER TOWELS	11/25/90	7	72	.54	38.88

Figure 14-45 Three example reports generated by the program that processes a sequential file between limits by the READ operation.

Report when low value is found, but not high value:

```
12/31/90                          ITEM LISTING                                  PAGE    1
  49:03

ITEM#           ITEM NAME              DATE    VENDOR#    QTY    COST/ITEM    DOLLAR AMT

 0019    ECONOMY PAPER TOWELS        11/28/90     4       108          .23         24.84

 0019 OR 0020 ......BEYOND END OF FILE......
```

Report when low or high values are not found:

```
12/31/90                          ITEM LISTING                                  PAGE    1
  49:43

ITEM#           ITEM NAME              DATE    VENDOR#    QTY    COST/ITEM    DOLLAR AMT

 0020 OR 0023 ......BEYOND END OF FILE......
```

(*Continued*)

Only one of the file maintenance functions that may be supported by the READ operation has been discussed. Others, including sequential file inquiry, update, and processing, may also be controlled by this method.

Regardless of the maintenance function supported, the READ operation requires that the demand file and the data that accesses it be sorted in the same order. Furthermore, similar to the matching records method, demand file access is a consecutive processing alternative that does not support the random access of a file as with the CHAINing method.

SUMMARY

The maintenance functions that support sequential disk files include the addition of records, inquiry, update, record deletion, and limits processing. Depending on the processing method used, sequential disk files may be consecutively or random processed.

The matching records method for the consecutive processing of a sequential file requires the assignment of matching fields to input items that are common to two or more input or update files. A maximum of nine matching fields (M1–M9) may be specified in a program to process two or more input or update files. The related fields must have the same attributes.

When the values in the matching fields are equal (match), an MR (matching record) indicator is automatically turned on to condition subsequent calculations and/or output. For matching records processing, the files used in the match must be sorted in the same order, or the run will cancel when the first out-of-sequence record is read. Processing always begins at the first record in the file, and control cannot return to the beginning of the file in the same run.

Sequential disk files may be random processed by the CHAINing method. The input or update file accessed by this method must be defined in the File Description instruction as a chained file (C in column 16) and have the letter R specified in column 28 to indicate that the file will be processed in a random mode.

A calculation statement that includes a CHAIN operation must be specified to access a record from the file. A resulting indicator is required in the High field, which turns on if the record is not found. The random processing of a sequential disk file is controlled by relative record number and not by a control or key field embedded in the body of the records. A relative record number is the record's position in the file as related to the first record. Consequently, for this processing method, the exact position of each record must be known to access it.

A sequential disk file may also be processed consecutively by a READ operation. The input or update file must be defined as a demand file (D in column 16) and be accessed by a READ instruction in calculations. Records are read from this file at calculation time instead of at input time, as controlled by the normal RPG processing cycle.

When more than one record is to be read from a file, the READ operation usually has to be included in a routine that controls iterative processing. In addition, an indicator must be specified in the Resulting Indicator Equal field to prevent runtime errors. Any of the maintenance functions may be controlled by the READ operation.

QUESTIONS

14-1. Name the maintenance functions that may be supported for sequential disk file processing.

14-2. Define the processing features of each of the maintenance functions named in Question 14-1.

14-3. By what RPG processing methods may the maintenance functions identified in Question 14-2 be controlled?

14-4. Explain the processing logic when two files are controlled by the *matching records method*. How must the files be organized to support matching records processing? Where in an RPG program is this order specified?

14-5. What are *matching fields*? Where and how are they identified? How many fields may be assigned as matching fields in a program?

14-6. Name the syntax requirements that must be followed for matching fields.

14-7. When the values in two or more matching fields match, what indicator is automatically turned on? What may this indicator be used for?

14-8. If the values in two or more matching fields match, is the primary or secondary file processed first? If the values do not match, which file is processed first?

14-9. In what order will the following records be processed when the matching records method is used? Assume TREMP# is included in the primary file and MSTEMP in the secondary file. Use the indicated letters to specify the processing order.

	TREMP#		MSTEMP
(a)	01234	(e)	01234
(b)	22222	(f)	01235
(c)	33212	(g)	41111
(d)	41111		

14-10. If three matching fields are specified for a match, how will the values of the fields be formatted in storage if M1 includes 18; M2, 44; and M3, 72?

14-11. Given below are the values for two matching fields. When will the MR indicator be turned on?

			Field Name	Storage Value
(a)	Primary file:	TRANACTS	TREMP#	17804
(b)	Secondary file:	EMPMASTR	MSTEMP	45102
(a)	Primary file:	TRANACTS	TREMP#	34512
(b)	Secondary file:	EMPMASTR	MSTEMP	34512

14-12. Refer to Question 14-11 and determine which file will supply the next record to be processed in examples a and b.

14-13. In a program that updates a sequential file, what new entries must be made in the Files Description coding to identify the file as an update file? Should the file to be updated be defined as a primary or secondary file? Explain your answer.

48 **14-14.** What, if anything, is wrong with the following input coding?

Line	Form Type	Filename or Record Name	Sequence	Record Identifying Indicator	Field Location From	Field Location To	Decimal Positions	RPG Field Name	Matching Fields or Chaining Fields
01Ø	I	TRANACTS	SM	Ø1					
02Ø	I				2	6	Ø	TCUST#	M1
03Ø	I				7	1Ø		TBRNCH	M3
04Ø	I				11	12		TSTATE	M2
05Ø	I				13	2Ø	2	TAMT	M4
06Ø	I	MASTER	SM	Ø2					
07Ø	I				2	5		MCUST#	M1
08Ø	I				6	8	Ø	MBRNCH	M2
09Ø	I				9	1Ø		MSTATE	M3
10Ø	I				11	18	2	MBALNC	M4

14-15. How does the random processing of a sequential disk file differ from consecutive processing?

14-16. What RPG method is required to support the random processing of a sequential disk file? Name the coding forms, fields, and entries to support this method of processing.

14-17. Explain the following terms and how they relate to the random processing of sequential disk files:

Chained File	CHAIN Operation
Chaining Field	Chaining File
(High) Resulting Indicator	Relative Record Number

14-18. Does a *relative record number* always relate to the identifying key or control field value for the record? Explain your answer

Examine the following coding and answer the related Questions 14-19 to 14-22.

Line	Form Type	Factor 1	Operation	Factor 2	Resulting Indicators High
01Ø	C	RECRD#	CHAIN	SEQFILE	99

14-19. The entry in Factor 1 is referred to as the ________.

14-20. Refer to Question 14-19, and explain what value must be included in the Factor 1 entry. Must the entry always be a field name?

14-21. The entry in Factor 2 is referred to as the ________.

14-22. The Resulting Indicator specified in High field turns on if the record ________ is found.

14-23. What is a *demand file*? In what coding form is a file defined as a demand file? How does the processing of a demand file differ from a file defined as primary (P in column 16) or secondary (S in column 16)?

14-24. Explain the processing logic for the READ operation. When are records read from the file controlled by the READ operation?

14-25. What coding forms, columns, and entries are required to control file processing by the READ operation?

Examine the following calculation form and answer Questions 14-26 to 14-27 related to the coding entries.

C Line (3–5)	Form Type (6)	Control Level (L0-L9, LR, SR, AN/OR) (7–8)	Indicators (9–17)	Factor 1 (18–27)	Operation (28–32)	Factor 2 (33–42)	Result Field Name (43–48)	Length (49–51)	Decimal Position (52)	Half Adjust (H) (53)	Resulting Indicators High (54–55)	Low (56–57)	Equal (58–59)
01Ø	C				READ	SEQFILE							9Ø

14-26. How must the file specified in Factor 2 be defined?

14-27. When does the Resulting Indicator specified in the Equal field turn on? What control must be provided in the program when this condition is tested?

14-28. How many records are read at one time by a single READ operation? When more than one record is to be accessed from a file by the READ operation, what control must be included in a program to support this processing?

EXERCISES

14-1. A sequentially organized master inventory file with the directory name ITEMFIL is stored on disk in the following record format:

FILE DEFINITION

SYSTEM Yours		DRAWN BY S. Myers
FILE NAME ITMFIL		DATE 12/31/90 REV. NO.0
CREATED BY S. Myers		FILE TYPE Disk
RECORD NAME None		KEY LENGTH None
RECORDING MODE Fixed	ORGANIZATION Sequential	SEQUENCE Ascending order
RECORD SIZE 11 bytes	BLOCKING FACTOR 20	BLOCKSIZE 220 bytes

FIELD DATA

FIELD NO.	FIELD NAME - DESCRIPTION	SIZE	CLASS C/P/Z/B	POSITION FROM	POSITION THRU	FORMAT/CONSTANT
1	Item Number	5	C	1	5	
2	Department Number	3	C	6	8	
3	Amount On Hand	5	P	9	11	

Write the File Description and Input Specifications to update the ITMFIL using the matching records method for sale and purchase transactions. Assign M1 to the item number field and M2 to the department number.

A sequential disk file UPDATES, which includes the transaction data to update the ITMFIL, is loaded in the following record format.

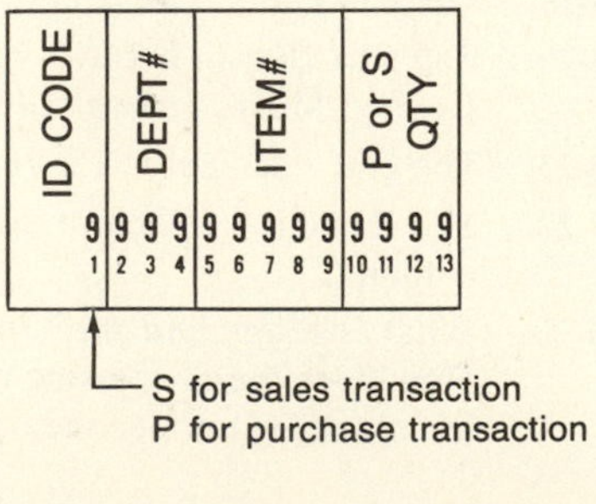

14-2. Write the calculations to update the file when a match is found. When MR is on, test the record code for a P or S. If the value is an S (sales transaction), subtract the transaction record quantity from the ITMFIL balance. For a purchase transaction (P in the code field), add the transaction quantity to the ITMFIL balance.

Provide for two count fields: one for the number of ITMFIL records updated and one for the number of transaction records with no matching ITMFIL record.

14-3. Write the output coding to update amount on hand field in the related ITMFIL file record when a match is found.

14-4. Refer to your completed coding for Exercises 14-1 and 14-2, and write the output coding to generate the following error report. Supply your own output file name.

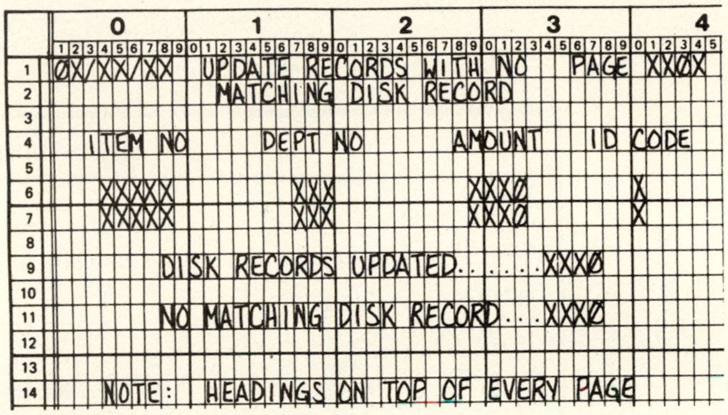
ØX/XX/XX UPDATE RECORDS WITH NO PAGE XXØX
MATCHING DISK RECORD
ITEM NO DEPT NO AMOUNT ID CODE
XXXXX XXX XXXØ X
XXXXX XXX XXXØ X
DISK RECORDS UPDATED...... XXXØ
NO MATCHING DISK RECORD... XXXØ
NOTE: HEADINGS ON TOP OF EVERY PAGE

14-5. Modify the coding completed for Exercises 14-1, 14-2, and 14-3 to update the ITMFIL by the CHAINing method.

14-6. Modify the coding completed for Exercises 14-1, 14-2, and 14-3 to update the ITMFIL by the READ operation.

14-7. Examine the following source listing and correct the logic and syntax errors:

```
... ... 1 ... ... 2 ... ... 3 ... ... 4 ... ... 5 ... ... 6 ... ... 7 ...
 * THIS PROGRAM BATCH UPDATES A SEQUENTIAL DISK FILE BY THE         EX147
 * MATCHING RECORDS METHOD WITH TWO MATCHING FIELDS                 EX147
H                                                                   EX147
FTRANACTSIS AF  47  47           DISK                               EX147
FSEQ13P1 UP DF 240  48           DISK                               EX147
FNOMATCHSO   F  47  47           DISK                               EX147
ITRANACTSSM  01                                                     EX147
I                                       1   1 TCODE                 EX147
I                                       2   5 ITEMNO  M1            EX147
I                                       6  30 TNAME           20    EX147
I                                      31  31 TVENDR          21    EX147
I                                      32  370TDATE   M2            EX147
I                                      38  400TQTY            22    EX147
I                                      41  472TCOST           23    EX147
I                                       1  47 RECORD                EX147
ISEQ13P1 SM  02                                                     EX147
I                                       1   1 CODE                  EX147
I                                       2   50ITEM#   M2            EX147
I                                       6  30 NAME                  EX147
I                                      31  31 VENDR#                EX147
I                                      32  370PDATE   M1            EX147
I                                     P 38  390QTY                  EX147
I                                     P 40  432COST                 EX147
I                                     P 44  482AMOUNT               EX147
C                   SETOF                    1011                   EX147
C   MR 02 01CODE    COMP 'D'                     10MSTR REC DEL?    EX147
C   MR 02 01TCODE   COMP 'D'                     11DELETE TRANS?    EX147
C   10                                                              EX147
COR 11              GOTO END                                        EX147
C   MR 01N22COST    MULT TQTY      AMOUNT          QTY CHANGE       EX147
C   MR 01N23TCOST   MULT QTY       AMOUNT          COST CHANGE      EX147
C   MR 01N22                                       COST AND QTY     EX147
CANN23 02   TCOST   MULT TQTY      AMOUNT          CHANGE           EX147
C           END     TAG                                             EX147
OSEQ13P1 D        01 MR                                             EX147
O                    11            1 'D'                            EX147
O                   N20  TNAME     30                               EX147
O                   N21  TVENDR    31                               EX147
O                   N22  TQTY      39P                              EX147
O                   N23  TCOST     43P                              EX147
O                        AMOUNT    48P                              EX147
ONOMATCHSD       NMR 02                                             EX147
O                        RECORD    47                               EX147
```

LABORATORY ASSIGNMENTS

Note: All the following program assignments require that a related sequential file from Chapter 13 has been created and loaded by the instructor or by you.

Laboratory Assignment 14-1: UPDATE OF A SEQUENTIAL FILE BY THE MATCHING RECORDS METHOD

Write an RPG program to update the sequential disk file created and loaded in Assignment 13-1. The format of that file (one to be updated for this assignment) is shown in the following File Definition form:

Master File Format:

FILE DEFINITION

SYSTEM Yours		DRAWN BY S. Myers
FILE NAME Defined in Lab13-1 assignment		DATE 11/30/92 REV. NO. 0
CREATED BY S. Myers		FILE TYPE Disk
RECORD NAME None		KEY LENGTH None
RECORDING MODE Fixed	ORGANIZATION Sequential	SEQUENCE Unordered
RECORD SIZE 53 bytes	BLOCKING FACTOR 16	BLOCKSIZE 848 bytes

FIELD DATA

FIELD NO.	FIELD NAME - DESCRIPTION	SIZE	CLASS C/P/Z/B	POSITION FROM	POSITION THRU	FORMAT/CONSTANT
1	Delete Code	1	C	1	1	D if deleted
2	Account Number	5	C	2	6	
3	Depositor's Name	24	C	7	30	
4	Branch Name	13	C	31	43	
5	State	2	C	44	45	
6	Balance	8	P	46	50	2 decimal positions
7	ID Code	3	C	51	53	BAL

The format of the records in the file that includes the update data is shown in the following record layout form:

Transaction File Format:

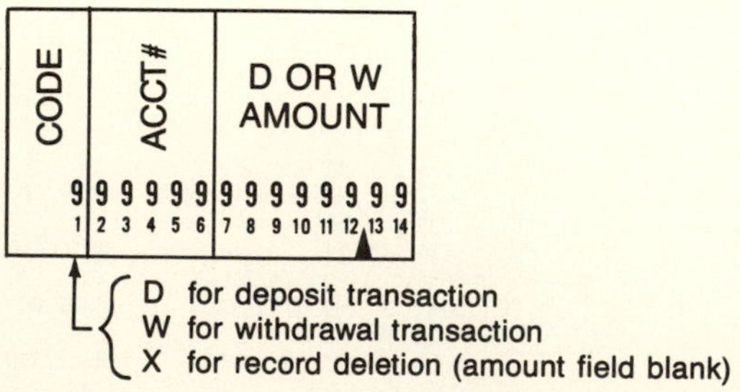

Processing: Assign the account number as the matching fields in the two files. For a match condition, add the update record amount to the master file balance if the transaction is a deposit, and subtract the amount if the transaction is a withdrawal. Store the new balance amount in the related master disk record.

If the transaction code is an X, tag the related master file record with the letter D and do not change any of the original field values.

Provide for a count of the number of master file records updated and the number of transaction records without a match. Output those values when end of file is sensed (see report for format). Transaction records that do not have a matching master record are to be loaded to another sequential disk file in *input record image*.

Report Design: Include coding in the program to generate the report shown in the following printer spacing chart:

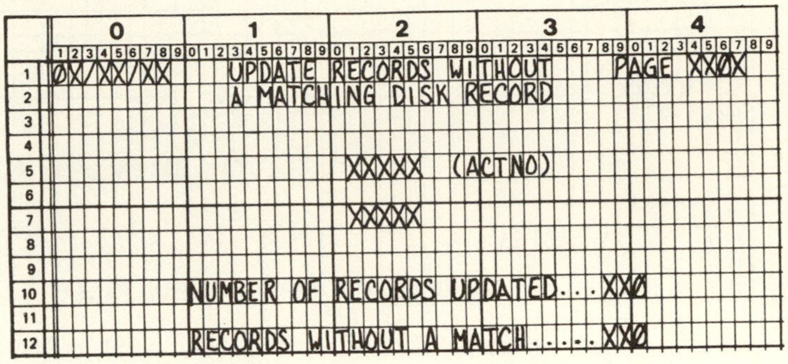

Transaction File Data:

Transaction Code Col 1	Account Number 2-6	Transaction Amount 7-14
D	34444	05000000
W	64321	00750000
W	74891	02100000
X	88397	00000000
D	91784	01000000

Note: The transaction file data above is sorted in ascending order by account number. Verify that the data in the master file created in Lab 13-1 (or loaded by your instructor) is in the same order. If it is not, use the system sort utility to sort it in the required ascending account number order.

To check the validity of the update process, print a utility listing (software supplied with most systems) of the master file before and after the program is run. In addition, print a utility listing of the error file.

Laboratory Assignment 14-2: UPDATING A SEQUENTIAL DISK FILE BY THE READ OPERATION

Refer to the program for Assignment 14-1 and rewrite it to process the master sequential disk file with the READ operation. If Assignment 14-1 was not completed, refer to the documentation included in that assignment to write this program. The transaction file for Assignment 14-1 may be used for this assignment.

Laboratory Assignment 14-3: LIMITS PROCESSING OF A SEQUENTIAL DISK FILE BY THE READ OPERATION

If Assignment 14-2 was completed, modify it to process the master file within account number limits. However, if it was not completed, refer to the documentation in Assignment 14-1 for the record formats of the two files.

If available on your system, use either CONSOLE, KEYBORD, or WORKSTN input for entering the lower and upper account numbers to access the master file within the specified record limits. Otherwise, include the lower and upper account numbers in a disk file.

Report Design:

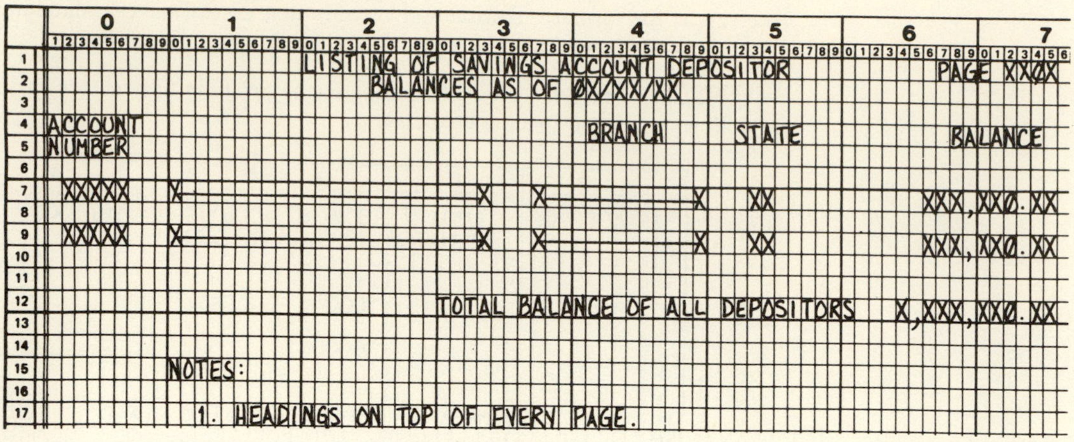

Process the file from account number 49814 to 74891 for one report and 55115 to 91784 for a second report.

Laboratory Assignment 14-4: UPDATING A SEQUENTIAL DISK FILE BY THE CHAINING METHOD

Refer to the program for Assignment 14-1 and rewrite it to process the master sequential disk file with the CHAINing method. If Assignment 14-1 was not completed, refer to the documentation included in that assignment to write this program. The transaction file is modified to include relative record numbers, which are used to access the master file, instead of account numbers. A listing of this data follows.

Transaction File Data:

Transaction Code Col 1	Relative Record# 2-6	Transaction Amount 7-14	References Account# (Ref only)
D	00004	01000000	91784
D	00001	05000000	34444
X	00003	00000000	88397
W	00009	03000000	99000
W	00002	00750000	64321

Note: For processing with the CHAIN operation the transaction file does not have to be sorted in a relative record number order or the master file in account number order.

References Account# column entries are to help reader identify the correct, if any, master record that was updated and is not a field in the transaction record.

Laboratory Assignment 14-5: UPDATING A SEQUENTIAL DISK FILE WITH TWO MATCHING FIELDS

Before this assignment can be completed, the sequential file created and loaded by Assignment 13-4 must exist. If it does not, you or your instructor must create and load it with the Assignment 13-4 input data.

Write an RPG program to update the sequential disk file created and loaded in Assignment 13-4. The format of that file (the one to be updated for this assignment) is shown in the following File Definition form:

Master File Format:

FILE DEFINITION

SYSTEM Yours		DRAWN BY S. Myers
FILE NAME Yours		DATE 1/15/91 REV. NO. 0
CREATED BY S. Myers		FILE TYPE Disk
RECORD NAME None		KEY LENGTH None
RECORDING MODE Fixed	ORGANIZATION Sequential	SEQUENCE Ascending (CUST#)
RECORD SIZE 99 bytes	BLOCKING FACTOR 5	BLOCKSIZE 495 bytes

FIELD DATA

FIELD NO.	FIELD NAME - DESCRIPTION	SIZE	CLASS C/P/Z/B	POSITION FROM	POSITION THRU	FORMAT/CONSTANT
1	Delete Code	1	C	1	1	D if deleted
2	Customer Number	4	C	2	5	
3	Customer Name	29	C	6	34	
4	Street Address	24	C	35	58	
5	City	15	C	59	73	
6	State	2	C	74	75	
7	Zip	5	P	76	78	
8	Account Balance	8	P	79	83	2 decimal positions
9	Balance Date	6	Z	84	89	
10	Store Number	4	P	90	92	
11	Telephone Number	10	P	93	98	
12	ID Code	1	C	99	99	Letter M

Either you or your instructor must build a file with the update data in the following record format:

Transaction File Format:

FILE DEFINITION

SYSTEM Yours		DRAWN BY S. Myers
FILE NAME Your own		DATE 1/20/91 REV. NO. 0
CREATED BY S. Myers		FILE TYPE Disk
RECORD NAME None		KEY LENGTH None
RECORDING MODE Fixed	ORGANIZATION Sequential	SEQUENCE Ascending-Cust#
RECORD SIZE 98 bytes	BLOCKING FACTOR 1	BLOCKSIZE 98 bytes

FIELD DATA

FIELD NO.	FIELD NAME - DESCRIPTION	SIZE	CLASS C/P/Z/B	POSITION FROM	POSITION THRU	FORMAT/CONSTANT
1	Customer Number	4	C	1	4	
2	Customer Name	29	C	5	33	
3	Street Address	24	C	34	57	
4	City	15	C	58	72	
5	State	2	C	73	74	
6	Zip	5	Z	75	79	
7	Telephone Number	10	Z	80	89	
8	Transaction Amount	8	Z	90	97	2 decimal positions
9	Transaction Code	1	C	98	98	S = Sale transaction
						P = Payment
						A = Other than S or P
						D = Delete record

Processing: Assign the customer number field in both files as the major matching field and the *first five characters* of the customer name as the minor matching field. Update is to occur when there is a match on the related field values in the two records.

To prevent a matching master record field from being updated with blanks or zeros when a transaction record field has no values, all the fields, except the customer number and name, must be checked on input for the absence of data.

Depending on the transaction code in the update records, perform the following functions when a match occurs:

A–Update master record fields with transaction record values. Master record balance amount is not changed.

S–Add the transaction sales amount to the master file balance. No other field values are to be changed.

P–Subtract the transaction payment amount from the master file balance. No other field values are to be changed.

D–Tag the master record in the deleted field with the letter D. No other field values are to be changed.

For transaction records that do not have a matching master record, write them to another sequential file in their input record image.

Check the validity of your update processing by printing a utility listing of your master file before updating and after. Also, to check the accuracy of any no-match condition, print a copy of the error file.

Transaction File Data:

Cust# 1-4	Customer Name 5-33	Address 34-57	City 58-72	State 73-74	Zip 75-79	Telephone# 80-89	Transaction Amount 90-97	Code 98
1234	JOHN FIRESTONE	9 PARK PLACE	BRIDGEPORT	CT	06611	2033781200		A
2345	WILLIAM GOODYEAR						01041879	P
3456	JAMES GOODRICH						05000000	S
4567	CLAUDE MICHELIN							D
5678	ANTHONY PIRELLI					2049990000		A
6789	TOYO KOGO	2 MAZDA ROAD						A
7777	BILL YOKOHOMA						00020000	P

Laboratory Assignment 14-6: MODIFICATION OF ASSIGNMENT 14-5 USING THE READ OPERATION

If Assignment 14-5 was completed, modify it to support updating by the READ operation. If it was not completed, refer to the documentation for that assignment and write the program using the READ operation instead of matching records.

chapter 15
Indexed-Sequential Disk File Creation, Loading, and Consecutive Processing

Chapters 13 and 14 presented sequential disk file processing and the RPG syntax for the loading and maintenance of that type of file organization. This chapter introduces the coding and processing methods associated with the creation, loading, and consecutive processing of *indexed-sequential* files. The term *indexed* will be used for any subsequent references to indexed-sequential file organization.

It was emphasized in Chapter 13 that sequential, indexed, and direct files have their own design characteristics, advantages, and disadvantages. As compared to sequential files, indexed files offer the following advantages.

1. Faster random processing because the file does not have to be searched from the beginning for inquiry, update, or delete functions. Individual records may be accessed by a key value and the related record address.
2. Sorted integrity of the file (index) is not destroyed when records are added.
3. Faster consecutive processing may be provided by beginning the reading of the file at a record other than the first one.
4. Multiple indexes may be supported (on some systems) that allow access to the file in different field orders without sorting.

Because of these advantages, master files—those that have a high incidence of maintenance activity and those that support an interactive or real-time environment—are usually organized as indexed.

Some of the disadvantages of indexed file organization include:

1. More disk space is required to support the index or indexes.
2. Because the indexes have to be searched for a record address, consecutive processing is slower than with sequential files. On some systems, this disadvantage may be overcome by defining the indexed file as sequential in the File Description form.
3. Approximately more than 10% adds to an indexed file will significantly increase processing time. This is called *file degradation*.

STRUCTURE OF INDEXED FILES

The physical differences between sequential, indexed, and direct file organizations were previously discussed in Chapter 13 (see Figure 13-5). It was pointed out that indexed files have two storage areas: an *index area* and a *prime data area*. Key values (employee numbers, part numbers, account numbers, and so forth) and the prime data area address of each related record are stored in the index. The data records, which are stored in the prime data area, must include the identifying key value. Figure 15-1 explains the structure of the index and prime data areas for indexed files.

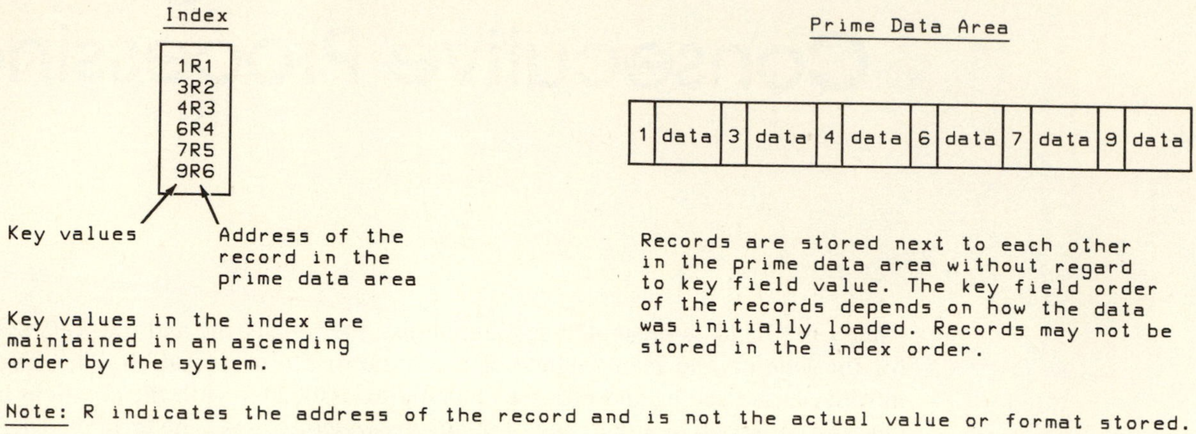

Figure 15-1 Organization of an indexed file (record addresses included in the index).

Some computer systems (IBM 370/4300 DOS series) do not support the file structure shown in Figure 15-1 but instead use cylinder and track indexes to identify the location of a record within the indexed file. This structure is illustrated and explained in Figure 15-2.

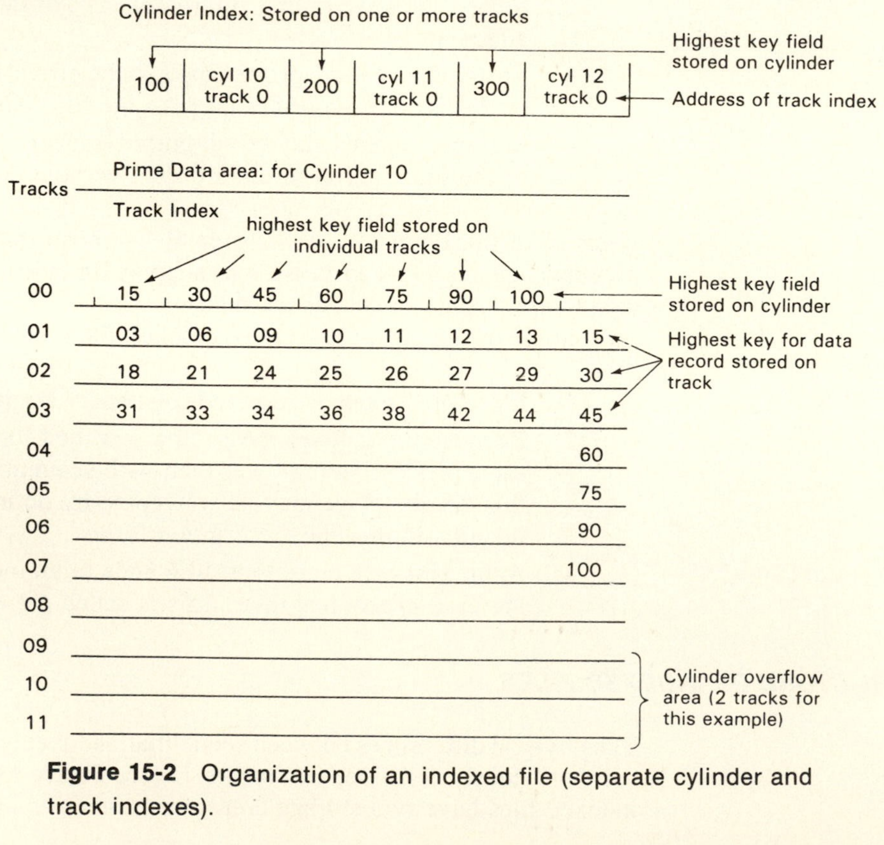

Figure 15-2 Organization of an indexed file (separate cylinder and track indexes).

IBM's AS/400 series supports a *table structure* for indexed files (*keyed files*) that is different from the two previous examples.

An application program is presented that creates and loads an indexed file from input data stored on a sequential disk file. The first version of the program controls the loading process when the input records are in an ascending key field value order. Another version shows how an RPG program may be modified to support the loading process when the input data is in an unordered key field sequence.

APPLICATION PROGRAM—LOADING AN INDEXED FILE

Documentation

The specifications for an RPG program that creates and loads an indexed file from the data stored in a sequential disk file are included in Figure 15-3.

PROGRAM SPECIFICATIONS Page 1 of 1

Program Name INDEXED FILE LOAD Program-ID CH15P1 Written By S. Myers

Purpose Creation and loading of an indexed file Approved By The Boss

Input files (directory names):

DATA15P1 (stored on disk)

Output files (directory names):

CUSTMSTR (stored on disk)

Processing Narrative:

Write a structured RPG program to create and load an indexed-sequential file from data stored in a sequential file which has been sorted in an ascending Account Number order.

Input to the program:

A supplemental record layout form is attached detailing the format of the records in the sequentially organized input file.

Processing:

Load all of the records in the sequential disk file to an indexed-sequential file

Output:

An attached record layout form details the record format for the indexed file (CUSTMSTR). Assign Account Number as the key field for this file.

Figure 15-3 Specifications for a program that creates and loads an indexed file (load data in key field order).

The system flowchart in Figure 15-4 indicates that the sequential disk file is input by the program to load an output disk file.

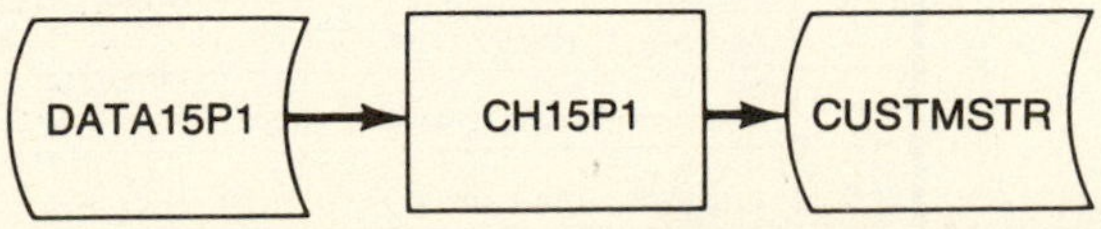

Figure 15-4 System flowchart for a program that creates and loads an indexed file (load data in key field order).

The format of the records in the sequential disk file stored with the load data and a listing of the file is shown in Figure 15-5.

	ACCT NO	ACCOUNT NAME	TRANS DATE	TRANS AMOUNT
9	9 9 9 9 9	9 9 9 9 9 9 9 9 9 9 9 9 9 9 9 9 9 9 9 9 9 9 9 9 9 9 9 9 9 9	9 9 9 9 9 9	9 9 9 9 9 9 9
1	2 3 4 5 6	7 8 9 10 11 12 13 14 15 16 17 18 19 20 21 22 23 24 25 26 27 28 29 30 31 32 33 34 35 36	37 38 39 40 41 42	43 44 45 46 47 48 49

↑ TRANSACTION CODE

Data File:

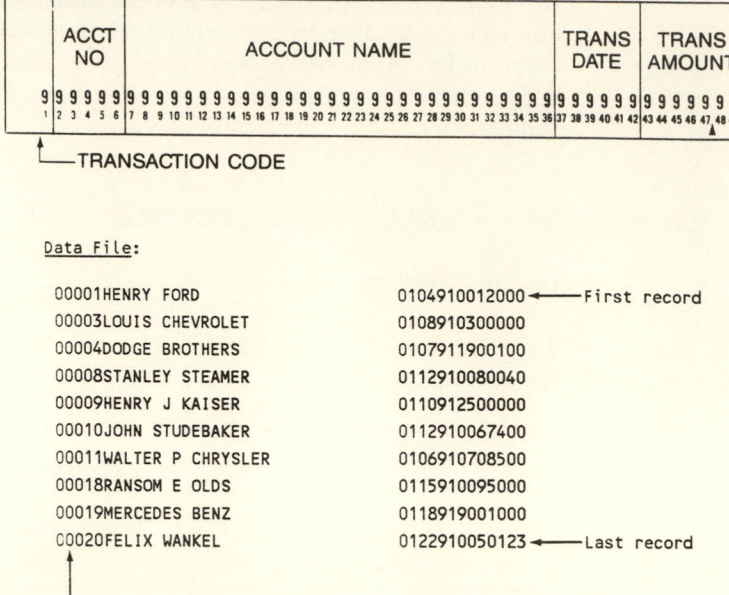

```
00001HENRY FORD              0104910012000<----First record
00003LOUIS CHEVROLET         0108910300000
00004DODGE BROTHERS          0107911900100
00008STANLEY STEAMER         0112910080040
00009HENRY J KAISER          0110912500000
00010JOHN STUDEBAKER         0112910067400
00011WALTER P CHRYSLER       0106910708500
00018RANSOM E OLDS           0115910095000
00019MERCEDES BENZ           0118919001000
C0020FELIX WANKEL            0122910050123<----Last record
↑
└─Account numbers (key field in the indexed file)
  in required ascending order
```

Figure 15-5 Record layout form and listing of the data stored in the sequentially organized input file.

The File Definition form in Figure 15-6 documents the file and field attributes of the indexed file to be created and loaded by the program. Supplemental to the file and field information, it is important that the key field (or fields) be identified. Indexed files are accessed by key fields; consequently, their size, type, and location in the body of the data records must be identified.

FILE DEFINITION

SYSTEM Yours		DRAWN BY S. Myers
FILE NAME CUSTMSTR		DATE 1/15/91 REV. NO. 0
CREATED BY S. Myers		FILE TYPE Disk
RECORD NAME None		KEY LENGTH 5 (ACCT#)
RECORDING MODE Fixed	ORGANIZATION Indexed	SEQUENCE Ascending (ACCT#)
RECORD SIZE 44 bytes	BLOCKING FACTOR 5	BLOCKSIZE 220 bytes

FIELD DATA

FIELD NO.	FIELD NAME - DESCRIPTION	SIZE	CLASS C/P/Z/B	POSITION FROM	POSITION THRU	FORMAT/CONSTANT
1	Delete Code	1	C	1	1	D if deleted
2	Account Number	5	C	2	6	Key field
3	Account Name	30	C	7	36	
4	Transaction Date (last)	7	P	37	40	
5	Account Balance	7	P	41	44	2 decimal positions

Figure 15-6 File Definition for the indexed file created and loaded by the application program.

Source Program Coding

A source listing of the RPG program that creates and loads a customer master file organized as indexed is presented in Figure 15-7.

```
... ... 1 ... ... 2 ... ... 3 ... ... 4 ... ... 5 ... ... 6 ... ... 7 ...
  * THIS PROGRAM CREATES & LOADS AN INDEXED-SEQUENTIAL DISK FILE      CH15P1
  * FROM INPUT RECORDS IN ASCENDING KEY FIELD ORDER.  BLOCKING &
  * PACKING ARE SPECIFIED FOR THE INDEXED-SEQUENTIAL FILE......
H
FDATA15P1IP  F  80  80             DISK
FCUSTMSTRO   F 220  44  5AI      2 DISK
IDATA15P1SM  01
I                                       1   1 TCODE
I                                       2   6 CUST#
I                                       7  36 NAME
I                                      37  400TDATE
I                                      43  492TAMT
OCUSTMSTRD         01
O                        TCODE      1
O                        CUST#      6
O                        NAME      36
O                        TDATE     40P
O                        TAMT      44P
```

Description of indexed file includes additional entries explained in Figure 15-8. (→ line 0006)

Input & output coding is identical to the loading of a sequential disk file

Key field must be included in the indexed record (→ line 0015)

Figure 15-7 Source listing of an RPG program that creates and loads an indexed file.

The File Description entries unique to the creation and loading of an indexed file are explained in Figure 15-8.

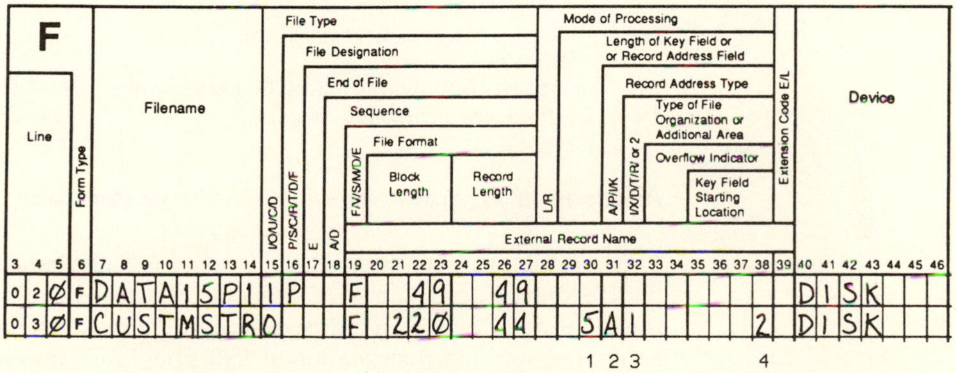

1. Columns 29-30 must contain the length of the key field. Key length may be from 1 to 99 bytes. Entry must be right-justified.

2. Column 31 must contain the letter A if the key is zoned decimal or alphanumeric, or a P if the key field is to be stored in a packed-decimal format. If the key field is specified as packed, it must also be defined as packed on the output form. This will load the key value in packed format in the index and in the body of the records.

3. Column 32 must contain the letter I to indicate that an indexed file is to be created.

4. Columns 35-38 must contain the beginning position of the key field in the body of the record. Entry must be right-justified.

Note: Fields entries not explained are identical to those discussed for sequential disk files.

Figure 15-8 File Description entries for the creation and loading of an indexed file.

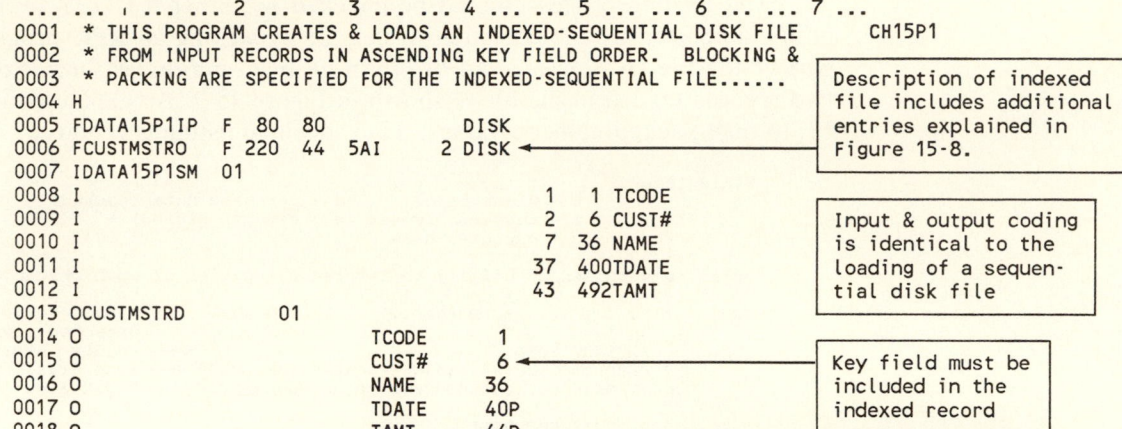

Because the input coding for the creation and loading of an indexed file is identical to that for sequential disk files, it is not detailed here. However, the key field must be included in the body of the records in the indexed file. If the key field was defined as packed in the File Description definition of the file (P in column 31), it must be specified as packed in the related output coding.

The loading process should be checked by either a COPY or DISPLAY utility supported by the computer system or by writing an RPG program to list part of the file. A *hexadecimal listing in an over-and-under format* of the first two records loaded in the file is shown in Figure 15-9. As explained in Chapter 13, to read packed numeric values, a hexadecimal listing is required.

```
Field legend:
              a - blank space        d - purchase date (packed)
              b - customer number    e - amount (packed)
              c - customer name

Ruler is supplied by utility to reference location of each character

RCDNBR  *... ... 1 ... ... 2 ... ... 3 ... ... 4 ...      Alphanumeric &
                                                          unpacked numeric
   1     00001HENRY FORD                          <------ values interpreted
        4FFFFFCCDDE4CDDC44444444444444444444 0111 0100 <------ Zone area
        00000185598066940000000000000000000 009F 020F <------ Digit area

   2     00003LOUIS CHEVROLET
        4FFF0FDDECE4CCCEDDDCE444444444444444 0181 0000 <------ Zone area
        000003364920385596353000000000000000 009F 300F <------ Digit area

        a b        c                          d    e

Notes:

  F in low-order digit bit of a packed numeric field indicates
    a positive value.
  On some systems the letter C is used to indicate a positive value.

  D in low-order digit bit of a packed numeric field indicates a
    negative value.

  4}  indicates a blank value
  0}
```

Figure 15-9 Utility listing in hexadecimal format of indexed file after it is loaded (first two records).

Application Program—Modified for Error Control

Indexed files will not support the loading (or addition) of records that have duplicate keys. Consequently, if duplicate records (same key value) are included in the input data to load an indexed file, program execution will halt or cancel. For computer systems that support a halt condition, an option may be taken that ignores the duplicate record and continues execution. With that control, however, duplicate records are not stored for later identification. For systems that do not support a halt when a duplicate record is read in the loading (or adding) process, program execution immediately cancels. In either case, however, procedures should be included in a program to override execution time cancellations caused by data errors.

The listing in Figure 15-10 illustrates the previous input file modified with records that include duplicate keys. A runtime error (halt or termination) is generated when the second 00003 is processed. The previous 00001 and 00003 records will have been loaded to the indexed file. For systems that support a halt condition, an option may be taken that will ignore the duplicate record and will continue loading the file until the second duplicate record is read (00019). The same option may be taken, the second 00019 record ignored, and record 00020 loaded to the file. For systems that terminate program execution, records with key values 00001 and 00003 will be loaded and the run will be cancelled when the first duplicate record (00003) is read.

```
  00001HENRY FORD                   0104910012000
  00003LOUIS CHEVROLET              0108910300000
┌→00003BARNEY OLDFIELD              0110910050000
│ 00004DODGE BROTHERS               0107911900100
│ 00008STANLEY STEAMER              0112910080040
│ 00009HENRY J KAISER               0110912500000
│ 00010JOHN STUDEBAKER              0112910067400
│ 00011WALTER P CHRYSLER            0106910708500
│ 00018RANSOM E OLDS                0115910095000
│ 00019MERCEDES BENZ                0118919001000
├→00019GUNNAR VOLVO                 0119910027750
│ 00020FELIX WANKEL                 0122910050123
│
└─Records with duplicate key value (file in ascending key
  value order)
```

Figure 15-10 Listing of the file that contains the load data modified to include duplicate key values.

To prevent either of these two error conditions, control may be included in an RPG program by a previously discussed method of processing (Chapter 9). Examine the source listing in Figure 15-11 and observe that Control Level Indicator L1 has been included with the definition of CUST#. Recall that this indicator is turned on only if a change is tested in the value of the related control field.

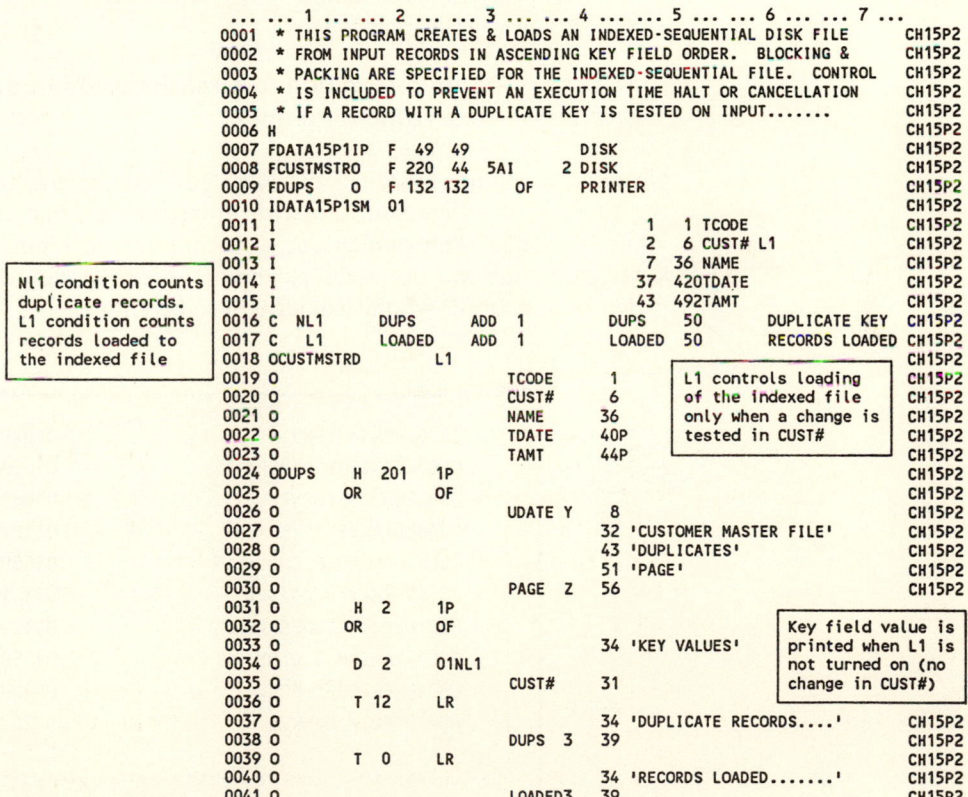

```
... ... 1 ... ... 2 ... ... 3 ... ... 4 ... ... 5 ... ... 6 ... ... 7 ...
 * THIS PROGRAM CREATES & LOADS AN INDEXED-SEQUENTIAL DISK FILE     CH15P2
 * FROM INPUT RECORDS IN ASCENDING KEY FIELD ORDER.  BLOCKING &     CH15P2
 * PACKING ARE SPECIFIED FOR THE INDEXED-SEQUENTIAL FILE.  CONTROL  CH15P2
 * IS INCLUDED TO PREVENT AN EXECUTION TIME HALT OR CANCELLATION    CH15P2
 * IF A RECORD WITH A DUPLICATE KEY IS TESTED ON INPUT.......       CH15P2
H                                                                   CH15P2
FDATA15P1IP  F  49  49             DISK                             CH15P2
FCUSTMSTRO   F 220  44  5AI      2 DISK                             CH15P2
FDUPS    O   F 132 132      OF     PRINTER                          CH15P2
IDATA15P1SM  01                                                     CH15P2
I                                            1   1 TCODE            CH15P2
I                                            2   6 CUST# L1         CH15P2
I                                            7  36 NAME             CH15P2
I                                           37  420TDATE            CH15P2
I                                           43  492TAMT             CH15P2
C  NL1      DUPS      ADD  1         DUPS    50      DUPLICATE KEY   CH15P2
C   L1      LOADED    ADD  1         LOADED  50      RECORDS LOADED  CH15P2
OCUSTMSTRD        L1                                                CH15P2
O                          TCODE      1                             CH15P2
O                          CUST#      6                             CH15P2
O                          NAME      36                             CH15P2
O                          TDATE     40P                            CH15P2
O                          TAMT      44P                            CH15P2
ODUPS     H  201    1P                                              CH15P2
O        OR         OF                                              CH15P2
O                          UDATE Y    8                             CH15P2
O                                    32 'CUSTOMER MASTER FILE'      CH15P2
O                                    43 'DUPLICATES'                CH15P2
O                                    51 'PAGE'                      CH15P2
O                          PAGE  Z   56                             CH15P2
O         H  2      1P
O        OR         OF
O                                    34 'KEY VALUES'
O         D  2      01NL1
O                          CUST#     31
O         T 12      LR
O                                    34 'DUPLICATE RECORDS....'     CH15P2
O                          DUPS  3   39                             CH15P2
O         T  0      LR                                              CH15P2
O                                    34 'RECORDS LOADED.......'     CH15P2
O                          LOADED3   39                             CH15P2
```

NL1 condition counts duplicate records. L1 condition counts records loaded to the indexed file

L1 controls loading of the indexed file only when a change is tested in CUST#

Key field value is printed when L1 is not turned on (no change in CUST#)

Note: Because L1 and NL1 are specified at detail time, the first record of any duplicate group will be loaded to the indexed file. If the control level indicator was specified at total time, the last record of the duplicate group would be loaded.

Figure 15-11 Source listing of program that loads an indexed file modified with error control.

Look at the output coding and notice that the L1 indicator conditions output (loading) to the indexed file. Because the L1 indicator is specified a detail time (D in column 15), the first record of any duplicates will be loaded to the file and not any others. Hence, a record will be loaded only when the value changes in the CUST# field, which will prevent a halt or cancellation of program execution when a record with a duplicate key is processed.

The printed report generated by the program, which identifies records that have duplicate key values and record counts of the number of records loaded and not loaded to the indexed file, is shown in Figure 15-12.

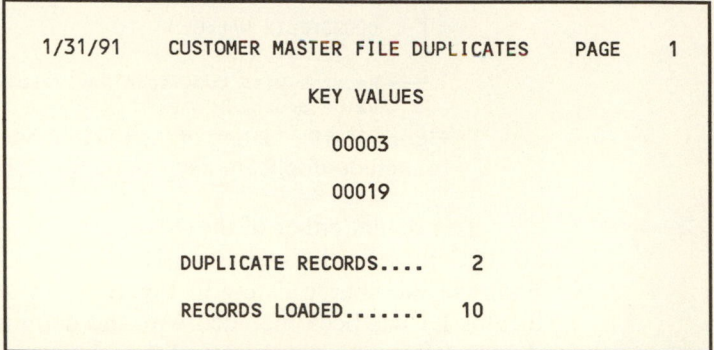

```
1/31/91    CUSTOMER MASTER FILE DUPLICATES    PAGE    1

                    KEY VALUES

                      00003

                      00019

            DUPLICATE RECORDS....    2

            RECORDS LOADED.......   10
```

Figure 15-12 Printed report generated by the program that loads an indexed file modified with error control.

Application Program-Modified to Load Records in an Unordered Key Value Sequence

On most computer systems, the RPG compiler includes a routine that supports the loading of an indexed file with input records that are in an unordered key value sequence. An examination of the data file in Figure 15-13 indicates that the key field values are not in an ascending order. Without the required RPG entry, program execution would cancel when the first out-of-sequence record (00003) was read.

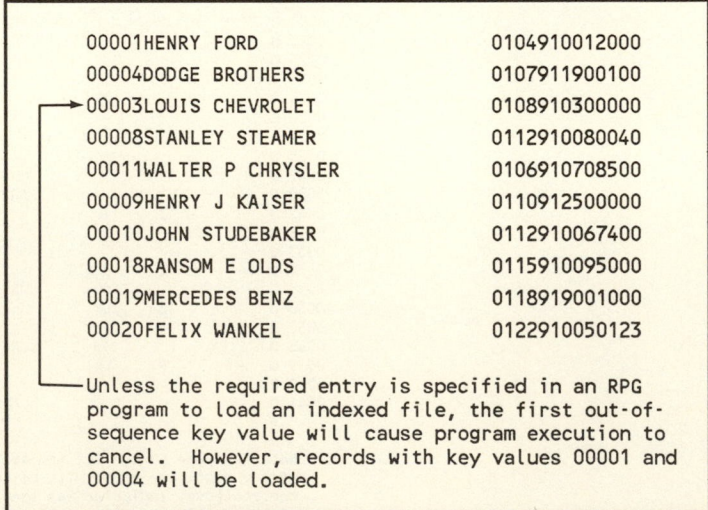

```
   00001HENRY FORD                0104910012000
   00004DODGE BROTHERS            0107911900100
 ->00003LOUIS CHEVROLET           0108910300000
   00008STANLEY STEAMER           0112910080040
   00011WALTER P CHRYSLER         0106910708500
   00009HENRY J KAISER            0110912500000
   00010JOHN STUDEBAKER           0112910067400
   00018RANSOM E OLDS             0115910095000
   00019MERCEDES BENZ             0118919001000
   00020FELIX WANKEL              0122910050123

 --Unless the required entry is specified in an RPG
   program to load an indexed file, the first out-of-
   sequence key value will cause program execution to
   cancel.  However, records with key values 00001 and
   00004 will be loaded.
```

Figure 15-13 Listing of the file that contains the load data in an unordered key value sequence.

The *only entry* required in an RPG program to support the loading of an indexed file with input records that are in an unordered key value sequence is included in the File Description definition for the indexed file. Figure 15-14 identifies the single entry. No additional entries or changes are required in the input, calculation, or output coding to support this loading process.

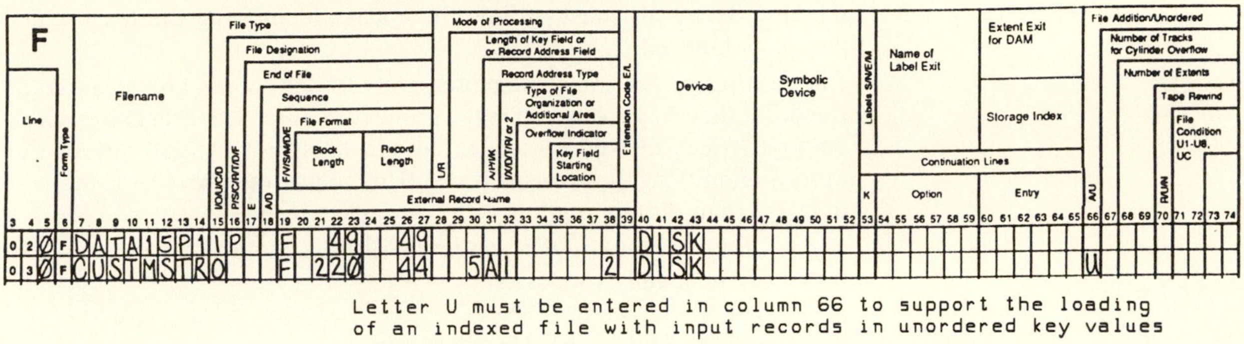

Figure 15-14 File description entry to support the loading of an indexed file with input records in an unordered key value sequence.

Regardless of the loading method, the system will maintain the index in an ascending key value order. However, the data records in the prime data area will be stored in the order to which they were initially loaded. The system-controlled processes followed when an indexed file is loaded with records in an unordered key value sequence are illustrated in Figure 15-15.

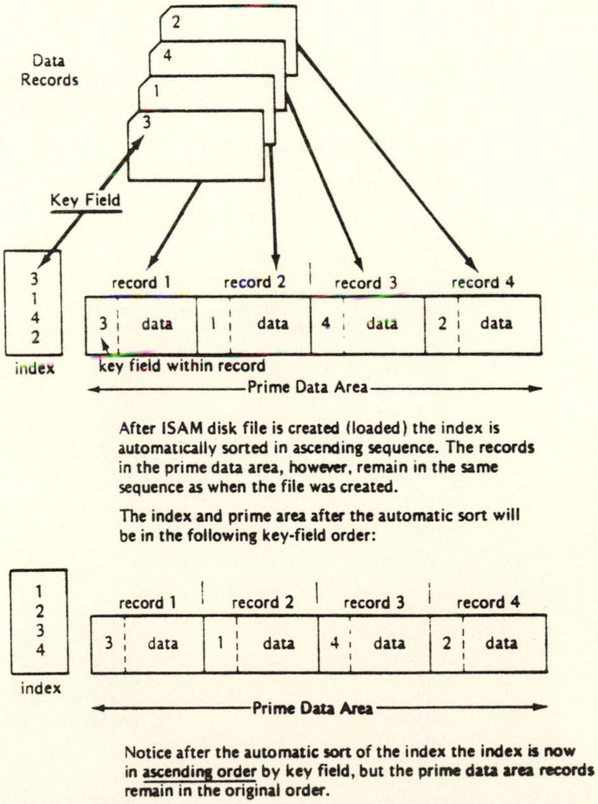

Figure 15-15 System-controlled process for loading an indexed file when the input records are in an unordered key value.

SEQUENTIAL PROCESSING OF AN INDEXED FILE

An indexed file may be read sequentially by any of the following methods:

1. *By key field (index) order.* All the records are accessed in accordance with their address location in the index. The File Description definition of the indexed file must include the entries identifying the file organization as indexed.
2. *Consecutively.* The index is ignored and all the records are accessed in the order that they are stored in the prime data area. The File Description coding defines the file as sequential and must not include any of the entries identifying the file as indexed. This sequential processing method is faster than the first option.
3. *Sequentially within key-field limits.* With this method an indexed file may be sequentially processed by:
   a. Using a limits record.
   b. Using the SETLL/READ operations.

Each of these sequential processing options is explained in the following paragraphs.

Sequential Processing by Key Field

The program shown in Figure 15-16 processes an indexed file in key field (index) order. Notice that all the attributes (i.e., key length, key type, file organization, and key start location) that define the file as indexed are specified in the File Description coding.

```
... ... 1 ... ... 2 ... ... 3 ... ... 4 ... ... 5 ... ... 6 ... ... 7 ...
 * THIS PROGRAM PROCESSES AN INDEXED FILE IN SEQUENTIAL KEY FIELD    CH15P3
 * INDEX (ORDER) AND GENERATES A PRINTED REPORT.................     CH15P3
H
FCUSTMSTRIP F 220  44  5AI     2 DISK<---------- Indexed file definition
FLISTING O  F 132 132     OF      PRINTER        includes entries speci-
ICUSTMSTRSM  01                                  fying it as indexed
I                                         1   1 TCODE
I                                         2   6 CUST#                CH15P3
I                                         7  36 NAME                 CH15P3
I                                      P 37  400TDATE                CH15P3
I                                      P 41  442BALANC               CH15P3
C           TOTAL     ADD  BALANC     TOTAL   82        TOTAL BALANCES CH15P3
OLISTING H  301   1P                                                 CH15P3
O       OR        OF                                                 CH15P3
O                         UDATE Y    8                               CH15P3
O                                   45 'CUSTOMER MASTER FILE'        CH15P3
O                                   53 'LISTING'                     CH15P3
O                                   75 'PAGE'                        CH15P3
O                         PAGE  Z   80                               CH15P3
O        H  2     1P                                                 CH15P3
O       OR        OF                                                 CH15P3
O                                    7 'CODE'                        CH15P3
O                                   15 'CUST#'                       CH15P3
O                                   41 'CUSTOMER NAME'               CH15P3
O                                   59 'DATE'                        CH15P3
O                                   73 'BALANCE'                     CH15P3
O        D  2     01                                                 CH15P3
O                         TCODE      6                               CH15P3
O                         CUST#     15                               CH15P3
O                         NAME      49                               CH15P3
O                         TDATE Y   61                               CH15P3
O                         BALANCA   76                               CH15P3
O        T 1      LR                                                 CH15P3
O                                   59 'TOTAL CUSTOMER BALANCES'     CH15P3
O                                   63 '....'                        CH15P3
O                         TOTAL A   76                               CH15P3
```

Figure 15-16 Listing of a program that sequentially processes an indexed file in key field (index) order.

The data file previously illustrated in Figure 15-13 is assigned as input to the program in Figure 15-16. An examination of the file listing indicates that the records were loaded in an unordered key sequence. However, because the file is defined as indexed, it is processed in the index and not prime data order. The report shown in Figure 15-17 indicates that the records are printed in ascending key value order.

```
1/31/91               CUSTOMER MASTER FILE LISTING                PAGE    1

CODE   CUST#              CUSTOMER NAME            DATE       BALANCE

  ──► 00001     HENRY FORD                        1/04/91       120.00
  ──► 00003     LOUIS CHEVROLET                   1/08/91     3,000.00
  ──► 00004     DODGE BROTHERS                    1/07/91    19,001.00
  ──► 00008     STANLEY STEAMER                   1/12/91       800.40
  ──► 00009     HENRY J KAISER                    1/10/91    25,000.00
  ──► 00010     JOHN STUDEBAKER                   1/12/91       674.00
  ──► 00011     WALTER P CHRYSLER                 1/06/91     7,085.00
  ──► 00018     RANSOM E OLDS                     1/15/91       950.00
  ──► 00019     MERCEDES BENZ                     1/18/91    90,010.00
  ──► 00020     FELIX WANKEL                      1/22/91       501.23

                              TOTAL CUSTOMER BALANCES....   147,141.63
```

When attributes for indexed file are included in the File Description definition of the file, it is processed in index order (ascending key)

Figure 15-17 Report generated by the program that sequentially processes an indexed file in key field (index) order.

Consecutive Processing Without Key Reference

If all the attributes defining the indexed file are omitted from the File Description definition of the file, the index will be ignored and the records will be processed in the order that they are stored in the prime data area. A listing of the previous program modified to support consecutive processing without key reference is included in Figure 15-18.

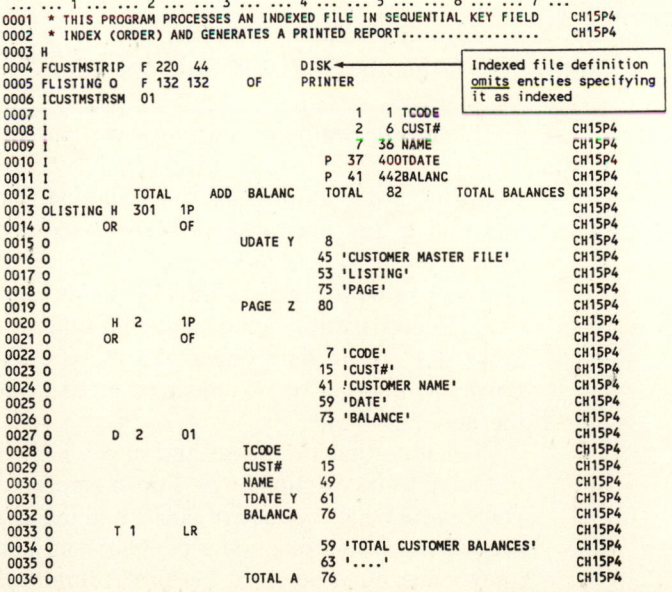

```
... ... 1 ... ... 2 ... ... 3 ... ... 4 ... ... 5 ... ... 6 ... ... 7 ...
 * THIS PROGRAM PROCESSES AN INDEXED FILE IN SEQUENTIAL KEY FIELD    CH15P4
 * INDEX (ORDER) AND GENERATES A PRINTED REPORT..................    CH15P4
H
FCUSTMSTRIP  F 220  44             DISK
FLISTING O   F 132 132      OF     PRINTER
ICUSTMSTRSM  01
I                                         1   1 TCODE
I                                         2   6 CUST#                CH15P4
I                                         7  36 NAME                 CH15P4
I                                       P  37  400TDATE              CH15P4
I                                       P  41  442BALANC             CH15P4
C           TOTAL     ADD  BALANC     TOTAL   82      TOTAL BALANCES CH15P4
OLISTING H  301    1P                                                CH15P4
O        OR        OF                                                CH15P4
O                             UDATE Y   8                            CH15P4
O                                      45 'CUSTOMER MASTER FILE'     CH15P4
O                                      53 'LISTING'                  CH15P4
O                                      75 'PAGE'                     CH15P4
O                             PAGE  Z  80                            CH15P4
O          H  2    1P                                                CH15P4
O        OR        OF                                                CH15P4
O                                       7 'CODE'                     CH15P4
O                                      15 'CUST#'                    CH15P4
O                                      41 !CUSTOMER NAME'            CH15P4
O                                      59 'DATE'                     CH15P4
O                                      73 'BALANCE'                  CH15P4
O          D  2    01                                                CH15P4
O                             TCODE     6                            CH15P4
O                             CUST#    15                            CH15P4
O                             NAME     49                            CH15P4
O                             TDATE Y  61                            CH15P4
O                             BALANCA  76                            CH15P4
O          T 1     LR                                                CH15P4
O                                      59 'TOTAL CUSTOMER BALANCES'  CH15P4
O                                      63 '....'                     CH15P4
O                             TOTAL A  76                            CH15P4
```

Indexed file definition omits entries specifying it as indexed

Figure 15-18 Listing of a program that consecutively processes an indexed file in prime data area order.

An examination of the report in Figure 15-19, generated by the program modified to process an indexed file consecutively, indicates that the records are not in an ascending key field value order. Remember that the file processed is the one that was illustrated in Figure 15-13, which was loaded with unordered keys.

```
1/31/91                 CUSTOMER MASTER FILE LISTING                PAGE   1

CODE  CUST#           CUSTOMER NAME             DATE       BALANCE

  ┌──►00001   HENRY FORD                      1/04/91      120.00
  ├──►00004   DODGE BROTHERS                  1/07/91   19,001.00
  │   00003   LOUIS CHEVROLET                 1/08/91    3,000.00
  │   00008   STANLEY STEAMER                 1/12/91      800.40
  │   00011   WALTER P CHRYSLER               1/06/91    7,085.00
  │   00009   HENRY J KAISER                  1/10/91   25,000.00
  │   00010   JOHN STUDEBAKER                 1/12/91      674.00
  │   00018   RANSOM E OLDS                   1/15/91      950.00
  │   00019   MERCEDES BENZ                   1/18/91   90,010.00
  │   00020   FELIX WANKEL                    1/22/91      501.23

                       TOTAL CUSTOMER BALANCES....  147,141.63

  └──── When attributes for indexed file are not included in the File Description
        definition of the file, it is processed as a sequential file (prime data
        area) order.
```

Figure 15-19 Report generated by the program that consecutively processes an indexed file in prime data area order.

Sequentially Processing an Indexed File Within Key Field Limits

A select group of records may be accessed sequentially from an indexed file by either of the following two methods:

Using a limits record
Using the SETLL/READ operations

Each of these methods is discussed separately in the following paragraphs.

Using a Limits Record. Examine the indexed file listing in Figure 15-20, and notice that the range of records to be processed is controlled by a record input from a *Record Address file*. The record must include two key fields: the first key value for the low limit of the range and a second key value for the upper limit. Records will be read sequentially from the low key value through the upper key value. More than one group of records may be accessed in the same run; however, another record must be input from the Record Address file specifying the new key limits.

Notice that the lower and upper key values in the Record Address file do *not* have to be existing keys. For example, look at Figure 15-20. If the lower key value were 00005 instead of 00003 and the upper key were 00017 instead of 00019, processing would begin at key 00008 and end at 00011. In any case, the low key limit value must begin in the first column of the record, and the high key limit entry must immediately follow. Only one set of keys may be specified per record. If any other data is included in the body of the record, it will be ignored.

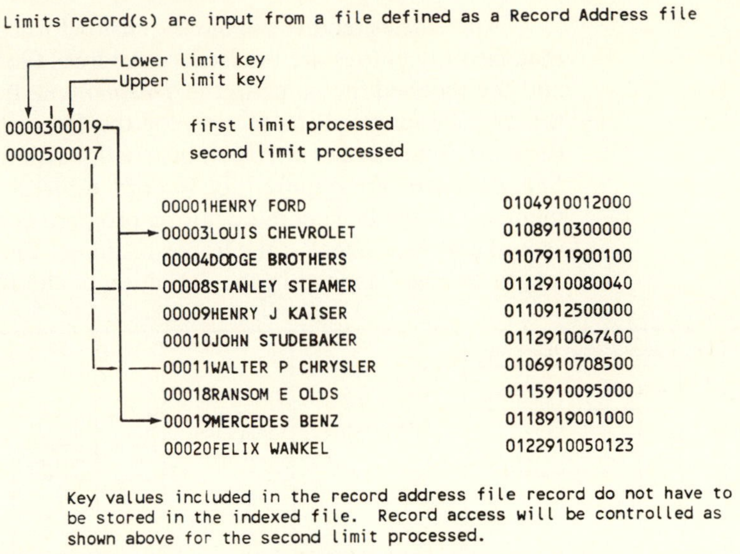

Figure 15-20 Logic of processing an indexed file between key field limits.

Furthermore, the key size defined for the Record Address file must be the same as the key size in the related indexed file. However, the keys stored in the two files may have different formats (zoned decimal and packed decimal). During program execution, the key format of the limits file will be changed into the key format of the indexed file.

Source Program Coding—Limits Processing Within Key Field Limits

The coding entries unique to the processing of an indexed file within key field limits are included only in the File Description and Extension Specifications. Figure 15-21 details the new entries that are required in the File Description form.

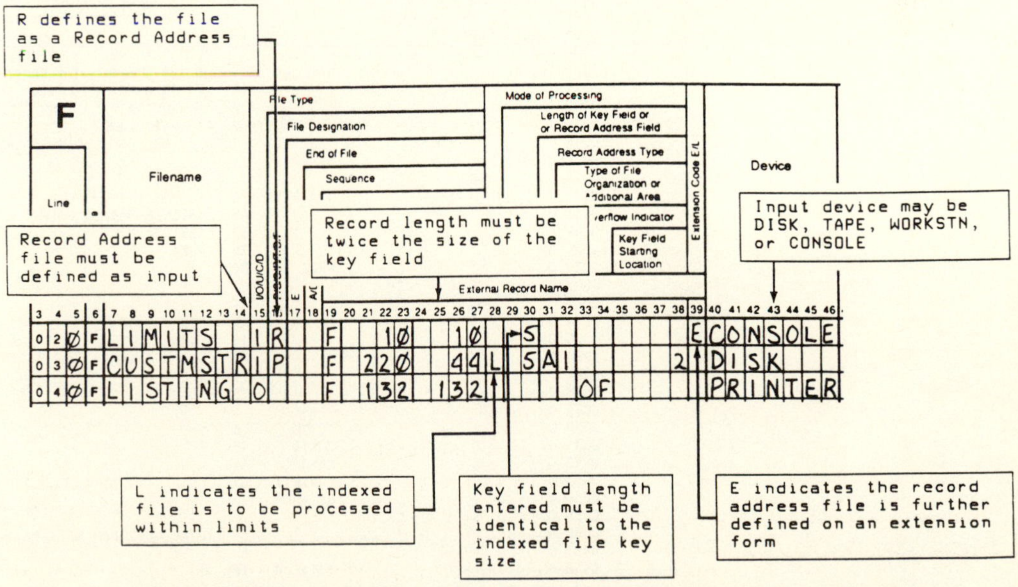

Figure 15-21 File Description coding for processing an indexed file within key field limits.

The entries required in the Extension form are shown in Figure 15-22. Notice that the only entries are the Record Address file name in the *From Filename* field and the indexed file name in the *To Filename* field. The letter E in column 39 of the File Description instruction for the Record Address file indicates that it is further defined in an Extension instruction. Similar to tables and arrays, *no Input Specifications* are required for Record Address files. If they are included, a terminal error will be generated during program compilation. The system knows the record and field sizes for the Record Address file from the key field and the record length entries included in the definition of the file.

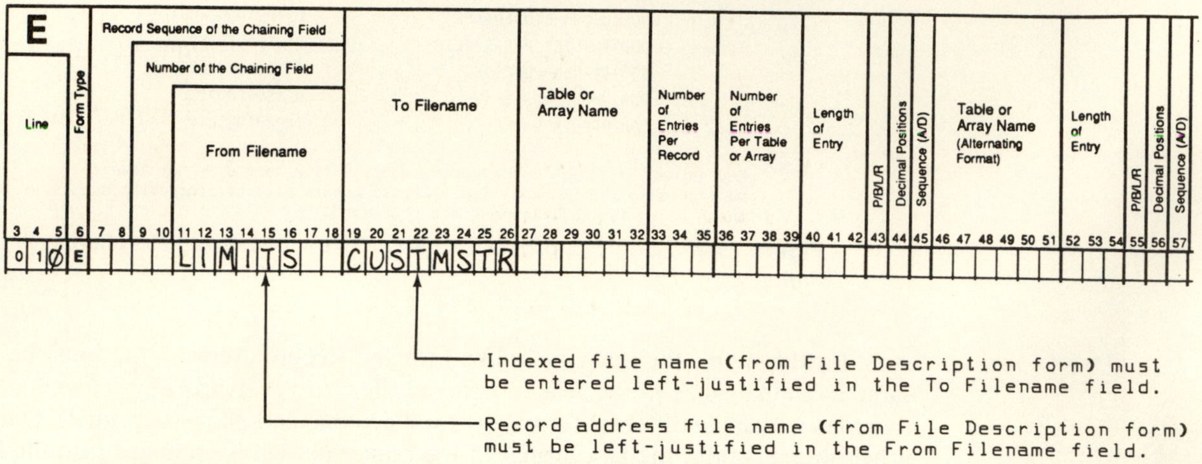

Figure 15-22 Extension Specifications coding for processing an indexed file within key field limits.

A listing of the complete source program that processes an indexed file between key field limits is illustrated in Figure 15-23.

```
... ... 1 ... ... 2 ... ... 3 ... ... 4 ... ... 5 ... ... 6 ... ... 7 ...
 * THIS PROGRAM PROCESSES AN INDEXED FILE WITHIN KEY FIELD LIMITS    CH15P6
 * AND GENERATES A PRINTED REPORT..................                  CH15P6
H                                                                    CH15P6
FLIMITS  IR  F  10  10  5       ECONSOLE      From and To key        CH15P6
FCUSTMSTRIP  F 220  44L 5AI    2 DISK         values are entered     CH15P6
FLISTING O   F 132 132     OF    PRINTER      by CONSOLE input       CH15P6
E    LIMITS  CUSTMSTR
ICUSTMSTRSM  01                                  Input coding is
I                                   1   1 TCODE  not supported for
I                                   2   6 CUST#  a Record Address
I                                   7  36 NAME   file
I                                P  37  400TDATE
I                                P  41  442BALANC                    CH15P6
C           TOTAL     ADD  BALANC   TOTAL   82      TOTAL BALANCES CH15P6
OLISTING H  301   1P                                                 CH15P6
O       OR        OF                                                 CH15P6
O                          UDATE Y    8                              CH15P6
O                                    45 'CUSTOMER MASTER FILE'       CH15P6
O                                    53 'LISTING'                    CH15P6
O                                    75 'PAGE'                       CH15P6
O                          PAGE  Z   80                              CH15P6
O          H  2   1P                                                 CH15P6
O       OR        OF                                                 CH15P6
O                                     7 'CODE'                       CH15P6
O                                    15 'CUST#'                      CH15P6
O                                    41 'CUSTOMER NAME'              CH15P6
O                                    59 'DATE'                       CH15P6
O                                    73 'BALANCE'                    CH15P6
O          D  2   01                                                 CH15P6
O                          TCODE      6                              CH15P6
O                          CUST#     15                              CH15P6
O                          NAME      49                              CH15P6
O                          TDATE Y   61                              CH15P6
O                          BALANCA   76                              CH15P6
O          T 1    LR                                                 CH15P6
O                                    59 'TOTAL CUSTOMER BALANCES'    CH15P6
O                                    63 '....'                       CH15P6
O                          TOTAL A   76                              CH15P6
```

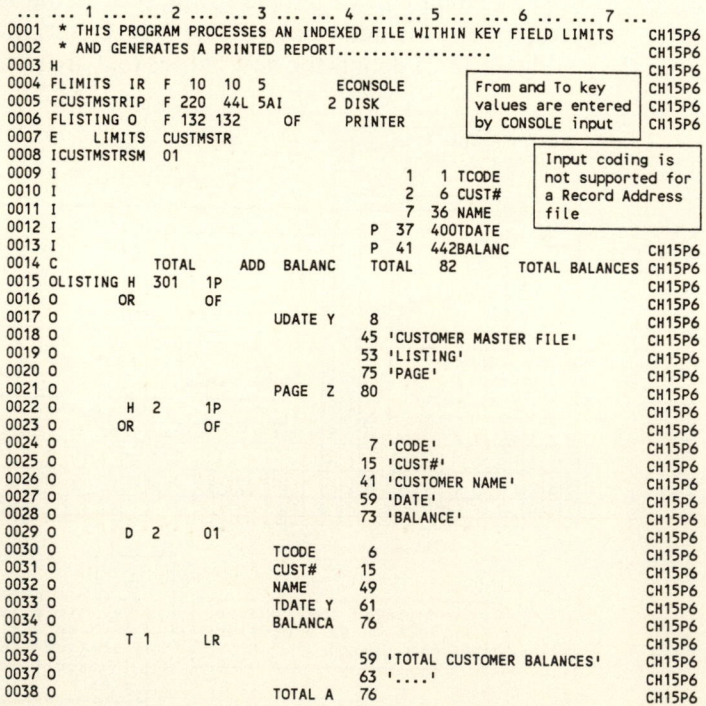

Figure 15-23 Source listing of a program that processes an indexed file within key field limits.

Notice that the program controlled the input of the *from* to *to* key fields by a CONSOLE file. Unlike previously discussed CONSOLE supported input files, a Record Address file does not require a record identification code entry or field definitions. The system supplies the prompts for the LOWER KEY and UPPER KEY entries. Any other input device supported by the system may be used to enter the key values.

The reports generated by the program that processes an indexed file within key field limits are presented in Figure 15-24. Both listings are the result of the key limit range that was illustrated in Figure 15-20. For the first report, the lower (00003) and upper (00019) key values are existing keys in the file, and the records are processed within that range. On the other hand, key value limits of 00005 and 00017 were entered which are not stored in the file. Consequently, the record with a key value greater than 00005 or 00008 is processed for the low limit and the record with a key less than 00017, or 00011 is processed through for a high key limit.

Report generated when key values 00003 and 00018 (keys in indexed file) are entered:

```
1/31/91                 CUSTOMER MASTER FILE LISTING                 PAGE    1

 CODE   CUST#              CUSTOMER NAME                DATE      BALANCE

        00003    LOUIS CHEVROLET                       1/08/91    3,000.00

        00004    DODGE BROTHERS                        1/07/91   19,001.00

        00008    STANLEY STEAMER                       1/12/91      800.40

        00009    HENRY J KAISER                        1/10/91   25,000.00

        00010    JOHN STUDEBAKER                       1/12/91      674.00

        00011    WALTER P CHRYSLER                     1/06/91    7,085.00

        00018    RANSOM E OLDS                         1/15/91      950.00

        00019    MERCEDES BENZ                         1/18/91   90,010.00

                                TOTAL CUSTOMER BALANCES.... 146,520.40
```

Report generated when key values 00005 and 00017 (keys not in indexed file) are entered:

```
1/31/91                 CUSTOMER MASTER FILE LISTING                 PAGE    1

 CODE   CUST#              CUSTOMER NAME                DATE      BALANCE

        00008    STANLEY STEAMER                       1/12/91      800.40

        00009    HENRY J KAISER                        1/10/91   25,000.00

        00010    JOHN STUDEBAKER                       1/12/91      674.00

        00011    WALTER P CHRYSLER                     1/06/91    7,085.00

                                TOTAL CUSTOMER BALANCES....  33,559.40
```

Figure 15-24 Reports generated by a program that processes an indexed file within key field limits.

Sequential Processing of an Indexed File Within Limits by the SETLL/READ Operations

The method by which the READ operation is used to process a sequential file was previously explained in Chapter 14. The same operation may be used to read an indexed file within limits (or sequentially). Accessed with a Set Lower Limit (SETLL) operation, processing times of the indexed file may be significantly reduced. Reading of the file begins at the record with a specified key value and not at the first record in the file. The syntax for the SETLL operation is detailed in Figure 15-25.

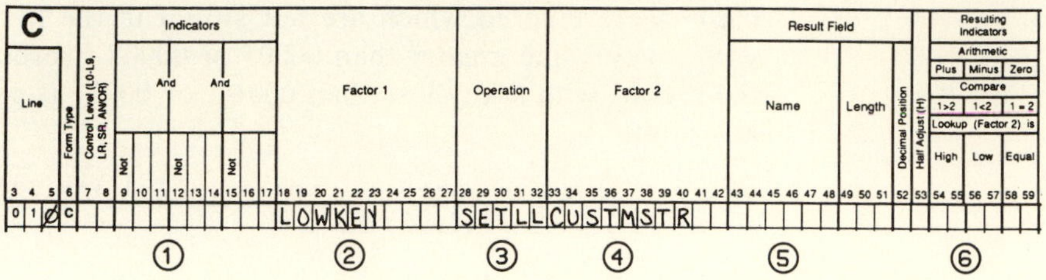

1. Total time and/or detail time indicators may condition a SETLL statement.
2. Factor 1 must contain a field name or literal that is the same length as the key size in the indexed file to be accessed.
3. SETLL word must be entered in Operation field.
4. Factor 2 must include the name of the indexed file to be limits processed. The indexed file must be defined in the File Description coding as a demand file (D in column 16) and include the letter L in column 28 to indicate that itis to be limits processed. Full-procedural files (F in column 16) may also be accessed with the SETLL operation. All other required entries must be included for the indexed file.
5. Result field not used.
6. Resulting indicators are not used. However, the RPG III/400 compilers on the IBM System/38 and AS/400's do support an indicator entry in the Equal field (columns 58-59). The indicator will turn on when the key value in the field or literal in Factor 1 is equal to a key in the indexed file.

   A record in the indexed file will be pointed to that has a key value equal to or greater than the field or literal value included in Factor 1.

   A READ (READE or READP) operation must follow a SETLL to retrieve the related record. The associated READ operation, however, does not have to immediately follow the SETLL. If a READ operation is executed before a SETLL operation, the SETLL will cause control to point to the first record in the file.

Figure 15-25 Syntax of the SETLL (set lower limits) operation.

Additional entries required in the File Description coding for the indexed file to support limits processing with the SETLL/READ operations are identified in Figure 15-26.

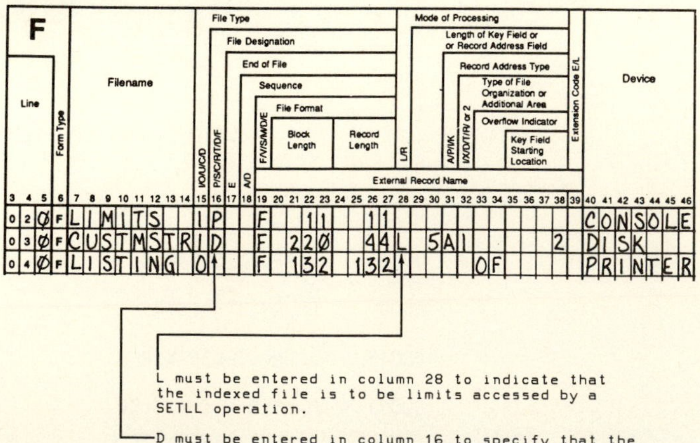

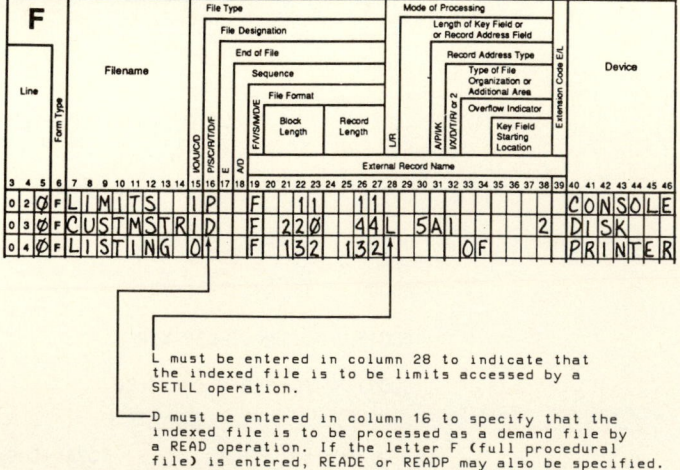

L must be entered in column 28 to indicate that the indexed file is to be limits accessed by a SETLL operation.

D must be entered in column 16 to specify that the indexed file is to be processed as a demand file by a READ operation. If the letter F (full procedural file) is entered, READE or READP may also be specified.

Figure 15-26 File Description entries required for the limits processing of an indexed file with the SETLL/READ operations.

The processing logic supported by the SETLL operation is shown in Figure 15-27. If an equal key is not found in the index of the indexed file, the SETLL operation will cause the pointer to point to the next highest key.

```
        SETLL points the search key value at a key stored in the index that
        is equal to or greater than the search key.

            00003...
                   .
sets processing    .      00001HENRY FORD                  0104910012000
  to begin here———→.....00003LOUIS CHEVROLET             0108910300000
                          00004DODGE BROTHERS              0107911900100
                          00008STANLEY STEAMER             0112910080040
                          00009HENRY J KAISER              0110912500000
                          00010JOHN STUDEBAKER             0112910067400
                          00011WALTER P CHRYSLER           0106910708500
                          00018RANSOM E OLDS               0115910095000
                          00019MERCEDES BENZ               0118919001000
                          00020FELIX WANKEL                0122910050123

        Sequential processing of the file from the SETLL position to an
        upper limit (or end of file) may be controlled by a READ, READE,
        or READP operation.
```

Figure 15-27 Processing logic of the SETLL operation.

The source listing of the program that sequentially processes an indexed file within key value limits using the READ/SETLL operations is presented in Figure 15-28.

```
... ... 1 ... ... 2 ... ... 3 ... ... 4 ... ... 5 ... ... 6 ... ... 7 ...
 * THIS PROGRAM PROCESSES AN INDEXED FILE WITHIN KEY FIELD LIMITS   CH15P7
 * WITH THE SETLL/READ OPERATIONS..................                 CH15P7
H
FLIMITS  IP  F  11  11          CONSOLE
FCUSTMSTRID  F 220  44L 5AI    2 DISK
FLISTING O   F 132 132     OF    PRINTER
ILIMITS  SM  01    1 CK
I                                  1   1 CODE                       CH15P7
I                                  2   6 LOWKEY                     CH15P7
I                                  7  11 HIKEY                      CH15P7
ICUSTMSTRSM  02                                                     CH15P7
I                                  1   1 TCODE                      CH15P7
I                                  2   6 CUST#                      CH15P7
I                                  7  36 NAME                       CH15P7
I                               P 37  400TDATE                      CH15P7
I                               P 41  442BALANC                     CH15P7
C            LOWKEY    SETLLCUSTMSTR                                CH15P7
C            AGAIN     TAG                                          CH15P7
C                      READ CUSTMSTR              90                CH15P7
C   90                 GOTO END                                     CH15P7
C            HIKEY     COMP CUST#              10  11 > OR =        CH15P7
C   10                                                              CH15P7
COR 11       TOTAL     ADD  BALANC    TOTAL   82       TOTAL BALANCES CH15P7
C   10                                                 PRINT IF FOUND CH15P7
COR 11                 EXCPT                           PRINT IF < OR =CH15P7
C   10                 GOTO AGAIN                                   CH15P7
C            END       TAG                                          CH15P7
OLISTING H  301    1P                                               CH15P7
O        OR        OF                                               CH15P7
O                         UDATE Y    8                              CH15P7
O                                   45 'CUSTOMER MASTER FILE'       CH15P7
O                                   53 'LISTING'                    CH15P7
O                                   75 'PAGE'                       CH15P7
O                         PAGE  Z   80                              CH15P7
O          H  2    1P                                               CH15P7
O        OR        OF                                               CH15P7
O                                    7 'CODE'                       CH15P7
O                                   15 'CUST#'                      CH15P7
O                                   41 'CUSTOMER NAME'              CH15P7
O                                   59 'DATE'                       CH15P7
O                                   73 'BALANCE'                    CH15P7
O          E  2    02                                               CH15P7
O                         TCODE      6                              CH15P7
O                         CUST#     15                              CH15P7
O                         NAME      49                              CH15P7
O                         TDATE Y   61                              CH15P7
O                         BALANCA   76                              CH15P7
O          T 1     LR                                               CH15P7
O                                   59 'TOTAL CUSTOMER BALANCES'    CH15P7
O                                   63 '....'                       CH15P7
O                         TOTAL A   76                              CH15P7
```

Lower and upper key values are entered via CONSOLE input

SETLL points to a key in the index that is = or > the key value in the Factor 1 field or literal. READ reads a record from the indexed file.

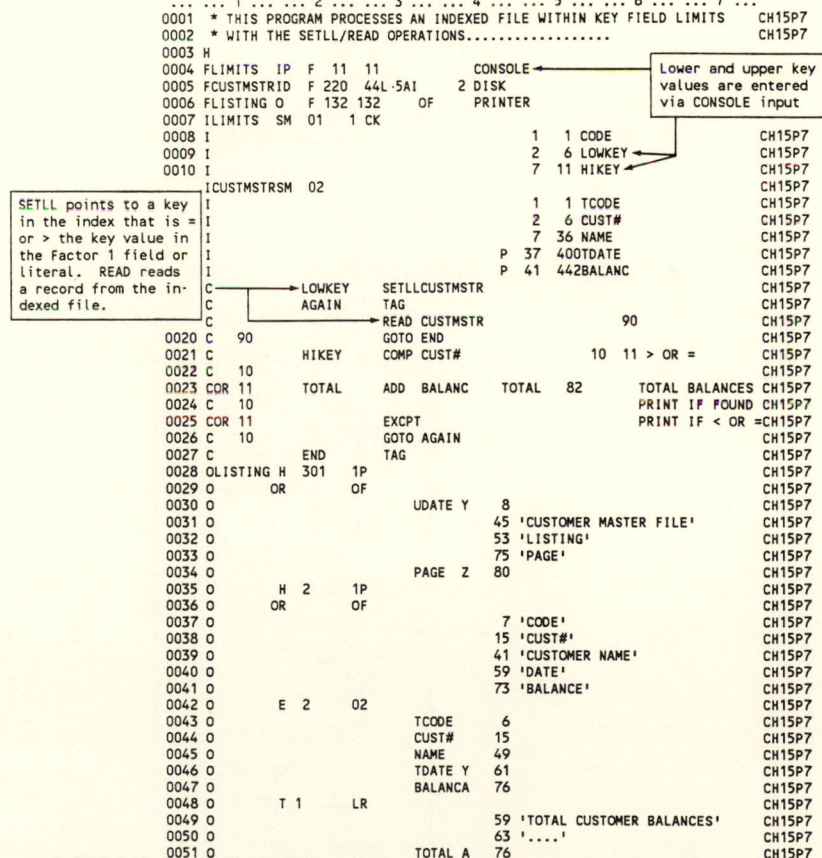

Figure 15-28 Source listing of a program that sequentially processes an indexed file within key limits by the READ/SETLL operations.

The calculations for the program are separately explained in Figure 15-29.

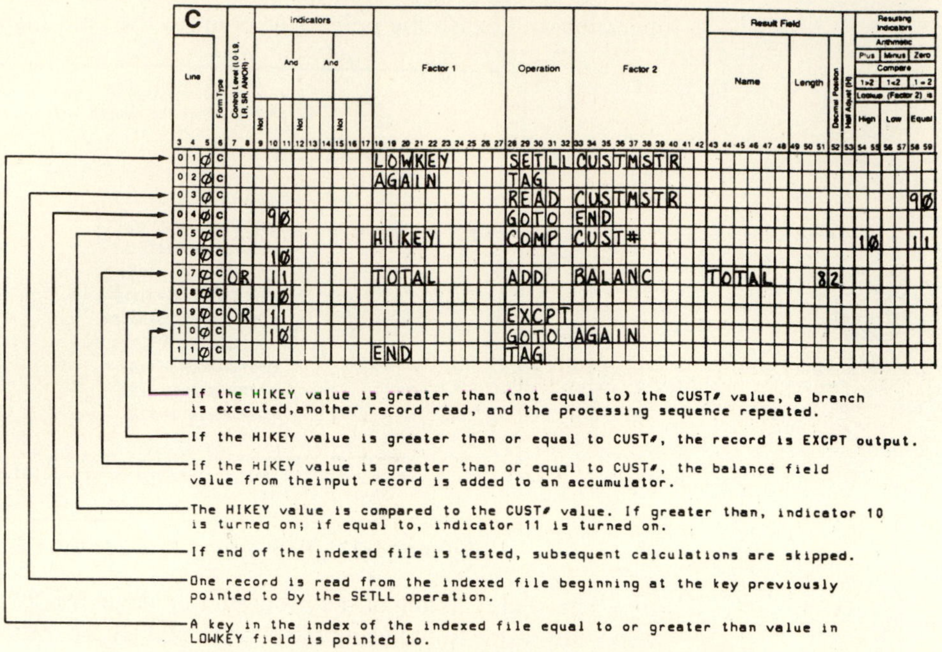

Figure 15-29 Calculations for the program that processes an indexed file within key limits by the SETLL/READ operations.

Reference to the flowchart in Figure 15-30 (or the program listing in Figure 15-28) indicates that output for each record is controlled at exception time. The EXCPT statement controls the printing of the data for each record within the looping routine. None of the other output instructions is modified in the program for exception output (E in column 15).

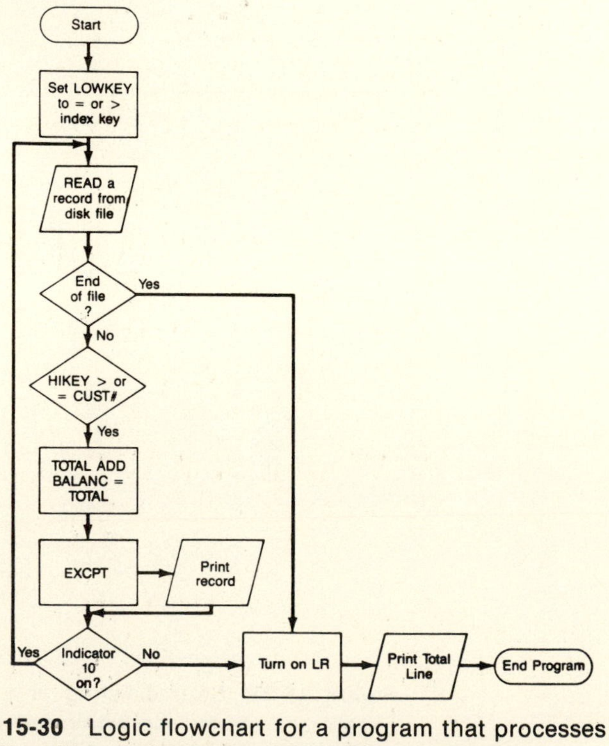

Figure 15-30 Logic flowchart for a program that processes an indexed file within limits by the SETLL/READ operations.

Two reports, one for records with a key value range of 00003 to 00019, and a second, for records 00008 to 00011, generated by the program are shown in Figure 15-31. Notice that key values 00003 and 00019 were entered and found in the index. However, 00005 and 00017 are not in the index. Consequently, a range of records from a key greater than 00005 (or 00008) and less than 00017 (or 00011) were read.

Report processed from key value 00003 to 00019 (key values 00003 and 00019 entered):

```
1/31/91                CUSTOMER MASTER FILE LISTING              PAGE    1

 CODE   CUST#              CUSTOMER NAME              DATE      BALANCE

        00003   LOUIS CHEVROLET                      1/08/91    3,000.00
        00004   DODGE BROTHERS                       1/07/91   19,001.00
        00008   STANLEY STEAMER                      1/12/91      800.40
        00009   HENRY J KAISER                       1/10/91   25,000.00
        00010   JOHN STUDEBAKER                      1/12/91      674.00
        00011   WALTER P CHRYSLER                    1/06/91    7,085.00
        00018   RANSOM E OLDS                        1/15/91      950.00
        00019   MERCEDES BENZ                        1/18/91   90,010.00

                        TOTAL CUSTOMER BALANCES....  146,520.40
```

Report processed from key value 00008 to 00011 (key values 00005 and 00017 entered):

```
1/31/91                CUSTOMER MASTER FILE LISTING              PAGE    1

 CODE   CUST#              CUSTOMER NAME              DATE      BALANCE

        00008   STANLEY STEAMER                      1/12/91      800.40
        00009   HENRY J KAISER                       1/10/91   25,000.00
        00010   JOHN STUDEBAKER                      1/12/91      674.00
        00011   WALTER P CHRYSLER                    1/06/91    7,085.00

                        TOTAL CUSTOMER BALANCES....   33,559.40
```

Figure 15-31 Reports generated by a program that processes an indexed file within a range of keys by the SETLL/READ operations.

FULL-PROCEDURAL FILES

A *full-procedural file* does not follow the normal RPG cycle for processing records, but instead reads records from an indexed (or direct) file only when a CHAIN, READ, READE, READP, or SETLL operation is executed. In addition to those operations, IBM's System/38 and AS/400 series of computers support OPEN, CLOSE, WRITE, DELET, READC, and SETGT operations for full-procedural files. The READE, READP, and SETGT operations are discussed in this chapter, and the others are introduced in Chapter 21.

Full-procedural files combine the processing functions of chained and demand files. They support both the random and sequential processing of an indexed (or direct file) by key field. If a file was not defined as full-procedural and if random and sequential processing were both required in the same program, the file would have to be defined twice in the File Description Specifications: once as a demand file (D in column 16) and again as a chained file (C in column 16). Only *one* file definition has to be included when the file is defined as full-procedural.

A full-procedural file may be defined as an *input* or *update* file and must be stored on a DISK device. Figure 15-32 details the syntax required for defining a file as full-procedural.

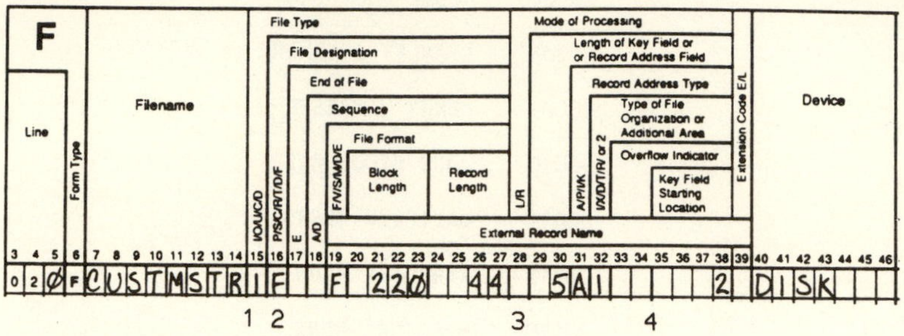

1. An indexed (or direct) file specified as full-procedural must be defined as an input (I in column 15) or update file (U in column 15).

2. Letter F must be entered in column 16 to define the file as full-procedural.

3. No entry is permitted in the Mode of Processing field (column 28).

4. All other entries related to the definition of an indexed file are required.

Note: Other than the column 15 and 16 entries and record length, the only entry for System/38 and AS/400 RPG III for indexed (keyed) files is a K in column 31. For nonkeyed files (sequential) the letter K is omitted. Other attributes for indexed (keyed) files are defined in the physical or logical file.

Figure 15-32 File Description syntax for defining an indexed file as full-procedural.

SETGT Operation (Set Greater Than)

The SETGT operation may be used only with full-procedural files. Similar to the SETLL operation, its function is to begin processing at some key in the index of an indexed file (or relative record number of a direct file) instead of at the first key. The SETGT and SETLL operations differ in that the SETGT automatically "points" to a key value higher than the search key value (Factor 1 entry). Remember that the SETLL operation points first to a key value equal to the search key, and then if it doesn't find it, to the next higher key. The SETGT operations immediately points to a key higher than the search key (Factor 1) value. Figure 15-33 explains the syntax of this operation.

In addition to a field name or literal, the figurative constant *LOVAL may be specified in Factor 1 of the SETGT statement so that processing will begin with the first record in the file. *HIVAL may be included in Factor 1 to position the pointer so that processing begins with the last record in the file (the file must be read backward by the READP operation).

The processing logic of the SETGT operation is illustrated in Figure 15-34.

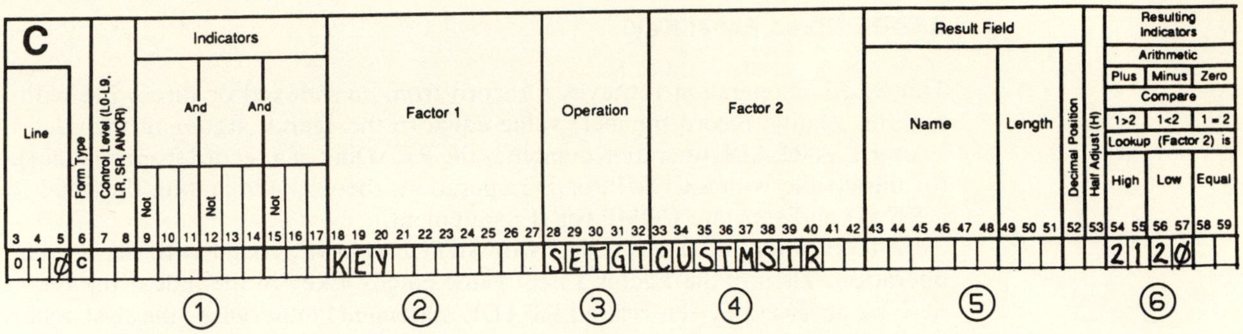

1. Total time and/or detail time indicators may condition a SETGT statement.

2. Factor 1 must contain a field name or literal that is the same length as the key size in the indexed file to be accessed.

3. SETGT word must be entered in Operation field.

4. Factor 2 must include the name of the indexed (or direct) file to be limits processed. The indexed (or direct) file must be defined in the File Description coding as a full-procedural file (F in column 16). The Mode of processing entry (R or L) in column 28 must be omitted. All other entries related to indexed or direct file must be included in the file definition.

5. Result field not used.

6. A Resulting Indicator may be specified in columns 54-55 which will turn on if a record is not found with a key or relative record number value greater than the search item specified in Factor 1. An indicator may be entered in columns 56-57 which will turn on if an error occurs during execution of the SETGT statement.

   A READ (READE or READP) operation must follow a SETGT to retrieve the related record from the file. The associated READ (READE or READP) operation, however, does not have to immediately follow the SETGT instruction.

   If the SETGT statement does not find a key value greater than the search argument, the file is positioned at the end.

Figure 15-33 Syntax for the SETGT operation.

SETGT points the search key value at a key stored in the index that is <u>greater than</u> the search key.

```
                     00003...
                         .
 sets processing         .   00001HENRY FORD               0104910012000
  to begin here          .   00003LOUIS CHEVROLET          0108910300000
                         .....00004DODGE BROTHERS          0107911900100
                              00008STANLEY STEAMER         0112910080040
                              00009HENRY J KAISER          0110912500000
                              00010JOHN STUDEBAKER         0112910067400
                              00011WALTER P CHRYSLER       0106910708500
                              00018RANSOM E OLDS           0115910095000
                              00019MERCEDES BENZ           0118919001000
                              00020FELIX WANKEL            0122910050123
```

Sequential processing of the file from the SETGT position to a lower (or beginning of file) or upper limit (or end of file) may be controlled by a READ, READE, or READP operation.

Figure 15-34 Processing logic of the SETGT operation.

READE (Read Equal Key)

The READE operation retrieves a record from an indexed or direct file with a key (or relative record number) value equal to the search argument included in Factor 1. A READE operation combines the READing of a record from an indexed (or direct) file with a COMP (or IF) operation, thereby eliminating the need for a READ and separate COMP (or IF) statement.

To position the file, a CHAIN or SETLL is always used with the READE operation. Then, if the Factor 1 item value equals a key in the index, the record may be accessed by the related READE statement. Otherwise, the first record in the file will be read, and if the key is not equal to the item value in Factor 1, the READE statement will fail. For any subsequent READE instructions to be successful, the file must be repositioned. Figure 15-35 details the syntax for the READE operation.

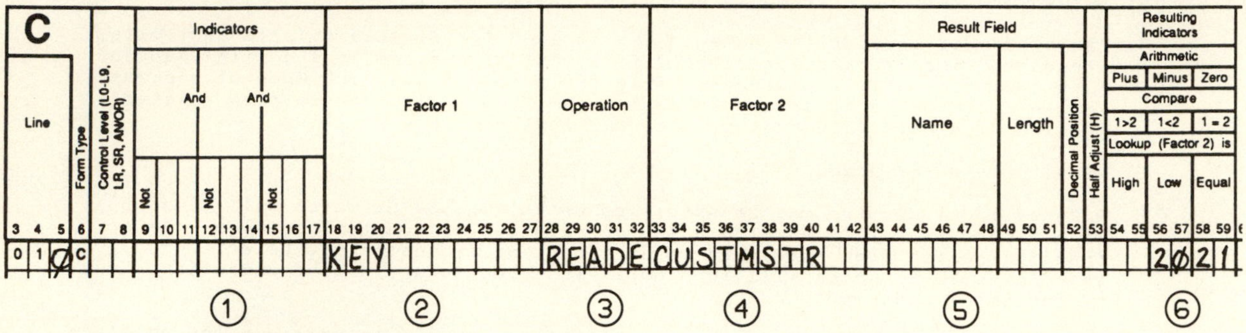

1. Total time and/or detail time indicators may condition a READE statement.

2. Factor 1 must contain a field name or literal that is the same length as the key size in the indexed file to be accessed.

3. READE word must be entered in Operation field.

4. Factor 2 must include the name of the indexed (or direct) file to be limits processed. The indexed (or direct) file must be defined in the File Description coding as a full-procedural file (F in column 16). For externally described files, E in column 19 of the File Description definition of the file (System/38 and AS/400 only), a record format name must be entered in Factor 2.

5. Result field not used.

6. A Resulting Indicator must be entered in columns 58-59 which will turn on if a record is not found with a key or relative record number value equal to the search item specified in Factor 1 or if an end of file condition occurs. An indicator may be entered in columns 56-57 which will turn on if an error condition occurs during execution of the READE statement.

   If a READE operation is not successful, the file must be repositioned by a SETLL, SETGT, or CHAIN operation or all subsequent READ, READE, or READP instructions will fail.

Figure 15-35 Syntax for the READE (Read Equal) operation.

The READE statement is useful for an indexed file that supports duplicate key values. In that environment, a group of records with the same key may be processed before an unequal condition is sensed. An example of how the READE operation is used and its processing logic are illustrated in Figure 15-36.

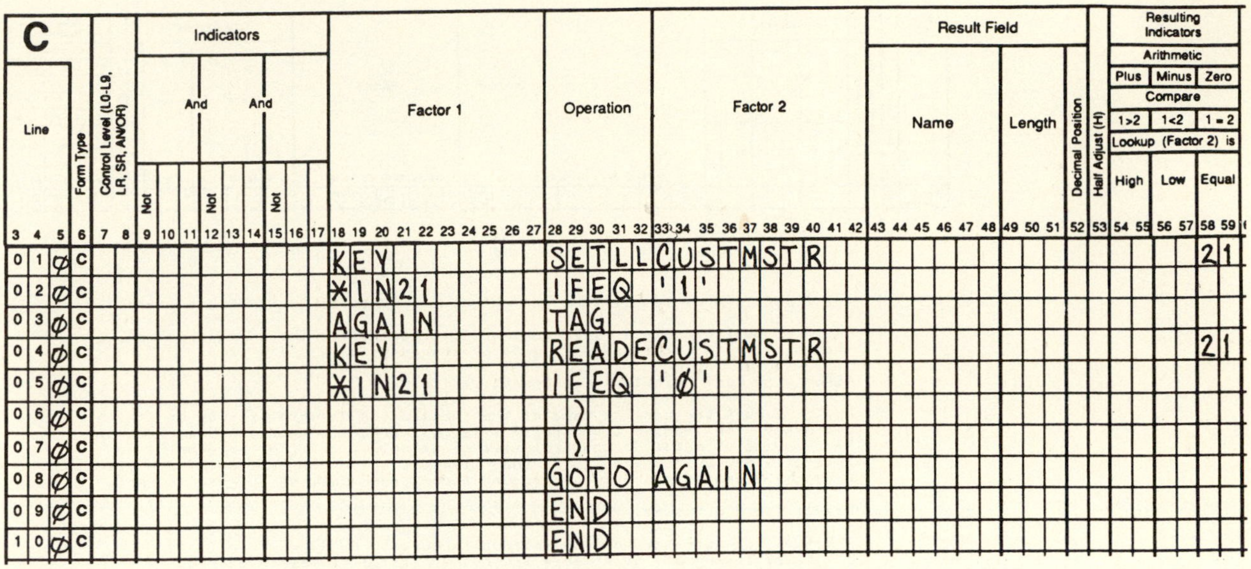

```
Line  Form  Factor 1   Operation  Factor 2    Resulting Indicators (Equal 58-59)
01ø   C     KEY        SETLL      CUSTMSTR    21
02ø   C     *IN21      IFEQ       '1'
03ø   C     AGAIN      TAG
04ø   C     KEY        READE      CUSTMSTR    21
05ø   C     *IN21      IFEQ       'ø'
06ø   C                }
07ø   C                }
08ø   C                GOTO       AGAIN
09ø   C                END
10ø   C                END
```

SETLL operation points to a key in the index that has the search key value.

If found, the READE statement reads a record for processing.

GOTO statement transfers control back to execute the READE statement again. When the value in the search argument is not equal to the key value of the next record read, the indicator specified in columns 58-59 turns on and the looping process ends. If the READE statement is to be executed again (with another search key value), the file must be repositioned with a CHAIN or SETLL.

```
00004............
                .
                .    00001HENRY FORD            0104910012000
                .    00003LOUIS CHEVROLET       0108910300000
                .....00004DODGE BROTHERS        0107911900100
                .....00004DODGE BROTHERS        0118910005000
                .....00004DODGE BROTHERS        0130910084500
                     00008STANLEY STEAMER       0112910080040
                     00009HENRY J KAISER        0110912500000
                     00010JOHN STUDEBAKER       0112910067400
                     00011WALTER P CHRYSLER     0106910708500
                     00018RANSOM E OLDS         0115910095000
                     00019MERCEDES BENZ         0118919001000
                     00020FELIX WANKEL          0122910050123
                          end-of-file
```

Figure 15-36 READE operation coding and processing logic.

READP Operation (Read Prior Record)

The READP operation controls the reading of a prior record from a full-procedural file. A CHAIN, SETLL, SETGT, READ, or READE must position the pointer at a record in the indexed or direct file before this operation may be executed. Then, the file may be processed backward until the required test condition is satisfied. The syntax for the READP operation is presented in Figure 15-37.

An example of how the READP operation controls processing is shown in Figure 15-38. Notice that the figurative constant *HIVAL is used to set the pointer at the end of the file. A routine included in calculations will process the file backward to the first record. Control may be included to process only one record or a select number; the entire file does not have to be read with a READP instruction.

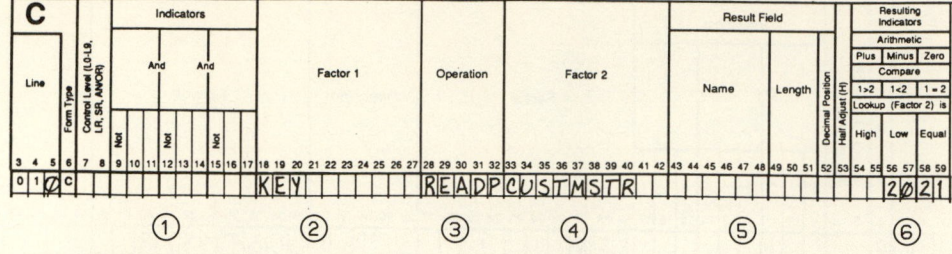

Line	Form Type	Control Level (L0-L9, LR, SR, AN/OR)	Indicators	Factor 1	Operation	Factor 2	Result Field Name	Length	Decimal Positions	Half Adjust (H)	Resulting Indicators High (54-55)	Low (56-57)	Equal (58-59)
01Ø	C			KEY	READP	CUSTMSTR						2Ø	21
			①	②	③	④	⑤						⑥

1. Total time and/or detail time indicators may condition a READP statement.
2. Factor 1 must contain a field name or literal that is the same length as the key size in the indexed file to be accessed.
3. READP word must be entered in Operation field.
4. Factor 2 must include the name of the indexed (or direct) file to be limits processed. The indexed (or direct) file must be defined in the File Description coding as a full-procedural file (F in column 16). For externally described files, E in column 19 of the File Description definition of the file (System/38 and AS/400 only), a record format name must be entered in Factor :
5. Result field not used.
6. A Resulting Indicator must be entered in columns 58-59 which will turn on if the beginning of the file is tested. An indicator may be entered in columns 56-57 which will turn on if an error condition occurs during execution of the READP statement.

   If a READP operation is not successful, the file must be repositioned by a SETLL, SETGT, or CHAIN operation or all subsequent READ, READE, or READP instructions will fail.

Figure 15-37 Syntax for the READP (Read Prior Record) operation.

Line	Form Type	Control Level	Indicators	Factor 1	Operation	Factor 2	Result Field Name	Length	Decimal Positions	Half Adjust (H)	High (54-55)	Low (56-57)	Equal (58-59)
01Ø	C			*HIVAL	SETGT	CUSTMSTR							
02Ø	C			LOOP	TAG								
03Ø	C				READP	CUSTMSTR							21
04Ø	C				(								
05Ø	C				(								
06Ø	C		N21		EXCPT								
07Ø	C		N21		GOTO	LOOP							

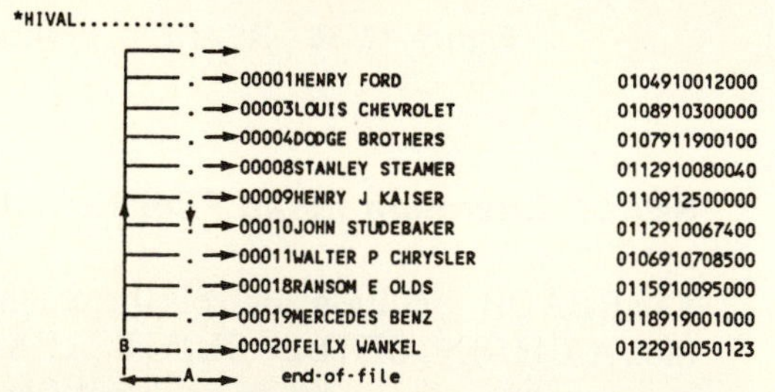

*HIVAL represents a key value of X'999...9F'. X indicates the hexadecimal value of the figurative constant and is not part of the value. The number of 9's supplied is determined by the size of the key field and the letter F in the low order position indicates a positive value.

A - Because *HIVAL was specified as the search argument (Factor 1), the pointer is set at end of file. Any field or literal may be specified in Factor 1 to point to a key in the index.

B - The READP operation reads the previous record. If all of the preceding records in the file are not to be processed, a comparison test must be included to determine when the low condition is satisfied. An iterative routine must be included in the program if more than one record is to be processed.

A valid indicator must be specified in columns 58-59 which will turn on when the beginning of the file is tested. An optional indicator may be included in columns 56-57 to test for an error condition.

Figure 15-38 READP (Read Prior Record) operation coding and processing logic.

SUMMARY

In addition to a prime data area, indexed-sequential files also include an index. The key values and the addresses of the records in the file are stored in the index.

As compared to sequential file organization, indexed-sequential files offer the following advantages:

1. Faster random processing.
2. Add records do not destroy the sorted integrity of the index.
3. Because processing may begin at a record other than the first one in the file, faster sequential processing is supported.
4. May be processed in different key field orders by alternate indexes.

Indexed files may be loaded with records in an ascending key value order or in an unordered key sequence. The data records in the prime data area will be stored in the order in which they are initially loaded. The index will always be maintained in an ascending key value order, however. Only one additional entry in the File Description definition of the file (letter U in column 66) is required to control the unordered loading of an indexed file.

Indexed files may be processed sequentially in key value order, thus defining the file in the File Description entries as an indexed file. In addition, the indexed file may be processed in prime data area order by defining the file as sequential in the file definition (all indexed file attributes are omitted). Either of these two methods is controlled by the RPG logic cycle.

An indexed file may also be processed sequentially within key field limits by a Limits Record or with the SETLL/READ operations. The Limits Record method, which is under the control of the RPG logic cycle, requires that a Record Address file be defined. A Record Address file contains one or more records that include only low and high key values. The indexed file will be processed sequentially from and to those key limits.

The RPG logic cycle for processing an indexed file sequentially may be overridden by defining it as a Demand file. When an indexed file is defined as a Demand file, a READ, READE, or READP operation must be included in calculations to read records sequentially from the file. The READE and READP operations may be used only with a full-procedural file. Only one record is read from an indexed file by a READ, READE, or READP operation. If more than one record is to be processed, an iterative (looping) routine that provides for multiple execution of the READ or READP statement must be included.

A full-procedural file (defined with an F in column 16 of the file definition) does not follow the normal RPG processing cycle. Records are read from a full-procedural file only when a CHAIN, READ, READP, or the like is executed. A SETLL (Set Lower Limit) or SETGT (Set Greater Than) operation may be used to position a file so that processing begins at a record other than the first one. The SETLL operation may be used with either nonprocedural or full-procedural files, whereas the SETGT operation may be specified only for full-procedural.

QUESTIONS

15-1. Explain how an indexed-sequential file differs structurally from a sequential file.

15-2. Name some of the advantages of indexed-file organization. Identify any disadvantages.

15-3. How should the following application data files be organized? Unless otherwise indicated, assume that all are stored on disk.

GENERAL LEDGER	BACKUP (on magnetic tape)
ACCOUNTS RECEIVABLE	INVENTORY
DAILY TRANSACTIONS	CHECKING ACCOUNTS

Support your answer with an explanation of why you selected a type of file organization.

15-4. What are record keys? Where are they stored? Identify some field names that are often used as record keys.

15-5. How does the computer locate a record from an indexed file?

15-6. What input data restrictions exist for loading an indexed-sequential file? How may the restriction(s) be controlled in an RPG program?

15-7. Write the File Description instruction to define an indexed file. Assume that the file name is ARMASTER, the record size is 200, the blocking factor is 10, and the key is a 9-byte alphanumeric that is to be stored beginning in the third position of the records in the indexed file. Also explain the function of each entry.

15-8. How would Question 15-7 be modified to support packed keys?

15-9. If an indexed file, defined with all of its attributes, is sequentially processed by the normal RPG logic cycle, in what order are the records accessed? If an indexed file is defined as sequential, in what order are the records accessed?

15-10. What is limits processing? By what methods may limits processing be controlled in an RPG program?

15-11. Refer to your answer for Question 15-10, and explain when records are read from the file by each of the limits processing methods.

15-12. What is a Record Address file? For which processing method named in Question 15-10 are they specified?

15-13. What coding forms are needed to limits process an indexed file when a Record Address file is specified?

15-14. Refer to the File Description form shown below and explain the function of each entry in the definition of the two files.

Line (3-5)	Form Type (6)	Filename (7-14)	File Type I/O/U/C/D (15)	File Designation P/S/C/R/T/D/F (16)	End of File E (17)	Sequence A/D (18)	File Format F/V/S/M/D/E (19)	Block Length (20-23)	Record Length (24-27)	Mode of Processing L/R (28)	Length of Key Field or of Record Address Field (29-30)	Record Address Type A/P/I/K (31)	Type of File Organization or Additional Area I/X/D/T/R/V or 2 (32)	Overflow Indicator (33-34)	Key Field Starting Location (35-38)	Extension Code E/L (39)	Device (40-46)
02Ø	F	RANGES	I	R			F	18	18		9					E	DISK
03Ø	F	CUSTMSTR	I	P			F	2ØØØ	1ØØ	L	9	A	I		2		DISK

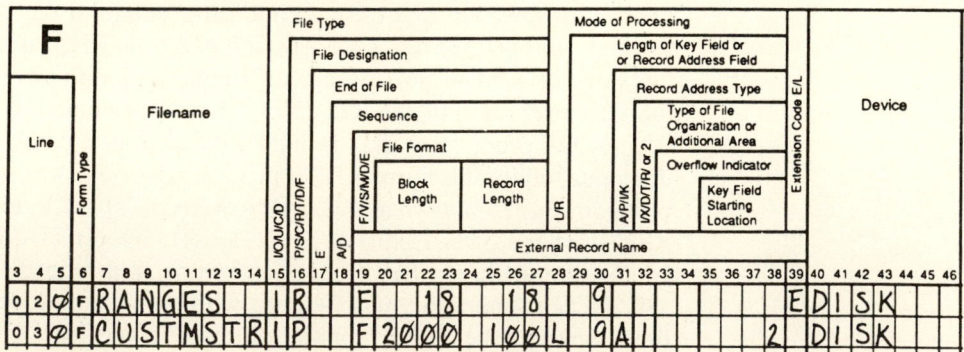

15-15. Determine what entries are required on any other form to support limits processing by the method indicated in Question 15-14.

15-16. How must record(s) in a Record Address file be formatted if they are stored on disk? Refer to Question 15-14 for any information you may need.

15-17. How many record limits may be processed during program execution?

15-18. Must the keys in a Record Address file be existing key values stored in the indexed file? Give an example to support your answer.

15-19. What is the function of the SETLL operation? Does the operation read records from an indexed file?

15-20. Write a SETLL statement to access the indexed file PARTMSTR with the search argument PART#.

15-21. What is the function of the READ operation? When in the RPG cycle are records read from an indexed file by this operation?

15-22. Write a READ instruction and assume that the indexed file to be processed is defined as ITEMMSTR in the program.

15-23. Explain the function of each entry in Question 15-22.

15-24. What additional entries (if any) are required in the definition of an indexed file to process it by a READ operation? Assume the file is defined as nonprocedural.

15-25. What controls must be included in an RPG program if more than one record is to be read by one READ operation?

15-26. Define a full-procedural file. How are indexed files defined as full-procedural?

15-27. Explain how processing controlled by a READE operation differs from a READ operation.

15-28. Identify the entries required for a READE instruction. What is the function of the Resulting Indicator(s)?

15-29. How does the processing supported by a SETGT operation differ from a SETLL operation?

15-30. Explain the processing features of the READP operation.

15-31. Identify the entries required for a READP statement. What is the function of the Resulting Indicator(s)?

15-32. Write the instruction(s) needed to process an indexed file backward from the last record to the first. Assume that the file name is STUDMSTR.

15-33. How must an indexed file be defined to process it with a SETGT, READE, or READP operation?

EXERCISES

15-1. An indexed-sequential disk file named INVMSTR is to be created as a master file for parts inventory. The file is to be loaded with data from a sequentially organized input disk file PART that has records stored in the following format:
Load the input records in disk file in the same field order. Define *part number* as the key file. Include a delete code field in the first position of the indexed file records and *pack* the quantity and cost fields. Assume that input records are in an ascending key field value order.

PART#	DESCRIPTION	QTY	CST/UNIT
9 9 9 9 9	9 9 9 9 9 9 9 9 9 9 9 9 9 9 9 9 9 9 9 9	9 9 9 9 9	9 9 9 9
1 2 3 4 5	6 7 8 9 10 11 12 13 14 15 16 17 18 19 20 21 22 23 24 25	26 27 28 29 30	31 32 33 34

15-2. If Exercise 15-2 was completed, modify your coding to prevent cancellation of program execution if a duplicate record is tested during the loading process.

15-3. Write the File Description instructions to sequentially process the indexed file created in Exercise 15-1. The file is to be processed in *index* order.

15-4. Modify the coding completed for Exercise 15-3 to process the indexed file in *prime data area* order.

15-5. Write an RPG program to *limits process* the indexed file created in Exercise 15-1 using the *limits record* method chart. Accumulate totals for quantity and records processed. The format of the report is shown in the following print chart. Notice that only Part Number, Description, and Quantity values are to be printed for each record processed.

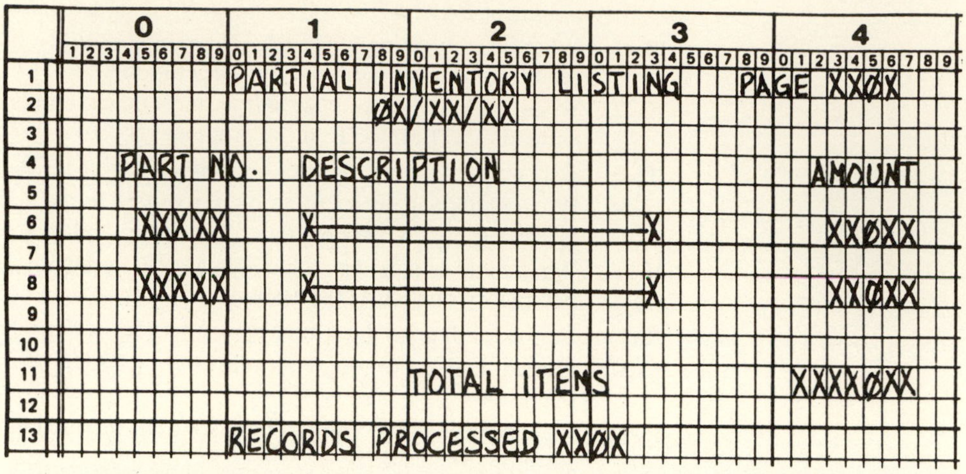

15-6. If Exercise 15-5 was completed, modify it to process the indexed file within key limits using the SETLL/READ operations method. On the other hand, if Exercise 15-5 was not completed, refer to the specifications for that assignment.

15-7. If Exercise 15-6 was completed, modify it to process the indexed file from the last record to the first. Otherwise, read to the specification included in Exercise 15-5 for the other requirements for this assignment.

15-8. Examine the following *partial* source listing and correct the logic and syntax errors:

```
... 1 ... ... 2 ... ... 3 ... ... 4 ... ... 5 ... ... 6 ... ... 7 ...EX158
 * THIS PROGRAM PROCESSES AN INDEXED FILE WITHIN KEY FIELD LIMITS    EX158
 * AND GENERATES A PRINTED REPORT..................                  EX158
H                                                                    EX158
FLIMITS  IP  F  10  10 10         CONSOLE                            EX158
FCUSTMSTRIR  F 220  44  5AI     2 DISK                               EX158
FLISTING O   F 132 132     OF     PRINTER                            EX158
E    CUSTMSTRLIMITS                                                  EX158
ICUSTMSTRSM  01                                                      EX158
I                                           1   1 TCODE              EX158
I                                           2   6 CUST#              EX158
I                                           7  36 NAME               EX158
I                                       P ·37  400TDATE              EX158
I                                       P  41  442BALANC             EX158
C          TOTAL      ADD  BALANC    TOTAL   82      TOTAL BALANCES EX158
OLISTING H  301    1P                                                EX158
O         OR       OF                                                EX158
```

15-9. Examine the following *partial* source listing and correct the logic and syntax errors:

```
... 1 ... ... 2 ... ... 3 ... ... 4 ... ... 5 ... ... 6 ... ... 7 ...EX159
 * THIS PROGRAM PROCESSES AN INDEXED FILE WITHIN KEY FIELD LIMITS    EX159
 * WITH THE SETLL/READ OPERATIONS..................                  EX159
H                                                                    EX159
FLIMITS  IP  F  11  11            CONSOLE                            EX159
FCUSTMSTRIS  F 220  44  5AI     2 DISK                               EX159
FLISTING O   F 132 132     OF     PRINTER                            EX159
ILIMITS  SM  01   1 CK                                               EX159
I                                           1   1 CODE               EX159
I                                           2   6 LOWKEY             EX159
I                                           7  11 HIKEY              EX159
ICUSTMSTRSM  02                                                      EX159
I                                           1   1 TCODE              EX159
I                                           2   6 CUST#              EX159
I                                           7  36 NAME               EX159
```

```
0016 I                                          P  37  400TDATE                EX159
0017 I                                          P  41  442BALANC               EX159
0018 C           LOWKEY    SETGTLIMITS                                         EX159
0019 C           AGAIN     TAG                                                 EX159
0020 C                     READ CUSTMSTR                                       EX159
0021 C                     GOTO END                                            EX159
0022 C           HIKEY     COMP CUST#                   10  11 > OR =          EX159
0023 C    10                                                                   EX159
0024 COR 11      TOTAL     ADD  BALANC    TOTAL   82          TOTAL BALANCES  EX159
0025 C    10                                                  PRINT IF FOUND  EX159
0026 COR 11                EXCPT                              PRINT IF < OR =EX159
0027 C    10               GOTO AGAIN                                          EX159
0028 C           END       TAG                                                 EX159
0029 OLISTING H  301    1P                                                     EX159
0030 O         OR       OF                                                     EX159
```

(Continued)

LABORATORY ASSIGNMENTS

Laboratory Assignment 15-1: CREATION OF A MASTER FILE FOR SAVINGS ACCOUNTS

Write an RPG to create a master file of savings accounts for a bank. The file is to be organized as indexed with Customer Number as the key. A sequential file includes the load data in the following record format:

FILE DEFINITION

SYSTEM Yours		DRAWN BY S. Myers
FILE NAME Yours		DATE 1/15/91 REV. NO. 0
CREATED BY S. Myers		FILE TYPE Disk
RECORD NAME None		KEY LENGTH None
RECORDING MODE Fixed	ORGANIZATION Sequential	SEQUENCE Ascending (ACCT#)
RECORD SIZE 85 bytes	BLOCKING FACTOR 1	BLOCKSIZE 85 bytes

FIELD DATA

FIELD NO.	FIELD NAME - DESCRIPTION	SIZE	CLASS C/P/Z/B	POSITION FROM	POSITION THRU	FORMAT/CONSTANT
1	Account Number	5	C	1	5	
2	Account Name	31	C	6	36	
3	Street	20	C	37	56	
4	City	16	C	57	72	
5	State	2	C	73	74	
6	Zip	5	Z	75	79	
7	Deposit Amount	6	Z	80	85	2 decimal positions

Processing: Load the indexed file records in the same field order as the input file. Include a delete code field in the first position, and pack the zip code and amount fields.

Include the necessary control(s) to prevent program cancellation (or halt on some systems) if an input record includes a duplicate key. The input data file must be in a sorted order by account number for this function to execute.

If a duplicate key is sensed, the first record of the group (detail time) is to be loaded to the file. Records with duplicate keys (total time) are to be identified in a printed report. Provide for a count of the number of records loaded to the indexed file and the number of duplicate records not loaded.

After the file is loaded, use the utility program on your system to check the results of the load process. Because the account balance and zip code fields are packed, a ''hex'' listing must be specified to interpret those field values. If a copy utility is not available, Assignment 15-2 may be completed to check the data in the indexed file.

Report Design:

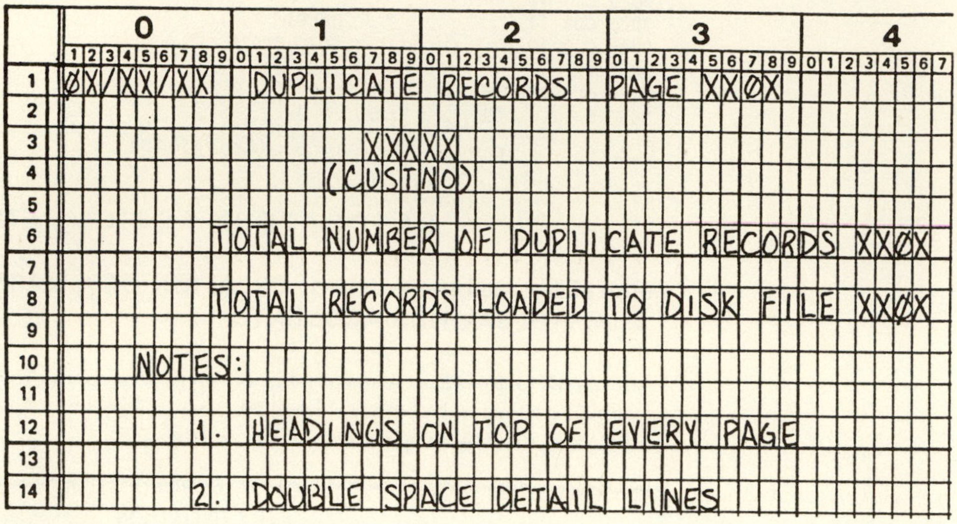
0
1
2
3
4
ØX/XX/XX DUPLICATE RECORDS PAGE XXØX
XXXXX
(CUSTNO)
TOTAL NUMBER OF DUPLICATE RECORDS XXØX
TOTAL RECORDS LOADED TO DISK FILE XXØX
NOTES:
1. HEADINGS ON TOP OF EVERY PAGE
2. DOUBLE SPACE DETAIL LINES

Input Data: Because Laboratory Assignments 15-2, 15-3, and 15-4 use the indexed file created by this program as input, a listing of the program or a file layout should be included with your documentation for this assignment.

Acct# Col 1-5	Account Name 6-36	Street 37-56	City 57-72	State 73-74	Zip 75-79	Deposit Amount 80-85
21345	JOHN DOE	212 ELM STREET	BRIDGEPORT	CT	06610	120000
31121	LOUISE LESSER	12 APPLES ROAD	BAHA	CA	92100	081299
48891	JUDY JOHNSON	114 EASY DRIVE	RALEIGH	NC	44410	006017
48891	DAVE HOOTEN	8 STRIKE LANE	LOS ANGELES	CA	90000	064111
51540	MARIE BLAKE	GREEN PASTURE RD	NEWARK	NJ	07733	940013
63141	JOSEPH WELCH	110 DILL STREET	NEW YORK	NY	10000	077777
71510	JOHN HINES	220 HIGH DRIVE	KEENE	ND	58847	000940

Laboratory Assignment 15-2: SEQUENTIAL PROCESSING OF THE SAVINGS ACCOUNTS MASTER FILE

Write an RPG program to sequential process the indexed file created in Assignment 15-1 in *index* order.

Master File Format: Refer to the documentation for the indexed file completed for Assignment 15-1.

Processing: Accumulate the account balance amount and print at last record (LR) time.

Report Design:

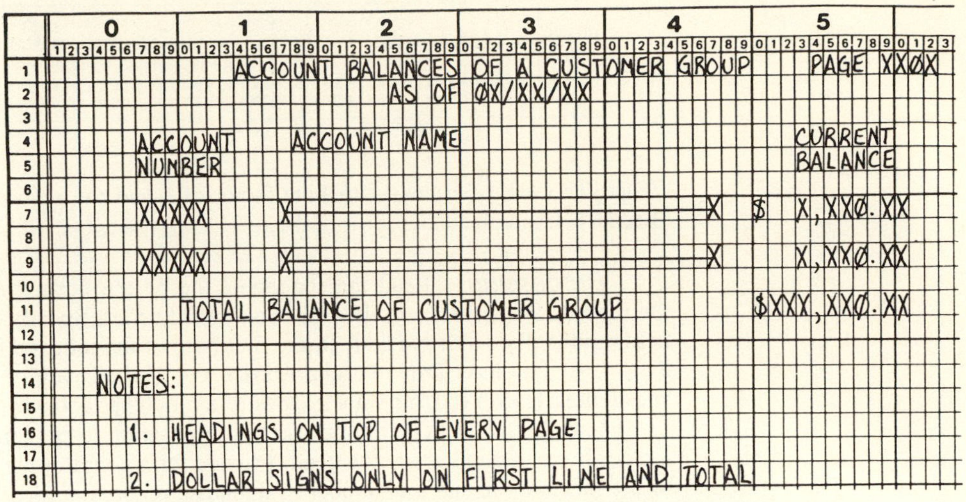

Laboratory Assignment 15-3: SEQUENTIAL PROCESSING OF THE SAVINGS ACCOUNT MASTER FILE BY THE LIMITS RECORD METHOD

Write an RPG program to sequentially process the indexed file created in Assignment 15-1 within limits by the Limits Record method (Record Address file). Generate two separate reports within the same program execution.

Input: Process the file first within key limits 48891 and 63141, and then from key 30000 through 80000. Input the limits keys via any input device supported on your system (i.e., DISK, DISKETTE, CONSOLE, KEYBORD, TAPE, or WORKSTN).

Report Design: Refer to Assignment 15-2 for the report format for this assignment.

Laboratory Assignment 15-4: SEQUENTIAL PROCESSING OF THE SAVINGS ACCOUNT MASTER FILE BY THE READ OPERATION

Write an RPG program to sequentially process the indexed file created in Assignment 15-1 within limits by the READ operation. Generate two separate reports within the same program execution.

Input: Process the file first within key limits 31121 and 51540, and then from key 20000 through 50000. Input the limits keys via any input device supported on your system (i.e., DISK, DISKETTE, CONSOLE, KEYBORD, TAPE, or WORKSTN).

Report Design: Use the report format for Assignment 15-2.

Laboratory Assignment 15-5: CREATION AND LOADING OF A CEREAL BRANDS MASTER INVENTORY FILE

Write an RPG program to create and load a cereal brands master inventory file as indexed-sequential. The input data is stored in a sequentially organized file with records in the format shown on the following page.

Format of Input Records:

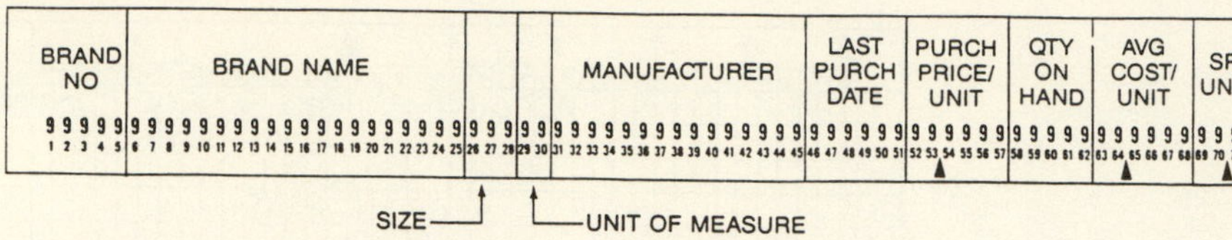

Note: The input file has a blocking factor of 1 and the records are stored in an ordered Brand Number sequence.

Processing: Read the sequential file by the normal RPG logic cycle, and load the records to the indexed file in the same field order. Specify Brand Number as the key field, and include a delete code in the first byte of the indexed file's records and *pack* the Size, Last Purchase Date, Purchase Price Per Unit, Quantity On Hand, Average Cost, and Selling Price Per Unit values. Specify a blocking factor of 20 for the indexed file.

Include the necessary controls in your program to prevent a runtime cancellation if a record with a duplicate key is read. Provide for a count of the number of records loaded to the indexed file and the number of duplicate records not loaded. Duplicate records are to be loaded to a sequential file in their input record image. In addition, generate the error report shown below:

Report Design:

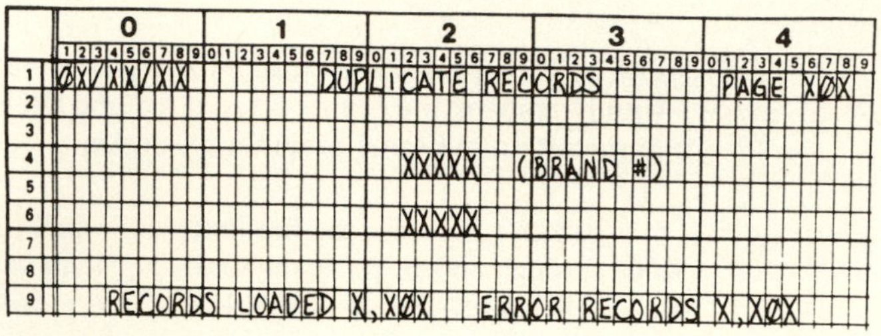

After the program is executed and the indexed (and sequential) files loaded, print a HEX listing of the indexed file to verify that the individual field values were stored correctly. If a COPY utility is not available to you, complete Assignment 15-6 and process the entire file by specifying that the key limits are from A0000 to Z9999. In addition, print a copy of the sequentially organized error file.

Input Data:

Brand# Col 1-5	Brand Name 6-25	Size 26-28	Measure 29-30	Manufacturer 31-45	Last Purchase Date 46-51	Last Purchase Price 52-57	Amount On Hand 58-62	Average Cost/Unit 63-68	SP Price/Unit 69-72
C1100	TOTAL	012	OZ	GENERAL MILLS	080791	016111	00360	016111	0183
C1134	KIX	014	OZ	GENERAL MILLS	080791	019990	00480	019990	0239
C2121	ET	014	OZ	GENERAL MILLS	080891	018750	00600	018750	0215
C4889	RAINBOW BRITE	011	OZ	RALSTON	081091	017000	00360	017000	0209
C4889	BRAN CHEX	014	OZ	RALSTON	081191	012899	00840	012899	0149
C5150	RICE CHEX	012	OZ	RALSTON	081191	014550	01200	014550	0169
C6314	RAISIN BRAN	020	OZ	KELLOGG	081291	018840	00960	018840	0209
C6550	CORN FLAKES	018	OZ	KELLOGG	081591	010000	02400	010000	0118
C6900	FROSTED FRAKES	010	OZ	KELLOGG	081591	010910	01800	010910	0129
C7000	GRAPE-NUT FLAKES	012	OZ	POST	081691	012788	02400	012788	0139
C7100	FRUIT & FIBER	014	OZ	POST	081891	016220	01200	016220	0189
C7440	ALPHA-BITS	015	OZ	POST	082091	017050	04800	017050	0195
C8000	CAP'N CRUNCH	016	OZ	QUAKER	082191	017233	06000	017233	0199
C8300	LIFE	015	OZ	QUAKER	082191	015000	02400	015000	0169
C8100	PUFFED WHEAT	006	OZ	QUAKER	082291	010000	12000	010000	0119

Laboratory Assignment 15-6: SEQUENTIAL PROCESSING OF THE CEREAL BRANDS MASTER FILE BY THE LIMITS RECORD METHOD

Write an RPG program to sequentially process the indexed file created in Assignment 15-5 within limits by the Limits Record method (Record Address file). Generate two separate reports within the same program execution.

Input: Process the file first within key limits C5150 and C8100, and then from key C2000 through C6000. Input the limits keys via any input device supported on your system (i.e., DISK, DISKETTE, CONSOLE, KEYBORD, TAPE, or WORKSTN).

Report Design:

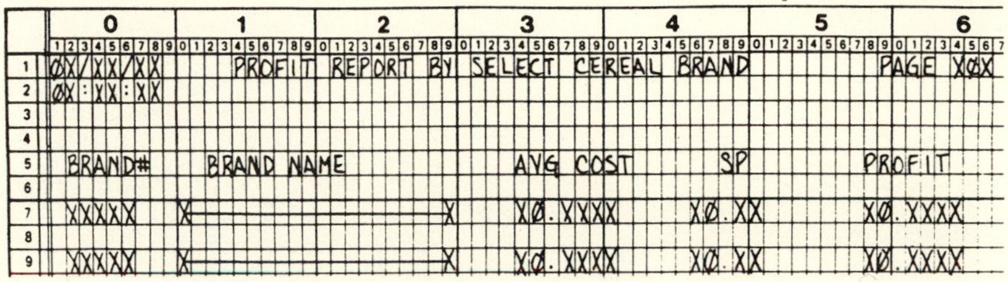

Laboratory Assignment 15-7: SEQUENTIAL PROCESSING OF THE CEREAL BRANDS MASTER FILE BY THE READ OPERATION

Write an RPG program to sequentially process the indexed file created in Assignment 15-5 within limits by the READ operation. Generate two separate reports within the same program execution.

Input. Process the file first within key limits C5150 and C8100, and then from key C2000 through C6000. Input the limits keys via any input device supported on your system (i.e., DISK, DISKETTE, CONSOLE, KEYBORD, TAPE, or WORKSTN).

Report Design. Use the report format for Assignment 15-6.

Laboratory Assignment 15-8: SEQUENTIAL PROCESSING OF THE CEREAL BRANDS MASTER FILE BY THE READP OPERATION

If the READP operation is supported by your system, modify Assignment 15-7 to process the indexed file with key limits by the READP operation. The file is to be read sequentially beginning with the last record through C6314. If Assignment 15-6 was not completed, use the print chart specified for that assignment for the report format for this program.

chapter 16
Indexed-Sequential File Maintenance

MAINTENANCE FUNCTIONS

After an indexed-file is created and loaded with data, the following maintenance functions are usually required:

1. Addition of data records
2. Record Inquiry
3. Record Update
4. Record Deletion
5. File Reorganization

Each of these maintenance functions will be explained and then controlled in separate RPG example programs. The indexed file loaded and defined as input for the programs in Chapter 15 will be used as the data base for the examples in this chapter.

File Addition

File addition may be defined as the loading of new records to an existing indexed (or sequential) file. The loading process differs for some systems. On most of the microcomputers and minicomputers, records are added after the last record stored in the file. Consequently, enough storage (usually expressed in record numbers or blocks) must be specified when the file is initially built. The addition of records to an indexed file in that environment is detailed in Figure 16-1. Even though the prime data area may not be in an ascending key sequence after one or more records are added to the file, the index is automatically maintained in the required ascending key value order.

For some mainframe systems, records are added in key order between existing records. When the track is full, records at the end are moved to an overflow (track or cylinder) area. In an IBM Virtual Storage Access Method (VSAM) environment, clusters (unused areas) are provided between groups of records for adds. Then, any add records are stored in its related cluster. For either scenario, the index is maintained in an ascending key value order.

```
        Add Records                                                Indexed File:

   A00002STUTZ BEARCAT         0201911643050.........  00001HENRY FORD              0104910012000
   A00006OTTO DIESEL           0205910083500....... .  00003LOUIS CHEVROLET         0108910300000
 ->A00002HENRY KAISER          0210912750000       . . 00004DODGE BROTHERS          0107911900100
|  A00023FERDINAND PORSCHE     0212910480125..... . .  00008STANLEY STEAMER         0112910080040
|  A00017HAROLD WINSTON        0226910010000... . . .  00009HENRY J KAISER          0110912500000
|->A00018RANSOM E OLDS         0228910090089  . . . .  00010JOHN STUDEBAKER         0112910067400
|                                             . . . .  00011WALTER P CHRYSLER       0106910708500
|                                             . . . .  00018RANSOM E OLDS           0115910095000
|                                             . . . .  00019MERCEDES BENZ           0118919001000
|    Records are added at the end of the file . . . .  00020FELIX WANKEL            0122910050123
|    in the order of the input file --------->. . . ...00002STUTZ BEARCAT           0201911643050
|                                             . . .....00006OTTO DIESEL             0205910083500
|                                             . .......00023FERDINAND PORSCHE       0212910480125
|                                             .........00017HAROLD WINSTON          0226910010000
|
 ----An attempt to add duplicate records (keys) to an indexed file that does not support
     duplicates will cause program execution to cancel or halt.

     Add records do not have to be in an ascending key value order.
```

Figure 16-1 Process of adding records to an indexed file (microcomputer and minicomputer environments).

APPLICATION PROGRAM—INDEXED FILE ADDITION

Documentation

An examination of the specifications in Figure 16-2 indicates that a program is to be completed that adds records stored in a sequential disk file to an existing indexed file.

PROGRAM SPECIFICATIONS Page 1 of 1

Program Name CUSTOMER MASTER ADDS **Program-ID** CH16P1 **Written By** S. Myers

Purpose Controls the addition of records **Approved By** The Boss

Input files (directory names):

DATA16P1 (stored on disk)

Output files (directory names):

CUSTMSTR (stored on disk)

ERRORS (stored on disk)

Processing Narrative:

Write an RPG program to add records to the customer master file (CUSTMSTR) with records stored in a sequentially organized transaction file (DATA16P1).

Input:

Supplemental record layout and file definition forms detail the file, record, and field information for the two files.

Processing:

Read the sequential file by the normal RPG processing cycle and add each record to the customer master file (CUSTMSTR). Include control in the program to prevent cancellation or halt of program execution when an attempt is made to add a record that has a key value equal to one already stored in the customer master file (CUSTMSTR).

Output:

Transaction records that do not have an existing key are to be added to the customer master file in that file's record format. Input records with duplicate keys are to be loaded to a sequentially organized disk file in the transaction file's record image.

Figure 16-2 Specifications for a program that adds records to an indexed file.

The system flowchart in Figure 16-3 shows that three disk files—a transaction file with the add records, the customer master file, to which the records are to be added, and an error file for duplicate records—are processed by the program.

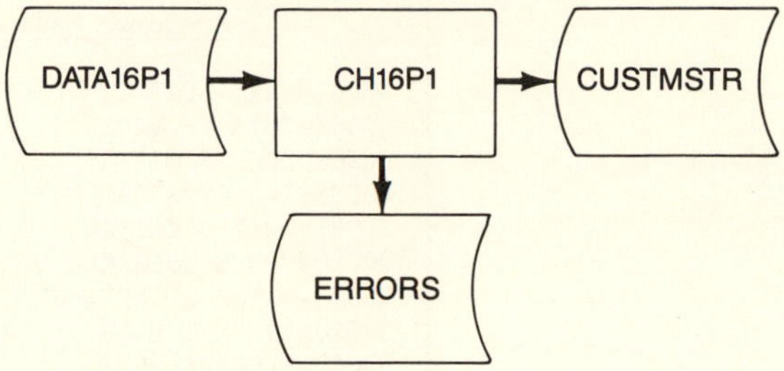

Figure 16-3 System flowchart for a program that adds records to the customer master file (indexed).

The format of the records in the transaction file and a listing of the add data are shown in Figure 16-4.

Add Records

```
┌→ A00002STUTZ BEARCAT          0201911643050
│  A00006OTTO DIESEL            0205910083500
├→ A00002HENRY KAISER           0210912750000
│  A00023FERDINAND PORSCHE      0212910480125
│  A00017HAROLD WINSTON         0226910010000
├→ A00018RANSOM E OLDS          0228910090089
│
└──Duplicate keys

Add records do not have to be in an ascending key value order.
```

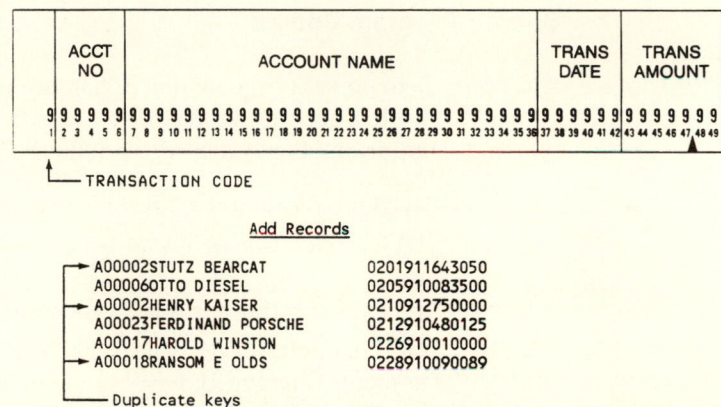

Figure 16-4 Record layout form and listing of the add data stored in the sequentially organized input file.

The File Definition form in Figure 16-5 documents the file, record, and field attributes of the customer master file (CUSTMSTR). All programs that reference

FILE DEFINITION

SYSTEM Yours		DRAWN BY S. Myers
FILE NAME CUSTMSTR		DATE 1/15/91 REV. NO. 0
CREATED BY S. Myers		FILE TYPE Disk
RECORD NAME None		KEY LENGTH 5 (ACCTS#)
RECORDING MODE Fixed	ORGANIZATION Indexed	SEQUENCE Ascending (ACCT#)
RECORD SIZE 44 bytes	BLOCKING FACTOR 5	BLOCKSIZE 220 bytes

FIELD DATA

FIELD NO.	FIELD NAME - DESCRIPTION	SIZE	CLASS C/P/Z/B	POSITION FROM	POSITION THRU	FORMAT/CONSTANT
1	Delete Code	1	C	1	1	D if deleted
2	Account Number	5	C	2	6	Key field
3	Account Name	30	C	7	36	
4	Transaction Date (last)	7	P	37	40	
5	Account Balance	7	P	41	44	2 decimal positions

Figure 16-5 File definition form for the customer master file processed by the adds program.

this file must specify the exact block, record, field sizes, and other attributes. A listing of the CUSTMSTR file before records are added is presented in Figure 16-6.

```
Customer Master File Listing

00001HENRY FORD                  0104910012000
00003LOUIS CHEVROLET             0108910300000
00004DODGE BROTHERS              0107911900100
00008STANLEY STEAMER             0112910080040
00009HENRY J KAISER              0110912500000
00010JOHN STUDEBAKER             0112910067400
00011WALTER P CHRYSLER           0106910708500
00018RANSOM E OLDS               0115910095000
00019MERCEDES BENZ               0118919001000
00020FELIX WANKEL                0122910050123
```

Figure 16-6 Listing of the customer master file before records are added.

Source Program Coding

The controls to prevent cancellation or halt of program execution when an attempt is made to write a record that has a key equal to one already stored in a file that does not support duplicate records include the following:

1. CHAIN operation for a nonprocedural or full-procedural file.
2. SETLL operation followed by a READ operation for a nonprocedural file.
3. SETLL operation for a full-procedural file.
4. WRITE operation (RPG III/400 only) for a full-procedural file. (Discussed in Chapter 21.)

Because the first method (CHAIN operation) is common to all systems, it is used in the example adds program to illustrate the control of errors during file addition.

A source listing of the program that adds records to the customer master file (CUSTMSTR) and includes error control is shown in Figure 16-7. The File Description, Input, Calculations, and Output Description entries for the adds program are discussed separately in the following sections.

```
... ... 1 ... ... 2 ... ... 3 ... ... 4 ... ... 5 ... ... 6 ... ... 7 ...
 * THIS PROGRAM ADDS RECORDS TO AN EXISTING INDEXED FILE (CUSTMSTR)  CH16P1
 * FROM RECORDS STORED IN A SEQUENTIAL DISK FILE.  CONTROL TO PRE-   CH16P1
 * VENT CANCELLATION (OR) HALT OF PROGRAM EXECUTION IS INCLUDED...   CH16P1
 * ADD RECORDS WITH AN EXISTING KEY IN THE CUSTOMER MASTER FILE      CH16P1
 * ARE LOADED TO A SEQUENTIAL DISK FILE IN INPUT RECORD IMAGE....    CH16P1
H                                                                    CH16P1
FDATA16P1IP  F  49  49           DISK
FCUSTMSTRUC  F 220  44R 5AI     2 DISK                         A
FERRORS  O   F  49  49           DISK
IDATA16P1SM  01
I                                        1   1 TCODE
I                                        2   6 CUST#                 CH16P1
I                                        7  36 NAME                  CH16P1
I                                       37  420TDATE                 CH16P1
I                                       43  492TAMT                  CH16P1
I                                        1  49 IMAGE
ICUSTMSTRSM  02
C           CUST#     CHAINCUSTMSTR             99   RECORD FOUND?
OCUSTMSTRDADD      99
O                          TCODE      1
O                          CUST#      6
O                          NAME      36
O                          TDATE     40P                             CH16P1
O                          TAMT      44P                             CH16P1
OERRORS  D       N99 02                                              CH16P1
O                          IMAGE     49                              CH16P1
```

Indexed file is defined as update, chained, and adds

CHAIN searches indexed file for an equal key. 99 turns on if key is not found

Records are added if a duplicate key was not found in the CUSTMSTR file

Add records with duplicate keys are loaded to an error file

Figure 16-7 Source listing of an RPG program that adds records to a customer master file (indexed).

APPLICATION PROGRAM—ADDS

File Description Coding

Figure 16-8 shows the additional syntax needed to control duplicate record errors by the CHAINing method. Notice that CUSTMSTR is defined as an Update (U in column 15) Chained (C in column 16) file. The R in the Mode of Processing field (column 28) specifies that the file is to be random processed and the letter A must be entered in column 66 to control adds processing.

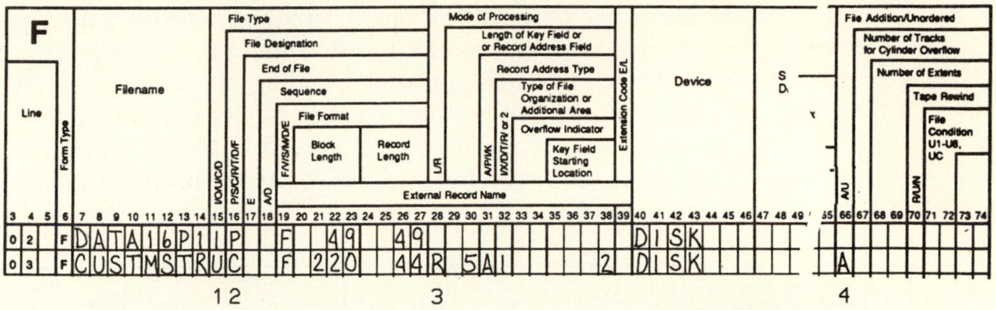

Explanation of Entries for the CUSTMSTR (Indexed) File:

1. U in column 15 defines the file in an update mode (both input and output)
2. C in column 16 defines the file as a chained file which must be random processed by the CHAIN operation.
3. R in column 28 indicates that the file is random processed. This mode of processing must be specified when the file is defined as U (update).
4. A in column 66 indicates that the addition of records to the file will be supported.

Figure 16-8 File Description coding for a program that adds records to an indexed file (CUSTMSTR) with error control.

Input Specifications Coding

An examination of the input form in Figure 16-9 indicates that the Record and Field Description instructions for the input file that contains the add records are specified. In addition, a Record Description statement is included for the

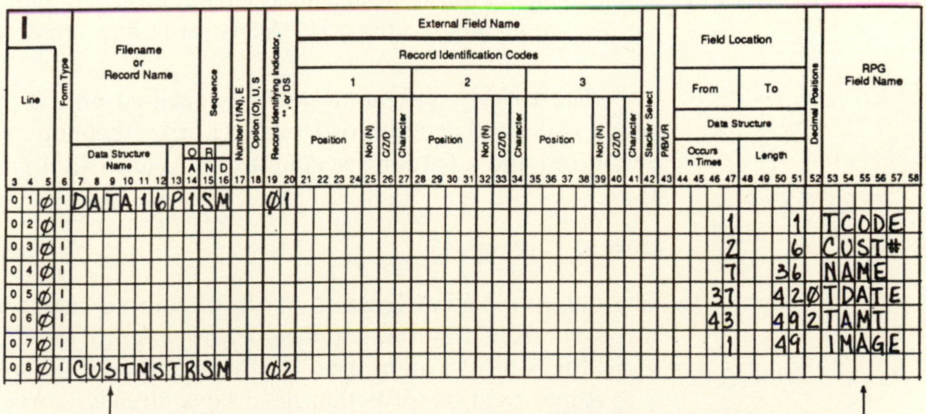

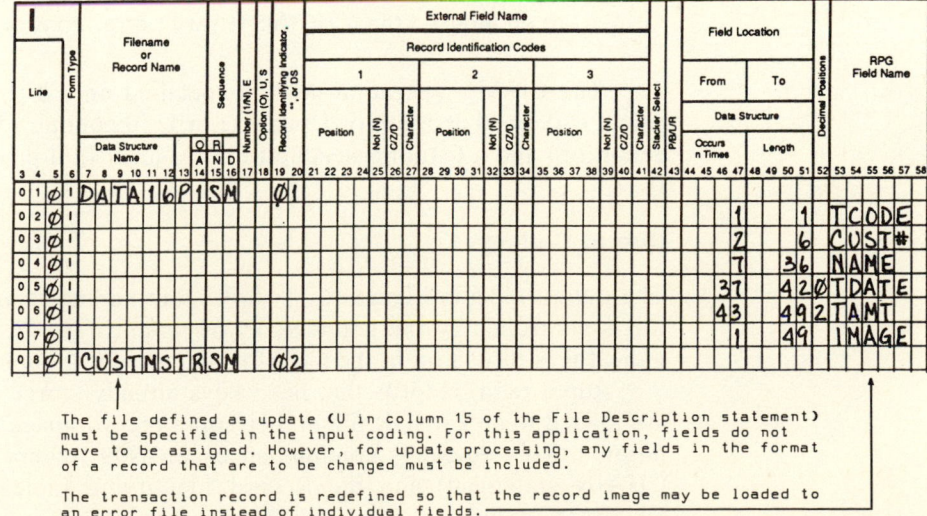

The file defined as update (U in column 15 of the File Description statement) must be specified in the input coding. For this application, fields do not have to be assigned. However, for update processing, any fields in the format of a record that are to be changed must be included.

The transaction record is redefined so that the record image may be loaded to an error file instead of individual fields.

Figure 16-9 Input coding for a program that adds records to an indexed file (CUSTMSTR) with error control.

CUSTMSTR file. When a file is defined as Update (U in column 15 of the File Description definition), it is processed as both input and output file. Consequently, the update files must be referenced in both the Input and Output Specifications. Because the CUSTMSTR file is CHAINed only to determine if a record with a duplicate key already exists, fields do not have to be defined. Notice, however, that on some systems this coding may result in a compilation error.

Calculation Coding

The CHAIN operation previously introduced in Chapter 14 is used to randomly access the CUSTMSTR file to determine whether a duplicate record exists. If the record (same key as the Factor 1 item) is not found, the resulting indicator 99 will turn on, which controls the adding of a record to the file. If a duplicate record is found, 99 will not turn on. For this example program, duplicate records are loaded to a sequentially organized disk file by an N99 condition. Figure 16-10 reviews the syntax for the CHAIN operation and explains its function in the adds program.

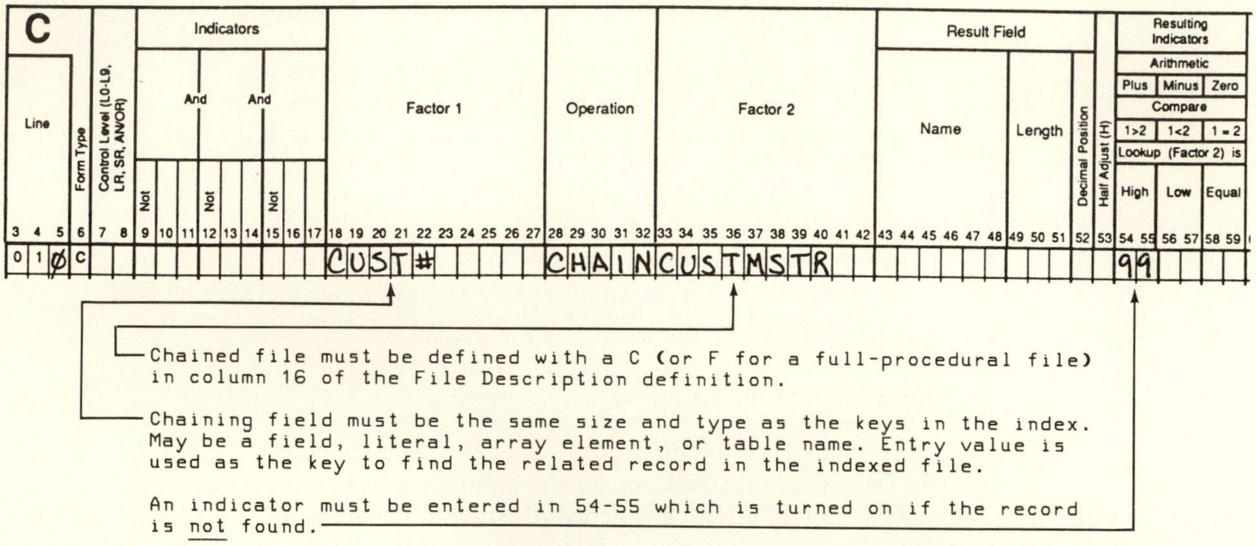

Figure 16-10 Calculation coding for a program that adds records to an indexed file (CUSTMSTR) with error control.

The CHAIN operation may be specified only if the chained file (Factor 2 entry) is defined as Input or Update (I or U in column 15 of the File Description definition) and a C (nonprocedural file) or an F (full-procedural files) in column 16.

Output Coding

The output form in Figure 16-11 shows that adding records to the CUSTMSTR file is controlled by the letters ADD in columns 16, 17, and 18, and that the 99 indicator is turned on in the CHAIN statement if a duplicate key is *not* found.

Input (add) records that have keys already stored in the CUSTMSTR file are loaded to an ERROR file in their input record image (no individual field definitions). This output is conditioned by an N99 (record found condition in the CHAIN statement) and the Record Identifying Indicator 02 assigned to the CUSTMSTR file.

A copy of the CUSTMSTR file after records are added is shown in Figure 16-12. The report is generated by program CH15P4 completed in Chapter 15.

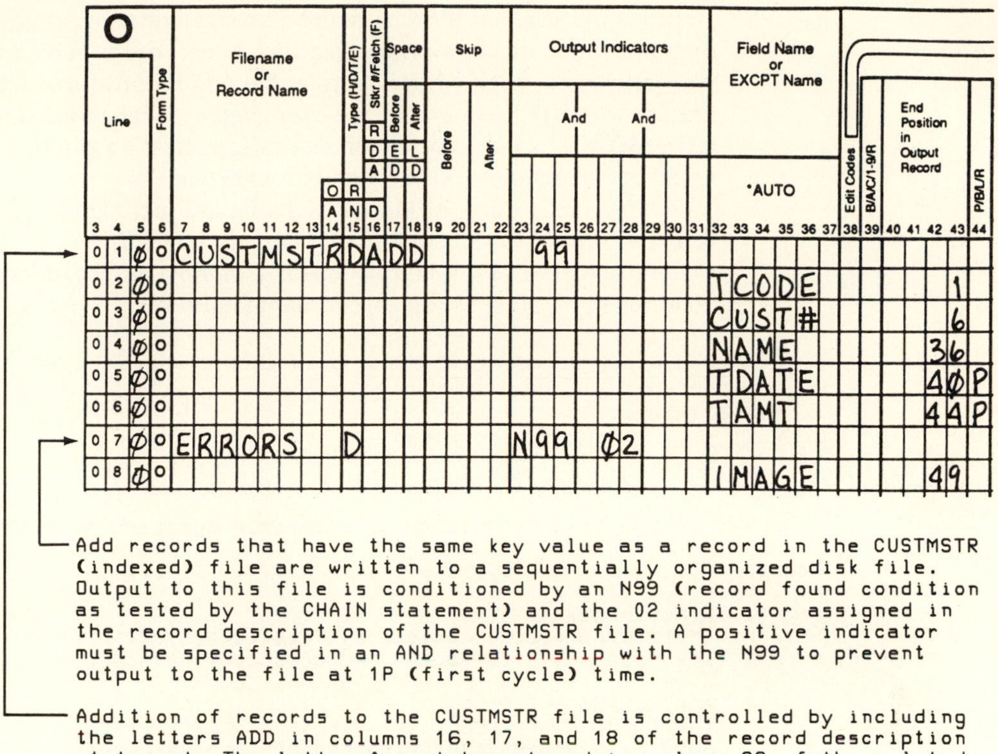

Add records that have the same key value as a record in the CUSTMSTR (indexed) file are written to a sequentially organized disk file. Output to this file is conditioned by an N99 (record found condition as tested by the CHAIN statement) and the 02 indicator assigned in the record description of the CUSTMSTR file. A positive indicator must be specified in an AND relationship with the N99 to prevent output to the file at 1P (first cycle) time.

Addition of records to the CUSTMSTR file is controlled by including the letters ADD in columns 16, 17, and 18 of the record description statement. The letter A must be entered in column 66 of the related File Description definition to execute the ADD function. Indicator 99 is turned by the CHAIN instruction when the key value in Factor 1 does not find the record in the CUSTMSTR file.

Figure 16-11 Output coding for a program that adds records to an indexed file (CUSTMSTR) with error control.

2/28/91 CUSTOMER MASTER FILE LISTING PAGE 1

CODE	CUST#	CUSTOMER NAME	DATE	BALANCE
	00001	HENRY FORD	1/04/91	120.00
	00003	LOUIS CHEVROLET	1/08/91	3,000.00
	00004	DODGE BROTHERS	1/07/91	19,001.00
	00008	STANLEY STEAMER	1/12/91	800.40
	00009	HENRY J KAISER	1/10/91	25,000.00
	00010	JOHN STUDEBAKER	1/12/91	674.00
	00011	WALTER P CHRYSLER	1/06/91	7,085.00
	00018	RANSOM E OLDS	1/15/91	950.00
	00019	MERCEDES BENZ	1/18/91	90,010.00
	00020	FELIX WANKEL	1/22/91	501.23
A	00002	STUTZ BEARCAT	2/01/91	16,430.50
A	00006	OTTO DIESEL	2/05/91	835.00
A	00023	FERDINAND PORSCHE	2/12/91	4,801.25
A	00017	HAROLD WINSTON	2/26/91	100.00

TOTAL CUSTOMER BALANCES.... 169,308.38

Figure 16-12 Report listing of the CUSTMSTR file after records are added (file defined as sequential in listing program).

Because the indexed file was defined as sequential in program CH15P4, the records are processed in a prime data (not index) order. This method of processing was purposely specified to illustrate that add records are stored at the end of the file in the IBM System/3X environments. If program CH15P4 had defined CUSTMSTR as indexed-sequential (its organization type), the records would be listed in an ascending key value (index) order.

Two hex listings of the ERROR file are included in Figure 16-13. The first is an *over-and-under* hexadecimal listing in EBCDIC code (supported on all IBM systems except PCs) and the second is a *side-by-side* hexadecimal listing in ASCII code (used by all other computer manufacturers).

```
Over-and-Under Hexadecimal Listing In EBCDIC Code:

Field legend:
                a - code field          d - purchase date
                b - customer number     e - amount
                c - customer name

Ruler is supplied by utility to reference location of each character

RCDNBR  *... ... 1 ... ... 2 ... ... 3 ... ... 4 ... ...     Alphanumeric &
                                                              unpacked numeric
     1  A|00002HENRY KAISER                                   values interpreted
        C|FFFFFCCDDE4DCCECD444444444444444444|FFFFFF|FFFFFFF|  Zone area
        1|000028559802192590000000000000000000|021091|2750000|  Digit area

     2  A|00018RANSOM E OLDS
        4|FFF0FDCDEED4C4DDCECE44444444444444|FFFFFF|FFFFFFF|  Zone area
        0|000189152240506342530000000000000000|022891|0090089|  Digit area

        a b          c                           d     e

Side-By-Side Hexadecimal Listing In ASCII Code:

0000   4130 3030 3032 4845  4E52 5920 4B41 4953    *A00002HENRY KAIS*
0010   4552 2020 2020 2020  2020 2020 2020 2020    *ER              *
0020   2020 2020 3032 3130  3931 3237 3530 3030    *    021091275000*
0030   3041 3030 3031 3852  414E 534F 4D20 4520    *0A00018RANSOM E *
0040   4F4C 4453 2020 2020  2020 2020 2020 2020    *OLDS            *
0050   2020 2020 2030 3232  3839 3130 3039 3030    *     02289100900*
0060   3839 0000 0000 0000  0000 0000 0000 0000    *89..............*
0070   0000 0000 0000 0000  0000 0000 0000 0000    *................*

                    Data interpreted in right-hand margin
```

Figure 16-13 Over-and-under hexadecimal listing in EBCDIC code and a side-by-side hexadecimal listing in ASCII code.

Not all programs that control the addition of records to an indexed file have to include duplicate record control. Within that processing environment, the file to be added to is defined as output and all syntax that is related to chaining is deleted.

APPLICATION PROGRAM—INDEXED FILE INQUIRY

Documentation

The specifications for a program that random accesses an indexed file (CUSTMSTR) for *inquiry only* is presented in Figure 16-14.

PROGRAM SPECIFICATIONS Page 1 of 1

Program Name CUSTOMER INQUIRY Program-ID CH16P2 Written By S. Myers

Purpose Inquiry individual customer accounts Approved By The Boss

Input files (directory names):

CONSOLE (CRT input)

CUSTMSTR (stored on disk

Output files (directory names):

Printed reports (individual customer accounts)

Processing Narrative:

Write an RPG program to inquiry the customer master file (CUSTMSTR).

<u>Input</u>:

Customer numbers are to be CONSOLE input. The attributes of the CUSTMSTR file are detailed in a supplemental File Definition form.

<u>Processing</u>:

Enter the customer numbers via CRT input and random access the CUSTMSTR file by the CHAIN operation.

<u>Output</u>:

When a customer's record is found in the CUSTMSTR file, print the data in the format shown in the supplemental print chart. If a customer's record is not found, print the CONSOLE entered customer number and the error message indicated in the print chart.

Figure 16-14 Specifications for indexed file (CUSTMSTR) inquiry program.

The system flowchart in Figure 16-15 indicates that two input files and a printer file are processed by the inquiry program. Search key values, which are input by CONSOLE control, random access the CUSTMSTR file for an equal key. If an equal key is found, the related record is read and the data printed.

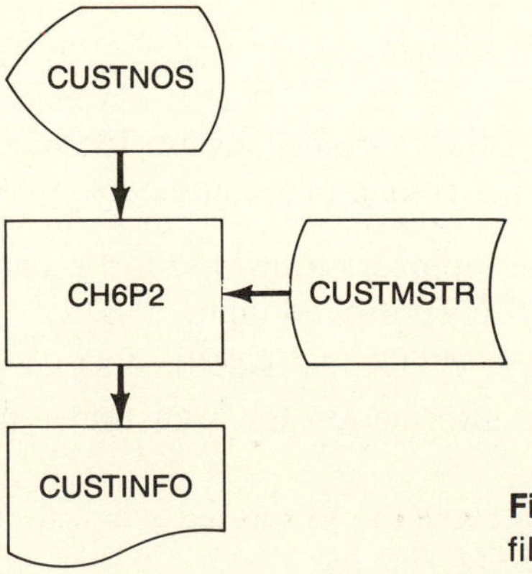

Figure 16-15 System flowchart for indexed file (CUSTMSTR) inquiry program.

Refer to Figure 16-5 for the attributes of the CUSTMSTR file.

The format of the printed report and listings for two customers and an error report generated when a customer is not found are presented in Figure 16-16.

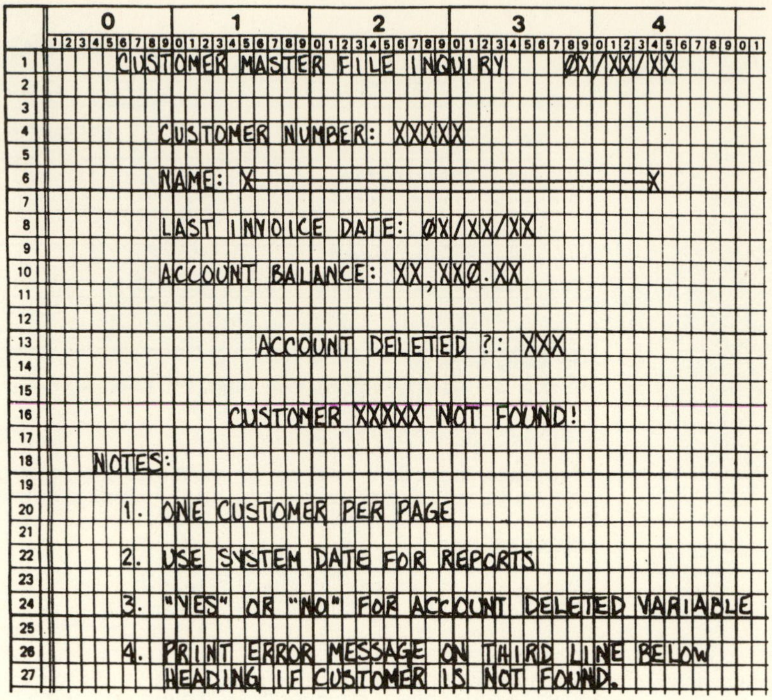


```
CUSTOMER MASTER FILE INQUIRY      2/28/91

   CUSTOMER NUMBER: 00023

   NAME: FERDINAND PORSCHE

   LAST INVOICE DATE:  2/12/91

   ACCOUNT BALANCE:  4,801.25

          ACCOUNT DELETED ?: NO
```

```
CUSTOMER MASTER FILE INQUIRY      2/28/91

   CUSTOMER NUMBER: 00009

   NAME: HENRY J KAISER

   LAST INVOICE DATE:  1/10/91

   ACCOUNT BALANCE: 25,000.00

          ACCOUNT DELETED ?: NO
```

```
CUSTOMER MASTER FILE INQUIRY      2/28/91

          CUSTOMER 00005 NOT FOUND!
```

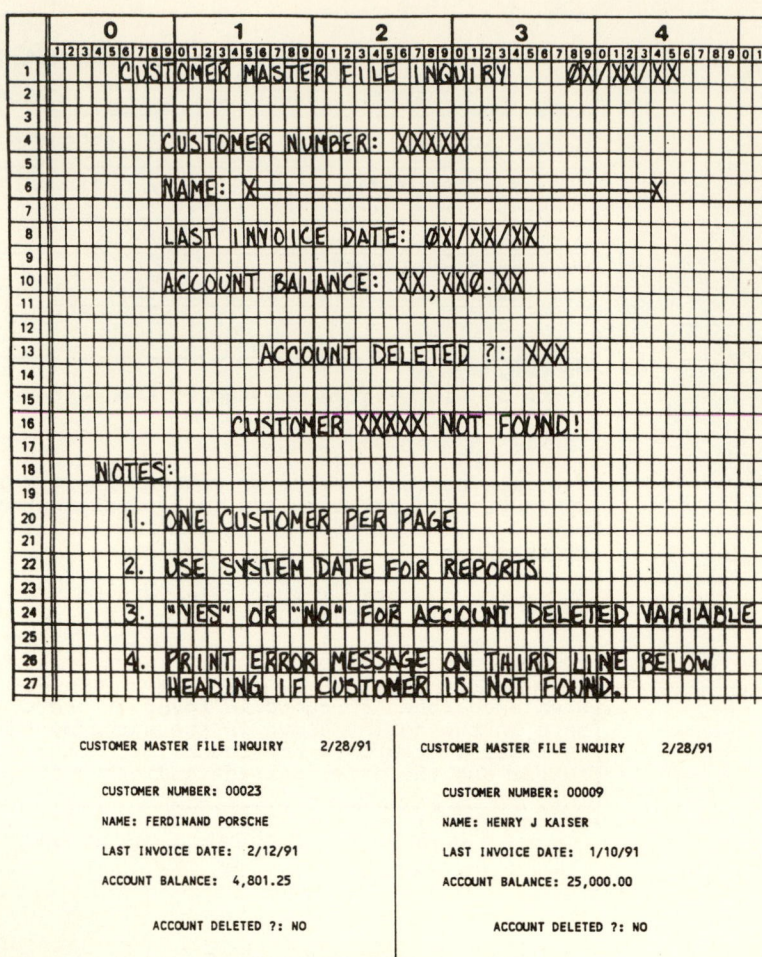

Figure 16-16 Report design and generated listings.

Source Coding

A source listing of the customer master file inquiry program is shown in Figure 16-17. The following coding procedures are used:

1. Customer number values used in a chaining field value are entered by CONSOLE controlled input.
2. The CUSTMSTR file is defined as an input *chained* file.
3. Account information for a customer found in the CUSTMSTR file is printed.
4. An error report is generated when a customer number is not found in the CUSTMSTR file.

```
... ... 1 ... ... 2 ... ... 3 ... ... 4 ... ... 5 ... ... 6 ... ... 7 ...
  * THIS PROGRAM RANDOM PROCESSES THE CUSTMSTR FILE FOR INQUIRY       CH16P2
 H                                                                    CH16P2
 FCUSTNOS IP  F   6   6            CONSOLE
 FCUSTMSTRIC  F 220  44R 5AI     2 DISK
 FINQUIRY O   F 132 132            PRINTER
 ICUSTNOS SM  01    1 CC
```

Indexed file is defined as input and chained

Figure 16-17 Source listing of the CUSTMSTR file inquiry program.

```
I                                            1   1 CODE
I                                            2   6 CUSTNO              CH16P2
ICUSTMSTRSM  02                                                        CH16P2
I                                            1   1 TCODE               CH16P2
I                                            2   6 CUST#               CH16P2
I                                            7  36 NAME                CH16P2
I                                        P  37  400TDATE               CH16P2
I                                        P  41  442BALANC
C           CUSTNO    CHAINCUSTMSTR               99    NOT FOUND?
C N99      TCODE     COMP 'D'                        30 EQUAL?
OINQUIRY H  301     1P
O                                       25 'CUSTOMER MASTER FILE'
O                                       33 'INQUIRY'
O                            UDATE Y    45                             CH16P2
O        D  2      02N99                                               CH16P2
O                                       24 'CUSTOMER NUMBER:'          CH16P2
O                            CUST#      30                             CH16P2
O        D  2      02N99
O                                       13 'NAME:'
O                            NAME       44
O        D  2      02N99
O                                       26 'LAST INVOICE DATE:'
O                            TDATE Y    35
O        D  2      02N99
O                                       24 'ACCOUNT BALANCE:'
O                            BALANCA    36                             CH16P2
O        D 1       02N99                                               CH16P2
O                                       33 'ACCOUNT DELETED ?:'        CH16P2
O                    30                 37 'YES'                       CH16P2
O                   N30                 37 'NO '
O        D  2      99
O                                       21 'CUSTOMER'
O                            CUSTNO     27
O                                       38 'NOT FOUND!'
```

Customer record is accessed by the CHAIN operation with CONSOLE entered CUSTNO.

When a customer record is found, data printed is controlled by the Record Identifying Indicator assigned to the CUSTMSTR file.

Error message is printed when a customer number is not found in the CUSTMSTR file

(*Continued*)

File Description Coding

Shown in Figure 16-18 is the syntax required to inquiry an indexed file by the CHAINing method. To support inquiry processing, the CUSTMSTR file must be defined as an input (I in column 15) Chained (C in column 16) file. The R in the Mode of Processing field (column 28) specifies that the file is to be random processed.

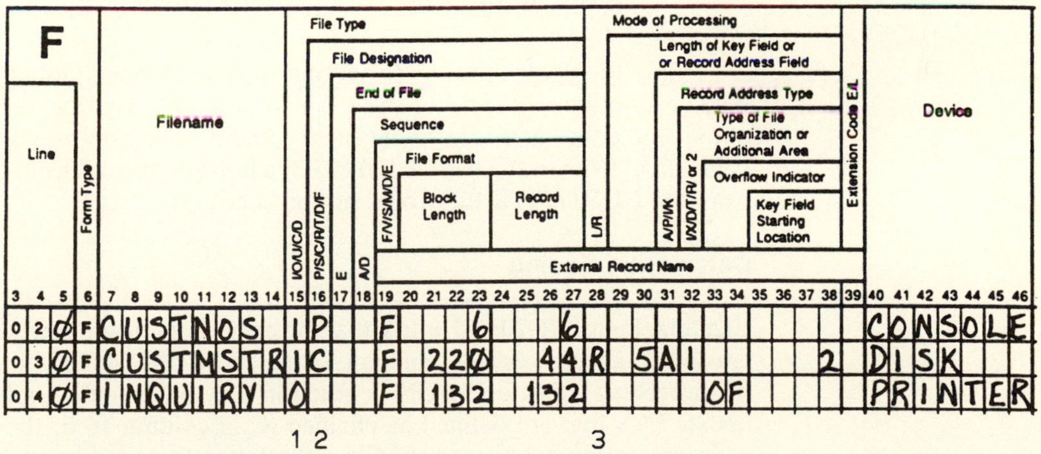

Explanation of Entries for the CUSTMSTR (Indexed) File:

1. I in column 15 defines the file as input.
2. C in column 16 defines the file as a chained file which must be random processed by the CHAIN operation.
3. R in column 28 indicates that the file is random processed. This mode of processing must be specified when the file is defined as U (update).

Figure 16-18 File Description coding for the CUSTMSTR file inquiry program.

Input Specifications Coding. As shown in Figure 16-19, the record and field description statements for the CONSOLE and CUSTMSTR files are defined in the input form. CUSTNO values, which are input by a CONSOLE file, are used in a CHAINing instruction to random access the CUSTMSTR file. Unlike sequential file processing, the customer number values do *not* have to be entered in ascending (or descending) order.

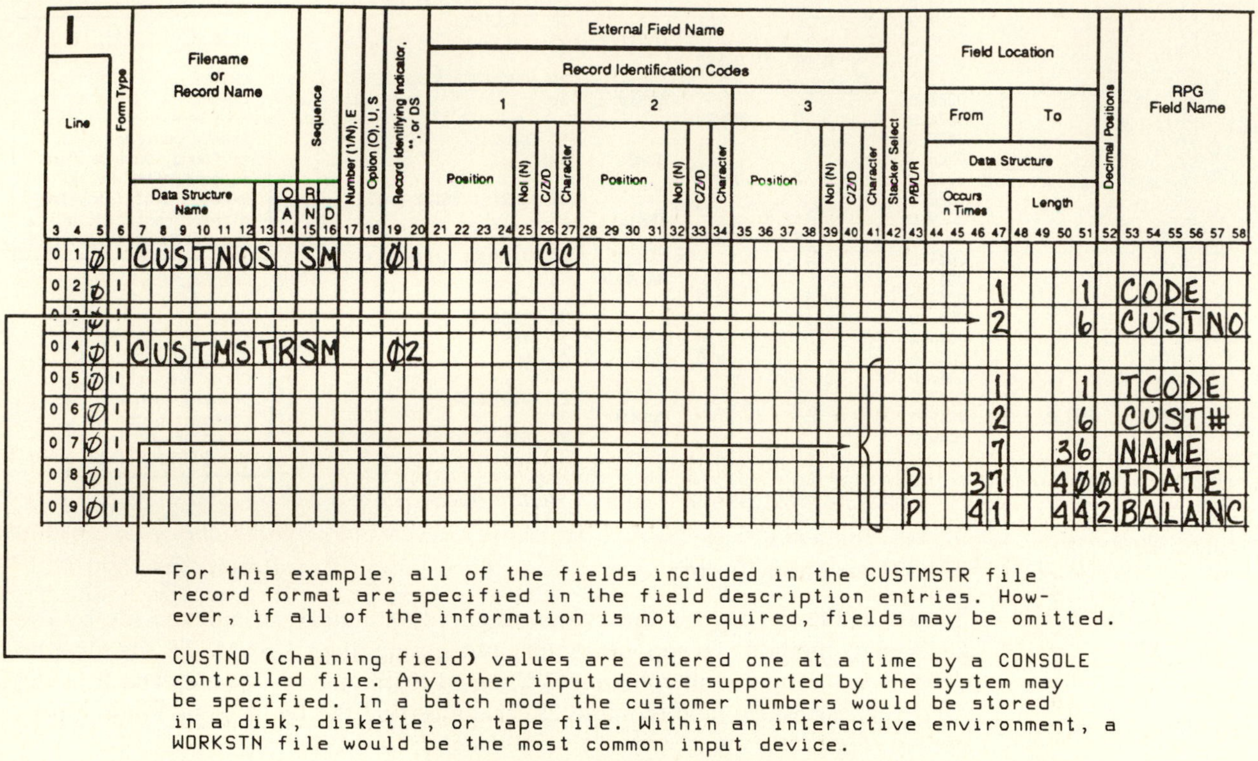
CUSTNOS SM 01 1 CC
1 1 CODE
2 6 CUSTNO
CUSTMSTRSM 02
1 1 TCODE
2 6 CUST#
7 36 NAME
P 37 400 TDATE
P 41 442 BALANC
For this example, all of the fields included in the CUSTMSTR file record format are specified in the field description entries. However, if all of the information is not required, fields may be omitted.
CUSTNO (chaining field) values are entered one at a time by a CONSOLE controlled file. Any other input device supported by the system may be specified. In a batch mode the customer numbers would be stored in a disk, diskette, or tape file. Within an interactive environment, a WORKSTN file would be the most common input device.

Figure 16-19 Input coding for CUSTMSTR inquiry program.

Only the fields required for output have to be specified in the CUSTMSTR field descriptions. In fact, for this example, the CUST# field is not required. The output for either a record *found* or *not found* condition may use the CUSTNO value input from the CONSOLE file. For a not-found condition, the CUST# value from the CUSTMSTR file would not be accessed.

Calculation Coding

Examine Figure 16-20 and notice that the previously introduced CHAIN operation is used to access records randomly from the CUSTMSTR file. Remember, for nonprocedural files, a CHAIN instruction may be specified only for input or for update files that are defined as chained (C in column 16 of the File Description definition). For full-procedural files, the letter F must be entered in column 16 instead of a C.

When the value in CUSTNO (CHAINing field) is equal to a key in the index of the CUSTMSTR file, the related master record data is extracted for processing and the indicator 99 specified in columns 54 to 55 will be off. If the key is not found, indicator 99 will be turned on. For this program, subsequent output is controlled by both conditions.

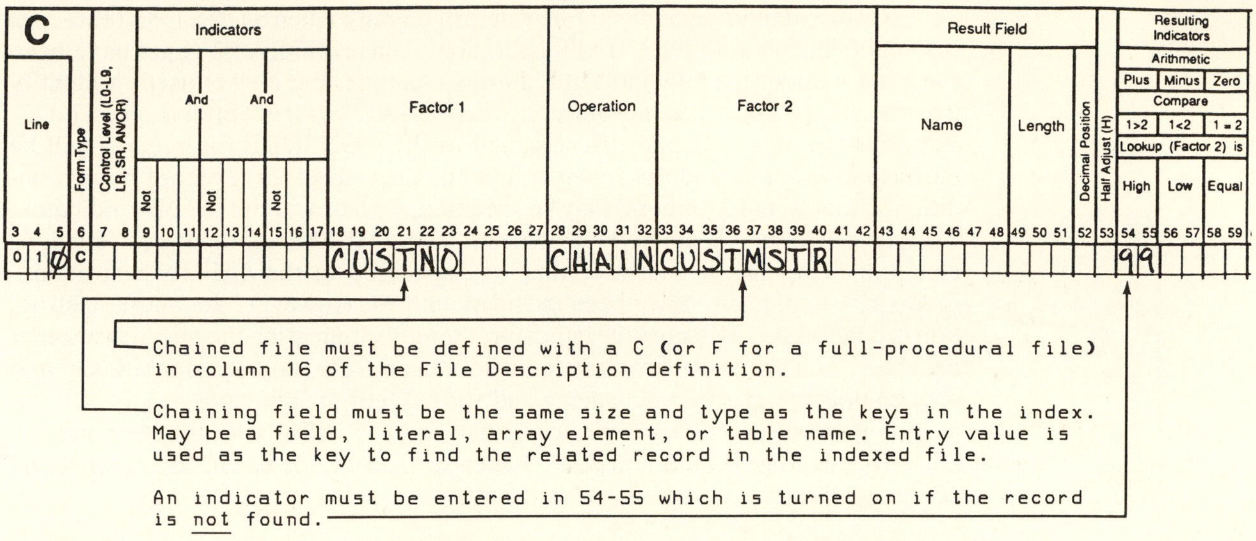

Figure 16-20 Calculation coding for CUSTMSTR inquiry program.

Output Coding

The output coding for the inquiry program is shown in Figure 16-21. Printed output for a successful CHAIN operation is conditioned by the record identifying indicator 02 assigned to the CUSTMSTR file and the N99 (99 off) indicator. If N99 was specified without the 02 indicator, the detail lines would print the constants on the report but not the variable field data. Recall that no record has been read during the first pass of the normal RPG processing cycle.

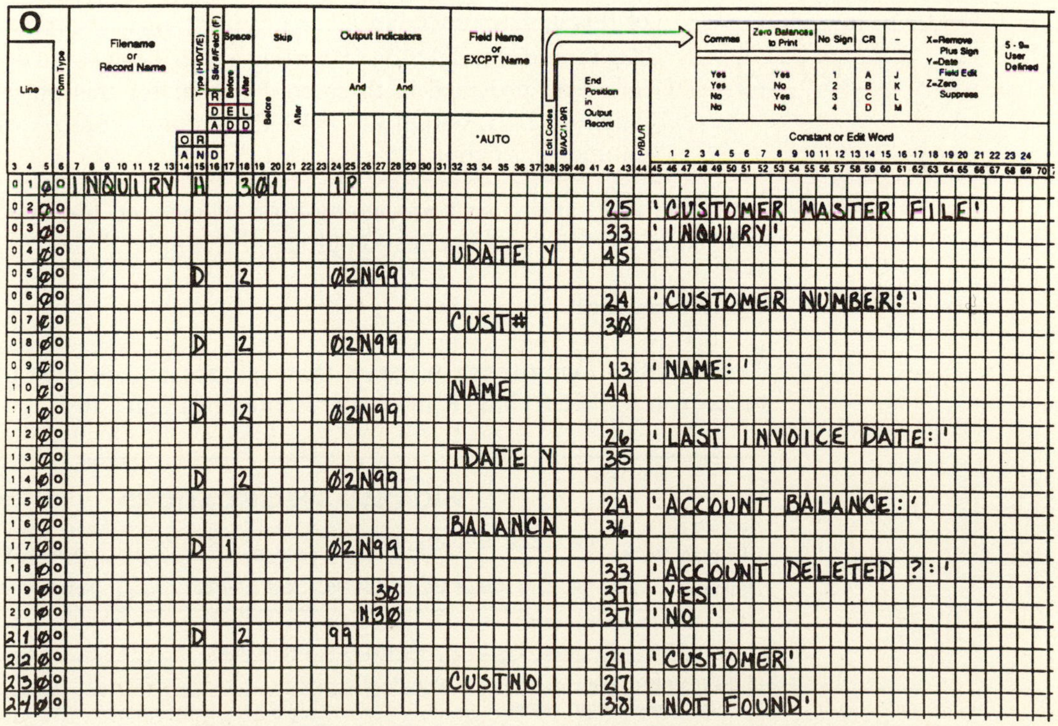

Figure 16-21 Output coding for the CUSTMSTR inquiry program.

Record identifying indicator 02 will turn on only when a CUSTMSTR record is found (same key) in the CHAIN operation. Consequently, 02 could have been specified without the N99 indicator. In this example, the N99 is used to identify that the 99 indicator does not turn on when CHAIN instruction is successful.

Furthermore, indicator 01, assigned to the CONSOLE file record, will be on for both a *found* and *not found* condition. Therefore, for a record *found* condition, either 01 or 02 (or both) may be specified, with or without the N99 indicator.

The error message, printed when a CUSTMSTR record is not found, is conditioned by the 99 indicator that was specified in the CHAIN instruction. Indicator 01 could also have been included with 99. However, the output instruction is conditioned by a *positive* indicator, thereby eliminating the need for another indicator. The use of unnecessary indicators in an RPG program is inefficient and may complicate program debugging and subsequent maintenance.

If Record Identifying Indicator 02 had been specified with the 99 indicator, the error message would not print. Indicator 02 will not be on for a *not-found chain condition.*

APPLICATION PROGRAM—INDEXED FILE UPDATE AND DELETE

The update function of file maintenance usually includes one or more of the following procedures:

1. Modify field values in the records of a file from input transaction data. A change in a customer's address and the correction of errors are examples of this update activity.
2. Access numeric data in a field (or fields) of a record and mathematically increase or decrease the original value with transaction data. A change in a customer's account balance to reflect a payment or sale is typical of this update procedure.
3. Tag records for deletion by writing a user-designated delete character(s) in a field provided in the record format for this purpose. The *logical* deletion (DEL output or DELET operation control) of records is also an update function.

The RPG syntax and processing logic of indexed file updating will be explained in the following application program example.

Documentation

The specifications for the program that updates and deletes (tagging method) records in the CUSTMSTR file are presented in Figure 16-22.

PROGRAM SPECIFICATIONS Page 1 of 2

Program Name CUSTOMER UPDATE/DEL Program-ID CH16P3 Written By S. Myers

Purpose Update and delete customer records Approved By The Boss

Input files (directory names):

UPDATES (Sequentially organized on disk)

CUSTMSTR (stored on disk)

Output files (directory names):

CUSTMSTR

ERRORS (Sequentially organized on disk)

Figure 16-22 Specifications for CUSTMSTR update and delete program.

Processing Narrative:

```
Write an RPG program to update and delete records in the customer
master file CUSTMSTR.

Input:

Data stored in the transaction file, UPDATES, is used to update or
delete records in the customer master file, CUSTMSTR.  The record
formats for each file are attached.

Test two of the transaction record fields for the following:

   1.  Transaction name field for blanks
   2.  Transaction date field for zeros

Processing:

Read the UPDATE file sequentially and update or delete records in the
CUSTMSTR file based on the following conditions:

   1.  If the transaction code is a D, retrieve the master file record
       and tag it with the letter D in position 1 of the record.  In
       addition, if the transaction date field is not zero, update the
       master record date with the new date.

   2.  If the transaction code is a U, retrieve the master record and
       perform one or more of the following:

         A.  Add the transaction amount to the master record balance.
             A positive value in the update amount field will add the
             amount to the master record balance.  A negative value
             will automatically subtract when the ADD operation is
             executed.  Any zero balance in the transaction amount
             field does not have to be tested.

         B.  If the name field in the transaction record is not blank,
             update the master record with the new name.

         C.  If the date field in the transaction record is not blank,
             update the master record with the new date.

message:

  1. A transaction record is not coded with a D or U.  Move
     BAD TRANSACTION CODE to the error message field.

  2. A master record not found.  Move CUSTOMER NOT FOUND to
     the error message field.

Note that the related error message is to be included in the format
of the error records.
```

(*Continued*)

The system flowchart in Figure 16-23 indicates that three disk files are processed by the update and delete program. Update data is stored in the one input file, and an output error file is provided for transaction records that do not have a valid identification code or CUSTMSTR file record. Because the CUSTMSTR file is both input and output, it is referenced in the flowchart with a double-arrowed line.

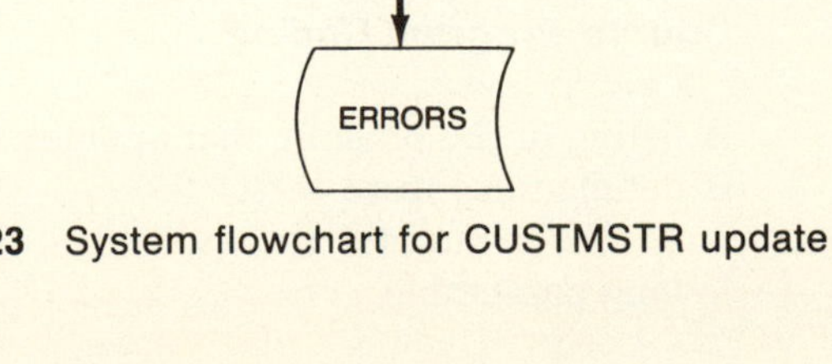

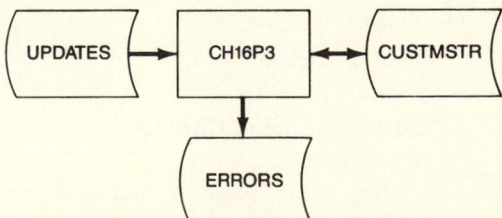

Figure 16-23 System flowchart for CUSTMSTR update and delete program.

A record layout form of the transaction file and a listing of the update data are shown in Figure 16-24.

The attributes of the CUSTMSTR file are presented in Figure 16-25.

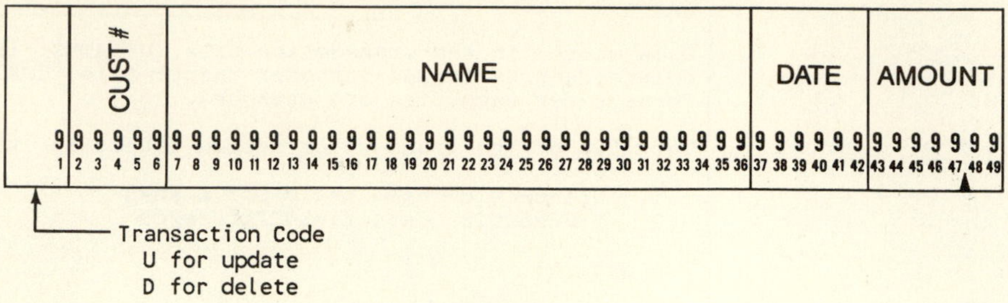

Update data:

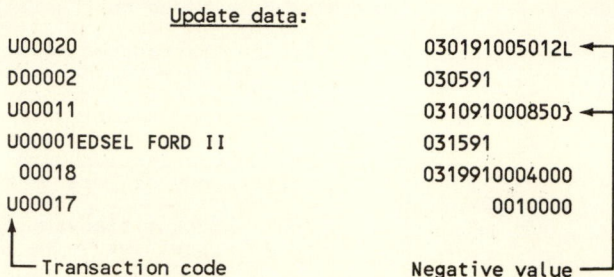

```
U00020                    030191005012L  <-
D00002                    030591
U00011                    031091000850}  <-
U00001EDSEL FORD II       031591
 00018                    0319910004000
U00017                          0010000
^
Transaction code          Negative value
```

Figure 16-24 Record layout form of the transaction file and listing of the update data.

FILE DEFINITION		
SYSTEM Yours		DRAWN BY S. Myers
FILE NAME CUSTMSTR		DATE 1/15/91 REV. NO. 0
CREATED BY S. Myers		FILE TYPE Disk
RECORD NAME None		KEY LENGTH 5 (ACCTS#)
RECORDING MODE Fixed	ORGANIZATION Indexed	SEQUENCE Ascending (ACCT#)
RECORD SIZE 44 bytes	BLOCKING FACTOR 5	BLOCKSIZE 220 bytes

FIELD DATA

FIELD NO.	FIELD NAME - DESCRIPTION	SIZE	CLASS C/P/Z/B	POSITION FROM	POSITION THRU	FORMAT/CONSTANT
1	Delete Code	1	C	1	1	D if deleted
2	Account Number	5	C	2	6	Key field
3	Account Name	30	C	7	36	
4	Transaction Date (last)	7	P	37	40	
5	Account Balance	7	P	41	44	2 decimal positions

Figure 16-25 File definition form for the CUSTMSTR file.

Source Program Coding

A listing of the program that updates and deletes records in the CUSTMSTR file is detailed in Figure 16-26.

The syntax for each specification type is individually discussed in the following paragraphs.

```
... ... 1 ... ... 2 ... ... 3 ... ... 4 ... ... 5 ... ... 6 ... ... 7 ...
 * THIS PROGRAM UPDATES THE CUSTMSTR FILE.  TRANSACTION RECORDS THAT CH16P3
 * THAT HAVE A MISSING ID CODE, OR INCORRECT ID CODE, OR CUSTOMER    CH16P3
 * NUMBER THAT IS NOT ON THE CUSTMSTR FILE ARE WRITTEM TO AN ERROR   CH16P3
 * FILE IN TRANSACTION RECORD IMAGE WITH RELATED ERROR MESSAGE.....  CH16P3
 *        TRANSACTION CODE D - TAG MASTER RECORD WITH D              CH16P3
 *        TRANSACTION CODE U - UPDATE MASTER RECORD NAME, DATE, AND  CH16P3
 *          AMOUNT FIELDS IF RELATED TRANSACTION RECORD HAS VALUES   CH16P3
 *          NEGATIVE AMOUNTS INCLUDE A MINUS SIGN OVER LOW ORDER BYTE CH16P3
H                                                                   CH16P3
FUPDATES IP  F  49  49           DISK                               CH16P3
FCUSTMSTRUC  F 220  44R 5AI     2 DISK                              CH16P3
FERRORS  O   F  73  73           DISK                               CH16P3
IUPDATES SM  01    1 CD                                             CH16P3
I        OR  02    1 CU                                             CH16P3
I        OR  03                                                     CH16P3
I                                  2   6 CUSTNO                     CH16P3
I                                  7  36 UPNAME     02    10        CH16P3
I                                 37  420UPDATE           11        CH16P3
I                                 43  492UPAMT      02              CH16P3
I                                  1  49 IMAGE      03              CH16P3
ICUSTMSTRSM  04                                                     CH16P3
I                                  7  36 NAME                       CH16P3
I                               P 37  400DATE                       CH16P3
I                               P 41  442BALANC                     CH16P3
C  N03      CUSTNO    CHAINCUSTMSTR            99    NOT FOUND?     CH16P3
C  N99 02   BALANC    ADD  UPAMT     BALANC                         CH16P3
 *                                                                  CH16P3
 * IF VALID TRANSACTION CODE AND MASTER RECORD IS FOUND, UPDATE     CH16P3
 * MASTER RECORD WITH RELATED TRANSACTION DATA....                  CH16P3
 *                                                                  CH16P3
OCUSTMSTRD        04                                                CH16P3
O                   01               1 'D'                          CH16P3
O                 02N10    UPNAME   36                              CH16P3
O                    N11   UPDATE   40P                             CH16P3
O                   02     BALANC   44P                             CH16P3
 *                                                                  CH16P3
 * IF BAD ID CODE OR CUST NOT FOUND, LOAD TRANS RECORD TO ERROR FILE CH16P3
 *                                                                  CH16P3
OERRORS  D        99                                                CH16P3
O        OR       03                                                CH16P3
O                          IMAGE    49                              CH16P3
O                   03              73 'BAD TRANSACTION CODE     '  CH16P3
O                   99              73 'CUSTOMER NOT FOUND       '  CH16P3
```

Figure 16-26 Source listing of the CUSTMSTR update and delete program.

File Description Coding

Detailed in Figure 16-27 is the File Description coding for the CUSTMSTR file update and delete program. Notice that CUSTMSTR is defined as an Update (U in column 15), Chained (C in column 16), indexed file that is to be random processed (R in column 28).

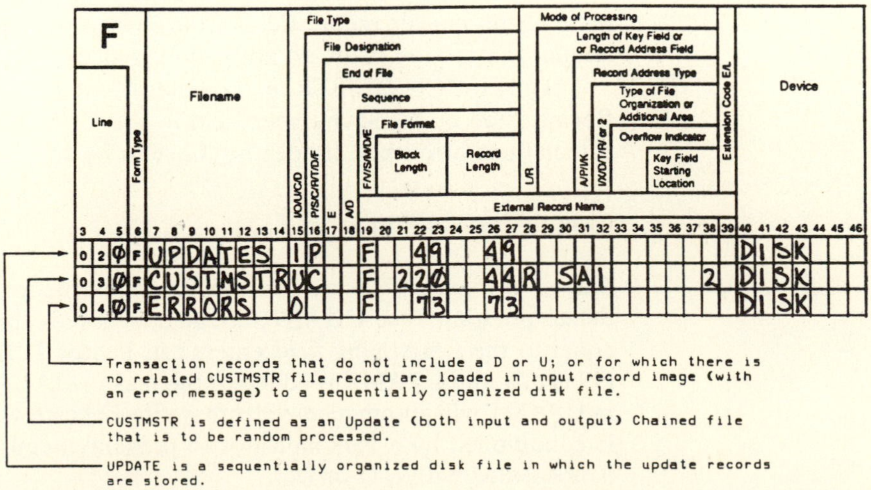

Figure 16-27 File Description coding for CUSTMSTR update and delete program.

Input Specifications

As shown in Figure 16-28, an OR relationship is specified for the two input record types in the transaction file (UPDATES). In addition, a catchall record type (03) is defined that prevents program cancellation (or halt) if an unidentified record is tested on input. Transaction records that have a missing or incorrect record identification code are loaded to a sequentially organized disk file in their input record image when the 03 indicator is on.

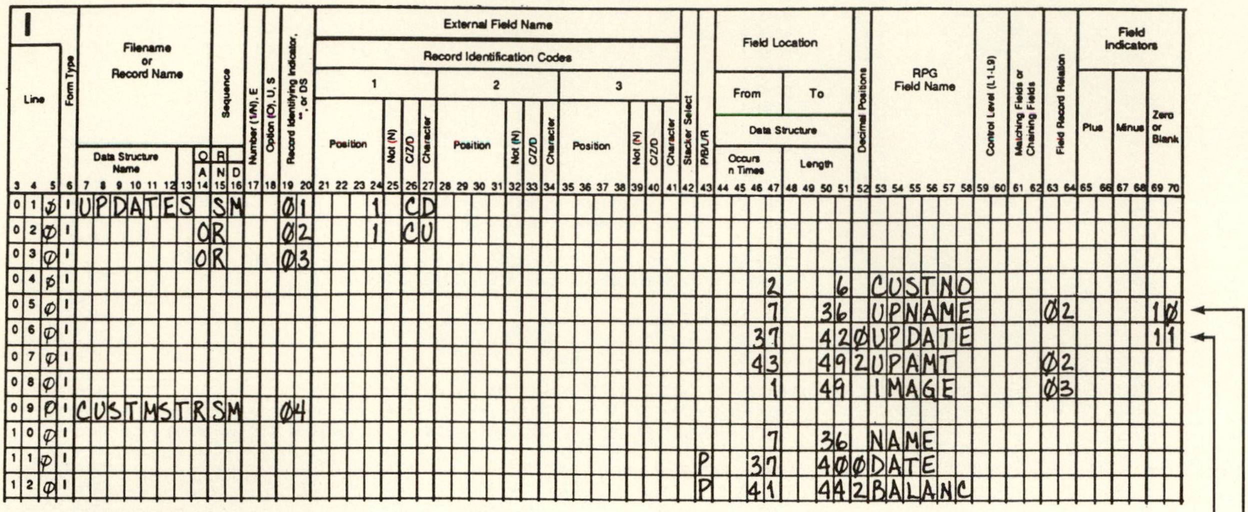

```
01 I UPDATES  SM 01   1 CD
02 I         OR  02   1 CU
03 I         OR  03
04 I                                   2   6 CUSTNO
05 I                                   7  36 UPNAME       02   10
06 I                                  37  420UPDATE            11
07 I                                  43  492UPAMT        02
08 I                                   1  49 IMAGE        03
09 I CUSTMSTRSM  04
10 I                                   7  36 NAME
11 I                                P 37  400DATE
12 I                                P 41  442BALANC
```

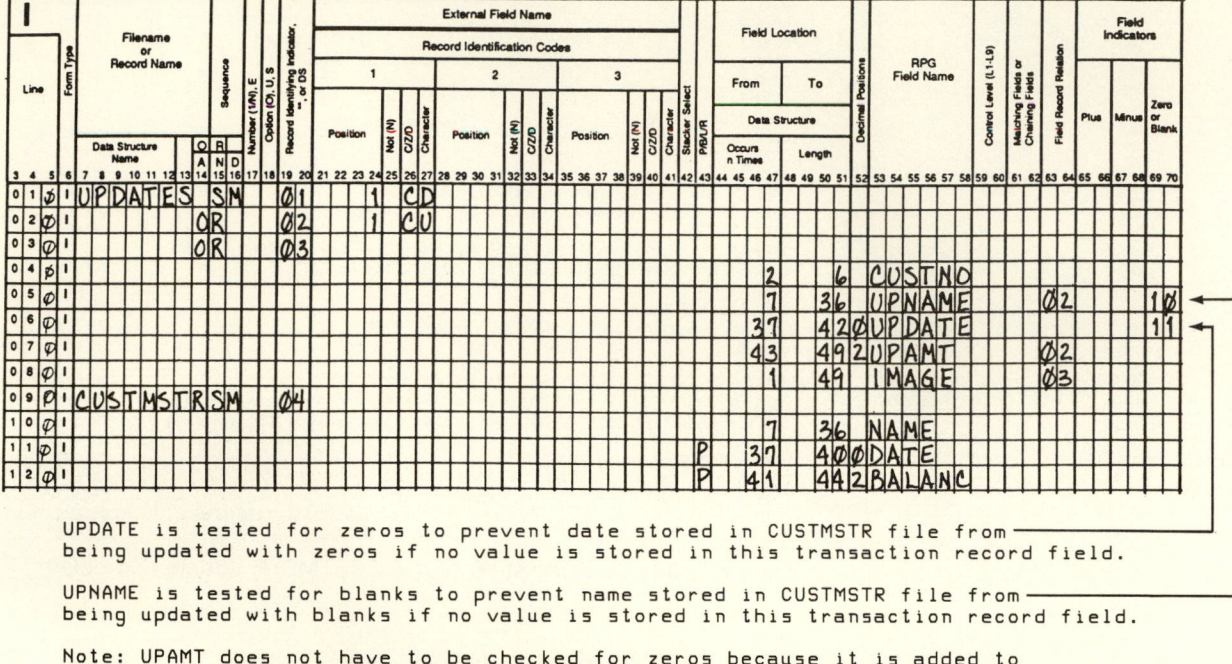

UPDATE is tested for zeros to prevent date stored in CUSTMSTR file from being updated with zeros if no value is stored in this transaction record field.

UPNAME is tested for blanks to prevent name stored in CUSTMSTR file from being updated with blanks if no value is stored in this transaction record field.

Note: UPAMT does not have to be checked for zeros because it is added to the CUSTMSTR BALANC field before that value is updated. Consequently, a zero value will not affect the original master file amount.

Figure 16-28 Input specifications for CUSTMSTR update and delete program.

Also notice that the transaction field UPNAME is tested for blanks and UPDATE is tested for zeros. The indicators (10 and 11) used to condition output prevent the master record fields from being updated with blanks or zeros if the related transaction fields do not include values.

Only the CUSTMSTR record fields needed in update processing are defined. Because the customer number field in the CUSTMSTR file is not required for calculations or output, it does not have to be specified.

Calculation Coding

Shown in Figure 16-29 are the calculation instructions included in the update and delete program. The CHAIN statement searches the CUSTMSTR file for a key equal to the CHAINing field entered in Factor 1. If the master record is found (99 is off), the UPAMT is added to the master BALANC value. A negative value in UPAMT will automatically decrease the balance value. The CHAIN instruction is conditioned by a N03 indicator to prevent execution if the transaction record is not coded with a U or D.

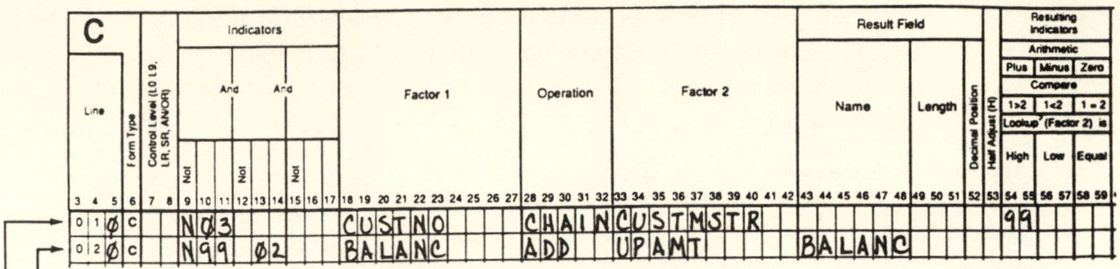

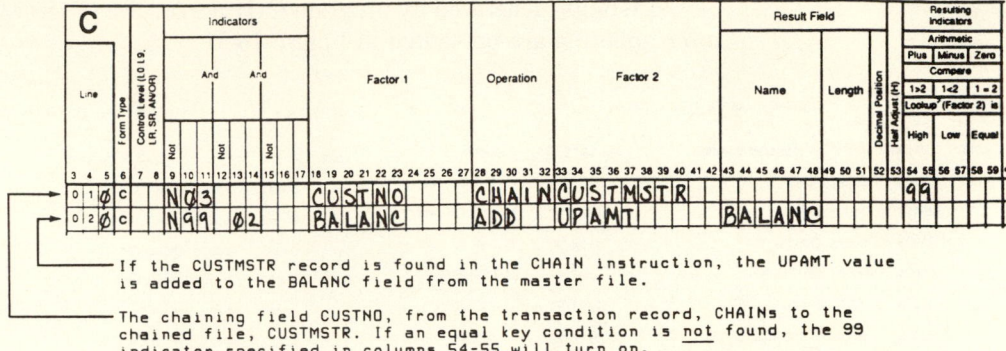

If the CUSTMSTR record is found in the CHAIN instruction, the UPAMT value is added to the BALANC field from the master file.

The chaining field CUSTNO, from the transaction record, CHAINs to the chained file, CUSTMSTR. If an equal key condition is <u>not</u> found, the 99 indicator specified in columns 54-55 will turn on.

Figure 16-29 Calculations for the update and delete program.

Output Coding

The output coding for the update and delete program is illustrated in Figure 16-30. As explained, the correct assignment of both Record Identifying and Resulting Indicators is important for control of the update, deletion, and error processes.

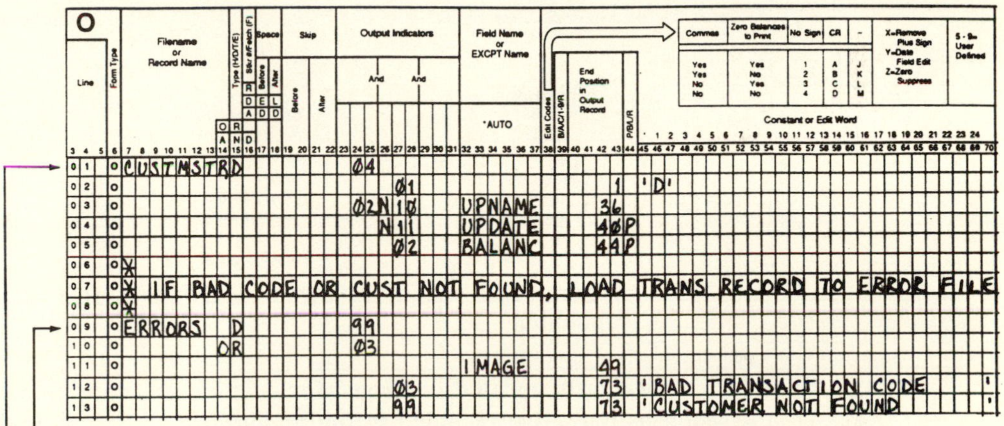

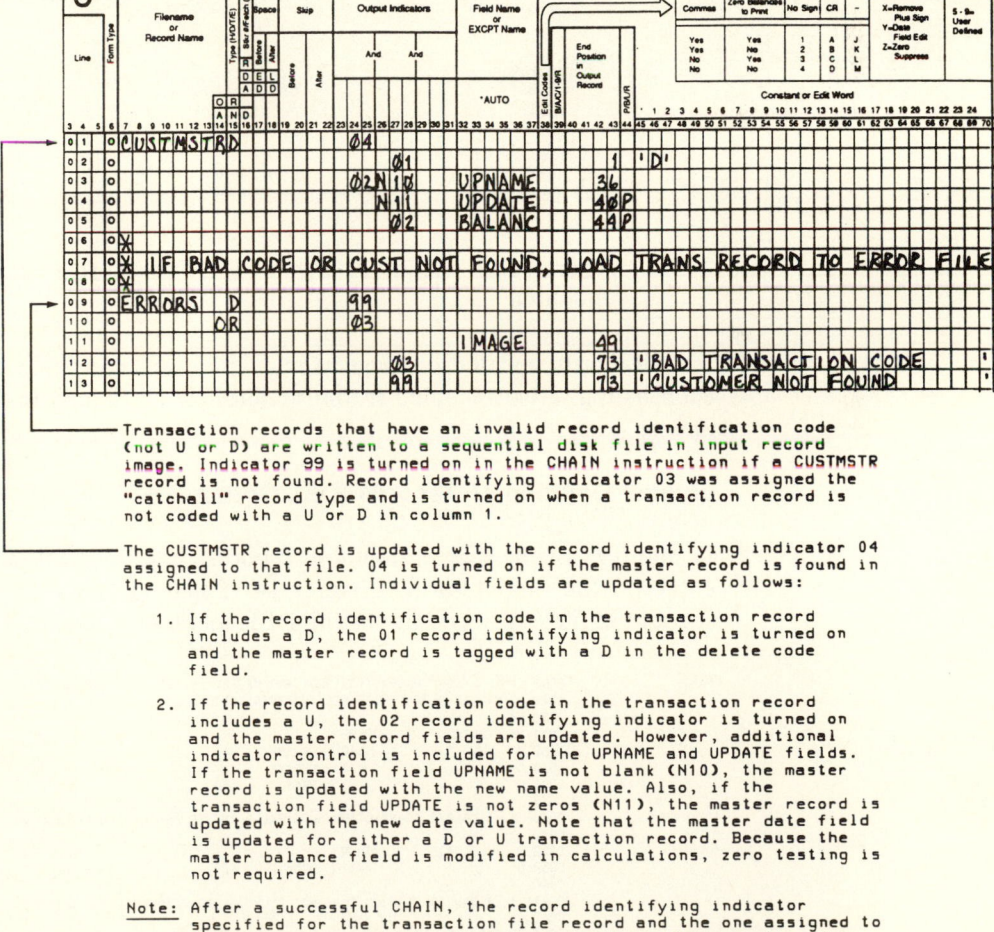

Transaction records that have an invalid record identification code (not U or D) are written to a sequential disk file in input record image. Indicator 99 is turned on in the CHAIN instruction if a CUSTMSTR record is not found. Record identifying indicator 03 was assigned the "catchall" record type and is turned on when a transaction record is not coded with a U or D in column 1.

The CUSTMSTR record is updated with the record identifying indicator 04 assigned to that file. 04 is turned on if the master record is found in the CHAIN instruction. Individual fields are updated as follows:

1. If the record identification code in the transaction record includes a D, the 01 record identifying indicator is turned on and the master record is tagged with a D in the delete code field.

2. If the record identification code in the transaction record includes a U, the 02 record identifying indicator is turned on and the master record fields are updated. However, additional indicator control is included for the UPNAME and UPDATE fields. If the transaction field UPNAME is not blank (N10), the master record is updated with the new name value. Also, if the transaction field UPDATE is not zeros (N11), the master record is updated with the new date value. Note that the master date field is updated for either a D or U transaction record. Because the master balance field is modified in calculations, zero testing is not required.

<u>Note:</u> After a successful CHAIN, the record identifying indicator specified for the transaction file record and the one assigned to the master file will be on at the same time. Consequently, the assignment of 04 and 01 or 04 and 02 is correct and required indicator control for this example.

Figure 16-30 Output coding for the update and delete program.

Listings (generated by program CH15P3) of the CUSTMSTR file *before* and *after* updating are presented in Figure 16-31.

3/31/91 CUSTOMER MASTER FILE LISTING PAGE 1

CODE	CUST#	CUSTOMER NAME	DATE	BALANCE	
	00001	HENRY FORD	1/04/91	120.00	◄
A	00002	STUTZ BEARCAT	2/01/91	16,430.50	◄
	00003	LOUIS CHEVROLET	1/08/91	3,000.00	
	00004	DODGE BROTHERS	1/07/91	19,001.00	
A	00006	OTTO DIESEL	2/05/91	835.00	
	00008	STANLEY STEAMER	1/12/91	800.40	
	00009	HENRY J KAISER	1/10/91	25,000.00	
	00010	JOHN STUDEBAKER	1/12/91	674.00	
	00011	WALTER P CHRYSLER	1/06/91	7,085.00	◄
A	00017	HAROLD WINSTON	2/26/91	100.00	◄
	00018	RANSOM E OLDS	1/15/91	950.00	
	00019	MERCEDES BENZ	1/18/91	90,010.00	
	00020	FELIX WANKEL	1/22/91	501.23	◄
A	00023	FERDINAND PORSCHE	2/12/91	4,801.25	

TOTAL CUSTOMER BALANCES.... 169,308.38

3/31/91 CUSTOMER MASTER FILE LISTING PAGE 1

CODE	CUST#	CUSTOMER NAME	DATE	BALANCE	
	00001	EDSEL FORD II	3/15/91	120.00	◄
D	00002	STUTZ BEARCAT	3/05/91	16,430.50	◄
	00003	LOUIS CHEVROLET	1/08/91	3,000.00	
	00004	DODGE BROTHERS	1/07/91	19,001.00	
A	00006	OTTO DIESEL	2/05/91	835.00	
	00008	STANLEY STEAMER	1/12/91	800.40	
	00009	HENRY J KAISER	1/10/91	25,000.00	
	00010	JOHN STUDEBAKER	1/12/91	674.00	
	00011	WALTER P CHRYSLER	3/10/91	7,000.00	◄
A	00017	HAROLD WINSTON	2/26/91	200.00	◄
	00018	RANSOM E OLDS	1/15/91	950.00	
	00019	MERCEDES BENZ	1/18/91	90,010.00	
	00020	FELIX WANKEL	3/01/91	:00	◄
A	00023	FERDINAND PORSCHE	2/12/91	4,801.25	

TOTAL CUSTOMER BALANCES.... 168,822.15

```
Upate data:
U00020                         030191005012L
D00002                         030591
U00011                         031091000850}
U00001EDSEL FORD II            031591
 00018                         0319910004000
U00017                               0010000

   Transaction code            Negative value
```

Figure 16-31 Report listings of the CUSTMSTR file before and after updating.

Records updated or tagged for deletion are identified by an arrowhead on each listing. Also included in the middle left of Figure 16-31 is a listing of the update data.

Logical Deletion of Records (DEL Option)

In addition to the tagging method, records may be deleted logically by a DEL entry on the output form. Chapter 14 explained the syntax of this option for sequential files. The coding for the DEL method is repeated here to illustrate its

```
 * IF VALID TRANSACTION CODE AND MASTER RECORD IS FOUND, UPDATE      CH16P4
 * MASTER RECORD WITH RELATED TRANSACTION DATA....                   CH16P4
 *                                                                   CH16P4
OCUSTMSTRD        02N99                                              CH16P4
O                   N10   UPNAME    36                               CH16P4
O                   N11   UPDATE    40P                              CH16P4
O                         BALANC    44P                              CH16P4
 *                                                                   CH16P4
 * IF DELETE TRANSACTION, LOGICALLY DELETE THE MASTER RECORD         CH16P4
 *                                                                   CH16P4
O         DDEL    01N99                                              CH16P4
O                   N11   UPDATE    40P                              CH16P4
 *                                                                   CH16P4
 * IF BAD ID CODE OR CUST NOT FOUND, LOAD TRANS RECORD TO ERROR FILE CH16P4
 *                                                                   CH16P4
OERRORS  D        99                                                 CH16P4
O        OR       03                                                 CH16P4
O                         IMAGE     49                               CH16P4
O                    03             73 'BAD TRANSACTION CODE    '    CH16P4
O                    99             73 'CUSTOMER NOT FOUND      '    CH16P4
```

Figure 16-32 Partial source listing of the update/delete program modified to logically delete records by the DEL method.

use with indexed files. A partial listing of the update and delete program modified to logically delete records by the DEL method is shown in Figure 16-32. Notice that the DEL entry is included in columns 16, 17, and 18 on a separate Record Description line. If it was included in an OR relationship with the record description for updates, both conditions would logically delete every record processed. When this method is used, a record logically deleted cannot be retrieved. The DEL method is supported on IBM's System/36 for all file organization types and on Digital's VAX RPG II for only indexed and direct files.

Indexed File Reorganization

File reorganization may include one or more of the following procedures:

1. *Purge* files of records tagged for deletion (or logically deleted by the DEL or DELET statements).
2. *Flush* out file overflow areas in systems that support them, and store all records in the prime data area.
3. *Key sort* records in the prime data area in index sequence. Some systems store added records at the end of the prime data area and not in the order of the index. This reorganization procedure sorts the records in the prime data area in index order.
4. *Resize* the file. If a file is too small or too large, some reorganization methods will provide more or less storage.
5. *Reformat* the records in a file. This process includes a change in the field sizes, locations, or inclusion in one or more record formats.
6. *Change* a file's organization type from one type to another.

Many systems include utilities that will perform most, if not all, of these reorganization processes. Any of them may be performed by a SORT/MERGE utility. However, there are specific utilities that control one or more reorganization procedures. For example, IBM's System/36 includes an ORGANIZE utility that controls the purging and key sort functions previously mentioned. Supplied with the software on IBM's System/38 and AS/400 is a RGZPFM (Reorganize Physical File Member) that purges logically deleted (with a DELET statement) records in a physical file member, and optionally resequences them according to an access path. On those two systems, a COPY utility must be used to remove from a physical file records that were tagged as deleted.

In an environment where a reorganization utility is not available (or in lieu of), an RPG program may be written to support any of the reorganization functions. The file to be reorganized is defined as input to the program and the reorganized file, as output.

File Maintenance in the System/38 and AS/400 Environments

In IBM's System/38 and AS/400 data base environments, indexed files are referred as *keyed* files and sequential as *nonkeyed*. Notice, however, that the structure of *keyed* and *nonkeyed* files is completely different from their counterparts. All data files processed by System/38s or AS/400s are defined as data base files. They offer considerably more flexibility in processing than the conventional files supported in a non-data-base environment.

RPG III and RPG/400 supported on the System/38 and AS/400 eliminates the requirement that the normal RPG logical cycle must always be followed in file maintenance programs. Record addition may now be controlled by a WRITE operation, update processing by an UPDAT operation, and the logical deletion of records by the DELET operation. Each of these operations and the syntax and the interactive loading of data base (physical) files will be explained in Chapters 19 to 21.

Alternative Index Files

Some computer systems support alternative indexes for index files. Alternative index files do not include data but only the addresses of the records in the related data file (physical file) in an ascending field order. The data is stored in the physical file from which the alternative index is built.

Alternative indexes are created to process a file in a field order other than the original key (primary index) sequence. For example, the indexed file processed in this chapter (and Chapter 15) was created with customer number as the primary index. By building an alternative index file for customer name, the data (physical) file may be processed sequentially or randomly by that field. The structure of an alternative index file and its relationship to a physical file is illustrated in Figure 16-33.

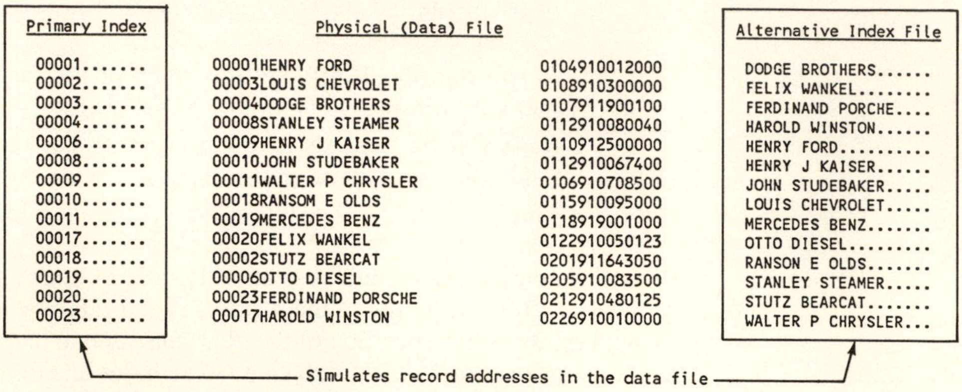

Note: Keys are stored in the indexes in an ascending order.

Figure 16-33 Relationship of an alternative index file to the related data (physical file).

Any field in the body of the record format may be used as the key(s) for alternative index file. Even though an alternative index file does not contain data, it is referred to as a file because it is created and stored separately from the primary index and prime data area.

An alternative index file may specify one data field as the key or a maximum of three noncontiguous fields as a composite key. The fields included in a composite key cannot overlap each other in the record format referenced.

The alternative index file example discussed here is supported only on IBM's System/36. Other systems that maintain alternative indexes have completely different build procedures and related RPG syntax.

Alternative index files control the same functions that the primary index supports, including the following:

1. Sequentially read records from the physical file in the alternative index file order.
2. Randomly read records from the physical file by the key(s) specified for the alternative index file.
3. Read records from the physical file within limits.

4. Update and delete records in the physical file by the key(s) specified for the alternative index file.
5. Add records to the physical file limited to the restrictions imposed by the alternative index file (i.e., duplicate keys supported or not supported).

An alternative index file is built on the System/36 by entering

BLDINDEX

which displays the screen shown in Figure 16-34. Note that each entry is explained at the bottom of the figure.

```
                         BLDINDEX Procedure                                  Optional-*

            Creates an alternative index for a physical file

Name of file to be created .....................................       CUSTNAME
Starting position for first field of key ....................1-4096    7
Length of first field .........................................1-120   30
Starting position for second field of key ...................1-4096          *
Length of second field ........................................1-120         *
Starting position for third field of key ....................1-4096          *
Length of third field .........................................1-120         *
Name of physical file ...........................................      CUSTMSTR
Creation date of physical file ..................................              *
Allow duplicate keys ...........................DUPKEY,NODUPKEY         DUPKEY
Preferred disk location ..................A1,A2,A3,A4,block number            *

Cmd3-Previous menu   Cmd4-Put on Job queue                         (c) 1985 IBM Corp.

Explanation of Entries:

Name of file to be created. Programmer-supplied name of alternative index.

Starting position for first field of key. Starting position of the field
within the body of the record used as the first key in the alternative index.

Length of first field. Length of the first alternative index field.

Starting position for second field of key. Only used when a composite
key is to be built. Specifies the starting position of the field within
the body of the record.

Length of second field. Length of the second alternative index field.

Starting position for third field of key. Only used when a composite
key is to be built. Specifies the starting position of the field within
the body of the record.

Length of third field. Length of the third alternative index field.

Name of physical file. Name of the physical file from which the alternative
index is to be built. The data is stored in this file and not in the
alternative index file. The term physical file used in the IBM System/36
environment does not refer to a data base file common to the System/38 or AS /400.

Creation date of physical file. Optional entry that indicates when the file
was created.

Allow duplicate keys. Specifies when duplicates keys are supported in the
alternative index.

Preferred disk location. Specifies which disk the alternative index will be
stored on. A1, indicates first disk; A2, second, and so on.
```

Figure 16-34 BLDINDEX (Build Alternative Index File) procedure screen (IBM System/36 only).

RPG Syntax to Support Alternative Index File Processing

The source listing in Figure 16-35 illustrates how the example update program that was shown in Figure 16-26 is modified to support processing of the CUSTMSTR file with the alternative index file CUSTNAME. Notice the term *physical file* used here to reference a data file is not the same physical file structure supported on IBM's System/38 or AS/400. Physical files with those systems are data base files that are built and defined externally from an RPG program. This topic will be thoroughly discussed in Chapter 19.

```
... ... 1 ... ... 2 ... ... 3 ... ... 4 ... ... 5 ... ... 6 ... ... 7 ...
 * THIS PROGRAM UPDATES THE CUSTMSTR FILE.  TRANSACTION RECORDS THAT CH16P5
 * THAT HAVE A MISSING ID CODE, OR INCORRECT ID CODE, OR CUSTOMER    CH16P5
 * NUMBER THAT IS NOT IN THE CUSTMSTR FILE ARE WRITTEM TO AN ERROR   CH16P5
 * FILE IN TRANSACTION RECORD IMAGE WITH RELATED ERROR MESSAGE.....  CH16P5
 *        TRANSACTION CODE D - TAG MASTER RECORD WITH D              CH16P5
 *        TRANSACTION CODE U - UPDATE MASTER RECORD NAME, DATE, AND  CH16P5
 *          AMOUNT FIELDS IF RELATED TRANSACTION RECORD HAS VALUES   CH16P5
 *          NEGATIVE AMOUNTS INCLUDE A MINUS SIGN OVER LOW ORDER BYTE CH16P5
H
FUPDATES IP  F  49  49              DISK
FCUSTNAMEUC  F 220  44R30AI       7 DISK
FERRORS  O   F  73  73              DISK
IUPDATES SM  01    1 CD
I        OR  02    1 CU
I        OR  03
I                                      2   6 CUSTNO                 CH16P5
I                                      7  36 UPNAME     02          CH16P5
I                                     37  420UPDATE           11    CH16P5
I                                     43  492UPAMT      02          CH16P5
I                                      1  49 IMAGE      03          CH16P5
ICUSTNAMESM  04                                                     CH16P5
I                                   P 37  400DATE                   CH16P5
I                                   P 41  442BALANC                 CH16P5
C   N03      UPNAME    CHAINCUSTNAME          99    NOT FOUND?
C   N99 02   BALANC    ADD  UPAMT     BALANC
 *
 * IF VALID TRANSACTION CODE AND MASTER RECORD IS FOUND, UPDATE
 * MASTER RECORD WITH RELATED TRANSACTION DATA....
 *                                                                  CH16P5
OCUSTNAMED         04                                               CH16P5
O                    01            1 'D'                            CH16P5
O                   N11   UPDATE   40P                              CH16P5
O                    02   BALANC   44P                              CH16P5
 *                                                                  CH16P5
 * IF BAD ID CODE OR CUST NOT FOUND, LOAD TRANS RECORD TO ERROR FILE CH16P5
 *                                                                  CH16P5
OERRORS  D         99                                               CH16P5
O        OR        03                                               CH16P5
O                         IMAGE    49                               CH16P5
O                    03            73 'BAD TRANSACTION CODE    '    CH16P5
O                    99            73 'CUSTOMER NOT FOUND      '    CH16P5
```

Alternative index file name must be specified to reference and process the physical file

Customer name field size (physical file) & starting position must be entered in related fields

Alternative index file name must be entered in Factor 2

Figure 16-35 Update program modified for processing with an alternative index file.

SUMMARY

Indexed file maintenance includes record addition, inquiry, deletion, and update. On some systems, add records are stored at the end of the file; on others, they are loaded into the prime data area in the index order of the keys. Unless a system supports duplicate records (same key value), any attempt to add a record with the same key value to an indexed file will abort or halt program execution. CHAINing to the file before the add statement is executed may be used to control a duplicate key error.

Indexed file inquiry is a random processing function that requires use of the CHAIN operation. If the value in the search field (Factor 1) is equal to a key in the index, the related record is accessed. Unlike sequential file inquiry, the processing of an index file does not require that the search keys be entered in an ascending relative record number.

Supplemental to the File Description entries that define a file as indexed, update processing requires that a U be entered in column 15, a C in column 16, and an R in column 28. The U entry processes the file as an input and output file. In the update process, a record is randomly accessed, modified, and then stored back to its original location. The CHAIN operation is used to find the record specified in the key value stored in the Factor 1 item. Records stored in a transaction file or input interactively do not have to be in an ascending or descending order.

Indexed file reorganization includes the purging, flushing, key sorting, resizing, reformatting, and changing of the records. The methods used to support this function often depend on the software supplied with the computer system.

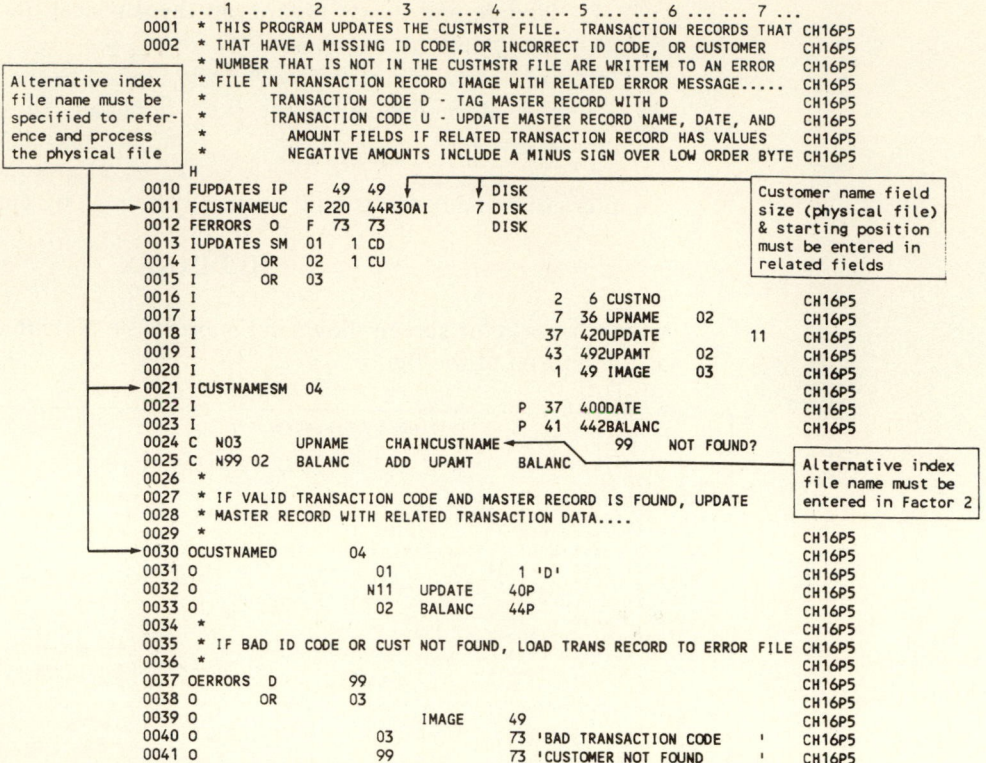

For example, an ORGANIZE utility is included with the software on IBM's System/36 that performs the purging and flushing functions. A RGZPFM (Reorganize Physical File Member) is included with the System/38 and AS/400 software to purge files of logically deleted records and resequences the files in accordance with an existing access path. If software unique to file reorganization is not available, the SORT/MERGE utility or an RPG program may be used to perform all the typical reorganization functions.

Operations included in RPG III/400, which are available only on IBM's System/38 and AS/400 computers, allow program control to override the normal RPG logical cycle in the maintenance of keyed files. The WRITE operation controls the loading and addition of records; the UPDAT operation, the update of records after they are found with a CHAIN or READ operation; and the DELET operation to control the logical deletion of records. Each of these operations will be discussed in Chapter 21.

Alternative index files may be built on some computer systems to process an index file in a field order other than that controlled by the primary index.

QUESTIONS

16-1. As compared to sequential files, what processing advantages do indexed files offer?

16-2. Name the physical areas of an indexed file. Explain what is stored in each area.

16-3. Name the maintenance functions that are supported for indexed files.

16-4. Where are add records loaded in an indexed file? Does your answer apply for all computer systems? Explain.

16-5. What specification form(s) and entries are required in an RPG program to support the addition of records to an indexed file?

16-6. Explain the restrictions for adding records to an indexed file. What coding may be included in an RPG program to control these restrictions? What happens if this control is not included?

16-7. Define the following terms:

CHAINing file	CHAINed file
CHAINing field	CHAIN (operation)
Sequential access	Random access

16-8. Explain file inquiry processing. What RPG specification forms are required to support file inquiry?

16-9. Modify the following File Description form to support inquiry processing:

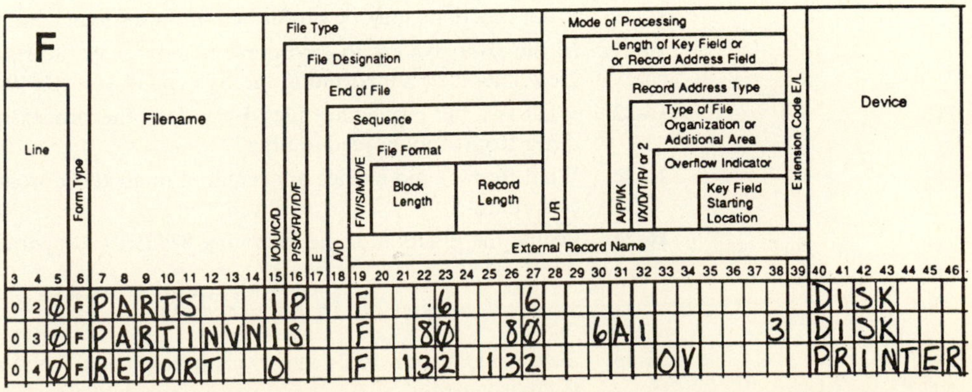

16-10. Modify the following File Description coding to support update processing:

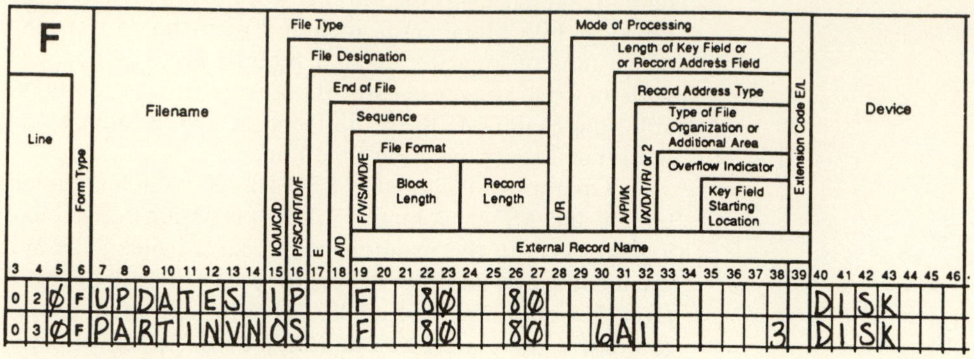

Refer to the following calculation statement and answer Questions 16-11 through 16-14:

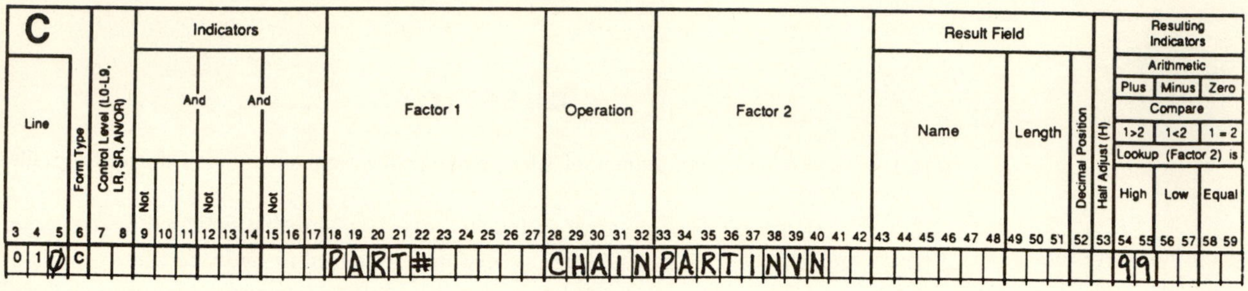

16-11. For which processing methods does the instruction in the foregoing calculation statement support?

16-12. What is the term for the entry in Factor 1?

16-13. What is the term for the entry in Factor 2?

16-14. When does the indicator specified in the High field (columns 54–55) turn on? Is the indicator optional? May it be specified in any other Resulting Indicator field?

16-15. Is an update file an input or output file? Explain the processing logic to support your answer.

16-16. Do all the fields in the record format of a chained file have to be specified in the related input Field Description? Explain your answer.

16-17. By what methods may records in an indexed file be deleted?

16-18. How is an indexed file defined for each of the record deletion methods identified in Question 16-17?

16-19. What entries are needed in an RPG program to control record deletion by the methods identified in Question 16-18?

16-20. What functions may be performed in the reorganization of an indexed file?

16-21. In the IBM System/36 environment, how may file reorganization be supported? How may it be supported in the System/38 and AS/400 environments?

16-22. What is a full-procedural file? How does the processing of a full-procedural file differ from a nonprocedural file?

16-23. What form(s) and entries are required in an RPG program to define a file as full-procedural?

16-24. Define the function of the following RPGIII/400 operations.

WRITE UPDAT DELET

16-25. Refer to Question 16-24 and explain how each function is supported in an RPG II environment.

16-26. Define an alternative index file. When are they necessary?

16-27. How are alternative index files created? What is stored in them?

16-28. Define the term *composite key*.

16-29. Identify the coding needed in an RPG program to support the processing of an index file by an alternative index file.

16-30. How does the System/36 term *physical file* differ from *physical files* in the System/38 and AS/400 environments?

EXERCISES

16-1. Write an RPG program to add records (without error checking) to an indexed file. The attributes of the file are detailed in the following File Definition form.

FILE DEFINITION

SYSTEM Yours		DRAWN BY S. Myers
FILE NAME None		DATE 3/1/91 REV. NO. 0
CREATED BY S. Myers		FILE TYPE Disk
RECORD NAME None		KEY LENGTH 5 bytes
RECORDING MODE Fixed	ORGANIZATION Indexed	SEQUENCE Key order
RECORD SIZE 32 bytes	BLOCKING FACTOR 1	BLOCKSIZE 32 bytes

FIELD DATA

FIELD NO.	FIELD NAME - DESCRIPTION	SIZE	CLASS C/P/Z/B	POSITION FROM	POSITION THRU	FORMAT/CONSTANT
1	Delete Code	1	C	1	1	D if deleted
2	Part Number	5	C	2	6	Key field
3	Part Description	20	C	7	26	
4	Quantity	5	P	27	29	
5	Cost per Unit	4	P	30	32	2 decimal positions

The format of the add records is shown below:

PART#	DESCRIPTION	QTY	CST/UNIT
9 9 9 9 9	9 9 9 9 9 9 9 9 9 9 9 9 9 9 9 9 9 9 9 9	9 9 9 9 9	9 9 9 9
1 2 3 4 5	6 7 8 9 10 11 12 13 14 15 16 17 18 19 20 21 22 23 24 25	26 27 28 29 30	31 32 ▲ 33 34

16-2. Modify the program completed for Exercise 16-1 to check the master file for a duplicate record before trying to add a record.

16-3. Refer to the master file attributes in Exercise 16-1, and write an RPG program to interactively *inquiry* the master file. Use CONSOLE input (or the device supported on your system) to enter the part number (CHAINing field) used to search the master file for a record that has an equal key. Assume output is to the printer in the input record image of the master file.

16-4. Refer to the master file attributes in Exercise 16-1, and write an RPG program to *update* the master file in a batch mode. The update data is stored on a sequential file in the same record format as the "add" record for Exercise 16-1 as shown on the following page.

PART#	DESCRIPTION	QTY	CST/ UNIT
9 9 9 9 9	9 9 9 9 9 9 9 9 9 9 9 9 9 9 9 9 9 9 9 9	9 9 9 9 9	9 9 9 9
1 2 3 4 5	6 7 8 9 10 11 12 13 14 15 16 17 18 19 20 21 22 23 24 25	26 27 28 29 30	31 32 33 34

16-5. Modify the program completed in Exercise 16-4 to logically delete records from the master file.

16-6. Assume that an alternative index file has been built on the master file created in Exercise 16-1 using the part description field as the key. Modify either the program completed for Exercise 16-3 or 16-4 to process the master file by the alternative index.

16-7. Examine the following source listing of a program that updates an indexed file and correct the syntax and logic errors.

```
... ... 1 ... ... 2 ... ... 3 ... ... 4 ... ... 5 ... ... 6 ... ... 7 ...
  * THIS PROGRAM UPDATES THE CUSTMSTR FILE.  TRANSACTION RECORDS THAT EX167
  * THAT HAVE A MISSING ID CODE, OR INCORRECT ID CODE, OR CUSTOMER    EX167
  * NUMBER THAT IS NOT ON THE CUSTMSTR FILE ARE WRITTEM TO AN ERROR   EX167
  * FILE IN TRANSACTION RECORD IMAGE WITH RELATED ERROR MESSAGE.....  EX167
  *       TRANSACTION CODE D - TAG MASTER RECORD WITH D              EX167
  *       TRANSACTION CODE U - UPDATE MASTER RECORD NAME, DATE, AND  EX167
  *         AMOUNT FIELDS IF RELATED TRANSACTION RECORD HAS VALUES   EX167
  *         NEGATIVE AMOUNTS INCLUDE A MINUS SIGN OVER LOW ORDER BYTE EX167
 H                                                                   EX167
 FUPDATES IP  F  49  49            DISK                              EX167
 FCUSTMSTROC  F 220  44  5AI     2 DISK                              EX167
 FERRORS  O   F  73  73            DISK                              EX167
 IUPDATES SM  01    1 CD                                             EX167
 I        OR  02    1 CU                                             EX167
 I        OR  03                                                     EX167
 I                                             2   6 CUSTNO          EX167
 I                                             7  36 UPNAME    02  10 EX167
 I                                            37  420UPDATE        11 EX167
 I                                            43  492UPAMT     02     EX167
 I                                             1  49 IMAGE     03     EX167
 C  N03      CUSTNO    CHAINCUSTMSTR              99    NOT FOUND?   EX167
 C  N99 02   BALANC    ADD  UPAMT     BALANC                         EX167
  *                                                                  EX167
  * IF VALID TRANSACTION CODE AND MASTER RECORD IS FOUND, UPDATE     EX167
  * MASTER RECORD WITH RELATED TRANSACTION DATA....                  EX167
  *                                                                  EX167
 OCUSTMSTRD        99                                                EX167
 O                   01                1 'D'                         EX167
 O                 02N10   UPNAME    36                              EX167
 O                   N11   UPDATE    40P                             EX167
 O                   02    BALANC    44P                             EX167
  *                                                                  EX167
  * IF BAD ID CODE OR CUST NOT FOUND, LOAD TRANS RECORD TO ERROR FILE EX167
  *                                                                  EX167
 OERRORS  D       N99 04                                             EX167
 O       OR       03                                                 EX167
 O                         IMAGE     49                              EX167
 O                   03              73 'BAD TRANSACTION CODE    '   EX167
 O                  N99              73 'CUSTOMER NOT FOUND      '   EX167
```

LABORATORY ASSIGNMENTS

The data file created for Assignment 15-1 must exist before the programs for Assignments 16-1, 16-2, 16-3, or 16-4 are executed. If the file is not stored, your professor will give you instructions on the procedures to follow.

Laboratory Assignment 16-1: ADDING RECORDS TO A SAVING ACCOUNTS MASTER FILE (INDEXED)

Write an RPG program to add records to the saving accounts master file created and loaded in Assignment 15-1.

Input: The attributes of the saving accounts master file are detailed in the following file definition form:

FILE DEFINITION

SYSTEM Yours		DRAWN BY S. Myers
FILE NAME Yours		DATE 3/1/91 REV. NO. 0
CREATED BY S. Myers		FILE TYPE Disk
RECORD NAME None		KEY LENGTH 5
RECORDING MODE Fixed	ORGANIZATION Indexed	SEQUENCE Key order
RECORD SIZE 82 bytes	BLOCKING FACTOR 1	BLOCKSIZE 82 bytes

FIELD DATA

FIELD NO.	FIELD NAME - DESCRIPTION	SIZE	CLASS C/P/Z/B	POSITION FROM	POSITION THRU	FORMAT/CONSTANT
1	Delete Code	1	C	1	1	D if deleted
2	Account Number	5	C	2	6	Key field
3	Account Name	31	C	7	37	
4	Street	20	C	38	57	
5	City	16	C	58	73	
6	State	2	C	74	75	
7	Zip Code	5	P	76	78	
8	Balance	6	P	79	82	2 decimal positions

The format of the add records follows:

FILE DEFINITION

SYSTEM Yours		DRAWN BY S. Myers
FILE NAME Yours		DATE 3/1/91 REV. NO. 0
CREATED BY S. Myers		FILE TYPE Disk
RECORD NAME None		KEY LENGTH None
RECORDING MODE Fixed	ORGANIZATION Sequential	SEQUENCE Unordered
RECORD SIZE 85 bytes	BLOCKING FACTOR 1	BLOCKSIZE 85 bytes

FIELD DATA

FIELD NO.	FIELD NAME - DESCRIPTION	SIZE	CLASS C/P/Z/B	POSITION FROM	POSITION THRU	FORMAT/CONSTANT
1	Account Number	5	C	1	5	
2	Account Name	31	C	6	36	
3	Street	20	C	37	56	
4	City	16	C	57	72	
5	State	2	C	73	74	
6	Zip Code	5	Z	75	79	
7	Deposit Amount	6	Z	80	85	2 decimal positions

Processing: Include the necessary controls in your program to prevent a runtime halt or termination when a duplicate record (same key value as master file) condition is tested in the adds process. Accumulate balance totals for all records added to the file. Include count fields for the number of records added and not added.

Output: Add to the indexed file the input records that do not have a duplicate key. Notice that zip code and amount fields are stored as *packed* in the master file. Also, generate a report in the following format:

Report Design:

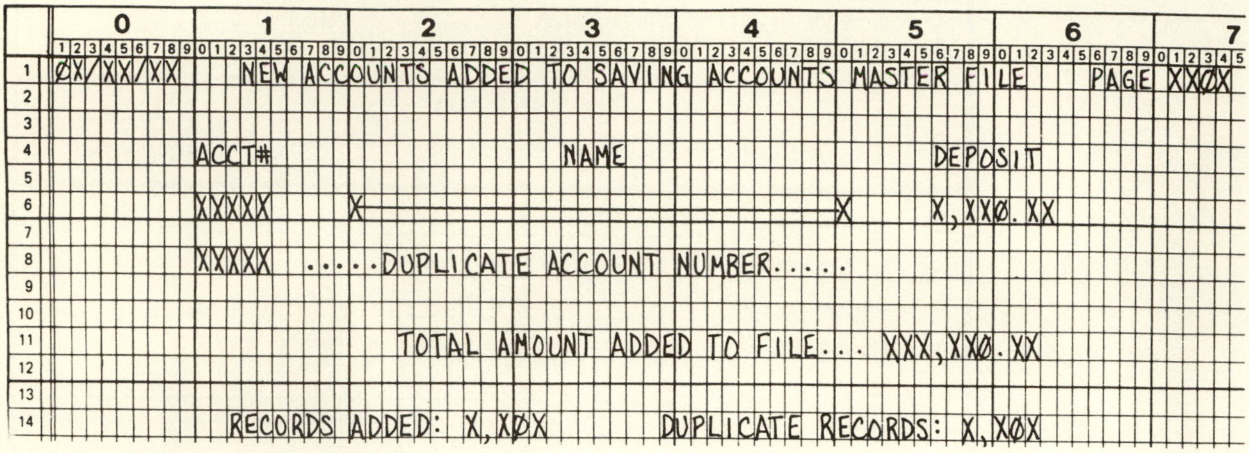

Adds Data:

Acct# 1-5	Account Name 6-36	Street 37-56	City 57-72	State 73-74	Zip 75-79	Deposit Amount 80-85
80000	SIDNEY GREENSTREET	10 CASTLE LANE	ALCATRAZ	CA	92220	100000
10000	PETER LORRE	9 DREARY DRIVE	HUNGRY	AL	99999	004500
71510	JOHN HINES	220 HIGH DRIVE	KEENE	ND	58847	075950
60000	BORIS KARLOFF	1 INNER SANCTUM	MISERABLE	AK	10000	549000

After program execution, print a hex listing (if available on your system) of the master file and check the format of the added records.

Laboratory Assignment 16-2: SAVING ACCOUNTS MASTER FILE INQUIRY

Write an RPG program to inquiry records from the Saving Accounts Master File.

Input: Enter account numbers (via CRT, KEYBORD, DISPLAY, or WORKSTN input) that are to be used as the CHAINing field to locate the related record in the Saving Accounts Master File. If any of these CRT devices are not available, include the account numbers in a sequential disk file. Enter account numbers 71510, 21345, 90000, and 80000. Refer to Lab 16-1 for the attributes of the Saving Accounts Master File.

Processing: Use the CHAIN operation to access records in the master file from the account numbers entered. If a master record is found, access all the field information.

Report Design: For each account number entered, generate a separate report in the format shown in the following printer spacing chart. When a master record is not found, print the report with the error message indicated.

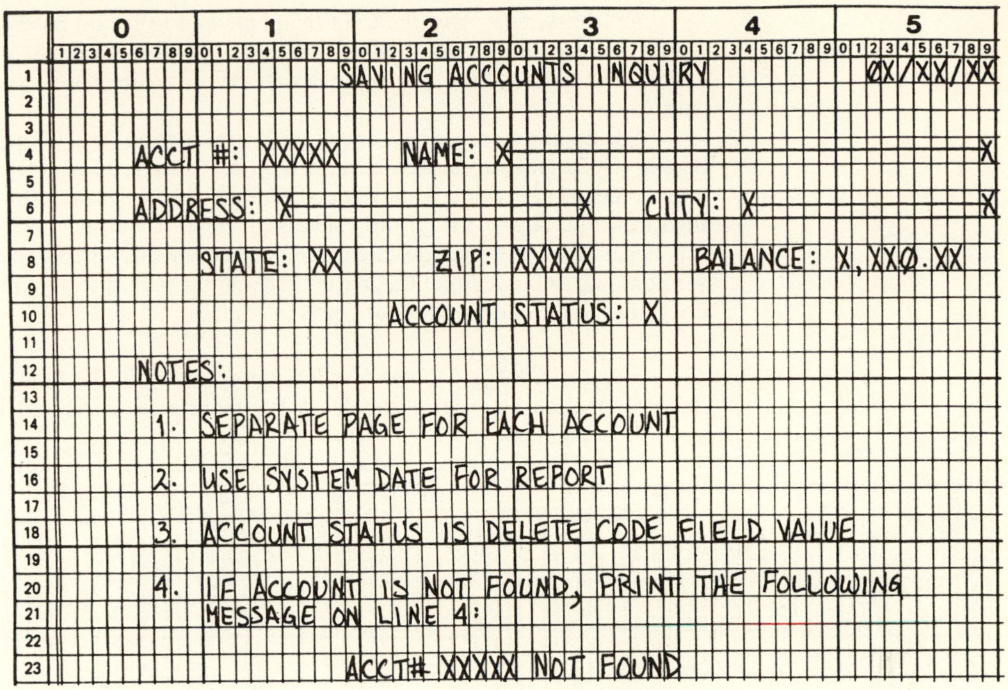

SAVING ACCOUNTS INQUIRY ØX/XX/XX
ACCT #: XXXXX NAME: X X
ADDRESS: X X CITY: X X
STATE: XX ZIP: XXXXX BALANCE: X,XXØ.XX
ACCOUNT STATUS: X
NOTES:
1. SEPARATE PAGE FOR EACH ACCOUNT
2. USE SYSTEM DATE FOR REPORT
3. ACCOUNT STATUS IS DELETE CODE FIELD VALUE
4. IF ACCOUNT IS NOT FOUND, PRINT THE FOLLOWING MESSAGE ON LINE 4:
ACCT# XXXXX NOT FOUND

Laboratory Assignment 16-3: SAVING ACCOUNTS MASTER FILE BATCH UPDATES AND DELETES

Write an RPG program to update and delete records (tagging method) in the Saving Accounts Master File.

Input: The format of the records in the sequential disk file that includes the update data is shown the following record layout form:

FILE DEFINITION

SYSTEM Yours		DRAWN BY S. Myers
FILE NAME Yours		DATE 3/15/91 REV. NO. 0
CREATED BY S. Myers		FILE TYPE Disk
RECORD NAME None		KEY LENGTH None
RECORDING MODE Fixed	ORGANIZATION Sequential	SEQUENCE Unordered
RECORD SIZE 86 bytes	BLOCKING FACTOR 1	BLOCKSIZE 86 bytes

FIELD DATA

FIELD NO.	FIELD NAME - DESCRIPTION	SIZE	CLASS C P Z B	POSITION FROM	POSITION THRU	FORMAT/CONSTANT
1	Transaction Code	1	C	1	1	U or D
2	Account Number	5	C	2	6	Chaining field
3	Account Name	31	C	7	37	
4	Street	20	C	38	57	
5	City	16	C	58	73	
6	State	2	C	74	75	
7	Zip Code	5	Z	76	80	
8	Transaction Amount	6	Z	81	86	2 decimal positions

Refer to the File Definition form included in Assignment 16-1 for the attributes of the Saving Accounts Master File.

Processing: Use the CHAINing method to locate records from the master file. Test the transaction code field for a U or D value. If the code value is U, perform the update procedures; if it is D, tag the master record as deleted and do not change any other field values.

For update transactions, check every transaction field (except account number) for blanks (alphanumeric) or zeros (numeric). If the field does not test as blanks or zeros, update the master record with the new value(s). Add the transaction amount to the balance field from the master file. If the value is positive, it will increase the account balance; if it is negative, it will decrease the balance when the add operation is executed. Because a zero amount will not affect the master account balance, the field in the transaction record does not have to be checked for zeros.

Report Design: Generate the report shown in the following print chart. Notice that only the master records updated are to be printed with the field values shown *before* and *after* updating.

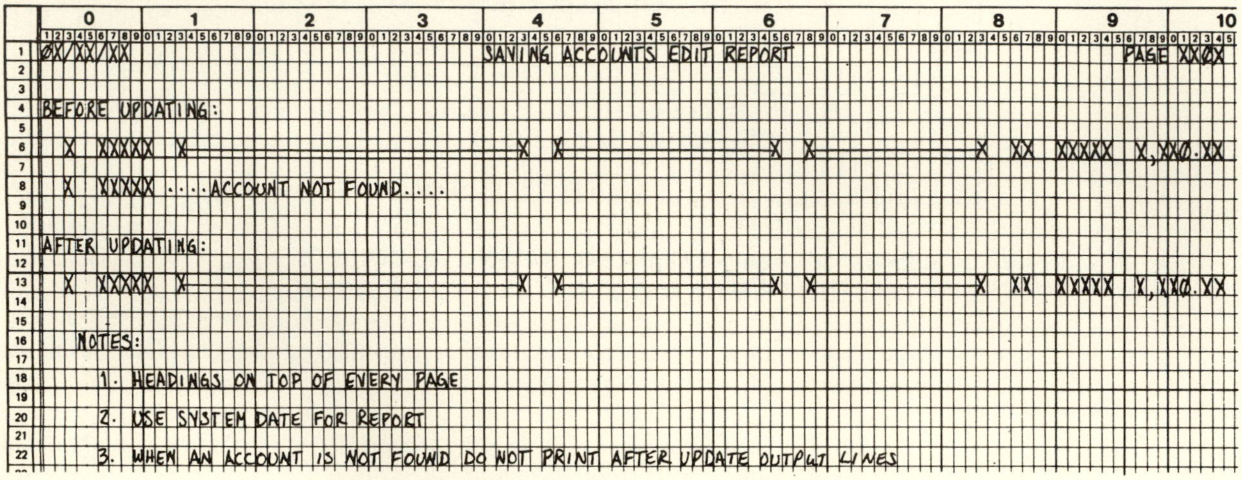

Update Data:

Trans. Code 1	Acct# 2-6	Account Name 7-37	Street 38-57	City 58-73	State 74-75	Zip 76-80	Deposit Amount 81-86
U	80000						200000
U	21345		10 ROSE TERRACE	TRUMBULL	VT	07779	
U	40000						015000
U	63141						07777P
D	48891						

Laboratory Assignment 16-4: LOGICAL DELETION OF RECORDS FROM THE SAVING ACCOUNTS MASTER FILE

If Assignment 16-3 was completed and if your system supports logical deletion processing, modify Assignment 16-3 to logically delete records from the Saving Accounts Master File.

Input: Enter account numbers (via CRT, KEYBORD, DISPLAY, or WORKSTN input) that are to be used as the CHAINing field to locate the related record in the Saving Accounts Master File. If any of these CRT devices are not available, include the account numbers in a sequential disk file and process in a batch mode. Delete records with account numbers 48891 and 80000.

Execute the inquiry program completed in Assignment 16-2 to validate that the two records have been logically deleted (the message ACCT# XXXXX NOT FOUND will be generated). If Assignment 16-2 was not completed, use the COPY utility supplied with your system to check the results of the deletion process. Notice, however, that some COPY utilities will output the logically deleted record(s). Consequently, you may get confusing results if a utility is used to check your processing results.

The data file created for Assignment 15-5 must exist before the programs for Assignments 16-5, 16-6, 16-7, and 16-8 are executed. If the file is not stored, your professor will give you instructions on the procedures to follow.

Laboratory Assignment 16-5: ADDING RECORDS TO THE CEREAL BRANDS INVENTORY FILE

Write an RPG program to add records to the cereal brands inventory file created and loaded in Assignment 15-5.

Input: The attributes of the cereal brands inventory file are detailed in the following File Definition form:

FILE DEFINITION

SYSTEM Yours		DRAWN BY S. Myers
FILE NAME Yours		DATE 3/31/91 REV. NO. 0
CREATED BY S. Myers		FILE TYPE Disk
RECORD NAME None		KEY LENGTH 5 bytes
RECORDING MODE Fixed	ORGANIZATION Indexed	SEQUENCE Key order
RECORD SIZE 63 bytes	BLOCKING FACTOR 20	BLOCKSIZE 1260 bytes

FIELD DATA

FIELD NO.	FIELD NAME - DESCRIPTION	SIZE	CLASS C/P/Z/B	POSITION FROM	POSITION THRU	FORMAT/CONSTANT
1	Delete Code	1	C	1	1	D if deleted
2	Brand Number	5	C	2	6	Key field
3	Brand Name	20	C	7	26	
4	Size of Item	3	P	27	28	
5	Unit of Measure	2	C	29	30	
6	Manufacturer	15	C	31	45	
7	Last Purchase Date	6	P	46	49	
8	Last Purchase Price Per Unit	6	P	50	53	4 decimal positions
9	Quantity On Hand	5	P	54	56	
10	Average Cost Per Unit	6	P	57	60	4 decimal positions
11	Selling Price Per Unit	4	P	61	63	2 decimal positions

The format of the add records follows:

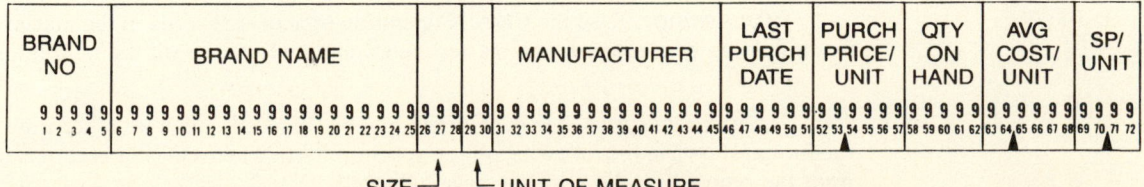

BRAND NO	BRAND NAME	SIZE	UNIT OF MEASURE	MANUFACTURER	LAST PURCH DATE	PURCH PRICE/ UNIT	QTY ON HAND	AVG COST/ UNIT	SP/ UNIT
9 9 9 9 9	9 9 9 9 9 9 9 9 9 9 9 9 9 9 9 9 9 9 9 9	9 9 9	9 9	9 9 9 9 9 9 9 9 9 9 9 9 9 9 9	9 9 9 9 9 9	9 9 9 9 9 9	9 9 9 9 9	9 9 9 9 9 9	9 9 9 9
1 2 3 4 5	6 7 8 9 10 11 12 13 14 15 16 17 18 19 20 21 22 23 24 25	26 27 28	29 30	31 32 33 34 35 36 37 38 39 40 41 42 43 44 45	46 47 48 49 50 51	52 53 54 55 56 57	58 59 60 61 62	63 64 65 66 67 68	69 70 71 72

Processing: Include the necessary controls in your program to prevent a runtime halt or termination when a duplicate record (same key value as master file) condition is tested in the adds process. Include count fields for the number of records added and not added (duplicate keys).

Output: Add to the indexed file the input records that do not have a duplicate key. Generate a report in the following format:

Report Design:

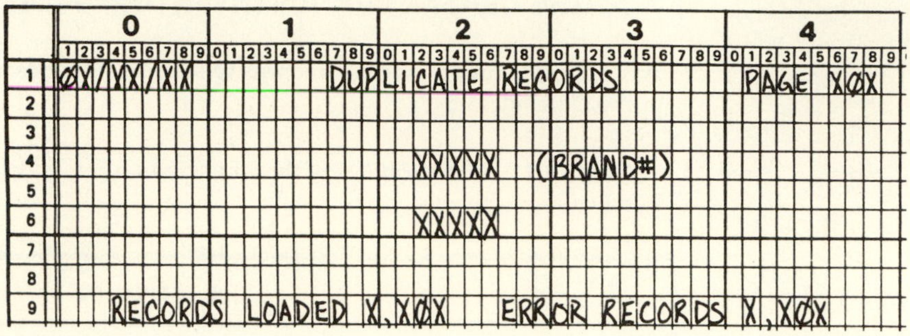

ØX/XX/XX
DUPLICATE RECORDS
PAGE XØX
XXXXX (BRAND#)
XXXXX
RECORDS LOADED X,XØX
ERROR RECORDS X,XØX

Adds Data:

Brand# 1-5	Brand Name 6-25	Size 26-28	Measure 29-30	Manufacturer 31-45	Last Purchase Date 46-51	Last Purchase Price 52-57	Amount On Hand 58-62	Average Cost/Unit 63-68	SP Price/Unit 69-72
C5200	SUN FLAKES	015	OZ	RALSTON	082292	019900	00600	019900	0219
C1134	CHEERIOS	020	OZ	GENERAL MILLS	082192	025500	12000	025500	0279
C9000	SHREDDED WHEAT SS	012	OZ	NABISCO	082492	011500	01080	011500	0125
C2200	PAC-MAN	013	OZ	GENERAL MILLS	082592	017899	24000	017899	0199

After program execution, print a hex listing (if available on your system) of the master file and check the format of the added records. If Assignment 15-6 or 15-7 was completed, one may be executed to validate the results of adds process.

Laboratory Assignment 16-6: CEREAL BRANDS INVENTORY FILE INQUIRY

Write an RPG program to inquiry records from the cereal brands inventory file.

Input: By CRT, KEYBORD, DISPLAY, or WORKSTN input, enter the brand numbers that are to be used as the CHAINing field to locate the related record in the cereal brands inventory file. If any of these CRT devices are not available, include the account numbers in a sequential disk file. Enter brand numbers C5150, C1100, C8500, and C9000. Refer to Assignment 16-5 for the attributes of the cereal brands inventory master file.

Processing: Use the CHAIN operation to access records in the master file from the brand numbers entered. If a master record is found, access all the field information.

Report Design: For each brand number entered, generate a separate report in the format shown in the following printer spacing chart. When a master record is not found, print the report with the error message indicated.

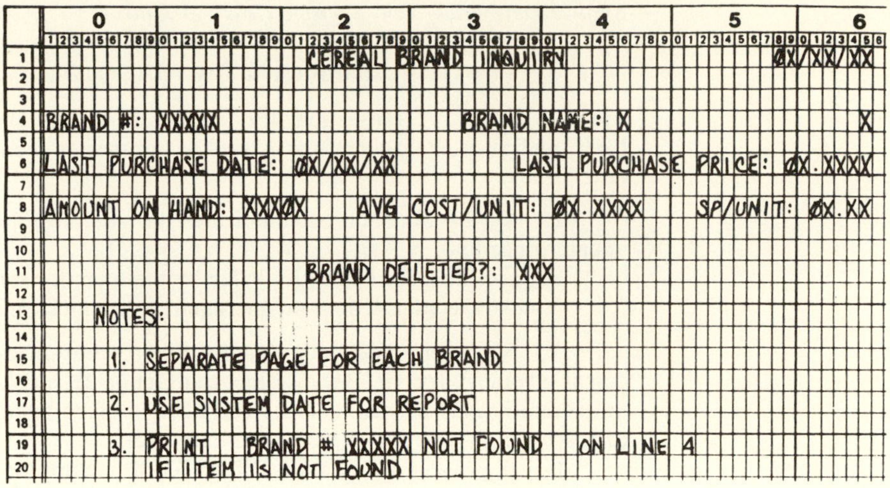

Laboratory Assignment 16-7: CEREAL BRANDS INVENTORY FILE BATCH UPDATES

Write an RPG program to update records in the cereal brands inventory file.

Input: The format of the records in the sequential disk file that includes the update data is shown the following record layout forms:

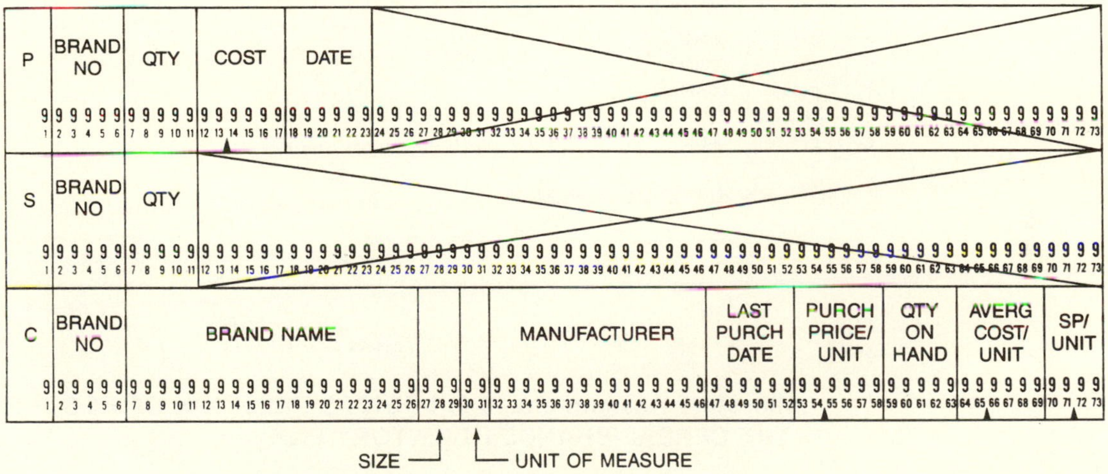

Refer to file definition form included in Assignment 16-5 for the attributes of the cereal brands inventory master file.

Processing: The following three separate update functions are to be performed:

1. A P code in the transaction record indicates a purchase transaction, which requires the following moving average cost computations:

Step 1: Determine Total Quantity and Cost After Purchase:

	Price/Unit ×	*Qty* =	*Total*
Values in master record	1.0000 ×	12,000 =	$12,000
Values in transaction record	1.1000 ×	8,000 =	8,800
Totals		20,000	$20,800

Step 2: Determine New Average Cost Per Unit:

Total Cost/Total Qty = 20,800/20,000 = 01.0400

For a P (purchase) transaction, the last purchase date last purchase price, quantity on hand, and average cost per unit values in the master record are to be updated with the new values.

2. An S transaction code indicates the sale of an item that requires the following update procedure:

Reduce the master quantity value by the quantity sold.

Note: Sales transactions do not require a recomputation of the average cost per unit.

3. A C transaction code requires a correction of one or more field values in the cereal inventory record. Because this transaction record format includes all the fields in the cereal brands master record, each field must be tested for the presence of a value (blank for alphanumeric and zeros for numeric).

If a field value in the transaction record is blank or zeros, it must not be used to update the cereal brands record. Only fields that have values other than blanks or zeros are used in this update process.

Note: This transaction type (C) includes only corrections of numeric field values and not sales or purchases.

Update Data:

DATA WITH TRANSACTION P or S IN COLUMN 1:

Trans Code 1	Brand# 2-6	Quantity 7-11	Transaction Amount 12-17	Purchase Date 18-23
P	C2121	00400	019000	091592
P	C8000	02000	017000	092192
S	C6550	00500		
S	C8900	10000		
S	C7440	00800		

DATA WITH TRANSACTION CODE C IN COLUMN 1:

Brand# 2-6	Brand Name 7-26	Size 27-29	Measure 30-31	Manufacturer 32-46	Last Purchase Date 47-52	Last Purchase Price 53-58	Amount On Hand 59-63	Average Cost/Unit 64-69	SP Price/Unit 70-73
C1100						017000			0190
C4889		012			081592				

Laboratory Assignment 16-8: LOGICAL DELETION OF RECORDS FROM THE CEREAL BRANDS INVENTORY FILE

Depending on what deletion method your system supports, write an RPG program to tag or logically delete records in the cereal brands inventory file.

Input: By CRT, KEYBORD, DISPLAY, or WORKSTN input, enter brand numbers that are to be used as the CHAINing field to locate the related record in the cereal brands inventory file. If any of those CRT devices are not available, include the brand numbers in a sequential disk file and process in a batch mode. Delete records with brand numbers C7000, C8300, and C1000.

Execute the inquiry program completed in Assignment 16-6 to validate that the two records have been tagged as deleted (letter D in column 1) or logically deleted. If the records were logically deleted, the error message BRAND # XXXXX NOT FOUND will print on the inquiry report. If the records were tagged as deleted, YES will print for the BRAND DELETED?: response. If Assignment 16-6 was not completed, use the COPY utility supplied with your system to check the results of the deletion process. Notice, however, that some COPY utilities will output the logically deleted record(s). Consequently, you may get confusing results from some utilities.

chapter 17

Direct and Addrout File Concepts and Processing

DIRECT FILE STRUCTURE

Direct files are uniquely different from sequential or indexed-sequential organizations. A direct file may be compared to a football stadium. When the stadium is built, its size limitations provide for a maximum number of seats, which may be numbered from 1 to *n* (*n* = maximum seat number). When fans buy tickets, they are assigned a prenumbered seat that they occupy for the event. Individuals are usually assigned seats according to their specific request for a location, or randomly by the ticket agent, and not always in a consecutive order. The seats are there, and the fans occupy them according to their ticket number.

A direct file parallels the same logic. When the file is created, the disk area assigned to the file is automatically cleared to blanks by the system software. Then, prenumbered record *slots* are assigned to the blanked disk area. The numbers for the slots are referred to as *relative record numbers*. They begin with 1 and go to a maximum number controlled by the space allocated to the file.

A relative record number refers the record's position in the file. For example, a record with a relative record number 1 is stored in the first slot of the file. A record with a relative record number 50 is stored in the fiftieth slot position, and so forth.

During the second step in the creation of a direct file, relative record numbers are automatically assigned to the slot positions *before* data is loaded. When the data is loaded, it is stored in the numbered slot previously created. Consequently, the control field in the logical record (e.g., employee number or part number) must relate to a relative record number allocated in the direct file area.

Because control or key fields in the load records must agree with a relative record number assigned in the file, serious restrictions are placed on the use of direct files in an application environment. It is difficult, if not sometimes impossible, to relate a control or key field to a relative record number. Later in the chapter, conversion formulas (algorithms) are presented that convert control or key field values to relative record numbers.

Figure 17-1 illustrates the processing logic for the creation and loading of a direct file. Notice the following features:

1. The disk area is cleared to blanks by the system software.
2. Slots are built for records in accordance with the logical record size specified in the RPG program. Then, relative record numbers, beginning with 1, are assigned to the slots.

3. An RPG load program writes the data records into the direct file slots from a field value that includes a relative record number.

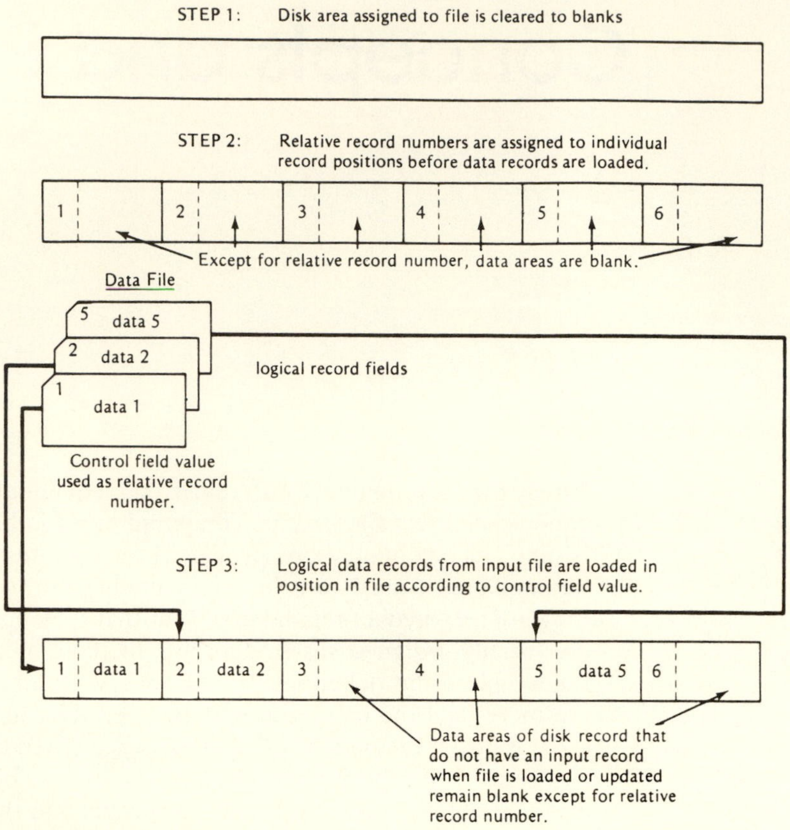

Figure 17-1 Processing logic of direct file creation and loading.

In Step 3 of Figure 17-1 direct file slots that do not have a related load record remain blank. The load records do not have to be in order and are randomly loaded and stored according to their relative record numbers. After the loading process is completed, records with control field values 1, 2, and 5 are stored in their related slots, and 3, 4, and 6 are blank.

APPLICATION PROGRAM—CREATING AND LOADING A DIRECT FILE

The specifications for an RPG program that creates and loads a direct file are explained in Figure 17-2.

The system flowchart in Figure 17-3 shows that one input file is read and two output files are loaded.

The format of the records in the sequential file that includes the load data and a listing of the file are shown in Figure 17-4.

Source Program Coding

Figure 17-5 shows the program that creates and loads a direct file with the data for a paper towel inventory. Notice the following syntax features of the program:

1. The direct file is defined in the File Description form as an output (column 15) CHAINed file (column 16) that is randomly processed (R in column 28).

PROGRAM SPECIFICATIONS Page 1 of 1

Program Name DIRECT FILE LOAD Program-ID CH17P1 Written By S. Myers

Purpose Create and load a towel inventory file Approved By The Boss

Input files (directory names):

DAT17P1 (Sequentially organized on disk)

Output files (directory names)

INVMSTR (Direct organization - stored on disk)

ERRORS (Sequentially organized on disk)

Processing Narrative:

Write an RPG program to create and load a direct file with error control.

Input:

The format of the load records stored in a sequentially organized disk file is detailed in the supplemental record layout form.

Processing:

Read the sequential file (DAT17P1) consecutively and CHAIN the item number from each record processed to the direct file (INVMSTR).

Output:

When a successful CHAIN is executed, write the input record to the related slot in the direct file in the same field format as the input record.

Numeric fields are not to be packed in the direct file.

If the CHAIN is not successful, write the input record to a sequential disk file in the input record image.

Validate the loading process by a utility listing of the direct and error files.

Figure 17-2 Specifications for a program that creates and loads a direct file for a paper towel inventory.

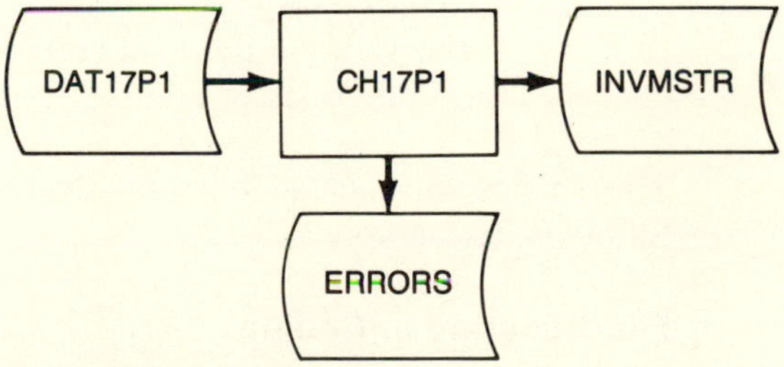

Figure 17-3 System flowchart for program that creates and loads a direct file.

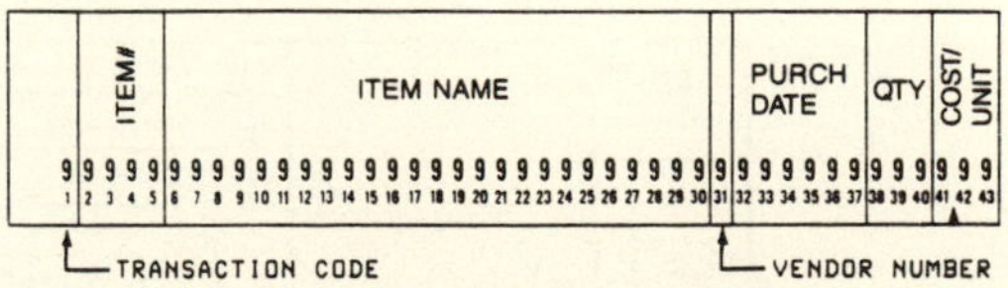

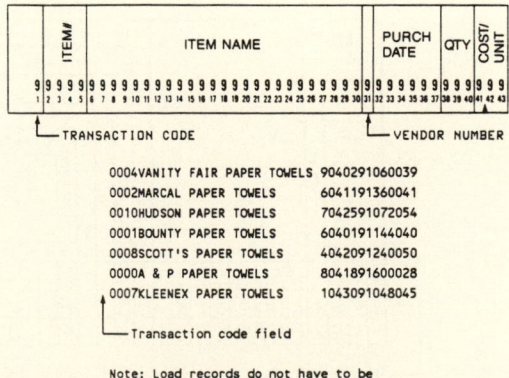

```
0004VANITY FAIR PAPER TOWELS 9040291060039
0002MARCAL PAPER TOWELS      6041191360041
0010HUDSON PAPER TOWELS      7042591072054
0001BOUNTY PAPER TOWELS      6040191144040
0008SCOTT'S PAPER TOWELS     4042091240050
0000A & P PAPER TOWELS       8041891600028
0007KLEENEX PAPER TOWELS     1043091048045
```

Transaction code field

Note: Load records do not have to be in relative record order.

Figure 17-4 Record layout form and listing of the data in the sequential (load) file.

```
... ... 1 ... ... 2 ... ... 3 ... ... 4 ... ... 5 ... ... 6 ... ... 7 ...
  * THIS PROGRAM CREATES AND LOADS A DIRECT FILE FROM DATA STORED IN  CH17P1
  * A SEQUENTIAL DISK FILE.  INPUT RECORDS WITHOUT A VALID RELATIVE   CH17P1
  * RECORD NUMBER ARE LOADED IN RECORD IMAGE TO A SEQUENTIAL DISK FILECH17P1
FDAT17P1 IP  F  43  43          DISK                                  CH17P1
FINVMSTR OC  F  43  43R         DISK                                  CH17P1
FERRORS  O   F  43  43          DISK                                  CH17P1
IDAT17P1 SM  01                                                       CH17P1
I                                         1   1 TCODE                 CH17P1
I                                         2   5 ITEM#                 CH17P1
I                                         6  30 NAME                  CH17P1
I                                        31  31 VENDR#                CH17P1
I                                        32  370PDATE                 CH17P1
I                                        38  400PQTY                  CH17P1
I                                        41  432ITMCST                CH17P1
I                                         1  43 RECORD                CH17P1
C           ITEM#     CHAININVMSTR                99    FIND SLOT     CH17P1
OINVMSTR D        N99 01                                              CH17P1
O                              TCODE      1                           CH17P1
O                              ITEM#      5                           CH17P1
O                              NAME      30                           CH17P1
O                              VENDR#    31                           CH17P1
O                              PDATE     37                           CH17P1
O                              PQTY      40                           CH17P1
O                              ITMCST    43                           CH17P1
OERRORS  D         99                                                 CH17P1
O                              RECORD    43                           CH17P1
```

Figure 17-5 Source listing of a program that creates and loads a direct file.

2. Slot (relative record) positions are located in the direct file by the CHAIN operation.
3. An input record is loaded to the direct file when the item number in a load record matches the relative record number of a slot (successful CHAIN).
4. If the value in the load record's item number does not find a slot with the same relative number, the input record is written to an error file.

The entries for each of the specification forms are separately explained in the following paragraphs.

File Description Coding

The File Description syntax related to the creation and loading of a direct file is detailed in Figure 17-6. In previous programs, only I (input)or U (update) files

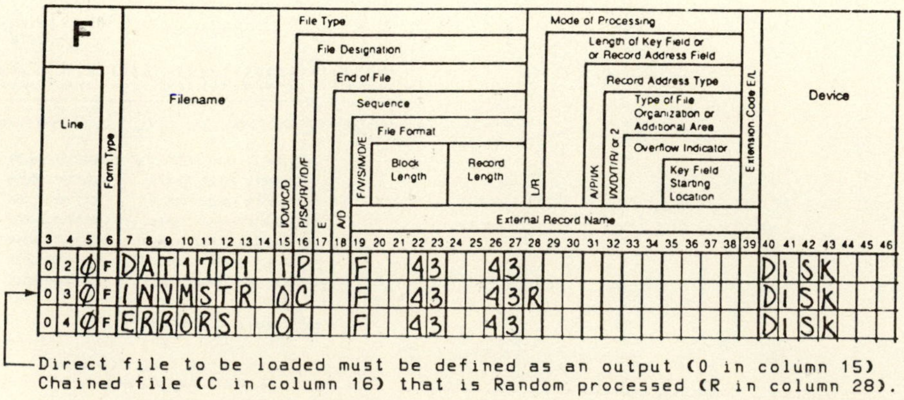

Figure 17-6 File Description coding for the program that creates and loads a direct file.

have been defined as CHAINed. Therefore, it may not seem logical to define an output file as CHAINed. However, as previously shown in Figure 17-1, the system software creates an area for the direct file; it then builds and numbers the slots before any records are loaded. For a load record to find its related slot, a CHAIN instruction must be executed. Finally, because any file organization type that is to be initially loaded with data must be defined as output, the direct file is defined with an O in column 15.

Input Specifications Coding

An examination of the input coding in Figure 17-7 shows that standard syntax is used to define the fields in the load records. The input record is redefined (columns 1–43) so that its exact image may be loaded to a sequential file for error conditions. Because the direct file is loaded in the same format as the input (load) records without packing the numeric fields, it could have been loaded as a record without field definitions. However, to support subsequent program maintenance, it is better documentation to identify each field in the direct file's record format.

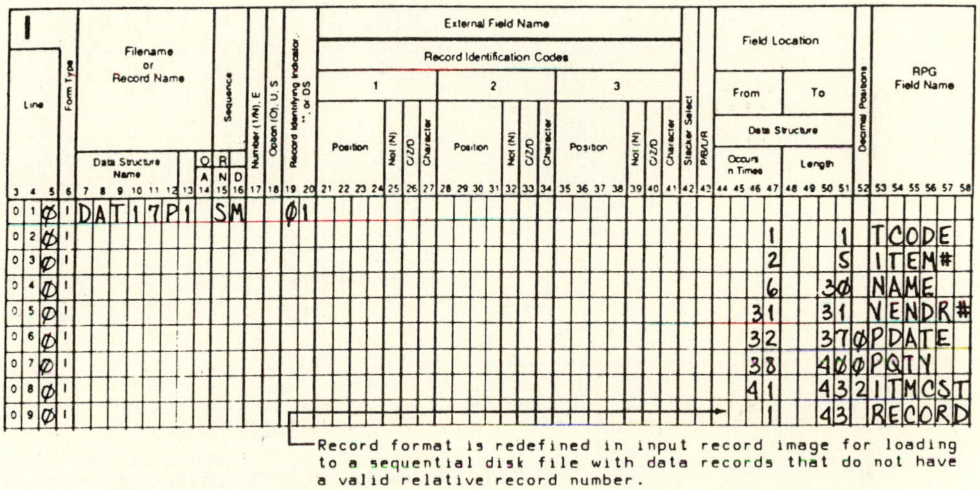

Figure 17-7 Input specifications coding for a program that creates and loads a direct file.

Calculation Specifications Coding

The direct file loading process is controlled by CHAINing the relative record numbers stored in the input records to the prenumbered slots previously built by the system during the creation process. Look at Figure 17-8. ITEM# (CHAINing

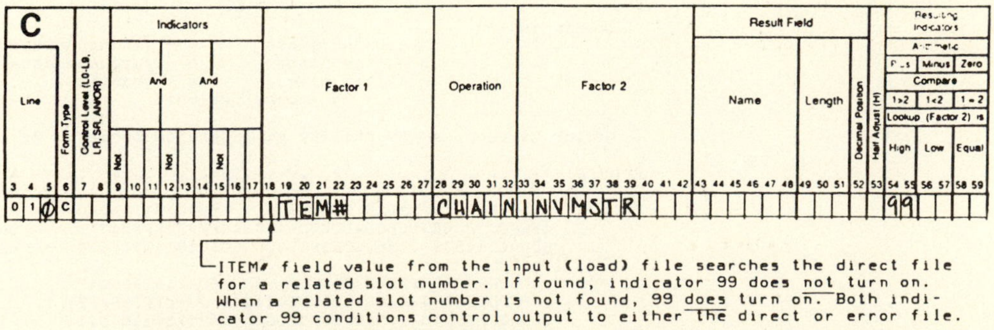

Figure 17-8 Calculation specifications coding for a program that creates and loads a direct file.

field) from the input record is CHAINed to the direct file INVMSTR. If a related slot number is found, indicator 99 is *not* turned on. When a slot is not found, the indicator *is* turned on. No other calculations are required for this program.

Output Specifications Coding

As shown in Figure 17-9, the loading of the direct file slots is controlled by the Record Identifying Indicator 01 and the Resulting Indicator N99 (not turned on in the CHAIN instruction when a slot is found). Loading of the error file is conditioned by the 99 indicator (turned on in the CHAIN instruction when a slot is not found).

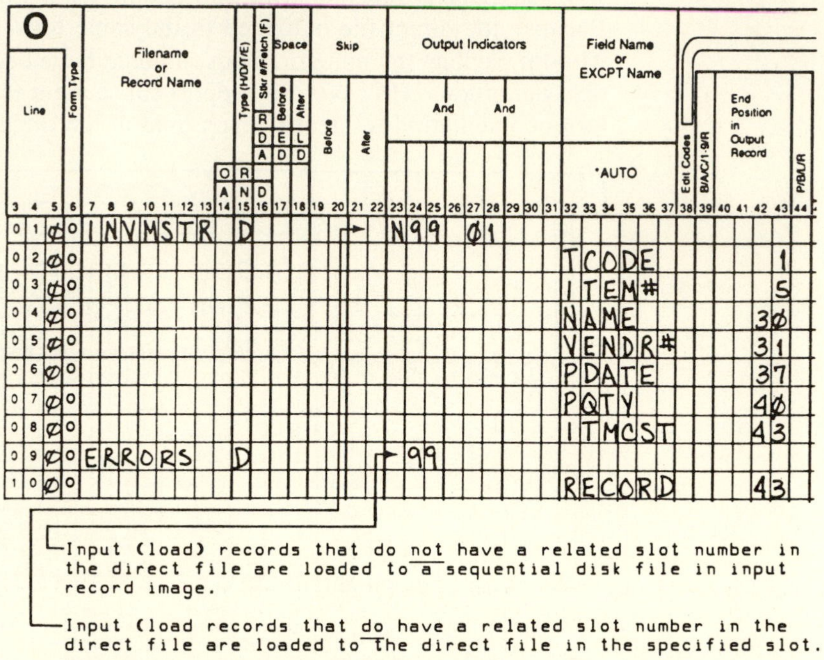

Figure 17-9 Output specifications coding for a program that creates and loads a direct file.

Results of Loading the Direct File

The over-and-under hexadecimal (EBCDIC code set) utility listing in Figure 17-10 shows that slot positions 000003, 000005, and 000006 were not loaded with data and are blank. This feature, which is unique to direct files, was discussed in

```
Field legend:
                        a - blank space        d - vendor number
                        b - item number        e - purchase date
                        c - item name          f - quantity
                              g - cost per unit

Ruler is supplied by utility to reference location of each character

RCDNBR  *... ... 1 ... ... 2 ... ... 3 ... ... 4 ..     Alphanumeric and
                                                        unpacked numeric
000001   0001BOUNTY PAPER TOWELS      6040191144040<---values interpreted
        4FFFFCDEDEE4DCDCD4EDECDE444444FFFFFFFFFFFFF<---Zone area
        0000126453807175903665320000006040191144040<---Digit area

000002   0002MARCAL PAPER TOWELS      6041191360041
        4FFFFDCDCDE4DCDCD4EDECDE444444FFFFFFFFFFFFF
        0000241931307175903665320000006041191360041
```

Figure 17-10 Hexidecimal listing (EBCDIC code set) of the direct file after it is loaded with data.

```
000003                                                    <--+
                                                              |
000004   0004VANITY FAIR PAPER TOWELS 9040291060039          +--Unused slot position
        4FFFFECDCEE4CCCD4DCDCD4EDECDE4FFFFFFFFFFFF           |   are allocated but
        0000451593806199071759036653209040291060039          |   contain no data
                                                              |
000005                                                    <--+
                                                              |
000006                                                    <--+

000007   0007KLEENEX PAPER TOWELS     1043091048045
        4FFFFDDCCDCE4DCDCD4EDECDE44444FFFFFFFFFFFF
        0000723555570717590366532000001043091048045

000008  |0008|SCOTT'S PAPER TOWELS      |4|042091|240|050|
       4|FFFF|ECDEE7E4DCDCD4EDECDE44444|4|FFFFFF|FFF|FFF|
       0|0008|23633D20717590366532000000|4|042091|240|050|
  ^
  |    a  b              c              d   e     f   g
  |
  +--- Relative record numbers are assigned by the system
```

(*Continued*)

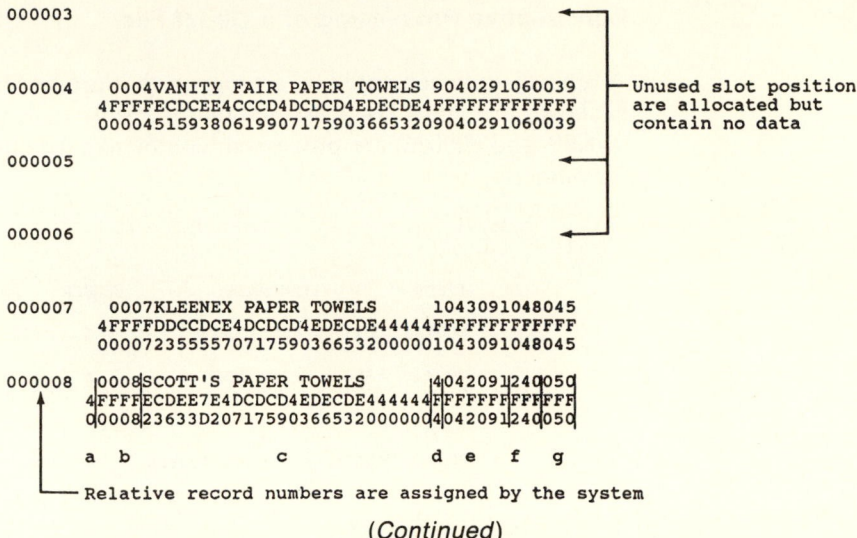

relation to Figure 17-1 with regard to prenumbered slots. Data may be subsequently loaded to the empty slot positions by update (not add) processing.

From the Figure 17-10 listing it should be obvious that the loading process for direct files differs from sequential and indexed-sequential file organization types in which the records are loaded next to each other in the prime data area. The utility listing of the sequentially organized error file in Figure 17-11 identifies the results of processing.

```
        Ruler is supplied by utility to reference location of each character

RCDNBR  *... ... 1 ... ... 2 ... ... 3 ... ... 4 ..     Alphanumeric and
                                                        unpacked numeric
     1   0010HUDSON PAPER TOWELS      7042591072054     values interpreted
        4FFFFCECEDD4DCDCD4EDECDE444444FFFFFFFFFFFF      Zone area
        000108442650717590366532000000704259107205 4    Digit area

     2   0000A & P PAPER TOWELS       6041191360041
        4FFFFC454D4DCDCD4EDECDE4444444FFFFFFFFFFFF
        0000010007071759036653200000006041191360041

Notes:

        Because control statements in the procedure to execute the direct
        file load program specified 8 records for the file, only 8 slots
        were created.  Hence, an input record with the relative record
        number 0010 could not be loaded.

        Because the first relative record number in a direct file is
        000001, the input record with a value of 0000 did not find a
        related slot and was consequently loaded to the error file.

        In a sequential file, records are loaded in a consecutive order.
        No unused record slots are stored between the records or at the
        end of the file.
```

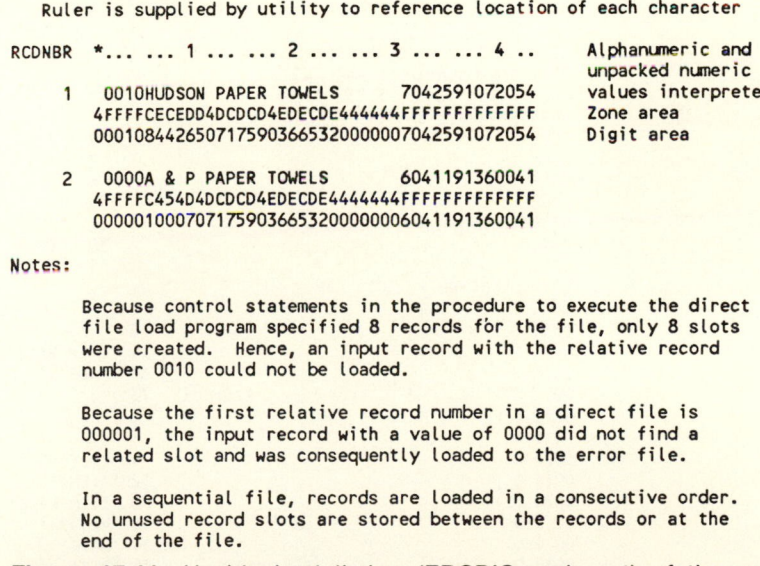

Figure 17-11 Hexidecimal listing (EBCDIC code set) of the sequentially organized error file.

Because the direct file does not have a beginning relative record number 000000, the input (load) record with an ITEM# value 0000 did not have a relative slot and was loaded to the error file. In addition, the OCL (Operation Control Language) statement for the definition of the direct file was specified with a RECORD parameter of eight records. Consequently, the input record with a relative record number of 0010 did not have a slot and was also written to the error file.

Consecutive Processing of a Direct File

A report listing generated by a program that processes a direct file consecutively is shown in Figure 17-12. Notice that the slots that do not contain data (000003, 000005, and 000006) are processed with blanks for alphanumeric fields and zeros for numeric.

```
4/30/91                    ITEM MASTER FILE LISTING                PAGE    1

CODE  ITEM#           ITEM NAME           VENDOR    DATE    QTY   COST/UNIT

      0001  BOUNTY PAPER TOWELS              6    4/01/91   144      .40

      0002   MARCAL PAPER TOWELS             6    4/11/91   360      .41

                                                  0/00/00     0      .00

      0004  VANITY FAIR PAPER TOWELS         9    4/02/91    60      .39

                                                  0/00/00     0      .00

                                                  0/00/00     0      .00

      0007  KLEENEX PAPER TOWLES             1    4/30/91    48      .45

      0008  SCOTT'S PAPER TOWELS             4    4/20/91   240      .50
```

Figure 17-12 Report listing of a direct file without blank record control.

To suppress the output of records (slots) that do not include data, the RPG program must include blank record control. Examine the source listing in Figure 17-13, and notice that Field Indicator 20 is assigned in the blank (zero) field on

```
... ... 1 ... ... 2 ... ... 3 ... ... 4 ... ... 5 ... ... 6 ...
 * THIS PROGRAM PROCESSES A DIRECT FILE CONSECUTIVELY......
FINVMSTR IP  F  43  43                 DISK<---------------
FLISTING O   F 132 132      OF         PRINTER
IINVMSTR SM  01
I                                       1   1 DCODE                CH17P2
I                                       2   5 ITEM#          20    CH17P2
I                                       6  30 NAME                 CH17P2
I                                      31  31 VENDR#               CH17P2
I                                      32  370DATE                 CH17P2
I                                      38  400QTY                  CH17P2
I                                      41  432ITMCST               CH17P2
OLISTING H  301     1P                                             CH17P2
O        OR         OF                                             CH17P2
O                          UDATE Y    8                            CH17P2
O                                    49 'ITEM MASTER FILE LISTING' CH17P2
O                                    68 'PAGE'                     CH17P2
O                          PAGE  Z   73                            CH17P2
O        H  2       1P                                             CH17P2
O        OR         OF                                             CH17P2
O                                     4 'CODE'                     CH17P2
O                                    12 'ITEM#'                    CH17P2
O                                    30 'ITEM NAME'                CH17P2
O                                    46 'VENDOR'                   CH17P2
O                                    54 'DATE'                     CH17P2
O                                    61 'QTY'                      CH17P2
O                                    73 'COST/UNIT'                CH17P2
 *                                                                 CH17P2
 * PRINT RECORD IF ITEM# VALUE IS NOT BLANK......................... CH17P2
 *                                                                 CH17P2
O        D  2     01N20                                            CH17P2
O                          DCODE      3                            CH17P2
O                          ITEM#     11                            CH17P2
O                          NAME      39                            CH17P2
O                          VENDR#    44                            CH17P2
O                          DATE  Y   55                            CH17P2
O                          QTY   1   61                            CH17P2
O                          ITMCST1   70                            CH17P2
```

File Description syntax for a direct file is identical to sequential organization

Figure 17-13 Source listing of a program that processes a direct file consecutively.

input. When ITEM# tests as blank (defined as alphanumeric), 20 will turn on. Reference to the output coding (line 30) indicates that detail output will be executed only when 20 is not on (N20 condition). This simple control prevents output of direct file records (slots) that have never been loaded or updated with data. The direct file INVMSTR is defined with syntax identical to that of a sequential file. Unlike indexed files, entries unique to direct files are not required in the File Description coding. The system will identify the file as direct from the job control language or attributes included in the file directory. The report generated by the RPG program that includes blank record control is illustrated in Figure 17-14.

```
4/30/91                    ITEM MASTER FILE LISTING               PAGE    1

CODE  ITEM#          ITEM NAME           VENDOR    DATE    QTY   COST/UNIT

      0001   BOUNTY PAPER TOWELS             6   4/01/91   144      .40

      0002   MARCAL PAPER TOWELS             6   4/11/91   360      .41

      0004   VANITY FAIR PAPER TOWELS        9   4/02/91    60      .39

      0007   KLEENEX PAPER TOWELS            1   4/30/91    48      .45

      0008   SCOTT'S PAPER TOWELS            4   4/20/91   124      .50
```

Figure 17-14 Report listing of a direct file with blank record control.

APPLICATION PROGRAM—DIRECT FILE INQUIRY

The specifications for an RPG program that random processes a direct file for inquiry are explained in Figure 17-15.

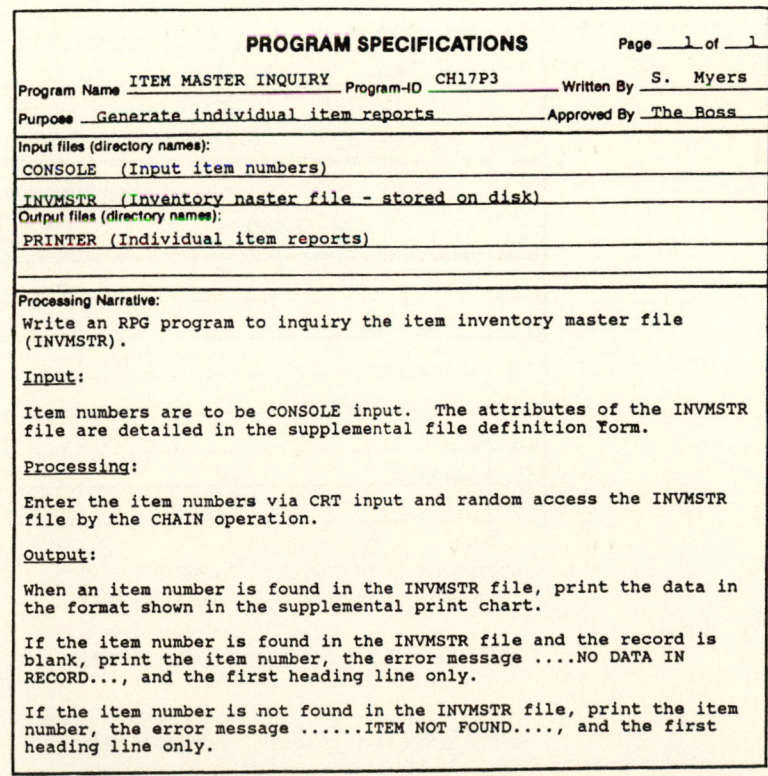

PROGRAM SPECIFICATIONS Page 1 of 1

Program Name ITEM MASTER INQUIRY Program-ID CH17P3 Written By S. Myers

Purpose Generate individual item reports Approved By The Boss

Input files (directory names):

CONSOLE (Input item numbers)

INVMSTR (Inventory naster file - stored on disk)

Output files (directory names):

PRINTER (Individual item reports)

Processing Narrative:

Write an RPG program to inquiry the item inventory master file (INVMSTR).

Input:

Item numbers are to be CONSOLE input. The attributes of the INVMSTR file are detailed in the supplemental file definition form.

Processing:

Enter the item numbers via CRT input and random access the INVMSTR file by the CHAIN operation.

Output:

When an item number is found in the INVMSTR file, print the data in the format shown in the supplemental print chart.

If the item number is found in the INVMSTR file and the record is blank, print the item number, the error message ....NO DATA IN RECORD..., and the first heading line only.

If the item number is not found in the INVMSTR file, print the item number, the error message ......ITEM NOT FOUND...., and the first heading line only.

Figure 17-15 Specifications for a program that random processes a direct file for inquiry.

The system flowchart in Figure 17-16 shows that a CRT supported file and the INVMSTR file are input to the program with a report as output.

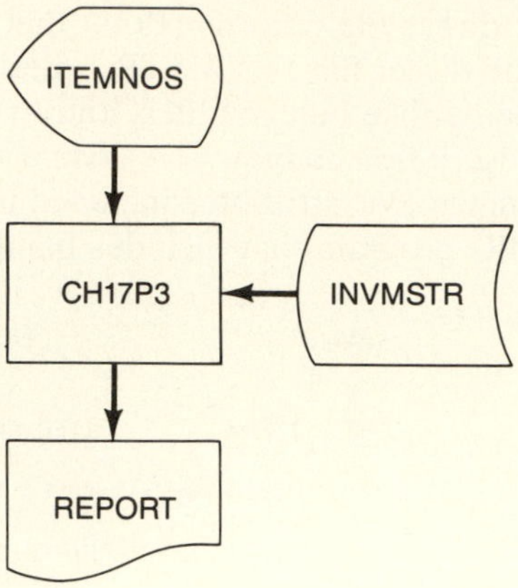

Figure 17-16 System flowchart for a program that random processes a direct file for inquiry.

A file definition form that identifies the attributes of the INVMSTR (direct) file is shown in Figure 17-17 with a nonhexadecimal listing of the stored data. As previously explained, the record gaps represent direct file slots that do not include data.

FILE DEFINITION

SYSTEM Yours		DRAWN BY S. Myers
FILE NAME INVMSTR		DATE 4/1/91 REV. NO. 0
CREATED BY S. Myers		FILE TYPE Disk
RECORD NAME None		KEY LENGTH 4 Rel Record #
RECORDING MODE Fixed	ORGANIZATION Direct	SEQUENCE Ascending - RR#
RECORD SIZE 43 bytes	BLOCKING FACTOR 1	BLOCKSIZE 43 bytes

FIELD DATA

FIELD NO.	FIELD NAME - DESCRIPTION	SIZE	CLASS C/P/Z/B	POSITION FROM	POSITION THRU	FORMAT/CONSTANT
1	Delete Code	1	C	1	1	D if deleted
2	Item Number	4	C	2	5	Relative Record No
3	Item Name	25	C	6	30	
4	Vendor Number	1	C	31	31	
5	Date	6	Z	32	37	
6	Quantity	3	Z	38	40	
7	Item Cost	3	Z	41	43	2 decimal positions

```
0001BOUNTY PAPER TOWELS      6040191144040
0002MARCAL PAPER TOWELS      6041191360041

0004VANITY FAIR PAPER TOWELS 9040291060039

0007KLEENEX PAPER TOWELS     1043091048045
0008SCOTT'S PAPER TOWELS     4042091240050
```

Blank lines represent slots (000003, 000005, and 000006) that do not contain data

Figure 17-17 File definition form describing the attributes of the INVMSTR (direct) file and listing of the stored data.

A printer spacing chart that details the report design and the three-item report generated by the direct file inquiry program are presented in Figure 17-18.

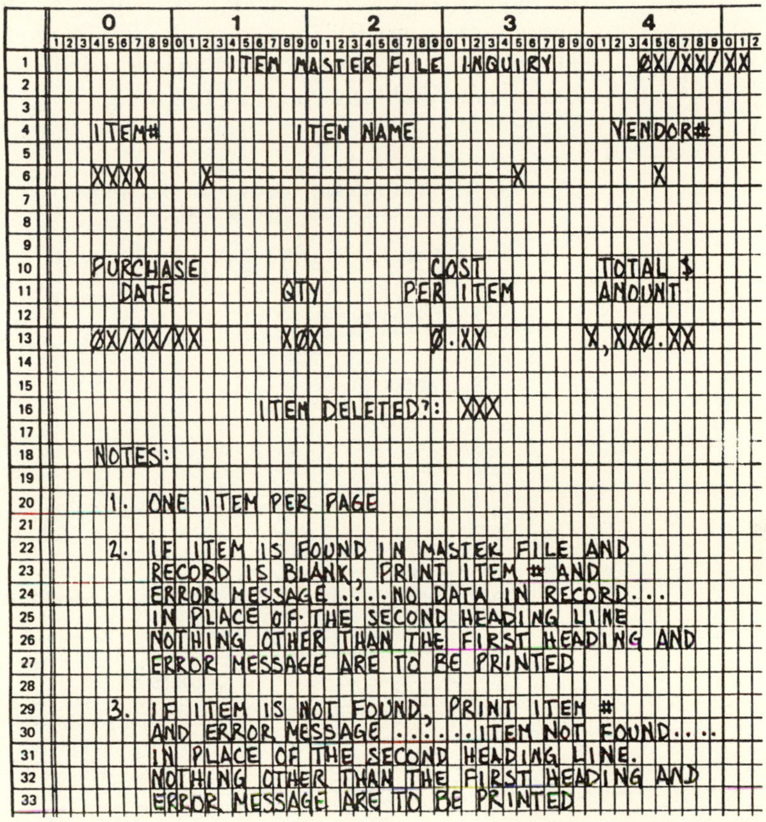


```
          ITEM MASTER FILE INQUIRY        4/30/91

ITEM#        ITEM NAME               VENDOR#

0002     MARCAL PAPER TOWELS            6

PURCHASE                COST       TOTAL $
  DATE                PER ITEM     AMOUNT

 4/11/91     360         .41        147.60

          ITEM DELETED?: NO
```

```
          ITEM MASTER FILE INQUIRY        4/30/91

0003   ....NO DATA IN RECORD...
```

```
          ITEM MASTER FILE INQUIRY        4/30/91

0000   ......ITEM NOT FOUND....
```

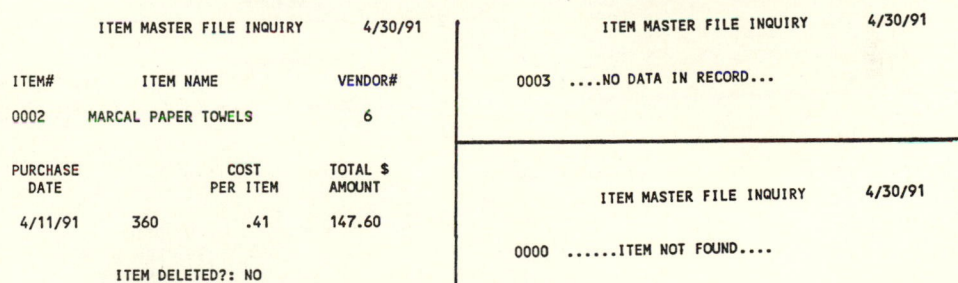

Figure 17-18 Report design and three report formats generated by the direct (INVMSTR) file inquiry program.

The three formats may be summarized as follows:

1. The report at the left is printed when a record is found and the direct file record includes data.
2. The report at the top right is generated when a record is found, but the direct file record has no data.
3. The report at the bottom right is printed when a record is not found in the direct file.

The three reports are printed on three separate pages. The grouping in Figure 17-18 is only for presentation.

Source Program Coding

A source listing of the program that random processes a direct file (INVMSTR) for inquiry is detailed in Figure 17-19. Other than the indicator assignments, which are unique to any RPG program, the syntax required to random process a direct file is identical to that needed for an indexed file. The coding forms for this program are separately discussed in the following paragraphs.

```
... ... 1 ... ... 2 ... ... 3 ... ... 4 ... ... 5 ... ... 6 ... ... 7 ...
 * THIS PROGRAM RANDOM PROCESSES A DIRECT FILE FOR INQUIRY           CH17P3
 * USING THE CHAINING METHOD...........................              CH17P3
H                                                                    CH17P3
FITEMNOS IP AF   5   5           CONSOLE                             CH17P3
FINVMSTR IC  F  43  43R          DISK                                CH17P3
FITEMINFOO   F 132 132           PRINTER                             CH17P3
IITEMNOS SM  01   1 CI                                               CH17P3
I                                        1   1 IDCODE                CH17P3
I                                        2   50RECRD#                CH17P3
IINVMSTR SM  02                                                      CH17P3
I                                        1   1 DCODE                 CH17P3
I                                        2   5 ITEM#          20     CH17P3
I                                        6  30 NAME                  CH17P3
I                                       31  31 VENDR#                CH17P3
I                                       32  370DATE                  CH17P3
I                                       38  400QTY                   CH17P3
I                                       41  432ITMCST                CH17P3
C           RECRD#    CHAININVMSTR              99                   CH17P3
C  N99      DCODE     COMP 'D'                      10               CH17P3
C  N99      QTY       MULT ITMCST    AMOUNT  62                      CH17P3
OITEMINFOD  301   N99 02                                             CH17P3
O        OR           99                                             CH17P3
O                                   37 'ITEM MASTER FILE INQUIRY'    CH17P3
O                          UDATE Y  51                               CH17P3
O        D  2     02N20                                              CH17P3
O                                    8 'ITEM#'                       CH17P3
O                                   27 'ITEM NAME'                   CH17P3
O                                   48 'VENDOR#'                     CH17P3
O        D  2     02N20                                              CH17P3
O                          ITEM#     7                               CH17P3
O                          NAME     36                               CH17P3
O                          VENDR#   45                               CH17P3
O        D  2     99                                                 CH17P3
O        OR       20                                                 CH17P3
O                          RECRD#    7                               CH17P3
O                      99           33 '......ITEM NOT FOUND....'    CH17P3
O                      20N99        33 '....NO DATA IN RECORD...'    CH17P3
O        D 11     02N20                                              CH17P3
O                                   11 'PURCHASE'                    CH17P3
O                                   32 'COST'                        CH17P3
O                                   47 'TOTAL $'                     CH17P3
O        D  2     02N20                                              CH17P3
O                                    9 'DATE'                        CH17P3
O                                   34 'PER ITEM'                    CH17P3
O                                   46 'AMOUNT'                      CH17P3
O        D  3     02N20                                              CH17P3
O                          DATE  Y  11                               CH17P3
O                          QTY   1  20                               CH17P3
O                          ITMCST1  33                               CH17P3
O                          AMOUNT1  46                               CH17P3
O        D  0     02N20                                              CH17P3
O                                   29 'ITEM DELETED?:'              CH17P3
O                      10           33 'YES'                         CH17P3
O                     N10           33 'NO '                         CH17P3
```

Figure 17-19 Source listing of program that random processes a direct file (INVMSTR) for inquiry.

File Description Coding

The File Description coding for the direct file inquiry program is shown in Figure 17-20. Notice that the key field entries, common to indexed files, are not included for direct files. In fact, the coding is identical to that required for sequential files when they are random processed by the CHAIN operation.

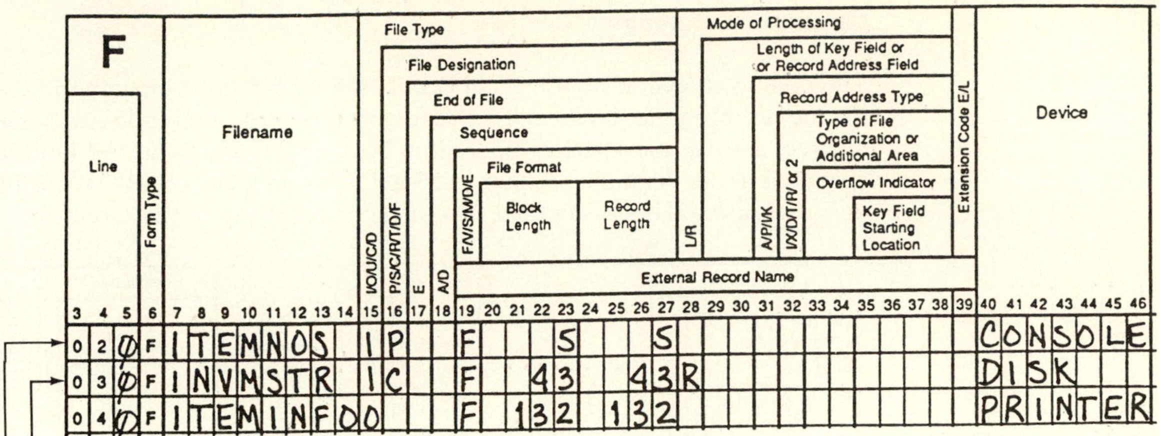

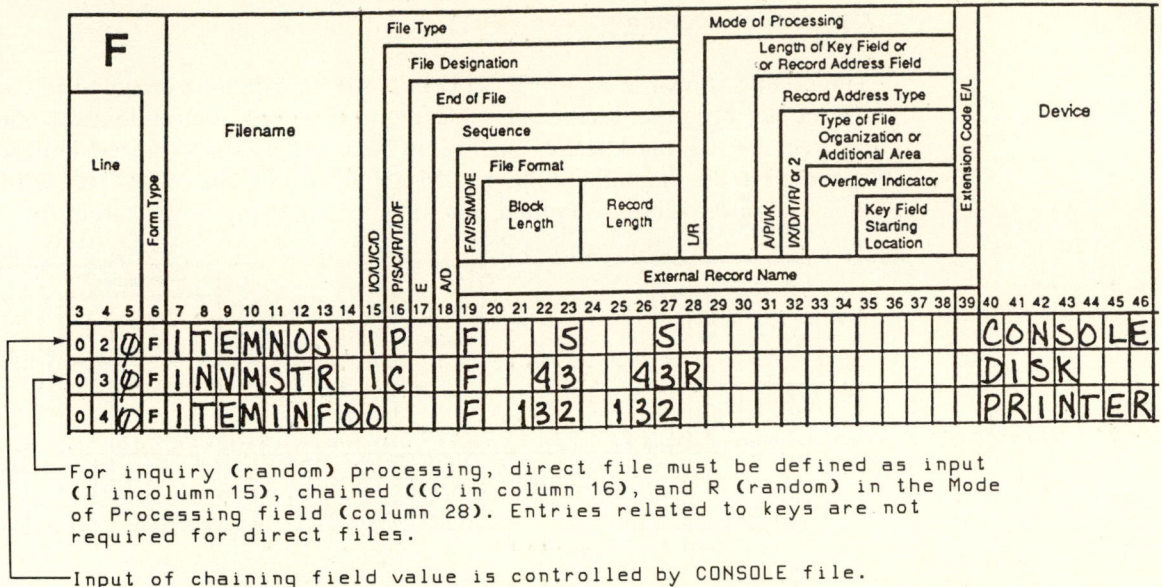

For inquiry (random) processing, direct file must be defined as input (I incolumn 15), chained ((C in column 16), and R (random) in the Mode of Processing field (column 28). Entries related to keys are not required for direct files.

Input of chaining field value is controlled by CONSOLE file.

Figure 17-20 File Description coding for a program that random processes a direct file for inquiry.

Input Coding

An examination of Figure 17-21 reveals that previously discussed RPG input coding is specified. Notice, however, that ITEM# is tested for blanks by the including indicator 20 in columns 69 to 70 with the field definition. The indicator conditions the printing of the error message . . . NO DATA IN RECORD . . . when a direct file record is found but contains no data.

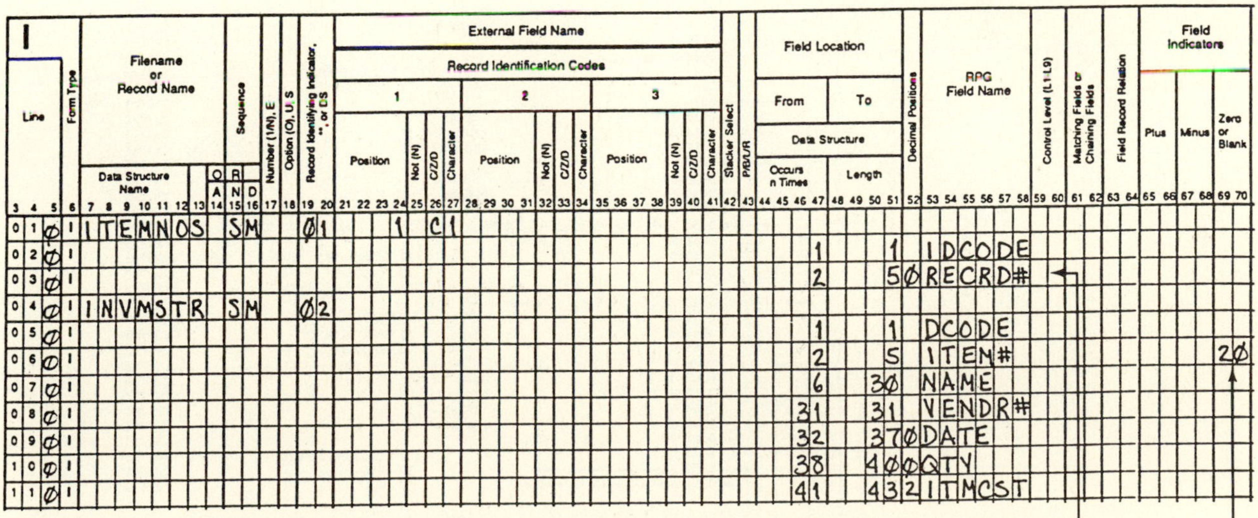

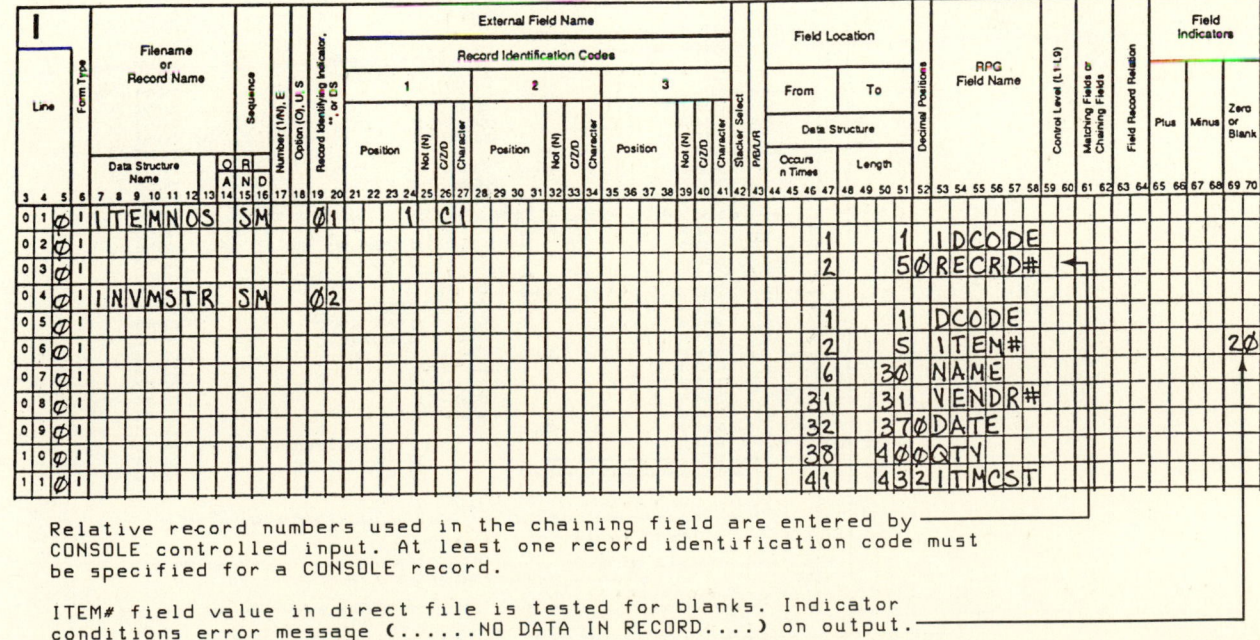

Relative record numbers used in the chaining field are entered by CONSOLE controlled input. At least one record identification code must be specified for a CONSOLE record.

ITEM# field value in direct file is tested for blanks. Indicator conditions error message (......NO DATA IN RECORD....) on output.

Figure 17-21 Input coding for a program that processes a direct file randomly for inquiry.

Calculation Coding

The coding shown in Figure 17-22 details the calculations included in the direct file inquiry program. Identical to indexed files, records are random accessed from a direct file by the CHAIN operation. Remember, the required indicator (99) specified in the High field (columns 54-55) turns on if the relative record number included in the CHAINing field (Factor 1) is not found in the direct file.

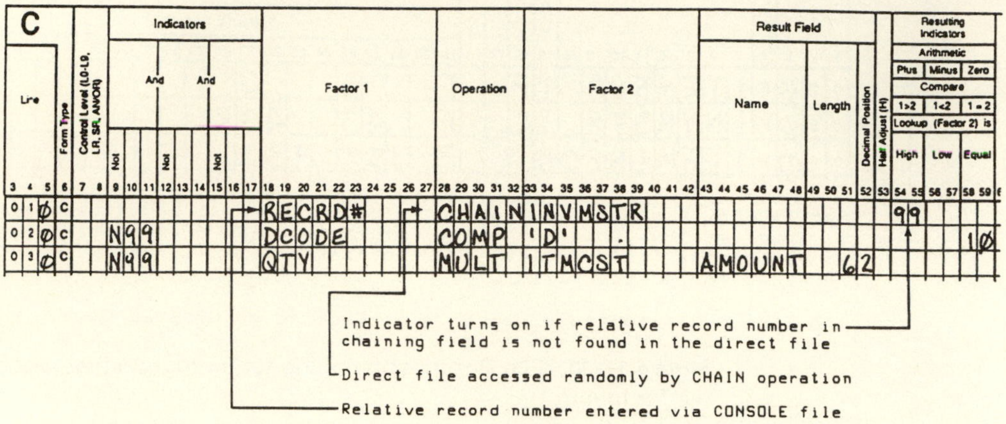

Figure 17-22 Calculation coding for a program that random processes a direct file for inquiry.

Output Coding

Figure 17-23 details the processing logic that controls the printing of the individual item reports.

```
OITEMINFOD  301  N99 02                                          CH17P3
O        OR         99                                           CH17P3
O                                 37 'ITEM MASTER FILE INQUIRY'  CH17P3
O                         UDATE Y 51                             CH17P3
O          D  2     02N20                                        CH17P3
O                                  8 'ITEM#'                     CH17P3
O                                 27 'ITEM NAME'                 CH17P3
O                                 48 'VENDOR#'                   CH17P3
O          D  2     02N20                                        CH17P3
O                         ITEM#    7                             CH17P3
O                         NAME    36                             CH17P3
O                         VENDR#  45                             CH17P3
O          D  2     99                                           CH17P3
O        OR         20                                           CH17P3
O                         RECRD#   7                             CH17P3
O                     99          33 '......ITEM NOT FOUND....'  CH17P3
O                     20N99       33 '....NO DATA IN RECORD...'  CH17P3
O          D 11     02N20                                        CH17P3
O                                 11 'PURCHASE'                  CH17P3
O                                 32 'COST'                      CH17P3
O                                 47 'TOTAL $'                   CH17P3
O          D  2     02N20                                        CH17P3
O                                  9 'DATE'                      CH17P3
O                                 34 'PER ITEM'                  CH17P3
O                                 46 'AMOUNT'                    CH17P3
O          D  3     02N20                                        CH17P3
O                         DATE  Y 11                             CH17P3
O                         QTY   1 20                             CH17P3
O                         ITMCST1 33                             CH17P3
O                         AMOUNT1 46                             CH17P3
O          D  0     02N20                                        CH17P3
O                                 29 'ITEM DELETED?:'            CH17P3
O                     10          33 'YES'                       CH17P3
O                    N10          33 'NO '                       CH17P3
```

Delete code field (DCODE) test in calculations determines whether YES or NO constant is printed.

Error messages are printed if relative record number is not found (99) or if the record is found but contains no data (20 AND N99).

Lines are printed if direct file record is found and contains data.

Line is printed for all conditions (record found and not found).

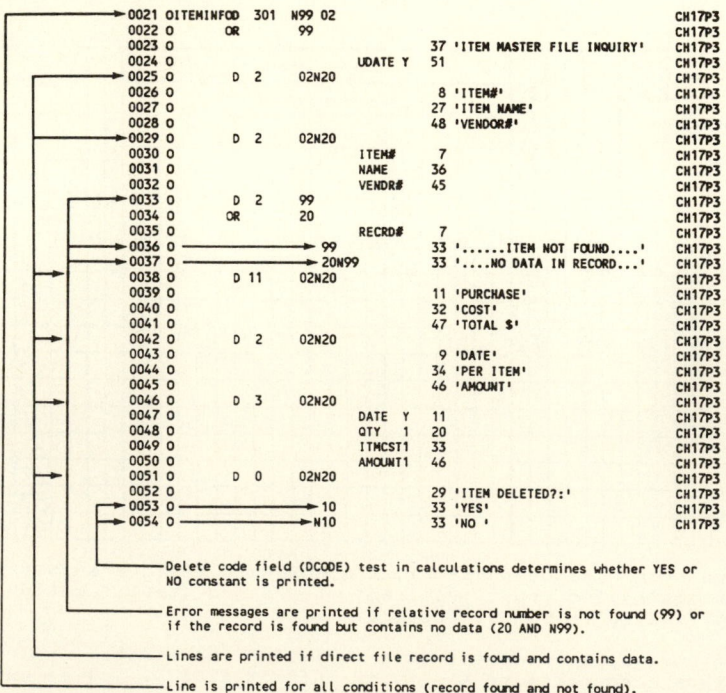

Figure 17-23 Output coding for a program that random processes a direct file for inquiry.

APPLICATION PROGRAM—DIRECT FILE UPDATE PROCESSING

Update maintenance processing has been previously discussed for sequential and indexed files. A record is accessed randomly from a disk or diskette file, stored, modified, and then written back to its original storage location. Identical to indexed files, direct files support update processing by the CHAINing method. Any file to be updated must be specified in the File Description definition as update (U in column 15). The following sections present the documentation, syntax, and logic for a program that updates a direct file.

Documentation

The specifications for an application program that updates and deletes (the tagging method) records from a direct file (INVMSTR) are detailed in Figure 17-24.

PROGRAM SPECIFICATIONS Page 1 of 2

Program Name ITEM MASTER UPDATE Program-ID CH17P4 Written By S. Myers

Purpose Update/delete records in INVMSTR file Approved By The Boss

Input files (directory names):

DAT17P4 (Sequential disk file) - transaction data

INVMSTR (Inventory master file) - Stored on disk)

Output files (directory names):

INVMSTR (Inventory master file)

ERRS174 (Sequential disk file) - Error records

Processing Narrative:

Write an RPG program to batch update the item inventory master file (INVMSTR).

Input:

Transaction records stored in a sequential disk file with the directory name DAT17P4 are used to batch update the item master inventory file which is organized as direct. Supplemental record layout forms for the transaction and master files are included with this documentation.

Processing:

Read the transaction file consecutively and for every record processed CHAIN to the INVMSTR file and perform one of the following routines:

Master record not found - Write the transaction record image to the error file ERRS174.

Master record found with no data - Update the master file record in the transaction record's image.

Master record found with data - Update the master record as follows

1. If the letter D is stored in the transaction record's code field, update the delete code field in the master record with a D. DO NOT CHANGE ANY OTHER FIELDS IN THE MASTER RECORD.

If not a delete transastion, do the following:

2. Update the master record date field with the transaction record date value.
3. Add the transaction quantity to the master quantity and update the master record with the new value.
4. Compute a new unit cost using the moving average method of inventory costing by the following procedure:

Figure 17-24 Specifications for a program that updates and deletes records in a direct file.

PROGRAM SPECIFICATIONS Page 2 of 2

Processing Narrative:

```
a. Multiply the transaction cost by the transaction quantity
   giving the transaction dollar amount.

b. Multiply the master cost by the master quantity giving
   master dollar amount.

c. Add the transaction dollar amount (step 4a) to the master
   dollar amount (step 4b) giving a total dollar amount.

d. Divide the total dollar amount (step 4c) by the total
   quantity (Step 3) giving a new average cost.  Update the
   master record with the new average cost.
```

Output:

```
Master file records are to updated or deleted (tagging method) when
the item number field in the transaction record finds the related
relative record number (slot) in the master file.

Transaction records that do not have a related master record are to
be loaded to a sequential disk file (ERRS174) in the transaction
file's record image.
```

(*Continued*)

The system flowchart presented in Figure 17-25 indicates that three files are processed by the program: one input disk file, a disk file (INVMSTR) specified as input and output (double-arrowed line), and a disk file as output.

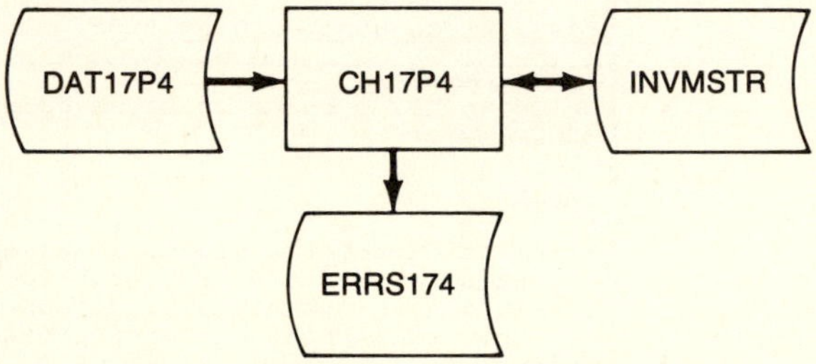

Figure 17-25 System flowchart for a program that updates and deletes records in a direct file.

The record layout form and file listing in Figure 17-26 identify the format of the transaction file, and the update and delete input data.

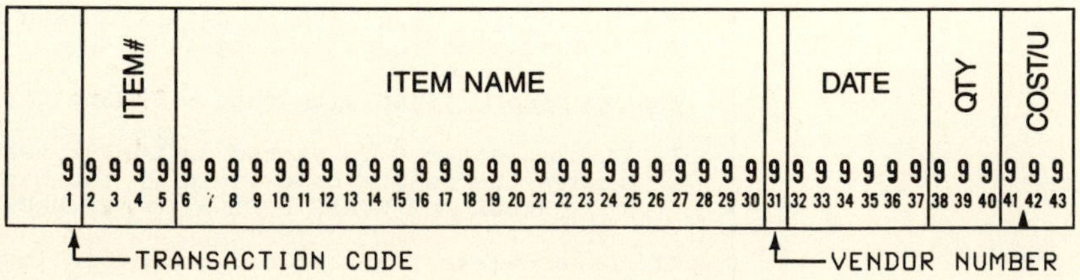

Transaction File Listing

```
 0004                     050191040042
 0009                     050591120037
D0002
 0006BRAVO PAPER TOWELS  2050391600035
```

Figure 17-26 Record layout form and listing of the transaction file records for the direct file update and delete program.

A file definition form that details the attributes of the direct file INVMSTR is included in Figure 17-27 with a listing of the records before update or delete processing.

FILE DEFINITION

SYSTEM Yours		DRAWN BY S. Myers
FILE NAME INVMSTR		DATE 4/1/91 REV. NO. 0
CREATED BY S. Myers		FILE TYPE Disk
RECORD NAME None		KEY LENGTH 4 Rel Record #
RECORDING MODE Fixed	ORGANIZATION Direct	SEQUENCE Ascending - RR#
RECORD SIZE 43 bytes	BLOCKING FACTOR 1	BLOCKSIZE 43 bytes

FIELD DATA

FIELD NO.	FIELD NAME - DESCRIPTION	SIZE	CLASS C/P/Z/B	POSITION FROM	POSITION THRU	FORMAT/CONSTANT
1	Delete Code	1	C	1	1	D if deleted
2	Item Number	4	C	2	5	Relative Record No
3	Item Name	25	C	6	30	
4	Vendor Number	1	C	31	31	
5	Date	6	Z	32	37	
6	Quantity	3	Z	38	40	
7	Item Cost	3	Z	41	43	2 decimal positions

```
0001BOUNTY PAPER TOWELS       6040191144040
0002MARCAL PAPER TOWELS       6041191360041

0004VANITY FAIR PAPER TOWELS 9040291060039      Blank lines represent slots
                                                (000003, 000005, and 000006)
                                                that do not contain data
0007KLEENEX PAPER TOWELS      1043091048045
0008SCOTT'S PAPER TOWELS      4042091240050
```

Figure 17-27 File definition form and data listing of the direct file INVMSTR for the direct file update and delete program.

Because the record format of the error file is identical to the transaction file, it is not shown here.

Source Program Coding

A source listing of the application program that updates and deletes (tagging method) records in the direct file INVMSTR is presented in Figure 17-28.

```
... ... 1 ... ... 2 ... ... 3 ... ... 4 ... ... 5 ... ... 6 ... ... 7 ...
 * THIS PROGRAM BATCH UPDATES AND DELETES (TAGGING METHOD) RECORDS   CH17P4
 * IN A DIRECT FILE (INVMSTR)......................................  CH17P4
H                                                                    CH17P4
FTRANACTSIP  F  43  43          DISK                                 CH17P4
FINVMSTR UC  F  43  43R         DISK                                 CH17P4
FNORECORDO   F  43  43          DISK                                 CH17P4
ITRANACTSSM  01                                                      CH17P4
I                                    1   1 TCODE                     CH17P4
I                                    2   5 ITEMNO                    CH17P4
I                                    6  30 TNAME                     CH17P4
```

Figure 17-28 Source listing of a program that updates and deletes (tagging method) records in a direct file.

```
I                                              31  31 TVENDR                CH17P4
I                                              32  370TDATE                 CH17P4
I                                              38  400TQTY                  CH17P4
I                                              41  432TCOST                 CH17P4
I                                               1  43 RECORD                CH17P4
IINVMSTR SM  02                                                             CH17P4
I                                               1   1 CODE                  CH17P4
I                                               2   5 ITEM#         20      CH17P4
I                                               6  30 NAME                  CH17P4
I                                              31  31 VENDR#                CH17P4
I                                              32  370DDATE                 CH17P4
I                                              38  400DQTY                  CH17P4
I                                              41  432DCOST                 CH17P4
C                         SETOF                     10                      CH17P4
C               ITEMNO    CHAININVMSTR              99                      CH17P4
C   20                                                                      CH17P4
COR 99                    GOTO END                                          CH17P4
C               TCODE     COMP 'D'                        10DELETE TRANS?   CH17P4
C   10                    GOTO END                                          CH17P4
 *                                                                          CH17P4
 * COMPUTE NEW AVERAGE COST PER UNIT - MOVING AVERAGE METHOD.........CH17P4
 *                                                                          CH17P4
C               TCOST     MULT TQTY      TAMT    62       TRANS $ AMT       CH17P4
C               DCOST     MULT DQTY      DAMT    62       MSTR $ AMT        CH17P4
C               TAMT      ADD  DAMT      NEWAMT  72       TOTAL $ TR & MRCH17P4
C               TQTY      ADD  DQTY      NEWQTY  30       TOT TQTY & DQTYCH17P4
C               NEWAMT    DIV  NEWQTY    NEWCST  32H      NEW AVG COST      CH17P4
C               END       TAG                                               CH17P4
 *                                                                          CH17P4
 * IF MASTER RECORD IS FOUND AND CONTAINS DATA, UPDATE QTY AND COST  CH17P4
 * FIELDS WITH NEW VALUES.  IF THE LETTER "D" IS STORED IN THE TRANS-CH17P4
 * ACTION CODE FIELD, WRITE "D" TO THE MASTER DELETE FIELD AND DO    CH17P4
 * NOT CHANGE ANY OTHER FIELDS IN THE MASTER FILE RECORD.........    CH17P4
 *                                                                          CH17P4
OINVMSTR D        02N20                                                     CH17P4
O                   10             1 'D'                                    CH17P4
O                  N10 TDATE      37                                        CH17P4
O                  N10 NEWQTY     40                                        CH17P4
O                  N10 NEWCST     43                                        CH17P4
 *                                                                          CH17P4
 * IF MASTER RECORD IS FOUND AND CONTAINS NO DATA, WRITE TRANSACTION CH17P4
 * RECORD TO MASTER FILE IN INPUT RECORD IMAGE...................    CH17P4
 *                                                                          CH17P4
O        D        02 20                                                     CH17P4
O                      RECORD     43                                        CH17P4
 *                                                                          CH17P4
 * IF A MASTER RECORD IS NOT FOUND, LOAD TRANSACTION RECORD TO       CH17P4
 * ERROR FILE IN INPUT RECORD IMAGE..............................    CH17P4
 *                                                                          CH17P4
ONORECORDD        99                                                        CH17P4
O                      RECORD     43                                        CH17P4
```

(Continued)

The coding for each of the specifications is separately discussed in the following paragraphs.

File Description Coding. A direct file (or any file organization type) to be updated must be defined as an update file (U in column 15) in the File Description definition. Also, when the CHAINing method is used for updating, the letter C must be specified in column 16 and the letter R in column 28. Other coding entries are common to the definition of a sequential file. Figure 17-29 explains the entries unique to the update and deletion processing of direct file.

Input Specification Coding. An examination of Figure 17-30 indicates that familiar RPG input coding is specified. Because the INVMSTR master file was defined as an Update file (both input and output), its record definition must be specified in the Input Specifications. For this program, all the fields from the INVMSTR record format are included. Only the fields that are used in the update process have to be specified, however. Hence ITEM#, NAME and VENDR# could have been omitted in this program.

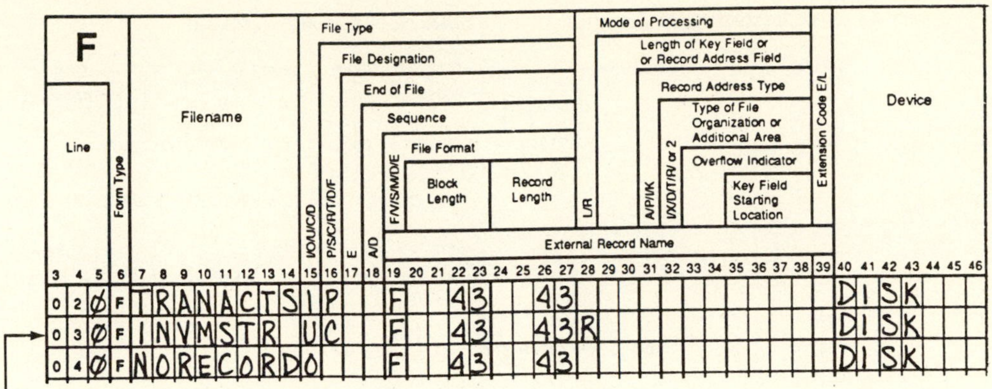

Update/delete processing of a direct file requires that it be defined as Update (U in column 15), CHAINed (C in column 16), and random processed (R in column 28). Other attributes are identical to those required for sequential files.

Figure 17-29 File description coding included in a program that updates and deletes records in a direct file.

```
... ... 1 ... ... 2 ... ... 3 ... ... 4 ... ... 5 ... ... 6 ... ... 7 ...
0007 ITRANACTSSM  01                                                CH17P4
0008 I                                        1    1 TCODE          CH17P4
0009 I                                        2    5 ITEMNO         CH17P4
0010 I                                        6   30 TNAME          CH17P4
0011 I                                       31   31 TVENDR         CH17P4
0012 I                                       32  370TDATE           CH17P4
0013 I                                       38  400TQTY            CH17P4
0014 I                                       41  432TCOST           CH17P4
0015 I                                        1   43 RECORD         CH17P4
0016 IINVMSTR SM  02                                                CH17P4
0017 I                                        1    1 CODE           CH17P4
0018 I                                        2    5 ITEM#       20 CH17P4
0019 I                                        6   30 NAME           CH17P4
0020 I                                       31   31 VENDR#         CH17P4
0021 I                                       32  370DDATE           CH17P4
0022 I                                       38  400DQTY            CH17P4
0023 I                                       41  432DCOST           CH17P4
```

After master record is found, ITEM# value is tested for a blank condition (indicator 20 in columns 69-70). If the field tests as blank (no data in direct file record), the transaction record image is written to the related slot in the direct file.

When the indicator does not turn on and the record is found in the direct file, only DDATE, DQTY, and DCOST fields are updated.

Figure 17-30 Input coding included in a program that updates and deletes (tagging method) records in a direct file.

Calculation Specifications Coding. The processing logic supported by the program indicates that when a successful CHAIN is executed and the direct file record found includes data, only the DDATE, DQTY, and DCOST are updated. New values for DQTY and DCOST must be computed, as explained previously in the program specifications (Figure 17-24). The sequence of calculation instructions followed when a successful CHAIN is executed and the direct file record includes data is detailed in Figure 17-31. Notice that the right margin includes the values in the Factor 1, Factor 2, and Result Fields after each instruction is executed.

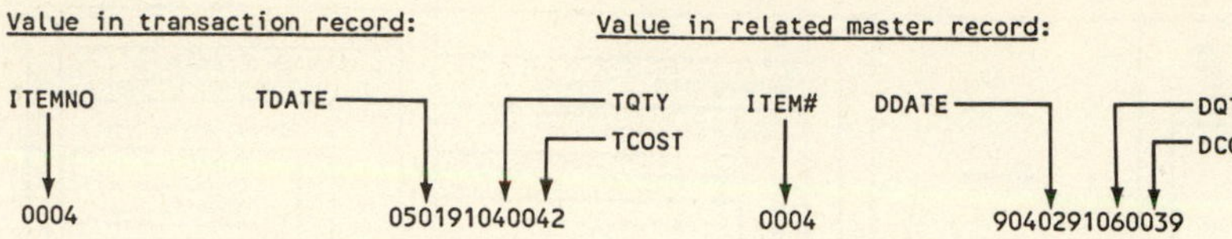


```
                                                               Value in items after execution
                                                                                    Result   INDICATORS
... ... 1 ... ... 2 ... ... 3 ... ... 4 ... ... 5 ... ...     Factor 1   Factor 2   Field       ON

C                     SETOF                  10                                                01
C           ITEMNO    CHAININVMSTR           99                                                01 02
C     20
COR   99              GOTO END                                                                 01 02
C           TCODE     COMP 'D'                   10                                            01 02
C     10              GOTO END                                                                 01 02
*
* COMPUTE NEW AVERAGE COST PER UNIT - MOVING AVERAGE METHOD.........
*
C           TCOST     MULT TQTY      TAMT    62             042        040        001680       01 02
C           DCOST     MULT DQTY      DAMT    62             039        060        002340       01 02
C           TAMT      ADD  DAMT      NEWAMT  72             001680     002340     004020       01 02
C           TQTY      ADD  DQTY      NEWQTY  30             040        060        100          01 02
C           NEWAMT    DIV  NEWQTY    NEWCST  32H            004020     100        040          01 02
C           END       TAG
```

▲ Indicates implied decimal

Figure 17-31 Calculations coding included in a program that updates and deletes (tagging method) records in a direct file.

Output Specifications Coding. The output coding for the direct file update and delete program is shown in Figure 17-32. Enough comments are included in the program to explain the output alternatives.

```
... ... 1 ... ... 2 ... ... 3 ... ... 4 ... ... 5 ... ... 6 ... ... 7 ...
 * IF MASTER RECORD IS FOUND AND CONTAINS DATA, UPDATE QTY AND COST  CH17P4
 * FIELDS WITH NEW VALUES.  IF THE LETTER "D" IS STORED IN THE TRANS-CH17P4
 * ACTION CODE FIELD, WRITE "D" TO THE MASTER DELETE FIELD AND DO    CH17P4
 * NOT CHANGE ANY OTHER FIELDS IN THE MASTER FILE RECORD.........    CH17P4
 *                                                                   CH17P4
OINVMSTR D        02N20                                              CH17P4
O                   10                 1 'D'                         CH17P4
O                  N10     TDATE      37                             CH17P4
O                  N10     NEWQTY     40                             CH17P4
O                  N10     NEWCST     43                             CH17P4
 *                                                                   CH17P4
 * IF MASTER RECORD IS FOUND AND CONTAINS NO DATA, WRITE TRANSACTION CH17P4
 * RECORD TO MASTER FILE IN INPUT RECORD IMAGE...................    CH17P4
 *                                                                   CH17P4
O        D        02 20                                              CH17P4
O                          RECORD     43                             CH17P4
 *                                                                   CH17P4
 * IF A MASTER RECORD IS NOT FOUND, LOAD TRANSACTION RECORD TO       CH17P4
 * ERROR FILE IN INPUT RECORD IMAGE..............................    CH17P4
 *                                                                   CH17P4
ONORECORDD        99                                                 CH17P4
O                          RECORD     43                             CH17P4
```

Figure 17-32 Output coding for a program that updates and deletes (tagging method) in a direct file.

Results of Update and Delete Processing

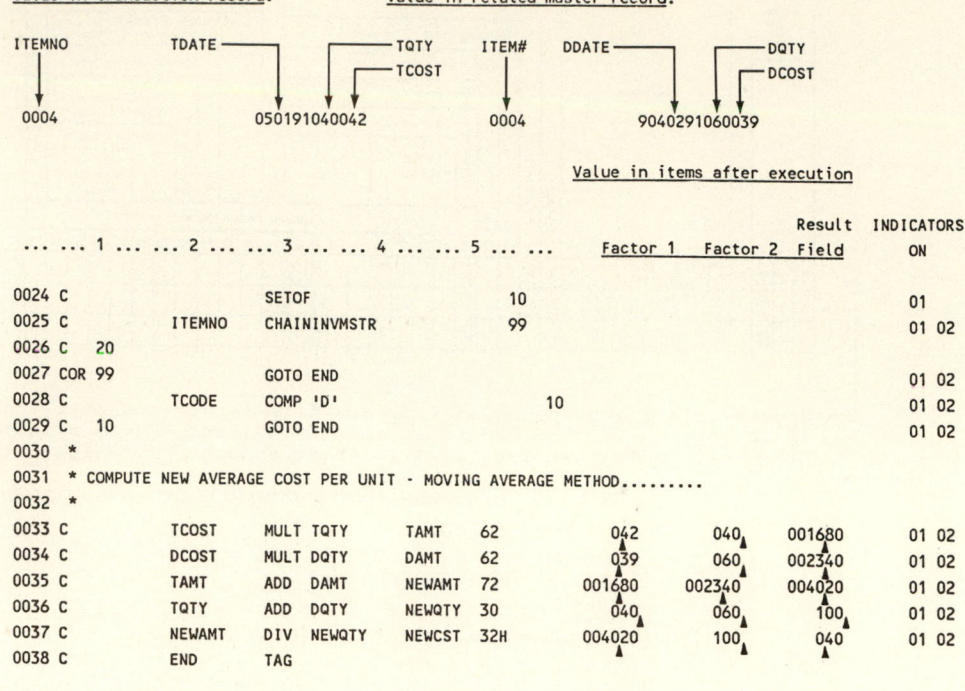

The results from execution of the direct file update and delete program are shown in the comparative listings in Figure 17-33. Records updated or tagged for deletion are identified on both reports. The reports are generated by program CH17P2 (Figure 17-13) previously introduced in this chapter.

5/31/91 ITEM MASTER FILE LISTING PAGE 1

CODE	ITEM#	ITEM NAME	VENDOR	DATE	QTY	COST/UNIT
	0001	BOUNTY PAPER TOWELS	6	4/01/91	144	.40
	0002	MARCAL PAPER TOWELS	6	4/11/91	360	.41
	0004	VANITY FAIR PAPER TOWELS	9	4/02/91	60	.39
	0007	KLEENEX PAPER TOWELS	1	4/30/91	48	.45
	0008	SCOTT'S PAPER TOWELS	4	4/20/91	124	.50

5/31/91 ITEM MASTER FILE LISTING PAGE 1

CODE	ITEM#	ITEM NAME	VENDOR	DATE	QTY	COST/UNIT
	0001	BOUNTY PAPER TOWELS	6	4/01/91	144	.40
D	0002	MARCAL PAPER TOWELS	6	4/11/91	360	.41
	0004	VANITY FAIR PAPER TOWELS	9	5/01/91	100	.40
	0006	BRAVO PAPER TOWELS	2	5/03/91	600	.35
	0007	KLEENEX PAPER TOWELS	1	4/30/91	48	.45
	0008	SCOTT'S PAPER TOWELS	4	4/20/91	124	.50

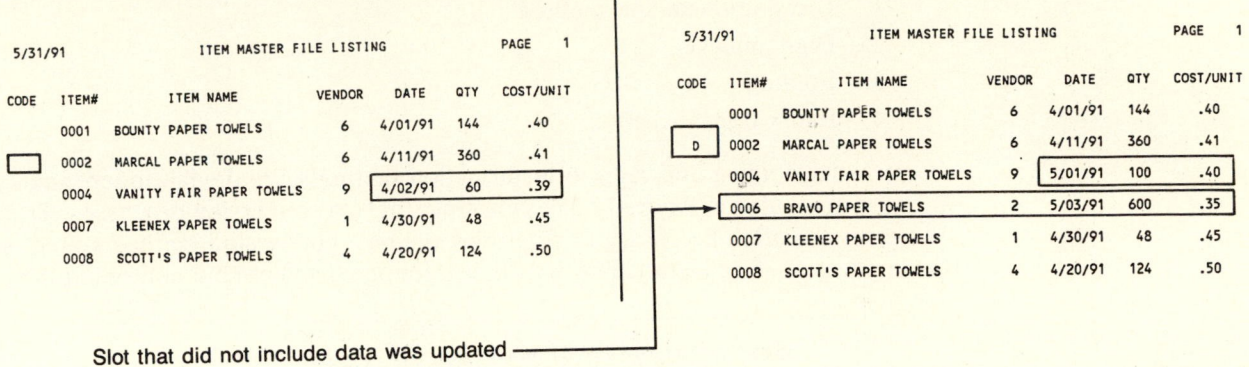

Slot that did not include data was updated

Figure 17-33 Comparative listings that show before and after results of update and delete processing.

A standard character utility listing (nonhexidecimal) of the error file shown in Figure 17-34 indicates that one record was loaded. Because the direct file was created to store only eight records (OCL control), the transaction record with an ITEMNO value of 0009 did not find a related slot in the CHAIN instruction and was written to the sequentially organized error file.

```
0009          050591120037
```

Figure 17-34 Nonhexidecimal utility listing of the error file defined in the direct file update and delete program.

The previous sections have discussed the creation, loading, inquiry, update, and deletion processing of direct files—but not addition maintenance. When a direct file is initially created, the system builds a number of slots based on the parameters (records, blocks, or tracks) specified by the job control language (OCL, JCL, or command language) included in a procedure or run unit. After the slots are assigned and before records are loaded, the system considers the file to be full of data. Consequently, the subsequent loading of new records to the unfilled slots is an update and *not* an adds procedure.

Indirectly Addressed Direct File

The direct file processing programs previously discussed have assumed that all the records were *directly addressable*. In other words, the relative record number in the load or update records related exactly to the slot positions allocated when the file was formatted by the system.

Sometimes, however, this exact relationship between the relative record number in the load or update date and the direct file may not exist. For example, customer numbers may range from 0001 to 9999 with only 4,000 of the possible numbers active. Without some conversion routine, 9,999 record slots would be allocated, with many unused positions. This would waste storage and increase processing times.

Any conversion routine presents two problems: (1) to use a method that reduces the size of the file to the allocated range of active relative record numbers, and (2) to develop the fewest number of *synonyms*. Synonyms are duplicate relative record numbers that may develop when a routine is used to change key field values to relative record numbers. Each of the problems is discussed in the following paragraphs.

Address Conversion. Some of the commonly used methods to convert keys to relative record numbers include the following:

1. Division/remainder method
2. Digit analysis
3. Folding
4. Radix transformation

Because the folding and radix transformation methods are device independent, they are presented in Figure 17-35 as examples of two conversion processes. Trial and error are often necessary to determine the best conversion method suited to the application. One method may be efficient for one data base but not for another.

```
Problem:  Convert customer numbers in the range 2500 to 9999 for
          relative file organization storage

Folding Conversion Method:  The key is split in two or more parts.

   Key field value: 7415

   Step 1:  Separate key value in half: 74 15

   Step 2:  Add the parts together: 74 + 15 = 89  relative file address


Radix transformation:  Radix 11 conversion

   Key field value:  2846

   Step 1: Multiply digits by related radix number power

               3              2              1           0
         (2 x 11  ) + (8 x 11 ) + (4 x 11 ) +  (6 x 11 )  =

          2662     +      968   +    44     +     6       =    3,680

         Drop the 3 and use 680 as relative address
```

Figure 17-35 Folding and radix transformation methods of converting key values to relative record addresses.

Synonym Control. The primary objective of any conversion process is to minimize the number of duplicate relative record addresses. However, it is usually inevitable that some key values will be converted to the same relative record address. Consequently, some provision must be made to store the synonyms when they occur.

Two commonly used methods for the storage of synonyms are *CHAINing* and *progressive overflow*. Both of these are complex and usually device-dependent. Therefore, you are advised to refer to the appropriate manufacturer's manuals for a comprehensive discussion of this control.

ADDROUT (ADDRESS OUTPUT) FILE CONCEPTS

An ADDROUT (Address Output) file is a record address that is generated by a Sort Utility program. One form of a record address file was discussed in Chapter 15 for the processing of an indexed file between limits.

Record address files created by a sort utility contain records in which the address (location) of the records in the file that was input to the sort are stored. In IBM's System/34 and 36 environments, records in the ADDROUT file are formatted as three bytes. For IBM's System /38 and AS/400 computers they are created as 4 bytes and on IBM mainframes (370, 4300, 3000 series), the ADDROUT file is built with 10 byte records.

After the ADDROUT file (record address) file is created, it is used to randomly process the related file in the new sequence without sorting. Any number of ADDROUT files may be created for a sequential, indexed, or direct file, but only one may be included in an RPG program.

As compared to *Tag-A-Long* sorts in which the output file *from* the sort is loaded with data from the input file(s) *to* the sort, ADDROUT files offer the following advantages:

1. They require less storage because only the relative record numbers of the sorted records are stored—not data from the input file.
2. They sort faster.
3. The original sequence of the input file to the sort is not destroyed, and many ADDROUT files may be created from one file. Thus, the base file may be processed in an ascending or descending order by any field(s) simply by creating additional ADDROUT files.

Processing Logic for ADDROUT Sorts

Figure 17-36 details the logic related to the creation and processing of an ADDROUT file. The sequence presented indicates the following:

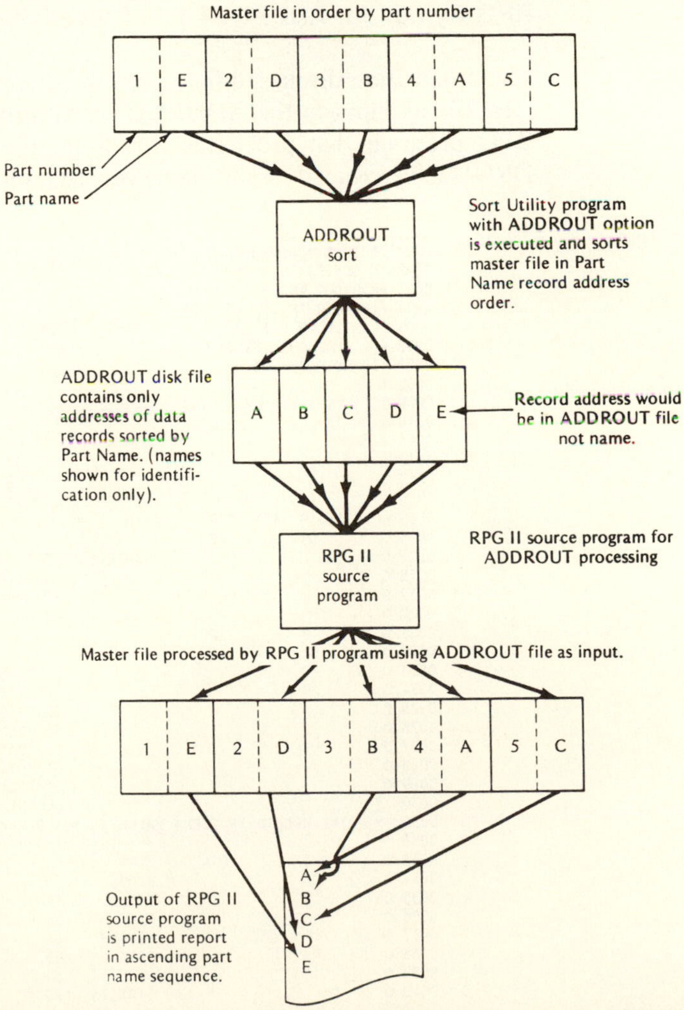

Figure 17-36 Steps required in the processing of an ADDROUT file by an RPG program.

1. An inventory file organized as direct includes records with only two fields—part number and name—and is input to the *Sort Utility* program.
2. A Sort Utility program specified with the ADDROUT option is executed and creates an ADDROUT file from the inventory file in ascending part name record address order.
3. The ADDROUT file is stored on disk with, depending on the system, 3, 4, or 10 byte records. The records include only the record address of the related records in the inventory file and no data.
4. An RPG program that includes the required syntax to process an ADDROUT file is executed. The record addresses in the ADDROUT file randomly process the inventory master file in part name order.
5. A report in part name order is generated by the RPG program.

Because the syntax for utility sorts is unique to almost every system it is not discussed here. However, IBM System/34 and 36 computers have identical sort utilities, and the one supplied (called REFORMAT) with the System/38 and AS/400 is basically the same. Other computer systems (including IBM) have a completely different syntax for their sort utilities. The RPG syntax required to process an ADDROUT file is presented in the following paragraphs.

RPG Syntax for ADDROUT File Processing

The application discussed here uses the direct file previously loaded by program CH17P1 as input to the ADDROUT sort utility program. A source listing of the RPG program that processes the direct file INVMSTR randomly by an ADDROUT file created in part name record address order is shown in Figure 17-37.

```
... ... 1 ... ... 2 ... ... 3 ... ... 4 ... ... 5 ... ... 6 ... ... 7 ...
 * THIS PROGRAM PROCESSES A DIRECT FILE RANDOMLY BY AN ADDROUT FILE  CH17P5
 * SORTED IN ASCENDING ORDER BY ITEM NAME..................          CH17P5
FADDROUT IR  F       3   3IT       EDISK                             CH17P5
FINVMSTR IP  F  43  43R  I          DISK                             CH17P5
FLISTING O   F 132 132     OF       PRINTER                          CH17P5
E    ADDROUT INVMSTR                                                 CH17P5
IINVMSTR SM  01                                                      CH17P5
I                                         1   1 DCODE                CH17P5
I                                         2   5 ITEM#          20    CH17P5
I                                         6  30 NAME                 CH17P5
I                                        31  31 VENDR#               CH17P5
I                                        32  370DATE                 CH17P5
I                                        38  400QTY                  CH17P5
I                                        41  432ITMCST               CH17P5
OLISTING H  301   1P                                                 CH17P5
O        OR       OF                                                 CH17P5
O                          UDATE Y    8                              CH17P5
O                                    49 'ITEM MASTER FILE LISTING'   CH17P5
O                                    68 'PAGE'                       CH17P5
O                          PAGE  Z   73                              CH17P5
O         H  2    1P                                                 CH17P5
O        OR       OF                                                 CH17P5
O                                     4 'CODE'                       CH17P5
O                                    12 'ITEM#'                      CH17P5
O                                    30 'ITEM NAME'                  CH17P5
O                                    46 'VENDOR'                     CH17P5
O                                    54 'DATE'                       CH17P5
O                                    61 'QTY'                        CH17P5
O                                    73 'COST/UNIT'                  CH17P5
 *                                                                   CH17P5
 * PRINT RECORD IF ITEM# VALUE IS NOT BLANK......................... CH17P5
 *                                                                   CH17P5
O         D  2    01N20                                              CH17P5
O                          DCODE      3                              CH17P5
O                          ITEM#     11                              CH17P5
O                          NAME      39                              CH17P5
O                          VENDR#    44                              CH17P5
O                          DATE  Y   55                              CH17P5
O                          QTY   1   61                              CH17P5
O                          ITMCST1   70                              CH17P5
```

Figure 17-37 Source listing of an RPG program that processes a direct file randomly by an ADDROUT file.

An examination of the source listing in Figure 17-37 indicates that new entries are included in the File Description instructions to support the processing of an ADDROUT (record address) file. An Extension Specification instruction is also specified. The coding for each of these types of forms is discussed in the following sections. Notice that input and output coding follows syntax common to RPG programs that generate reports.

File Description Coding—ADDROUT File Processing

Figure 17-38 shows the syntax required to define and process a direct (sequential or indexed) file randomly with an ADDROUT (record address) file.

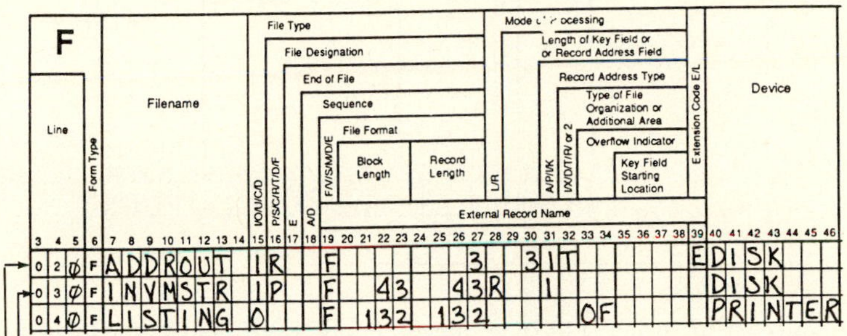

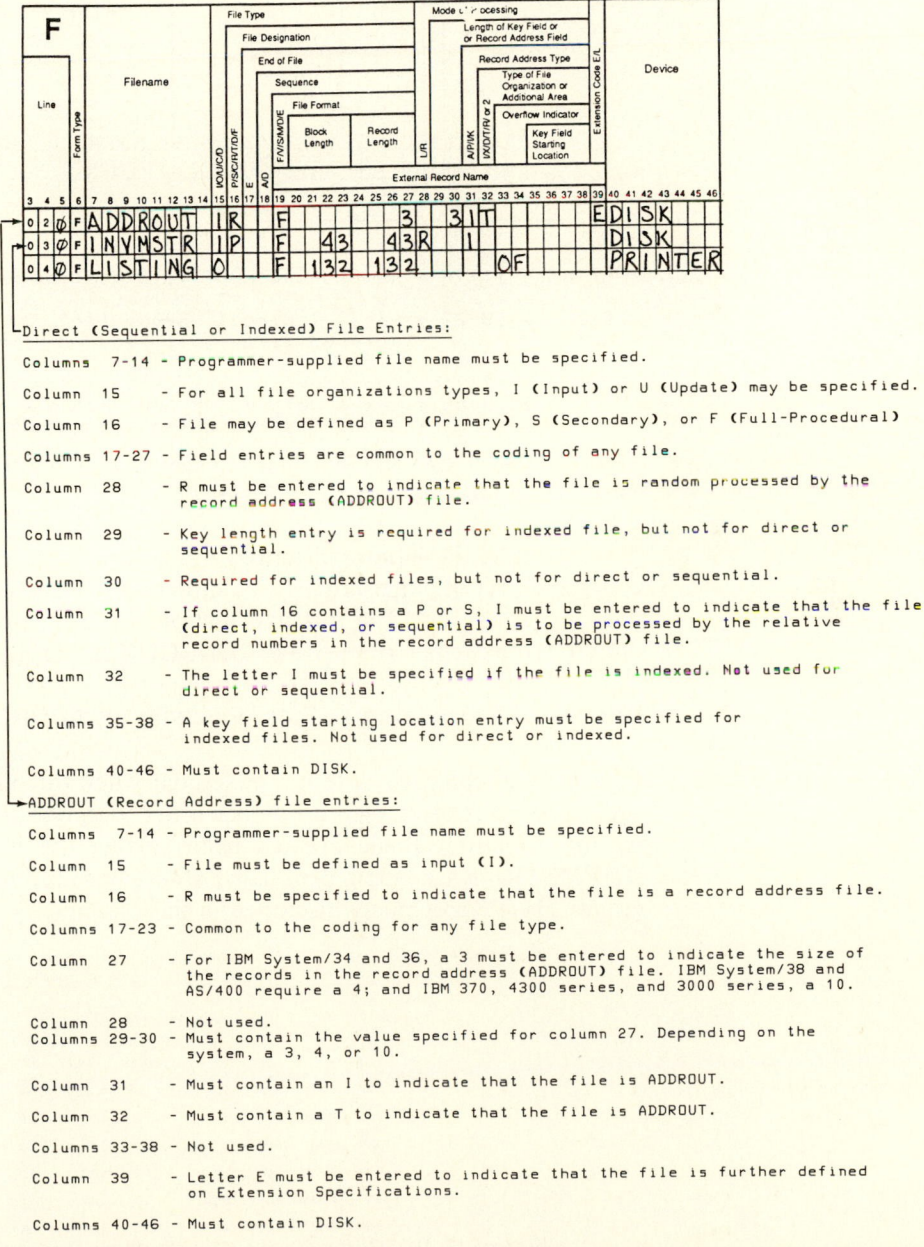

Direct (Sequential or Indexed) File Entries:

Columns 7-14 - Programmer-supplied file name must be specified.

Column 15 - For all file organizations types, I (Input) or U (Update) may be specified.

Column 16 - File may be defined as P (Primary), S (Secondary), or F (Full-Procedural)

Columns 17-27 - Field entries are common to the coding of any file.

Column 28 - R must be entered to indicate that the file is random processed by the record address (ADDROUT) file.

Column 29 - Key length entry is required for indexed file, but not for direct or sequential.

Column 30 - Required for indexed files, but not for direct or sequential.

Column 31 - If column 16 contains a P or S, I must be entered to indicate that the file (direct, indexed, or sequential) is to be processed by the relative record numbers in the record address (ADDROUT) file.

Column 32 - The letter I must be specified if the file is indexed. Not used for direct or sequential.

Columns 35-38 - A key field starting location entry must be specified for indexed files. Not used for direct or indexed.

Columns 40-46 - Must contain DISK.

ADDROUT (Record Address) file entries:

Columns 7-14 - Programmer-supplied file name must be specified.

Column 15 - File must be defined as input (I).

Column 16 - R must be specified to indicate that the file is a record address file.

Columns 17-23 - Common to the coding for any file type.

Column 27 - For IBM System/34 and 36, a 3 must be entered to indicate the size of the records in the record address (ADDROUT) file. IBM System/38 and AS/400 require a 4; and IBM 370, 4300 series, and 3000 series, a 10.

Column 28 - Not used.
Columns 29-30 - Must contain the value specified for column 27. Depending on the system, a 3, 4, or 10.

Column 31 - Must contain an I to indicate that the file is ADDROUT.

Column 32 - Must contain a T to indicate that the file is ADDROUT.

Columns 33-38 - Not used.

Column 39 - Letter E must be entered to indicate that the file is further defined on Extension Specifications.

Columns 40-46 - Must contain DISK.

Figure 17-38 File Description coding to process a direct file randomly with an ADDROUT file.

Extension Specifications Coding—ADDROUT File Processing

The letter E in column 39 in the File Description entry for the ADDROUT (record address) file indicates that the file is further defined in an Extension Specification instruction. Identical to all record address files, the attributes of the record format in an ADDROUT file are defined in File Description and Extension statements and *not* in input. Figure 17-39 explains the entries required to support the processing of a direct (sequential or indexed) file randomly by an ADDROUT file.

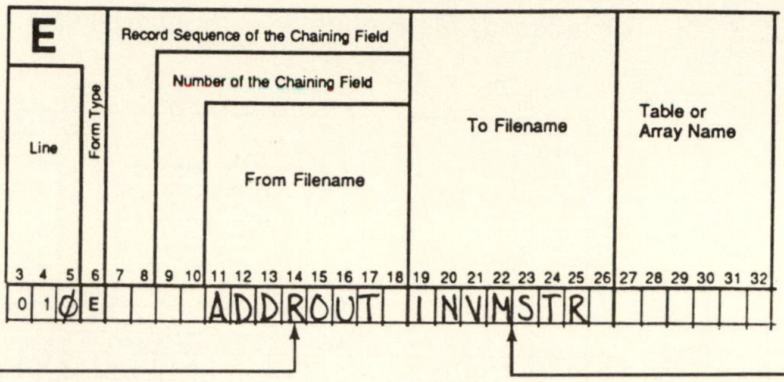

Columns 11-18 - Name of ADDROUT file must be entered left-justified.

Columns 19-26 - Name of direct, sequential, or indexed file must be entered left-justified.

Note: The Extension form further defines the ADDROUT file. Record attributes were defined in the record and key length entries in the File Description definition of the file.

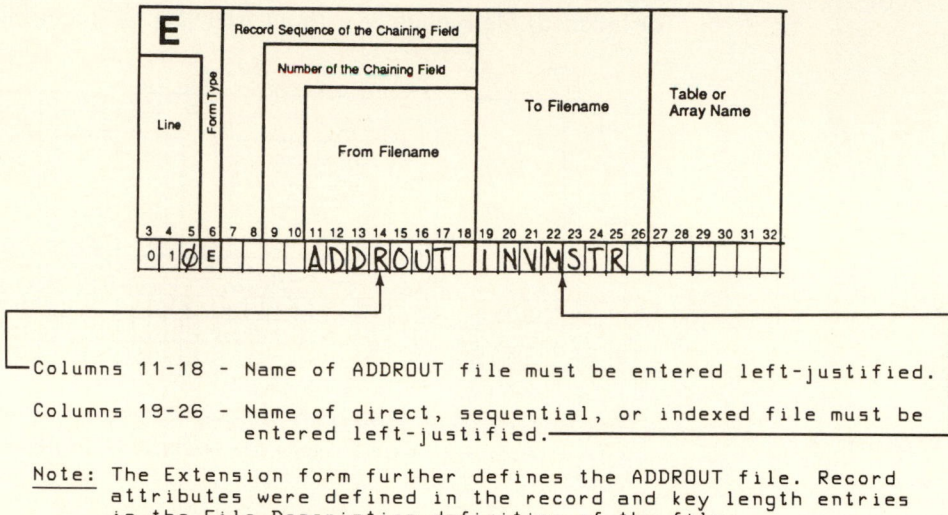

Figure 17-39 Extension Specification syntax required to process a direct (sequential or indexed) file randomly by an ADDROUT file.

Because the input and output (no calculations) coding are identical to the program (CH17P2) that processes a direct file consecutively to generate a report, they are not included in this explanation. In any case, input, calculations, and output syntax is not affected by ADDROUT file processing.

Results of Processing a Direct File with an ADDROUT File

Figure 17-40 compares a report generated when the direct file is processed consecutively in relative record number order with one that is randomly processed by the ADDROUT file created from sorting the item master inventory file (INVMSTR) in ascending item name order. Both reports were generated by program CH17P2 previously discussed in this chapter.

Report generated when direct file is consecutively processed:

5/31/91 ITEM MASTER FILE LISTING PAGE 1

CODE	ITEM#	ITEM NAME	VENDOR	DATE	QTY	COST/UNIT
	0001	BOUNTY PAPER TOWELS	6	4/01/91	144	.40
D	0002	MARCAL PAPER TOWELS	6	4/11/91	360	.41
	0004	VANITY FAIR PAPER TOWELS	9	5/01/91	100	.40
	0006	BRAVO PAPER TOWELS	2	5/03/91	600	.35
	0007	KLEENEX PAPER TOWELS	1	4/30/91	48	.45
	0008	SCOTT'S PAPER TOWELS	4	4/20/91	124	.50

Figure 17-40 Comparative reports generated by consecutively processing a direct file by relative record number and randomly processing with ADDROUT file control.

```
0006  BRAVO PAPER TOWELS       2  5/03/91  600   .35

0007  KLEENEX PAPER TOWELS     1  4/30/91   48   .45

0008  SCOTT'S PAPER TOWELS     4  4/20/91  124   .50
```

Report generated when direct file is randomly processed by an ADDROUT file created by sorting the INVMSTR in ascending order by item name:

```
5/31/91            ITEM MASTER FILE LISTING            PAGE   1

CODE  ITEM#      ITEM NAME            VENDOR   DATE    QTY  COST/UNIT

      0001  BOUNTY PAPER TOWELS          6   4/01/91   144     .40

      0006  BRAVO PAPER TOWELS           2   5/03/91   600     .35

      0007  KLEENEX PAPER TOWELS         1   4/30/91    48     .45

 D    0002  MARCAL PAPER TOWELS          6   4/11/91   360     .41

      0008  SCOTT'S PAPER TOWELS         4   4/20/91   124     .50

      0004  VANITY FAIR PAPER TOWELS     9   5/01/91   100     .40
```

(*Continued*)

The System/38 and AS/400 Environments

Direct files are not supported in the System/38 or AS/400 environments. However, nonkeyed files on those systems may be processed as if they were structured as direct. A record may be located by its relative position in the file similar to direct file organization.

ADDROUT files are created on the System/38 and AS/400 computers by a REFORMAT utility that has syntax almost identical to that of the Sort Utility supported by the System/34 and 36. However, because a *Physical File* may be processed by any field(s) through *Logical Files*, sorting has limited use in those environments.

SUMMARY

Direct files are created with slots to which relative record numbers are assigned starting with 000001. The maximum number of slots is controlled by an OCL (or JCL) statement included in a procedure. Records loaded to a direct file must have relative record numbers that match the system-supplied slot numbers. Because of this limitation, direct files are not widely used for storage of data related to accounting or business applications. It is difficult to assign customer numbers, account numbers, and so forth to a direct file's relative record numbers.

Direct files may be processed consecutively or randomly for inquiry, update, and delete maintenance. Similar to indexed files, direct files are randomly processed by the CHAINing method. However, because there is no index for direct files, they may be randomly processed faster.

Record addition, common to sequential and index files, is not supported for direct files. Record slots that were not loaded when the file was initially created are filled with data by update and *not* by adds processing.

Because identifying fields as customer number, student number, social security number, part number, and so forth do not usually relate to a relative number in a direct file, the use of direct files in the application environment is limited. If a key field in a transaction record is not directly addressable (i.e., has the same relative record number), conversion routines have been developed to convert a control field to a related relative record number.

A *Synonym* problem may develop, however, when the conversion formula creates two different key fields for the same relative record number. Procedures have also been developed to control this problem. However, the maintenance problems that may occur often discourages the use of direct files.

ADDROUT files are created from the output of a Sort Utility program. The records in an ADDROUT file contain only the record addresses of the records in the related file and no data. Depending on the computer system, the records may be 3, 4, or 10 bytes in length. Any number of ADDROUT files may be created from one sequential, indexed, or direct file. However, if records are added to the base file, all the ADDROUT sorts must be executed again.

In an RPG program, the ADDROUT file must be defined as a record address file that randomly processes the file from which it was created. Changes in the File Description syntax and the inclusion of an Extension Specification instruction are required for ADDROUT file processing.

System/38 and AS/400 computers do not support direct file organization. However, it may be simulated by processing a nonkeyed file by the relative location of the records. Because of logical files, sorting is not commonly done on those systems.

QUESTIONS

17-1. As compared to sequential and indexed files, what processing advantages do direct files offer?

17-2. Name the physical area(s) of a direct file and explain what is stored in the area(s).

17-3. What is the sequence of steps for creating a direct file?

17-4. As related to direct files, explain the term *slots*. What determines how many slots are created in a direct file?

17-5. How are records loaded to a direct file? After the file is created, how are new records added?

17-6. Identify anything wrong with the following File Description coding to create and load a direct file.

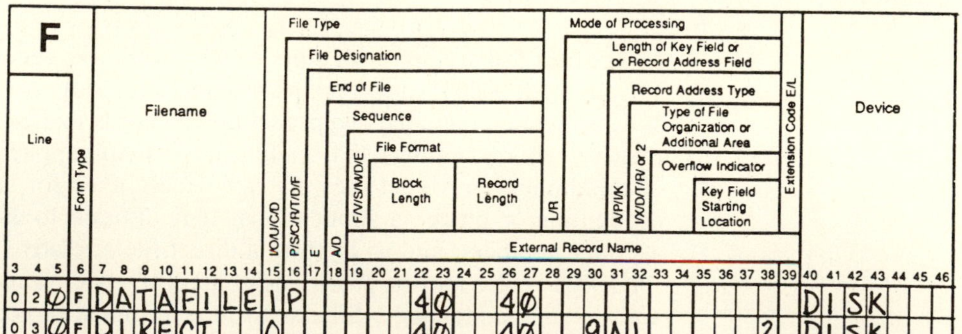

17-7. What entry is required in calculations to load a direct file? Explain the function of this instruction.

17-8. What maintenance functions may be specified for a direct file?

17-9. Explain the term *directly addressable direct file*. What problem is presented if a direct file is not directly addressable?

17-10. What methods are available to process a direct file that is indirectly addressable? What may occur in the conversion process?

17-11. As related to direct files, explain the *synonym* problem. What may be done to support this problem?

17-12. How are direct files supported on the System/38 and AS/400?

17-13. How are ADDROUT files created? What is included in the records of an ADDROUT file? What is the record size?

17-14. How many ADDROUT files may be related to one data file? Which types of file organizations may be the input to a sort program that creates an ADDROUT file?

17-15. As compared to *Tag-A-Long* sorts, what are the advantages of ADDROUT sorts?

17-16. What is the function of ADDROUT files?

Questions 17-28 are related to the following illustration and to the ADDROUT file (line 020).

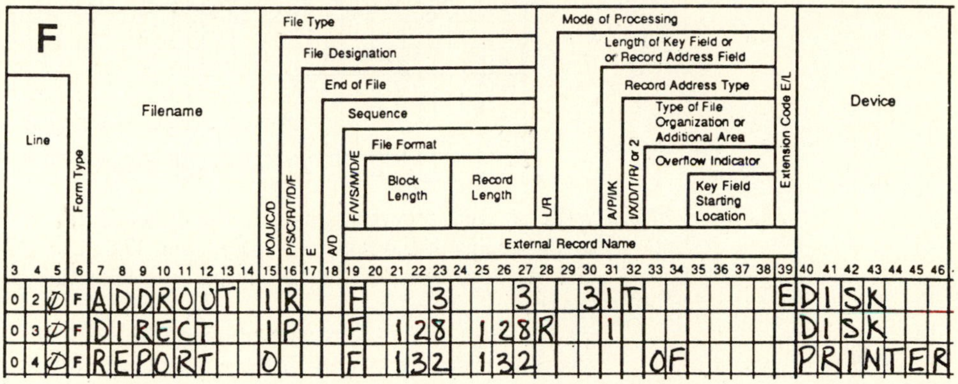

17-17. In addition to being defined as I (input), may an ADDROUT file be defined as O (output) or U (update)?

17-18. What does the letter R in column 16 indicate?

17-19. May the record size specified be larger or smaller?

17-20. What does the entry in column 30 represent?

17-21. What does the letter I in column 31 indicate?

17-22. What does the letter T in column 32 specify?

17-23. What is the function of the letter E in column 39?

17-24. Are the entries included in the ADDROUT file definition common to all types of file organizations?

Questions 25-29 are related to the direct file (line 030).

17-25. For ADDROUT file processing, does the base file have to be defined as Primary (P in column 15)?

17-26. What is the function of the letter R in column 28?

17-27. What is the function of the letter I in column 31?

17-28. For sequential or indexed files, are any of the entries shown omitted or supplemented?

EXERCISES

17-1. Write the File Description and input coding to create a direct file. A sequential disk file NEWACTS contains the data to load the direct file MASTCUST. An output file, ERRORS must be provided for a listing of input records that do not have a matching relative record number. The format of the records in the input file NEWACTS follows. Store all the fields in the same order as the input record format. Specify a blocking factor of 10.

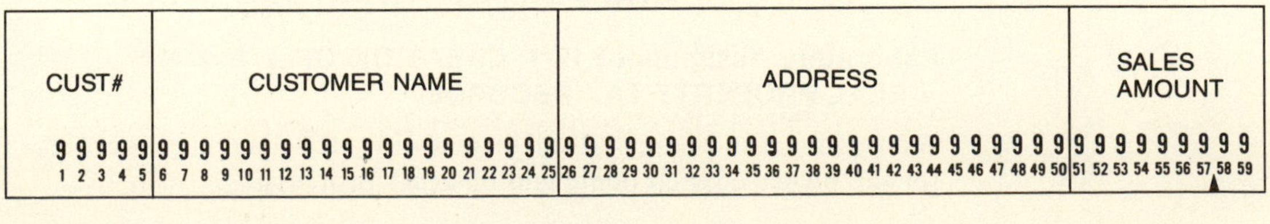

17-2. Refer to Exercise 17-1 and complete the calculations and output to load the direct file.

17-3. Refer to Exercises 17-1 and 17-2 and complete the output coding for the report format that follows:

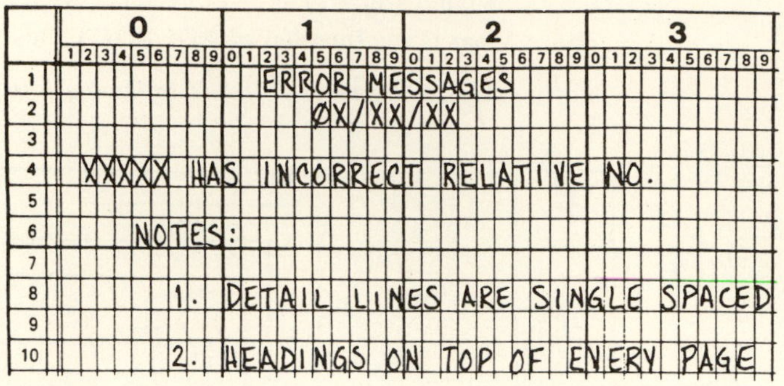

17-4. Write an RPG program to update the direct file MASTCUST created and loaded by the coding in Exercises 17-1, 17-2, and 17-3. Use UPDATES for the sequential disk file that contains the update records with the same format as NEWCUST (Exercise 17-1).

After a direct file record is found, the customer number field in the master record is tested for blanks. If there are blanks, a new customer is identified and the transaction record image is loaded to the related slot in the direct file. If there are no blanks, update the direct file with fields in the transaction record that have values. For transaction records that do not have a matching direct file record, load them to a sequential disk file in the input record image.

17-5. Assume that an ADDROUT file was created by a sort utility program in a descending balance order from the MASTCUST file created in Exercises 17-1 through 17-3. Write an RPG program to process the MASTCUST file randomly by the ADDROUT file and generate the report that follows:

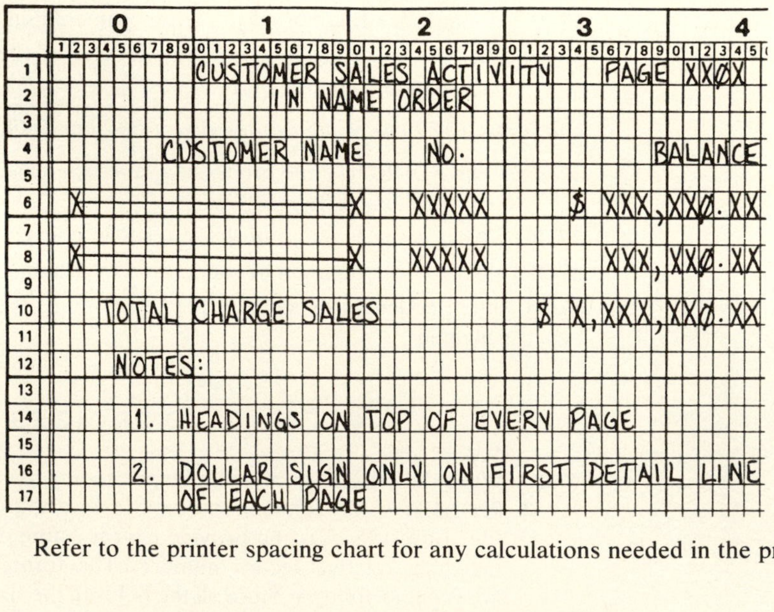

Refer to the printer spacing chart for any calculations needed in the program.

LABORATORY ASSIGNMENTS

Laboratory Assignment 17-1: CREATION OF A TOWN'S REAL PROPERTY TAX RECORDS

A direct file is to be created and loaded with a town's real property tax information for the owner of each home and business property.

Input: Stored in a sequential disk file is the input data to load the direct file in the following format:

TAX NO.	TAXPAYER'S NAME	ADDRESS	
9 9 9 9 9	9 9 9 9 9 9 9 9 9 9 9 9 9 9 9 9 9 9 9 9	9 9 9 9 9 9 9 9 9 9 9 9 9 9 9 9 9 9 9 9	9 9 9 9 9 9
1 2 3 4 5	6 7 8 9 10 11 12 13 14 15 16 17 18 19 20 21 22 23 24 25	26 27 28 29 30 31 32 33 34 35 36 37 38 39 40 41 42 43 44 45	46 47 48 49 50 51

ASSESSED AMOUNT ──────────↑

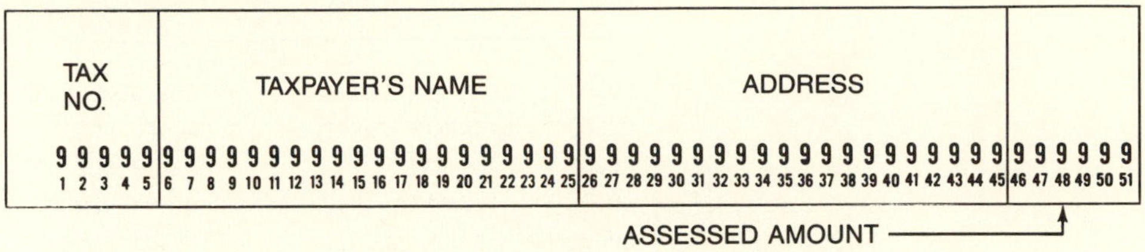

Processing: Read the sequential file consecutively and use the taxpayer's number as the CHAINing field to find a related relative record number in the direct file. If one is found, load the input record's fields to the related slot in the direct file. In addition, the following eight additional fields must be initialized to zeros and provided for in each direct file record:

Field Description	Unpacked Length
First quarter payment date	6
First quarter payment amount	5
Second quarter payment date	6
Second quarter payment amount	5
Third quarter payment date	6
Third quarter payment amount	5
Fourth quarter payment date	6
Fourth quarter payment amount	5

All the input record fields and those created in calculations are to be stored next to each other. All numeric fields except the taxpayer's number are to be packed.

Provide for two counters—one for the number of records loaded to the direct file and another for those that do not have a matching relative record number. Refer to the print chart for the size of those fields. In addition, load the error records to a sequential disk file in the input record image.

Report Design: The format of the report is shown in the following printer spacing chart. Only the input records that have a matching direct file relative record number are to be printed.

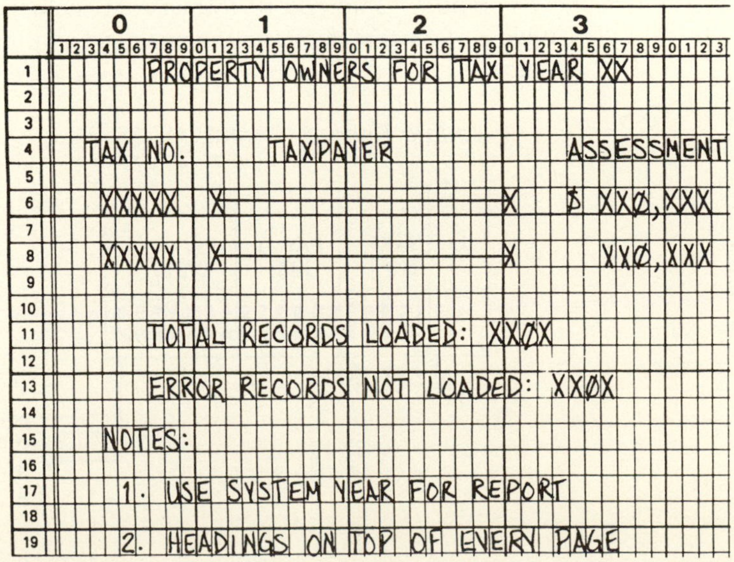

Input Data:

Tax Number 1-5	Taxpayer's Name 6-25	Address 26-45	Assessment Amount 46-51
00001	SEAN MAILLET	19 ROSEWOOD LANE	035000
00002	LAWRENCE FARRELL	1 LAUREL ROAD	027900
00005	PAUL GREGORY	7 PARK RIDGE ROAD	041012
00006	RICHARD SWANSON	40 WINDY RIDGE	067184
00008	MICHAEL DURGAS	8 TASHUA PLACE	082933
00000	SVEN ANDERSON	22 LAKEVIEW ROAD	110569

Laboratory Assignment 17-2: CONSECUTIVE PROCESSING OF A DIRECT FILE

Write an RPG program to consecutively process the direct file created in Assignment 17-1. Use the same report format as was used for that assignment. Do not print any records that include blanks in the tax number field.

Laboratory Assignment 17-3: INQUIRY OF A DIRECT FILE

Write an RPG program to randomly process the direct file created in Assignment 17-1. Access taxpayers with tax numbers 00001, 00003, and 00008. Use the same report format that was used for Assignment 17-1. Enter the tax numbers via CRT control (CONSOLE, KEYBORD, or WORKSTN device). If CRT input is not available on your system, load the tax numbers in a sequentially organized disk file and process in a batch mode.

Laboratory Assignment 17-4: UPDATE OF A DIRECT FILE

Write an RPG program to update the direct file created in Assignment 17-1 with data from a sequential disk file.

Input: Two record formats are included in the transaction file: one for update of current taypayer accounts and another for new taxpayers. The formats follow:

Update Record Format:

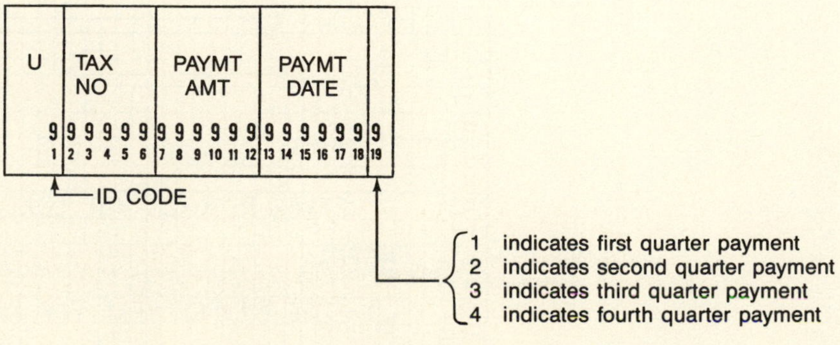

New Customer Record Format:

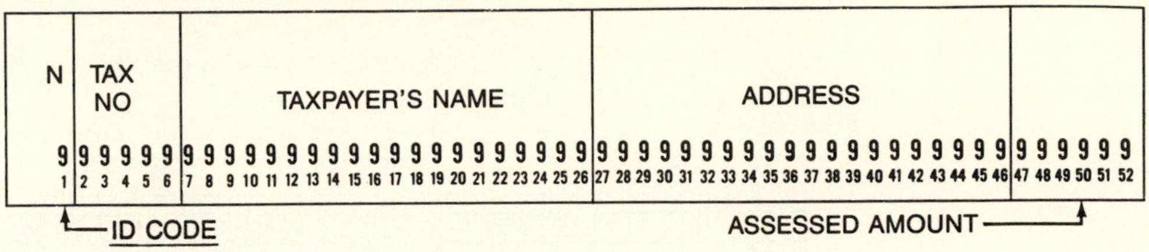

Direct File Format:

FILE DEFINITION

SYSTEM YOURS		DRAWN BY S. Myers
FILE NAME YOURS (From Lab 17-1)		DATE Any / REV. NO. 0
CREATED BY S. Myers		FILE TYPE Disk
RECORD NAME None		KEY LENGTH 5
RECORDING MODE Fixed	ORGANIZATION Direct	SEQUENCE Relative Record #
RECORD SIZE 77 bytes	BLOCKING FACTOR 1	BLOCKSIZE 77 bytes

FIELD DATA

FIELD NO.	FIELD NAME - DESCRIPTION	SIZE	CLASS C/P/Z/B	POSITION FROM	POSITION THRU	FORMAT/CONSTANT
1	Taxpayer's Number	5	C	1	5	Relative Record #
2.	Taxpayer's Name	20	C	6	25	
3	Taxpayer's Address	20	C	26	45	
4	Assessment Amount	6	P	46	49	
5	First Quarter Payment Date	6	P	50	53	
6	First Quarter Payment	5	P	54	56	
7	Second Quarter Payment Date	6	P	57	60	
8	Second Quarter Payment	5	P	61	63	
9	Third Quarter Payment Date	6	P	64	67	
10	Third Quarter Payment	5	P	68	70	
11	Fourth Quarter Payment Date	6	P	71	74	
12	Fourth Quarter Payment	5	P	75	77	

Processing: Use the tax number to CHAIN to the direct file. If a record is found, do one of the following:

1. If the transaction is for a current taypayer, update the payment date and amount field in the direct file record.
2. If the transaction is for a new taxpayer, update all the fields in the direct file.

Load any transaction records that do not have a matching relative record number to a sequential disk file in input record image.

Accumulate the total for the number of existing accounts update, number of new taxpayers, and the total quarterly payments received, which will be printed in the report. Refer to the printer spacing chart that follows for required field sizes.

Report Design: In addition to the update of the direct file, the program must generate the following report format:

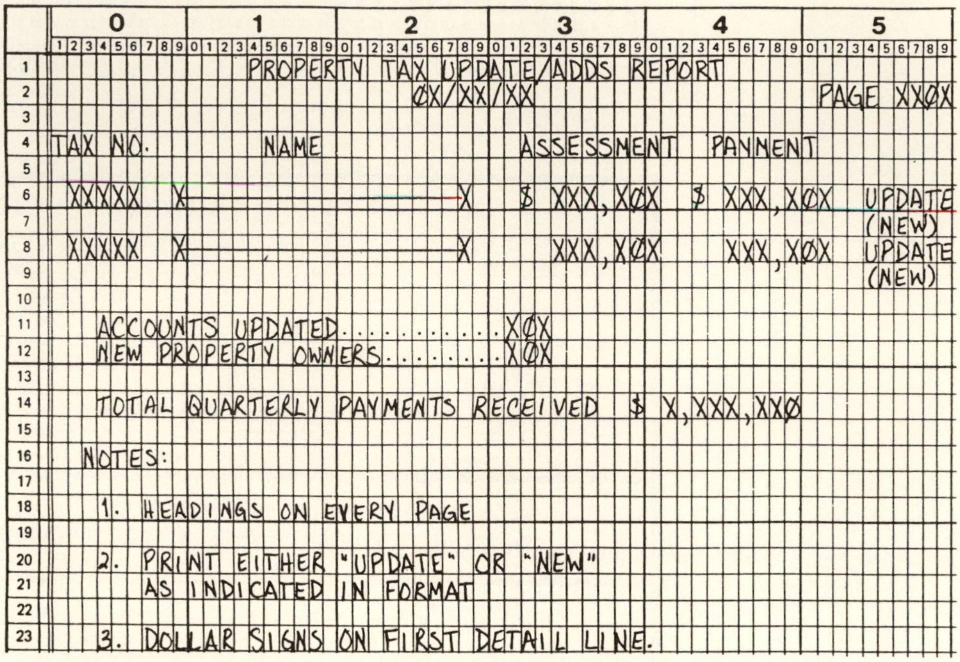
PROPERTY TAX UPDATE/ADDS REPORT
ØX/XX/XX
PAGE XXØX
TAX NO.
NAME
ASSESSMENT
PAYMENT
XXXXX X X $ XXX,XØX $ XXX,XØX UPDATE (NEW)
XXXXX X X XXX,XØX XXX,XØX UPDATE (NEW)
ACCOUNTS UPDATED..........XØX
NEW PROPERTY OWNERS........XØX
TOTAL QUARTERLY PAYMENTS RECEIVED $ X,XXX,XXØ
NOTES:
1. HEADINGS ON EVERY PAGE
2. PRINT EITHER "UPDATE" OR "NEW" AS INDICATED IN FORMAT
3. DOLLAR SIGNS ON FIRST DETAIL LINE.

Input Data:

Update Data:

ID Code 1-1	Tax No 2-6	Payment Date 7-12	Payment Amount 13-18	Quarter 19-19
U	00001	050191	000350	1
U	00002	050591	000300	2
U	00005	051091	000402	2
U	00006	051191	000615	3
U	00008	012291	001123	4

New Accounts:

ID Code 1-1	Tax No 2-6	Taxpayers's Name 7-26	Address 27-46	Assessment 47-52
N	00003	JERRY FURMAN	18 EAGLE PASS LANE	861111
N	00007	ERIC FELDER	44 HAITIAN BLVD	222100
N	00009	THOMAS PARKER	8 MADISON STREE	019914

Laboratory Assignment 17-5: CREATION OF AN ADDROUT FILE

Your computer's software utility has to be used to create an ADDROUT file from the direct file built and loaded in Assignment 17-1. Consequently, your instructor may have created the ADDROUT file (in which case this assignment is completed) or you may have to learn the syntax of your system's sort utility and create it yourself. In any case, your instructor will advise you. The direct file created in Assignment 17-1 must be sorted in descending order by the assessment amount.

Laboratory Assignment 17-6: RANDOMLY PROCESSING A DIRECT FILE BY AN ADDROUT FILE

Assignments 17-1 and 17-5 must be completed before this assignment is started. Write an RPG program to randomly process the direct file built and loaded in Assignment 17-1 by the ADDROUT file created in Assignment 17-5.

Processing: Process the direct file randomly by using the ADDROUT file, and print only the records that have data. Remember that your system will determine the size of the records (3, 4, or 10 bytes) in the ADDROUT file.

Accumulate totals for the number of property owners, and total all the assessments. Refer to the printer spacing chart that follows for the sizes of total fields.

Report Design: The program is to generate the following report format:

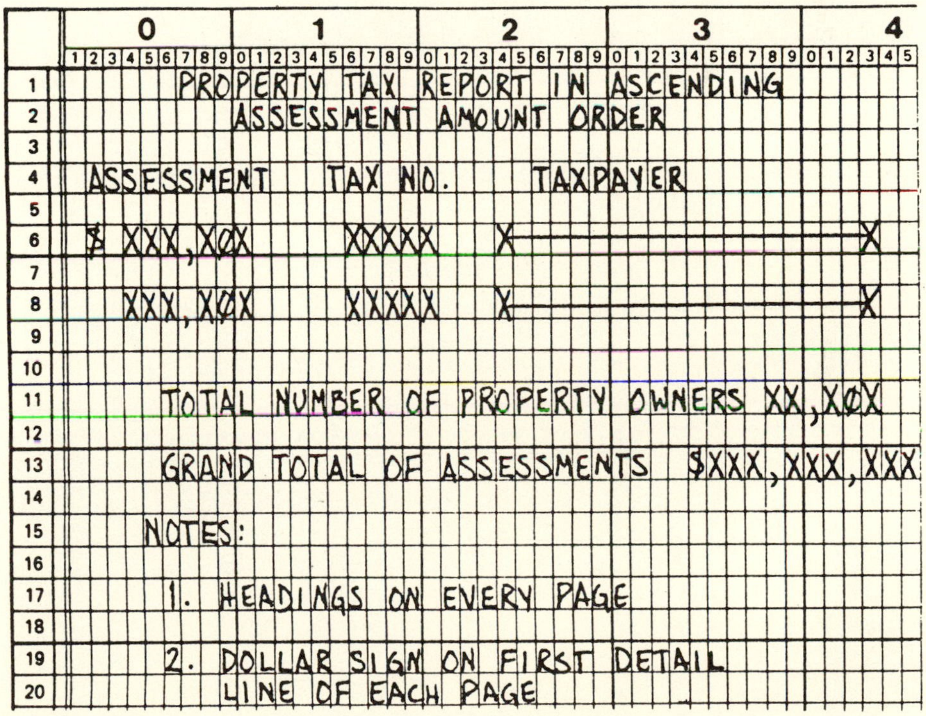
PROPERTY TAX REPORT IN ASCENDING
ASSESSMENT AMOUNT ORDER
ASSESSMENT
TAX NO.
TAXPAYER
$ XXX,XØX
XXXXX
X
X
XXX,XØX
XXXXX
X
X
TOTAL NUMBER OF PROPERTY OWNERS XX,XØX
GRAND TOTAL OF ASSESSMENTS $XXX,XXX,XXX
NOTES:
1. HEADINGS ON EVERY PAGE
2. DOLLAR SIGN ON FIRST DETAIL LINE OF EACH PAGE

chapter 18
Interactive RPG II (System/36/34)

Previous chapters have explained RPG II, III and 400 coding methods centered around batch processing that used disk input/output and printer files. Today's state-of-the-art technology usually requires the use of a workstation (WORKSTN) file for maintenance functions. CONSOLE and KEYBORD files, which are supported by CRTs and keyboards, were discussed in previous chapters. Those types of files simulate the interactive environment, but they do not give the control that separate WORKSTN files provide. For example, it is impossible to display a full screen with a CONSOLE file and then selectively modify field values for update processing. CONSOLE or KEYBORD controlled files are satisfactory to initiate inquiry or limits processing, but they have limited use in interactive update and delete maintenance.

A WORKSTN file permits users to interact with a disk file from one or more workstations at the same time. A program that controls the processing of one workstation is called a *single requestor terminal (SRT)* program. An RPG program that can process requests from more than one workstation at the same time from *one* copy of the object program in storage is referred to as a *multiple requestor terminal (MRT)* program.

The system flowchart in Figure 18-1 illustrates the processing logic of SRT and MRT environments. Notice that for both conditions, only one copy of the RPG object program is in storage. However, the program that supports SRT processing controls only one workstation, whereas the MRT program controls four. Syntax included in an RPG program determines whether SRT or MRT processing is to be supported.

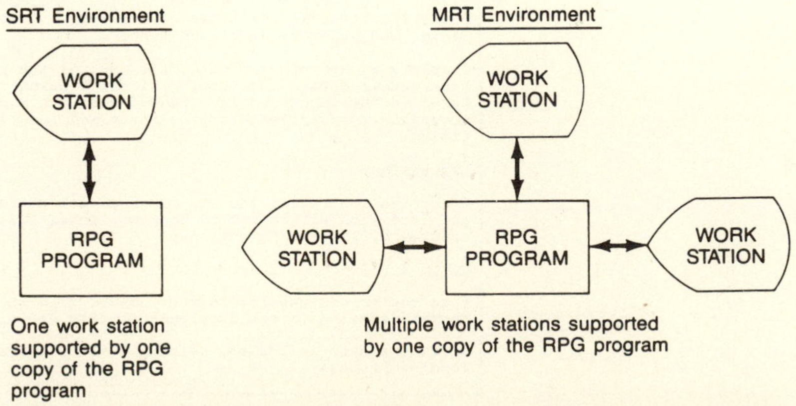

Figure 18-1 Single Requestor (SRT) and Multiple Requestor (MRT) Terminal environments.

STEPS FOR DEVELOPING AN INTERACTIVE RPG II PROGRAM

The steps required to develop an RPG program that supports interactive processing with a workstation (WORKSTN) file are the following:

1. Design a screen format on a CRT form or printer spacing chart.
2. Enter the instructions to support the screen format using the syntax supported by either SEU (Source Entry Utility) or SDA (Screen Design Aid). Compile, debug, and generate an object member. All screens developed in this chapter will be created with SEU.
3. Write an RPG program to control the processing of the WORKSTN file.
4. Write a procedure to execute the RPG program.

Three example interactive RPG programs that support SRT workstation processing are presented in this chapter. The first program adds records to an indexed file; the second provides for file inquiry; and the third controls file update and delete maintenance.

APPLICATION WORKSTN FILE PROGRAM—INDEXED FILE ADDITION

The specifications for an interactive RPG program that adds records to an indexed file are presented in Figure 18-2.

PROGRAM SPECIFICATIONS Page 1 of 1

Program Name PAYROLL FILE LOAD Program-ID CH18P1 Written By S. Myers

Purpose Interactive loading of a payroll file Approved By The Boss

Input files (directory names):

CH18P1FM (Screen name - CH18P1SC)

Output files (directory names):

DATA18P1 (Stored on disk)

Processing Narrative:

Write an interactive RPG program to load an indexed file with employee payroll data,

Input:

Use the BLDFILE utility, and create an indexed file shell with the attributes included in the supplemental file definition form.

Using either the SEU or SDA utility, enter the instructions for an interactive screen that will support the input of data for the loading of the employee payroll file (DATA18P1). An attached CRT layout form details the screen design. Include the display attributes specified in the notes on the form. Compile the screen file, debug, and generate an object member.

Complete an RPG program that will control the processing of the interactive screen and loading of the indexed file (DATA18P1). Refer to the input buffer, created when the screen file was successfully compiled, for the sizes and location of the screen fields.

Processing:

Under the control of the RPG program, enter the data interactively and load each screen record to the indexed file shell previously created by the BLDFILE utility.

Output:

Load the screen records to the indexed file (DATA18P1) in the format detailed in the supplemental file definition form.

After the data is loaded, print a utility listing to validate the loading process.

Figure 18-2 Specifications for an interactive RPG program that adds records to an indexed file.

The system flowchart shown in Figure 18-3 indicates that the RPG program controls the input of data from a workstation file and adds the records to a disk file.

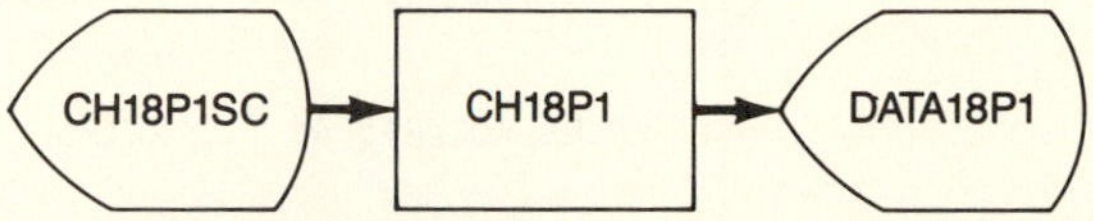

Figure 18-3 System flowchart for an interactive RPG program that adds records to an indexed file.

WORKSTN File Screen Format. WORKSTN File screen formats may be designed on either the special form shown in Figure 18-4 or on a printer spacing chart. Because most CRTs support only 80 columns and 24 lines, consideration must be given to this restriction. Examine the screen layout form in Figure 18-4 and notice the following features in the design of the screen:

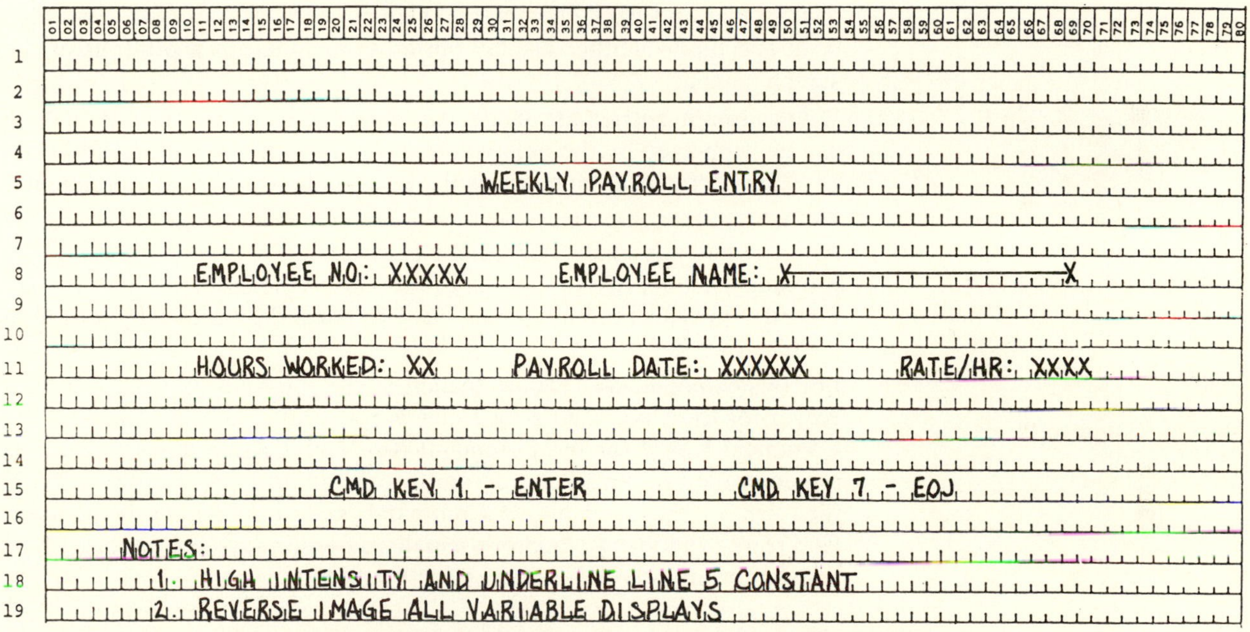

Figure 18-4 WORKSTN file screen layout for a program that adds records to an indexed file.

1. Because line 1, column 1 is reserved for system control, it cannot be used.
2. Editing numeric fields for interactive entry, addition, deletion, and update of data is not recommended because edit characters have to be removed before the values are loaded to the disk, diskette, or tape file. With inquiry processing, however, editing may be specified.
3. When a screen format is coded, reference is made to the beginning position of the constant and variable field. This differs from RPG source program coding in which output is referenced by the end position of the constant or variable.

A printout of the screen as it appears when the program is executed and after data is entered is shown in Figure 18-5. An input screen displayed before data is entered is referred to as a *blank screen* even though it usually includes constants (prompts).

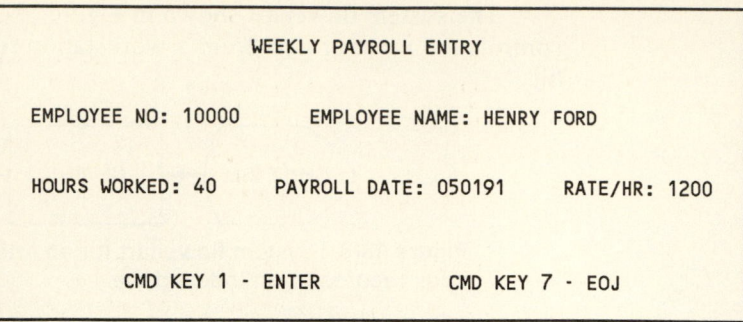

```
                    WEEKLY PAYROLL ENTRY

EMPLOYEE NO: 10000       EMPLOYEE NAME: HENRY FORD

HOURS WORKED: 40     PAYROLL DATE: 050191     RATE/HR: 1200


         CMD KEY 1 - ENTER             CMD KEY 7 - EOJ
```

Figure 18-5 Display of the filled-in screen (before command key 1 is pressed and the record loaded to the file).

The following features are related to this interactive screen:

1. The sizes of the variable items are identified as reverse image (light background and dark characters). Column separators could have also been specified. Neither display option is included in a printout of the screen's image.
2. When prompt entries are made, any attempt to enter more data than can be supported by the field will result in a buzzer sound. In addition, any field defined as numeric will prevent the entry of a nonnumeric value.
3. After an entry is made, the cursor is advanced to the next prompt by pressing the ENTER key. At any time during the entry process for the record, a previous prompt value may be changed by returning to it with a backspace key.
4. For this example, records are loaded to the file by pressing Command Key 1 (or the Command Key and 1 Key). End of job is controlled by Command Key 7 (or the Command Key and 7 Key). These functions are controlled in the RPG program through input from the WORKSTN file. Any of the available 24 Command Keys could have been used. Company or industry standards usually determine what Command Key is used for an interactive processing function.

A listing of the source document data that is input to the adds program by the interactive screen shown in Figure 18-5 and then added to the indexed file is shown in Figure 18-6.

Emp#	Employee Name	Hours	Payroll Date	Hourly Rate
10000	HENRY FORD	40	050191	1200
11000	LOUIS CHEVROLET	35	050191	1450
12000	WALTER CHRYSLER	32	050191	1800
13000	BENJAMIN DODGE	42	050191	1280
14000	WILLIAM BRICKLIN	45	050191	1900
15000	JOHN STUDEBAKER	30	050191	1000
16000	STANLEY STEAMER	37	050191	1950
17000	RANSOM E OLDS	35	050191	1550

Figure 18-6 Listing of source document data input to the adds program via interactive screen control.

The File Definition of the indexed file created by the BLDFILE utility supplied with the System/34 and 36 computers is presented in Figure 18-7. The

FILE DEFINITION			
SYSTEM System 36 or 34		DRAWN BY S. Myers	
FILE NAME DATA18P1		DATE 5/01/91	REV. NO. 0
CREATED BY S. Myers		FILE TYPE Disk	
RECORD NAME None		KEY LENGTH 5 bytes	
RECORDING MODE Fixed	ORGANIZATION Indexed	SEQUENCE Key order	
RECORD SIZE 38 bytes	BLOCKING FACTOR 1	BLOCKSIZE 38 bytes	

FIELD DATA

FIELD NO.	FIELD NAME - DESCRIPTION	SIZE	CLASS C/P/Z/B	POSITION FROM	POSITION THRU	FORMAT/CONSTANT
1	Delete Code	1	C	1	1	D if deleted
2	Employee Number	5	Z	2	6	Key field
3	Employee Name	20	C	7	26	
4	Hours Worked	2	Z	27	28	
5	Payroll Date	6	Z	29	34	
6	Hourly Rate	4	Z	35	38	2 decimal positions

Figure 18-7 File Definition of the indexed file processed by the RPG adds program.

BLDFILE utility creates only an empty shell for the file with a record or block size specified by the RECORD or BLOCK clause in an OCL statement in a procedure. Field sizes and locations in the body of the records are defined in the related RPG program. Because the file created for this application is indexed, the key size and beginning position of the key in the body of the records must also be included in the prompt screen for the BLDFILE utility.

In the paragraphs that follow, the syntax and procedures necessary to complete an interactive RPG program that controls the addition of records to an indexed file are presented.

Procedures Used to Create a WORKSTN File. After a screen format is designed, System/34 and 36 have two utilities for entering the coded instructions. The Screen Design Aid (SDA) utility allows the programmer to "paint" the screen design on the CRT without first coding the instructions. Then, the SDA utility translates the screen entries to instructions supported by the SCREEN FORMAT GENERATOR utility (SFGR).

The other method for entering a source code for a WORKSTN file is by the Source Entry Utility (SEU). Depending on the programmer's experience, this method may require that the instructions for the WORKSTN file be first coded on a special form (Display Screen Format Specifications) before entering them. Because SDA is a unique and standalone utility, the SEU method for building WORKSTN files will be explained. Any information regarding SDA, however, may be found in separate IBM-supplied manuals.

WORKSTN File Syntax. Shown in Figure 18-8 is a printout of the completed WORKSTN file screen for the adds program. The image was generated by a test screen function in the SDA utility. Even though the screen was coded with SEU, after it is successfully compiled, it may be tested with SDA. The asterisks represent variable field positions that do not appear on the user's screen but are printed by the SDA test function for identification and validation.

```
2
A


                              3
                      WEEKLY PAYROLL ENTRY

      4       5                 6                  7
  EMPLOYEE NO: *****     EMPLOYEE NAME: ********************

      8           9          10          11           12      13
  HOURS WORKED: **     PAYROLL DATE: ******      RATE/HR: ****


                 14                          15
          CMD KEY 1 - ENTER           CMD KEY 7 - EOJ
```

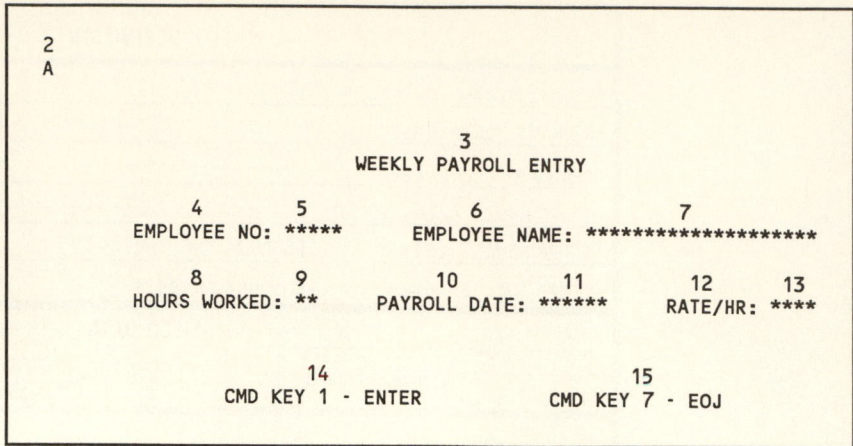

Figure 18-8 Printout of WORKSTN file screen generated by the SDA utility test function.

Included in Figure 18-8 are numbers above each constant and variable that relate to the sequence numbers (columns 1–5) of the instructions in the completed Display Screen Format Specifications form shown in Figure 18-9. An explanation of the syntax of each instruction is included at the bottom of Figure 18-9. Notice that not all the fields on the Display Screen Format form are used for this application. For a comprehensive discussion of the function of every field, refer to the related IBM manual.

IBM

System/34 Display Screen Format Specifications

Second Edition Use this coding sheet only to define display screen formats for WSU and $SFGR. This coding sheet could contain typographical errors.

GX21-9253-1 U/M 050* Printed in U.S.A. *No. of sheets per pad may vary slightly.

Sequence Number (1–5)	Form Type (6)	Format Name (7–14)	Start Line Number (17–18)	Number of Lines to Clear (19–20)	Enable Function Keys (27)	Enable Command Keys (28)	Key Mask (64–79)
ØØØØ1	S	CH18P1SC	Ø1	24	Y	Y	AG

Sequence Number (1–5)	Form Type (6)	WSU Field Name (7–12)	Field Length (15–18)	Line Number (19–20)	Horizontal Position (21–22)	Output Data (23)	Input Allowed (26)	Data Type (27)	Mandatory Fill (28)	Mandatory Entry (29)	Protect Field (37)	High Intensity (39)	Nondisplay (43)	Reverse Image (45)	Underline (47)	Constant Type (56)	Constant Data (57–79)
ØØØØ2	D		1	1	3	Y	Y				Y		Y			C	A
ØØØØ3	D		2Ø	5	3Ø	Y						Y			Y	C	WEEKLY PAYROLL ENTRY
ØØØØ4	D		12	8	11	Y										C	EMPLOYEE NO:
ØØØØ5	D	EMP#	5	8	24		Y	N	Y					Y			
ØØØØ6	D		14	8	35	Y										C	EMPLOYEE NAME:
ØØØØ7	D	NAME	2Ø	8	5Ø		Y			Y				Y			
ØØØØ8	D		13	11	11	Y										C	HOURS WORKED:
ØØØØ9	D	HOURS	2	11	25		Y	N		Y				Y			
ØØØ1Ø	D		13	11	32	Y										C	PAYROLL DATE:
ØØØ11	D	DATE	6	11	46		Y	N	Y					Y			
ØØØ12	D		8	11	57	Y										C	RATE/HR:
ØØØ13	D	RATE	4	11	66		Y	N		Y				Y			
ØØØ14	D		17	15	19	Y										C	CMD KEY 1 - ENTER
ØØØ15	D		15	15	47	Y										C	CMD KEY 7 - EOJ

Figure 18-9 Completed Display Screen Format Specifications for the adds program.

S Section

Sequence Number	
00001	Format Name (Columns 7-14): Programmer-supplied screen record name (more than one screen format (record) may be included in a screen file) is entered in this field. Name may be eight characters and must begin with an alphabetic character. Screen record name for this application is CH18P1SC.
	Start Line Number (Columns 17-18): Specifies the CRT line where the screen format will begin to display. The 01 entry indicates that the screen will display beginning on line 1.
	Number of Lines to Clear (Columns 19-20): Provides for the clearing of the screen before output. The 24 entered indicates that all 24 lines on the CRT will be cleared before the screen is displayed. For applications in which two screens are displayed at one time, a number smaller than 24 must be specified for the second screen.
	Enable Command Keys (Column 28): Letter Y indicates that Comamnd Keys specified in the Key Mask (Columns 64-79) are to be "enabled" (made functional) for screen to program control. Command Keys relate to indicators. For example, Command Key KA turns on indicator 01; KB, indicator 02, and so forth. Depending on the terminal design, Command Keys may be included in a top row of keys on the keyboard, or a Comamnd Key and associated number key must both be pressed. For this screen record, Command Key A, for KA (indicator 01) and G, for KG (indicator 07) are "enabled".
	Blink Cursor (Column 29-30): Letter Y indicates that cursor will blink at the first prompt position when screen is displayed.
	Key Mask (Columns 64-79): Letters A and G indicate that Command Keys KA and KG are to be "enabled" (functional) for screen to program control. Any of the available 25 Command Keys (K0 is not supported) may be used. A company's programming standards may determine which Command Keys are to be used for specific controls. For this application, KA is used to control the writing of a record to the indexed file and KG controls end of job processing.

D Section

Sequence Number	
00002	Field Length (Columns 15-18): Defines the length of the field specified in columns 7-12 or the constant entered in columns 57-79. The 1 entry indicates the size of the constant specified in column 57.
	Starting Location-Line Number (Columns 19-20): Refers to the line number on which the field or constant entry is to entered. 1 indicates that the letter A is to be entered on line 1 of the screen record.
	Starting Location-Horizontal Position (Columns 21-22): Specifies the column in which the field value or constant is to begin. 3 indicates that the constant A is to be entered in column 3. This entry and the Line Number entry above indicate that the constant A is to be entered on line 1 column 3
	Output Data (Columns 23-24): Letter Y in this field allows the field value or constant to be displayed on the screen. For this example screen, the constant A will be output.
	Input Allowed (Column 26): Y in this field allows variable data or constants to be input from the screen record to the RPG program. Note that the constant A will be passed to the RPG program and defined as a Record Identification Code to determine which screen record is currently processed. Any character or characters may be used to code the screen record.
	Protect Field (Columns 37-38): Y entered here prevents the field value or constant defined in this statement from being changed by input or output processing.
	Nondisplay (Columns 43-44): Y entry indicates that value defined in this instruction is not to be visible to the operator.
	Constant Type (Column 56): Letter C indicates there is a constant entered in the Constant Data field (Columns 57-79). If an edit code was specified in columns 57-79, this entry must be omitted. Editing of numeric fields is sometimes specified for inquiry only processing.
	Constant Data (Columns 57-79): Letter A in column 57 is the constant defined and controlled by the previous entries in this statement. For this example, the letter A is used to define the screen record. Input from the CRT is processed as a record and the controlling program must test this code to determine which screen record is currently being processed.
00003	Follows the same coding logic as sequence line 00002 except the constant, WEEKLY PAYROLL ENTRY, is 20 long and begins on line 5 column 30. Because the constant is only to be displayed and not input to the program, it is defined with a Y in column 23 and nothing in column 27. The Y in column 39 indicates that the constant will be displayed in a high intensity mode and the Y in column 47 supports underlining of the constant when it is displayed. Note that high intensity or underlining will not be included in a printout of the screen image.
00004	Same coding logic for the constant on sequence line 00003 except that high intensity and underlining are not specified.
00005	Field Name (Columns 7-12): EMP# is a programmer-supplied variable field name used to transfer data from the screen to the RPG program or from the program to the screen. The field size and location in the screen record will be identified in the input and output buffers that are automatically built when the screen is successfully compiled. How these buffers are used will be discussed later.
	When the screen record is displayed, the high intensity option specified with this statement will identify the size of the EMP# field.
	Field Length (Columns 15-18): Defines the length of the field specified in columns 7-12. 5 indicates that EMP# is 5 bytes.
	Line Number (Columns 19-20): 8 indicates the field value is to be displayed on line 8.

(*Continued*)

Horizontal Position (Columns 21-22): Entry indicates that field value will be displayed beginning in column 24.

Output Data (Columns 23-24): Not used for variables that are only input from the screen to the RPG program.

Input Allowed (Column 26): Y entry supports input from the screen to the program.

Data Type (Column 27): Letter N indicates screen input/output field (EMP#) is defined as numeric. On input, any attempt to enter a non-numeric character will result in a buzzer sound and the cursor will not advance to the next prompt.

Reverse Image (Columns 45-46): Y entry in this field causes the field area to display in a reverse image (light background with black letters on a monochrome CRT)

00006 Except for line and column locations, this instruction follows the same coding logic as sequence line 00003.

00007 Except for line and column locations, this instruction follows the same coding logic as sequence line 00005. Note, however, that the field is defined as alphanumeric by the omission of an entry Data Type field (column 27).

00008 Except for line and column locations, this instruction follows the same coding logic as sequence line 00004.

00009 Except for line and column locations, this instruction follows the same coding logic as sequence line 00005. Note that this field is defined as numeric by the N entry in the Data Type field column 27.

00010 Except for line and column entries, this instruction follows the same coding logic as sequence line 00004.

00011 Except for line and column entries, this instruction follows the same coding logic as sequence line 00005.

00012 Except for line and column entries, this instruction follows the same coding logic as sequence line 00004.

00013 Except for line and column entries, this instruction follows the same coding logic as sequence line 00005.

00014 and 00015 Except for the line and column entries, this instruction follows the same coding logic as sequence line 00002. Note that the only attribute is the Y in the Output Data field (columns 23-24). This purpose of these constants is to inform the operator on how to enter a record and to end the job.

(Continued)

Figure 18-9 is divided into S and D sections. The S section defines the attributes of the record (screen), and the D section defines the attributes of the constants and data fields included in the screen record.

As mentioned previously, the SEU (Source Entry Utility) method of entering the source code was used and not SDA (Screen Design Aid). Two methods to enter the source code under SEU control are by displaying the related specifications form by pressing Command Key 3, which displays a Forms Menu. Option 23 must be selected for the S section and 24 for the D section formats. Both formats display the fields horizontally.

A more convenient method for entering a source code with SEU is with Forms Menu option 35 for the S section format and 36 for the D section. Figure 18-10 shows the S and D section formats displayed by selecting options 35 and 36 on the Forms Menu. Notice how the prompt for each field in the S and D sections of the Display Screen Format Specifications is easily referenced. The circled values are entries made by the programmer.

Forms Menu Option 35 (S Section format):

```
SEQ #          0001   FORM TYPE        (S) FORMAT NAME (CH18P1SC)   WSU FORMAT ID
START LINE     (01)   LINES TO CLEAR  (24) LOWERCASE                RETURN INPUT
RESET KEYBD           SOUND ALARM          BLINK CURSOR             ERASE INPUT
OVERRIDE              SUPPRESS INPUT       WSU START                WSU END
REQUIRED              REPEAT               PRIORITY                 PREPROCESS
REVIEW RECORD IDS                    INSERT RECORD IDS
FUNCTION KEYS         COMMAND KEYS     (Y)KEY MASK     (AG)
```

Forms Menu Option 36 (D Section format):

```
  SEQ NO  0006     FORM TYPE(D)      FLD NAME  (EMP#)       FLD LEN(0005)
LINE #        (5)POSITION     24 OUTPUT DATA(Y) ALLOW INPUT(Y) DATA TYPE      (N)
MAND ENT         MAND FILL        SELF CHK         ENABLE DUP       WSU EDIT
POS CURSOR       ADJUST/FILL      CTL FLD EXIT     AUTO REC ADV     COL SEP
PROTECT FLD      BLINK FLD        UNDERLINE        NON-DISPLAY      REVERSE IMAGE(Y)
HIGH INTEN
CONST TYPE         CONSTANT                                      CONTINUATION
```

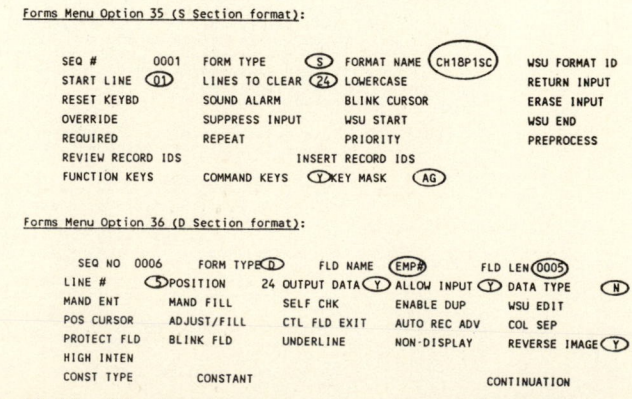

Figure 18-10 Displays for Forms Menu option 35 (S section format) and option 36 (D section format).

Compilation of the Display Format Member. After the source code for the screen file (display format source member) is entered and saved, it is compiled by entering the statement detailed in Figure 18-11.

```
FORMAT CREATE,CH18P1FM,SEMLIB,CH18P1FM,SEMLIB,1

  1       2       3         4        5       6   7
```

The function of each entry in this "free-format" statement is as follows:

1 - FORMAT: Calls the $SFGR (Screen Format Generator) utility to compile the source program and generate an object member.

2 - CREATE: Specifies that a screen object will be created. Other functions for this entry include UPDATE and ADD.

3 - CH18P1FM: Name of the display format load (object) member.

4 - SEMLIB: Name of the library in which the display format load member is to be stored. A successful compilation (no terminal errors) will store the load member in this library.

5 - CH18P1FM: Name of the display format source member. May be a defined with a name different than the display format load member.

6 - SEMLIB: Name of the library in which the display format source member is stored. May not be the same library as the display format load member.

7 - 1: Number of display formats in the source member. 1 to 255 record formats may be included in one source and load member.

Figure 18-11 Free-form statement for compiling a display source member.

In lieu of entering the statement shown in Figure 18-11, a prompt menu may be displayed by entering the word FORMAT and pressing ENTER. This OCL statement will display the menu shown in Figure 18-12. Notice that all the entries included in the free-form statement are presented for easy reference.

```
                         FORMAT PROCEDURE                          Optional-*

            Processes source statements for $SFGR display formats


Format generation option  . . . . . . CREATE,ADD,DELETE,UPDATE  CREATE
Name of display format load member  . . . . . . . . . . . . . . CH18P1FM
Name of library to contain load member . . . . . . . . . . . . . SEMLIB
Name of display format source member  . . . . . . . . . . . . . CH18P1FM
Name of library containing source member  . . . . . . . . . . . SEMLIB
Number of display formats in source member  . . . . . . . 1-255  1
To replace an existing load member ,
  enter REPLACE . . . . . . . . . . . . . . . . . . . .. REPLACE  REPLACE     *
Halt on error messages . . . . . . . . . . . . . . HALT,NOHALT  NOHALT
Print option  . . . . . . . . . . . . . . PRINT,NOPRINT,PARTIAL  PRINT



Cmd2-Page back       Cmd4-Put on job queue                     COPR IBM Corp. 1983
```

Figure 18-12 FORMAT statement prompt menu.

The source listing generated from compilation of the display format member by either FORMAT method is presented in Figure 18-13. An explanation of sections A and B is included at the bottom of the listing.

An explanation of the input buffer area is included in Figure 18-14.

```
....+....1....+....2....+....3....+....4....+....5....+....6....+....7....+....8

     SCH18P1SC  0124       YY                                  AG
     D            1 1 3Y  Y          Y     Y            CA
     D           20 530Y               Y       Y        CWEEKLY PAYROLL ENTRY
     D           12 811Y                                CEMPLOYEE NO:
     DEMP#        5 824   YNY                Y
     D           14 835Y                                CEMPLOYEE NAME:
     DNAME       20 850   Y  Y               Y
     D           131111Y                                CHOURS WORKED:
     DHOURS       21125   YN Y               Y
     D           131132Y                                CPAYROLL DATE:
     DDATE        61146   YNY                Y
     D            81157Y                                CRATE/HR:
     DRATE        41166   YN Y               Y
     D           171519Y                                CCMD KEY 1 - ENTER
     D           151547Y                                CCMD KEY 7 - EOJ

INPUT BUFFER DESCRIPTION
FIELD NAME    LENGTH      START       END

                  1          1          1
  EMP#            5          2          6
  NAME           20          7         26
  HOURS           2         27         28
  DATE            6         29         34
  RATE            4         35         38

  No Observation Errors
  No Warning Errors
  No Fatal Errors
```

Section A

The source listing of the display format member in the same format as the Screen Specifications Form. Relative position of each entry is referenced by the ruler included at the top of the listing. Compile time terminal and warning errors will be included in the body of the listing.

Section B

The section entitled, INPUT BUFFER DESCRIPTION, specifies the location of the input fields (*from screen to program*) in the INPUT BUFFER created in the compilation process. The exact location of each field is included in the Input Specifications of the related RPG program so that data may be passed from the display format member (input) to the program for processing.

Because this application includes only the input of data, no OUTPUT BUFFER is included. For update processing, the display format member listing will include both input and output buffers.

Figure 18-13 Display format member listing and input buffer.

Input Buffer Structure

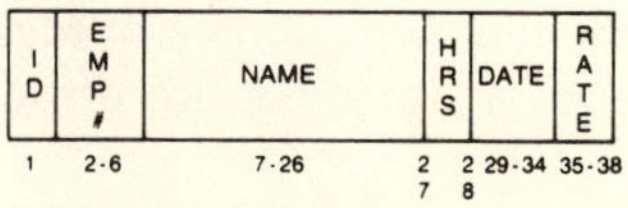

Notes:

1. Position 1 of INPUT BUFFER represents the display format member record type. To identify the record, letter A was specified in screen coding (line 1 column 3). This field must be referenced in the RPG program as a record identification entry to determine which display format member record is to be processed. One display format member may include a maximum of 255 record formats.

2. The exact FROM and TO field locations in the INPUT BUFFER must be specified in the Input Specifications of the related RPG program. Field names in the program, however, do not have to be the same as those in the display format member.

Figure 18-14 INPUT BUFFER area generated during compilation of the display format member for index file addition program.

RPG Source Program Coding—Indexed File Addition

The processing logic controlled by the RPG program that adds records to an indexed file previously built by the BLDFILE utility is detailed in Figure 18-15.

A source listing of the interactive program that adds records to an indexed file is presented in Figure 18-16.

An examination of the program shows that new syntax and processing features are included in the instructions. These entries are discussed separately in the following paragraphs.

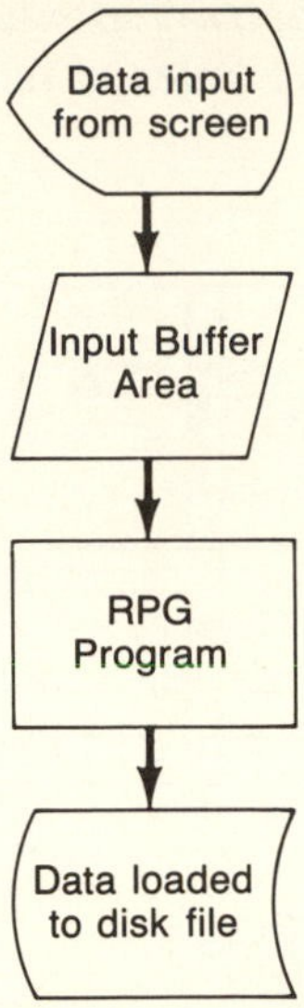

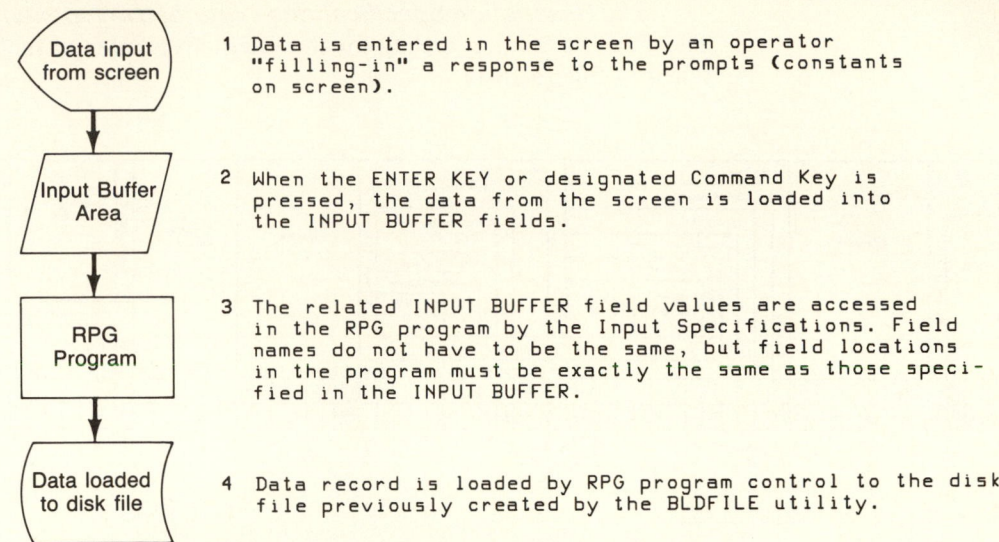

1 Data is entered in the screen by an operator "filling-in" a response to the prompts (constants on screen).

2 When the ENTER KEY or designated Command Key is pressed, the data from the screen is loaded into the INPUT BUFFER fields.

3 The related INPUT BUFFER field values are accessed in the RPG program by the Input Specifications. Field names do not have to be the same, but field locations in the program must be exactly the same as those specified in the INPUT BUFFER.

4 Data record is loaded by RPG program control to the disk file previously created by the BLDFILE utility.

Figure 18-15 Processing logic controlled by the RPG program that adds records to an indexed file.

```
H                                                                    CH18P1
 *                                                                   CH18P1
 * THIS PROGRAM LOADS/ADDS RECORDS TO AN INDEXED FILE INTERACTIVELY  CH18P1
 * SYSTEM/36 & 34 ENVIRONMENTS....................................   CH18P1
 *                                                                   CH18P1
FCH18P1FMCD  F  81  81            WORKSTN                            CH18P1
FDATA18P10   F  38  38  5AI      2 DISK                    A         CH18P1
 *                                                                   CH18P1
 * FIELDS DEFINITIONS MUST MATCH SCREEN'S INPUT BUFFER DESCRIPTION   CH18P1
 * FIELD SIZES AND LOCATION MUST MATCH, BUT NAMES MAY BE DIFFERENT   CH18P1
 *                                                                   CH18P1
ICH18P1FMSM  01   1 CA                                               CH18P1
I                                              2   60EMP#            CH18P1
I                                              7  26 NAME            CH18P1
I                                             27  280HOURS           CH18P1
I                                             29  340DATE            CH18P1
I                                             35  382RATE            CH18P1
C           AGAIN     TAG                                            CH18P1
C                     SETON                     80    SCREEN CONTROL CH18P1
C                     EXCPT                           DISP BLANK SCRNCH18P1
C                     SETOF                     80    OFF SCREEN CONTCH18P1
C                     READ CH18P1FM                   READ SCRN DATA CH18P1
C   KG                GOTO QUIT                       EOJ?           CH18P1
C   KA                EXSR PROCES                     SR - FILE LOAD CH18P1
C                     GOTO AGAIN                      GET BLANK SCRN CH18P1
C           QUIT      TAG                                            CH18P1
C                     SETON                     LR    EOJ            CH18P1
C           PROCES    BEGSR                                          CH18P1
C                     SETON                     04    FILE LOAD CONTLCH18P1
C                     EXCPT                           WRITE DISK RECDCH18P1
C                     SETOF                     04    OFF WRITE CONTLCH18P1
C                     ENDSR                                          CH18P1
 *                                                                   CH18P1
 * DISPLAYS BLANK SCREEN (CONSTANTS & PROMPTS)...................    CH18P1
 *                                                                   CH18P1
OCH18P1FME        80                                                 CH18P1
O                                        K8 'CH18P1SC'               CH18P1
 *                                                                   CH18P1
 * CONTROLS LOADING OF DISK RECORDS..............................    CH18P1
 *                                                                   CH18P1
ODATA18P1EADD      04                                                CH18P1
O                                         1 ' '                      CH18P1
O                          EMP#       6                              CH18P1
O                          NAME      26                              CH18P1
O                          HOURS     28                              CH18P1
O                          DATE      34                              CH18P1
O                          RATE      38                              CH18P1
```

Figure 18-16 Source listing of a program that adds records to an indexed file by screen controlled input.

File Description Specifications—Interactive Indexed File Adds Program. The File Description coding for the interactive indexed file adds program is detailed in Figure 18-17.

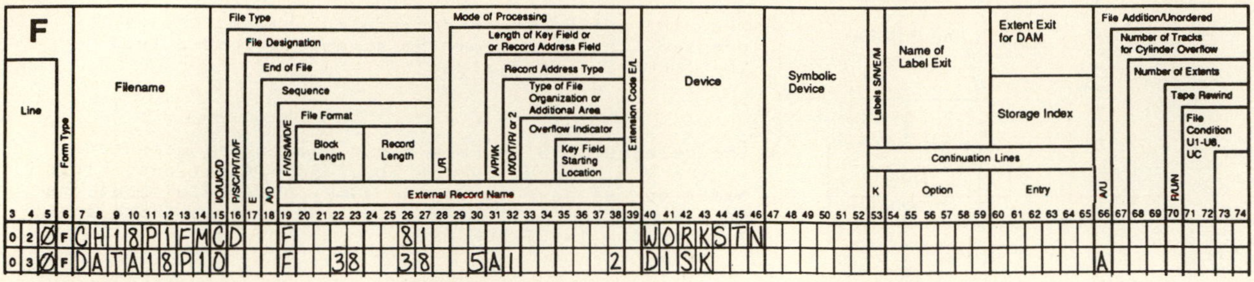

<u>Coding for WORKSTN file:</u>

<u>Line 020:</u>

Filename (cols 7-14) — Name of the display format member (file) must be entered in this field.

File Type (col 15) — C, for Combined file (both input and output), must be specified in this field for WORKSTN files.

File Designation (col 16) — P (primary) or D (demand) must be entered in this field. If this field contains a P, the WORKSTN file is automatically read during input time of the RPG program cycle. If a WORKSTN file is defined as primary, no secondary (S) files may be specified in the program.

D defines the file as a demand file by which the records are read during calculations by one of the READ operations. Record identifying indicators are not automatically set off in demand file processing.

File Format (col 19) — Must include an F to indicate that all of the records from the WORKSTN file have all the same length.

Block Length (cols 20-23) — Must be blank.

Record Length (cols 24-27) — Must include the length of the longest record in the display format member.

Device (cols 40-46) — Must contain the device name WORKSTN.

File Condition (cols 71-71) — External indicators (U1-U8) may be specified in this field.

<u>Coding for Indexed file:</u>

<u>Line 030:</u>

See Chapter 15 for an explanation of the syntax for adding to an indexed file.

Figure 18-17 File Description coding for interactive indexed file adds program.

Input Specifications—Interactive Indexed File Adds Program. Examine the relationship of the input coding to the Input Buffer Description in Figure 18-18, and notice that the unnamed field position (1–1) in the INPUT BUFFER DESCRIPTION represents the display format member identification code (letter A in line 1, column 3), which is specified as a Record Identification Code in the RPG program. This entry identifies the display record format defined.

Field locations in the Input Specifications relate to the START and END positions in the INPUT BUFFER DESCRIPTION. The field names included in the program and screen do not have to be the same.

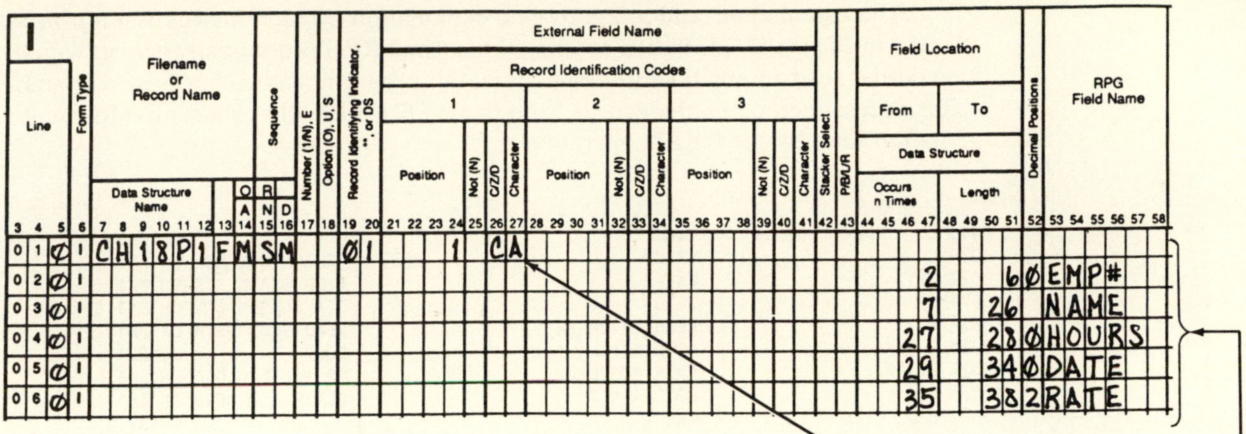

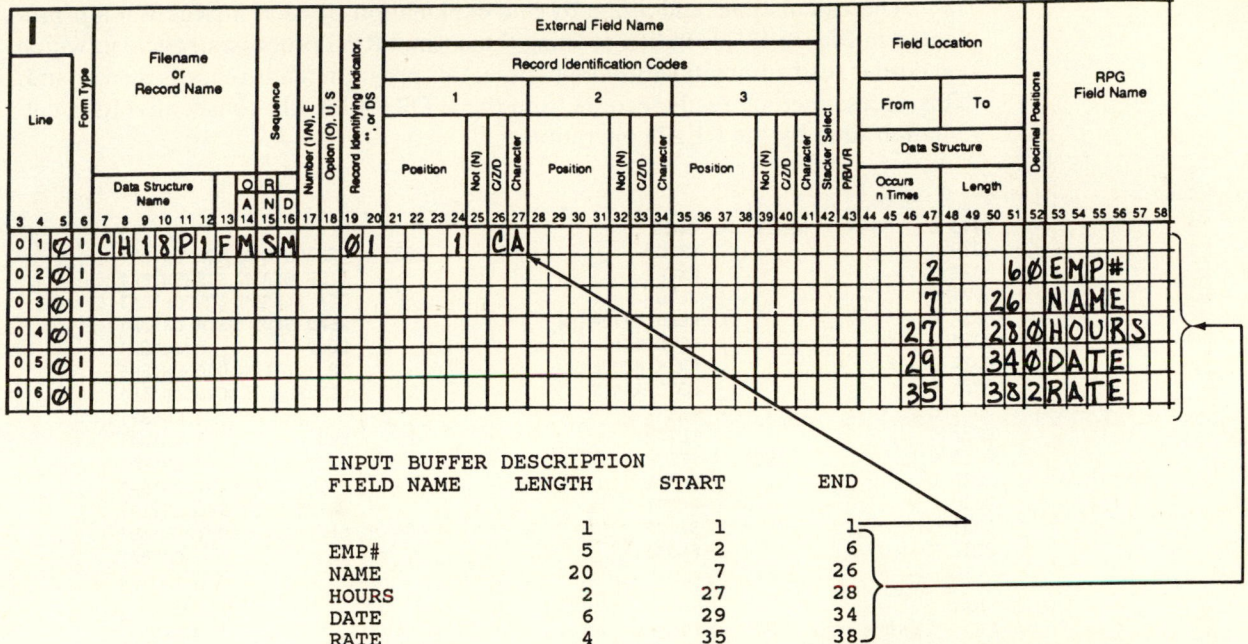

```
INPUT BUFFER DESCRIPTION
FIELD NAME     LENGTH      START      END

                  1           1         1
EMP#              5           2         6
NAME             20           7        26
HOURS             2          27        28
DATE              6          29        34
RATE              4          35        38
```

Figure 18-18 Input Specifications coding and relationship to INPUT BUFFER (interactive indexed file adds program).

Calculation Specifications—Interactive Indexed File Adds Program. A flowchart of the processing logic controlled by the calculation statements included in the interactive adds program is shown in Figure 18-19.

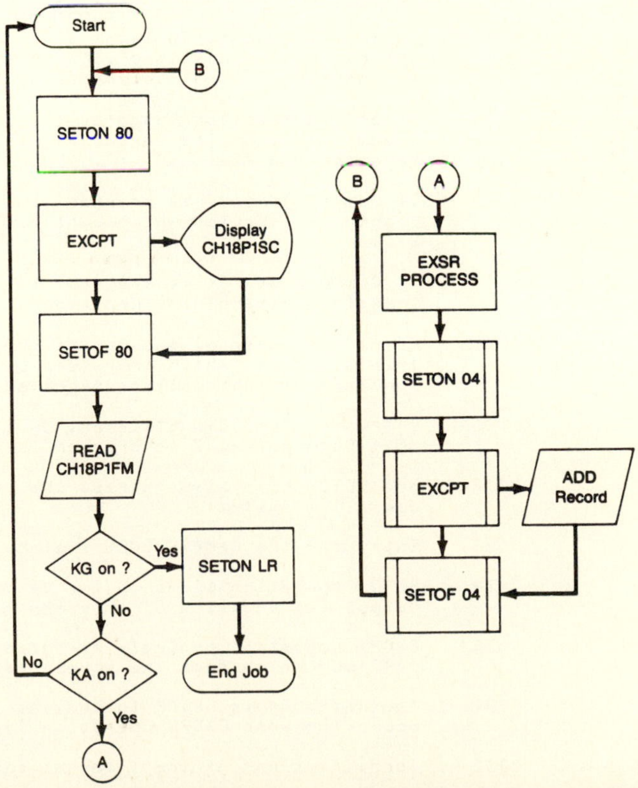

Figure 18-19 Flowchart of the processing controlled by the calculations included in the interactive adds program.

The calculations and a line-by-line explanation of each instruction are presented in Figure 18-20. In lieu of using the normal RPG processing cycle in which a record is read automatically at input time, this program reads records on demand. This access method reads records from the WORKSTN file consecutively at calculation time by the READ operation.

```
... ... 1 ... ... 2 ... ... 3 ... ... 4 ... ... 5 ... ... 6 ... ... 7 ...
0018 C            AGAIN     TAG                                     CH18P1
0019 C                      SETON                     80  SCREEN CONTROL CH18P1
0020 C                      EXCPT                         DISP BLANK SCRNCH18P1
0021 C                      SETOF                     80  OFF SCREEN CONTCH18P1
0022 C                      READ CH18P1FM                 READ SCRN DATA CH18P1
0023 C   KG                 GOTO QUIT                     EOJ?           CH18P1
0024 C   KA                 EXSR PROCES                   SR - FILE LOAD CH18P1
0025 C                      GOTO AGAIN                    GET BLANK SCRN CH18P1
0026 C            QUIT      TAG                                          CH18P1
0027 C                      SETON                     LR  EOJ            CH18P1
0028 C            PROCES    BEGSR                                        CH18P1
0029 C                      SETON                     04  FILE LOAD CONTLCH18P1
0030 C                      EXCPT                         WRITE DISK RECDCH18P1
0031 C                      SETOF                     04  OFF WRITE CONTLCH18P1
0032 C                      ENDSR                                        CH18P1
```

Line No.

0018 Entry for GOTO statement on line 0025 which controls subsequent displays a new screen (blank screen) for entry or end of job response.

0019 Indicator 80 is turned on which controls output of a blank screen. Note that a "blank screen" is a display format that includes only the prompts (constants). Operator enters required data which is referred to as a "filled-in" screen.

0020 This EXCPT operation transfers control to an exception type output record (E in column 15) conditioned by the 80 indicator. Output lines 0036 and 0037 (Figure 18-16) are executed by this statement which causes the screen record CH18P1SC to be displayed. CH18P1SC is the record defined in the display format member CH18P1FM.

0021 This SETOF operation turns off the 80 indicator to prevent the output instruction conditioned with that indicator from being executed when the next EXCPT instruction (line 0030) is executed.

0022 After the operator responds to the blank screen's prompts, the READ operation reads the variable data and the status of the two command keys (KA and KG).

0023 If Command Key 07 is pressed, the KG indicator is turned on and a branch is executed which controls end of job processing (lines 26 and 27).

0024 If Command Key 01 is pressed, the KA indicator is turned on which transfers control to the internal subroutine PROCES.

0025 After the internal subroutine PROCES is executed, control returns to this statement which transfers control back to line 0018 and the sequence of instructions repeated.

0026 Entry for the GOTO statement on line 0023. Control is transferred here when Command Key 7 is pressed to end the job.

0027 The SETON LR statement ends the job and returns control back to the operating system.

0028 Entry for the EXSR PROCES statement on line 0024.

0029 SETON operation turns on the 04 indicator which controls exception output and addition of a screen record to the indexed file.

0030 EXCPT operation controls exception type output on lines 0041 through 0047 add which adds the screen record to the indexed file.

0031 Indicator 04 is SETOF to prevent this exception type output record from occurring when EXCPT operation for redisplay of the screen is executed.

0032 Identifies end of the internal subroutine.

Figure 18-20 Calculations included in the interactive indexed file adds program.

Notice also that the end of the job is controlled in calculations by a SETON LR statement. Unlike disk, diskette, or tape files, an end-of-file record is not stored in a WORKSTN file to flag end-of-job processing. End-of-job control must be determined by an operator's response. In this program, end-of-job processing is executed when the operator presses Command Key 7. This command key turns on indicator KA (defined in the screen format), which conditions a GOTO statement that transfers control to a SETON LR instruction that ends the job immediately. If, however, any additional instructions had been conditioned at LR time, they would be executed before the program ended.

Output-Format Specifications—Interactive Indexed File Adds Program. Examine the coding form in Figure 18-21, and notice that all output is conditioned at exception time (E in column 15). The following two functions are controlled by the output coding:

1. A blank screen (displayed with prompts) is displayed by the instructions on lines 010 and 020. The K8 entry (End Position in Output Record, columns 40–43) on line 020 defines the length of the screen record name (not the file name) included in the CONSTANT area. If the screen record name was six characters, K6 would be specified.
2. The output instructions on line 060 to 120 control the addition of records to the indexed file. Because the file "shell" was previously created by the BLDFILE utility, records may be loaded to the file only by adds processing. If the file was created and loaded by an RPG program, the syntax related to adds maintenance would be omitted.

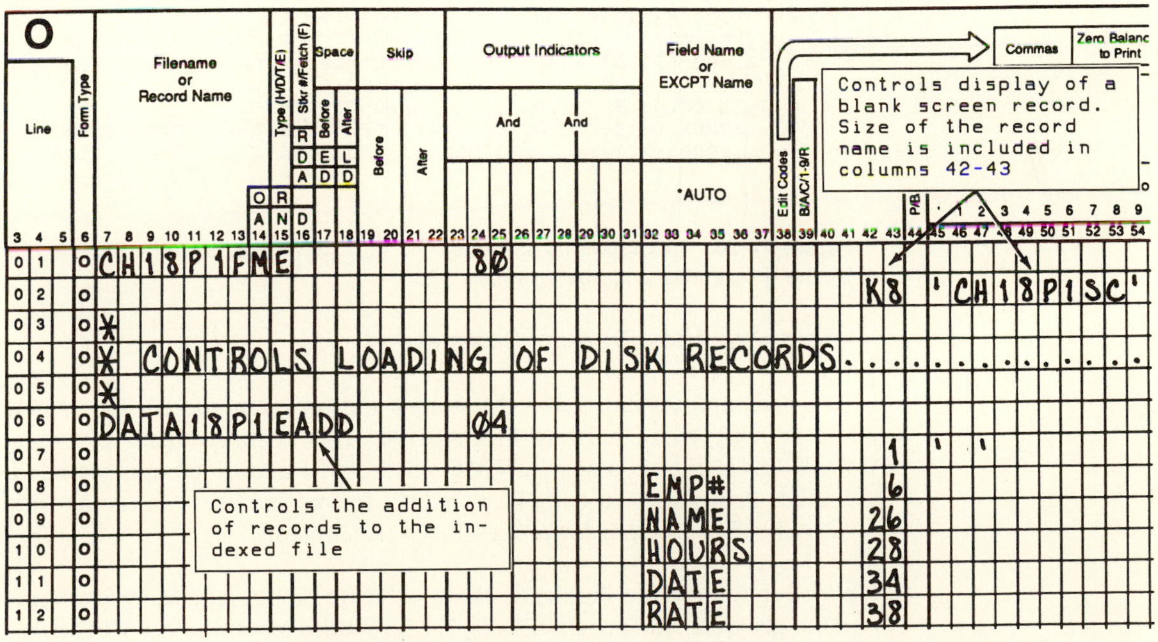

Figure 18-21 Output instructions included in the interactive indexed file adds program.

The relationship of the output coding for blank screen control and the displayed screen are shown in Figure 18-22. Until the operator presses Command Key 1 (add a record) or 7 (ends the job), the screen will be displayed.

A hexadecimal listing of the first two records added to the indexed file is illustrated in Figure 18-23.

```
... ... 1 ... ... 2 ... ... 3 ... ... 4 ... ... 5 ... ... 6 ... ... 7 ...

* DISPLAYS BLANK SCREEN (CONSTANTS & PROMPTS)..................   CH18P1
*                                                                  CH18P1
OCH18P1FME        80                                               CH18P1
O                              K8 'CH18P1SC'                       CH18P1
```

```
                     WEEKLY PAYROLL ENTRY

  EMPLOYEE NO:              EMPLOYEE NAME:

  HOURS WORKED:           PAYROLL DATE:               RATE/HR:


        CMD KEY 1 - ENTER              CMD KEY 7 - EOJ
```

Figure 18-22 Relationship of the output coding for screen control to the blank screen displayed—indexed file adds program.

```
Field legend:
               a - blank space        d - hours worked
               b - employee number    e - payroll date
               c - employee name      f - hourly rate

Ruler is supplied by utility to reference location of each character

RCDNBR  *... ... 1 ... ... 2 ... ... 3 ... ...      Alphanumeric &
                                                    unpacked numeric
   1     10000HENRY FORD          400501911200  <-- values interpreted
        4FFFFFCCDDE4CDDC4444444444FFFFFFFFFFFF  <-- Zone area
        0100008559806694000000000040050191120 0 <-- Digit area

   2     11000LOUIS CHEVROLET     350501911450
        4FFF0FDDECE4CCCEDDDCE44444FFFFFFFFFFFF      Zone area
        01100036492038559635300000350501911450      Digit area

        a  b           c            d   e     f
```

Figure 18-23 Hexadecimal listing of the first two records in the indexed file loaded by the interactive adds program.

Interactive Adds Program Summary

This program has illustrated the syntax and program control for adding records interactively to an existing indexed file. The syntax related to the coding of WORKSTN files common to IBM's System/34 and 36 computers has been discussed. Procedures to compile a display format member source and interface it with an RPG program for processing were explained.

Interactive file inquiry is the next topic discussed. Modifications required in the previous add program's display format member and the RPG program syntax to support interactive file inquiry will be identified.

APPLICATION PROGRAM—INTERACTIVE INDEXED FILE INQUIRY

The program specifications in Figure 18-24 explain the processing requirements for the interactive inquiry of the indexed file used as the data base for the program examples included in this chapter.

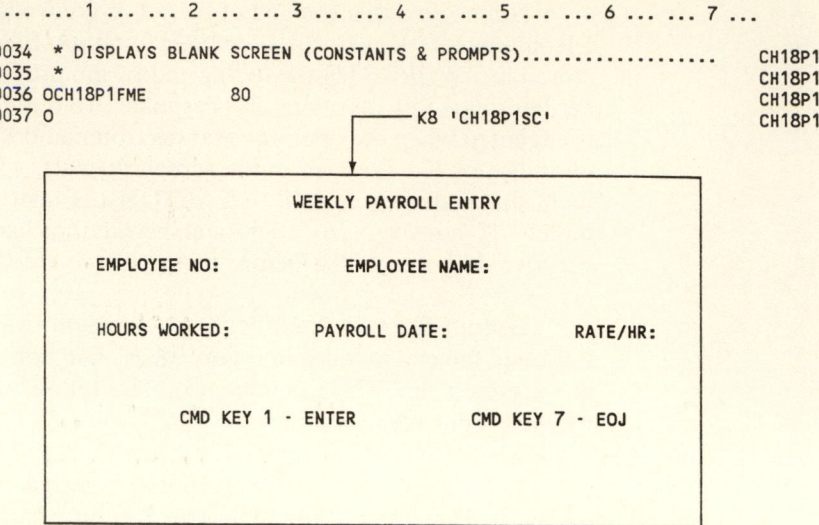

PROGRAM SPECIFICATIONS Page 1 of 1

Program Name INTERACTIVE INQUIRY Program-ID CH18P2 Written By S. Myers

Purpose Interactive inquiry of payroll file Approved By The Boss

Input files (directory names):

DATA18P1 (stored on disk)

CH18P2FM (display format member) screen record CH18P2S1

Output files (directory names):

CH18P2FM (display format member) screen record CH18P2S2

Processing Narrative:

Write an interactive RPG program to inquiry the employee weekly payroll file (DATA18P1).

Input:

Use either SEU or SDA to enter the code for a WORKSTN file (display format member) that includes the two screen formats shown in the attached CRT layout forms. The attributes are specified at the bottom of each form. Compile, debug, and test the display format member.

Processing:

Complete an RPG program that processes both screens. The first screen controls the entry of an employee number (key field) which is used in the program to CHAIN to the payroll file and access the related employee's record.

Entry of a key field value and end-of-job processing are to be controlled from the first screen. Specify Command Key 7 for end-of-job control and the ENTER key for all other processing.

Test the delete code field (position 1 in the payroll record) for the letter D. If an equal condition is tested, display the constant YES next with the prompt RECORD DELETED? in the second screen record format. If not equal to the letter D, display NO .

Output:

When a successful CHAIN is executed. display the second screen with the field values from the accessed employee's record. For an unsuccessful CHAIN, display the error message EMPLOYEE NOT FOUND! in the first screen.

Figure 18-24 Specifications for a program that controls interactive inquiry of an indexed file.

The system flowchart shown in Figure 18-25 indicates that the program controls the processing of an input screen file and an output screen file. For this program example, both screen formats are included as records in the same display format member (WORKSTN file). Hence, the names in the display symbols are screen record names and not display format member names. The record formats could have been in separate files. However, when more than one screen record is related to an application, it is common practice to include them in one display format member (WORKSTN file).

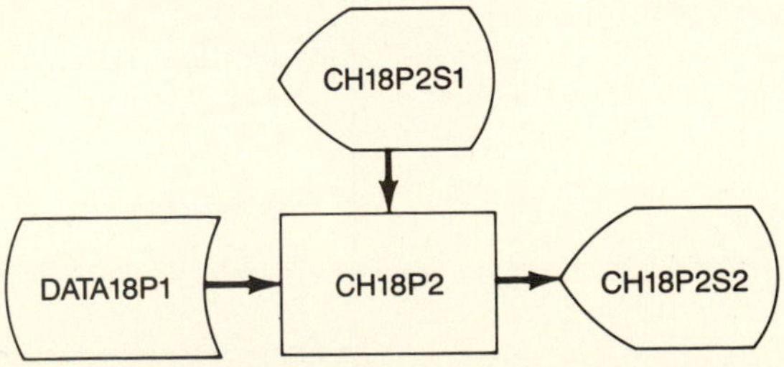

Figure 18-25 System flowchart for a program that controls interactive inquiry of an indexed file.

WORKSTN File—Interactive Inquiry Program

A display format member (WORKSTN file) includes the two screen record formats CH18P2S1 and CH18P2S2. The design and coding of each is discussed separately in the following paragraphs.

Screen Format—CH18P2S1. The format of the first screen is shown in Figure 18-26. Its function is to control the input of an employee number that is used in the RPG program to CHAIN to the indexed file and to access a related employee record. If the employee number is not found, the error message EMPLOYEE NOT FOUND! is displayed on this screen and the second screen is not processed. The notes at the bottom of Figure 18-26 specify the screen attributes and controls.

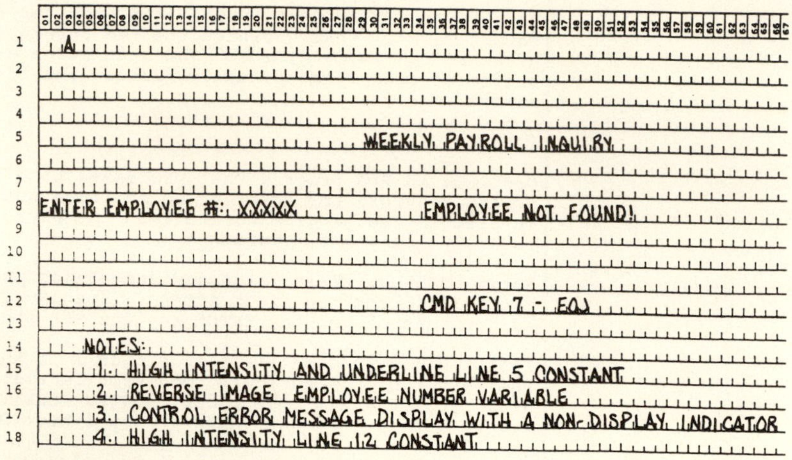
A
WEEKLY PAYROLL INQUIRY
ENTER EMPLOYEE #: XXXXX
EMPLOYEE NOT FOUND!
CMD KEY 7 - EOJ
NOTES:
1. HIGH INTENSITY AND UNDERLINE LINE 5 CONSTANT
2. REVERSE IMAGE EMPLOYEE NUMBER VARIABLE
3. CONTROL ERROR MESSAGE DISPLAY WITH A NON-DISPLAY INDICATOR
4. HIGH INTENSITY LINE 12 CONSTANT

Figure 18-26 WORKSTN file CH18P2FM screen layout CH18P2S1 for interactive inquiry program.

A printout of the actual screen when an EMPLOYEE # is entered but before the ENTER key is pressed is shown in Figure 18-27. A screen display is also included in the same figure to illustrate the result when the entered EMPLOYEE # is not found in the indexed file.

```
Blank Screen Display (before EMPLOYEE # is entered):

                              WEEKLY PAYROLL INQUIRY

ENTER EMPLOYEE #:

                                 CMD KEY 7 - EOJ

Screen Display (after an invalid EMPLOYEE # is entered):

                              WEEKLY PAYROLL INQUIRY

ENTER EMPLOYEE #: 12345          EMPLOYEE NOT FOUND!

                                 CMD KEY 7 - EOJ
```

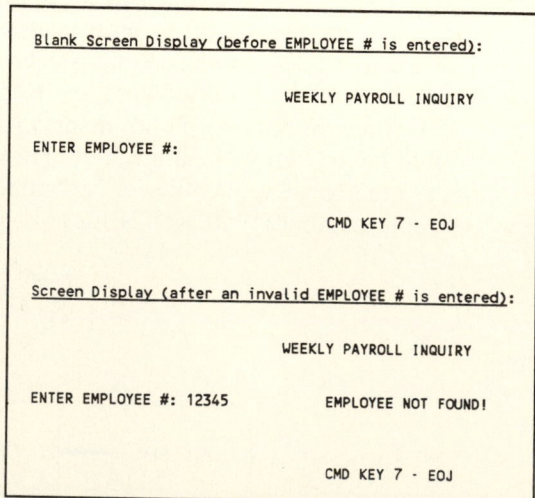

Figure 18-27 Example displays of the first screen (CH18P2S1) included in the interactive inquiry program.

The coding for the first screen (CH18P2S1) including the display format member CH18P2FM is presented in the Display Screen Format Specifications form in Figure 18-28. A detailed explanation of each coding line is also included.

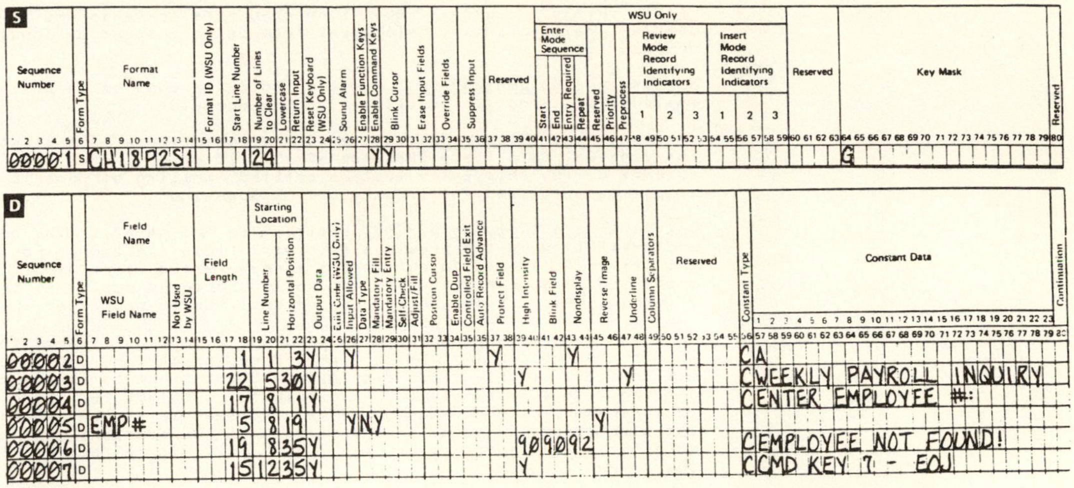

S Section

Sequence Number

00001 Format Name (Columns 7-14): Programmer-supplied screen record name (more than one screen format (record) may be included in a screen file) is entered in this field. Name may be eight characters and must begin with an alphabetic character. Screen record name for this application is CH18P2S1.

Start Line Number (Columns 17-18): Specifies the CRT line where the screen format will begin to display. The 01 entry indicates that the screen will display beginning on line 1.

Number of Lines to Clear (Columns 19-20): Provides for the "clearing" of the screen before output. The 24 entered indicates that all 24 lines on the CRT will be cleared before the screen is displayed. For applications in which two screens are displayed at one time, a number smaller than 24 must be specified for the second screen.

Enable Command Keys (Column 28): Letter Y indicates that Command Keys specified in the Key Mask (Columns 64-79) are to be "enabled" (made functional) for screen to program control. Command Keys relate to indicators. For example, Command Key KA turns on indicator 01; KB, indicator 02, and so forth. Depending on the terminal design, Command Keys may be included in a top row of keys on the keyboard, or a Command Key and associated number key must both be pressed. For this screen record, Command Key G, for KG (indicator 07) is "enabled".

Blink Cursor (Column 29-30): Letter Y indicates that cursor will blink at the first prompt position when screen is displayed.

Key Mask (Columns 64-79): Letter G indicates that Command Key KG is to be "enabled" (functional) for screen to program control. Any of the available 25 Command Keys (KO is not supported) may be used. A company's programming standards may determine which Command Keys are to be used for specific controls. For this application, KG controls end of job processing.

D Section

Sequence Number

00002 Field Length (Columns 15-18): Defines the length of the field specified in columns 7-12 or the constant entered in columns 57-79. The 1 entry indicates the size of the constant specified in column 57.

Starting Location-Line Number (Columns 19-20): Refers to the line number on which the field or constant entry is to be entered. 1 indicates that the letter A is to be entered on line 1 of the screen record.

Starting Location-Horizontal Position (Columns 21-22): Specifies the column in which the field value or constant is to begin. 3 indicates that the constant A is to be entered in column 3. This entry and the Line Number entry above indicate that the constant A is to be entered on line 1 column 3

Output Data (Columns 23-24): Letter Y in this field allows the field value or constant to be displayed on the screen. For this example screen, the constant A will be output.

Figure 18-28 Completed Display Screen Format Specifications for the first screen record for the interactive inquiry program.

Input Allowed (Column 26): Y in this field allows variable data or constants to be input from the screen record to the RPG program. Note that the constant A will be passed to the RPG program and defined as a Record Identification Code to determine which screen record is currently processed. Any character or characters may be used to code the screen record.

Protect Field (Columns 37-38): Y entered here prevents the field value or constant defined in this statement from being changed by input or output processing.

Nondisplay (Columns 43-44): Y entry indicates that value defined in this instruction is not to be visible to the operator.

Constant Type (Column 56): Letter C indicates there is a constant entered in the Constant Data field (Columns 57-79). If an edit code was specified in columns 57-79, this entry must be omitted. Editing of numeric fields is sometimes specified for inquiry only processing.

Constant Data (Columns 57-79): Letter A in column 57 is the constant defined and controlled by the previous entries in this statement. For this example, the letter A is used to define the screen record. Input from the CRT is processed as a record and the controlling program must test this code to determine which screen record is currently being processed.

00003 Follows the same coding logic as sequence line 00002 except the constant, WEEKLY PAYROLL INQUIRY, is 22 long and begins on line 5 column 30. Because the constant is only to be displayed and not input to the program, it is defined with a Y in column 23 and nothing in column 26. The Y in column 39 indicates that the constant will be displayed in a high intensity mode and the Y in column 47 supports underlining of the constant when it is displayed. Note that high intensity or underlining will not be included in a printout of the screen image.

00004 Same coding logic for the constant on sequence line 00003 except that high intensity and underlining are not specified.

00005 Field Name (Columns 7-12): EMP# is a programmer-supplied variable field name used to transfer data from the screen to the RPG program or from the program to the screen. The field size and location in the screen record will be identified in the input and output buffers that are automatically built when the screen is successfully compiled. How these buffers are used will be discussed later.

When the screen record is displayed, the reverse image option specified with this statement will identify the size of the EMP# field.

Field Length (Columns 15-18): Defines the length of the field specified in columns 7-12. 5 indicates that EMP# is 5 bytes.

Line Number (Columns 19-20): 8 indicates the field value is to be displayed on line 8.

Horizontal Position (Columns 21-22): Entry indicates that field value will be displayed beginning in column 19.

Output Data (Columns 23-24): Not used for variables that are only input from the screen to the RPG program.

Input Allowed (Column 26): Y entry supports input from the screen to the program.

Data Type (Column 27): Letter N indicates screen input/output field (EMP#) is defined as numeric. On input, any attempt to enter a nonnumeric character will result in a buzzer sound and the cursor will not advance to the next prompt.

Mandatory Fill (Column 28): Y entry in this field requires that all of the field positions must be filled with data before the cursor will advance to the next prompt.

Reverse Image (Columns 45-46): Y entry in this field causes the field area to display in a reverse image (light background with black letter on a monochrome CRT)

00006 The constant EMPLOYEE NOT FOUND! is displayed on line 8 beginning in column 35 when a successful CHAIN is not completed to the indexed file. Indicators 90 and 92 control how and when the constant will be displayed. When indicator 92 is turned off (because of an unsuccessful CHAIN) in the program, the error message will be displayed. In addition, indicator 90 is turned on which causes the error message to be displayed in a high intensity and blinking image.

00007 Except for line number, column position, and underline control, this instruction follows the same coding logic as sequence line 00003.

(*Continued*)

A listing of the screen record CH18P2S1 generated by compilation of the display format member CH18P2FM is shown in Figure 18-29. Notice that the all-inclusive screen file (CH18P2FM) is compiled and not all of the record formats that may be included in the structure.

```
....+....1....+....2....+....3....+....4....+....5....+....6....+....7....+....8

 SCH18P2S1   124        YY                                  G
 D            1 1 3Y  Y            Y     Y             CA
 D           22 530Y                 Y         Y       CWEEKLY PAYROLL INQUIRY
 D           17 8 1Y                                   CENTER EMPLOYEE #:
 DEMP#        5 819    YNY                      Y
 D           19 835Y                 909092            CEMPLOYEE NOT FOUND!
 D           151235Y                 Y                 CCMD KEY 7 - EOJ

INPUT BUFFER DESCRIPTION
FIELD NAME    LENGTH      START       END

                 1           1          1
 EMP#            5           2          6

INDICATORS USED

 90 92
```

<u>Section A</u>

The source listing of the display format member in the same format as the Screen Specifications Form. Relative position of each entry is referenced by the ruler included at the top of the listing. Compile time terminal and warning errors will be included in the body of the listing.

<u>Section B</u>

The section entitled, INPUT BUFFER DESCRIPTION, specifies the location of the input fields *(from screen to program)* in the INPUT BUFFER created in the compilation process. The exact location of each field is included in the Input Specifications of the related RPG program so that data may be passed from the display format member (input) to the program for processing.

Because this application includes only the input of data, no OUTPUT BUFFER is included. The second screen (CH18P2S2) for this inquiry program will require only an OUTPUT BUFFER and no input.

Figure 18-29 Display format member (CH18P1FM) listing of the CH18P2P1 screen record format—inquiry program.

Screen Format CH18P2S2—Inquiry Program. The design of the second screen included in the display format member CH18P2FM is presented in Figure 18-30. Only when the employee number value, entered in the first screen, executes a successful CHAIN to the indexed file is this screen format displayed.

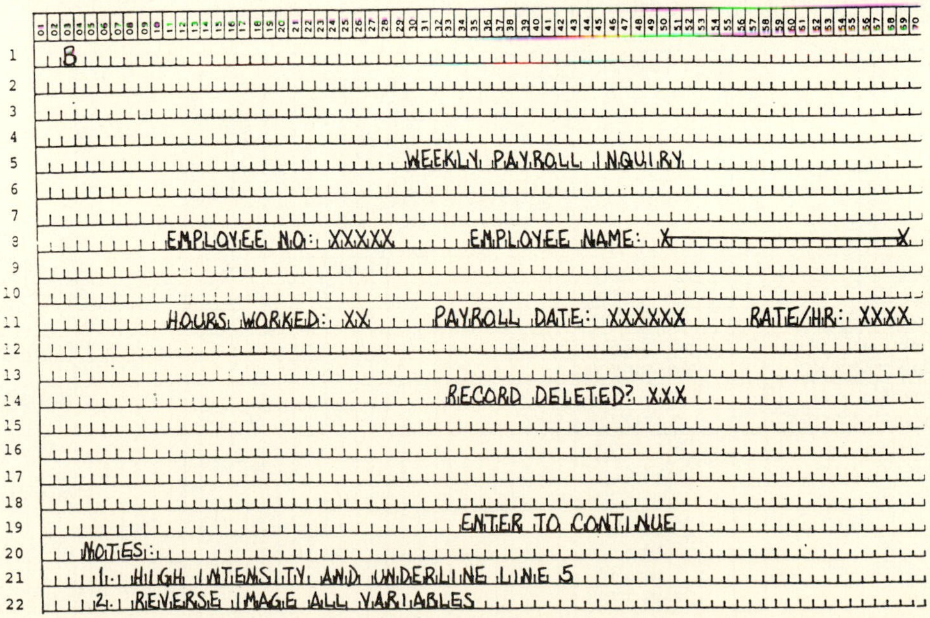

Figure 18-30 WORKSTN file CH18P2FM screen layout CH18P2S2 for interactive inquiry program.

A display of the screen record CH18P2S2 after a successful CHAIN (employee number found) is executed to the indexed file is shown in Figure 18-31. The variable field values are accessed from the indexed file's related record.

```
                         WEEKLY PAYROLL INQUIRY

        EMPLOYEE NO: 10000        EMPLOYEE NAME: HENRY FORD

        HOURS WORKED: 40      PAYROLL DATE: 050191      RATE/HR: 1200

                           RECORD DELETED? NO



                           ENTER TO CONTINUE
```

Figure 18-31 Display of the second screen (CH18P2S2) after a successful CHAIN is executed to the indexed file—inquiry program.

The coding for the second screen (CH18P2S2) is included in the display Screen Format Specifications shown in Figure 18-32. Because the entries follow the same syntax included in the screens explained in Figures 18-9 and 18-28, a line-by-line explanation is omitted. However, do notice that the variable field names are now specified as Output Data (Y in column 23) instead of as Input Allowed (Y in column 26).

Sequence Number (1–5)	Form Type (6)	Format Name (7–14)	Start Line Number (17–18)	Number of Lines to Clear (19–20)	Enable Function Keys (27)	Enable Command Keys (28)	Key Mask (57–)
ØØØØ1	S	CH18P2S2	1	24	Y	Y	A

Sequence Number (1–5)	Form Type (6)	Field Name (7–14)	Field Length (15–18)	Line Number (19–20)	Horizontal Position (21–22)	Output Data (23)	Input Allowed (26)	Protect Field (37)	High Intensity (39)	Nondisplay (43)	Reverse Image (45)	Underline (47)	Constant Type (56)	Constant Data (57–)
ØØØØ2	D		1	1	3	Y	Y	Y		Y			C	B
ØØØØ3	D		22	5	30	Y			Y			Y	C	WEEKLY PAYROLL INQUIRY
ØØØØ4	D		12	8	11	Y							C	EMPLOYEE NO:
ØØØØ5	D	EMP#	5	8	24	Y					Y			
ØØØØ6	D		14	8	35	Y							C	EMPLOYEE NAME:
ØØØØ7	D	NAME	2Ø	8	5Ø	Y					Y			
ØØØØ8	D		13	11	11	Y							C	HOURS WORKED:
ØØØØ9	D	HOURS	2	11	25	Y					Y			
ØØØ1Ø	D		13	11	32	Y							C	PAYROLL DATE:
ØØØ11	D	DATE	6	11	46	Y					Y			
ØØØ12	D		8	11	57	Y							C	RATE/HR:
ØØØ13	D	RATE	4	11	66	Y					Y			
ØØØ14	D		15	14	33	Y							C	RECORD DELETED?
ØØØ15	D	STATUS	3	14	49	Y					Y			
ØØØ16	D		17	19	33	Y							C	ENTER TO CONTINUE

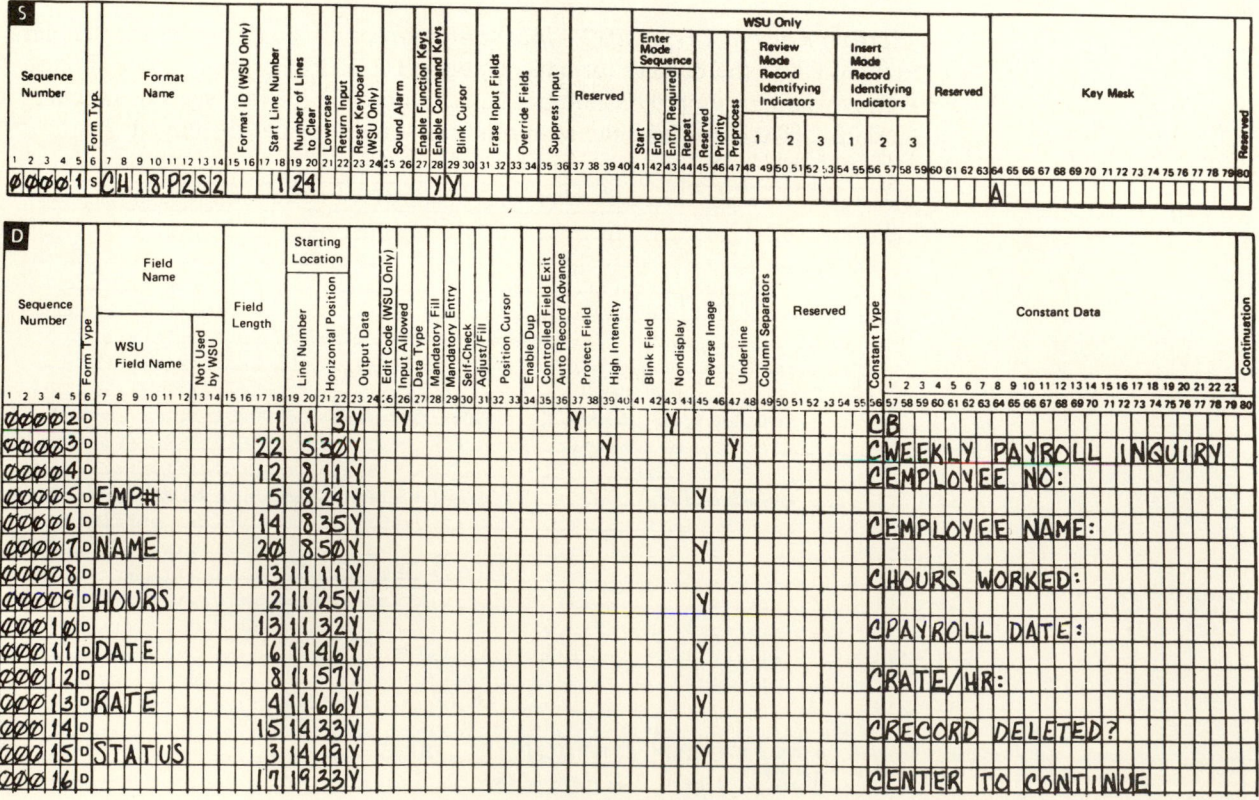

Figure 18-32 Completed Display Screen Format Specifications for the second screen record CH18P2S2—inquiry program.

The data (employee number) for the first screen in this display format member is input from the CRT to the program and, therefore, is defined as Input Allowed (Y in column 26). Data in the second screen is output from the program to the CRT and does not provide for input. Inquiry processing should not include the option to make changes to field values.

A compilation listing of the screen record CH18P2S2 is shown in Figure 18-33. Notice that an Output Buffer Description is included in the listing. This section was generated by defining the fields (i.e., EMP#, DNAME, DHOURS, DATE, RATE, and STATUS) included in the screen record as Output Data (Y in column 23). The length and end position of each field are referenced in the RPG program that processes the screen record. Because the screen's identification code (letter B) is defined as Input Allowed (Y in column 26), an INPUT BUFFER DESCRIPTION is also created.

```
....+....1....+....2....+....3....+....4....+....5....+....6....+....7....+....8

SCH18P2S2   124        YY                                    A
D             1 1 3Y  Y          Y     Y                     CB
D            22 530Y                  Y       Y              CWEEKLY PAYROLL INQUIRY
D            12 811Y                                         CEMPLOYEE NO:
DEMP#         5 824Y                        Y
D            14 835Y                                         CEMPLOYEE NAME:
DNAME        20 850Y                        Y
D            131111Y                                         CHOURS WORKED:
DHOURS        21125Y                        Y
D            131132Y                                         CPAYROLL DATE:
DDATE         61146Y                        Y
D             81157Y                                         CRATE/HR:
DRATE         41166Y                        Y
D            151433Y                                         CRECORD DELETED?
DSTATUS       31449Y                        Y
D            171933Y                                         CENTER TO CONTINUE

EXECUTION TIME OUTPUT BUFFER DESCRIPTION
FIELD NAME     LENGTH       START        END

  EMP#            5           1           5
  NAME           20           6          25
  HOURS           2          26          27
  DATE            6          28          33
  RATE            4          34          37
  STATUS          3          38          40

INPUT BUFFER DESCRIPTION
FIELD NAME     LENGTH       START        END

                  1           1           1

  No Observation Errors
  No Warning Errors
  No Fatal Errors
```

Figure 18-33 Display format member (CH18P1FM) listing of the CH18P2P2 screen record format—inquiry program.

The structure of the OUTPUT BUFFER DESCRIPTION for the CH18P2S2 screen record generated when the display format member is successfully compiled is presented in Figure 18-34.

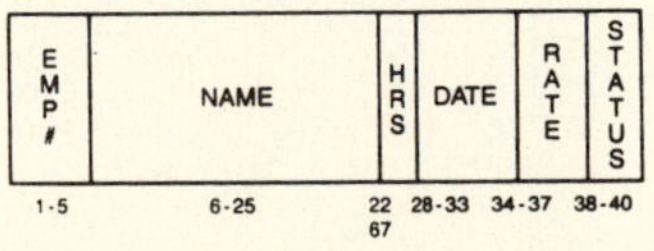

Note: The END position in the OUTPUT BUFFER is specified in the Output Specifications in the RPG program to store value in the related buffer area for display. Field names in the program do not have to be the same as those in the display format member.

Figure 18-34 Structure of the Output Buffer area for the CH18P2S2 screen record format—inquiry program.

Source Program Coding—Interactive Inquiry Program

The file processing logic controlled by the interactive RPG inquiry program is detailed in Figure 18-35.

1. When the program is executed, the first screen is displayed. Operator enters an EMP# and presses ENTER.

2. Indexed file is CHAINed to by EMP#.

3. If the EMP# is not found, a screen defined error message is displayed in the first screen (CH18P2S1).

4. If the EMP# is found, the second screen is displayed with the indexed record's field values.

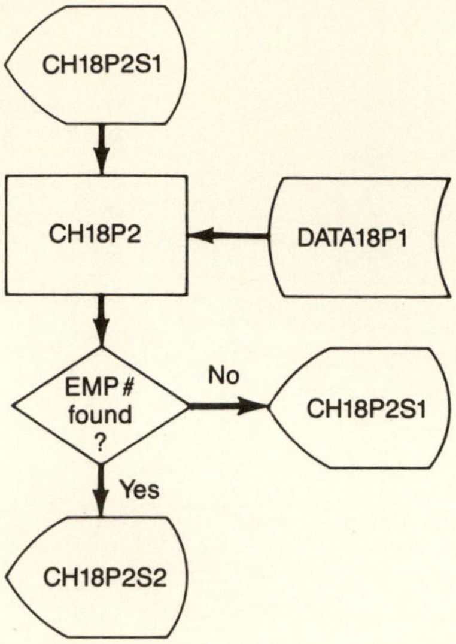

Figure 18-35 Processing logic controlled by the interactive inquiry program.

A source listing of the interactive inquiry program is presented in Figure 18-36.

The instructions included in each of the specification types are explained in the following paragraphs.

```
... ... 1 ... ... 2 ... ... 3 ... ... 4 ... ... 5 ... ... 6 ... ... 7 ...
H                                                                   CH18P2
 *                                                                  CH18P2
 * THIS PROGRAM INQUIRIES AN INDEXED FILE INTERACTIVELY..........   CH18P2
 * SYSTEM/36 & 34 ENVIRONMENTS...................................   CH18P2
 *                                                                  CH18P2
FCH18P2FMCD  F  81  81           WORKSTN                            CH18P2
FDATA18P1IC  F  38  38R 5AI     2 DISK                              CH18P2
 *                                                                  CH18P2
 * INPUT DEFINITION OF THE 1ST & 2ND SCREEN FORMATS.  BECAUSE 2ND   CH18P2
 * SCREEN IS DEFINED WITH OUTPUT ONLY FIELDS, NO INPUT FIELDS ARE   CH18P2
 * DEFINED.......................................................   CH18P2
ICH18P2FMSM  01   1 CA                                              CH18P2
I                                        2   60EMP#                 CH18P2
I           SM  03   1 CB                                           CH18P2
IDATA18P1SM  02                                                     CH18P2
I                                        1    1 DCODE               CH18P2
I                                        2   60EMP#                 CH18P2
I                                        7   26 NAME                CH18P2
I                                       27  280HOURS                CH18P2
I                                       29  340DATE                 CH18P2
I                                       35  382RATE                 CH18P2
C                     SETON                     92    NON-DISP MSG  CH18P2
C           AGAIN     TAG                                           CH18P2
 *                                                                  CH18P2
C                     SETON                     80    1ST SCRN INDR. CH18P2
C                     EXCPT                           DISP 1ST SCREENCH18P2
C                     SETOF                     80    OFF 1ST SCRN INCH18P2
 *                                                                  CH18P2
C                     READ CH18P2FM                   READ 1ST SCREENCH18P2
C   KG                GOTO EOJ                        EOJ?          CH18P2
C           EMP#      CHAINDATA18P1             90    GET DISK RECORDCH18P2
C   90                SETOF                     92    DISP ERROR MSG CH18P2
 *                                                                  CH18P2
C  N90                EXSR PROCES                     2ND SCRN SR   CH18P2
C                     GOTO AGAIN                      GET 1ST SCRN  CH18P2
C           EOJ       TAG                                           CH18P2
C                     SETON                     LR    END JOB       CH18P2
```

Figure 18-36 Source listing of the interactive inquiry program.

```
C           PROCES    BEGSR                                        CH18P2
C                     SETON                        92    STOPS MSG DISP CH18P2
C           DCODE     COMP 'D'                       91DELETE TEST    CH18P2
C   91                MOVE 'YES'     STATUS  3       RECORD DELETED CH18P2
C  N91                MOVE 'NO '     STATUS          NOT DELETED    CH18P2
 *                                                                  CH18P2
C                     SETON                        04    2ND SCRN INDR  CH18P2
C                     EXCPT                              DISP 2ND SCREENCH18P2
C                     SETOF                        04    SETOF 2ND SCRN CH18P2
 *                                                                  CH18P2
C                     READ CH18P2FM                      HOLDS 2ND SCRN CH18P2
C                     ENDSR                                         CH18P2
 *                                                                  CH18P2
 * DISPLAY 1ST SCREEN FOR EMP# ENTRY............................    CH18P2
 *                                                                  CH18P2
OCH18P2FME        80                                                CH18P2
O                                  K8 'CH18P2S1'                    CH18P2
 * DISPLAY FILLED-IN INQUIRY (2ND) SCREEN.......................    CH18P2
 *                                                                  CH18P2
OCH18P2FME        04                                                CH18P2
O                                  K8 'CH18P2S2'                    CH18P2
O                        EMP#       5                               CH18P2
O                        NAME      25                               CH18P2
O                        HOURS     27                               CH18P2
O                        DATE      33                               CH18P2
O                        RATE      37                               CH18P2
O                        STATUS    40                               CH18P2
```

(*Continued*)

File Description Specifications—Interactive Inquiry Program. The File Description Specifications coding for the interactive inquiry program is explained in Figure 18-37.

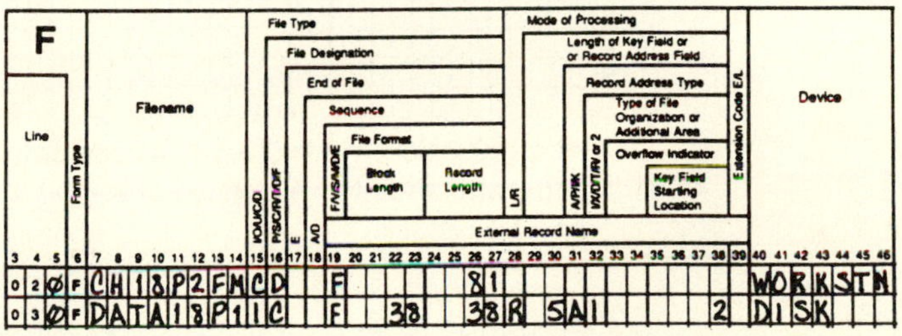

<u>Coding for WORKSTN file:</u>

<u>*Line 020:*</u>

Filename (cols 7-14)	Name of the display format member (file) must be entered in this field.
File Type (col 15)	C, for *Combined file* (both input and output), must be specified in this field for WORKSTN files.
File Designation (col 16)	P (primary) or D (demand) must be entered in this field. If this field contains a P, the WORKSTN file is automatically read during input time of the RPG program cycle. If a WORKSTN file is defined as primary, no secondary (S) files may be specified in the program. D defines the file as a demand file by which the records are read during calculations by one of the READ operations. Record identifying indicators are not automatically set off in demand file processing.
File Format (col 19)	Must include an F to indicate that all of the records from the WORKSTN file have all the same length.
Block Length (cols 20-23)	Must be blank.
Record Length (cols 24-27)	Must include the length of the longest record in the display format member.
Device (cols 40-46)	Must contain the device name WORKSTN.

<u>Coding for Indexed file:</u>

<u>*Line 030:*</u>

File Type (col 15)	I entry indicates the file is to be processed as input.
File Designation (col 16)	C entry indicates the file is to be processed as a CHAINED file.

Mode of Processing R entry indicates the file is to be random processed

See Chapter 15 for an explanation of the entries that define the attributes of an indexed file

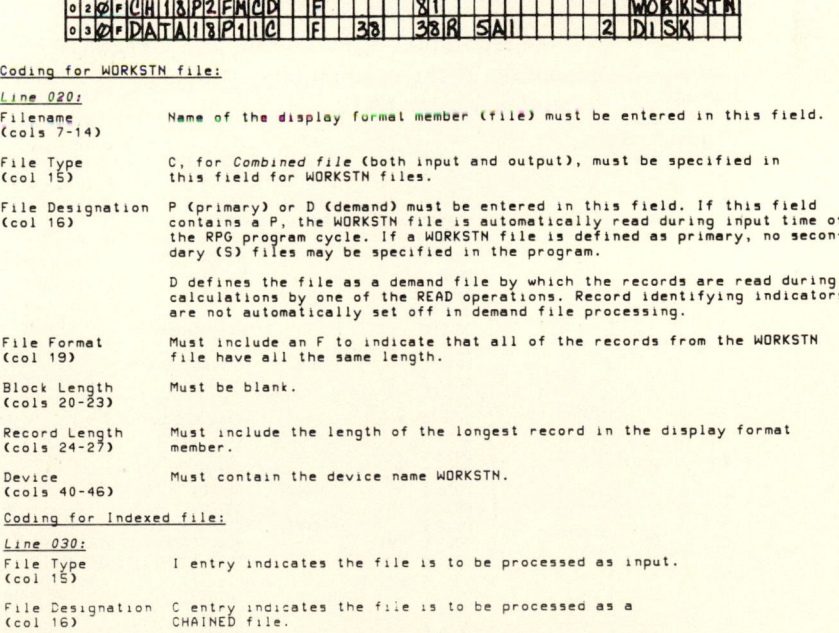

Figure 18-37 File Description coding for the interactive inquiry program.

Input Specifications—Interactive Inquiry Program. The relationship of the first screen record processed by the interactive inquiry program to the input coding is detailed in Figure 18-38. Remember that the first screen includes only one input field (EMP#) and the identification code (A). The record code (B) for the second screen, which is displayed when the related employee number record is found in the indexed file, is also defined. However, because the second screen's fields are defined as output only, they are not specified on input. Also included in the input coding is the definition of the indexed file record format.

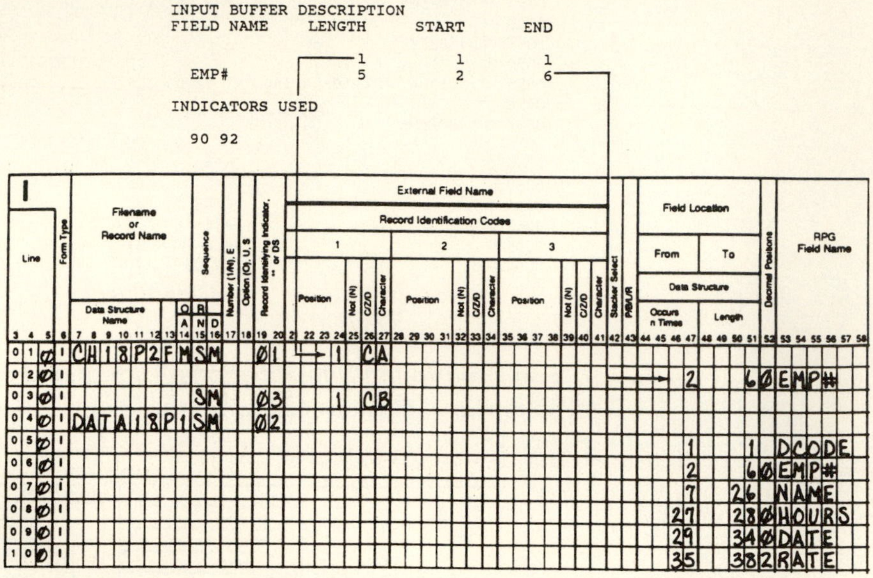

Figure 18-38 Input Specifications coding for the interactive inquiry program and its relationship to the INPUT BUFFER for the first screen record.

Calculation Specifications—Interactive Inquiry Program. A detailed explanation of the calculations included in the interactive inquiry program is presented in Figure 18-39.

```
... ... 1 ... ... 2 ... ... 3 ... ... 4 ... ... 5 ... ... 6 ... ... 7 ...
C                   SETON                     92   NON-DISP MSG   CH18P2
C          AGAIN    TAG                                           CH18P2
*                                                                 CH18P2
C                   SETON                     80   1ST SCRN INDR. CH18P2
C                   EXCPT                          DISP 1ST SCREENCH18P2
C                   SETOF                     80   OFF 1ST SCRN INCH18P2
*                                                                 CH18P2
C                   READ CH18P2FM                  READ 1ST SCREENCH18P2
C   KG              GOTO EOJ                       EOJ?           CH18P2
C          EMP#     CHAINDATA18P1             90   GET DISK RECORDCH18P2
C   90              SETOF                     92   DISP ERROR MSG CH18P2
*                                                                 CH18P2
C  N90              EXSR PROCES                    2ND SCRN SR    CH18P2
C                   GOTO AGAIN                     GET 1ST SCRN   CH18P2
C          EOJ      TAG                                           CH18P2
C                   SETON                     LR   END JOB        CH18P2
C          PROCES   BEGSR                                         CH18P2
C                   SETON                     92   STOPS MSG DISP CH18P2
C          DCODE    COMP 'D'                     91DELETE TEST    CH18P2
C   91              MOVE 'YES'     STATUS  3       RECORD DELETED CH18P2
C  N91              MOVE 'NO '     STATUS          NOT DELETED    CH18P2
*                                                                 CH18P2
C                   SETON                     04   2ND SCRN INDR  CH18P2
C                   EXCPT                          DISP 2ND SCREENCH18P2
C                   SETOF                     04   SETOF 2ND SCRN CH18P2
*                                                                 CH18P2
C                   READ CH18P2FM                  HOLDS 2ND SCRN CH18P2
C                   ENDSR                                         CH18P2
```

Figure 18-39 Calculation Specifications coding for the interactive inquiry program.

Line No.

0022 Indicator 92, which was specified in the first screen record to control the nondisplay of the error message (refer to Figure 18-27, line 00006, columns 43-44), is turned on so that the error message will not display when the screen appears on the CRT.

0023 Entry for GOTO statement on line 0035 which controls subsequent displays of the first screen (CH18P2S1) for entry of an employee number or end of job response.

0025 Indicator 80 is turned on which controls ouput of the first prompt screen for input of an employee number and, if the employee number is not found in the indexed file, an error message.

0026 This EXCPT operation transfers control to an exception type output record (E in column 15) conditioned by the 80 indicator. Output lines 0053 and 0054 are executed by this statement which causes the screen record CH18P2S1 to be displayed for entry of an employee number or end of job response. CH18P2S1 is one of the two record formats defined in the display format member CH18P2FM.

0027 This SETOF operation turns off the 80 indicator to prevent the output instructions conditioned with that indicator from being executed when the next EXCPT instruction (line 0045) is executed.

0029 After the operator responds to the first screen's prompt (enters an employee number), the READ operation reads the variable data and tests the status (on or off) of the command key KG.

0030 If Comamnd Key 7 is pressed, the KG indicator is turned on and a branch is executed which controls end of job (LR) processing (lines 36 and 37).

0031 If ENTER is pressed (instead of Command Key 7), the EMP# entered from the first screen (CH18P2S1) is included in a CHAIN instruction which randomly searches the indexed file for an equal key value.

0032 If the CHAIN instruction is not successful (indicator 90 turned on), indicator 92 which was specified in the screen coding to prevent the constant EMPLOYEE NOT FOUND! from always being displayed, is turned off. This instruction causes the error message to be displayed when an employee number is not found in the indexed file.

0034 If an employee number is found in the indexed file, this instruction transfers control to the internal subroutine PROCES on line 0038.

0035 After the internal subroutine is executed, the GOTO statement transfer control to line 0023 which repeats the instructions that redisplay the first screen for entry of an employee number or end of job response.

0036 Entry for the GOTO statement line 30 which is executed if the operator pressed Command Key 7 (turned on indicator KG) to pass control to the instruction on line 0037 to end the job.

0037 SETON operation turns on the LR indicator to end the job and return control back to the operating system.

0038 Entry for the EXSR PROCES statement on line 0034.

0039 Stops any previous error message display in the first screen.

0040 COMP operation tests the value of the delete code field in the related indexed file record.

0041 If the delete code field value is a D, indicator 91 included in the previous instruction is turned on and the constant YES is moved to a field (STATUS) in the second screen (CH18P2S2).

0042 If the delete code field value is not a D, indicator 91 is not turned on in the COMP instruction on line 40 and the constant NO is moved to the STATUS field in the second screen (CH18P2S2).

0044 Indicator 04 is SETON to condition the exception output instructions on lines 0057-0064 which controls display of the second screen "filled-in" with data.

0045 EXCPT operation controls exception type output on lines 0057 through 0064 which displays the "filled-in" second screen (CH18P2S2).

0046 Indicator 04 is SETOF to prevent this exception type output from executing when the EXCPT operation on line 026 is executed after a loop occurs for a redisplay of the first screen.

0048 This READ operation holds the display of the second screen until the operator presses the ENTER key. Without this statement, the second screen display format would flash on the CRT and not hold for examination.

0049 Indicates the end of the internal subroutine.

(*Continued*)

Output Specifications—Interactive Inquiry Program. The relationship of the Outpuut Specifications coding and the second screen's output buffer are shown in Figure 18-40. Recall that the second screen (CH18P2S2) was coded to control the output of both constants and variables. Consequently, the fields from an indexed file record are defined on input with the field names included in the screen record format. When an indexed file record is found, the values are automatically passed from the file to the screen. On the other hand, if the field names included in the screen record were not used to define the indexed file records, MOVE operations would have to be included to move the data from the disk record to the related screen fields for display.

```
EXECUTION TIME OUTPUT BUFFER DESCRIPTION
FIELD NAME     LENGTH      START       END

  EMP#              5          1         5
  NAME             20          6        25
  HOURS             2         26        27
  DATE              6         28        33
  RATE              4         34        37
  STATUS            3         38        40

CH18P2S2 (second screen) output coding:

 ... ... 1 ... ... 2 ... ... 3 ... ... 4 ... ... 5 ... ... 6 ... ... 7

0057 OCH18P2FME         04
0058 O                                   K8 'CH18P2S2'
0059 O                          EMP#      5
0060 O                          NAME     25
0061 O                          HOURS    27
0062 O                          DATE     33
0063 O                          RATE     37
0064 O                          STATUS   40
```

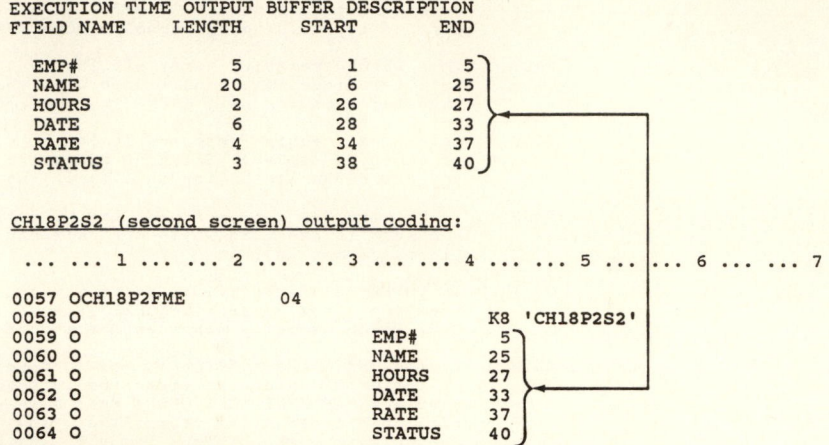

Figure 18-40 Output Specifications coding for the interactive inquiry program and its relationship to the OUTPUT BUFFER for the second screen record.

A program that controls interactive update of an indexed file is presented next. Because the screen formats and RPG program control are almost identical to the inquiry program, only the modifications will be detailed.

APPLICATION PROGRAM—INTERACTIVE INDEXED FILE UPDATE

The specifications in Figure 18-41 explain the processing requirements for a program that updates an indexed file interactively.

PROGRAM SPECIFICATIONS Page 1 of 1

Program Name PAYROLL FILE UPDATE Program-ID CH18P3 Written By S. Myers

Purpose Interactive update of payroll file Approved By The Boss

Input files (directory names):

DATA18P1 (stored in disk)

CH18P3FM (display format member) screen records CH18P3S1 & CH18P3S2

Output files (directory names):

CH18P3FM (display format member) screen record CH18P3S2

DATA18P1 (stored on disk)

Processing Narrative:

Write an interactive RPG program to update the payroll file.

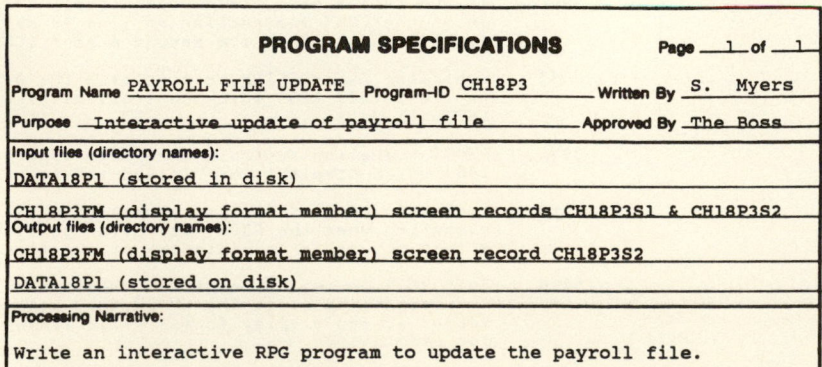

Figure 18-41 Specifications for a program that controls the interactive update of an indexed file.

```
Input:

Using either SEU or SDA, enter the coding for a WORKSTN file (dis-
play format member) that includes the two screen formats shown in
the attached CRT layout forms.  The attributes are specified at
the bottom of each from.  Compile, debug, and test the display for-
mat member.

Processing:

Complete an RPG program that processes both screen formats.  The
first screen controls the entry of an employee number (key field)
which is used in the program to CHAIN to the indexed file to access
the related employee's record.  The second screen format, which is
to override the first, is displayed when a successful CHAIN is ex-
ecuted.  If the CHAIN is not successful (an employee number not
found in the file), an error message is to be displayed in the
first screen.

To prevent modifying the EMPLOYEE NO value in the second screen,
control the cursor in the second screen so that it positions at
the EMPLOYEE NAME prompt and not the EMPLOYEE NO.  With the ex-
ception of EMPLOYEE NO, any other field in the second screen may
be updated.

Records are to be tagged for deletion by entering a letter D for
the DELETE CODE prompt.

In the second screen, update and delete processing is to be control-
led by the ENTER key.  Also, specify Command Key 1 to allow the
operator to ignore any response to the second screen and prevent
file update.  Under both conditions, control is to return to the
first screen for an end-of-job or an employee number entry response.
In the coding of first screen, specify Command Key 7 to end the
job.
```

(Continued)

The system flowchart shown in Figure 18-42 indicates that the update program controls the processing of an input screen file and an output screen file. However, because there is only one screen format member (file) with two screen records, the record names are specified in the display symbols instead of the file name. The double-headed arrowed line connecting the program and the disk file indicates that it is an input-output file. Also, because the second screen format outputs and inputs data to the program, it is referenced with a double-headed arrowed line.

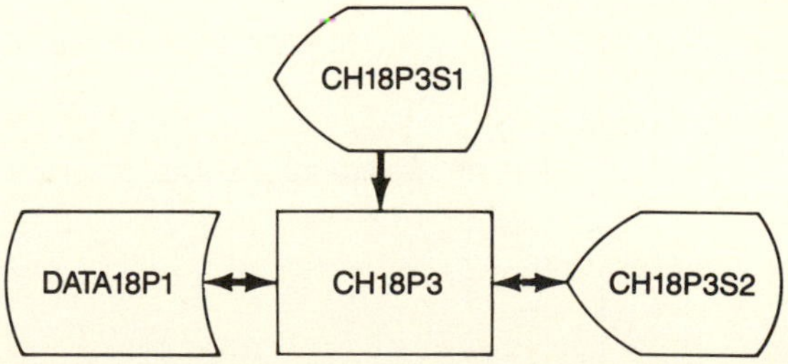

Figure 18-42 System flowchart for a program that controls interactive update of an indexed file.

WORKSTN File—Interactive Update Program

The display format member CH18P3FM includes two screen formats—CH18P3S1 and CH18P2S2. The attributes of each are discussed in the following sections.

Screen Format—CH18P3S1. The format of the first screen is shown in Figure 18-43. Its function is to control the input of an employee number that is used in the RPG program to CHAIN to the index file and access the related employee record. The error message, EMPLOYEE NOT FOUND!, is also included in the coding to identify an employee number that is not found in the index file. Included at the bottom of the form in Figure 18-43 are the supplemental screen attributes and controls.

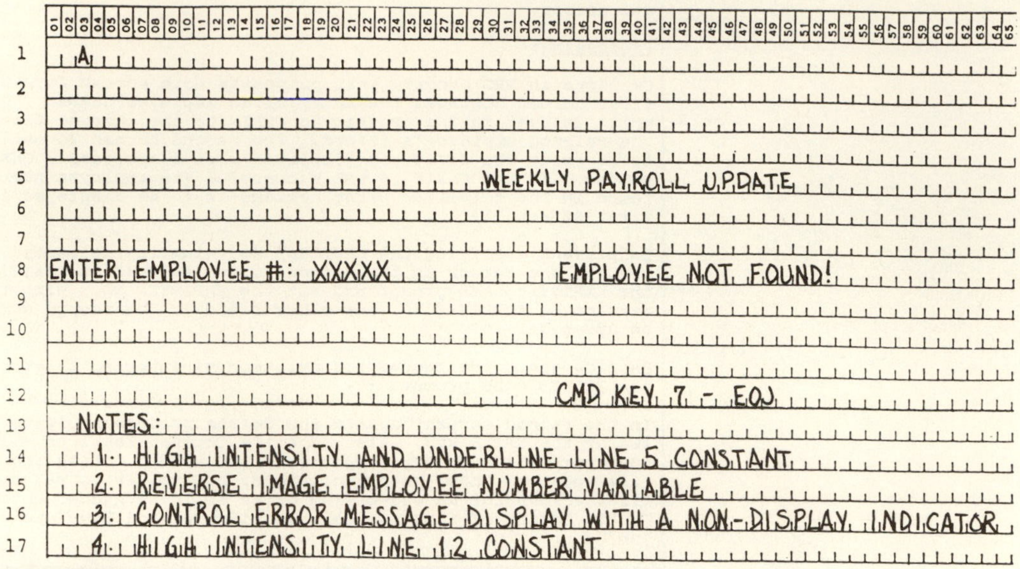
A
WEEKLY PAYROLL UPDATE
ENTER EMPLOYEE #: XXXXX
EMPLOYEE NOT FOUND!
CMD KEY 7 - EOJ
NOTES:
1. HIGH INTENSITY AND UNDERLINE LINE 5 CONSTANT
2. REVERSE IMAGE EMPLOYEE NUMBER VARIABLE
3. CONTROL ERROR MESSAGE DISPLAY WITH A NON-DISPLAY INDICATOR
4. HIGH INTENSITY LINE 12 CONSTANT

Figure 18-43 WORKSTN file CH18P3FM screen layout CH18P3S1 for the interactive update program.

A printout of the screen display after an employee number is entered and before the ENTER key is pressed is shown at the top of Figure 18-44. At the bottom of the figure is a display of the screen after the ENTER key is pressed, the employee number not found in the indexed file, and the error message displayed.

```
Blank Screen Display (before EMPLOYEE # is entered):

                                          WEEKLY PAYROLL UPDATE

              ENTER EMPLOYEE #: 10000

                                                CHD KEY 7 - EOJ

Screen Display (after an invalid EMPLOYEE # is entered):

                                          WEEKLY PAYROLL UPDATE

              ENTER EMPLOYEE #: 12345      EMPLOYEE NOT FOUND!

                                                CHD KEY 7 - EOJ
```

Figure 18-44 Example displays of the first screen (CH18P3S1) included in the interactive update program.

The coding for the first screen (CH18P3S1) included in the display format member CH18P3FM is detailed in the Display Screen format Specifications form in Figure 18-45. Except for the constant WEEKLY PAYROLL INQUIRY, which has been changed to WEEKLY PAYROLL UPDATE, the coding is identical to that of Figure 18-28. Consequently, a detailed explanation of the screen's syntax is omitted.

A compilation listing of the screen record CH18P3S1 is shown in Figure 18-46. Remember that the format member CH18P3FM is compiled and not an individual screen record.

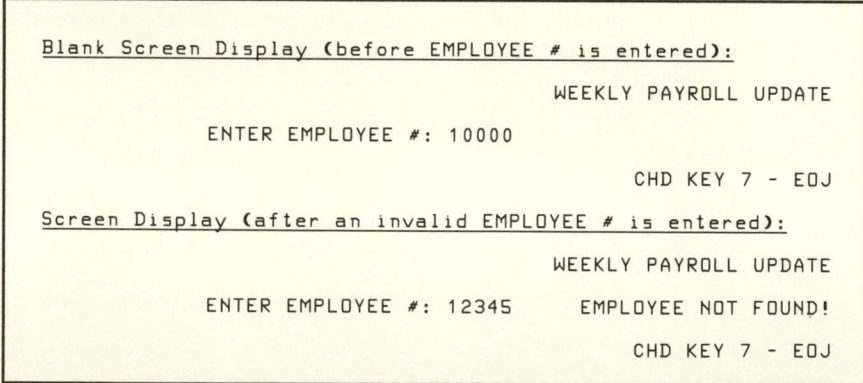

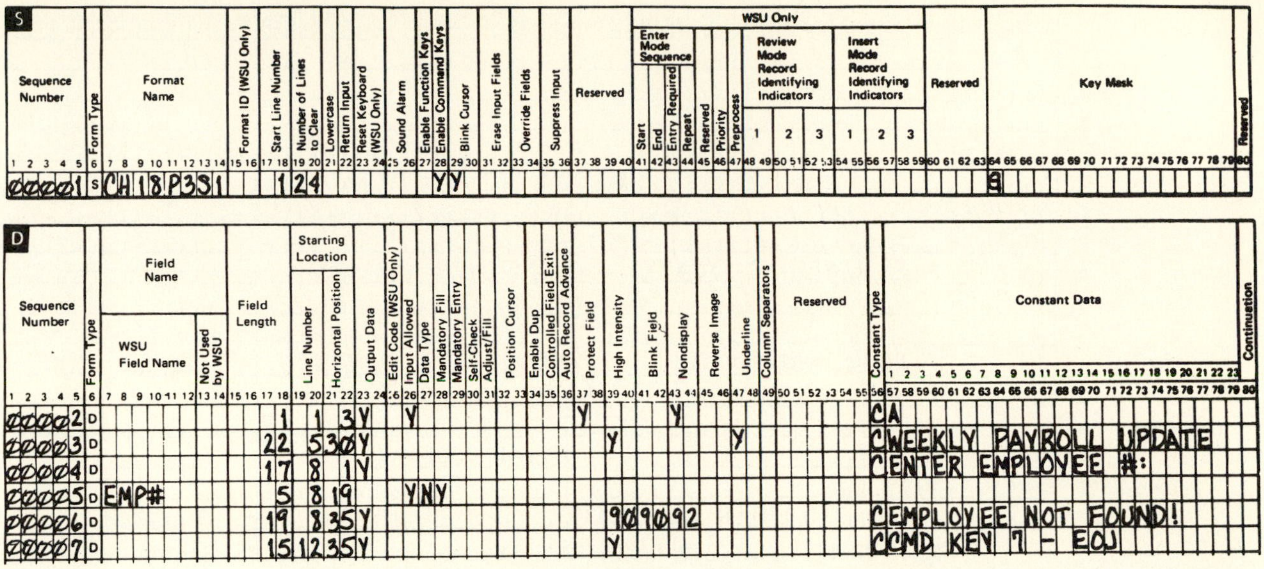

Figure 18-45 Completed Display Screen Format Specifications for the first screen record for the interactive update program.

```
....+....1....+....2....+....3....+....4....+....5....+....6....+....7....+....8

     SCH18P3S1    124         YY                                      G
     D             1 1 3Y  Y             Y     Y              CA
     D            22 530Y                  Y        Y         CWEEKLY PAYROLL UPDATE
     D            17 8 1Y                                     CENTER EMPLOYEE #:
     DEMP#         5 819   YNY                        Y
     D            19 835Y                 909092              CEMPLOYEE NOT FOUND!
     D            151235Y                  Y                  CCMD KEY 7 - EOJ

INPUT BUFFER DESCRIPTION
FIELD NAME     LENGTH      START        END

                  1          1           1
  EMP#            5          2           6

INDICATORS USED

  90 92
```

Section A

The source listing of the display format member in the same format as the Screen Specifications Form. Relative position of each entry is referenced by the ruler included at the top of the listing. Compile time terminal and warning errors will be included in the body of the listing.

Section B

The section entitled, INPUT BUFFER DESCRIPTION, specifies the location of the input fields (*from screen to program*) in the INPUT BUFFER created in the compilation process. The exact location of each field is included in the Input Specifications of the related RPG program so that data may be passed from the display format member (input) to the program for processing.

Because this application includes only the input of data, no OUTPUT BUFFER is included. The second screen (CH18P3S2) for this update program will require both INPUT and OUTPUT BUFFERs.

Figure 18-46 Display format member (CH18P3FM) listing of the CH18P3S1 screen record format—inquiry program.

Screen Format CH18P3S2—Update Program. The design of the second screen (CH18P3S2) included in the format member CH18P3FM is illustrated in Figure 18-47. During program execution, this screen is displayed only after an

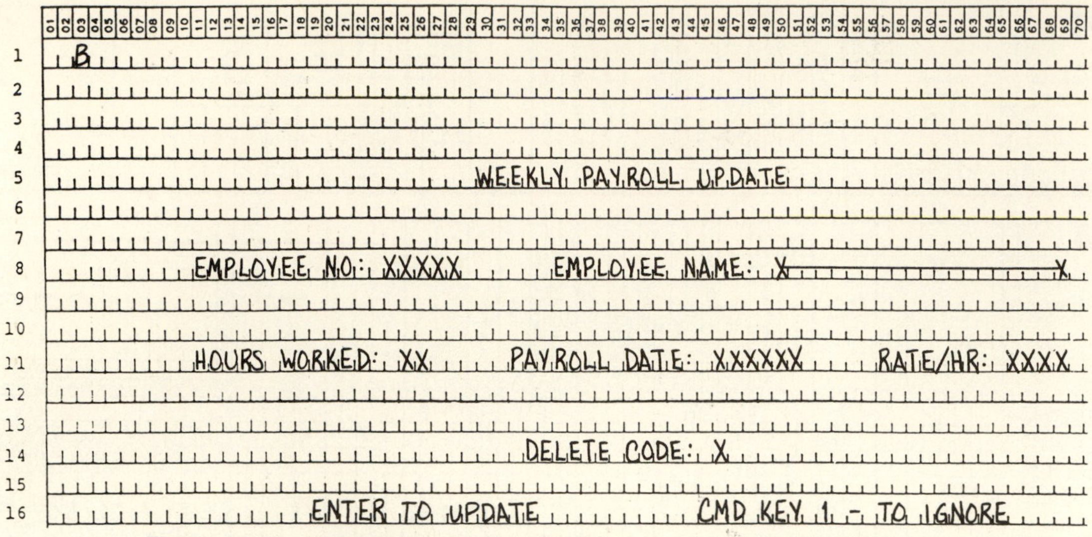

Figure 18-47 WORKSTN file CH18P3FM screen layout CH18P3S2 for interactive update program.

employee number has been entered in response to the first screen prompt and a successful CHAIN to the indexed file executed.

A display of the screen record CH18P3S2 after a successful CHAIN (employee number found) is executed to the indexed file is presented in Figure 18-48. The variable data displayed is accessed from the related indexed file's record. Because this application controls update processing, the screen values may be changed and the record written back to the file.

```
                         WEEKLY PAYROLL UPDATE


           EMPLOYEE NO: 10000      EMPLOYEE NAME: HENRY FORD


           HOURS WORKED: 40     PAYROLL DATE: 050191     RATE/HR: 1200


                              DELETE CODE:




                ENTER TO UPDATE                CMD KEY 1 - TO IGNORE
```

Figure 18-48 Display of the second screen (CH18P3S2) after a successful CHAIN is executed to the indexed file—update program.

The coding for the second screen (CH18P3S2) is shown in Figure 18-49. Again, because the coding is almost identical with that explained for the second screen for the inquiry program, a detailed explanation is omitted. However, the following additions should be noted:

1. All variable fields are defined to allow the input of data by the letter Y entry in column 26. This entry is in addition to the Y in the output data entry in column 23. Update processing requires the input of data to and output from the screen, hence, the reason for the input-output control.
2. Command Key 1 (letter A in the Key Mask field—S section) has been made operational to allow the operator to change his or her mind and not update the current record. This control will be explained in more detail when the calculations for this program are introduced.

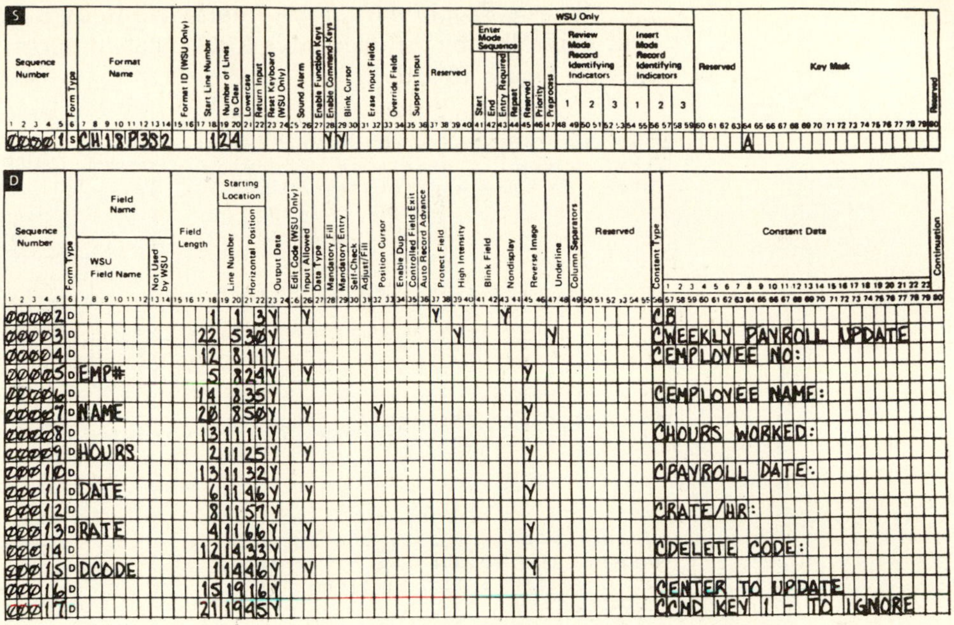

Figure 18-49 Completed Display Screen Format Specifications for the second screen record CH18P3S2—update program.

An examination of the compilation listing for the second screen (CH18P3S2) (see Figure 18-50) indicates that OUTPUT and INPUT DESCRIPTION buffers are generated. With the exception of the extra unnamed position (identification code) in the first byte of the record defined in the INPUT BUFFER DESCRIPTION, both formats include the same field names. The creation of two almost identical buffers is necessary because the fields were defined as input and output in the screen's syntax.

```
....+....1....+....2....+....3....+....4....+....5....+....6....+....7....+....8

     SCH18P3S2   124        YY                               A
     D             1 1 3Y Y           Y     Y           CB
     D            22 530Y               Y       Y       CWEEKLY PAYROLL UPDATE
     D            12 811Y                               CEMPLOYEE NO:
     DEMP#         5 824Y Y                   Y
     D            14 835Y                               CEMPLOYEE NAME:
     DNAME        20 850Y Y     Y             Y
     D            131111Y                               CHOURS WORKED:
     DHOURS        21125Y Y                   Y
     D            131132Y                               CPAYROLL DATE:
     DDATE         61146Y Y                   Y
     D             81157Y                               CRATE/HR:
     DRATE         41166Y Y                   Y
     D            121433Y                               CDELETE CODE:
     DDCODE        11446Y Y                   Y
     D            151916Y                               CENTER TO UPDATE
     D            211945Y                               CCMD KEY 1 - TO IGNORE

EXECUTION TIME OUTPUT BUFFER DESCRIPTION
FIELD NAME    LENGTH      START        END

  EMP#             5          1          5
  NAME            20          6         25
  HOURS            2         26         27
  DATE             6         28         33
  RATE             4         34         37
  DCODE            1         38         38

INPUT BUFFER DESCRIPTION
FIELD NAME    LENGTH      START        END

                   1          1          1
  EMP#             5          2          6
  NAME            20          7         26
  HOURS            2         27         28
  DATE             6         29         34
  RATE             4         35         38
  DCODE            1         39         39
```

Figure 18-50 Display format member (CH18P3FM) listing of the CH18P3P2 screen record format—update program.

Source Program Coding—Interactive Update Program. The processing logic controlled by the interactive RPG update program is presented in the flowchart in Figure 18-51.

1. When the program is executed, the first screen is displayed. Operator enters an EMP# and presses ENTER.

2. Indexed file is CHAINed to by EMP#.

3. If the EMP# is not found, a screen defined error message is displayed in the first screen (CH18P3S1).

4. If the EMP# is found, the second screen is displayed with the indexed record's field values for update.

5. If Command Key 1 is pressed by the operator, control returns to the first screen display.

   If ENTER key is pressed by the operator, control updates the displayed record.

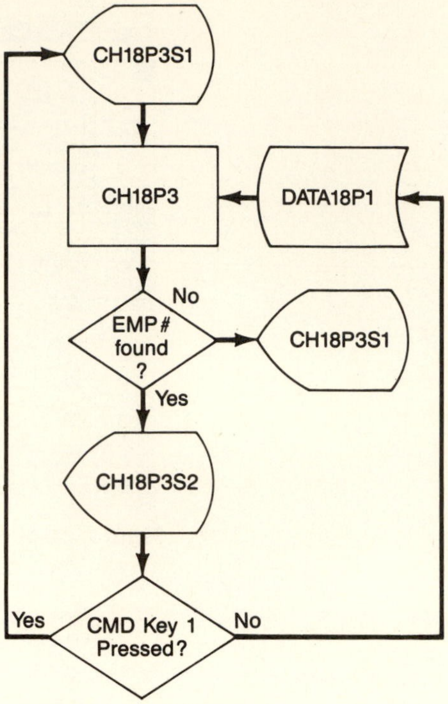

Figure 18-51 Processing logic controlled by the interactive update program.

A source listing of the interactive update program is shown in Figure 18-52.

The syntax for each of the specification types is separately discussed in the following sections.

```
... ... 1 ... ... 2 ... ... 3 ... ... 4 ... ... 5 ... ... 6 ... ... 7 ...
H                                                                       CH18P3
 * THIS PROGRAM UPDATES AN INDEXED FILE INTERACTIVELY............       CH18P3
 * SYSTEM/36 & 34 ENVIRONMENTS...................................       CH18P3
 *                                                                      CH18P3
FCH18P3FMCD  F  81  81            WORKSTN                               CH18P3
FDATA18P1UC  F  38  38R 5AI     2 DISK                                  CH18P3
 *                                                                      CH18P3
 * INPUT DEFINITION OF THE 1ST & 2ND SCREEN FORMATS.                    CH18P3
ICH18P3FMSM  01   1 CA                                                  CH18P3
I                                          2   60EMP#                   CH18P3
I       SM  03   1 CB                                                   CH18P3
I                                          2   60EMP#                   CH18P3
I                                          7  26 NAME                   CH18P3
I                                         27  280HOURS                  CH18P3
I                                         29  340DATE                   CH18P3
I                                         35  382RATE                   CH18P3
I                                         39  39 DCODE                  CH18P3
 *                                                                      CH18P3
 * DEFINITION OF UPDATE FILE'S DISK RECORD.......................       CH18P3
IDATA18P1SM  02                                                         CH18P3
I                                          1   1 DCODE                  CH18P3
I                                          2   60EMP#                   CH18P3
I                                          7  26 NAME                   CH18P3
I                                         27  280HOURS                  CH18P3
I                                         29  340DATE                   CH18P3
I                                         35  382RATE                   CH18P3
C                     SETON                     92      NON-DISP MSG    CH18P3
C           AGAIN     TAG                                               CH18P3
 *                                                                      CH18P3
```

Figure 18-52 Source listing of the interactive update program.

```
0030 C                       SETON                     80     1ST SCRN INDR. CH18P3
0031 C                       EXCPT                            DISP 1ST SCREENCH18P3
0032 C                       SETOF                     80     OFF 1ST SCRN INCH18P3
0033  *                                                                      CH18P3
0034 C                       READ CH18P3FM                    READ 1ST SCREENCH18P3
0035 C   KG                  GOTO EOJ                         EOJ?           CH18P3
0036 C            EMP#       CHAINDATA18P1             90     GET DISK RECORDCH18P3
0037 C   90                  SETOF                     92     DISP ERROR MSG CH18P3
0038  *                                                                      CH18P3
0039 C  N90                  EXSR PROCES                      2ND SCRN SR    CH18P3
0040 C                       GOTO AGAIN                       GET 1ST SCRN   CH18P3
0041 C            EOJ        TAG                                             CH18P3
0042 C                       SETON                     LR     END JOB        CH18P3
0043 C            PROCES     BEGSR                                           CH18P3
0044 C                       SETON                     92     STOPS MSG DISP CH18P3
0045  *                                                                      CH18P3
0046 C                       SETON                     04     2ND SCRN INDR  CH18P3
0047 C                       EXCPT                            DISP 2ND SCREENCH18P3
0048 C                       SETOF                     04     SETOF 2ND SCRN CH18P3
0049  *                                                                      CH18P3
0050 C                       READ CH18P3FM                    HOLDS 2ND SCRN CH18P3
0051  * UPDATE DISK RECORD CONTROL - IGNORE IF CMD KEY 1 (KA) IS PRESSED     CH18P3
0052  *                                                                      CH18P3
0053 C  NKA                  SETON                     98     UPDATE IND.    CH18P3
0054 C  NKA                  EXCPT                            UPDATE RECORD  CH18P3
0055 C                       SETOF                     98     OFF UPDATE IND.CH18P3
0056 C                       ENDSR                                           CH18P3
0057  *                                                                      CH18P3
0058  * DISPLAY 1ST SCREEN FOR EMP# ENTRY.............................       CH18P3
0059 OCH18P3FME         80                                                   CH18P3
0060 O                                  K8 'CH18P3S1'                        CH18P3
0061  * DISPLAY FILLED-IN UPDATE (2ND) SCREEN........................        CH18P3
0062 OCH18P3FME         04                                                   CH18P3
0063 O                                  K8 'CH18P3S2'                        CH18P3
0064 O                        EMP#       5                                   CH18P3
0065 O                        NAME      25                                   CH18P3
0066 O                        HOURS     27                                   CH18P3
0067 O                        DATE      33                                   CH18P3
0068 O                        RATE      37                                   CH18P3
0069 O                        DCODE     38                                   CH18P3
0070  *                                                                      CH18P3
0071  * UPDATE DISK RECORD............................................       CH18P3
0072 ODATA18P1E         98                                                   CH18P3
0073 O                        DCODE      1                                   CH18P3
0074 O                        EMP#       6                                   CH18P3
0075 O                        NAME      26                                   CH18P3
0076 O                        HOURS     28                                   CH18P3
0077 O                        DATE      34                                   CH18P3
0078 O                        RATE      38                                   CH18P3
```

(*Continued*)

File Description Specifications—Interactive Update Program. Figure 18-53 includes the File Description coding for the interactive update program. The only syntax change needed in the previously discussed inquiry program to support file update is in column 15 of the indexed file's definition. For update processing, the letter U is required in that field instead of an I.

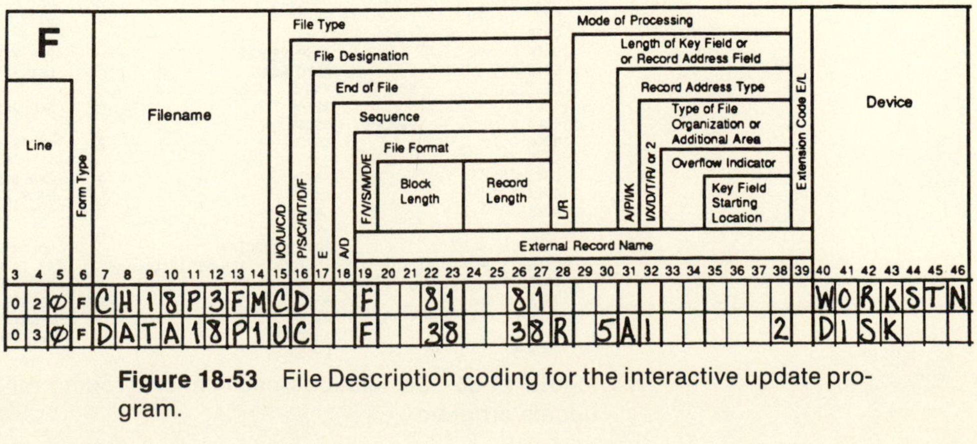

Figure 18-53 File Description coding for the interactive update program.

Input Specifications—Interactive Update Program. The relationship of the separate INPUT BUFFERS created for the two screens included in the CH18P3FM format member to the input coding is shown in Figure 18-54. The other input statements define the attributes of the indexed file's record format and related fields.

```
First screen's (CH18P3S1) input buffer:

    INPUT BUFFER DESCRIPTION
    FIELD NAME     LENGTH        START        END

                        1            1          1
      EMP#              5            2          6

Second screen's (CH18P3S2) input buffer:

    INPUT BUFFER DESCRIPTION
    FIELD NAME     LENGTH        START        END

                        1            1          1
      EMP#              5            2          6
      NAME             20            7         26
      HOURS             2           27         28
      DATE              6           29         34
      RATE              4           35         38
      DCODE             1           39         39

Program's related input coding:

...  ... 1 ... ... 2 ... ... 3 ... ... 4 ... ... 5 ... ... 6 ... ... 7 ...

 * INPUT DEFINITION OF THE 1ST & 2ND SCREEN FORMATS.             CH18P3
ICH18P3FMSM  01    1 CA                                          CH18P3
I                                         2   60EMP#             CH18P3
I          SM  03    1 CB                                        CH18P3
I                                         2   60EMP#             CH18P3
I                                         7  26 NAME             CH18P3
I                                        27  280HOURS            CH18P3
I                                        29  340DATE             CH18P3
I                                        35  382RATE             CH18P3
I                                        39  39 DCODE            CH18P3
```

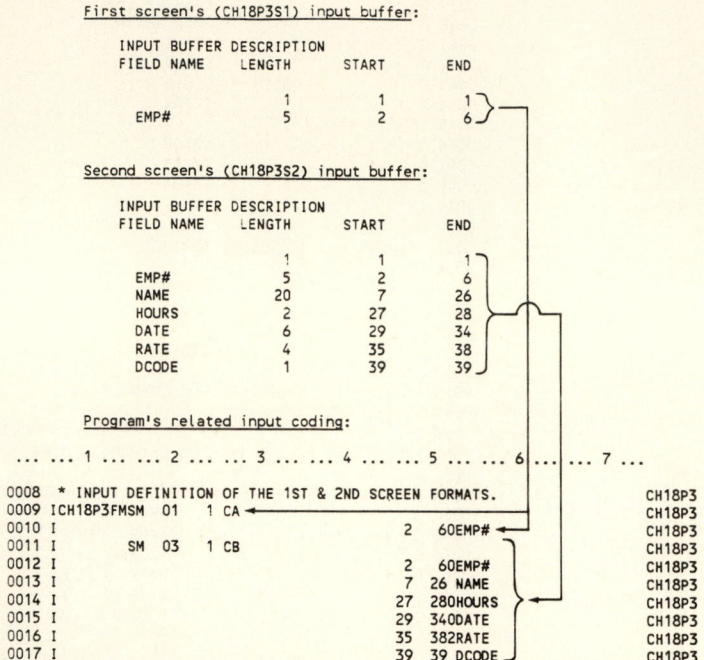

Figure 18-54 Relationship of the INPUT BUFFERS for two screens included in format member CH18P3FM—update program.

Calculation Specifications—Interactive Update Program. A line-by-line explanation of the calculations included in the interactive update program is presented in Figure 18-55.

```
...  ... 1 ... ... 2 ... ... 3 ... ... 4 ... ... 5 ... ... 6 ... ... 7 ...

C                    SETON                     92    NON-DISP MSG   CH18P3
C           AGAIN    TAG                                            CH18P3
 *                                                                  CH18P3
C                    SETON                     80    1ST SCRN INDR. CH18P3
C                    EXCPT                           DISP 1ST SCREENCH18P3
C                    SETOF                     80    OFF 1ST SCRN INCH18P3
 *                                                                  CH18P3
C                    READ CH18P3FM                   READ 1ST SCREENCH18P3
C   KG               GOTO EOJ                        EOJ?           CH18P3
C           EMP#     CHAINDATA18P1             90    GET DISK RECORDCH18P3
C   90               SETOF                     92    DISP ERROR MSG CH18P3
 *                                                                  CH18P3
C  N90               EXSR PROCES                     2ND SCRN SR    CH18P3
C                    GOTO AGAIN                      GET 1ST SCRN   CH18P3
C           EOJ      TAG                                            CH18P3
C                    SETON                     LR    END JOB        CH18P3
C           PROCES   BEGSR                                          CH18P3
C                    SETON                     92    STOPS MSG DISP CH18P3
 *                                                                  CH18P3
C                    SETON                     04    2ND SCRN INDR  CH18P3
C                    EXCPT                           DISP 2ND SCREENCH18P3
C                    SETOF                     04    SETOF 2ND SCRN CH18P3
 *                                                                  CH18P3
C                    READ CH18P3FM                   HOLDS 2ND SCRN CH18P3
 * UPDATE DISK RECORD CONTROL - IGNORE IF CMD KEY 1 (KA) IS PRESSED CH18P3
 *                                                                  CH18P3
C  NKA               SETON                     98    UPDATE IND.    CH18P3
C  NKA               EXCPT                           UPDATE RECORD  CH18P3
C                    SETOF                     98    OFF UPDATE IND.CH18P3
C                    ENDSR                                          CH18P3
```

Figure 18-55 Calculation Specifications coding for the interactive update program.

Line No.

0027 Indicator 92, which was specified in the first screen record to control the nondisplay of the error message (refer to Figure 18-27, line 00006, columns 43-44), is turned on so that the error message will not display when the screen appears on the CRT.

0028 Entry for GOTO statement on line 0040 which controls subsequent displays of the first screen (CH18P2S1) for entry of an employee number or end of job response.

0030 Indicator 80 is turned on which controls output of the first prompt screen for input of an employee number and, if the employee number is not found in the indexed file, an error message.

0031 This EXCPT operation transfers control to an exception type output record (E in column 15) conditioned by the 80 indicator. Output lines 0059 and 0060 are executed by this statement which causes the screen record CH18P3S1 to be displayed for entry of an employee number or end of job response. CH18P3S1 is one of the two record formats defined in the display format member CH18P3FM.

0032 This SETOF operation turns off the 80 indicator to prevent the output instructions conditioned with that indicator from being executed when the next EXCPT instruction (line 0062 and 0072) are executed.

0034 After the operator responds to the first screen's prompt (enters an employee number), the READ operation reads the variable data and tests the status (on or off) of the command key 7 (KG indicator).

0035 If Command Key 7 is pressed, the KG indicator is turned on and a branch is executed which controls end of job (LR) processing (lines 41 and 42).

0036 If ENTER is pressed (instead of Command Key 7), the EMP# entered from the first screen (CH18P3S1) is included in a CHAIN instruction which randomly searches the indexed file for an equal key value.

0037 If the CHAIN instruction is not successful (indicator 90 turned on), indicator 92 which was specified in the screen coding to prevent the constant EMPLOYEE NOT FOUND! from always being displayed, is turned off. This instruction causes the error message to be displayed when an employee number is not found in the indexed file.

0039 If an employee number is found in the indexed file, this instruction transfers control to the internal subroutine PROCES on line 0043.

0040 After the internal subroutine is executed, the GOTO statement transfers control to line 0028 which repeats the instructions that redisplay the first screen for entry of an employee number or end of job response.

0041 Entry for the GOTO statement line 35 which is executed if the operator pressed Command Key 7 (turned on indicator KG) to pass control to the instruction on line 0041 to end the job.

0042 SETON operation turns on the LR indicator to end the job and return control back to the operating system.

0043 Entry for the EXSR PROCES statement on line 0039.

0044 Stops any previous error message display in the first screen.

0046 Indicator 04 is SETON to condition the exception output instructions on lines 0062-0069 which controls display of the second screen "filled-in" with data.

0047 EXCPT operation controls exception type output on lines 0062 through 0069 which displays the "filled-in" second screen (CH18P3S2).

0048 Indicator 04 is SETOF to prevent this exception type output from executing when the EXCPT operation on line 031 is executed after a loop occurs for a redisplay of the first screen.

0050 This READ operation holds the display of the second screen until the operator presses the ENTER key. Without this statement, the second screen display format would flash on the CRT and not hold for examination.

0053 If command key 1 is not pressed (NKA), indicator 98 is SETON to condition exception output that updates the current disk record.

0054 If command key 1 is not pressed (NKA), EXCPT operation is executed which controls the output instructions on line 0072-0078 which update a disk record.

0055 Indicator 98 is SETOF to prevent that output from executing when loop is executed and first screen is redisplayed.

0056 ENDSR indicates end of the PROCES subroutine.

(Continued)

Output Specifications—Interactive Update Program. Figure 18-56 illustrates the relationship of the Output Buffer generated for the second screen (CH18P3S2) and the output instructions in the program. Output coding on program lines 0059 and 0060 control the display of the first screen for which there is no Output Buffer. The instructions on the Output Specifications lines 0072 through 0078 support the update of the indexed file record currently being processed.

Second screen's (CH18P3S2) output buffer:

```
EXECUTION TIME OUTPUT BUFFER DESCRIPTION
FIELD NAME     LENGTH     START       END

  EMP#              5         1         5
  NAME             20         6        25
  HOURS             2        26        27
  DATE              6        28        33
  RATE              4        34        37
  DCODE             1        38        38
```

Program's related output coding:

```
... ... 1 ... ... 2 ... ... 3 ... ... 4 ... ... 5 ... ... 6 ... ... 7 ...

0058  * DISPLAY 1ST SCREEN FOR EMP# ENTRY...........................................   CH18P3
0059 OCH18P3FME         80                                                              CH18P3
0060 O                                      K8 'CH18P3S1'                               CH18P3
0061  * DISPLAY FILLED-IN UPDATE (2ND) SCREEN.......................................   CH18P3
0062 OCH18P3FME         04                                                              CH18P3
0063 O                                      K8 'CH18P3S2'                               CH18P3
0064 O                        EMP#           5                                          CH18P3
0065 O                        NAME          25                                          CH18P3
0066 O                        HOURS         27                                          CH18P3
0067 O                        DATE          33                                          CH18P3
0068 O                        RATE          37                                          CH18P3
0069 O                        DCODE         38                                          CH18P3
0070  *                                                                                 CH18P3
0071  * UPDATE DISK RECORD..........................................................   CH18P3
0072 ODATA18P1E         98                                                              CH18P3
0073 O                        DCODE          1                                          CH18P3
0074 O                        EMP#           6                                          CH18P3
0075 O                        NAME          26                                          CH18P3
0076 O                        HOURS         28                                          CH18P3
0077 O                        DATE          32P                                         CH18P3
0078 O                        RATE          35P                                         CH18P3
```

Figure 18-56 Relationship of OUTPUT BUFFER for the second screen (CH18P3S2) to the output coding—update program.

Note that the same names were specified in the program for the fields defined in the second screen and those in the disk record. Sometimes it may expedite program debugging and maintenance if different field names are used for a screen and related disk file record formats. With that method, however, MOVE statements have to be included in the program to move data from the disk record to the screen record and then, for updating, from the screen record to the disk record.

Processing Results—Interactive Update Program. The top section of Figure 18-57 presents the second screen filled with data from the indexed file after a successful CHAIN instruction in the program is executed. In the lower section is a display of the same screen after an operator has entered the update information and before he/she has pressed ENTER.

As indicated at the bottom of the screen displays, the current disk record is updated by pressing the ENTER key. The operator has the option of overriding the update process by pressing Command Key 1. Observe that HOURS WORKED was changed from 45 to 46 and RATE/HR from 1900 to 2000.

```
Screen display before update data is entered:

                    WEEKLY PAYROLL UPDATE

EMPLOYEE NO: 14000      EMPLOYEE NAME: WILLIAM BRICKLIN

HOURS WORKED: 45     PAYROLL DATE: 050191     RATE/HR: 1900

                         DELETE CODE:



    ENTER TO UPDATE                 CMD KEY 1 - TO IGNORE
```

```
Screen display after update data is entered:

                    WEEKLY PAYROLL UPDATE

EMPLOYEE NO: 14000      EMPLOYEE NAME: WILLIAM BRICKLIN

HOURS WORKED: 46     PAYROLL DATE: 050191     RATE/HR: 2000

                         DELETE CODE:



    ENTER TO UPDATE                 CMD KEY 1 - TO IGNORE
```

Figure 18-57 Displays of the second screen before and after an operator has entered update data.

For this application, validation of the record updated may be performed by one of the following methods:

1. Access and display the updated record by execution of the inquiry program (CH18P2).
2. Access and display the updated record by execution of the update program (CH18P3).
3. A utility listing of the record or file section where the record is stored.

Shown in Figure 18-58 is a display of the updated record generated by the execution of the previously discussed inquiry program CH18P2.

```
                    WEEKLY PAYROLL INQUIRY

EMPLOYEE NO: 14000      EMPLOYEE NAME: WILLIAM BRICKLIN

HOURS WORKED: 46     PAYROLL DATE: 050191     RATE/HR: 2000

                       RECORD DELETED? NO



                       ENTER TO CONTINUE
```

Figure 18-58 Display of the updated record after it was written back to the disk file and random accessed by the inquiry program (CH18P2).

SUMMARY

The screen and RPG program syntax introduced in this chapter relate to the IBM System/36 and 34 environments. Interactive screens are created on those systems by either SEU (Source Entry Utility) or SDA (Screen Design Aid) utilities. Because SEU relates to the coding procedures closely followed for RPG programs (the filling-in of forms or an editor screen), it is used in the examples instead of SDA. You may find, however, that SDA is faster and easier and you should therefore consult an IBM manual on that subject.

After the syntax for a display format member (screen file) is entered (with SEU or SDA), it is compiled by executing a Screen Format Generator utility. Debugging procedures are similar to those followed for RPG programs.

A display format member may include more than one record format (different screens). Design considerations of the application will usually determine how many screen records are required.

Display format members (screen files) are defined in the File Description Specifications as input (I in column 15), combined (C in column 16), and with the device name WORKSTN.

INPUT and/or OUTPUT BUFFERS are automatically generated in the compilation of the display format member for each screen record. A screen that controls only the entry of data from the screen to the RPG program, as in loading or adding to a disk file, will generate only an INPUT BUFFER. On the other hand, a screen that supports only the output of data from a program (e.g., a file for inquiry processing) will create only an OUTPUT BUFFER. Screen records that provide for interactive update processing will generate both INPUT and OUTPUT BUFFERs.

The exact location and size of each field in the buffers must be referenced on the input and/or output coding in the RPG program. However, the field names included in the screen record(s) and the program may differ. For that coding method, MOVE statements have to be specified to move the data from the screen to the program, and vice versa.

Display of the records included in a display format member is controlled in an RPG program that specifies the length of the screen name with a Kn entry, right-justified in columns 40 to 43, and with the screen name enclosed in apostrophes in the CONSTANT field area.

All the program examples discussed in this chapter follow the same structure. Screen and disk output are controlled by the EXCPT operation. End of job control is initiated by a Command Key 7 entry (from the screen), which causes processing to branch to a sequence of instructions that SETON LR and return control back to the operating system.

QUESTIONS

18-1. Explain the processing principles associated with interactive processing.

18-2. What are the programming steps necessary to develop an interactive RPG program?

18-3. Explain the coding procedures required in the design, coding, and compilation of a *display format member*.

18-4. What are the two methods of entering a source code for a display format member on System/36 and 34?

18-5. Examine the following Display Screen Format Specifications and explain the coding entries included for each line:

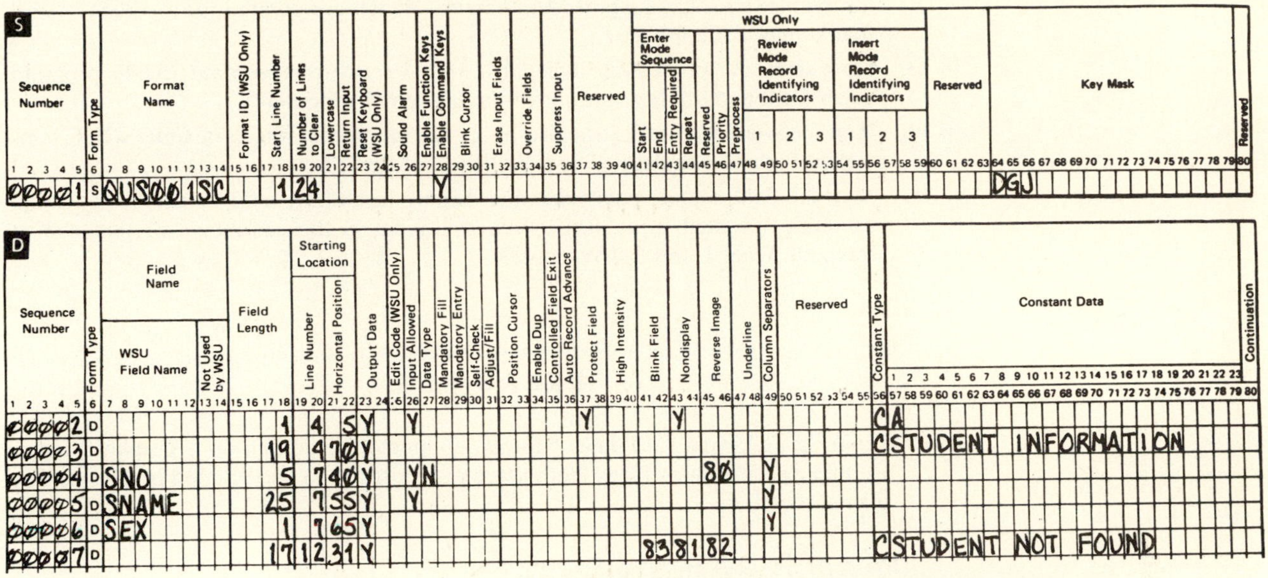

18-6. What sections are included in the screen listing generated by the $SFGR system utility when the display format member is successfully compiled?

18-7. What is the function of the OUTPUT and INPUT BUFFERs included in a display format member's source listing?

18-8. What is the function of the following OCL command? Explain the meaning of each entry.

FORMAT UPDATE, EX001FM, DEMOLIB, EX001SC, DEMOLIB

18-9. Define the function of each entry in the following File Description instruction.

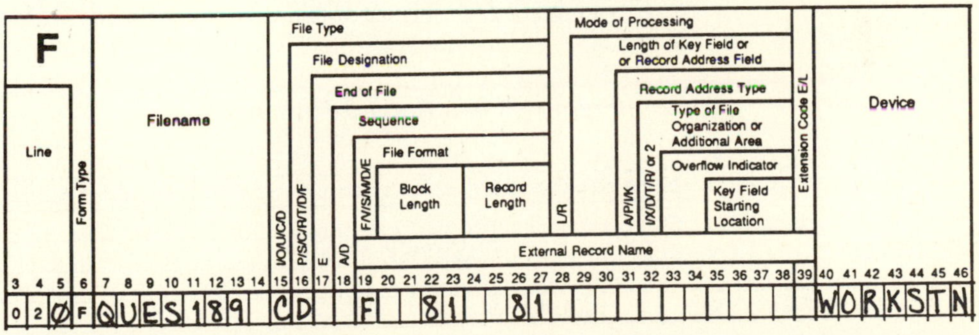

18-10. What are Command Key indicators? Where are they defined in an interactive program? Where are they specified? What is their function?

18-11. Explain the meaning of the following output instruction:

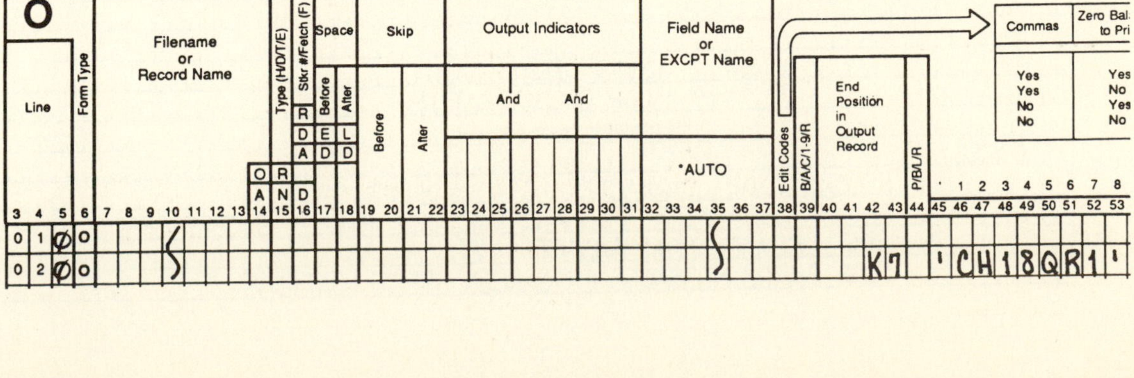

18-12. Will an INPUT and/or an OUTPUT BUFFER be created for a screen record that supports only the addition of records to a disk file? Which buffers are created for a screen record that supports file inquiry? Which are created for a screen record that supports file update?

18-13. How does the processing logic of a *single requestor terminal* (*SRT*) program differ from a *multiple requestor terminal (MRT)* program?

18-14. How does a program's structure differ for the processing of a CONSOLE controlled file and one defined as a WORKSTN file?

18-15. May the field names specified in the display format member record be the same as those specified in an RPG program? What is the advantage of this coding method? What is the disadvantage?

EXERCISES

18-1. From the following CRT layout forms, complete the coding on a Display Screen Format Specifications form. Both screen records are to be included in one display format member.

Prompt Screen Record Format:

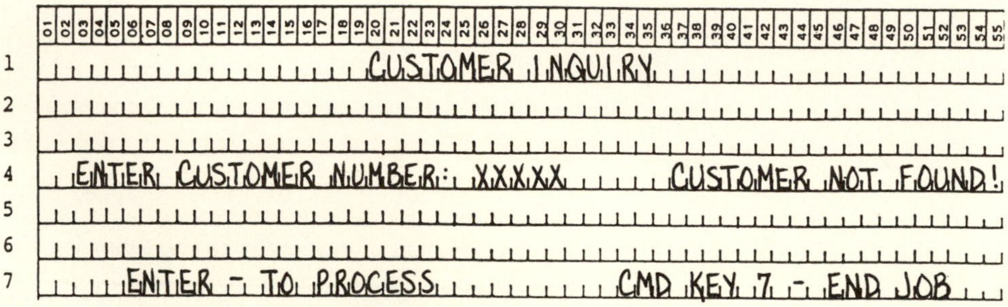

Inquiry Screen Record Format:

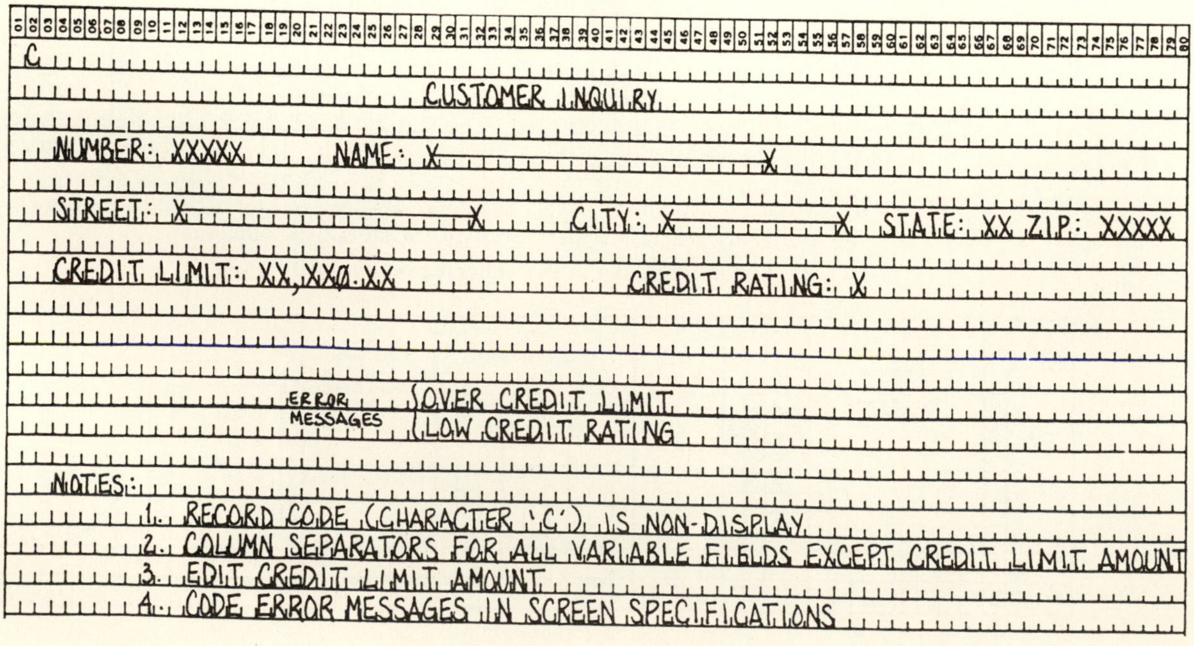

C
CUSTOMER INQUIRY
NUMBER: XXXXX
NAME: X X
STREET: X X
CITY: X X
STATE: XX ZIP: XXXXX
CREDIT LIMIT: XX,XXØ.XX
CREDIT RATING: X
ERROR MESSAGES
OVER CREDIT LIMIT
LOW CREDIT RATING
NOTES:
1. RECORD CODE (CHARACTER 'C') IS NON-DISPLAY
2. COLUMN SEPARATORS FOR ALL VARIABLE FIELDS EXCEPT CREDIT LIMIT AMOUNT
3. EDIT CREDIT LIMIT AMOUNT
4. CODE ERROR MESSAGES IN SCREEN SPECIFICATIONS

18-2. Based on the information in the Customer Master file included in the File Definition form shown below, complete the File Description coding for a program that processes the interactive screen shown in Exercise 18-1. Name the display format member EX181FM (information from Exercise 18-1).

FILE DEFINITION			
SYSTEM System/36		DRAWN BY S. Myers	
FILE NAME CUSTOMER		DATE 10/1/91	REV. NO. 0
CREATED BY S. Myers		FILE TYPE Disk	
RECORD NAME None		KEY LENGTH 6	
RECORDING MODE Fixed	ORGANIZATION Indexed	SEQUENCE Key order	
RECORD SIZE 73 bytes	BLOCKING FACTOR 1	BLOCKSIZE 73 bytes	

FIELD NO.	FIELD NAME - DESCRIPTION	SIZE	CLASS C/P/Z/B	POSITION FROM	POSITION THRU	FORMAT/CONSTANT
1	CUSTOMER NUMBER	6	C	1	6	Key Field
2	CUSTOMER NAME	24	C	7	30	
3	ADDRESS	20	C	31	50	
4	CITY	13	C	51	63	
5	STATE	2	C	64	65	
6	ZIP	5	P	66	68	
7	CREDIT LIMIT	7	P	69	72	
8	CREDIT RATING	1	C	73	73	Codes:
						N = Over Limit
						L = Low Rating
						Blank = Good Rating

18-3. Code the program's input coding for the indexed file defined in Exercise 18-2. Also include the coding for the screen field attributes described in the following INPUT BUFFER generated when the screen coded in Exercise 18-1 was compiled.

INPUT BUFFER DESCRIPTION

FIELD NAME	LENGTH	START	END
	1	1	1
CUST#	6	2	7

18-4. Refer to Exercises 18-1 and 18-3, and complete the calculations to process the display format member's screen records and inquiry the disk file.

18-5. Complete the output coding for the program developed in the previous exercises. Refer to the following OUTPUT BUFFER for the related information:

EXECUTION TIME OUTPUT BUFFER DESCRIPTION

FIELD NAME	LENGTH	START	END
CUSTNO	6	1	6
NAME	24	7	30
STREET	20	31	50
CITY	13	51	63
STATE	2	64	65
ZIP	5	66	70
LIMIT	9	71	79
RATING	1	80	80

18-6. Write the System/36 or 34 OCL procedure to execute the program, and process the screen and disk files.

18-7. The source listing of a display format member after it has been compiled follows. Identify, explain, and correct all the errors to insure a successful compilation.

```
  SOURCE INPUT SCREEN FORMAT SOURCE SPECIFICATIONS

  ERRORSSC- SOURCE MEMBER NAME

0001 SERRORSSC  0125        Y                                   GK
SYS-5064 W VALUE SPECIFIED IN NUMBER OF LINES TO CLEAR ENTRY EXCEEDS THE NUMBER OF LINES ON THE SCREEN.
0002 D         00010204Y  Y             Y            CC
0003 D         00160229Y                             CCUSTOMER INQUIRY
0004 D         00070403Y                             CNUMBER:
0005 DCUSNO    00070409Y  YN                Y
SYS-5102 T THIS FIELD OCCUPIES A SCREEN POSITION ALREADY DEFINED BY A PREVIOUS FIELD IN THIS FORMAT.
0006 D         00050422Y                             CNAME:
0007 DNAME     00000428Y  Y                 Y
SYS-5090 T VALUE SPECIFIED IN FIELD LENGTH ENTRY IS ZERO.
0008 D         00070603Y                             CSTREET:
0009 DSTREET   00220611Y  Y                 Y
0010 D         00050639Y                              CITY:
0011 DCITY     00130600Y  Y                 Y
SYS-5097 T VALUE SPECIFIED IN HORIZONTAL POSITION ENTRY IS ZERO.
0012 D         00060660Y                             CSTATE:
0013 DSTATE    00020667                     Y
SYS-5150 T NEITHER INPUT NOR OUTPUT WAS SPECIFIED FOR THIS FIELD.
0014 D         00040670Y                             CZIP:
0015 D         00050675Y  YN                Y
0016 D         00130803Y                             CCREDIT LIMIT:
0017 DLIMIT    00070817Y  YN                Y
0018 D         00140843Y                             CCREDIT RATING:
0019 DRATING   00010858Y  Y                 Y
0020 D         00181128Y              90Y            CCUSTOMER NOT FOUND
0021 D         00171228Y              91Y            COVER CREDIT LIMIT
0022 D         00181328Y              92Y            CLOW CREDIT RATING


  EXECUTION TIME OUTPUT BUFFER DESCRIPTION

  FIELD                        START        END
  NAME            LENGTH       POSITION     POSITION

  STREET            22            1            22
                     5           23            27
  LIMIT              7           28            34
  RATING             1           35            35

  INPUT BUFFER DESCRIPTION

  FIELD                        START        END
  NAME            LENGTH       POSITION     POSITION

                     1            1             1
  STREET            22            2            23
                     5           24            28
  LIMIT              7           29            35
  RATING             1           36            36
```

LABORATORY ASSIGNMENTS

Laboratory Assignment 18-1: CREATING AND LOADING AN INDEXED FILE INTERACTIVELY

Complete an RPG program to load a master parts inventory file in accordance with the following screen and disk file documentation. Using your own design, complete a CRT layout form based on the information included in the suggested screen format. The error message, DUPLICATE KEY!, is to be displayed if a record with the same part number has previously been loaded to the file.

Display Format Member Record Design:

```
0X/XX/XX                    PARTS INVENTORY                   ENTRY/ADDS

  PART NUMBER:  XXXXX            PART NAME: XXXXXXXXXXXXXXXXXXXX

  AMT ON HAND: XXXXXX  AVG COST: XXXXXXX  AMT ON ORDER: XXXXXX

  AMT ALLOCATED: XXXXXX     EOQ: XXXXXX   SAFETY STOCK: XXXXXX

  LEAD TIME: XXX DAYS                   WAREHOUSE LOCATION: XXXX


       ENTER - LOAD RECORD                CMD KEY 7 - EOJ
```

Determine the attributes of each field included in the screen record by referring to the File Definition form that follows.

Record Format of the Master Parts Inventory File:

FILE DEFINITION

SYSTEM Yours		DRAWN BY S. Myers
FILE NAME MASTER PARTS INVENTORY		DATE 10/29/91 REV. NO. 0
CREATED BY S. Myers		FILE TYPE Disk
RECORD NAME None		KEY LENGTH 5 bytes
RECORDING MODE Fixed	ORGANIZATION Indexed	SEQUENCE Key
RECORD SIZE 69 bytes	BLOCKING FACTOR 1	BLOCKSIZE 69 bytes

FIELD DATA

FIELD NO.	FIELD NAME - DESCRIPTION	SIZE	CLASS C/P/Z/B	POSITION FROM	POSITION THRU	FORMAT/CONSTANT
1	Delete Code	1	C	1	1	D = deleted
2	Part Number	5	C	2	6	Key field
3	Part Name	20	C	7	26	
4	Amount On Hand	6	Z	27	32	0 decimal positions
5	Amount On Order	6	Z	33	38	0 decimal positions
6	Average Cost	7	Z	39	45	2 decimal positions
7	Amount Allocated	6	Z	46	51	0 decimal positions
8	Economic Order Quantity	6	Z	52	57	0 decimal positions
9	Safety Stock	6	Z	58	63	0 decimal positions
10	Lead Time	3	Z	64	66	0 decimal positions
11	Warehouse Location	3	C	67	69	

Data for Assignment 18-1:

Part#	Part Name	Amount On Hand	Avg Cost	Amount On Order	Amount Allocated	EOQ	Safety Stock	Lead Time	Warehouse Location
A2345	AC SPARK PLUG	000000	0000075	012000	005000	001440	002000	014	ABC
B6789	FRAM OIL FILTERS	004000	0000324	001200	001875	001200	000500	031	DEF
C5555	POINT SETS	000500	0000227	000000	000000	001000	002000	015	AAA
D9876	LOCKING GAS CAP	000325	0000455	001000	000400	001000	000400	090	GHI
E3459	LIQUID CAR WASH	010224	0000125	000000	050000	004000	003000	015	

Laboratory Assignment 18-2: INTERACTIVE INQUIRY OF THE MASTER PARTS INVENTORY FILE

Assignment 18-1 *must* be completed before this assignment is started. Modify Assignment 18-1 to control interactive inquiry of the master parts inventory file. Include a second screen record in the existing display format member for Assignment 18-1 that will function as a prompt screen to enter a part number. Its suggested format follows:

```
0X/XX/XX                  PARTS INVENTORY                 INQUIRY

     ENTER PART NUMBER: XXXXX          PART NOT FOUND!

               ENTER - TO CONTINUE        CMD KEY 7 - EOJ
```

The error message, PART NOT FOUND!, is to be displayed when the part number entered is not found in the master parts inventory file. Modify the screen format completed (second screen for this assignment) for Assignment 18-1 as follows:

1. Change the constant (first line) from ENTRY/ADDS to INQUIRY.
2. Include the delete code field at the end of the existing display record format.
3. Modify the screen coding to support only the output of data (from the program to the screen record).
4. Include a message in the second screen to press ENTER to continue.

Inquiry part numbers A2345, C5555, and F7890 and print a copy of the screen with the PRINT key.

Laboratory Assignment 18-3: INTERACTIVE UPDATE/DELETE OF THE MASTER PARTS INVENTORY FILE

Assignment 18-2 *must* be completed before this assignment is started. Modify Assignment 18-2 to control interactive update and deletion (tagging method) of the master parts inventory file. The changes to the screens are:

First and Second Screens:

1. Change the constant INQUIRY to UPDATE/DELETE.

Second Screen:

2. Modify the screen coding to support the input and output of data.
3. In addition to the ENTER key control for updating, include a command key so that the operator may return to the first screen without executing an update.

Refer to the File Definition form included with Assignment 18-1 for the attributes of the master parts inventory disk file.

Update Data:

Delete Code 1	Part# 2-6	Part Name 7-26	Amount On Hand 27-32	Amount On Order 33-38	Avg Cost 39-45	Amount Allocated 46-51	EOQ 52-57	Safety Stock 58-63	Lead Time 64-66	Warehouse Location 67-69
	D9876									GHH
	A2345		007000							
D	E3459									
	D9876			003000		001400				

Note: Fields that do not have update values are <u>not</u> to be changed when screen is displayed with data from the related disk record.

Validate the update process by accessing the records updated or deleted by execution of this program (or Assignment 18-2).

chapter 19
Physical Files (AS/400 and System/38)

TYPES OF DATA BASE FILES

An *externally described file* is one in which the record and field descriptions are defined outside of a program. The two types supported on the AS/400 are *physical* and *logical* files. Physical files are explained in this chapter and logical files in Chapter 22.

Similar to disk files on non-data based computer system, physical files contain the actual data records. The attributes of the records may be data base defined or program defined. If they are data base defined, the field definitions are specified outside of a program. For *program defined* files, the field attributes must be included in the program in the traditional RPG II way.

Physical files may be organized as *arrival sequence* or *key sequence* files. The type of organization determines the access path followed when the file is processed.

An *arrival sequence* file is similar to the standard sequential organization file in which keys are not specified. Records, which are processed in the order that they were loaded, may be read, written, and updated using sequential or relative record processing methods. Direct file organization is not supported on the AS/400 or System/38. The processing methods unique to that file type, however, may be simulated for arrival of key-sequenced files.

A *key sequence* file is similar to the familiar indexed sequential file organization in which one or more fields may be specified as a key. Processing features unique to this kind of file organization are the following:

1. Records may be accessed sequentially in key value order or randomly by the value of a key.
2. Records may be accessed in arrival sequence order (ignores key value order).
3. Composite keys may be defined by specifying more than one field within the body of a record. These fields need not be contiguous.
4. Any field in the body of the record may be specified as a key field after the file is created. However, a logical file must be used to process the physical file by the new key(s).
5. In addition to standard sequential and random processing, files may be read backward or accessed by a relative record number.
6. The next record that is lower or higher than the specified key value may be accessed.

BUILDING A PHYSICAL FILE

The steps followed for building a physical file are the following:

1. Design a record format based on some application criteria.
2. Write the code on a Data Description Specifications (DDS) form.
3. Enter the DDS statements via SEU and save.
4. Compile, debug, and store the error-free physical file object format.

Record Format Design

Unlike the file organization types common to the traditional computer system, the AS/400 Physical File structure will support only *one* record format. Consequently, when designing a user-system, this restriction must be considered. Note, however, that multiple record processing may be simulated by *non-joined* and *joined logical* files which are related to two or more physical files.

The record design shown in Figure 19-1 will be used as the documentation source to define; first, an *arrival sequence* and then, a *keyed sequence* physical file.

FILE DEFINITION

SYSTEM AS/400		DRAWN BY S. Myers	
FILE NAME P1PF1		DATE 3/1/91	REV. NO. 0
CREATED BY S. Myers		FILE TYPE Physical	
RECORD NAME P1PF1R		KEY LENGTH None	
RECORDING MODE Fixed	ORGANIZATION Arrival	SEQUENCE None	
RECORD SIZE 75 bytes	BLOCKING FACTOR 1	BLOCKSIZE 75 bytes	

FIELD DATA

FIELD NO.	FIELD NAME - DESCRIPTION	SIZE	CLASS C/P/Z/B	POSITION FROM	POSITION THRU	FORMAT/CONSTANT
1	CUST#	5	C	1	5	
2	NAME	20	C	6	25	
3	STREET	20	C	26	45	
4	CITY	20	C	46	65	
5	STATE	2	C	66	67	
6	ZIP	5	P	68	70	
7	BALANC	8	P	71	75	

Figure 19-1 Example Physical File record format.

THE DATA DESCRIPTION SPECIFICATIONS (DDS) FORM

Physical File-Arrival Sequence Organization

All physical file formats (arrival and keyed sequence) are usually written on Data Description Specifications forms before the code is entered via CRT.

A form completed for the example arrival sequence physical file is illustrated and explained in Figure 19-2.

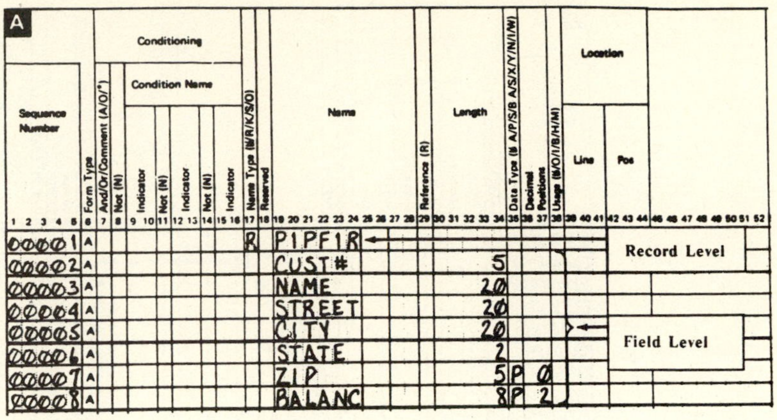

Only the fields related to the example arrival sequence physical file are explained below:

Column 6 - The letter A must be included in every statement. Entry of the DDS code via SEU will automatically supply this value.

Record level (Line 00001):

Name Type

Column 17 The letter R must be included to indicate the entry defines the physical file's record name. Only one record format may be defined for a physical file.

Columns 19-28 Programmer-supplied record name is entered left-justified in this field. Record names must be 10 characters or less and begin with an alphabetic character or one of the special characters @, $, and #. All of the other characters in the record name may be A-Z, 0-9, @, $, #, and underscore _. Embedded blanks are not permitted.

Field level (Lines 00002 to 00008):

Name

Columns 19-28 Programmer-supplied field names (CUST#, NAME, STREET, CITY, STATE, ZIP, and BALANC must be left-justified in this field. For physical files that are processed by RPG/400 programs, field sizes are limited to six characters and the underscore character is not supported. Otherwise the same syntax restrictions imposed on record names apply to field names. Note that the field names specified become a permanent part of the data base and must be referenced exactly as formatted in any high-level languages that process the file.

Length

Columns 30-34 Unless the field is being referenced from a Field Reference file, every field must be defined with a length. For packed fields, the unpacked size is specified. The field length entry must be right-justified in the Length field.

Data Type

Column 35 The data types specified for this field are:

Numeric Types	Alphanumeric Type
P - Packed Decimal	A - Any character supported by the system
S - Zoned Decimal	
B - Binary	
F - Floating Point	

If the entry is omitted, and columns 36-37 (Decimal Positions) are blank, the default is A. If columns 36-37 are not blank (include the number from 0 to 9), the default will be P.

Fields CUST# through STATE are defined as a character type (letter) with ZIP and BALANCE defined as packed by the letter P.

Columns 38-44, which includes fields for Usage and Location, are related to Display files. The Functions field (columns 45-80) supports 26 keywords that are valid for physical files. None are specified for this example, however, when other DDS supported file types are discussed, some of the keywords will be introduced.

Figure 19-2 Completed Data Description Specifications form for example arrival sequence physical file.

Physical File-Key Sequence Organization

Except for key definition requirements, the DDS coding for a keyed sequence physical file is similar to an arrival sequence. The DDS coding for the arrival sequence file previously shown in Figure 19-2 is modified in Figure 19-3 to define it as a keyed sequence physical file.

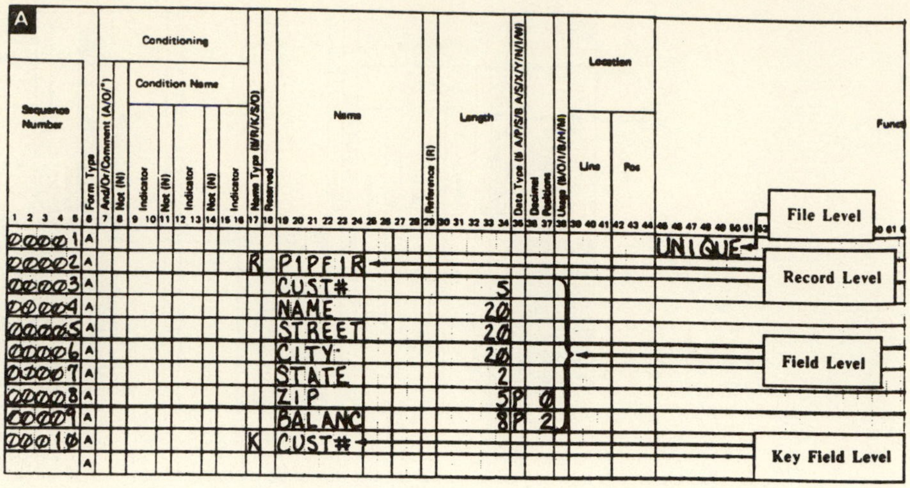

Only the fields related to the example keyed sequence physical file are explained below. Those common to both file organization types were explained in Figure 19-2.

Column 6 - The letter A must be included in every statement. Entry of the DDS code via SEU will automatically supply this value.

File level (Line 00001):
Functions

Columns 45-80 The file level keyword **UNIQUE** specifies that the key sequence file is not to support duplicate keys. During program execution, if a load or an add record has a key value the same as one that is already stored in the file, a runtime error will be flagged. If **UNIQUE** is omitted, records with duplicate keys will be supported. When the physical file is subsequently processed, the duplicate records will be accessed in a **FIFO** (first in, first out) order. However, the duplicate records may be accessed in a last in, first out order by specifying the keyword **LIFO** at the file level.

Record level (Line 00002): Explained in Figure 19-2.

Field level (Lines 00003-00009): Explained in Figure 19-2.

Key field level (Line 00010):
Name type
Column 17 The letter **K** indicates that the related NAME entry is the key field for the key sequence file.
Name
Columns 19-28 Items defined as key fields must be fields previously defined in the record format. Any number of key fields may be specified. The order of the key fields indicates how the composite key is built. The first key field specified places that value as the high-order segment with the last key field, as the low-order segment. Because the key fields were previously defined at the field level, length, data type, and decimal position entries are omitted.

Figure 19-3 Completed Data Description Specifications form for example keyed sequenced physical file.

DDS Function Field Keywords

Only one function field entry, the keyword UNIQUE, has been discussed for physical files. A total of 26 keywords are available in the definition of a physical file. They are the following:

ABSVAL	DIGIT	REFFLD
ALIAS	EDTCDE	REFSHIFT
ALTSEQ	EDTWRD	SIGNED
CHECK	FLTPCN	TEXT
CMP	FORMAT	UNIQUE
COLHDG	LIFO	UNSIGNED
COMP	NOALTSEQ	VALUES
DESCEND	RANGE	ZONE
DFT	REF	

When specified for a physical file, any of these keywords must be entered in the Functions field (columns 45–80). Some may be used only at the file, record, or field level. Examples showing how a few of the keywords are used are illustrated in Figure 19-4.

A

Sequence Number (1–5)	Form Type (6)	Name Type (17)	Name (19–28)	Length (30–34)	Data Type (35)	Decimal Positions (36–37)	Functions (45–80)
00001	A						LIFO
00002	A	R	P1PF1R				TEXT('CUSTOMER MASTER')
00003	A		CUST#	5			COLHDG('CUSTOMER' 'NUMBER')
00004	A		NAME	20			COLHDG('CUSTOMER NAME')
00005	A		STREET	20			
00006	A		CITY	20			
00007	A		STATE	2			
00008	A		ZIP	5	P	0	
00009	A		BALANC	8	P	2	EDTCDE(J)
00010	A	K	CUST#				DESCEND

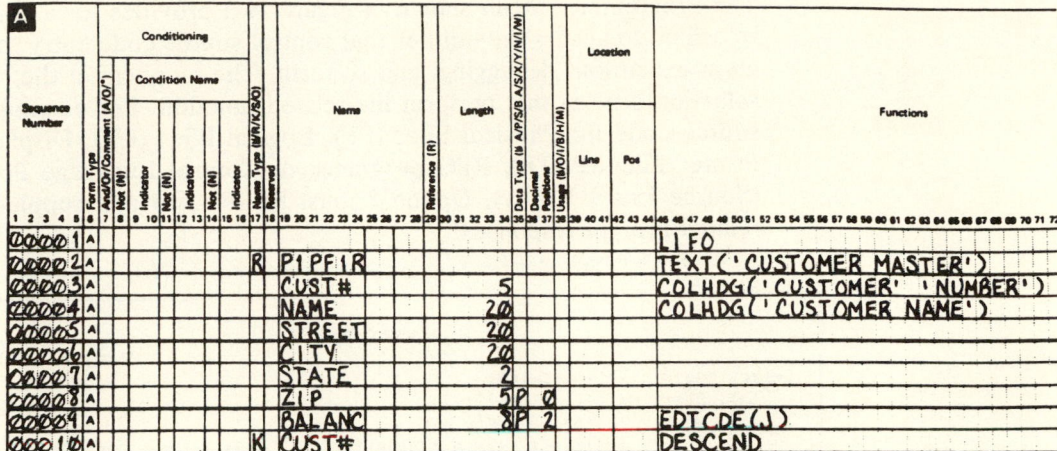

Line 00001 **LIFO**

Specifies that the keyed file which supports records with duplicate keys is to be processed in a last in, first out mode. In other words the last duplicate record loaded will be the first processed. If this keyword is omitted, the file will process the duplicate records in a **FIFO** (first in, first-out) mode.

Line 00002 **TEXT('CUSTOMER MASTER')**

A record or field level keyword that provides additional documentation for a record or field. The text, that must be enclosed in parenthesis and single quotes, will be included with the related field name on any source listing that includes the physical file. A maximum of 50 characters may be specified.

Line 00003 **COLHDG('CUSTOMER' 'NUMBER')**

A field level keyword (column heading) that may be used as a field label or prompt in a screen design aid (SDA) utility, data file utility (DFU), and query utility. If **COLHDG** is not specified and the field is reference in one of the named utilities, the default will be the field name.

The example shown will center NUMBER under CUSTOMER. Each heading line for a field must be enclosed in single quotes. A maximum of three lines of 20 characters each is supported.

If **TEXT** is not specified and **COLHDG** is, **COLHDG** will control the functions of both keywords.

Line 00004 **COLHDG('CUSTOMER NAME')**

Because the entire constant is enclosed in only one set of single quotes, it will appear as one heading.

Under most circumstances, **COLHDG** functions would be included for all of the fields in the body of the physical file record.

Line 00009 **EDTCDE(J)**

This keyword provides the same edit code control as RPG. The letter J, enclosed in parenthesis, will edit the numeric field with zero suppression, insertion of a decimal, comma(s), and a negative sign after the low-order digit if the value is negative.

Note that the editing function will not be performed for physical file loading or maintenance functions. It is only operational for Display and Printer files and does not modify the physical file data.

Any **EDTCDE** entry may be overridden in a Display or Printer file by specifying the keyword DLTEDT.

Line 00010 **DESCEND**

This keyword must be specified at the key field level. When used it will process the physical file in a descending key value sequence instead of the ascending sequence default. If the keyword is not specified, the records will be accessed in ascending key value order.

Figure 19-4 Examples of physical file keyword usage.

ENTERING DDS PHYSICAL FILE CODE

The Programmer Menu (AS/400 Format)

The Programmer Menu shown in Figure 19-5 provides for a convenient method by which to access the utilities that control source code entry, compilation, program execution, debugging, and so forth. The numbers at the left side relate to selection criteria that perform the related function. For example, to enter DDS source code for Physical Files (PF), Logical Files (LF), Display Files (DSPF), Printer Files (PRTF), RPG programs, or Control Language Programs by SEU (Source Entry Utility), Option 8 must be selected and supplemented with the related prompt responses.

```
                              Programmer Menu
                                                         System:   SVMCBPT
 Select one of the following:
      1. Start Data File Utility
      2. Work with AS/400 Query
      3. Create an object from a source file     object name, type, pgm for CMD
      4. Call a program                          program name
      5. Run a command                           command
      6. Submit a job                            (job name), , , (command)
      7. Go to a menu                            menu name
      8. Edit a source file member               (srcmbr), (type)
      9. Design display format using SDA         (srcmbr), ,(mode)
     90. Sign off                                (*nolist, *list)

 Selection . . . . .    8             Parm . . . .    p1pf1
 Type  . . . . . . .    PF            Parm 2 . . .
 Command . . . . . .

 Source file . . . .    stan          Source library . . . . . . .   cemyers400
 Object library  . .    cemyers400    Job description  . . . . . .   cemyers

 F3=Exit        F4=Prompt             F6=Display messages     F10=Command entry
 F12=Previous   F14=Work with submitted jobs                  F18=Work with output
```

The prompts to call **SEU** (Source Entry Utility) for **DDS** code entry for a Physical File are explained below:

Option: 8 must be entered to call the **SEU** utility.

Type: Programmer-supplied Physical File name (limited to 8 characters for RPG) must be entered for this prompt. p1pf1 is entered for this example (may be lower or upper case characters).

Parm: **PF** must be entered for Physical File source entry. The entry calls the related SEU screen format.

Parm 2: Used for Option 1 (DFU app) and Option 2 (Query app). Not used for PF create.

Command: Control language statement may be entered for this prompt. Execution is controlled by Option 5 (Execute command). For example, in lieu of using Option 8 and the Parm and Type options, the Physical File could be cvreated and compiled by entering the command CRTPF for this prompt and pressing Command Key 4. A sequence of response screens will display to define the attributes of the file. All of the default attributes may be taken or specific attributes may be changed (file size and so forth).

Prompts for Source file, Source library, Object library, and Job description are usually included in the user's logon profile. However, any of them may be changed as needed.

The Enter key must be pressed to display an SEU format for DDS PF entry. Sign off from this menu is controlled by Option 90. Prompts Parm, Type, Parm 2 and Command must be blank for Sign off to execute.

Command key options are included at the bottom of the screen to control processing options.

The PROGRAMMER MENU may be accessed from any AS/400 display that has a Command Line by typing **STRPGMMNU** and pressing Enter.

Figure 19-5 Programmer Menu (AS/400 format) filled in to call SEU for Physical File code entry.

Entering the DDS Code for a Physical File with SEU

After the prompts are completed to create a physical file format and the ENTER key is pressed, the SEU screen shown in Figure 19-6 will display.

```
EDIT     US W:1     Mbr: SOURCE                     Scan:
FMT PF .....A..........T.Name++++++RLen++TDpB......Functions++++++++++++++++++
       ****BEGINNING OF DATA****
.......
       ********END OF DATA*******
```

Figure 19-6 SEU EDIT screen (A format) for DDS physical file code entry.

Notice that the second line begins with the identifying format (FMT PF). The remainder of the line duplicates the fields on the DDS form. For example, the five dots after FMT PF represent the sequence number (columns 1–5) on the form; A in column 6 gives the form type, and so forth. Statements are entered horizontally by aligning the field entry with the column header. Pressing the ENTER key stores the instructions and moves the "******* END OF DATA *******" logo down one line. Figure 19-7 illustrates the EDIT screen after all the example physical file statements have been entered.

```
EDIT     US W:1     Mbr: SOURCE                     Scan:
FMT PF .....A..........T.Name++++++RLen++TDpB......Functions++++++++++++++++++
       ****BEGINNING OF DATA****
            A                                      UNIQUE
            A          R P1PF1R
            A            CUST#          5A
            A            NAME          20A
            A            STREET        20A
            A            CITY          20A
            A            STATE          2A
            A            ZIP            5P 0
            A            BALANC         8P 2
            A          K CUST#
       *******END OF DATA*******
```

Figure 19-7 Filled-in SEU EDIT screen with example PF code.

Another method that some programmers find more convenient is to use prompt line control. Prompt line entry is initiated by entering P on a statement line and pressing the ENTER key.

A prompt line (for the format type) with field headers will display at the bottom of the screen as shown in Figure 19-8. Right-justification of number field entries is automatically supported when the FIELD EXIT key is pressed. After

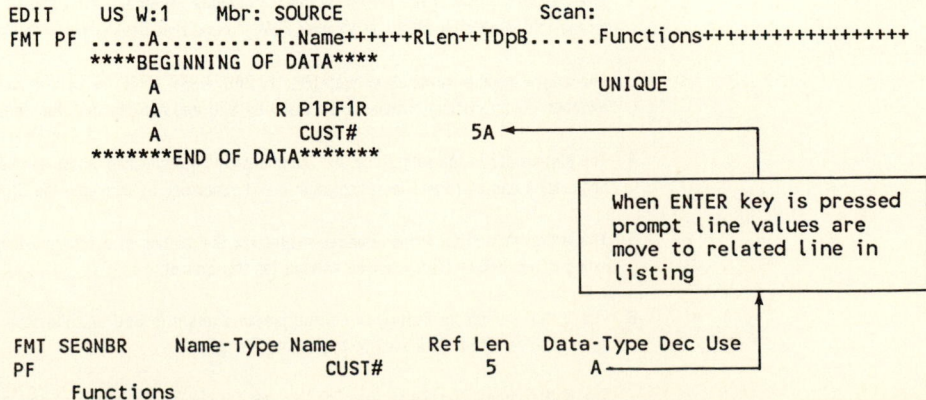

```
EDIT     US W:1     Mbr: SOURCE                     Scan:
FMT PF .....A..........T.Name++++++RLen++TDpB......Functions++++++++++++++++++
       ****BEGINNING OF DATA****
            A                                      UNIQUE
            A          R P1PF1R
            A            CUST#          5A <-------------------+
       *******END OF DATA*******                               |
                                            +--------------------------------+
                                            | When ENTER key is pressed      |
                                            | prompt line values are         |
                                            | move to related line in        |
                                            | listing                        |
                                            +--------------------------------+
                                                               ^
FMT SEQNBR    Name-Type Name        Ref Len   Data-Type Dec Use |
PF                      CUST#            5        A ------------+
     Functions
```

Figure 19-8 Filled-in SEU prompt line format for DDS physical file code entry.

all the values for the statement are entered, the ENTER key is pressed, and the statement is moved to its related location in the top section of the screen and the prompt line is blanked out. This sequential entry of the source code will continue at the option of the programmer. With either method (free-form or prompt), any syntax errors will be displayed when the ENTER key is pressed. Any corrections must be made before the statement is moved and stored.

The *insertion* of a line between existing lines is performed by placing the cursor above the line where the inserted line is to be entered, typing IP at the beginning of the statement and pressing the ENTER key. After the prompt line is completed and the ENTER key is pressed, the new statement is inserted in the specified location. Line insertion using the free-form method is executed by specifying the letter I at the beginning of the previous statement and pressing the ENTER key. A blank line will be displayed to enter the statement.

A line may be *deleted* by typing the letter D at the beginning of a statement. Consecutive lines may be deleted from the listing by typing DD at the beginning of the first line and DD at the beginning of the last line of the group to be deleted.

After all the source code for the physical file is entered, Command Key 3 is pressed to exit from SEU EDIT screen into an SEU EXIT menu. The screen shown in Figure 19-9, which gives the programmer *exit options*, will be displayed.

```
                                  Exit

   Type choices, press Enter.

     Change/create member . . . . . . .   Y              Y=Yes, N=No
       Member . . . . . . . . . . . . .   P1PF1          Name
       File . . . . . . . . . . . . . .   STAN           Name
         Library . . . . . . . . . . . .  CEMYERS400     Name
       Text . . . . . . . . . . . . . .   Customer File

       Resequence member . . . . . . . .  Y              Y=Yes, N=No
         Start . . . . . . . . . . . . .  0001.00        0000.01 - 9999.99
         Increment . . . . . . . . . . .  01.00          00.01 - 99.99

     Print member . . . . . . . . . . .   N              Y=Yes, N=No

     Return to editing . . . . . . . . .  N              Y=Yes, N=No

     Go to member list . . . . . . . . .  N              Y=Yes, N=No


   F3=Exit        F5=Refresh       F12=Previous
```

1. The **EXIT** screen is displayed if Command Key 3 is pressed when in SEU.
2. The variables shown in the Exit menu are the defaults. **Member, File,** and **Library** names are accessed by the entries on the PROGRAMMER MENU or through PDM (Programmer Development Method). A **Text** entry provides documentation.
3. The source member currently entered (PF, LF, RPG, DSPF, PRTF, or CLP) is saved by the Y default for **Change/create member**. If an existing member is accessed by SEU and not changed, the default here will be an N (No).
4. The statements in the source file will automatically be sequenced unless the default Y is overridden with an N. Sequencing and statement incrementation may be modified by changing the **Start** and **Increment** prompts.
5. The N (No) default for **Print member** suppresses the printing of a source listing (before compilation). If a source listing is required, Y (Yes) must be entered for this prompt.
6. The N (No) default for **Return to editing** prevents return to SEU and the source file currently entered. Y (Yes) must be entered to return SEU back to the source listing.
7. The N (No) default for **Go to member list** will not display the names of any members in the current library. Y (Yes) must be entered to display a member list.

Figure 19-9 SEU EXIT screen (AS/400 format).

When the ENTER Key is pressed, control is returned to the Programmer Menu. At this step of data base development, the physical file source member is usually compiled. Again, this is a different procedure from that of the traditional computer system in which record formats are not compiled but are either hard-coded in the source program or included as a source code COPY member. With either method, the object program will include the record format.

In the AS/400 and System/38 environments, the physical file format is stored separately as a source member and object member mutually exclusive from any high-level language program. The physical file's record format is called in during program compilation and becomes an integral part of the object program.

Physical File Format Compilation

When control returns to the Programmer Menu, all the original prompt entries are retained, unless changed on the SEU EXIT menu. The physical file is compiled by entering a 3 in response to the Option prompt (Create object) and pressing the ENTER key.

The two listings shown in Figure 19-10 are generated when the physical file is compiled. The first includes the header information related to the physical file and lists the source member format exactly as created. A second listing, which is printed immediately after the first, is called an EXPANDED SOURCE. It supplements the original source with the COLHDG keywords for each field and identifies field lengths and the beginning position of each field in the output buffer. During program execution, input and output buffers are automatically built for all physical files processed. It is important to note that after the physical file is loaded, subsequent compilation will delete all the data in the file.

```
File Name . . . . . . . . . . . . . . . . . . . . . :   P1PF1
  Library name  . . . . . . . . . . . . . . . . . . :   CEMYERS400
File attribute  . . . . . . . . . . . . . . . . . . :   Physical
Source file containing DDS  . . . . . . . . . . . . :   STAN
  Library name  . . . . . . . . . . . . . . . . . . :   CEMYERS400
Source member containing DDS  . . . . . . . . . . . :   P1PF1
Source member last changed  . . . . . . . . . . . . :   09/20/91    6:30:00
Source listing options  . . . . . . . . . . . . . . :   *SOURCE     *LIST       *NOSECLVL
DDS generation severity level . . . . . . . . . . . :   20
File type . . . . . . . . . . . . . . . . . . . . . :   *DATA
Authority . . . . . . . . . . . . . . . . . . . . . :   *CHANGE
Text  . . . . . . . . . . . . . . . . . . . . . . . :   customer master
Compiler  . . . . . . . . . . . . . . . . . . . . . :   IBM AS/400 Data Description Processor

                                        Data Description Source

SEQNBR  *...+....1....+....2....+....3....+....4....+....5....+....6....+....7....+....8  Date

   100       A                                      UNIQUE                                09/20/91
   200       A          R P1PF1R                                                          09/20/91
   300       A            CUST#          5A                                               09/20/91
   400       A            NAME          20A                                               09/20/91
   500       A            STREET        20A                                               09/20/91
   600       A            CITY          20A                                               09/20/91
   700       A            STATE          2A                                               09/20/91
   800       A            ZIP            5P 0                                             09/20/91
   900       A            BALANC         8P 2                                             09/20/91
  1000       A          K CUST#                                                           09/20/91

                                          EXPANDED SOURCE
                                                                                         FIELD  BUFFER POSITION
SEQNBR  *...+....1....+....2....+....3....+....4....+....5....+....6....+....7....+....8  LEN     OUT      IN

   100       A                                      UNIQUE
   200       A          R P1PF1R
   300       A            CUST#          5A         COLHDG('CUST#')                         5       1
   400       A            NAME          20A         COLHDG('NAME')                         20       6
   500       A            STREET        20A         COLHDG('STREET')                       20      26
   600       A            CITY          20A         COLHDG('CITY')                         20      46
   700       A            STATE          2A         COLHDG('STATE')                         2      66
   800       A            ZIP            5P 0       COLHDG('ZIP')                           3      68
   900       A            BALANC         8P 2       COLHDG('BALANC')                        5      71
  1000       A          K CUST#
```

Figure 19-10 Listings generated from compilation of the example physical file data base format.

Building a Physical File Without Record or Field Definitions

A physical file may be defined without record and field descriptions by the CRTPF (create physical file) command. This control language statement may be entered from the Programmer Menu by specifying 5 as the Option and CRTPF on the command line. After Command Key 4 is pressed, the prompt screens shown in Figure 19-11 will display. Most of the prompts shown in the two screens in Figure 19-11 have default values specified. However, the programmer may change any entry as needed. For a complete explanation of each prompt line, the Control Language manual should be referenced.

```
                    Create Physical File (CRTPF) Prompt        +++
Enter the following:
  Physical file name:              FILE        R   ______
    Library name:                                     QGPL
  Source file containing DDS:      SRCFILE     P   *FILE
    Library name:                                     *LIBL
  Source member containing DDS:    SRCMBR      P   ________
  Record length, if no DDS:        RCDLEN      P
  Source listing options:          OPTION      P   ________

  DDS generation severity level:   GENLVL          ____
  File type (*DATA *SRC):          FILETYPE        *DATA
  Member name, if desired:         MBR             *FILE
  Expiration date for members:     EXPDATE         *NONE
  Maximum number of members:       MAXMBRS         1
  Access path maintenance:         MAINT           *IMMED
  Access path recovery:            RECOVER         ________
  Force keyed access path:         FRCACCPTH       *NO
  Member size:                     SIZE
    Initial number of records:                     10000
    Increment number of records:                   1000
    Maximum number of increments:                  3
  Allocate storage (*NO *YES):     ALLOCATE        *NO
```

```
                    Create Physical File (CRTPF) Prompt

Contiguous storage?              CONTIG        *NO
Preferred storage unit:          UNIT          *ANY
Nbr of rcds to force a write:    FRCRATIO      *NONE
Max file wait in sec:            WAITFILE      *IMMED
Max record wait in sec:          WAITRCD       60
Share open data path?            SHARE         *NO
Max % deleted records allowed:   DLTPCT        *NONE
Check record format level ID?    LVLCHK        *YES
Public authority                 PUBAUT
  (*NORMAL *ALL *NONE):                        *NORMAL
Text 'description':              TEXT          SRCMBRTXT
```

Figure 19-11 CRTPF CL command generated parameter screens to create a physical file.

When a physical file is built without a DDS code, two parameters that must be responded to are the physical file name (FILE) entry on line 1 of the first screen and the record length (RCDLEN) entry on line 6 of the same screen. Defaults may be taken for the remaining prompts in both screens 1 and 2.

Notice that the CRTPF command functions are automatically executed when the previously discussed method of building a DDS file and then creating an object member for it by selecting Option 3 on the Programmer Menu is followed. Unless some of the defaults on the parameter screens have to be changed, the create physical file (CRTPF) functions are transparent to the programmer.

Displaying Attributes of a Physical File

The attributes of a physical file may be displayed by the DSPFD (display file description) command. If the Programmer Menu is used to execute the command after Option 5 is selected, DSPFD is entered on the command line and Command Key 4 is pressed. The screen shown in Figure 19-12 will be displayed with default values for every parameter except the file name (FILE). Any default value may be changed at the option of the programmer. After the ENTER key is pressed, the attributes of the physical file are displayed.

```
              Display File Description (DSPFD) Prompt
Enter the following:
  File or generic* name:              FILE       R   ________
    Library name:                                       *USRLIBL
  Type of info to display:            TYPE       P   *ALL
                                      + for more     __________
  Output (*  *LIST *NONE):            OUTPUT     P   *
  File attributes:                    FILEATR    P   *ALL
                                      + for more     ______
  File to receive output:             OUTFILE    P   *NONE
    Library name:                                       ________
  Member to receive output:           OUTMBR     P   *FIRST
  File location:                      SYSTEM     P   *LCL
```

Figure 19-12 Display File Description (DSPFD) prompt screen.

Displaying Field Attributes of a Physical File (DSPFFD)

The field attributes of a physical file (names, sizes, types, output buffer locations, and so forth) may be determined by the DSPFFD command. Again, if the Programmer Menu is used to control commands, Option 5 is selected, DSPFFD is entered on the Command line, and Command Key 4 is pressed, then the screen shown in Figure 19-13 will display. After the programmer responds to the file name (FILE) entry and presses ENTER, the field attributes of the physical file are displayed.

```
          Display File Field Description (DSPFD) Prompt
Enter the following:
  File or generic* name:              FILE       R   ________
    Library name:                                       *USRLIBL
  Output (*  *LIST *NONE):            OUTPUT     P   *
  File to receive output:             OUTFILE    P   *NONE
    Library name:                                       ________
  Member to receive output:           OUTMBR     P   *FIRST
  File location:                      SYSTEM     P   *LCL
```

Figure 19-13 Display file field description (DSPFFD) prompt screen.

QUESTIONS

19-1. What is an externally defined file? What two types are supported on the AS/400 and System/38?

19-2. Explain the differences between a data base and a program defined file. How are the field attributes included in an RPG program for each method?

19-3. What organization types are supported for physical files?

19-4. Refer to Question 19-3, and explain the processing features of each organization type.

19-5. Explain the term *composite key*.

19-6. Explain how a physical file may be processed by any field included in the file in an ascending or descending order. "Sorting" is not an acceptable answer.

19-7. Name the steps followed for building a physical file.

19-8. What form is used to code a physical file? For an arrival sequence file, what are the logical levels of coding? What are they for a key sequence file?

19-9. How many record formats may be included in a physical file?

19-10. What is the function of nonjoined and joined logical files?

19-11. What type of physical file is shown in the following figure? Explain the meaning of each entry.

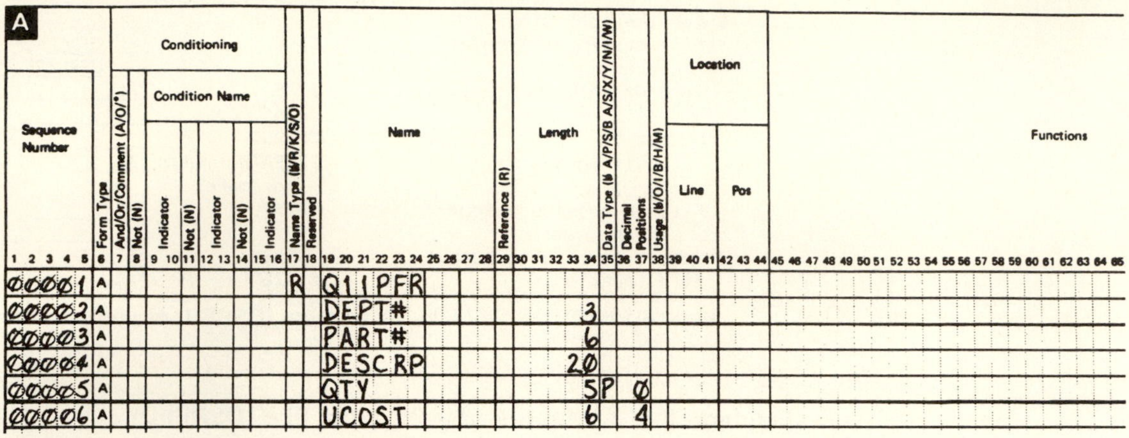

Sequence Number (1–5)	Form Type (6)	Name Type (17)	Name (19–28)	Length (30–34)	Data Type (35)	Decimal Positions (36–37)
ØØØØ1	A	R	Q11PFR			
ØØØØ2	A		DEPT#	3		
ØØØØ3	A		PART#	6		
ØØØØ4	A		DESCRP	20		
ØØØØ5	A		QTY	5	P	Ø
ØØØØ6	A		UCOST	6		4

19-12. Refer to Question 19-11, and notice that some of the fields do not include an entry in column 35. What is the default type for these fields?

19-13. Refer to Question 19-11, and explain the function of the letter P in column 35 for the QTY field. What does the length entry for this field type refer to?

19-14. Rewrite the coding in the Question 19-11 to define a key sequence file. Assume that duplicate keys are not to be supported and that DEPT# and PART# are to be specified as a composite key.

19-15. What is the function of the following physical file keywords?

```
COLHDG    EDTWRD   REFFLD
DESCEND   LIFO     TEXT
EDTCDE    REF      UNIQUE
```

19-16. What entries are needed on the Programmer Menu to call the utility to enter the DDS code for a physical file?

19-17. Name the utility used to enter the DDS code for a physical file. What is a prompt line in this utility?

19-18. After the source code for a physical file is entered, explain the procedures that must be followed to exit from the utility and prepare the physical file for execution.

19-19. How many listings are generated when Option 3 is selected from the Programmer Menu for the compilation of a physical file? Briefly explain how the listings differ.

19-20. What Control Language command is executed when Option 3 is selected from the Programmer Menu?

19-21. Under what circumstances does the CRTPF command have to be explicitly specified?

19-22. What is the CL command used to display the attributes of a physical file? Name the CL command needed to display the field attributes of a physical file.

EXERCISES

19-1. From the following record layout form, write the DDS coding to define a Physical File organized as arrival sequence. Include a TEXT function for the record level and COLHDGs for the field level. ZIP and CREDIT LIMIT fields are to be defined as packed.

	CUST#	CUSTOMER NAME	ADDRESS	CITY	STATE	ZIP	CREDIT LIMIT	
9	9 9 9 9 9 9 9	9 9 9 9 9 9 9 9 9 9 9 9 9 9 9 9 9 9 9 9 9 9 9 9	9 9 9 9 9 9 9 9 9 9 9 9 9 9 9 9 9 9 9 9	9 9 9 9 9 9 9 9 9 9 9 9 9	9 9	9 9 9 9 9	9 9 9 9 9 9 9	9
1	2 3 4 5 6 7 8	9 10 11 12 13 14 15 16 17 18 19 20 21 22 23 24 25 26 27 28 29 30 31 32	33 34 35 36 37 38 39 40 41 42 43 44 45 46 47 48 49 50 51 52	53 54 55 56 57 58 59 60 61 62 63 64 65	66 67	68 69 70 71 72	73 74 75 76 77 78 79	80

DELETE CODE (position 1) CREDIT CODE (position 80)

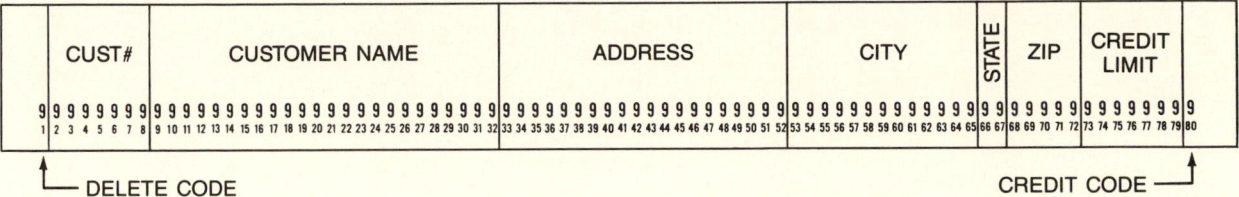

19-2. Refer to Exercise 19-1 and rewrite the DDS coding to define the Physical File in a key sequence organization. Specify CUST# as the key field. Define the file so that it will not support duplicate keys and include the control that will process the data in a descending key value order.

LABORATORY ASSIGNMENT

Laboratory Assignment 19-1: PARTS INVENTORY MASTER FILE

From the following record layout form, write the DDS coding to create a physical file that is to be defined as key sequenced. Duplicate keys are not to be supported. Part Number is to be specified as the key field. Fields that are to be stored in an internally packed decimal format are identified on the record layout form. Complete the following steps for this assignment.

1. Complete the DDS coding for the physical file. Include a TEXT entry for the record and key level entries and COLHDG for all field level entries.
2. Enter the DDS code via SEU, compile, and keep your listings.

Note: Retain this lab assignment!!!! It is the data base for assignments in Chapters 20 and 21.

Physical File Format:

FILE DEFINITION

SYSTEM Yours		DRAWN BY S. Myers
FILE NAME Yours		DATE 3/1/91 REV. NO. 0
CREATED BY S. Myers		FILE TYPE Physical
RECORD NAME Yours		KEY LENGTH 5 bytes
RECORDING MODE Fixed	ORGANIZATION Keyed	SEQUENCE Ascending by key
RECORD SIZE 54 bytes	BLOCKING FACTOR 1	BLOCKSIZE 54 bytes

FIELD DATA

FIELD NO.	FIELD NAME - DESCRIPTION	SIZE	CLASS C/P/Z/B	POSITION FROM	POSITION THRU	FORMAT/CONSTANT
1	Part number	5	C	1	5	Key field
2	Part Name	20	C	6	25	
3	Amount on hand	6	P	26	29	
4	Amount on order	6	P	30	33	
5	Average cost per unit	7	P	34	37	2 decimal positions
6	Amount allocated	6	P	38	41	
7	Economic order quantity	6	P	42	45	
8	Safety stock	6	P	46	49	
9	Lead time	3	P	50	51	
10	Warehouse location	3	C	52	54	

chapter 20
Display Files (AS/400 and System/38)

Interactive screen formats (DSPF) may be built by the following two methods:

1. Complete DDS coding forms and enter code via SEU.
2. Design and code screen using Screen Design Aid Utility (SDA).

Either approach allows the programmer to use SEU to update a screen format. However, because SDA is a standalone utility that has syntax and procedures unique to its control, it is not presented in this text. Instead, the SEU method of entering a source code that was previously introduced in Chapter 19 is followed for the creation of display files.

CREATING AN INTERACTIVE SCREEN (DSPF FILE)

The steps required to create a DSPF file using SEU are:

1. Design screen format on a layout form (or print chart).
2. Code screen format on DDS forms.
3. Enter DDS screen code via SEU.
4. Compile, debug, and test.

The screen format shown in Figure 20-1 is used as the I/O medium to load, add, delete, inquiry, and update records in the Physical File (P1PF1) built in Chapter 19.

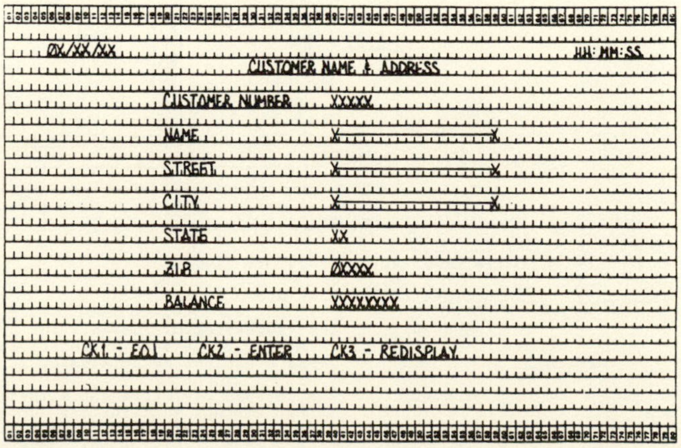

Figure 20-1 Design format for the interactive screen that controls I/O functions for the Physical File built in Chapter 19.

DDS Coding for Interactive Screens (DSPF File)

Similar to the coding for physical files, the DDS form is also used to code Display Files (DSPF). Figure 20-2 presents the completed DDS form for the screen design previously shown in Figure 20-1. As compared to physical files, notice that considerably more entries are required. The entries in file, record, and field levels for the DSPF file shown in Figure 20-2 are discussed separately in supporting figures.

Sequence Number	Form Type	Conditioning	Name Type	Name	Length	Data Type	Decimal Positions	Usage	Line	Pos	Functions
00001	A										PRINT
00002	A										CA01(01)
00003	A										CF02(02)
00004	A										CA03(03)
00005	A		R	P1SC1R							
00006	A								2	6	DATE
00007	A										EDTCDE(Y)
00008	A								2	69	TIME
00009	A								3	30	'CUSTOMER NAME & ADDRESS'
00010	A								5	20	'CUSTOMER NUMBER'
00011	A			CUST#	5			B	5	40	DSPATR(CS)
00012	A	99									ERRMSG('CANNOT ADD DUPLICATE KEY')
00013	A								7	20	'NAME'
00014	A			NAME	20			B	7	40	DSPATR(CS)
00015	A			STREET	20			B	9	40	DSPATR(CS)
00016	A								9	20	'STREET'
00017	A								11	20	'CITY'
00018	A			CITY	20			B	11	40	DSPATR(CS)
00019	A								13	20	'STATE'
00020	A			STATE	2			B	13	40	DSPATR(CS)
00021	A								15	20	'ZIP'
00022	A			ZIP	5	S	0	B	15	40	DSPATR(CS)
00023	A								17	20	'BALANCE'
00024	A			BALANC	8	S	2	B	17	40	DSPATR(CS)
00025	A								20	10	'CK1 - EOJ CK2 - ENTER CK-
00026	A										3 - REDISPLAY'

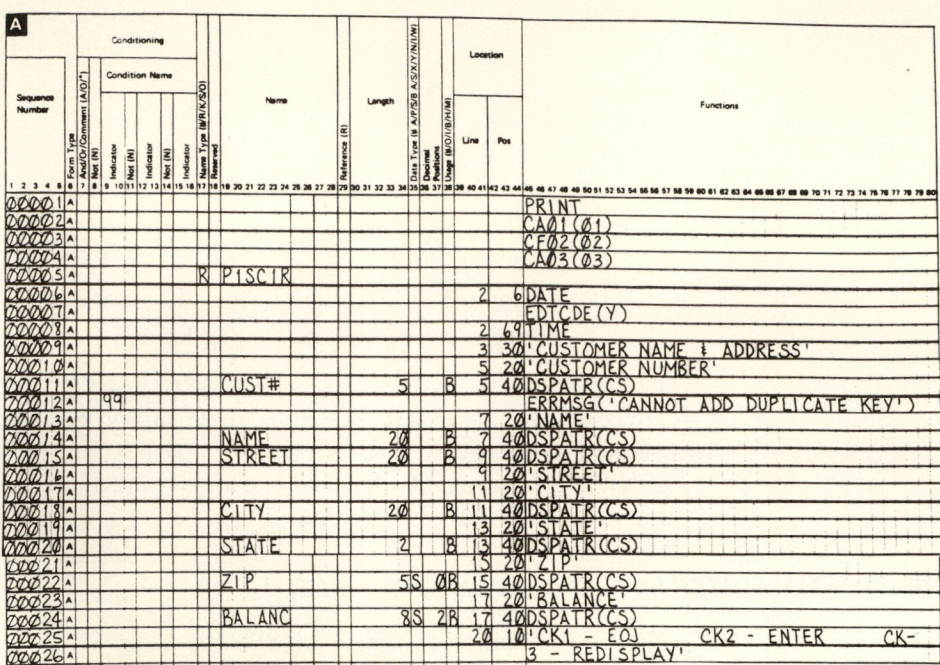

Figure 20-2 DDS coding for example interactive screen (DSPF File).

DSPF File Level Syntax

Figure 20-3 details the file level entries in the example DSPF.

Sequence Number	Form Type	Functions
00001	A	PRINT
00002	A	CA01(01)
00003	A	CF02(02)
00004	A	CA03(03)

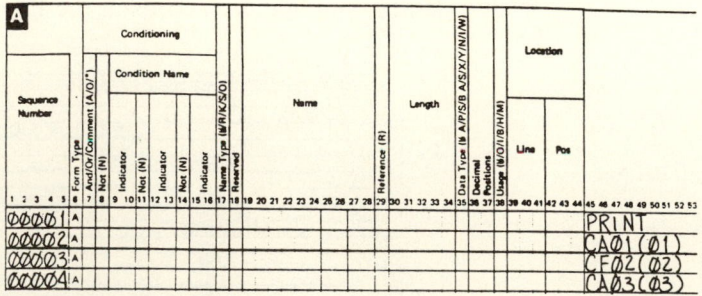

File Level (Lines 00001 to 00004)

Functions (Columns 45-80)

Line 00001 The keyword PRINT controls the printing of a displayed screen when the PRINT key is pressed on the keyboard. Without this entry the screen image could not be printed at the operator's discretion.

Line 00002 The keyword CA01 (Command Attention key) assigns the Command Key 1 to some screen control function and turns on indicator 01 for use in an RPG program. Command Attention keys 01 through 24 may be assigned at the file or record level. They do not, however, provide for the transmission of input data from a screen.

Figure 20-3 File level coding for the example DSPF file.

The format of a CA keyword is shown below:

```
                CAnn[(response-indicator ['text'])]
Command key ——/              └—Indicator assigned    \——Text is optional
on keyboard                      will be turned on to
                                 control a function in
                                 the RPG program
```

Note that the response-indicator specified does not have to be the same number assigned as the CA key.

When a CA key is pressed during program execution, all other command keys are turned off.

CA01(01) will be used to control end of job processing in the example RPG program introduced in Chapter 21.

Line 00003 — The keyword CF02 (Command Function key) assigns the Command Key 2 to some screen control function and turns on indicator 02 for use in an RPG program. Command function keys 01 through 24 may be assigned at the file or record level. The Command Function keyword (CF) differs from the Command Attention keyword (CA) in that it does provide for the transmission of modified input data from a screen.

The format of a CF keyword is shown below:

```
                CFnn[(response-indicator ['text'])]
Command key ——/              └—Indicator assigned    \——Text is optional
on keyboard                      will be turned on to
                                 control a function in
                                 the RPG program
```

Note that the response-indicator specified does not have to be the same number assigned for the CF key.

When a CF key is pressed during program execution, all other command keys are turned off.

CF02(02) will be used to control the writing of records to the Physical File in the RPG program introduced in Chapter 21.

Line 00004
Columns 45-80 — Refer to the definition of line 00002 for a description of the CA keyword. When the Command key 03 is pressed by an operator, indicator 03 will turn which will control the redisplay of a screen in the RPG program introduced in Chapter 21.

(*Continued*)

DSPF Record Level Syntax

Unlike physical files, where only one record format may be defined, display files (DSPF) support a maximum of 1,024. Any one record format may support no more than 32,763 bytes as the combined field and indicator length. Figure 20-4 shows the Record Level coding included in the example display file DSPF.

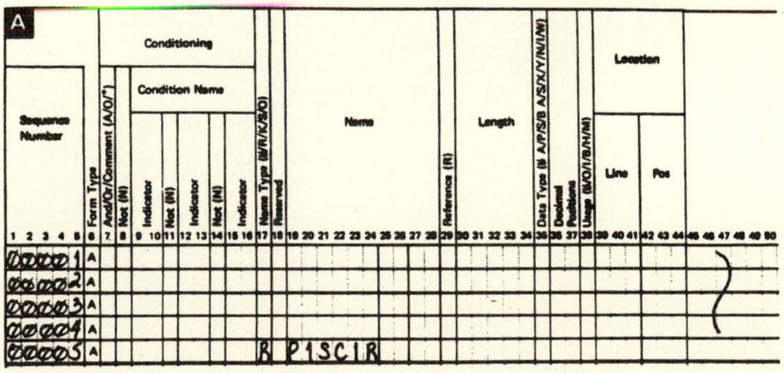

Record level (line 000005)

Name Type
Column 17 — The letter R must be specified to indicate that the entry in the following Name field is a record format.

Name
Columns 19-28 — Programmer-supplied record name is entered left-justified in this field. Record names must be 10 characters or less and begin with an alphabetic character or one of the special characters &, $, #. All of the other characters in the record name may be a combination of A-Z, 0-9, &, $, #, or underscore _. Embedded blanks are not permitted.

A maximum of 1024 record formats may be supported in one display file. Any record format may include no more than 32,763 bytes.

Figure 20-4 Record level coding for the example DSPF.

DPSF Field Level Syntax

Because of the number of new syntax concepts associated with display files (DSPF), the explanation of the field level entries is detailed in three separate figures (Figures 20-5 through 20-7).

System Date and Time (DATE/TIME). The keyword DATE accesses the system date in an MMDDYY format. Standard date editing (i.e., MM/DD/YY) is not included and must be separately specified.

System time, which is accessed by the keyword TIME, displays or prints in an HH:MM:SS format. Notice that the colons (:) are automatically inserted. An explanation of how these keyword entries are used in the example Display File is included in Figure 20-5.

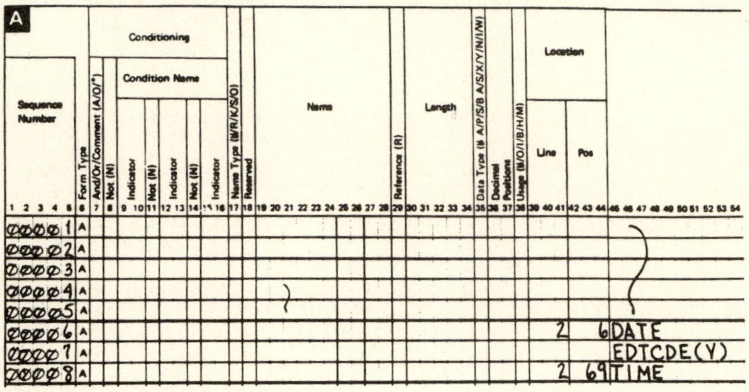

Field level (lines 00006-00008)

Line 00006

Location - Line

Columns 39-41 — The 2 right-justified in this field indicates the line on which the value will be displayed.

Location - Pos

Columns 42-44 — The 6 right-justified in this field indicates the starting position of the field or constant value that will be displayed on the line specified in the Line field.

Columns 45-80 — The keyword DATE accesses the system date in a MMDDYY format and will display the value in accordance with the Location field entries. Note that DATE is predefined as a six byte numeric field.

Line 00007

Functions

Columns 45-80 — The keyword EDTCDE controls editing of DATE or any numeric field specified in the Name field entry. Edit codes specified within parentheses are identical to those supported by RPG (1, 2, 3, 4, A, B, C, D, J, K, L, M, Y, and Z). EDTCDE(Y) edits the DATE value by suppressing the leading zero for months 01 through 09 and inserts two slashes (/) in an MM/DD/YY format. The keyword (EDTCDE) may be included on the same line as the item edited or immediately follow on the next line as in the example shown.

When unique editing is required, as for social security or telephone numbers, the keyword, EDTWRD, may be used. Again, the structure of an EDTWRD is identical to the RPG syntax for edit words. The example shown below illustrates how DATE is edited using EDTWRD.

```
EDTWRD('0 /  /  ')
```

Line 00008

Location

Columns 38-44 — Line and starting position locations are specified for the TIME value

Functions

Columns 45-80 — The keyword TIME accesses the system time in an HH:MM:SS format. Because the colons (:) are included in the TIME value, an edit code or edit word is not needed. Because TIME is redefined as a numeric field, the edit string specified may be modified with any EDTWRD format.

Figure 20-5 DATE and TIME keyword entries in the example display file.

DSPF Constants and Field Entries (Field Level). The following six syntax features detailing the next segment of the example display file are shown in Figure 20-6.

1. Line and column display references for all constants and fields.
2. DSPF syntax for constants that are displayed when file is executed.
3. Use of a predefined physical file field name (CUST#).
4. Display attributes controlled by the DSPATR keyword.
5. Error control (duplicate keys) for the loading or addition to the physical file defined as supporting only UNIQUE keys.
6. Assignment of an indicator, turned on in an RPG III program when an attempt to WRITE a record with a key that is already stored in the physical file.

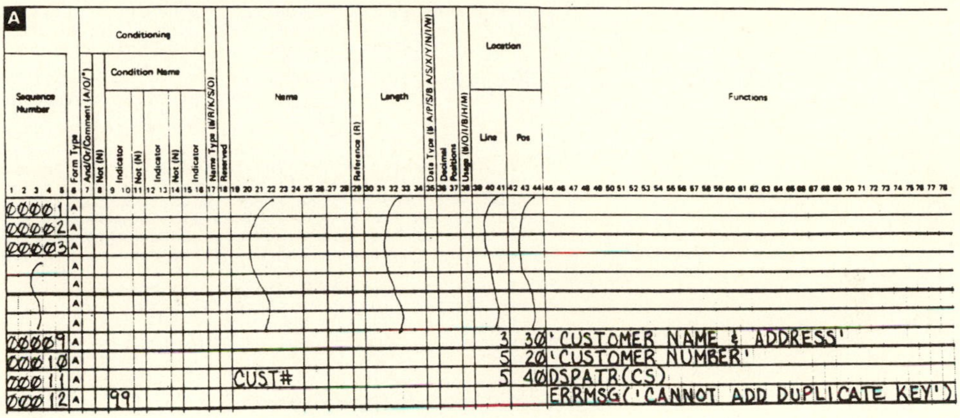

Lines
00009 to 00010

Location

Columns 38-44 — Indicates the line and column locations where the constants will display.

Columns 45-80 — Any constants must be enclosed in single quotes and will display exactly as they are specified in the DSPF coding. Display attributes (DSPATR) including reverse image, highlighting, underlining, blinking, and so forth may be specified for any constant or field.

Line 00011

Name

Columns 19-28 — The field name, CUST#, from the physical file is entered here. Independent fields may be also defined in a Display File.

Length

Columns 30-34 — The size of CUST# field is entered here. Note that the size of any fields previously defined in a physical file do not have to be repeated in the DSPF format if the following keyword is specified at the file level.

REF([library-name/]data-base-file-name [record-format-name])

Also, the attributes of individual fields may be accessed from any Physical File by the following field level keyword:

REFFLD([record-format-name/]referenced-field-name [{*SRC | [library-name/] data-base-file-name}])

If the program that supports the DSPF file is executing in the same library as the Physical File and the PF field name is used, the keyword may be shortened to the following format:

REFFLD(P1PF1)

Note that the letter R must be specified in the Reference field (column 29) to access the attributes of any field referenced from the related PF when the keywords REF and REFFLD are used.

Usage

Column 38 — The B specified indicates that the field is defined both as an input and an output field. Values may be input from the screen to a program or output from a program to a screen as required in update or deletion processing.

Other options include:

O - Output from a program to the screen as required by inquiry processing.

I - Input from the screen to a program as required by data entry proing or adding records to an existing file.

Figure 20-6 Constants, PF field name, display attribute, and error message control included in the example display file.

Location

Columns 39-44 Line and Pos entries define the line and starting position of the field value.

Functions

Columns 45-80 Any display attributes assigned to the field or constant are specified by the DSPATR keyword. The letter CS enclosed in parentheses indicates that column separators will be placed in the body of the field when it is displayed as shown below for the five-byte CUST# field:

| | | | | |

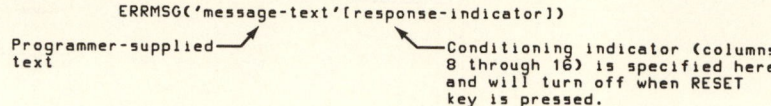

Other display attributes are discussed later in the chapter.

Line 00012

Functions

Columns 45-80 The ERRMSG keyword controls the display of any error condition specified within the parentheses and single quotes. A conditioning indicator(s) must be specified in columns 8 through 16, which is turned on when the error condition is flagged during execution of an RPG program, controls the display of the error message.

The format of the ERRMSG keyword is illustrated below:

ERRMSG('message-text'[response-indicator])

Programmer-supplied text ↗ ↖ Conditioning indicator (columns 8 through 16) is specified here and will turn off when RESET key is pressed.

For the example shown, indicator 99 will be turned on in an RPG program if an attempt is made to WRITE a record with a key already stored in the file. When the related error is tested, the programmer-supplied text in the body of the ERRMSG keyword will display in reverse-image at the bottom line of the screen and the cursor will move to the input field that generated the error. The RESET key must be pressed to continue.

If more than one ERRMSG keyword is specified and the errors tested occur at the same time, only the first ERRMSG text will be displayed.

(Continued)

The remainder of the DDS coding for the example display file (DSPF) is detailed in Figure 20-7. Notice that except for the two numeric fields specified on lines 22 and 24, the syntax and processing logic for constants and the fields from the physical file have been previously discussed.

A

Sequence Number	Form Type	Name	Length	Data Type	Decimal Positions	Usage	Line	Pos	Functions
00001	A								PRINT
	A								
	A								
	A								
00013	A						7	20	'NAME'
00014	A	NAME	20			B	7	40	DSPATR(CS)
00015	A	STREET	20			B	9	40	DSPATR(CS)
00016	A						9	20	'STREET'
00017	A						11	20	'CITY'
00018	A	CITY	20			B	11	40	DSPATR(CS)
00019	A						13	20	'STATE'
00020	A	STATE	2			B	13	40	DSPATR(CS)
00021	A						15	20	'ZIP'
00022	A	ZIP	5	S	0	B	15	40	DSPATR(CS)
00023	A						17	20	'BALANCE'
00024	A	BALANC	8	S	2	B	17	40	DSPATR(CS)
00025	A						20	10	'CK1 - EOJ CK2 - ENTER CK-
00026	A								3 - REDISPLAY'

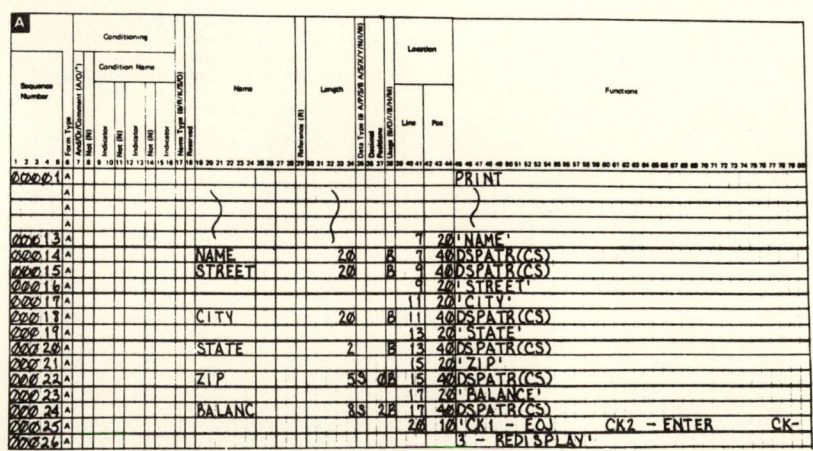

Lines 00013 to 00024

Name

Columns 19-28 NAME, STREET, CITY, STATE, ZIP, and BALANC are fields defined in the Physical File (P1PF1). New names may be assigned for the related field(s) if the keyword ALIAS or REFFLD is used.

Length

Columns 30-34 The length of the Physical File's fields must be specified unless the keyword REF or REFFLD is used. When the attributes of a field are referenced by one of these keywords, the letter R must be entered in column 29.

Data Type

Column 35 This entry does not determine the type of field defined (an entry in positions 36 and 37 does that), but refers to the keyboard shift attributes that limit what may be keyed into the field. The valid Data Type entries for Display Files are:

Figure 20-7 Remaining constants, PF field names, display attributes, and numeric fields included in the example Display File.

Entry	Keyborad Assignment	Data Type Supported
Blank	Zoned decimal Alphanumberic	If an entry (0-9) is specified in 36-37 If no entry is specified in 36-37
X	Alphabetic only	Characters A-Z, comma, period, dash and space
A	Alphanumeric	Any character supported is valid
S	Numeric	Sign position is provided in low-order position in a displayed field. FIELD - key must be pressed to tag input value as negative. Only numbers 0-9 are valid for this keyboard shift entry.
Y	Numeric	The numbers 0-9, decimal point, comma, plus, minus, and space are valid characters for this entry. In addition to the positions for numbers, one more is included in the body of the display field. Consequently, a minus sign and decimal position entry may not be specified together. A negative sign may be assigned to the value by pressing the FIELD - key when entering the field, which does not require a screen position. Any comma or decimal point included in the input value is deleted by CPF. Spaces in the value are replaced by zeros.
N	Numeric	All characters are valid for this entry. The displayed length of the input field is one more than the size specified in positions 30-34 if the field is an unedited input-capable field and the decimal position field entry is greater than 0.
I		This entry inhibits any keyboard entry. An error will be issued if the cursor is in a field assigned with this entry and a key is pressed.

Notice in the DDS coding for the example display file that NAME, STREET, CITY, and STATE are specified as A type (default) values by the absence of an entry in this field. ZIP and BALANC are defined as signed numeric by the letter S entry.

Lines 25-26

Functions

Columns 45-80 Notice that the constant on line 00025 does not include a low-order quote. Instead, a minus sign (a plus sign may also be used) is specified indicating that the statement is continued on line 00026. Also note that the continuation on line 00026 does not have a beginning quote but does include a terminating one.

(Continued)

ENTERING DDS DISPLAY FILE CODE

The Programmer Menu discussed before may also be used to access the Source Entry Utility (SEU) to enter the DDS source code for a display file (DSPF). Figure 20-8 shows the entries needed. Observe that 8 is entered as the selection; a programmer-supplied display file name (P1SC1SM) is entered in the Parm prompt, and DSPF is entered in the Type field. All other entries are defaults that may be changed as needed by the programmer. The Command Key options at the bottom of the menu provide for the processing functions indicated.

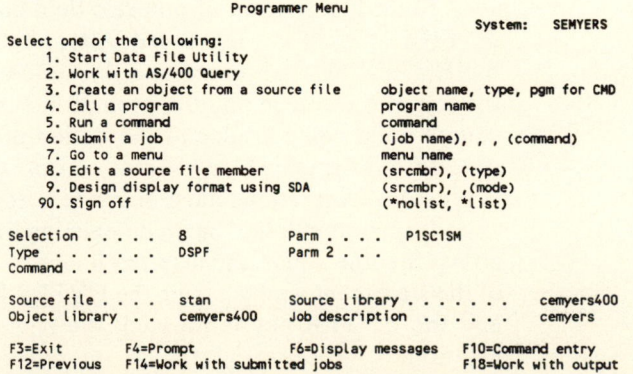

```
                              Programmer Menu
                                                       System:   SEMYERS
Select one of the following:
     1. Start Data File Utility
     2. Work with AS/400 Query
     3. Create an object from a source file    object name, type, pgm for CMD
     4. Call a program                         program name
     5. Run a command                          command
     6. Submit a job                           (job name), , , (command)
     7. Go to a menu                           menu name
     8. Edit a source file member              (srcmbr), (type)
     9. Design display format using SDA        (srcmbr), ,(mode)
    90. Sign off                               (*nolist, *list)

Selection . . . . .   8             Parm . . . .   P1SC1SM
Type  . . . . . . .   DSPF          Parm 2 . . .
Command . . . . . .

Source file . . . .   stan          Source library . . . . . . .   cemyers400
Object library  . .   cemyers400    Job description  . . . . . .   cemyers

F3=Exit         F4=Prompt              F6=Display messages     F10=Command entry
F12=Previous    F14=Work with submitted jobs                   F18=Work with output
```

Figure 20-8 Programmer Menu "filled-in" to call SEU for Display File code entry.

Entering the DDS Code for a Physical File

After the prompts are completed to create a display file format and the ENTER key is pressed, the SEU screen shown in Figure 20-9 will display. Notice that the second line begins with an identification that it is a display file format (FMT DP). The remainder of the line duplicates the field positions on the DDS form for DSPF.

```
 EDIT    US W:1     Mbr: SOURCE                      Scan:
 FMT DP .....Aan01n02n03T.Name++++++RLen++TDpBLinPosFunctions+++++++++++++++++
          ****BEGINNING OF DATA****
.......
          *******END OF DATA*******
```

Figure 20-9 SEU EDIT screen (A format) for DDS display file code entry.

Remember from the discussion of physical file DDS code entry, that a prompt line entry method may be used. Prompt line entry is initiated by entering the letter P on the first entry line and pressing the ENTER key. A prompt line (for the related format type) with field headers will display at the bottom of the screen as shown in Figure 20-10.

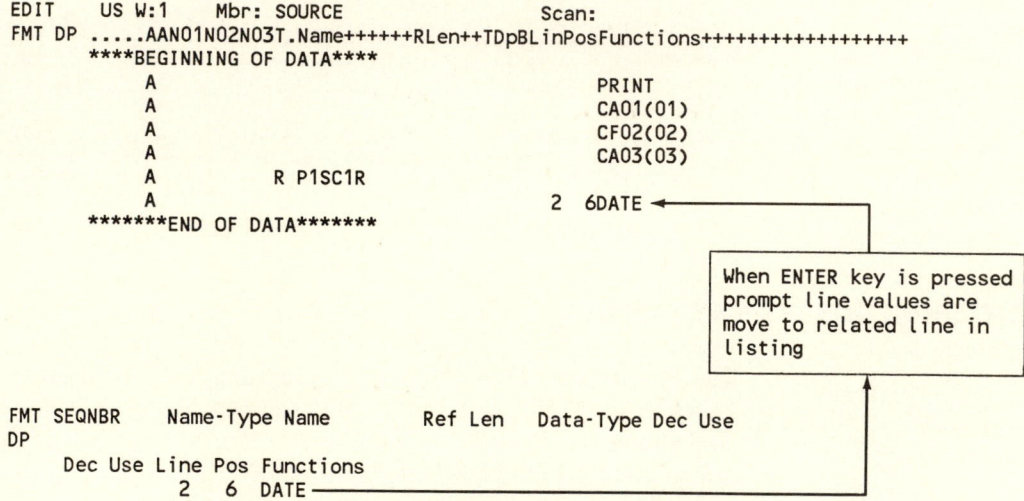

```
EDIT    US W:1     Mbr: SOURCE                      Scan:
FMT DP .....AAN01N02N03T.Name++++++RLen++TDpBLinPosFunctions+++++++++++++++++
       ****BEGINNING OF DATA****
            A                                   PRINT
            A                                   CA01(01)
            A                                   CF02(02)
            A                                   CA03(03)
            A          R P1SC1R
            A                               2  6DATE <-----------+
       *******END OF DATA*******                                  |
                                                    +-------------------------+
                                                    | When ENTER key is pressed|
                                                    | prompt line values are   |
                                                    | move to related line in  |
                                                    | listing                  |
                                                    +-------------------------+
                                                                  ^
FMT SEQNBR    Name-Type Name        Ref Len   Data-Type Dec Use   |
DP                                                                |
     Dec Use Line Pos Functions                                   |
               2   6  DATE -------------------------------------------+
```

Figure 20-10 "Filled-in" SEU prompt line format for DDS Display File code entry.

Right-justification of numeric field entries is automatically supported when the FIELD EXIT key is pressed. After all the values for the statement are entered, the ENTER key is pressed and the statement is moved to its related location at the top of the screen and the prompt line is blanked out. This sequential entry of source code will continue at the option of the programmer. With either method (free-form or prompt), any syntax errors will be displayed when the ENTER key is pressed. Corrections must be made before the statement is moved and stored.

Insertion of a line between existing lines is performed by placing the cursor above the line where the inserted line is to be entered, typing IP at the beginning of the statement, and pressing the ENTER key. After the prompt line is completed and the ENTER key is pressed, the new statement is inserted in the specified location.

Line insertion using the free-form method is executed by specifying the letter I at the beginning of the previous statement and pressing the ENTER key. A blank line will be provided to enter the statement. A line may be *deleted* by typing the letter D at the beginning of a statement. Consecutive lines may be deleted from the listing by typing DD at the beginning of the first line to be deleted and DD at the beginning of the last line of the group to be deleted.

After all the source code for the Physical File is entered, Command Key 3 is pressed to exit from the SEU EDIT screen into an SEU EDIT menu. The SEU EDIT screen shown in Figure 20-11 gives the programmer the "exit options" indicated on the Exit screen. Notice that the default is to change or create a member and resequence the member (Y in the selection column). The Member, File, and Library names are carried over from the entries made in the Programmer Menu. For the Text prompt, the name of the application may be entered.

```
                              Exit

Type choices, press Enter.

  Change/create member . . . . . . .   Y             Y=Yes, N=No
    Member . . . . . . . . . . . . .   P1SC1SM       Name
    File . . . . . . . . . . . . . .   STAN          Name
      Library . . . . . . . . . . . .  CEMYERS400    Name
    Text . . . . . . . . . . . . . .   Accounts Receivable Entry

    Resequence member . . . . . . . .  Y             Y=Yes, N=No
      Start . . . . . . . . . . . . .  0001.00       0000.01 - 9999.99
      Increment . . . . . . . . . . .  01.00         00.01 - 99.99

  Print member  . . . . . . . . . . .  N             Y=Yes, N=No

  Return to editing . . . . . . . . .  N             Y=Yes, N=No

  Go to member list . . . . . . . . .  N             Y=Yes, N=No


F3=Exit        F5=Refresh      F12=Previous
```

Figure 20-11 SEU EXIT menu.

The ENTER key exits from this screen and returns control back to the Programmer Menu. Key F5 redisplays a fresh version of the SEU EXIT menu. Pressing F12 will return control back to the SEU EDIT screen.

Identical to physical files, RPG programs, and CL programs, display files are compiled by returning to the Programmer Menu and selecting option 3 (Create an object from a source file) and pressing the ENTER key.

The two listings shown in Figure 20-12 are generated from the compilation. Any syntax errors (warnings and terminal) will be identified in the first listing. The second listing will be included only if there are no terminal errors.

The first listing shown in Figure 20-12 includes header information related to the display file and lists the source member format exactly as created. A second listing, called an EXPANDED SOURCE, supplements the original source with information about field lengths, and includes the output and input buffer positions for every field and indicator.

After a display file is successfully compiled and an object member generated, it may be processed by an RPG program. The fields specified in the example DSPF were defined with a B usage, which provides for the input of data from and/or output to the screen.

```
File Name . . . . . . . . . . . . . . . . . . . . . . :   P1SC1SM
  Library name  . . . . . . . . . . . . . . . . . . . :   CEMYERS400
File attribute  . . . . . . . . . . . . . . . . . . . :   Display
Source file containing DDS  . . . . . . . . . . . . . :   STAN
  Library name  . . . . . . . . . . . . . . . . . . . :   CEMYERS400
Source member containing DDS  . . . . . . . . . . . . :   P1SC1SM
Source member last changed  . . . . . . . . . . . . . :   09/20/91    6:30:00
Source listing options  . . . . . . . . . . . . . . . :   *SOURCE     *LIST       *NOSECLVL
DDS generation severity level . . . . . . . . . . . . :   20
File type . . . . . . . . . . . . . . . . . . . . . . :   *DATA
Authority . . . . . . . . . . . . . . . . . . . . . . :   *CHANGE
Text  . . . . . . . . . . . . . . . . . . . . . . . . :   Accounts Receivable Entry
Compiler  . . . . . . . . . . . . . . . . . . . . . . :   IBM AS/400 Data Description Processor

                                     Data Description Source

SEQNBR  *...+....1....+....2....+....3....+....4....+....5....+....6....+....7....+....8  Date

   100       A                                      PRINT                                09/20/91
   200       A                                      CA01(01)                             09/20/91
   300       A                                      CF02(02)                             09/20/91
   400       A                                      CA03(03)                             09/20/91
   500       A          R P1SC1R                                                         09/20/91
   600       A                                  2  6DATE                                 09/20/91
   700       A                                      EDTCDE(Y)                            09/20/91
   800       A                                  2 69TIME                                 09/20/91
   900       A                                  3 30'CUSTOMER NAME & ADDRESS'            09/20/91
  1000       A                                  5 20'CUSTOMER NUMBER'                    09/20/91
  1100       A            CUST#          5A  B  5 40DSPATR(CS)                           09/20/91
  1200       A  99                                  ERRMSG('CANNOT ADD DUPLICATE KEY')   09/20/91
  1300       A                                  7 20'NAME'                               09/20/91
  1400       A            NAME          20A  B  7 40DSPATR(CS)                           09/20/91
  1500       A            STREET        20A  B  9 40DSPATR(CS)                           09/20/91
  1600       A                                  9 20'STREET'                             09/20/91
  1700       A                                 11 20'CITY'                               09/20/91
  1800       A            CITY          20A  B 11 40DSPATR(CS)                           09/20/91
  1900       A                                 13 20'STATE'                              09/20/91
  2000       A            STATE          2A  B 13 40DSPATR(CS)                           09/20/91
  2100       A                                 15 20'ZIP'                                09/20/91
  2200       A            ZIP            5S 0B 15 40DSPATR(CS)                           09/20/91
  2300       A                                 17 20'BALANCE'                            09/20/91
  2400       A            BALANC         8S 2B 17 40DSPATR(CS)                           09/20/91
  2500       A                                 20 10'CK1 - EOJ      CK2 - ENTER      CK- 09/20/91
  2600       A                                      2 - REDISPLAY'                       09/20/91

                              * * * * *  E N D   O F   S O U R C E  * * * * *
```

```
                                        Expanded Source
                                                                                        Field    Buffer position
SEQNBR  *...+....1....+....2....+....3....+....4....+....5....+....6....+....7....+....8 Length    Out      In

   100                                              PRINT CA01(01 CF02(02) CA03(03)
                                                    DSPSIZ(*DS3)
            * OPTION INDICATOR OUTPUT BUFFER POSITIONS -
            *  *IN99 0001
            * RESPONSE INDICATOR INPUT BUFFER POSITIONS -
            *  *IN01 0001   *IN02 0002   *IN03 0003
   500       A          R P1SC1R
   600       A                                  2  6DATE EDTCDE(Y)                         8
   800       A                                  2 69TIME                                   8
   900       A                                  3 30'CUSTOMER NAME & ADDRESS'             23
  1000       A                                  5 20'CUSTOMER NUMBER'                     15
  1100       A            CUST#          5A  B  5 40DSPATR(CS)                             5        2        4
  1200       A  99                                  ERRMSG('CANNOT ADD DUPLICATE KEY')
  1300       A                                  7 20'NAME'                                 4
  1400       A            NAME          20A  B  7 40DSPATR(CS)                            20        7        9
  1500       A            STREET        20A  B  9 40DSPATR(CS)                            20       27       29
  1600       A                                  9 20'STREET'                               6
  1700       A                                 11 20'CITY'                                 4
  1800       A            CITY          20A  B 11 40DSPATR(CS)                            20       47       49
  1900       A                                 13 20'STATE'                                5
  2000       A            STATE          2A  B 13 40DSPATR(CS)                             2       67       69
  2100       A                                 15 20'ZIP'                                  3
  2200       A            ZIP            5S 0B 15 40DSPATR(CS)                             5       69       71
  2300       A                                 17 20'BALANCE'                              7
  2400       A            BALANC         8S 2B 17 40DSPATR(CS)                             8       74       74
  2500       A                                 20 10'CK1 - EOJ      CK2 - ENTER      CK-  47
  2500       A                                      2 - REDISPLAY'
```

Figure 20-12 Listings generated from compilation of the example Display File format.

Testing a Display Record Format

Testing a record format in a display file (object member) may be performed by the Screen Design Aid (SDA) utility. SDA is accessed through the Programmer Menu by selecting Option 9 and pressing the ENTER key. The Selection Menu shown in Figure 20-13 will be displayed in which the programmer may select one of the three processing options.

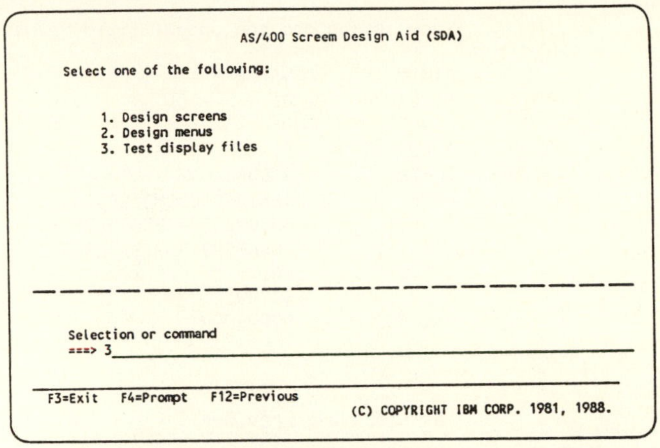

Figure 20-13 Screen Design Aid Selection Menu.

For testing a previously compiled display record format, Option 3 must be selected. This option provides for the following:

1. It tests record formats in the display file to observe how they appear on the screen.
2. It tests any data validation checks of the input fields.
3. It displays the contents of the input buffer that pass data and indicator control to the related RPG program.
4. It tests output fields and conditioning indicators.

To advance to the next prompt screen, press ENTER. The test display file screen shown in Figure 20-14 will display to which the user must respond to the prompts for the display file, Library, and Record to be tested. An entry (or entries) may be made for the additional records to display prompt if the display file includes more than one record format and any others are to be tested. Notice that the required prompts have been included in Figure 20-14.

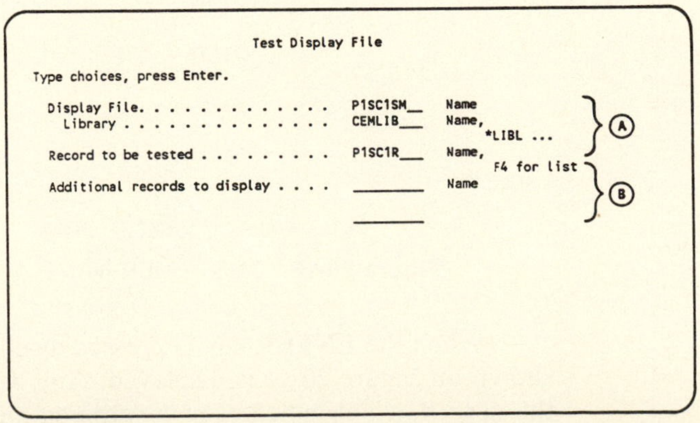

Figure 20-14 Test display file screen with required entries.

If the name of the display record format to be tested is not known, a list of the record names in the display file may be generated by pressing the F4 key.

Pressing the ENTER key again will display the Set Test Output Data prompt screen presented in Figure 20-15.

```
                         Set Test Output Data

Record . . . :    P1SC1R

Type indicators and output field values, press /enter.

Field          Value
*IN01          0:
*IN02          0:
*IN03          0:
CUST#          BBBBB:
NAME           BBBBBBBBBBBBBBBBBBBB:
STREET         BBBBBBBBBBBBBBBBBBBB:
CITY           BBBBBBBBBBBBBBBBBBBB:
STATE          BB:
ZIP            99999:
BALANC         99999999:

                                                          More...

F3=Exit    F12=Previous
```

Figure 20-15 Set Test Output Data Display format.

Data may be entered into any or all of the fields for testing. The indicators assigned to the Command Attention and Command Function keys (i.e., *IN01, *IN02, and *IN03) are also listed in this test screen. Their status defaults to '0', which indicates ''off'' in binary. The user may test the ''on'' condition by entering a 1 in the Value response column.

Pressing the ENTER key again will display the exact image of the display file's record format which is shown in Figure 20-16. Any field values or indicator conditions entered in the Set Test Output Data prompt screen will be included in this display. For additional testing, the user has the option of entering data in this screen.

```
                 CUSTOMER NAME AND ADDRESS

          CUSTOMER NUMBER     BBBBB

          NAME                BBBBBBBBBBBBBBBBBBBB

          STREET              BBBBBBBBBBBBBBBBBBBB

          CITY                BBBBBBBBBBBBBBBBBBBBB

          STATE               BB

          ZIP                 99999

          BALANC              99999999

   CK1 - EOJ         CK2 - ENTER         CK3 - REDISPLAY
```

Figure 20-16 CUSTOMER NAME AND ADDRESS screen display.

When the ENTER key is pressed again, the Display Test Input Data screen shown on Figure 20-17 is displayed. Any data previously entered will appear in this screen, which indicates to the programmer what and how the values are stored in the fields of the screen's input record format.

```
                          Display Test Input Data

Record . . . :    P1SC1R

Type indicators and input field values.

Field           Value
*IN01           0:
*IN02           0:
*IN03           0:
CUST#           BBBBB:
NAME            BBBBBBBBBBBBBBBBBBBB:
STREET          BBBBBBBBBBBBBBBBBBBB:
CITY            BBBBBBBBBBBBBBBBBBBB:
STATE           BB:
ZIP             99999:
BALANC          99999999:
                                                              More...
Press Enter to continue



F3=Exit    F12=Previous    fF14=Display input buffer
```

Figure 20-17 Display Test Input Data screen.

At this point in the test procedure, if key F14 is pressed, the Display Test Input Buffer screen illustrated in Figure 20-18 will be displayed. This screen format presents the input buffer format supported by the RPG program that processes the display file.

```
                          Display Test Input Buffer


     .... ....1.... ....2.... ....3.... ....4.... ....5.... ....6.... ....7
   1 00000BBBBBBBBBBBBBBBBBBBBBBBBBBBBBBBBBBBBBBBBBBBBBBBBBBBBBBBBBBBBBB999
   2 9999999999
   3
   4
   5
   6
   7
   8
   9
  10
  11
  12
  13
  14
  15
  16
                                                                  Bottom
Press Enter to continue


F3=Exit    F12=Previous
```

Figure 20-18 Display Test Input Buffer screen.

After the last test screen is displayed, the programmer has one of the following processing options:

1. Press F3 to exit from the test routine.
2. Sequentially, exit by:
   a. Press ENTER to return to the Display Test Input Data screen.
   b. Press F12 to return to the Test Display File display.
   c. Press F12 to return to the Screen Design Aid (SDA) menu.

Display Attributes (DSPATR keyword)

Display attributes are controlled in a display file by the DSPATR keyword. The functions included are blinking, column separators, high intensity, nondisplay, position cursor, reverse image, underline, protect field, and modified data tag. Each of these attributes is explained in Figure 20-19.

Display Attribute	Meaning	Explanation
BL	Blinking Field	Field (or constant) will blink when displayed.
CS	Column Separator	Places a vertical line at the left and right of every character in the body of the field. Separators will always be displayed for the item.
HI	High Intensity	Highlights the field (or constant) when it is displayed.
ND	Nondisplay	Prevents field (or constant) from being displayed. Often used for passwords and other security-sensitive data.
PC	Position Cursor	Positions the cursor at the first (high-order) position of the related field. If specified for more than one field, the cursor will position at the first field defined with this attribute.
RI	Reverse Image	Reverses the image of this field (or constant) from the screen's image. For example, if the screen is light-on-dark, the field will display as dark-on-light, or vice versa.
UL	Underline	Underlines a field or constant. All input-capable fields (I or B Usage), default to underlining. This default may be overridden with a CHGINPDFT keyword specified at the File or Record level. If column separators (CS) are included as a display attribute for an item, and underlining is not suppressed, the displayed value will be difficult to read.
PR	Protect	Prevents the work station user from entering data into an input capable field (I or B Usage).
MDT	Set Modified Data Tag	Insures that a field value is read from the screen.

Figure 20-19 Display Attribute (DSPATR) keyword functions.

The relationship of some of the DSPATR attributes with the displayed results are shown in Figure 20-20. Note that more than one logically related attribute may be specified for a field or constant.

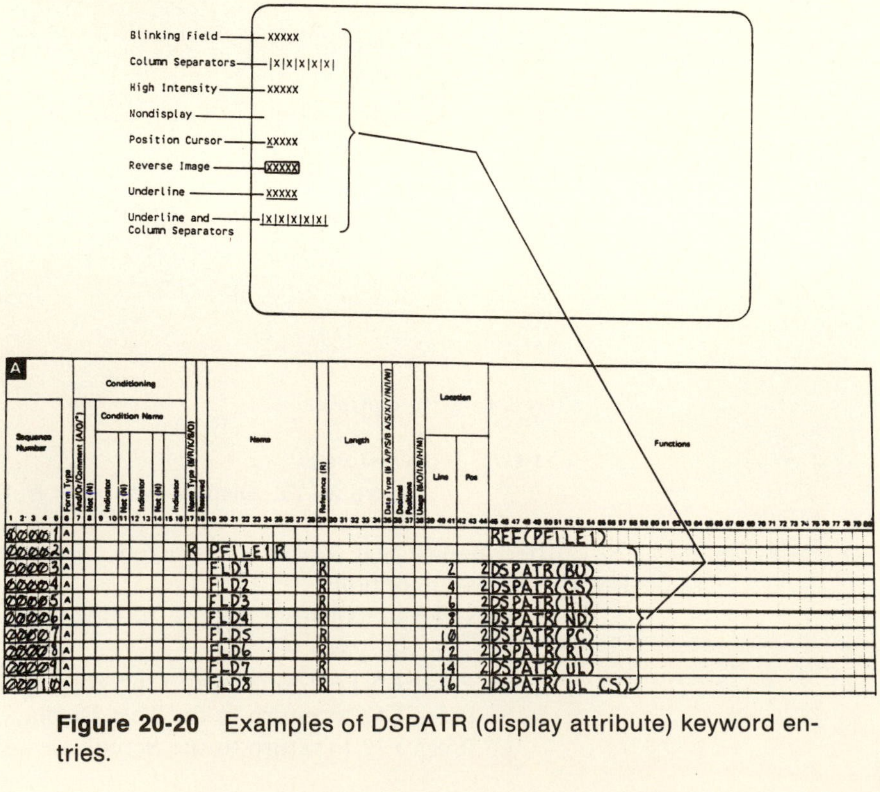

Figure 20-20 Examples of DSPATR (display attribute) keyword entries.

Display File Keywords

All the keywords supported by display files (DSPF) are listed in Figure 20-21 by functional groups.

For an explanation of the keywords, consult Appendix C in the *IBM Control Program Facility Reference Manual—Data Description Specifications*. Some of the keywords have been discussed, others related to validity checking and subfiles will be introduced in later chapters.

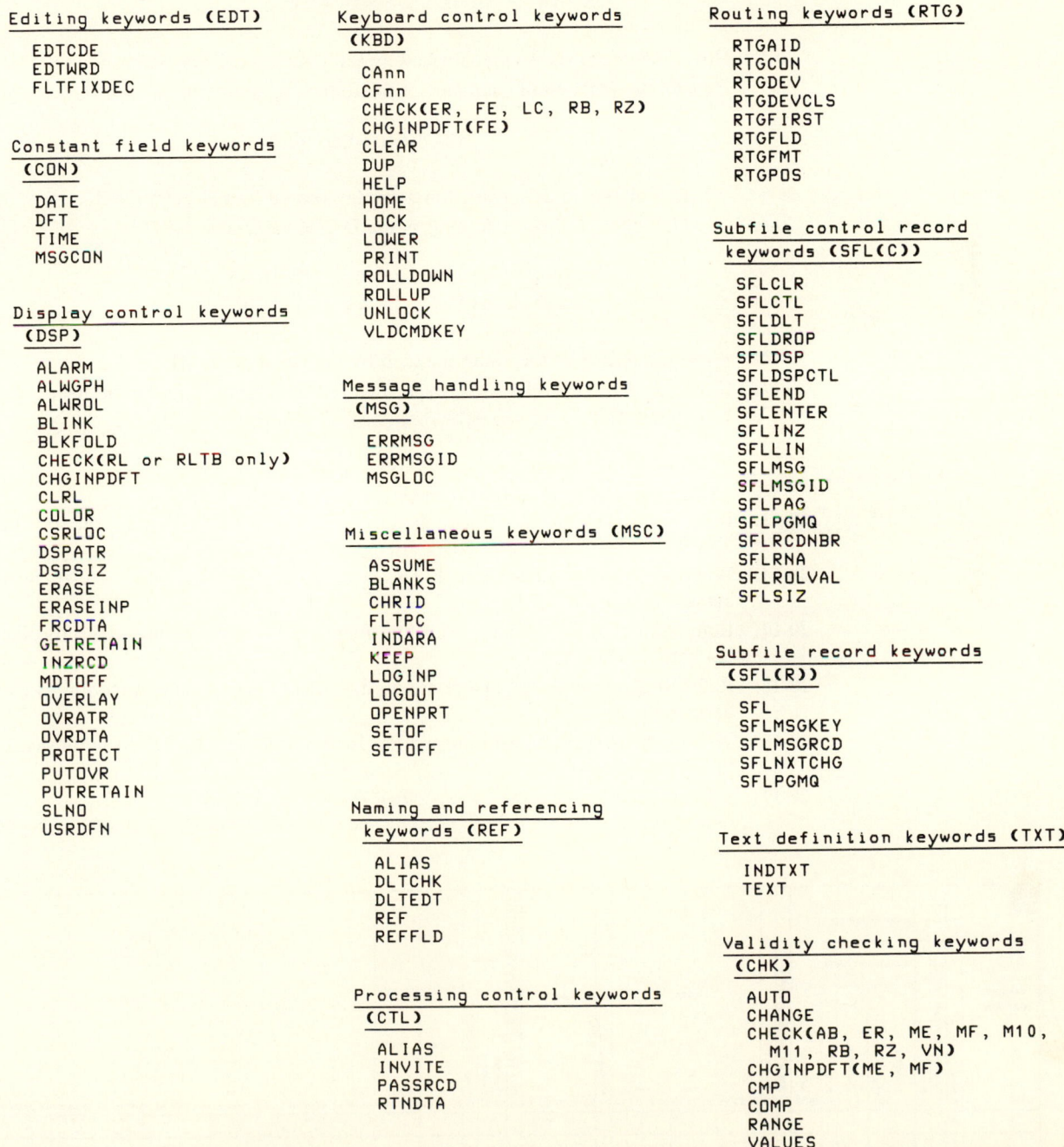

```
Editing keywords (EDT)
  EDTCDE
  EDTWRD
  FLTFIXDEC

Constant field keywords
(CON)
  DATE
  DFT
  TIME
  MSGCON

Display control keywords
(DSP)
  ALARM
  ALWGPH
  ALWROL
  BLINK
  BLKFOLD
  CHECK(RL or RLTB only)
  CHGINPDFT
  CLRL
  COLOR
  CSRLOC
  DSPATR
  DSPSIZ
  ERASE
  ERASEINP
  FRCDTA
  GETRETAIN
  INZRCD
  MDTOFF
  OVERLAY
  OVRATR
  OVRDTA
  PROTECT
  PUTOVR
  PUTRETAIN
  SLNO
  USRDFN

Keyboard control keywords
(KBD)
  CAnn
  CFnn
  CHECK(ER, FE, LC, RB, RZ)
  CHGINPDFT(FE)
  CLEAR
  DUP
  HELP
  HOME
  LOCK
  LOWER
  PRINT
  ROLLDOWN
  ROLLUP
  UNLOCK
  VLDCMDKEY

Message handling keywords
(MSG)
  ERRMSG
  ERRMSGID
  MSGLOC

Miscellaneous keywords (MSC)
  ASSUME
  BLANKS
  CHRID
  FLTPC
  INDARA
  KEEP
  LOGINP
  LOGOUT
  OPENPRT
  SETOF
  SETOFF

Naming and referencing
keywords (REF)
  ALIAS
  DLTCHK
  DLTEDT
  REF
  REFFLD

Processing control keywords
(CTL)
  ALIAS
  INVITE
  PASSRCD
  RTNDTA

Routing keywords (RTG)
  RTGAID
  RTGCON
  RTGDEV
  RTGDEVCLS
  RTGFIRST
  RTGFLD
  RTGFMT
  RTGPOS

Subfile control record
keywords (SFL(C))
  SFLCLR
  SFLCTL
  SFLDLT
  SFLDROP
  SFLDSP
  SFLDSPCTL
  SFLEND
  SFLENTER
  SFLINZ
  SFLLIN
  SFLMSG
  SFLMSGID
  SFLPAG
  SFLPGMQ
  SFLRCDNBR
  SFLRNA
  SFLROLVAL
  SFLSIZ

Subfile record keywords
(SFL(R))
  SFL
  SFLMSGKEY
  SFLMSGRCD
  SFLNXTCHG
  SFLPGMQ

Text definition keywords (TXT)
  INDTXT
  TEXT

Validity checking keywords
(CHK)
  AUTO
  CHANGE
  CHECK(AB, ER, ME, MF, M10,
    M11, RB, RZ, VN)
  CHGINPDFT(ME, MF)
  CMP
  COMP
  RANGE
  VALUES
```

Figure 20-21 DSPATR keyword attributes listed by functional groups. (Courtesy of IBM.)

QUESTIONS

20-1. What are display files? For what processing functions are they used?

20-2. By what methods may display files be created?

20-3. How many record formats may be included in a display file?

20-4. Explain the procedures for entering the DDS coding for a display file.

20-5. Explain the function of the following display file keywords:

```
PRINT   DSPATR   EDTWRD   DATE
CAnn    ERRMSG   REF      TIME
CFnn    EDTCDE   REFFLD
```

20-6. How does the processing controlled by the CAnn and CFnn keywords differ?

20-7. Explain the function of each part of the following keyword:

CA04 (04 'Update Record')

20-8. Where may the fields specified in a display record format be defined?

20-9. In which of the following formats is the DATE value accessed?

```
(a) YYMMDD     (c) MMDDYY
(b) DDMMYY     (d) YYDDD
```

20-10. Write the format of the value supplied by the keyword TIME.

20-11. If the keyword DSPATR (CS) is specified for a field, how will the following value be displayed?

00001099

20-12. Refer to a DDS form and explain the function of the following Data Type (position 35) entries: blank, A, S, Y, N, I.

20-13. When is an entry needed in columns 36 to 37 of the DDS form for display file syntax?

20-14. Refer to a DDS form and explain the function of the following usage (position 38) entries: O; I; B.

20-15. Refer to Question 20–14 and relate a physical file maintenance function to each usage entry.

20-16. What is the purpose of the Line and Pos field entries on the DDS form for display files?

20-17. What levels of coding may be specified for a display file?

Questions 20-18 through 20-20 relate to the following DDS DSPF coding segment:

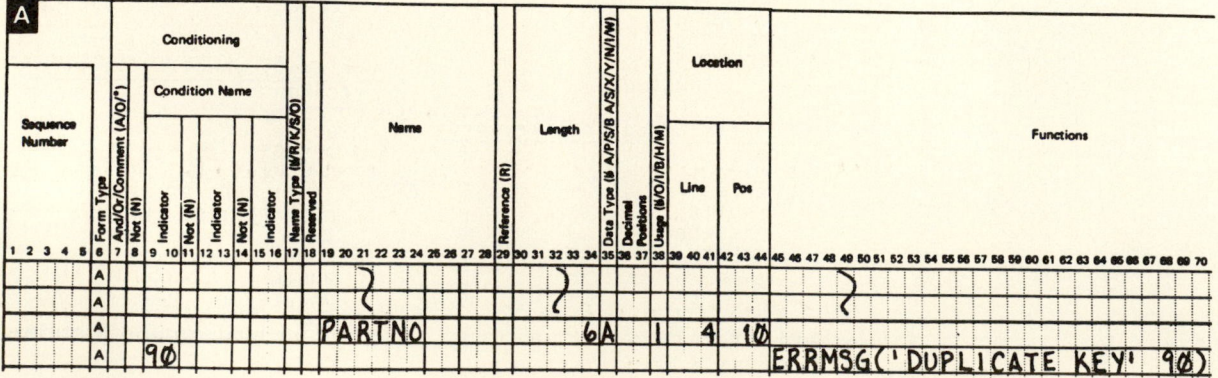

Sequence Number (1–5)	Form Type (6)	And/Or/Comment (7)	Conditioning: Not/Indicator (8–16)	Name Type (17)	Reserved (18)	Name (19–28)	Reference (29)	Length (30–34)	Data Type (35)	Decimal Positions (36–37)	Usage (38)	Line (39–41)	Pos (42–44)	Functions (45–70)
	A					~		~						~
	A													
	A					PARTNO		6	A		I	4	10	
	A		90											ERRMSG('DUPLICATE KEY' 90)

20-18. What is the purpose of the indicator specified in positions 9 and 10? Where and under what conditions is it turned on?

20-19. What happens if 90 is turned on?

20-20. How is 90 turned off?

20-21. If more than one ERRMSG keyword is included in a display file, and more than one error occurs as the same time, how many messages will display? Where on the screen does a message (or messages) display?

20-22. Explain the function that the following display attributes control:

```
BL   ND   UL
CS   PC
HI   RI
```

20-23. Write a keyword that specifies BL, HI, and UL attributes for a field.

20-24. Write a keyword to access the attributes of ITEM# from the physical file INVENTRY stored in the library ITEMLIB.

20-25. Explain the procedure for testing a Display Record Format.

EXERCISES

20-1. Write, enter, and compile a display file (DSPF) for the following screen design format. The display attributes for the constants and fields are specified on the form.

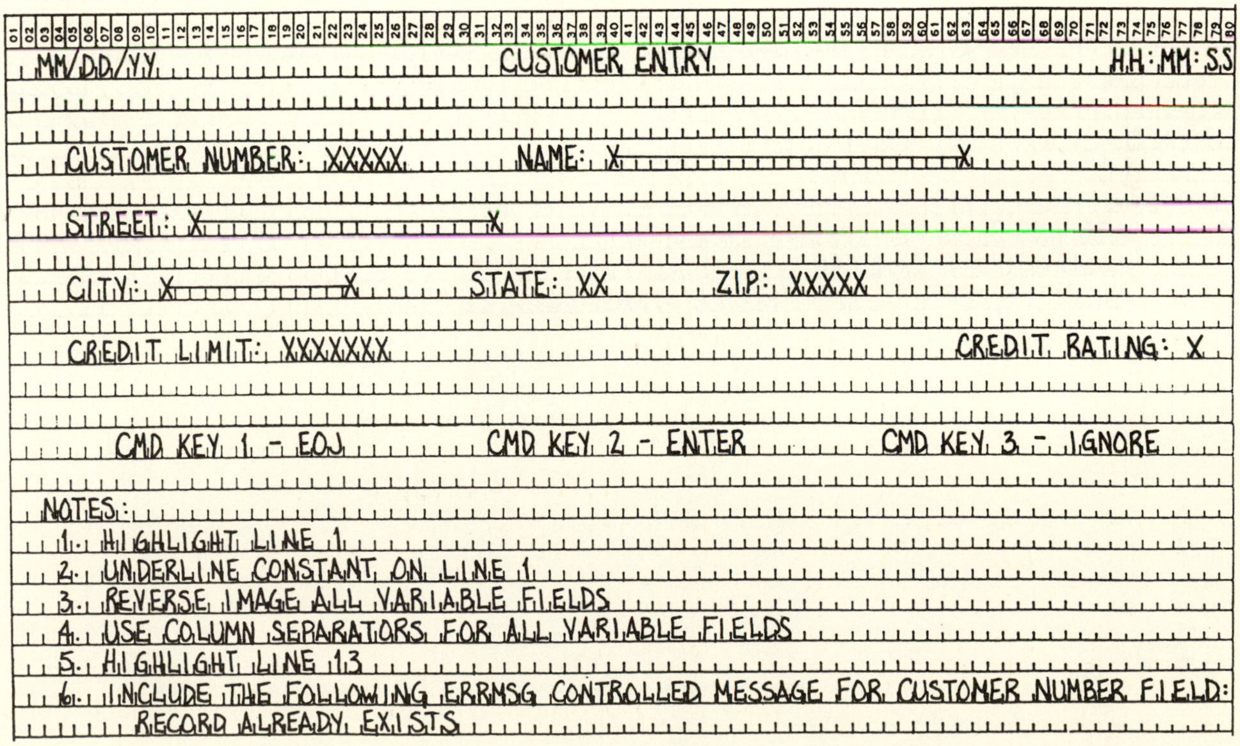
MM/DD/YY
CUSTOMER ENTRY
HH:MM:SS
CUSTOMER NUMBER: XXXXX
NAME: X
X
STREET: X
X
CITY: X
X
STATE: XX
ZIP: XXXXX
CREDIT LIMIT: XXXXXXX
CREDIT RATING: X
CMD KEY 1 - EOJ
CMD KEY 2 - ENTER
CMD KEY 3 - IGNORE
NOTES:
1. HIGHLIGHT LINE 1
2. UNDERLINE CONSTANT ON LINE 1
3. REVERSE IMAGE ALL VARIABLE FIELDS
4. USE COLUMN SEPARATORS FOR ALL VARIABLE FIELDS
5. HIGHLIGHT LINE 13
6. INCLUDE THE FOLLOWING ERRMSG CONTROLLED MESSAGE FOR CUSTOMER NUMBER FIELD:
RECORD ALREADY EXISTS

Note that this assignment relates to the exercises in Chapter 19. The screen completed here is the input medium to load data into the physical file created in Exercise 20-2. An RPG III/400 program that interfaces the screen and the physical file will be assigned as an Exercise in Chapter 21.

LABORATORY ASSIGNMENTS

Laboratory Assignment 20-1: INTERACTIVE SCREEN FOR THE LOADING OF A PARTS MASTER INVENTORY FILE

NOTE THAT THIS ASSIGNMENT IS A CONTINUATION OF ASSIGNMENT 20-1. From the following screen design, write, enter, and compile a display file. The required display attributes are specified in the layout form. After the screen is successfully compiled, test it with the SDA utility. An RPG program for assignment 21-1 will interface this display file and the physical file completed for Laboratory Assignment 20-1 to control the interactive loading of data to the file.

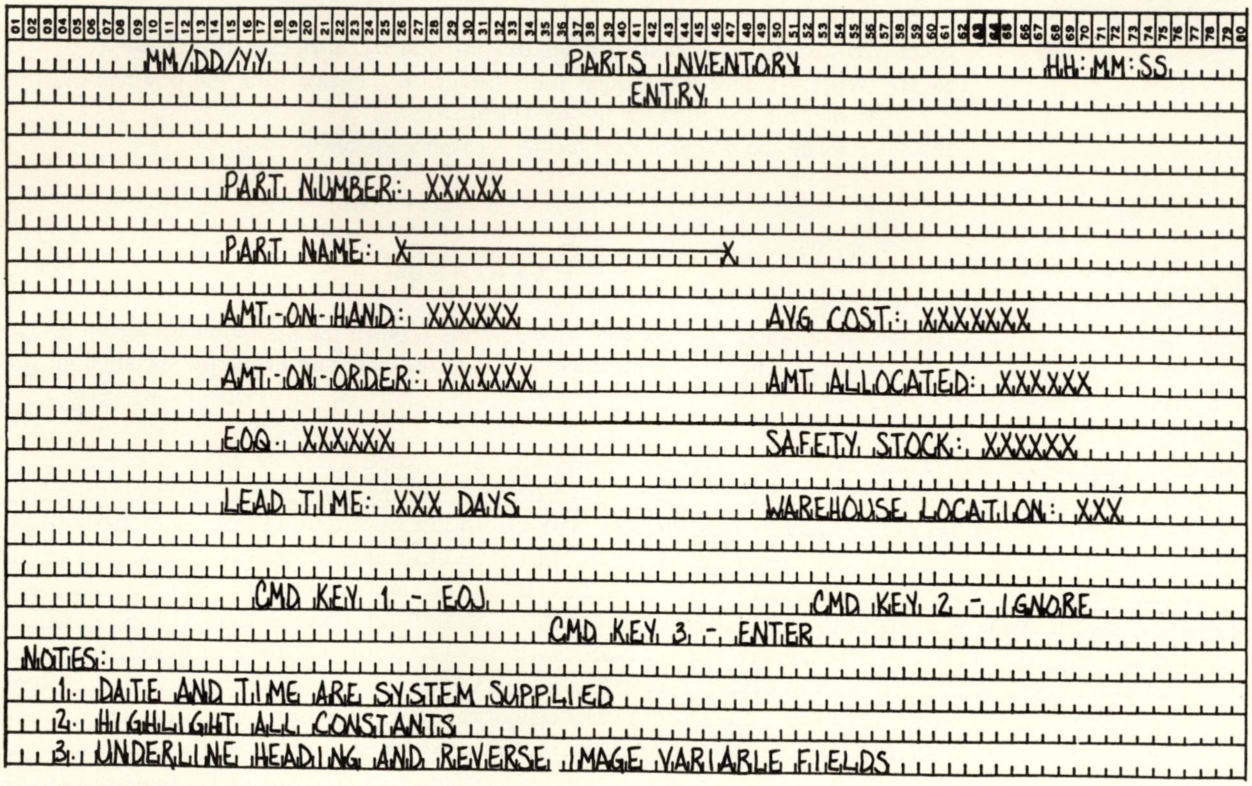

chapter 21
RPG III/400 Interactive Processing

The following structured RPG/400, III, and II (System/36) operations have been previously introduced in the chapters indicated:

DO (Do)	Chapter 6	IFxx (If/Then)	Chapter 6
DOWxx (Do While)	Chapter 6	ELSE (Else Do)	Chapter 6
DOUxx (Do Until)	Chapter 6	END (End)	Chapter 6
CASxx	Chapter 7		

Because the programs presented in this chapter include these structured operations, a review of the them in their related chapters may be required.

Other operations required in RPG/400 or III programs that process physical (PF) and display files (DSPF) are introduced in this chapter. Included are the EXFMT, WRITE, UPDAT, and DELET statements. Also presented are an explanation and examples of the RPG/400 and III syntax and procedures for the processing of WORKSTN (workstation) and physical files.

EXFMT (EXECUTE FORMAT)

The EXFMT operation is valid only for WORKSTN files defined as a combined file (C in position 15); full procedural file (F in position 16); and externally defined file (E in position 19) in the File Description Specifications. An EXFMT operation is a combined WRITE (to the screen) followed by a READ (from the screen) statement. Note that separate WRITE and READ statements may be specified in lieu of an EXFMT instruction. The syntax of this operation is detailed in Figure 21-1.

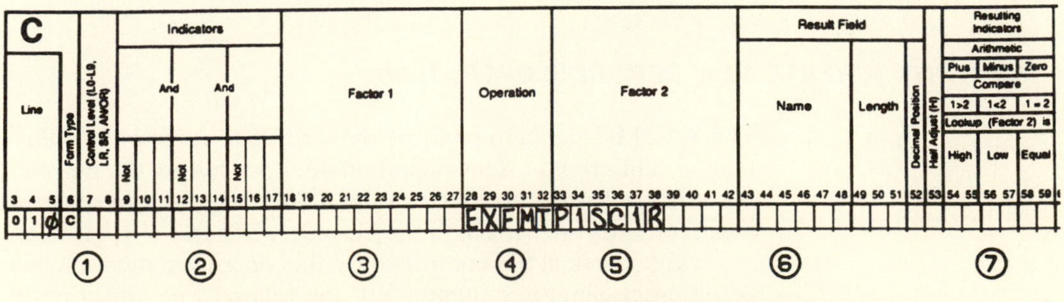

1. Control level indicators (L1-L9 & LR) may specified at total time.

2. Conditioning indicators may be specified at detail time.

Figure 21-1 Syntax of the EXFMT (Execute Format) operation.

3. Factor 1 is not used.

4. EXFMT operation must be entered in the operation field.

5. A display file's record format name must be entered left-justified in Factor 2. Because a DSPF may include more than one record format, the file name cannot be specified.

6. Result field is not used.

7. An optional indicator may be specified *only* in the Low field (columns 56-57) for error control. When used, the indicator will be set on if an error occurs during the WRITE cycle of the EXFMT operation.

(*Continued*)

An explanation of the File Description Specification entries that support this operation is presented in Figure 21-2.

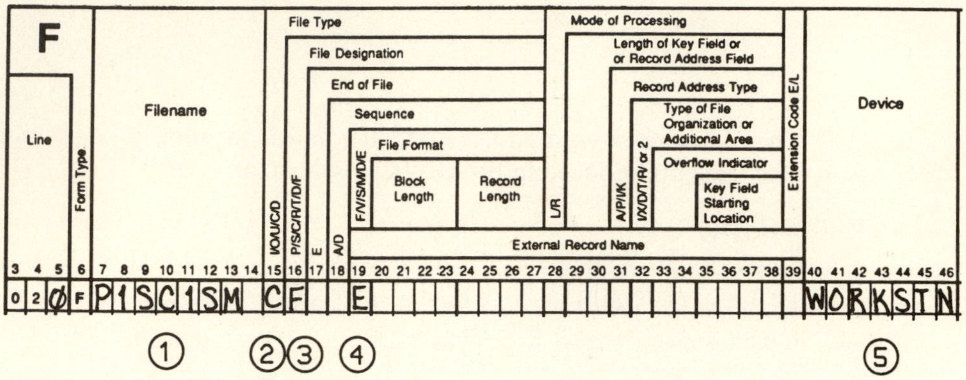

1. File name entry must be left-justified in field. For WORKSTN (workstation) files, the entry must specify a display file name (DSPF).

2. The letter C in column 16 indicates that the file must be processed as both an input and output file.

3. The letter F in column 17 indicates that the display file is a *full-procedural* file. A full-procedural file is not processed by the normal RPG cycle. For example, to read from a display file (screen), the EXFMT or READ operation has to be used; and to write to a display file, an EXFMT or WRITE operation must be specified.

4. The letter E in column 19 indicates that the record format(s) in the display file are *externally defined*. An eternally defined file is one in which the record and field attributes are defined outside of the RPG program and not in the Input Specifications as in a *program-defined* file.

   Because the display file is externally defined, other usually required file attributes as block length, record length, and so forth are not specified.

5. WORKSTN is the predefined Device name for workstation supported files. The entry must be entered left-justified in the Device field.

Figure 21-2 File Description entries required for a WORKSTN file.

THE WRITE (CREATE NEW RECORDS) OPERATION

The WRITE operation controls the writing of records to a Physical File in a file load or add process. This operation does not follow the normal RPG cycle where records are loaded or added to the file as they are consecutively processed. Instead, records are written to the file only when the WRITE operation is executed.

The physical file controlled by this operation must include the letter A (for ADD processing) in column 66 of the related File Description Specification instruction. The syntax of this operation is explained in Figure 21-3.

Three example programs that load a physical file interactively with different controls are introduced in the following paragraphs. All the programs load the

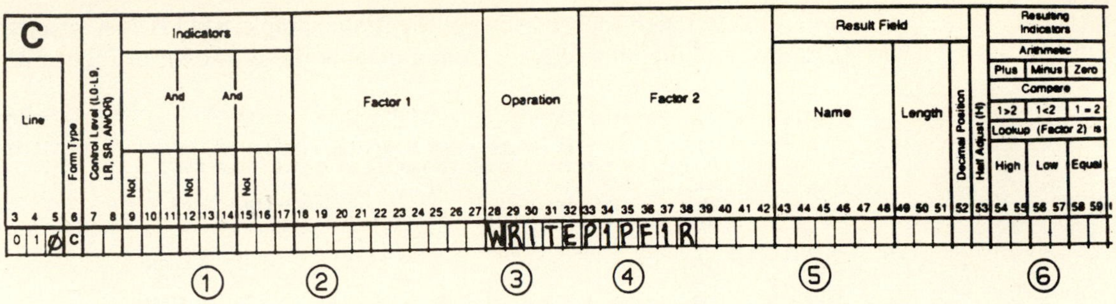

1. Any detail or total time RPG indicators may be used to condition the WRITE instruction.

2. Factor 1 is never used.

3. The WRITE operation controls the writing of a new record to be written to a disk file. Performs add function from calculation without need for any output instructions.

4. Factor 2 must contain a file name or record format name. If a file name is used, a *data structure* name must be entered in the Result Field. When a record format is referenced here, the fields are defined by a DDS supported data base.

5. Result Field is used only if Factor 2 contains a file name. Name of data structure would be entered here. Otherwise, this field must be blank.

6. A Resulting Indicator may be entered in columns 56 and 57, which will turn on if the WRITE operation does not execute successfully.

Figure 21-3 Syntax of the WRITE operation.

physical file built in Chapter 19 interactively through data entered by the display file created in Chapter 20 under RPG program control.

RPG PROGRAM THAT INTERACTIVELY LOADS A PHYSICAL FILE (EXAMPLE 1)

The first example program to load a physical file interactively includes the following controls:

EXFMT operation	WRITE operation
CABxx operation	*INxx
CASxx operation	Data Structure

A flowchart of the processing logic for the program is presented in Figure 21-4.

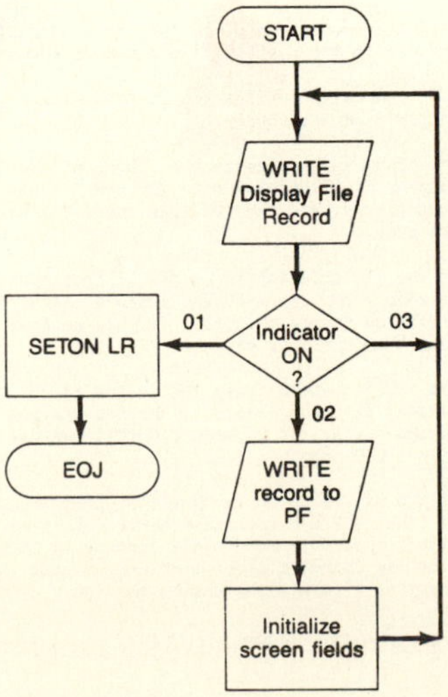

Figure 21-4 Processing logic flowchart for first example RPG III/400 program that loads a physical file from a display file.

A detailed source listing of the first example RPG III/400 program that loads a physical file interactively from a display file is shown in Figure 21-5.

```
SEQNBR  *... ... 1 ... ... 2 ... ... 3 ... ... 4 ... ... 5 ... ... 6 ... ... 7 ... ... 8

  100        * THIS PROGRAM LOADS A PHYSICAL FILE INTERACTIVELY WITH REPETITIVE  CH21P1
  200        * SCREEN DISPLAY CONTROLLED BY A GOTO OPERATION................     CH21P1
  300        *                                                                   CH21P1
  400       FP1SC1SM CF  E                    WORKSTN                            CH21P1
  500       FP1PF1SM O   E           K        DISK                     A         CH21P1
  600       I            DS                                                      CH21P1
  700       I                                         1   5 CUST#                CH21P1
  800       I                                         6  25 NAME                 CH21P1
  900       I                                        26  45 STREET               CH21P1
 1000       I                                        46  65 CITY                 CH21P1
 1100       I                                        66  67 STATE                CH21P1
 1200       I                                         1  67 BLANK                CH21P1
 1300       C           AGAIN     TAG                                            CH21P1
 1400       C                     EXSR HOUSEK                    HOUSEKEEP SR    CH21P1
 1500       C                     EXFMTP1SC1R                    DISPLAY SCREEN  CH21P1
 1600       C           *IN01     CABEQ'1'       EOJ             EOJ CONTROL     CH21P1
 1700       C           *IN03     CABEQ'1'       AGAIN           CANCEL INPUT    CH21P1
 1800       C           *IN02     CASEQ'1'       SUBWTE          WRITE SR        CH21P1
 1900       C                     END                            ENDS CAS        CH21P1
 2000       C                     GOTO AGAIN                     REDSPLY CTRL    CH21P1
 2100       C           EOJ       TAG                                            CH21P1
 2200       C                     SETON                     LR   END OF JOB      CH21P1
 2300        *                                                                   CH21P1
 2400       C           HOUSEK    BEGSR                          BEGIN HOUSE SR  CH21P1
 2500       C                     MOVE *BLANKS   BLANK           INIT ALPH FLDS  CH21P1
 2600       C                     MOVE *ZEROS    ZIP             INIT ZIP        CH21P1
 2700       C                     MOVE *ZEROS    BALANC          INIT BALANC     CH21P1
 2800       C                     ENDSR                          END HOUSE SR    CH21P1
 2900        *                                                                   CH21P1
 3000       C           SUBWTE    BEGSR                          BEGIN WRITE SR  CH21P1
 3100       C                     WRITEP1PF1R               99   WRITE PF RECORDCH21P1
 3200       C                     ENDSR                          END WRITE SR    CH21P1
```

SEQNBR

400 - Work station file (created in Chapter 20) is defined as a combined (C in position 15), full-procedural (F in column 16), and externally defined (E in column 19) file. Device name (WORKSTN) is entered in columns 40-46.

500 - Physical File (created in Chapter 19) is defined as an output (O in column 15), externally defined (E in column 19), and a keyed file (K in column 31). DISK is specified as the device name.

The letter A in column 66 supports the addition of records to the file. Because the Physical File was previously created, any records loaded to the file are processed as "add" records. Consequently, the letter A entry is always required for the initial and subsequent loading of a physical file.

600 to
1200 - A data structure that includes the alphanumeric fields from the display file record is specified. The entry on line 1200 redefines the individual subfields in the data structure as one subfield. Because the fields in the display file record format were defined as B type (both input and output), they will not be initialized to blanks and zeros after a record is entered. Consequently, the fields must be initialized in the RPG program (lines 2500-2700). Redefining the five alphanumeric subfields as one subfield within the data structure reduces the number of MOVE statements required.

1300 - Entry point of CABEQ statement on line 1700 and the GOTO statement one line 2000.

1400 - EXSR statement controls branch to a subroutine that initializes the fields defined in the display file's record format.

1500 - EXFMT operation WRITEs the Display File record P1SC1R to the screen and READs the record from the screen.

1600 - The *IN01 keyword tests the status of the 01 indicator which is turned on in the display file and passed to the RPG program if Command Key 1 is pressed. Remember that the keyword CA01(01) was specified at the File Level in the display file's DDS code.

If the 01 indicator is ON ('1'), program control will branch to the EOJ TAG statement on line 2100 and execute the SETON instruction which turns on the LR indicator to end the job. If this control was not included, the files would remain in the OPEN state.

1700 - The *IN03 keyword tests the status of the 03 indicator which is turned on in the display file and passed to the RPG program if Command Key 03 is pressed. Again, remember that the keyword CA03(03) was specified at the File Level in the display file's DDS code.

If the 03 indicator is ON ('1'), program control will branch to the TAG statement on line 1300 and then pass control to line 1500 which will redisplay the display file's record format. This control is included in the program so that the operator may change his/her mind and not add the current record (cancel) to the physical file without ending the job.

Figure 21-5 First example RPG III/400 program that loads a Physical File from a Display File.

```
1800 - The *IN02 keyword tests the status of the 02 indicator which is turned on in the
       display file and passes to the RPG program if Command Key 2 is pressed. The ON
       or OFF status of this indicator is controlled by the CF02(02) keyword specified
       at the file level in the display file's DDS coding.

       If the 02 indicator is ON ('1'), program control will execute the CASEQ state-
       ment and exit to the internal subroutine, SUBWTE.

       Data is not passed by the 01 and 03 indicators, because a CAnn (Command
       Attention) keyword was specified for this control in the Display File. However,
       because the 02 indicator controls the processing that requires the reading of
       data from the Display File, a CFnn (Command Function) keyword had to be
       specified for this processing function.

1900 - The required END operation indicates the end of a single or group of CASxx
       statements. Note the END statement is not related to CABxx statements.

2000 - After Command Key 2 is pressed, indicator 02 is turned on, and the subroutine
       SUBWTE executed, program control will return to the GOTO statement following the
       END statement on line 1900 and branch to the TAG on line 1300. The display
       record fields will be initialized (line 1400) and the EXFMT instruction on line
       1500 will redisplay the screen for additional data entry or end of the job
       response.

2100 to
2200 - The TAG statement on line 2100 is the entry point for the CABEQ statement on
       line 1600. This branching is controlled when an operator presses Command Key
       1, which turns on the 01 indicator.

       The SETON statement on line 2200 turns on the LR indicator which ends the job.
       If this control was not included, the files would remain in an OPEN condition.

2400 to
2800 - The MOVE statements in this subroutine initialize the display file's record
       fields before the screen is displayed.

       The MOVE *BLANKS instruction on line 2500 initializes the subfield that rede-
       fined all of the alphanumeric subfields in the data structure to blanks.

       The MOVE *ZEROS instructions on line 2600 and 2700 individually initialize the
       numeric fields to zeros. Note that one subfield could have been specified in
       the data structure to redefine two numeric subfields as one subfield. Then,
       only one MOVE statement would be needed. In any case, however, a subfield
       defined as numeric may not be greater than 15 bytes.

3000 to
3100 - The BEGSR instruction on line 3000 is the entry point for the CASEQ statement on
       line 3100.

       A record is written to the physical file by the WRITE operation on line 3100.
       Either the file or record format name may be specified in Factor 2. Indicator
       99 in positions 56-57 will turn on if the WRITE is unsuccessful; as for a
       DUPLICATE KEY error.

3200 - The ENDSR operation indicates the end of the internal subroutine. Program
       control will return back to line 2000. Then the GOTO statement will branch
       control
       back to the TAG statement on line 1300 and continue the initialization and
       display processes.
```

(*Continued*)

Notice that the RPG example program listing shown in Figure 21-5 did not include any Input or Output Specifications. Because the Display and Physical Files were both specified as *externally defined* (E in column 19 of the File Description form), their record and field attributes do not have to be included in the program's source code.

Compilation of the source program generates a listing that integrates the attributes of the externally defined files in their related specification (input and output) locations. This listing is shown in Figure 21-6.

```
*...+....1....+....2....+....3....+....4....+....5....+....6....+....7....+....8

100  FP1DF1SM CF  E                   WORKSTN
      RECORD FORMAT(S); LIBRARY SEMLIB FILE P1DF1SM
             EXTERNAL FORMAT P1SC1R RPG NAME P1SC1R

200  FP1PF1   O   E          K        DISK
      RECORD FORMAT(S); LIBRARY SEMLIB FILE P1PF1
             EXTERNAL FORMAT P1PF1R RPG NAME P1PF1R

A000000   INPUT  FIELDS FOR RECORD P1SC1R FILE P1DF1SM FORMAT P1SC1R
A000001                                      1   1 *IN01              END OF JOB
A000002                                      2   2 *IN02              ADD RECORD
A000003                                      3   3 *IN03              REDISPLAY
A000004                                      4   4 *IN99              CANNOT ADD DUPLICATE RECORD
```

Figure 21-6 Listings generated from compilation of the RPG III/400 source program.

```
A000005                                                5   9 CUST#
A000006                                               10  29 NAME
A000007                                               30  49 STREET
A000008                                               50  69 CITY
A000009                                               70  71 STATE
A000010                                               72  760ZIP
A000011                                               77  842BALANC
    300  I        DS                                                                            05/29/91
    400  I                                             1   5 CUST#                              05/29/91
    500  I                                             6  25 NAME                               05/29/91
    600  I                                            26  45 STREET                             05/29/91
    700  I                                            46  65 CITY                               05/29/91
    800  I                                            66  67 STATE                              05/29/91
    900  I                                             1  67 BLANK                              05/29/91

   1000  C           AGAIN     TAG                                                              05/29/91
   1100  C                     EXSR HOUSEK                                                      05/29/91
   1200  C                     EXFMTP1SC1R                                                      05/29/91
   1300  C           *IN01     CABEQ'1'       EOJ                EOJ CONTROL                    05/29/91
   1400  C           *IN03     CABEQ'1'       AGAIN              DO NOT ADD                     05/29/91
   1500  C           *IN02     CABEQ'1'       SUBWTE             WRITE SR                       05/91/91
   1600  C                     END                               END CAS GROUP                  05/29/91
   1700  C                     GOTO AGAIN                                                       05/29/91
   1800  C                     EOJ       TAG                                                    05/29/91
   1900  C                     SETON                        LR   END OF JOB        1            05/29/91
   2000   *                                                                                     05/29/91
   2100  C           HOUSEK    BEGSR                                                            05/29/91
   2200  C                     MOVE *BLANKS   BLANK              INIT ALPHA FLDS                05/29/91
   2300  C                     MOVE *ZEROS    ZIP                INIT NUM FLD                   05/29/91
   2400  C                     MOVE *ZEROS    BALANC             INIT NUM FLD                   05/29/91
   2500  C                     ENDSR                                                            05/29/91
   2600   *                                                                                     05/29/91
   2700  C           SUBWTE    BEGSR                                                            05/29/91
   2800  C                     WRITEP1PF1R                  99 WRITE RECORD      2            05/29/91
   2900                        ENDSR                                                            05/29/91
B000000  OUTPUT  FIELDS FOR RECORD P1SC1R FILE P1DF1SM FORMAT P1SC1R.                           05/29/91
B000001                      *IN99     1  CHAR    1                                  CANNOT ADD DUPLICATE RECORD
C000000  OUTPUT  FIELDS FOR RECORD P1PF1R FILE P1PF1 FORMAT PFPF1R.
C000001                      CUST#     5  CHAR   20
C000002                      NAME     25  CHAR   20
C000003                      STREET   45  CHAR   20
C000004                      CITY     65  CHAR   20
C000005                      STATE    67  CHAR    2
C000006                      ZIP      70P PACK  5,0
C000007                      BALANC   75P PACK  8,2
```

(*Continued*)

The blank screen displayed from execution of the program is shown in Figure 21-7. The vertical lines, which are column separators and do not print, are included here only to indicate field sizes. Reverse image is often used in lieu of column separators; a reverse image also will not appear in a printout of the screen image. The Command Key options listed at the bottom of the screen indicate the processing functions that may be controlled by the operator. As previously explained, each Command Key turns on an indicator that controls the related sequence in the RPG program.

```
08/11/91                                                        14:30:00
                         CUSTOMER NAME & ADDRESS

                CUSTOMER NUMBER    | | | | | |

                NAME               | | | | | | | | | | | | | | | | | | | | |

                STREET             | | | | | | | | | | | | | | | | | | | | |

                CITY               | | | | | | | | | | | | | | | | | | | | |

                STATE              | | |

                ZIP                | | | | | |

                BALANCE            | | | | | | | | |

                CK1 - EOJ     CK2 - ENTER     CK3 - REDISPLAY
```

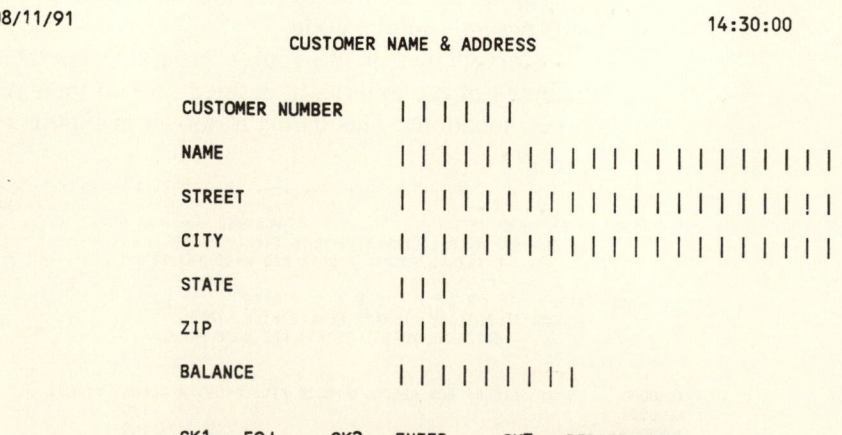

Figure 21-7 Screen display generated by an RPG program that controls the interactive loading of records to a physical file.

FIRST MODIFIED PROGRAM EXAMPLE 2 (IF/ELSE CONTROL)

The RPG/400/III program example previously discussed is only one of many structured coding approaches that may be followed by a programmer. In the paragraphs that follow, two modified versions of the example program are presented. The first includes IFxx/ELSE operations and the second, the DOUxx operation. The syntax for both of these operations was previously introduced in Chapter 6.

The source listing for the first modified program that controls the necessary decision-making functions by IFxx/ELSE statements is presented in Figure 21-8. All the other program's processing features were previously discussed in the first example.

```
SEQNBR  *... ... 1 ... ... 2 ... ... 3 ... ... 4 ... ... 5 ... ... 6 ... ... 7 ... ... 8

  100        * THIS PROGRAM LOADS A PHYSICAL FILE INTERACTIVELY WITH IF/ELSE    CH21P2
  200        * CONTROL.....................................................     CH21P2
  300        *                                                                  CH21P2
  400       FP1SC1SM CF  E                  WORKSTN                             CH21P2
  500       FP1PF1SM O   E           K      DISK                   A            CH21P2
  600       I            DS                                                     CH21P2
  700       I                                      1   5 CUST#                  CH21P2
  800       I                                      6  25 NAME                   CH21P2
  900       I                                     26  45 STREET                 CH21P2
 1000       I                                     46  65 CITY                   CH21P2
 1100       I                                     66  67 STATE                  CH21P2
 1200       I                                      1  67 BLANK                  CH21P2
 1300       C           AGAIN     TAG                                           CH21P2
 1400       C                     EXSR HOUSEK                 INITIALIZE SR  CH21P2
 1500       C                     EXFMTP1SC1R                 DSPLY SCREEN   CH21P2
 1600       C           *IN01     IFEQ '1'                    EOJ ?          CH21P2
 1700       C                     SETON                  LR   END JOB        CH21P2
 1800       C                     ELSE                        NOT EOJ        CH21P2
 1900       C           *IN03     IFEQ '1'                    DO NOT WRITE   CH21P2
 2000       C                     GOTO AGAIN                  BRNCH & DSPLY  CH21P2
 2100       C                     ELSE                        NO3 TEST       CH21P2
 2200       C                     CAS          SUBWTE         EXIT TO SUBRTN CH21P2
 2300       C                     END                         ENDS CAS       CH21P2
 2400       C                     GOTO AGAIN                  BRNCH & DSPLY  CH21P2
 2500       C                     END                         FOR LNE 1600 IFCH21P2
 2600       C                     END                         FOR LNE 1300 IFCH21P2
 2700        *                                                               CH21P2
 2800       C           HOUSEK    BEGSR                                      CH21P2
 2900       C                     MOVE *BLANKS BLANK          INIT ALPHA FLDSCH21P2
 3000       C                     MOVE *ZEROS  ZIP            INIT NUM FIELD CH21P2
 3100       C                     MOVE *ZEROS  BALANC         INIT NUM FIELD CH21P2
 3200       C                     ENDSR                       END OF SUBRTN  CH21P2
 3300        *                                                               CH21P2
 3400       C           SUBWTE    BEGSR                       BEGIN SUBRTN   CH21P2
 3500       C                     WRITE P1PF1R                WRITE REC TO PFCH21P2
 3600       C                     ENDSR                                      CH21P2
```

SEQNBR

400 - Work station file (created in Chapter 20) is defined as a combined (C in position 15), full-procedural (F in column 16), and externally defined file (E in column 19) file. Device name (WORKSTN) is entered in columns 40-46.

500 - Physical File (created in Chapter 20) is defined as an output (O in column 15), externally defined (E in column 19), and a keyed file (K in column 31). DISK is specified as the device name.

The letter A in column 66 supports the addition of records to the file. Because the Physical File was previously created, any records loaded to the file are processed as "add" records. Consequently, the letter A entry is always required for the initial and subsequent loading of a Physical File.

600 to
1200 - A data structure that includes the alphanumeric fields from the display file record is specified. The entry on line 1200 redefines the individual subfields in the data structure as one subfield. Because the fields in the display file record format were defined as B type (both input and output), they will not be initialized to blanks and zeros after a record is entered. Consequently, the fields must be initialized in the RPG program (lines 2900-3100). Redefining the five alphanumeric subfields as one subfield within the data structure reduces the number of MOVE statements required.

1300 - Entry point of the GOTO statements on lines 2000 and 2400.

1400 - EXSR statement controls branch to a subroutine that initializes the fields defined in the display file's record format.

1500 - EXFMT operation WRITEs the Display File record P1SC1R to screen and READs the record from the screen.

Figure 21-8 Source listing of the first modified program that controls the decision-making functions by IFxx/ELSE statements.

1600 to
1700 - The IF statement tests the status of the 01 indicator which is turned on in the display file and is passed to the RPG program if Command Key 1 is pressed. The keyword CA01(01) was specified at the File Level in the Display File's DDS code for this control.

If 01 indicator is ON ('1'), the IF statement test is "true" and the SETON LR instruction on line 1700 will be executed to end the job.

1800 - If the IF statement test on line 1600 is "false", statements 1900-2600 will be executed by this related ELSE group.

1900 to
2000 - This IF statement tests the status of the 03 indicator which is turned on in the display file and passed to the RPG program if Command Key 03 is pressed, Again, remember that the keyword CA03(03) was specified at the File Level in the display file's DDS code to control the "ON" or "OFF" status of the 03 indicator. If the 03 indicator is ON ('1'), the GOTO statement on line 2000 will pass program control to the TAG statement on line 1300, execute the initialization subroutine on line 1400 and then redisplay the display file's record format by executing the EXFMT statement on line 1500. This control is included in the program so that the operator may change his/her mind and not add the record to the Physical File without having to end the job.

2100 to
2400 - If the IF statement test on line 1900 is "false", the unconditional CAS statement on line 2200 branches control to the subroutine SUBWTE on lines 3400-3600 to WRITE the input record to the physical file.

After the subroutine SUBWTE is executed, control returns to the GOTO statement on line 2400 which transfers control back to line 1300 and the initialization and display cycle continued until end of job is indicated.

Note in the previous program example, Command Key 2 (indicator 02) was explicitly specified in the program to control execution of the SUBWTE routine. It is used here by default. If the operator presses command Key 2, indicator 02 will be on and not 01 or 03. Screen prompts remind the operator of the Command Key options.

2500 - This END operation is related to the IFEQ statement on line 1900.

2600 - This END operation is related to the IFEQ statement on line 1600.

2800 to
3200 - The MOVE statements in this subroutine initialize the display file's record fields before the screen is displayed.

3400 to
3500 - A record is written to the Physical File by the WRITE statement on line 3500. Either the file or record format name may be specified in Factor 2. Indicator 99 in positions 56-57 will turn on if the WRITE is unsuccessful; as when a DUPLICATE KEY error is sensed.

3600 - The ENDSR operation transfers control from this subroutine back to line 2400 which causes program control to branch and repeat the initialization and display cycle.

(Continued)

SECOND MODIFIED PROGRAM (DOU CONTROL)

The original example program used CASxx and CABxx statements to control the decision-making functions; the first modified program used IFxx/ELSE statements. A second modified version of the example program incorporates the DOUxx (Do Until) operation. The syntax for this operation has been previously explained in Chapter 6.

The source listing of the second modified version of the application program that loads a physical file interactively is illustrated in Figure 21-9. All the program functions including end of job control, writing a record to the physical file, and redisplay of the screen are directly controlled within the DOUxx group.

```
SEQNBR  *... ... 1 ... ... 2 ... ... 3 ... ... 4 ... ... 5 ... ... 6 ... ... 7 ... ... 8

   100        * THIS PROGRAM LOADS A PHYSICAL FILE INTERACTIVELY WITH DOUxx      CH21P3
   200        * (DO UNTIL) CONTROL........................................       CH21P3
   300        *                                                                  CH21P3
   400       FP1SC1SM CF  E                    WORKSTN                           CH21P3
   500       FP1PF1SM O   E           K        DISK                    A         CH21P3
```

Figure 21-9 Source listing of the second modified version of the application program that loads a Physical File and is controlled by the DOUxx operation.

```
600    I        DS                                               CH21P3
700    I                                   1   5 CUST#           CH21P3
800    I                                   6  25 NAME            CH21P3
900    I                                  26  45 STREET          CH21P3
1000   I                                  46  65 CITY            CH21P3
1100   I                                  66  67 STATE           CH21P3
1200   I                                   1  67 BLANK           CH21P3
1300   C        *IN01     DOUEQ'1'                   CMD KEY 1 EOJ' CH21P3
1400   C        AGAIN     TAG                                    CH21P3
1500   C                  EXSR HOUSEK                INITIALIZE SR  CH21P3
1600   C                  EXFMTP1SC1R                DSPLY SCREEN   CH21P3
1700   C        *IN03     CABEQ'1'       AGAIN       CANCEL ADD     CH21P3
1800   C        *IN02     CASEQ'1'       SUBWTE      EXIT TO ADD SR CH21P3
1900   C                  END                        FOR CASEQ      CH21P3
2000   C                  END                        FOR DOUEQ      CH21P3
2100   C                  SETON                  LR  END JOB        CH21P3
2200    *                                                        CH21P3
2300   C        HOUSEK    BESGR                      BEGIN HOUSEK SRCH21P3
2400   C                  MOVE *BLANKS   BLANK       INIT ALPHA FLDSCH21P3
2500   C                  MOVE *ZEROS    ZIP         INIT NUM FIELD CH21P3
2600   C                  MOVE *ZEROS    BALANC      INIT NUM FIELD CH21P3
2700   C                  ENDSR                      END HOUSEK SR  CH21P3
2800    *                                                        CH21P3
2900   C        SUBWTE    BEGSR                      BEGIN ADD SR   CH21P3
3000   C                  WRITEP1PF1R             99 WRITE REC TO PFCH21P3
3100   C                  ENDSR                      END ADD SR     CH21P3
```

SEQNBR

400 to
1200 - Same as program examples previously detailed in Figures 21-5 and 21-8.

1300 - DOUEQ statement identifies beginning of a DOU group. Because the test for this operation is made at the related END statement on line 2000, instructions within the DOUEQ group will be executed at least once.

1400 to
1900 - Same as program examples previously detailed in Figures 21-5 and 21-8.

2000 - Relational test for DOUEQ statement on line 1300 is made at this related END operation. When the condition in the DOUEQ statement tested as true, program control will pass to the statement following this END operation.

(Continued)

SUMMARY OF THE THREE VERSIONS OF THE INTERACTIVE LOAD PROGRAM

The original version of the application program that loads a physical file interactively incorporated the CAS and CAB operations. The RPG syntax for externally defined files, display file processing, and the WRITE operation were introduced in the first example. It was emphasized that an RPG program does not have to include any Input or Output Specifications when the files (physical, display, logical, and printer files) are externally defined. During compilation, however, the record and field attributes from those files are included in the compiled source listing.

The first modified version of the application program introduced the use of the IF and ELSE structured operations. Other syntax and processing features common to the original program were included.

Finally, the second modified version of the application program used the DOUxx operation to control the major processing functions. Other calculation instructions included some of those specified in the original and first modified versions of the application program.

The three RPG III and RPG/400 program versions of the same application are only some of the many approaches available. Coding procedures and program structure are usually developed at the discretion of the programmer.

An application program that controls the maintenance procedures common to physical files is now discussed.

APPLICATION PROGRAM—PHYSICAL FILE MAINTENANCE

The maintenance procedures associated with physical files (or any data file type) are the addition, update, and deletion of records in the file. Inquiry and limits processing are not considered maintenance functions but processing options. A program is presented that includes the addition, update, and deletion maintenance of the physical file previously created and loaded with data.

Documentation

The specifications presented in Figure 21-10 explain the maintenance procedures that are to be controlled by this program.

PROGRAM SPECIFICATIONS Page 1 of 2

Program Name CUSTOMER FILE MAINT. Program-ID CH21P4 Written By S. Myers

Purpose Addition, update, and delete maintenance Approved By The Boss

Input files (directory names):

```
P1PF1 (Customer Master File - record format P1PF1R)
P1DF1 (Display File - record formats P1DF1S1 and P1DF1S2)
```

Output files (directory names):

```
P1PF1 (Customer Master File - record format P1PF1R)
P1DF1 (Display File - record formats P1DF1S1 and P1DF1S2)
```

Processing Narrative:

```
Write a structured RPG 400/III program to control the addition, up-
date, and logical deletion of records in a physical file that stores
customer information (P1PF1).

Input/Output:

The attributes of a physical file stored on disk are detailed in the
supplemental file definition form.  To control update and deletion
processing, the file must be defined in the File Description statement
as an update file (U in column 15).

Enter the coding, compile, and test the display screens shown in the
attached CRT form.  The first screen, which is used to enter a cust-
omer number, must provide for the display of the following error
messages:

                    DUPLICATE KEY - CANNOT ADD RECORD!
                    RECORD NOT FOUND - CANNOT UPDATE!
                    RECORD NOT FOUND - CANNOT DELETE!

Note the following program controls are to be included in the design
and syntax of the second screen:

        Command Key 1 - End of job control
        Command Key 2 - Record addition
        Command Key 3 - Prevent update/deletion processing
        Command Key 4 - Record Update
        Command Ley 5 - Record Deletion (logical)
```

Figure 21-10 Specifications for a program that interactively controls addition, update, and deletion maintenance.

Note that the heading of the second screen (see format) is to indicate which processing mode the program is currently controlling.

Addition Processing:

For addition processing, if the customer number is found, a record cannot be added. This is because the file was originally created as UNIQUE, which prevents the addition of records with key values already stored in the file (DUPLICATE KEY error). If a customer number is not found, however, the second screen will display, data

Processing Narrative:

may be entered, and the record added to the file. Command key 2 is to control record addition.

Update Processing:

For update processing, if the customer number is found, the second screen is displayed and any field, execpt customer number, may be changed. Command key 4 is to control update processing.

Deletion (Logical) Processing:

For logical deletion processing the related record is to be extracted from the file, no changes made, and the record logically deleted by Command Key 5 control.

Even though it is not required, use indicators that relate to the Command Key specified (i.e. indicator 01 for Command Key 1, and so forth)

(*Continued*)

Figure 21-11 is a system flowchart that identifies the files related to this application.

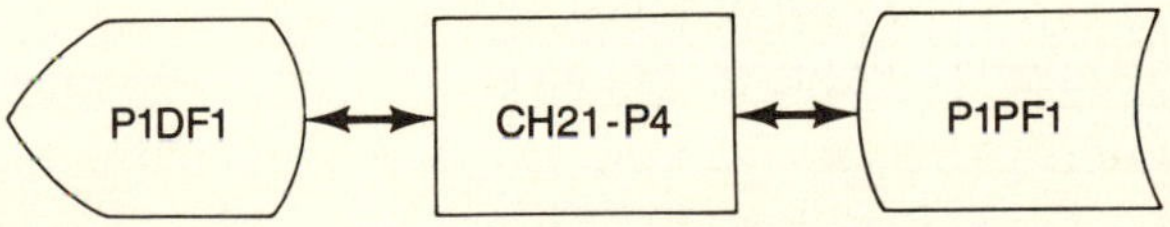

Figure 21-11 System flowchart for a program that interactively controls maintenance of a physical file.

Detailed in the File Definition form in Figure 21-12 are the attributes of the physical file processed by this application program.

FILE DEFINITION

SYSTEM AS/400		DRAWN BY S. Myers
FILE NAME P1PF1		DATE 8/11/91 REV. NO. 0
CREATED BY S. Myers		FILE TYPE Physical
RECORD NAME P1PF1R		KEY LENGTH 5 bytes
RECORDING MODE Unique	ORGANIZATION Keyed	SEQUENCE CUST#
RECORD SIZE 75 bytes	BLOCKING FACTOR 1	BLOCKSIZE 75 bytes

FIELD DATA

FIELD NO.	FIELD NAME - DESCRIPTION	SIZE	CLASS C/P/Z/B	POSITION FROM	POSITION THRU	FORMAT/CONSTANT
	P1PF1R					Record name
1	CUST#	5	C	1	5	Key field (unique)
2	NAME	20	C	6	25	
3	STREET	20	C	26	45	
4	CITY	20	C	46	65	
5	STATE	2	C	66	67	
6	ZIP	5	P	68	70	
7	BALANC	8	P	71	75	2 decimal positions

Figure 21-12 File Definition of the physical file maintained by the application program.

A listing of the data in the physical file before any maintenance is performed is shown in Figure 21-13.

```
12345KAREL APPEL          20 AMSTERDAM AVENUE NEW YORK             NY0745000125000
23456GEORGES BRAQUE       300 ST CLAIR STREET TRENTON              NJ0550100010000
34567PAUL CEZANNE         44 RUE PIGALLE      STAMFORD             CT0651808190000
45678MARC CHAGALL         222 QUAIL AVENUE    BRIDGEPORT           CT0666600092600
56789EDGAR DEGAS          10 ROSE TERRACE     WESTPORT             PA0777700784599
67890MAX ERNST            1 FRANKFURT DRIVE   FRANKFORT            KY0555100050000
78900BUCKMINSTER FULLER   999 PARK AVENUE     NEW YORK             NY0755503300010
89000JULIO GONZALEZ       101 SMITH LANE      GREENWICH            CT0644400065478
90000HECTOR HYPPOLITE     888 PEACHTREE AVENUEATLANTA              GA0333212000000
91000PIERRE JEANERET      90 CHATEAU DRIVE    GENEVA               NY0777700000945
```

Figure 21-13 Listing of the data in the physical file before maintenance.

As indicated in the program specifications, the display file includes two screen records. The design of the first screen, which is used to enter a customer number and either identify one of the specified processing errors or display the second screen, is shown in Figure 21-14.

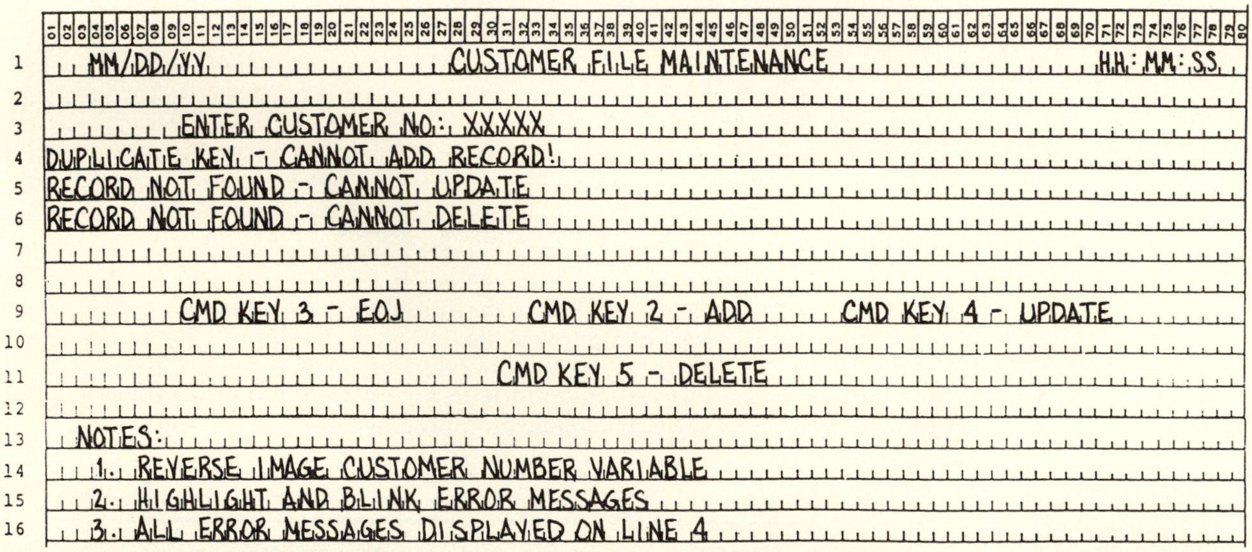

Figure 21-14 Format of the first screen record included in the display file for the interactive maintenance program.

Two printouts of the image of screen record 1 (P1DF1S1) are included in Figure 21-15. The first is a display of the screen after a customer number is entered

Screen image after a customer number is entered:

```
8/11/91               CUSTOMER FILE MAINTENANCE               14:30:00

              ENTER CUSTOMER NO: 12345




              CMD KEY 3 - EOJ       CMD KEY 2 - ADD       CMD KEY 4 - UPDATE

                                    CMD KEY 5 - DELETE
```

Figure 21-15 Display of two screen record 1 images generated during program execution.

Screen image after customer number is entered, command key 2 pressed, and a duplicate record found in the customer file:

```
8/11/91                  CUSTOMER FILE MAINTENANCE                  14:30:00


          ENTER CUSTOMER NO: 12345
DUPLICATE KEY - CANNOT ADD RECORD!




          CMD KEY 3 - EOJ        CMD KEY 2 - ADD        CMD KEY 4 - UPDATE

                                 CMD KEY 5 - DELETE
```

(Continued)

and before a Command Key is pressed. The second display shows the screen after a customer number is entered, Command Key 2 pressed for addition processing, and a DUPLICATE RECORD! error identified. Notice that reverse image and highlight attributes do not appear on a screen printout.

Display File Screen Record 1 (P1DF1S1) Syntax

The syntax for screen 1 (P1DF1S1) is included in the Data Description Specifications form detailed in Figure 21-16. Notice that the keyword MSGLOC(04) has been specified on the first line of screen record 1 coding. This command indicates that the messages controlled by the ERRMSG keywords are to be displayed on line 4 (beginning in column 1). If MSGLOC was not specified, any message displayed by an ERRMSG keyword will default to line 24 (beginning in column 1).

Sequence Number (1–5)	Form Type (6)	Conditioning Indicator (9–10)	Name Type (17)	Name (19–28)	Length (30–34)	Usage (38)	Location Line (39–41)	Location Pos (42–44)	Functions (45–80)
00001	A								MSGLOC(04)
00002	A								PRINT
00003	A								CA03(03 'END OF JOB')
00004	A								CF02(02 'ADD RECORD')
00005	A								CF04(04 'UPDATE RECORD')
00006	A								CF05(05 'DELETE RECORD')
00007	A		R	P1DF1S1					
00008	A						1	3	DATE EDTCDE(Y)
00009	A						1	28	'CUSTOMER FILE MAINTENANCE'
00010	A						1	71	TIME
00011	A						3	10	'ENTER CUSTOMER NO:'
00012	A			CUST#	5	I	3	29	DSPATR(RI)
00013	A	90							ERRMSG('DUPLICATE KEY - CANNOT ADD-
00014	A								RECORD!' 90) DSPATR(HI BL)
00015	A	91							ERRMSG('RECORD NOT FOUND - CANNOT -
00016	A								UPDATE' 91) DSPATR(HI BL)
00017	A	92							ERRMSG('RECORD NOT FOUND - CANNOT -
00018	A								DELETE' 92) DSPATR(HI BL)
00019	A						9	10	'CMD KEY 3 - EOJ CMD KEY 2-
00020	A								- ADD CMD KEY 4 - UPDATE'
00021	A						11	31	'CMD KEY 5 - DELETE'

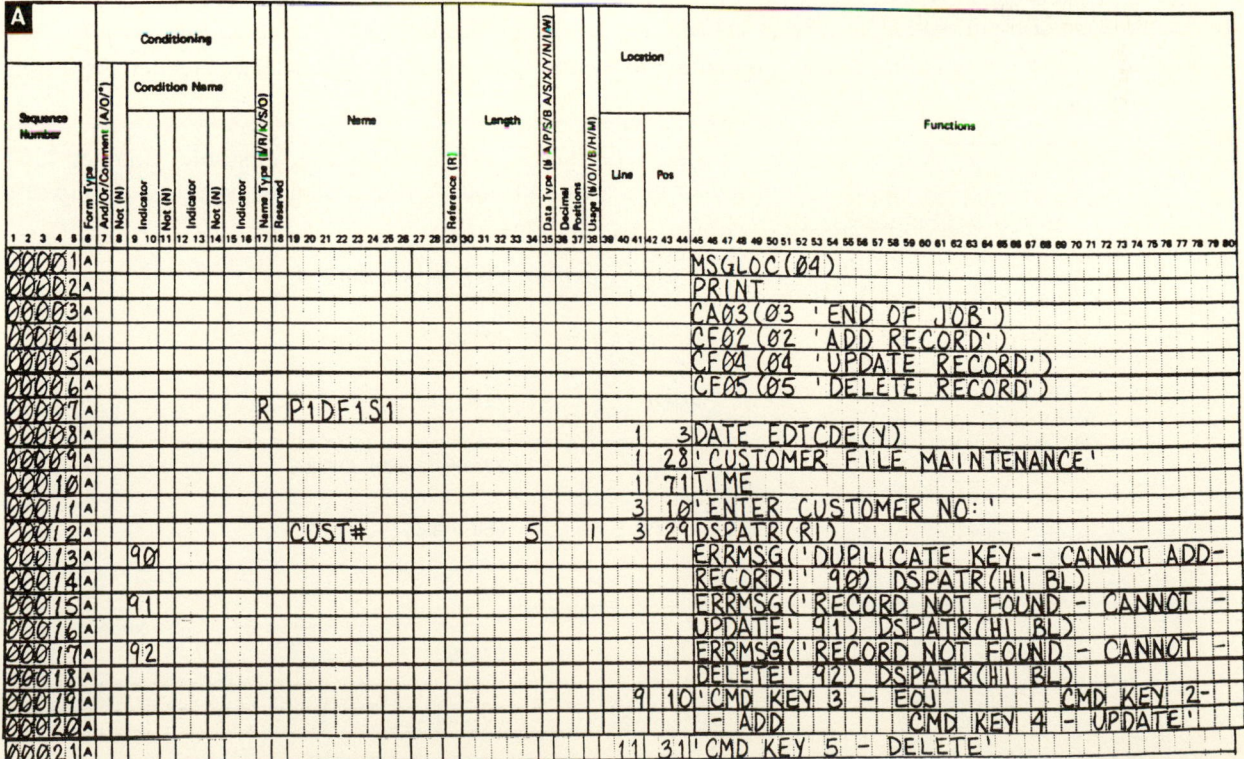

Figure 21-16 Data Description Specifications coding for screen record 1 (P1DF1S1) in the display file P1DF1.

The format of the second screen record (P1DF1S2) included in the display file (PFDF1) is illustrated in Figure 21-17. This screen is displayed only if one of the errors indicated in the first screen record is not generated. If add maintenance is requested, a blank screen will be displayed to permit entering of the data for an add record. If update or delete maintenance is requested, the second screen will be displayed with the field values from the related customer's record.

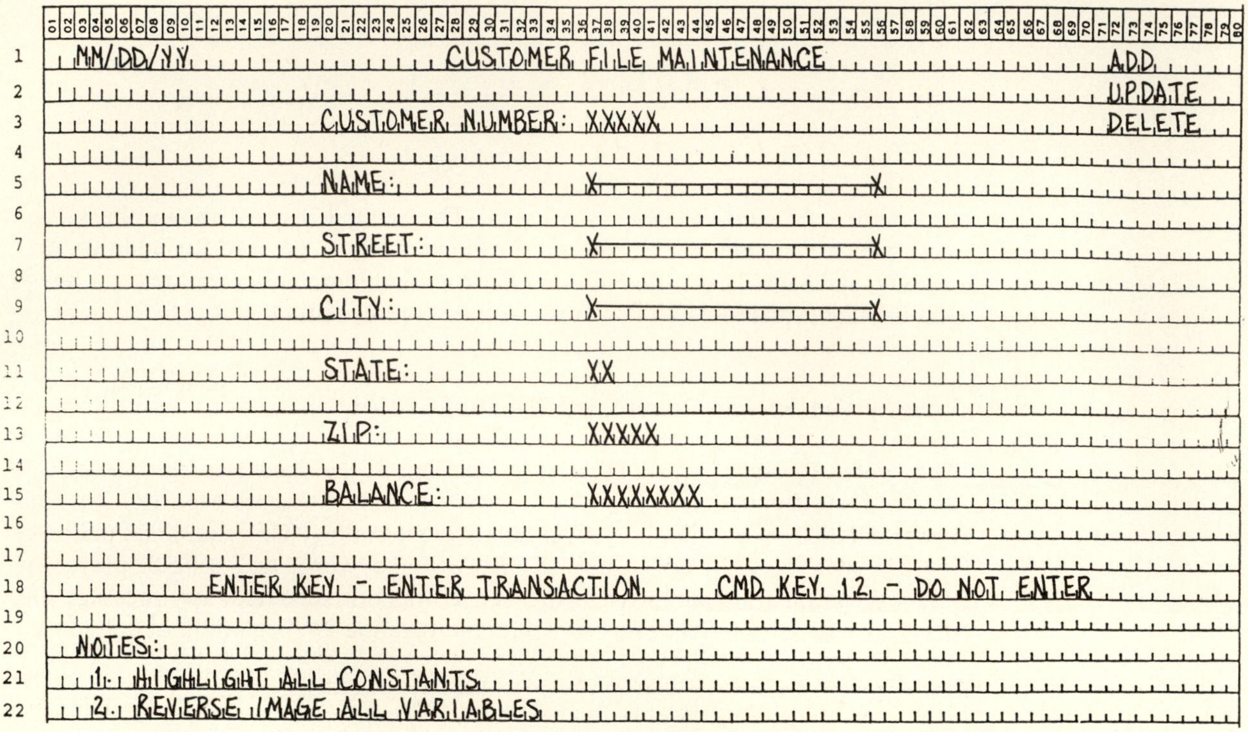

Figure 21-17 Format of the second screen record (P1DF1S2) included in the display file (P1DF1).

A display of the second screen record (P1DF1S2) after customer number 12345 is entered from the first screen and update processing is specified is shown in Figure 21-18.

```
8/11/91              CUSTOMER FILE MAINTENANCE                UPDATE

                   CUSTOMER NUMBER: 12345

                   NAME:            KAREL APPEL

                   STREET:          20 AMSTERDAM AVENUE

                   CITY:            NEW YORK

                   STATE:           NY

                   ZIP:             07450

                   BALANCE:         00125000


             ENTER KEY - ENTER TRANSACTION     CMD KEY 12 - DO NOT ENTER
```

Figure 21-18 Display of screen record 2 (P1DF1S2) image.

Display File Screen Record 2 (P1DF1S2) Syntax

The syntax for screen record 2 (P1DF1S2) included in the display file (P1DF1) is presented in Figure 21-19.

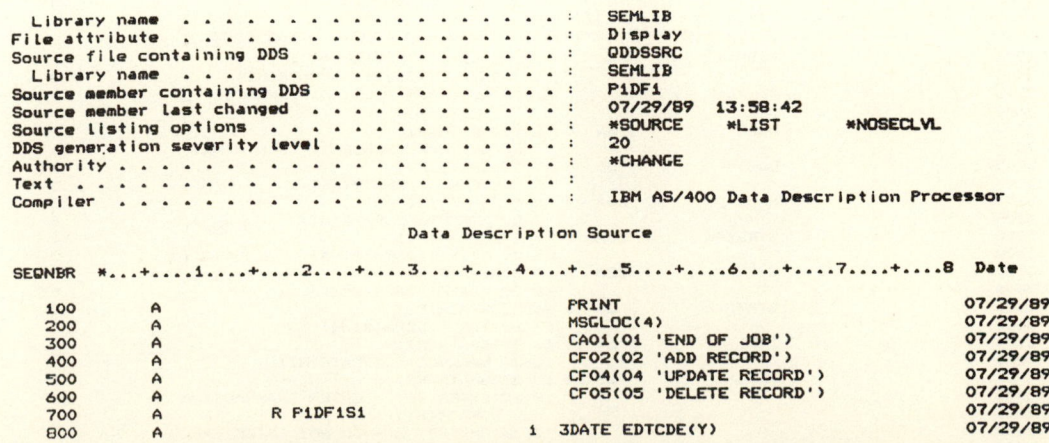

```
00001A                                   PRINT
00002A                                   CA03(03 'REDISPLAY')
00003A          R P1DF1S2
00004A                                 1  3DATE EDTCDE(Y) DSPATR(HI)
00005A                                 1 28'CUSTOMER FILE MAINTENANCE'
00006A                                     DSPATR(HI)
00007A            MODE           6   O 1 72DSPATR(RI)
00008A                                 3 20'CUSTOMER NUMBER:' DSPATR(HI)
00009A            CUST#          5   O 3 37DSPATR(RI PR)
00010A                                 5 20'NAME:' DSPATR(HI)
00011A            NAME          20   B 5 37DSPATR(RI PC)
00012A                                 7 20'STREET:' DSPATR(HI)
00013A            STREET        20   B 7 37DSPATR(RI)
00014A                                 9 20'CITY:' DSPATR(HI)
00015A            CITY          20   B 9 37DSPATR(RI)
00016A                                11 20'STATE:' DSPATR(HI)
00017A            STATE          2   B11 37DSPATR(RI)
00018A                                13 20'ZIP:' DSPATR(HI)
00019A            ZIP            5Y 0B13 37DSPATR(RI)
00020A                                15 20'BALANCE:' DSPATR(HI)
00021A            BALANC         8S 2B15 37DSPATR(RI)
00022A                                18 12'ENTER KEY - ENTER TRANSACTION'
00023A                                     DSPATR(HI)
00024A                                18 46'CMD KEY 03 - DO NOT ENTER'
00025A                                     DSPATR(HI)
```

Figure 21-19 Data Description Specifications coding for screen record 2 (P1DF1S2) in the display file P1DF1.

The source listings generated from compilation of the display file (P1DF1) shown in Figure 21-20 includes the syntax for the two screen records (P1DF1S1 and P1DF1S2).

```
  Library name . . . . . . . . . . . . . . . . . . :   SEMLIB
File attribute . . . . . . . . . . . . . . . . . . :   Display
Source file containing DDS . . . . . . . . . . . . :   QDDSSRC
  Library name . . . . . . . . . . . . . . . . . . :   SEMLIB
Source member containing DDS . . . . . . . . . . . :   P1DF1
Source member last changed . . . . . . . . . . . . :   07/29/89   13:58:42
Source listing options . . . . . . . . . . . . . . :   *SOURCE    *LIST     *NOSECLVL
DDS generation severity level . . . . . . . . . . :   20
Authority . . . . . . . . . . . . . . . . . . . . :   *CHANGE
Text . . . . . . . . . . . . . . . . . . . . . . . :
Compiler . . . . . . . . . . . . . . . . . . . . . :   IBM AS/400 Data Description Processor

                              Data Description Source

SEQNBR  *...+....1....+....2....+....3....+....4....+....5....+....6....+....7....+....8  Date

   100       A                                      PRINT                                07/29/89
   200       A                                      MSGLOC(4)                            07/29/89
   300       A                                      CA01(01 'END OF JOB')                07/29/89
   400       A                                      CF02(02 'ADD RECORD')                07/29/89
   500       A                                      CF04(04 'UPDATE RECORD')             07/29/89
   600       A                                      CF05(05 'DELETE RECORD')             07/29/89
   700       A          R P1DF1S1                                                        07/29/89
   800       A                                    1  3DATE EDTCDE(Y)                     07/29/89
```

Figure 21-20 Source listings generated by completion of the display file (P1DF1).

```
 900     A                                   1 28'CUSTOMER FILE MAINTENANCE'        07/29/89
1000     A                                   1 71TIME                               07/29/89
1100     A                                   3 10'ENTER CUSTOMER NO:'               07/29/89
1200     A              CUST#        5   I   3 29DSPATR(RI)                         07/29/89
1300     A  90                                  ERRMSG('DUPLICATE KEY - CANNOT ADD- 07/29/89
1400     A                                        RECORD!' 90) DSPATR(HI BL)        07/29/89
1500     A  91                                  ERRMSG('RECORD NOT FOUND - CANNOT-  07/29/89
1600     A                                        UPDATE' 91)                       07/29/89
1700     A  92                                  ERRMSG('RECORD NOT FOUND - CANNOT-  07/29/89
1800     A                                        DELETE' 92)                       07/29/89
1900     A                                   9 10'CMD KEY 1 - EOJ       CMD KEY 2-  07/29/89
2000     A                                       - ADD        CMD KEY 4 - UPDATE'   07/29/89
2100     A                                  11 31'CMD KEY 5 - DELETE'               07/29/89
2200     A          R P1DF1S2                                                       07/29/89
2300     A                                      CA03(03 'REDISPLAY')                07/29/89
2400     A                                   1  3DATE EDTCDE(Y) DSPATR(HI)          07/29/89
2500     A                                   1 28'CUSTOMER FILE MAINTENANCE'        07/29/89
2600     A                                      DSPATR(HI)                          07/29/89
2700     A              MODE         6   O   1 72DSPATR(RI)                         07/29/89
2800     A                                   3 20'CUSTOMER NUMBER:' DSPATR(HI)      07/29/89
2900     A              CUST#        5   O   3 37DSPATR(RI)                         07/29/89
3000     A                                   5 20'NAME:' DSPATR(HI)                 07/29/89
3100     A              NAME        20   B   5 37DSPATR(RI PC)                      07/29/89
3200     A                                   7 20'STREET' DSPATR(HI)                07/29/89
3300     A              STREET      20   B   7 37DSPATR(RI)                         07/29/89
3400     A                                   9 20'CITY:' DSPATR(HI)                 07/29/89
3500     A              CITY        20   B   9 37DSPATR(RI)                         07/29/89
3600     A                                  11 20'STATE' DSPATR(HI)                 07/29/89
3700     A              STATE        2   B  11 37DSPATR(RI)                         07/29/89
3800     A                                  13 20'ZIP:' DSPATR(HI)                  07/29/89
3900     A              ZIP          5Y OB  13 37DSPATR(RI)                         07/29/89
4000     A                                  15 20'BALANCE:' DSPATR(HI)              07/29/89
4100     A              BALANC       8S 2B  15 37DSPATR(RI)                         07/29/89
4200     A                                  18 12'ENTER KEY - ENTER TRANSACTION'    07/29/89
4300     A                                        DSPATR(HI)                        07/29/89
4400     A                                  18 46'CMD KEY 3 - DO NOT ENTER'         07/29/89
4500     A                                        DSPATR(HI)                        07/29/89
```

```
                                        Expanded Source
                                                                                   Field      Buffer position
SEQNBR  *...+....1....+....2....+....3....+....4....+....5....+....6....+....7....+....8 length      Out     In

        *DS3                                 MSGLOC(04)
 100                                         PRINT CA01(01 'END OF JOB') +
 400                                         CF02(02 'ADD RECORD') +
 500                                         CF04(04 'UPDATE RECORD') +
 600                                         CF05(05 'DELETE RECORD')
                                             DSPSIZ(*DS3)
     * Option indicator output buffer positions:
     *  *IN90 0001   *IN91 0002   *IN92 0003
     * Response indicator input buffer positions:
     *  *IN01 0001   *IN02 0002   *IN04 0003   *IN05 0004   *IN90 0005
     *  *IN91 0006   *IN92 0007
 700           R P1DF1S1
 800                                     1  3DATE EDTCDE(Y)                        8
 900                                     1 28'CUSTOMER FILE MAINTENANCE'           25
1000                                     1 71TIME                                  8
1100                                     3 10'ENTER CUSTOMER NO:'                  18
1200              CUST#        5A   I    3 29DSPATR(RI)                            5                 8
1300      90                                 ERRMSG('DUPLICATE KEY - CANNO  ADD -
1300                                         RECORD!' 90) DSPATR(HI BL)
1500      91                                 ERRMSG('RECORD NOT FOUND - CANNOT U-
1500                                         PDATE' 91)
1700      92                                 ERRMSG('RECORD NOT FOUND - CANNOT D-
1700                                         ELETE' 92)
1900                                     9 10'CMD KEY 1 - EOJ       CMD KEY 2 - -  62
1900                                         ADD        CMD KEY 4 - UPDATE'
2100                                    11 31'CMD KEY 5 - DELETE'                  18
     * Response indicator input buffer positions:
     *  *IN01 0001   *IN02 0002   *IN03 0005   *IN04 0003   *IN05 0004
2200           R P1DF1S2                     CA03(03 'REDISPLAY')
2400                                     1  3DATE EDTCDE(Y) DSPATR(HI)             8
2500                                     1 28'CUSTOMER FILE MAINTENANCE' +         25
2600                                         DSPATR(HI)
2700              MODE         6A   O    1 72DSPATR(RI)                            6         1
2800                                     3 20'CUSTOMER NUMBER:' DSPATR(HI)         16
2900              CUST#        5A   O    3 37DSPATR(RI)                            5         7
3000                                     5 20'NAME:' DSPATR(HI)                    5
3100              NAME        20A   B    5 37DSPATR(RI PC)                         20        12      6
3200                                     7 20'STREET' DSPATR(HI)                   6
3300              STREET      20A   B    7 37DSPATR(RI)                            20        32      26
3400                                     9 20'CITY:' DSPATR(HI)                    5
3500              CITY        20A   B    9 37DSPATR(RI)                            20        52      46
3600                                    11 20'STATE' DSPATR(HI)                    5
3700              STATE        2A   B   11 37DSPATR(RI)                            2         72      66
3800                                    13 20'ZIP:' DSPATR(HI)                     4
3900              ZIP          5Y OB    13 37DSPATR(RI)                            5         74      68
4000                                    15 20'BALANCE:' DSPATR(HI)                 8
4100              BALANC       8S 2B    15 37DSPATR(RI)                            8         79      73
4200                                    18 12'ENTER KEY - ENTER TRANSACTION' +     29
4300                                         DSPATR(HI)
4400                                    18 46'CMD KEY 3 - DO NOT ENTER' +          24
4500                                         DSPATR(HI)
```

(Continued)

SOURCE PROGRAM CODING—INTERACTIVE CUSTOMER FILE MAINTENANCE PROGRAM

A listing of the RPG 400/III source program that performs interactive maintenance (record adds, updates, and deletes) of the customer file (P1PF1) is presented in Figure 21-21. An explanation of the coding included in the program for each of the maintenance functions is separately presented in the following sections.

```
SEQNBR *... ... 1 ... ... 2 ... ... 3 ... ... 4 ... ... 5 ... ... 6 ... ... 7 ... ... 8

             * THIS PROGRAM CONTROLS FILE MAINTENANCE (ADDS, UPDATES, & LOGICAL  CH21P4
             * DELETION) ON THE CUSTOMER FILE.............................      CH21P4
             *                                                                   CH21P4
            FP1DF1   CF  E                    WORKSTN                            CH21P4
            FP1PF1   UF  E           K        DISK                      A        CH21P4
            I            DS                                                      CH21P4
            I                                        1   5 CUST#                 CH21P4
            I                                        6  25 NAME                  CH21P4
            I                                       26  45 STREET                CH21P4
            I                                       46  65 CITY                  CH21P4
            I                                       66  67 STATE                 CH21P4
            I                                        1  67 BLANK                 CH21P4
            C           *IN01     DOUEQ'1'                        EOJ CONTROL    CH21P4
            C           AGAIN     TAG                                            CH21P4
            C                     EXSR HOUSEK                     INITIALIZE SR  CH21P4
            C                     EXFMTP1DF1S1                    DSPLY SCREEN   CH21P4
            C           *IN02     CASEQ'1'       ADDSR            ADDS SR        CH21P4
            C           *IN04     CASEQ'1'       UPSR             UPDATE SR      CH21P4
            C           *IN05     CASEQ'1'       DELSR            DELETE SR      CH21P4
            C                     END                             FOR CASEQ      CH21P4
            C                     END                             FOR DOUEQ      CH21P4
            C                     SETON                     LR    END JOB        CH21P4
             *                                                                   CH21P4
            C           HOUSEK    BEGSR                                          CH21P4
            C                     MOVE *BLANKS   BLANK            INIT ALPHA FLDSCH21P4
            C                     MOVE *ZEROS    ZIP              INIT NUM FIELD CH21P4
            C                     MOVE *ZEROS    BALANC           INIT NUM FIELD CH21P4
            C                     ENDSR                           END OF SUBRTN  CH21P4
             *                                                                   CH21P4
            C           ADDSR     BEGSR                           BEGIN ADD SR   CH21P4
            C           CUST#     SETLLP1PF1                    90CHECK FOR DUP  CH21P4
            C   N90               MOVE 'ADD   '  MODE             DSPLY MODE     CH21P4
            C   N90               EXFMTP1DF1S2                    DSPLY 2ND SCRN CH21P4
            C           *IN03     CABEQ'1'       AGAIN            DO NOT ADD     CH21P4
            C   N90               WRITEP1PF1R                     ADD RECORD     CH21P4
            C                     ENDSR                           END ADD SR     CH21P4
             *                                                                   CH21P4
            C           UPSR      BEGSR                           BEGIN UPDATE SRCH21P4
            C           CUST#     CHAINP1PF1                91    FIND RECORD    CH21P4
            C   N91               MOVE 'UPDATE'  MODE             DSPLY MODE     CH21P4
            C   N91               EXFMTP1DF1S2                    DSPLY 2ND SCRN CH21P4
            C           *IN03     CABEQ'1'       AGAIN            DO NOT UPDATE  CH21P4
            C   N91               UPDATP1PF1R                     UPDATE RECORD  CH21P4
            C                     ENDSR                           END UPDATE SR  CH21P4
             *                                                                   CH21P4
            C           DELSR     BEGSR                           BEGIN DELETE SRCH21P4
            C           CUST#     CHAINP1PF1                92    FIND RECORD    CH21P4
            C   N92               MOVE 'DELETE'  MODE             DSPLY MODE     CH21P4
            C   N92               EXFMTP1DF1S2                    DSPLY 2ND SCRN CH21P4
            C           *IN03     CABEQ'1'       AGAIN            DO NOT DELETE  CH21P4
            C   N92               DELETP1PF1R                     DELETE RECORD  CH21P4
            C                     ENDSR                           END DELETE SR  CH21P4
```

Figure 21-21 Source listing of the interactive customer file maintenance program.

Adds Maintenance

Records are added at the end of an existing physical file in the AS/400 or System/38 environments. The File Description definition of the file must include the letter A in column 66. The addition of records to a physical file may be controlled in the program by the normal RPG cycle in which addition processing occurs at output time by specifying the letters ADD in columns 16, 17, and 18 of the record description section of the Output Specifications. With this method, the physical file may be specified as either program or externally defined (E in column 19 of the related file description statement), but not as full-procedural.

Addition processing by the second method requires that the physical file be defined as full-procedural (F in column 16 of the File Description statement) and as either program or externally defined. Records are added to the file at calculation time by a WRITE operation (previously explained in this chapter).

The coding included in the maintenance program for addition processing is detailed in Figure 21-22.

```
SEQNBR *... ... 1 ... ... 2 ... ... 3 ... ... 4 ... ... 5 ... ... 6 ... ... 7 ... ... 8

  1600      C               EXFMTP1DF1S1                   DSPLY SCREEN   CH22P4
  1700      C         *IN02 CASEQ'1'      ADDSR            ADDS SR        CH22P4
   .                          .
   .                          .
   .                          .
  3000      C         ADDSR BEGSR                          BEGIN ADD SR   CH22P4
  3100      C         CUST# SETLLP1PF1                   90CHECK FOR DUP  CH22P4
  3200      C  N90          MOVE 'ADD   '                  DSPLY MODE     CH22P4
  3300      C  N90          EXFMTP1DF1S2                   DSPLY 2ND SCRN CH22P4
  3400      C         *IN03 CABEQ'1'      AGAIN            DO NOT ADD     CH22P4
  3500      C  N90          WRITEP1PF1R                    ADD RECORD     CH22P4
  3600      C               ENDSR                          END ADD SR     CH22P4
```

Line #

1600 The EXFMT operation displays the first record format in the display file

1700 If Command Key 2 option is pressed as a response to the first screen format, the CASEQ statement transfers control to the ADDSR subroutine which begins on line 3100.

3000 ADDSR BEGSR statement is the entry statement for the adds subroutine.

3100 The SETLL statement checks the index to determine if the customer number entered from the first screen format is stored in the customer file. If the record is stored (indicator 90 turned on) the error message DUPLICATE KEY - CANNOT ADD RECORD! will be displayed in the first screen and the second screen will not be accessed.

This procedure of validating as to whether the add record's key is already stored is more efficient for two reasons. First, the second screen does not have to be displayed and filled-in with data before finding that a record with the same key (CUST#) is already stored in the file. Second, the CHAIN operation requires more processing time and resources then the SETLL operation and should be reserved for update, deletion, and inquiry processing in which a record must be accessed and displayed.

3200 If the key value entered from the first screen is not found in the file (indicator 90 not on), the literal ADD is moved to the MODE field defined in the second screen record. This instruction will display the current processing mode in the second screen.

3300 If the key value entered from the first screen is not found in the file (indicator 90 not on), the EXFMT statement displays the second screen format for the entry of the data for an add record.

3400 The CABEQ statement is executed if the operator presses Command Key 03 after the second screen is displayed. This control cancels the addition of the record and transfers control back so that the first screen may be redisplayed and the processing cycle con-tinued or end-of-job executed.

3500 If an equal key was not found in the execution of the SETLL statement (indicator 90 not on) and Command Key 03 was not pressed by the operator, the record is written (added) to the customer file by the WRITE statement.

3600 The ENDSR operation indicates the end of the ADDSR subroutine.

Figure 21-22 Subroutine for addition processing.

Update Maintenance

Update processing may be controlled in a program by two methods. One is by the normal RPG logic cycle in which updating occurs at output time by explicitly specifying output statements. The second is with the UPDAT operation, which updates the current record being processed at calculation time. Figure 21-23 explains the syntax of the UPDAT operation.

An explanation of the statements included in the subroutine that controls update processing is presented in Figure 21-24. An UPDAT statement requires

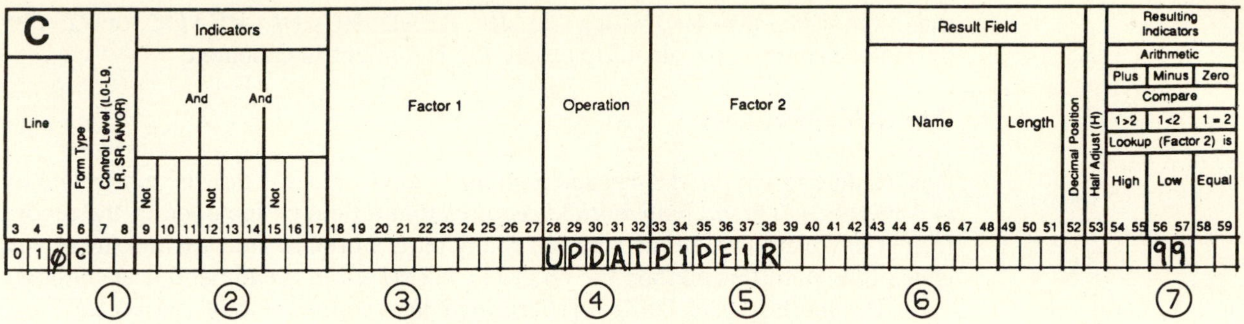

1. Any total time (L0-L1 & LR) RPG indicator may be used to condition an UPDAT instruction.

2. Any detail time RPG indicator(s) may be used to condition an UPDATE instruction.

3. Factor 1 is never used.

4. The UPDAT operation modifies (updates) the last record retrieved for processing. A successful READ, READE, READP, READC, or CHAIN operation must have been executed (record accessed) on the related file before this operation may be performed.

5. Factor 2 must include the name of a file or record format. A record format name is required for *externally defined* files. A file name must be specified in this field for *program defined* files.

6. The Result Field must include a data structure name if a filename is specified in Factor 2. This field must be blank if Factor 2 includes a physical file record name.

7. An optional indicator may be specified in Resulting Indicator columns 56-57 which will turn on if an error is detected during the UPDAT process.

Figure 21-23 Syntax of the UPDAT operation.

```
SEQNBR *... ... 1 ... ... 2 ... ... 3 ... ... 4 ... ... 5 ... ... 6 ... ... 7 ... ... 8

 1600      C                   EXFMTP1DF1S1                    DSPLY SCREEN   CH21P4
                                 .
 1800      C           *IN04   CASEQ'1'      UPSR              UPDATE SR      CH21P4
                                 .
                                 .
                                 .
 3800      C           UPSR    BEGSR                           BEGIN UPDATE SRCH21P4
 3900      C           CUST#   CHAINP1PF1               91     FIND RECORD    CH21P4
 4000      C   N91             MOVE 'UPDATE'  MODE             DSPLY MODE     CH21P4
 4100      C   N91             EXFMTP1DF1S2                    DSPLY 2ND SCRN CH21P4
 4200      C           *IN03   CABEQ'1'       AGAIN            DO NOT UPDATE  CH21P4
 4300      C   N91             UPDATP1PF1R                     UPDATE RECORD  CH21P4
 4400      C                   ENDSR                           END UPDATE SR  CH21P4
```

Line#

1600 The EXFMT operation displays the first record format in the display file.

1800 If Command Key 4 option is pressed as a response to the first screen format, this CASEQ statement transfers control to the UPSR subroutine which begins on line 3800.

3800 UPSR BEGSR is the entry statement for the update subroutine.

3900 The CUST# value entered from the first screen is used in the CHAIN statement. If the record is found, indicator 91 will not be turned on. Note that in the CHAIN operation, the physical file name is used and not the record name.

4000 If the key value entered from the first screen is found in the file (indicator 91 not on), the literal UPDATE is moved to the MODE field defined in the second screen record. This instruction will display the current processing mode in the second screen.

4100 If a successful CHAIN is executed (indicator 91 not on), the second screen is displayed with the values from the related customer record. The operator has the option of ignoring the update by pressing Command Key 03 or may press the ENTER key to execute update of the current record..

4200 If Command Key 03 is pressed by the operator after the second screen is displayed, control is transferred to repeat the processing cycle. This control will prevent the update function from executing.

4300 If the CUST# value is found in the file, the second screen is displayed and if Command Key 03 is not pressed, the updated record will be written back to the physical file.

Note that the physical file's record name must be specified with the UPDAT operation and not the filename.

4400 The ENDSR operation indicates the end of the UPSR subroutine.

Figure 21-24 Subroutine for update processing.

that a record be accessed with a CHAIN, READ, READE, READC, or READP operation from the physical file before the statement is executed.

Delete Maintenance

Record deletion in the AS/400 and System/38 environments may be controlled by two methods. The *tagging method* requires that a field be included in the record format in which some predetermined character is stored to indicate that the record is deleted. With this method the record is still stored in the file and is accessible.

The method of deleting a record *logically* requires use of the DELET operation in which records are deleted by storing a "null byte" in the first byte. After a record is logically deleted, it cannot be accessed. Any subsequent adds to the file may store the new record in the slot previously occupied by the deleted record. The syntax for the DELET operation is detailed in Figure 21-25.

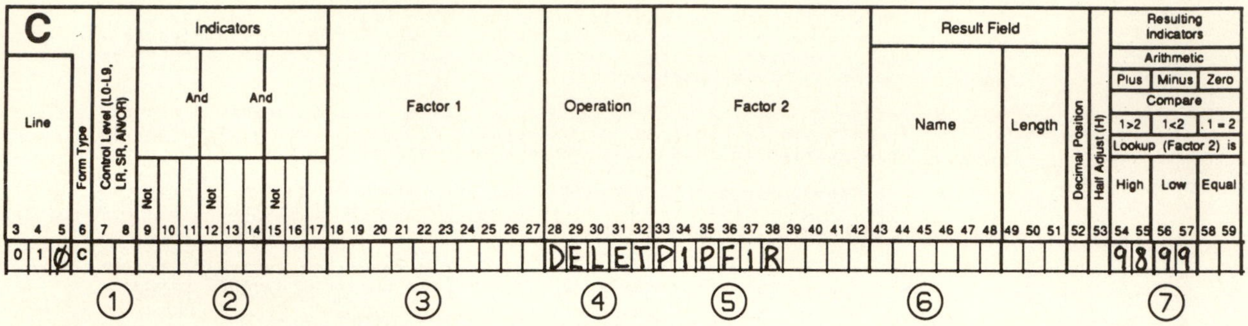

1. Any total time (L0-L1 & LR) RPG indicator may be used to condition a DELET instruction.

2. Any detail time RPG indicator(s) may be used to condition a DELET instruction.

3. Factor 1 may contain a field name or literal that includes a search argument value that identifies the record to be deleted. If no entry is included in this field, the current record is deleted.

4. The DELET operation logically deletes a record in a physical file. If Factor 1 includes an entry, the value specified in that field or literal is deleted. On the other hand, if Factor 1 does not contain an entry, a successful READ, READE, READP, READC, or CHAIN operation must have been executed (record accessed) on the related file before this operation may be performed.

5. Factor 2 must include the name of a file or record format. A record format name is required for *externally defined* files. A file name must be specified in this field for *program defined* files.

6. The Result Field is never used.

7. If Factor 1 has an entry, an indicator must be specified in Resulting Indicator columns 54-55. The indicator is turned on if the record with the search argument (key or relative record number) value is not found in the file.

   If Factor 1 does not contain an entry, an optional indicator may be specified in Resulting Indicator columns 56-57 which will turn on if an error is detected during the DELET process.

Figure 21-25 Syntax of the DELET operation.

The subroutine included in the interactive maintenance program that controls the logical deletion of records in the customer file is shown in Figure 21-26. Unless a key field is specified in Factor 1 of the DELET statement, the record to be logically deleted must have been previously accessed by a CHAIN, READ, READE, READC, or READP operation.

```
SEQNBR  *... ... 1 ... ... 2 ... ... 3 ... ... 4 ... ... 5 ... ... 6 ... ... 7 ... ... 8

 1600      C                    EXFMTP1DF1S1                      DSPLY SCREEN   CH21P4
   .                                 .
   .                                 .
 1900      C          *IN05     CASEQ'1'       DELSR              DELETE SR      CH21P4
   .                                 .
   .                                 .
   .                                 .
 4600      C          DELSR     BEGSR                             BEGIN DELETE SRCH21P4
 4700      C          CUST#     CHAINP1PF1               92       FIND RECORD    CH21P4
 4800      C   N92              MOVE 'DELETE'  MODE               DSPLY MODE     CH21P4
 4900      C   N92              EXFMTP1DF1S2                      DSPLY 2ND SCRN CH21P4
 5000      C          *IN03     CABEQ'1'       AGAIN              DO NOT DELETE  CH21P4
 5100      C   N92              DELETP1PF1R                       DELETE RECORD  CH21P4
 5200      C                    ENDSR                             END DELETE SR  CH21P4
```

Line

1600 The EXFMT operation displays the first record format in the display file.

1900 If Command Key 5 option is pressed as a response to the first screen format, this CASEQ statement transfers control to the DELSR subroutine which begins on line 4600.

4600 DELSR BEGSR is the entry statement for the delete subroutine.

4700 The CUST# value entered from the first screen is used in the CHAIN statement. If the record is found, indicator 92 will not be turned on. Note that in the CHAIN operation, the physical file name is used and not the record name.

4800 If the key value entered from the first screen is found in the file (indicator 92 not on), the literal DELETE is moved to the MODE field defined in the second screen record. This instruction will display the current processing mode in the second screen.

4900 If a successful CHAIN is executed (indicator 92 not on), the second screen is displayed with the values from the related customer record. The operator has the option of ignoring the update by pressing Command Key 03 or may press the ENTER key to execute a logical deletion of the current record.

5000 If Command Key 03 is pressed by the operator after the second screen is displayed, control is transferred to repeat the processing cycle. This control will prevent the delete function from executing.

5100 If the CUST# value is found in the file, the second screen is displayed and if Command Key 03 is not pressed, the logically deleted record will be written back to the physical file.

Note that the physical file's record name must be specified with the DELET operation and not the filename.

5200 The ENDSR operation indicates the end of the DELET subroutine.

Figure 21-26 Subroutine for deletion processing.

End-of-Job Control

End-of-job processing is controlled in the interactive maintenance program by pressing Command Key 1 from the first screen record. Coding in the program continues processing selected maintenance until the indicator (01), controlled by Command Key 1, is turned on. Figure 21-27 details the statements included in the program for end-of-job control.

```
SEQNBR  *... ... 1 ... ... 2 ... ... 3 ... ... 4 ...  ... 5 ... ... 6 ... ... 7 ... ... 8
   .                                 .
   .                                 .
 1300      C          *IN01     DOUEQ'1'                          CMD KEY 1 EOJ  CH21P4
   .                                 .
   .                                 .
 1600      C                    EXFMTP1DF1S1                      DSPLY SCREEN   CH21P4
   .                                 .
```

Figure 21-27 End-of-job control.

```
  .              .
  .              .
2100    C        END                           FOR DOUEQ    CH21P4
2200    C        SETON                  LR     END JOB      CH21P4
  .              .
  .              .
```

Line

1300 The DOUEQ statement will process the "DO Group" (lines 1300-2100) at least once. The relational test in the DOUEQ statement is made at the related END statement on line 2100 and not at the DOUEQ instruction. Indicator 01 is turned on by the operator when Command Key 01 is pressed for the end of job option in the first screen record.

1600 The EXFMT statement displays the first screen record from which the operator (by pressing a specific Command Key) may end the job or request one of the three maintenance functions.

2100 The END statement identifies the end of the "DO Group". The relational test is not made at DOUEQ statement but at the related END operation. Control will branch back to line 1300 and continue the processing sequence if the test specified in the DOUEQ statement is "false". If the DOUEQ statement is "true" (indicator 01 is "ON"), processing will exit the DO Group and continue with the following statement on line 2200.

2200 The SETON statement turns on the LR indicator which ends the job. Control is passed to this statement from the END statement on line 2100 when Command Key 1 (indicator 01 turned on) is pressed in the first screen.

(*Continued*)

The results of maintenance processing are identified in Figures 21-28 and 21-29. A hexidecimal copy of the customer file *before* maintenance is shown in Figure 21-28. This listing is generated by the CPYF (Copy File) utility, which is explained later in this chapter.

```
RCDNBR  *...+... 1 ...+... 2 ...+... 3 ...+... 4 ...+... 5 ...+... 6 ...+... 7 ...+...

    12  12345KAREL APPEL          20 AMSTERDAM AVENUE NEW YORK              NY á
        FFFFFDCDCD4CDDCD444444444FF4CDEECDCCD4CECDEC4DCE4EDDD444444444444DE0400200
        12345219530177530000000002001423594140155545055608692000000000000005875F0150F

     2  23456GEORGE BRAQUE        300 ST CLAIR STREET TRENTON               NJ &
        FFFFFCCDDCC4CDCDEC4444444FFF4EE4CDCCD4EEDCCE4EDCDEDD4444444444444DD05100100
        23456756975029184500000003000230331990239553039553650000000000000005150F0000F

     3  34567PAUL CEZANNE         44 RUE PIGALLE       STAMFORD             CT é±
        FFFFFDCED4CCECDDC44444444FF4DEC4DCCCDDC444444EECDCDDC444444444444CE05800100
        34567714303591555000000004409450797133500000023146694000000000000003361F0890F

     4  45678MARC CHAGALL         222 QUAIL AVENUE     BRIDGEPORT           CT Ā?  k-
        FFFFFDCDC4CCCCCDD44444444FFF4DECCD4CECDEC4444CDCCCCDDDE4444444444CE06600960
        45678419303817133000000002220841930155545000029947576930000000000003366F0020F

     5  56789EDGAR DEGAS          10 ROSE TERRACE      WESTPORT             PA Ÿ"  dß¤
        FFFFFCCCCD4CCCCE444444444FF4DDEC4ECDDCCC44444ECEEDDDE444444444444DC07700859
        56789547190457120000000001009625035991350000065237693000000000000007177F0749F

     6  67890MAX ERNST            1 FRANKFURT DRIVE    FRANKFORT            KY ¡   &
        FFFFFDCE4CDDEE44444444444F4CDCDDCEDE4CDCEC444CDCDDCDDE44444444444DE05100500
        67890417059523000000000001069152649304995500069152669300000000000002855F0000F

     7  78900BUCKMINSTER FULLER   999 PARK AVENUE      NEW YORK             NY ¡¬
        FFFFFCECDDCDEECD4CEDDCD44FFF4DCDD4CECDEC44444DCE4EDDD444444444444DE05503000
        78900243249523590643359009990719201555450000055608692000000000000005875F0301F

     8  89000JULIO GONZALEZ       101 SMITH LANE       GREENWICH            CT à|  Ãå±
        FFFFFDEDCD4CDDECDCE444444FFF4EDCEC4DCDC444444CDCCDECCC44444444444CE04400648
        89000143960765913590000001010249380315500000079555693800000000000003364F0057F

     9  90000HECTOR HYPPOLITE     888 PEACHTREE AVENUEATLANTA               GA
        FFFFFCCCEDD4CEDDDDCEC4444FFF4DCCCCEDCC4CECDECCEDCDEC4444444444444CC03202000
        90000853369088776393500008880751383955015554513315310000000000000007133F1000F

    10  91000PIERRE JEANERET      90 CHATEAU DRIVE     GENEVA               NY Ÿ"   m¬
        FFFFFDCCDDC4DCCDCDCE44444FF4CCCECCE4CDCEC4444CCDCEC44444444444444DE07700095
        91000795995015155953000009003813514049955000075555100000000000000005877F0004F
```

Figure 21-28 Hexidecimal copy of the customer file *before* maintenance.

A hexidecimal format copy of the file after maintenance is performed is illustrated in Figure 21-29. The following record maintenance has been completed:

Customer 12345 (record deleted)
Customer 15555 (record added)
Customer 67890 (balance changed from 000050000 to
000020000

```
RCDNBR  *...+... 1 ...+... 2 ...+... 3 ...+... 4 ...+... 5 ...+... 6 ...+... 7 ...+...

    11  15555PABLO PICASSO       1 ARTISAN PLACE     SPAIN               IL
        FFFFFDCCDD4DCCCEED4444444F4CDECECD4DDCCC44444EDCCD444444444444444CD22200100
        15555712360793122600000001019392150731350000027195000000000000000009322F0000F

     2  23456GEORGE BRAQUE       300 ST CLAIR STREET TRENTON             NJ &
        FFFFFCCDDCC4CDCDEC4444444FFF4EE4CDCCD4EEDCCE4EDCDEDD4444444444444DD05100100
        23456756975029184500000003000230331990239553039553650000000000000005150F0000F

     3  34567PAUL CEZANNE        44 RUE PIGALLE      STAMFORD            CT é±
        FFFFFDCED4CCECDDC44444444FF4DEC4DCCCDDC444444EECDCDDC444444444444CE05800100
        34567714303591555000000004409450797133500000023146694000000000000003361F0890F

     4  45678MARC CHAGALL        222 QUAIL AVENUE    BRIDGEPORT          CT Ā?  k-
        FFFFFDCDC4CCCCCDD44444444FFF4DECCD4CECDEC4444CDCCCCDDDE4444444444CE06600960
        45678419303817133000000002220841930155545000299475769300000000000003366F0020F

     5  56789EDGAR DEGAS         10 ROSE TERRACE     WESTPORT            PA Ÿ"  dß¤
        FFFFFCCCCD4CCCCE444444444FF4DDEC4ECDDCCC44444ECEEDDDE444444444444DC07700859
        56789547190457120000000001009625035991350000065237693000000000000007177F0749F

     6  67890MAX ERNST           1 FRANKFURT DRIVE   FRANKFORT           KY ¡
        FFFFFDCE4CDDEE4444444444F4CDCDDCEDE4CDCEC444CDCDDCDDE44444444444DE05100200
        67890417059523000000000001069152649304995500069152669300000000000002855F0000F

     7  78900BUCKMINSTER FULLER  999 PARK AVENUE     NEW YORK            NY ¡¬
        FFFFFCECDDCDEECD4CEDDCD44FFF4DCDD4CECDEC44444DCE4EDDD444444444444DE05503000
        78900243249523590643359009990719201555450000055608692000000000000005875F0301F

     8  89000JULIO GONZALEZ      101 SMITH LANE      GREENWICH           CT à|  Àà±
        FFFFFDEDCD4CDDECDCE444444FFF4EDCEC4DCDC444444CDCCDECCC44444444444CE04400648
        89000143960765913590000001010249380315500000079555693800000000000003364F0057F

     9  90000HECTOR HYPPOLITE    888 PEACHTREE AVENUEATLANTA             GA
        FFFFFCCCEDD4CEDDDDCEC4444FFF4DCCCCEDCC4CECDECCEDCDEC4444444444444CC03202000
        90000853369088776393500008880751383955015554513315310000000000000007133F1000F

    10  91000PIERRE JEANERET     90 CHATEAU DRIVE    GENEVA              NY Ÿ"    m¬
        FFFFFDCCDDC4DCCDCDCE44444FF4CCCECCE4CDCEC4444CCDCEC444444444444444DE07700095
        91000795995015155953000009003813514049955000075555100000000000000005877F0004F
```

Figure 21-29 Hexidecimal copy of the customer file *after* maintenance.

Maintenance Program Summary

The file maintenance program previously discussed provides for the interactive control of adds, update, and logical deletion processing.

A display file that includes two screen records is controlled by the program. The first screen record provides for the entry of a customer number and Command Key selections to control end of job, addition, update, deletion, and error processing.

A second screen, which displays only if a customer number is not found in the file for addition processing or is found for update and deletion maintenance, controls the selected file maintenance function.

The program is written in a structured format with the coding for each maintenance function included in a separate internal subroutine. To further support the RPG 400/III structured format, the DOU, CAS, and CAB operations control the decision-making functions. File access is provided by the WRITE, UPDAT, SETLL, CHAIN, and DELET statements instead of being under the control of the normal RPG logic cycle. Processing with any of these operations requires that the related disk file be defined as full-procedural (F in column 16).

UTILITIES FOR PHYSICAL FILE ACCESS

During the testing phase, or for the subsequent maintenance of a Physical File, individual records or groups of records frequently have to be accessed from file for examination. An RPG 400/III could be written to support this processing, but a different program (or versions of a program) would have to be provided for almost every file stored on the system. Obviously, this would be impractical.

To support the functions associated with COPYing or viewing of the records in a Physical File, the AS/400 software includes the CPYF (Copy File) and DSPPFM (Display Physical File Member) utilities. The CPYF file utility is accessed by selecting Option 5 on the Programmer's Menu and typing CPYF on the Command Line. Command Key 4 must be pressed to display a series of prompt screens that provide for a number of processing options. The operator selects the required functions and returns to the Programmer's Menu by pressing Command Key 3. All the options selected from the prompt screens are displayed in a free-form format on the Command line as shown in Figure 21-30. The choice of options for this example generated the hexidecimal listings shown in Figures 21-28 and 21-29. If the user remembers the command entries, he may enter it directly without referencing the prompt menus.

```
Free Form CPYF Command:

CPYF FROMFILE(SEMLIB/P1PF1) TOFILE(*PRINT) OUTFMT(*HEX)

  1         2                   3              4

1 - Calls the Copy File Utility.

2 - The FROMFILE keyword identifies the file to be copied (P1PF1)
    and the library that it is stored in (SEMLIB).

3 - The TOFILE keyword identifies to where the output is to directed.
    *PRINT indicates that output is to be printed.

4 - The OUTFMT keyword specifies the format of the output.  *HEX
    will generate the output in an over-and-under hexidecimal format.
```

Figure 21-30 CPYF (Copy File) command generated by selections from the prompt menus.

The DSPPFM utility is controlled by a series of prompts that provide for differing display formats (e.g., Over-and-Under, Side-by-Side, and so forth). Unlike the CPYF utility, DSPPFM supports display output only. Individual screen displays, however, may be printed by pressing the PRINT key.

QUESTIONS

21-1. What is the function of the EXFMT operation? With what kinds of files must it be used?

Examine the following coding and answer Questions 21-2 through 21-4:

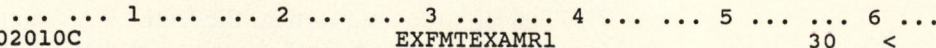

```
... ... 1 ... ... 2 ... ... 3 ... ... 4 ... ... 5 ... ... 6 ...
02010C                     EXFMTEXAMR1                30   <
```

21-2. What does the Factor 2 entry EXAMR1 refer to?

21-3. What occurs if the instruction is executed successfully?

21-4. When does the indicator (30) specified in columns 56 and 57 turn on?

Examine the following coding form and answer Questions 21-5 through 21-9:

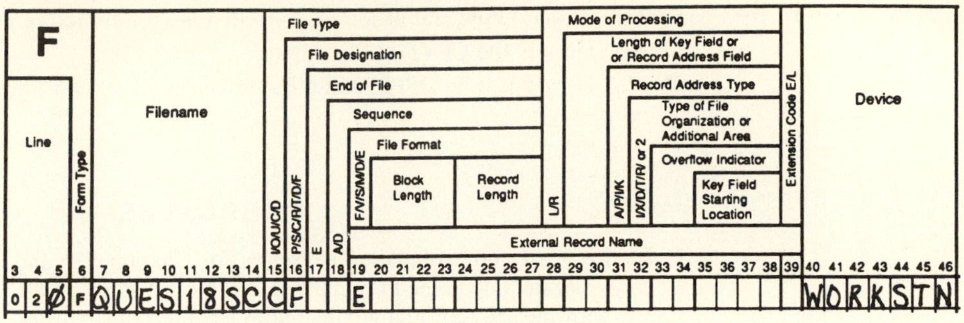

21-5. What type of file does the entry in columns 7 to 14 represent?

21-6. What is the function of the letter C in column 15?

21-7. What control is supported by the letter F in column 16?

21-8. What is the function of the letter E in column 19. If a letter F had been specified instead of the E, what would that indicate?

21-9. What physical device is supported by the WORKSTN device name?

21-10. Explain the function of the WRITE statement. What must be specified in Factor 2 of this instruction? For which devices is it valid?

21-11. Name the classification of errors that may occur during the execution of a WRITE instruction. How may a processing error be identified?

21-12. What is the function of the UPDAT operation?

21-13. How must a physical file be defined that is to be processed with an UPDAT instruction?

Examine the following coding and answer Questions 21-14 through 21-16:

```
... ... 1 ... ... 2 ... ... 3 ... ... 4 ... ... 5 ... ... 6 ...
02010C                   UPDATPFP2R                   30   <
```

21-14. What does the entry in Factor 2 (columns 33 to 42) refer to? May some other entry be specified?

21-15. Under what conditions is the Result Field (column 43 to 48) used in an *UPDAT* instruction?

21-16. When does the indicator specified in columns 56 to 57 turn on? May other Resulting Indicators be used in an UPDAT statement?

21-17. Explain the processing that must be executed before an UPDAT instruction is performed.

21-18. What is the function of the DELET operation?

21-19. How must a physical file be defined that is to be processed with a DELET instruction?

Examine the following coding and answer Questions 21-20 through 21-24:

```
... ... 1 ... ... 2 ... ... 3 ... ... 4 ... ... 5 ... ... 6 ...
02010C                   DELETPFP2R                   30   <
```

21-20. What does the entry in Factor 2 (columns 33 to 42) refer to? May some other entry be specified?

21-21. Under what conditions is the Result Field (column 43 to 48) used in a DELET instruction?

21-22. When does the indicator specified in columns 56 to 57 turn on? May other Resulting Indicators be used in a DELET statement?

21-23. Explain the processing that must be executed before a DELET instruction is performed.

21-24. Refer to your answer for Question 21-23. How may a DELET instruction be formatted to eliminate that processing?

21-25. Explain how end of job is controlled in an interactive program.

21-26. How is the CPYF utility initiated?

21-27. How does the DSPPFM utility differ from the CPYF utility?

EXERCISES

21-1. Refer to your completed exercises for Chapters 19 and 20 and write an RPG III program to load the Physical File created in Chapter 19 (Exercise 19-1) interactively with the Display File completed in Chapter 20 (Exercise 20-1)

LABORATORY ASSIGNMENTS

Laboratory Assignment 21-1: PART INVENTORY MASTER FILE

Write an RPG III/400 program to load the physical file created in Assignment 19-1 for Chapter 19 from input controlled by the Display File created in Assignment 20-1 for Chapter 20. The input data, which is to be entered via the display file, follows:

Input Data:

Part#	Part Name	Amount On Hand	Amount On Order	Avg/Cost Unit	Amount Allocated	EOQ	Safety Stock	Lead Time	Warehouse Location
A2345	AC SPARK PLUG	000000	012000	0000075	005000	001440	002000	014	ABC
B6789	FRAM OIL FILTERS	004000	001200	0000324	001875	001200	000500	031	DEF
C5555	POINT SETS	000500	000000	0000227	000000	001000	002000	015	AAA
D9876	LOCKING GAS CAP	000325	001000	0000455	000400	001000	000400	090	GHI
E3459	LIQUID CAR WASH	010224	000000	0000125	050000	004000	003000	015	BBB

Verify the loading process by printing a hexidecimal listing of the physical file data.

Laboratory Assignment 21-2: PARTS INVENTORY MASTER FILE REPORT (USING THE RPG LOGIC CYCLE)

Write an RPG program to generate a report in the format that follows. Use the physical file loaded in Assignment 21-1 as input to the program. Code the program so that the normal RPG logic cycle is followed (i.e., 1P and overflow indicators).

Report Design:

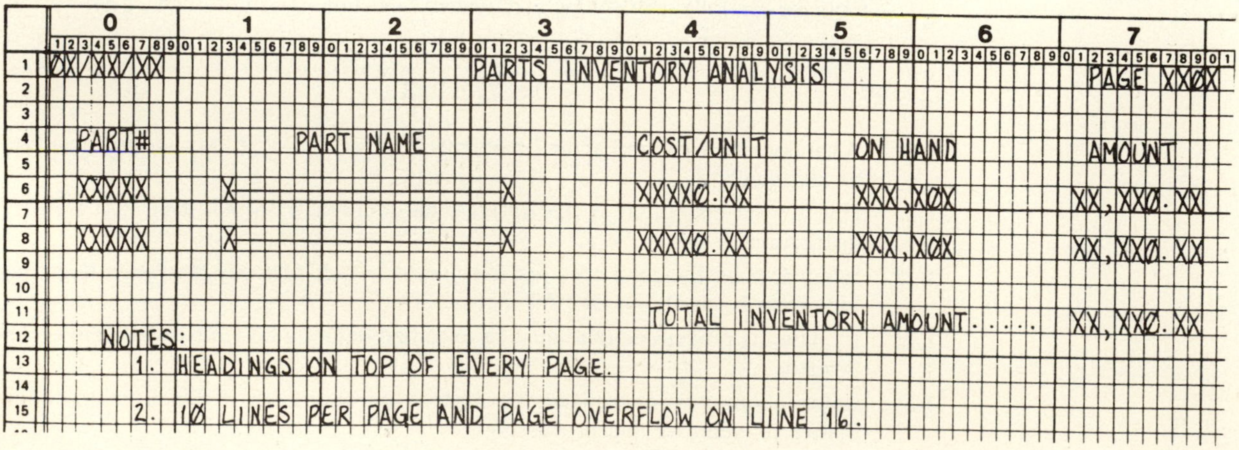

Laboratory Assignment 21-3: PART INVENTORY MASTER FILE REPORT (WITHOUT THE RPG LOGIC CYCLE)

Modify the program in Assignment 21-2 to generate the report to override the normal RPG logic cycle by including EXCPT and RPG III/400 operations (i.e., IF/ELSE) to control page overflow. 1P or Overflow indicators are *not* to be specified in the program.

Laboratory Assignment 21-4: PARTS INVENTORY MASTER FILE MAINTENANCE

Because the physical file must include data, Assignment 21-1 must have been completed before this assignment is started.

Write an RPG III/400 program to control addition, inquiry, update, and logical deletion maintenance to the Part Inventory Master File.

Physical File: The physical file created in Assignment 19-1 and loaded in Assignment 21-1 *does not* have to be modified for this assignment.

Display File: The display file created in Assignment 20-1 must be modified to include another (prompt) screen record in the following format:

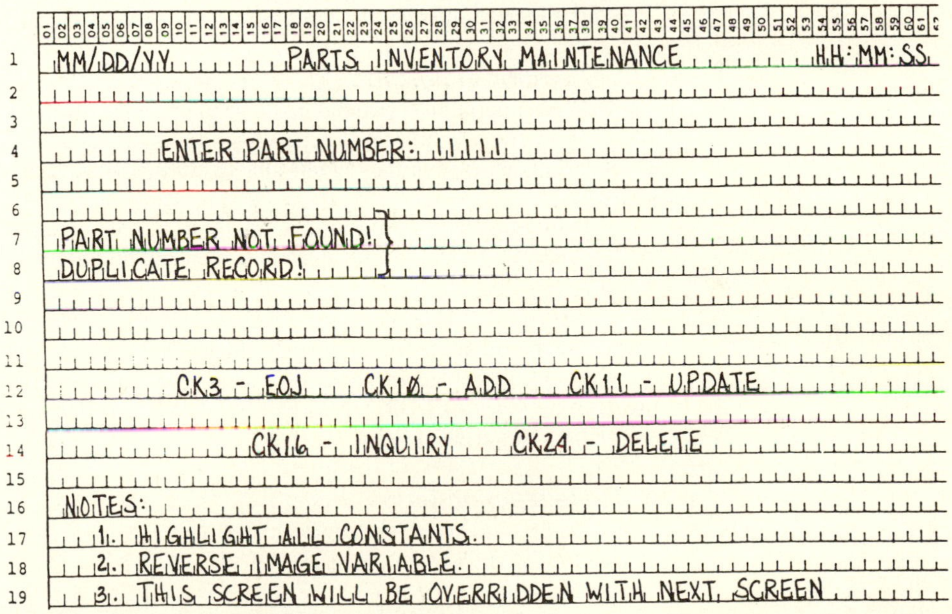

MM/DD/YY PARTS INVENTORY MAINTENANCE HH:MM:SS
ENTER PART NUMBER:
PART NUMBER NOT FOUND!
DUPLICATE RECORD!
CK3 - EOJ CK1Ø - ADD CK11 - UPDATE
CK16 - INQUIRY CK24 - DELETE
NOTES:
1. HIGHLIGHT ALL CONSTANTS.
2. REVERSE IMAGE VARIABLE.
3. THIS SCREEN WILL BE OVERRIDDEN WITH NEXT SCREEN.

When the program is executed, this screen record is to be displayed first. An operator must enter a PART NUMBER to display the second screen for a selected file maintenance function. For update, inquiry, and deletion processing, the related part number must be found in the physical file to display the second screen record. On the other hand, for addition maintenance, the related part number must not be found (unique key condition) to support this function and display the second screen for entry.

In addition, the screen record in the display file completed for Assignment 20-1 must be modified to include the following features:

1. Replace the ENTRY constant on line 2 with a 7-byte field to which, depending on the processing mode, the literal UPDATE, ADDS, INQUIRY, OR DELETE will be moved and displayed. On the basis of the option selected from the prompt screen, this control is to be included in the program.
2. If not previously defined, all variable fields (except part number) in the Assignment 20-1 screen record must be specified with a usage of B (column 38 of the DDS form) to support both input and output processing.

3. Except for the redisplay option, delete all the other Command Key options from the Assignment 20-1 screen record. The related maintenance function is to be executed from this screen by the ENTER key.

End-of-job control and the maintenance function selected will be controlled from the prompt screen by command keys.

Maintenance Processing:

Addition: The part number for the record to be added is entered in the prompt screen. If an equal key is not found, the blank (second) screen is to be displayed for entering values for the adds record. If an existing key is found, display the error message DUPLICATE RECORD! on line 7 of the screen and do not display the second screen record. For this function, display the variables in the second screen in *reverse image*.

Update: The part number for the record to be updated is entered from the prompt screen. If the record is found in the physical file, display the second screen record with the related field values included. With the exception of part number, every other field may be changed. Protect the part number, and position the cursor at the second field.

If an equal key is not found in the physical file, display the error message RECORD NOT FOUND! on line 7 of the prompt screen, and do not display the second screen record. For this function, display the variables in the second screen in *reverse image*.

Deletion (Logical): The part number for the record to be logically deleted by the DELET operation is entered in the prompt screen. If the record is found in the physical file, display the second screen record with the field values included. In the second screen, display the variables in the default image. All fields are to be protected so they cannot be changed.

If an equal key is not found in the physical file, display the error message RECORD NOT FOUND! on line 7 of the prompt screen and do not display the second screen record.

Inquiry: The part number for the inquiry record is to be entered in the prompt screen. If the record is found, display the second screen record with the field values from the physical file record included. If an equal key is not found in the physical file, display the error message RECORD NOT FOUND! on line 7 of the prompt screen. Specify *reverse image* for the variables.

Transaction Data:

	Adds Data		Update Data	
	Transaction #1	Transaction #2	Transaction #1	Transaction #2
Part#	A4444	C5555	F6666	A2345
Part Name	ICE SCRAPPER	DRI-GAS	ICE SCRAPPER	AC SPARK PLUGS
Amt-on-hand	000360	001440	000360	000500
Amt-on-order	000000	000000	000144	004500
Avg-cost/unit	0000112	0000075	0000115	
Amt-allocated	000000	000000	000000	000000
EOQ	000000	000480		
Safety Stock	000024	000500	000030	
Lead time	030	010		031
Location	AAA	EEE		ACE

Any fields without transaction data are not to be changed

Inquiry Keys

A2345, A4444, and E3458

Records to Delete

B6789 and A2344

Laboratory Assignment 21-5: SALESPERSON MASTER FILE

This assignment requires the following:

1. Creation of a keyed physical file (salesperson master file) that is to support only unique keys.
2. Creation of a display file (your own design) that supports interactive loading of the physical file created in step 1.
3. Completion of an RPG III/400 program to load the data via the display file created in step 2 to the physical file built in step 1.
4. Entering of the physical file data interactively.

Step 1: Create the Physical File. Create the physical file based on the following field attributes:

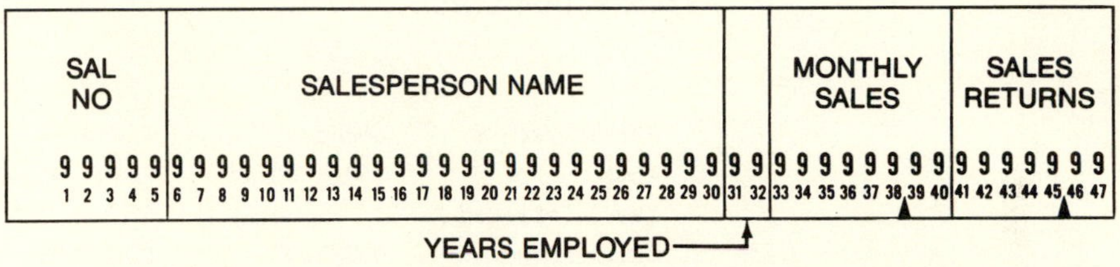

The salesperson number is to be defined as the key, and only unique keys are to be supported.

Step 2: Design and Create a Display File. Design and create a display file that will provide for the input of all the fields included in the physical file. Include end-of-job, WRITE, and redisplay controls. Provide for the error message DUPLICATE KEY to identify a duplicate key condition during the interactive loading process.

Step 3: Write an RPGIII/400 Load Program. Write an RPG III/400 program to load the physical file created in step 1 by input of data from the display file completed in step 2. The physical and display files must have been successfully compiled before the RPG program is compiled!

Step 4: Execute the Program and Enter the Following Data Interactively:

Salesman Number	Name	Years Employed	Sales Amount	Sales Returns
11111	SIEGFRIED HOUNDSTOOTH	4	01125050	0100000
11112	FELIX GOODGUY	1	02800000	0000000
22222	OTTO MUTTENJAMMER	6	10000000	0000000
33333	HANS OFFENHAUSER	1	00250000	0070000
44444	BARNEY OLDFIELD	3	00190000	0000000
55555	WILLIAM PETTY	2	02200000	0000000

Step 5: Physical File Validation. Use the CPYF utility, and print a hexidecimal listing of the physical file after it is loaded. Delineate field boundaries to validate file loading results.

Laboratory Assignment 21-6: SALESPERSON MASTER FILE MAINTENANCE

Write an RPG III/400 program to provide for add, update, deletion (logical), and inquiry maintenance to the Salesperson Master File created in Assignment 21-5.

Display File Requirements: Create a copy of the display file completed for Assignment 21-5 and include another screen record for a prompt screen of your own design. When the program is executed, this screen is to be displayed first. For all the maintenance functions, the salesperson number is to be entered from this screen. End of job, adds, update, deletion, and inquiry are to be controlled from this screen record. Consequently, the appropriate Command Key controls must be included in this display record format.

Modify the original (created for Assignment 21-5) screen record to control the input and output of data and only the option to cancel the related function. All other command key options are to be deleted. Adds, update, and inquiry of the physical file are to be controlled from this screen record by the ENTER key.

RPG Program Requirements: Complete an RPG program to process the display file and provide the indicated maintenance to the physical file. Use RPG III/400 coding and internal subroutines, and omit any conditioning indicators in columns 7 to 17.

Transaction Data:

Adds Data

Salesperson #	66666	44444
Name	JAMES BOND	PERRY MASON
Years Employed	1	1
Sales Amount	00075000	00099000
Sales Returns	0000000	0000000

Update Data

Salesperson #	66666	33333	77777
Name			
Years Employed		2	
Sales Amount		00050000	00098500
Sales Returns	0025000		

Any fields without transaction data are not be be changed

Inquiry Keys

Inquiry salesperson numbers: 66666, 11111, 23456

Records to Delete

Logically delete records with salesperson numbers: 4444 and 12340

Validate update and deletion processing by inquiry processing the related records after the transaction is executed.

chapter 22
Logical Files (AS/400 and System/38)

A *logical file* is a data base file that is used to access the data stored in one or more physical files. The features unique to logical files include the following:

1. Logical files do not contain data.
2. Access paths (indexes) may be built by logical files to process the data stored in one or more physical files in an arrival sequence or in any single or multiple field (key) value order.
3. Any physical file may be processed by any number of logical files.
4. Two or more logical files may share the same access path.
5. Omit and select criteria may be specified in a logical file to process only the required physical file data.
6. A logical file may include multiple record formats. Each format, however, must relate to one or more physical files and include at least one key field.
7. Any one logical file with multiple record formats may process the data from more than one physical file as though all the data were stored in the same physical file.
8. A logical file with multiple record formats may be used to process the data from more than one physical file. The physical file record formats accessed may be of different lengths.
9. During processing, a physical file's field attributes may be changed by a logical file. However, the data stored in the physical file will not be modified.

Logical files may be specified as either a *nonjoin* or *join*. A *nonjoin* logical file processes each record individually from one or more physical files. *Join* logical files, however, create a single record from the selected fields from two or more physical files.

The type of logical file (nonjoin or join) specified is determined in the related DDS coding. In the following text, the processing logic and DDS syntax for *nonjoin logical* files are introduced first, followed by the coding requirements associated with *join logical* files.

NONJOIN LOGICAL FILES (ONE RECORD FORMAT)

All logical files are formatted and defined by DDS coding. The DDS coding for *nonjoin* logical files is specified in the following order:

1. File level entries (optional)
2. Record level entries
3. Field level entries (optional)
4. Key field level entries (optional)
5. Select/omit level entries (optional)

Accessing One Physical File by a Logical File

Processing Logic. In the traditional computer environment, keyed files are processed in an order different from the base index by either sorting the file with a Sort/Merge utility or by specifying alternate indexes when the file is initially created. Logical files eliminate the restrictions imposed by those methods by building access paths that process a Physical File(s) by any select field or fields included in the Physical File's record format.

Figure 22-1 illustrates the logic associated with processing of a Physical File (created with CUST# as the key) by a Logical File that will process it in a STATE code order. The term *access path* refers to a separate index built and maintained by the related logical file.

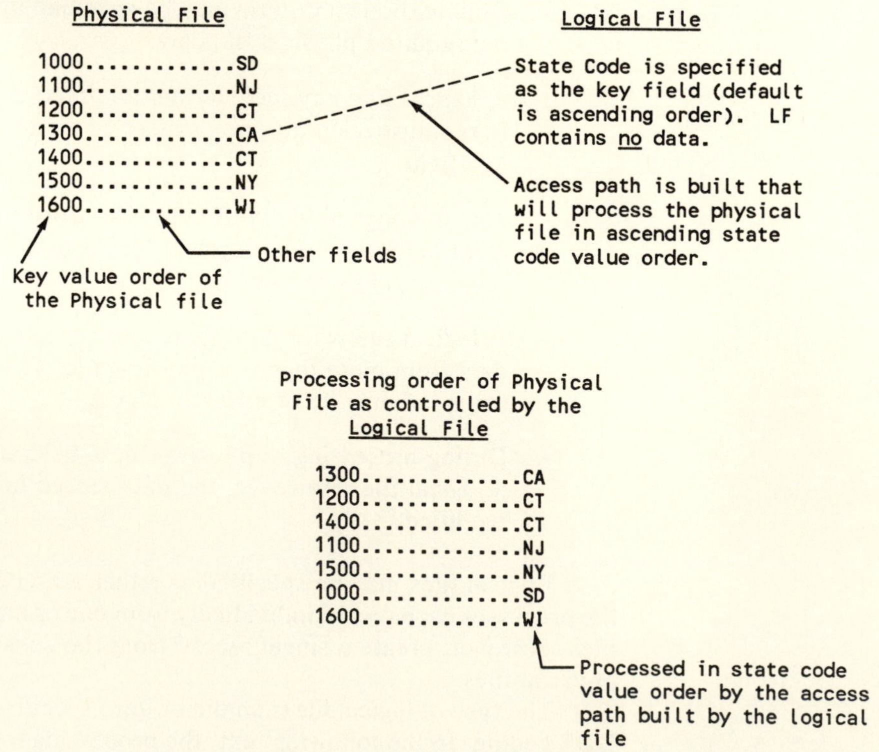

Figure 22-1 Processing logic of the access path created by a Logical File (one record format).

Data Description Specifications Coding (Nonjoin Logical File)

Logical files (LF) are created according to DDS syntax that is entered and stored via SEU. LF must be entered in the TYPE field on the Programmer's Menu to initiate the required SEU format. Similar to physical and display files, logical files must be compiled and an object member created. Figure 22-2 details the syntax to control the processing shown in Figure 22-1.

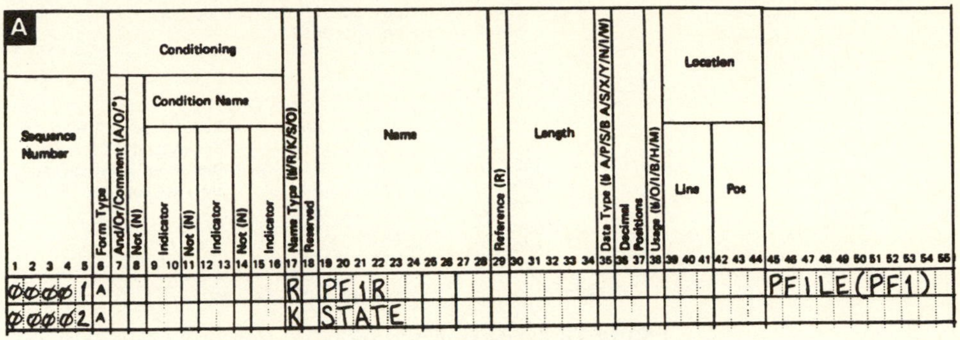

Line 00001: Unless a FORMAT keyword is specified indicating the physical file record name, the related record name must be entered (left-justified) in columns 19-28.

The PFILE keyword defines the file as a nonjoin logical file. The general format of PFILE is presented below:

```
PFILE(physical-file-name[library-name]....
```

The libray-name extension is optional. If omitted, the library list at file creation time is used.

A maximum of 32 physical files may be referenced with one PFILE keyword.

The format used in this example is detailed below:

```
             PFILE(PF1)
Keyword--------^    ^------Physical file name that contains the
                           data to be processed by the access path
                           built by the logical file
```

Line 00002: The K in column 17 and STATE in columns 19-28 specifies the key field which builds the access path to the physical file. After the logical file is successfully compiled, this access path will be created. When the program that processes the logical file is executed, the physical file's records will be accessed in ascending STATE field value order. If descending order was required, the keyword DESCEND must be specified in columns 45-80 with the key field entry.

NOTE: Because no fields are specified in the logical file record format, all of the field values from the physical file's records are accessed.

Figure 22-2 DDS syntax for a logical file that processes one physical file in a STATE code order.

RPG Program Control of a Nonjoin Logical File

An RPG 400/III program that processes the logical file shown in Figure 22-2 is detailed in Figure 22-3. Because the logical file is designated a primary (P in column 16) of the File Description instruction (line 100), it will access the related physical file consecutively in an ascending key value (STATE code) order.

If the physical file were to be random processed, the letter P must be replaced by an F (full-procedural file). Then, operations including CHAIN, READ, READE, READC, READP, SETLL, SETGT, DELET, and WRITE could be supported by the program. Because the logical and printer files are externally defined, no input or output instructions are required in the program. Calculations must include instructions to control page overflow and any report computations.

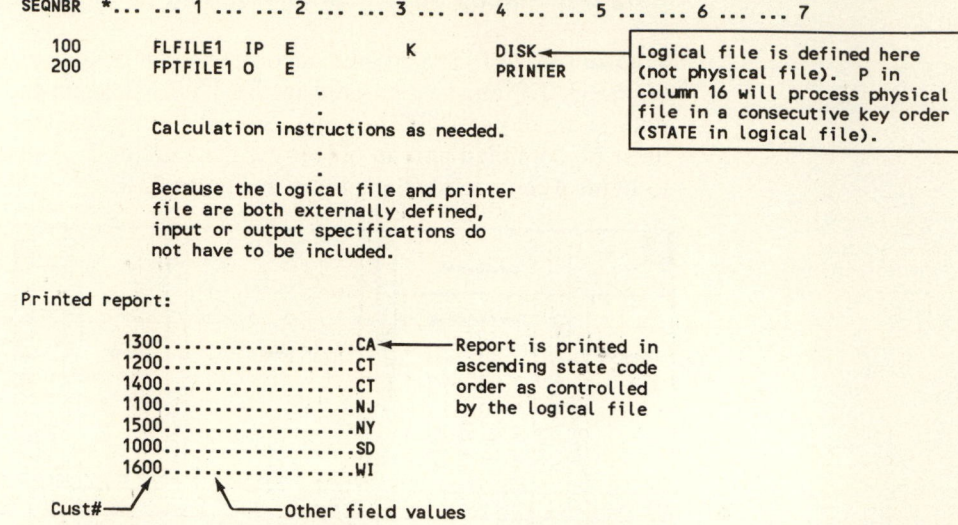

```
SEQNBR  *... ... 1 ... ... 2 ... ... 3 ... ... 4 ... ... 5 ... ... 6 ... ... 7

 100        FLFILE1  IP  E           K        DISK<-------  Logical file is defined here
 200        FPTFILE1 O   E                    PRINTER       (not physical file).  P in
                             .                              column 16 will process physical
                             .                              file in a consecutive key order
            Calculation instructions as needed.             (STATE in logical file).
                             .
                             .
            Because the logical file and printer
            file are both externally defined,
            input or output specifications do
            not have to be included.

Printed report:

        1300...................CA<--------Report is printed in
        1200...................CT         ascending state code
        1400...................CT         order as controlled
        1100...................NJ         by the logical file
        1500...................NY
        1000...................SD
        1600...................WI
Cust#---/       \------Other field values
```

Figure 22-3 RPG III/400 program that processes one logical file that accesses one physical file consecutively.

Accessing More Than One Physical File with a Nonjoin Logical File

More than one physical file may be accessed with one logical file. If the record formats are not common to all the physical files, separate PFILE keywords must be specified. Figure 22-4 details the processing logic that supports the access of two physical files that have differing record formats. The records are merged for processing in the order that the physical files are specified in the logical file.

```
        PF1                              PF2

1000MICKEY MOUSE..........       1000MEN'S .............
1100DONALD DUCK...........       1000WOMEN'S WEAR.......
1200BUGS BUNNY............       1000SMALL APPLIANCES...
                                 1100GARDEN EQUIPMENT...
                                 1200CHILDREN'S WEAR....
                                 1200FURNITURE..........

              Processing order of the Physical
                Files as controlled by the
                       Logical File

             1000MICKEY MOUSE..........      Records from the physical
             1000MEN'S WEAR............      files are merged in their
             1000WOMEN'S WEAR..........      common key value order
             1000SMALL APPLIANCES......
             1000WOMEN'S WEAR..........
             1100DONALD DUCK...........
             1100GARDEN EQUIPMENT......
             1200BUGS BUNNY............
             1200CHILDREN'S WEAR.......
             1200FURNITURE.............
```

Figure 22-4 Processing logic for two physical files that have different record formats with one logical file.

The DDS coding for the logical file that controls the processing of the two physical files is presented in Figure 22-5.

A partial listing of the RPG 400/III program that processes the logical file that accesses two physical files with different record formats is shown in Figure 22-6. The coding is identical to that explained for the processing of one physical file. The merging of the records from the two physical files is controlled by the logical file and not by the program.

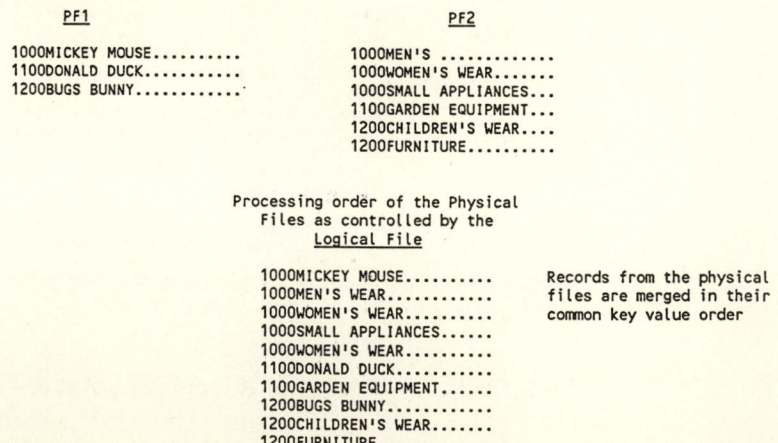

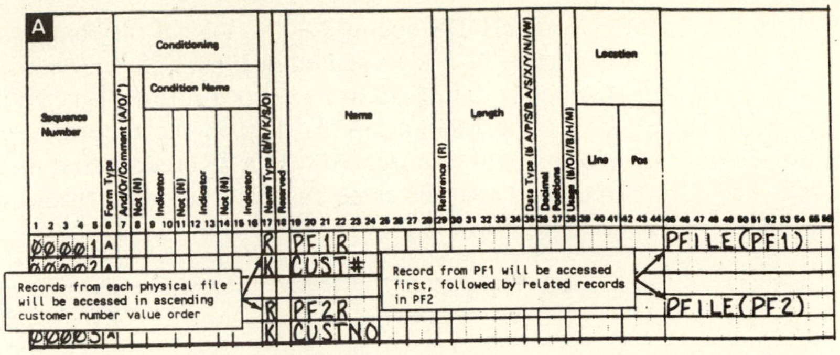

Figure 22-5 DDS coding for a logical file that processes two physical files that have different record formats.

```
SEQNBR  *... ... 1 ... ... 2 ... ... 3 ... ... 4 ... ... 5 ... ... 6 ... ... 7

   100       FLFILE2  IP  E            K         DISK        Logical file is defined here
   200       FPTFILE2 O   E                      PRINTER     (not physical file).  P in
                          .                                  column 16 will process the
                          .                                  physical files in a consecutive
             Calculation instructions as needed.             customer number key value order.
                          .                                  First physical file specified
                          .                                  in logical file will be pro-
             Because the logical file and printer            cessed first, followed related
             file are both externally defined,               record(s) in the second physi-
             input or output specifications do               cal file.
             not have to be included.

Printed report:

             1000 MICKEY MOUSE..........
             1000 MEN'S WEAR............
             1000 WOMEN'S WEAR..........
             1000 SMALL APPLIANCES......     Records from each file are
             1100 DONALD DUCK...........     merged.  The first physical
             1100 GARDEN EQUIPMENT......     file specified in the logical
             1200 BUGS BUNNY............     file is processed first.
             1200 CHILDREN'S WEAR.......
             1200 FURNITURE.............
```

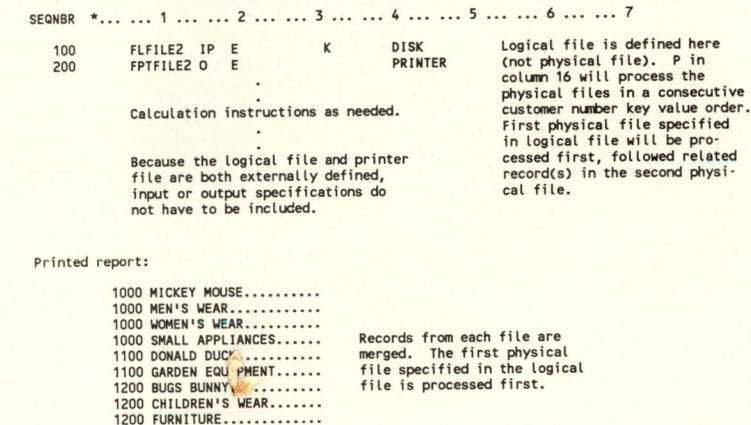

Figure 22-6 RPG III/400 program that processes one logical file that accesses two physical files.

Merging Records from Two Physical Files and Resequencing One Physical File

The example illustrated in Figure 22-7 details the processing logic for a *nonjoin* logical file that accesses two physical files by a common key and then resequences the records in the second physical file.

```
        PF1                                    PF2

1000MICKEY MOUSE..........       1000MEN'S WEAR.........910901
1100DONALD DUCK...........       1000WOMEN'S WEAR.......911012
1200BUGS BUNNY............       1000SMALL APPLIANCES...910831
                                 1100GARDEN EQUIPMENT...911001
                                 1200CHILDREN'S WEAR....911002
                                 1200FURNITURE..........910920

                  Processing order of the Physical
                     Files as controlled by the
                            Logical File

                  1000MICKEY MOUSE..........
                  1000SMALL APPLIANCES......910831
                  1000MEN'S WEAR............910901
                  1000WOMEN'S WEAR..........911012
                  1100DONALD DUCK...........
                  1100GARDEN EQUIPMENT......911001
                  1200BUGS BUNNY............
                  1200FURNITURE.............910920
                  1200CHILDREN'S WEAR.......911002

Physical files processed                       Second physical file is
in a merged ascending                          processed in ascending
customer no key order                          date order within each
                                               customer group
```

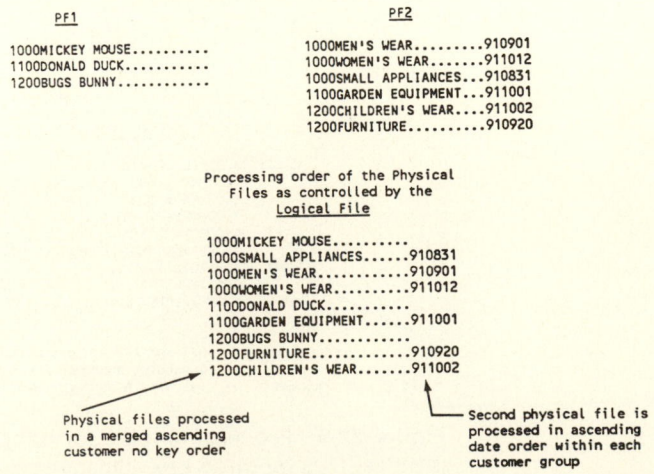

Figure 22-7 Processing logic for a logical file that processes two physical files by a common key field and then resequences the second physical file within the group.

The DDS coding for the logical file that controls the processing explained in Figure 22-7 is presented in Figure 22-8. Because the physical file PF1 does not include a date field in its record format, an *NONE word must be specified to offset the related DATE field in the record format of PF2. Then the merging process will be executed with a PF1 record first, followed by any number of related records (with the same customer number) from the PF2 file in an ascending date order.

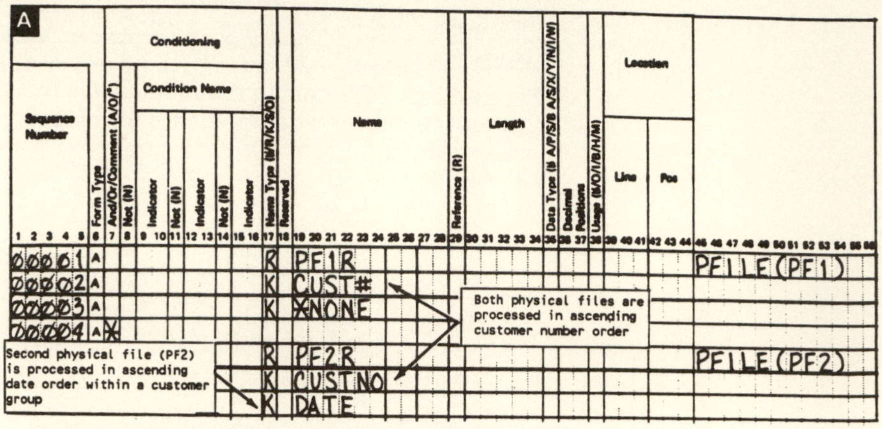

Figure 22-8 DDS coding for a logical file that processes two physical files by a common key and then resequences the records in the second physical file by a second key.

Merging Records from Two Physical Files and Resequencing Both Files Within Two Groups

Figure 22-9 details the processing logic associated with the processing of two physical files and the resequencing of both files within two groups. Notice that STATE is related only to PF1, CUST# to both files, and DATE only to PF2.

```
PF1                                      PF2

1000MICKEY MOUSE..........CA             1000MEN'S WEAR.........910901
1100DONALD DUCK...........CT             1000WOMEN'S WEAR.......911012
1200BUGS BUNNY............CT             1000SMALL APPLIANCES...910831
                                         1100GARDEN EQUIPMENT...911001
                                         1200CHILDREN'S WEAR....911002
                                         1200FURNITURE..........910920

              Processing order of the Physical
                  Files as controlled by the
                         Logical File

          CA...1000MICKEY MOUSE..........
               1000SMALL APPLIANCES......910831
               1000MEN'S WEAR............910901
               1000WOMEN'S WEAR..........911012
          CT...1100DONALD DUCK...........
               1100GARDEN EQUIPMENT......911001
          CT...1200BUGS BUNNY............
               1200FURNITURE.............910920
               1200CHILDREN'S WEAR.......911002

PF1 processed in ascend-   PF1 and PF2 are processed in   PF2 is processed in as-
ing state code order.      ascending customer number or-  cending date order within
field is not included      der within each state group.   a customer number group.
in PF2.
```

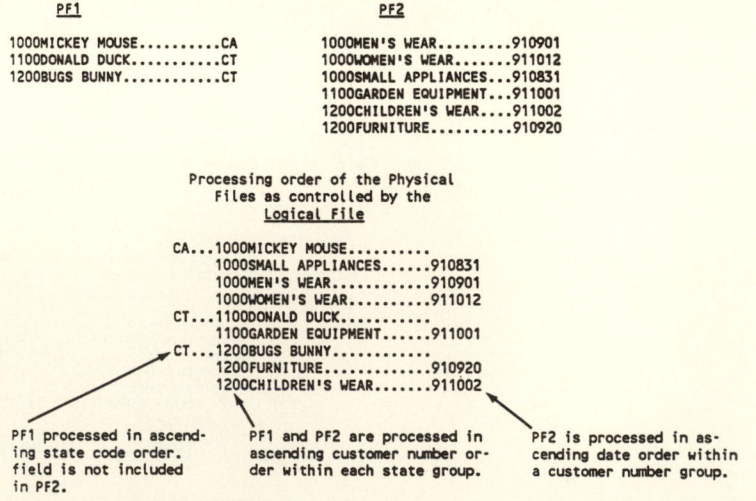

Figure 22-9 Processing logic for a logical file that processes two physical files by three key fields.

The DDS coding that supports the processing shown in Figure 22-9 is detailed in Figure 22-10. When a related key field is missing in one of the physical files, the special word *NONE is included in that position. The effect of this coding on the order of processing is as follows:

Physical File	Key Position in DDS Coding 1	2	3
PF1	STATE	CUST#	*NONE
PF2	*NONE	CUSTNO	DATE

The processing sequence may be parallel to that of sorting, with STATE/*NONE as the major field level, CUST#/CUSTNO as the intermediate field level, and *NONE/DATE as the minor field level.

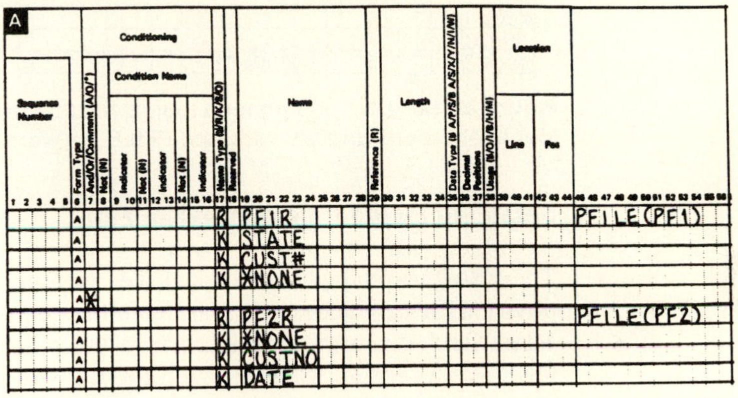

Figure 22-10 DDS coding for a logical file that processes two physical files by three key fields.

Multiple Physical Files Accessed with One Logical File Record

When a logical file record accesses more than one physical file in a single PFILE keyword, the record formats must be identical to each physical file. In the example shown in Figure 22-11, two physical files that include transaction records for two separate weeks are merged and processed in an ascending customer number order and a descending date order within a customer group.

```
WEEK1                                  WEEK2

1100JEWELRY.........910825             1000MEN'S SHOES........910901
1000MEN'S SHOES.....910826             1000WOMEN'S WEAR.......910912
1200CARPETING.......910827             1000SMALL APPLIANCES...910930
1000COSMETICS.......910828             1100GARDEN EQUIPMENT...910902
                                       1200CHILDREN'S WEAR....910905
                                       1200FURNITURE..........910920

                 Processing order of the Physical
                   Files as controlled by the
                          Logical File

                 1000SMALL APPLIANCES......910930
                 1000WOMEN'S WEAR..........910912
                 1000MEN'S WEAR............910901
                 1000COSMETICS.............910828
                 1000MEN'S SHOES...........910826
                 1100GARDEN EQUIPMENT......910902
                 1100JEWELRY...............910825
                 1200FURNITURE.............910920
                 1200CHILDREN'S WEAR.......910905
                 1200CARPETING.............910828

Physical files are processed in              Physical files are pro-
a merged ascending customer                  cessed in a descending
number order (major field)                   date order within each
                                             merged customer number
                                             group
```

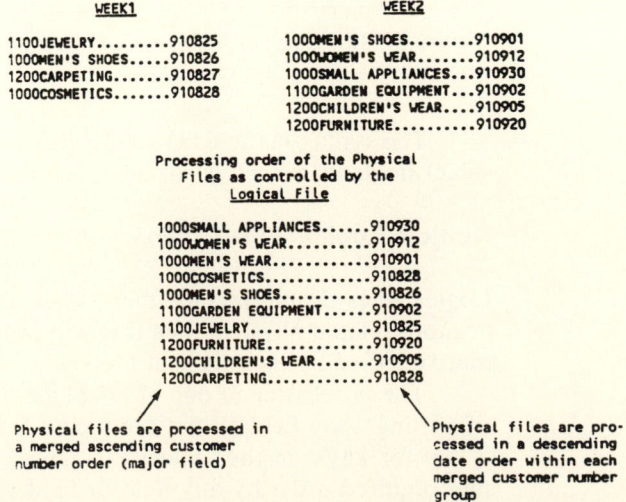

Figure 22-11 Processing logic for the access of two physical files with identical record formats by a logical file that includes one PFILE keyword.

The syntax included in a logical file to support the merging of two physical files that have identical record formats is detailed in Figure 22-12. The first file specified in the PFILE keyword will be processed first.

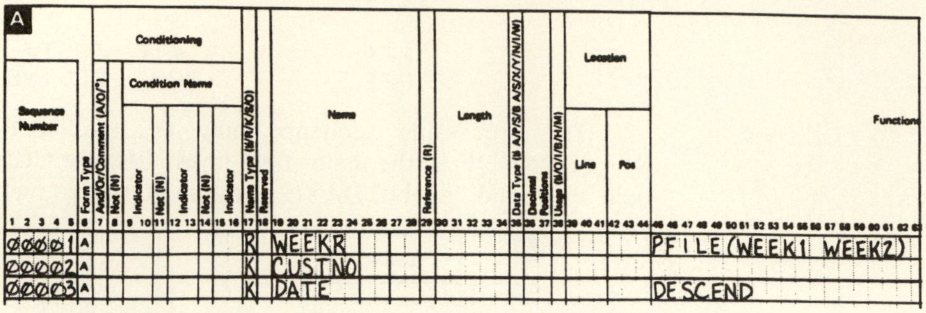

Figure 22-12 DDS coding for a logical file that processes two physical files that have identical record formats with one PFILE keyword.

Selecting Fields from a Physical File

The previous examples of logical files have assumed that all the fields from the physical files are accessed. This default action may be changed by specifying only select fields from the physical file in the related logical file record format. The DDS syntax for a logical file with this control is shown in Figure 22-13.

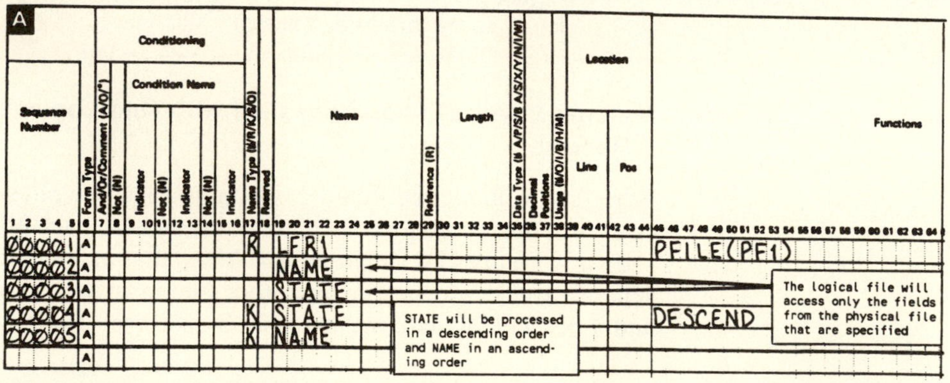

Figure 22-13 Logical file syntax for accessing only select fields from a physical file and not the complete record format.

The syntax in the RPG 400/III program to process a logical file that accesses select fields from a physical file is identical to the examples previously shown.

Nonjoin Logical File Summary

Logical files do not include data. Their function is to build access paths to one or more related physical files that will process the data in an order different from that specified by the physical file(s).

The processing of one physical file by a logical file may be compared to that of sorting. Any field(s) that are included in the physical file may be specified as a key (or keys) in the logical file. This control will process the physical file in any required order by any field or field values.

In addition, the base key sequence of a physical file may be ignored and the file processed in an arrival sequence by a logical file. This processing is controlled by not specifying any key field in the related logical file.

Unless otherwise controlled in an RPG III/400 program, the records from two or more physical files are sorted and merged in an order controlled by fields referenced as keys in the logical file.

Nonjoin logical files may specify more than one record format. If two or more physical files with *different* record formats are to be accessed by a logical file, separate PFILE keywords must be specified. When the record formats are the same, only one PFILE keyword is required. A maximum of 32 physical files may be referenced in one PFILE keyword.

When two or more physical files with different record formats are accessed by a logical file, *NONE may be specified as a key field substitute for any of the following conditions:

1. The related key fields from the physical files do not have the same attributes.
2. The key fields from the physical files have the same attributes, but they are not to be merged and sequenced together.

APPLICATION PROGRAM—PROCESSING THREE PHYSICAL FILES WITH A NONJOIN LOGICAL FILE

The specifications presented in Figure 22-14 detail the processing requirements for an RPG 400/III program that reads a logical file that accesses three physical files.

PROGRAM SPECIFICATIONS Page 1 of 1

Program Name Credit card report Program-ID CH22P1 Written By S. Myers

Purpose Generate a credit card activity report Approved By The Boss

Input files (directory names):

Physical Files CUSMAST, CUSTRAN, and CUSPAID

Logical File CUSHIST

Output files (directory names):

Printed Report

Processing Narrative:

Create a logical file that will access the three physical files, CUSMAST, CUSTRAN, and CUSPAID in an ascending order by customer number and transaction date. Complete an RPG III/400 program to process the logical file and generate a report that includes information from all of the physical files.

Input:

An access path is to be built by a logical file that processes the three physical files in a customer number/transaction date composite key order. Because the CUSMAST record format does not include a transaction date field, the keyword *NONE is to be substituted in the composite key for that file.

Customer number and transaction date are to be used as the keys for the CUSTRAN file and customer number and payment date for the CUSPAID file.

For all of the composite keys, customer number is the major key element (specified first) and date the minor.

The CUSMAST file includes address, credit limit, and beginning balance for each account. CUSTRAN contains records for charge transactions that have occurred for each account. CUSPAID includes records that store information for payments on account.

Include each physical file's record format name in the input specifications (columns 7-14). Assign a unique record identifying indicator to each record format and specify the related customer number field with the control level indicator L1.

Processing:

Define the logical file in a File Description statement as an input, primary, and externally defined keyed file. The logical file is to be processed by the normal RPG cycle (not with a READ operation). Include separate internal subroutines in the program for charge and payment processing. Determine the ending balance for each account by adding charge amounts to the beginning balance and subtracting payments.

Output:

Generate the report format shown in the supplemental printer spacing chart. The printing of each customer group is to be controlled at L1 time.

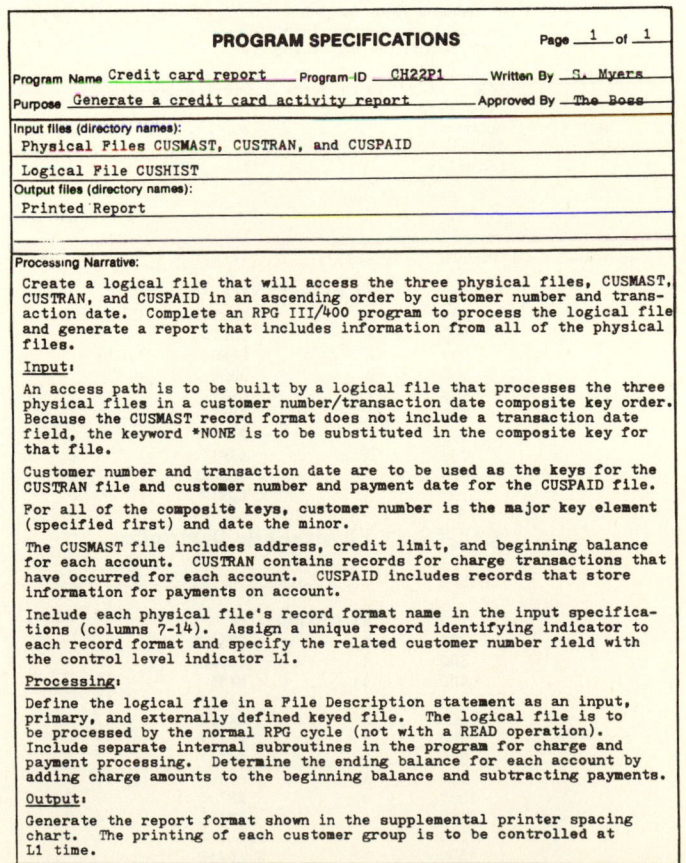

Figure 22-14 Specifications for an RPG 400/III program that processes a logical file that accesses three physical files.

The system flow chart in Figure 22-15 shows that three physical files, CUSMAST, CUSTRAN, and CUSPAID, are accessed by the logical file CUSHIST, which is read by the program CH22P1.

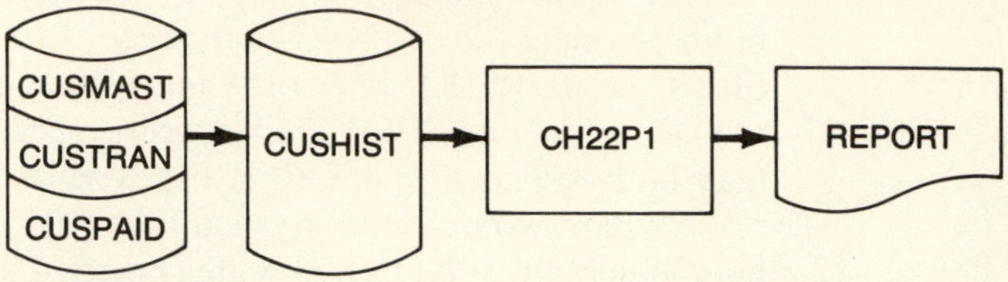

Figure 22-15 System flowchart for an RPG 400/III program that processes a logical file that accesses three physical files.

Figure 22-16 shows the record formats for the three physical files (CUSMAST, CUSTRAN, and CUSPAID) accessed by the logical file CUSHIST. Because the Data Description (top section) is identical for all the physical files (except for the file name), it has been omitted from the CUSTRAN and CUSPAID listings. Observe that all the files have the customer number as the major key field with CUSTRAN and CUSPAID defined with transaction date as a minor key field.

CUSTMAST Physical File Description:

```
File Name . . . . . . . . . . . . . . . . . . . . . :   CUSMAST
  Library name  . . . . . . . . . . . . . . . . . . :   CEMYERS400
File attribute  . . . . . . . . . . . . . . . . . . :   Physical
Source file containing DDS  . . . . . . . . . . . . :   STAN
  Library name  . . . . . . . . . . . . . . . . . . :   CEMYERS400
Source member containing DDS  . . . . . . . . . . . :   CUSHIST
Source member last changed  . . . . . . . . . . . . :   08/11/93    7:33:59
Source listing options  . . . . . . . . . . . . . . :   *SOURCE     *LIST       *NOSECLVL
DDS generation severity level . . . . . . . . . . . :   20
File type . . . . . . . . . . . . . . . . . . . . . :   *DATA
Authority . . . . . . . . . . . . . . . . . . . . . :   *CHANGE
Text  . . . . . . . . . . . . . . . . . . . . . . . :   customer master
Compiler  . . . . . . . . . . . . . . . . . . . . . :   IBM AS/400 Data Description Processor

                              Data Description Source

SEQNBR  *...+....1....+....2....+....3....+....4....+....5....+....6....+....7....+....8  Date

   100       A* CUSTMAST FILE                                                         08/11/93
   200       A            R MASTR                                                     08/11/93
   300       A              CUST#          5                                          08/11/93
   400       A              NAME          15                                          08/11/93
   500       A              ADDR          20                                          08/11/93
   600       A              CITY          10                                          08/11/93
   700       A              STATE          2                                          08/11/93
   800       A              ZIP            5  0                                       08/11/93
   900       A              LIMIT          5  0                                       08/11/93
  1000       A              BEGBAL         7  2                                       08/11/93
  1100       A            K CUST#                                                     08/11/93
```

CUSTRAN Physical File Description:

```
SEQNBR  *...+....1....+....2....+....3....+....4....+....5....+....6....+....7....+....8  Date

   100       A* CUSTRAN FILE                                                          08/11/93
   200       A            R CHARGR                                                    08/11/93
   300       A              CUSTNO         5                                          08/11/93
   400       A              NAME          15                                          08/11/93
   500       A              PAYEE         12                                          08/11/93
   600       A              PADDR         15                                          08/11/93
   700       A              PCITY         12                                          08/11/93
   800       A              PSTAT          2                                          08/11/93
   900       A              PZIP           5  0                                       08/11/93
  1000       A              AMT            7  2                                       08/11/93
  1100       A              CDATE          6  0                                       08/11/93
  1200       A            K CUSTNO                                                    08/11/93
  1300       A            K CDATE                                                     08/11/93
```

Figure 22-16 Record formats of the physical files accessed by logical file CUSHIST.

CUSPAID Physical File Description:

```
SEQNBR  *...+....1....+....2....+....3....+....4....+....5....+....6....+....7....+....8  Date

  100* CUSPAID FILE                                                                       08/11/93
  200                R PAIDR                                                              08/11/93
  300                  CUSTN          5                                                   08/11/93
  400                  NAME          15                                                   08/11/93
  500                  PAMT           7  2                                                08/11/93
  600                  PDATE          6  0                                                08/11/93
  700                K CUSTN                                                              08/11/93
  800                K PDATE
```

(Continued)

A printer chart that details the format of the report and a listing generated by the program that processes a nonjoin logical file are presented in Figure 22-17.

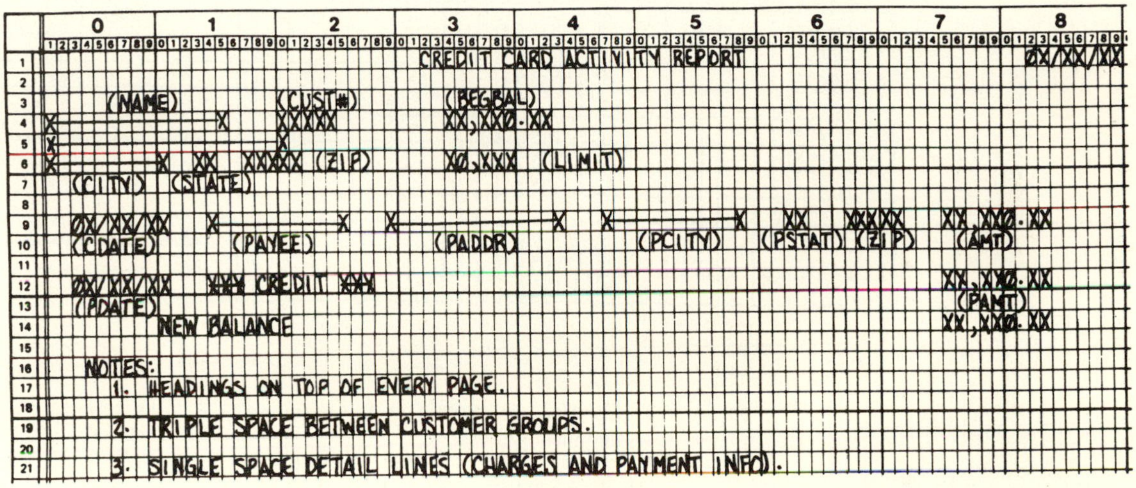

```
                        CREDIT CARD ACTIVITY REPORT                 8/15/91


HENRY FORD          10000             3,250.00
10 DEARBORN AVENUE
HARTFORD    CT  06100                 10,000


   8/09/91     *** CREDIT ***                                                320.00
   8/11/91     FAGAN'SXXXXX    200 BOSTON AVE    STRATFORD     CT    06497    85.25
   8/15/91     STONEHENGE      RTE 7             WILTON        CT    06640   120.00

          NEW BALANCE                                                      3,135.25


LOUIS CHEVROLET  11000                1,950.15
15 MOTOR PLACE
BRIDGEPORT  CT                        2,000


   8/01/91     *** CREDIT ***                                                 20.00

          NEW BALANCE                                                      1,930.15


HORACE DODGE       12000              2,478.89
9 CHASSIS BOULEVARD
NEW HAVEN    CT   06601               3,000


   8/04/91     CALDORS         HAWLEY LANE CTR   TRUMBULL      CT    06601   100.00

          NEW BALANCE                                                      2,578.89


WALTER CHRYSLER  13000                  500.00
30 SPARKPLUG LANE
STRATFORD    CT   06497             1,500


   8/05/91     *** CREDIT ***                                                 75.00

          NEW BALANCE                                                       425.00
```

Figure 22-17 Printer spacing chart and report generated by the program that processes a nonjoin logical file.

Nonjoin Logical File Syntax

The syntax for the *nonjoin* logical file that accesses three physical files is explained in Figure 22-18.

Sequence Number (1–5)	Form Type (6)	And/Or/Comment (A/O/*) (7)	Name Type (b/R/K/S/O) (17)	Name (19–28)	Functions (45–)
00100	A		R	MASTR	PFILE(CUSMAST)
00200	A		K	CUST#	
00300	A		K	*NONE	
00400	A	*			
00500	A		R	CHARGR	PFILE(CUSTRAN)
00600	A		K	CUSTNO	
00700	A		K	CDATE	
00800	A	*			
00900	A		R	PAIDR	PFILE(CUSPAID)
01000	A		K	CUSTN	
01100	A		K	PDATE	

SEQUENCE NUMBER

100 The record format (MASTR) in the physical file CUSMAST is included left-justifed in columns 19-28. A PFILE(CUSTMAST) keyword identifies the physical file accessed.

A different physical file record format may be referenced in columns 19-28 if the FORMAT keyword is specified after the PFILE keyword statement as shown below:

```
              FORMAT(MASTER)
                   ↑   ↑
         keyword───┘   └───physical file name
```

200 CUST# is defined as one of the key fields by which the physical file (CUSMAST) will be accessed. This field matches the customer number fields in the other physical file record formats.

300 Because the other physical files are accessed by two key fields, the keyword *NONE must be specified for the CUSMAST file to indicate that the record format does not have a matching second key (date) field. CUST# will be processed as the major field and *NONE as the minor. Because the *NONE value will always be spaces, the records from this file will be processed first for the customer group.

500 The record format (CHARGR) in the physical file CUSTRAN is included left-justifed in columns 19-28. A PFILE(CUSTRAN) keyword identifies the physical file accessed.

600 CUSTNO is defined as one of the key fields by which the physical file (CUSTRAN) will be accessed. This field matches the customer number fields in the other physical file record formats.

700 The value of the date field (*NONE, CDATE, PDATE) in each physical file record will determine the order in which the records are processed. CDATE is defined in the CHARGR record format as the minor key field.

900 The record format (PAIDR) in the physical file CUSMAST is included left-justifed in columns 19-28. A PFILE(CUSPAID) keyword identifies the physical file accessed.

Figure 22-18 Syntax for a nonjoin logical file that accesses three physical files.

1000 CUSTN is defined as one of the key fields by which the physical file (CUSPAID) will be accessed. This field matches the customer number fields in the other physical file record formats.

1100 The value of the date field (*NONE, CDATE, PDATE) in each physical file record will determine the order in which the records are processed within the customer group. PDATE is defined in the PAIDR record format as the minor key field.

(Continued)

The first listing (Expanded Listing not shown) generated from compilation of the nonjoin logical file processed by the application program is presented in Figure 22-19.

```
File Name . . . . . . . . . . . . . . . . . . . . . . :   CUSHIST
  Library name  . . . . . . . . . . . . . . . . . . . :   CEMYERS400
File attribute  . . . . . . . . . . . . . . . . . . . :   Logical
Source file containing DDS  . . . . . . . . . . . . . :   STAN
  Library name  . . . . . . . . . . . . . . . . . . . :   CEMYERS400
Source member containing DDS  . . . . . . . . . . . . :   CUSHIST
Source member last changed  . . . . . . . . . . . . . :   08/09/91    7:53:14
Source listing options  . . . . . . . . . . . . . . . :   *SOURCE     *LIST       *NOSECLVL
DDS generation severity level . . . . . . . . . . . . :   20
File type . . . . . . . . . . . . . . . . . . . . . . :   *DATA
Authority . . . . . . . . . . . . . . . . . . . . . . :   *CHANGE
Text  . . . . . . . . . . . . . . . . . . . . . . . . :   customer history
Compiler  . . . . . . . . . . . . . . . . . . . . . . :   IBM AS/400 Data Description Processor

                                  Data Description Source

SEQNBR  *...+....1....+....2....+....3....+....4....+....5....+....6....+....7....+....8  Date

   100       A          R MASTR                     PFILE(CUSMAST)                   08/09/91
   200       A          K CUST#                                                      08/09/91
   300       A          K *NONE                                                      08/09/91
   400       A*                                                                      08/09/91
   500       A          R CHARGR                    PFILE(CUSTRAN)                   08/09/91
   600       A          K CUSTNO                                                     08/09/91
   700       A          K CDATE                                                      08/09/91
   800       A*                                                                      08/09/91
   900       A          R PAIDR                     PFILE(CUSPAID)                   08/09/91
  1000       A          K CUSTN                                                      08/09/91
  1100       A          K PDATE                                                      08/09/91
```

Figure 22-19 First listing (expanded not shown) generated from compilation of the nonjoin logical file.

The processing logic controlled by the nonjoin logical file read by the application program is presented in Figure 22-20.

```
    CUSMAST               CUSTRAN                CUSPAID

10000............     10000.......081191     10000.......080991
11000............     12000.......080491     11000.......080191
12000............     10000.......081591     13000.......080591
13000............

                  Order the records are processed

                  10000          -  CUSMAST record
                  10000080991    -  CUSPAID record
                  10000081191    -  CUSTRAN record
                  10000081591    -  CUSTRAN record
                  11000          -  CUSMAST record
                  11000080191    -  CUSPAID record
                  12000          -  CUSMAST record
                  12000080491    -  CUSTRAN record
                  13000          -  CUSMAST record
                  13000080591    -  CUSPAID record
```

The logical file controls the processing of the three physical files in ascending customer number order and in an ascending date order within each customer group. Because the value of the *NONE field for the CUSMAST record is spaces, a record from the master file is processed first for each customer group. Then, the records from the other two physical files are selected for processing in a date value order.

Figure 22-20 Processing logic for the application program that accesses a nonjoin logical file.

Source Program Coding

A source listing of the application program that reads a logical file that accesses three physical files is detailed in Figure 22-21.

```
SEQUENCE   *...1....+....2....+....3....+....4....+....5....+....6....+....7...*
NUMBER

     100   FCUSHIST IP  E           K        DISK
     200   FQSYSPRT O   F     132     OF     PRINTER
     300   IMASTR       01
     400   I                                                CUST# L1
     500   ICHARGR      02
     600   I                                                CUSTNOL1
     700   IPAIDR       03
     800   I                                                CUSTN L1
     900   C           *INL1     IFEQ '1'                          CTRL BREAK?
    1000   C                     Z-ADDBEGBAL    OWED     72        STORE BEGBAL
    1100   C                     EXCPTHDGING                       CUST ADDR
    1200   C                     END                               ENDS IF GRP
    1300   C           *IN02     CASEQ'1'       CHARSR             CHARGE SR
    1400   C           *IN03     CASEQ'1'       PAYTSR             PAID SR
    1500   C                     END                               ENDS CAS GRP
    1600    *
    1700   C           CHARSR    BEGSR                             BEGIN CHG SR
    1800   C                     EXCPTCHARGE                       PRINT CHG LINE
    1900   C                     ADD  AMT       OWED               ADD TO BALNC
    2000   C                     ENDSR
    2100    *
    2200   C           PAYTSR    BEGSR                             BEGIN PAID SR
    2300   C                     EXCPTPAYMT                        PRINT PAID LNE
    2400   C                     SUB  PAMT      OWED               SUB FROM BALNC
    2500   C                     ENDSR
    2600   OOSYSPRT H  301   1P
    2700   O        OR       OF
    2800   O                                    51 'CREDIT CARD ACTIVITY'
    2900   O                                    58 'REPORT'
    3000   O                         UDATE Y   80
    3100   O        E  1             HDGING
    3200   O                         NAME      15
    3300   O                         CUST#     24
    3400   O                         BEGBAL1   42
    3500   O        E  1             HDGING
    3600   O                         ADDR      20
    3700   O        E  3             HDGING
    3800   O                         CITY      10
    3900   O                         STATE     14
    4000   O                         ZIP       21
    4100   O                         LIMIT 1   39
    4200   O        E  1             CHARGE
    4300   O                         CDATE Y   10
    4400   O                         PAYEE     25
    4500   O                         PADDR     43
    4600   O                         PCITY     58
    4700   O                         PSTAT     63
    4800   O                         PZIP      71
    4900   O                         AMT   1   83
    5000   O        E  1             PAYMT
    5100   O                         PDATE Y   10
    5200   O                                   27 '*** CREDIT ***'
    5300   O                         PAMT  1   83
    5400   O        T 13       L1
    5500   O                                   20 'NEW BALANCE'
    5600   O                         OWED  1   83
```

Sequence Number

100 -
200 The *logical file* (CUSHIST) is defined as processed by the normal RPG logic cycle (P in column 16) and externally defined (E in column 19). In addition, the letter K in column 31 defines the file as keyed.

300 -
800 Entries in the File/Record Name field (columns 7-14) reference the related physical file record names (MASTR, CHARGR, and PAIDR). The field names specified (CUST#, CUSTNO, and CUSTN) are included to L1 control level break processing.

900 The status of the L1 control level indicator is tested by this IF statement. If "ON", the heading lines (HDGING) for the next customer group is output by the EXCPT operation on line 1100.

1000 - The BEGBAL value is saved by moving it into the new field OWED which is incremented by charges and decremented by paid transactions.

Figure 22-21 Source listing of an application program that reads a nonjoin logical file that accesses three physical files.

1100 - The EXCPT instruction controls the printing of a line which includes the values in NAME, CUST#, and BEGBAL.

1200 - This END operation indicates end of the IF statement on line 900.

1300 - The status of Record Identifying Indicator (02) is tested. If it is "ON", the internal subroutine CHARSR is branched to where charge transactions are processed.

1400 - The status of Record Identifying Indicator (03) is tested. If it is "ON", the internal subroutine PAYTSR is branched to where payment transactions are processed.

1500 - A required END operation indicates the end of the CAS group.

1700 -
2000 The CHARGR subroutine, which is executed when a CHARGR record is processed (02 indicator turned on by input control), controls the printing of a CHARGE record at exception time. The ADD instruction on line 1900 increments the beginning balance (OWED) by the transaction amount.

2200 -
2500 The PAYTSR subroutine, which is executed when a PAIDR record is processed (03 indicator turned on by input control), controls the printing of a PAYMT record at exception time. The SUB instruction on line 2400 decreases the beginning balance (OWED) by the transaction amount.

2600 -
5300 The first line of the report is controlled at 1P (first page) time with automatic overflow control included (OF). Exception lines (3100, 3500, 3700, 4200, and 5000) control the printing of the variable data.

5400 -
5600 Total time output is controlled by the L1 indicator assigned to each control field (CUST#, CUSTNO, and CUSTN) in the input specifications. When the value in one of the control fields changes, an L1 control break is executed which controls the output of this print line.

(*Continued*)

JOIN LOGICAL FILES

Join Logical Files concatenate the fields from the records in two or more physical files and process them as one record. The advantages of Join Logical Files include the following:

1. *Increased productivity.* Because multiple READ operations are not required with Join Logical Files, the coding in RPG 400/III programs is simplified.
2. *Improved performance.* Because a Join Logical File builds only one record for processing, program performance is improved. Only one READ (or CHAIN) operation has to be specified instead of the multiple READs (or CHAINs) required for nonjoin logical file processing. Furthermore, if a program has fewer open data paths, the job's *PAG* (Process Access Group) size is reduced. This saves main storage and facilitates faster program loading.
3. *More flexible database.* As compared to Nonjoin Logical Files, Join Logical Files parallel the design and processing features related to a true database structure. Hence, more complex accesses may be built around the existing database.

Features of Join Logical Files. The features unique to *join* logical files supported by IBM's AS/400 and System/38 computers are the following:

1. Join logical files are READ only files and may not be used in update processing.
2. Join logical files support only inner and left outer joins. Outer join processing is not supported.

3. They may reference from two to 32 physical files. The physical files specified may be in key or arrival sequence. A common key (or keys) is not required to link the files. In addition, because the same physical file may be specified as the base file more than once, it may be joined to itself.
4. Any key field specified must be included in the primary file.
5. Select/omit criteria may be specified for any field in a Join Logical File.

Join Logical File Keywords. The steps in building a Join Logical File include the following:

1. Name all the physical files that will be accessed by the Join Logical File.
2. Specify the fields that will relate the physical files to each other.
3. Define all the fields from each physical file that will be included in the Join Logical File's record format.

The creation of a join logical file depends on a knowledge of the seven keywords: JFILE, JOIN, JFLD, JREF, JDUPDEQ, JDFTVAL, and DYNSLT. The function and syntax of each of these keywords are explained in the following paragraphs.

JFILE Keyword (Record Level): This record level (which requires the letter R in column 17 of the Data Description statement) keyword is used to identify the physical files to be accessed in a Join Logical File. At least two physical files and no more than 32 may be specified in one JFILE keyword.

The general format of the JFILE keyword follows:

```
JFILE(physical-file-name[.library-name]...)
```

The first file included in a JFILE keyword is called the primary file, and it is this file from which the join processing starts.

When formatting a JFILE keyword, the physical file that has the smallest number of data records should be specified first (as the primary file). The sequence in which the physical files are specified in the JFILE keyword can affect performance and the results of join logical file processing.

JOIN Keyword (Join Level): The JOIN keyword is required in the coding for a join logical file to join two physical files for processing. If three physical files are accessed by the join logical file, two JOIN keywords must be specified; if four physical files are accessed, three JOIN statements must be included, and so forth. The general format of a JOIN keyword is as follows:

```
JOIN(from-file to-file)
```

The from-file and to-file entries may be the names of two physical files that were included in the JFILE keyword, or their relative numbers. In the first example following, relative numbers 1 and 2 are used in the alternative coding in the JOIN keyword. To join the third file to the master file, the second example uses 1 and 3.

```
JFILE(CUSMAST CUSTRAN CUSPAID)
```

The JOIN keyword may be formatted as:

```
JOIN(CUSMAST CUSTRAN) -or- JOIN(1 2)
```

and

```
JOIN(CUSMAST CUSPAID) -or- JOIN(1 3)
```

When duplicate physical file names are specified in a JFILE keyword, the JOIN keyword must use the relative number format. Definition of the JOIN keyword requires that the letter J be included in column 17 of the DDS statement.

JFLD Keyword (Join Level): A JFLD keyword identifies the from-field and the to-field that will join two physical files. The related fields must have the same attributes (type, size, and decimal positions), but they do not need to have the same name. Any from-field and to-field that do not have the same attributes may be redefined in the join logical file. Any fields specified in a JFLD keyword must have been defined in the related physical file. Consequently, join fields do not have to be defined in the join logical file. The general format of the JFLD keyword is:

```
JFLD(from-field-name to-field-name)
```

Notice that only two fields may be specified in a JFLD keyword. If the physical files are to be joined by other fields, then additional JFLD keywords must be defined.

JREF Keyword (Field Level): The JREF keyword is used when the physical files accessed by the join logical file have some or all of the same field names. JREF is used to identify the physical file in which the field is related. The general format of the JREF keyword is:

```
JREF(file-name | relative-file-number)
```

A file name or the relative position of the file's name in the JFILE keyword may be included in the JREF statement. The related field name must be entered in the Name field (columns 19–28) of the DDS statement.

JDUPSEQ Keyword (Join Level): A JDUPSEQ keyword specifies the order in which the records from physical files that have duplicate join fields will be processed. The general format of the JDUPSEQ keyword is:

```
JDUPSEQ(sequencing-file-name[*DESCEND])
```

If *DESCEND is included in the keyword, the duplicate records (same field value) will be retrieved in a descending order instead of an ascending default order.

JDFTVAL Keyword (File Level): The JDFTVAL keyword enables primary file records that do not have matching secondary file records to be included in the join. Without the JDFTVAL keyword, any primary file record that did not have a matching secondary file record would be skipped. The general format of the JDFTVAL keyword is:

```
JDFTVAL
```

DYNSLT Keyword (File Level): The DYNSLT keyword is required when the JDFTVAL key word is specified in a join logical file. When specified, it causes record selection to occur when a record is read instead of after it is stored. The general format of the DYNSLT keyword is:

```
DYNSLT
```

Join Logical File DDS Coding Examples. The DDS coding for the first join logical file example is shown in Figure 22-22. Two physical files (HISTORY and courses) are accessed by the join logical file and joined by student number fields that are common to both files. The processing result indicates that the physical files are retrieved in an ascending student number order. Multiple records from the COURSES file are grouped within their related student number.

The processing results in Figure 22-22 do not indicate a printed report but only the order in which the records from the physical files are retrieved by the join logical file. Only one record will be read from the HISTORY (primary) file and stored. Then, one or more records will be retrieved from the COURSES file in an *arrival* sequence until the student number changes.

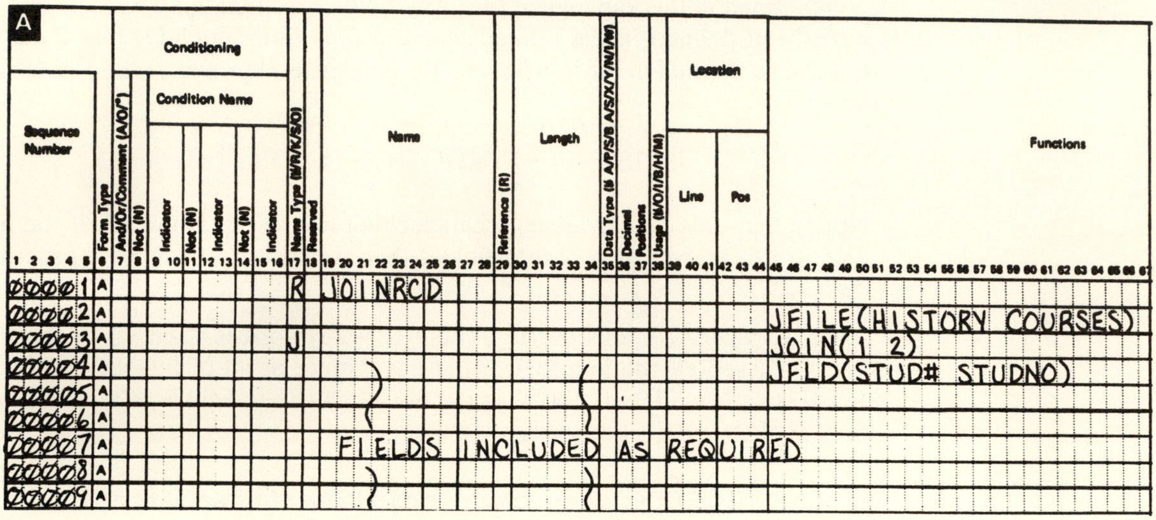

A
Conditioning
Condition Name
Sequence Number
Form Type
And/Or/Comment (A/O/*)
Not (N)
Indicator
Name Type (B/R/K/S/O)
Reserved
Name
Reference (R)
Length
Data Type (b A/P/S/B A/S/X/Y/N/I/W)
Decimal Positions
Usage (b/O/I/B/H/M)
Location
Line
Pos
Functions
00001 A R JOINRCD
00002 A JFILE(HISTORY COURSES)
00003 A J JOIN(1 2)
00004 A JFLD(STUD# STUDNO)
00005 A
00006 A
00007 A FIELDS INCLUDED AS REQUIRED
00008 A
00009 A


```
HISTORY File        COURSES File

STUD#               STUDNO  DATE

100                 200     052092
200                 300     122391
300                 200     122091
                    100     052091
                    200     122392


            Processing Results

            STUD#      DATE

            100        052091
            200        052092
            200        122091
            200        122392
            300        122391
             ^           ^
Processed by the JFLD--+  +-----Processed in an
keyword in an ascending        arrival sequence
STUD# number order
```

Figure 22-22 Join logical file coding and processing results—Example 1.

The DDS coding for the second Join Logical File example is shown in Figure 22-23. Two physical files (HISTORY and COURSES) are accessed by the join logical file and joined by student number fields that are common to both files. In addition, the JDUPSEQ(DATE) statement accesses the records from the COURSES file in an ascending date order within a student group as shown in the processing results in Figure 22-23.

As shown in Figure 22-23, the only change in the join logical file syntax from example 1 is the addition of a JDUPSEQ keyword. When more than one record

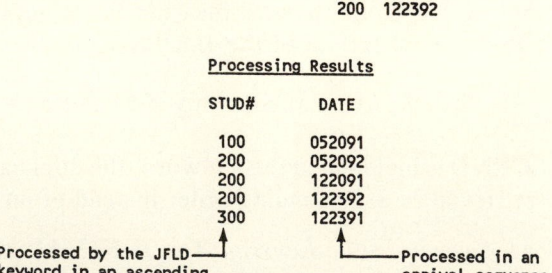

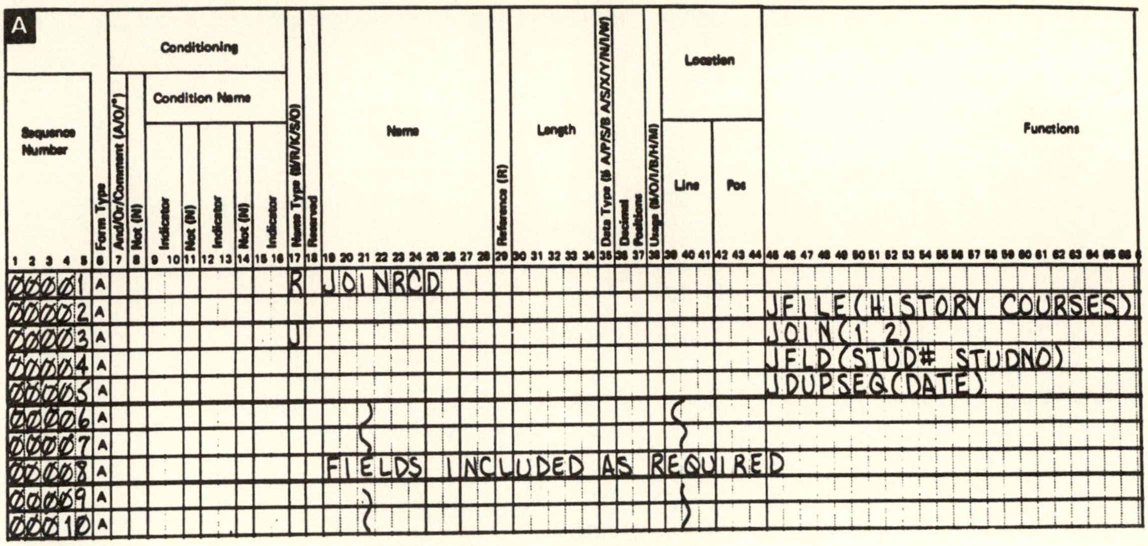
A
Conditioning
Condition Name
Sequence Number
Form Type
And/Or/Comment (A/O/*)
Not (N)
Indicator
Name Type (B/R/K/S/O)
Reserved
Name
Reference (R)
Length
Data Type (b A/P/S/B A/S/X/Y/N/I/W)
Decimal Positions
Usage (B/O/I/B/H/M)
Location
Line
Pos
Functions
00001 A R JOINRCD
00002 A JFILE(HISTORY COURSES)
00003 A J JOIN(1 2)
00004 A JFLD(STUD# STUDNO)
00005 A JDUPSEQ(DATE)
00006 A
00007 A
00008 A FIELDS INCLUDED AS REQUIRED
00009 A
00010 A

HISTORY File

STUD#
100
200
300

COURSES File

STUDNO	DATE
200	052092
300	122391
200	122091
100	052091
200	122392

Processing Results

STUD#	DATE
100	052091
200	122091
200	052092
200	122392
300	122391

Processed by the JFLD keyword in an ascending STUD# number order (STUD# column)

Processed by the JDUPSEQ keyword in an ascending date order within a student group (DATE column)

Figure 22-23 Join logical file coding and processing results—Example 2.

for a student is retrieved from the COURSES file, the JDUPSEQ(DATE) keyword indicates that the records from that file are to be processed in an ascending date order within the related student number group.

If you will relate the HISTORY file record to the miles digit on an automobile's speedometer and regard the COURSES records as incrementations of tenths of a mile, you may have a clearer understanding of join logical file processing.

APPLICATION PROGRAM—PROCESSING TWO PHYSICAL FILES WITH A JOIN LOGICAL FILE

An application program that processes two physical files with a join logical file is presented in the following paragraphs. Except for only one transaction file, the documentation for this application is identical to that of the previously discussed nonjoin logical file program. Consequently, only the format of the transaction (TRANS) physical file is presented in the source listing in Figure 22-24.

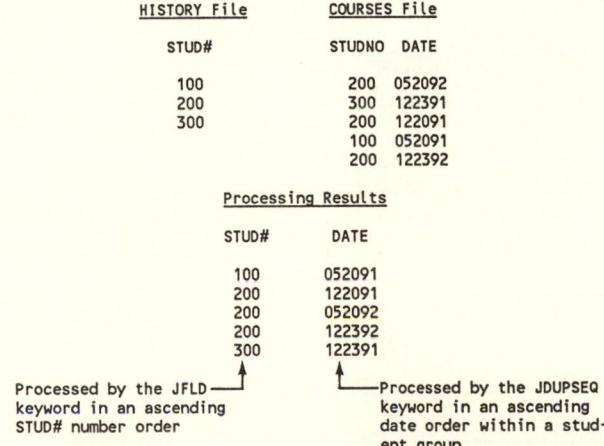

```
TRANS Physical File Description:

SEQNBR  *...+....1....+....2....+.....3....+....4....+....5

   100       A          R CHARGR
   200       A            CUSTNO         5
   300       A            NAME          15
   400       A            PAYEE         12
   500       A            PADDR         15
   600       A            PCITY         12
   700       A            PSTAT          2
   800       A            PZIP           5S 0
   900       A            AMT            7S 2
  1000       A            DATE           6S 0
  1100       A            CODE           1
  1200       A          K CUSTNO
  1300       A          K DATE
```

Figure 22-24 Format of the transaction file.

Join Logical File Syntax

Figure 22-25 details the syntax for the join logical file processed by the application program. Notice the sequence in which the join logical file keywords are specified. Syntax errors will result in compilation if the keywords are not specified in the indicated order.

Sequence Number	Form Type	Name Type	Name	Functions
00001	A			JDFTVAL
00002	A	R	CHISTR	
00003	A			JFILE(CUSMAST TRANS)
00004	A	J		JOIN(CUSMAST TRANS)
00005	A			JFLD(CUST# CUSTNO)
00006	A			JDUPSEQ(DATE)
00007	A		NAME	JREF(1)
00008	A		CUST#	
00009	A		BEGBAL	
00010	A		ADDR	
00011	A		CITY	
00012	A		STATE	
00013	A		ZIP	
00014	A		LIMIT	
00015	A		DATE	
00016	A		PAYEE	
00017	A		PADDR	
00018	A		PCITY	
00019	A		PSTAT	
00020	A		PZIP	
00021	A		AMT	
00022	A		CODE	
00023	A	K	CUST#	

Sequence Number

```
00001  The JDFTVAL statement controls the processing of a primary (physical) file
       record when the secondary (physical) file does not have a related record
       (same key field value(s)).
```

Figure 22-25 Syntax for a join logical file that accesses two physical files.

00002 The letter R in column 17 identifies this entry as the join logical files's record format. Unlike nonjoin logical files, this entry is cannot be a record name from one of the physical files.

Only one record format name may be specified for a join logical file.

00003 The JFILE keyword joins CUSMAST and TRANS for access by the join logical file. This entry must be made at the record level; on the same line as the record name or as a separate entry on the next coding line.

The first file specified in the JFILE keyword is the primary file and the other file the secondary.

00004 The letter J must be entered in column 17 with a JOIN keyword. This entry identifies which pair of physical files are to be joined for processing. At least one JOIN keyword is required in a join logical file.

00005 The JFLD keyword joins the two files specified in the preceding JOIN statement by common fields (customer numbers). This entry must immediately follow a related JOIN keyword.

00006 The JDUPSEQ(DATE) controls the processing of records from the TRANS file in an ascending transaction date order within the customer group.

00007
to
00022 Because the NAME field is included in the record formats of the CUSMAST and TRANS files, a JREF(1) keyword must be specified to indicate from which physical file the value is to be used. The 1 entry included with the JREF keyword, indicates the file referenced by its relative position in the JFILE keyword.

The fields to be included in the join logical file processing are specified in these entries. Lines 00007 through 00014 include fields from the CUSMAST file with the remaining entry fields from the TRANS file.

00023 CUST# is defined as the key field which will cause the join logical file to process both files in ascending customer number order. However, because of the JDFTVAL keyword, transactions record will be accessed in an ascending date order within the customer group.

(Continued)

The first listing (expanded not shown) generated from compilation of the join logical file is presented in Figure 22-26.

```
File Name . . . . . . . . . . . . . . . . . . . . . :  CHISTORY
  Library name  . . . . . . . . . . . . . . . . . . :  CEMYERS400
File attribute  . . . . . . . . . . . . . . . . . . :  Logical
Source file containing DDS  . . . . . . . . . . . . :  STAN
  Library name  . . . . . . . . . . . . . . . . . . :  CEMYERS400
Source member containing DDS  . . . . . . . . . . . :  CHISTORY
Source member last changed  . . . . . . . . . . . . :  08/23/91  16:26:43
Source listing options  . . . . . . . . . . . . . . :  *SOURCE    *LIST      *NOSECLVL
DDS generation severity level . . . . . . . . . . . :  20
File type . . . . . . . . . . . . . . . . . . . . . :  *DATA
Authority . . . . . . . . . . . . . . . . . . . . . :  *CHANGE
Text  . . . . . . . . . . . . . . . . . . . . . . . :  join file
Compiler  . . . . . . . . . . . . . . . . . . . . . :  IBM AS/400 Data Description Processor

                              Data Description Source

SEQNBR  *...+....1....+....2....+....3....+....4....+....5....+....6....+....7....+....8  Date

   100       A                                  JDFTVAL                         08/16/91
   200       A          R CHISTR                                                08/16/91
   300       A                                  JFILE(CUSMAST TRANS)            08/16/91
   400       A          J                       JOIN(CUSMAST TRANS)             08/16/91
   500       A                                  JFLD(CUST# CUSTNO)              08/16/91
   600       A                                  JDUPSEQ(DATE)                   08/16/91
   700       A            NAME                  JREF(1)                         08/16/91
   800       A            CUST#                                                 08/16/91
   900       A            BEGBAL                                                08/16/91
  1000       A            ADDR                                                  08/16/91
  1100       A            CITY                                                  08/16/91
  1200       A            STATE                                                 08/16/91
  1300       A            ZIP                                                   08/16/91
  1400       A            LIMIT                                                 08/16/91
  1500       A            DATE                                                  08/16/91
  1600       A            PAYEE                                                 08/16/91
  1700       A            PADDR                                                 08/16/91
  1800       A            PCITY                                                 08/16/91
  1900       A            PSTAT                                                 08/16/91
  2000       A            PZIP                                                  08/16/91
  2100       A            AMT                                                   08/16/91
  2200       A            CODE                                                  08/16/91
  2300       A          K CUST#                                                 08/16/91
```

Figure 22-26 First listing (expanded not shown) generated from compilation of the join logical file.

The processing logic controlled by the join logical file read by the application program is detailed in Figure 22-27.

```
        CUSMAST                 TRANS

   09000............     10000.......090191
   10000............     10000.......090591
   11000............     10000.......090791
   12000............     11000.......090191
   13000............     12000.......091091
                         13000.......090591

               Order the records are processed

    In storage, the first matching records (same customer number)
    from each file are processed as one record (concatenated):

                      10000|090191
           CUSMAST ---^      ^--- TRANS

 Because another record for CUST# 10000 is read from the TRANS file,
 the first record from the CUSMAST file remains in storage.  The second
 record from the TRANS file concatenates with the CUSMAST record for
 processing:

                      10000|090591·
           CUSMAST ---^      ^--- TRANS

 Note that customer number 09000 in the CUSMAST file does not have a
 matching record in the TRANS file.  Because JDFTVAL value was specified
 in the join logical file format, the CUSMAST record will processed.
 Without that key word entry, the 09000 record would not be accessed.
```

Figure 22-27 Processing logic that accesses three physical files.

Source Program Coding

The source listing of the RPG 400/III program that reads a join logical file that processes two physical files is detailed in Figure 22-28.

```
SEQUENCE  *...1....+....2....+....3....+....4....+....5....+....6....+....7...*
NUMBER

          FCHISTORYIP  E           K        DISK
          FQSYSPRT O   F     132      OF     PRINTER
          ICHISTR      01
          I                                            CUST# L1
          C           *INL1     IFEQ '1'                          CTRL BREAK?
          C                     Z-ADDBEGBAL    OWED    72         SAVE BEGBAL
          C                     EXCPTHDGING                       CUST HDG INFO
          C                     END                               ENDS IF GRP
          C           CODE      CASEQ'C'       CHARSR             CHARGE SR
          C           CODE      CASEQ'P'       PAYTSR             PAYMNT SR
          C                     END                               ENDS CAS GRP
           *
          C           CHARSR    BEGSR                             BEGIN CHG SR
          C                     EXCPTCHARGE                       PRINT CHG LINE
          C                     ADD  AMT       OWED               ADD TO BALNC
          C                     ENDSR
           *
          C           PAYTSR    BEGSR                             BEGIN PAID SR
          C                     EXCPTPAYMT                        PRINT PAID LNE
          C                     SUB  PAMT      OWED               SUB FROM BALNC
          C                     ENDSR
          OOSYSPRT H  301   1P
          O        OR       OF
          O                                  51 'CREDIT CARD ACTIVITY'
          O                                  58 'REPORT'
          O                        UDATE Y   80
          O          EF 1          HDGING
          O                        NAME      15
          O                        CUST#     24
          O                        BEGBAL1   42
          O          EF 1          HDGING
          O                        ADDR      20
          O          EF 3          HDGING
```

Figure 22-28 Source listing of an application program that reads a join logical file that accesses two physical files.

```
3400  O                         CITY      10
3500  O                         STATE     14
3600  O                         ZIP       21
3700  O                         LIMIT 1   39
3800  O        EF 1             CHARGE
3900  O                         DATE  Y   10
4000  O                         PAYEE     25
4100  O                         PADDR     43
4200  O                         PCITY     58
4300  O                         PSTAT     63
4400  O                         PZIP      71
4500  O                         AMT   1   83
4600  O        EF 1             PAYMT
4700  O                         DATE  Y   10
4800  O                                   27 '*** CREDIT ***'
4900  O                         AMT   1   83
5000  O        TF13     L1
5100  O                                   20 'NEW BALANCE'
5200  O                         OWED  1   83
```

Sequence Number	
100 - 200	The *logical file* (CHISTORY) is defined as processed by the normal RPG logic cycle (P in column 16) and externally defined (E in column 19). In addition, the letter K in column 31 defines the file as keyed. Output is directed to a printer file.
300	Entries in the File/Record Name field (columns 7-14) reference the related physical file record name CHISTR from the CUSMAST file. Because a concatenated record is created in storage for processing, only the record format for the primary file has to be specified.
400	The CUST# field in the CHISTR record format in the physical file CUSMAST is specified with an L1 control level indicator. The L1 indicator turns on when the value on CUST# changes which controls subsequent calculation and output processing.
500 - 800	The status of the L1 indicator is tested by an IFEQ instruction. If L1 is "on" (turned on by a change in CUST#), statements 600 and 700 are executed. The BEGBAL value is saved by moving it into the new field OWED which is incremented by charges and decremented by payment transactions. This EXCPT instruction controls the printing of three exception lines with data from the CUSMAST file. Because it is conditioned at detail time by an L1 indicator, it is executed only when the value in CUST# changes. The END operation indicates the end of the IF statement.
900 - 1100	The CODE field from the TRANS file record is tested for the letter C (charge transaction). If the test is true, control branches to the CHARSR subroutine where the calculations for a charge transaction are executed. If the first CASEQ test is not true, the CASEQ statement on line 1000 is executed. If this test is true, control branches to the PAYTSR subroutine where calculations for a payment transaction are executed. The required END operation on line 1100 indicates end of the CAS group.
1300 - 1600	The CHARGR subroutine, which is executed when a charge record is processed (CODE equal to C), controls the printing of a CHARGE record at exception time. The ADD instruction on line 1500 increments the beginning balance (OWED) by the transaction amount.
1800 - 2100	The PAYTSR subroutine, which is executed when a payment record is processed (CODE equal to P), controls the printing of a PAYMT record at exception time. The SUB instruction on line 2000 decrements the beginning balance (OWED) by the transaction amount.
2200 - 4900	The first line of the report is controlled at 1P (first page) time with automatic overflow control included (OF). Exception lines (2700, 3100, 3300, 3800, and 4600) control the printing of the variable data.
5000 - 5200	Total time output is controlled by the L1 indicator assigned to the control field CUST# in the input specifications. When the value in CUST# changes, an L1 control break is executed which controls the output of this print line. L1 is also turned on at LR time which controls the printing of the last customer group when end of file is sensed.

(*Continued*)

Because an additional record was included in the customer master file (CUSMAST), the report generated in Figure 22-29 by the program that reads a join logical file is not the same as the one previously shown for the nonjoin file application. Otherwise, the formats are identical.

```
                     CREDIT CARD ACTIVITY REPORT                         8/15/91

STANLEY STEAMER  09000          100.00
22 ANTIQUE LANE
STRATFORD   CT                2,500


          NEW BALANCE                                                          100.00

HENRY FORD       10000        3,250.00
10 DEARBORN AVENUE
HARTFORD    CT  06100        10,000

 8/09/91     *** CREDIT ***                                                    320.00
 8/11/91     FAGAN'SXXXXX   200 BOSTON AVE    STRATFORD      CT   06497         85.25
 8/15/91     STONEHENGE     RTE 7             WILTON         CT   06640        120.00

          NEW BALANCE                                                        3,135.25

LOUIS CHEVROLET  11000        1,950.15
15 MOTOR PLACE
BRIDGEPORT  CT                2,000

 8/01/91     *** CREDIT ***                                                     20.00

          NEW BALANCE                                                        1,930.15

HORACE DODGE     12000        2,478.89
9 CHASSIS BOULEVARD
NEW HAVEN   CT  06601         3,000

 8/04/91     CALDORS        HAWLEY LANE CTR   TRUMBULL       CT   06601        100.00

          NEW BALANCE                                                        2,578.89

WALTER CHRYSLER  13000          500.00
30 SPARKPLUG LANE
STRATFORD   CT  06497         1,500

 8/05/91     *** CREDIT ***                                                     75.00

          NEW BALANCE                                                          425.00
```

Figure 22-29 Report generated by the application program that reads a join logical file.

QUESTIONS

22-1. Name some of the processing functions for which logical files are used.

22-2. As compared to the sorting of files, what are the advantages of logical files?

22-3. Is data stored in a logical file? On what specifications form is the syntax for a logical file included? Does the compilation of a logical file delete the data in the related physical file(s)?

22-4. Name the two types of logical files. How do they differ in processing logic?

22-5. When a logical file references one or more physical files, what is automatically built by each logical file to control processing?

22-6. What is the function of a PFILE keyword?

Examine the following DDS coding and answer Question 22-7 through 22-12:

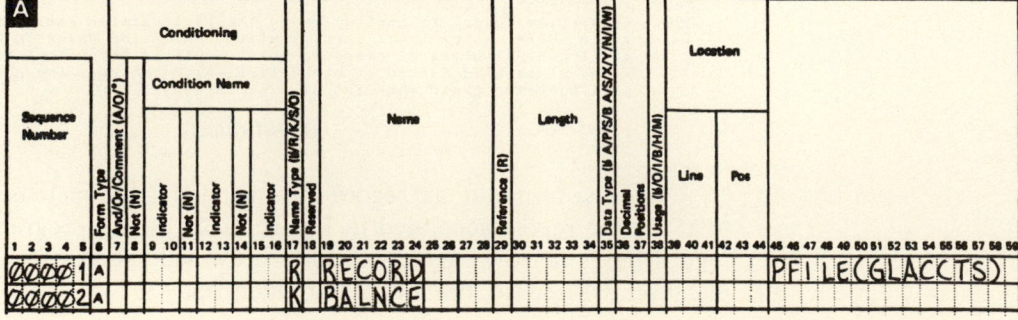

Sequence Number (1–5)	Form Type (6)	And/Or/Comment (7)	Not (8)	Indicator (9–10)	Not (11)	Indicator (12–13)	Not (14)	Indicator (15–16)	Name Type (17)	Reserved (18)	Name (19–28)	Reference (29)	Length (30–34)	Data Type (35)	Decimal Positions (36–37)	Usage (38)	Location Line (39–41)	Location Pos (42–44)	Functions (45–)
00001	A								R		RECORD								PFILE(GLACCTS)
00002	A								K		BALNCE								

22-7. What is the function of the letter R in column 17 of line 1?

22-8. What does the entry in the Name field (columns 19–28) reference?

22-9. What does the entry GLACCTS in the PFILE keyword reference?

22-10. Explain the function of the entry on line 2.

22-11. In what order will the physical file be processed?

22-12. What fields will be accessed in the record format of the physical file?

Examine the following DDS coding and answer Questions 22-13 through 22-16:

Sequence Number (1–5)	Form Type (6)	And/Or/Comment (A/O/*) (7)	Not (N) (8)	Indicator (9–10)	Not (N) (11)	Indicator (12–13)	Not (N) (14)	Indicator (15–16)	Name Type (b/R/K/S/O) (17)	Reserved (18)	Name (19–28)	Reference (R) (29)	Length (30–34)	Data Type (b A/P/S/B A/S/X/Y/N/I/W) (35)	Decimal Positions (36–37)	Usage (b/O/I/B/H/M) (38)	Location Line (39–41)	Location Pos (42–44)	(45–56)
00001	A								R		LFR1								PFILE(PF1)
00002	A																		FORMAT(PF1)
00003	A								K		ACCT#								DESCEND
00004	A	*																	
00005	A								R		LFR2								PFILE(PF2)
00006	A																		FORMAT(PF2)
00007	A								K		ACCT#								DESCEND

22-13. How many physical files will be accessed by the nonjoin logical file?

22-14. What is the function of the FORMAT keyword?

22-15. Where are the field names in columns 19 to 28 defined?

22-16. What is the function of the DESCEND keyword?

Examine the following DDS coding and answer Questions 22-17 through 22-19:

Sequence Number (1–5)	Form Type (6)	And/Or/Comment (A/O/*) (7)	Not (N) (8)	Indicator (9–10)	Not (N) (11)	Indicator (12–13)	Not (N) (14)	Indicator (15–16)	Name Type (b/R/K/S/O) (17)	Reserved (18)	Name (19–28)	Reference (R) (29)	Length (30–34)	Data Type (b A/P/S/B A/S/X/Y/N/I/W) (35)	Decimal Positions (36–37)	Usage (b/O/I/B/H/M) (38)	Location Line (39–41)	Location Pos (42–44)	(45–57)
00001	A								R		GLRECD								PFILE(GLEDER)
00002	A								K		ACCT#								
00003	A								K		*NONE								
00004	A	*																	
00005	A								R		TRRECD								PFILE(GLTRAN)
00006	A								K		ACTNO								
00007	A								K		TDATE								

22-17. How many physical files are accessed by the nonjoin logical file?

22-18. What is the function of the *NONE keyword on line 3?

22-19. Within an account group, which of the physical files will be processed first, second, and third? What controls this processing?

22-20. Explain the function of the following join logical file keywords:

```
JFILE   JFLD   JDUPSEQ
JOIN    JREF   DYNSLT
```

22-21. Identify the level of the join logical file keywords listed in Question 22-20—file, record, or field.

Examine the following DDS coding and answer Questions 22-22 through 22-24:

Sequence Number	Form Type	And/Or/Comment (A/O/*)	Not (N)	Indicator	Not (N)	Indicator	Not (N)	Indicator	Name Type (W/R/K/S/O)	Reserved	Name	Reference (R)	Length	Data Type	Decimal Positions	Usage	Line	Pos	Functions
00001	A								R		JRECRD								JFILE(SUMMARY ITEMS)
00002	A								J										JOIN(SUMMARY ITEMS)
00003	A																		JFLD(INV# INV#)
00004	A										CUST#								
00005	A										INV#								JREF(1)
00006	A										DESCRP								
00007	A										QTY								
00008	A										UCOST								

22-22. How many record formats are being joined into one record? Which physical file is considered primary?

22-23. By what value and order will the physical files be processed?

22-24. What is the function of the JREF(1) keyword?

22-25. How would a JDFTVAL keyword control change the processing of the physical files?

EXERCISES

22-1. Based on the format of following two physical files, write a nonjoin logical file to access them:

```
SALEMAST      MTHSALS

SALM#         SALNUM
SNAME         CUST#
SALYTD        SALAMT
              SDATE
```

Process the physical files in ascending salesperson number and descending sales date (SDATE) order within each salesperson group.

22-2. Write the File Description and Calculation Specifications to control processing the nonjoin logical file. Accumulate the sales amount (SALAMT) field value for each MTHSALS record processing. Assume that output of a salesperson group is to be controlled at L1 time. Output specifications are not required for this exercise.

22-3. Refer to Exercise 22-1 and modify the coding to access the physical files by a join logical file.

22-4. Refer to exercise 22-3 and modify the RPG program to process the join logical file created in Exercise 22-3.

LABORATORY ASSIGNMENTS

Laboratory Assignment 22-1: ACCESS OF TWO PHYSICAL FILES BY A NONJOIN LOGICAL FILE

Step 1: Laboratory assignments for Chapters 19, 20, and 21 must have been completed before this assignment is started. If the assignments were not completed, time may be saved by creating the physical file shell (parts inventory) and loading it with data by the data file utility (DFU). Refer to Chapter 19 for the attributes of the file and Chapter 21 for the data.

Step 2: A second physical file that has to be created and loaded with data is unique to this assignment. Its attributes and data are detailed in the following sections.

Physical File Record Format (Transaction File):

FILE DEFINITION

SYSTEM Yours		DRAWN BY S. Myers
FILE NAME Yours		DATE Yours / REV. NO. 0
CREATED BY S. Myers		FILE TYPE Disk
RECORD NAME Yours		KEY LENGTH 5 bytes
RECORDING MODE Fixed	ORGANIZATION Keyed	SEQUENCE Key order
RECORD SIZE 13 bytes	BLOCKING FACTOR 1	BLOCKSIZE 13 bytes

FIELD DATA

FIELD NO.	FIELD NAME - DESCRIPTION	SIZE	CLASS C/P/Z/B	POSITION FROM	POSITION THRU	FORMAT/CONSTANT
1	TRCODE	1	C	1	1	S or P
2	PARTNO	5	C	2	6	Key field
3	TRAMT	5	P	7	9	0 decimal positions
4	TDATE	6	P	10	13	

Data for the Transaction File:

Transaction Code 1-1	Partno 2-6	Transaction Amount 7-11	Transaction Date 12-17
P	A2345	00144	041591
S	B6789	00200	041091
S	E3459	00060	040291
P	D9876	01200	040191
P	B6789	00100	040191
S	A2345	00036	040591

Note the field positions specified indicate the input size when loading the physical file. Transaction amount and date are packed when store in the file and use less storage positions then shown here.

Step 3: Design and code a display file to provide for the input of the transaction data, and write the RPG program to control the loading process. An alternative method is to create the physical file shell and use the Data File Utility (DFU) to load the data to the file.

Step 4: Create a nonjoin logical file that will access the part inventory master file and the transaction file in an ascending order by part number and ascending order by transaction date within each part number.

Step 5: Write an RPG 400/III program to process the nonjoin logical file and generate the following report. The following calculations are required for the report:

1. For a purchase transaction, increase the amount-on-hand value.
2. For a sales transaction, decrease the amount-on-hand value.

Report Design:

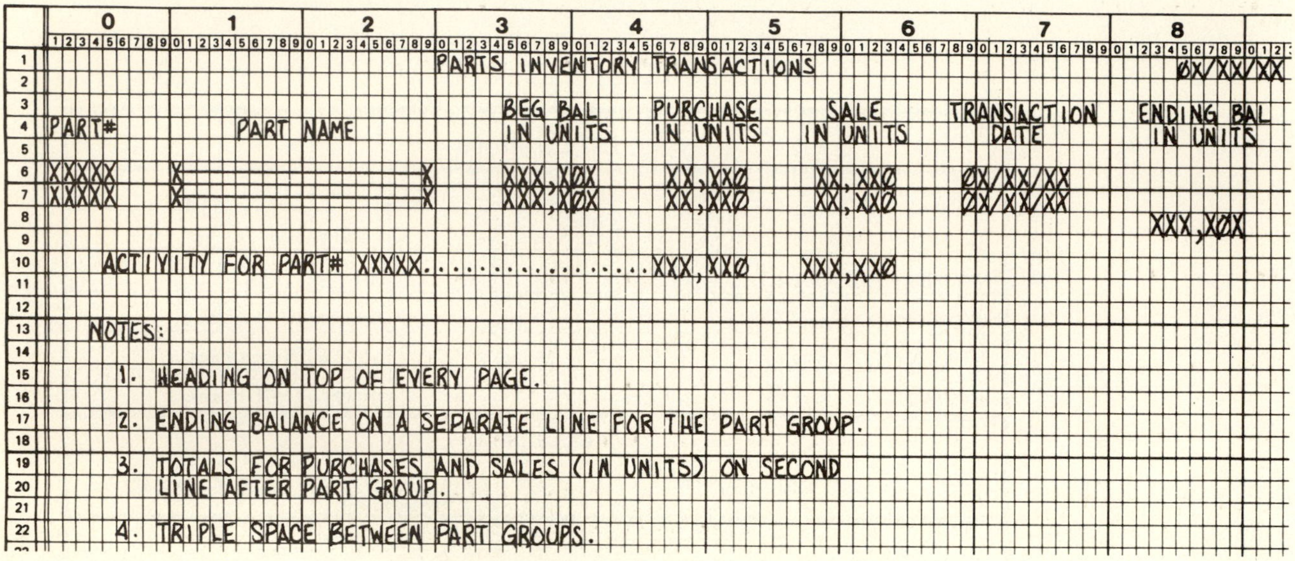
PARTS INVENTORY TRANSACTIONS
ØX/XX/XX
BEG BAL IN UNITS
PURCHASE IN UNITS
SALE IN UNITS
TRANSACTION DATE
ENDING BAL IN UNITS
PART#
PART NAME
XXXXX
XXX,XØX
XX,XXØ
ØX/XX/XX
XXX,XØX
ACTIVITY FOR PART# XXXXX.................XXX,XXØ XXX,XXØ
NOTES:
1. HEADING ON TOP OF EVERY PAGE.
2. ENDING BALANCE ON A SEPARATE LINE FOR THE PART GROUP.
3. TOTALS FOR PURCHASES AND SALES (IN UNITS) ON SECOND LINE AFTER PART GROUP.
4. TRIPLE SPACE BETWEEN PART GROUPS.

Laboratory Assignment 22-2: ACCESS OF TWO PHYSICAL FILES BY A JOIN LOGICAL FILE

If Assignment 22-1 was completed, modify it to process the physical files by a join logical file. On the other hand, if the previous lab was not completed, refer to its specifications (steps 1, 2, 3, 4, and 5) to complete this assignment.

chapter 23
Printer Files (AS 400 and System/38)

Traditionally, printer output is specified in an RPG program by Output-Format Specifications coding. A review of the syntax for this control is discussed in the following paragraphs.

STANDARD RPG SYNTAX FOR PRINTED REPORTS

Using the field attributes from the example Physical File loaded in Chapter 19, the report design shown in Figure 23-1 has been formatted. The standard RPG

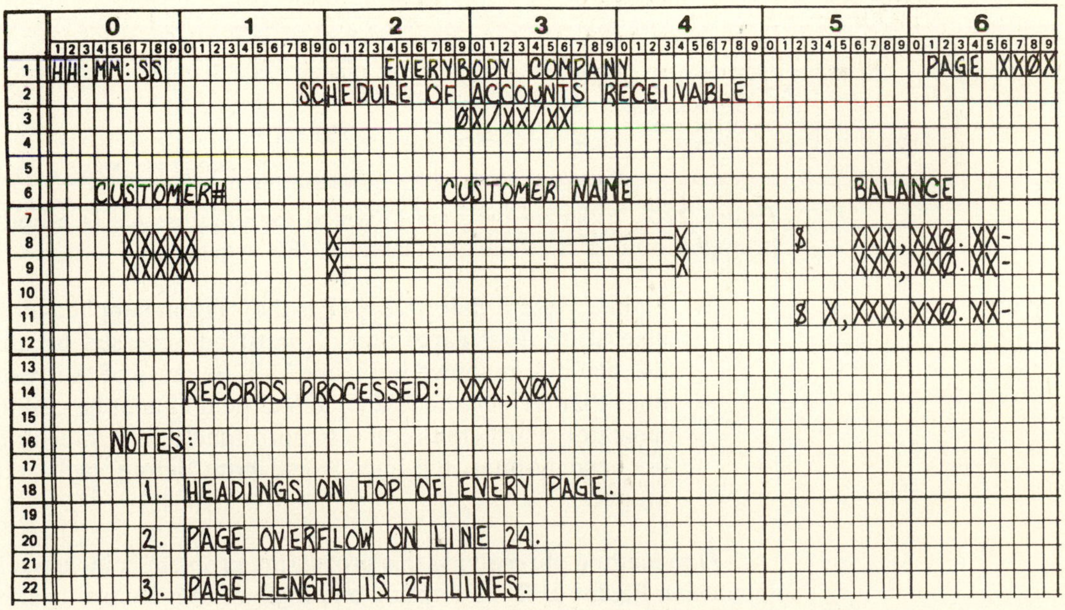

Figure 23-1 Report design for continuing example program.

syntax for this report design is summarized in the program example in Figure 23-2. When examining the program, recall the following syntax rules related to RPG controlled printer output:

1. The output record lines must be specified in an H (Heading), D (Detail), and T (Total) time sequence. Exception time lines (E) may be specified before or after the other line types.

2. Advancing to the top of a page is controlled by a Skip Field entry (Before in columns 19–20, or After in columns 21–22). Page overflow is controlled by specifying an overflow indicator (OA-OG and OV) in columns 33 to 34 of the File Description Specifications and on the output form with the related print line(s).

```
*...1....+....2....+....3....+....4....+....5....+....6....+....7....+...*
FP1PF1   IP  F                   DISK
FREPORT  O           132     OF     LPRINTER
LREPORT   22FL 200L
IP1PF1   SM  01
I                                               1   5 CUST#
I                                               6  25 NAME
I                                              26  45 STREET
I                                              46  65 CITY
I                                              66  67 STATE
I                                             P 68  700ZIP
I                                             P 72  752BALANC
C  N10                 EXSR TIMSUB
C           TOTAL      ADD  BALANC     TOTAL   92
C           RECRDS     ADD  1          RECRDS  60
C           TIMSUB     BEGSR
C                      SETON                       10OF
C                      TIME            HHMMSS  60
C                      ENDSR
OREPORT  D  106   OF
O                         HHMMSS    8 '  :  :  '
O                                  40 'EVERYBODY COMPANY'
O                                  64 'PAGE'
O                         PAGE  Z  69
O        D  1     OF
O                                  37 'SCHEDULE OF ACCOUNTS'
O                                  48 'RECEIVABLE'
O        D  3     OF
O                         UDATE Y  36
O        D  2     OF
O                                  12 'CUSTOMER#'
O                                  40 'CUSTOMER NAME'
O                                  62 'BALANCE'
O        D  0     OF
O                                  52 '$'
O        DF 1     01
O                         CUST#    10
O                         NAME     44
O                         BALANCJ  66
O        T  1     LR
O                                  52 '$'
O                         TOTAL J  66
O        T  2     LR
O                                  27 'RECORDS PROCESSED:'
O                         RECRDSZ  35
```

Controls page length and overflow line location

Physical file attributes are program-defined

Conditioning with N10 prevents execution of subroutine after the first record is processed

System time is accessed and OF and 10 are turned on. OF controls all hdgs and 10 prevents execution of subroutine for every record processed

OF controls printing of first and subsequent page headings. TIME value is not available at 1P time

Fetch overflow (F in column 16) controls the printing of all output conditioned by OF before the detail line is printed

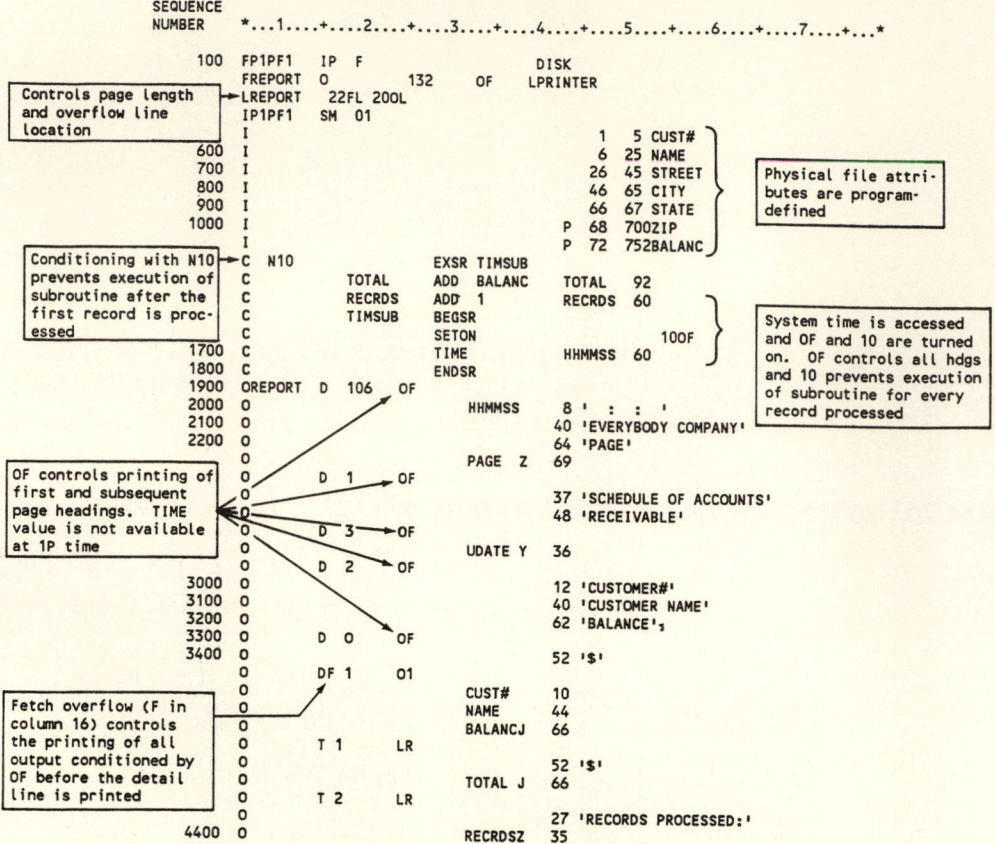

Figure 23-2 Example program in which the physical file is program-defined and printed output is controlled by standard RPG syntax.

3. Unlike system date (UDATE), the system-supplied time is not available at 1P (first page) time. It must be accessed by an instruction in calculations as shown in Figure 23-2. Because of this restriction, output lines that include the related TIME field cannot be conditioned by a 1P indicator. Furthermore, if a Record Identifying Indicator was specified for heading lines, the lines would print before each detail record was output.

One method of resolving this processing problem is included in the program detailed in Figure 23-2. The syntax and logic of this control is explained below.

1. An internal subroutine includes the following statements:

```
N10         EXSR TIMSUB


      TIMSUB BEGSR
             SETON                         10OF
             TIME          HHMMSS 60
             ENDSR
```

After the first record is read, the SETON operation turns on indicators 10 and OF. Indicator 10, which is specified as N10, conditions the EXSR statement to prevent subsequent execution of the subroutine after the first record is processed. Because 10 is never set off, it will remain on for the job.

2. The OF (overflow) indicator is set on to control the printing of the heading lines. However, output conditioned by the OF indicator will not occur until the Detail line (3500) is executed and fetches (F in column 16) the overflow lines before printing its values.
3. The results of this control are shown in the report in Figure 23-3. Notice in the figure that the heading lines print before the first detail line. Then, after the first data record is processed, the OF indicator is automatically turned off before the next record is read. Any subsequent page overflow will occur only when the overflow line (24 for this example) is sensed and turns on OF.
4. Because the fetch overflow option is specified (F in column 16 of the detail line), the status of the overflow indicator is tested when the detail line is executed. If OF is on, page overflow will occur, the heading lines will print, and then the current detail line. On the other hand, if the OF indicator is off, only the detail line will be output.

In the program example in Figure 23-2, the Physical File is *program-defined* and not *externally defined*. Consequently, the record's field attributes are included in the Input Specifications.

The report generated by the example program is shown in Figure 23-3. A page length of 22 lines and page overflow on line 20 were specified in the program by a Line Counter Specification instruction. This form type is not required for reports printed on stock paper of standard size.

```
13:32:54              EVERYBODY COMPANY                     PAGE    1
                  SCHEDULE OF ACCOUNTS RECEIVABLE
                             9/01/91

 CUSTOMER#              CUSTOMER NAME                 BALANCE

   12345             KAREL APPEL                $      1,250.00
   23456             GEORGES BRAQUE                      100.00
   34567             PAUL CEZANNE                     81,900.00
   45678             MARC CHAGALL                        926.00
   56789             EDGAR DEGAS                       7,854.99
   67890             MAX ERNST                           500.00
   78900             BUCKMINSTER FULLER               33,000.10
   89000             JULIO GONZALEZ                      654.78

. . . . . . . . . . . . . . . . . . . . . . . . . . . . . . . . . . .

13:32:54              EVERYBODY COMPANY                     PAGE    2
                  SCHEDULE OF ACCOUNTS RECEIVABLE
                             9/01/91

 CUSTOMER#              CUSTOMER NAME                 BALANCE

   90000             HECTOR HYPPOLITE           $    120,000.00
   91000             PIERRE JEANERET                       9.45
   92000             WASSILY KANDINSKY               375,000.00
   93000             CHARLES CORBUSIER                   250.00

                                                $    621,445.32

           RECORDS PROCESSED:        12
```

Figure 23-3 Printed report generated from example program shown in Figure 23-2.

PRINTER FILES (PRTF)

Instead of hard-coding the report formats in the Output-Format Specifications of an RPG III/400 program, you can *externally define* them. Similar to Physical Files and Display Files, report formats may be coded using DDS by specifying PRTF (Printer File) for the type selection on the Programmer Menu. The syntax is entered, debugged, and compiled by exactly the same procedures described for the other DDS file types. As compared to hard-coded report formats, PRTF (Printer Files) offer the following advantages:

1. RPG programs include less coding and are therefore easier to maintain.
2. If more than one program uses the same report format, the coding does not have to be duplicated in each program.
3. Modifications have to be made to only one source member and not to every program that references the report format.
4. Because the RPG built-in processing cycle for output control cannot be followed, page overflow, line count, and page numbering must be controlled by programmer-supplied statements. This requirement eliminates many of the problems associated with RPG controlled printed output. For example, overflow lines cannot be specified with Exception Lines (E in column 15) for standard RPG controlled output. In addition, programmer-controlled output parallels the logic familiar to procedure-oriented languages such as COBOL, BASIC, and so forth.

Printer File Keywords

The keywords valid for Printer Files (PRTF) are listed in Figure 23-4. For a comprehensive discussion of all the valid PRTF keywords, refer to the Data Description Specifications manual. Only those specified in the example Printer File are summarized in the following paragraphs.

ALIAS	DRAWER	REFFLD
BLKFOLD	EDTCDE	SKIPA
CHRID	EDTWRD	SKIPB
CPI	FLTFIXDEC	SPACEA
CVTDTA	FLTPCN	SPACEB
DATE	INDARA	TEXT
DFNCHR	INDTXT	TIME
DFT	MSGCON	TRNSPY
DLTEDT	PAGNBR	UNDERLINE
	REF	

Figure 23-4 Valid keywords for Printer Files (PRTF).

DATE Keyword. DATE is a field-level keyword that accesses and prints the current job date. The standard format is MMDDYY, which may be edited by an EDTCDE (Edit Code) or EDTWRD (Edit Word) keyword.

EDTCDE Keyword. EDTCDE (Edit code) is a field-level keyword that controls the editing of output capable numeric fields. The edit code options, which are identical to those available in RPG, include 1, 2, 3, 4, A, B, C, D, J, K, L, M, Y, and Z. Examples of the syntax and edited results for three EDTCDE keywords are shown in Figure 23-5.

The table presented in Figure 23-6 summarizes all the valid EDTCDE (Edit Code) keyword options and their editing functions. An EDTCDE (or EDTWRD) is valid only for numeric fields specified as a Data Type S (signed) or blank (numeric only) in position 35 of the DDS form.

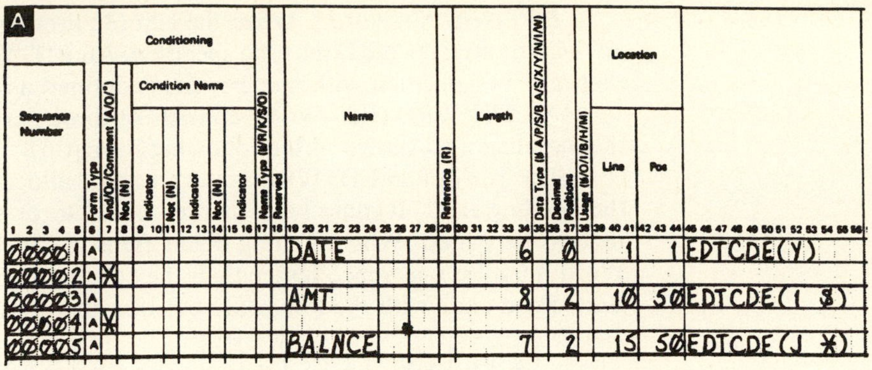

Line #	Value in Storage	EDTCDE Specified	Edited Result
00001	090191	Y	9/01/91
00003	00150000	1 $	$1,500.00
00005	000250}	J *	***25.00-

Notes:

1. Line 00003 coding controls a floating dollar sign. a separate EDTWRD (Edit Word) or constant must be specified for a fixed $.

2. } indicates negative 0.

Figure 23-5 EDTCDE keyword and edited result examples.

Edit Code	Commas	Decimal Point	Sign for Negative Balance	Entry in Column 21 of Control Specification: D or Blank	I	J	Zero Suppress
1	Yes	Yes	No sign	.00 or 0	,00 or 0	0,00 or 0	Yes
2	Yes	Yes	No sign	Blanks	Blanks	Blanks	Yes
3		Yes	No sign	.00 or 0	,00 or 0	0,00 or 0	Yes
4		Yes	No sign	Blanks	Blanks	Blanks	Yes
A	Yes	Yes	CR	.00 or 0	0,00 or 0	Yes	
B	Yes	Yes	CR	Blanks	Blanks	Blanks	Yes
C		Yes	CR	.00 or 0	,00 or 0	0,00 or 0	Yes
D		Yes	CR	Blanks	Blanks	Blanks	Yes
J	Yes	Yes	-(minus)	.00 or 0	,00 or 0	0,00 or 0	Yes
K	Yes	Yes	-(minus)	Blanks	Blanks	Blanks	Yes
L		Yes	-(minus)	.00 or 0	,00 or 0	0,00 or 0	Yes
M		Yes	-(minus)	Blanks	Blanks	Blanks	Yes
X[1]							
Y[2]							Yes
Z							Yes

[1] The X code performs no editing.

[2] The Y code suppresses the leftmost zero only. The Y code edits a three- to six-digit field according to the following pattern:

nn/n
nn/nn
nn/nn/n
nn/nn/nn

Figure 23-6 Summary of all valid EDTCDE codes and editing functions.

EDTWRD Keyword. When the edit requirements cannot be satisfied by an EDTCDE, an EDTWRD must be specified. An EDTWRD is a field-level keyword that may be specified with numeric fields defined as Data Type S or blank.

An EDTWRD (Edit Word) consists of three parts: the body, the status, and the expansion as shown in the following format:

The *body* of an EDTWRD is the area that allocates space for the digits from the sending field. It must be formatted equal to or greater than the size of the field to be edited. When floating dollar signs are included, the body of the Edit Word must be one space larger than the related numeric field. The body of the Edit Word ends with the low-order position that may be replaced by a digit.

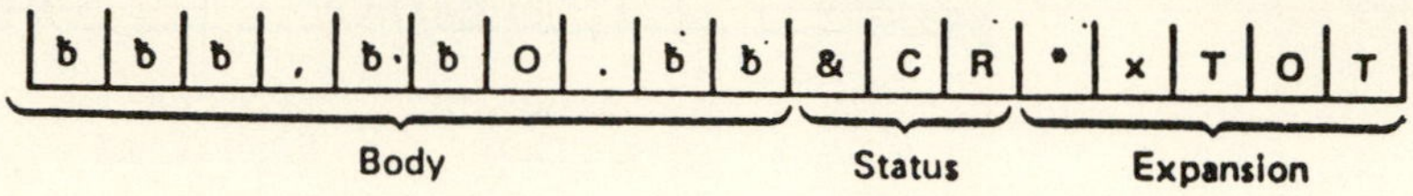

The *status* is an optional part of an EDTWRD that immediately follows the body and supports a minus sign or a CR (credit) symbol. If the numeric field value is negative and a minus sign is included in this area, a minus sign will print (or display) after the low-order digit. On the other hand, if CR is specified and the value is negative, CR will print or display in the area. When the field value is positive (a plus sign), blanks will print in the positions allocated to the status section. If a minus sign or credit symbol is not specified, a status entry is not part of an EDTWRD.

The *expansion* area of an EDTWRD begins after the status section, or after the body if status is not specified. The characters included in this area will print or display every time the instruction is executed; it does not depend on the field value. Blanks are not permitted in the expansion area. If blanks are required, they must be specified by ampersands (&). Examples of EDTWRD formats and their edited results are shown in Figure 23-7. In addition to the parentheses, EDTWRDs must also be enclosed in single quotes.

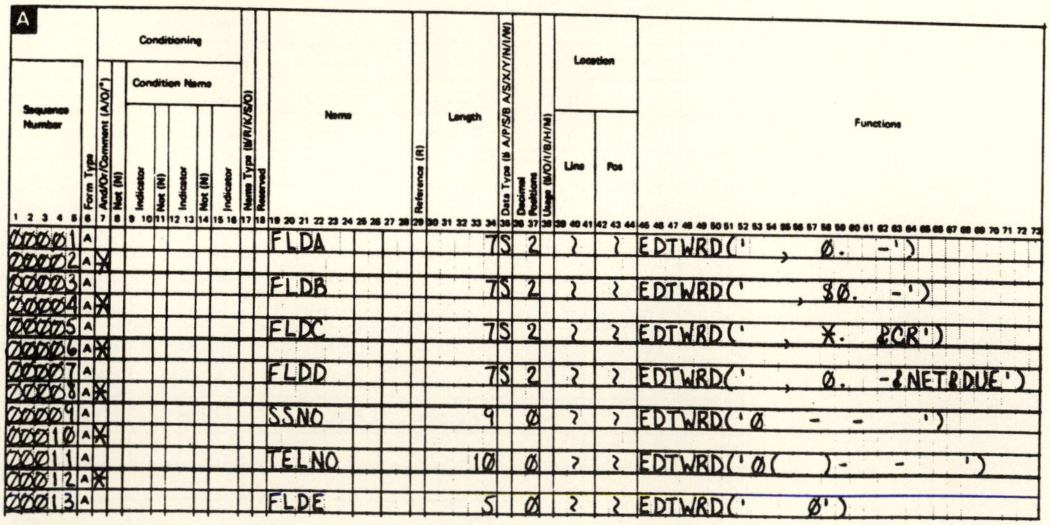

Sequence Number	Data Value in Storage	EDTWRD Format	Edited Result	Comments
00001	010000}	'bb,bb0.bb-'	1,000.00-	Minus will print only when value is negative. 0 in the body of the edit word indicates extent of zero suppression.
00003	0000199	'bbb,b$0.bb'	$1.99	Floating $ sign requires extra high-order digit position in edit word format. A fixed dollar sign is specified by placing it in the extra-high order position.

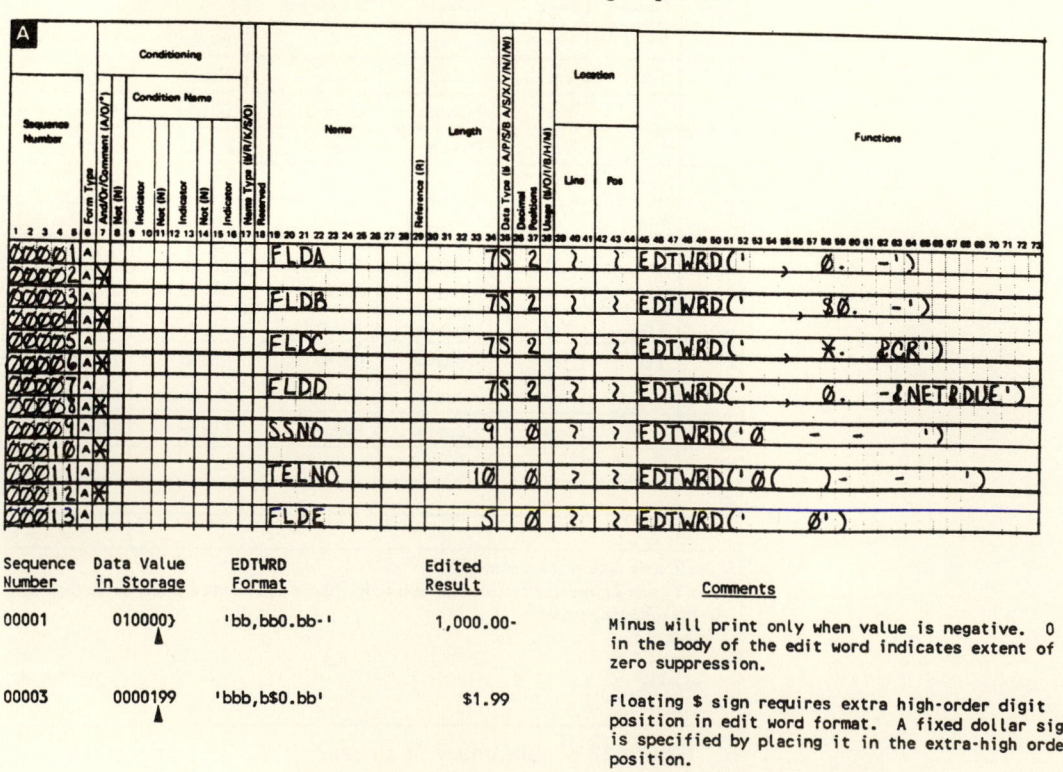

Figure 23-7 EDTWRD formats and editing example.

00005	000004R ▲	'bb,bb*.bb&CR'	******.49 CR	Asterisk replaces all high-order zeros with asterisks to the extent of its location in the body of the edit word. The ampersand provides a space after the status part. CR prints because the value is negative (R = -9). If the value was positive two spaces would be included in those positions.
00007	1250000 ▲	'bb,bb0.bb-&NET&DUE'	12,500.00 NET DUE	Because the value is positive, the minus sign does not print. The space after the status and in the expansion part, are controlled by ampersands. NET DUE, which is in the expansion area, follows the status for this example. If a status was not specified, the expansion value would follow the body. Regardless of the value of the edited item, the expansion entry will print.
00009	011223333	'0bbb-bb-bbbb'	011-22-3333	To prevent suppression of the leading zero in the social security number, a 0 must be specified in an extra high-order position in the body of the edit word.
00011	2039998888	'0(bbb)-bbb-bbbb'	(203)-999-8888	To prevent suppression of the leading parenthesis, a 0 must be specified in an extra high-order position in the body of the edit word.
00012	00000 ▲	'bbbb0'		Complete zero suppression may be specified by placing a 0 in the low-order position in the body of an edit word.

b's in body part of edit word indicate spaces.

▲ indicates implied decimal position in stored value

(*Continued*)

PAGNBR (Page Number) Keyword. The PAGNBR keyword predefines a 4-byte numeric integer field. Its value is automatically initialized to zeros when the program is executed and is incremented by 1 before printing a page. Page numbers are not incremented beyond 9999, but PAGNBR may be reset to 1 by conditioning the related instruction with an indicator. Figure 23-8 illustrates two coding examples of the PAGNBR keyword.

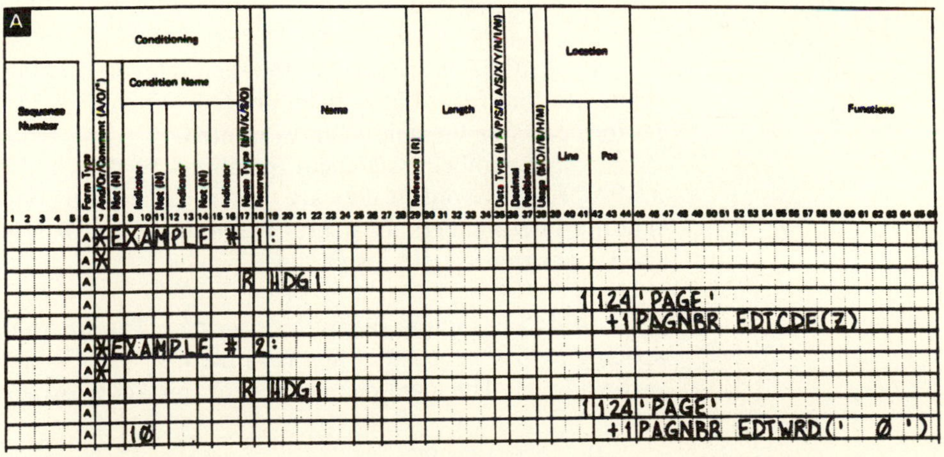

Example 1:

The constant PAGE is optional. The +1 entry in the Pos field indicates the number of spaces to be included between the previous constant or field and the beginning of the field or constant currently defined. Also notice that EDTCDE(Z) is specified to suppress leading zeros in the PAGNBR value.

Example 2:

The constant PAGE and PAGNBR value locations are identical to Example 1. However, here the PAGNBR line is conditioned by an indicator (10). Regardless of the ON or OFF status of the indicator, the PAGNBR value will be incremented and printed on every page. When the status of the indicator changes (from ON to OFF or OFF to ON), the PAGNBR value will be rest to 1 and automatic incrementation continued. To illustrate how an EDTWRD may be used for PAGNBR editing, it is specified for this example.

Figure 23-8 Examples of the PAGNBR keyword.

SKIPA (Skip After) Keyword. The SKIPA (Skip After) keyword, which may be specified at the file, record, or field level, controls skipping to a specific line *after* one or more lines are printed. If the specified line number has been passed, control will advance the paper to the next page and begin printing on the line indicated. When SKIPA is specified at the file level, skipping will be performed *after* all the records defined in the PRTF have been printed. If SKIPA is assigned at the record level, skipping will be performed *after* all the lines related to the record format are printed. Finally, when SKIPA is included at the field level, skipping will be executed *after* the related field value is printed.

SKIPB (Skip Before) Keyword. The SKIPB (Skip Before) keyword may be specified at the file, record, or field level. It controls skipping to a specified line before the next line is printed. If the designated line has been passed, control will advance the paper to the next page and begin printing on the specified line. When SKIPB is specified at the file level, skipping will be performed *before* all the records defined in the PRTF have been printed. If SKIPB is assigned at the record level, skipping will be performed *before* any of the lines related to the record format are printed. Finally, when SKIPB is included at the field level, skipping will be executed *before* the related field value is printed.

SPACEA (Space After) Keyword. The SPACEA keyword controls line spacing *after* a record or line is printed. It may be specified only at the record or field level. The valid parameters for this keyword are as follows:

0	No spacing
1	Space one line
2	Space two lines
3	Space three line

If SPACEA is specified at the record level, spacing occurs *after* all the lines related to that record have been printed. When used at the field level, spacing is performed *after* the field value is printed.

A line number assignment (positions 39–41) cannot be specified along with a SPACEA keyword. If they are used together, the compilation of the PRTF will flag the line numbers as errors. If line numbers or a SPACEA keyword is not used, overprinting will result.

SPACEB (Space Before) Keyword. The SPACEB keyword controls line spacing *before* a record or line is printed. It may be specified only at the record or field level. The valid parameters for this keyword are as follows:

0	No spacing
1	Space one line
2	Space two lines
3	Space three line

If SPACEB is specified at the record level, spacing occurs before the first line related to that record is printed. When used at the field level, spacing is performed before the field value is printed.

A line number assignment (positions 39–41) cannot be specified along with a SPACEB keyword. If they are used together, the compilation of the PRTF will flag line numbers as errors. If a line number or the SPACEB keyword is not specified, overprinting will result.

Examples of SKIPA, SKIPB, SPACEA, SPACEB Keywords Control

The parameter included with a SKIPA, SKIPB, SPACEA, or SPACEB keyword is coded in the following general format:

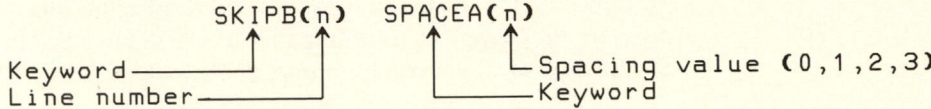

```
             SKIPB(n)  SPACEA(n)
                  ↑  ↑    ↑    ↑
Keyword ──────────┘  │    │    └─Spacing value (0,1,2,3)
Line number ─────────┘    └──────Keyword
```

Coding examples and the processing functions of the SKIPB and SPACEA keywords are illustrated in Figure 23-9.

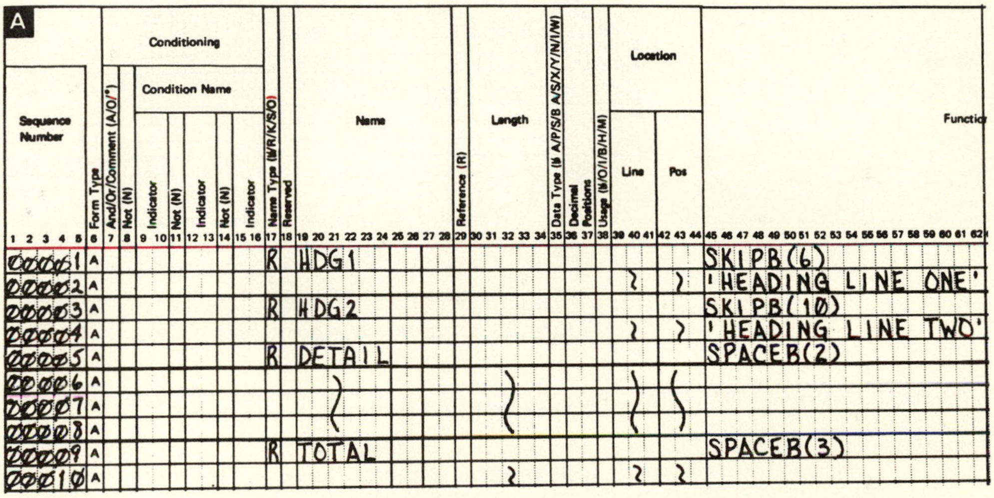

Previous Page

Line No On Page	Value Printed	Keyword Specified	Comments
Line 6	HEADING LINE ONE	SKIPB(6)	If printer carriage is beyond line 6 on the previous page, paper will advance to line 6 of the next page before printing the line.
Line 10	HEADING LINE TWO	SKIPB(10)	Keyword advances paper to line 10 of the same page before printing the line.
Line 12	DETAIL LINE	SPACEB(2)	Keyword advances the paper two lines before printing a detail line.
	.		
	.		
	.		
	TOTAL LINE	SPACEB(3)	Keyword advances paper three lines before printing the total line.

Notes:

1. Any combination of SKIPA, SKIPB, SPACEA, and SPACEB may be specified to meet page and line requirements.
2. Execution of skipping and spacing is controlled in an RPG III/400 program by referencing the related PRTF file record and/or field name.

Figure 23-9 SKIPB and SPACEB syntax and processing functions.

TIME (Current System Time)

TIME is a field-level-only keyword that prints the current system time as a constant in an edited HH:MM:SS format. Other edited formats may be specified by an EDTWRD or user-defined Edit Code. Conditioning indicators may be used to control the printing of a specific TIME value format. Figure 23-10 shows two examples of the syntax and processing results for this keyword. An application program that accesses a Printer File (PRTF) instead of including RPG III Output Specifications to generate a report is introduced in the following sections.

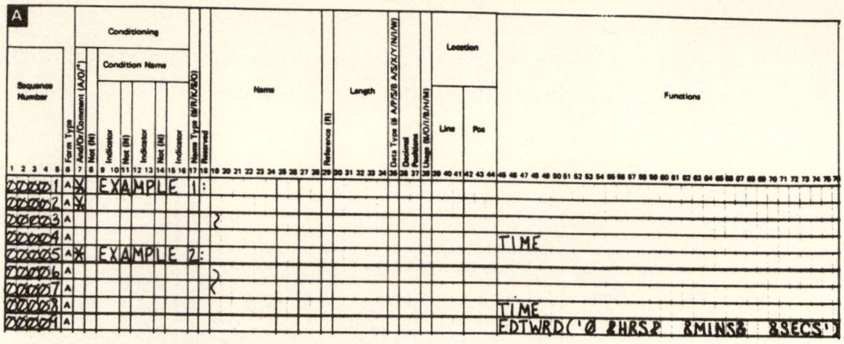

Assuming the system time is 123045, the time format printed for the two examples is as follows:

Example 1: 12:30:45 (Colons are system-supplied)

Example 2: 12 HRS 30 MINS 45 SECS (EDTWRD required for this format)

Figure 23-10 Syntax and processing results for the TIME keyword.

Continuing Example Application Program

This example program generates a report from the Physical File created in Chapter 19 and loaded interactively in Chapter 21. The report design previously shown in the printer spacing chart in Figure 23-1 is repeated in Figure 23-11 for easier reference. The field sizes specified were defined in the Physical File.

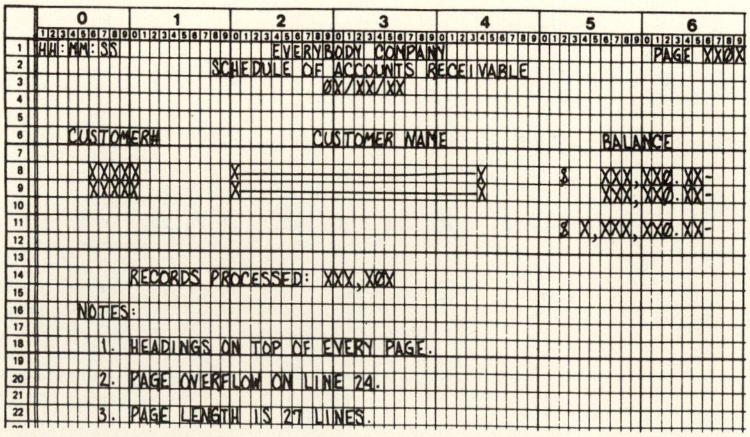

Figure 23-11 Report design for continuing example program.

Printer File (PRTF) Syntax

The Printer File (PRTF) syntax for the report design illustrated in Figure 23-11 is detailed in the Data Description Specifications in Figure 23-12.

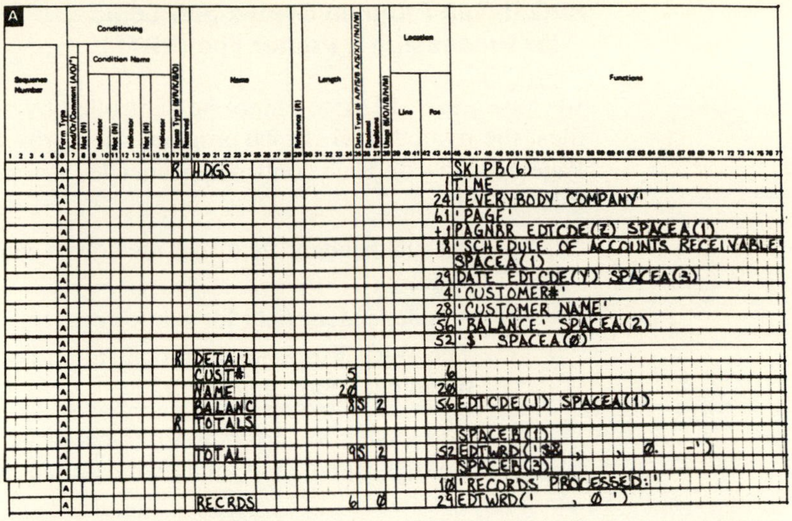

Figure 23-12 Data Description Specifications coding for example Printer File (PRTF).

A source listing of the example PRTF (generated by Option 3—Create Object) on the Programmer Menu is illustrated in Figure 23-13. Also included in the figure is the relationship of the line control provided by the SKIPB, SKIPA, and SKIPB keywords to the printed report.

```
SEQNBR *...+....1....+....2....+....3....+....4....+....5....+....6....+....7....+....8

  100    A        R HDGS                        SKIPB(6)
  200    A                                      1TIME
  300    A                                     24'EVERYBODY COMPANY'
  400    A                                     61'PAGE'
  500    A                                     +1PAGNBR EDTCDE(Z) SPACEA(1)
  600    A                                     18'SCHEDULE OF ACCOUNTS RECEIVABLE'
  700    A                                       SPACEA(1)
  800    A                                     29DATE EDTCDE(Y) SPACEA(3)
  900    A                                      4'CUSTOMER#'
 1000    A                                     28'CUSTOMER NAME'
 1100    A                                     56'BALANCE' SPACEA(2)
 1200    A                                     52'$' SPACEA(0)
 1300    A        R DETAIL
 1400    A          CUST#          5            6
 1500    A          NAME          20           20
 1600    A          BALANC         8S 2        56EDTCDE(J) SPACEA(1)
 1700    A        R TOTALS
 1800    A                                       SPACEB(1)
 1900    A          TOTAL          9S 2        52EDTWRD('$& ,   , 0.  -')
 2000    A                                       SPACEB(3)
 2100    A                                     10'RECORDS PROCESSED:'
 2200    A          RECRDS         6 0         29EDTWRD('  ,  0 ')
```

```
Printed Report:                                            Keyword/PRTF Line Ref

13:32:54            EVERYBODY.COMPANY              PAGE    1<-SKIPB(6)  Line 100
           SCHEDULE OF ACCOUNTS RECEIVABLE<-------------------SPACEA(1) Line 500
                       9/01/91<-------------------------------SPACEA(1) Line 700


  CUSTOMER#            CUSTOMER NAME               BALANCE<---SPACEA(3) Line 800
                                                              SPACEA(0) LINE 1200
    12345             KAREL APPEL             $     1,250.00<-SPACEA(2) Line 1100
    23456             GEORGES BRAQUE                  100.00<-SPACEA(1) Line 1600
    34567             PAUL CEZANNE                 81,900.00      "        "
    45678             MARC CHAGALL                    926.00      "        "
    56789             EDGAR DEGAS                   7,854.99      "        "
    67890             MAX ERNST                       500.00      "        "
    78900             BUCKMINSTER FULLER           33,000.10      "        "
    89000             JULIO GONZALEZ                  654.78      "        "

. . . . . . . . . . . . . . . . . . . . . . . . . . . . . . . . . . . .

13:32:54            EVERYBODY COMPANY              PAGE    2<-SKIPB(6)  Line 600
           SCHEDULE OF ACCOUNTS RECEIVABLE <------------------SPACEA(1) Line 500
                       9/01/91<-------------------------------SPACE(1)  Line 700


  CUSTOMER#            CUSTOMER NAME               BALANCE<---SPACEA(3) Line 800
                                                              SPACEA(0) Line 1200
    90000             HECTOR HYPPOLITE        $   120,000.00<-SPACEA(2) Line 1100
    91000             PIERRE JEANERET                   9.45<-SPACEA(1) Line 1600
    92000             WASSILY KANDINSKY           375,000.00      "        "
    93000             CHARLES CORBUSIER               250.00      "        "

                                              $   621,445.32<-SPACEB(1) Line 1800


      RECORDS PROCESSED:      12<-----------------------------SPACEB(3) Line 2000


     Note: The keyword/line references indicate position of printer carriage
           after related statement is executed.
```

Figure 23-13 Relationship of SKIPB, SPACEA, and SPACEB line control to the printed report.

RPG III/400 Program Syntax and Logic for Processing a Printer File (PRTF)

Because page overflow cannot be controlled by an overflow indicator for PRTF files, the related RPG III/400 program must provide for this processing function. Page overflow and line control items needed in a program that processes a Printer File follow:

1. An independent field that includes a value for the number of lines per page.
2. A independent field for a line counter.
3. The WRITE operation to control output of Printer File record formats (heading, detail, and total).

The processing logic for program-controlled page overflow and line type control (headings, detail, and total) is illustrated in the flowchart in Figure 23-14.

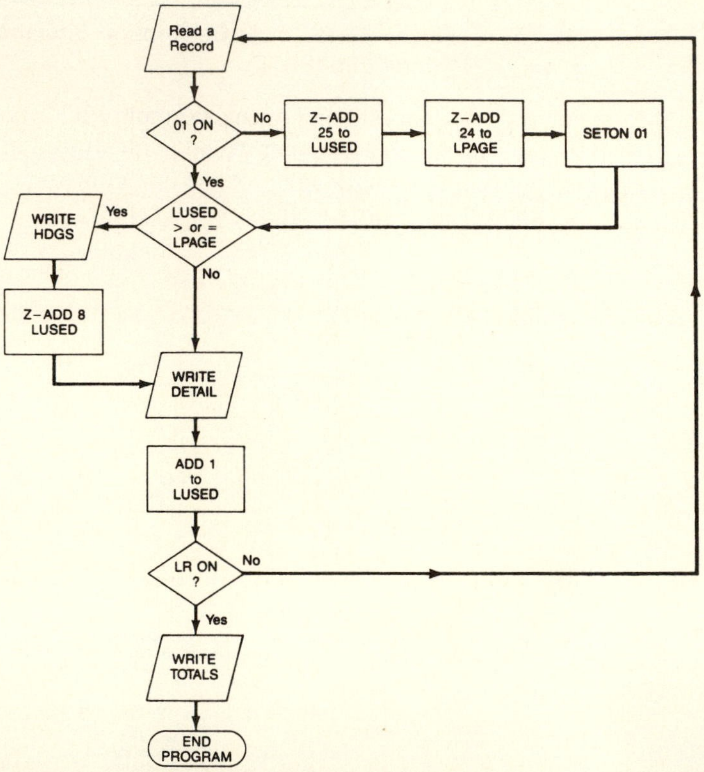

Figure 23-14 Processing logic flowchart and related RPG III/400 coding that controls page overflow and line type output.

A source listing of the program that processes a Printer File (PRTF) is detailed in Figure 23-15. Notice the following syntax features:

1. Printer File is specified as externally defined (E in column 19 of the File Description Specifications).
2. WRITE statements are used to output related PRTF record formats (HDGS, DETAIL, and TOTAL).
3. Page overflow decision-making is controlled in the program.
4. IF statements instead of conditioning indicators are used to control decision-making functions and processing.
5. Output Specifications are omitted in the program.

```
*... ... 1 ... ... 2 ... ... 3 ... ... 4 ... ... 5 ... ... 6 ... ... 7 ... ... 8

     FP1PF1SM IP  E           K        DISK
     FP1PTR1SMO   E                    PRINTER
     C           *IN01     IFEQ '0'                        IND. 01 TEST         If group is performed
     C                     Z-ADD25        LUSED   20       LINE COUNTER         only for first record
     C                     Z-ADD24        LPAGE   20       LINES/PAGE           processed.
     C                     SETON                      01   CTRL PAGE INIT
     C                     END                             ENDS IF GROUP
     C           LUSED     IFGE LPAGE                      PAGE OVFLW TEST      Headings are written
     C                     WRITEHDGS                       WRITE HDGS           only when > or = test
     C                     Z-ADD8         LUSED            CHANGE CTR           is true.
     C                     END                             ENDS IF GROUP
     C                     WRITEDETAIL                     WRITE DETL RCRD      Detail line is written
     C                     ADD  1         LUSED            INCREMENT CTR        for every record read.
     C                     ADD  BALANC    TOTAL            TOTAL BALANCES       Total line is written
     C                     ADD  1         RECRDS           TOTAL RECORDS        after end of file is
     CLR                   WRITETOTALS                     WRITE AT EOF         sensed and LR turns on.
```

Figure 23-15 Source listing of program that processes the example Printer File.

Printer File (PRTF) Command Parameters

External parameters for Printer Files are assigned by the CRTPRTF (Create Printer File) command. Controls including formsize, lines per inch, characters per inch, overflow, forms alignment, print quality, and so forth may be specified by a series of prompt screens generated by the CRTPRTF command.

All the options available with this command are shown in Figure 23-16. The heavy lined paths for each option represent the default value. The lower and lighter lined paths indicate the other processing options that may be selected by the programmer. Some of the options are valid, however, only if the printer model(s)

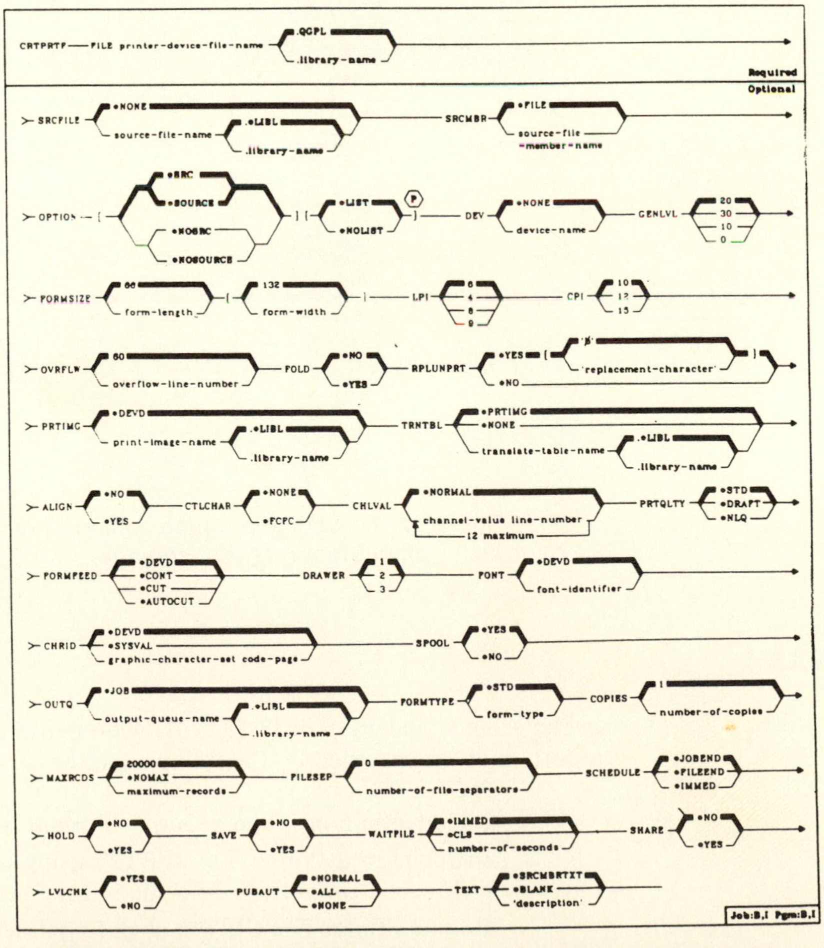

Figure 23-16 CRTPRTF (Create Printer File) command parameters. (Courtesy of IBM)

interfaced with the system supports them. For example, line printers do not support many of the optional features.

The format of the CRTPRTF options illustrated in Figure 24-16 does not represent the design of the prompt screens generated by this command. It is only a diagram of the command syntax that lists the processing options available. Diagrams for the syntax of all the commands are included in an IBM publication entitled *Programming Reference Summary (SC21–7734–7).*

Printer File (PRTF) Shells

In lieu of including the syntax for a printed report in a PRTF, many programmers may prefer to follow standard RPG Output Specifications coding procedures. Normally, this would prevent many of the options available with the CRTPRTF from being specified. This problem may be resolved by creating a PRTF shell by the CRTPRTF command (with parameters) and include *no* DDS syntax in the Printer File member. The coding for the report would be included in the Output Specifications of the RPG program. A detailed source listing in Figure 23-17 explains the RPG III/400 syntax associated with this method.

PRTF "shell" created by CRTPRTF command. Because report coding is program-defined, record size must be specified. (→ 200)

In lieu of SETON operations, MOVEs are used to turn on related indicators. Turning on 10 prevents the subroutine from executing again. (→ 800, 900)

Unlike UDATE, TIME value must be accessed by a calculation instruction. (→ 1000, 1300)

```
SEQNBR *... ... 1 ... ... 2 ... ... 3 ... ... 4 ... ... 5 ... ... 6 ... ... 7 ... ... 8
  100        FP1PF1   IP  E                    DISK
  200        FP1PTR2SMO   F     132      OF    PRINTER
  300        C            *IN10     CASEQ'0'    TIMSUB              XEQ IF 10 OFF
  400        C                      END                             ENDS CAS GROUP
  500        C                      ADD  BALANC TOTAL    92         ACCUMULATE
  600        C                      ADD  1      RECRDS   60         RECRD COUNT
  700        C            TIMSUB    BEGSR
  800        C                      MOVE '1'    *IN10               TURN ON 10
  900        C                      MOVE '1'    *INOF               TURN ON OF
 1000        C                      TIME        HHMMSS   60         ACCESS TIME
 1100        C                      ENDSR
 1200        OP1PTR2SMH  106   OF
 1300        O                          HHMMSS    8 '  :  :  '
 1400        O                                   40 'EVERYBODY COMPANY'
 1500        O                                   64 'PAGE'
 1600        O                          PAGE  Z  69
 1700        O         H  1     OF
 1800        O                                   37 'SCHEDULE OF ACCOUNTS'
 1900        O                                   48 'RECEIVABLE'
 2000        O         H  3     OF
 2100        O                          UDATE Y  36
 2200        O         H  2     OF
 2300        O                                   12 'CUSTOMER#'
 2400        O                                   40 'CUSTOMER NAME'
 2500        O                                   62 'BALANCE'
 2600        O         H  0     OF
 2700        O                                   52 '$'
 2800        O         DF 1
 2900        O                          CUST#    10
 3000        O                          NAME     44
 3100        O                          BALANCJ  66
 3200        O         T 1      LR
 3300        O                                   52 '$'
 3400        O                          TOTAL J  66
 3500        O         T 2      LR
 3600        O                                   27 'RECORDS PROCESSED:'
 3700        O                          RECRDS   35 '    , 0 '
```

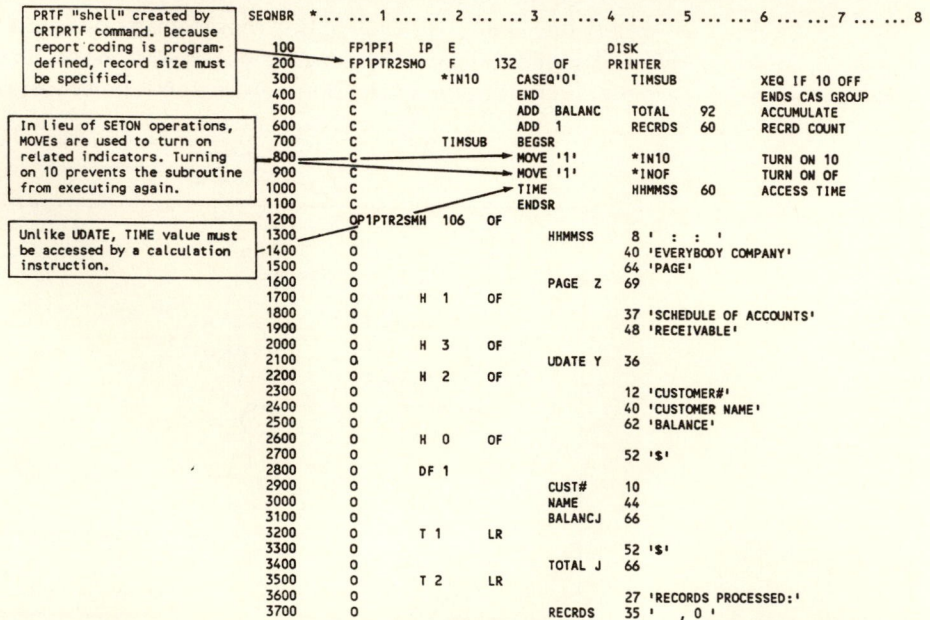

Figure 23-17 Source program coding when PRTF is specified as a shell (without report format coding).

SUMMARY

In the AS/400 and System/38 RPG III/400 environments, the syntax for printed reports may be specified by the following alternatives:

1. Included in a program's Output-Format Specifications.
2. Included in a Printer File (PRTF) using unique DDS syntax. Page overflow control must be specified in the related RPG III/400 program.
3. Build a Printer File (PRTF) shell to define attributes (i.e., print quality, font type, and so forth) not assignable in standard RPG coding. The syntax for the report is coded in Output-Format Specifications.

Page overflow indicators (OA-OG, OV) and control are not supported by Printer Files (PRTF). Those functions must be included as instructions in the Calculation Specifications.

QUESTIONS

23-1. What are Printer Files?

23-2. As compared to standard RPG Output Specifications coding for reports, what are the advantages of Printer Files? Are there any disadvantages?

23-3. How are Printer Files created?

23-4. Where and how are Printer Files defined in an RPG III/400 program?

23-5. What is the function of each of the following Printer File keywords?

DATE	EDTWRD	SPACEB
SPACEA	SKIPA	SKIPB
TIME	PAGNBR	EDTCDE

23-6. Where in the DDS form are the keywords in Question 23-5 specified?

23-7. In what format is the DATE value accessed?

23-8. In what format is the TIME value accessed?

23-9. What is the maximum value that may be specified with the SPACEA and SPACEB keywords?

23-10. What is the result of processing if SKIPB(06) is specified and the printer carriage is on line 1? On line 10?

23-11. Format EDTCDE keywords to generate the indicated edited result for the following examples.

	Value in Storage	Edited Output	EDTCDE Format
a.	00000▲00	.00	
b.	092291	9/22/91	
c.	125000▲0}	125,000.00-	
d.	000000▲00		

▲Indicates implied decimal position

23-12. Format EDTWRD keywords to generate the indicated edited result for the following examples.

	Value in Storage	Edited Output	EDTWRD Format
a.	00150▲00	$ 150.00	
b.	00150▲00	$150.00	
c.	011223333	011-22-3333	
d.	011223333	011 22 3333	
e.	2038380601	(203)-838-0601	
f.	000009▲00	*****9.00 CREDIT	
g.	00001	1	
h.	093091	9/30/91	
i.	2500▲0}	2,500.00-	

▲Indicates implied decimal position

Assume all dollar values are to include commas in the EDTWRD when large enough

23-13. How is page overflow controlled in an RPG program when Printer Files are used for report formats?

23-14. Explain the processing logic of the following calculation instructions.

```
*... ... 1 ... ... 2 ... ... 3 ... ... 4 ... ... 5 ... ... 6

     C           *IN10     IFNE '1'
     C                     Z-ADD55        LCOUNT  20
     C                     Z-ADD54        PAGLEN  20
     C                     MOVE '1'       *IN10
     C                     END
```

23-15. Explain the processing logic of the following calculation instructions.

```
*... ... 1 ... ... 2 ... ... 3 ... ... 4 ... ... 5

     C           LCOUNT    IFGE PAGLEN
     C                     WRITEHDINGS
     C                     MOVE 06        LCOUNT
     C                     END
     C                     WRITEDETLIN
     C                     ADD  2         LCOUNT
     CLR                   WRITETOLINE
```

23-16. Refer to Question 23-15 and explain where HDINGS, DETLIN, and TOLINE are defined. How are they defined? What general syntax is included in each?

23-17. What is the function of the CRTPRTF command? Name some of the controls that may be specified by this command.

23-18. Under what conditions may the syntax for a report be included in the Output Specifications and a related Printer File be specified in the File Description Specifications?

EXERCISES

These are continuing exercises. The physical file was built in Exercise 19-1, the display file in Exercise 20-1, and the RPG program in Exercise 21-1.

23-1. From the following Printer Spacing Chart, write the DDS coding for a Printer File (PRTF). Refer to your completed physical file coding for Exercise 19-1 for field attributes.

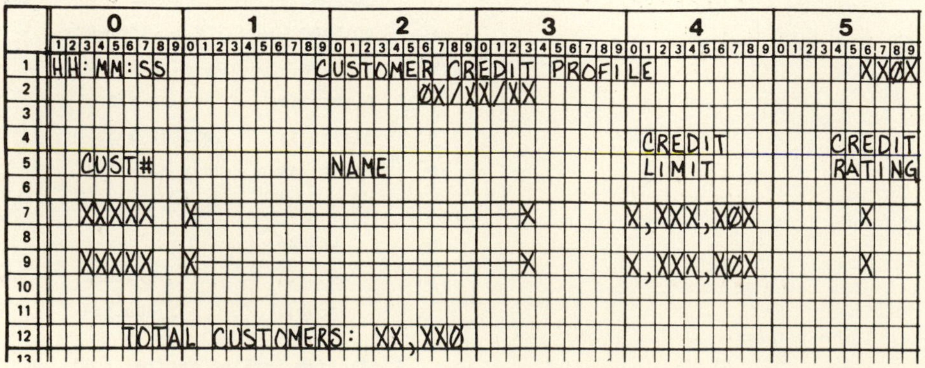

23.2 Write an RPG III program to process the Printer File completed in Exercise 23-1.

LABORATORY ASSIGNMENTS

Laboratory Assignment 23-1: PARTS INVENTORY STATUS REPORT

Assignments 19-1, 20-1, and 21-1 must have been completed and the data loaded to the physical file before the program for this assignment is executed.

From the following printer spacing chart, write the DDS coding for a Printer File (PRTF) and complete an RPG III/400 program to process it and generate the required report. Refer to your completed Physical File coding Assignment 19-1 to determine the field names and attributes.

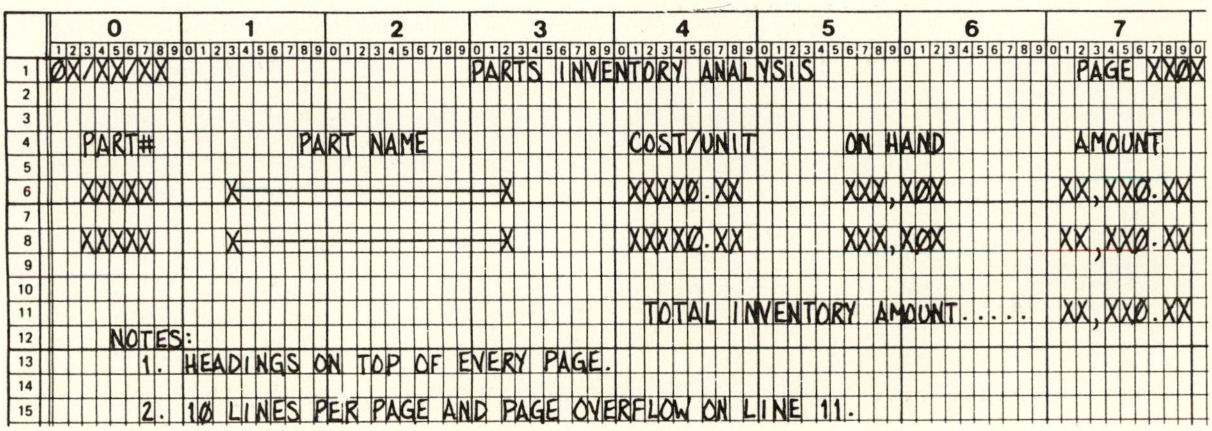
ØX/XX/XX PARTS INVENTORY ANALYSIS PAGE XXØX
PART# PART NAME COST/UNIT ON HAND AMOUNT
XXXXX X X XXXXØ.XX XXX,XØX XX,XXØ.XX
XXXXX X X XXXXØ.XX XXX,XØX XX,XXØ.XX
TOTAL INVENTORY AMOUNT..... XX,XXØ.XX
NOTES:
1. HEADINGS ON TOP OF EVERY PAGE.
2. 1Ø LINES PER PAGE AND PAGE OVERFLOW ON LINE 11.

Laboratory Assignment 23-2: COMMISSION REPORT

If Lab Assignment 21–5 was completed (Physical File created and loaded), write an RPG/400 program to control all of the processing specified to generate the report detailed in *Lab Assignment 6–1*. Use a *Printer File* for the report format.

If Lab Assignment 21–5 has not been completed, create a Physical File, Display File, and an RPG/400 program to load the data. In lieu of this, the DFU utility may be used to load the data to the Physical File which will eliminate the need to create a Display File and RPG/400 program.

chapter 24
Subfiles (AS/400 and System/38)

A *subfile* is a group of records that is loaded and read from or written to a display device file. Examples of subfile applications follow:

1. For inquiry processing, a subfile may be created to which a group of records read from a physical file are loaded.
2. For update processing, a subfile may be used to store a group of records read from a physical file. All or select records may be updated. Under control of an RPG III/400 program (READC operation), only the changed records are written back to the physical file.
3. For adds processing, a subfile may be built to load the new records that may be edited before adding them to an existing physical file.
4. For deletion processing, a subfile may be created to load a group of records that may be logically deleted or tagged for deletion.

The processing logic for subfiles included in RPG programs that control inquiry, update, or deletion maintenance is detailed in Figure 24-1.

To control subfile processing, the following sequence of operations must be included in an RPG III/400 program.

1. For inquiry, addition, update, and delete maintenance, records are read from a physical file and written to a subfile one at a time until the subfile is full or until end of file is sensed in the input (physical) file.

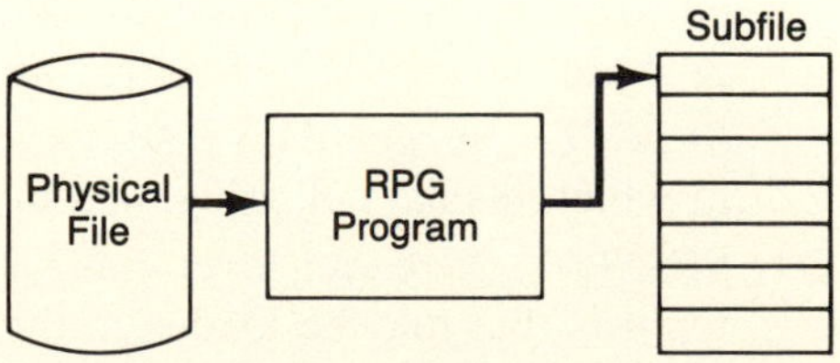

2. After the subfile is full or the input file at end, all of the records in the subfile are displayed by one operation.

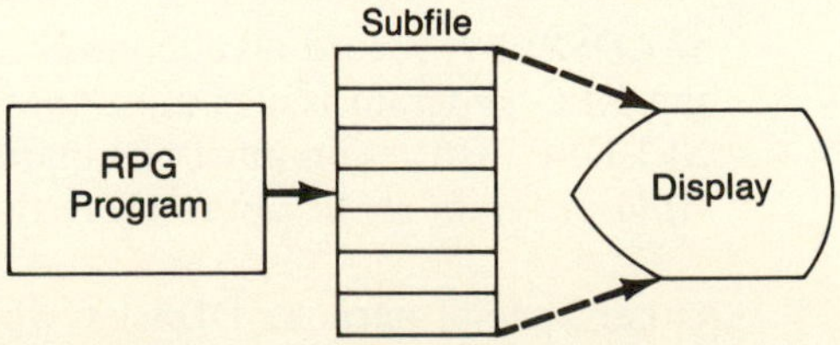

Figure 24-1 Subfile processing logic.

3. Depending on the maintenance application, the displayed records may be individually reviewed, changed, or deleted.

4. For addition, update, and deletion processing, each record may read from the subfile and the related physical file modified accordingly.

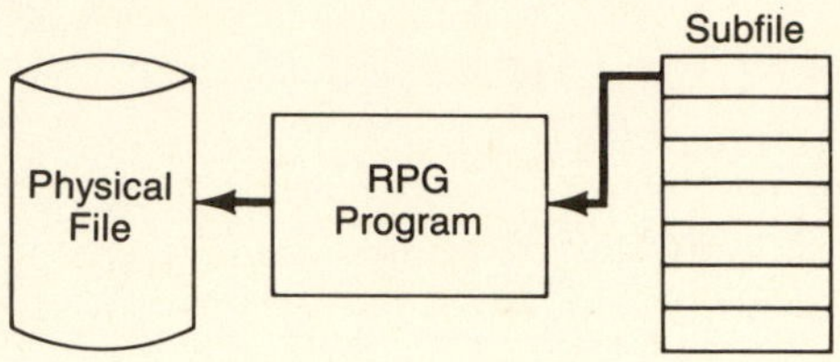

Note: In lieu of the procedure illustrated, add records may be loaded directly to a subfile from a display file that supports input.

(*Continued*)

Similar to any display file, subfiles are coded as DDS specifications using either SEU (Source Entry Utility) or SDA (Screen Design Aid). All subfiles must include a *subfile record format* and a related *subfile control record format* in the DDS coding. The function of each format is explained below.

The *subfile record format* defines the fields in the subfile record. RPG programs that control subfile processing use the subfile record format to read the subfile (input), write records to the subfile (output), and perform update operations to the subfile. Processing of the subfile record format is performed between the subfile and the RPG program. The display is not changed on operations to a subfile record format.

The *subfile control record* format describes any heading syntax and controls unique subfile functions such as size, clearing, and initialization. DDS coding requires that the *subfile record format* description precede the control record format instructions. An RPG program must access the control record format in order to write the complete subfile to the display unit and to read the subfile from the display unit.

The minimum Data Description Specification (DDS) keywords required in the definition of a subfile are SFL, SFLCTL, SFLSIZ, SFLPAG, and SFLDSP. The function of each is explained in the following paragraphs.

SFL: A record level keyword that specifies the subfile record format, which consists of variable data items. The instructions for this format must immediately precede the subfile control record format.

SFLCTL: A record level keyword that specifies the subfile control record format in which display, clearing, and initialization functions are controlled.

SFLSIZ: A record level control record keyword that specifies the number of records that may be loaded in the subfile. The maximum allowed for a subfile is 9999.

SFLPAG: A record level control record keyword that specifies the number of records that may be displayed on the CRT at the same time.

SFLDSP: A record level control record keyword that displays the subfile when the RPG program issues an output operation to the control record format. The SFLDSP instruction must be conditioned by one or more indicators set on in the RPG program at the appropriate time in the processing cycle.

Other special purpose DDS keywords for subfiles that must be specified at the record level in the control record format include the following:

SFLCLR: Clears a subfile of all records before new records are loaded. The subfile is *not* deleted by execution of this keyword, only cleared.

SFLINZ: Initializes all records in a subfile. Alphanumeric fields are initialized with blanks and numeric fields with zeros.

SFLDLT: Deletes a subfile. It is used when more than one subfile is controlled by an RPG program and one or more are no longer needed. Because the number of subfiles that may be active at any time is limited to 24, this keyword may be specified to delete subfiles so that others may be included in the processing cycle.

SFLDSPCTL: Displays constants and fields defined within the control record instruction format. This keyword is usually conditioned by an indicator that is turned on in an RPG program at the appropriate time in the processing cycle.

SFLEND: A record level control record keyword that displays a plus sign in the lower, rightmost area of the screen. The plus sign indicates that more records are stored in the subfile than can display at one time on the screen. Pressing the Roll Up key displays the next group of records in the subfile. A plus sign will not display if there are no more records in the subfile. Recall that the number of records displayed on the screen is controlled by the value included with the SFLPAG keyword. SFLEND is usually conditioned by an indicator.

SFLRNA: This keyword is used with SFLINZ for program-controlled initialization of a subfile with no active records. A workstation user may key data into the related blank subfile records. SFLRNA must be specified when the SFLINZ keyword is included in the coding of a subfile.

SFLMSG: Specifies a subfile record error that is included in the control record format and displays on the error message line (default 24) unless the location is changed by a MSGLOC keyword.

SFLDROP: Controls the folding of records when they are too long to display at one time on the screen. This keyword is used with a command key that the workstation operator may press to display the folded format of the subfile record.

For an explanation of the function of other subfile keywords, SFLROLVAL, SFLNXTCHG, SFLRCDNBR, SFLLIN, SFLMSGRCD, and SFLPGMQ, refer to the system's *CPF Reference Manual–DDS*. Use of many of these keywords will be seen in the presentation of three application programs that include subfiles for inquiry, update, and the adds maintenance of a physical file.

SUBFILE APPLICATION PROGRAM—INQUIRY PROCESSING

The specifications for a program that processes a subfile for the inquiry of a physical file are detailed in Figure 24-2.

The system flowchart shown in Figure 24-3 indicates that the program accesses records from a physical file and stores them in a subfile for review.

The structure of the physical file (P1PF1) processed by the subfile inquiry application program is shown in Figure 24-4. Also included is a listing of the data stored in the file.

The design of the prompt screen included in the display file is shown in Figure 24-5.

The format of the subfile, which is displayed when the inquiry program is executed, is illustrated in Figure 24-6. Notice that Xs represent the size and location of the variable field data. As shown in the last section of Figure 24-6, the Xs are replaced with field values when the subfile is executed under program control.

PROGRAM SPECIFICATIONS Page 1 of 1

Program Name PF Inquiry Program-ID CH24P1 Written By S. Myers

Purpose Inquiry of a PF utilizing a subfile Approved By The Boss

Input files (directory names):

P1PF1 (Physical File Keyed/Unique)

Output files (directory names):

SFINQ (Display File)

Processing Narrative:

Write an RPG program to inquiry a group of records from a physical file utilizing a subfile.

Input:

Create a display file that includes a prompt screen, a subfile record format, a subfile control record format, and a command line record. The designs of the prompt screen and subfile are included in supplemental forms.

The prompt screen, which will be executed first, is included for the entering of a customer number. The entry specifies the record at which reading of the physical file is to begin.

The subfile must be coded with the subfile record definition first followed by the subfile control record statements.

Processing:

Read the physical file (beginning at the customer number entered) and sequentially write the records out to a subfile. The loading process is to continue until the subfile is full or the physical file is "at end".

Output:

Output from the program to a subfile which is to support only inquiry processing. Define the subfile to store 10 records with 6 per page.

Figure 24-2 Specifications for an application program that controls the inquiry file with a subfile.

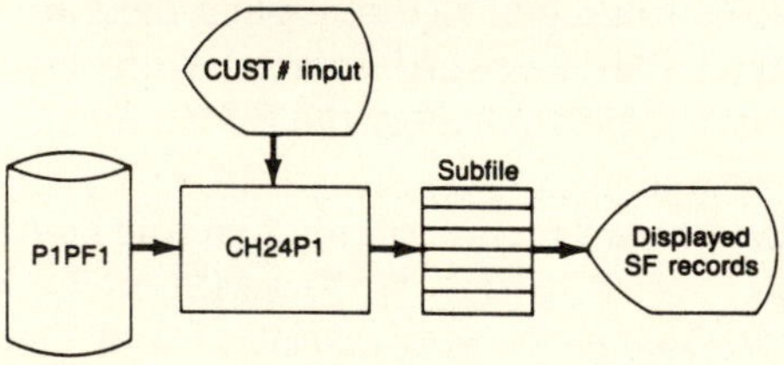

Figure 24-3 System flowchart for a program that accesses records from a physical file for inquiry with subfile control.

FILE DEFINITION

SYSTEM Yours		DRAWN BY S. Myers
FILE NAME P1PF1		DATE 8/11/91 REV. NO. 0
CREATED BY S. Myers		FILE TYPE Physical
RECORD NAME P1PF1R		KEY LENGTH 5 bytes
RECORDING MODE Fixed	ORGANIZATION Keyed	SEQUENCE Ascending Key
RECORD SIZE 75 bytes	BLOCKING FACTOR 1	BLOCKSIZE 75 bytes

FIELD DATA

FIELD NO.	FIELD NAME - DESCRIPTION	SIZE	CLASS C/P/Z/B	POSITION FROM	POSITION THRU	FORMAT/CONSTANT
1	CUST#	5	C	1	5	Key field (unique)
2	NAME	20	C	6	25	
3	STREET	20	C	26	45	
4	CITY	20	C	46	65	
5	STATE	2	C	66	67	
6	ZIP	5	P	68	70	
7	BALANC	8	P	71	75	2 decimal positions

Figure 24-4 Physical file (P1PF1) structure and listing of the stored data processed by the subfile inquiry program.

```
12345KAREL APPEL            20 AMSTERDAM AVENUE NEW YORK          NY0745000125000
23456GEORGES BRAQUE         300 ST CLAIR STREET TRENTON           NJ0550100010000
34567PAUL CEZANNE           44 RUE PIGALLE      STAMFORD          CT0651808190000
45678MARC CHAGALL           222 QUAIL AVENUE    BRIDGEPORT        CT0666600092600
56789EDGAR DEGAS            10 ROSE TERRACE     WESTPORT          PA0777700784599
67890MAX ERNST              1 FRANKFURT DRIVE   FRANKFORT         KY0555100050000
78900BUCKMINSTER FULLER     999 PARK AVENUE     NEW YORK          NY0755503300010
89000JULIO GONZALEZ         101 SMITH LANE      GREENWICH         CT0644400065478
90000HECTOR HYPPOLITE       888 PEACHTREE AVENUEATLANTA           GA0333212000000
91000PIERRE JEANERET        90 CHATEAU DRIVE    GENEVA            NY0777700000945
```

(*Continued*)

PROMPT Screen Design:

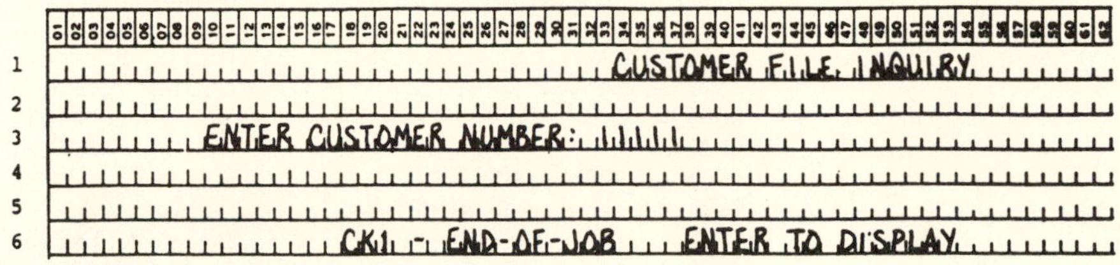

CRT Display (with customer number entered):

```
                    CUSTOMER FILE INQUIRY

ENTER CUSTOMER NUMBER: 10000


        CK1 - END-OF-JOB    ENTER TO CONTINUE
```

Figure 24-5 Prompt screen for subfile inquiry program.

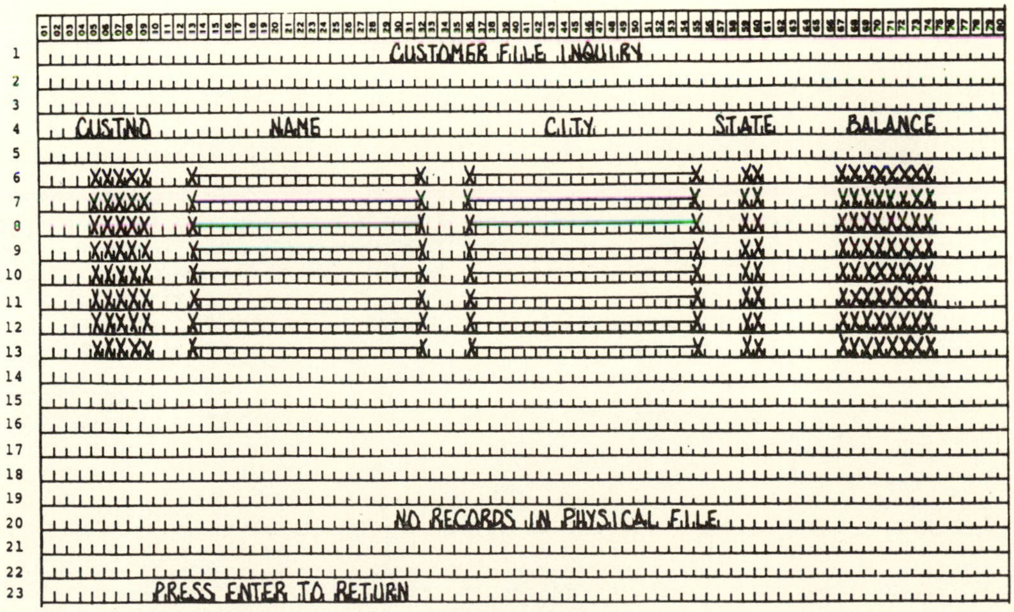


```
                         CUSTOMER FILE INQUIRY


CUSTNO          NAME                CITY         STATE      BALANCE

 12345   KAREL APPEL          NEW YORK            NY       00125000
 23456   GEORGES BRAQUE       TRENTON             NJ       00010000
 34567   PAUL CEZANNE         STAMFORD            CT       08190000
 45678   MARC CHAGALL         BRIDGEPORT          CT       00092600
 56789   EDGAR DEGAS          WESTPORT            PA       00784599
 67890   MAX ERNST            FRANKFORT           KY       00050000
 78900   BUCKMINSTER FULLER   NEW YORK            NY       03300010
 89000   JULIO GONZALEZ       GREENWICH           CT       00065478     +
```

Figure 24-6 Display format of the subfile controlled by the inquiry program.

Subfile DDS Syntax—Inquiry Program

The instructions for a subfile may be explicitly entered with SEU (Source Entry Utility) or be generated by SDA (Screen Design Aid) through a series of prompt screens. In any case, the structure of the subfile and the function of its keywords are the same. Common to the method used in the previous System/38 and AS/400 chapters, the entering of DDS source code via SEU will be followed.

A listing of the display file (SFINQ), which includes record formats for the prompt screen (PROMPT), subfile record (SM01SFR), subfile control record (SM01CTL), and command message record (CMDLINE) is presented in Figure 24-7. An explanation of the function of each instruction is also included.

```
... ... 1 ... ... 2 ... ... 3 ... ... 4 ... ... 5 ... ... 6 ... ... 7 ...
0001 A                                      PRINT
0002 A                                      REF(P1PF1)
0003 A* PROMPT SCREEN..........
0004 A          R PROMPT
0005 A                                      CA01(01 'END OF JOB')
0006 A                                  1 34'CUSTOMER FILE INQUIRY'
0007 A                                  3 10'ENTER CUSTOMER NUMBER:'
0008 A            CUSTNO         5   I  3 33
0009 A                                  6 18'CK1 - END-OF-JOB'
0010 A                                  6 38'ENTER TO DISPLAY'
0011 A* SUBFILE DEFINITION.....
0012 A          R SMO1SFR                   SFL
0013 A            CUST#     R        O  6  5
0014 A            NAME      R        O  6 13
0015 A            CITY      R        O  6 36
0016 A            STATE     R        O  6 59
0017 A            BALANC    R        O  6 67
0018 A* CONTROL RECORD.........
0019 A          R SMO1CTL                   SFLCTL(SMO1SFR)
0020 A                                      SFLSIZ(10)
0021 A                                      SFLPAG(8)
0022 A  80                                  SFLCLR
0023 A  81                                  SFLDSP
0024 A  81                                  SFLDSPCTL
0025 A  81                                  SFLEND
0026 A                                      OVERLAY
0027 A                                  1 30'CUSTOMER FILE INQUIRY'
0028 A                                  4  4'CUSTNO'
0029 A                                  4 20'NAME'
0030 A                                  4 43'CITY'
0031 A                                  4 57'STATE'
0032 A                                  4 68'BALANCE'
0033 A          R CMDLINE
0034 A  70                             20 30'NO RECORDS IN PHYSICAL FILE'
0035 A                                 23 10'PRESS ENTER TO RETURN'
```

Line

0001 The keyword PRINT allows use of the Print Key to print a copy of the screen image.

0002 The keyword REF references the field attributes in the physical file P1PF1.

0003-0010 The instructions included in this group relate to a prompt screen in which the operator enters a customer number to begin an inquiry of the physical file or end-of-job processing.

0012 An R in column 17 defines this entry as the name of the subfile record format. In columns 19-28, a programmer-supplied name for the subfile record format is included. In addition, the keyword SFL must be entered (at the record level) in the Functions field (columns 45-80) to identify this entry as a subfile record format.

Figure 24-7 SEU syntax for display file (SFLINQ) (includes record formats PROMPT, SM01SFR, SM01CTL, and CMDLINE).

0013-
0017 The physical file (P1PF1) field attributes included in the subfile record format are referenced by the letter R in column 29. Individual field line (columns 39-41) and column locations (columns 42-44) are specified for each field entry. Because this subfile only supports inquiry processing, the letter O (output from the program to the screen) is specified in the Usage field (column 38) for all of the data items.

0019 The letter R in column 17, programmer-supplied name SM01SFR (columns 19-28), and supporting keywords define this entry as the subfile control record format.

The SFLCTL(SM01SFR) keyword defines the record format as the control record for the subfile record SM01SFR specified on line 12.

0020 The SFLSIZ(10) keyword defines the size of the subfile. For this example, the file will store a maximum of 10 records. Note that subfiles may be defined to store 9,999 records.

0021 The SFLPAG(8) keyword determines how many subfile records are to be displayed at one time on the screen. This value specified does not include the constants or variables that may be described in the subfile control record.

0022 The SFLCLR keyword clears the subfile before it is loaded. Indicator 80 is turned on in the RPG program and the clearing function is performed when the control record is executed by an EXFMT SM01CTL instruction.

0023 The SFLDSP keyword displays the subfile record values when indicator 81 is set on in the RPG program. The number of records displayed on the screen is determined by the SFLPAG keyword.

0024 SFLDSPCTL displays any constants and variable included in the subfile control record (SM01CTL) when indicator 81 is set on in the RPG program.

0025 SFLEND controls the display of a + (plus sign) to the right of the last subfile record displayed on the screen. The + sign indicates that more records are included on the following page. When there are no more records in the subfile, the + sign does not display. This keyword is executed when indicator 81 is set on in the RPG program.

0026 The OVERLAY keyword controls the overlaying of the control record format (SM01CTL) over the record CMDLINE constants included in lines 34-35 when they are displayed on the screen. Without this keyword, the constants included on the comamnd line (CMDLINE) would be written over (not displayed) when the EXFMT SM01CTL statement is executed.

0027-
0032 The constants included in these statements are displayed when an EXFMT SM01CTL statement that controls the display of the subfile control record is executed.

0033 - Display of the constants included in the CMDLINE record format are controlled by a WRITE CMDLINE statement in the RPG program. Note that this record format is displayed before the subfile control record is displayed by the EXFMT SM01CTL instruction.

0034 - Indicator 70, set on in the RPG program by a READ statement when no records are stored in the physical file, conditions the constant NO RECORDS IN PHYSICAL FILE. Display of this constant is controlled by the WRITE CMDLINE statement in the RPG program. If 70 is on, the error message will display, otherwise, it will not.

0035 - The constant PRESS ENTER TO RETURN display is controlled by the WRITE CMDLINE statement in the RPG program. It will always appear at the bottom of the current screen.

(*Continued*)

Notice the following two important coding features in the syntax of the subfile:

1. The keyword OVERLAY is included in the subfile control record format so that the subfile's variables and constants will not erase the message lines (CMDLINE format) after they are displayed. In the RPG program, the message line(s) is/are displayed by a WRITE statement before the subfile control record format (SM01CTL) is executed by an EXFMT operation. Because processing is so fast, the sequence of the record displays will not be seen by the operator. All the variables in the subfile

record (one page) and constants in the subfile control record and command line appear to display simultaneously.

2. A separate record format (CMDLINE) must be included for the command line constants (error and action messages) and is displayed before the other subfile record formats.

The relationship of the subfile record, control record, and command line record formats are illustrated in Figure 24-8. The subfile control record (SM01CTL) includes the constants (two heading lines) and control keywords; the subfile record (SM01SFR) defines variable fields and stores the data; and the command record (CMDLINE) file defines the message lines. All these subfile components are displayed simultaneously in the RPG program by either a WRITE or EXFMT operation.

```
... ... 1 ... ... 2 ... ... 3 ... ... 4 ... ... 5 ... ... 6 ... ... 7 ...
A                                           PRINT
A                                           REF(P1PF1)
A* PROMPT SCREEN..........
A          R PROMPT
A                                           CA01(01 'END OF JOB')
A                                       1 34'CUSTOMER FILE INQUIRY'
A                                       3 10'ENTER CUSTOMER NUMBER:'
A            CUSTNO         5   I   3 33
A                                       6 18'CK1 - END-OF-JOB'
A                                       6 38'ENTER TO DISPLAY'
A* SUBFILE DEFINITION.....
A          R SMO1SFR                        SFL
A            CUST#     R        O   6  5
A            NAME      R        O   6 13
A            CITY      R        O   6 36
A            STATE     R        O   6 59
A            BALANC    R        O   6 67
A* CONTROL RECORD.........
A          R SMO1CTL                        SFLCTL(SMO1SFR)
A                                           SFLSIZ(10)
A                                           SFLPAG(8)
A  80                                       SFLCLR
A  81                                       SFLDSP
A  81                                       SFLDSPCTL
A  81                                       SFLEND
A                                           OVERLAY
A                                       1 30'CUSTOMER FILE INQUIRY'
A                                       4  4'CUSTNO'
A                                       4 20'NAME'
A                                       4 43'CITY'
A                                       4 57'STATE'
A                                       4 68'BALANCE'
A          R CMDLINE
A  70                                  20 30'NO RECORDS IN PHYSICAL FILE'
A                                      23 10'PRESS ENTER TO RETURN'
```

```
                         CUSTOMER FILE INQUIRY

CUSTNO        NAME                  CITY            STATE     BALANCE

 12345   KAREL APPEL           NEW YORK              NY     00125000
 23456   GEORGES BRAQUE        TRENTON               NJ     00010000
 34567   PAUL CEZANNE          STAMFORD              CT     08190000
 45678   MARC CHAGALL          BRIDGEPORT            CT     00092600
 56789   EDGAR DEGAS           WESTPORT              PA     00784599
 67890   MAX ERNST             FRANKFORT             KY     00050000
 78900   BUCKMINSTER FULLER    NEW YORK              NY     03300010
 89000   JULIO GONZALEZ        GREENWICH             CT     00065478    +

               PRESS ENTER TO RETURN
```

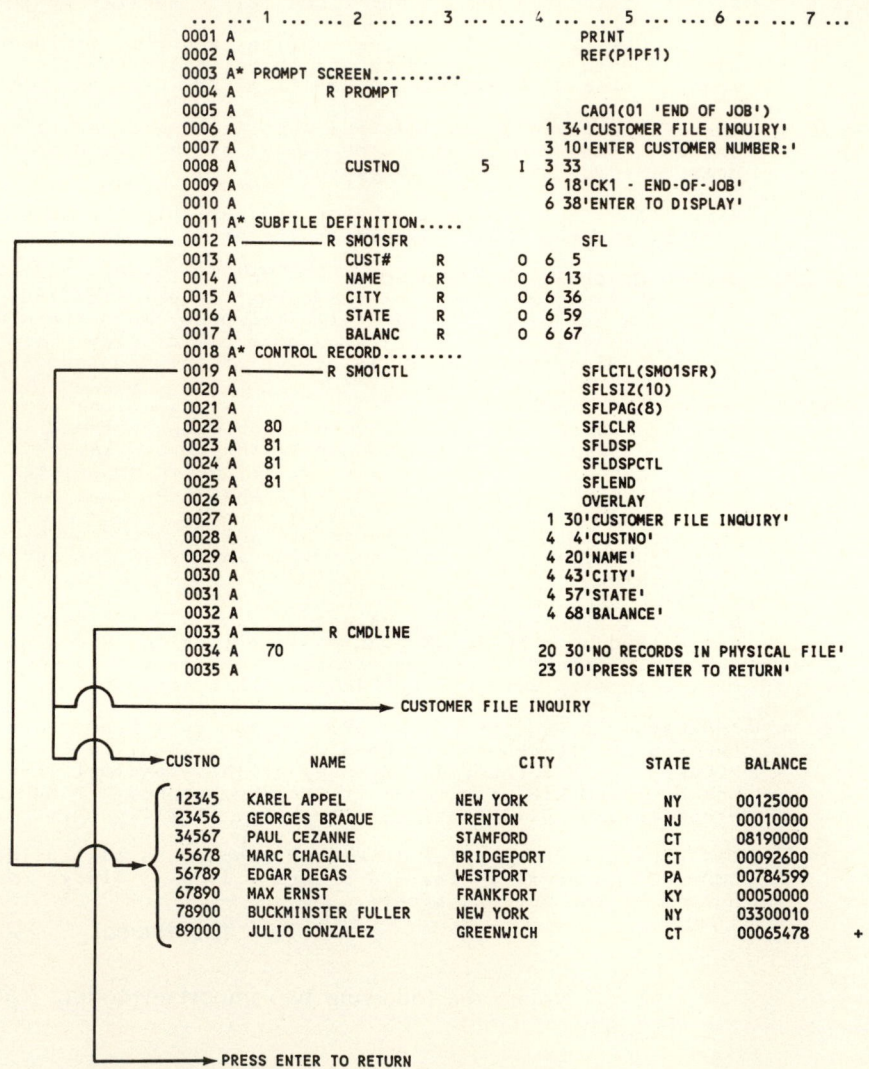

Figure 24-8 Relationship of subfile coding to subfile display.

Subfile RPG Source Coding—Subfile Inquiry Program

A line-by-line explanation of the function of each instruction supplements the RPG source listing in Figure 24-9.

```
... ... 1 ... ... 2 ... ... 3 ... ... 4 ... ... 5 ... ... 6 ... ... 7 ...
0001  * CUSTOMER MASTER INQUIRY WITH A SUBFILE.....                     CH24P1
0002 H                                                                  CH24P1
0003 FSFINQ   CF  E                    WORKSTN                          CH24P1
0004 F                                        SFRRN1KSFILE SM01SFR      CH24P1
0005 FP1PF1   IF  E           K        DISK                             CH24P1
0006 C                     EXFMTPROMPT                     DSP PROMPT SCRNCH25P1
0007 C           *IN01     DOWEQ'0'                        EOJ CONTROL    CH24P1
0008 C                     MOVE '1'       *IN80            SF CLEAR CNTRL CH24P1
0009 C                     WRITESM01CTL                    XEQ SF CLEAR   CH24P1
0010 C                     MOVE '0'       *IN80            TURN OFF IND.  CH24P1
0011 C                     Z-ADD0         SFRRN1  40       INIT RCRD CTR  CH24P1
0012 C                     SETOF                       707181TURN OFF INDTRSCH25P1
0013 C           CUSTNO    SETLLP1PF1                      SET PF POINTER CH24P1
0014 C                     READ P1PF1                    70 READ A PF RCRDCH25P1
0015 C           *IN70     IFEQ '0'                        NO RECORDS TESTCH25P1
0016  *                                                                 CH24P1
0017  * IF ONE OR MORE RECORDS ARE STORED IN THE PHYSICAL FILE, LOAD THE  CH24P1
0018  * SUBFILE UNTIL END OF PHYSICAL FILE OR SUBFILE IS FULL....         CH24P1
0019  *                                                                 CH24P1
0020 C           *IN71     DOWEQ'0'                        CONTROLS LOAD  CH24P1
0021 C                     ADD  1         SFRRN1           INCREMENT RRN  CH24P1
0022 C                     WRITESM01SFR                  71 LOAD RCD TO SFCH25P1
0023 C  N71                READ P1PF1                    71 READ ANOTHER  CH24P1
0024 C                     END                             END LINE 20 DOWCH25P1
0025 C                     END                             END LINE 15 IF CH24P1
0026  *                                                                 CH24P1
0027  * DISPLAY SUBFILE ON SCREEN OR MSG IF NO RECORDS IN PHYSICAL FILE   CH24P1
0028  *                                                                 CH24P1
0029 C                     WRITECMDLINE                    DSP CMD LINES  CH24P1
0030 C                     MOVE '1'       *IN81            SF DSP INDICTR CH24P1
0031 C                     EXFMTSM01CTL                    DSP SUBFILE    CH24P1
0032 C                     MOVE '0'       *IN81            TURN OFF 81    CH24P1
0033 C                     EXFMTPROMPT                     DSP PROMPT SCRNCH25P1
0034 C                     END                             END LINE 7 DOW CH24P1
0035 C                     SETON                     LR    EOJ CONTROL    CH24P1
```

Line

0003 The display file, which includes formats for the PROMPT screen, subfile record format, and subfile control record, is specified as a combined, full-procedural, externally defined workstation file.

0004 The K in column 53 indicates that this instruction is a continuation of the previous one.

The SFRRN1 entry in columns 47-52 specifies a field to which relative record numbers of records written to the subfile are stored and incremented.

The SFILE keyword in columns 54-59 specifies that this statement is related to a subfile.

The SM01SFR entry in columns 60-65 specifies the name if the subfile, included in the display file SFINQ, is processed by this program.

0005 - The physical file, P1PF1, is specified as an input, full-procedural, externally defined keyed disk file.

0006 - EXFMT statement displays the PROMPT screen record for entry of a customer number or end-of-job control.

0007 - If command key 1 (EOJ control) is not pressed as a response to the PROMPT screen (indicator 01 not turned on), the DOWEQ statement will control execution of statements 0007 through 0034. Additional inquiries may be made to the physical file until the operator presses command key 1 to end the job.

0008 - Indicator 80, specified with the SFLCLR keyword in the subfile control record format, is turned on so that the subfile may be cleared when the statement on line 0009 is executed.

0009 - The subfile's control record, SM01CTL, is written to clear the subfile.

0010 - Indicator 80, which controlled clearing of the subfile, is turned off.

Figure 24-9 Detailed source listing of an RPG program that processes a subfile for the inquiry of a physical file.

0011 - The relative record number counter, specified with the file description coding for the display file on line 0004, is defined and initialized to zero.

0012 - A housekeeping instruction that turns off the control indicators.

0013 - The SETLL positions the file pointer at the customer number value entered via the PROMPT screen. If the customer number is not found in the physical file, the pointer is positioned at the next highest key value.

0014 - The READ statement reads the first record from the physical file, P1PF1. Indicator 70 will be turned on if no records are stored in the disk file.

0015 - The IFEQ statement tests the status of the 70 indicator which was specified with the READ statement on line 0014. If the indicator is "on", program control will branch over the following DOWEQ group and displays the subfile (lines 0029 and 0030) with an error message that indicates that the FILE CONTAINS NO RECORDS.

0020 - Within the DOWEQ group, indicator 71 is turned on if the subfile is full or if the physical file is at end. This iterative process, which controls loading of the subfile, continues until indicator 71 is turned "on" by one of the described conditions.

0021 - The relative record number counter, SFRRN1, specified in the File Description statements for the subfile (line 0004), is incremented by 1 when a physical file record is loaded to the subfile. When this counter is greater than the number of records specified in the SFLSIZ keyword in DDS coding for the subfile, loading of the subfile will stop and subsequent statements executed.

0022 - The WRITE statement writes a record to the subfile in the relative record position as determined by the value in SFRNN1. If the value in SFRNN1 is 1, the current record is written to the first record position in the subfile. When the value in SFRNN1 is 2, the record is written to the second record position in the subfile; and so forth. Indicator 71, specified in columns 58-59, will turn on when the subfile is full.

0023 - If indicator 71 was not turned in the previous instruction, this READ statement, which is included within the DOWEQ group, reads records from the physical file until the subfile is full (previous statement) or the physical file is at "end". Indicator 71, specified in columns 58-59, will turn on when the physical file is at end.

0024 - A required END statement indicates the end of the DOWEQ instruction on line 0020.

0025 - A required END statement indicates the end of the IFEQ instruction on line 0015.

0029 - The WRITE CMDLINE instruction displays the constants included in the display file's record format CMDLINE. Note that the error message NO RECORD IN PHYSICAL FILE included in this format will only display if indicator 70 is on.

0030 - Indicator 81, which conditions the SFLDSP, SFLDSPCTL, and SFLEND keywords in the subfile's DDS coding, is turned on. When the EXFMT statement in line 30 is executed, indicator 81 controls display of the subfile control record format entries, subfile record field values, and the continuation symbol.

0031 - The EXFMT statement here displays the subfile records and the constants and variable in the subfile's control record format. If indicator 81 was not previously turned on (line 0029) nothing would display. The comments for the line 0029 statement explained how the 81 indicator controls the keywords related to the display of the subfile record and control record formats.

0032 - Indicator 81 which controlled display of the subfile, is turned off.

0033 - The PROMPT screen is displayed again so that the operator may continue processing of the physical file with another inquiry or end the job.

0034 - This required END statement is related to the DOWEQ statement on line 0007.

0035 - The SETON operation turns on indicator LR which ends the job and returns control back to the operating system.

(Continued)

The processing logic of the RPG program that executes a subfile for inquiry of a physical file is detailed in the flowchart shown in Figure 24-10.

An examination of the source listing in Figure 24-9 and the related line-by-line explanation shows that previously discussed RPG III/400 syntax unique to

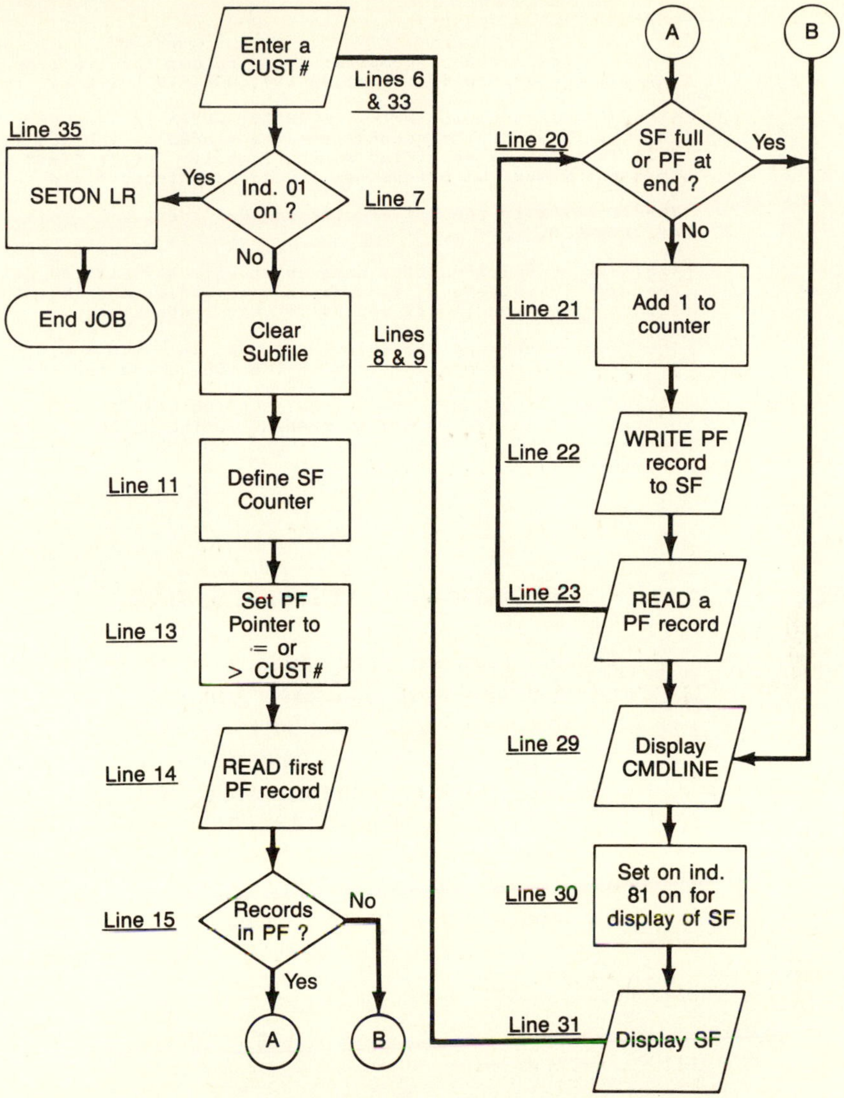

Figure 24-10 Processing logic flowchart for subfile inquiry program.

interactive processing has been included. Other than the WRITE and EXFMT statements that control the display of the subfile components, the only unfamiliar coding is included in a *continuation line* for the File Description entries for the WORKSTN file. An explanation of this instruction segment is presented in Figure 24-11.

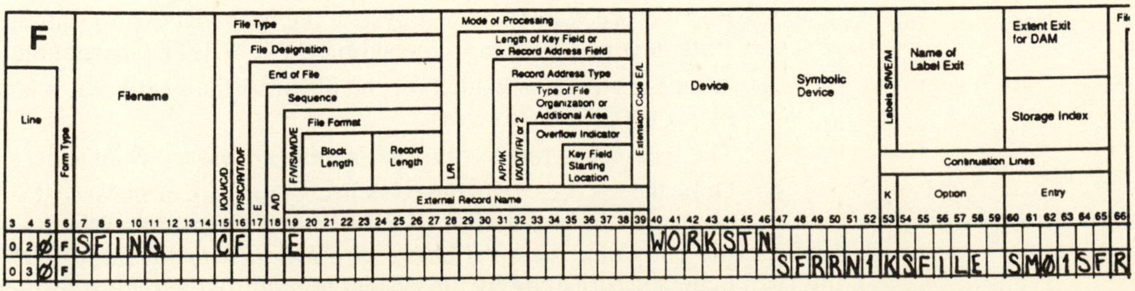

Figure 24-11 File Description entries that define a WORKSTN (display) file that includes a subfile.

Line

020 SFINQ is defined as a combined (C in column 15), full-procedural (F in column 16), externally defined (E in column 19), WORKSTN (display) file.

030 A programmer-supplied entry (SFRRN1), which is used as a record counter to indicate in what location the record is to be stored in the subfile and "flags" when the subfile is full, is specified in the Symbolic Device field (columns 47-52). Note that this entry must be defined as a numeric integer field in the RPG program.

The letter K in the K field (column 53) identifies this instruction as a continuation of line 020.

The keyword SFILE must be entered in Option field (columns 54-59) to specify that the WORKSTN (display) file includes a subfile and that the entries in this instruction are related to its definition and processing.

The programmer-supplied entry, SM01SFR, in columns 60-66, is the name of the subfile record format defined in the DDS coding for the subfile.

NOTE: THE FIELD NAMES ON THE CONTINUATION LINE (i.e. Symbolic Device, Labels, Option, and so forth) HAVE NO DIRECT MEANING TO THE DEFINITION OF A SUBFILE. THE LOCATION OF THE ENTRIES DETERMINES THEIR FUNCTION AND IS INTERPRETED BY THE RPG COMPILER ACCORDINGLY.

(*Continued*)

SUBFILE APPLICATION PROGRAM—UPDATE PROCESSING

Instead of accessing and updating one physical file record at a time, subfiles may be effectively used to access a group of records for selective changes. The processing is similar to functions supported by some third-party utilities, such as REVUE, except that it is controlled by a user RPG program. Perhaps more important, however, is that the displayed records are in a format specifically designed for and familiar to the end user, who is not typically a programmer.

The system flowchart illustrated in Figure 24-12 details the processing sequence controlled by an RPG program that updates a physical file via a subfile. An explanation of the processing steps are detailed in the following paragraphs:

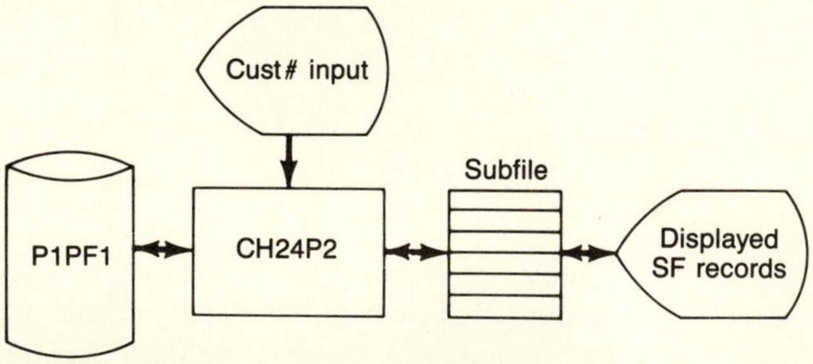

Figure 24-12 System flowchart for an RPG program that updates a physical file with subfile control.

1. Records are read from the physical file in the RPG program by a READ statement and written to the subfile by a WRITE instruction.
2. After the subfile is loaded (or the physical file is at end), it is displayed by an EXFMT instruction.
3. The user scans the records and makes necessary changes.
4. Only the records that have been changed are processed by the RPG program with a READC (Read Change) operation. When any byte in the body of a record is changed, a *Modified Data Tag* (*MDT*) is automatically turned on by the system to identify the record for update processing. Therefore, if only one record is changed in the subfile, that record is processed in the update of the physical file and not every record

in the subfile. This feature saves both input and output resources and processing time.

5. The SCUST# field from each record read by the READC instruction is used to CHAIN to the physical file and locate the address of the record before it is updated by an UPDAT operation.

DDS Coding—Subfile Update Program

Modifications to the DDS coding for the subfile inquiry application to support update processing are identified in Figure 24-13 and explained in the following paragraphs.

Instead of specifying the physical file's field names that were used in the inquiry program, new fields have been defined in the subfile's record format. This is a necessary change because once the physical file's records are accessed and loaded to the subfile their storage addresses have been lost and the records must be randomly accessed again before updating.

If the same field names were used in both the physical file and subfile definitions, the second access of the physical file's records would replace any changed subfile values and the physical file's records would be updated with their original field values.

Consequently, it is necessary to move the physical file's field values to the subfile fields before loading the subfile and, then, after modifying records in the subfile, move the subfile field values to their related physical file fields before updating the physical file.

Another change needed in the DDS coding to support update processing is in the Usage (column 38) field for the subfile record data items in which B (both input and output) is specified instead of O (output only). This entry controls both the output of field values from the program to the screen and input from the screen to the program.

The last change in the DDS coding replaces the constants on lines 0006 and 0026 from CUSTOMER FILE INQUIRY to CUSTOMER FILE UPDATE.

```
... ... 1 ... ... 2 ... ... 3 ... ... 4 ... ... 5 ... ... 6 ... ... 7 ...
0001 A                                      PRINT
0002 A                                      REF(P1PF1)
0003 A* PROMPT SCREEN..........
0004 A          R PROMPT
0005 A                                      CA01(01 'END OF JOB')
0006 A                                  1 34'CUSTOMER FILE UPDATE'
0007 A                                  3 10'ENTER CUSTOMER NUMBER:'
0008 A            CUSTNO         5   I  3 33
0009 A                                  6 18'CK1 - END-OF-JOB'
0010 A                                  6 38'ENTER TO DISPLAY'
0011 A* SUBFILE DEFINITION.....
0012 A          R SM02SFR                   SFL
0013 A            SCUST#    R        B  6  5REFFLD(CUST#) DSPATR(PR)
0014 A            SNAME     R        B  6 13REFFLD(NAME) DSPATR(PC)
0015 A            SCITY     R        B  6 36REFFLD(CITY)
0016 A            SSTATE    R        B  6 59REFFLD(STATE)
0017 A            SBALAN    R        B  6 67REFFLD(BALANC)
0018 A* CONTROL RECORD.........
0019 A          R SM02CTL                   SFLCTL(SM02SFR)
0020 A                                      OVERLAY
0021 A                                      SFLSIZ(10)
0022 A                                      SFLPAG(8)
0023 A  80                                  SFLCLR
0024 A  81                                  SFLDSP
0025 A  81                                  SFLDSPCTL
0026 A  81                                  SFLEND
0027 A                                  1 30'CUSTOMER FILE UPDATE'
0028 A                                  4  4'CUSTNO'
0029 A                                  4 20'NAME'
0030 A                                  4 43'CITY'
0031 A                                  4 57'STATE'
0032 A                                  4 68'BALANCE'
0033 A          R CMDLINE
0034 A  70                             20 30'NO RECORDS IN PHYSICAL FILE'
0035 A                                 23 10'PRESS ENTER TO RETURN'
```

Field names unique to the subfile are specified. Physical file is referenced for the attributes.

To support update processing, Usage field entry is changed from O to B.

Constants changed from CUSTOMER FILE INQUIRY to CUSTOMER FILE UPDATE

Figure 24-13 DDS subfile coding to support the update processing of a physical file.

RPG Source Coding—Subfile Update Program

An examination of the RPG program in Figure 24-14 indicates that coding for the update processing of a physical file via subfile control is similar to the previously discussed inquiry application. Any changes and additions to convert the inquiry program to support update processing are identified in comments included in the right-hand margin.

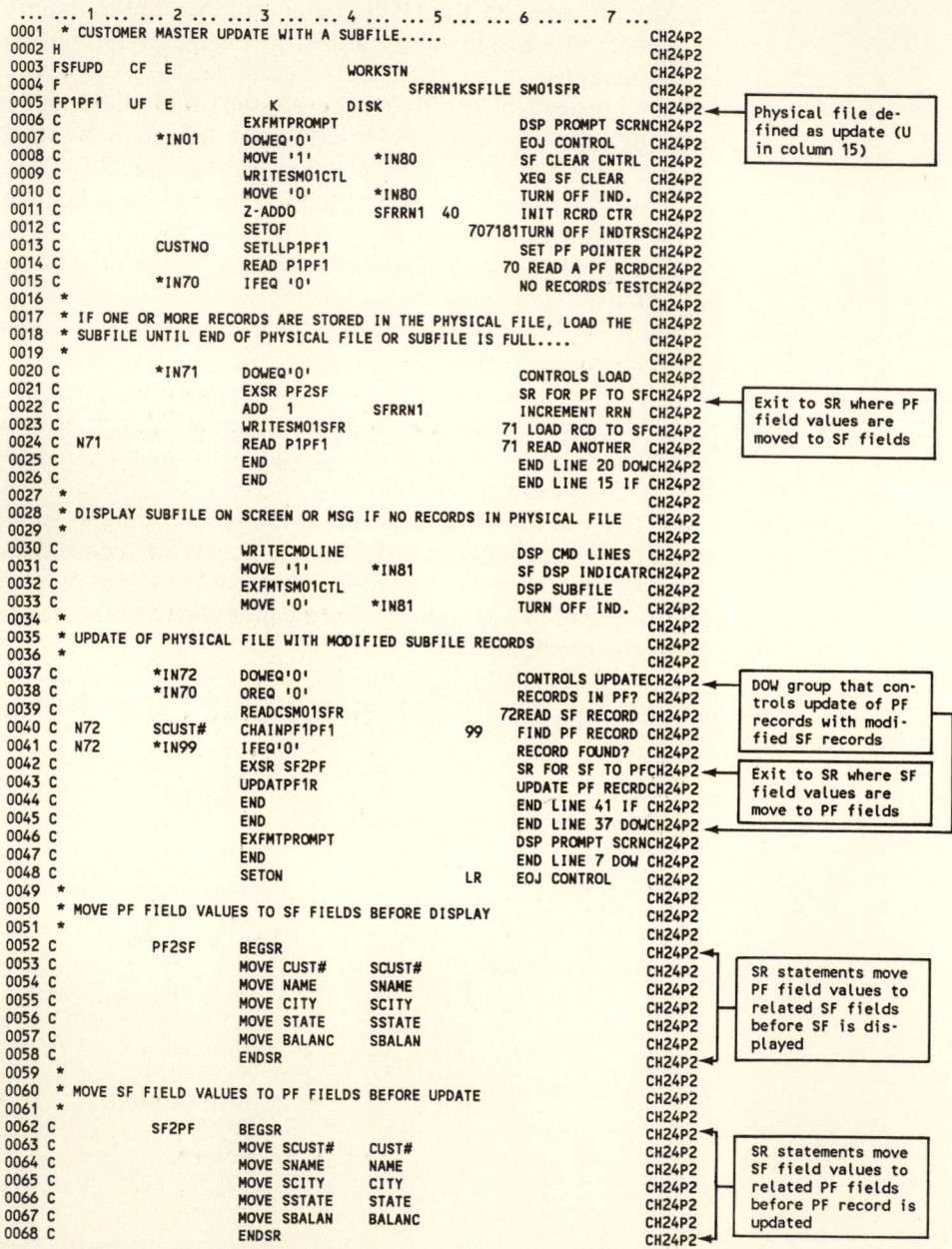

```
 ... ... 1 ... ... 2 ... ... 3 ... ... 4 ... ... 5 ... ... 6 ... ... 7 ...
0001  * CUSTOMER MASTER UPDATE WITH A SUBFILE.....                      CH24P2
0002 H                                                                  CH24P2
0003 FSFUPD   CF  E                    WORKSTN                          CH24P2
0004 F                                        SFRRN1KSFILE SM01SFR      CH24P2
0005 FP1PF1   UF  E           K        DISK                             CH24P2
0006 C                     EXFMTPROMPT                  DSP PROMPT SCRNCH24P2
0007 C           *IN01     DOWEQ'0'                     EOJ CONTROL    CH24P2
0008 C                     MOVE '1'       *IN80         SF CLEAR CNTRL CH24P2
0009 C                     WRITESM01CTL                 XEQ SF CLEAR   CH24P2
0010 C                     MOVE '0'       *IN80         TURN OFF IND.  CH24P2
0011 C                     Z-ADD0         SFRRN1  40    INIT RCRD CTR  CH24P2
0012 C                     SETOF                    707181TURN OFF INDTRSCH24P2
0013 C           CUSTNO    SETLLP1PF1                   SET PF POINTER CH24P2
0014 C                     READ P1PF1                 70 READ A PF RCRDCH24P2
0015 C           *IN70     IFEQ '0'                     NO RECORDS TESTCH24P2
0016  *                                                                 CH24P2
0017  * IF ONE OR MORE RECORDS ARE STORED IN THE PHYSICAL FILE, LOAD THE  CH24P2
0018  * SUBFILE UNTIL END OF PHYSICAL FILE OR SUBFILE IS FULL....       CH24P2
0019  *                                                                 CH24P2
0020 C           *IN71     DOWEQ'0'                     CONTROLS LOAD  CH24P2
0021 C                     EXSR PF2SF                   SR FOR PF TO SFCH24P2
0022 C                     ADD  1         SFRRN1        INCREMENT RRN  CH24P2
0023 C                     WRITESM01SFR               71 LOAD RCD TO SFCH24P2
0024 C  N71                READ P1PF1                 71 READ ANOTHER  CH24P2
0025 C                     END                          END LINE 20 DOWCH24P2
0026 C                     END                          END LINE 15 IF CH24P2
0027  *                                                                 CH24P2
0028  * DISPLAY SUBFILE ON SCREEN OR MSG IF NO RECORDS IN PHYSICAL FILE   CH24P2
0029  *                                                                 CH24P2
0030 C                     WRITECMDLINE                 DSP CMD LINES  CH24P2
0031 C                     MOVE '1'       *IN81         SF DSP INDICATRCH24P2
0032 C                     EXFMTSM01CTL                 DSP SUBFILE    CH24P2
0033 C                     MOVE '0'       *IN81         TURN OFF IND.  CH24P2
0034  *                                                                 CH24P2
0035  * UPDATE OF PHYSICAL FILE WITH MODIFIED SUBFILE RECORDS           CH24P2
0036  *                                                                 CH24P2
0037 C           *IN72     DOWEQ'0'                     CONTROLS UPDATECH24P2
0038 C           *IN70     OREQ '0'                     RECORDS IN PF? CH24P2
0039 C                     READCSM01SFR               72READ SF RECORD CH24P2
0040 C  N72      SCUST#    CHAINPF1PF1              99  FIND PF RECORD CH24P2
0041 C  N72      *IN99     IFEQ'0'                      RECORD FOUND?  CH24P2
0042 C                     EXSR SF2PF                   SR FOR SF TO PFCH24P2
0043 C                     UPDATPF1R                    UPDATE PF RECRDCH24P2
0044 C                     END                          END LINE 41 IF CH24P2
0045 C                     END                          END LINE 37 DOWCH24P2
0046 C                     EXFMTPROMPT                  DSP PROMPT SCRNCH24P2
0047 C                     END                          END LINE 7 DOW CH24P2
0048 C                     SETON                    LR  EOJ CONTROL    CH24P2
0049  *                                                                 CH24P2
0050  * MOVE PF FIELD VALUES TO SF FIELDS BEFORE DISPLAY                CH24P2
0051  *                                                                 CH24P2
0052 C           PF2SF     BEGSR                                        CH24P2
0053 C                     MOVE CUST#     SCUST#                        CH24P2
0054 C                     MOVE NAME      SNAME                         CH24P2
0055 C                     MOVE CITY      SCITY                         CH24P2
0056 C                     MOVE STATE     SSTATE                        CH24P2
0057 C                     MOVE BALANC    SBALAN                        CH24P2
0058 C                     ENDSR                                        CH24P2
0059  *                                                                 CH24P2
0060  * MOVE SF FIELD VALUES TO PF FIELDS BEFORE UPDATE                 CH24P2
0061  *                                                                 CH24P2
0062 C           SF2PF     BEGSR                                        CH24P2
0063 C                     MOVE SCUST#    CUST#                         CH24P2
0064 C                     MOVE SNAME     NAME                          CH24P2
0065 C                     MOVE SCITY     CITY                          CH24P2
0066 C                     MOVE SSTATE    STATE                         CH24P2
0067 C                     MOVE SBALAN    BALANC                        CH24P2
0068 C                     ENDSR                                        CH24P2
```

Physical file defined as update (U in column 15)

Exit to SR where PF field values are moved to SF fields

DOW group that controls update of PF records with modified SF records

Exit to SR where SF field values are move to PF fields

SR statements move PF field values to related SF fields before SF is displayed

SR statements move SF field values to related PF fields before PF record is updated

Figure 24-14 Source listing of an RPG program that processes a subfile for the update of a physical file.

The instructions (lines 0037–0045) that control the update processing of the physical file are detailed separately in Figure 24-15.

```
0035  * UPDATE OF PHYSICAL FILE WITH MODIFIED SUBFILE RECORDS           CH24P2
0036  *                                                                 CH24P2
0037 C           *IN72     DOWEQ'0'                       CONTROLS UPDATECH24P2
0038 C           *IN70     OREQ '0'                       RECORDS IN PF? CH24P2
0039 C                     READCSM01SFR                  72READ SF RECORD CH24P2
0040 C  N72      SCUST#    CHAINPF1PF1             99     FIND PF RECORD CH24P2
0041 C  N72      *IN99     IFEQ'0'                        RECORD FOUND?  CH24P2
0042 C                     EXSR SF2PF                     SR FOR SF TO PFCH24P2
0043 C                     UPDATPF1R                      UPDATE PF RECRDCH24P2
0044 C                     END                            END LINE 41 IF CH24P2
0045 C                     END                            END LINE 37 DOWCH24P2
```

Line

0037
0038 - The DOWEQ group is performed while there are changed records in the subfile (indicator 72 off - assigned to the READC instruction on line 0039).

In addition, OR statement on line 0028 prevents the DOWEQ group from being executed if the READ statement on line 14 determines that no records are stored in the physical file (indicator 70 turned on for end-of-file condition).

0039 The READC operation reads only the subfile records that have been *changed*. When processing determines that there are no more changed records in the subfile, indicator 72, specified in the Equal field (columns 58-59), will automatically be turned on. Note that any subfile records not changed are not processed by the READC operation.

0040 The customer number value of a changed subfile record is used to CHAIN to the physical file record so that the related record address is found before it is updated. Processing of the subfile automatically begins at the first changed record.

0041 This IFEQ statement test is included to determine if the CHAIN on line 0040 was successful (indicator 99 off and the related physical file record found).

0042 When the IFEQ test on line 0041 is true, the subroutine which moves the subfile field values to their related physical file fields is executed.

0043 The UPDAT statement updates the current physical file record with the related and changed subfile record.

0044 This END operation determines the end of the IFEQ statement on line 0042.

0045 This END operation indicates the end of the DOWEQ statement on line 0037. Unlike the DOU operation, the relational test is made at the DOW statement and not at its related END operation.

Figure 24-15 DOWEQ group that controls the update of a physical file from changed subfile records.

READC (Read Next Modified Record)

The syntax of the READC (Read Next Modified Record) operation is explained in Figure 24-16.

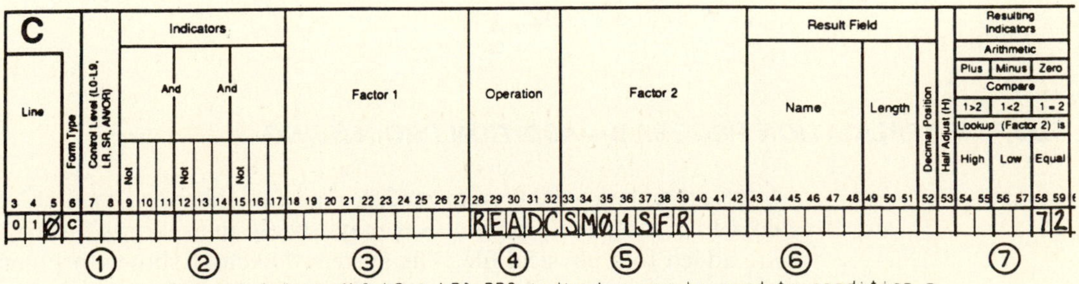

1. Any total time (L0-L9 & LR) RPG indicator may be used to condition a READC instruction.

2. Any detail time RPG indicator(s) any be used to condition a READC instruction.

3. Factor 1 must be blank (not used).

Figure 24-16 Syntax of the READC (Read Next Modified Record) operation.

```
4. READC operation name must be specified in the Operation field.

5. The subfile record format name that was specified in the Entry
   field (columns 60-65) of the continuation line for the File Des-
   cription definition of the WORKSTN file must be entered left-
   justified in Factor 2.

6. Result field must be blank (not used).

7. Resulting indicator > field (columns 54-55) must be blank (not used).

   An optional indicator may be entered in the resulting indicator <
   field (columns 56-57) to test for an error condition when the opera-
   tion is executed.

   A required indicator must be entered in the resulting indicator =
   field (columns 58-59) that is set on when there are no more changed
   records (end-of-file condition) in the subfile.
```

(Continued)

Results of the subfile update processing are shown in Figure 24-17. The top section shows that one subfile record has been changed; the bottom section is a redisplay of the same data after the physical file record is updated. Again, the only physical file record updated is the one changed in the subfile; the others are ignored by the READC instruction in the update process.

Subfile Records Changed Before Update Is Executed:

CUSTOMER FILE UPDATE

CUSTNO	NAME	CITY	STATE	BALANCE	
12345	KAREL APPEL	NEW YORK	NY	00125000	
23456	GEORGES BRAQUE	TRENTON	NJ	00020000	◄ Changed from 10000
34567	PAUL CEZANNE	STAMFORD	CT	08190000	to 20000
45678	MARC CHAGALL	BRIDGEPORT	CT	00092600	
56789	EDGAR DEGAS	WESTPORT	PA	00784599	
67890	MAX ERNST	FRANKFORT	KY	00069000	◄ Changed from 50000
78900	BUCKMINSTER FULLER	NEW YORK	NY	03300010	to 69000
89000	JULIO GONZALEZ	GREENWICH	CT	00065478	+

After Physical File Records Are Updated (Records Recalled from Physical File):

CUSTOMER FILE UPDATE

CUSTNO	NAME	CITY	STATE	BALANCE	
12345	KAREL APPEL	NEW YORK	NY	00125000	
23456	GEORGES BRAQUE	TRENTON	NJ	00020000	◄ Record changed
34567	PAUL CEZANNE	STAMFORD	CT	08190000	
45678	MARC CHAGALL	BRIDGEPORT	CT	00092600	
56789	EDGAR DEGAS	WESTPORT	PA	00784599	
67890	MAX ERNST	FRANKFORT	KY	00069000	◄ Record changed
78900	BUCKMINSTER FULLER	NEW YORK	NY	03300010	
89000	JULIO GONZALEZ	GREENWICH	CT	00065478	+

Figure 24-17 Before and after results of updating a physical file with a subfile.

SUBFILE APPLICATION PROGRAM—ADDITION PROCESSING

Interactive data validation procedures may be enhanced by first loading the input data to a subfile. Then, the user may review the records for errors before they are added to a physical file. The system flowchart shown in Figure 24-18 details the file processing associated with the addition of records to a physical file via a subfile. The sequence of processing steps shown in Figure 24-18 are controlled by the RPG program and include the following:

1. Records are input via a separate display file record format and loaded to the subfile.

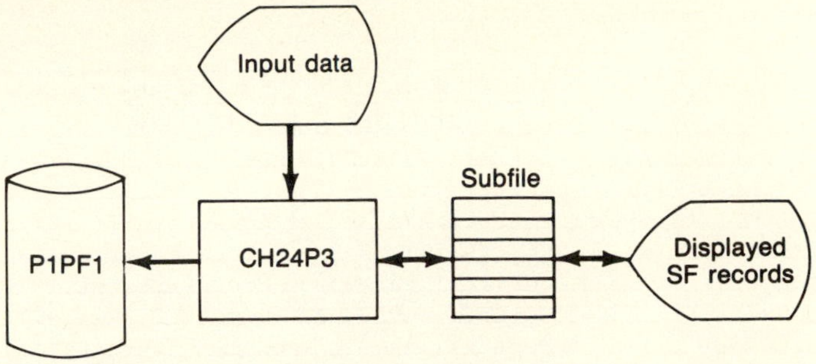

Figure 24-18 System flowchart for an RPG program that adds records to a physical file via a subfile.

2. The subfile is displayed and the records are reviewed by the user. Any necessary changes are made.
3. The subfile records are added to the physical file.

DDS Coding—Subfile Adds Program

Formats of the four records, SFADDR, SM03SFR, SM03CTL, and CMDLINE included in the display file SFLADD are shown in Figure 24-19. The constants defined on line 23 of the subfile are defined as the fourth record format in the display file.

A source listing and a line-by-line explanation of the DDS coding of the display file SFADD processed by the subfile addition program is detailed in Figure 24-20. Notice that three keywords not used in the previous subfile programs have been specified in this application. Included is the subfile record keyword,

SFADDR Record Format:

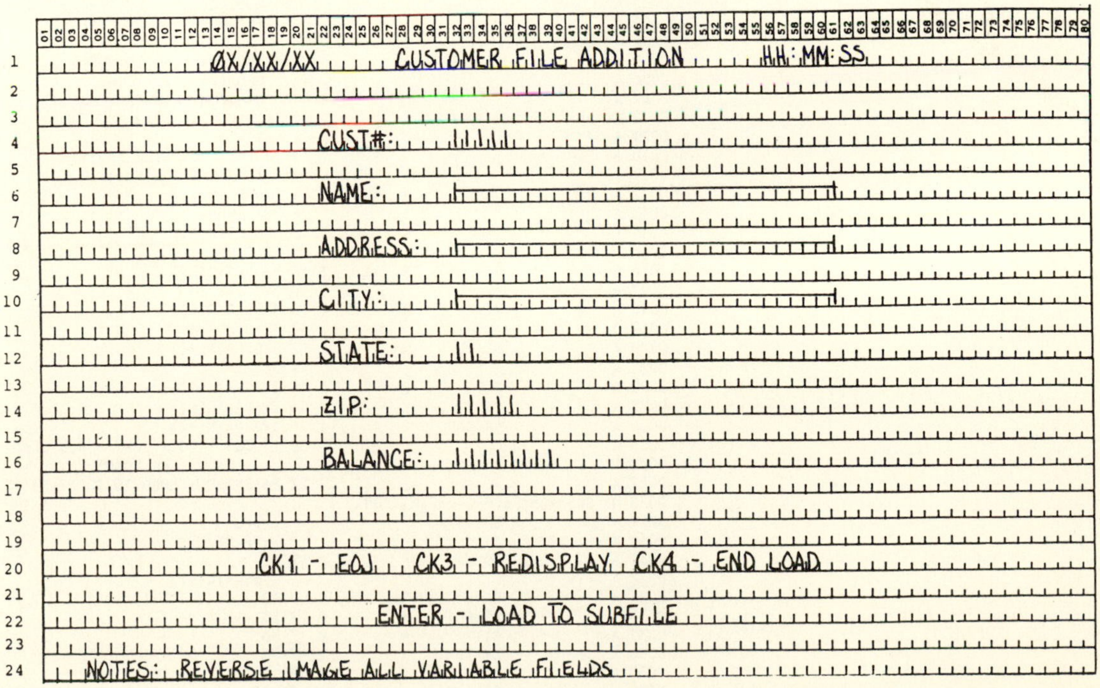

ØX/XX/XX CUSTOMER FILE ADDITION HH:MM:SS
CUST#:
NAME:
ADDRESS:
CITY:
STATE:
ZIP:
BALANCE:
CK1 - EOJ CK3 - REDISPLAY CK4 - END LOAD
ENTER - LOAD TO SUBFILE
NOTES: REVERSE IMAGE ALL VARIABLE FIELDS

Figure 24-19 Record formats defined in the display file SFLADD.

Subfile Record Formats:

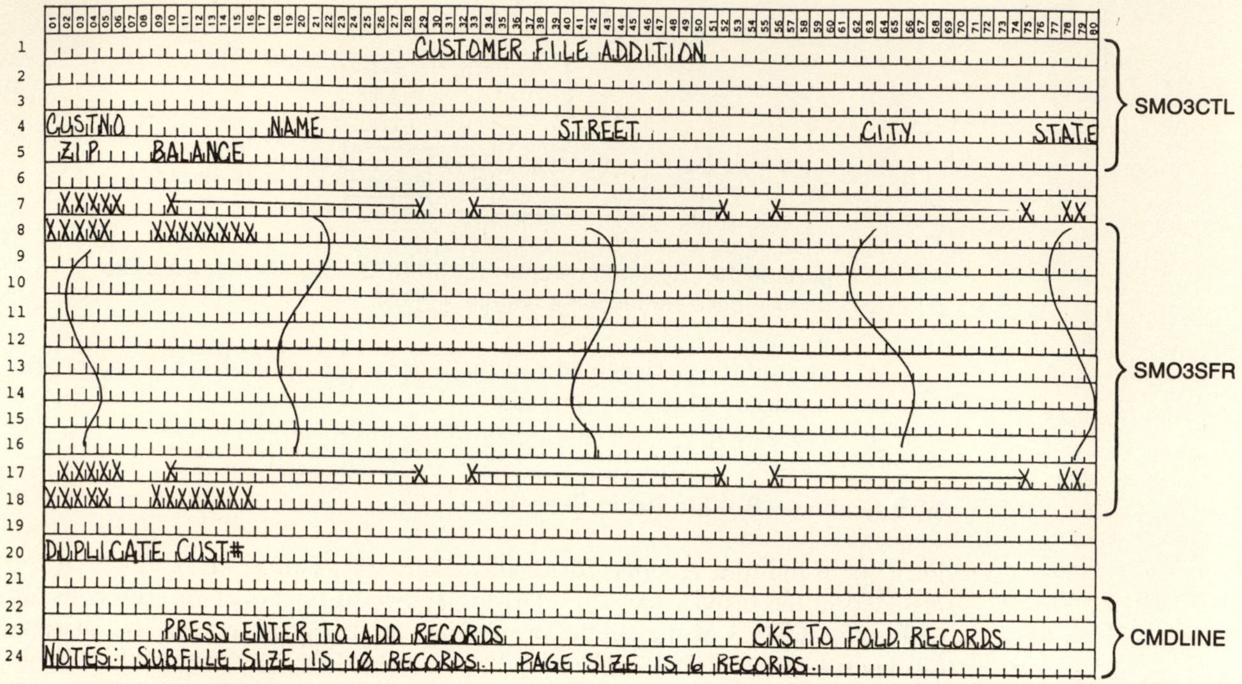

(Continued)

SFLNXTCHG and the subfile control record keywords SFLNRA and SFLINZ. The function of each is explained in the text that supplements Figure 24-20.

```
... ... 1 ... ... 2 ... ... 3 ... ... 4 ... ... 5 ... ... 6 ... ... 7 ...
A                                         PRINT
A                                         MSGLOC(20)
A                                         REF(P1PF1)
A* ENTRY SCREEN..........
A           R SFADDR                      CA01(01 'END OF JOB')
A                                         CF03(03 'REDISPLAY')
A                                         CA04(04 'END SF LOAD')
A                                     1 14DATE EDTCDE(Y)
A                                     1 56TIME
A                                     1 28'CUSTOMER FILE ADDITION'
A                                     4 22'CUST#:'
A             CUST#      R         I  4 32DSPATR(RI)
A                                     6 22'NAME:'
A             NAME       R         I  6 32DSPATR(RI)
A                                     8 22'STREET:'
A             STREET     R         I  8 32DSPATR(RI)
A                                    10 22'CITY:'
A             CITY       R         I 10 32DSPATR(RI)
A                                    12 22'STATE:'
A             STATE      R         I 12 32DSPATR(RI)
A                                    14 22'ZIP:'
A             ZIP        R         I 14 32DSPATR(RI)
A                                    16 22'BALANCE:'
A             BALANC     R         I 16 32DSPATR(RI)
A                                    20 17'CK1 - EOJ   CK3 - REDISPLAY-
A                                            CK4 - END LOAD'
A                                    22 26'ENTER - LOAD TO SUBFILE'
A* SUBFILE RECORD DEFINITION.....
A           R SMO3SFR                     SFL
A                                         SFLNXTCHG
A             CUST#      R         B  7  2
A   99                                    DSPATR(RI)
A             NAME       R         B  7 10
A             STREET     R         B  7 33
A             CITY       R         B  7 56
A             STATE      R         B  7 78
A             ZIP        R         B  8  1
A             BALANC     R         B  8  9
A* CONTROL RECORD DEFINITION......
```

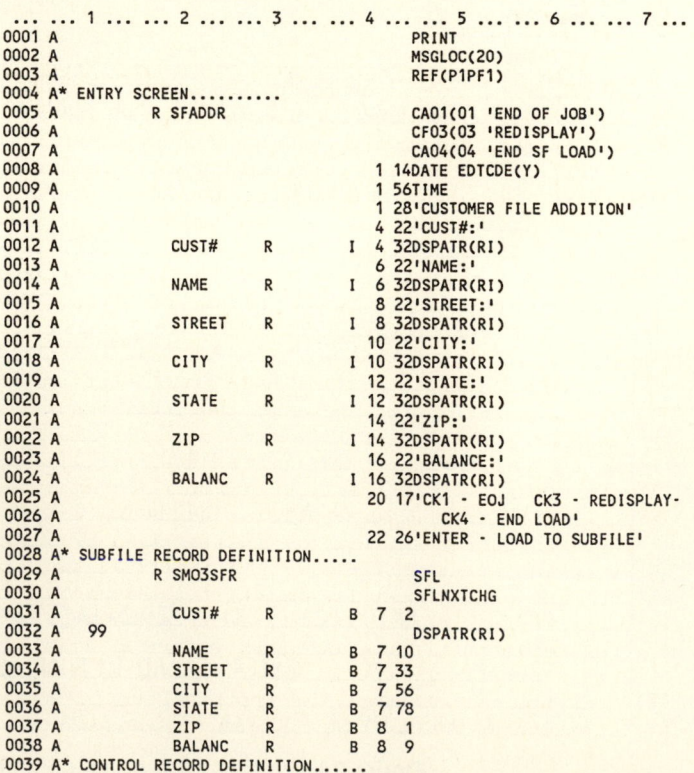

Figure 24-20 DDS coding for the display file that supports the subfile addition program.

```
0040 A          R SM03CTL                     SFLCTL(SM03SFR)
0041 A                                        OVERLAY
0042 A                                        SFLRNA
0043 A                                        SFLSIZ(10)
0044 A                                        SFLPAG(6)
0045 A    80                                  SFLCLR
0046 A    80                                  SFLINZ
0047 A    81                                  SFLDSP
0048 A    81                                  SFLDSPCTL
0049 A    81                                  SFLEND
0050 A                                        SFLDROP(CF05)
0051 A    99                                  SFLMSG('DUPLICATE CUST#' 99)
0052 A                                    1 29'CUSTOMER FILE ADDITION'
0053 A                                    4  1'CUSTNO'
0054 A                                    4 18'NAME'
0055 A                                    4 40'STREET'
0056 A                                    4 63'CITY'
0057 A                                    4 76'STATE'
0058 A                                    5  2'ZIP'
0059 A                                    5  9'BALANCE'
0060 A          R CMDLINE
0061 A                                   23 10'PRESS ENTER TO ADD RECORDS'
0062 A                                   23 55'CK5 TO FOLD RECORDS'
```

Line

0001 PRINT keyword supports printing of a screen image when the print key is pressed.

0002 MSGLOC(20) keyword specifies that SFLMSG text, DUPLICATE CUST#, (line 0051) is to display on line 20 instead of line 24, the default line for error messages.

0003 The field attributes of the physical file P1PF1 are referenced by the REF(P1PF1) keyword.

0005-
0007 The entry screen record, SFADDR, is defined with its related controlling command keys. CA01 controls end of job processing in the RPG program; CF03, redisplays this screen without adding the record to the subfile; and CA04, allows the operator to stop loading of the subfile.

0008
0027 - These instructions define the screen record that supports the entry of data and subsequent loading to the subfile.

0029 - Record, SM03SFR, is defined as a subfile record format by the SFL keyword.

0030 - Keyword, SFLNXTCHG, enables a READC instruction in an RPG program to identify all of the subfile records as changed.

0031 -
0038 Physical file fields are referenced in these instructions. Because the physical file was defined as supporting only UNIQUE keys, any attempt to add a record with a duplicate key will cause a WRITE error. Indicator 99, assigned to the WRITE instructions (columns 56-57) in the RPG program, identifies this error by turning on which is used here to highlight the CUST# value in the related subfile record.

0040 The SFLCTL(SM03SFR) keyword defines record format SM03CTL as the subfile control record related to the subfile record SM03SFR.

0041 OVERLAY prevents the previously displayed record format (CMDLINE) from being erased when this record format is output. Because the processing of the subfile control record, subfile record, and command record are so fast, it will appear as if they display simultaneously.

0042 Keyword SFLRNA allows the program to initialize the subfile with no active records. This keyword is used in conjunction with SFLINZ which actually performs the initialization function.

0043 SFLSIZ(10) specifies that the subfile is to store a maximum of 10 records. Note that a subfile may store 9,999 records.

0044 SFLPAG(6) specifies that 6 records are to be displayed on each page of the subfile.

0045 SFLCLR clears the subfile area before the subfile is created. This action is performed in the RPG program when indicator 80 is turned on and the subfile control record executed by a WRITE statement.

0046 SFLINZ performs the initialization of alphanumeric fields to blanks and numeric fields to zeros in all of the subfile's records with one operation when indicator 80 is turned on in the RPG program and the subfile control record is executed.

Because the READC operation (not READ) is used to read records from a subfile, the records must be changed to support this function. When the input records are added to a subfile initialized by a SFLINZ operation, they are flagged as changed and may then be processed by a READC instruction. For this program example, all of the subfile records are added to a physical file.

Without the SFLRNA/SFLINZ keywords, none of the subfile records would be identified as changed. Consequently, no records would be read by a READC operation and none added to the physical file.

(*Continued*)

0047 -
0049 Indicator 81, turned on in the RPG program, conditions the following subfile functions:

SFLDSP - Displays the subfile records.
SFLDSPCTL - Displays the constants and any variables specified in the subfile control record format.
SFLEND - Displays a + (plus sign) to the right of the last subfile record on the current page indicating that another page of records are stored in the subfile.

0050 The SFLDROP(CF05) keyword controls the folding of subfile control and record formats when the constants and/or variables require a display of more than 80 columns on a standard CRT. The command function or attention key specified with this keyword (CF05 for this example) must be pressed to cause the subfile records to change from a truncated to a folded format (continued on next line specified). Note that the constants in the control record format will automatically wrap to the line specified. However, a command key must be pressed to cause the subfile record's field values to continue on to another line.

Notice in the control record format, lines 0058 and 0059, that the constants ZIP and BALANCE are defined on line 5 immediately below the other constants on line 4.

Refer to the subfile record format, lines 0037 and 0038, and notice that the variables ZIP and BALANC are defined to display on line 8 below the other related field variables on line 7.

The line location in the subfile record identifies the location of the first record. Other records are sequentially displayed on subsequent lines of the page as defined by the SFLPAG keyword.

0051 SFLMSG performs the same function as a ERRMSG keyword. When the WRITE statement in the RPG program attempts to add a record that has a key value already stored in the physical file, indicator 99 specified in columns 56-57 of the WRITE statement will be turned on. Because this keyword is conditioned by the 99 indicator, the message DUPLICATE CUST# will be displayed on line 20 as specified by the MSGLOC(20) keyword. Indicator 99, which is included in the parentheses of the SFLMSG keyword, turns off the indicator when any key is subsequently pressed. Identical to the ERRMSG keyword, the default line for the message included with the SFLMSG keyword is line 24.

0052 -
0059 Column headings are defined in these instructions. When the subfile control record format is executed by an EXFMT instruction, the headings will be displayed in their specified locations.

0060 -
0062 - Record format CMDLINE includes constants that are displayed at the bottom of the subfile to inform the operator what actions to take to add the subfile records to the physical file or fold the truncated field values on to the next display line.

(Continued)

RPG Source Coding—Subfile Addition Program

A detailed source listing of the RPG program that controls addition to a physical file via a subfile is presented in Figure 24-21.

```
... ... 1 ... ... 2 ... ... 3 ... ... 4 ... ... 5 ... ... 6 ... ... 7 ...
 * CUSTOMER MASTER FILE ADDITION WITH SUBFILE CONTROL......         CH24P3
H                                                                   CH24P3
FSFADD   CF  E                    WORKSTN                           CH24P3
F                                      SFRRN1KSFILE SM03SFR         CH24P3
FP1PF1   O   E           K        DISK                      A       CH24P3
 *                                                                  CH24P3
 * LOAD SUBFILE WITH RECORDS ENTERED VIA ENTRY SCREEN......         CH24P3
 *                                                                  CH24P3
C           AGAIN     TAG                                           CH24P3
C           *IN71     DOUEQ'1'                        DOU SF IS FULL CH24P3
C           *IN04     OREQ '1'                        OR STOP BY OPERCH24P3
C                     EXSR HOUSEK                     HOUSEKEEPING SRCH24P3
C                     EXFMTSFADDR                     FILL-IN SCREEN CH24P3
C           *IN01     CABEQ'1'       EOJ              EOJ?           CH24P3
C           *IN03     CABEQ'1'       AGAIN            DO NOT ENTR RCDCH24P3
C           *IN04     IFEQ '0'                        LOAD SF?      FCH24P3
C                     ADD  1         SFRRN1           INCRMENT SF CTRCH24P3
C                     WRITESM03SFR                  71LOAD RCD TO SF CH24P3
C                     END                             END LINE 15 IF CH24P3
C                     END                             END LINE 10 DOUCH24P3
 *                                                                  CH24P3
 * DISPLAY SUBFILE & COMMAND RECORDS......                          CH24P3
 *                                                                  CH24P3
C                     WRITECMDLINE                    DISPLAY CMDLINECH24P3
C                     MOVE '1'       *IN81                          CH24P3
```

Figure 24-21 Source listing of an RPG program that processes a subfile for the addition of records to a physical file.

```
0026 C                 EXFMTSMO3CTL                        DISPLAY SF     CH24P3
0027 C                 MOVE '0'      *IN81                                CH24P3
0028  *                                                                   CH24P3
0029  * ADD SUBFILE RECORDS TO PHYSICAL FILE......                        CH24P3
0030  *                                                                   CH24P3
0031 C                 Z-ADD1        SFRRN1                INIT. SF CTR   CH24P3
0032 C                 READCSMO3SFR                      72READ 1ST SF RCDCH24P3
0033 C         *IN72   DOWEQ'0'                            DOW NOT END SF CH24P3
0034 C                 WRITEP1PF1R                     99  ADD RCD TO PF  CH24P3
0035 C                 ADD  1        SFRRN1                INCRMENT SF CTRCH24P3
0036 C                 READCSMO3SFR                      72 READ A SF RCD CH24P3
0037 C                 END                                 END LINE 31 DOWCH24P3
0038 C                 EXSR CLEAR                          CLEAR SF       CH24P3
0039 C                 GOTO AGAIN                          REPEAT SF LOAD CH24P3
0040 C         EOJ     TAG                                                CH24P3
0041 C                 SETON                          LR   END OF JOB     CH24P3
0042  *                                                                   CH24P3
0043  * SUBROUTINE TO INITIALIZE ENTRY SCREEN FIELDS TO BLANKS & ZEROS    CH24P3
0044  *                                                                   CH24P3
0045 C         HOUSEK  BEGSR                                              CH24P3
0046 C                 MOVE *BLANKS  CUST#                                CH24P3
0047 C                 MOVE *BLANKS  NAME                                 CH24P3
0048 C                 MOVE *BLANKS  STREET                               CH24P3
0049 C                 MOVE *BLANKS  CITY                                 CH24P3
0050 C                 MOVE *BLANKS  STATE                                CH24P3
0051 C                 MOVE *ZEROS   ZIP                                  CH24P3
0052 C                 MOVE *ZEROS   BALANC                               CH24P3
0053 C                 ENDSR                                              CH24P3
0054  *                                                                   CH24P3
0055  * SUBROUTINE TO CLEAR SUBFILE & INITIALIZE RECORD COUNTER......      CH24P3
0056  *                                                                   CH24P3
0057 C         CLEAR   BEGSR                                              CH24P3
0058 C                 MOVE '1'      *IN80                                CH24P3
0059 C                 WRITESMO3CTL                        CLEAR SUBFILE  CH24P3
0060 C                 MOVE '0'      *IN80                                CH24P3
0061 C                 Z-ADDO        SFRRN1  40            INITIAL. SF CTRCH24P3
0062 C                 SETOF                        7172                  CH24P3
0063 C                 ENDSR                                              CH24P3
```

Line #

0009 TAG for related GOTO statement on line 39.

0010 -

0011 DOUEQ group of instructions are performed until the subfile is full (indicator 71) or the operator presses command key 4 (indicator 04) to stop loading of the subfile.

0012 Control is passed to the HOUSEK subroutine where the SFADDR screen format fields are initialized to blanks and zeros.

0013 EXFMT instruction displays record format SFADDR for the entry of adds data.

0014 If command key 1 is pressed, control is passed to line 0040 and the job is stopped by the SETON LR statement on line 0041.

0015 If the operator changes his/her mind about entering the current record, command key 3 may be pressed which will pass control back to line 0009 to continue the process of entering new data or ending the job.

0016 When the IFEQ test is true (indicator 4 off), the instructions on lines 0017 through 0019 will be executed.

0017 Subfile relative record counter SFRRN1 is incremented by 1.

0018 The WRITE statement controls loading of the current screen record to a subfile record position as determined by the current value in the SFRRN1 counter. Indicator 71, entered in the equal field (columns 58-59), will turn on when the subfile is full. The indicator is specified in the DOU statement on line 0010 as one of the conditions that determines when loading of the subfile is to stop.

0019 END operation ends the IFEQ statement on line 0016.

0020 END operation ends the DOUEQ group (lines 0010 through 0020). The equal test specified in the DOUEQ statement on line 0010 is made at this END operation.

0024 The CMDLINE record format line constants are displayed by this WRITE statement.

(*Continued*)

0025 Indicator 81, which controls the display of the subfile record and control record formats, is turned on.

0026 EXFMT statement displays the subfile control record constants and subfile record variables. Indicator 81, which was turned on line 25, conditioned the subfile's keywords (SFLDSP, SFLDSPCTL, and SFLEND) in the DDS coding for this control.

0027 Indicator 81 is turned off.

0031 Subfile record counter (SFRRN1) is reinitialized to 1 so that reading of the subfile will begin at the first record.

0032 This READC statement reads the first record from the subfile record format (SM03SFR). If no records are stored in the subfile, indicator 72, specified in the equal field (columns 58-59) will turn on. Indicator 72 is included in the test for the following DOWEQ statement (line 0032) to determine when to end the writing of subfile records to the physical file.

Note that only the READC operation may be used to read subfile records and not a READ or READP operation.

0033 The DOWEQ group controls the reading of subfile records and loading of the physical file with them until end of the subfile is tested (indicator 72 is on).

0034 The WRITE statement adds the current subfile record at the end of the physical file.

0035 The subfile relative record counter is incremented by 1.

0036 Another record is read from the subfile by the READC statement.

0037 END operation ends the DOWEQ group. When this statement is executed, control is passed back to the DOWEQ statement on line 0033 where the test is made to determine the processing alternatives.

0038 This EXSR instruction branches program control to a subroutine where the subfile is cleared before the entry screen (line 0012) is displayed again and another group of subfile records entered.

0039 Control is passed back to line 0009 and processing sequence continued.

0040 Related TAG operation for CABEQ instruction on line 0014.

0041 SETON LR statement ends the job and returns control back to the operating system.

0045 -
0053 The SFADDR entry screen fields are cleared in this subroutine before the screen is displayed for the entry of data.

0057 -
0063 This subroutine includes instructions that clear the subfile (lines 0058-0059), initialize the subfile relative record counter (line 0061), and turn off resulting indicators (line 0062).

(Continued)

Execution of the subfile addition program generates the screen displays illustrated in Figure 24-22. The first screen shown (SFADDR) supports the entry of data to load the subfile, and the second shows a display of the subfile after it is loaded. Under control of the subfile display, the user has the option to move the cursor to any record and modify one or all the field values. To see the truncated subfile record values (ZIP and BALANC), the operator must press command key 5. This action folds the two hidden field values onto the next line for review and/or change. As was previously explained in Figure 24-20, folding the subfile record values is controlled by the SFLDROP keyword in the subfile's control record format (SM03CTL).

A display of the physical file (P1PF1) generated by the CPYF (Copy File) or DSPPFM (Display Physical File Member) will show that the "add" records are stored at the end of the file in the order they were loaded.

Displayed SFADDR Record Format :

```
12/01/91        CUSTOMER FILE ADDITION        11:15:00

        CUST#:      20000
        NAME:       PAUL GAUGUIN
        STREET:     12 TAHITI PLACE
        CITY:       PACIFIC
        STATE:      CA
        ZIP:        09900
        BALANCE:        10012


CK1 - EOJ   CK3 - REDISPLAY  CK4 - END LOAD
        ENTER - LOAD TO SUBFILE
```

DisplayedSM03CTL, SM03SFR, and CMDLINE Subfile Record Formats:

```
                    CUSTOMER FILE ADDITION

CUSTNO          NAME              STREET              CITY          STATE
 ZIP    BALANCE

 20000   PAUL GAUGUIN        12 TAHITI PLACE         PACIFIC          CA
09900 00010012
 35000    EDWARD MONET       4 IMPRESSIONIST ROAD    MILAN            PA
04444 00089500
 40000    HENRI MATISSE      44 RUE PIGALLE          FRANCE           KY
07777 00034910
 90000    PIERRE RENOIR      96 MONTCLAIR DRIVE      PARIS            NY
01111 00100000                                                           +



PRESS ENTER TO ADD RECORDS                CK5 TO FOLD RECORDS
```

Figure 24-22 CRT displays of the entry and subfile screen records after the addition program is executed.

QUESTIONS

24-1. Define a subfile as related to the AS/400 and System/38 environments.

24-2. For what processing functions may a subfile be used?

24-3. How may a subfile be created?

24-4. Name the minimum number of record formats that must be included in the definition of a subfile. In what order must they be specified?

24-5. Refer to Question 24-4 and explain the function of each record format.

24-6. What is the minimum number of keywords that must be included in the definition of a subfile?

The following subfile terms relate to Questions 24-7 through 24-21:
Match the following keywords to their related definition:

```
a. SFL       e. SFLDSP   i. SFLRNA      m. SFLMSG
b. SFLCTL    f. SFLCLR   j. SFLDSPCTL   n. SFLDROP
c. SFLSIZ    g. SFLINZ   k. SFLEND      o. SFLNXTCHG
d. SFLPAG    h. SFLDLT   l. SFLLIN
```

24-7. ____ Deletes a subfile from the current processing environment.

24-8. ____ Used in conjunction with another keyword that actually performs the initialization of a subfile's field values.

24-9. ____ Specifies the number of spaces between columns of subfile records when the subfile is displayed horizontally.

24-10. ____ Determines the number of records that may be stored in the subfile.

24-11. ____ Indicates the number of subfile records that may be displayed on the screen at one time.

24-12. ____ Specifies that the record format defined is a subfile control record format.

24-13. ____ Controls display of the records stored in the subfile record format.

24-14. ____ Initializes alphanumeric fields in the subfile to blanks and numeric fields to zeros.

24-15. ____ Supports the folding of truncated subfile record format field values.

24-16. ____ Identifies the subfile record format.

24-17. ____ Controls display of the constants and variables defined in the subfile control record format.

24-18. ____ Identifies on the CRT that more records are included in the subfile.

24-19. ____ Is the control record format keyword that supports the display of an error message.

24-20. ____ Enables RPG program to identify subfile records that have been modified.

24-21. ____ Clears the subfile of all records.

24-22. For inquiry processing, what Usage must be assigned to the subfile record's fields? What Usage is specified for update and for addition processing?

24-23. What RPG operation is used to read records from a subfile? In what resulting indicator field(s) must the indicator(s) be specified? What is the function of the indicator(s)?

Examine the following File Description Specifications and answer Questions 24-24 through 24-27.

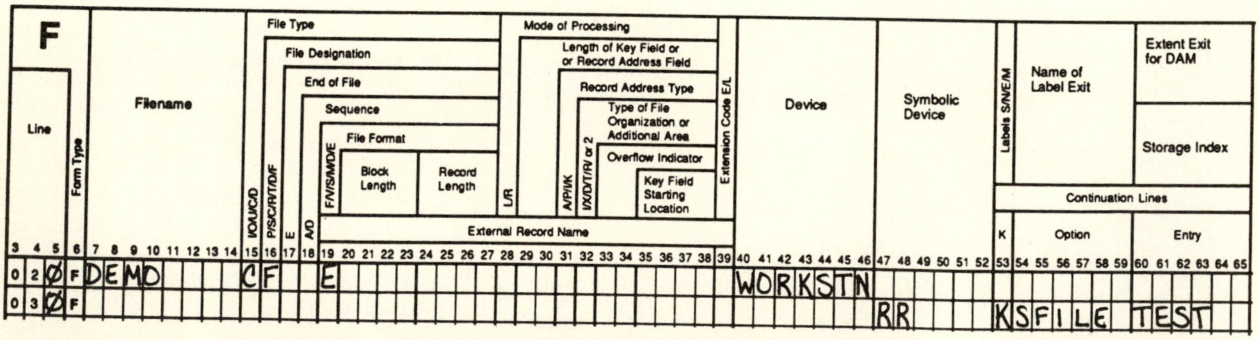

24-24. Explain the function of the RR entry in the Symbolic Device field in an RPG program.

24-25. What is the purpose of the letter K in column 53?

24-26. The SFILE entry in the Option field (columns 54-59) indicates what?

24-27. What does the TEST entry in the Entry field (columns 60-65) represent?

24-28. When a subfile is cleared, is the control record format or the subfile record format included in the WRITE statement?

24-29. When a subfile is displayed, is the control record format or the subfile record format included in the EXFMT statement?

24-30. Name the RPG operation that loads records to a subfile. What is the function of the indicator(s) that must be specified in the resulting indicator field(s)? In which resulting indicator field(s) must it be included?

EXERCISES

24-1. On the basis of the attributes of the following physical file, (SALTRANS record format SALR), write a display file, named SFLINQ, that includes a prompt screen and the necessary subfile record formats. The subfile is to support inquiry processing of the physical file.

Field Name	*Size*	*Type*	*Decimal Positions*
SALNUM	4	A	
CUST#	5	A	
SALAMT	8	P	2
SDATE	6	P	0

The format of the prompt screen, which is to be named ENTER, follows:

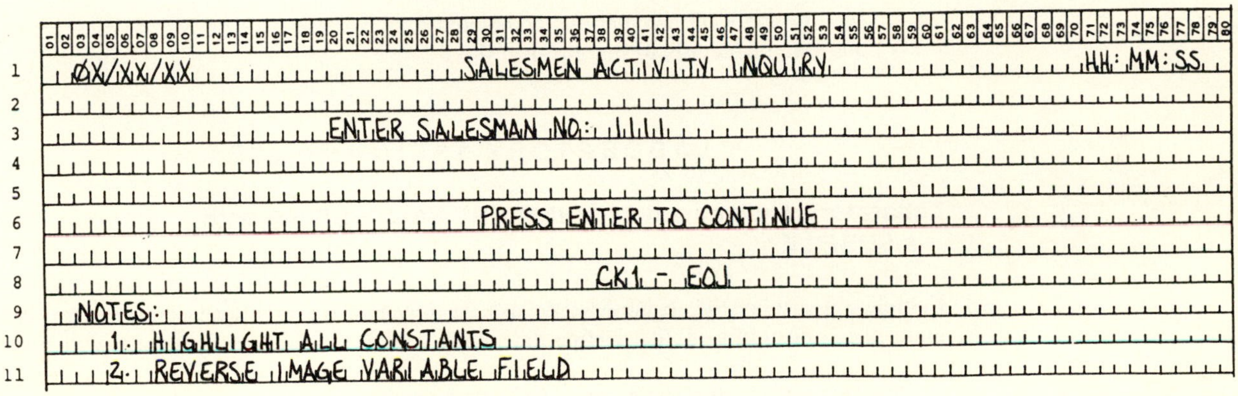

ØX/XX/XX SALESMEN ACTIVITY INQUIRY HH:MM:SS
ENTER SALESMAN NO: ||||
PRESS ENTER TO CONTINUE
CK1 - EOJ
NOTES:
1. HIGHLIGHT ALL CONSTANTS
2. REVERSE IMAGE VARIABLE FIELD

The design of the subfile follows:

Assign SFINQR to the subfile record format; SFINQC, to the subfile control record format; and, INFOR to the subfile command record format.

24-2. Refer to Exercise 24-1 and write the File Description coding to process the display and physical files. Use RRN1 for your subfile relative record counter. How will the File Description coding be modified to support update and addition maintenance?

24-3. Refer to Exercises 24-1 and 24-2 and write the RPG calculations to inquiry the physical file under the control of a subfile.

24-4. Refer to Exercise 24-1 and modify the record formats in the display file to support update processing of the physical file via the subfile.

24-5. Refer to Exercises 24-2 and 24-4 and modify the RPG calculations to support update processing of the physical file via the subfile.

24-6. Modify the display file completed for Exercise 24-1 or 24-3 to support the entry of data for the addition of records to the physical file. Design your own entry screen and include all the fields in the physical file's record format.

24-7. Modify the RPG calculations completed for Exercise 24-2 or 24-5 to support the addition of records to the physical file.

LABORATORY ASSIGNMENTS

Laboratory Assignment 24-1: INQUIRY PROCESSING with a SUBFILE

Complete a display file to inquiry process the physical file created in Assignment 19-1 under the control of a subfile. Define the subfile so that it will store 12 records with 5 per page.

The physical file for Assignment 19-1 must have been created and loaded with data before this assignment is started.

Format of the Physical File (Repeated from Chapter 19):

FILE DEFINITION

SYSTEM Yours		DRAWN BY S. Myers
FILE NAME Yours		DATE 3/1/91 REV. NO. 0
CREATED BY S. Myers		FILE TYPE Physical
RECORD NAME Yours		KEY LENGTH 5 bytes
RECORDING MODE Fixed	ORGANIZATION Keyed	SEQUENCE Ascending by key
RECORD SIZE 54 bytes	BLOCKING FACTOR 1	BLOCKSIZE 54 bytes

FIELD DATA

FIELD NO.	FIELD NAME - DESCRIPTION	SIZE	CLASS C/P/Z/B	POSITION FROM	POSITION THRU	FORMAT/CONSTANT
1	Part number	5	C	1	5	Key field
2	Part Name	20	C	6	25	
3	Amount on hand	6	P	26	29	
4	Amount on order	6	P	30	33	
5	Average cost per unit	7	P	34	37	2 decimal positions
6	Amount allocated	6	P	38	41	
7	Economic order quantity	6	P	42	45	
8	Safety stock	6	P	46	49	
9	Lead time	3	P	50	51	
10	Warehouse location	3	C	52	54	

Physical File Data (Repeated from Chapter 21, Assignment 21-1):

Part#	Part Name	Amount On Hand	Amount On Order	Avg Cost/ Unit	Amount Allocated	Economic Order Qty	Safety Stock	Lead Time	Warehouse Location
A2345	AC SPARK PLUGS	000000	018000	0000075	005000	000150	002000	014	ABC
B6789	FRAM OIL FILTRS	004000	001200	0000325	000480	001200	000500	031	DEF
C5555	POINT SETS	000600	000000	0000850	000000	000100	000100	015	AAA
D9876	LOCKING GAS CAP	000024	000012	0000499	000012	000012	000012	090	GHI
E3459	LIQUID CAR WASH	000360	000120	0000179	000480	000072	000200	016	BBB

The record formats to be included in the display file are detailed in the following CRT layout forms.

Prompt Screen Format:

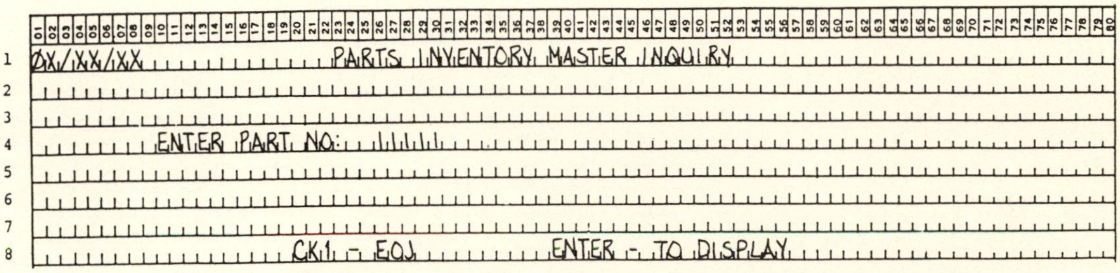

Subfile Formats (Record, Control, and Command):

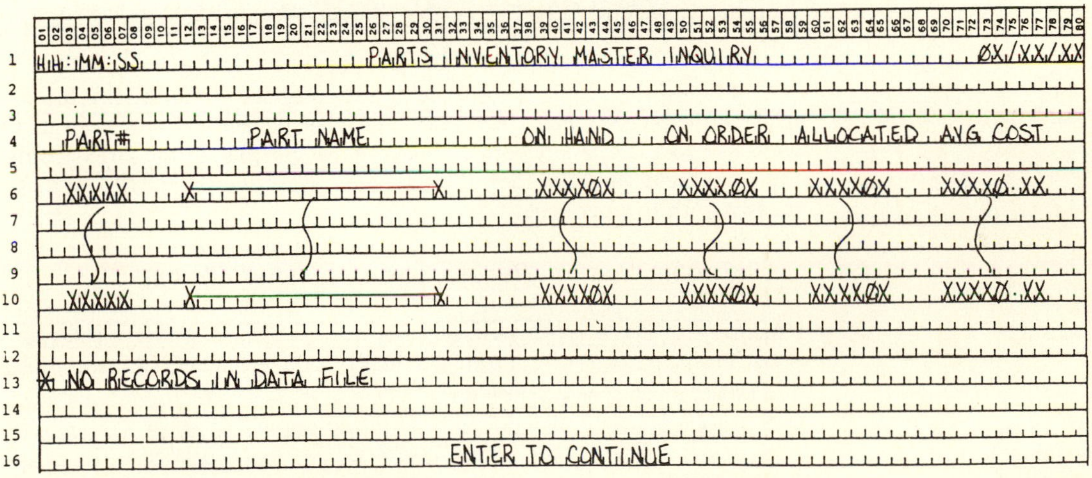

Laboratory Assignment 24-2: UPDATE PROCESSING WITH A SUBFILE

Modify the display file and RPG program completed for Ássignment 24-1 to support update processing of the physical with subfile control. Numbers of records to be stored in the subfile and displayed per page are not to be changed. To prove the results of the updates, generate hexidecimal listings of the physical file *before* and *after* processing.

Update Data:

Part #	Part Name	Amount On Hand	Amount On Order	Avg Cost/ Unit	Amount Allocated
A2345 .	...	018000 ...	000000	..	002000
B6789 .	FRAM OIL FILTERS ...	...	....	0000370 ..	
C5550 .	...	...	004000 ...	..	
E3459 .	...	000480 ...	000000 ...	..	

Note: Only change the related fields in the physical file that include corresponding update data.

Laboratory Assignment 24-3: ADDITION PROCESSING WITH A SUBFILE

Refer to completed Assignments 24-1 or 24-2, and modify the display file and RPG program to support the addition of records to the physical file with subfile control. Replace the prompt screen with an entry screen in the following format:

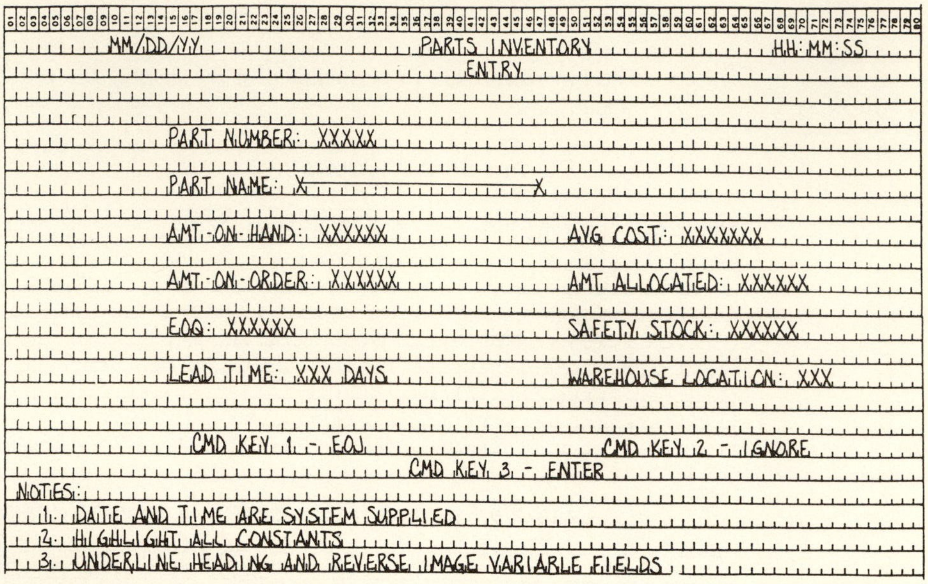

Modify the subfile record and control formats in the display file to include all the fields in the physical file. Unless the CRT available supports a screen that is 132 columns wide, the SFLDROP keyword will have to be specified in the DDS coding to display the truncated field values in the subfile records. Describe the subfile so that it will store 10 records with five per page.

Subfile Control, Record, and Command Formats:

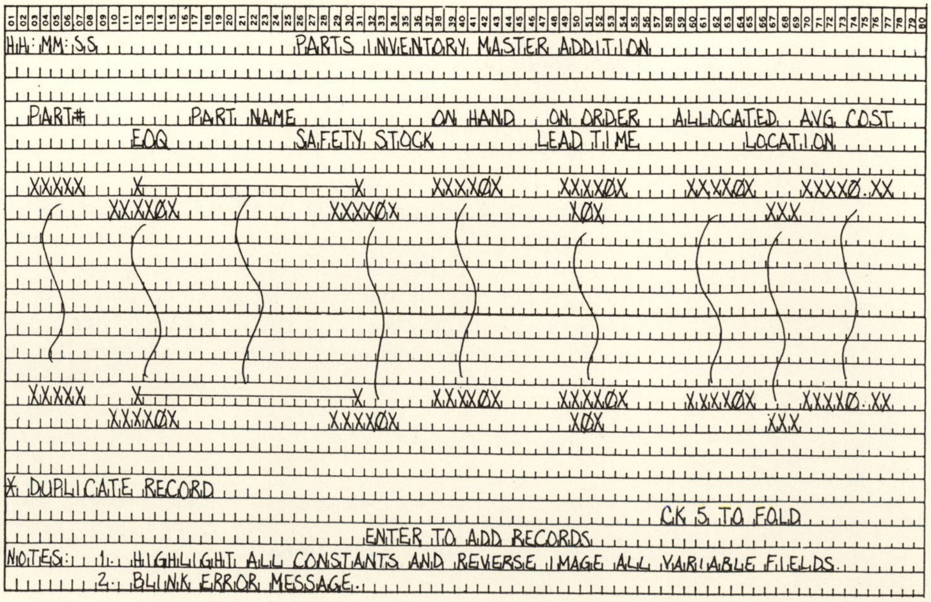

HH:MM:SS
PARTS INVENTORY MASTER ADDITION
PART#
PART NAME
ON HAND
ON ORDER
ALLOCATED
AVG COST
EOQ
SAFETY STOCK
LEAD TIME
LOCATION
XXXXX X X XXXXØX XXXXØX XXXXØX XXXXØ.XX
XXXXØX XXXXØX XØX XXX
XXXXX X X XXXXØX XXXXØX XXXXØX XXXXØ.XX
XXXXØX XXXXØX XØX XXX
X DUPLICATE RECORD
CK 5 TO FOLD
ENTER TO ADD RECORDS
NOTES: 1. HIGHLIGHT ALL CONSTANTS AND REVERSE IMAGE ALL VARIABLE FIELDS.
2. BLINK ERROR MESSAGE.

Adds Data:

	Transaction #1	Transaction #2	Transaction #3
Part#..........	A1000	C5000	D9876
Part Name......	PRESTONE DE-ICER....	CHAMOIS (LARGE)....	LOCKING GAS CAP
Amt-on-hand....	000000	000000	000000
Amt-on-order...	000144	000120	000144
Avg-cost/unit..	0000259	0000675	0000115
Amt-allocated..	000000	000012	000000
EOQ............	000144	000120	000024
Safety Stock...	000100	000024	000012
Lead time......	010	015	090
Location.......	SSS	EFG	GHI

Index

T

U

W

X

Y

Z

NOW YOU CAN DO YOUR RPG III or 400 PROGRAMMING ON AN IBM PC COMPATIBLE MICROCOMPUTER!

Read about the special purchase offer(s) on the previous page for an:

RPG/400 IBM PC Compatible Compiler